A Lithuanian Bibliography

A check-list of books and articles held by the
major libraries of Canada and the United States.

Adam & Filomena Kantautas

The University of Alberta Press   1975

First published by
The University of Alberta Press
Edmonton, Alberta, Canada.   1975

Copyright © 1975 The University of Alberta Press

ISBN   0-88864-010-2

Printed in Canada by
Printing Services of The University of Alberta

TABLE OF CONTENTS

Page

FOREWORD

Multiculturalism as a national policy has been adopted fairly recently by the Canadian government. The policy is intended to encourage racial groups to take pride in the cultural heritage they or their parents brought to this country, to preserve the best of it so that in time the amalgamation of cultures may create a new and richer Canadian culture. In any cultural programme relating to a specific ethnic group the first requisite is a catalogue of its written heritage. Adam and Filomena Kantautas have anticipated the current interest by preparing a bibliography of Lithuanian culture.

Interest in this bibliography will not be confined to Canada, but will be international. The problems of relations between East and West in Europe will continue to disturb international politics for a long time to come. To the student of Eastern European affairs Lithuania is an important case study of a small country wedged between Slavic and Western culture, and currently dominated by the Soviets.

Historically, Lithuania played a role beyond its present borders, for until the beginning of the 19th century its boundaries extended east over Belorussia, and for four centuries Lithuania was linked politically with Poland. At the same time it is one of the Baltic nations, and like Latvia and Estonia suffered greatly in World War II, being overrun first by the Russians then by German armies, and was finally submerged in the Soviet Union. The Western nations still retain diplomatic relations with a Lithuanian government in exile, for they are reluctant to acknowledge the Russian conquest as final.

An examination of the contents of this bibliography reveals the comprehensive scope of the topics covered, and also the frequency with which Lithuanian life and politics touch on neighbouring nations, or have significance for an understanding of their problems of preserving a national identity under the Soviet hegemony. The books and articles listed are in several languages, an indication of how widely the compilers searched.

The bibliographer who would compile a bibliography must invest heavily of his time and money, and must exercise patience and pertinacity. Mr. and Mrs. Adam Kantautas have been engaged for over a decade in the collection of information on Lithuania. Now the scholar interested in the Lithuanian nation or in Lithuanians in America will benefit by the dedication of two bibliographers to a colossal task.

Bruce Peel
Edmonton
June, 1974

INTRODUCTION

This bibliography has been compiled in response to a growing interest in the affairs of Eastern Europe. It lists materials dealing with all aspects of Lithuania, its people, history, culture, literature, language, and cultural life.

The purpose of this work is:

   (a) To present a checklist of material relating to Lithuania, held in Canadian and American Libraries.

   (b) To assist scholars, librarians and general readers in locating the material described above.

The availability of desired material is of great importance to any researcher. This is why location symbols have been given, showing which libraries possess the item. A book may be of very great value and importance, but if none of the libraries surveyed owns it, it is not included.

It comprises monographs, pamphlets, serials, periodicals, government documents, League of Nations and United Nations documents, and articles on Lithuania in almost all European languages. Neighbouring countries are also included if the works are relevant. In addition to the sources mentioned above, the bibliography includes the oldest source material, old texts as well as belles-lettres, and covers material published up to December 31, 1971. A few works published since that date have been included because of their importance.

This reference book is not a guide to any single view or partisan opinion, but includes books representing all points of view on the subject. The researcher will have to approach the publications included in the bibliography with a critical eye for the accuracy of the facts they contain, and for the objectivity of the works as a whole. It is also necessary to be aware of two distinct types of writing which express different points of view on Lithuanian problems. They include:

   (a) Studies and reports prepared by foreign observers.

   (b) Publications which present the Lithuanian point of view.

The bulk of the material is of a scholarly nature, though some popular works and belles-lettres have been included. The criteria for inclusion varied with the topic under survey, taking into consideration the obvious fact that some subject areas or specific topics are heavily represented, while others receive less coverage, or are rarely discussed at all. The relative importance of the material was considered, and quite frequently it was necessary to include popular works and even publications of rather poor quality, just to provide some information on less usual but important topics.

This bibliography has been arranged by broad subject areas. Each of the major headings is subdivided further, as need arises, into smaller and more specific subject headings or topics. Within each subdivision, works are listed alphabetically by author or title. Author and title indexes have been provided. The author index also lists editors, translators, illustrators, and their pseudonyms. "See" and "See also" references are made for variant forms of names and pseudonyms. The analytical table of contents and the author and title indexes refer to item numbers only, and not to page numbers.

Each entry presents the essential bibliographic description of a book. It contains entry number, author, title, edition (if any), place of publication, publisher, date of publication, and the number of pages or volumes. Information which has to be included in the entry, but which is not on the title page of the work, is placed in square brackets. Additional notes have been provided only where clarification was necessary or additional information desirable. In order to avoid repetition in the typing of headings for the entries which follow each other, a unit of three hyphens is used. In cases where the subheadings change, the whole entry is retyped. The second unit of three hyphens is used to replace the title, if it is identical up to the period, collon, or semicollon in the title.

The following principals have governed the choice of forms of authors' names:

(a) Wherever possible, the form of entry used by the Library of Congress is followed. When the Library of Congress does not have the publication, the entry of the particular library has been accepted.

(b) When two different persons have identical surnames and Christian names, their birth and death dates are included in the entry.

(c) If a person has changed his surname and or Christian name during his lifetime, and the libraries have used both forms, then the latest form is used with "see" references given in the author index.

(d) Only in a few unusual cases have two forms of the author's surname been used, because of special circumstances. In such cases "see also" references are given for both forms of the surname.

(e) Books written under pseudonyms are entered under the real names of their authors. The pseudonym is then given after the title, and a "see" reference from pseudonym to real name in the author index. Exception is made when real name is unknown or when the pseudonym has become fixed in literary history.

(f) The name of the author of a periodical article is given exactly as it appears in the periodical.

For the benefit of readers not familiar with the Estonian, Finnish, Latvian and Lithuanian languages, English translations of the titles have been added to the main entries for works in those languages, with the exception of belles-lettres. Works in the Cyrillic alphabet are transliterated according to the rules of the Library of Congress but without the diacritical marks.

The entry is completed by giving the call number of the book and location symbols of all the libraries which have this particular title. The location symbols are the same as those in the National Union Catalog of the Library of Congress, and have been used with their permission. It should be emphasized that the call number given for a work is that assigned by the library appearing _first_ in the list of location symbols. Other libraries may well have assigned a slightly different call number.

Articles from serials and periodicals show the call number and location symbol only if there is no more than one item from the periodical in question. If several articles from the same serial or periodical are cited, then a note is made referring the reader to the complete list of serials consulted, where full details on locations, holdings, and call number will be found. Holdings of serials or periodicals are indicated by volume number or year of publication. A hyphen between numbers or dates indicates an inclusive range. A hyphen after the date or volume number indicates that the library has a continuous run from that point.

Many works have been listed under more than one subject area in this bibliography, since they are concerned with more than one subject. In these cases a brief entry appears under the second and successive subject areas, with a cross-reference to the main entry.

ACKNOWLEDGMENTS

We are indebted to many people for their assistance, advice, cooperation and encouragement in compiling this bibliography. It is a great pleasure for us to express our special gratitude to all of them.

We wish in particular to thank Dr. Arthur G. McCalla, Vice-President (Academic) of the University of Alberta, Dr. Henry Kreisel, Vice-President (Academic) of the University of Alberta, and Mr. Bruce B. Peel, Librarian to the University of Alberta, for enabling us to carry through our research by approving a sabbatical leave for Adam Kantautas, so that we could visit the major Canadian and United States libraries.

Special thanks are extended to Dr. Jonas Balys, Library of Congress, Washington, D. C., and Dr. Vincas Maciūnas, University of Pennsylvania Library, Philadelphia, for their valuable advice and suggestions, and for giving us access to their private card catalogues on Lithuanian materials, as well as for constructive criticism.

We wish also to express our gratitude to Miss Mary E. P. Henderson, Director of the Library School, University of Alberta, Edmonton, for valuable advice in the planning stages of this bibliography.

We also acknowledge the assistance of Mrs. Livia Fricke and Miss Lidia Sorobej who helped to transcribe bibliographic information at the original stages of compilation, Dr. Paul Gudjurgis for indexing, proofreading and checking and Doreen Youngs (Mrs. C. W. Youngs) for the typing of the manuscript.

For permission to use required materials from printed library catalogues, and to use the symbols of American libraries from the National Union Catalog, we owe a debt of gratitude to the Library of Congress, the Trustees of the British Museum, and the H. W. Wilson Company.

We are also grateful to the Lithuanian Research Institute, Inc., New York, N.Y., for permission to use and consult their publication Lithuania and Lithuanians.

We are indebted to many librarians, associate librarians, and heads of reference departments, who were kind enough to answer our letters, who sent us Xerox copies of catalogue cards on Lithuanian topics, or who granted us access to their libraries and helped us in collecting the material we needed.

The libraries we visited is as follows:

ALKA Museum Library, R. F. D. 2, Putnam, Conn.
Balzekas Museum of Lithuanian Culture, Chicago, Ill.
Brown University, Providence, R. I.
Case Western Reserve University, Cleveland, Ohio
Catholic University of America, Washington, D. C.
Columbia University, New York, N. Y.
Duke University, Durham, N. C.
Edmonton Public Library, Edmonton, Alta.

Free Library of Philadelphia, Pa.

Harvard University, Cambridge, Mass.

Hoover Institution on War, Revolution and Peace,
   Stanford, Calif.

Immaculate Conception Convent Library, Putnam, Conn.

Library of Congress, Washington, D. C.

Library of Congress Union Catalog, Washington, D. C.

Library of Lithuanian Musicology, Chicago, Ill.

Lithuanian Jesuit Fathers Library, Chicago, Ill.

Marian Fathers, Marianapolis, Thompson, Conn.

New York Public Library, New York, N. Y.

North Dakota State University, Fargo, N. D.

Northwestern University, Evanston, Ill.

Princeton University, Princeton, N. J.

Rutgers University, New Brunswick, N. J.

St. Casimir Convent Library, Chicago, Ill.

Seattle Public Library, Seattle, Wash.

Simon Fraser University, Vancouver, B. C.

Toronto Public Library, Toronto, Ont.

University of Alberta, Edmonton, Alta.

University of British Columbia, Vancouver, B. C.

University of California, Berkeley, Calif.

University of California at Los Angeles, Calif.

University of Chicago, Chicago, Ill.

University of Florida, Gainesville, Fla.

University of Manitoba, Winnipeg, Man.

University of Minnesota, Minneapolis, Minn.

University of North Carolina, Chapel Hill, N. C.

University of North Dakota, Grand Forks, N. D.

University of Pennsylvania, Philadelphia, Pa.

University of Pittsburgh, Pittsburgh, Pa.

University of Saskatchewan, Regina, Sask.

University of Saskatchewan, Saskatoon, Sask.

University of Toronto, Toronto, Ont.

University of Virginia, Charlottesville, Va.

University of Washington, Seattle, Wash.

University of Wisconsin, Madison, Wis.

Yale University, New Haven, Conn.

York University, Toronto, Ont.

The following important libraries were kind enough to give us information of their holdings of Lithuanian material by correspondence.

Boston Public Library, Boston, Mass.

Brandeis University, Waltham, Mass.

Brooklyn Public Library, Brooklyn, N. Y.

Carnegie Library of Pittsburgh, Pittsburgh, Pa.

Chicago Public Library, Chicago, Ill.

Cleveland Public Library, Cleveland, Ohio

Cornell University, Ithaca, N. Y.

Dalhousie University, Halifax, N. S.
Emory University, Atlanta, Ga.
Geological Survey of Canada, Ottawa, Ont.
Indiana State Library, Indianapolis, Ind.
Indiana University, Bloomington, Ind.
John Crerar Library, Chicago, Ill.
John Hopkins University, Baltimore, Md.
Kent State University Library, Kent, Ohio
Library of Parliament, Ottawa, Ont.
Louisiana State University, Baton Rouge, La.
McGill University, Montreal, Que.
McMaster University, Hamilton, Ont.
Memorial University, St. John's Nfd.
Milwaukee Public Library, Milwaukee, Wis.
National Library of Canada, Ottawa, Ont.
New York University, New York, N. Y.
Newberry Library, Chicago, Ill.
Oklahoma State University, Enid, Okla.
Pennsylvania State University, University Park, Pa.
Purdue University, Lafayette, Ind.
Queen's University, Kingston, Ont.
Southern Methodist University, Dallas, Tex.
Syracuse University, Syracuse, N. Y.
University of Alabama, University, Ala.
University of Arkansas, Fayetteville, Ark.
University of Buffalo, Buffalo, N. Y.
University of Cincinnati, Cincinnati, Ohio
University of Colorado, Boulder, Colo.
University of Georgia, Athens, Ga.
University of Hawaii, Honolulu, Hawaii
University of Houston, Houston, Tex.
University of Idaho, Moscow, Ida.
University of Illinois, Urbana, Ill.
University of Iowa, Iowa City, Iowa.
University of Kansas, Lawrence, Kan.
University of Maine, Orono, Me.
University of Massachusetts, Amherst, Mass.
University of Missouri, Columbia, Mo.
University of Nebraska, Lincoln, Neb.
University of Nevada, Reno, Nev.
University of New Brunswick, Fredericton, N. B.
University of New Hampshire, Durham, N. H.
University of New Mexico, Albuquerque, N. M.
University of Notre Dame, Notre Dame, Ind.
University of Oklahoma, Norman, Okla.
University of Oregon, Eugene, Or.
University of South Carolina, Columbia, S. C.

University of South Dakota, Vermillion, S.D.
University of Tennessee, Knoxville, Tenn.
University of Texas, Austin, Tex.
University of Utah, Salt Lake City, Utah.
University of Vermont, Burlington, Vt.
University of Waterloo, Waterloo, Ont.
University of Western Ontario, London, Ont.
University of Wyoming, Laramie, Wyo.
West Virginia University, Morgantown, W.Va.

The appearance of this bibliography has been made possible with the help of grants from the Federal Government, Secretary of State, Multicultural Projects Program; The Province of Alberta, Dept. of Culture, Youth and Recreation; The Institute of Lithuanian Studies, Inc., Arlington, Mass.; The Lithuanian Canadian Foundation, Toronto, Ont. and The Lithuanian Canadian Community, National Executive, Toronto, Ont.; and The Lithuanian Foundation, Chicago, Ill.

ANALYTIC TABLE OF CONTENTS

NOTES TO THE ANALYTIC TABLE OF CONTENTS

The broad subject headings of this bibliography require little or no comment. In some cases, however, the use of terms or arrangement of material require some explanation. The subject areas concerned are discussed in alphabetical order.

Agriculture. This has been divided into two sections. The first subdivision includes materials that deal chiefly with the economic and social aspects of agriculture. The second subdivision contains only works dealing with the land reform from the earliest period. The subdivision on Land Tenure, however, will be found in the section on Society. Technological works on husbandry, cultivation, crops, soils, etc., are not included.

Archaeology. This section is reserved for works which describe the planning of archaeological research, actual excavations, or other specific archaeological research. Works which synthesize the results of archaeological research, so as to present a picture of the earliest times, have been placed in Prehistory.

Architecture. The first subdivision, Urban architecture, also includes the architecture of churches. The second subdivision, Rural Architecture, includes primitive rural architecture, such as farm buildings and the like.

Bibliographic aids. All bibliographies are listed here with the exception of bibliographies on history, folklore, language and literature, which are located under those subjects.

Biography. This subdivision contains pure biographies and also works which cover the authors' literary works, their criticism and their lives. Works of the latter type are also included under literature, art and music.

Description and travel. The last four subdivisions of General Works contain works of all types describing Lithuania, as follows: (1) General description and travel; (2) Travel guides, mostly for tourists; (3) Ancient travel reports by foreign travellers; and (4) Pictorial works. Some of the works might as easily have been placed in the section on Local History.

Economy. Works on the economic situation in Lithuania, and on its economic relations with other countries from the earliest times, have been listed here. Statistical data on economic life is placed in the subdivision Statistics under General reference aids.

General reference aids. All dictionaries appear only in this section of the bibliography.

General works. Treatises, pamphlets, and general essays on all aspects of life are listed here, with the addition of such special aspects as the National Awakening. Works on the Baltic countries in general are listed if they contain material on Lithuania.

History--Soviet Lithuania. Pure historical events are contained in two subdivisions: Treatises and textbooks, and Lithuania. Materials on semi-historical events of that period are placed in the subdivision on Communism in Lithuania.

Languages. There are special subdivisions for works on the Indo-European, Baltic and Prussian languages. The more important linguistic studies of geographical names are also included under General reference aids. All dictionaries and glossaries appear under General reference aids, in the Dictionaries subdivision.

Literature. Three basic subdivisions have been used: Bibliographies, History and criticism, and Belles lettres, which are further subdivided as needed. Belles lettres are included for two reasons (although it is not customary to include them in this kind of bibliography): first, departments of comparative literature in North America quite often question the existence of a representative Lithuanian literature; and secondly, general readers (chiefly Lithuanians) are eager to know where they can obtain Lithuanian belles lettres for reading or study.

It is difficult to subdivide Lithuanian literature into clearly separated periods; for instance, some authors lived through the period of Russian occupation before the First World War, then the period of Independent Lithuania, and most recently in Soviet Lithuania. The arrangement arrived at is sometimes a compromise; some writers have been assigned to Soviet Lithuanian literature, while others have been placed in the earlier periods.

Lithuanians Abroad. This subdivision is part of the section on People, and it encompasses all the activities of Lithuanians living outside Lithuania, such as their intellectual and social life, and political activities. The problems of displaced persons and their activities are also located here.

Manners and customs. Creativity belonging to folklore, and Lithuanian folk art (weaving, crafts, ornaments, carvings, etc.) are placed in the subdivision Ancient folk culture (XIII.3.d.) rather than under Anthropology and ethnography (VI.4).

Serials. This section lists all the newspapers, periodicals, annuals, almanacs and publications of learned institutions.

State. The Lithuanian state has changed its form during the centuries. At first it was a loosely joined country made up of a number of duchies. Later these united and it became a kingdom. Then it changed into a

Grand Duchy, and remained so until 1795, when Russia occupied it. In 1918 it became a republic and existed as such until 1940. During this time a great many systems of government existed and a great number of laws were enacted; works on all of these are included in the State section of this bibliography.

Because this material is very extensive, more subdivisions have been required to accommodate it. The Lietuvos Statutas and Kazimiero tei-synas are singled out because of their great importance in the legal world, not only in Lithuania.

It will be seen that Lithuania conducted active foreign relations mainly with neighbouring countries. The most acute problems confronting Lithuanian diplomacy were the territorial questions of Klaipeda (Memel) and Vilnius (Vilna); these are accordingly segregated from the listings for general diplomatic relations.

Of a few treaties with other countries, two only are of signifi-cance: the Personal Union, a treaty concluded with Poland by Jogaila, the Grand Duke of Lithuania (Treaty of Krevo, 1385); and the treaty of Lublin of 1569, by which a Lithuanian-Polish Commonwealth was established.

ABBREVIATIONS

a.M. am Main, on the Main River
a.S. an der Salle, on the Salle
    River
Abdr. Abdruck, reprint, offprint
afd. afdeling, -en, chapter, chap-
    ters, part, parts
akad. akademiia, akademia, academy
A.L.R.K. Amerikos lietuvių katalikų
    federacija, Federation of Ame-
    rican Lithuanian Catholics
& and, et, und.
apr. aprel', April
arr. arranger, arranged
Assoc. Association
ats. atsakingasis, responsible
ats. red. atsakingasis redaktorius,
    editor-in-chief
atsak. red. atsakingasis redaktorius
    editor-in-chief
Aufl. Auflage, edition, issue, prin-
    ting
augm. augmenté, enlarged
Ausg. Ausgabe, edition, printing
avg. avgust, August

b-vė, -s, bendrovė, bendrovės, com-
    pany, company's
bal. balandis, April
Bd. Band, volume
bd. bind, volume
bearb. bearbeitet, revised, rewrit-
    ten, edited.
Bibl. Biblioteka, library
birž. birželis, June
boktr. boktrykeri, Printing house
bzw. beziehungsweise, respectively

cm. centimeter
col. coloured
comp. compiler
corr. corrected
czerw. czerwiec, June

dek. dekabr', December
der. derevnia, village
dop. dopolnenie, supplement
dr. drugie, others
Druk. Drukarnia, Printing house

ed., ed. edition, edition, editor.
ekon., ekonom. ekonomicheskoe, eco-
    nomic
ESSR Estonskaia SSR, Estonian Soviet
    Socialist Republic
et al. et alii, and others
etc. et cetera, and so forth

fasc. fascicle, fascicule, part,
    number.

facsim. facsimile
fevr. fevral', February
fold. folded

g. god, year
g. gorod, city, town
gg. gody, years
gaz. gazeta, gazety, newspaper, news-
    papers.
geg. gegužis, May
geogr. geograficheskii, geografiches-
    koi, geographical
Ger. Germany
ges. gesammelt, collected
gł. główny, main chief, principal,
    central
glav. glavnyi, main, chief, prin-
    cipal, central
Gos. gosudarstvennyi, gosudarstven-
    noe, state, national
Gos. izd. polit. i nauch. lit-ry Go-
    sudarstvennoe izdatel'stvo po-
    liticheskoi i nauchnoi litera-
    tury, Publishing house of the
    political and scientific lite-
    rature
Gos. sots.-ekon. izd-vo Gosudarst-
    vennoe sotsialistichesko-eko-
    nomicheskoe izdatel'stvo, Pub-
    lishing house of the socio-eco-
    nomic literature
Gos. ucheb.-pedagog. izd-vo Gosu-
    darstvennoe uchebno-pedagogi-
    cheskoe izdatel'stvo, Publi-
    shing house of educational li-
    terature
GPO Government Printing Office
Govt. Print. Off. Government Prin-
    ting Office
gr. gruodis, December
grudz. grudzień, December
Gub. tip. Gubernskaia tipografiia,
    Provincial Publishing House

Hft. Heft, part, number, issue
Hl. Heilige, holy
H.M.S.O. His (Her) Majesty's Statio-
    nary Office
H.M. Stationary Off. His (Her) Ma-
    jesty's Stationary Office
Hr. Hrabia, Earl
hrsg. herausgegeben, edited, pub-
    lished, edited
hum. humanitarinių, humanities'

i dr. i drugie, and others
ianv. ianvar', January
ill., illius. illiustratsiia, illius-
    trirovannyi, illustration,
    illustrations, illustrated
illus illustration, -s, illustrated

im.	imienia (Polish), imeni (Rus-
	sian), name, of the name
Imp., Imperat.	Imperator, impera-
	torskii, imperatorskaia, im-
	peratorskoe, imperial, Empe-
	ror
imp., impr.	imprimé, imprimerie,
	imprimeur, printed, printing,
	printing firm, printer
in-t	institut, institute
in-tov	institutov, of the insti-
	tutes
Inaug.-Diss.	Inaugural-Dissertation,
	inaugural dissertation
introd.	introduction
ispr.	ispravlennyi, corrected, re-
	vised
izd.	izdanie, edition
izdat.	izdatel', editor
izd-vo	izdatel'stvo, printing firm,
	publishing house, publisher

Jg., Jahrg.	Jahrgang, year, annual
	publication
jun., Jr.	junior

Kais.	kaiserlih, -e, imperial
khud.	khudozhnik, artist
khudozh.	khudozhestvennaia, khudo-
	zhestvennoi, khudozhestvennyi,
	artistic
	khudozhestvennoe proizvedenie,
	work of art
khudozh. lit-ra, khudozh. lit-ry,
	khudozhestvennaia literatura,
	khudozhestvennoi literatury,
	belle-lettres, of belles-
	lettres
Kl. Litauen	Klein Litauen, Lithua-
	nia Minor
KLHMMTI	Kaunas.	Lietuvos hidrotech-
	nikos ir melioracijos mokslinio
	tyrimo institutas
KLTSRVRB	Kaunas.	Lietuvos TSR Vals-
	tybinė respublikinė biblioteka
KLVA	Kaunas.	Lietuvos Veterinarijos
	akademija
KLVKKI	Kaunas.	Lietuvos Valstybi-
	nis kūno kultūros institutas
KLZUA	Kaunas.	Lietuvos Žemės ūkio
	akademija
kn.	knyga, kniga, knyha, book, vo-
	lume
Korp.	Korporacija, fraternity
KPI	Kaunas.	Politechnikos institu-
	tas
KPID	Kaunas.	Politechnikos insti-
	tutas. Darbai
kpt.	kapitan, captain
król.	królewski, królewskiego,
	royal
Ks.	Książę, Księcia, Duke, Duke's
ks.	ksiądz, księdza, priest, priest's
Księg.	Księgarnia, Book store
KSIIMK	Akademiia nauk SSSR.	Insti-
	tut arkheologii.	Kratkie soob-
	shcheniia o dokladakh i pole-

vykh issledovaniakh Instituta
	istorii material'noi kul'tury
KUB	Kaunas.	Universitetas.	Biblio-
	teka
KUBS	Kaunas.	Universitetas.	Bota-
	nikos sodas
KUHMF	Kaunas.	Universitetas.	Hu-
	manitarinių mokslų fakultetas
KUHMFD	Kaunas.	Universitetas.	Hu-
	manitarinių mokslų fakultetas.
	Darbai
KUMeFD	Kaunas.	Universitetas.	Me-
	dicinos fakultetas.	Darbai
KUMGFD	Kaunas.	Universitetas.	Ma-
	tematikos-gamtos fakultetas.
	Darbai
Kun.	Kunigas, priest, reverend
KUTF	Kaunas.	Universitetas.	Tei-
	sių fakultetas
KUTFD	Kaunas.	Universitetas.	Tei-
	sių fakultetas.	Darbai
KUTFF	Kaunas.	Universitetas.	Teo-
	logijos-filosofijos fakultetas
KUTFFD	Kaunas.	Universitetas.	Teo-
	logijos-filosofijos fakultetas.
	Darbai
KVČDM	Kaunas.	Valstybinis M.K.
	Čiurlionio vardo dailės muzie-
	jus
KVDKM	Kaunas.	Vytauto Didžiojo kul-
	tūros muziejus
KVDKMČG	Kaunas.	Vytauto Didžiojo
	kultūros muziejus.	M.K. Čiur-
	lionies galerija
KVDKMES	Kaunas.	Vytauto Didžiojo
	kultūros muziejus.	Etnogra-
	fijos skyrius
kwiec.	kwiecień, April

l.	leaves
lapkr.	lapkritis, November
latv.	latviiskii, latviiskoi, Lat-
	vian
LCSB	Lithuania.	Centralinis sta-
	tistikos biuras
leid.	leidinys, publikation, issue
lip.	lipiec, July
listop.	listopad, November
litov.	litovskii, litovskaia, li-
	tovskoi, Lithuanian
lit-ra, lit-ry	literatura, litera-
	tury, literature, of litera-
	ture
L.K.M.	Lietuvių katalikų mokslo aka-
	demija, Lithuanian Catholic
	Academy of Sciences
LKMAM	Lietuvių katalikų mokslo aka-
	demija, Rome.	Metraštis
LKMASD	Lietuvių katalikų mokslo
	akademija.	Suvažiavimo darbai
LLGM	Litauische Literarische Ge-
	sellschaft, Tilsit.	Mittei-
	lungen
LLS	Lithuania.	Laws, statutes, etc.
LMP	Lithuania.	Ministras Pirmi-
	ninkas
LSM	Lithuania.	Švietimo ministerija
LSMKLK	Lithuania.	Švietimo minis-
	terija.	Knygų leidimo komisija

L.S.D.P. Lietuvos Socialdemokratų
    Partija
LTSR Lietuvos Tarybų Socialistinė
    Respublika
LTSRAMMD Lietuvos TSR Aukštųjų mo-
    kyklų mokslo darbai
LTSRKR Lietuvos TSR Knygų rūmai
LTSRMA Lietuvos TSR Mokslų akadem
    ja, Vilna
LTSRMAAD Lietuvos TSR Mokslų aka-
    demija, Vilna. Archyviniams
    dokumentams skelbti redak-
    cija
LTSRMABiID Lietuvos TSR Mokslų aka-
    demija, Vilna. Biologijos ins-
    titutas
LTSRMABI Lietuvos TSR Mokslų akade-
    mija, Vilna. Botanikos insti-
    tutas
LTSRMACB Lietuvos TSR Mokslų aka-
    demija, Vilna. Centrinė bib-
    lioteka
LTSRMACBBB Lietuvos TSR Mokslų aka-
    demija, Vilna. Centrinė biblio-
    teka. Bibliotekininkystė ir
    bibliografija
LTSRMAD Lietuvos TSR Mokslų akade-
    mija, Vilna. Darbai
LTSRMAEI Lietuvos TSR Mokslų aka-
    demija, Vilna. Ekonomikos
    institutas
LTSRMAEID Lietuvos TSR Mokslų aka-
    demija, Vilna. Ekonomikos
    institutas. Darbai
LTSRMAGGI Lietuvos TSR Mokslų aka-
    demija, Vilna. Geologijos ir
    geografijos institutas
LTSRMAGGICPXIX Lietuvos TSR Mokslų
    akademija, Vilna. Geologijos
    ir geografijos institutas.
    Collected papers for the XIX In-
    ternational Geographical Con-
    gress
LTSRMAGGICPXXI Lietuvos TSR Mokslų
    akademija, Vilna. Geologijos
    ir geografijos institutas. Col-
    lected papers for the XXI ses-
    sion of the International Geo-
    logical Congress
LTSRMAGGIMP Lietuvos TSR Mokslų
    akademija, Vilna. Geologijos
    ir geografijos institutas.
    Moksliniai pranešimai
LTSRMAII Lietuvos TSR Mokslų aka-
    demija, Vilna. Istorijos in-
    stitutas
LTSRMAIID Lietuvos TSR Mokslų aka-
    demija, Vilna. Istorijos ins-
    titutas. Darbai
LTSRMAIILKI Lietuvos TSR Mokslų
    akademija, Vilna. Istorijos
    institutas. Iš lietuvių kul-
    tūros istorijos
LTSRMALKLI Lietuvos TSR Mokslų aka-
    demija, Vilna. Lietuvių kalbos
    ir literatūros institutas
LTSRPAD Lietuvos TSR Paminklų ap-
    saugos ir kraštotyros drau-
    gija

m. miasto, miasta, city, city's
    town, town's
m. metai, year, years, annual pub-
    lication
mar. marzec, March
Min. Ministerstwo, ministerstvo,
    Department, ministry
Min. Obr. Nar. Ministerstwo Obrony
    Narodowej, Department of De-
    fense
muz. muzika, muzikos, music

Nakł. Nakład, edition, impression
narod. narodowa, narodowej,
Nar. narodowa, narodowej, state,
    national
nauch. nauchnyi, nauchnoi, scienti-
    fic
nauch.-tekh. nauchno-tekhnicheskoe,
    -oi, scientific technical
Nauczyciel. Nauczycielstwa, Tea-
    chers'
n.d. no date of publication
nd. nauja dalis, new series
n.F., N.F., NF., neue Folge, new
    series
no. numero, number, -s
nouv. nouveau, nouvelle, new
n.p. no publisher, no place
Nr. Nummer, number
nr. nummer, numeris, number
n.s., ns new series
ns. nouvelle serie
numb. numbered
N.Y. New York
N.T. New Testament

Obr. Obrony, obrona, defense
obrabot. obrabotana, edited,
    compiled
obshch. obshchii, common, general
Okr. Szk. Okręg Szkolny, School
    District
okt. oktiabr', October
oprac. opracował, edited
orig. original
otd-nie otdelenie, Division, Branch
    Section
O.T. Old Testament
otv. red. otvetstvennyi redaktor,
    editor-in-chief

p. page, -s
part. col. partly coloured
pazdz. pazdziernik, October
Pa. Pennsylvania
per. perevod, translation
perer. pererabotana, -yi, revised
philos.-histor. Classe philosophisch-
    historische Classe, philosophy
    and history section
pirm. pirmininkas, chairman
Pol. Polska, Poland
polit. politicheskii, politicheskoi,
    political

polsk. polskiego, Polish
port., ports, portrait, -s
Pow. Powiat, Powiatów, County
Pr. Preussen, Prussia
prov. proverennyi, proverennoe,
  revised, corrected.
przeł. przelozył, translated by
pt. part
pts parts
PZHP Powszechny Zjazd Historyków
  Polskich

r. rok, year
red. redagowany, redakcja, redak-
  tsiia, redaktsiei, edited,
  editorial office
red. redaktorius, redaktor, editor
Reg. Rath. Regierungsrat, Councilor
  to the Government
rev. revised
rhein. rheinisch, -e, -en, Rhine
rhein. Fuss rheinisch Fuss, Rhine
  foot (measure)
rugp. rugpiūtis, August
rugs. rugsėjis, September

s. seria, series
sąs. sąsiuvinys, fascicle, part,
  issue, number
saus. sausis, January
SDPiL Socjaldemokracja Królewstwa
  Polskiego i Litwy
sent. sentiabr', September
ser. serija, series
sér. série, series
ser. series
śierp. śierpień, August
Skł. Skład, Publisher, Publishing
  house
sobr. sobranie, collection
sobr. sochinenii sobranie sochinenii, Collected works
Soed. Shtat. Siev. Ameriki Soed-
  nionnye Shtaty Sievernoi Ameriki, v Soednionnykh Shtatakh Sievernoi Ameriki, United States
  of North America
sots. sotsialisticheskaia, -oi, socialist
sots.-ekon. sotsial'no-ekonomiches-
  koi, -kogo, social economic
sov. sovetskaia, -oi, Soviet
sp. spauda, spaustuvė, publishing,
  printing firm
sp. sk. spaudos skyrius, Publishing
  section
Społdz. Społdzielnica, Cooperative
specred. specialusis redaktorius,
  special editor
St. Saint
st. stat'ia, article
Stow., Stowarz. Stowarzyszenie,
  Stowarzyszenia, Association
Stowarz. Nauczyciel. Polskiego Stowarzyszenie Nauczycielstwa Polskiego, Polish Teachers' Association

stycz. styczen, January
Sv.-Dukh. Sviatogo Dukha, Holu Spi-
  rit, Holy Ghost
Sw. Swiety, swietego, Saint, of the
  Saint

T., Th., Teil, Theil, part
T., t. tom, tomas̄, tome, volume
tip. tipografiia, tipografia, printing firm
tłumacz. tłumaczyl, translated by
Tow. Towarzystwo, Association
t.p. title page
t.p. tak potem, and so forth
tr. translated, translator
t-va, t-vo tovarichestva, tovarichestvo, Association, Society
tzw. tak zwany, -a, -e, -i, so
  called

u. und, and
u,A. und Andere, and others
übers. übersetzt, translated
Übers. Übersetzer, translator
ucheb.-pedagog. uchebno-pedagogi-
  cheskoe, teaching
umgearb. umgearbeitet, revised
unacc. unaccounted
univ. universitetskaia, universitet,
  University, University's
unver., unverand. unverandert,
  unchanged, unaltered
utg. utgiven, edited
utg. utgave, edition
uzup. uzupelnione, enlarged

v., vol. volume, -s
vas. vasaris, February
verm. vermehrte, enlarged
verb. verbessert, improved, revised
VEZMLL Valstybinė enciklopedijų,
  žodynų ir mokslo literatūros
  leidykla
VGLL Valstybinė grožinės literatūros leidykla
Vilen. Vilenskago, Vilenskogo,
  of Vilnius
voen. voennyi, voennoe, voennoi,
  military
VPMLL Valstybinė politinės ir mokslinės literatūros leidykla
V.R.M. Vidaus Reikalų Ministerija,
  Department of Interior
vstup. vstupitel'nyi, introductory
vstup. stat'ia vstupitel'naia
  stat'ia, introduction, indro-
  ductory article
Vyp., vyp. vypusk, issue, number,
  part, fascicle, edition
Vyr. redaktorius Vyriausias redaktorius, Editor-in-chief
VPSh. Vyschaia Partiinaia Shkola,
  University of the Communist
  Party

VUBMBM Vilna. Universitetas. Bib-
     lioteka. Mokslinės bibliotekos
     metraštis
VUMD Vilna. Universitetas. Mokslo
     darbai

wrzes. wrzesien, September
wyd. wydał, wydanie, edited,edi-
     tion
wydawn. wydawnictwo, publishing
     house

X. Książę, Księstwo, Duke, Duchy
XX Księży, Księże, priests'
     priests

yr year

zesz. zeszyt, fascicle, part
ZMNP Zhurnal ministerstva narodna-
     go prosveshcheniia (Russia,
     Ministerstvo narodnogo pro-
     sveshcheniia. Zhurnal)

LIST OF SYMBOLS FOR CANADIAN
AND AMERICAN LIBRARIES

CANADIAN LIBRARIES

ALBERTA

CaACU University of Calgary
CaAE   Edmonton Public Library
CaAEU University of Alberta,
       Edmonton

BRITISH COLUMBIA

CaBVa   Vancouver Public Library
CaBVaS Simon Fraser University,
        Vancouver
CaBVaU University of British
        Columbia, Vancouver
CaBVi   Victoria Public Library
CaBViP Provincial Library, Victoria

MANITOBA

CaMW   Winnipeg Public Library
CaMWU University of Manitoba,
       Winnipeg

NEW BRUNSWICK

CaNBFU University of New Brunswick,
        Fredericton

NOVA SCOTIA

CaNSHD Dalhousie University, Halifax

ONTARIO

CaOG Guelph Public Library
CaOH Hamilton Public Library

CaOHM McMaster University, Hamilton
CaOKF Canadian Army Staff College,
       Kingston
CaOKQ Queen's University, Kingston
CaOKQL --- Law Library
CaOL   London Public Library
CaOLU University of Western
       Ontario, London
CaOLUM --- Medical Library
CaOOAg Department of Agriculture,
       Main Library, Ottawa
CaOOG Geological Survey of Canada,
       Ottawa
CaOOGB Water Sector Library, Depart-
       ment of Energy, Mines and
       Resources, Ottawa
CaOON National Science Library,
       National Research Council,
       Ottawa (Formerly National
       Research Council)
CaOOND Department of National De-
       fence, Departmental Libra-
       ry, Ottawa
CaOONL National Library of Canada,
       Ottawa
CaOONM National Museum of Canada,
       Ottawa
CaOOP Library of Parliament,
       Ottawa
CaOOSC Supreme Court of Canada,
       Ottawa
CaOOU University of Ottawa
CaOTP Toronto Public Library, Me-
       tropolitan Bibliographic
       Centre
CaOTR Ryerson Institute, Toronto
CaOTU University of Toronto
CaOTY York University, Toronto
CaOWA University of Windsor
CaOWtU University of Waterloo
CaWtU Obsolete. See CaOWtU

QUEBEC

CaQMAI	Arctic Institute of North America, Montreal
CaQMM	McGill University, Montreal
CaQMU	Université de Montreal

SASKATCHEWAN

CaSRU	University of Saskatchewan, Saskatoon. Regina Campus
CaSSU	University of Saskatchewan, Saskatoon

UNITED STATES LIBRARIES

ALABAMA

AAP	Auburn University, Auburn
AMAU	Air University, Maxwell Air Force Base, Montgomery
AU	University of Alabama, University

ARIZONA

AzTeS	Arizona State University, Tempe
AzU	University of Arizona, Tucson

CALIFORNIA

C	California State Library, Sacramento
CBPac	Pacific School of Religion, Berkeley
CL	Los Angeles Public Library
CLL	Los Angeles County Law Library, Los Angeles
CLS	California State College at Los Angeles
CLSU	University of Southern California, Los Angeles
CLSU-H	---Hancock Library of Biology and Oceanography
CLU	University of California, Los Angeles
CMthL	University of California, Lick Observatory, Santa Cruz
CPT	California Institute of Technology, Pasadena
CS	Sacramento City-County Library
CSaT	San Francisco Theological Seminary, San Anselmo
CSd	San Diego Public Library
CSf	San Francisco Public Library
CSfA	California Academy of Sciences, San Francisco
CSmH	Henry E. Huntington Library, San Marino
CSt	Stanford University, Palo Alto

CSt-H	---Hoover Institution on War, Revolution and Peace
CSt-Law	---Law Library
CStoC	University of the Pacific, Stockton
CU	University of California, Berkeley
CU-A	University of California, Davis
CU-I	University of California, Irvine
CU-M	University of California Medical Center, San Francisco
CU-Riv	University of California, Riverside
CU-S	University of California, San Diego

COLORADO

Co	Colorado State Library, Denver
CoAT	Obsolete. See CoAlC
CoAlC	Adams State College, Alamosa
CoCC	Colorado College, Colorado Springs
CoD	Denver Public Library
CoDGS	U.S. Geological Survey, Federal Center, Denver
CoDM	Medical Society of the City and County of Denver
CoDPS	Denver Public Schools, Professional Library
CoDU	University of Denver
CoFS	Colorado State University, Fort Collins
CoFcS	ULS symbol for CoFS
CoGrS	Colorado State College, Greeley
CoU	University of Colorado, Boulder

CONNECTICUT

CtH	Hartford Public Library
CtHC	Hartford Seminary Foundation, Hartford
CtHT	Trinity College, Hartford
CtHW	ULS symbol for CtHT-W
CtPAM	ALKA Museum, Putnam, Conn.
CtPI	Immaculate Conception Convent, Putnam, Conn.
CtTMF	Marian Fathers, Thompson, Conn.
CtU	University of Connecticut, Storrs
CtW	Wesleyan University, Middletown
CtY	Yale University, New Haven
CtY-AO	---American Oriental Society Library. (Obsolete See CtY)
CtY-D	---Divinity School
CtY-L	---Law Library
CtY-M	---Medical School
CtY-OS	---Obsolete. See CtY

DISTRICT OF COLUMBIA
WASHINGTON, D. C.

DA	Obsolete. See DNAL
DAFM	Obsolete. See DNLM
DAL	U.S. Army Library, Pentagon Building
DAS	U.S. Environmental Sciences Services Administration, Atmospheric Sciences Library, Silver Spring
DAU	American University
DBB	U.S. Bureau of the Budget
DCE	Obsolete. See DSI
DCU	Catholic University of America
DCU-H	---Hyvernat Collection
DCaE	Canadian Embassy
DD	ULS symbol for DDC
DDC	Dominican House of Studies, Immaculate Conception Convent
DDO	Dumbarton Oaks Research Library of Harvard University
DF	Obsolete. See DI
DGL	ULS symbol for DCI-G
DGS	Obsolete. See DI-GS
DHEW	U.S. Department of Health, Education and Welfare
DI	U.S. Department of the Interior Library
DI-GS	---Geological Survey Library
DL	U.S. Department of Labor.
DLC	U.S. Library of Congress
DLC-L	---Law Library
DLC-P4	---Priority 4 Collection
DLL	Lithuanian Legation, Washington, D.C.
DN	U.S. Department of the Navy
DNAL	U.S. National Agricultural Library
DNLM	U.S. National Library of Medicine
DNW	U.S. National War College, Fort McNair
DS	U.S. Department of State Library (Division of Library and Reference Services
DSG	Obsolete. See DNLM
DSG	ULS symbol for DNLM
DSI	Smithsonian Institution
DSI-E	Bureau of American Ethnology Library. Obsolete See DSI
DSI-M	Obsolete. See DSI
DT	U.S. Department of the Treasury
DW	Obsolete. See DNW
DWB	Obsolete. See DAS

DELAWARE

DeU	University of Delaware, Newark

FLORIDA

FMU	University of Miami, Coral Gables
FTS	University of South Florida, Tampa
FTS	ULS symbol of FTaSU
FTaSU	Florida State University, Tallahassee
FU	University of Florida, Gainesville

GEORGIA

GA	Atlanta Public Library
GEU	Emory University, Atlanta
GU	University of Georgia, Athens

HAWAII

HH	Hawaii State Library System, Honolulu
HU	University of Hawaii, Honolulu

ILLINOIS

IC	Chicago Public Library
ICA	Art Institute of Chicago
ICAC	American College of Surgeons, Chicago
ICBM	Balzekas Museum of Lithuanian Culture, Chicago
ICCC	St. Casimir Convent, 2601 West Marquette Road, Chicago
ICD	DePaul University, Chicago
ICF	Chicago Natural History Museum, Chicago
ICHi	Chicago Historical Society
ICI	Illinois Institute of Technology, Chicago
ICIU	University of Illinois at Chicago Circle, Chicago
ICJ	John Crerar Library, Chicago
ICLJF	Lithuanian Jesuit Fathers, Chicago
ICLLM	Library of Lithuanian Musicology, Chicago
ICM	Obsolete. See ICMe
ICMILC	Midwest Inter-Library Center, Chicago. (Obsolete. See ICRL)
ICMcC	McCormick Theological Seminary, Chicago
ICMe	Meadville Theological School, Chicago
ICN	Newberry Library, Chicago
ICP	Obsolete. See ICMcC
ICR	ULS symbol for ICA
ICRL	Center for Research Libraries, Chicago, (Formerly Midwest Inter-Library Center)
ICS	ULS symbol for ICAC
ICT	Chicago Theological Seminary, Chicago

ICU	University of Chicago
IEG	Garrett Theological Seminary, Evanston
IEN	Northwestern University, Evanston
IEN-L	---Law Library, Chicago
IMS	ULS symbol for IMunS
IMunS	Saint Mary of the Lake Seminary, Mundelein
IU	University of Illinois, Urbana

IOWA

IaAS	Iowa State University of Science and Technology, Ames
IaCfT	University of Northern Iowa, Cedar Rapids
IaU	University of Iowa, Iowa City

IDAHO

IdB	Boise Public Library
IdPI	Idaho State University, Pocatello
IdPS	Obsolete. See IdPI
IdU	University of Idaho, Moscow

INDIANA

In	Indiana State Library, Indianapolis
InLP	Purdue University, Lafayette
InNU	ULS symbol for InNd
InNd	University of Notre Dame, Notre Dame
InU	Indiana University, Bloomington
InU-L	---Law Library
InU-A	---Archives of Traditional Music

KANSAS

KAS	Saint Benedict's College, Atchison
KMK	Kansas State University, Manhattan
KPT	Kansas State College of Pittsburg
KT	Topeka Public Library
KU	University of Kansas, Lawrence
KU-M	---School of Medicine, Kansas City

KENTUCKY

KyLo	Louisville Free Public Library
KyLx	Lexington Public Library
KyMdC	Midway Junior College and Pinkerton High School, Midway

KyU	University of Kentucky, Lexington
KyU-N	---Northern Center, Covington

LOUISIANA

L	Louisiana State Library, Baton Rouge
LNHT	Tulane University, New Orleans
LU	Louisiana State University, Baton Rouge
LU-L	---Law Library

MASSACHUSETTS

MA	Amherst College, Amherst
MB	Boston Public Library
MBA	American Academy of the Arts and Sciences, Boston
MBAt	Boston Atheneum
MBC	American Congregational Association, Boston
MBCo	Countway Library of Medicine (Harvard-Boston Medical Libraries), Boston
MBM	Obsolete. See MBCo
MBN	Boston Museum of Science
MBU	Boston University
MBdAF	U.S. Air Force Cambridge Research Center, Bedford
MBrigStJ	Obsolete. See MBtS
MBtS	Saint John's Seminary, Brighton
MCM	Massachusetts Institute of Technology, Cambridge
MH	Harvard University, Cambridge
MH-A	---Arnold Arboretum
MH-AH	---Andover-Harvard Theological Library
MH-BA	---Graduate School of Business Administration
MH-BH	---Blue Hill Observatory
MH-G	---Gray Herbarium
MH-I	---Isham Library of Early Instrumental Music
MH-L	---Law School
MH-M	---Obsolete. See MBCo
MH-O	---Astronomical Observatory, Phillips Library
MH-P	---Peabody Museum
MH-PA	---Graduate School of Public Administration
MH-Z	---Museum of Comparative Zoology
MMeT-F	Tufts University, Medford. Fletcher School of Law and Diplomacy
MNS	Smith College, Northampton
MShM	Mount Holyoke College, South Hadley
MU	University of Massachusetts, Amherst
MWA	American Antiquarian Society, Worcester
MWC	Clark University, Worcester
MWalB	Brandeis University Waltham

MWelC   Wellesley College, Wellesley
MWhB   Marine Biological Labora-
         tory, Wodds Hole
MWiW   Williams College, Williams-
         town

MARYLAND

MdBE   Enoch Pratt Free Library,
         Baltimore
MdBJ   Johns Hopkins University,
         Baltimore
MdBJ-W   ---William H. Welch Me-
         dical Library
MdBP   Peabody Institute, Baltimore
MdBT   Towson State College, Balti-
         more
MdBU   University of Baltimore
MdBW   ULS symbol for MdBJ-W
MdU   University of Maryland,
         College Park

MAINE

MeB   Bowdoin College, Brunswick
MeKPF   Franciscan Fathers, Kenne-
         bunkport
MeWC   Colby College, Waterville

MICHIGAN

Mi   Michigan State Library,
         Lansing
MiD   Detroit Public Library
MiD-A   Obsolete. See MiDA
MiD-B   Detroit Public Library. Bur-
         ton Historical Collection
MiDA   Detroit Institute of Arts
MiDU   University of Detroit
MiDW   Wayne State University,
         Detroit
MiEM   Michigan State University,
         East Lansing
MiHM   Michigan Technological Uni-
         versity, Houghton
MiU   University of Michigan, Ann
         Arbor
MiU-A   ---Asia Library
MiU-L   ---Law Library
MiU-G   ---Bureau of Government Li-
         brary. See MiU

MINNESOTA

MnCS   Saint John's University,
         Collegeville
MnHi   Minnesota Historical So-
         ciety, Saint Paul
MnRM   Mayo Clinic and Foundation,
         Rochester
MnU   University of Minnesota,
         Minneapolis
MnU-L   ---Law Library

MISSOURI

MoK   Kansas City Public Library
MoKL   Linda Hall Library, Kansas
         City
MoS   Saint Louis Public Library
MoSA   Obsolete. See MoSU
MoSB   Missouri Botanical Garden,
         Saint Louis
MoSM   Mercantile Library Associ-
         ation, Saint Louis
MoSU   Saint Louis University,
         Saint Louis
MoSW   Washington University, Saint
         Louis
MoU   University of Missouri,
         Columbia

MISSISSIPPI

MsSM   Mississippi State Universi-
         ty, State College
MsU   University of Mississippi,
         University

MONTANA

MtBC   Montana State University at
         Bozeman
MtBuM   Montant College of Mineral
         Science and Technology,
         Butte
MtU   University of Montana at
         Missoula

NEW YORK

N   New York State Library,
         Albany
NB   Brooklyn Public Library
NBC   Brooklyn College, Brooklyn
NBG   Brooklyn Botanic Garden
NBM   Medical Research Library
         of Brooklyn
NBu   Buffalo and Erie County Pub-
         lic Library, Buffalo
NBuB   Buffalo Society of Natural
         Sciences, Buffalo Museum
         of Science
NBuC   State University of New York
         College at Buffalo
NBuG   Grosvenor Reference Division
         Buffalo and Erie County
         Public Library, Buffalo
NBuU   State University of New York
         at Buffalo
NBuU-L   ---Law Library
NCH   Hamilton College, Clinton
NFQC   Queens College, Flushing
NGrnUN   Obsolete. See NNUN
NHC   Colgate University, Hamilton
NHi   New York Historical Society,
         New York
NIC   Cornell University, Ithaca
NIC-A   ---Obsolete. See NIC
NJQ   Queens Borough Public Li-
         brary, Jamaica
NN   New York Public Library

NNA	American Geographical Society, New York	NbU	University of Nebraska, Lincoln
NNAHI	Augustinian Historical Institute, New York		
NNAN	American Numismatic Society, New York		**NORTH CAROLINA**
NNB	Association of the Bar of the City of New York	NcC	Public Library of Charlotte & Mecklenburg County, Charlotte
NNC	Columbia University, New York	NcD	Duke University, Durham
NNC-L	---Law Library	NcD-L	---School of Law
NNC-T	---Teachers College	NcGU	University of North Carolina at Greensboro
NNCFR	Council on Foreign Relations, New York	NcGW	Obsolete. See NcGU
NNCL	Consulate General of Lithuania, New York	NcRS	North Carolina State University at Raleigh
NNE	Engineering Societies Library, New York	NcU	University of North Carolina, Chapel Hill
NNF	Fordham University, New York		
NNG	General Theological Seminary of the Protestant Episcopal Church, New York		**NORTH DAKOTA**
NNHi	ULS symbol for NHi	NdFA	North Dakota State University, Fargo
NNJ	Jewish Theological Seminary of America, New York	NdU	University of North Dakota, Grand Forks
NNM	American Museum of Natural History, New York		
NNMM	Metropolitan Museum of Art, New York		**NEW HAMPSHIRE**
NNN	ULS symbol for NNNAM	NhD	Dartmouth College, Hanover
NNNAM	New York Academy of Medicine	NhU	University of New Hampshire, Durham
NNQ	Obsolete. See NJQ		
NNRI	Obsolete. See NNRU		
NNRU	Rockefeller University, New York		
NNU	New York University Libraries, New York		**NEW JERSEY**
NNU-H	---University Heights Library	NjP	Princeton University, Princeton
NNU-W	---Washington Square Library	NjPT	Princeton Theological Seminary, Princeton
NNUH	United Hospital Fund of New York, Reference Library, New York	NjR	Rutgers-The State University, New Brunswick
NNUN	United Nations, New York		
NNUN-W	---Woodrow Wilson Memorial Library		**NEW MEXICO**
NNUT	Union Theological Seminary, New York	NmU	University of New Mexico, Albuquerque
NPV	Vassar College, Poughkeepsie		
NR	Rochester Public Library		
NRCR	Colgate-Rochester Divinity School, Rochester		**NEVADA**
NRU	University of Rochester	NvU	University of Nevada, Reno
NSU	ULS symbol for NSyU		
NStBU	Saint Bonaventure University, Saint Bonaventure		
NStC	Obsolete. See NStBU		**OHIO**
NSyU	Syracuse University, Syracuse		
NWM	U.S. Military Academy, West Point	OC	Public Library of Cincinnati and Hamilton County, Cincinnati
NYBT	Boyce Thompson Institute for Plant Research, Yonkers	OCH	Hebrew Union College, Jewish Institute of Religion, Cincinnati
		OCL	ULS symbol for OCLloyd
	NEBRASKA	OCLloyd	Lloyd Library and Museum, Cincinnati
NbHi	Nebraska State Historical Society, Lincoln	OCU	University of Cincinnati
NbOU	University of Nebraska at Omaha	OCX	Xavier University, Cincinnati
		OCl	Cleveland Public Library

OClCS	Obsolete. See OClW
OClMA	Cleveland Museum of Art
OClND	Notre Dame College, Cleveland
OClW	Case Western Reserve University, Cleveland
OCoB	Battelle Memorial Institute, Columbus
ODW	Ohio Wesleyan University, Delaware
OEac	East Cleveland Public Uni-Library
OKentU	Kent State University, Kent
OLak	Lakewood Public Library
OO	Oberlin College, Oberlin
OOxM	Miami University, Oxford
OU	Ohio State University, Columbus
OYesA	Antioch College, Yellow Springs

OKLAHOMA

OkS	Oklahoma State University, Stillwater
OkU	University of Oklahoma, Norman

OREGON

Or	Oregon State Library, Salem
OrAshS	Southern Oregon College, Ashland
OrCA	Obsolete. See OrCS
OrCS	Oregon State University, Corvallis
OrMonO	Oregon College of Education, Monmouth
OrP	Library Association of Portland
OrPR	Reed College, Portland
OrPS	Portland State College, Portland
OrSaW	Williamette University, Salem
OrStbM	Mount Angel College, Saint Benedict
OrU	University of Oregon, Eugene
OrU-L	---Law Library

PENNSYLVANIA

PAtM	Muhlenberg College, Allentown
PBL	Lehigh University, Bethlehem
PBm	Bryn Mawr College, Bryn Mawr
PCamA	Alliance College, Cambridge Springs
PEL	Lafayette College, Easton
PHC	Haverford College, Haverford
PKsL	Longwood Gardens Library, Kennett Square
PNortHi	Historical Society of Montgomery County, Norristown
PP	Free Library of Philadelphia
PPA	Athenaeum of Philadelphia
PPAN	Academy of Natural Sciences, Philadelphia

PPAP	Obsolete. See PPAmP
PPAmP	American Philosophical Society, Philadelphia
PPC	College of Physicians of Philadelphia
PPCCH	Chestnut Hill College, Philadelphia
PPCI	Curtis Institute of Music Philadelphia
PPD	Drexel Institute of Technology, Philadelphia
PPDrop	Dropsie College for Hebrew and Cognate Learning, Philadelphia
PPE	Obsolete. See PPPL
PPF	Franklin Institute, Philadelphia
PPFr	Friends' Free Library of Germantown, Philadelphia
PPG	German Society of Pennsylvania, Philadelphia
PPGi	Girard College, Philadelphia
PPL	Library Company of Philadelphia
PPLT	Luthern Theological Seminary, Krauth Memorial Library, Philadelphia
PPLas	LaSalle College, Philadelphia
PPM	Mercantile Library, Philadelphia (No longer in existence)
PPPD	Philadelphia Divinity School (Formerly Divinity School of the Protestant Episcopal Church)
PPPL	Philadelphia Board of Public Education, Pedagogical Library
PPPM	Philadelphia Museum of Art
PPPlay	Plays and Players Club, Philadelphia
PPT	Temple University, Philadelphia
PPTU	Obsolete. See PPT
PPULC	Union Library Catalogue of Pennsylvania, Philadelphia
PPWILP	Women's International League for Peace and Freedom. Friends Historical Library, Swarthmore College, Swarthmore
PPWa	Wagner Free Institute of Science, Philadelphia
PPWe	Westminster Theological Seminary, Philadelphia
PPeSchw	Schwenckfelder Historical Library, Pennsburg
PPi	Carnegie Library of Pittsburgh
PPiU	University of Pittsburgh
PR	Reading Public Library
PSC	Swarthmore College, Swarthmore
PSc	Scranton Public Library
PSt	Pennsylvania State University, University Park
PU	University of Pennsylvania, Philadelphia
PU-FA	---School of Fine Arts

PU-L ---Biddle Law Library
PU-MU ---University Museum
PU-Penn ---Penniman Library of
Education
PU-W ---Wharton School of Finance and Commerce
PV Villanova University, Villanova
PWcT Obsolete. See PWcS

RHODE ISLAND

RP Providence Public Library
RPB Brown University, Providence

SOUTH CAROLINA

ScU University of South Carolina, Columbia

SOUTH DAKOTA

SdU University of South Dakota, Vermillion

TENNESSEE

TMG Goodwyn Institute, Memphis
TNF Fisk University, Nashville
TNJ Joint University Libraries, Nashville
TNJ-M ---Vanderbilt School of Medicine and Nursing
TNV Obsolete. See TNJ
TNV-M Obsolete. See TNJ-M
TONS Obsolete. See TOU
TOU Oak Ridge Associated Universities, Oak Ridge
TU University of Tennessee, Knoxville

TEXAS

TxDaM Southern Methodist University, Dallas
TxHMC Houston Academy of Medicine
TxHR Rice University, Houston
TxHU University of Houston
TxLT Texas Technological College, Lubbock
TxU University of Texas, Austin

UTAH

ULA Utah State University, Logan
UPB Brigham Young University, Provo
UU University of Utah, Salt Lake City

VIRGINIA

VHS ULS symbol for ViHdsC
VRT Obsolete. See ViRUT
VU Obsolete. See ViU
ViHdsC Hampden-Sydney College, Hampden-Sydney
ViRUT Union Theological Seminary, Richmond
ViU University of Virginia, Charlottesville
ViU-L ---Law Library

VERMONT

VtU University of Vermont and State Agricultural College, Burlington

WISCONSIN

WHi State Historical Society of Wisconsin, Madison
WM Milwaukee Public Library
WMM Marquette University, Milwaukee
WMUW University of Wisconsin, Kenwood Campus, Milwaukee
WU University of Wisconsin, Madison

WASHINGTON

Wa Washington State Library, Olympia
WaE Everett Public Library
WaPS Washington State University, Pullam
WaS Seattle Public Library
WaSp Spokane Public Library
WaSpG Gonzaga University, Spokane
WaT Tacoma Public Library
WaTC University of Puget Sound, Tacoma
WaU University of Washington, Seattle
WaU-L ---Law Library
WaWW Whitman College, Walla Walla

WEST VIRGINIA

WvU West Virginia University, Morgantown

WYOMING

WyU University of Wyoming, Laramie

LIBRARIES IN OTHER COUNTRIES

BM British Museum Library, London, W.C.1., England

BN Bibliotheque National, Paris, France

Fr.NaU Université de Nancy, Nancy, France

Fr.TEV École Veterinaire, Toulouse, France

Ger.BU Universitäts-Bibliothek, Bonn, Germany

Ger.HoLI Landwirtschaftliches Institut, Hohenheim, Germany

Ger.JeU Universitäts-Bibliothek, Jena, Germany

Ger.KIW Institut für Weltwirtschaf, Kiel, Germany

Ger.LU Universitäts-Bibliothek, Leipzig, Germany

Ger.TU Universitäts-Bibliothek, Tübingen, Germany

LSC Science Library, Science Museum, London, England

BIBLIOGRAPHY

I. BIBLIOGRAPHIC AIDS

I.1. GENERAL BIBLIOGRAPHIES

1. ANGRABAITIS, Juozas. Suskaita arba statistika visų lietuviszkų knygų atsaustų [sic] Prusuose nuo 1864 metų iki pabaigai 1896 metų. [Statistics on all Lithuanian books printed in Prussia from 1864 to the end of 1896] Suraszė A. Jonas Zanavikutis. Tilžė, 1897. 55 p. Bound with Zauniutė, Marta. Priedas prie statistikos lietuviškų knygų. Plymouth, Pa., 1900; and Žilius, Jonas. Suskaita arba statistika visų lietuviškų knygų, atspaustų Amerikoje. Plymouth, Pa., 1900. Collective cover title for the three works: Statistika lietuviškų knygų spaustų užsieniuose... nuo 1864 iki 1900 metų. Z2514.L4Z2 DLC PU PPULC

2. BALTISCHE STAATEN UND FINLAND; eine Bibliographie. Leipzig, 1936-40. 4 v. in 3. Irregular. Published with the cooperation of the Institut für osteuropäische Wirtschaft der Universität Königsberg and the Wirtschaftsinstitut für Russland und die Oststaaten. Title varies: 1936-Mar. 1937, Memelgebiet und Baltische Staaten; Aug.1937-1939, Memelgebiet (Ostpr.), Baltische Staaten und Finnland. Vol. 1-4 include citations of publications from 1931. Z2531. B3 DLC ICU(1) NN

3. DIE BALTISCHEN LÄNDER UND DER Ostseeraum. [Hannover] Gesellschaft zur Förderung der west-östlichen Begegnung in Europa, 1964. In Europäische Begegnung; Beiträge zum west-östlichen Geschpräch (Hannover), Sept.1964, Hft.9. 947.4.B216 PU

4. BALTRAMAITIS, Silvestras. Bibliograficheskii obzor litovskich povremennykh izdanii za 1898 god. In Zhivaia starina (Sanktpeterburg), v.8, no. 3-4, 1898, p. 477-479. See serials consulted.

5. --- Sbornik bibliograficheskikh materialov dlia geografii, etnografii i statistiki Litvy. S prilozheniem spiska litovskikh i drevne-prusskikh knig s 1553 [sic] po 1891 g. Sanktpeterburg, Tip. V. Bezobrazova i Komp., 1891-92. viii, 289, 96 p. Includes: Spisok litovskikh i drevne-prusskikh knig. Slav 6295.4 MH

Z2537.B218 DLC ICLJF NN PU

6. --- Sbornik bibliograficheskikh materialov dlia geografii, istorii prava, statistiki i etnografii Litvy. S prilozheniem spiska litovskikh i drevne-prusskikh knig s 1553 [sic] po 1903 g. Izd. 2. Sanktpeterburg, Tip. V. Bezobrazova, 1904. xii, 616, 218 p. (Russkoe geograficheskoe obshchestvo. Zapiski po otdeleniiu etnografii, v.25, vyp.1) Z2537.B22 1904 DLC CaOTU ICJ ICN IU MH NN NcU NNC

7. --- Spisok litovskikh i drevne-prusskikh knig, izdannykh 1553 [sic] po 1891 god. Sanktpeterburg, Tip. V. Bezobrazova i Komp., 1892. 96 p. Bound with His Sbornik bibliograficheskikh materialov. Sanktpeterburg, 1891-92. Z2537.B218 DLC ICLJF MH NN PU

8. BALYS, Jonas. Lithuania and Lithuanians; a selected bibliography. New York, N.Y., Published for the Lithuanian Research Institute by F.A. Praeger [1961] x, 190 p. (Books that matter) Z2537.B3 DLC AzU CLU CU CSt-H CaAEU CaBVaU CaBVaS CaMWU CaOHM CaOTP CaOTU CaOTY CtPAM CaOWtU CtY CoU FU GU HU IC In InNd IdU ICU IEN LU MH MnU NIC NN NcD NbU NdFA NcU NSyU OC1 OkU PP PPi PU RPB ScU VtU WaU WU TxHU

9. --- The more important works on the Baltic States; a survey of the last ten years. In Lituanus (Brooklyn, N.Y.), v.8, no.4, 1962, p. 110-119. See serials consulted.

10. BEZZENBERGER, Adalbert. Zur litauischen Bibliographie. In Altpreussische Monatsschrift (Königsberg in Pr.), v.17, 1880, p. 195-208. See serials consulted.

11. BIBLIOGRAFIJA [A bibliography on Lithuania Minor] In Lithuanian Research Institute, New York. Mažoji Lietuva. New York, N.Y., 1958. p. 115-121, 145-149, 207-210, 252-255. DK511.L2L715 DLC CaAEU CaOTU CLU CtY NN NSyU

12. BIRŽIŠKA, Vaclovas. Aleksandrynas; senųjų lietuvių rašiusių prieš 1865 metus, biografijos, bibliografijos ir biobibliografijos [Aleksandrynas; biographies, bibliographies, and bio-bibliographies of old Lithuanian authors to 1865]

2

Chicago, Ill., Išleido JAV LB Kultūros fondas, 1960-65. 3 v. (Kultūros fondas. Leidinys, 8 [etc.]) At
head of title: Lituanistikos institutas. PG8703.B53 DLC CaAEU CaOONL
CaOTU CtTMF CtY ICBM ICLJF ICU MH
MnU NcD NjP PPiU PU WU WaU

13. --- Bibliografija, 1905-1909
[Bibliography, 1905-1909] Kaunas,
1935. 44 p. illus. Z1001.B53b CLU

14. --- Lietuvių bibliografija,
1547-1904 [Lithuanian bibliography,
1547-1904] Kaunas, 1924-29. 3 v.
in 1. Microfilm. Original at University of Pennsylvania. Detached
from Knygos, no.4-6, 7-9, 1924-29.
Film 5521 Z Lib. School CU Film 337
NIC NNC (Film) Film 248 PU WU(microfilm)

15. --- Lietuvių bibliografija
Lithuanian bibliography] Kaunas,
Švietimo Ministerijos leidinys,
1924-39, 5 pts. in 4 v. (Supplement to Knygos no.4-10) Covers publications from 1547 to 1910. Z2537.
K74 DLC(V.1-2 unclassified; v.3-4
(no.8-10)) BM MH(v.2-3, v.3, microfilm) CU(microfilm) NNC(v.1-3 on
microfilm)

16. --- Mažosios Lietuvos rašytojai [The writers of Lithuania Minor
and their works] In Aidai (München)
no.18, 1948, p. 352-360. See serials consulted.

17. --- Selected bibliography on
Lithuania: Lithuania and Lithuanians
mirrored in the books. [Washington,
D.C., Library of Congress, 1952]
52 leaves. DLC-Slav.Div.(microfilm)

18. BOOKS ON LITHUANIA. In Lithuanian World Directory. Ed. A. Simutis. New York, N.Y. [1958] p. 112-
116. DK511.L223S5 1958 DLC CLU MH
PU

19. BRESLAU. OSTEUROPA-INSTITUT.
Osteuropäische Bibliographie. Bres-
lau, Priebatsch, 1921-26. 3 v.
Z2483.B84 DLC CaAEU(microfiche) PU

20. BRÜCKNER, Alexander. Lituanica. In Archiv für slavische Philologie (Berlin), 1882-1891, v.6, p.
601-612; v.8, p. 303-312; v.13, p.
212-224, 311-314. See serials consulted.

21. CATALOGUE DES LIVRES LITHUA-
niens imprimés de 1864 à 1899 hors
de Russie;ou,les Impressions lithuaniennes sous interdites. Paris, Imprimerie A. Reiff, 1900. 28 p.
491.922B.C282 PU

22. CHICAGO. UNIVERSITY. HUMAN
RELATIONS AREA FILES. Bibliography
of Lithuania. New Haven, Conn.,HRAF,
1956. 45 leaves. (Behavior science
bibliographies) Z2514.L4C53 NIC CoU
HU MH-P

23. DOBRIANSKII, Flavian Nikolaevich. Putevoditel' po Vilenskoi
publichnoi biblioteke. Vil'na, Tip.
A.IA. IAlovtseva, 1879. viii, 71 p.
Z939.V61D6 DLC

24. GOLDAS, M. Tarybų Lietuva
(1940-1965); literatūros rodyklė.
[Soviet Lithuania, 1940-1965; bibliography. Vyr. redaktorius K. Meškaus-
kas] Vilnius, 1965. 203 p. Z2537.
G6 DLC CaAEU InNd MH PU

25. HELLMANN, Manfred. Zu neueren
litauischen Veröffentlichungen. In
Zeitschrift für Ostforschung (Marburg), v.1, no.1, 1952, p. 120-126;
no.3, p. 446-449. Publications of
Lithuanian émigrés in Germany since
1945. See serials consulted.

26. HILL, Frank J., comp. Lithuanian bibliography, publications in
English. Waterbury, Conn., 1938.
20 leaves. Typescript. X698-938h
CtY

27. --- Lithuanian bibliography.
In Bulletin of Bibliography and Dra-
matic Index, v.17, no.1(152), Jan.-
Apr. 1940 p. 6-7. Z1007.B94 v.17
DLC CLU CU CaQMM CaOTU CaBVa CaBViP
CoU CtY IEN IaU IU KU MB MH MoU NIC
NN NNC NcD NcU NjP OCl OClW OrU PPi
PU RPB WaU

28. HORNA, Dagmar, ed. Current
Research on Central and Eastern Eu-
rope. New York, N.Y., Mid-European
Studies Center, Free Europe Committee
1956. xviii, 251 p. (Free Europe
Committee. Mid-European Studies Cen-
ter. Publication,no.28) Z2483.H6
DLC CU CSt-H CtY CaAEU GEU FTaSU ICU
IU KyU InU MH-PA NN NcU NjP OU PPiU
RPB WU

29. JONAITIS, B., comp. Lithuanian books and books on Lithuanian
affairs published abroad in 1964. In
Lituanistikos darbai (Chicago, Ill.)
v.1, 1966, p. 191-203. See serials
consulted.

30. --- Lithuanian books and books
on Lithuanian affairs published a-
broad in 1965. In Lituanistikos
darbai (Chicago, Ill.) v.1, 1966,
p. 204-217. See serials consulted.

31. --- A selected bibliography on
the Baltic countries for the years
1962-1963. In Lituanistikos darbai

(Chicago, Ill.), v.1, 1966, p. 155-190. See serials consulted.

32. JURČIUKONIENĖ, A. Bibliografinis-informacinis darbas Vilniaus Universiteto bibliotekoje. [Bibliographic work in the library of the University of Vilnius] In LTSRAMMD: Bibliotekininkystės ir bibliografijos klausimai (Vilnius), v.1, 1961, p. 19-34. See serials consulted.

33. JUREVIČIUS, Stanislovas. Lituanica lenkiszkoje kalboje t.y.: suraszymas nekurių lenkiszkų knygų apie Lietuvą, jos istoriją, kalbą, literatūrą ir t.t. [By] s. Jurjevičius. In Apszwieta (Tilsit) 1892, p. 473-485. BM(P.P.-Tilsit) ICCC.

34. KEBLIENĖ, S. Užsienio rašytojai lietuvių kalba, 1940-1967; bibliografinė rodyklė. [Foreign authors in Lithuanian language] Vilnius, 1970. 318 p. At head of title: Lietuvos TSR Valstybinė respublikinė biblioteka. Z2537.K DLC

35. KEIT, Ernst. Bibliographie zur Landeskunde, 1939-1943. In Altpreussische Forschungen (Königsberg in Pr.), v.17-20, 1940-1943. See serials consulted.

36. KISINAS, Izidorius, comp. Lietuviškų knygų sistematinis katalogas; rinkoje esančios knygos. [A systematic catalogue of Lithuanian books in print. Kaunas] Spaudos fondas [1938] xvi, 1159 p. Z2539.K55 DLC CtY ICCC ICBM ICLJF MB MH(microfiche) NN PU

37. KNYGOS; bibliografijos ir kritikos žurnalas. [Books; a journal of bibliography and criticism. Ed. Vaclovas Biržiška] Kaunas, Švietimo Ministerijos Knygų leidimo komisija, 1922-39. 10 no. Z2537.K74 DLC BM (1-8) MH(4-9) NN(1-8) PPiU PU(1-6)

38. KNYGOS SAVOS SPAUDOS, išleistos "Lietuvos" [Lithuanian books published by "Lietuva". Chicago, Ill., n.d.] Catalogue of books published until 1915 in United States. 002.Ll LCLJF

39. KONCEVIČIUS, Jonas. Zur litauischen Bibliographie. [By] J. Koncewicz. In LLGM, v.1, no.3, 1880, p. 160-161; v.2, 1882, p. 12-22; also In Altpreussische Monatsschrift (Königsberg in Pr.), v.17, 1880, p.572-575. See serials consulted.

40. LIETUVIŲ BIBLIOGRAFINĖ TARNYBA, MEMMINGEN. Lietuvių knyga tremtyje, 1945-1948. [The Lithuanian book in exile, 1945-1948] Neumünster, Ger., International Exchange Agency Correspondence and Advertisement

[1948] 52 p. 002.LK ICLJF

41. LIETUVIŲ IŠEIVIŲ SPAUDOS METraštis. Lithuanian in exile bibliography yearbook. Chicago, JAV LB Kultūros fondas, 1966. 62 p. Supersedes Knygų lentyną and superseded by Užsienio lietuvių spaudos metraštis. Z2537.L43 DLC CaOTU(1-) NN NjP

42. LIETUVIŲ SPAUDOS METRAŠTIS. Yearbook of the Lithuanian press. 1968- . Chicago, JAV LB Kultūros fondas. Supersedes Užsienio lietuvių spaudos metraštis. Z2537.L46 DLC

43. LIETUVOS TSR BIBLIOGRAFIJA. Serija A: Knygos lietuvių kalba. [Lithuanian National Bibliography. Series A: Books in Lithuanian language. Ats. redaktorius A. Ulpis] Vilnius, Mintis, 1969- . Partial contents.--T.1. Knygos lietuvių kalba, 1547-1861. Z2537.L47 DLC CaAEU CaOONL CtPAM MH PU

44. LIETUVOS TSR KNYGŲ RŪMAI. Didžiojo tėvynės karo laikotarpio Lietuvos TSR spauda, 1941-1944; valstybinė bibliografija. [Soviet Lithuanian press during the Second World War, 1941-1944. Ats. redaktorius A. Ulpis] Vilnius, 1955. xiv, 270 p. 891.92.BL625 PU

45. --- KNYGŲ METRAŠTIS; valstybinė bibliografija. [Yearbook of the books; a National bibliography] Kaunas, Valstybinė enciklopėdijų, žodynų ir mokslo literatūros leidykla, 1947-56. 10 v. Quarlerly (except 1948, annual) Superseded in 1957 by Spaudos metraštis. Z2537.L48 DLC

46. --- Lietuvos TSR spauda; valstybinė suvestinė bibliografija,1940-1955. [Soviet Lithuanian publishing; a cummulative National bibliography, 1940-1955. Sudarė E. Urniežiūtė, T. Čyžas, A. Ulpis, J. Aleksandravičienė, E. Lebedienė ir A. Bučienė. Ats. redaktorius A. Ulpis] Vilnius, VPMLL, 1962. 2 v. Z2537.L53 DLC CU CaAEU CaOONL CtY DNAL ICU IU MH NN NNC PPiU TxHU WU

47. LIETUVOS TSR MOKSLŲ AKADEMIJA, VILNA. CENTRINĖ BIBLIOTEKA. Lietuvos TSR Mokslų akademijos ir jos Mokslo darbuotojų leidinių bibliografija; knygos, 1941-1954. [Bibliography of publications of the Lithuanian SSR Academy of Sciences and its associates: books, 1941-1954. Comp. by J. Basiulis et al. Ed. by T. Adomonis et al.] Vilnius, 1956. 88 p. Z5055.L52L5 DLC CaAEU ICU MH NN NNC NIC NcD PPiU WaU CtY InU

48. --- Lietuvos TSR Mokslų akademijos ir jos darbuotojų knygų ir straipsnių bibliografija, 1955. [Bibliography of publications of the Lithuanian SSR Academy of Sciences and its associates: books and articles, 1955. Comp. by J. Basiulis] Vilnius, Laikraščių ir žurnalų leidykla, 1957. 104 p. Z5055.L52L5 DLC CaAEU ICU InU MH NN NcD PPiU PU WaU

49. --- ---, 1956-1957. Vilnius, Laikraščių ir žurnalų leidykla, 1959, 232 p. Z5055.L52L5 1956 DLC CaAEU ICU InU MH NN NcD PPiU PU WaU

50. --- ---, 1958. Vilnius, Laikraščių ir žurnalų leidykla, 1961. 235 p. Z5055.L52L5 1958 DLC CaAEU CtY ICU InU MH NN NNC NcD PPiU PU WaU

51. --- ---, 1959. Vilnius, Laikraščių ir žurnalų leidykla ir spaustuvė, 1961. 247 p. Z5055.L52L5 1959 DLC CaAEU CtY DNAL ICU InU MH NN NIC NNC NcD PPiU PU WaU

52. --- ---, 1960. Vilnius, Laikraščių ir žurnalų leidykla,1962. 222 p. Z5055.L52L5 1960 DLC CaAEU CtY DNAL ICU InU MH NN NIC NcD PPiU PU

53. --- ---, 1961. Vilnius, Laikraščių ir žurnalų leidykla, 1963. 184 p. Z5055.L52L5 1961 DLC CaAEU CtY DNAL InU ICU MH NN NIC NcD NjP PPiU PU

54. --- ---, 1962. Vilnius, Laikraščių ir žurnalų leidykla, 1964. 201 p. Z5055.L52L5 1962 DLC CtY DGS DNAL ICU InU MH MH-Z NN NIC NcD NjP PPiU PU

55. --- Lietuvos TSR Mokslų akademijos leidinių bibliografija, 1963. [Bibliography of publications of the Lithuanian SSR Academy of Sciences, 1963] Vilnius, 1965. 190 p. Z5055.L52L5 1963 DLC CaAEU CtY DNAL ICU InU MH MH-Z NN NIC NNC NcD NjP PPiU PU RPB WU WaU

56. --- ---, 1964. Vilnius, 1966. 206 p. Z5055.L52L5 1964 DLC CtY DNAL ICU InU MH NN NIC NcD NjP PPiU PU WU

57. --- ---, 1965. Vilnius, 1967. 238 p. Z5055.L52L5 1965 DLC CtY DNAL ICU InU MH NIC NN NcD NjP PPiU PU WU

58. --- ---, 1966. Vilnius, 1968. 291 p. Z5055.L52L5 1966 DLC CtY DNAL ICU InU MH NIC NN NcD NjP PPiU PU WU WaU

59. --- ---, 1967. Vilnius, 1969. Z5055.L52L5 1967 DLC CtY DNAL ICU InU MH NIC NN NcD NjP PPiU PU WU WaU

60. --- ---, 1968. Vilnius, 1970. Z5055.L52L5 1968 DLC CtY DNAL ICU InU MH NIC NN NNC NcD NjP PPiU PU WU WaU

61. LIETUVOS TSR SPAUDA; valstybinė suvestinė bibliografija. [Lithuanian SSR publications; a cumulative National Bibliography] 1940/55- . Vilnius, VPMLL. Issued by Lietuvos TSR Knygų rūmai. Z2537.L53 DLC CaAEU CtY CtPAM MH NN NcD PPiU TxHU WU

62. LITHUANIA. CONSULATE. NEW YORK. Short list of English references on Lithuania. Prepared by Consulate General of Lithuania. [New York, N.Y., 1938] 7 leaves. (BTE p.v. 489)NN

63. LITHUANIAN PUBLICATIONS IN THE United States. In Lists of foreign language publications in the United States. New York, N.Y., Common Council for American Unity [1959] 5 leaves (unpaged) Z9653.5.A1A6 1959 DLC

64. NAUJOS KNYGOS. [New books] 1- ; 1959- . Vilnius. Bimonthly 1959-1966; monthly, 1967- . Unclass. DLC(1961-)

65. PRINZHORN, FRITZ. Lithuania. In Europa-Bibliographie, 8: Ostland, v.1, 1939-1942. Leipzig, Harrassowitz, 1944. p. 11-38. Z1009.B45 DLC

66. PRINZHORN, FRITZ AND MANFRED HELLMANN. Schrifttum über Litauen, 1928-1938. In Deutsches Archiv für Landes- und Volksforschung, v.3, 1939, p. 217-252. DD1.D5 v.3 DLC

67. ROBINSON, David F. Lithuanian books in the British Museum, 1578-1937. In General Linguistics (Lexington, Ky.), v.10, no.2, 1970, p. [75]-96. See serials consulted.

68. RUŽANCOVAS, Aleksandras. Lietuvių knyga tremtyje; 1945-1949 metų bibliografija. [The Lithuanian book in exile; bibliography for the years 1945-1949] In Naujienos (Chicago, Ill.), 1959, no.50,133,174,192,227, 292; 1960, no.31 and 67. F71.L714 N ICN PU(yr 20-35,37-44)

69. --- Lietuvių išeivių 1958 metų bibliografija. [A bibliography of Lithuanian books published in exile, 1958] In Knygų lentyna (Danville, Ind.), no.2(116), March-April 1960, p. 29-40. See serials consulted.

70. RUŽANCOVAS, Aleksandras and Bronius Kviklys. Lietuvos išeivių

1959 metų knygų bibliografija. [A bibliography of Lithuanian books published in exile, 1959] In Knygų lentyna (Danville, Ind.), no.1(115), Jan.-Feb. 1960, p. 2-14; and no. 2(116), March-April 1960, p. 25-28. See serials consulted.

71. SCHRIFTEN IN LITAUISCHER SPRA-che. In LLGM, 1900, p. 493-529. See serials consulted.

72. ŠIRVYDAS, Vytautas. Amerikos lietuvių knygos, 1875-1904. [Books of American Lithuanians, 1875-1904] In Bagdanavičius, V.J. Kovos metai dėl savosios spaudos. Chicago, 1957. p. 239-296. PN5278.L5B3 DLC CaAEU OCl

73. ŠLIŪPAS, Jonas. Lietuviszkie-ji rasztai ir rasztininkai. Rasz-liszka peržvalga parengta Lietuvos Mylėtojo. Tilžėje, Kaszta Baltimo-rės M.D.L.M. draugystės, 1890. 234 p. ports. 891.92.HS135 PU ICLJF ICCC CtTMF NNC

74. SPAUDOS METRAŠTIS. Lietuvos TSR valstybinės bibliografijos orga-nas. [Yearbook of the press. Ats. redaktorius A. Ulpis] Vilnius, Min-tis [etc.] 1957- . Monthly. Su-persedes Knygų metraštis and Žurna-lų ir laikraščių straipsnių metraš-tis. In Lithuanian and Russian. CU(1964-) MH([1960]-) NNC(1966-) PU([1962]-)

75. STANKA, Elena. Lithuania; a selected bibliography, with brief history survey. Washington, D.C., 1958. vi, 124 leaves. 2 maps. Thesis (M.S.)--Catholic University of America. Z2537.S77 DLC also Mic 6193Z DLC

76. STANKIEWICZ, Maurycy. Biblio-grafia litewska od r. 1547 do 1701. Kraków, Gebethner, 1889. xvi, 74 p. (Studya bibliograficzne nad litera-turą litewską, t.2) BM(11840.d.57.) ICN MH NN

77. --- Studya bibliograficzne nad literaturę litewską. Wiadomość o biblii litewskiej drukowanej w Lon-dynie 1663 roku, i o wrzekomym jei tłómaczu S.B. Chylińskim. Kraków, Gebethner, 1886-89. 2 v. BM MH(2) ICN NN(2)

78. STEPONAITIS, Vytautas. Lietu-vos bibliografijos pirmas papildymas, 1927-1940 m. [The first supplement to the Lithuanian bibliography, 1927-1940] Kaunas, 1944. 141 p. 75.475.St48 PU

79. --- Lituanica; lietuvių raštai kitomis kalbomis. [Lituanica; Lithu-anian works in foreign languages] In Bibliografijos Žinios (Kaunas), v.15, no.6, p. 164-172. Z2537.B58 DLC BM ICU NN PU

80. --- Vilniaus lietuvių spauda, 1919-1928. [Lithuanian publishing in Vilnius, 1919-1928] Kaunas, Vilniui vaduoti sąjunga, 1931. 138 p. (Vil-niui vaduoti sąjungos leidinys, nr. 48) PN5279.V5S7 DLC PU

81. THOMSON, Erik. Baltische bib-liographie. 1945- . Würzburg, Hol-zner Verlag, 1957- . (Ostdeutsche Beiträge aus dem Göttinger Arbeits-kreis, Bd.5,23)(Der Göttinger Arbeits-kreis. Veröffentlichungen, nr.173, 269) Z2531.T5 DLC CLU CSt CU CaBVaU CoU DS InU ICU KU MH MiU MdBJ NN NNC NIC NjR

82. UNITED STATES. LIBRARY OF CON-GRESS. PROCESSING DEPARTMENT. East European accessions list. v.1- ; Sept./Oct. 1951- . Washington, D.C. Government Printing Office. Title varies. Z881.A1U35 DLC(1-) AzU(1-) CaOON(1-) DH(7-) FU(1-) IaU(1-) ICJ(1-) MnRM([1],2-3) NN(1-) NcD(1-) OU(1-) PPT(1-) WM(1-)

83. URBŠIENĖ, Marija (Mašiotaitė) Lituanica, 1933. Offprint from Bib-liografijos Žinios. Kaunas, 1934. 947.52.Url3 PU; also in Bibliografi-jos Žinios (Kaunas), 1934. See se-rials consulted.

84. ---- Lituanica, 1934 ir 1935 m. papildymai. [Supplements to Litua-nica, 1934 and 1935. Offprint from Bibliografijos Žinios. Kaunas, 1936. 947.52B.Url3 PU; also in Bibliogra-fijos Žinios (Kaunas), 1936. See se-rials consulted.

85. VILNA. LIETUVOS TSR VALSTYBI-NĖ RESPUBLIKINĖ BIBLIOTEKA. Tarybų Lietuva, 1940-1955; rekomenduojamo-sios literatūros rodyklė. [Soviet Lithuania, 1940-1955; a list of re-commended literature. Sudarė Vytau-tas Steponaitis] Kaunas, 1955. 74 p. Lithuanian and Russian. Z2537. V5 DLC MH PU

86. UŽSIENIO LIETUVIŲ SPAUDOS MET-raštis. Lithuanian publications abroad, 1967. Sudarė Z. Ašoklis [et al.] Chicago, Ill. JAV LB Kul-tūros fondas, 1968. 64 p. Z2537.L54 PU CaOTU

87. ZAUNIUTĖ, Marta. Priedas prie statistikos lietuviškų knygų, ats-paustų Prūsuose nuo 1864 m. iki pa-baigai 1899 m., knygos neužrašytos statistikoj Zanavykučio ir knygos bei laikraščiai išleisti nuo 1896 m. iki 1900 m. Surinko Marta Zauniutė.

Sutaisė ir parengė į spaudą Jr. Jonas. [Supplement and continuation for the years 1896-1900 of the Lithuanian books published in Prussia] Plymouth, Pa., Spauda "Vienybės Lietuvninku," 1900. 15 p. Bound with Angrabaitis, Juozas. Suskaita arba statistika visų lietuviszkų knygų atsaustų [sic] Prusuose nuo 1864 metų iki pabaigai 1896 metų. Tilžė, 1897. Collective cover-title for the three works reads: Statistika lietuviškų knygų spaustų užsieniuose... nuo 1864 metų iki 1900 metų. Z2514.L4Z2 DLC PU PPULC

88. ŽILIUS, Jonas. Suskaita arba statistika visų lietuviszkų knygų, atspaustų Amerikoj nuo pradžios lietuviszkos Amerikon emigracijos iki 1900 metų. Surazsė Jr. Jonas [pseud. Books published in the United States from the beginning of printing in Lithuanian till 1900] Plymouth, Pa., Spauda "Vienybes lietuvninkų", 1900. 35 p. "Iszleista kasztais Paryžiaus parodos fondo" Bound with Angrabaitis, Juozas. Suskaita arba statistika visų lietuviszkų knygų. Tilžėje, 1897. Z2514.L4Z2 DLC PU PPULC

I.2. SUBJECT BIBLIOGRAPHIES

89. ABRAMAVIČIUS, Vladas and J. Šliubauskienė. Kova už Tarybų valdžią Lietuvoje, 1818-1940 m; rankraščių bibliografinė rodyklė. [The struggle for Soviet government in Lithuania, 1918-1940; a bibliography of manuscripts] In LTSRMACBBB, v.1, 1961, p. 23-130. See serials consulted.

90. ANTONIEWICZ, Jerzy. Polskie badania archeologiczne nad Bałtami, 1945-1957. In Rocznik Olsztynski (Olsztyn), v.1, 1958, p. 295-317. See serials consulted.

91. BAGDANAVIČIUS, Vytautas. Lietuviška materialistinė raštija iki nepriklausomybės paskelbimo. Literary activity of Lithuanian materialists from 1904 till 1918. In LKMAM, v.2, 1966, p. 145-207. See serials consulted.

92. BALYS, Jonas. Lithuanian narrative folksongs; a description of types and a bibliography. Washington, D.C., 1954. 144 p. (A Treasury of Lithuanian folklore, 4) ML3695.B3 DLC CLU CaAEU KU MH NN PU

93. GEOLOGICHESKAIA IZUCHENNOST' SSSR. 1- ; 19 - . facsim., maps. Issued by Komissiia po geologicheskoi izuchennosti SSSR of the

Akademiia nauk SSSR. Editor: D.V. Nalivkin. Partial contents.--T.43. Litovskaia SSSR, 1800/1955- . QE276.G415 DLC CaOTU DI-GS MH PU

94. INTERNATIONAL ASSOCIATION OF SCIENTIFIC HYDROLOGY. Hidrologinė bibliografija: Lietuva. Bibliographie hydrologique: Lithuanie, 1934-1938. Kaunas, 1935-39. 5 pts. (Its International bibliography of Hydrology, pt. 12) Z6004.P5I735 CaOTU DLC(1935-1939) NN(1932-1937)

95. IVINSKIS, Zenonas. Senovės lietuvių religijos bibliografija. [A bibliography of ancient Lithuanian religion] Kaunas, 1938. 156 p. Reprint from Soter. 947.52.Iv54.2 PU; also in Soter (Kaunas), 1935-1937, no.21-25. See serials consulted.

96. JAKŠTAS, P. Lietuvos karinė spauda, 1918-1938. [Publications of the military Lithuanian press, 1918-1938] Kaunas, 1938. 48 p. Offprint from Mūsų žinynas (Kaunas), v.35, no.11-12, 1938, p. 803-847. U4M8 v.35 DLC NN; see also serials consulted.

97. JURČIUKONIENĖ, A. Tarybų Lietuvos aukštosios mokyklos; bibliografija, 1940-1969. [The High-Schools of Soviet Lithuania; bibliography, 1940-1969] Vilnius, 1971. 418 p. At head of title: Lietuvos TSR Aukštojo ir specialiojo vidurinio mokslo ministerija. Mokslinis metodikos kabinetas. Sudarė A. Jurčiukonienė. Paruošė Vilniaus V. Kapsuko universiteto mokslinė biblioteka. LA853.148J8 DLC

98. KIRSNYS, Vytautas. Lietuvos kurortai; bibliografinė rodyklė, 1711-1967. [Lithuanian resorts; a bibliography, 1711-1967] Sudarytojai: V. Kirsnys ir D. Baronienė. Vilnius, 1969. 204 p. Z6675.B33L55 CaOTU

99. KOLUPAILA, Steponas. Bibliography of Hydrometry. Notre Dame, Ind., University of Notre Dame Press, 1961. xxiii, 975 p. Z5853.H9K6 DLC CSt CU CaAEU CaBVaU FU IaU IU IdU ICU KU MiU MB MnU NIC NNC NbU NjP NjR NRU OCl OU OCU PPF TxU ViU WU WaU

100. --- Hidrologinė bibliografija: Lietuva. Bibliographie hydrologique de l'année 1934-1940; Lithuanie. Kaunas, 1935-41. 7 pts. In International Association of Scientific Hydrology. International bibliography of hydrology, pt. 12. Z6004.P5I735 CaOTU DLC NN

101. --- Hidrologinė bibliografija, 1934-1940. In Žemėtvarka ir melioracija (Kaunas), pts.1-5, 1935-1939; and in Bibliografijos žinios (Kaunas), pts.6-7, 1940-1941. See serials consulted.

102. LITHUANIAN SSR. LIAUDIES ŪKIO TARYBA. CENTRINĖ-TECHNINĖ BIBLIOTEKA, VILNA. Medžio apdirbimo pramonės gamybos procesų mechanizavimas; bibliografinė rodyklė. [Mechanization and automation of the processes in the lumber industry; a bibliography] Vilnius, 1961. 177 p. Z7914.W8L5 DLC

103. --- Sintetinių medžiagų panaudojimas lengvoje pramonėje; bibliografinė rodyklė. [The use of synthetic products in light industry; a bibliography. Sudarytoja M. Samuolytė] Vilnius, 1962. 69 p. Z7914.T3L5 DLC

104. LITHUANIAN SSR. SVEIKATOS APSAUGOS MINISTERIJA. Lietuviškoji medicininė bibliografija, 1940-1957. [Lithuanian medical bibliography, 1940-1957] Vilnius, 1960. ZWB.100.L5L MH

105. LITOVSKAIA SSR; period 1800-1955, vyp.1: Pechatnye raboty. Vil'nius, 1962. 257 p. illus., ports., facsims. (Geologicheskaia izuchennost' SSSR, t.43) QE276.G415 t.43, 1800-1955, v.1 DLC DI-GS MH

106. LITOVSKAIA SSR; period 1956-1960. Vil'nius, Mintis, 1964. illus., facsims., maps. (Geologicheskaia izuchennost' SSSR, t.43) QE276.G415 t.43, 1956-1960 DLC

107. MATULAITYTĖ, S. Astronomai; bibliografinė rodyklė. [Astronomers; a bibliography] Mokslinis redaktorius ir įžanginio straipsnio autorius P. Slavėnas. Vilnius, 1965. 79 p. (Tarybų Lietuvos mokslininkai) Z5155.L5M3 DLC

108. MID-EUROPEAN LAW PROJECT. Legal sources and bibliography of the Baltic States (Estonia, Latvia, Lithuania) by Johannes Klesment [and others] Vladimir Gsovski, general editor. New York, N.Y., Published for Free Europe Committee, by Praeger [c1963] 197 p. (Praeger publications in Russian history and world Communism, no.23) KU B2M62 CaAEU CaOONL CaOTU CaOTY DLC FU MnU NcD NcU PU

109. NAUJOKAITIS, Pranas. Pedagogika ir metodika, 1940-1965; bibliografija. [Pedagogics and methodology, 1940-1965; a bibliography] Kaunas, Šviesa, 1968. 390 p. Z5811.34 DLC

110. OKINSHEVICH, Leo. The law of the Grand Duchy of Lithuania; background and bibliography. New York, N.Y., Research Program on the USSR, 1953. 53 p. DK1.E35 no.32 DLC MnU NN PU

111. PAGIRIENĖ, L. Lietuvos TSR archeologija, 1940-1967; bibliografinė rodyklė. [Soviet Lithuanian archaeology, 1940-1967; a bibliography] Vilnius, 1970. At head of title: Lietuvos TSR Valstybinė respublikinė biblioteka. Sudarė L. Pagirienė. Z2537.P34 DLC

112. RUŽANCOVAS, Aleksandras. Biografija ir istorija užjūrių lietuvių periodikoje. [Biography and history in Lithuanian periodicals in exile] In Tautos praeitis (Chicago, Ill.), v.1, pt.1, 1959, p. 116-127. See serials consulted.

113. --- Lietuvių išeivių katalikų religinė knyga; 1948-1958 metų bibliografija. Bibliographie lituanienne à l'étranger. In LKMAM, v.1,1965, p. 225-271. See serials consulted.

114. --- Lietuvių išeivių katalikų knyga; 1959-1965 metų bibliografija. Bibliographie lituanienne à l'étranger. In LKMAM, v.2, 1966, p. 297-328. See serials consulted.

115. --- Lietuvos karo bibliografija, 1917-1922. [Lithuanian military bibliography, 1917-1922] Kaunas, Krašto apsaugos ministerija, Karo mokslo skyrius, 1923. 89 p. Z6725. L7R9 DLC CtY DW

116. --- Mažosios Lietuvos reikalai lietuvių tremtinių spaudoje;1945-1949 metų bibliografija. [The affairs of Lithuania Minor in the Lithuanian press in exile; a bibliography] In Tautos praeitis (Chicago, Ill.), v.1, no.1, 1959, p. 127-131. See serials consulted.

117. ŠAPIRAITĖ, Sara. Lietuvos botanikos bibliografija, 1800-1965. [A bibliography of Lithuanian botany] Mokslinis redaktorius Kazys Brundza. Vilnius, 1971. 527 p. At head of title: Lietuvos TSR Mokslų akademijos Centrinė biblioteka. Z5358.L5S3 PU

118. SITNIKAITĖ, A. Lietuvos geologijos bibliografija, 1800-1965. [A bibliography of Lithuanian geology, 188-1965] Vilnius, 1970. 275 p. Z6034.L5S5 PU DLC

119. SZAMEITAT, Max. Bibliogra-

phie des Memellandes. Würzburg,
Holzner-Verlag, 1957. x, 248 p. (Ost-
deutsche Beiträge aus dem Göttinger
Arbeitskreis, Bd. 7) Z2537.S96 DLC
CLU CU DS ICU IEN MH MiU NN NNC PU WJ

120. TARYBINIS VILNIUS; rekomenduojamos literatūros rodyklė. [Soviet
Vilnius; a bibliography of recommended literature. Sudarė Ona Kriukelienė, Elena Daunaravičiūtė ir Kazė
Šiaudinienė] Vilnius, Viešoji A. Mickevičiaus vardo biblioteka, 1966.
156 p. Z2514.V5T3 DLC

121. TYSZKIEWICZ, Eustachy. Ein
Blick auf die Quellen der Archäologie
Littauens. In Baltische Studien
(Stettin), v.13, no.2, 1847. See
serials consulted.

122. URBŠIENĖ, Marija (Mašiotaitė).
Klaipėdos krašto bibliografija. [A
Bibliography of the Klaipėdos kraštas
(Memel territory)] In Mūsų žinynas
(Kaunas), no.103, 1933. See serials
consulted.

123. --- Sąrašas aktualių knygų ir
rašinių apie Vilnių ir Vilniaus kraštą. [A list of relevent books and
articles on the city and region of
Vilnius] Kaunas, 1939. 42 p.
947.52.Url3.2 PU

124. --- Suvalkų trikampis ir raštai apie jį. [The triangle of Suvalkai and literature concerning it]
Kaunas, 1939. 24 p. Offprint from
"Lietuvos žinios" 947.52.Url3.2 PU

125. VILNA. LIETUVOS TSR VALSTY-
BINĖ RESPUBLIKINĖ BIBLIOTEKA. Buities kultūra; rekomenduojamosios literatūros sąrašas. [Home economics;
a bibliography] Vilnius, 1965. 25 p.
Z5775.V53 DLC MH

126. --- Muzikinė literatūra, 1959-
1963; rodyklė. [Musical literature,
1959-1963; a bibliography] Vilnius,
1965. 265 p. ML120.L6V54 DLC PU

127. --- Muzikalinė literatūra,
1946-1965. [The Musical literature,
1946-1965] Vilnius, 1968. 107 p.
Sudarė: E. Juodis.

128. VILNA. UNIVERSITETAS. VALSTY-
BINĖ MOKSLINĖ MEDICINOS BIBLIOTEKA.
Lietuviškoji medicininė bibliografija.
[A Lithuanian medical bibliography,
1940-1963. Sudarė V. Šimkūnas et
al.] Vilnius, Valstybinė mokslinės
medicinos biblioteka, 1959-65. 3 v.
Z6661.L75V5 DLC(2-) MH DNLM(1-)

129. YLA, Stasys, 1908- . Lietuvių apologetinės literatūros bibliografija, 1904-1914. [A bibliography
of Lithuanian apologetic literature,
1904-1914] Kaunas, 1935. 53 p.
947.5.Y2 CtTMF

I.3. BIBLIOGRAPHIES OF INDIVIDUAL
AUTHORS

130. ČIURLIONYTĖ-KARUŽIENĖ, Valerija. Mikalojus Konstantinas Čiurlionis; bibliografija. [A Bibliography of M.K. Čiurlionis] Vilnius,
Vaga, 1970. 682 p. At head of
title: Valerija Čiurlionytė-Karužienė, Simonas Egidijus Juodis, Vladas
Žukas. Z8171.C57 DLC PU

131. GIMBUTAS, Jurgis. Bibliografija; Stepono Kolupailos svarbesnie-
ji darbai. [A Bibliography of the
most important works of Steponas Ko-
upaila] In LKMAM, v.4, 1968, p.
542-546. See serials consulted.

132. HLEB-KOSZAŃSKA, Helena. Centre de documentation sur Joachim Lelewel à la bibliotèque de l'Université de Wilno. Wilno, [Drukarnia Artystyczna "Grafika"] 1937. 15 p.
illus., port. (Wydawnictwa Biblioteki
Uniwersyteckiej w Wilnie, nr. 12)
Z818.V76H DLC CtY

133. KISINAS, Izidorius. Antano
Smetonos bibliografija ir bio-biblio-
grafija, 1874-1934. La bibliographie
et la bio-bibliographie de Antanas
Smetona. [Klaipėda, 1935] xlix, 609
p. illus., ports. (Švietimo ministerijos leidinys, nr.452)
Z8819.97.K5 DLC CtTMF PU

134. --- E.A. Volterio bibliografija. [A Bibliography of E.A. Volter]
In Tauta ir žodis (Kaunas), v.5,
1928, p. 316-385. See serials consulted.

135. --- Prof. Mykolo Biršiškos
bibliografija. [A Bibliography of
the works of M. Biržiška] In Biržiška, Mykolas. Iš mūsų kultūros ir literatūros istorijos. Kaunas, 1931-
38. v.1, p. [3]-85; v.2, p. [1]-85.
PG8703.B48 DLC CU ICU MH OCl(1) PU

136. --- Prof. Vaclovo Biržiškos
bibliografija. [A Bibliography of
the works of V. Biržiška] In Praeitis (Kaunas), v.3, 1940. See
serials consulted.

137. LANKUTIS, Jonas. E. Mieželaičio kūrinių ir literatūros apie jo
kūrybą bibliografija. [A Bibliography of the works of E. Mieželaitis]
In the author's E. Mieželaičio poezija. Vilnius, 1965. p. 203-269.
PG.8721.M45Z7 DLC CtY MH PU

138. LEBEDIENĖ, Elena. Kristijono Donelaičio bibliografija. [A Bibliography of the works of Kristijonas Donelaitis] Vilnius, Vaga, 1964. 381 p. Z8236.3.L4 DLC CaAEU CtY PU

139. MERKELIS, Aleksandras. Vaižgantika; bibliografija. [A Bibliography of J. Tumas-Vaižgantas] In Bibliografijos žinios (Kaunas), v.4, 1931. See serials consulted.

140. SALYS, Antanas. Prof. K. Būgos rašto palikimas. [A Bibliography of the works of Prof. K. Būga] In Tauta ir žodis (Kaunas), v.3, 1925, p. 563-577. See serials consulted.

141. ŠČESNULEVIČIUS, Kazimieras. Mokslingo miškininko Antano Rukuižos spausdintų darbų sąrašas. [A Bibliography of the works of Antanas Rukuiža] Chicago, Ill. 1965. 14 p. illus. L 002Sč ICLJF

142. VILNA. LIETUVOS TSR VALSTYBINĖ RESPUBLIKINĖ BIBLIOTEKA. Antanas Vienuolis, 1882-1957; rekomenduojamuosios literatūros rodyklė. [Antanas Vienuolis; a bibliography of recommended literature] Sudarė Birutė Mituzienė. Kaunas, 1960. 56 p. Z8942.315.V35 DLC PU

143. --- Eduardas Mieželaitis; rekomenduojamosios literatūros rodyklė. [Eduardas Mieželaitis; a bibliography of recommended literature] Sudarė: V. Vilmonytė. Kaunas, 1962. 45 p. port. (Tarybų Lietuvos rašytojai) Z8574.2.V5 DLC

144. --- Jovaras; rekomenduojamosios literatūros rodyklė. [Jovaras; a bibliography of recommended literature] Vilnius, 1964. 37 p. At head of title: Lietuvos TSR Valstybinė respublikinė biblioteka. B. Knizikevičienė. Z8467.799.V5 DLC MH

145. --- Liudas Gira, 1884-1946; rekomenduojamosios literatūros rodyklė. [Liudas Gira; a bibliography of recommended literature] Kaunas, 1957. 73 p. 891.92.G448.yM PU

146. --- Petras Cvirka, 1909-1949; rekomenduojamosios literatūros rodyklė. [Petras Cvirka; a bibliography of recommended literature] Sudarė J. Ragauskas. Kaunas, 1958. 80 p. 891.92.C888.vR PU

147. --- Salomėja Neris gyvenime ir kūryboje; parodos katalogas, 1946. VII.7-1946.VII.21. [Salomėja Neris her life and works; a catalogue...] Kaunas, Valstybinė grožinės literatūros leidykla [1946] 29 p. illus. PG8721.N4Z93 DLC

148. VITKAUSKIENĖ, Patricija and Vladas Žukas. Antanas Strazdas; bibliografija. [Antanas Strazdas; a bibliography of his works] Vilnius, Vaga, 1969. 243 p. ports., music. Z8849.78.V5 DLC

149. ZINKEVIČIUS, Zigmas. K. Būgos spausdintų raštų bibliografija.. [A Bibliography of the works of K. Būga] In Būga, Kazimieras. Rinktiniai raštai. Vilnius, 1961. v.3, p. 963-1003. PG8509.B8 DLC CU CaAEU CtPAM ICLJF IEN ICU MH NN NB NBuU(1-2) NjP PPiU PU TxU

150. ŽUKAS, Vladas. Julius Janonis; bibliografinė rodyklė. [Julius Janonis; a bibliography of his works. Sudarė: V. Žukas. Spec. red. V. Kubilius et al.] Vilnius, 1965. 214 p. Z8449.4.Z8 DLC MH PU

151. --- Konstantino Jablonskio bibliografija. [A Bibliography of the works of K. Jablonskis] In LTSRAMMD: Bibliotekininkystės ir bibliografijos klausimai (Vilnius), v.4, 1965, p. 155-206. See serials consulted.

152. --- Medžiaga Žemaitės bibliografijai. [Žemaitė: a bibliography of her works] In LTSRAMMD: Bibliotekininkystės ir bibliografijos klausimai (Vilnius), v.5, 1966, p. 177-213. See serials consulted.

153. --- Salomėjos Nėries kūrinių ir literatūros apie ją bibliografija. [A Bibliography of the works of S. Nėris] In Literatūra ir kalba (Vilnius), v.4, 1959, p. 351-503. See serials consulted.

154. --- V. Mykolaičio spausdintų darbų bibliografija. [A Bibliography of the works of V. Mykolaitis] In LTSRAMMD: Literatūra (Vilnius), v.11, pt.1, 1969, p. 66-89. See serials consulted.

I.4 LIBRARY CATALOGUES, AND GUIDES TO COLLECTIONS

155. DZIKOWSKI, Mikołaj, comp. Katalog atłasów Biblioteki Uniwersyteckiej w Wilnie. Ze szczególnym uwzględnieniem zbiorów J. Lelewela. Wilno, 1934-40. 1 v. (Biblioteka Uniwersytecka w Wilnie. Wydawnictwa, 8) Map Room MH X327.W74W CtY BM

156. ELLIS, FIRM, BOOKSELLERS, LONDON. A catalogue of a remarkable collection of books & manuscripts relating to Russia, Poland, Finland, Lithuania, Latvia, &c., many of great

rarity, including some early speci-
mens of printing in Slavonic. On
sale by Messrs. Ellis. London,
Ellis, 1929. [ii], 138 p. facsims.
Catalogue no. 262. 016.947.E15 NbU

157. HANOVER. NIEDERSÄCHISCHE
LANDESBIBLIOTHEK. Katalog des
Schrifttums über die baltischen Sta-
aten. Hannover, 1971. 2 v.
Z2531.H3 PU

158. KIEL. UNIVERSITÄT. INSTITUT
FÜR WELTWIRTSCHAFT. BIBLIOTHEK. Re-
gionenkatalog; Litauen. Boston,
Mass., G.K. Hall, 1967. v. 27, p.
453-493. Z929.K52 1967 v.27 DLC
CaAEU

159. LIETUVOS TSR MOKSLŲ AKADEMIJA.
VILNA. CENTRINĖ BIBLIOTEKA. Lietuvos TSR Mokslų akademijos, Centrinės
bibliotekos atlasų ir žemėlapių katalogas. [A Catalogue of atlases and
maps in the Central Library of the
Academy of Sciences of Lithuanian
SSR. Sudarė K. Čepienė] Vilnius,
1969. 343 p. Map room MH NN

160. LITAUISCHE LITERARISCHE GESELL-
schaft, Tilsit. Bibliothek. Katalog
der Bibliothek. Tilsit, O. v. Mauderode, 1892. 38 p. Z2514.L4T5 DLC
MiU NN(1-3)

161. MACIŪNAS, Vincas. Lituanisti-
ka Pensilvanijos universiteto bibliotekoje. Lithuanian books and books
in foreign languages concerning Lithuania in University of Pennsylvania
Library, Philadelphia, Pa. Chicago,
Lietuvių profesorių draugija Amerikoje, 1964. 119 p. 016.9475 M1891
PP PU CtPAM ICLJF InU NNC

162. MACIŪNAS, Vincas and Kostas
Ostrauskas. The Šaulys Collection;
books on Lithuania. In Library
Chronicle (Philadelphia, Pa.), v.20,
1954, p. 35-46. See serials consulted.

163. MŪSŲ RAŠTAI. [Our book catalogue. Kaunas] Šv. Kazimiero draugija [1938] 32 p. illus.
L 002 ŠK ICLJF

164. NOMMIK, Tonia. A guide to the
Baltic collection in the Waterloo Lu-
theran University Library. Waterloo,
Ont., 1967. 26 p. CaOWtL DLC

165. PAUKSZTIS, J.J., & CO., BROOK-
LYN, N.Y. Catalogue of Lithuanian
books. Katalogas knygų išleistų
"Vienybės Lietuvininkų" ir visų kitų
lietuviškų spaustuvių, gaunamų pas
J.J. Pauksztis & Co., Brooklyn, N.Y.
[Brooklyn, N.Y.] 1914. 128 p.
Z2514.L4Z97 1914 PU

166. PAUKSZTIS, J.J., & CO., PLY-
MOUTH, PA. Catalogue of Lithuanian
literature. Katalogas knygų išleistų "Vienybės Lietuvininkų" ir visų
kitų...[Plymouth, Pa., 1906] 29,
[4] p. Z2537.Z9P3 DLC

167. PODROBNYI KATALOG IZDANII VI-
lenskoi komissii dlia razbora drevnikh aktov, Vilenskago TSentalnago
arkhiva, Vitebskago TSentralnago
arkhiva, Vilenskoi Publichnoi biblioteki i Vilenskago Uchebnago okruga,
vyshedshykh v sviet s 1865 po 1905
god. Vil'na, Tip. A.G. Syrkina,
1905. 25 p. Z2514.W5P6 DLC PU

168. PUZINAITĖ, V. and Leonas Vladimirovas. Senojo Vilniaus universiteto katalogai. [The catalogues of
the old University of Vilnius] IN
Vilna. Universitetas. Biblioteka.
Mokslinės bibliotekos metraštis,
1957. (Vilnius), 1958, p. 19-[31]
Z821.7.V5 1957 DLC InU NN PU

169. ŠV. KAZIMIERO DRAUGIJOS LEIDI-
NIŲ sąrašas su recenzijomis. [A list
of publications of the Šv. Kazimiero
society] Kaunas, Šv. Kazimiero draugija, 1924. 28 p. 002.ŠK ICLJF

170. VILNA. PUBLICHNAIA BIBLIOTEKA.
Sistematicheskii katalog Russkago
otdieleniia biblioteki. Pechataniem
zaviedyvali D. Stolypin i F. Dobrianskii. Vil'na, Tip. I. IAlovtsera
i F. Vainshteina, 1879-80. 2 v. in 1.
Z2491.V6 DLC

--- Pervoe-chetvertoe pribav-
lenie. Vil'na, Tip. A.G. Syrkina,
1888-1907. 4 v. in 2.
Z2491.V6 Suppl. DLC CtY(4)

171. VILNA. PUBLICHNAIA BIBLIOTEKA.
MUZEI DREVNOSTEI. Katalog predmetov
Muzeia drevnostei, nastoiashchago pri
Vilenskoi publichnoi bibliotekie.
Sostavil F. Dobrianskii. Vil'na,
Tip. O.S. Bliumovicha, 1879. 118 p.
Yudin AM60.V4 DLC

172. --- --- 2. izd.Vil'na, Tip. O.
S. Bliumovicha, 1885. 272 p.
Yudin AM60.V4 1885 DLC

173. VILNA. UNIVERSITETAS. BIBLIO-
TEKA. Senoji lietuviška knyga Vil-
niaus universitete; leidinių iki
1800 m. bibliografijos rodyklė. [A
Bibliography of rare books in the
University of Vilnius. Sudarė Feigel-
manas. Ats. red. L. Vladimirovas]
Vilnius, 1959- . illus., facsims.
Z940.7.V5 DLC ICU CaOOLN MH NNC PU

I.5. BIBLIOGRAPHIES OF SERIALS

174. BALTRAMAITIS, Silvestras. Spisok litovskikh zhurnalov, izdannykh vnie Rossii v 1883-1896 gg. In Zhivaia starina (Sanktpeterburg), v.5, no.3-5, 1895, p. 505-506. See serials consulted.

175. BIRŽIŠKA, Vaclovas. The American Lithuanian press from 1875 to 1910. [Washington, D.C., Library of Congress, Photoduplication Services] 1952. 282 leaves. Ms. in the Library of Congress, Slavic Division. Microfilm copy (negative) of typescript. 1366 entries. Microfilm 7100Z DLC MnU NN PU WaU

176. BRUOŽIS, Ansas. Prūsų lietuvių laikraščiai. [The Prussian-Lithuanian newspapers. By] A. B. Klaipėdiškis [pseud.] In Draugija (Kaunas), 1914, p. 69-82. See serials consulted.

177. KISINAS, Izidorius. Lietuvos ir užsienio lietuvių kolonijų 1935 m. periodika. Péridioques parus en 1935 en Lithuanie et chex [sic] les lithuaniens hors Lithuanie. Kaunas, 1936. 22 p. Offprint from Bibliografijos žinios. BM(Ac.1157.c/4.) In Bibliografijos žinios (Kaunas), v.9, no.3, 1936, p. 99-111. See serials consulted.

178. LAVINSKAS, Frank. Amerikos lietuvių laikraščiai, 1879-1955. The Lithuanian press in U.S.A. Long Island City, N.Y., Author [c1956] 191 p. illus., ports. PN4885.L54L3 DLC CLU CtPAM CtY CU ICBM IEN MH PU

179. LIETUVOS TSR KNYGŲ RŪMAI. Lietuvos TSR periodika, 1940-1950; jubiliejinis leidinys. [Lithuanian S.S.R. periodicals, 1940-1950] Vilnius, Valstybinė politinės ir mokslinės literatūros leidykla, 1952. 77 p. Z6956.L5L47 DLC

180. LIETUVOS TSR PERIODINIŲ LEIDINIŲ metraštis; valstybinė bibliografija. [Yearbook of the Lithuanian S.S.R. periodical publications; a national bibliography. Ats. redaktorius A. Ulpis] Vilnius, Lietuvos TSR Knygų rūmai, 1953-55. 4 v. Annual. Z6956.L5L5 DLC(1951-)

181. THE LITHUANIAN AMERICAN PRESS. In Lithuanian Bulletin (New York) v.8, no.7-12, 1950, p. 19-20. See serials consulted.

182. NEW YORK PUBLIC LIBRARY. A list of Russian, other Slavonic and Baltic periodicals in the New York Public Library; comp. by Herman Rosenthal. New York, N.Y., New York Public Library, 1916. iii, 36 p. 016.05.Z454 NNC NN

183. RUŽANCOVAS, Aleksandras. Lietuvos periodika, 1929-1930. [Lithuanian periodical press, 1929-1930] Kaunas, Varpo bendrovės spaustuvė, 1930. 15 p. 947.59.R94L WaU CU

184. --- Lietuvos periodinė spauda 1928 metais. Die Presse Litauens im Jahre 1928. Kaunas, 1929. 15 p. Balt 8040.10 MH

185. --- Nepriklausomos Lietuvos periodika, 1929-1930 m. [Lithuanian periodical press, 1929-1930) In Bibliografijos žinios (Kaunas), v.3, p. 50-63, 94-95, 118-119, 159, 191. See serials consulted.

186. SCATTERED NUMBERS OF LITHUANIAN underground newspapers, published between 1942-1944. n.p., 1942-44. 111 pieces. Includes an index prepared by Algirdas Vokietaitis, and a facsim. of the title pages of the newspapers represented. D802.L5S25 DLC

187. TAUTVILAS, Danutė Dana J. The Lithuanian press in America. Washington, D.C., 1961. 127 leaves. Thesis (M.S.) --Catholic University of America. PN4885.L54T3 DLC MH(microfilm)

I.6. INDEXES TO PERIODICAL ARTICLES

188. BALTRAMAITIS, Casimir V. Lithuanian affairs; an index of the New York Times on subjects pertaining to Lithuania and Lithuanians. New York, N.Y., Lithuanian Press Club, 1945. xxxi, 136 leaves. Reproduced from type-written copy. DK511.L27B3 DLC AzU CSt CSt-H CU CtY CtPAM FU FMU In IdU ICJ IU IaU ICN InU ICU IEN MH MB MNU MdBJ MnU NN NmU NjP NvU NB NNC NIC OCl OkU PU ScU TxDaM VtU WU WaS WaU

189. LIETUVOS TSR KNYGŲ RŪMAI. Lietuvos TSR žurnalų ir laikraščių straipsniai; valstybinė bibliografija. [National bibliography of articles of the Soviet Lithuanian press, 1944-1948. Ats. redaktorius A. Ulpis] Vilnius, 1954-56. 3 v. Superseded by "Spaudos metraštis" in 1957; Supersedes "Lietuvos TSR žurnalų ir laikraščių straipsnių metraštis" AI 19.L5Z8 DLC MH(1940-1941)

190. LIETUVOS TSR MOKSLŲ AKADEMIJA,

VILNA. CENTRINĖ BIBLIOTEKA. Lietuvos TSR Mokslų akademijos darbuotojų straipsnių bibliografija, 1945-1954. [Bibliography of articles by the members of the Lithuanian S.S.R. Academy of Sciences, 1945-1954. Sudarė J. Basiulis and A. Sitnikaitė] Vilnius, 1960. 405 p. Z5055.L52L5 1945-1954 DLC CaAEU ICU INU MH NN NNC NcD PP1U PU WaU

191. ŽURNALŲ IR LAIKRAŠČIŲ STRAIPSnių metraštis; Lietuvos TSR Valstybinės bibliografijos organas. [An annual index of periodical articles] Vilnius, LTSRKR, 1947-56. 5 v. Title varies: vol.1, 1947, Lietuvos TSR Žurnalų ir laikraščių straipsnių metraštis; 1954-1956, Lietuvos TSR Žurnalų ir laikraščių straipsniai. Superseded by "Spaudos metraštis" in 1957. AI 19.L5Z8 DLC(1944-1956) NNC(1944 45-)

I.7. BIBLIOGRAPHIES OF MANUSCRIPTS

192. DOBRIANSKII, Flavian Nikolaevich. Opisanie rukopisei Vilenskoi Publichnoi biblioteki tserkovno-slavianskikh i russkikh. Vil'na, Tip. A.G. Syrkina, 1882. 533 p. Z6621.V765D6 DLC CSt-H MH NN

193. LIETUVOS TSR MOKSLŲ AKADEMIJA, VILNA. CENTRINĖ BIBLIOTEKA. Lietuvos TSR Mokslų akademijos rankraštinių darbų ir disertacijų bibliografija, 1946-1956. [A Bibliography of manuscripts and theses at the Lithuanian S.S.R. Academy of Sciences, 1946-1956. Sudarė V. Abramavičius and K. Čepienė] Vilnius, 1958. 158 p. RC16.378475L625 NNC(Xerox copy) Z5055.L52L53 DLC MH PU

194. --- Rankraščių rinkiniai; Lietuvos TSR Mokslų akademijos Centrinės bibliotekos XI-XX amžių rankraščių fondų trumpa apžvalga. [Collection of manuscripts; a brief review of manuscripts from the 11th to 20th centuries in the Central Library of the Lithuanian S.S.R. Academy of Sciences. Sudarė V. Abramavičius. Redakcinė kolegija: S. Brašiškis, J. Galvydis ir A. Ivaškevičius, atsakingasis redaktorius] Vilnius [Laikraščių ir žurnalų leidykla] 1963. 289 p. facsims. Z6621.L72 DLC CU CtPAM CtY ICU MH NN PU

195. --- Revoliucinis judėjimas Lietuvoje ir Baltarusijoje, 1905-1907 metais; Lietuvos TSR Mokslų akademijos Centrinės bibliotekos rankraščių aprašas. [The revolutionary movement in Lithuania and White Russia, 1905-1907; an annotated list of manuscripts

in the Central library of the Lithuanian S.S.R. Academy of Sciences. Sudarė N.A. Leškovič; redakcinė kolegija: S. Brašiškis et al.] Vilnius, 1958. 120 p. DK511.L25L5 DLC IU MH NN

196. SALYS, Antanas. Kretingos vienuolyno lietuviškieji rankraščiai. [The Lithuanian manuscripts in the monastery of Kretinga] In Svietimo darbas (Kaunas), no.1, 1927, p. 16-24. See serials consulted.

197. VILENSKAIA KOMISSIIA DLIA RAZbora i izdaniia drevnikh aktov. Sbornik paleograficheskikh snimkov s drevnikh gramot i aktov khraniashchikhsia v Vilenskom TSentral'nom arkhivie i Vilenskoi Publichnoi bibliotekie. Vyp.1: 1432-1549 GG. Vil'na, Tip. A.G. Syrkina, 1884. 1 v. Z115.R9V5 DLC BM NN PU

198. VILNA. PUBLICHNAIA BIBLIOTEKA. Opisanie rukopis'nago otdeleniia. Vil'na, Tip. A.G. Syrkina, 1895-1906. 5 v. Z6621.V762 DLC MH(1-4) NN OCl

199. --- Rukopis'noe otdelenie Vilenskoi Publichnoi biblioteki. Vil'na, Izd. Vilenskoi biblioteki, 1871. 1 v. Yudin Z6621.V5 DLC

200. VOLTER, Eduard Aleksandrovich. Beschreibung der handschriftlichen Abteilung der Wilnaer öffentlichen Bibliothek. In LLGM, v.4, 1899, p. 459-463. See serials consulted.

201. ZELENIN, Dimitrii Konstantinovich. Obzor rukopis'nykh materialov arkhiva Vsesoiuznogo geograficheskogo obshchestva o narodakh Pribaltiki (Latyshi, Litovtsi, Esty) In Sovetskaia etnografiia (Moskva), no.6-7, 1947, p. 254-274. See serials consulted.

202. ŽUKAS, Vladas. Lietuviški ir su Lietuva susiję rankraščiai Lenkijos bibliotekose. [Lithuanian and manuscripts relating to Lithuania in Polish libraries] In VUBMBM, 1958-1959. Vilnius, 1961. p. 217-248. Z821.7.V5 DLC InU MH NN PU

I.8. BIBLIOGRAPHIES OF DISSERTATIONS

LIETUVOS TSR MOKSLŲ AKADEMIJA, VILNA. CENTRINĖ BIBLIOTEKA. Lietuvos TSR Mokslų akademijos rankraštinių darbų ir disertacijų bibliografija, 1946-1956. Vilnius, 1958. See entry no. 193.

203. --- Medicinos daktarų disertacijos, apgintos arba pripažintos

Vilniaus Universitete, 1793-1842 metais; bibliografinė rodyklė. [Doctoral dissertations in medicine defended and accepted by the University of Vilnius in the years 1793-1842: a bibliographic index. Sudarė A. Bielinis; redakcinė kologija: S. Brašiškis et al.] Vilnius, 1958. 131 p. illus. Lithuanian and Russian. Z.6661.L75L5 DLC DNLM NN NNC-M PU

204. PETRAUSKIENĖ, Zofija and P. Valentėlienė. Lietuvos TSR mokslininkų disertacijos, 1945-1968; bibliografija. [Dissertations of Soviet Lithuanian scientists, 1945-1968] Vilnius, 1971. 490 p. At head of title: Lietuvos TSR Mokslų akademijos Centrinė biblioteka. Vilniaus Valstybinio V. Kapsuko universiteto Mokslinė biblioteka. Z5055.R9L55 DLC CaAEU PU

I.9. BIBLIOGRAPHIES OF BIBLIOGRAPHIES

205. BALYS, Jonas. Baltic encyclopedias and biographical directories. In The Quarterly Journal of the Library of Congress. (Washington,D.C.) v.22, no.3, 1966, p. 270-275. See serials consulted.

206. --- Bibliography of Baltic bibliographies. [Chicago, Ill., 1969-71. 52 p.] Detached from Lituanistikos darbai (Chicago, Ill.), v.2, 1969, p. 141-186 and Naujoji viltis (Chicago, Ill.), no.2, 1971, p. 115-120. Z2531.B19 CaAEU; also In Lituanistikos darbai (Chicago, Ill.), v.2, 1969, p. 141-186. See serials consulted.

207. MORKŪNAITĖ, Ž., comp. Tarybų Lietuvos mokslinėse bibliotekose sudarytų bibliografinių sąrašų suvestinė rodyklė. [A list of the bibliographies compiled by Soviet Lithuanian research libraries] Vilnius, 1965. 90 p. Z2537.M6 DLC

I.10. LITHUANIAN BIBLIOGRAPHY, ITS HISTORY AND CRITICISM

208. BIRŽIŠKA, Vaclovas. Lietuviškos bibliografijos istorija. [History of Lithuanian bibliography] Kaunas, "Bibliografijos žinių" priedas, 1944. 16, 49-80 p. (Bibliotekininko parankinė, 3) Microfilm F1877 NNN(letters N-Z)

209. LIROV, V. P. Problema ob"ekta bibliografii lituaniki. In

LTSRAMMD: Bibliotekininkystės ir bibliografijos klausimai (Vilnius), v.3, 1964, p. 27-60. See serials consulted.

210. ŽUKAS, Vladas. Karlovičiaus darbas "Lietuvių bibliografijos bandymas" [The work of Karlovičius "The attempt of Lithuanian bibliography"] In VUBMBM, 1957. Vilnius, 1958, p. 50-[62] Z821.7.V5 DLC InU NN PU

211. --- S. Baltramaičio kraštotyros bibliografijos darbų vertinimas ir II. dalies paruošimas. [Evaluation of the bibliographic works on description and travel by S. Baltramaitis] In LTSRAMMD: Bibliotekininkystės ir bibliografijos klausimai (Vilnius), v.1, 1961, p. 111-122. See serials consulted.

212. --- S. Baltramaičio lietuvių spaudos bibliografija. [The Bibliography of Lithuanian publications by S. Baltramaitis] In LTSRCBBB, v.1, p. 131-190. See serials consulted.

213. --- S. Baltramaičio lietuvių spaudos ir rankraščių bibliografijos darbai. [The bibliographic works on Lithuanian publications and manuscripts by S. Baltramaitis] In VUBMBM, Vilnius, 1961, p. 43-68. See serials consulted.

II. GENERAL REFERENCE AIDS

II.1. ENCYCLOPEDIAS

214. ENCYCLOPEDIA LITUANICA. [Edited by Simas Sužiedėlis] Boston, Mass., J. Kapočius, Lithuanian Encyclopedia Press, 1970- . 6 v. illus., ports., facsims. DK511.L2E5 DLC C CL CLU CaACU CaAE CaAEU CaBVaU CaOONL CaOOP CaOLU CaOTU CSt CSt-H CU-A Cu-S CU CoD CtPAM CtY FTaSU ICL ICIU IEN ICU InU InNd L MB MBU MdBE MiDW MnU MH N NBuU NNC NNU NbOU NcD NcU NjP NRU NvU OClW OKentU OU PP PPi PSt PU TxU WMUW WU

215. LIETUVIŠKOJI ENCIKLOPEDIJA. [Lithuanian encyclopedia] Kaunas, Spaudos Fondas [1933-1944] 9 v. Covers letters A-I. No more published. AE60.L5 DLC(1-4) DLL(1-8) CtPAM(1-4) ICCC(1-8) InU(1-9) NN(1-4) OCl(1-7) PU(1-8) WU(1)

216. LIETUVIŲ ENCIKLOPEDIJA. [Lithuanian encyclopedia] Boston, Mass. Lietuvių enciklopedijos leidykla, 1953-69. 36 v. illus., ports., maps. Publisher: Juozas Kapočius. AE60. L5L5 DLC CaAEU CaOTP CaOTU CLU CU CtY DNLM IC ICCC ICU InU IU KU MH

MnU NN NNC NcU NRU OCl OU PSt PU WaU

217. MAŽOJI LIETUVIŠKOJI TARYBINĖ
enciklopedija. [Little Soviet Lithuanian encyclopedia. Ed. by J. Matu-
lis] Vilnius, Mintis, 1966-71. 3 v.
illus. DK511.L2M33 DLC CaOTU CtY
CtPAM GU ICBM ICU InU IU NNC NjP PU

II.2. DIRECTORIES, HANDBOOKS AND MANUALS

218. AMERIKOS LIETUVIŲ RYMO KATA-
likų kunigų sąjunga. Žinynas.
[Directory] South Boston, Mass.,
Darbininkas, 1918. 1 v. illus.
325.2475.Am35 PU NN

219. CATALOGUS CUSTODIAE LITUANIAE
Sancti Casimiri Fratrum Minorum.
Kennebunkport, Me., 1971. 1 v.
MeKPF

220. CATALOGUS UNIO CLERI LITUANI
in U.S.A. Paruoštas Kun. Vytauto
Pikturnos. n.p., Lux Christi, 1954.
1 v. CtPAM

221. ELENCHUS SACERDOTUM LITUANO-
rum in variis statibus pro A.D.
195 - . [n.p., Kunigų vienybė JAV]
Irregular. CtPAM(1955-)PU(1966, 1970)

222. KARININKŲ METRAŠTIS. [Offi-
cers' annual] 1- ; Kaunas, Kariuomenės štabo Rikiuotės skyrius, 1932-
40. The yearbook was an official
directory of the Ministry of defence.
U11.L5K3 DLC

223. LIETUVOS EKSPORTAS IR EKSPOR-
teriai. Lithuanian export and exporters. 1927- . Kaunas. illus.,
ports., map, tables. Annual. Lithuanian, French, English, and German.
HF3635.7.L48 DLC CtPAM NN(1929-1931)
RPB WaU(1930)

224. LIETUVOS TELEFONŲ ABONENTŲ SĄ-
rašas. [Lithuania's telephone direc-
tory] Kaunas. HE9275.7.L5 DLC(1922,
1924,1925,1936)

225. LITHUANIA. The Diplomatic
and consular services. In A collection of the diplomatic and consular
laws and regulations of various countries. Ed. by A.H. Feller [and] M.O.
Hudson. Washington, D.C., 1933.
p. 769-785. JX1632.F4 DLC

226. LITHUANIA. SVEIKATOS DEPAR-
TAMENTAS. Lietuvos medicinos, veterinarijos ir farmacijos personalo ir
įstaigų sąrašas. [Directory of Lithuania's medical, veterinarian, and
pharmaceutical professions] Kaunas,
Varpas, 1925. 98 p. R713.67.L5A5 DLC

227. LITHUANIA. UŽSIENIŲ REIKALŲ
MINISTERIJA. Liste du corps diplo-
matique accredité à Kaunas avec an-
nexe contenat la list des consuls
généraux, consuls et vice-consuls
en Lithuanie. Kaunas [1924] 1 v.
JX1806.6.A23 DLC

228. --- Žinynas. [Directory of
the Ministry of Foreign Affairs]
Kaunas. Annual. JX1808.6.A25
DLC(1929,1931,1933) MH PU(1929)

229. METRAŠTIS LIETUVIŲ BIZNIO RO-
dyklė. Classified annual directory
of the Lithuanian business. Chicago, Ill., 1920-31. Title varies:
1920, Metinė lietuvių biznio knyga;
1928/29, Biznio ir informacijų knyga. (*TLA)NN(1920-1923,1925,1928/
29,1931)

230. SIMUTIS, Anicetas, ed. Pasaulio lietuvių žinynas. Lithuanian
world directory. New York, N.Y.,
Lithuanian Chamber of Commerce,1953.
366 p. illus. DK511.L223S5 DLC
ICLJF MH PU

231. --- --- 2d ed. New York,N.Y.,
Lithuanian Chamber of Commerce, 1958.
464 p. illus., ports. DK511.L223S5
1958 DLC CLU CU CSt-H CtPAM CtY
CaAEU CaOTP CaOTU GU ICCC IC InNd
IU LU MH MnU NB NNC NBuU OCl PU

232. REKLAITIS, Povilas. Rytinei
Europai tirti dokumentacijos ir informacijos centrai Vokietijos Fede-
ralinėje Respublikoje ir jų reikšmė
lituanistikai. Dokumentations- und
Informationszentren zur Erforschung
des östlichen Europas in der Bundesrepublik Deutschlands und ihre Bedeutung für die Litauenkunde. In
Lituanistikos darbai (Chicago, Ill.)
v.2, 1969, p. 35-65. Bibliography:
61-64. Summary in German. See serials consulted.

233. VILNIUS; adresai ir informa-
cijos. [Vilnius directory] Vilnius,
Vilniaus miesto vykdomasis komitetas.
DK651.V4V43 DLC(1960-) MH(1960)

234. VIL'NIUS; kratkaia adresno-
spravochnaia kniga. 1- ; 1957- .
Vil'nius, Upravlenie mestnogo khoziaistva, Vil'niusskii gorodskoi ispolnitel'nyi komitet. DK651.V4V346
DLC(1957,1960,1964-) NIC(1960)

235. VILNIUS; trumpa adresų-infor-
macijos knyga, 1957 m. rugpiūčio 1d.
duomenimis. [Vilnius directory]
Vilnius, 1957. 256 p. 914.75.V715
PU

II.3. DICTIONARIES, GLOSSARIES, ETC.

II.3.a. BILINGUAL, POLYGLOT, ETC.

236. ALMINAS, Kazys. Vokiškai lietuviškas žodynas. Deutsch-litauisches Wörterbuch. Kaunas, Valstybinė leidykla, 1943. xvi, 687 p. PG8681.G5A8 1943 DLC

237. AMBROZEWICZ, Józef. Polsko-Litewsko-Rosyjski słownik. Warszawa, Księg. H. Wajnera [1907] 552 p. PC491.A49 CtY

238. ANGLŲ-LIETUVIŲ KALBŲ ŽODYNAS. [English-Lithuanian dictionary. Sudarė autorių kolektyvas: V. Baravykas ir D. Šlapoberskis] Vilnius, VPMLL, 1953. 368 p. Contains about 20,000 words. PG8679.A6 DLC CaAEU

239. --- Apie 30,000 žodžių. Vilnius, 1958. 589 p. PG8679.A57 1958 PU

240. --- Apie 20,000 žodžių. [Chicago, Ill.] Terra [1960] 368 p. NN

241. --- Apie 30,000 žodžių. [Sudarė A. Laučka ir A. Dantaitė] Chicago, Terra, 1959. 583 p. PG8679.A57 1959 DLC CaOTU IU NNC OCl

242. --- --- 2., pataisytas ir papildytas leidimas. Apie 30,000 žodžių. Vilnius, 1961. 595 p. PG8679.A59 1961 DLC CSt CaAEU DS OClW WU

243. BARONAS, Jonas. Rusiškai lietuviškas žodynas. Russko-litovskii slovar'. Kaunas, Sakalo bendrovės leidinys, 1924. 576 p. PG8682.B3 DLC BM CtY TxU

244. --- Rusų lietuvių žodynas. Antras naujai parašytas kirčiuotas leidimas. Russko-litovskii slovar'. Novoe izdanie s udareniami. Kaunas, Sakalas, 1933. 630 p. PG8682.R8B3 1933 PU

245. --- --- Kaunas, Sakalas,1933. Nandeln, Lichtenstein, Krauss Reprint Ltd., 1968. 630 p. 3297.218.4 MH

246. BARONAS, Jonas. Rusų-lietuvių kalbų žodynas. Russko-litovskii slovar'. Paruošė Vaclovas Baronas ir V. Galinis. Ats. redaktorius J. Macaitis. Sudarytas panaudojant spausdintą ir rankraštinę medžiagą kurią surinko J. Baronas. Vilnius, Mintis, 1967. 2 v. PG8682.R8R8 1967 DLC CaAEU CaBVaU CaOTU CoU OClW PU WU

247. BUSCH, Arndt and Teodoras Chomskas. Lietuviškai vokiškas žo-

dynas praktikos ir mokyklos reikalams sudarė A. Bušas ir T. Chomskas. Litauisch-deutsches Wörterbuch für den Hand- und Schulgebrauch. Dal.1. Berlin und Leipzig, G. Neuner, 1927. 305 p. PG8681.B8 DLC BM ICU MH MnU NN

248. DAS ELBINGER DEUTSCH-PREUSSIsche Vokabular. 17 Tafeln in Lichtdruck. Hrsg. Namens der Altertumsgesellschaft Prussia von A. Bezzenberger... und W. Simon. Königsberg in Pr., In Commission bei W. Koch, 1897. [4] p. 17 facsims. German and Prussian in parallel columns. From the codex Neumannianus of the Elbinger Stadtbibliothek. Sp 491.91.El.13 PU DLC

249. FULST, K., A. SCHOLZ and Jurgis Talmantas. Litauisch-deutsches Wörterbuch. Lietuviškai vokiškas žodynas. Kaunas, Valstybinė leidykla [1943] xlviii, 605 p. Published only v.1 (A-N) PG8681.G5F8 DLC ICLJF PU

250. GAILIUS, Viktoras and M. Šlaža. Vokiškai-lietuviškas žodynas. Deutsch-litauisches Wörterbuch. Klaipėda, Rytas, 1932. xii, 628 p.

251. GAILIUS, Viktoras. Vokiškai-lietuviškas žodynas. Deutsch-litauisches Wörterbuch. Tübingen, Patria [1948] xiv, 1181 p. PG8681.G5G3 DLC MH PU

252. HAACK, Friedrich Wilhelm. Vocabvlarivm litthvanico-germanicvm, et germanico-litthvanicvm, darin alle im Neuen Testament und Psalter befindliche Wörter nach dem Alphabeth enthalten sind; nebst einem Anhang einer kurtzgefassten litthauischen Grammatic. Halle, S. Orbau [1730] 336 p. Bonaparte Collection no. 13434 ICN BM

253. HERLITAS, J.A. English-Lithuanian dictionary. Klaipėda, Rytas, 1931. xvi, 399 p. 491.92.H26 CaOTP CtTMF MiD NN NNC OCl PU

254. JOKANTAS, Kazys. Lotyniškai-lietuviškas žodynas. [Latin-Lithuanian dictionary] Kaunas, Spindulio bendrovės spaustuvė, 1936. x, 1096 p. 473.1.J672 PU CtPAM

255. JUŠKA, Antanas. Litovskii slovar' A. IUshkevicha s tolkovaniem slov na russkom i pol'skom iazykakh. Sanktpeterburg, Izdanie Otdieleniia russkago iazyka i slovesnosti Imperatorskoi akademii nauk, 1904-22. 3 v. PG8678.I8 DLC CtPAM ICBM KU (t.1, v.2; t.2, v.1) MH(2-3) PU

256. KARECKAITĖ, Aldona. Trumpas

mokyklinis vokiečių-lietuvių ir lie-
tuvių-vokiečių kalbų žodynas. Sudarė A. Kareckaitė, H. Kazlauskaitė,
V. Kazlauskaitė. [A short German-
Lithuanian and Lithuanian-German dic-
tionary] Kaunas, Valstybinė pedagoginės literatūros leidykla, 1963.
301 p. PG8681.G5K3 DLC

257. KIŠENINIS ŽODYNĖLIS LIETUVIŠ-
kai-angliškas ir angliškai-lietuviškas. A dictionary of the English
and Lithuanian languages. Chicago,
Ill., 1911. 151 p. BM(12976.a.31.)
NN

258. KURSCHAT, Alexander Theodor.
Litauisch-deutsches Wörterbuch. The-
saurus linguae Lituanicae. Hrsg.
von Wilhelm Wissmann und Erich Hof-
mann. Unter Mitwirkung von Armin
Kurschat und Hertha Krick. Göttin-
gen, Vandenhoeck & Ruprecht, 1968- .
PG8681.G5K78 DLC CaAEU CaBVaS CaBVaU
CaOHM CaOTY CaOWtU CoU CtY IEN ICU
InNd GU MH MU NBuU NIC NjP NjR PU
RPB TxU WU

259. KURSCHAT, Friedrich. Wörter-
buch der litauischen Sprache. Halle,
Buchhandlung des Waisenhauses, 1870-
83. 3 v. in 2. Contents.--T.1,
Bd.1-2. Deutsch-littauisches Wörter-
buch.--T.2. Littauisch-deutsches
Wörterbuch. PG8681.K8 DLC CLU(2)
CaBVaU CaQMM CtPAM CtY IEN(2) ICU
ICN IaU KU MH MB MdBJ NN NNC NjP PU
TxU WU

260. LALIS, Antanas. Lenkų ir lietuvių kalbos žodynas. [Polish-Lithu-
anian dictionary] Vilnius, 1919.
331 p. PG8682.P6L3 PU

261. LALIS, Anthony. Lietuviškos
ir angliškos kalbų žodynas. A dictionary of the English and Lithuanian
languages. Sutaišė Antanas Lalis.
Chicago, Ill., Turtu ir spauda "Lietuvos", 1903. 2 v. PG8679.L3 DLC
CaBVaU(1903-1905) CaOTU CaQMM ICN
ICU(1903-1905) MnU(1903-1915)
NN(1903-1905) PU(1903-1905)

262. --- --- 2., mažuma taisytas
ir papildytas spaudimas. [2d corr.
and enlarged ed.] Chicago, Ill.,
Turtu ir spauda "Lietuvos", 1905.
2 v. in 1. PG8679.L32 DLC CSt CSt-H
CaOTP ICLJF ICS MBC NN NNC NcU(2) OO

263. --- --- 3., iš naujo taisytas
ir gausiai papildytas spaudimas.
[3d corr. ed.] Chicago, Ill., Turtu
ir spauda "Lietuvos", 1911. 2 v.
in 1. PG8679.L33 DLC CtTMF IaU
NB(1910-1915) NNC(1911-1915) OCl TxU
WaS

264. --- --- Reprint. Chicago,

Ill., Turtu ir spauda "Lietuvos",
1915. 2 v. in 1. PG8679.L33 1915
DLC CaOTP CaOTU FU InNd ICJ MA MiU
MH MoU NIC NcU NjP NSyU OCl PU TU
RPB

265. LEMCHENAS, Chackelis. Russko
litovskii slovar'. 2. izd. ispr. i
dop. Vil'nius, Gos. izd-vo polit. i
nauch. lit-ry Litovskoi SSR, 1955.
903 p. PG8682.R8L4 1955 DLC PU

266. --- Trumpas rusų-lietuvių
kalbų žodynas. [A short Russian-
Lithuanian dictionary] Vilnius,
VPMLL, 1957. 440 p. PG8682.R8L42
DLC CaAEU ICU OKentU PU TxU

267. --- Trumpas mokyklinis rusų-
lietuvių kalbų žodynas. Kratkii
shkol'nyi russko-litovskii slovar'.
Kaunas, 1960. 555 p. PG8682.R8L417
DLC CaAEU PU

268. --- --- Apie 20,000 žodžių.
[2., pataisytas leidimas. 2d. corr.
ed.] Kaunas,Šviesa, 1968. 576 p.
PG8682.R8L417 1968 DLC

269. LENKŲ-LIETUVIŲ KALBŲ ŽODYNAS.
Apie 50,000 žodžių. Sudarė A. Vait-
keviciūtė. [A Polish-Lithuanian dic-
tionary] Vilnius, Mintis, 1964.
627 p. PG8682.P6L4 DLC CaAEU CaOTU
PU

270. LIETUVIEŠŲ-LATVIEŠŲ VARDNĪCA.
Ap 50,000 vardu. [Lithuanian-Lat-
vian dictionary. About 50,000 words]
Redigējis J. Balkevičs. Rīgā, Lat-
vijas valsts izdevnieciba, 1964.
915 p. At head of title: A. Bojāte,
V. Subatnieks. PG8681.L3L5 DLC CtY

271. LIETUVIŠKAI-ŽYDIŠKAI ŽODYNAS.
[Lithuanian-Yddish dictionary] Su-
rinko broliai Kolodnai. Redagavo
ir lietuviškai tekstą apdirbo St.
Dabušis. Kaunas, 1923. 243, viiip.
PG8681.Y5L5 PU

272. LIETUVIŲ-ANGLŲ KALBŲ ŽODYNAS.
Apie 27,000 žodžių. [Lithuanian-
English dictionary. About 27,000
words] Redagavo I. Karsavinaitė ir
D. Šlapoberskis. Vilnius, VPMLL,
1960. 511 p. At head of title: B.
Piesarskas, B. Svecevičius.
PG8679.L55 DLC CLU CSt CU CaAEU DS
IaU ICU MH NIC NNC NjP PU RPB WU WaU

273. LIETUVIŲ-PRANCŪZŲ KALBŲ ŽODY-
nas; apie 25,000 žodžių. [Lithua-
nian-French dictionary; about 25,000
words] Vilnius, VPMLL, 1962. 647 p.
At head of title: I. Karsavina, S.
Kairiūkštytė. PG8681.F7L5 DLC CaQMM
CaSSU CtY NN PU

274. LIETUVIŲ-RUSŲ KALBŲ ŽODYNAS;

apie 37,000 žodžių. [Lithuanian-Russian dictionary; about 37,000 words] Redagavo Ch. Lemchenas. Vilnius, VPMLL, 1962. 747 p. At head of title: A. Lyberis. PG8682.R8L49 DLC CLU CtY InU MH MiDW NN NIC NNC NcD PPiU PU

275. ---; apie 50,000 žodžių. [Lithuanian-Russian dictionary; about 50,000 words] Redagavo Ch. Lemchenas. Vilnius, Mintis, 1971. 893 p. At head of title: A. Lyberis. PG8682.R8L9 1971 PU

276. LIETUVIŲ-RUSŲ KALBŲ ŽODYNAS, skiriamas mokyklai; apie 22,000 žodžių. [Lithuanian-Russian dictionary for the school; 22,000 words] Vilnius, VPMLL, 1956. 391 p. At head of title: V. Kozuchinas ir A. Lyberis. PG8682.R8L5 DLC CaAEU CtY DS InU IU NN OU PU

277. LOTYNŲ-LIETUVIŲ KALBŲ ŽODYNAS; apie 20,000 žodžių. 2. pataisytas ir papildytas leidimas. [Latin-Lithuanian dictionary...] Vilnius, VPMLL, 1958. 696 p. PA2365.L5L6 1958 DLC PU

278. LOUGAS, Vello. Leedu-eesti sonaraamat. [Lithuanian-Estonian dictionary] Tallinn, Valgus, 1969. 447 p. PH625.L6 PU

279. MIELCKE, Christian Gottlieb. Littauisch-deutsches und deutsch-littauisches Wörterbuch. Nebst einer Nachschrift des Herrn Prof. Kant. Königsberg in Pr., Hartung, 1800. 16 p.l., 352, 576, [4], 280 p. Hvc32.M58 CtY CLSU MdBP NN PBm PU

280. MIEŽINIS, Mikolas. Lietuviszkai-latviszkai-lenkiszkai-rusiszkas žodynas. [Lithuanian-Latvian-Polish-Russian dictionary] Tilžė, M. Noveskis, 1894. 292 p. PG8678.M63 ICU BM(12975. i. 25.) CtTMF MH PU

281. NESSELMANN, Georg Heinrich Ferdinand. Wörterbuch der littauischen Sprache. Königsberg in Pr., Gebrüder Bornträger, 1851. xi,555 p. PG8681.G5N45 DLC CaOHM CtY ICN IEN ICU MB MH MnU NN NIC NjP PU

282. NIEDERMANN, Max. Wörterbuch der litauischen Schriftsprache, Litauisch-Deutsch. Bearb. von Max Niedermann, Alfred Senn, Franz Brender und Anton Salys. Heidelberg, C. Winter, 1932 [i.e. 1926-1932]-1968. 5 v. (Indogermanische Bibliothek. 5. Abt. Baltische Bibliothek, Bd. 3) PG8681.G5N55 CLU CSt-H CU CaAEU CaBVaS CaBVaU CaOHM CaOTU HU ICN ICU InNd IEN LCA LU MH MnU MoU MiU MB NIC NN NNC NcD NcU NBuU NjP OClW OU

PPiU PU RPB TxU ViU WaU WU

283. PAŠKEVIČIUS, Juozas. Lietuviškai-vokiškas žodynas. [Lithuanian-German dictionary] Augsburg, Ger. Sudavija, 1947. viii, 734 p. BM(12977. a. 42.) ICCC ICLJF

284. PESSIS, Jerzy. Lietuviškai-lenkiškas parankusis žodynėlis. [Lithuanian-Polisch dictionary] Warszawa, 1907. 190 p. 491.923.P2 CtTMF BM

285. PĖTERAITIS, Vilius. Lietuviškai angliškas žodynas. Lithuanian-English dictionary. [Nördlingen, Ger.] M. Sutkevičius [1948] xv,579 p. PG8679.P38 1948 DLC CSt CU MiD NN OCl PU

286. --- --- 2d edition. Chicago, Ill., Lietuviškos knygos klubas, 1960. xv, 586 p. PG8679.P38 1960 DLC AzU CSt CaAEU CaBVaS CaBVaU CoU CaOONL CaMWU CaOTP CaOTU CaOLU CtY CtPAM HU IEN InNd ICU KU LU MH MU NN NIC NNC NjP NB NcD PU RPB TxU WaU WU

287. --- --- [New York, N.Y., P. Shalom, 1967] xvi, 416 p. PG8679.P38 1967 CaOTY CoU InNd

288. --- Mažasis lietuviškai-angliškas žodynas su tartimi. The concise Lithuanian-English dictionary. [München] M. Sutkevičius [1949] xvi, 419 p. PG8679.P383 DLC CaNSHD CaOOP MiD NN PU

289. PEWTRESS, Harry Howard. Marlborough's English-Lithuanian and Lithuanian-English dictionary. Ed. by H.H. Pewtress... and T. Gerikas. London, E. Marlborough & Co., [1939] 383 p. PG 8679.P7 DLC CLU CSt CU CaBVaS CaBVaU CaOTP CaOTU CaQMM DWB DAFM IC ICJ LU MH MnU MB NN NjP OCl OClW PPiU PU WaS WU

290. PRANCŪZŲ-LIETUVIŲ KALBŲ Žodynas; apie 25,000 žodžių. [French-Lithuanian dictionary] Sudarė E. Juškienė et al. Ats. redaktorius D. Šlapoberskis. Vilnius, VPMLL, 1957. 553 p. PG8681.F7P7 DLC PU

291. RADAUSKAS, Henrikas. Lenkiškai lietuviškas žodynas. [Polish-Lithuanian dictionary] Kaunas, Spaudos Fondas, 1939. 297 p.

292. RĪTERIS, Jānis. Lietuviškai-latviškas žodynas. [Lithuanian-Latvian dictionary] Rīgā, Autora izdevums, 1929. viii, 1368 p. PG8682.L4R5 DLC BM(12977. aa. 1.) NjP PU WU

293. ROSEN, S. IA. Russko-litov-

skii slovar'. Pod redaktsiei B.A. Larina. Moskva, Ogiz, Gos. izdatel'stvo inostrannykh i natsional'nykh slovarei,1941. 327 P. 491.92.R722r WaU PU

294. RUHIG, Philipp. Littauisch-deutsches und deutsch-littauisches lexicon...Nebst einer historischen Betrachtung der littauischen Sprache: wie auch einer gründlichen Grammatick. Königsberg in Pr., J.H. Hartung, 1747. 2 v. in 1. Bonaparte Collection no. 13468 ICN MH

295. --- Littauisch-deutsches und deutsch-littauisches Wörterbuch, worin das vom Pfarrer Ruhig ehemals herausgegebene zwar zum Grunde gelegt aber mit sehr vielen Wörtern, Redens-Arten und Sprüchwörtern zur Hälfte vermehret und verbessert worden von C.G. Mielcke. Nebst einer Nachscrift des Herrn Professor Kant. Königsberg in Pr., Hartung, 1800. 2 v. in 1. Bonaparte Collection no. 13453 ICN NNC NN

296. --- Littauisches Wörterbuch; Auszug der Wurzel aus dem Wörterbuch von Ruhig, herausgegeben von Mielcke. Königsberg in Pr., 1800. [111] p. Manuscript. 3297.9 MH

297. SABALIS, Stasys. Lietuvių-esperanto kalbų Žodynėlis; apie 5,000 žodžių. [Lithuanian-Esperanto dictionary] Vilnius, Profleidykla, 1960. 99 p. PM8238.L5S3 DLC PU

298. ŠAKELĖ-PUIŠYS, St. Lotynų-lietuvių kalbos žodynas. [Latin-Lithuanian dictionary] Vilkaviškis, Spaustuvė "Progresas", 1924. 96 p. Hvc32.Sa29 CtY

299. SAURUSAITIS, Peter. An abridged dictionary of the English-Lithuanian language. Waterbury, Conn., Author, 1899. xii, 188 p. PG8679.S3 DLC MH NN OCl

300. SCHOLZ, A. and Jurgis Talmantas. Deutsch-litauisches Taschenwörterbuch. Memel, Verfasser, 1929. viii, 444 p. PG8681.G5S4 DLC ICLJF

301. SEREISKIS, Benjaminas. Lietuviškai-rusiškas žodynas. [Lithuanian-Russian dictionary] Kaunas, A. Lapino ir G. Volfo leidinys, 1933. xxxii, 1096 p. PG8682.R8S3 CaAEU(1969 ed.) CaBVaU CtY ICU(1969 ed.) MH MnU NN(1969 ed.) PU

302. --- Trumpas lietuviškai rusiškas žodynas. [A concise Lithuanian-Russian dictionary] Sudarė V. Kosuchinas ir K. Ulvydas. [Kaunas] Valstybinė enciklopedijų žodynų ir mokslo literatūros leidykla, 1948.

313 p. PG8681.R9S4 DLC PU

303. SIEBEN-SPRACHEN-WÖRTERBUCH: deutsch-polnisch, russisch, weissruthenisch, litauisch, lettisch, jiddisch. Hersg. im Auftrage des Oberbefehlshaber Ost. Leipzig, A. Spamer [1918] 419 p. PG331.85 DLC BM(12902. i. 32.)

304. ŠLAPELIS, Jurgis. Kirčiuotas lenkiškas lietuvių kalbos žodynas. [Accented Polish-Lithuanian dictionary] Vilnius, Author, 1938. 608 p.

305. --- --- 2. leidimas. Vilnius, 1940. PG8682.P6S55 1940 PU

306. --- Lietuvių ir rusų kalbų žodynas. [Lithuanian-Russian dictionary] Vilnius, 1921-26. 320 p. 491.923.S1 CtTMF

307. --- --- Vilnius, 1931. 320 p. PG8681.S8Z35 PU NjP

308. ŠLAPOBERSKIS, D. Vokiečių-lietuvių kalbų žodynas; apie 60,000 žodžių ir posakių. [German-Lithuanian dictionary] Vilnius, Valstybinė politinės ir mokslinės literatūros leidykla, 1963. 1037 p. PG8681.G5S55 DLC

309. TALMANTAS, Jurgis. Lietuvių-lenkų kalbų žodynas. [Lithuanian-Polish dictionary] Vilnius, Valstybinė politinės ir mokslinės literatūros leidykla, 1955. 349 p. PG8682.L4T3 DLC PU

310. TANANEVICZ, Michael J. Kišeninis žodynėlis, lietuviškai-angliškas ir angliškai-lietuviškas. [Pocket dictionary, Lithuanian-English and English-Lithuanian] Milwaukee, Wis., 1911. 160 p. ICJ

311. --- --- 2. leidimas. [Milwaukee, Wis., C.N. Caspar Co., 1921] 160 p. NN

312. --- --- 3. padidinta laida. Milwaukee, Wis., Book Emporium, 1927. 160 P. PG8679.T3 1927 DLC

313. --- --- 2. padidinta laida. Chicago, Turtu ir spauda Tananevičios, 1921. [Xerox copy, 1971] 160 p. PG8679.T3 1971 PU

314. TRAUTMANN, Reinhold. Baltisch-slavisches Wörterbuch. Göttingen, Vandenhoeck & Ruprecht, 1923. viii, 382 p. PG8091.T7 DLC IU OCU OU PBm PU

315. --- --- 2., unveränd. Aufl. (Unveränd.Nachdruck der 1. Aufl. von 1923) Göttingen, Vandenhoeck und Ruprecht, 1970. PG8093.T7 1970

CaOTU CaAEU CaMWU

316. VĖGĖLĖ, Adolfas and Jonas Strazdas. Karmannyi russko-litov-skii slovar'. Izd. 3-e. Kišeninis rusiškas-lietuviškas žodynėlis. 3. leidimas. Kaunas, Švyturio bendrovė, 193-. 252 p. Ht35.L7V52c CtY

317. VOKIEČIŲ-LIETUVIŲ KALBŲ ŽO-dynas. [German-Lithuanian diction-ary] Sudarytojas-vertėjas D. Šlapo-berskis. Vilnius, VPMLL, 1954. 382 p. PG8681.G5V6 PU

318. ŠIRVYDAS, Konstantinas. Dic-tionarium trium linguarum, in usum studiosae inventutis auctore Con-stantino Szyrwid... Tertia editio recognita & aucta. Vilnae, Typis Academicis Societatis Jesu, 1642. 540 p. Polish-Latin-Lithuanian dictionary for use of students. PG8681.P5S55 1642a PU (Photo-mechanical reproduction)

II.3.b. SPECIAL AND SUBJECT DICTIONARIES

319. ANSKAITIS, Vincas and Mar-celinas Kilas. Rusų-lietuvių kalbų žemės ūkio terminų žodynas. [Rus-sian-Lithuanian dictionary of agri-cultural terms] Vilnius, Mintis, 1971. 362 p. S411.A57 PU

320. ČEIČYS, Jonas. Melioracijos terminų žodynas. [A dictionary of land-reclamation terms] Vilnius, VPMLL, 1960. 382 p. TC970.C4 DLC PU

321. DAUKŠAS, Kazys. Chemijos žo-dynas. [Dictionary of chemistry] Vilnius, VPMLL, 1960. 449 p. QD5.D3 DLC PU

322. GORBACHEVSKII, Nikita Ivan-ovich. Slovar' drevniago aktovago iazyka Sievero-Zapadnago kraia i TSarstva Pol'skago. Vil'na, Tip. Zaka, 1874. xix, 397 p. 947.52.G853 PU NN

323. GREAT BRITAIN. WAR OFFICE. GENERAL STAFF. GEOGRAPHICAL SECTION Short glossary of Lithuanian. Pro-visional edition. London, 1943. 3 p. G108.L5G7 1943 DLC

324. GUDELIS, Vytautas. Geologi-jos ir fizinės geografijos terminų žodynas. [A Russian-Lithuanian dictionary of terms in geology and physical geography] Vilnius, VPMLL, 1956. 219 p. QE5.G78 DLC NN PU

325. ĮVARDAI, ARBA TERMINAI, priimti terminologijos komisijos.

[Terms as adapted by the Commission of Terminology. Kaunas] Sakalas, 1924. 144 p. PG8685.I93 1924 CaAEU PU

326. JUREVIČIUS, A. Aiškinamasis tekstilės terminų žodynas. [Inter-pretative dictionary of the termin-ology in textiles] Vilnius, [Res-pubublikinis mokslinės-techninės informacijos ir propagandos insti-tutas, 1962- . TS1309.J8 DLC PU

327. KAMANTAUSKAS, Viktoras. Trumpas kalbos netaisyklingumų ir barbarizmų žodynėlis. [A concise dictionary of irregularities and barbarisms in the Lithuanian lan-guage] Kaunas, Valstybės spaustuvė, 1928. 78 p. 491.922.K127 PU CtY

328. --- --- Kaunas, Šyturio ben-drovės leidinys, 1930-31. 2 v. 491.925.K ICCC

329. KAUNAS. LIETUVOS VALSTYBINIS KŪNO KULTŪROS INSTITUTAS. Sportinių terminų žodynas. [A dictionary of sports terms] Sudarė V. Stepon-aitis. Vilnius, VPMLL, 1959. 338 p. GV11.K3 DLC PU

330. KAUNAS. POLITECHNIKOS IN-STITUTAS. Rusų-lietuvių kalbų po-litechninis žodynas. [Russian-Li-thuanian technical dictionary] Re-dakcinė kolegija: A. Novodvorskis [et al.] Vilnius, VPMLL, 1959. 515 p. T9.K22 DLC BM CaAEU CtY PU

331. KRUTULYS, Antanas. Trumpas, muzikos žodynas. Redagavo St. Yla. [A concise dictionary of music] Vilnius, VPMLL, 1960. 207 p. illus. music. 491.92.K948 PU CtY

332. LIETUVOS TSR MOKSLŲ AKADEMI-JA, VILNA. BOTANIKOS INSTITUTAS. Botanikos terminų žodynas. Sudarė Botanikos žodyno komisija. Reda-gavo: J. Dagys, vyr. redaktorius, A. Lekavičius ir V. Mališauskienė. [A dictionary of botanical terms] Vilnius, Mintis, 1965. 660 p. At head of title: Lietuvos TSR Mokslų akademijos Botanikos institutas ir Lietuvos TSR botanikų draugija. Bibliography: p. 655-660. QK9.L66 DLC CtPAM IEN MH PU

333. LIETUVOS TSR MOKSLŲ AKADEMI-JA, VILNA. ENERGETIKOS IR ELEKTRO-TECHNIKOS INSTITUTAS. TERMINILOGI-JOS KOMISIJA. Automatika. [Auto-mation] Kaunas, 1960- . (Its Technikos terminai, 1) TJ212.5.L54 DLC

334. --- Hidroenergetika. [Dic-tionary of terms in water power] Kaunas, 1960- . (Its Technikos

terminai, 3) TC147.L5 DLC

335. --- Šiluminė technika. [Dictionary of terms in heat engineering] Kaunas, 1960- . (Its Technikos terminai, 4) TJ260.A1L5 DLC

336. --- Tekstilė. (Dictionary of terms in textiles] Kaunas, 1960- . (Its Technikos terminai, 2) TS1309.L58 DLC

337. LIETUVOS TSR MOKSLŲ AKADEMIJA, VILNA. FIZIKOS IR MATEMATEMATIKOS INSTITUTAS. Fizikos terminų žodynas. [Dictionary of terms in physics] Redaktorius P. Brazdžiūnas. Vilnius, VPMLL, 1958. 122 p. (Its Publikacija, nr. 1) Q60.L495 no.1 DLC CU CtPAM PU

338. LIETUVOS TSR MOKSLŲ AKADEMIJA, VILNA. ISTORIJOS IR TEISĖS INSTITUTAS. Teisinių terminų žodynas. [Dictionary of juridical terms] Sudarė A. Žiurlys, Redakcinė kolegija: J. Bulavas [et al.] Vilnius, VPMLL, 1954. 238 p. DLC-L

339. LIETUVOS TSR MOKSLŲ AKADEMIJA, VILNA. LIETUVIŲ KALBOS IR LITERATŪROS INSTITUTAS. Literatūros terminų žodynas. [Dictionary of literary terms] Sudarė: J. Petronis, V. Vanagas ir A. Zalatorius. Vilnius, VPMLL, 1962. 80 p. PN44.5.L5 DLC CtY MH PU

340. LITHUANIA. KRAŠTO APSAUGOS MINISTERIJA. Kariškas lietuviškai-rusiškas ir rusiškai-lietuviškas žodynėlis. [A concise military dictionary of Lithuanian-Russian and Russian-Lithuanian] Kaunas, Krašto apsaugos ministerijos Literatūros skyriaus leidinys, 1919. 106 p. U25.L64 1919 DLC

341. MARGERIS, Algirdas. Amerikos lietuviai ir angliškųjų skolinių žodynas, 1872-1949. [The American Lithuanians and a dictionary of borrowings from the English language] Chicago, Ill., Author 1956 [i.e. 1958] 366 p. ports. E184.L7M3 DLC ICBM NNC PU

342. MEŠKAUSKAS, Kazys, ed. Rusiškai-lietuviškas ekonomikos terminų žodynas. [Russian-Lithuanian dictionary of economic terms] Vilnius, Mintis, 1966. 290 p. HB61.M4 DLC MH NN

343. NEČIŪNAS, Vytautas. Basic affixes and word roots for medical terminology. Kaunas, 1967. 128 p. English and Lithuanian. R121.N35 DLC

344. NOVODVORSKIS, Andrius. Ang-lų-lietuvių kalbų politechninis žodynas; apie 10,000 įvairių technikos terminų. [English-Lithuanian technological dictionary] Vilnius, VPMLL, 1958. 172 p. T9.N6 DLC PU

345. RUSŲ-LIETUVIŲ-ANGLŲ KALBŲ skaičiavimo technikos terminų žodynas. [Russian-Lithuanian-English dictionary of mathematical terms. Redaktorius Ch. Lemchenas] Vilnius, Mintis, 1971. 597 p. TK7885.A2R87 PU

346. SCHMALSTIEG, William Riegel and Antanas Klimas. Lithuanian-English glossary of linguistic terminology. [University Park] Dept. of Slavic Languages, Pennsylvania State University, 1971. vi, 115 p. P29.S3 DLC PU

347. ŠLAPELIS, Jurgis. Svetimų ir nesuprantamų žodžių žodynėlis. [A concise dictionary of international terms] Tilžė, 1907. 110 p. 491.92.S1.12 PU(Xerox copy 1967)

348. SLOVAR' RUSSKIKH I LITOVSKIKH sokrashchenii. Sostavil G. Feigel'sonas [i dr.] Rusiškų ir lietuviškų santrumpų žodynas. Vil'nius, Gos. izd-vo polit. i khudozh. nauch. lit-ry, 1960. 436 p. PG8686.S55 DLC CaAEU CtY PU

349. TARPTAUTINIŲ ŽODŽIŲ ŽODYNAS. [Dictionary of international terms] Vertė O. Deveikienė, J. Kabelka ir Ch. Lemchenas. Vilnius, Mintis, 1969. 806 p. PG8684.T3 PU CaAEU

350. TIMOFEEV, Leonid Ivanovich. Literatūros mokslo terminų žodynėlis. [Dictionary of literary terms] Vertė ir lietuviškus pavyzdžius parinko J. Vildžiūnas. Kaunas, Valstybinė pedagoginės literatūros leidykla, 1961. 205 p. 803.T485.LF PU MH

351. VAILIONIS, Liudas ir Jonas Dagys. Lietuviškas botanikos žodynas. [Lithuanian dictionary of botany] Kaunas, 1938. 40,598 p. 491.922.V194 PU

352. ŽIUGŽDA, Juozas, ed. Tarptautinių žodžių žodynas. [Dictionary of international words] Sudarė K. Boruta, Pr. Čepėnas, A. Sirutytė-Čepėnienė. Redagavo J. Žiugžda. Klaipėda, Sakalas, 1936. 1064 p. PG8675.Z58 MB

353. YLA, Stasys, 1908- . Liturginės terminologijos klausimu; atsakymas Mažojo Maldyno kritikui. [On the terminology in liturgy...] Putnam, Conn., 1953. 92 p. BX1977.L85Y55 DLC CtTMF PU

II.3.c. DICTIONARIES WITH DEFINI-TIONS IN SAME LANGUAGE

354. BENDER, Harold Herman. A Li-thuanian etymological index, based upon Brungmann's Grundriss and the etymological dictionaries of Uhlen-beck (Sanskrit), Kluge (German), Feist (Gothic), Berneker (Slavic), Walde (Latin), and Boisacq (Greek). Princeton, N.J., Princeton Univer-sity Press, 1921. xvii, 307 p. PG8663.B4 DLC CLU CSt CU CaOTU CoCC CoDU CoU CtY IC ICJ IaU ICU ICBM MB MH MnU MiU NB NIC NN NNC NjP NjR OClW OCU OrU PP PU TxU WU WaU

355. BŪGA, Kazimieras. Lietuvių kalbos žodynas. [Lithuanian dic-tionary] Kaunas, Švietimo ministe-rija, 1924-1925. 2 pts. (cxlix,82p.) PG8675.B9 InU BM CU IEN ICU IU NjP PPULC PU; also in His Rinktiniai raštai, v.3, 1961, p. 9-483. PG8509.B8 v.3 DLC CU CaAEU CtPAM CtTMF IEN ICLJF ICU MH NN NjP PPiU PU TxU

356. FRAENKEL, Ernst. Litauisches etymologisches Wörterbuch. Heidel-berg, C. Winter, 1962-65 [c1955] 2 v. (Indogermanische Bibliothek. 2. Reihe: Wörterbücher) PG8663.F7 DLC CSt CaAEU CaBVaU CaBVaS CaOLU CaOTU CaQMM CoU CtY HU IaU InNd IEN ICU KU LU MH MU NBuU NcU NcD NIC NN NNC PU RPB TxU ViU WaU

357. LIETUVIŲ KALBOS ŽODYNAS. [Dictionary of the Lithuanian lan-guage. Ed. by Balčikonis et al.] Kaunas; Vilnius, 1941-66. 7 v. in 8. At head of title: Lietuvos TSR Mokslų akademija. Lietuvių kalbos ir literatūros institutas. PG8675.L48 DLC CtPAM NjP PU CtY ICU (1-2) KU(4) MH(1-7) NN(1-3)

358. --- [2d ed. Redakcinė kole-gija: J. Kruopas et al.] 2. leidi-mas. Vilnius, Mintis, 1968- . At head of title: Lietuvos TSR Mokslų akademija. Lietuvių kalbos ir lite-ratūros institutas. PG8675.L49 DLC CaAEU CaOONL CtY ICU MH MU NN NjP PPiU PU

359. LIETUVIŲ KALBOS RAŠYBOS ŽO-dynas; rašyba, skyryba, kirčiavimas, lyčių vartojimas, lietuvių kalbos tarmės, vardynas, žodynas. [Ortho-graphic dictionary of the Lithuanian language... Ed. by K. Gasparavičius et al.] Kaunas, VEŽMLL, 1948. 438 p. PG8545.L5 DLC MH(microfilm)

360. LIETUVOS TSR MOKSLŲ AKADEMI-JA, VILNA. LIETUVIŲ KALBOS IR LITE-RATŪROS INSTITUTAS. Dabartinės lie-tuvių kalbos žodynas; apie 45,000 žodžių. [Dictionary of the Lithua-nian language; about 45,000 words] Redakcinė kolegija: J. Balčikonis, K. Korsakas, J. Kabelka, J. Kruopas (atsak. redaktorius), A. Lyberis, K. Ulvydas. Vilnius, VPMLL, 1954. xvi, 990 p. PG8675.L5 DLC CLU CU CaAEU CaOTP CaOTU CoU CtTMF CtY ICU KU MH MnU NIC NN NNC NSyU NcD PU TxU

361. LYBERIS, Antanas. Lietuvių kalbos sinonimų žodynas. [Diction-ary of the Lithuanian language sy-nonyms] Kaunas, Valstybinė pedago-ginės literatūros leidykla, 1961. 293 p. PG8667.L9 DLC CSt CaAEU CtPAM CtY ICU MH NN PU

362. SKARDŽIUS, Pranas. Lietuvių kalbos vadovas; tartis ir rašyba, kirčiavimas, kalbos dalykai, žodynas. [A guide to standard Lithuanian...] Bielefeld, Lietuvių tremtinių ben-druomenė, 1950. 606 p. PG8675.S5 DLC CaOTP CaQMM CtPAM CtY ICCC ICLJF MH MiD MnU NB NN NNC NjP OCl PP1U PU TxU

II.4. STATISTICS

363. ARSEN'EV, Konstantin Ivano-vich. Statisticheskiie ocherki Rossii. Sanktpeterburg, Tip.I. Akademii nauk, 1848. [10], 503 p. DK17.Z DLC CU(microfilm) KU OOxM

364. KAUNAS. STATISTIKOS BIURAS. Biuletenis. Nr.1- ; 1935- . Kaunas. Tables. HA1448.L5K32 DLC

365. --- Kauno miesto statistikos metraštis. Annuaire statistique de la ville de Kaunas, 1934- . Kaunas, 1935- . Lithuanian and French. HA1448.L5K3 DLC(2-4)

366. LACHNICKI, Ignacy Emmanuel. Statystyka gubernii litewsko-grod-zieńskiej. Wilno, J. Zawadzki, 1817. 88, x p. 947.52.L114 PU

367. LAPTOVAS, M. A. Agricultural statistics in Lithuania. Rome, Printing office of the Internation-al Institute of Agriculture, 1926. 31 p. (International Institute of Agriculture. Bureau of General sta-tistics. Organization of Agricul-tural statistics in various coun-tries, no.1) 251.In840r no.1 DNAL

368. LEAGUE OF NATIONS. Interna-tional trade statistics, 1931-1938. Geneva, League of Nations, 1933-39. Annual. HF499.L4 DLC

369. LITHUANIA. CENTRALINIS STA-
TISTIKOS BIURAS. 297-nių darbininkų, tarnautojų ir valdininkų šeimų
biudžetų tyrinėjimo Lietuvoje 1936-
1937 metų rezultatai. Resultats de
l'enquête organisée en Lithuanie
durant les années 1936-1937, sur
les budgets de 297 familles ouvri-
ères, d'employés et de fonction-
naires. Kaunas, Centralinis statistikos biuras, 1939. 135 p. plates.
HD7035.6.A52 DLC BM(S.c. 140/11.)
MH NN NjP PP PU

370. --- Lietuva skaitlinėmis;
diagramų albumas. [Lithuania in
figures. Kaunas, Finansų ministerijos leidinys, 1924] 1 v. (unpaged,
chiefly illus.) In, Lithuanian,
French and English. HA1448.L5A53
DLC ICU NbU NN NNC PU

371. --- Lietuva skaitmenimis
1918-1928 m. La Lithuanie en
chiffres 1918-1928. Diagramų albomas. [Kaunas] Finansų ministerija
[1929] 184 p. illus., map, tables,
diagrs. Text in Lithuanian and
French in parallel columns.
HA1448.L5A5 1928 DLC BM CLU CSt-H
CaAEU CtPAM ICCC IU MH NN NNC PU
RPB WaU

372. --- Lietuvos apgyventos vie-
tos. Pirmojo visuotinojo Lietuvos
gyventojų 1923 m. surašymo duomenys.
[Inhabited areas of Lithuania; results of the first general census of
1923] Kaunas, Finansų ministerija,
1925. viii, 735 p. tables.
HA1448.L5A5 DLC BM NN NNC PU

373. --- Lietuvos gyventojai; 1923
m. rugsėjo 17 d. surašymo duomenys.
Population de la Lithuanie; données
du recensement du 17 septembre 1923.
Kaunas, Finansų ministerija [1926]
lxix, 311 p. tables, graphs. In
Lithuanian and French. HA1448.L5A4
DLC MH MH-BA NN PU

374. --- Lietuvos pasėlių plotų ir
gyvulių surašymas 1935 m. birželio
mėn. 30 d. Recensement des super-
ficies ensemencées et du cheptel vivant en Lithuanie le 30 juin 1935.
Kaunas, Centralinis statistikos biuras, 1936. 69 p. maps., tables,
diagrs. HD1995.L5A52 DLC BM NN NNC

375. --- Lietuvos statistikos metraštis. Annuaire statistique de
la Lithuanie. Kaunas, 1927-39.
12 v. Annual. HA1448.L5A25 DLC
CtPAM(1927-1928, 1930-1934, 1936)
CtTMF(1938) DNAL DS MH-BA MH-L(1927-
1938) NN NcD NNC NjP OCl(1927-1928,
1937) PP PU(2-12) WaU(1927-1928)

376. --- Lietuvos užienio prekyba,
1924-1938. Commerce exterieur de la
Lithuanie en 1924-1938. Kaunas,
1925-39. 15 v. tables. HF208.6.A3
DLC BM(1924-1935) CtPAM(1929-1930,
1932-1937) DNAL(1924-1938) ICU(1929)
MH NN NNC(1930-1935, 1937) NjP

377. --- Statistikos biulentis.
Bulletin de statistique. Kaunas,
1924-40. Monthly. Text in Lithuanian, French, and English. HA1448.
L5A3 DLC CtPAM(1924-1927, 1928-1932,
1935-1937) CLU(1924-1931, 1935-1940)
CtY(1924, 1925) DNAL DLC(1924-1927)
MH-L(1, no.3-12, 2-) NN(1-) NNC NjP
(1924-1934)

378. --- Statistikos žinios apie
Lietuvą ligi karui 1914 m. [Statis-
tics on Lithuania until World War I)
Kaunas, Sokolauski, 1919. 200 p.
DK511.L717 InNd CSt-H CtTMF PU

379. --- Valstybės statistikos kalendorius 1937. The Lithuanian Government Statistical Almanac 1937.
[Kaunas, 1937] viii, 517 p. illus.
Lithuanian and English. Issued also
in Lithuanian and German.
HA1448.L5A27 DLC BM DL MH NjP NN

380. --- Visuotinis Lietuvos žemės
ūkio surašymas 1930... Recensement
agricole en Lithuanie, le 30 décembre
1930. Kaunas, 1932-33. 4 v.
S242.L35A5 1930 DLC CLU CtPAM(1,3-4)
DNAL NN

381. LITHUANIA. FINANSŲ MINISTE-
RIJA. Lietuva skaitlinėmis; diagramų albomas. La Lithuanie en chiffres;
album de diagrammes. Kaunas, Valstybės spaustuvė, 1924. [3],p. 39 col.
diagrs. HC337.L5A6 1924a DLC CLU
CSt-H IU NjP

382. LITHUANIA. MIŠKŲ DEPARTAMEN-
TAS. Lietuvos miškų statistika.
Statistique forestière de la Lithu-
anie, 1937. Kaunas, 1939. Only
vol. 1 published. SD83.L5A3 DLC
DNAL

383. LITHUANIA IN FIGURES. 1- ;
196- . Vilnius, Gintaras. illus,
tables. Compiled by Jonas Pocius.
HA1448.L5A48 InU IU KU MH

384. LITHUANIAN INFORMATION BUREAU.
Quelques données statistiques sur la
Lithuanie. Paris, 1919. 4 p. (Dé-
légation de Lituanie à la Conference
de la Paix, pt.V: 1)
D643.A7DP5L7 CSt-H

385. LITHUANIAN S.S.R. CENTRINĖ
STATISTIKOS VALDYBA. 20 let Sovet-
skoi Litvy; statisticheskii sbornik.
Vil'nius, Gosstatizdat, Litovskoe
otd-nie, 1960. 351 p. illus. A1448.
L5A557 DLC IU MH NNC OrU ViU

386. --- 25 let Sovetskoi Litvy: statisticheskii sbornik. [V podgotovke sbornika uchastie prinimali: S.T. Belianskii i dr. Perevod s litovskogo] Vil'nius, Statistika, Litovskoe otd-nie, 1965. 270 p. col. illus., fold. col. map. HA1448. L5A357 DLC CSt-H CaBVaU MH WU

387. --- Ekonomika i kul'tura Litovskoi SSR; statisticheskii ezhegodnik. 1- ; 1965- . Vil'nius, Statistika, Litovskoe otd-nie. HA1448.L5A319 DLC CaAEU ICU(1967) IU KU(1967) MH(1968-) OrU

388. --- Ekonomika i kul'tura Litovskoi SSR; statisticheskii sbornik posviashchennyi 50-letiiu Velikogo Oktiabria. Vil'nius, Statistika, 1967. 415 p. HA1448.L5L5583 DLC CaAEU CaBVaU CaOTU CtY ICU InU IU MH NIC NNC NcD NcU PU TU NiU WU

389. --- Lietuvos TSR ekonomika ir kultūra; statistikos metraštis. Ekonomika i kul'tura Litovskoi SSR; statisticheskii ezhegodnik. 1- ; 1963- . Vilnius, Statistika, tables. HA1448.L5A316 DLC(1963-) MB CaAEU(1963) CaBVaU CaOTU CSt-H CtY ICU InU(1967-) KU(1967-) MH(1963-) MiU(1963-) PU(1963-) ViU WU(1967-)

390. --- Lietuvos TSR ekonomika ir kultūra; statistinių duomenų rinkinys, skirtas Didžiojo Spalio penkiasdešimtosioms metinėms. [Soviet Lithuanian economy and culture... Rinkinį parengė Centralinės statistikos valdybos kolektyvas... ir galutinai jį suredagavo B. Dubasovas] Vilnius, Statistika, 1967. 414 p. HA1448.L5A558 DLC MH

391. --- Lietuvos TSR liaudies ūkio plano vykdymo pagrindiniai rodykliai... Osnovnye pokazateli vypolneniia narodno-khoziaistvennogo plana po Litovskoi SSR. Kaunas, 1941. XX1818 Ger. KIW (1941, Jan.-April) No more published.

392. --- Lietuvos TSR skaičiais. [Lithuanian SSR in figures] 1- ; 1958/62- . Vilnius, Valstybinė statistikos leidykla, 1962- . HA1448.L5A317 DLC NIC PU WU

393. --- Lietuvos TSR žemės ūkis; trumpas statistikos duomenų rinkinys. [Soviet Lithuanian agriculture...] Vilnius, 1966. 63 p. XM458 MH

394. --- Prosveshchenie i kul'tura Litovskoi SSR; statisticheskii sbornik. Vil'nius, Statistika, 1964. 207 p. L466.L5B3 1964 DLC CU ICU IU InU MH ViU

395. --- Tarybų Lietuvai 25 metai; statistikos duomenų rinkinys. [Twenty-five years of Soviet Lithuania; a collection of statistical information] Vilnius, Statistika, 1965. 263 p. col. illus., fold. col. map. HA1448.L5A5595 DLC CU CaAEU CaOTU IU KU

396. --- Tarybų Lietuvos dvidešimtmetis; statistinių duomenų rinkinys. [Twenty years of Soviet Lithuania; a collection of statistical information] Vilnius, Valstybinė statistikos leidykla, 1960. 349 p. illus., map. HA1448.L5A5594 DLC CaOTU CtY ICU InU MH NIC PPiU PU WU WaU

397. LITOVSKAIA SSR V TSIFRAKH; kratkii statisticheskii sbornik. 1- ; 1962- . Vil'nius, Gosstatizdat; Litovskoe otd-nie, 1963- . HA1448.L5A318 DLC(1962-) CSt-H CaAEU(1962-) MH(1962-) NNC

398. MÜLLER, Ernst Ferd. Statistisches Handbuch für Kurland und Litauen, nebst übersichten über Livland und Estland... mit einem bibliographischen Anhang zur Wirtschaftskunde Russlands. Jena, G. Fischer, 1918. xv, 211 p. tables, fold. maps. (Schriften des Instituts für ostceutsche Wirtschaft in Königsberg, hft.4) Bibliography: p.[179]-205. HA1448.B3M8 DLC Cst-H CaOTU CU CtY IU NNC PU

399. MUSTEIKIS, Antanas, ed. Lietuvos žemės ūkis ir statistika. [Statistics of Lithuanian agriculture] Dillingen, Ger., "Mūsų kelias", 1948. 233 p. and 143 p. of tables. HA1448.L5M8 DLC ICLFJ PU

400. NARODNOE KHOZIAISTVO LITOVSKOI SSR; statisticheskii sbornik. 1- ; 1957- . Vil'nius, Gosstatizdat; Litovskoe otd-nie. tables. Issued by the Lithuanian SSR. Centrinė statistikos valdyba. HA1448. L5A33 DLC(1957-) CLU CSt-H CU CtY DNAL(1961-) IaU ICU IU(1957, 1961, 1965) KU(1959-1965) MH(1957-) NIC NN NNC NcU

401. --- kratkii statisticheskii sbornik. 1960- . Vil'nius, Gosstatizdat, Litovskoe otd-nie. Issued by TSentral'noe statisticheskoe upravlenie of Sovet Ministrov Litovskoi SSR. HA1448.L5A32 DLC CSt-H CtY IU NcD NSyU OrU WaU

402. OSTLAND. REICHSKOMMISSAR. Ostland in Zahlen. Gesamtbearbeitung: Gottfried Müller; statistische Unterlagen: Jekob Jureviz. Riga, 1942. xiv, 166 p. (Its Strukturbericht über das Ostland, T.1) Lithuania covered on p. 114-52. HA1448.B308 1942 DLC CSt-H PU

403. --- Statistische Berichte für das Ostland. Nov./Dec., 1941-Mai/Juli 1944. Riga, 1942-44. HA1448.B307 DLC BM

404. PAMIATNAIA KNIZHKA GRODNENSKOI gubernii. Izdanie Grodnenskago gubernskago statisticheskago komiteta. Grodno. Annual. (QCA)NN(1905)

405. PAMIATNAIA KNIZHKA KOVENSKOI gubernii. 1845- . Kovna, Gubernskii statisticheskii komitet. Annual. DK511.K55P32 DLC MH(1897) NN(1894-) PU(1881-1882, 1888-1889, 1893, 1897, 1905-1906, 1910)

406. POCIUS, Jonas. Present-day Lithuania in figures. [English version by Vl. Grodzenskis] Vilnius, Gintaras, 1971. 128 p. HA1448.L5P6 PU

407. RIMKA, Albinas. Lietuvos ūkis prieš Didįjį karą. [The Lithuanian economy before World War I] Vilnius, Švyturio spaustuvė, 1918. 115 p. tables. (Lietuvių mokslo draugijos leidinys, 20) Bibliography: p. [112]-115. HC337.L5R5 DLC CtTMF InNd MH PU

408. --- Lietuvos ūkis; statistikos tyrinėjimai. [The Lithuanian economy...] 2. leidimas. Kaunas, Švyturys, 1922. 134 p. 530.9475.R464 PU ICLJF

409. SUWALKI, RUSSIA (GOVERNMENT) Pamiatnaia knizhka Suvalskoi gubernii. 18 - . Sostavil i izdal M. I. Kirkor. Suvalki, Tip. Gubernskago pravleniia. Annual. DK511.S9K DLC NN

410. VILNA. CENTRALNE BIURO STATYSTYKI. Rocznik statystyczny Wilna. 1921/28- . Annuaire statistique de Wilno. Wilno. Annual. HA1458.V5A3 DLC NN

411. VILNA (GOVERNMENT) VILENskii gubernskii statisticheskii komitet. Istoricheskii-statisticheskie ocherki Vilenskoi gubernii. Vil'na, 1852-53. 2 v. BM(10292. bbb.1.)

412. --- Sbornik istoriko-statisticheskikh materialov po Vilenskoi gubernii. Redaktor M. Gusev. Vil'no, 1863. viii, 262 p. BM(10290. cc.4.)

413. VISA LIETUVA; informacinė knyga. [A statistical book of information on Lithuania] 1- ; 1922- . Kaunas, Spaudos fondas. Irregular. Issued by Centralinis statistikos biuras. Kaunas, Editor

V. Ruzgas. In Lithuanian and German. HC337.L7A2 ICU CtPAM(1922) CSt-H(1925) DLC(1922,1925,1931) PU(1925)

414. WALTER, Eginhard. Das Baltikum in Zahlen: Estland, Lettland, Litauen, Memelgebiet... Königsberg in Pr., Institut für osteuropäische Wirtschaft, 1937. xiv, 64 p. tables, map. Bibliography: p. 41-59. HC337.A13W3 DLC CU MH PU

415. ŽEMĖS ŪKIO RŪMAI, KAUNAS. Žemės ūkio sąskaitybos rezultatai. [Agricultural statistics] 1932/33- . Kaunas. S469.L5Z4 DLC

II.5. GAZETTEERS, GEOGRAPHIC DICTIONARIES

416. FALK, Knut Olaf. Wody Wigierskie i Huciańskie; studium toponomastyczne. Uppsala, Almquist & Wiksell, 1941. 2 v. illus., fold. map. Bibliography: p. [234]-243. PG8662.F3 DLC CtY ICU(1) IU MH NNC NjP(1) PU

417. FENZLAU, Walter. Die deutschen Formen der litauischen Orts- und Personennamen des Memelgebiets. Halle a.S., M. Niemeyer, 1936. 154 p. map. (Zeitschrift für Mundartforschung. Teutonista. Beiheft, 13) PF5001.Z371 no.13 CLU CU CaAEU CtY DLC ICU OCU OU

418. GAUSE, Fritz. Neue Ortsnamen in Ostpreussen seit 1800. Königsberg in Pr., Kommissionsverlag Gräfe und Unzer, 1935. 120 p. table. 947.52.G235 PU CtY WU

419. GERULLIS, Georg. Die altpreussischen Ortsnamen, gesammelt und sprachlich behandelt von Georg Gerullis. Berlin ind Leipzig, Vereinigung wissenschaftlicher Verleger, 1922. 286 p. DD308.G4 DLC ICU MiU MH NN NjP PU

420. LIETUVOS TSR MOKSLŲ AKADEMIJA, VILNA. LIETUVIŲ KALBOS IR LITERATŪROS INSTITUTAS. Lietuvos TSR upių ir ežerų vardynas. [Directory of the rivers and lakes of the Lithuanian SSR. Sudarė: B. Savukynas, et al. Redagavo: E. Grinaveckienė (ats. redaktorė), J. Senkus] Vilnius, VPMLL, 1963. xix, 225. Preface also in German and Russian. DK511.L2I426 DLC CtY ICU MH NN PPiU PU

421. SCHMITTLEIN, Raymond. Études sur la nationalité des Aestii. I. Toponymie lituanienne. Bade, Édi-

tions art et science, 1948. 4 v.
(320 p.) illus., maps. Bibliography: p. 19-49. DK511.B295S3 DLC
CtY InU KU MH NNC NcU(1) NjR PU

422. --- Toponymie lituanienne.
Bade, Éditions art et science,1948.
319 p. illus., maps, facsim. (His
Études sur la nationalité des Aestii, t.1) 929.4.Sch57 MnU

423. SPROGIS, Jānis. Geograficheskii slovar' drevnei Zhomoits-
koi zemli XVI stolietiia, sost. po
40 aktovym knigam Rossienskago zemskago suda, Ivan IAkovlevich Sprogis.
Vil'na, Tip. I. IA. IAlovtsera,1888.
xix, 362 p. 911.47503.Sp8g IU NN
PU(film 423)

424. TARVYDAS, Stasys. Lietuvos
vietovardžiai. [Place names of Li-
thuania] Vilnius, VPMLL, 1958. 55
p. PG8662.T35 PU

425. UNGER, Hellmuth. Neues Orts-
namenverzeichnis von Ostpreussen mit
den alten und neuen Ortsnamen. Königsberg in Pr., Gräfe und Unzer,
1938. 168 p. 947.52.Un33.2 PU

426. UNITED STATES. BOARD OF GEO-
GRAPHICAL NAMES. Directions for the
treatment of geographical names in
Lithuania. [Washington,D.C., 1944]
3 numb. leaves. (Its Special publications, 14) G105.U544 no.14 DLC

427. VANAGAS, Aleksandras. Aukš-
tutinės Padneprės hidronimija ir
baltų praeitis. [The names of rivers and lakes in the area of the Upper Dniepr and the past of the Bal-
ts] In Lietuvių kalbotyros klausimai (Vilnius), v.7, 1964, p. 207-
220. See Serials consulted.

428. --- Lietuvos TSR hidronimų
daryba. [The formation of the Lithuanian hydronyms] Vilnius, Mintis, 1970. 428 p. maps. At head
of title: Lietuvos TSR Mokslų akademija. Lietuvių kalbos ir literatūros institutas. Summaries in German and Russian. PG8662.V3 DLC PU

429. VODOPALAS, Antanas. Vardai
dumblynams ir durpynams. [The names for marshes and peat-bogs] Chicago,Ill., Lietuvių miškininkų sąjunga išeivijoj, 1966. 80 p.
910.5.V ICBM

II.6. BIOGRAPHIES

II.6.a. GENERAL BIOGRAPHIES

430. AMERIKOS LIETUVIŲ VARDYNAS;
Jungtinių Amerikos Valstybių žinomes-
nių lietuvių biografinės žinios.
[American Lithuanian directory] Su
K. Pakšto įvadu. Los Angeles, Calif.,
Lietuvių dienos, 1953. 279 p.
E184.L7A7 DLC CaOTU CtPAM CtTMF ICU
InNd MH NN NNC OCl PU

BIRŽIŠKA, Vaclovas. Aleksandrynas; senųjų lietuvių rašytojų,
rašiusių prieš 1865 m. biografijos.
Chicago, 1960-65. See entry no.12.

431. --- Lietuvių rašytojų kalendorius. [Almanac of Lithuanian au-
thors] Tübingen, Patria [1946] 263
p. (Mūsų rašytojai ir raštai, 1)
PG8709.B5 DLC ICLJF PU

432. BRUOŽIS, Ansas. Mažosios Lietuvos buvusieji rašytojai. [The
writers of the Lithuania Minor] Tilžėje, "Spaudos" spaustuvė, 1920. 125
p. ports. Author's pseudonym: Prabočių Anūkas, at head of title.
891.92R.B835 PU CtTMF MiD OCl PPULC

433. DAMBRAUSKAS, Aleksandras. Už-
gesę žiburiai; biografijų ir nekro-
logų rinkinys. [A collection of biographies and obituaries] Parašė A-
domas Jakštas [pseud.] Redagavo ir
jo 70 metų sukakties paminėjimą pridėjo J. Tumas. Kaunas, Zavišos ir
Steponavičiaus spaustuvė, 1930. xvi,
[502] p. illus., ports. (Lietuvių
katalikų mokslo akademijos leidinys,
1) 891.92H.D183 PU CtTMF ICLJF OCl

434. GELUMBIS, Francis A. Who's
who and what among our great men.
[New York, N.Y., 1926] 79 p.
L 970.9.ŽE ICLJF NN

435. GOŠTAUTAS, Stasys. Antologia
biográfica del arte lituano. Medellín, Colombia, Editorial Bedout,
1959. 246 p. illus. N6995.L5G6
DLC CLU CtPAM CtY PU

436. HARRISON, Ernest John, ed.
Who's who in Lithuania. In His Li-
thuania, 1928. London, 1928. p.240-
257. DK511.L27H3 DLC AzU BM CLU CSt
CU CaOLU CaQMM CtY FU IEN ICU ICN
InNd KU MH MnU MoU NB NbU NN NNC NjP
NjR NSyU OCl OClW OrU PP PPiU PU RPB

437. LIETUVOS ALBUMAS. [Berlin,
O. Elsner, 1921] 435 p. (chiefly
illus.) Lithuanian and English cap-
tions. DK511.L28A1L72 CaAEU ICBM
ICLJF NN PPi PU RPB

438. LITHUANIA. STEIGIAMASIS SEIMAS. Trumpos Steigiamojo seimo narių biografijos su atvaizdais.[Brief biographies with portraits of the members of the Constituent Diet] Klaipėda, Lithuania, 1924. 71 p. 947.52.L713 PU

439. MŪSŲ POETAI, 1956-1957. [Our poets, 1956-1957] Vilnius, VGLL, 1957. [28] p. ports. PG8709.M8 DLC MH

440. PINNEBERG, GER. BALTIC UNIVERSITY. Who is who at the Baltic University; biographies of the professors and teachers. [Pinneberg, Ger., 1949] 176 p. LF3194.P54A3 1949 DLC CtY BM PU

441. PRIALGAUSKAS, Vincentas. Żywoty biskupów wileńskich. Petersburg, Nakład autora, 1860. 3 v. in 1. 970.31.PR ICLJF

442. RUSECKAS, Petras. Mūsų įžymieji žmonės. [Our famous men] 1-ji dalis: nuo Duonelaičio ligi Baranausko. Kaunas, Spaudos fondas, 1934. 155 p. illus., ports. No more published. 491.922.R893 PU CtTMF

443. TARYBŲ LIETUVOS RAŠYTOJAI. [Writers of Soviet Lithuania] Vilnius, VGLL, 1957. 572 p. ports. PG8701.T3 DLC CtY NN PU

444. --- Sudarė A. Sinjoras. Redakcinė kolegija: A. Venclova, J.Marcinkevičius, ir J. Lankutis. Vilnius, Vaga, 1967. 601 p. ports. PG8701.T3 1967 DLC CtY ICU MH MU NN PU

445. TUMAS, Juozas. Aplink nepriklausomybės veikėjus. [On the men working for the Lithuania's independence] Vilnius, 1919. 239 p. 891.92T832A PU

446. --- --- Kaunas, Švyturio bendrovės leidinys, 1922. 239 p. (Vaižganto raštai, t.4) CT1215.L5T8 DLC PU

447. ŽILEVIČIUS, Juozas. Lietuvių muzikų vardynas. [A biographic dictionary of Lithuanian musicians. Chicago, Ill.] Leidžia A. L. Vargonininkų bei kitų muzikų sąjunga [1955-] ports. Published as part 3 of Muzikos žinios. ML302.Z69 CaAEU

448. ZINGHAUS, Viktor. Führende Köpfe der Baltischen Staaten; 31 Porträts. Kaunas; Leipzig, Pribačis, 1938. ix, 273 p. ports. Lithuanians: p.1-96. DK511.B3Z5 DLC PU

II.6.b. INDIVIDUAL BIOGRAPHIES

449. ABRAMAVIČIUS, Girša. Tiesos beieškant; iš Liudo Adomausko gyvenimo. [Searching for the truth; from the life of Liudas Adomauskas. Literatūrinis bendradarbis A. Beriozovas] Vilnius, Valstybinė politinės ir mokslinės literatūros leidykla, 1960. 101 p. HX315.65.A8A3 DLC

450. ABRAMAVIČIUS, Vladas. Valerii Vrublevskii, 1836-1908. Moskva, Mysl', 1968. 157 p. illus. At head of title: V. E. Abramavichiius, V. A. Diakov. DK436.5.W7A16 CaAEU

451. ABRAMAVIČIUS, Vladas. Valerijonas Vrublevskis. Vilnius, VPMLL, 1958. 102 p. illus. At head of title: Lietuvos TSR Mokslų akademija. Centrinė biblioteka. DK436.5.W7A65 DLC

452. ADOMONIS, Tadas. Jonas Mikėnas. Vilnius, Vaga, 1969. 62 p. illus. NK4210.M55A35 PU

453. AIDAI. Maironis; jo gimimo šimtmečiui paminėti. [Brooklyn, N.Y. 1963] 214 p. illus, facsim., ports. PG8721.M3Z58 DLC CLU CaAEU CaOONL CtTMF ICLJF

454. ALANTAS, Vytautas, ed. Antanas Vanagaitis, jo gyvenimas ir veikla. [Antanas Vanagaitis, his life and activities. Cleveland, Ohio] J.J. Balčiūnas [1954] 192 p. illus. ML410.V24A6 DLC CaOONL ICLJF MiD NN OCl PU

455. ALEKNA, Antanas. Žemaičių vyskupas Motiejus Valančius. [Motiejus Valančius, Bishop of Žemaitija (Samogitia)] Klaipėda, Spauda Lituanijos" [1922 283 p. port. (Šv. Kazimiero draugijos leidinys, nr. 341) 491.922.T232.yA PU BM CtTMF ICLJF PU OCl

456. ALEKSAITĖ, Irena. Borisas Dauguvietis; režisūros bruožai. [Borisas Dauguvietis as stage-manager] Vilnius, Mintis, 1966. 243 p. illus., ports. PN2728.D28A7 DLC PU

457. ALŠĖNAS, Pranys. Martynas Jankus, Mažosios Lietuvos patrijarchas; gyvenimas, darbai ir likimo lemties vingiai. [Martynas Jankus; his life and works] Toronto, Ont. [J.J. Bachunas, 1967] 394 p. illus. CT1215.L5A4 DLC CaAEU ICLJF

458. AMBRAZAS, Algirdas. Kompozitorius Juozas Gruodis; gyvenimo ir kūrybos bruožai. [Juozas Gruodis, the composer; his life and works]

Kaunas, Valstybinė pedagoginės literatūros leidykla, 1960. 60 p.
ports., music. ML410.G945A4 DLC

459. ANTANINA DAMBRAUSKAITĖ, LI-
thuanian opera singer. Munich,1948.
66, 10 p. illus., ports. NNCL

460. ATSIMINIMAI APIE A. VIENUOLĮ.
[Recollections on A. Vienuolis. Redakcinė komisija: A. Venclova (pirm.)
M. Sluckis, J. Stonys] Vilnius, VGLL
1963. 437 p. illus., ports., facsims. PG8721.V5A93 DLC CaAEU CaAEU
PU

461. ATSIMINIMAI APIE PETRĄ CVIRKĄ
[Recollections on Petras Cvirka. Redakcinė komisija: J. Baltušis, V. Galinis, A. Venclova (pirm.). Sudarė:
Mickienė] Vilnius, Vaga, 1969. 659p.
illus., port. PG8721.C8Z57 DLC CaAEU

462. ATSIMINIMAI APIE V. MONTVILĄ.
[Recollections on V. Montvila. Re-
dakcinė komisija: J. Lankutis, J.
Macevičius, T. Tilvytis] Vilnius,
Vaga, 1966. 469 p. illus.
PG8721.M56Z6 PU DLC

463. ARKIVYSKUPAS JURGIS MATULEVI-
čius. [Marijampolė] Marijonai, 1933.
309 p. illus., ports.
BX4705.M4295A8 DLC ICLJF OCl PU

464.AUGUSTAITIS, Jonas. Antanas
Smetona ir jo veikla. [Antanas Smetona and his public life] Chicago,
Ill., Chicagos lietuvių draugija,
1966. 154 p. 947.5L.Sm35A PU

465. BACHUNAS, Juozas J. Vincas
S. Jokubynas. [Sodus, Mich., Author,
1954] 12 p. illus. E184.L7J6 DLC
ICLJF

466. BARONAS, Aloyzas. Šviesa ir
kelias; Prelato Igno Albavičiaus gyvenimo ir veiklos bruožai. [Monsig.
Ignas Albavičius, his life and work]
Chicago, Ill., Draugas, 1954. 155 p.
ports., plates. BV4462.5.A32B2
IMunS KMK PU PPULC

467. BASANAVIČIUS, Jonas. Autobiografija. In Lietuvių tauta (Vilnius), v.5, 1935, p.5-195. See serials consulted.

468. --- Mano gyvenimo kronika.
[The chronicle of my life] In Lietuvių tauta (Vilnius), v.2, pt.4;
v.3-4, 1919-1932, p. 5-195. See
serials consulted.

469. BIČIŪNAS, Vytautas Pranas.
Kunigas Jonas Katelė ir jo laikai,
1831-1908. [Rev. Jonas Katelė and
his epoch] Kaunas, Kun. Katelės
mirties sukaktuvėms minėti komite-

tas, 1934. 295 p. illus., ports.,
facsims. 947.52.K157.yB PU ICLJF
OCl

470. --- M.K. Čiurlionis. Kaunas,
Lietuvių dailės draugija, 1927. 32 p.
illus., port. Electrostatic reproduction The New York Public Library.
947.52.C497.yB PU NN

471. --- Vinco Krėvės likimo keliais; pastabos ir komentarai. [Some
commentaries about V. Krėvė] Kaunas,
Spaudė Akc. bendrovė "Rytas", Klaipėdoje, 1930. 87 p. 891.92.K889L.
yB PU

472. BINKIS, Kazys. Antanas Smetona, 1874-1934; šešių dešimčių metų sukaktuvėms paminėti. [A commemoration of the 60th birthday of Antanas Smetona] Illus. by Petras
Rimša. Kaunas [Vyriausias minėjimo
komitetas] 1934. 64 p. illus.
DK511.L27B5 DLC PU

473. BIRŽIŠKA, Mykolas. Antanas
Baranauskas. In Lietuvių enciklopedija. Boston, Mass., 1954. v.2, p.
185-191. See entry no.216.

474.--- Antanas Klementas; lietuvių rašytojas pradžioje XIX-ojo amžiaus. [Antanas Klementas; a Lithuanian writer] Vilnius, M. Kuktos
spaustuvė, 1910. 39 p. Offprint
from Lietuvių tauta. PG8721.K59Z59
DLC CtTMF OCl

475. --- Antoni Klement, pisarz
litewski w początku w. XIX. M. Bir-
žyszka. Z litewskiego tłumacz. St.J.
[pseud.] Wilno, Wydawn. "Mildy",
1921. 62 p. PG8721.K585Z62 PU

476. --- Barono gyvenimas ir raštai. [Baronas; his life and works]
Kaunas, Dirva, 1924. 107 P.
491.922.B232.yB PU

477. --- Daukantas Simanas. Kaunas, 1937. 11 p. illus., ports.
"Atspausta iš Lietuviškosios enciklopedijos VI tomo, 2 sąsiuvinio."
947.52.D69.yB PU For holdings see
entry no.215.

478. --- Donelaičio gyvenimas ir
raštai, su kalbos paaiškinimais.
[Donelaitis; his life and works]
3. leidimas. Kaunas, Vairo bendrovė, 1927. 216 p. illus., ports.
491.922.D717.yB PU BM CtTMF

479. BIRŽIŠKA, Vaclovas. Abraham
Kulvietis, the first Lithuanian hu-
manist. Pinneberg, Ger., 1947. 30 p.
(Contributions of Baltic Universi-
ty, 47) AS182.P5 no.47 DLC ICU NNC
PU PPULC

480. ---- Iš Vyskupo Valančiaus
veiklos. [From the activities of
Bishop Valančius] In Mūsų senovė
(Kaunas), v.2, 1938, p.355-371.
See serials consulted.

481. --- Jonas Basanavičius. In
Lietuvių enciklopedija, Boston,Mass.,
v.2, 1954. p. 241-247. AE60.L5L5
v.2 DLC CaAEU CU; see entry no.216.

482. --- Vyskupo Motiejaus Valančiaus biografijos bruožai. [The
biographical outline of Bishop Motiejus Valančius. Brooklyn, N.Y.,
1952] 99 p. BX4705.V27B5 DLC
CaOONL OCl PU

483. BIRŽIŠKA, Vaclovas and Juozas
Brazaitis. Donelaitis Kristijonas...
ir jo "Metai" [Donelaitis,Kristijo-
nas and his "Seasons"] In Lietuvių
enciklopedija, Boston, Mass., v.5,
1955, p. 115-120. See entry no.216.

484. BRAZAITIS, Juozas. Juozas
Tumas-Vaižgantas; kunigas, visuomenės veikėjas... [Juozas Tumas-Vaižgantas; priest, author, etc.,] In
Lietuvių enciklopedija, Boston, Mass.,
1965, v.32, p.27-34. See entry
no.216.

485. --- Maironis-Mačiulis; prelatas, spaudos draudžiamojo laikotarpio
didžiausias poetas. [Jonas Mačiulis-
Maironis...the great Lithuanian poet]
In Lietuvių enciklopedija, Boston,
Mass., 1959. v.17, p.11-116. See
entry no.216.

486. BRONIUS KAZYS BALUTIS; jo gy-
venimas ir darbai. [The life of B.
K. Balutis. Spaudai paruošė Vytautas
Širvydas] Sodus, Mich., J.J. Bachu-
nas, 1951. 128 p. illus., ports.
DK511.L27B7 DLC ICLJF MB NN PU

487. BUDREIKA, Eduardas. Architek-
tas Laurynas Stuoka-Gucevičius, 1753-
1798. [Architect Laurynas Stuoka-
Gucevičius] Vilnius, VPMLL, 1954.
165 p. illus., ports. Bibliography:
p. 147-158. NA1199.G8B8 DLC PU
PPULC

488. --- Lietuvos klasicizmo architektūros kūrėjas Laurynas Stuoka-Gucevičius, 1793-1798. [Laurynas Stuoka-Gucevičius the founder of Lithuanian classical architecture] Kaunas,
Mintis, 1965. 25 p. port., 31 p.
of illus., facsims, plans.
NA1199.G8B8 DLC

489. BUDRYS, Stasys. Bronius Pundžius. Vilnius, Mintis, 1969. 124
p. NB699.P8B8 PU

490. --- Gediminas Jakubonis. Vilnius, VGLL, 1963. 31 p. Summaries

and lists of legends in French, English and Russian. NB699.J8B8 DLC

491. --- Juozas Kėdainis. Vilnius,
VPMLL, 1960. xi p. 25 plates.
(Lietuvių Tarybinių dailininkų mono-
grafijos) Sp 735.75.K236.yB PU MH

492. --- Juozas Zikaras, 1884-1944.
Vilnius, VPMLL, 1960. 142 p. illus.
NB955.Z5B8 DLC PU

493. --- Robertas Antinis. Vilnius, Vaga, 1968. 56 p. illus., 28
leaves of illus. (Lietuvių Tarybinių dailininkų monografijos)
NB699.A49B8 DLC PU

494. BUGE, Jacques. Milosz en
quête du divin. Paris, Nizet, 1963.
319 p. PQ2625.I558Z7B88 CaAEU DLC
IU MH OU WU

495. --- O.V. de Milosz, 1877-1939.
Paris, A. Silvaire [1959] 222 p.
illus. (Oeuvres complètes de O.V.
de L. Milosz, t.0) Textes réunis
par Jacques Buge et André Silvaire.
PQ2625.I558Z6 DLC CaAEU

496. BULOTA, Jonas. A. Jasutis;
gyvenimo ir kūrybos bruožai. [A.
Jasutis; his life and works] Vilnius, VGLL, 1961. 336 p. PG8721.
J33Z6 PU MH

497. BŪTĖNAS, Julius and Jonas
Kruopas. Kalbininkas Kazimieras Būga. Vilnius, VPMLL, 1955. 34 p.
491.92.B866.yB PU

498. --- Povilas Višinskis. Kaunas, J. Būtėnas, 1936. 214 p. front,
ports. 947.52.V823.yB PU OCl PPULC

499. --- Vincas Kudirka. [Kaunas]
Autoriaus leidinys, 1937. 198 p.
16 plates (incl. ports., facsims)
Bibliography: p. [186]-194.
491.922.K953.yB PU CtTMF PPULC

500. --- Žemaitė. Kaunas, Spaudos
fondas [1938] 227 p. ports. A biography with bibliography. 491.922.
Z98.yB PU BM CtTMF MiD OCl PPULC

501. --- Žemaitės gyvenimas. [The
life of Žemaitė] Kaunas, VPMLL,
1947. 76 p. 891.92.Z99.yB PU DLC

502. ČIBIRAS, Kazimieras. Arkivyskupas Jurgis Matulevičius. [Archbi-
shop Jurgis Matulevičius] Marijampolė, Marijonų spaustuvė, 1933. 309
p. 947.520.M4 CtTMF

503. --- Gyvenimo menininkė Marija
Pečkauskaitė. [Marija Pečkauskaitė;
a biography] Kaunas, 1937. 132 p.
Xerox copy 1970. PG8721.P4Z62 1970
PU CtTMF

504. CIEPIEŃKO-ZIELIŃSKA, Donata. Emilia Plater. [Warszawa] Książka i Wiedza [1966] 297 p. illus. (Świa- towid-biblioteczka popularno-nauko- wa) DK511.L28P55 PU MH

505. ČIURLIONYTĖ, Jadvyga. Atsi- minimai apie M.K. Čiurlionį. [Re- collections on M.K. Čiurlionis] Vilnius, Vaga, 1970. 334 p. illus. music, port. ND699.C6C5 PU CaOTU

506. DAMBRAUSKAITĖ, Roma. Ieva Simonaitytė. Vilnius, Vaga, 1968. 218 p. PG8721.S5Z72 PU CtPAM PPULC

507. DAMBRAUSKAS, Aleksandras. Jo malonybė naujas Žemaičių vysku- pas Pranciškus Karevičius, jo kon- sekracija Peterburge, kelionė Kau- nan ir sutiktuvės Kaune. [His grace, the Bishop Franciškus Karevičius, thenew Bishop of Žemaitija (Samogi- tia), his consecretion in Sanktpeter- burg, etc.] Kaunas, Šv. Kazimiero draugija, 1914. 84 p. illus. L Bl.KAR ICLJF CtTMF ICBM

508. --- Vyskupas Gasparas Cirtau- tas. [Bishop Gasparas Cirtautas] Kaunas, Šv. Kazimiero draugija, 1913. 31 p. (Šv. Kazimiero draugijos lei- dinys, nr.144) L Bl.CIR ICLJF PU

509. DAMBRIŪNAS, Leonardas. Žy- maus kalbininko sukaktis. [The anni- versary of the noted linguist Jan Otrębski] In Lituanistikos darbai (Chicago, Ill.), v.1, 1966, p.94-103. "Jono Otrembskio Baltų kalbotyros raštų bibliografija":p.96-103. (103 entries) See serials consulted.

510. DEMBSKIS, Vladislovas. Ar vyskupas Valančius nebuvo vilingu lietuvybei? [Was Bishop Valančius playing a double game on the Lithu- anian question?] Chicago, Ill., iš- leista kaštais "Susivienyjimo lietu- vių laisvamanių", 1901. 37 p. (Bib- lioteka Susivienyjimo lietuvių lais- vamanių, nr.3) 891.92.V232A PU CtY

511. DIDYSIS JO NUOTYKIS; prof. J. Eretas tarnyboje Lietuvai. [Prof. J. Eretas in the service for Lithu- ania. Spaudai paruošė J. Brazaitis. Brooklyn, N.Y., 1971] 288 p. Issued by the Friends of Prof. J. Eretas. DK511.L28E7 PU

512. DIDŽIAI GERBIAMO VISUOMENINKO kunigo Prano M. Jūro, Šv. Pranciš- kaus parapijos klebono, sidabrinio kunigystės jubiliejaus atsiminimui, 1922-1947. [Silver jubilee of Rev. P.M. Juras' priesthood] Lawrence, Mass., 1947. 1 v. (unpaged) illus. BX4705.J83D5 DLC

513. DINEIKA, Karolis. Lietuvos karžygys Antanas Juozapavičius; psi- chologiški bruožai. [The Lithuanian hero Antanas Juozapavičius] Kaunas, Vyriausiojo štabo Karo mokslo valdy- bos leidinys, 1926. 29 p. illus. DK511.L26D5 DLC

514. DONELAITIS, Kristijonas. Do- nelaičio gyvenimas ir raštai; su kal- bos paaiškinimais. [The life and works of K. Donelaitis] 3. leidimas. Kaunas, Vairo bendrovės leidinys, 1927. 216 p. illus. 891.928D ICCC

515. DOVYDAITIS, Pranas. Profe- sorius Juozas Eretas. In Ateitis (Kaunas), 1934, p. 435-448. See se- rials consulted.

516. ERETAS, Juozas. Kazys Pakš- tas; tautinio šauklio odisėja, 1893- 1960. Roma, LKMA, 1970. xvi, 372 p. illus. (Negęstantieji žiburiai, t.3) Summary in German. Bibliography: p. [329]-340. DK511.L28P3 DLC PU

517. --- Rėzos santykiai su Goe- the. [The relations between Rhesa and Goethe] In Athenaeum (Kaunas), v.9, no.2, 1938. See serials con- sulted.

518. --- Stasys Šalkauskis, 1886- 1941. [Brooklyn, N.Y., Ateitininkų federacija, 1960] xxiii, 278 p. B4745.S34E7 CaOTU CLU CtY DLC ICLJF NN OC1 PU

519. --- Šalkauskis idėjų keliais. [Šalkauskis as philosopher and thin- ker] In LKMASD, t.4, p. [175]-209. See serials consulted.

520. FESTSCHRIFT ADALBERT BEZZEN- berger zum 14. April 1921 dargebra- cht von seinen Freunden und Schülern. Göttingen, Vandenhoeck & Ruprecht, 1921. 16, 172 p. 409.6.F437 PU

521. GALAUNĖ, Paulius. Tapytojas Juozas Oleškevičius, 1777-1830. [Artist painter Juozas Oleškevičius] Kaunas, Valstybės spaustuvė, 1927. 22 p. 947.5201.yG PU

522. GALINIS, Vytautas. Antanas Venclova; monografinė apybraiža. [Antanas Venclova; a monograph] Vil- nius, VGLL, 1958. 202 p. ports. Bibliography: p. 199-[208] PG8721. V4Z68 DLC

523. GAUDRIMAS, Juozas. Balys Dva- rionas. Moskva, Sovetskii kompozi- tor, 1960. 29 p. ML410.D98G4 DLC MH

524. GIMBUTAS, Jurgis. Prof. Dr. Steponas Kolupaila. In LKMAM, t.4,

1968, p. 533-546. See serials consulted.

525. GINEITIS, Leonas. Kristijonas Donelaitis ir jo epocha. [Kristijonas Donelaitis and his era] Vilnius, VPMLL, 1964. 381 p. Ed. by K. Doveika. Summary in Russian. Bibliography: p. 363-376. PG8721. D7Z68 ICU CtY CtPAM DLC NN PU

526. GIRA, Liudas. Dvi seserys Ivanauskaitės. [Two sisters Ivanauskaitės] In Židinys (Kaunas), no.4-6, 1929, p. 315-324,418-428. See serials consulted.

527. GIRDVAINIS, J. V., ed. Aušrininkas Jonas Šliūpas; medžiaga jo biografijai ir Lietuvos kultūros istorijai. [Jonas Šliūpas and the materials for his biography] Kaunas, 1934. 116. PN5355.L5G5 DLC CtTMF PU

528. GRIGAS, Kazys. Simonas Daukantas lietuvių tautosakos rinkėjas, leidėjas ir vertintojas. [Simonas Daukantas; the collector, publisher, and evaluator of Lithuanian folk-lore] In LTSRMAIILKI, v.1, 1958, p. 270-286. See serials consulted.

529. GRINEVIČIUS, Adomas. Apie kun. Adomą Grinevičių. Philadelphia, Pa., Žvaigždės spauda, 1926. 31 p. 891.92.G887 PU

530. GRINIUS, Jonas. O.V. Milašius-poetas. Kaunas, Vytauto Didžiojo Universitetas, Teologijos-filosofijos fakulteto leidinys, 1930. 196 p. illus. PQ2625.I558Z72 DLC BM MH NN PU

531. GRINIUS, Kazys. Atsiminimai ir mintys. [Memoirs and reflections] Tübingen; Chicago, Ill., Patria; Dr. Kazio Griniaus komitetas, 1947-62. 2 v. DK511.L27G77 DLC CaAEU CaOTP(1) CaOTU CtPAM CtY MH MiD(1) NN(1) OC1 (1) PU

532. --- Medžiaga L. Ivinskio biografijai. [Material on the biography of L. Ivinskas] Vilnius, 1908. 23 p. 947.520.D4 CtTMF

533. --- Petras Kriaučiūnas. In His Atsiminimai ir mintys. Tübingen, Ger., 1947. v.1, p. 37-57. DK511.L27G77 DLC CaAEU CtY MiD NN OC1 PU

534. GRUODIS, Juozas. Straipsniai, laiškai, užrašai. Amžininkų atsiminimai. [Articles, letters, notes, and recollections about Juozas Gruodis] Vilnius, Vaga, 1965. 394 p. illus., facsims, ports.

ML410.G945A3 DLC PU

535. GUDYNAS, Pranas. Kai prabyla medis; monografinė apybraiža apie liaudies menininką Juozą Laurinkų. [About the folk artist Juozas Laurinkus] Vilnius, VPMLL, 1959. 91 p. illus. NK9798.L3G8 DLC OKentU

536. --- Petras Kalpokas. Kaunas, Valstybinė pedagoginės literatūros leidykla, 1962. 37 p. illus., col. plates. MH

537. GULBINAS, Konstantinas. Das pädagogische Lebenswerk der litauischen Dichterin Marija Pečkauskaitė. München, F. Schöningh, 1971. 173 p. Bibliography: p. [161]-171. LA2375. L52P44 DLC PU

538. GUSTAITIS, Motiejus. Kunigas Antanas Tatarė; pirmutinis Suvalkų gubernijos švietėjas. Vilnius, Lietuvių mokslų draugija, 1913. 48 p. BM(1156.h/4.) CtTMF; also in Lietuvių tauta (Vilnius), v.2, no.2, 1913. See serials consulted.

539. --- Petras Kriaučiūnas; gyvenimas, raštai, dokumentai. [The life, works, and documents of Petras Kriaučiūnas] Kaunas, Dirvos bendrovės leidinys, 1926. 160 p. illus. 491.922.K892.yG PU OC1

540. IEŠMANTA, Albinas. Kudirka; rašytojo siluetas aukštesniajai mokyklai. [Vincas Kudirka; a biografical sketch for use in the High-Schools] Kaunas, Dirvos bendrovės leidinys, 1927. 67 p. PG8721.K8Z73 DLC CtTMF

541. IVAŠKEVIČIUS, Adolfas. Kazimir Semenovich i ego kniga "Velikoe iskusstvo artillerii. Chast' pervaia." A. Ivashkiavichius. Vil'nius, Mintis, 1971. 65 p. TR268.5.S53I85 PU

542. IVINSKIS, Zenonas. Merkelis Giedraitis; arba, Lietuva dviejų amžių sąvartoje. [Bishop Merkelis Giedraitis; a biography] In Aidai (Kennebunkport, Me.), 1951, no.3, p. 110-120; no.4(39), p. 163-170;no.5 (40), p.207-215; no.6(41),p.254-263; no.7(42), p.317-324. See serials consulted.

543. JABLONSKIS, Konstantinas. Papildomos žinios apie Mikalojų Daukšą. [Supplementary information about Mikalojus Daukša] In Archivum philologicum (Kaunas), v.4, 1933, p.64-85. See serials consulted.

544. JANULAITIS, Augustinas. Adomas Mickevyčia; 1798-1855; jo gyve-

nimas, raštai ir darbai. [Adam Mickiewicz; his life and works] Plymouth, Pa., Spauda "Vienybės Lietuvninkų," 1902. 40 p. 891.85.M583.yJ
PU

545. --- Emilija Plateraitė. In
Lietuvių tauta (Vilnius), v.1, no.2,
1908. See serials consulted.

546. --- Ignas Danilevičius; Lietuvos ir jos teisės istorikas. [Ig-
nas Danilevičius; the historian of
Lithuania and its law] Kaunas, 1932.
231 p. (Kaunas. Universitetas.
Teisių fakultetas. Darbai, T.6, kn.
15) See serials consulted.

547. --- Kun. Liudvikas Adomas Ju-
cevičius, Lietuvos rašytojas. Vilnius, 1910. 40 p. 947.5.T4 CtTMF

548. --- Mikalojus Akelaitis. Vilnius, Mintis, 1969. 93 p. (Lietuvos TSR Mokslų akademija. Istorijos
institutas. Acta historica lituanica, 3) Summary in Russian.
PG8721.A43Z72 PU MH

549. --- Simanas Daukantas. Vilnius, 1913. 46 p. 947.520.D4 CtTMF

550. JASAITIS, Domas. Mykolas
Krupavičius visuomenininkas, politikas, kovotojas. [Mykolas Krupavičius; the statesman, politician and
fighter for the Lithuanian cause]
In Tėvynės sargas (Chicago, Ill),
no.2(12), 1955, p.1-21. See serials
consulted.

551. JASAITIS, Juozas. Gabrielė
Petkevičaitė-Bitė. Vilnius, Vaga,
1972. 303 p. PG8721.P43Z7 PU

552. JASINSKAS, Kazys. Stasys
Vainiūnas. Vilnius, VPMLL, 1960.
62 p. illus., ports. ML410.
V163J4 DLC PU

553. JO EKSCELENCIJA KAUNO ARKIVYS-
kupas Metropolitas dr. Juozapas Skvireckas; 80 metų sukakties proga. [Bi-
ography of Abp. Metropolitan Dr. J.J.
Skvireckas. Comp. by Bronius Zume-
ris] Melbourne, Australia, P. Vase-
ris, 1953. 40 p. BX4705.S6615J6
DLC ICLJF PU

554. JONAITIS, Stanley. Jean Mauclère and Lithuania. Ann Arbor, University of Michigan, 1958. iii,247
p. Microfilm AC-1, no.58-7735 DLC
NN

555. JOVAIŠAS, Albinas. Liudvikas
Rėza. Vilnius, Vaga, 1969. 358 p.
illus., port, facsims. PG8517.R5J6
DLC PU

556. JULIUS JANONIS; atsiminimai,

archivinė medžiaga, straipsniai.
[Memoirs of Julius Janonis] Vilnius,
Vaga, 1966. 614 p. illus. (Literatūra ir kalba, 8) See serials
consulted.

557. JUODAKIS, Virgilijus. Balys
Buračas. Vilnius, Vaga, 1971. 26
p., 160 plates. GN21.B87J8 PU

558. JUOZAPAVIČIUS, Pranas. Ado-
mas Mickevičius in Kaunas] Vilnius,
Mintis, 1970. 62 p. PG7185.M51J85
PU

559. JUOZAS NAUJALIS; straipsniai,
laiškai, dokumentai, amžininkų atsiminimai, etc. [Memoirs of Juozas
Naujalis] Sustatė Ona Narbutienė.
Vilnius, Vaga, 1968. 333 p. illus.,
port., music. Bibliography: p. 318-
[324], 325. 805.NJ ICLJF

560. JUOZO TŪBELIO GYVENIMO IR
veiklos bruožai. [Juozas Tūbelis;
his life and works] Jo 10 metų mi-
nisteriavimo sukakčiai paminėti spaudai paruošė Kauno Tautininkų laikraš-
tininkų apylinkė. Kaunas, Pažangos
bendrovė, 1936. 68 p. 947.5.Z67 PU

561. JURGĖLA, Peter Vincent. Spar-
nuoti lietuviai Darius ir Girėnas;
jų gyvenimas ir pirmasis skridimas
per atlantą iš Amerikos Lietuvon.
[Darius and Girėnas; their life and
the first Lithuanian trans-Atlantic
flight] Chicago, Ill., 1935 [c1934]
383 p. illus., ports., map.
TL539.J8 DLC CtTMF CaOONL ICLJF NN
OKentU PU

562. JURGELIONIS, Kleofas. Antanas Vienožinskis ir jo dainos. [An-
tanas Vienožinskis and his songs]
Scranton, Pa., Spauda ir lėšos "Laisvosios minties," 1911. 947.52.B833.2
PU

563. JURGINIS, Juozas. Mikalojus
Katkus. Vilnius, VGLL, 1963. 280
p. illus.CtY MH

564. JUSTINAS TUMĖNAS; [jubilieji-
nis leidinys. Redagavo ir išleido
Vanda Tumėnienė-Mingailaitė] Chicago, Ill., 1959. 174 p. illus.,
ports. PG8721.T8Z75 DLC ICLJF MiD
NN PU

565. KAIRIŪKŠTIS, Vytautas. Kajetonas Sklėrius-Šklėrys, 1876-1932.
Kaunas, Lietuvių dailininkų sąjunga
[1938] xvi, 64 p. 947.52Sk43.yK PU

566. KAPSUKAS, Vincas. Jono Biliūno biografija. Philadelphia,Pa.,
"Kovos", 1917. 127 p. port. (Lietuvių darbininkų literatūros draugijos leidinys, nr.2) PG8721.B47Z7

DLC CtTMF NN OKentU PU

567. KARVELIENĖ, Paulina (Kalvaitytė). Gyvenimo vingiais; autobiografiniai atsiminimai. [Autobiography of Paulina Karvelienė] Chicago, Ill.,Lietuviškos knygos klubas, 1963-68. 2 v. CT1218.K345A3 DLC ICLJF MiD PU

568. KAVOLIŪNAS, Vladas. Gyvenimas pašvęstas dainai. [Life dedicated to the song] Vilnius, VPMLL, 1963. 103 p. illus., facsims, ports. ML420.P47K4 DLC

569. KAZIMIERAS BARŠAUSKAS. Vilnius, Mintis, 1969. 267 p. 267 p. illus., port. CtPAM

570. KOVAS, Nykolas R., ed. Antanina Dambrauskaitė. [Antanina Dambrauskaitė, Lithuanian opera singer] München, 1948. 66 p. AS27.8.D183K PU

571. KRISTIJONAS DONELAITIS; pranešimai, straipsniai, archyvinė medžiaga. [Essays, articles and archival material on Kristijonas Donelaitis] Vilnius, Vaga, 1965. 547 p. illus. (Literatūra ir kalba, 7) Summary in Russian. See serials consulted.

572. KRUPAVIČIUS, Mykolas. Jonas Basanavičius, didis tėvynės meilės mokytojas. [Jonas Basanavičius the great teacher of patriotism] Kaunas, 1927. 17 p. illus. B1.BAS ICLJF

573. --- Kunigas, dievo ir žmogaus tarnyboje. [A priest in the service of God and man] Chicago, Ill., Lietuviškos knygos klubas, 1961] 723 p. ICLJF OCL PPULC

574. KUBILIUS, Vytautas. Julius Janonis. Vilnius, Vaga, 1962. 435p. illus. PG8721.J3Z77 DLC ICLJF MH

575. --- --- 2. pataisytas leidimas. Vilnius, Vaga, 1970. 307 p. illus. PG8721.J35Z77 1970 CaOTU

576. KUBILIUS, Vytautas. Teofilis Til'vitis; kritiko-biograficheskii ocherk. Avtorizovannyi perevod s litovskogo I. Kaplanasa. Moskva, Sovetskii pisatel', 1958. 154 p. PG8721.T55Z737 PU

577. KUČAS, Antanas. Kunigas Antanas Staniukynas; 100 metų sukakčiai nuo jo gimimo paminėti. [Rev. A. Staniukynas and the commemoration of his hundredth birthday] Roma, Lietuvių katalikų mokslo akademijos leidinys, 1965. xvi, 208 p. illus., ports. (Negęstantieji žiburiai, t.2)

Bibliography: p.[191]-195. BX4705.S797K8 DLC CaAEU CaOONL PU

578. KUČINSKAS, Antanas. Profesorius kun. dr. Jonas Totoraitis. In Athenaeum (Kaunas), v.4, 1933, p.1-16. See serials consulted.

579. KŪJUS, Mykolas Kristupas. Dr. Jurgis Sauerveinas; jo gyvenimas,veikla ir raštai. [Dr. J. Sauerveinas; his life, activities and works] In KUHMF. Darbai ir dienos, v.6, 1937. p.5-105. See serials consulted.

580. KUN. PR. M. JURAS, ŠV. TĖVO monsinjoras. n.p., 1951. 32 p. 947.520.J5 CtTMF

581. KUNIGAS PETRAS KRAUJELIS; straipsnių rinkinys. Vilnius, 1937. 120 p. 947.520.K11 CtTMF

582. KUZMICKIS, Zigmantas. Motiejus Valančius politiškas auklėtojas. [M. Valančius as a political educator] In Vairas (Kaunas), no.7-8, 1935, p.257-267. See serials consulted.

583. LABANAUSKAITĖ, Ona. Arkivyskupas Jurgis Matulevičius. Putnam, Conn., Immaculate Conception Convent Press, 1949. 53 p. illus. BX4705. M4295L3 DLC CaOONL CtTMF ICLJF PU

584. LAPELIS, Petras. Prelatas Kazimieras Šaulys. Vaidevutis-Lapelis [pseud.] So. Boston, Mass., 1949. 66 p. 947.520.Š2 CtTMF

585. LEBEDYS, Jurgis. Mikalojus Daukša; monografija. Vilnius, VGLL, 1963. 422 p. facsims., Port. BX4705.D277L4 DLC CaAEU CaOTU CtY ICLJF NN PU

586.--- Simonas Stanevičius; monografija. [Vilnius] VGLL, 1955. 331 p. facsims. Bibliography: p.316-[322] 891.92.St27.yL PU ICLJF NN

587. LELIS, Jonas. Blyškiosios pabaisos atradėjas F.R. Šaudinis; 100-siomsgimimo metinėms. Vilnius, Mintis, 1971. 101 p. QL31.S35L4 PU

588. LIETUVOS ATGIMIMO PATRIARCHO d-ro Jono Basanavičiaus gyvenimo vaizdų albumas su biografija. [An album and biography of the Lithuanian patriarch Dr. J. Basanavičius] Surinko, spaudai paruošė ir redagavo Kostas Radziulis. Kaune, V.D.U. Studentų "Šarūno" korporacija, 1937. 79p. illus., ports. DK511.L28B3 DLC

589. LIETUVOS TSR MOKSLŲ AKADEMIJA VILNA. BOTANIKOS INSTITUTAS. Jurgis Pabrėža, 1771-1849. [Ats. redak-

torius V. Petrauskas] Vilnius, Mintis, 1972. 121 p. At head of title: Lietuvos TSR Mokslų akademija. Botanikos institutas ir Lietuvos botanikų draugija. DK511.L28P25 PU

590. LITHUANIAN POPULIST PEASANT UNION. Dr. Kazys Grinius. Documentation in commemoration on June 24, 1955 at the Carnegie Endowment International Center in New York City [in cooperation with the International Peasant Union] New York, N.Y., 1955. 37 p. illus. (International Peasant Union documents, 11) Soc 827.41.20(11) MH

591. LIULEVIČIUS, Vincentas, ed. Jurgis Krasnickas; 50 metų mirties sukakčiai atminti. [Chicago, Ill.] Studentų ateitininkų sąjunga [1972] 192 p. DK511.L28K7 PU

592. MACIŪNAS, Vincas. Lietuvių kalbai skirtas gyvenimas; keli bruožai ir prisiminimai apie Antaną Salį. [Biography of Antanas Salys. Chicago, Ill., 1972] 19 leaves, ports. Xerox copy of clippings from "Draugas" (Chicago, Ill.), no. 254,260,266, 1972. PG8517.S3M3 PU

593. --- Mykolas Biržiška; 70 metų amžiaus sukakties proga. [On the occasion of the seventieth anniversary of Mykolas Biržiška] In Aidai (Kennebunkport, Me.), no.7(41), 1952, p. 302-310. See serials consulted.

594. --- Naujoji dokumentinė medžiaga apie Antaną Strazdą. [New source material on the Lithuanian poet A. Strazdas] In Lituanistikos darbai (Chicago, Ill.), v.1, 1966, p. 3-18. Summary in English. See serials consulted.

595. --- Pluoštas duomenų apie Antaną Strazdą. [Some biographic information on Antanas Strazdas. Sodus, Mich., Išleido J.J. Bačiūnas-Bachunas, 1967] 137 p. PG8721. S75Z77 DLC PU

596. --- Krėvė, Vincas. In Lietuvių enciklopedija. Boston, 1958. v.13, p. 75-81. For holdings see entry no.216.

597. MACKONIS, Jonas. Antanas Žmuidzinavičius. In Žmuidzinavičius, Antanas. Antanas Žmuidzinavičius, TSRS liaudies dailininkas. Vilnius, 1957. p. 7-23,25-42. ND699.Z6A43 PU CtPAM CtTMF ICLJF

598. MACKEVIČIUS, Rapolas. Daktaras Jonas Basanavičius. Vilnius,

[1930. 64 p.] OCL

599. MAKAROV, Aleksandr Nikolaevich. Eduardas Mezhelaitis [Mieželaitis] Moskva, Sovetskii pisatel', 1966. 197 p. PG8721.M45Z42 PU CaAEU CaOTU NN

600. MAKNICKAS, Vytautas. Gabrielis Landsbergis-Žemkalnis. Kaunas, KUHMF. (Darbai ir dienos, t.5) See serials consulted.

601. MALDEIKIS, Petras, ed. Vytautas Endziulaitis. Chicago, Ill., [M. Gylienė, S. Treigienė ir J. Maldeikienė] 1965. 106 p. 947.5.M293 PU

602. MANELIS, Vitas. Kan. Fabijono Kemėšio veikla nepriklausomoje Lietuvoje. [The activity of Monsig. F. Kemėšis in the independent Lithuania] In Vytis (Chicago, Ill.),no. 11, 1956, p.7-8. See serials consulted.

603. MATEJA, Tadeusz. Podwójne życie Jerzego Giedroycia. Malmö, Sweden, Nasz Znak, 1965. 100 p. illus., facsims. DK440.5.G5M33 DLC

604. MATULAITIS, Kazimieras Aloyzas. Arkivyskupas Pranciškus Karevičius; jo asmens ir veiklos bruožai [Archbishop P. Karevičius, his life and works] In LKMASD, t.6, 1969, p.277-[297] See serials consulted.

605. MATULIONIS, Balys. ed. Generolo gydytojo Vlado Nagiaus-Nagevičiaus gyvenimo ir darbų apžvalga. [Vladas Nagevičius, his life and works] Putnam, Conn., V. Nagevičienė, 1962. 374 p. illus., ports. Bibliography: p.166-167. Summary in English. DK511.L28N35 DLC CaAEU PU CtPAM CtTMF CtY ICLJF MiD NN NNC OCl

606. MATUSAS, Jonas. Motiejus Valančius kaip istorikas. [Bp. M. Valančius as historian] Senovė (Kaunas), v.4, 1938, p.3-24. See serials consulted.

607. MAŽVYDAS, Martynas. Martynas Mažvydas, pirmosios lietuviškos knygos autorius, jo mirties 400 metų sukakčiai paminėti. [A work to commemorate the quartocentenniary of the first book in Lithuanian and its author Martynas Mažvydas] Chicago, Ill., Pedagoginis lituanistikos institutas, 1963. 111 p. facsim. A facsim. p.17-95 of the first known book printed in Lithuania a translation of Luther's catechism. The hymns are accompanied by the music. Wing fZP fac.5549481.47 ICN CaOONL MH-AH NN

608. MERKELIS, Aleksandras. Antanas Smetona; jo visuomeninė, kultūrinė ir politinė veikla. [A. Smetona; his cultural and political activities] New York, N.Y., Amerikos lietuvių tautinės sąjungos leidinys, 1964. xiii, 740 p. illus., ports. Bibliography: p.727-732. DK511. L28S6M56 ICU CaOTP CaOTU CtY ICLJF

609. --- Iš Vydūno vaikystės ir jaunystės. [From the childhood and youth of Vydūnas] In Aidai (Kennebunkport, Me.), no.4, 1953, p.159-167. See serials consulted.

610. --- Jonas Jablonskis. In Kalba (Kaunas), v.2, 1930, p.7-36. See serials consulted.

611. --- Juozas Tumas-Vaižgantas. Chicago, Ill., J. Karvelis, 1955. [16], 398 p. illus., ports. PG8721.T77Z77 DLC CaAEU CaOTU CtPAM CtTMF ICLJF NN PU

612. --- Vincas Kudirka. In Lietuvių enciklopedija. Boston, Mass., 1958. v.13, p.278-284. For holdings see entry no.216.

613. --- Vydūnas, jo 80 metų amžiaus sukakčiai paminėti. [Vydūnas to commemorate his eightieth birthday] Detmold, Ger., "Mūsų kelio" leidinys, 1948. 80 p. 491.922. St78.yM PU CtTMF ICLJF

614. MERKYS, Vytautas. Liudvikas Janavičius. Vilnius, Vaga, 1964. 228 p. illus., facsims, ports. CT1218.J3M4 DLC CtY PU

615. --- Simonas Daukantas. Vilnius, Vaga, 1972. 333 p. DK511.L28D37 DLC

616. MIKUTAITIS, Petras. Julius Janonis; gyvenimas ir kūryba. [Julius Janonis; his life and works] Kaunas, Valstybinė pedagoginės literatūros leidykla, 1941. 253 p. ports. NN

617. --- --- Kaunas, Valstybinė pedagoginės literatūros leidykla, 1959. 113 p. PG8721.J3Z79 DLC

618. MILUKAS, Antanas. Petras Kriaučiūnas. [A. Miluko paskaita 1924 m. Petrinėse] Philadelphia, Pa., Žvaigždės spauda, 1927. 26 p. 891.92.K892.yM PU

619. --- Vyskupo Motiejaus Valančiaus darbai. [Achievements of Bishop M. Valančius] Philadelphia, Pa., Pranaičių Julės leidinys, 1925. 63 p. 891.92.V332A PU

620. MILUKIJADA, ARBA NEPAPRASTO dzūko viršžmogiški nuopelnai ir juodesnis už pragarą tiems nuopelnams pavydas, ir atsiliepimas į Susiv. L. R.K.A. sąnarius. [Rev. A. Milukas; his life and works] n.p., nd. 37 p. Bound with Dokumentas apie lotyniškas litaras. 891.92H.0687 PU

621. MINGĖLA, Vladas. Kun. Antanas Milukas, jo gyvenimas ir darbai. [Rev. A. Milukas, his life and works] Detroitas, [Kun. Antano Miluko monografijai leist komitetas] 1962. 384 p. illus., ports., map, facsims. E184.L7M55 DLC CtPAM CtTMF CaOONL ICLJF PU

622. MIŠKINIS, Antanas. Neužmirštamas Vaižgantas. [Unforgetable Vaižgantas] In Pergalė (Vilnius), no.10, 1969, p.95-117. See serials consulted.

623. MOCKUS, Kazys. Mykolas Krupavičius. In Aidai (Kennebunkport, Me.), no.8(34), 1950, p.345-351. See serials consulted.

624. MOTIEJUS VALANČIUS; Žemaičių vyskupas ir rašytojas. [M. Valančius, Bishop of Žemaitija (Samogitia) In Lietuvių enciklopedija. Boston, Mass., 1965, v.32, p.523-531. AE60. L5L5 v.32 DLC CU CaAEU See entry no. 216.

625. MUŠINSKAS-MUŠAITIS, Antanas, ed. Vladislava Grigaitienė, 1919-1934, jos 15 metų scenos darbo sukaktuvėms paminėti. [V. Grigaitienė and her fifteenth anniversary as an opera singer] Kaunas, Daina, 1934. 31 p. 947.52.G873.yM PU

626. MŪŠOS DOBILAS; kunigui J.Lindei-Dobilui atminti. [Rev. J. Lindė-Dobilas, his life and works] Panevėžys, 1936. 112 p. 947.520.L3 CtTMF

627. MYKOLAS ŠLEŽEVIČIUS. [Contributors: Julius Butėnas, Mečys Mackevičius et al. Ed. by Antanas Rūkas. Chicago, Ill.] Terra [1954] 343 p. illus., ports, facsim. DK511.L28S55 DLC CaAEU CtTMF ICLJF NN PU

628. NARBUTIENĖ, Ona. Juozas Naujalis; straipsniai, laiškai,dokumentai, amžininkų atsiminimai, Etc. [J. Naujalis, his life and works... Sudarė ir paaiškinimus parašė Ona Narbutienė] Vilnius, Vaga, 1968. 334 p. music, 9leaves of illus. Bibliography: p.[315]-[324]-325. ML410N287N4 DLC PU

629. NEZABITAUSKIS, Adolfas. Jonas Basanavičius. Kaunas, 1938. 542 p.

947.520.B8 CtTMF

630. ORINTAITĖ, Petronėlė. Ką laumės lėmė; atsiminimai apie Salomėją Nėrį, 1904-1945. [Reminiscences about Salomėja Nėris. Chicago, Ill.] Chicagos Lietuvių literatūros draugijos leidinys, 1965. 234 p. ports. PG8721.N4Z8 DLC CaOTU

631. PALIONYTĖ, Dana. Valanda su kompozitorium Antanu Račiūnu. [One hour with composer A. Račiūnas] Vilnius, Vaga, 1970. 91 p. ML410.R122P3 PU

632. PEČIULIONIS, M. Suvalkų mieste 1882-1914 metais Juozą Marčiukaitį prisimenant. [Recalling Juozas Marčiukaitis in Suvalkai] In Lietuvos žinios (Kaunas), no.67-68, 1932. See serials consulted.

633. PERVYI AERONAVT LITVY; Aleksandras Grishkiavichius i ego kniga "Parolet zhmudina." Vil'nius, 1971. 80 p. DK511.L28G74 PU

634. PETRAS CVIRKA GYVENIME IR KŪryboje. [P. Cvirka; his life and works. Redakcinė komisija: K. Korsakas, J. Šimkus, A. Venclova. Paruošė K. Vairas-Račkauskas] Vilnius, VGLL, 1953. 178 p. illus. PG8721.C8Z75 DLC

635. PEURSEM, Jan Henrik van. President Smetona, door mr. J.H. van Peursem. ['s-Gravenhage, Philatelie en geschiedenis, 1936] 23 p. illus., port. (Philatelie en geschiedenis, no.17) HE6183.P42 no.17 DLC BM PU

636. PRANSKUS, Bronius. Pranas Vaičaitis. Vilnius, VPMLL, 1956. 37 p. 891.92.V188.yP PU MH OKentU

637. PREIKŠAS, Kazys. Kazys Preikšas. [Sudarė M. Katliauskas ir J. Lebedys. Ats. redaktorius G. Zimanas] Vilnius [Mintis] 1964. 350 p. illus., ports. DK511.L27P67 DLC PU

638. PŠIBILIAUSKIENĖ, Sofija (Ivanauskaitė). Autobiografija...iš praeities. Lazdynų Pelėda [pseud.] In Her Raštai. Vilnius, 1954. v.1. PG8721.P7 v.1 DLC

639. PUTVINSKIS, Vladas. Vladas Putvinskis-Putvys; jo gyvenimas ir parinktieji raštai. [V. Putvinskis-Putvys; his life and works] Redagavo A. Marcinkevičius. Kaunas, 1933-1934. 2 v. Vol.1 never published. 947.5.P985 PU(2) CtTMF(2)

640. PUZINAS, Jonas. Tadas Daugirdas ir jo darbai. Offprint from Lietuviškoji enciklopedija. Kaunas,

1937. t.3 For holdings see entry no.215.

641. RASTENIS, Vincas. Bronius K. Balutis; Lietuvos Respublikos nepaprasto pasiuntinio ir įgalioto ministro Didžiojoj Britanijoj 75 metų sukakties minėjime, 1955 m. kovo 14 d., New Yorke Vinco Rastenio pasakyta kalba. Sodus, Mich., J.J. Bachunas, 1965. 16 p. DK511.L28B3 PU

642. RĖKLAITIS, Kazimieras. Il servo di Dio Giorgio Matulewich-Matulevičius; profilo biografico. Roma, Postulazione Generale[1955] 51 p. illus. Bl.MAT ICLJF

643. RIMANTAS, Juozas. Žemaitė, gyvenime ir kūryboje. [Žemaitė; her life and works] Vilnius, VGLL, 1956. 249 p. illus., facsims. 891.92.Z99.yZ PU NN

644. RIMAŠAUSKAS, Jonas. Kunigas kan. Antanas Petraitis. [Redagavo Stasys Džiugas] Chicago, Ill., 1955 23p. 922.2.P442R PU

645. RIMKA, Albinas and Mikas Petrauskas. Vincas Kudirka; jo gyvenimas, darbai ir visuomenės pažiūros. [V. Kudirka; his life and works] Chicago, ill., 1915. 35 p. 891.92.K952.yR PU CtTMF

646. RIMŠA, Petras. Petras Rimša pasakoja. [Surašė Juozas Rimantas] Vilnius, VGLL, 1964. 384 p. illus., ports. NB699.R5A2 DLC PU

647. RIŠKUS, Jonas. Liaudies dainius Antanas Strazdas. Vilnius, VPMLL, 1957. 37 p. At head of title: Lietuvos TSR Politinių ir mokslinių žinių skleidimo draugija. PG8721.S75Z8 DLC OKentU PU

648. RŪKAS, Antanas. Vienišo žmogaus gyvenimas; Juozo Adomaičio-Dėdės Šerno gyvenimo bruožai. [An outline of the life and works of J. Adomaitis. Chicago, Ill.] Amerikos lietuvių istorijos draugijos leidinys, [162] 206 p. illus. E184.L7A3 DLC ICLJF

649. RUKUIŽA, Antanas. Prof. Dr. h.c. Povilas Matulionis; gyvenimas ir darbai. [P. Matulionis; his lile and works] Chicago, Ill., Lietuvių profesorių draugija Amerikoje, 1960. 83 p. illus., ports., maps. (Lietuvių profesorių draugijos Amerikoje leidinys, nr.1) SD129.M33R8 DLC CtPAM ICLJF PU

650. ŠALKAUSKIS, Stasys. 15 metų kultūrinėje Lietuvos tarnyboje. [15 years of service in the cultural

field in Lithuania] In Židinys(Kaunas), v.20, 1934. p.193-211, 34-50. See serials consulted.

651. SALOMĖJA NĖRIS,1904-1945. [Paruošė K. Vairas-Račkauskas. Dailininkas V. Bačėnas] Vilnius, VGLL, 1955. 213 p. (chiefly illus.,ports) PG8721.N4Z84 DLC BM

652. SAMULIONIS, Algis Romualdas. Balys Sruoga, dramaturgijos ir teatro kritikas. [B. Sruoga the critic of drama and theatre] Vilnius, Mintis, 1968. 176 p. PG8721.S68Z87 DLC

653. SENN, Alfred. Vincent Krėvė and Lithuanian folklore. In Halle, Morris, comp. For Roman Jacobson, essays on the occasion of his sixtieth birthday... The Hague, 1956. p.444-448. P26.J3 DLC CU CtY CSt IU InU ICN ICU KyU MB MH MiU MoU MdBJ NIC NN NNC NcD OClW OrU PU PPiU RPB TxU TU WU WaU

654. --- --- Offprint from For Roman Jacobson, essays...Q 891.92. K689.yS PU

655. SENN, Alfred Erich. Garlawa: a study in émigré intrigue, 1915-17. In Slavic review (Menasha, Wis.), v.45, 1967, p.411-425. See serials consulted.

656. SERAPINAS, Rapolas. Vilius Storasta (Vydūnas, pseud.) In Lietuvių enciklopedija. Boston, Mass., 1965. v.33, p.519-524. For holdings see entry no.216.

657. ŠIMONIS, Kazys. Gyvenimo nuotrupos; atsiminimai. [Fragments from my life; memoirs] Vilnius, 1959. 206 p. illus. ND699.S516A2 PU CtPAM NN

658. --- --- 2. leidimas. Vilnius, Vaga, 1966. 194 p. illus. ND699. S516A2 1966 DLC

659. ŠIRVYDAS, Vytautas, ed. Juozas O. Širvydas, 1875-1935; biografijos bruožai. [Biographical outline of J.O. Širvydas] Cleveland,Ohio, Dirvos spauda, 1941. 493 p. illus., ports. E184.L7S5 DLC CSt-H CaOONL CtPAM CtTMF MiD NN PU

660. ŠLIOGERIS, Vaclovas. Antanas Smetona; žmogus ir valstybininkas, atsiminimai. [A. Smetona; a man and a ststesman...Sodus, Mich., J. Bachunas] 1966. 181 p. illus.,ports. 947.52.Sm35S PU CaAEU ICLJF

661. ŠLIUPAS, Jonas, ed. Kunigas Vladislovas Dembskis; jo gyvenimas, raštai ir darbai. [Rev. V. Dembskis;

his life and works. Edited by John Szlupas] New York, N.Y., Spauda "Tėvynės", 1916. 156 p. illus. 891.92.D393.yK PU CtTMF DLC ICLJF NN

662. SRUOGA, Balys and J. Žadeikis. Kipras Petrauskas. Kaunas, Tulpė, 1939. 215 p. illus., ports. 947.52.P455.yS PU

663. STAKNYS, Alina. Lithuanian poet, writing in French, O.V. Milosz-Milašius. In Lituanus(Brooklyn,N.Y.) v.5, no.2, June 1959, p.50-57. See serials consulted.

664. STASYS PILKA; jauna kūryba. [S. Pilka; his theatrical life] Chicago, Ill., 1928. 32 p. illus. L Bl.PIL ICLJF

665. STASYS ŠIMKUS; straipsniai, dokumentai, laiškai, amžininkų atsiminimai. [S. Šimkus; his life and works. Comp. by D. Palionytė] Vilnius, Vaga, 1967. 494 p. illus., port. 805.Sm ICLJF CtPAM

666. STOČKUS, Bronius. Rėzos charakteris ir jo lietuvybė. [Rhesa's character and his Lithuanian feelings] In Athenaeum (Kaunas), v.5, 1934, p.1-33. See serials consulted.

667. STONYS, Juozas. Antanas Vienuolis. Vilnius, VGLL, 1957. 84 p. PG8721.V5Z85 DLC PU

668. STOROST, Wilhelm. Kalėjimas-laisvėjimas. [W. Storost in the concentration camp in Germany] Detmold, Ger., Lietuvos skautų sąjungos brolijos valdyba, 1947. 72 p. Bl.VYD ICLJF

669. STRASZEWICZ, Józef. Emilie Plater, sa vie et sa mort, avec une préface de M.Ballanche. Paris, Chez l'éditeur, 1835. xvi, 356 p. port. DK435.5.P4S8 DLC ICBM

670. --- The life of Countess Emily Plater. Tr. by J.K. Salomonski. New York, N.Y., J.F. Trow, 1842. 285 p. ports. DK435.5.P4S82 DLC MU NBuG NN ViU

671. SUŽIEDĖLIS, Simas. Kunigas Jonas nuo Kryžiaus; kunigo Jono Švagždžio biografijos metmens. [A short biography of Rev. J. Švagždys] Brooklyn, N.Y., 1956. 286 p. illus. BR1725.S87S8 DLC CtPAM CtTMF ICLJF MH-AH NN OCl PU

672. TALKO-HRYNCEWICZ, Julian. Wandalin Szukiewicz jako prehistoryk Litwy. In Wiadomości Archeologiczne (Warszawa), v.5, zesz.1-2, 1920, p.65-76. See serials consulted.

673. TERCIJONAS, Vincas. Dr. K. Grinius; gydytojas ir visuomeninin-kas, 1866-1926. Kaunas, 1927. 59 p. BM(010795. ee. 59.)

674. TOTORAITIS, Jonas. Žemaičių vyskupas Aleksandras Gorainis ir di-dysis maras. [The Bishop of Žemaitija (Samogitia) A. Gorainis and the Great Plague in Lithuania] In Lietuvos praeitis (Kaunas), v.1, no.2, 1941, p.604-614. See serials consulted.

675. TUMAS, Juozas. Antanas Baranauskas, 1835-1902. Kaunas, 1924. 117 p. 947.520.B6 CtTMF

676. --- Broliai Juzumai-Juzumavičiai ir Kazimieras Skrodzkis. [A biography of brothers Juzumai-Juzumavičiai and Kazimieras Skrodzkis] Kaunas, 1924. 68 p. 491.922.T832.2 CtTMF ICCC

677. --- Kun. Juozapas Silvestras Dovydaitis-Šiaulėniškis Senelis 1825-1882; paskaita. Kaunas, 1924. 43 p. Xerox copy, 1970. PG8721.D742.T85 1970 PU

678. --- Vincas Kudirka-Vincas Kapsas. Kaunas, "Varpo" bendrovės leidinys, 1924. 42 p. 491.922. K953.yE PU CtTMF

679. URBONAVIČIUS, Kazimieras. Kun. J. Navickas; jo gyvenimas ir asmens bruožai. [By] Jonas Kmitas, [pseud. Rev. J. Navickas; his life and works] Chicago, Ill., T.T. Marijonų leidinys, 1943. 128 p. illus. ports. BX4705.N32U7 DLC CtTMF ICLJF PU

680. VAILOKAITIS, Jonas. Vyskupas Antanas Baranauskas. Seinai, 1911. 51 p. 891.92.B229.yV PU

681. VAIŠNORA, Juozas. Arkivyskupas J. Matulevičius Vilniuje. [Archbishop J. Matulevičius in Vilnius] In Matulevičius, Jurgis. Užrašai. London, 1953. p.137-214. BX4705.M4295A3 DLC CtTMF

682. --- Dievo tarnas arkivyskupas Jurgis Matulaitis. [God's servant Abp. J. Matulaitis. Putnam, Conn., Nek. Prasidėjimo seserys, 1953] 23 p. L Bl.MAT ICLJF

683. VAITKUS, Mykolas. Mūsų ryto saulė Maironis. [Reminiscences about Maironis] In His Nepriklausomybės saulėj, 1918-1940; atsiminimai. London, 1969. v.5, pt.3, p.5-64. PG8721.V322Z52 PU

684. --- Salomėja Nėris. In His

Nepriklausomybės saulėj, 1918-1940; atsiminimai. London, 1969. v.7, pt.3, p.147-210. PG8721.V322Z52 PU

685. VANAGAS, Vytautas. Antanas Strazdas. Vilnius, Vaga, 1968. 397 p. illus., port., facsims. PG8721.S75Z9 DLC ICLJF PU

686. --- Nauja archyvinė medžiaga apie A. Strazdą. [New archival documents about A. Strazdas. Su dokumentų publikacija] In Literatūra ir kalba (Vilnius), v.5, 1961, p.435-464. See serials consulted.

687. VARPAS. Dr. K. Griniaus jubiliejinis numeris 1926 m. ["Varpas" issue in honour of Dr. K. Grinius] Kaunas, 1926. 947.5.G887.yV PU

688. --- Vinco Kudirkos jubiliejinis numeris 1924 m. lapkritys. [Varpas issue in memory of Vincas Kudirka] Kaunas, 1924. 891.92.K852.yV PU CtTMF

689. VENCLOVA, Antanas, ed. Salomėja Nėris, poetės atminimui. [Kaunas] VGLL, [1946] 190 p. illus. PG8721.N4Z9 DLC

690. VENGRIS, Antanas. Kastantas Glinskis; gyvenimo ir kūrybos apybraiža. [An outline of the life and works of K. Glinskis] Vilnius, Mintis, 1965. 117 p. illus., ports. PN2728.G65V4 DLC PU

691. --- Petras Kubertavičius. Sudarė ir paruošė A. Vengris. Vilnius, Mintis, 1970. 184 p., 32 leaves of illus. PN2725.L5V4 DLC PU

692. VIENOŽINSKIS, Justinas. Straipsniai, dokumentai, laiškai, amžininkų atsiminimai. [J. Vienožinskis; his life and works. Knygą parengė Irena Kostkevičiūtė] Vilnius, Vaga, 1970. xii, 277 p. ND699.V55A3 PU

VILNA. LIETUVOS TSR VALSTYBINĖ RESPUBLIKINĖ BIBLIOTEKA. Salomėja Nėris gyvenime ir kūryboje; parodos katalogas. [Kaunas. 1946] See entry no.147.

693. VINCAS AMBROZEVIČIUS. Vincent W. Ambroze (75 metų sukakčiai); autobiografija. [Redaktorius Vytautas Širvydas] Sodus, Mich., J.J. Bachunas, 1942. [19] p. E184.L7A55 PU

694. VISVALDA, A. Lituanica II. ir Atlanto nugalėtojas P. Vaitkus. [Lituanica the Second and its pilot P. Vaitkus] Kaunas, 1935. 32 p. 947.520.V6 CtTMF

695. VYSKUPAS PRANAS BRAZYS.
Brooklyn, N.Y., 1969. 87 p.
BX1559.L5V35 PU

696. YLA, Stasys, (1913-). Juozas
Mažeika. [Užsitarnavę artistai Lietuvos SSR] Vilnius, Lietuvos TSR
teatro draugija, 1968. 70, [8] p.
illus. (Scenos meistrai) ML420.
M339Y5 DLC

697. ZABORSKAITĖ, Vanda. Maironis.
Vilnius, Vaga, 1968. 518 p. illus.
PG8721.M3Z9 PU CU CtY DLC

698. ZAJANČKAUSKAS, Kajetonas.
Nuo piemenelio iki arkivyskupo; ar-
kivysk. Jurgio Matulevičiaus biografija. [A biography of Abp. J. Matulevičius. Marijampolė] Marijonai,
[1939] 110 p. illus. L Bl.MAT
ICLJF CtTMF

699. ŽEKAITĖ, Janina. Antanas
Vienuolis. Vilnius, VPMLL, 1956.
32 p. 891.92.Z89.yZ PU

700. ŽIDONIS, Geneviève Irene.
O.V. de L. Milosz; sa vie, son oeuv-
re, son rayonnement. Paris, O. Per-
rin [1951] 293 p. port. Bibliography: p.275-280. PQ2625.I558Z95
DLC CaAEU CtY IaU IU MH NN

701. ŽILEVIČIUS, Juozas. Česlovas
Sasnauskas. [A monograph about Č.
Sasnauskas, a notable composer] 2d
ed. Brooklyn, N.Y., L.E. Joffre Voi-
sekauska, 1953. 126 p. illus.
927.8.S78Z PU CtTMF ICLJF

702. ŽILIUS, Jonas. Kun. A. Burba;
jo gyvenimas ir darbai. [Rev. A.Bur-
ba; his life and works] Mažas pamin-
klėlis nuo "S.L.A." Parašė Jr.-Jonas
[pseud] Plymouth, Pa., Spaustuvėj
S.L.A., 1898. 29 p. ports.
(*Q p.v. 124)NN CtTMF

703. ZINKEVIČIUS, Zigmas and Kabelka, Jonas. Kazimieras Būga; gyvenimas ir mokslo darbai. [K. Būga; his
life and works] In Būga, Kazimieras.
Rinktiniai raštai. Vilnius, 1958.
v.1, p.13-100. PG8509.B8 v.1 DLC
CaAEU

704. ZINKUS, Jonas. Vaižgantas-
kunigas ir Vaižgantas - žmogus. In
Komunistas (Vilnius), no.9, 1969,
p.46-54. See serials consulted.

705. ŽIUGŽDA, Juozas. Antanas
Mackevičius, Lietuvos valstiečių vadovas kovoje prieš carizmą ir dvari-
ninkus. [A. Mackevičius the leader
of the struggle against czarism and
landlords] Vilnius, VPMLL, 1951.
56 p. 947.5.Z68 PU

706. ŽMUIDZINAVIČIUS, Antanas.
Antanas Ionasovich Zhmuidzinavichius
Moskva, Sovetskii khudozhnik, 1953.
64 p. illus. ND699.Z6A42 DLC

707. --- Antanas Žmuidzinavičius;
Lietuvos TSR liaudies dailininkas.
[A monograph about A. Žmuidzinavi-
čius, a notable artist] Vilnius,
VPMLL, 1957. 157 p. illus. Text
also in Russian. ND699.Z6A43 PU
CtPAM CtTMF ICCC ICLJF

708. --- Paletė ir gyvenimas. [Pa-
lette and life. Autoriaus iliustra-
cijos] Vilnius, VGLL, 1961. 414p.
illus., plates, ports. ND699.Z6A2
DLC NN PU

709. ŽYMANTIENĖ, Julija (Beniuše-
vičiūtė). Autobiografija. Kaunas,
VGLL, 1946. 123 p. PG8721.Z9Z5
1946 DLC PU

II.6.c. GENEALOGY OF NOBLE FAMILIES

710. AVIŽONIS, Konstantinas. Die
Entstehung und Entwicklung des li-
tauischen Adels bis zur litauisch-
polnischen Union 1385. Berlin, Emil
Ebering, 1932. vi, 174 p. (Histo-
rische Studien, Hft.223). Bibliogra-
phy: p.[156]-174. 900.H628 v.223
NNC BM CU CaOTU GU IdU IEN InU IU KU
MH MiU MnU NN NIC NcU NcD NjP NSyU
UU WU WaU

711. BARTOSZEWICZ, Julian. Het-
mani polscy i Koronni i Wielkiego
Księstwa Litewskiego. Wizerunki zebrane i rysowane przez Wojciecha
Gersona. Warszawa, 1862-[65] 2pts.
27 ports. Slav 5300.4 MH

712. BARTOSZEWICZ, Kazimierz. Ra-
dziwiłłowie. Początek i dzieje rodu
typy i charaktery... Warszawa, Księgarnia J. Czernieckiego [1927] 320p.
DLC-P4 MH

713. BONIECKI, Adam Józef Feliks.
Herbarz polski. Wiadomości history-
czno-geneologiczne o rodach szla-
checkich. Ułożył i wydał Adam Boniecki. Warszawa, Gebethner i Wolff,
1899-[1915] 16 v. CR2060.B6 DLC MH
NN PU

714. --- Poczet rodów w Wielkim
Księstwie Litewskim w XV i XVI wieku. Warszawa [J. Berger] 1887. xv,
425, xlix p. illus., tables.
CS886.B65 DLC NN MH PPULC PU

715. BRODOWSKI, Samuel. Żywoty
hetmanów Królewstwa Polskiego i Wielkiego Księstwa Litewskiego; z mate-

ryałów po Samuelu Brodowskim w Podkolcach znalezionych. Wyd. Żegota Pauli. Lwów, Nakł. J. Malikowskiego, 1850. 314 p. illus. Original title: Buława sławna w obozie i w senacie. Slav 5380.105 MH

716. CHODYNICKI, Kazimierz. Geneza dynastii Giedymina. In Kwartalnik Historyczny (Lwów), v.40, 1926, p. 541-566. Dl.K85 DLC CU CtY MH MnU NN; see also serials consulted.

717. CHODŹKO, Leonard Jakób Borejko. Historya domu Rawitów-Ostrowskich, związana z dziejami Polski, Litwy, Prus i Rusi, składających Rzeczpospolitą Polską między latami 1190-1650. Z przedmową Karola Widmana. Lwów [Nakł. K. Ostrowskiego] 1871-73. 2 v. CS879.08C54 ICU CtY

718. GLINKA, Jan. Ród Klausucia w wiekach 13-16. Ze studiów nad kształtowaniem się i różnicowaniem społecznym bojarstwa litewskiego. In Studia Źródłoznawcze (Warszawa), v.4, 1959, p. 85-107; v.5, 1960, p. 35-55. D13.S853 DLC MH NN WU WaU

719. DIE HISTORISCHE STELLUNG DES Hauses Radziwill. Berlin, In Commission bei R.v. Decker, 1892. 109 p. 4DD2601 DLC

720. JAKŠTAS, Juozas. Naujausi Gedimino dinastijos kilmės tyrinėjimai. [The latest research on the origin of the dynasty of Gediminas] In Lietuvos praeitis (Kaunas), v.1, 1940, p. 29-56. See serials consulted.

721. IURGEVICH, Vladimir Norbertovich. Opyt ob"iasneniia imen kniazei litovskikh. Moskva, 1882. 29 p. (Chteniia v Imperatorskom Obshchestvie istorii i drevnostei rossiiskikh pri Moskovskom Universitetie, t.126, otd. II.) 947.0b7 v.126 NNC

722. KIRKOR, Stanisław. Poczet Kirkorów ułożony chronologicznie. Londyn, 1969. 89 p. CS879.K55 1969 PU

723. --- Uwagi ogólne o genealogii rodziny Kirkorów litewskich. Londyn, 1969. 52 p. CS879 1969a PU

724. KOJAŁOWICZ, Wojciech Wijuk. Herbarz rycerstwa W.X. Litewskiego tak zwany Compendium... Wydanie "Herolda Polskiego" [Ed. by Franciszek Piekosiński] Kraków; Wilno, Czas; J. Zawadzki, 1897. iv, 527 p. illus. 897.52.K827 PU BM(09915.bb.5.) CaAEU CtY MH NN

725. --- Herbarz szlachty Wielkiego Księstwa Litewskiego zwany Nomenclator. Wyd. Franciszek Piekosiński. In Herold Polski (Kraków), 1905, p. 1-208; 1906, p. 209-320. See serials consulted.

726. KOŚCIALKOWSKI, Stanisław. Antoni Tyzenhauz, podskarbi narodowy litewski. Londyn, Wydawn. Społeczności Akademickiej Univ. Stefana Batorego w Londynie, 1970. 1 v. illus. DK511.L28T9 PU CaTOU MH

727. KOTŁUBAI, Edward. Życie Janusza Radziwiłła na Birżach i Dubinkach. Wilno i Witebsk, M. Mindelsohn, 1859. viii, 460 p. DK511. L28R27 DLC

728. LABARRE DE RAILLICOURT, Dominique. Les grands-ducs de Lithuanie; maison de Gedymin et leurs descendants. [Paris] L'auteur, 1965. 23p. illus., ports., tables. DK511.L23L3 DLC MH NN PU

729. ŁOWMIAŃSKI, Henryk. Wykaz wywodów szlachectwa na Litwie. In Miesięcznik Heraldyczny (Warszawa), 1939, v.18, no.1, p.1-7. See serials consulted.

730. MAŁACHOWSKI, Piotr Nałęcz. Zbiór nazwisk szlachty z opisem herbów własnych-familiom zostaiącym w Królewstwie Polskim i Wielkim Xięstwie Litewskim. Łuck, Druk J.K.Mci i Rzeczypospolitej, 1790. 2 v. CR2064.M3 WU

731. --- --- Ułożony, poprawiony i powtórnie do druku podany. Lublin, Drukarnia Ks. Trynitarzy, 1805. 3 v. Bb2b BO5M CtY NN

732. NIESIECKI, Kasper. Herbarz Polski. Powiększony dodatkami z późniejszych autorów rękopismów...przez J.N. Bobrowicza. Leipzig, Breitkopf & Härtel, 1839-46. 10 v. illus. CS874.N6 DLC InU MB NN

733. NOWAKOWSKI, Tadeusz. Die Radziwills. Die Geschichte einer grossen europäischen Familie. [Nach dem polnischen Manuscript übersetzt von Janusz von Pilecki und Józef Hahn] München, R. Piper [1966] 427 p. illus. CS879.R3 1966 DLC PU

734. ORIGO REGIS JAGYELO ET WYTHOldi ducum Lithuaniae. In Russia. Arkheograficheskaia komissiia. Polnoe sobranie russkikh letopisei. Sanktpeterburg, 1907. v.17, p. 219-226. DK70.A53 v.17 DLC NN

735. PIEKOSIŃSKI, Franciszek Ksawery. Heraldyka polska wieków średnich. Kraków, Nakł. Akademii Umie-

jętności, 1899. 486 p. illus., coats of arms. Bb26899P CtY DLC MH PU

736. PORAI-KOSHITS, Ivan Antonovich. Istoricheskii razskaz o litovskom dvorianstvie. Sanktpeterburg, Tip. Eduarda Pratsa, 1858. xii, 175 p. illus. 947.52.P927 PU NN

737. POTOCKI, Wacław. Poczet herbów szlachty Korony Polskiej i Wielkiego Xięstwa Litewskiego... Tudzież starożytność domów. Rodowitość familiey. Kraków, A. Schedel, 1696. 14, 741 p. BM(9917. h. 13.)

738. RADZIWIŁŁ, Bogusław. Żywot Księcia B. Radziwiłła... Wyd. A. Popliński. Poznań, 1840. 211 p. BM(10790. bb. 6.)

739. SEMKOWICZ, Władysław. O litewskich rodach bojarskich zbratanych ze szlachtą polską w Horodle r. 1413. In Miesięcznik Heraldyczny (Warszawa), v.6, 1913, p. 143-145, 176-190; v.7, 1914/15, p. 7-16, 51-59, 96-103; and continuation in Rocznik Towarzystwa Heraldycznego (Warszawa), v.5-9, 1920-1929. See serials consulted.

740. --- Tradycya o kniaziewskim pochodzeniu Radziwiłłów w swietle krytyki historycznej. In Kwartalnik Historyczny (Lwów), v.24, 1920. See serials consulted.

741. --- W sprawie początków szlachty na Litwie i jej ustroju rodowego. In Kwartalnik Historyczny (Lwów), v.29, 1915, p. 224-256. See serials consulted.

742. STADNICKI, Kazimierz. Bracia Władysława Jagiełły Olgierdowicza, króla Polski, Wielkiego Xięcia Litwy. Jako dalszy ciąg "Synów Giedymina". Z tablicami genealogicznemi ... Lwów, A. Vogel, 1867. viii, 416 p. tables. DK511.L23S8 CU CoU ICU ICLJF NN PU WU

743. --- Dodatki i poprawki do dzieła:"Bracia Władysława Jagiełły" i "Olgierd i Kiejstut", wydawanych we Lwowie... 1867-1870. Lwów, Nakł. s. Igła, 1873. 38 p. 947.52.Stl3.4 PU

744. --- Olgierd i Kiejstut, synowie Giedymina W. Xięcia Litwy. Lwów, Gubrinowicz i Schmidt, 1870. 3, 213, xxi p. 947.52.Stl3.2 PU CtY ICLJF ScU

745. --- Synowie Giedymina. Wydanie drugie przerobione i poprawione. Lwów, 1849-53. 2 v. facsims, tables. 947.52.Stl3 PU BM(18790. dd. 11.)

746. --- --- Wyd. nowe. Lwów, Nakł. Ign. Stadnickiego, 1881. 272 p. DK511.L28G4 DLC

747. STECKI, Henryk. Rodowody książąt i królów polskich oraz wielkich książąt litewskich. Przez H. S. Petersburg, 1861. [5], 27 geneal. tables. CS874.S75 PU

748. SZYDŁOWSKI, Stefan von. Verzeichnis der polnischen und litauischen Familien, die den erblichen Titel eines Fürsten, Markgrafen, Grafen und Freiherren tragen, mit kurzen genealogischen Angaben über dies Familie. Budapest, Officina-Druckerei, [n.d.] 123 p. DK413.8.S999 InNd

749. WDOWISZEWSKI, Zygmunt. Genealogia Jagiellonów. [Warszawa] 1968. 230 p. DK413.1.W35 PU

750. WIĘCKOWSKA-MITZNEROWA, Wanda. Karol Chodkiewicz. Warszawa, Książka i Wiedza, 1959. 412 p. illus. (Światowid; biblioteczka popularna naukowa) DK430.2.C5W5 DLC BM MiD

751. --- --- [Wyd. 2.] Warszawa, 1965. 315 p. DK430.2.C5W5 1965 PU

752. WOLFF, Józef. Kniaziowie litewsko-ruscy od końca czternastego wieku. Warszawa, 1895. xxv, 698 p. Slav 6575.6 MH BM(9902. i. 32.)

753. --- Pacowie. Senatorowie i kniaziowie litewscy. Petersburg, w druk. F. Suszczyńskiego, 1885. x, 377 p. ports., coats of arms, geneal. tables. 947.52.W833.2 PU

754. --- Ród Gedimina. Dodatki i poprawki do dzieł K. Stadnickiego: "Synowie Gedymina", "Olgierd i Kiejstut" i "Bracia Władysława Jagiełły" Kraków, w druk. W.L. Anczyca, 1886. vii, 171 p. geneal. tables. DK511. L28G44 DLC PU

755. --- Senatorowie i Dygnitarze Wielkiego Księstwa Litewskiego 1386-1795. Kraków, w druk. W.L. Anczyca, 1885. vii, 354 p. DK511.L28A1 1885 DLC BM(9902. f. 13.)

III. GENERAL WORKS

III.1. BALTIC COUNTRIES IN GENERAL

756. ANDERSON, Herbert Foster. Borderline Russia. London, The Cresset Press, 1942. [6], 238 p. Information pertaining to Lithuania is on p. 142-200. DK267.A58 DLC CU CaAEU CaVaU CaOTU CtY InNd KU MBat

NN NNC NcD OClW

757. BALTIC AMERICAN SOCIETY. The Baltic republics; what they are, what they have. New York, N.Y., 1922. 8 leaves. (GMC p.v.1, no.1) NN

758. BALTIC AND SCANDINAVIAN COUNtries; a survey of the peoples and states on the Baltic with special regard to their history, geography, and economics. Gdynia, Poland, The Baltic Institute, 1935-39. 5 v. illus., plates, ports., diagrams. 3 nos. a year. D965.A1B3 DLC CLSU CaBVaU CoU CtY DAU DDO ICU IU In MB MH MiU MnU NN NNC NcD NjP NR NcU OCl OCU OU PPULC PU PUW WU

759. THE BALTIC STATES AND THE SOviet Union; reprinted from a report to the Council of Europe, with a preface and supplementary comments. Stockholm, Supreme Committee for Liberation, 1962. 52 p. (Problems of the Baltic, 1) DK511.B3B19 CaAEU

760. BALTISCHE GESELLSCHAFT IN DEUTSCHLAND. Die baltischen Völker in ihrer europäischen Verpflichtung; sechs Vorträge. Redaktion von Hans v. Rimscha. Hannover-Döhren, Ger., H. v. Hirschheydt, 1958. 63 p. DK511.B3B285 DLC PU

761. BALTISKA KOMMITTÉN. Ha de rätt att leva? Inför de Baltiska kommittén, med illustrationer och planscher. Stockholm, H. Geber [1943] 351 p. illus., maps, plates, ports. DK511.B3B3 DLC DS NcD

762. BILMANIS, Alfreds. Baltic essays. Washington, D.C., Latvian Legation, 1945. 267 p. illus., map. Bibliography: p. 222-256. DK511.B3B48 DLC AU CU CaAEU CaBVaU CaBViP CaQMM CoCC CoDU CoD CtY DNAL IaU IdPS IdU MeB Mi NcD OrU OU PPT PPULC PU ViU WaS WyU

763. --- The Baltic States and the problem of the freedom of the Baltic Sea. Washington, D.C., The Press Bureau of the Latvian Legation, 1943. 71 leaves, maps. DK511.B3B5 1943a DLC CaAEU NN

764. --- Baltic States and World peace and security organization; facts in review. [Washington, D.C. The Latvian Legation, 1945] 67 p. illus., map. Bibliography: p. 64-67. DK511.B3B515 DLC CoAT CoCC CtY MB MeB NN NIC PPULC PU WaU-L

765. --- The Baltic States in post-war Europe. Washington, D.C., The Press Bureau of the Latvian Legation, 1943. v, 86 p. maps. DK511.B3B52 DLC CU CaBVaU CoCA IEN NBuG NN NSyU OrU PPULC PU UU ViU WyU

BUTLER, Ralph. The new eastern Europe. London, 1919. See entry no. 867.

766. CAMENA D'ALMEIDA, Pierre Joseph. Les États Baltes. In his Etats de la Baltique; Russie 1932, p. 17-33. DK511.B28 C2 CaAEU CaBVaU CtY DS IEN ICLJF MB MiU NN NcU OrU OU PPULC PU PPAmP TxU

767. DELLINGSHAUSEN, Eduard. Die baltischen Landesstaaten unter russischer Herrschaft 1710-1918 und die gegenwärtige Lage im Baltikum. Langensalza, Ger., H. Beyer, 1926. 39 p. (Schriften zur politischen Bildung. 5. Reihe: Grenzlande, Heft 4) DK511.B3D37 DLC CSt-H NN

768. DIUSHEN, Boris V. Respubliki pribaltiki; Estoniia, Laviia, Litva. Berlin, Russkoe Universal'noe izdvo, 1921. 60, [2] p. (Vseobshchaia biblioteka, 15) DK511.B3D5 CU NN NIC RPB

769. ECKARDT, Julius Wilhelm Albert von. Baltische und russische Culturstudien aus zwei Jahrhunderten. Leipzig, Duncker & Humblot, 1869. xiv, 552 p. DK511.B28E2 DLC CtY ICJ PPG PU

770. --- Die baltischen Provinzen Russlands. Politische und kulturgeschichtliche Aufsätze. 2., verm. Aufl. Leipzig, Duncker & Humblot, 1869. xii, 460 p. DK511.B28E3 1869 DLC CtY ICJ NN

771. EICHHOLZ, Alvin C. The Baltic States; Estonia, Latvia and Lithuania. A short review of resources, industry, finance, and trade. [Washington, D.C., U.S. Govt. Print. Off., 1928] 11, 64 p. maps, tables. (United States Bureau of Foreign and Domestic Commerce. Trade information bulletin, 569) Lithuania: p. 45-64. HC243.E5 DLC IU ICU KU MoU MiU OO OCl OU PP TxU WaU

772. ENGELHARDT, Alexis, Freiherr von. Die deutschen Ostseeprovinzen Russlands, ihre politische und wirtschaftliche Entwicklung. 2. Aufl. München, Ger., G. Müller, 1916. ix, 278 p. DK511.B3E7 1916a DLC

773. ERCKERT, Roderich von. Vzgliad na istoriiu i etnografiiu zapadnykh gubernii Rossii. Sanktpeterburg, 1863-64. 2 v. atlas. BM(10291. f. 1. + 14000. d. 12.)

774. EHRET, Joseph. Baltisches Schicksal. Basel, 1970. 39 p. DK511.B3E46 PU

775. --- Die vergessenen Balten. Basel; Luzern, 1969. 11 p. Off-print from "Civitas" DK511.B3E45 PU

776. FRIEDERICHSEN, Maximilian Hermann. Die ostbaltischen Rand-staaten, Estland, Lettland und Li-tauen. In Handbuch der geographi-schen Wissenschaft. Fritz Klute, ed. Mitteleuropa, Osteuropa in Na-tur, Kultur und Wissenschaft. Pots-dam, Ger., Athenaion, 1933, Bd. 8 p. 278-320. illus., map. G115.H4E6 Bd.8 DLC CtY ICU IU IEN ICJ MiU MH MnU NbU OCl OClW OCU PPAN TxU

777. --- Países bálticos. Tra-ducción del alemán por Carlos de Salas. Barcelona, Editorial Labor [1930] 199 p. (Colección labor. Biblioteca de iniciación cultural, Sección 7: Geografía) Bibliography: p. [192]-196. DK706 DLC TxU

778. GAIGALAT, Wilhelm. Die li-tauisch-baltische Frage. Berlin, Verlag der Grenzboten, 1915. 24 p. DK511.L2G3 CU CSt CSt-H CaAEU CtY MH NN PU

779. GEHRMANN, Karlheinz. Die baltischen Staaten, eine Brücke zwischen Ost und West. Berlin, O. Stollberg [1939] 96 p. illus., maps. (Bücherei Länder und Völker, hrsg. von der Gesellschaft für Länderkunde, 6) DK511.B3G4 DLC MH NNC

780. GENTIZON, Paul. Voyage aux pays occupés de l'Est. Montreaux, Les Éditions du mois Suisse [1944] 87 p. D802.B3G4 DLC NcD

781. GIBBONS, John. Keepers of the Baltic gates. London, R. Hale, Ltd., 1939. 252 p. D965.G455 DLC PU

782. GIMBUTAS, Marija (Alseikaité) Ancient Baltic lands. In Interna-tional Journal of Slavic Linguistics and Poetics ('s-Gravenhage), v.6, 1963, p. 65-102. See serials consulted.

783. GLOGER, Kurt. Baltikum. [Ber-lin] Edwin Runge Verlag, 1938. 160 p. illus., maps, plates, port. DK511.B5G5 DLC CU MH MiU NN NNC PU

784. GOETZ, Bruno. Die Balten und ihre Aufgabe. In Preussische Jahrbücher (Berlin), v.162, 1915, p. 85-97. See serials consulted.

785. HALE, Robert. The Baltic provinces; report of the Mission to Finland, Esthonia, Latvia, & Lithu-ania on the situation in the Baltic provinces. Washington, D.C., Govt. Print. Off., 1919. (United States. Congress. Senate. 66th Cong., 1st sess., S.doc. no.105, 1919) Cong. Doc. 7610, no.105 PP

786. HALTENBERGER, Michael. Die baltischen Länder. Leipzig, F. Deuticke, 1929. vi, 77 p. illus., tables, maps. (Enzyklopaedie der Erdkunde. Teil [24]) Bibliography: p. 67-70. 914.74.H168 PU NN

787. HEHN, Jürgen von. Die balti-schen Lande; Geschichte und Schi-cksal der baltischen Deutschen. Kitzingen am Main, Ger., Holzner-Verlag, 1951. 24 p. illus. (Der Göttinger Arbeitskreis. Schriften-reihe, Heft 17) DK511.B3H34 DLC InU MH NN NcD PU TxU

788. HOLST, Niels von. Balten-land. Berlin, Deutscher Kunstver-lag [1937] 111 p. illus., map. DK511.B28H65 DLC CU CtY OClMA

789. KOEPPEN, Petr Ivanovich. Über den Ursprung, die Sprache und Literatur der litauischen oder let-tischen Völkerschaften. Aus dem Russischen übersetzt von Peter v. Schröter. In Magazin der lettisch-literarischen Gesellschaft (Mitau), v.3, 1829, p. 1-112. See serials consulted.

790. KÜRBS, Friedrich. Die osteur-opäischen Staaten: Polen, Litauen, Lettland, Estland, als Staats- und Wirtschaftskörper. Stuttgart, F. Enke, 1931. vii, 266 p. Lithuania: p. 92-143. DK511.B3K8 DLC DS MiU NN

791. LÉOUZON LE DUC, Louis Antoine. La Baltique. Paris, L. Hachette, 1855. vi, 548 p. DL617.L4 DLC

792. MIGLIORINI, Elio. Finlandia e Stati Baltici. Roma, 1937. 222 p. (Publ. dell'Istituto per l'Europa orientale, ser. 2, t.30) DLC NN

793. --- Note geografiche sulle condizioni attuali degli Stati Baltici. I. Lituania. In Società geografica italiana, Rome. Bolet-tino. Ser. 6, v.9, no.7-8, 1932, p. 459-499. illus. maps. See serials consulted.

794. --- Paesi del Baltico; La Li-tuania e il suo popolo. In Le Vie del mondo (Milano), v.7, no.8, 1939, p. 775-790. See serials consulted.

795. PARROT, Johann Leonhard von. Versuch einer Entwicklung der Sprache, Abstammung, Geschichte,

Mythologie und bürgerlichen Verhältnisse der Liwen, Lätten, Eesten; mit
Hinblick auf einige benachbarte Ost-
seevölker... Neue Ausgabe mit...
einer topographischen Karte des Landes... und einem polyglotten Atlas.
Berlin, C.J. Klemann, 1839. vi,
[38], 418, [298] p. and atlas of
49 leaves., map. Bonaparte Collection no. 2002 2lii ICN

796. PULLÈ, Giorgio. Le repub-
liche Baltiche... La Lituania. In
Geografia universale ilustrata. II.
Gli Stati Scandinavici e Baltici...
Torino, Unione tipografico-editrice
torinese, 1935. p. 193-205.
G115.G54 DLC NNC

797. PUNGA, Kh.A. Nashi pribaltiiskie sosedi; Finlandiia, Estoniia,
Latviia, Litva. Moskva, Gosudarstvennoe izdatel'stvo, 1927. 64 p.
map. DK511.B3P8 DLC CSt-H

798. REPUBLICA; sive, Status regni
Poloniae, Lituaniae, Prussiae, Li-
voniae, etc... Alessandro Guagnino.
Lugduni Batavorum, ex officina El-
zeviriana, 1627. [8], 450, [13] p.
DK405.R43 DLC BM CaBVaU CaOTU ICBM
ICLJF NN

799. --- Lugduni Batavorum, ex
officina Elzeviriana, 1642. 417 p.
BM(568. a. 8.) CaOTU

800. ROYAL INSTITUTE OF INTERNA-
TIONAL AFFAIRS. INFORMATION DEPART-
MENT. The Baltic States; a survey
of political and economic structure
and the foreign relations of Es-
tonia, Latvia, and Lithuania...
London, Oxford University Press,
1938. 194 p. map. DK511.B3R6 DLC
CU CaBVaU CaOHM CaQMM CaOTU NIC NN
NNC NcD OCl OCU OU PBm PPi PU PSc
WaU

801. --- --- Westport, Conn.,
Greenwood Press [1970] 194 p. map.
Reprint of 1938 ed. DK511.B3R6
1970 DLC CaAEU

802. RUHL, Arthur Brown. New
masters of the Baltic. New York,
N.Y., E.P. Dutton & Co., [1921] xii,
239 p. illus., plates, map ports.
DK511.B3R7 DLC ClU CU CSt-H CaNSHD
CaOTU CaQMM CtY ICLJF ICU IEN IU
ICJ MB MiU MoU NN NNC NjP NcD NbU
OCl OClW OU PU RPB TxU

803. SHUSTIKOV, Nikolai Ivanovich.
Latviiskaia SSR, Litovskaia SSR, Estonskaia SSR; uchenyi material.
Moskva, 1958. 127 p. maps. At head
of title: Vysshaia partiinaia shkola
pri TSK KPSS. Kafedra ekonomicheskoi i politicheskoi geografii SSSR i
zarubezhnykh gosudarstv. DK511B28S5

DLC DS IU

804. SPECKEL, Anna Maria. Medi-
terráneo báltico; traducción y pró-
logo de I. de A. Madrid, Espasa-
Calpe, 1942. 190 p. illus., plates
DK511.B28S63 DLC

805. TISSOT, Louis. La Baltique,
situation des pays riverains de la
Baltique, importance économique et
stratégique de la "Mediterranée du
Nord", préface de Georges Blondel.
Paris, Payot, 1940. 262 p. illus.,
maps, diagrms, (Collection de documents et de témoignages pour servir
à l'histoire de notre temps)
DK511.B3T54 DLC CaAEU IaU ICU PU

806. TORNIUS, Valerian Hugo. Die
Baltischen Provinzen. Leipzig und
Berlin, B.G. Teubner, 1915. 104 p.
(Aus Natur und Geisteswelt, Bd. 542)
DK511.B28T6 DLC CaAEU NN

807. --- --- 3. Aufl. Leipzig und
Berlin, B.G. Teubner, 1918. vi, 111
p. illus., maps. (Aus Natur und
Geisteswelt, Bd. 542) DK511.B28T6
1918 DLC CU DW PU

808. TUMAS, Juozas. Aplink Baltiją; kas jau yra pajūryje ir kas dar
norėtų ten būti. [The Baltic Pro-
vinces] Vilnius, "Švyturio" spaustuvė, 1919. 95 p. Author's pseud.:
Vaižgantas. DK46.T77 InNd CtTMF
ICLJF

809. VALTERS, Nikolaus. Ein Versuch die baltische Zukunft zu deu-
ten. In Acta Baltica (Königstein
im Taunus), v.1, 1961, p. 180-214.
See serials consulted.

810. WALLROTH, Erich. Die Baltischen Provinzen und Litauen; Bericht
der Handelskammer zu Lübeck. [Be-
richtserstater; Syndikus E. Wallroth]
Lübeck, 1915. 59 p. Q 947.52.W157
PU

811. WALTER, Eginhard. Estland,
Lettland, Litauen; das Gesicht der
Baltischen Staaten. Berlin, Steini-
ger-Verlage, 1939. 204 p. illus.,
maps, diagr. Lithuania: p. 123-202.
DK511.B28W3 DLC CSt-H CaAEU CaBVaU
CaNBFU ICU InI MH NN NNC WU WaU

812. WIKBERG, Sven. Från bärn-
stenskusten och ordensriddarnas land;
reseanteckningar och studier i Ostpreussen, Litauen och Lettland...
Stockholm, H. Geber [1931] 147 p.
illus., maps, plates, port. Bibliography: p. [146]-147. 914.W64 MnU

813. WRONKA, Johannes. Kurland
and Litauen, Ostpreussens Nachbarn.
Freiburg in Br., und St. Louis, Mo.,

Herder, 1917. xii, 176 p. plates, map. DK511.C6W7 DLC BM CSt-H DW MH MU NIC

III.2. LITHUANIA IN GENERAL
III.2.a. GENERAL STUDIES

814. BENDORIUS, Antanas. Lietuva; kraštas gyventojai, kultūra. [Lithuania; country, its people and culture. Chicago] Sūduva [1952] 176 p. illus., map. DK511.L2B38 DLC BM CtTMF ICBM ICLJF NN OCl PPULC PU

815. BENEDICTSEN, Åge Meyer. Lithuania, "The awakening of a nation"; a study of the past and present of the Lithuanian people. Translation from the Danish language. Copenhagen, E.H. Petersen, 1924. 247 p. illus., ports., maps. Originally published 1895 under the title: Et folk, der vaagner. Kulturbillede fra Litaven. DK511.L2B4 DLC CLU CSt-H CU CaBVaU CoU CtY ICU IaU ICJ MH MiU MoU NN NNC NcU OCl OO OU OrU PP PPULC PR PU WaS WaU

816. BRANGIOJI TĒVYNĒ; lietuvių rašytojai, menininkai, mokslininkai apie tėvynę. [Dear homeland; Lithuanian authors, artists, scientists about homeland. Vilnius, VGLL, 1952. 366 p. illus. PG8713.B7 DLC KU

817. BŪGA, Kazimieras. Lietuvių tauta ir kalba bei jos artimieji giminaičiai. [Lithuanian nation and its language and kinsmen] In His Rinktiniai raštai. Vilnius, 1961. v.3, p. 85-282. PG8509.B8 DLC CU CaAEU CtPAM CtTMF ICLJF ICU IEN MH NN NjP PPiU PU TxU

818. BUTKUS, Tadas. Take a look at Soviet Lithuania. [Translated by V. Grodzenskis] Vilnius, Mintis, 1964. 114 p. illus., maps, plates. DK511.L2B813 DLC CLU CU CaOTU ICBM IEN IU InU MH MoU RPB

819. CHAMBON, Henri de. La Lithuanie moderne. Paris, Éditions de la revue parlamentaire [1933] 308 p. illus., maps. DK511.L27C45 DLC BM CaAEU CaBVaU CaOOP CaOTU CtY ICU IaU InU KU MH NN NNC NjP PU WaU

820. CHASE, Thomas George. The story of Lithuania...with a forward by William Henry Chamberlin. New York, N.Y., Stratford House, Inc., 1946. xiii, 392 p. illus., maps. Bibliography: p.351-359. DK511.L2C4 DLC AzU CU CaOKQ CaOTU CoU CtPAM CtY IaU ICN ICU ICBM IdU IEN InU InNd IU

KU LU MB MH MoU MtU MnU MeU NIC NN NNC NcD NbU NBuU NjP NjR OCl OClW OrU PPi PI RPB ScU SdU TU TxU WaU WyU

821. CHICAGO. UNIVERSITY. DIVISION OF SOCIAL SCIENCES. Lithuania in the last 30 years, prepared at the University of Chicago. Faculty Supervisory Committee: Bert F. Hoselitz, Chauncy D. Harris [and] George B. Carson. Editor: Benedict V. Maciuika. Contributors: Anton W. De Porte, Benedict V. Maciuika [and] Luitgard Wundheiler. New Haven, Conn., Printed by Human Relations Area Files, 1955. vi, 411 p. maps, diagrs., tables. (Human Relations Area Files, Inc. Subcontractor's monograph, HRAF-18) DK511.L2C5 DLC CU CSt-H CaQMM CaOTU CoU CtY HU ICN IEN ICU IU MH-P NN NNC NIC NbU NcU NBuU NjR NSyU OkU PU TxU ViU WU

822. DANILEVIČIUS, Eugenijus. Lithuania in questions and answers. Vilnius, Gintaras, 1970. 246 p. illus., maps. DK511.L2D313 CaOTU

823. GAIGALAT, Wilhelm. La Lithuanie, le territoire occupé, la population et l'orientation de ses idées. Traduction et préface d'Adam Vilimovicz. Genève, Édition Atar [1918] 272 p. illus., maps. DK511.L2G1373 CSt-H CSt BM ICU MH NNC

824. GARGASAS, Petras. Litovskaia SSR. Moskva, Gos. izd-vo geogr. lit-ry, 1960. 126 p. illus., maps. DK511.L2G45 DLC IU InU MH NNC WU WaU

825. GLOGAU, Karl Wilhelm Otto. Littauen und die Littauer; gesammelte Skizzen. Tilsit, Reyländer, 1869. 219 p. DK511.L2G54 NIC BM MH PU

826. HARRISON, Ernest John, ed. Lithuania, 1928. Edited and compiled by E.J. Harrison. London, Hazell, Watson & Viney, 1928. xv, 383 p. illus. map. Includes Who's who in Lithuania: p.240-257. Lithuanian bibliography: p.266-277. DK511.L27H2 DLC AzU BM CLU CU CSt CaOLU CaQMM CoU CtY FU ICJ ICN ICLJF ICU IEN InNd KU LU MH MnU MoU NIC NB NN NNC NjP NjR NSyU NbU OCl OClW OO OCU OU OrU PP PPL PBm PPiU PU RPB TxU WU WaU

827. JELÍNEK, Edvard. Črty litovské... Praha, J. Otto, 1886. 197 p. (Salonni bibliotéka. Čislo 43) (*QW)NN

828. JURGINIS, Juozas. Legendos apie lietuvių kilmę. [Legends about Lithuanian origin] Vilnius, Vaga, 1971. 198 p. DK511.L21J8 PU

829. KRAŠTOTYRA; leidinys skirtas

Tarybų valdžios atkūrimo Lietuvoje 25-mečiui. [Kraštotyra; an issue on occasion of the twenty fifth anniversary of the reinstatement of Soviet government in Lithuania. Vyr. redaktorius B. Vaitkevičius] Vilnius, LTSRPAD, 1966. 236 p. DK511.L27K65 PU

830. KRAŠTOTYRA; leidinys skirtas Tarybų valdžios penkiasdešimtmečiui. [Kraštotyra; an issue on occasion of the fiftieth anniversary of Soviet Government. Vyr. redaktorius B.Vaitkevičius] Vilnius, LTSRPAD, 1967. 284 p. DK511.L27K66 PU

831. KRAŠTOTYRA. [Vyr. redaktorius Bronius Vaitkevičius. Spaudai parengė Domas Butėnas et al.] Vilnius, LTSRPAD, 1969. 361 p. illus., maps, ports. DK511.L27K67 PU

832. KRASZEWSKI, Józef Ignacy. Litwa: starożytne dzieje, ustawy, język, wiara, obyczaje, pieśni, przysłowia, podania i t.d. Warszawa, W druk. S. Strabskiego, 1847-50. 2 v. DK511. L2K72 DLC CU CtY ICLJF InU KU MH NN PU

833. KRAUSE, August Gotthilf. Litthauen und dessen Bewohner in Hinsicht der Abstammung, der volkstümlichen Verwandschaft und Sprache. Königsberg in Pr., Hartung, 1834. 168p. 947.5.K86 PU BM(12976. c. 23.)

834. KVIKLYS, Bronius. Mūsų Lietuva; krašto vietovių istoriniai, geografiniai, etnografiniai bruožai. [Our Lithuania... Boston] Lietuvių enciklopedijos leidykla [1964-68] 4 v. illus., ports., maps. DK511. L2K9 PU CaAEU CaOTP CaOTU CaOONL CtPAM ICBM ICU

835. LAVOIX, Vincent. Quand la lumière nous vient du nord ou les enseignements de l'expérience lituanienne. Paris, Éditions littéraires de France, 1938. 190 p. DK511. L2L414 CSt-H BM DLL MH NN PU

836. LIETUVA. [Lithuania] In Lietuvių enciklopedija. Boston, Mass., 1968. v.15. 807 p. For holdings see entry no.216.

837. LIETUVOS TSR MOKSLŲ AKADEMIJA, VILNA. Litovskaia SSR. [Otvetstvennye redaktory: K.K. Beliukas, IU.I. Bulavas, I.V. Komar] Moskva, Gos. izd-vo geogr. lit-ry, 1955. 389,[3]p. illus., maps. DK511.L2L414 DLC CSt-H CU CaBVaU CaOKQ CaOTU HU ICU IU InU MH MnU NIC NcD NjP NSyU PU TU WaU

838. MAUCLÈRE, Jean. Gens et routes de Lithuanie. Paris, A. Redier [1931] 247 p. DK511.L2M25 DLC CaAEU

MH PU

839. MICHALONIS, LITUANUS. Apie totorių, lietuvių ir maskvėnų papročius; dešimts įvairaus turinio fragmentų. De moribus tartarorum, lituanorum et moschorum... Nunc primum per I. Iac. Grasserum ex manuscripto authentico edite. Par Michalonis Lituani. Vilnius, Vaga, 1966. 136p. facsims. DK511.L23M62 1966 CaAEU InU PU

840. ŠVIESA. Lithuania, past and present. [By the editorial staff of Šviesa] New York, N.Y., American Lithuanian Literary Association, 1965. 188 p. maps. DK511.L2S825 DLC CLU CSt CoU IC MU MeU NcD NjR NcU NvU OCl PPi RPB TxU TxHU WaS

841. VIJEIKIS, Vladas. Lietuva mano tėvų žemė. [Lithuania my homeland] Chicago, Ill., Tėviškėlė, 1961. 430 p. (chiefly illus.) maps, ports. DK511.L2V42 DLC CaOTP ICBM NN

842. VOZKA, Jaroslav. Litva; klič k situaci ve východní Evropě. Předmluva od poslance Jaromíra Nečase. Praha, O. Girgal, 1933. 204 p. plates., ports., map. DK511.L25V97 CSt-H CSt CtY InU NN NNC PU

843. VSTRECHA S LITVOI. [Sostavili B. Zalesskaia i G. Gerasimov] Vil'nius, Vaga, 1965. 257 p. illus., ports. DK511.L27V7 DLC IU KU MH PU

844. WIELHORSKI, Władysław. Das heutige Litauen. Litwa współczesna. Berlin, 1941. 241 p. (Publikationsstelle Berlin-Dahlem. Polnische Reihe. Bücher und grössere Aufsätze, 209). DK511.L2W52 DLC CaAEU

845. --- Litwa etnograficzna; przyroda, jako podstawa gospodarcza, rozwój stosunków narodościowych. Wilno, Wydawn. Wileńskiego Biura Informacyjnego, 1928. 215 p. maps. (Materjały do sprawy litewskiej, t.3)

846. --- Litwa współczesna. Warszawa, Tow. Wiedzy Wojsk., 1938. 254 p. (Biblioteka służby geograficznej, t.17) Bibliography: p. 251-254. DK511.L2W515 DLC PU

847. ZWECK, Albert. Litauen; eine Landes- und Volkskunde. Stuttgart, Hobbing und Buchle, 1898-1901. viii, 452 p. illus., plates, maps. (Ostpreussen. Land- und Volkskunde, 1, 5, 9, 12, 15) MH PU

III.2.b. MINOR WORKS

848. ALEKSA-ANGARIETIS, Zigmas. Stabmeldiška Lietuva; iš artimos praeities. [The pagan Lithuania...] So. Boston, Mass., Keleivis, 1912. 32 p. 285.1.A126 PU MH

849. AŠMYS, Mikelis. Land und Leute in Litauen von M. Aschmies. Mit 9 Abbildungen und einer Karte. Breslau, Priebatsch's Verlagsbuchhandlung. [1918] 86 p. plates, map. DLC-4 DNW NbU NjP PPULC PU

850. L'AVENIR DE LA LITHUANIE ET de la Russie Blanche. Notes revues et approuvées par la Délégation des Conseils nationaux polonais. Varsovie, 1919. 8 p. NN

851. AVIŽONIS, Konstantinas. Lietuvių kilimo iš Romėnų teorija XV ir XVI a. [The theory on the Lithuanian origin from the Romans] Kaunas, 1939. 31 leaves. DK511.Z9 1939 CtY KU(Photocopy)

852. BARTUŠKA, Vincas and Juozas Purickis. Litauen und seine Provinzen Suvalkai und Gardinas. Lausanne, 1918. 32 p. map. BM(8095. f. 39.)

853. BASANAVIČIUS, Jonas. Lietuviszkai trakiszkos studijos. [Lithuanian studies] Shenandoah, Pa., Dirva, 1898. 123 p. 947.5.B272 PU CtTMF NNC

854. BENEDICTSEN, Åge Meyer. Det genfoedte Litaven. In Savickis, Jurgis, ed. Lysskaer; en samling politiske og oekonomiske afhandlinger om Litauen. København, E.H. Petersen, 1919. DK511.L2S26 InU

855. BIRULIA, K. V. Kratkii geograficheskii, estestvenno-istoricheskii i ekonomicheskii obzor Kovenskoi gubernii. [3d. ed.] Ponevezh, 1909. 39 p. DK511.K55B5 1909 DLC

856. BIULETYN LITEWSKI. Nr.1. d. 28 czerwca 1919 r. Warszawa. No more published. ICBM

857. BOHUSZ, Franciszek Ksavery M. O początkach narodu i języka litewskiego; rozprawa... na publicznym posiedzeniu... Towarzystwa Warszawskiego Przyjaciół Nauk w roku 1806. d.12 grudnia czytana. Warszawa, 1808. 207 p. 491.922.B634 PU(Xerox) NN(orig.)

858. BOSSIN, André. La Lithuanie. Préface de M. Michel Lheritier, avec huit planches hors-text... par M. Gudaitis. Paris,Rieder, 1933. 120 p. illus., plates, maps. (Les états contemporaines) Bibliographie: p. [115]-118. DK511.L27B65 DLC BM CtY CaOTU GU ICBM IaU OO PPULC PU WU WaU

859. BROCHER, Gustave. Essais sur les principales nationalités de Russie; leur histoire, leurs revendications, leur littérature. Lausanne, Russie Libre [1918] iv, 128 p. plates, ports., map. Includes chapter: "Les Lithuaniens" DK33.B7 DLC PPULC NN

860. BRÜCKNER, Aleksander. Polacy a Litwini; język i literatura. In Polska i Litwa w dziejowym stosunku. Warszawa, 1914. p.343-392. DK418. 5.L5P6 DLC BM CU CSt-H

861.--- Slaven und Litauer. In Chantepie de la Saussaye, Pierre Daniel. Lehrbuch der Religionsgeschichte. Tübingen, 1925. Bd.2, p.506-539. BL80.C46 1925 v.2 DLC CaAEU OCL

862. BÜSCHING, Anton Friedrich. Korolevstvo Pol'skoe i Velikoe Kniazhestvo Litovskoe s prisoedinennymi k... zemliami. Iz Bishingovoi geografii perevel s niemetskago Fedor Rogenbuke. Sanktpeterburg, Imp. Akademiia Nauk, 1775. 224 p. 947.52. B665 PU

863. BUREAU D'INFORMATIONS DE LITUANIE, LAUSANNE. [Pamphlets] Lausanne, 1917-19. 7 pts. BM(8095.g.28)

864. BUTKUS, Tadas. Lytovs'ka RSR. Kyiv, Vyd-vo polit. lit-ry Ukrainy, 1966. 85 p. illus. HC337.L5B DLC

865. --- Poznakom'tes' s Sovetskoi Litvoi. [Perevod D. Gel'pernasa] Vil'nius, Mintis, 1965. 100 p. illus., maps. DK511.L2B817 DLC IU InU KU MH NNC NIC PP1U ViU

866. --- Trumpai apie Tarybų Lietuvą. [Briefly about Soviet Lithuania] Vilnius, VPMLL, 1960. 151 p. illus., maps, ports. DK511.L2B8 DLC ICBM NN

867. BUTLER, Ralph. The new Eastern Europe. London, Longmans, Green and Co., 1919. vii, 176 p. Reprinted in part from various periodicals. DK46.B8 DLC CLU CSt CSt-H CU CaAEU CaOKQ CaMWU DN GU IEN ICU InNd ICJ InU IU KU MB MH MiU MoU NIC NB NN NNC NbU NBuU NjP NcD NcU NjR OO OU OCl OClW PP1 PPULC PU TxU ViU

868. CAMOGLIO, Costantino. Lietuva kankinė. [Lithuania the martyr] Translated from Italian by Dr. P.M. Kaunas, Vilniui vaduoti sąjungos leidinys, 1929. 16 p. 970.31.ŽE ICLJF CtMF ICCC ICBM

869. --- Lituania martire. Roma, Ediz. di Camicia Rossa, 1928. 41 p. 947.52.C145.2 PU

870. --- La questione lituana... Prefazione del generale Ezio Garibaldi. Roma, Arti-Grafiche V. Locchi, 1930. 143 p. DK511.L27C35 DLC CSt-H CoU NN PPiU PU WaU

871. CHODŹKO, Leonard Jakób Borejko. La Pologne historique, littéraire monumentale et pittoresque... Paris, Au Bureau Central, 1835-1837. 3 v. Extensive information on Lithuania given by F. Vrotnovski, and on Lithuanian folksongs by A. Sovinski. DK414.C49 DLC CtY IU MB MH MiU NN NIC NcD PU

872. --- --- 2. éd. Paris, Au Bureau central [Impr. de H. Fournier et Cie] 1842. 472, xxxii, p. illus., plates, ports., maps, music. DK414.C495 DLC

873. --- --- 3. éd. Paris, Au Bureau central [Impr. de H. Fournier et Cie] 1843. [8], 472 [32], xxxii p. illus., plates, map, plans, facsim. DK414.C5 DLC

874. --- --- 5. éd. Paris, Au Bureau central, 1844. [8], 472, xxxii p. illus., plates, maps. DK414.C54 DLC

875. --- --- 7. éd. Paris, Bureau des publications historiques, 1847-1848. 1 v. ports., plates. MB

876. --- Relazione storica, politica, geografica, legislativa, scientifica, letteraria, & c. della Pollonia antiqua e moderna. Traduzione italiana. Livorno, G.P. Pozzolini, 1831. 2 v. in 1. DK414.C55 ICU

877. THE CLAIM OF LITHUANIA. Glasgow, 1919. BM(08028. df. 3.)

878. CONFERENCE DES NATIONALITÉS, 3d, LAUSANNE, 1916. DELEGATION LITHUANIENNE. La question lithuanienne. Mémoire présenté par la Délégation Lithuanienne à la 3-me Conférence des Nationalités, Lausanne, les 27-29 juin 1916. Lausanne, Bureau d'Information de Lithuanie, 1916. 15 p. illus., maps. (Union des Nationalités. Office Central. Publications, 22) JC311.A2C74 1916g CSt-H DLC

879. DABRILA, Jurgis. Lietuva tautų kovoj už būvį. [Lithuania in the struggle of nations for survival] Kaunas, 1934. 220 p. 947.5.D112 PU

880. DREVLIANSKII, P. Ocherki zhmudi. In Panteon (Sanktpeterburg, v.19, no.1, 1855, p. 29-72. See serials consulted.

881. ERSS, Adolfs. Lietuva; celojuma iespaidi un piezimes. Rīga, "Latvju kultura", 1930. 215 p. illus., port, maps, plates. DK511.L2E8 CU NN WaS

882. GABRYS, Juozas. L'État lituanien et Mitteleuropa. Lausanne, 1917. 15 p. Offprint from "Pro Lituania" 1917, no.10. 947.52.0113.4 PU

883. --- Lietuvių tautos memorialas, induotas Tautų (Rasių) Kongresui Londone liepos 26-29 d. 1911 m. Vertimas iš prancūzų kalbos. Chicago, Draugo spaustuvėje, 1911-1913. 2 pts in 1 v. DK511. L713G1141 InNd(pt.2) NN(pt.1) PU

884. --- Mémoire sur la nation lithuanienne. Présenté... au premier Congrès des Races... Avec traduction anglaise... Par Jerzy Gabrys. Paris, 1911. 50 p. Bw91.65 CtY BM(10106. i. 2.(4))

885. --- A memorandum upon the Lithuanian nation, presented by J. Gabrys at the first Races Congress, London, 26-29 July, 1911. Paris, Imprimerie de la Cour d'Appel, 1911. 24 p. Issued also under title: A sketch of the Lithuanian nation. DK511.L2G3 DLC ICN IC ICU InNd MB NN OO OCl RPB

886. GARGASAS, Petras. Lithuanian SSR. Washington, D.C., JPRS, 1961. 126 p. maps. (United States. Joint Publications Research Service, 9536. Scholarly book translation series, no.148) DK511.L2G46 CaOHM (Photocopy)

887. GATTERER, Johann Christoph. An prussorum, lituanorum ceterorumque populorum letticorum originem a Sarmatia liceat... Detached from Commentationes Societatis regiae Gottingensis. 1793-1794 (Hist.-phil) v.12, p. 116-272. 947.52.G225 PU also in Gesellschaft der Wissenschaften zu Göttingen. Commentationes Societatis... Gottingae, 1793-1794, v.12, p. 116-272. AS182. G781 v.12 DLC

888. GEČYS, Kazys. Katalikiškoji Lietuva. [Catholic Lithuania] Chicago, Ill., Draugo spaustuvė, 1946. xii, 575 p. map. Bibliography: p. 536-556. BX1559.L5G4 DLC CtTMF ICCC ICLJF InND MH PU

889. GEOGRAFICHESKOE OBSHCHESTVO SSSR. Geografichesko-statistiches-kii slovar' Rossiiskoi Imperii. Sostavil... P. Semenov. Sanktpeter-burg, 1863-85. 5 v. Lithuania in vol. 2(1865), p. 650-658; vol. 3 (1869), p. 62-64. DK14.G4 DLC(1-5) CaAEU(1-3)

890. GERMANY. PUBLIKATIONSSTELLE BERLIN-DAHLEM. Litauische Pres-seauszüge. Berlin-Dahlem, 1935-44. Irregular. AP95.L5G4 DLC (1935-40)

891. GOL'DSHTEIN, Severian Mavrik' evich. Pol'sko-litovskiia drevnos-ti. Lektsii, chitanniia v Impera-torskom arkheologicheskom institu-tie. Sanktpeterburg, Tip. Soikina, 1913. 227 p. JN6745.A81G6 CU NN

892. GUAGNINO, Alessandro. De Li-tuanae gentis origine et moribus... In Respublica; sive, Status regni Poloniae, Lituaniae, Prussiae... Lugduni Batavorum, 1627. DK405.R43 DLC BM CaBVaU NN

893. HARRISON, Ernest John. Li-thuania; a review. London, Eyre & Spottiswoode [1925?] 51 p. illus., ports., maps. DK511.L2H28 DLC CU ICLJF MH NN PU WaU

894. --- Lithuania: land of Gods. In Aryan Path (Bombay), v.14, no.8, 1943, p. 349-357. See serials con-sulted.

895. HERTMANOWICZ, Joseph John. The Lithuanians. [Chicago, Ill., E.A. Russel, 1920] 16 p. F54948.41 ICN ICBM MeU NN

896. --- Litwini i polacy. Lietu-viaj ir lenkaj... Chicago, Ill., Nakładem Oświaty Związku Nar. Pol., 1906. 65 p. (*QO p.v. 82, no.1)NN

897. IVINSKIS, Zenonas. In de-fense of West European culture. In Lituanus (Brooklyn, N.Y.) no.4(9), 1956, p. 7-9. See serials consulted.

898. JUNGFER, Victor. Alt-Litau-en; ein Darstellung von Land und Leuten, Sitten und Gebräuchen. Berlin und Leipzig, G. Neuner, 1926. 143 p. Bibliography: p. 137-140. DK511.L2J77 CU CLU InU MH MiU MnU NN NjP OCl PU WaU

899. --- Hinter den Seen, hinter den Wäldern; Bilder litauischen Volkstums. Königsberg in Pr.,Gräfe und Unzer, 1932. 166 p. plates. DK511.L2J9 CLU PU

900. KANNER, L. F. Litva. [Lenin-grad] Gazetno-zhurnal'noe i knizhnoe izd-vo Leningradskago Soveta RK i KD, 1938. 68 p. map. DK511.L2K3 DLC KU NN

901. KOLUPAILA, Steponas. Lietu-va; gintaro ir kryžių šalis. La Lithuanie-pays de l'ambre et des croix. Offprint from Žemėtvarka ir melioracija. Kaunas, 1935. 19 p. 947.52.P192 PU also in Žemėtvarka ir melioracija (Kaunas), nr.2, 1935, p. 5-24, illus. See serials con-sulted.

902. KRAMÁŘ, Karl. Die Ankunft der Germanen, Litauer und Slaven aus der Uhrheimat am Altaj. Berlin, K. Stieglmaier, 1916. 144 p. illus., map. Q 947.K862 PU

903. KRZYWICKI, Ludwik. Żmudź starożytna. Dawni Zmudzini i ich warownie. Warszawa, Nakł. Księg. Naukowej, 1906. ii, 89 p. 947.52. K949 PU BM(10292. dd. 7.) CtTMF MH

904. KUČAS, Antanas. Lithuania. In Catholic encyclopedia. New York, N.Y., 1957. v.18, suppl. 2. 9 columns unpaged. BX841.C25 DLC CaAEU

905. KUDRINSKII, F. A. Litovtsy; obshchii ocherk. Vil'na, Tip. Rus-skii pochin, 1905. 70 p. 947.52. K9536 PU

906. LIETUVA; kraštas ir tauta. [Lithuania; country and nation. Re-dagavo A. Stanys] Augsburgas, Ger., 1946. 62 p. illus. DK511.L2L42 DLC PU

907. LIETUVIŲ TAUTA. [The Lithua-nian nation] Vilnius, Lietuvių mokslo draugija, 1919-32. (Lietu-vių mokslo draugijos raštai, kn.2, dal.4; kn.3-4) BM(Ac.1156.h.)

908. LINKSCH, Erich. Litauen und die Litauer; einführende Betrachtun-gen. Stuttgart, Z. Schrader, 1917. 57 p. DK511.L2L756 CSt-H DLC PU

909. LITHUANIA. European confe-rence on rural life, 1939. Nation-al monographs drawn up by govern-ments. Lithuania. Geneva, 1939. 47 p. illus. (Series of League of Nations publications. European Con-ference on Rural Life, 12) HD105.E8 1939a no.12 CLU CSt CSt-H CaBVaS CaOLU DLC ICU InU IU LU NBuU NSyU OkU PPi PU RPB TxDaM TxU ViU

910. LITHUANIA, COUNTRY AND NATION. [Edited by A. Stanys] Augsburg, Ger. [Community of the Lithuanian DPs] 1946. 62 p. illus., map. DK511. L2L48 DLC CSt-H CtY MH

911. LITHUANIAN AMERICAN COMMUNITY OF THE U.S.A. CHICAGO DISTRICT. Lithuania. [Chicago, Ill. 1960. 16 p.] illus., maps. Ref. Pams CLU NN

912. LITHUANIAN INFORMATION SERVICE. Living in freedom; a sketch of independent Lithuania's achievements. [Augsburg, Ger. 1949] 95 p. illus., plates. DK511.L2L5 NIC CSt ICBM IEN MB PU

913. LITOVSKAIA LITERATURA, LItovskii iazyk, litovskoe gosudarstvo... In Entsiklopedicheskii slovar'. Sanktpeterburg, 1896. v.34, p. 815-830. AE55.E61 v.34 CaAEU DLC

914. LITOVSKAIA SOVETSKAIA SOTSIAlisticheskaia Respublika. In Bolshaia Sovetskaia entsiklopediia. Moskva, 1954. v.25, p. 248-279. AE55.B62 v.25 DLC CaAEU CSt GU MU OCU NN OOxM

915. MEILLET, Antoine. Pologne et Lithuanie. In France. Comité d'études. Travaux. Paris, 1919. v.2, p.[329]-339. D650.T4F8 v.2 DLC NNC .

916. MÉMOIRE SUR LA LITHUANIE, Genève, le 10 décembre 1920... [Genève, Imp. Atar, 1920] 19 p. DK511. L2M4 DLC BM(8095. gg. 6. (1.)) PU

917. MILANČIUS, Jurgis. Lietuvos žvaigždutė 1907. [The Lithuanian little star] Parašė Dzūkas Trakietis. Vilnius, M. Kuktos spaustuvė, 1907.   4 p. (Vievjo vaistininko lejdinijs pirmas) 891.923M ICBM

918. MILOSZ, Oscar Vladislas. Conférence de M. O.W. Lubicz-Milosz à la salle de la Société de Geographie, Paris, 29 mars, 1919. Paris, 1919. 12 p. D643.A7 DP617.M661 CSt-H

919. MORTENSEN, Hans. Litauen. Grundzüge einer Landeskune. Hamburg, de Gruyter & Co., 1926. xvii, 321 p. (Quellen und Studien. Osteuropa Institut in Breslau. Abt. 5, Heft 1) DK511.L2M7 DLC CU CSt-H ICJ InU MB NN NjP NSyU PU

920. A NEW ACCOUNT OF POLAND AND Lithuania describing their governments, palatinates, provinces, religion, language, habits... London, H. Rhodes, 1702. [12], 130 p. DK405. N48 DLC

921. NOREM, Owen Joseph Christoffer. Timeless Lithuania. Chicago, Ill., Amerlith Press, 1943. 299 [i.e. 301] p. illus., plates, maps. DK511.L27N6 DLC CU CSt CSt-H CaAEU

CaOOP CaQMM CtPAM CoU CtY GU IEN IU ICU IaU ICBM InNd InU KyU MH MnU NN NNC NbU NdU OCl OClW OO PP PU TxU ViU

922. OPISANIE ZHMUDSKOI ZEMLI V 1554 g. In Arkheograficheskii sbornik dokumentov otnosiashchikhsia k istorii Sievero-Zapadnoi Rusi. Vil'na, Vilenskaia komissiia dlia razbora i izdaniia drevnikh aktov, 1870. v.8. DK511.L21A7 v.8 DLC CLU CSt-H MH MH-L NN

923. PAKŠTAS, Kazys. Lithuania and World War II. Chicago, Ill., [Lithuanian Cultural Institute] 1947. 80 p. map. Bibliography: p. 78-80. DK511.L2P17 CLU CU CSt-H CaAEU CaOTU DLC IU InNd KU MH NN NNC PU

924. POPOV, IA. Litovtsy, zhmudiny i latyshi. In Priroda i liudi (Sanktpeterburg), no.5, 1878, p. 1-44. (*QCA)NN

925. POWELL, Edward Alexander. Embattled borders; eastern Europe from the Balkans to the Baltic. New York; London, The Century Co., [1928] xx 374 p. front., plates, ports., maps. D443.P65 DLC CSt-H MB MiU NN OCl PP PPL PPM PU PPA

926. --- Lithuania. In his Thunder over Europe. New York, N.Y. 1931. p. 109-125. D443.P66 DLC DAL InU   NcC NjN OCl PP PPL PU

927. --- Undiscovered Europe. New York, N.Y., I. Washburn, 1932, 320 p. maps. Lithuania: p. 184-220. D921.P685 DLC WaS

928. PUZINAS, Jonas. Lietuvių kilmės teorijos amžių būvyje. [Theories on the origin of the Lithuanians] Chicago, Ill., 1950. p. 194-244. Offprint from Literatūra. DK511.L22P8 PU

929. R., G. Razskazy o Litvie i litovtsakh. Moskva, Tip. I.D. Sytina, 1896. 101 p. 947.52.Sn53 PU

930. RACKUS, Aleksander Michaels. Guthones (the Goths) kinsmen of the Lithuanian people. Chicago, Ill., Press of "Draugas", 1929. 432 p. illus., plates. English and Lithuanian. Bibliography: p. 408-411. D137.R15 DLC CSt CaAEU CtPAM CtTMF CtY ICJ InNd MH NNC NIC NjR NjP PP WU

931. RINK, Eucharius Gottlieb. Das verwirrte Pohlen;... eine Beschreibung aller polnischen und littauischen Herzoge und Könige, nebst des Landes, Städte und Provinzen.

Frankfurth, Bey C. Riegel, 1711.
[16], 676 [i.e. 976] 112 p. map,
plates, ports. Rare Books and
Special Collections CaOTU

932. RITTIKH, Aleksandr Fedorovich
Obizhennyi krai. Sanktpeterburg,
Tip. T-va "Elektro-tip. N. IA,
Stoikovoi", 1911. 50 p. map DK508.
7.R61 ICU

933. ROZENTAL', Rassa Eduardovna.
Litovskaia SSR; [kratkie svedeniia
o prirode, naselenii i khoziaistve]
Moskva, Gos. izd-vo geogr. lit-ry,
1959. 79 p. illus. DK511.L2R6 DLC
CaAEU NIC NNC NcU

934. RUBINSHTEIN, K. I. Litva.
Moskva, Gos Sots.-ekon. izd-vo,
1940. 106 p. maps. DK511.L2R8
DLC CSt-H

935. SAVICKIS, Jurgis., ed. Lysskaer; en samling politiske og
oekonomiske afhandlinger om Litauen
... København, E.H. Petersen, 1919.
103 p. illus., ports., maps.
DK511.L2S26 InU

936. SILVANTO, Reino. Liettua,
muinoin ja nyt. Helsingissä, Otava
[1920] 176 p. illus., ports.,
maps. DK511.L2S5 InU

937. SLEINIS, Indrikis. Mūsu kai-
miņu valstis un Baltijas jūra. Igau-
nija, Lietuva un Polija. [Our neigh-
bour countries and the Baltic Sea.
Estland, Lithuania and Poland]
Rīgā, A. Gulbis, 1934. 81 p. illus.,
diagrs, tables, maps. (*QYN p.v.
130)NN

938. ŠLIŪPAS, Jonas. Essay on the
past, present and future of Lithuania. [By] J. Szlupas. Stockholm,
Svenska Andelsförlaget [1928] 88 p.
map. DK511.L2S85 DLC NN OO

939. --- Lietuvių protėviai Mažojoje Azijoje nuo senovės iki jie
pateko po valdžia Persų. [Lithua-
nian forefathers in Asia Minor]
Parašė Lietuvos Mylėtojas [pseud.]
Chicago, Ill., Spauda "Lietuvos",
1899. 283 p. illus., fold. maps,
tables. DS63.S9 DLC CaOTP ICLJF PU
RP WaS

940. --- Lithuania in retrospect
and prospect. [By] John Szlupas.
New York, N.Y., The Lithuanian Press
Association of America, 1915. 97 p.
illus., map. DK511.L2S8 DLC CU CSt-H
CLU CtY ICN ICJ ICBM KU NIC NB NN
NNC NSyU OCl PU RP WaS

941. STRUNGE, Mogens. Litaviske
studier. København, 1938-39. 155

p. DK511.L2S74 PU

942. STUDIA HISTORICA W 35-LECIU
pracy naukowej Henryka Łowmiańskiego. [Tom przygotowany przez Aleksandra Gieysztora et al.] Warszawa, Państwowe Wydawn. Naukowe,
1958. 438 p. illus., port., maps.
D6.S796 DLC CtY ICU MnU NN NIC NNC

943. TARVYDAS Stasys. Litva. [Av-
tory: S.S. Tarvydas i A.B. Basali-
kas. Otv. redaktory: K.K. Bieliukas i M.I. Rostovtsev] Moskva
[Mysl'] 1967. 285 p. illus., maps,
col. plates. (Sovietskii Soiuz;
geograficheskoe opisannie) DK511.
L2T3 DLC CaAEU CaOLU CaOWtU CaOTU
CaSSU CoU CtY IaU InU MnU NIC NNC
NSyU NcD NhU NcU NjP PPiU PU ViU WU
WaU

944. THURSTON, Theodore S. Lithuanian history, philology and grammar. With assistance of Corine Coulson. Chicago, Ill., Printed by Peoples Printing Co., 1941. 39 p.
DK511.L2T5 PU

945. TROTS'KYI, Mykola. Litovtsi.
Vidanie Soiuza vyzvoleniia Ukrainy.
Viden', 1917. 19 p. Nkd68R7+1 1917
CtY NNC WU

946. VAITIEKŪNAS, Vytautas. Lithuania. Prepared by the Committee for
a Free Lithuania. New York, N.Y.,
1965. 47 p. maps. (Assembly of
Captive European Nations. Booklets,
v.58) DR48.5.A845 no.58 CSt-H CaAEU
CaOONL CaOTU DLC IaU ICBM InU IU MH
MH-L NIC NB NcU NjR PU

947. --- --- 2nd revised ed. New
York, N.Y., Lithuanian National Foundation, 1968. 64 p. maps, tables.
Bibliography: p.64-[65] DK511.L713V3
1968 InNd PU

948. VETLOV, I. Litva. Moskva,
Moskovskii rabochii, 1928. 52 p.
(Nashi sosedi) DK511.L23V4 DLC NNC
NN

949. VILENSKAIA KOMISSIIA DLIA RAZ-
BORA I IZDANIIA DREVNIKH AKTOV. Zapiski Vilenskoi arkheologicheskoi
komissii... pod redaktsieiu A. Kirkora i M. Guseva. Pamiętniki Kommissji
archeologicznej Wileńskiej...pod redakcją M. Balińskiego i L. Kondrato-
wicza. Częśc 1. Wilno, 1856. viii,
59 p. Russian and Polish. WR89 CtY
BM

950. VILNA. (GOVERNMENT) GUBERNSKII
STATISTICHESKII KOMITET. Cherty iz
istorii i zhizni litovskago naroda...
Vil'na, 1854. 149 p. col. front.
16377.936 NjP NNC MH

951. WANKLYN, Harriet Grace. The Baltic group; regional introduction ... Lithuania. In His The Eastern Marchlands of Europe. London, 1941. pt.1. J53.W185 CaQMM CaAEU MH NN

952. WESTENBERGER, Hans. Litauen; Entstehung und wirtschaftspolitische Lage. Eine führung. In Osteuropa (Berlin), Jahrg.2, 1926/27, p.261-274. (*GLA)NN

953. WILNO. WILEŃSKIE BIURO INFORMACYJNE. Najważniejsze dane o państwie litewskiem. Wilno, 1926. 16 p. map. BM(olo290. df. 17.)

954. ZECHLIN, Erich. Litauen. In Politische Handwörterbuch. Leipzig, 1923. v.2, p.46-61. 947.52.Z34.2 PU(Photocopy)

955. --- Litauen und seine Probleme. Leipzig, B.G. Teubner [1916] [257]-286 columns. Sonderabdruck aus dem 10. Jahrgang der Internationalen Monatsschrift für Wissenschaft, Kunst und Technik. DK511.L2Z4 CU CSt-H ; also in Internationale Monatsschrift für Wissenschaft, Kunst und Technik (Leipzig), Jahrg.10, Heft3, 1916, p.[257]-286. AP30.17 v.10 DLC CSt ICU IaU InU MB MH MiU MnU NIC NN NjP PU WU

956. ŽILIUS, Jonas. Palemonas ir jo padermė. [Palemonas and his lineage] Padavimus surinko ir paaiškino Jonas Jonila Žilius. Klaipėda, Ryto bendrovės spaustuvė, 1928. 68p. 491.922.Z67.3 PU

957. ŽIUGŽDA, Juozas, ed. Už socialistinę Lietuvą. [For socialist Lithuania] Vilnius, VPMLL, 1960. 294 p. Balt 8180.25 MH

958. ZUBRAS, Albertas. People of the amber land. Melbourne, Australian Lithuanian Student Society, 1968. 96 p. DK511.B3Z8 PU

III.3. NATIONAL AWAKENING AND THE ROAD TOWARDS INDEPENDENCE

959. ALSEIKA, Danielius. Lietuvių tautinė idėja istorijos šviesoje. [Lithuanian national movement from the historical point of view] Vilnius "Motus", 1924. 125, [3] p. OCl PU

960. AMBRAZEVIČIUS, Juozas. Simonas Daukantas lietuvių tautinės sąmonės evoliucijoje. [Simonas Daukantas in the evolution of Lithuanian consciousness] In Židinys (Kaunas), v.23, no.2, 1936, p.129-139. See

serials consulted.

961. BASANAVIČIUS, Jonas. Iš Didžiojo Vilniaus Seimo istorijos. [On the great assembly of Vilnius] J. S-lius,[pseud.] Vilnius, "Ruch" spaustuvė, 1925. 23 p. 947.52. B292.2 PU PPULC

BENEDICTSEN, Åge Meyer. Lithuania, "The awakening of a nation". Copenhagen, 1924. See entry no.815.

962. BEZZENBERGER, Adalbert. Der Werdegang des litauischen Volkes. In Vierteljahrsschrift für Sozial- und Wirtschaftsgeschichte (Leipzig), v.13, 1916, p.1-40. See serials consulted.

963. BIRŽIŠKA, Mykolas. Lietuvių tautos kelias; į naująjį gyvenimą. [The road of the Lithuanian nation; toward a new life] Los Angeles, Calif., Lietuvių dienos] 1952-53. 2 v. port. DK511.L2B5 DLC CLSU CaOTU CaOTP CtPAM CtTMF CtY ICCC ICLJF MB MH MiD NN OCl PPULC PU

964. ČEGINSKAS, Kajetonas Julius. Lietuvių tautos atgimimo pradmenys; žvilgsnis į tautinį atgimimą. [The rudiments of the Lithuanian national awakening] In Bagdanavičius, V.J. Kovos metai dėl savosios spaudos. Chicago, Ill., 1957. p.77-111. PN5278.L5B3 DLC CaAEU OCl

965. DAMBRAUSKAS, Aleksandras. Głos litwinów do młodej generacyi magnatów, obywateli i szlachty na Litwie. [Moskva, 1902] 32 p. Slav 6295.03 MH

966. --- --- Wyd. 2., powiększone i poprawione. Kowno, Druk. Sokołowskiego i Estrina, 1906. 28 p. 947.52.D183 PU CtTMF MH

967. THE DESTINY OF LITHUANIA. In Polish Review (London), v.1, 1917, p.115-131. See serials consulted.

968. EXPOSÉ SOMMAIRE DU DÉVELOPpement de la conscience nationale lithuanienne dans le passé et le présent. [n.p.] 1916. 22 p. DK511. L2E8 DLC

969. GABRYS, Juozas. Le problème des nationalités et la paix durable. Lausanne, Librairie centrale des nationalités, 1917. 185 p. D645.G3 DLC BM(6916.c.18.)

970. GIMŽAUSKAS, Silvestras. 1885 meto priesżauszris. [The national awakening before 1885] Kraków, W.Ł. Anczyc, 1886. 29 p. DK511.L25G53 1971 PU(Xerox copy)

971. HELLMANN, Manfred. Die litauische Nationalbewegung im 19. und 20. Jahrhundert. In Zeitschrift für Ostforschung (Marburg), v.2, no.1, 1953, p. 66-106. See serials consulted.

972. HERBAČIAUSKAS, Juozas Albinas. Odrodzenie Litwy wobec idei polskiej. Kraków, 1905. 79 p. Preface also in Lithuanian. DK511. L2H38 DLC

973. HERTMANOWICZ, Joseph John. Ruch wszechlitewski. Chicago, Ill., Drukiem Zgody, 1907. 62 p. (*C p.v.3520)NN

974. JANOWSKI, Ludwik. Les théories néo-lithuaniennes et la vérité historique. Lausanne, Impr. de la Société Suisse de publicité, 1916. 12 p. (La Pologne et la guerre, 5) BN(8o M.17407(5))

975. KAIRYS, Steponas. Lietuvių tautinio atgimimo sąjudis. [The Lithuanian nationalawakening] In His Lietuva budo. New York, N.Y., 1957. p. 216-260. DK511.L25K3 DLC CaAEU CtY MH OCl PU

976. KAUPAS, V. Die Presse Litauens; unter Berücksichtigung des nationalen Gedankens und der öffentlichen Meinung. I. Vom Anfang bis zum Jahre 1904. Klaipėda, Rytas, 1934. vii, 223 p. PN5355.L7K2 InU PU

977. KUNIGAI KOVOJE SU CARO VALdžia. [The clergy in a struggle against the czarist rule] Kaunas, Šviesos spaustuvė, 1919. 26 p. illus. 970.7KU ICLJF

978. LIULEVIČIUS, Vincentas. Lietuvos laisvės idėjos raida, 1795-1918. [The development of the idea for independence from 1795 till 1918] In Aidai (Kennebunkport, Me.), no.2 (137), 1961, p. 49-58. See serials consulted.

979. NIKOL'SKII, Aleksandr. K voprosu o sovremennom natsional'nom vozrozhdenii litovtsev i otnoshenii ikh k russkim i poliakam. Smolensk, Tipo-lit. S. Gurevich, 1908. 27 p. 947.52.N587 PU

980. OCHMAŃSKI, Jerzy. Litewski ruch narodowo-kulturalny w XIX wieku, do 1890. Białystok [Państwowe Wydawnictwo Naukowe] 1965. 201 p. (Prace Białostockiego Towarzystwa Naukowego, 5) AS262.B47A14 DLC CU CaBVaU InU KU MH NNC NjP PU WU

981. PÉLISSIER, Jean. Les principaux artisans de la renaissance nationale lituanienne; hommes et choses de Lituanie. Lausanne, Bureau d'informations de Lituanie, 1918. iv, 326 p. DK511.L25P3 DLC CSt-H ICJ InU MH NN PU WU

982. PENKAUSKAS, Pranas. Lietuvių tautos dvasia istorijos šviesoje. [The spirit of the Lithuanian nation through the ages] Kaunas, Šviesos spaustuvė, 1919. 20 p. illus. 970.9.PE ICLJF

983. PETRIKA, Antanas. Lietuvių tautinio atbudimo pionieriai. [Pioneers of the Lithuanian national awakening. Brooklyn, N.Y., Laisvės spauda, 1939] 318 p. ports. (Amerikos lietuvių darbininkų literatūros draugija. Leidinys, nr.44) 891.92H.P448 PU ICLJF MH NN OKentU

984. PUZINAS, Jonas. Vorgeschichtsforschung und Nationalbewusstsein in Litauen. Kauen, Progresas, 1935. viii, 134 p. Thesis (Ph.D)-University of Heidelberg. CC105. L5P88 DLC CtY MH NN NNC NjP PU

985. RIMKA, Albinas. Lietuvių tautos atgimimo socialiniai pagrindai ir "Auszros"-"Varpo" gadynės (1883-1893) socialekonominiai raštai [The social principles of the reviving Lithuanian nation and the socioeconomic writings of the Auszra and Varpas period] Kaunas, 1932. 139p. (Kaunas. Universitetas. Teisių fakultetas. Darbai. T.6, kn.3) See serials consulted.

986. RÖMERIS, Mykolas. Litwa; studyum o odrodzeniu narodu litewskiego. Lwów, Polskie Tow. Nakładowe, 1908. 438 p. fold. map. DK511.L25R6 DLC BM(8093. c. 42.) ICU MH NN

987. RUSECKAS, Petras. Į laisvę; iš mūsų atgijimo istorijos. [From the history of Lithuania's awakening] Kaunas, 1919. 31 p. 947.5.R893.2 PU ICLJF OCl

988. ŠLEŽAS, Paulius. Kražių įvykių reikšmė tautiniam susipratimui. [Importance of the massacre of Kražiai on the national awakening] In Židinys (Kaunas), v.10, no.12, 1933, p.506-519. See serials consulted.

989. ŠLIŪPAS, Jonas. Lietuvystės praeitis, dabartis ir ateitis; istoriszkai-socialogiszkas pieszinys. [The past, present and future of the Lithuanian nation] Baltimore, Md., 1897. 83 p. 947.5.Sl35.5 PU WaS

990. SMETONA, Antanas. Atgimstant. [Awakening Lithuania] Kaunas, Spindulio bendrovės spaustuvė, 1930.

322 p. illus. (His Raštai, t.3)
081.S ICCC

991. --- Šviesos takais. [On the
road to enlightenment] Kaunas, Spindulio bendrovės spaustuvė, 1930.
358 p. illus. (His Raštai, t.2)
081.S ICCC

992. --- Vienybės gairėmis. [On
the path of unity] Kaunas, Spindulio bendrovės spaustuvė, 1930. 320p.
illus. (His Raštai, t.1) 081.S
ICCC

993. STAKAUSKAS, Juozapas. Lietuviškoji sąmonė Seinų seminarijoje.
[Lithuanian consciousness in the Seminary of Seinai] In Tiesos kelias
(Kaunas), no.9, 1939, p.322-329;
no.6, 1940, p.238-243. See serials
consulted.

994. --- Lietuviškosios minties
pasireiškimas Žemaičių seminarijoje.
[The manifestation of Lithuanian
thought at the Theological Seminary
in Žemaitija (Samogitia) In Tiesos
kelias (Kaunas), no.,11-12, 1938,
p.751-756, 823-828; no.1-3,5,7-8,
1939, p.28-35, 105-109, 181-185,
354-364, 551-554. See serials consulted.

995. --- Lietuvių kalbos kelias į
Žemaičių kunigų seminariją. [The
way of Lithuanian language into the
Theological Seminary in Žemaitija
(Samogitia)] In Tiesos kelias (Kaunas), no.7-11, 1937, p.340-356, 442-
450, 533-537,592-597; no.1, 1938,
p.16-28. See serials consulted.

996. --- Valančiaus laikų lietuviškas darbas. [The Lithuanian national activities at the time of Valan-
čius] In Tiesos kelias (Kaunas),
no.3-4,7-8,11, 1938 p.133-144, 203-
212, 503-515, 740-750. See serials
consulted.

997. STAUGAITIS, Justinas. Lietuvos Nepriklausomybės aušra. [At the
dawn of Lithuania's independence]
In Naujoji romuva (Kaunas), no.9-10,
1937, p. 193-198. See serials consulted.

998. STOROST, Wilhelm. Mūsų užda-
vinis. 2. leidimas. Tilžė, Rūta,
1921. 188 p. DK511.L22S7 1921 DLC
NN(1911 ed.)

999. STUKAS, Jack J. Awakening
Lithuania; a study on the rise of
modern Lithuanian nationalism...
Madison, N.J., Florham Park Press
[1966] xiii, 187 p. maps, ports.
Bibliography: p. 175-183. DK511.
L212S75 DLC CaAEU CaOTU CtY ICU InNd

InU MnU NN NjP PP PU

1000. --- The rise of modern Lithuanian nationalism. New York, N.Y.
1966. 203 leaves. Thesis (Ph.D)-
New York University. DK511.L2S78
CaOHM(Microfilm copy-positive) NNU

1001. TIJŪNAITIS, Stasys. Lietuvos atgijimas. [The awakening of
Lithuania] Seinai, Laukaičio, Dvaranausko ir Narjausko spaustuvė, 1911.
103 p. illus., ports. 947.52T447
PU PPi

1002. TOTORAITIS, Jonas. Lietu-
vos atgijimas. [The awakening of
Lithuania] Chicago, Ill., Draugas,
1921. 128 p. DK511.L25T6 DLC CaAEU
CaOONL CtTMF ICBM ICJ ICLJF InNd MH
PU

1003. TRUMPA, Vincas. Simonas
Daukantas, historian and pioneer of
the Lithuanian national rebirth. In
Lituanus (Chicago, Ill.), v.11, no.1,
1965, p. 5-17. See serials consulted.

1004. VOLDEMARAS, Augustinas. Natsional'naia bor'ba v Velikom Kniazhestve Litovskom v XV i XVI vekakh.
A.I. Voldemar. In Akademiia nauk
SSSR. Otdelenie russkago iazyka i
slovesnosti. Izvestiia. (Petrograd),
Vtoraia seriia, T.14, 1910, kn.3, p.
160-198. See serials consulted.

1005. WIELHORSKI, Władysław. Wa-
runki rozwoju świadomości narodowej
Litwinów i powstania współczesnego
państwa litewskiego 1861-1920. In
PZHP Pamiętnik VI. Referaty (Lwów),
1935, t.1, p. 126-143. See serials
consulted.

III.4. CULTURAL, INTELLECTUAL, AND
SOCIAL LIFE IN GENERAL

1006. AISTIS, Jonas. Apie laiką
ir žmones. [Of the time and people.
Chicago, Ill.] Terra [195-] 249 p.
PG8721.A4A7 DLC CaAEU CtTMF CaOONL
CaOTU MiD NN OCl PU

1007. ALEKSA, Jonas. Lietuvių
tautos likimo klausimu. [On the
destiny of the Lithuanian nation]
Kaunas, 1925. 2 v. Contents.--T.1.
Lietuvos kaimas ir žemės ūkis.--T.2.
Lietuviškų gyvenimo kelių beieškant.
DK511.L2A65 DLC(2) CtTMF(1-2) CtY(1)
ICCC(1-2) OCl(2)

1008. BARKAUSKAS, Antanas. Kaimas,
kultūra, buitis. [Rural life, culture...] Vilnius, Mintis, 1967.
263 p., 24 leaves of illus.

DK511.L2B36 DLC IEN

1009. BUJACK, Georg. Das erste Trinium des Comitees der ostpreussischen und littauischen Stände. Königsberg in Pr., 1887-88. 2 v.

1010. CAPPELLER, Carl. Kaip senėji lětuvininkai gyveno. Aufzeichnungen aus dem Kreise Stallupönen mit Anmerkungen und Wörterbuch. Hrsg. von der Litauischen literarischen Gesellschaft zu Tilsit. Heidelberg, Carl Winter, 1904. v, 75 p. PG8698.C36 ICU BM(Ac. 8964/2.) CtY ICU IEN InU MH MnU MiU NN NSyU PPULC PU WU

1011. --- Leben und Gebräuche der alten preussischen Litauer; Aufzeichnungen aus dem Kreise Stallupönen. 2 d ed. Holland, Oberländer, [1925] 64 p. DK511.L2C1 CLU MH

1012. THE CENTRAL EUROPEAN REVIEW. Special Lithuanian number; a detailed account of Lithuanian cultural and economic life. London, [1927] 53 p. illus., maps, tables. DK511.L2C4 DLC CSt-H CU CaQMM CtY MH MiU MoU TxU WU

1013. CHMIELOWSKI, Piotr. Liberalizm i obskurantyzm na Litwie i Rusi, 1815-1823. Z przedmową Bronisława Chlebowskiego. Warszawa, S. Sikorski, 1898. 163 p. port. (Biblioteka Dzieł Wyborowych, no. 21) DK511.L25C4 CSt CaOTU CtY ICU IU MiU MoU NIC PU WU KU

1014. ČIURLIONIENĖ, Sofija (Kymantaitė. Lietuvoje; kritikos žvilgsnis į Lietuvos inteligentiją. [A critical look at the Lithuanian intellectuals] Vilnius, 1910. 83 p. DK511.L212C53 PU CtTMF

1015. DABRILA, Jurgis. Lietuvos inteligentijos apsnūdimo priežastys ir pabudimo galimybė. [The causes of the apathy of the Lithuanian intelligentsia] Progreso meteoras [pseud.] Kaunas, 1928. 30 p. 891.92.D112L PU

1016. GAIGALAT, Wilhelm. Litauen, das besetzte Gebiet, sein Volk und dessen geistige Strömungen. Frankfurt a M., Frankfurter Vereinsdruckerei, 1917. 179 p. illus., plates, port., fold. map. DK511.G12 CLU CSt-H ICJ MnU NN NjP PU TxU

1017. IVINSKIS, Zenonas. Geschichte des Bauernstandes in Litauen von den ältesten Zeiten bis zum Anfang des XVI. Jahrhunderts: Beiträge zur sozialen und wirtschaftlichen Entwicklung des Bauernstandes in Litau-

en im Mittelalter. Berlin, E. Ebering, 1933. 264 p. (Historische Studien, 236) Bibliography: p. [7]-16. DK511.L2319 CLU CaOTU-(Reprint 1965) CtY GU IEN IU MnU NNC NIC NcD NjP-(Reprint 1965) NN NSyU OU PU WU WaU

1018. --- Iki šioliniai lietuvių kultūros tyrinėjimai; bibliografiškai-kritiška apžvalga. [Research on Lithuanian cultural history...] In Aidai (Brooklyn, N.Y.), no.1(126), 1960, p. 22-29. See serials consulted.

1019. JANULAITIS, Augustinas. Aus dem sozialen und wirtschaftlichen Kämpfen in Litauen. In Die Neue Zeit (Stuttgart), v.34, pt.2, 1916, p. 429-435, 493-498. See serials consulted.

1020. JAROSZEWICZ, Józef. Obraz Litwy pod względem jej cywilizacji, od czasów najdawniejszych do końca wieku XVIII. Wilno R. Rafałowicz, 1844-45. 3 v. in 1. DK511.L2J36 DLC BM PU

1021. JUCEWICZ, Ludwik Adam. Litwa pod względem starożytnych zabytków, obyczajów i zwyczajów skreślona przez Ludwika z Pokiewia [pseud.] Wilno, Nakł. R. Rafałowicza, 1846. 381 p. DK511.L212J73 CU BM CtY PU

1022. JUNGFER, Victor. Kulturbilder aus Litauen; ein Beitrag zur Erkenntnis des litauischen Volkstums. Berlin; Leipzig [etc.] F. Würtz, 1918. 144 p. (Litauische Bücherei, Bd.1) DK511.L2J7 DLC BM ICJ NN PU

1023. JURGINIS, Juozas. Renesansas ir humanizmas Lietuvoje. [The renaissance and humanism in Lithuania] Vilnius, Vaga, 1965. 286 p. DK511.L212J8 DLC ICBM ICU NN PU

1024. KALIŃSKI, Wilhelm. Dziennik 1787-1788. Opracował Łukasz Kurdybach. Wrocław, Zakł. Narod. im Ossolinskich, 1968. xxix, 89 p. (Pracownia Dziejów Oświaty Polskiej Akademii Nauk. Archiwum Dziejów Oświaty, tom 4) Slav 6595.65 MH

1025. KAMIENIECKI, Witold. Społeczeństwo litewskie w XV wieku. Warszawa, Nakł. Tow. Naukowego Warszawskiego, 1947. 125, iii p. (Towarzystwo Naukowe Warszawskie. Wydział II. Nauk Historycznych, Społecznych i Filozoficznych. [Wydawnictwa]) DK511.L2K27 DLC CSt CU CtY CoU InU InNd KU MH NNC PU WU

1026. KAUNIETIS, Senas, pseud. Litauischer Kulturkampf. Zum Verhältnis zwischen Regierung, Parteien und Kirche in Litauen. Danzig, Danziger Zeitungsverlags-Gesellschaft, 1930. 20 p. (BTE p.v.251) NN

1027. KOT, Stanisław. La réforme dans le Grand-Duché de Lithuanie; facteur d'occidentalisation culturelle. Bruxelles, 1953. 65 p. illus. "Extrait de l'Annuaire de l'Institut de Philologie et d'histoire Orientales et Slaves, tome 12 (1952)" DK511.L2K6 CaBVaU ICN IdU NNC ICBM

1028. KULTŪRŲ KRYŽKELĖJE. [In the crossroads of culture. Redakcinė kolegija: J. Jurginis ir kiti. Vilnius, Mintis, 1970] 240 p. DK511.L212K8 DLC

1029. LIETUVOS TSR MOKSLŲ AKADEMIJA, VILNA. EKONOMIKOS INSTITUTAS. Ketvirtis amžiaus socializmo keliu. [A quarter of a century towards socialism. Vyr. redaktorius K. Meškauskas] Vilnius, Mintis, 1965. 334 p. illus. DK511.L27L4943 DLC CSt-H IU CtY MH

1030. DAS LITAUEN-BUCH; eine Auslese aus der Zeitung der 10. Armee. Zeitung der 10. Armee, 1918. 195 p. illus., plates, ports., maps, facsims. DK511.L2L3 CaBVaU InU NN PU

1031. LITHUANIAN INFORMATION BUREAU, WASHINGTON, D.C. Sidelights on life in Lithuania. Washington, D.C. [1918] 14, [1] p. illus. 947.5.L776 CSt ICLJF In ICN IEN MiU MH OrU PU TxU

1032. MARTÍNEK, Vojtěch. Z Litvy a o Litvě. Praha, 1926. 186 p. (Aventinum, sv.133) 947.52.M363 PU BM(010290. eee. 57.)

1033. MATULIS, Anatole C. Lithuanian culture in modern German prose literature: Hermann Sudermann, Ernst Wiechert, Agnes Miegel. [Lafayette, Ind.] Purdue University, 1966. 166 p. DK511.L163M44 CaAEU DLC InNd KyU PU

1034. ---Lithuanian culture in the prose works of Hermann Sudermann, Ernst Wiechert, and Agnes Miegel. [East Lansing, Mich.] 1963. iii, 343 leaves. Thesis—Michigan State University. Microfilm copy of typescript. Ann Arbor, Mich., University Microfilms, 1966. 1 reel. Film 10270 IaU InNd

1035. MATUSZEWICZ, Marcin. Pamiętniki Marcina Matuszewicza, kasztelana Brzesko-litewskiego, 1714-1765.

Wyd. A. Pawiński. Warszawa, Gebethner i Wolff, 1876. 4 v. DK434.8.M44A3 ICU BM(10790. g. 17.)

1036. MAUCLÈRE, Jean. Le rayonnement de la France en Lithuanie. Le Raincy, S. et O., Éditions Claires [1946] 47 p. DK511.L212M35 PU CSt-H ICLJF

1037. MEYER, Åge. Et folk, der vaagner; kulturbileder fra Litaven. København, Gyldendalske Boghandels Forlag, 1895. 259. illus. DK511.L212M49 CtY MnU

1038. PAPLAUSKAS-RAMŪNAS, Antanas. Iš sutemų i aušrą. [From dusk to dawn; the Lithuanian cultural awakening] [Toronto, Ont., Author, 1967] 453 p. illus. DK511.L212P34 PU InNd CaOONL

1039. PIGOŃ, Stanisław. Z dawnego Wilna; szkice obyczajowe i literackie. Wilno, Wydawn. Magistratu miasta Wilna, 1929. 167 p. (Biblioteczka Wileńska, nr.2) DK651.V4B47 no.2 DLC CaOTU MH PU

1040. POŽARSKAS, Mykolas. Cultural life in Lithuania. Vilnius, Gintaras, 1966. 96 p. illus., ports. DK511.L212P58 DLC ICU IU MH

1041. --- Das kulturelle Leben Litauens. [Von] M. Požarskas. [Übersetzer: J. Beržas] Vilnius, Gintaras, 1967. 96 p. illus. DK511.L212P6 DLC MU

1042. --- Kultūros augimas Tarybų Lietuvoje šeštajame penkmetyje. [The growth of cultural life in Soviet Lithuania during the sixth five-year plan] Vilnius, VPMLL, 1956. 61 p. DK511.L27P6 DLC

1043. RAILA, Bronys. Dialogas su lietuviais. [A dialogue with Lithuanians. Boston, Mass.] Lietuvių enciklopedijos leidykla [1970] 560 p. (Akimirksnių kronikos, 2) DK511.L223R3 PU DLC CaAEU

1044. RIMANTAS, Juozas. V.D. Universiteto studentų gyvenimas. [The life of students in the University of Lithuania. By] J. Slapšinskas. Kaunas, 1933. 46 p. 370.S7 CtTMF

1045. RÖMERIS, Mykolas. Stosunki etnograficzno-kulturalne na Litwie. Kraków, 1905. 41 p. Offprint from Krytyka. 947.52.R663.6 PU BM(10107. gg. 6.(2.)) MH

1046. SABALIŪNAS, Leonas. Lithuania in crisis; nationalism to communism, 1939-1940. Bloomington, Ind.,

University Press[1972] xxi, 293 p. DK511.L27S2 PU

1047. ŠALČIUS, Matas. Dešimt metų tautiniai-kultūrinio darbo Lietuvoje, 1905-1915. [Ten years of national and cultural work in Lithuania] Chicago, Ill., Spauda "Lietuvos", 1917. 99 p. illus., ports (Tėvynės mylėtojų draugijos leidinys,nr.26) DK511.L2S25 DLC CSt-H CtTMF CtY ICLJF NN OCl PU

1048. ŠALKAUSKIS, Stasys. Sur les confins de deux mondes; essai synthétique sur le problème de la civilisation nationale en Lituanie. .. Genève, Édition "Atar" [1919] 271 p. plates, ports. DK511.L2S3 DLC BM InU MH PU

1049. SIRVAITIS, Casimir Peter. Religious folkways in Lithuania and their conservation among the Lithuanian immigrants in the United States; a study with conclusions on acculturation. Washington, D.C., Catholic University of America Press, 1952. vii, 49 p. (Catholic University of America. Studies in sociology; abstract series, v.3) BR937.L3S5 DLC CaAEU IU NB NN NNC NcD PU

1050. SRUOGIENĖ, Vanda (Daugirdaitė). Lietuvos kultūros istorijos bruožai; paskaitos, skaitytos Pedagoginiame lituanistikos institue 1960-61 m. [The outline of the Lithuanian cultural history...] Chicago, Ill., Padagoginis lituanistikos institutas, 1962. 109 p. DK511.L212S65 DLC CaAEU CaOONL CtPAM MH PU

1051. STOROST, Wilhelm. Die Lebenswelt im Preussischen Litauen ums Jahr 1770 nach den Dichtungen des Pfarrers Christian Donelaitis mit ihrer völkischen Bedeutung. Kassel-Mattenberg, Ger., Verlagskommission des Hilfsausschusses für Klein-Litauen, 1948. 50 p. illus. 891.92. D713.yS PU ICBM

1052. --- Ein Nachlass schlichter litauischer Menschen. Kassel, Ger., Aistia, 1948. 28 p. 891.92.St78N PU BM(12592. a. 73.)

1053. --- Sieben hundert Jahre deutsch-litauischer Beziehungen: kulturhistorische Darlegungen... [Von] Vydūnas, [pseud.] Tilsit, Rūta-Verlag, 1932. 478 p. illus., plates, maps. 914.78.St78 PU CaOTU NNC

1054. SZYDŁOWSKI, Stefan von. Der polnische und litauische Hochadel.

Budapest, 1944. 123 p. Bibliography: p. 120-123. CS874.S8 DLC CLU CtY InNd

1055. TUMAS, Juozas. Šeimos vėžiai .... [The family's cancer By] Vaižgantas [pseud.] Kaunas, 1929. 256 p. (Vaižganto raštai, t. 15) 891.93V39 CtTMF

1056. VAITKUS, Mykolas. Nepriklausomybės saulėj; 1918-1940, atsiminimai... [Under the sun of Independence, 1918-1940, memoirs...] London, Nida Press [1968-69] 3 v. (Nidos knygų klubo leidinys, 66, 69, 72) PG8721.V322Z52 PU CaOTU

1057. WASILEWSKI, Zygmunt. Mickiewicz i Słowacki jako czlonkowie towarzystwa litewskiego. Warszawa, Nakład Gebethnera i Wolffa, 1921. viii, 343 p. C158.M626 Wa PCamA

1058. WIELHORSKI, Władysław. Litwini, Białorusini i Polacy w dziejach kultury Wielkiego Księstwa Litewskiego. In Alma Mater Vilnensis ...(Londyn), część 3, zesz.2, 1951, p.[21]-157. See serials consulted.

1059. ZALESKI, Bronisław. Z życia litwinki [Heleny Skirmunttowej, 1827-1874] z listów i notatek. Poznań, J.I. Kraszewski, 1876. 282 p. BM(o10790. g.44.)

III.5. DESCRIPTION AND TRAVEL, GENERAL

1060. BABICKAS, Petras. Lietuva vasarą. [Lithuania in the summer] Kaunas, 1934. 80 p. 914.47B2 CtTMF

1061. --- Lithuania. Traducido por Leonardas Sruoga. Buenos Aires, Argentinos lietuvių balsas, 1947. 32p. 914.78.B112S PU

1062. BARANAUSKAS, Albinas. Kalvos ir lankos; tolimo Suvalkijos kampelio žmonės ir gamta. [The people and the nature of a distant corner in Suvalkija. Putnam, Conn., 1959] 155 p. 891.92.B229K PU

1063. BAYE, Joseph de. En Lithuanie; souvenirs d'une mission. Paris, Librarie Nilson, 1905. 47 p. illus. Balt 8519.05 MH

1064. BONOSKY, Phillip. Beyond the borders of myth, from Vilnius to Hanoi. New York, N.Y., Praxis Press, 1967. 223 p. DK511.L2B6 DLC CtY IU IaU MH NN NNC NjP WU

1065. CALLIAS, Suzanne de. Aux pays des femmes-soldats; Finlande, Esthonie, Danemark, Lithuanie, par Suzanne de Callias et de Blanche Vogt. Paris, Fasquelle [1931] 190p. illus., port., plates. D921.C34 CaOOP

1066. ČIA UŽAUGAU. [Here I have grown up. Autoriai: J. Degutytė et al.] Vilnius, VGLL, 1961. 391 p. illus. DK511.L2C55 DLC PU

1067. DAVIES, Ellen Chievers. A wayfarer in Estonia, Latvia and Lithuania. New York, N.Y., McBride, 1937. xi, 280 p. front., plates, map. Lithuania: p.177-273. DK511. E5D3 1937 DLC CSt-H CU CaOTP CoU IC IaU MH MoU NN NNC NB NbU NcD NjP OU OCl Or OrP PP PPi TxU Wa WaS WaT

1068. FRIEDERICHSEN, Maximilian Hermann. Landschaften und Städte Polens und Litauens. Beiträge zu einer regionalen Geographie. [Berlin, Gea Verlag] 1918. x, 133 p. illus., plates, map. (Veröffentlichungen der Landeskundlichen Kommission beim Kaiser. deutschen Gouvernement Warschau. Beiträge zur polnischen Landeskunde. Reihe B.[Bd.4]) DK407.F8 DLC CU CaAEU CtY ICJ InU PU

1069. GABRYS, Juozas. Trumpas Lietuvos aprašymas. [A brief sketch of Lithuania] Vilnius, "Vilniaus žinių" spaustuvė, 1905. 54 p. illus. WA11116 CtY CtTMF

1070. --- --- 2., leidimas. Kovno, Ona Vitkauskytė, 1913. 104 p. NN

1071. GLOGER, Zygmunt. Dolinami rzek; opisy podróży wzdłuż Niemna, Wisły, Bugu i Biebrzy. Warszawa, F. Hösick, 1903. 218 p. illus. 947.52.G513.3 PU

1072. GRIGAT, Martin. Die Memelniederung; die Natur des Landes. Königsberg in Pr., Gräfe und Unzer, 1931. 163 p. plates, tables, maps. (Königsberg. Universität. Geographisches Institut. Veröffentlichungen. Ausser der Reihe. Nr.5) Bibliography: p.133-147. MH NN

1073. GUDELIS, Vytautas. Kuršių Nerija. [Couronian sand dunes] Vilnius, Mintis, 1970. 71 p. illus. Summary in English and Russian. DK511.C6G78 DLC

1074. HOESICK, Ferdynand. Wilno i Krzemieniec; wrażenia z dwóch wycieczek literackich pod znakiem Słowackiego. Warszawa, Trzaska, Everet i Michalski [1933] 151 p. His Pisma zbiorowe, t.3) Slav 7123.2.882 MH

1075. KOLUPAILAITĖ, Evelina. Baidare per 35 ežerus. [Canoeing through 35 lakes] In Ateitis (Kaunas), no.11-12, 1937, p.394-398, 460-466. See serials consulted.

1076. KONDRATOWICZ, Ludwik. Niemen od źródeł do ujścia... Przez W. Syrokomla [pseud.] Wilno, A. Ass, 1861. 172 p. BM(10290. b. 8.)

1077. KURAITIS, Dan. Anapus geležinės uždangos. [On the other side of the iron-curtain] Chicago, Ill., 1959. 237 p. illus. 914.5K ICBM

1078. --- Magiškuoju kilimu į Vilnių; 1962 metų kelionės į Lietuvą įspūdžiai. [On the magic carpet to Vilnius...] Chicago, Ill., Chicagos lietuvių literatūros draugijos leidinys [1962] 331 p. illus. DK511. L27K77 DLC PU

1079. LIETUVA-LITAUEN. Kaunas, Handels-, Industrie- und Handwerkerkammer, 1938. 20 p. illus. 914.5L ICBM

1080. LIETUVOS ŠAULIŲ SĄJUNGA. Į Lietuvą Vytauto Didžiojo metais. [go to Lithuania during the year of Vytautas the Great] Kaunas, 1930. 95 p. illus. DK511.L2L422 DLC CU CtTMF ICLJF WaU

1081. ŁOPALEWSKI, Tadeusz. Między Niemnem a Dźwiną; ziemia wileńska i nowogródzka. Przedmowę napisał Aleksander Prystor. Poznań, Wydawn. Polskie [1938?] 234 p. illus., map, ports. (Cuda Polski) DK511.L2L8 DLC IU NIC PU

1082. --- --- Posłowie Antoniego Bogusławskiego. [2. wyd.] Londyn, Tern (Rybitwa Book) [1955] 256 p. illus. (Cuda Polski) DK511L2L66 1955 CU CaBVaU CaOTU MH

1083. MARGERIS, Algirdas. Amerikiečio įspūdžiai Lietuvoje, 1931. Algirdas Šeštokas Margeris. [The impressions of an American in Lithuania] Kaunas, Spaudos fondas, 1932. 429 p. DK511.L2M37 PU CtTMF MH OKentU

1084. --- 150 dienų Tarybų Lietuvoje. [150 days in Soviet Lithuania] Chicago, Ill., Amerikos lietuvių literatūros draugijos leidinys, 1961. 380 p. illus. T 914.75M CaOTP ICBM OKentU

1085. MATUTIS, Anselmas. Nemuno vingiuose. [Along the bends of the Nemunas] Vilnius, VPMLL, 1959. 305p. illus. DK511.L2M245 DLC ICBM ICLJF PU

1086. MAUCLÈRE, Jean. Sous le
ciel pâle de Lithuanie. Paris, Plon
[1926] 1x, 212 p. illus., fold.
maps. DK511.L27M3 CSt BM CaOOP DLC
ICBM IaU IU NN OCH PU

1087. MĘKARSKA, Józefa. Wędrówka
po ziemiach wschodnich Rzeczypospolitej. Londyn, Nakł. Stowarzyszenia
Polskich Kombatantów, 1966. 123 p.
illus., plates, maps. DK507.2.M4
DLC CaBVaU CaOTU KU MH NNC

1088. METEL'SKII, Georgii Vasil'-
evich. Au pays du Niemen. [Tr. du
Russe par H. Lusternik] Moscou,
Éditions en langues etrangeres, 1959.
250 p. illus., fold. map.
914.75.,589v.F CaNBFU DLC DS

1089. --- Lietuvos keliais. [Along
the Lithuanian roads] Vilnius, VPMLL,
1955. 218 p. illus. DK511.L2M43
DLC

1090. --- Lithuania, land of the
Niemen. Tr. from the Russian by
George H. Hanna. Moscow, Foreign
languages publishing house, 1959.
273 p. illus. DK511.L2M443 DLC BM
CSt-H CaOLU CaOWtU CtY DS ICD InU IU
InNd MH MtU MnU MU NIC NN NcU NSyU
NvU OrU TNJ WaU

1091. --- V kraiu Nemana. Moskva,
Molodaia gvardiia, 1957. 298 p.
illus., maps. (Geograficheskaia
nauchno-khudozhestvennaia seriia.
Nasha Rodina) DK511.L2M44 DLC BM
ICU IU INU HU MH NN NcU OrU

1092. MIZARA, Rojus. Apie tave,
gimtoji žemė. [About you, my native
land] Vilnius, VGLL, 1962. 268 p.
illus. DK511.L2M67 DLC

1093. NARBUTAS, Jonas Vytautas.
Anapus linijos. [On the other side
of the demarcation line] Kaunas,
1936. 103 p. 914.47.N1 CtTMF

1094. NEWMAN, Bernard. Baltic
roundabout. London, R. Hale, 1948.
280 p. plates, maps. DK511.B3N38
DLC

1095. OSTANKOVICH, N.N. Ekskur-
siia po Litvie. Sanktpeterburg,
1907. In Istoricheskii Viestnik
(Sanktpeterburg), t.107, 1907, p.
586-612. See serials consulted.

1096. OSTLAND. REICHSKOMMISSAR.
Auf Informationsfahrt im Ostland,
Reiseeindrücke deutscher Schriftlei-
ter. Sonderdruck des Reichskommissars für das Ostland Pressechef, Riga. [Riga, 1944] 307 p. illus.,
port. D802.B3 08 DLC

1097. PAMATYKIME LIETUVĄ! [Let's
visit Lithuania] Kaunas, Turizmo
sąjunga, 1930. 108 p. illus. G2PAM
ICLJF

1098. PRANAITYTĖ, Julė. Viešnagė
Šeštokuose. [A visit to the town
of Šeštokai] Philadelphia, Pa.,
[n.d.] 211 p. 914.47.P7 CtTMF

1099. ROSENHEYN, Max. Aus Litau-
en. In His Reise-Skizzen aus Ost-
und Westpreussen. Danzig, Kafemann,
1858. Bd.2, p. 121-136. BM(10250.
aa. 4.)

1100. ROSTOVTSEV, Mikhail Ivano-
vich. V kraiu iantaria i slantsa.
Moskva, Prosveshchenie, 1965. 202 p.
DK511.B28R65 DLC ViU

1101. SACKS, Abraham A. An excursion to Lithuania. New York, N.Y.,
Hudson Bay Press, 1934. xiv, 308 p.
front., plates, map. DK511.L2S24
DLC CaAEU ICBM IU NB OCl PPiU NNC

1102. SAVICKIS, Jurgis. En rejse
gennem Litauen. Forord af Georg
Brandes. København, Jespersen, 1919.
80 p. illus., port., map, facsims.
309.Z Box 308 NNC

1103. SCHLICHTING, Richard. Bil-
der aus Litauen; im Auftrage des
Chefs und unter Mitarbeit zahlrei-
cher Herren der Militärverwaltung
Litauen. Bearbeitet von R. Schlich-
ting und Leutnant Hans Osman. 2.er-
weiterte Auflage. Kowno, Kownoer
Zeitung, 1917. 168 p. illus.
DK511.L26S34 CSt-H BM(10290. ff. 29.)
CaAEU CSt NN NjP PU

1104. SLUCHEVSKII, Konstantin Konstantinovich. Po sievero-zapadnu
Rossii. Sanktpeterburg, Marks,
[1897] 2 v. Lithuania: v.2, p.397-
437. G1SLU ICLJF

1105. SOVETSKII SOIUZ. Geograficheskoe opisanie v 22 tomakh. Litva. Otv. red. K.K. Bieliukas. Moskva, Mysl', 1967. 285 p. illus.
DK511.L2S6 MU

1106. SPAULL, Hebe. The Baltic
States: Latvia, Lithuania & Estonia.
London, A. & C. Black, 1931. ix, 80
p. col. front., plates, map.
DK511.B28S6 DLC CLU CSt-H CtY CaQMM
In InU ICU KU MnU NN NNC

1107. STRUCK, Hermann and Herbert
Eulenberg. Skizzen aus Litauen,
Weissrussland und Kurland, von Her-
mann Struck und Herbert Eulenberg.
Berlin, G. Stilks, 1916. 125 p.,
60 plates. DK507.S92s CLU CSt-H
MH NN NmU OCH OCl PU TxHU

1108. VENCIENĖ, Viktorija. Ameri-
kiečiai Lietuvoje. [Americans in
Lithuania] SO. Boston, Mass., "Sandaros" spauda ir lėšos, 1922. 58 p.
DK511.L2V4 DLC OCl

1109. VILAINIS, Adomas. Čia mūsų
žemė. [Here is our land] Chicago,
Ill., 1950. 104 p. 914.5V ICBM

1110. --- Žemaičių žemėje; reportažai iš kelionių Lietuvoje. [In
the country of Žemaitija (Samogitia)
reports from voyages in Lithuania]
Chicago, Ill., 1952. 132 p. illus.
DK511.L2V44 DLC ICBM ICLJF PU

1111. VILNA. WOJEWÓDZKI KOMITET
REGIONALNY. Wilno i ziemia wileńska; zarys monograficzny. Wilno,
1930-37. 2 v. illus., ports., map,
facsims. DK651.V4A57 DLC CtY NNC PU

1112. ZAMIECHATEL'NOSTI SIEVERO-
Zapadnago kraia. Vil'na, Vilenskii
uchebnyi okrug, 1868. 1 v. illus.
DK511.L2Z24 ICU(1)

III.6. TRAVEL GUIDES

1113. BARKAUSKAS, Pranas and Aleksandras Vabalas, eds. Vadovas po
Lietuvą. [Traveller's guide to Li-
thuania] Kaunas, Lietuvos turizmo
draugija, 1938. 380 p. maps, plan,
947.52.B242 PU BM CtTMF PPULC

1114. BROGA, L. and Eugenijus Danilevičius, comp. Lietuvos TSR turistinis žemėlapis. [Tourist map
of the Lithuanian SSR] Vilnius,
VPMLL, 1963. 101 p. illus., col.
maps. G2135.B7 1963 DLC PU

1115. --- Turistskaia karta Litovskoi SSR. Perevod s litovskogo iazyka. Vilnius, VPMLL, 1963. 72 p.
illus., col. maps. G2135.B72 1963
DLC

1116. DANILEVIČIUS, Eugenijus.
Po okolicach Wilniusa; marsruty tu-
rystyczne. [Przeł. T. Mockienė]
Przez Eug. Danilewiczius. Wilnius,
Państwowe Wydawn. Literatury Poli-
tycznej i Naukowej, 1963. 119 p.
DK511.V4D37 DLC

1117. --- Vilniaus apylinkėmis;
turistiniai maršrutai. [Travels in
the vicinity of Vilnius] Vilnius,
VPMLL, 1962. 102 p. map. DK511.
V4D3 PU DLC MH NN

1118. DOBRIANSKII, Flavian Nikolaevich. Vil'na i eia okrestnosti;
putevoditel' i istoricheskaia spra-

vochnaia kniga. Vil'na, Tip. A.G.
Syrkina, 1883. xv, 318 p.
947.52.D653 1883 PU

1119. --- Staraia i novaia Vil'na.
Izd. 3. Vil'na, Tip. A.G. Syrkina,
1904. viii, 286 p. 1st ed. 1883 has
title: Vil'na i eia okrestnosti.
DK651.V4D6 1904 DLC PU

1120. FÜHRER DURCH KOVNO. Kovno,
Verlag Kovnoer Zeitung, 1916. 68 p.
947.52.F952 PU

1121. FÜHRER DURCH WILNA. Wilna,
1916. 947.52.F953 PU

1122. GAILIUS, P. Palydovas.
[A guide] Kaunas, 1922. 93 p.
charts, maps. 914.5G ICBM

1123. GIZBERT, W. Wilno; przewodnik ilustrowany po mieście i okolicach z planem miasta i dodatkami.
Wilno, A. Żukowski i W. Borkowski,
1910. 268, 34 p. illus., col.plan.
(*QR)NN

1124. JAROCKI, Stanisław. Okolice
Wilna; przewodnik turystyczny. Wilno, J. Zawadzki, 1925. 80 p. illus.,
map. 947.52.J295 PU NNC

1125. JURGINIS, Juozas and Vladis-
lovas Mikučianis. Vilnius, Tarybų
Lietuvos sostinė. [Vilnius; the ca-
pital of Soviet Lithuania] Vilnius,
VPMLL, [1956] 173 p. illus. DK651.
V4J8 DLC CaAEU ICLJF MH NN NNC PU

1126. KAZRAGIS, Algirdas. Žemaičių kalneliais. [Through the hills
of Žemaitija (Samogitia)] Vilnius,
Mintis, 1968. 126 p. illus. DK511.
S24K38 DLC CtY PU

1127. KELIONIŲ VADOVAS. [Travel-
ler's guide. By A. Dembinskas et al.]
Vilnius, Mintis, 1970. 344 p. illus.
G155.L5K4 DLC

1128. KEŽINAITIS, Petras. Aplink
Kauną; turistinės kelionės po Kauno
miesto pakraščius ir priemiesčius, jo
artimesniąsias bei tolimesniąsias
apylinkes. [Around Kaunas; touristic
travels in the suburbs and the vici-
nity] Vilnius, Mintis, 1966. 96 p.
DK651.K125K42 DLC ICBM NN

1129. --- Okrestnosti Kaunasa.
[Per. s litovskogo I. Fridaitė. Khud.
Vl. Norkus. Vil'nius, Gos. izd-vo
polit. i nauch. lit-ry, Litovskoi
SSR, 1959] 125 p. illus. DK651.
K125K4 DLC MH WaU

1130. KIRKOR, Adam Honory. Przewodnik; Wilno i koleje żelazne z
Wilna do Petersburga i Rygi, oraz do

granic na Kowno i Warszawę. Wilno, Nakładem autora, 1862. xxi, 297 p. illus., map. 970.31.Ki ICLJF NN

1131. --- Przewodnik historyczny po Wilnie i jego okolicach. Wyd.2, przejrzane i powiększone. Wilno, J. Zawadzki, 1880. 308 p. 947.52. K634 PU

1132. KŁOS, Juljusz. Wilno; przewodnik krajoznawczy. Wilno, Oddział Wileńskiego Polsk. Tow. Krajoznawczego, 1923. ix, 260 p. illus. DK651.V4K57 CaOTU ICLJF

1133. --- Wyd.2., całkowcie i uzupełnione. Wilno, Wydawn. Oddziału Wileńskiego Polsk. Tow. Krajoznawczego-Touring-Klubu, 1929. 947.52. K695 PU NN

1134. --- --- Wyd.3., poprawione po zgonie autora. Wilno, [Wydawn. Oddziału Wileńskiego Polsk. Tow. Krajoznawczego, 1937. 323 p. illus. DK651.V4K57 1937 DLC CaBVaU NNC PU

1135. KONDRATAS, B. Veisėjų ežerais. [Through the lakes of Veisėjai] Vilnius, Mintis, 1970. 83 p. DK511.V35K6 PU

1136. KONDRATAS, M. Dubysa. [The Dubysa river] Vilnius, VPMLL, 1961. 63 p. (Maršrutas, nr.6) DK511. D9K6 DLC PU

1137. KONDRATOWICZ, Ludwik. Wycieczki po Litwie w promieniach od Wilna do Oszmiany- do Kiernowa- do Kowna przez Władysława Syrokomlę [pseud.] Wilno, Autor, 1857-60. 2 v. 947.52.K837 PU(2)

1138. KULWIEĆ, E. Troki; przewodnik. Wilno, Wydawn. Polsk. Tow. Krajoznawczego, Oddział w Wilnie, 1939. 41 p. Bound with Wołłosewicz, S. Ziemia Wileńska. 947.52.W835.3 PU

1139. LIETUVOS AUTOMOBILIŲ KLUBAS. Lithuania; guiding facts for tourists. [Kaunas] Automobile Club of Lithuania [1930] 80 p. illus., fold.map, diagrams. DK511.L713L713aL InNd CU ICBM ICLJF MB MH NcU OCl PP PU WaU

1140. LIETUVOS TURIZMO DRAUGIJA. Litauen. [Hrsg. vom Turistenverein Litauens. Kaunas, 1937.] 40 p. DK511.L2L52 PU

1141. LITHUANIA. [Kaunas, Lithuanian Tourist Association, 1937] 32 p. illus., map. DK511.L2L47 DLC PU

1142. MACEIKA, Juozas. Vadovas po Vilnių. [A guide to places in and

surrounding Vilnius. Vilnius, VPMLL, 1960] 385 p. illus. Bibliography: p. 349-352. DK651.V4M3 DLC ICBM ICLJF MH PU

1143. --- Vil'nius; putevoditel' po gorodu. [Perevod s litovskogo D. Gel'pernas. Vil'nius, Gos. izdvo polit. i nauch. lit-ry, Litovskoi SSR, 1962] 390 p. illus. DK651.V4M37 DLC ViU

1144. MATIUKAS, Antanas. Po Zarasų krašta. [Through the district of Zarasai. Vilnius, Mintis, 1967] 95 p. illus., col. maps. DK511. Z365M3 DLC MH

1145. MEDONIS, Ar. Turistu o Vil'niuse. [Perevod s litovskogo O.Kaplanasa i M. Shul'kinasa] Vil'nius, Mintis, 1965. 218 p. illus., maps. DK651.V4M417 DLC ViU

1146. --- Turistui apie Vilnių. [Traveller's guide to Vilnius] Vilnius, Mintis, 1965. 176 p. illus., maps. DK651.V4M4 PU DLC NN PU

1147. --- Vilnius; a pocket-book for tourists. [Translated from Lithuanian by Vl. Grodzenskis. Edited by M. Ginsburgas] Vilnius, Mintis, 1966. 191 p. illus. DK651.V4M413 DLC MH

1148. NEVARDAUSKAS, Alfonsas. Pajūriais, pamariais. [Along the sea coast. Chicago, Ill., 1963] 317 p. illus., ports., maps. DK511.K77N45 DLC PU

1149. OBELIENIUS, J. Kur bėga Šešupė. [There flows Šešupė river] Vilnius, VPMLL, 1961. 49 p. (Maršrutas, nr.4) DK511.S3902 DLC ICBM

1150. --- Merkiu per pietryčių Lietuvą. [On the river Merkys through South Eastern Lithuania] Vilnius, VPMLL, 1961. 55 p. illus. fold. map. (Maršrutas, nr.5) DK511.M426 02 DLC

1151. PALYDOVAS, ARBA KAS REIKIA žinoti lietuviui grižtančiam tėvynėn. [A guide; or, What a Lithuanian should know when returning to his homeland] Kaunas, 1922. 112 p. illus., fold. col. plan. DK511. L2P37 DLC CtY ICJ ICLJF PU

1152. PUTEVODITEL' PO PRIBALTIKE. Kursbuch für das Baltikum. Kowno, 1922. 1 v. maps. DK511.B25P8 DLC

1153. RAMANAUSKAS, Antanas. Žemaitijos keliais. [On the roads of Žemaitija (Samogitia)] Vilnius, VPMLL, 1958. 140 p. (Chiefly illus.)

DK511.L2R3 DLC ICBM ICLJF NN PU

1154. ROUBA, Napoleon. Przewodnik po Litwie i Białejrusi. Wilno, [1910] 215 p. 947.52.R733 PU BM(10292. h. 25.)

1155. ŠALŪGA, R. Vilnius, svarbiausios žinios turistui. [Vilnius; essential information for the tourist] Vilnius, VPMLL, 1957. 86 p. (chiefly illus.) DK651.V4S34 DLC ICBM ICLJF

1156. UŽDAVINYS, Vincas. Po Vilniaus apylinkes. [A guide to places surrounding Vilnius] Vilnius, VPMLL 1958. 184 p. illus. DK651.V4U9 DLC ICBM ICLJF IU OKentU PU

1157.--- V okrestnostiakh Vil'niusa. [Perevod s litovskogo M. Shtarkene] Vil'nius, Gos. izd-vo polit. i nauch. lit-ry, 1958. 180 p. illus. DK651.V4U9 DLC CaOTU

1158. VADOVĖLIS PO PALANGĄ IR apylinkes. [A guide through the town of Palanga and its vicinity] Klaipėda, 1922. 23 p. 914.47.V1 CtTMF

1159. VIL'NA V KARMANIE. Izd.2. Vil'na, Izdanie M. Tassel'krauta, 1915. 220 p. map. DK651.V4V4 1915 DLC

1160. VINOGRADOV, Aleksandr Aleksandrovich. Putevoditel' po gorodu Vil'nie i ego okrestnostiam. Vil'na, Tip. Shtaba Vilenskago voen. okruga, 1904. 2 v. in 1. DK651. V4V46 DLC

1161. ŽADEIKIS, Povilas. Introducing Lithuania; an economic-historical outline and hints for tourists. New York, N.Y., 1929? 64 p. map. 308 Z Boz 744 NNC ICBM NN NjP PU

1162. --- --- 2d rev. ed. New York, N.Y., 1933. 64 p. illus., map. DK511.L273 DLC OCl PU

1163. ZAHORSKI, Władysław. Przewodnik po Wilnie. Wilno, J. Zawadzki, 1910. 295 p. illus., maps, plans. NN

1164. --- --- Wyd. 3, przejrzane i uzupełnione. Wilno, 1923. x,180 p. illus., fold. plan. MH

1165. --- --- Wyd. 5, poprawione i uzupełnione przez Marję Łowmiańską. Wilno, J. Zawadzki, 1935. 200 p. illus., map. DK511.V4Z2 1935 CaBVaU

1166. ZEITUNG DER 10. ARMEE. Ich weiss Bescheid; kleiner Soldatenführer durch Wilna, zusammengestellt von der Armeezeitung A.-O.-K.10. Wilna, Verlag Armeezeitung der A.-O. -K.10., 1916. 29 p. 947.52.Z37 PU

III.7. ANCIENT TRAVEL REPORTS BY FOREIGN TRAVELLERS

1167. BRAND, Johann Arnhold von. Reysen durch die Marck Brandenburg, Preussen... Wesel, J. von Wesel, 1702. 516 p. 947.52.B737 PU BM(590. a. 34.)

1168. CELLARIUS, Andreas. Regni Poloniae Magnique Ducatus Lithuaniae omniumque regionum juri polonico subjectorum novissima descriptio. Amstelodami, Aedipius Janssonius Valckenier, 1659. 605 p. tables, maps. 947.52.C334 PU BM(572. a 12.)

1169. HEBERSTEIN, Sigismund. Comentarii della Moscovia et perimente della Russia... come sonode Tartari, Lithuani, Poloni, & altri... Venetia, Gioan. Battista Pedrezzano, 1550. [8], 90 leaves. plates, map. (*KB 1550)NN

1170. KLIMAS, Petras. Ghillebert de Lannoy in medieval Lithuania; voyages and embassies of an ancestor of one of America's great presidents. New York, N.Y., The Lithuanian American Information Center, 1945. 96 p. illus., geneal. tables, plates, ports., maps, facsims. An introduction and translation from the Lithuanian by C.R. Jurgėla. Bibliography: p. 95-96. DC102.8.L3K552 DLC CLU CSt CtY ICBM ICN ICU IEN IU InNd InUMH MnU MoU NIC NN NNC NBuU NcD NcU OCl OCU PU WaS WU

1171. --- Vieno prancūzo įspūdžiai Lietuvoje Vytauto laikais. [The Frenchman's impressions from the voyage to Lithuania] In Židinys (Kaunas), v.11, no.3(63), 1930, p. 232-245. See serials consulted.

1172. KOT, Stanisław. Die Reise eines Schweizers in Polen im 16. Jahrhundert. In Schweizerische Zeitschrift für Geschichte (Zürich), v.8, no.2, 1958, p. 193-221. See serials consulted.

1173. LANCASTER (DUCHY) ENGLAND. Expeditions to Prussia and the Holy Land made by Henry Earl of Derby (afterwards King Henry IV.) in the years 1390/91 and 1392/93; being the account kept by his treasurer during

two years. Edited from the origi-
nals by Lucy Toulmin Smith. [West-
minster, Printed for the Camden Society, 1894. cxiv, 360, 16 p.
(Camden Soc. Publications. ns., no.
52) (CA Camden)NN

1174. LELEWEL, Joachim. Guillebert de Lannoy et ses voyages en
1413-1414 et 1421, commentés en
français et en polonais. Bruxelles; Poznań, A. Vandale; J.K. Žu-
pański, 1844. ii, 46 p. In Lannoy, Guillebert de. Guillebert de
Lannoy et ses voyages. (BTH)NN MH

1175. PRUTZ, Hans. Rechnungen
über Heinrich von Derby's Preussen-
fahrten 1390-91 und 1392. Leipzig,
Dunker und Humblot, 1893. civ,
226 p. (Verein für die Geschichte
der Provinz Ost- und Westpreussen.
Publikationen) BM(Ac. 7351/5.)

1176. VAIČIULAITIS, Antanas. Vi-
duramžių poetas Machaut Lietuvoj.
[The medieval poet Machaut in Lithu-
ania] In Židinys (Kaunas), v.16,
no.2, 1939, p.181-190. See serials
consulted.

1177. ZAJĄCZKOWSKI, Stanisław.
Wilhelm de Machaut i jego wiadomości do dziejów Polski i Litwy w XIV
w. In Kwartalnik Historyczny (Lwów)
v. 43, 1929, p.217-228. See serials consulted.

III.8. DESCRIPTION AND TRAVEL,
PICTORIAL WORKS

1178. AUGUSTINAS, Vytautas. Li-
thuania. Lietuva 2. laida. Brooklyn,
N.Y., Ateitis, c1955] 119 p.(chief-
ly illus.) Lithuanian and English;
added title page in Lithuanian.
First edition published in 1951 un-
der title: Our country Lithuania.
DK511.L2A8 1955 DLC CaAEU CaOTP ICJ
ICBM IaU ICLJF InNd NB NbU NdU NN
NNC WaS

1179. --- Our country Lithuania.
New York, N.Y., [Leidykla Vaga]
1951. 115 p. (chiefly illus.) Lithuanian and English. DK511.L2A8
DLC CtPAM ICBM NN OC1 PU

1180. BABICKAS, Petras. Gintaro
krantas. [The Amber coast] Dailininkas Vladas Vijeikis. 3. papildytas leidimas. Chicago, Ill., Tėviškėlė, 1958. 96 p. (chiefly illus.)
maps. DK511.K77B3 1958 DLC CaOTP
CtTMF ICBM ICLJF PU

1181. --- Picturesque Lithuania...

Chicago, Ill., [ViVi Printing] 1958.
104 p. illus. plates, maps. Title
and text in English, Lithuanian, and
Spanish. DK511.L212B3 DLC CtPAM
ICBM PU

1182. BALČIŪNAS, A. and A. Milke-
vičius. Kaunas. [Kaunas] Šviesa,
1968. 1 v. illus. DK651.K125B34
DLC CaBVaS

1183. BALSYS, Al. Kaunas. [Fo-
tografavo ir išleido Al. Balsys.
Kaunas, Author, 192-] 62 p. illus.
947.52.B216 PU ICBM ICLJF

1184. GINTARINIS PAJŪRIS. The
amber coast. [Nuotraukos: P. Karpavičius. Eilioutas tekstas: Eug. Ma-
tuzevičius] Vilnius, Mintis, 1965.
[48] p. (chiefly illus) DK511.L2G6
DLC

1185. GUDELIS, Vytautas. Kuršių
Nerija ir Marios. [The Curonian
sand dunes and the Bay] Vilnius,
VPMLL, 1960. 17 p., 195 p. of
illus. (Lietuvos gamtos vaizdai)
DK511.C6G8 DLC CaOTP CtPAM ICBM
ICLJF PU

1186. HOLLER, Alfred. Wilna.
Wilno, 1917. 1 v. (chiefly illus.)
1638.472 NjP

1187. ISTORINĖS LIETUVOS ALBUMAS.
[The album of historical Lithuania]
[n.p.] 1959. 1 v. (chiefly illus.)
947.5.I CaOTP CtPAM

1188. JUKNEVIČIUS, D. Zarasai-
ežerų kraštas. [Zarasai the counry
of lakes. Kaunas] VPMLL [1957]
123 p. (chiefly illus.) fold. col.
map. DK651.Z36J8 DLC ICBM ICLJF

1189. JUKNEVIČIUS, J. Anykščiai
ir jų apylinkės. [Anykščiai and
its vicinity] Vilnius, VPMLL, 1959.
25 p. illus., map. DK651.A63J8
DLC PU

1190. KAKIES, Martin. Die Kuri-
sche Nehrung in 144 Bildern. Leer
(Ostfriesland), G.Rautenberg, 1960.
1 v. (unpaged, chiefly illus.) map.
Q 914.75.K127 PU NN

1191. ---, ed. Von Memel bis
Trakehnen in 144 Bildern. Leer
(Ostfriesenland), G. Rautenberg,
1960. 1 v. (chiefly illus.)
Q 943.11.K127 PU

1192. KARPAVIČIUS, P. Kaunas,
Mintis, 1966. [2], 40 p. of col.
illus. DK651.K125K28 DLC ICBM

1193. KLAIPĖDOS DIENA. [The Klaipėda day. Fotonuotraukos B. Alekna-

vičius. Sudarytojas ir teksto autorius S. Krivickas] Vilnius, Mintis,
1969. 96 p. illus. DK651.M29K56
PU DLC

1194. KONDRATENKA, B. Po Druski-
ninkus ir apylinkes. [Traveller's
guide to Druskininkai] Vilnius,
Mintis, 1968. 144 p. illus., maps.
DK651.D7K65 DLC

1195. KRIVICKAS, S. Lietuvos fotografija. [Lithuania in pictures]
Vilnius, Vaga, 1967. 1 v. (chiefly
illus.) 795Kr ICBM

1196. KUDABA, Česlovas. Ignalinos apylinkės. [The district of
Ignalina. Tekstas Č. Kudabos. Nuotraukos V. Sparnaičio] Vilnius,
Mintis, 1967. [72] p. (chiefly
col. illus.) DK511.I35K8 DLC

1197. KUNČIUS, Algimantas. Senojo Vilniaus vaizdai. [Views of the
old city of Vilnius. Dailininkas
V. Kalinauskas] Vilnius [Mintis]
1969. 255 p. of illus. Lithuanian,
English, and Russian. DK651.V4K85
DLC CtPAM ICBM PU

1198. LIETUVA, ŠALIS GRAŽIOJI.
[Lithuania, a beautiful country.
Albumą sudarė ir tekstus parašė P.
Pukys. Dailininkas V. Kalinauskas]
Vilnius, VPMLL, 1960. 1 v. (chief-
ly illus.) DK511.L2L4215 DLC ICLJF

1199. LIETUVA, ŠALIS MANO BRAN-
gioji. [Lithuania, my dear country.
Meninė dalis J. Firinausko. Tekstai
V. Šalčiūno. Weilheim-Teck, Ger.,
Atžalynas, n.d.] 88 p. illus.
G2Lie ICLJF

1200. LIETUVA VAIZDUOSE. Views
of Lithuania. [Hanau, Ger., L.T.B.
Hesseno apygardos komiteto leidinys,
1949] 1 v. (chiefly illus.), maps.
DK511.L212L47 DLC

1201. LIETUVOS FOTOGRAFIJA. [Li-
thuania in pictures. Sudarytojas
Skirmantas Valiulis] Vilnius, Vaga,
1971. 1 v. (chiefly illus.)
TR650.L54 PU

1202. LIETUVOS PILIAKALNIAI. [Li-
thuania's mounds] Vilnius, Mintis,
1967. 13 plates. (*QY)NN

1203. LITHUANIAN SOVIET SOCIALIST
Republic. [Moscow, Novosti Press
Agency Publishing House, 1967] 56
p., 32 leaves of illus. DK511.L2L73
DLC CaAEU CaOTU FU IaU InNd KU MH
NSyU NcD NcU PPiU TU ViU

1204. LITUANIA ILUSTRADA. [Reda-
tores: Rachel Portella Audenis e

Petras Babickas] Rio de Janeiro,
Frikas Mejeris, 1954. 131 p.
914.75.L720 1954 PU

1205. MATUTIS, Anselmas and Vytautas Stanionis. Dainava. [District
of Dainava] A. Matučio tekstas.
V. Stanionio fotonuotraukos. Vilnius, VPMLL, 1958. 237 p. illus.
914.75.M439.2 PU ICCC ICLJF

1206. MEDONIS, Ar. Baltijos pa-
jūriu. [Along the Baltic Sea coast]
Vilnius, VPMLL, 1962. [46] p. map.
illus. DK511.B28M38 DLC

1207. --- Druskininkai. [Vil'nius
Gos. izd-vo polit. i nauch. lit-ry
Litovskoi SSR, 1961] 1 v. (unpa-
ged, chiefly illus.) DK651.D7M4
DLC PU

1208. --- Po Sūduvą. [Through the
district of Sūduva. Nuotraukos P.
Karpavičiaus] Vilnius, VPMLL, 1962.
103 p. illus., ports. DK511.S9M4
DLC MH PU

1209. --- Trakai. [The town of
Trakai. Vilnius, VPMLL, 1957] 64 p.
illus. G2.Tra ICLJF

1210. --- --- 3. papildytas leidimas. Vilnius, Mintis, 1965. 58p.
illus. map. DK651.T69M4 1965 DLC
NN PU

1211. --- --- Khudozhnik L. Skers-
tonaite. [Perevod s litovskogo A.
Berman] Vil'nius, Gos. izd-vo polit. i nauch. lit-ry Litovskoi SSR,
1961. 62 p. illus. DK651.T69M4
1961 DLC

1212. --- Vilnius. [A pictorial
account of Vilnius] Vilnius, VGLL,
1960. 261 p. 914.5.Me ICBM

1213. MEŠYS, Juda. Klaipėda. [Ci-
ty of Klaipėda. Vilnius, 1963] [32]
p. (chiefly illus.) 914.25.M565 PU
CU NIC NcD OU

1214. --- --- [Perevod s litovs-
kogo] Vil'nius, Mintis, 1964. 92 p.
illus. DK651.M29M47 DLC NN

1215. --- Kurshiu Neringa. [The
Curonian sand dunes] Vil'nius, Gos.
izd-vo polit. i nauch. lit-ry Litovskoi SSR, L959. 123 p. illus.,
fold. map. DK511.K77M47 DLC

1216. --- Kuršių Neringa. [The
Curonian sand dunes] Vilnius,VPMLL,
1957. 123 p. (chiefly illus.)
DK511.K77M4 DLC ICBM ICLJF

1217. MILUKAS, Antanas. Lietuviškas albumas. [Lithuanian album]

Shenandoah, Pa., Spaustuvėje V.J.
Stagaro & Co., 1900. 3 v. illus.
Lithuanian and English. 891.92.
M649 PU ICLJF MH NN OCl RP

1218. MOŚCICKI, Henryk. Wilno.
Fotografje J. Bułhaka, okłada według rysunku R. Ruszczyca. Warszawa, F. Hoesick, 1922. 72 p. front.
plates. DK651.V4M6 CaBVaU NN OCl
PU

1219. PAČESA, R. and J. Sideravičius. Kapsukas-Sūduvos širdis.
[The town of Kapsukas (Marijampolė)
heart of Sūduva] Vilnius, Mintis,
1970. 45 p., 64 p. of illus.
914.5P ICBM

1220. RAKAUSKAS, Romualdas and
Antanas Sutkus. Šalis ta Lietuva
vadinas. [This is the country of
Lithuania. Skyrių tekstas Sigito
Gedos. Vilnius, Mintis, 1970] l v.
(chiefly illus.) DK511.L2R34 PU

1221. --- Vilniaus šiokiadieniai.
[Vilnius on the week-days] Vilnius,
Mintis, 1965. 258 p. (chiefly
illus) DK651.V4R3 DLC ICBM PU

1222. REPUBLIQUE SOCIALISTE SO-
vietique de Lithuania. [Moscou,
Éditions de l'agence de presse "Novosti", 1967. 64 p., 32 leaves of
illus. DK511.L2R44 DLC

1223. ŠAPOKA, Adolfas. Lithuania
through the ages. [Translated by
O. Saulaitienė. München,] T.J.
Vizgirda [1948] 62, [97] p. illus.
ports., maps. (Lithuania, country
and nation, 1) DK511.L2S335 DLC CLU
CaAEU CaMWU CaOTP CtPAM CtTMF CtY IU
ICLJF InU MH NB NN NNC OClW PU WyU

1224. DAS SCHÖNE LITAUEN. Wilna,
1918. 20 plates. Q 947.52.G694 PU

1225. SUTKUS, Antanas. Senojo
Vilniaus fragmentai. [The old Vilnius in pictures] Vilnius, Mintis,
1968. 16 plates. Fogg Art Mus. MH
NN

1226. THOMSON, Erik. Baltikum;
eine Erinnerung gesehen in 96 Auf-
nahmen. Landeskundliche Einfürung
von Erik Thomson. Frankfurt am
Main, W. Weidlich, 1963. 118 p.
(chiefly illus.) G q447.4.885 OCl
PU

1227. UŽDAVINYS, Vincas, ed. Laisvoji Lietuva be Vilniaus. [Free
Lithuania without Vilnius] Kaunas,
Vilniui vaduoti sąjunga, 1935. 120p.
illus. GeVil ICLJF ICBM

1228. --- Vilniaus krašto vaizdų

albumas. [Vilnius region album]
Kaunas, Vilniui vaduoti sąjunga,
1934. 112 p. illus. G2Vil
ICLJF ICBM

1229. VILAINIS, Adomas, ed. Istorinės Lietuvos albumas. Album of
historical Lithuania. Chicago, Ill.,
Nemunas, 1959. 268 p. illus.
DK511.L2V43 DLC ICBM ICLJF NNC OCl

1230. VILNIAUS ETIUDAI. Vil'nius-
kie etiudy. Vilniaus scetches. Eilės Vl. Mozuriūno. Nuotraukos Vl.
Sparnaičio. Vilnius, Mintis, 1967.
48 p. (chiefly illus.) Balt 8100.04
MH

1231. VILNIUS [RUDENĮ] Vilnius
in autumn. Vilnius, Mintis, 1964.
50 p. (chiefly col. illus.) DK651.
V4V446 DLC

1232. VILNIUS [VAKARE] Vilnius
at night. [Sudarė O. Aleksa. Vilnius, Mintis, 1965] l v. (chiefly
illus, part. col.) DK651.V455 DLC

1233. VIZGIRDA, Tadas J., ed.
Vilnius the capital of Lithuania;
105 illustrations. [München, Author,
1948] 62 p. illus., plans, 63
plates. (Lithuania, country and nation, 2) DK651.V4V48 DLC CaOONL
CtY DCU DGU ICLJF ICU IEN MB MH MiD
NICNN NNC NjP OCl PP PPT PU RPB

1234. VYTAUTO DIŽIOJO MIRTIES 500
metų sukaktuvėms paminėti albumas,
1430-1930. [Album in commemoration
of the 500th anniversary of Vytautas
the Great] Ed. H. Serafinas. Kaunas, Spindulio spaustuvė, 1933.
474 p. illus. XL 970.9Se CtPAM
ICLJF

1235. ZGIRSKIS, Česlovas, comp.
Lietuva šiandien. [Lithuania today.
Sudarė Česlovas Zgirskis. Dailinin-
kas Vytautas Kalinauskas. Vilnius,
Mintis] 1964. l v. (chiefly illus,
part. col.) DK511.L2Z45 DLC CaOTP
CtTMF ICU NIC NcD PU

1236. ŽILIUS, Jonas. Albumas
lietuviškos parodos Paryžiuje, 1900
metuose. [The album of the Lithuanian exhibition in Paris, 1900] Jonas Žilinskas. Plymouth, Pa., Spauda "Vienybės Lietuvninkų", 1902.
22 p. diagr., illus. 572.9475Z67
PU

IV. SERIALS

IV.1. DAILY NEWSPAPERS

1237. DARBO LIETUVA. Nr.1-134;
liepos 16-spalio 31, 1940. Kaunas,
1940. 134 no. Daily. Superseded
by Tarybų Lietuva. OKentU(1-134)

1238. DIENOS ŽINIOS. Augsburg,
Ger., 1946-49. CtPAM(1946, 1949)
OKentU(no.[652-732])

1239. DRAUGAS; lietuvių katalikų
laikraštis. 1- ; liepa 1909- .
Wilkes Barre, Pa.; Chicago, Ill.
Weekly; daily since 1916. See serials consulted.

1240. XX AMŽIUS. Kaunas, Ryto
bendrovė, 1936-40. Daily. CtTMF(
1936-1940) DLL NNCL OKentU(1937, no.
263,285)

1241. KATALIKAS; Amerikos lietuvių dienraštis. Chicago, Ill.,1899-
1917. Weekly; daily since 1914.
(*QYC)NN(1914)

1242. KLAIPĖDOS ŽINIOS; politikos,
ekonomijos ir kultūros dienraštis.
Klaipėda, 1924-26. Daily. Supersedes Prūsų Lietuvininkų Balsą.
PU(1924, no.1-252)

1243. LAISVĖ. Boston, Mass.;Brook-
lyn, N.Y., 1911- . Weekly; twice
a week, 1911-1919; daily since 1919;
twice a week since 1958. F71.L717L
PU(30-34; 1941- june 1944)

1244. LIETUVA. Gruodžio 6, 1892-
gegužės 8, 1920. Chicago, Ill.,
1892-1920. Weekly; daily.
BN(1900, no.1-52) ICRL(Aug.31, 1917-
Oct. 1918; Nov. 1918-May 8, 1920)
NN(1917-Jan.1919) PU(1925-1928; in-
complete; microfilm)

1245. LIETUVA. Nr.1-2704; sausis 1919-sausio 31, 1928. Kaunas,
1919-28. Daily. PU[1925-1928] NN

1246. LIETUVOS AIDAS. Metai 1-2,
nr.1-214; rugsėjis 1917-gruodis
1918. Vilnius, 1917-18. See serials consulted.

1247. --- Metai 1(3)-13(15); vasario 1, 1928-birželio 15, 1940.
Kaunas, Pažangos bendrovė, 1928-40.
Supersedes "Lietuva" and also previously published "Lietuvos Aidas"
Superseded by "Darbo Lietuva" See
serials consulted.

1248. LIETUVOS ŽINIOS; politikos,
visuomenės ir literatūros laikraštis. Birželio 19, 1909-rugpiūčio 15,
1915 (Vilnius); vasario 16, 1922-
rugpiūčio 1, 1940. Vilnius; Kaunas,
1909-40. Twice a week; three times
a week; daily. See serials consulted.

1249. LIETUWOS KELEIVIS; wyriau-
sias kraszto lietuwių dienrasztis.
Sausis 1924-kovas 1939. Klaipėda,
1924-39. 3 no. a week; daily.
CtPAM(1927-1928)

1250. NAUJIENOS. 1- ; vasario
19, 1914- . Chicago, Ill., Lithuanian News Publishing Co. Weekly;
daily. See serials consulted.

1251. RYTAS. Gruodžio 15,1923-ba-
landžio 4, 1936. Kaunas, Žaibo bendrovė, 1923-36. Daily. CtTMF(1932-
1935)

1252. TARYBŲ LIETUVA. Spalio 1,
1940-birželio 21, 1941; liepa 1,
1944- . Kaunas; Vilnius, Lietuvos
Aukščiausios tarybos prezidiumas.
Daily. Suspended June 21, 1941-
July 1, 1944. CtPAM(1940-1941)
CtTMF(1940) OKentU(1940, no.1-9,11-
52,54-65; 1941,no.1-8)

1253. VIENYBĖ. Metai 1- ; vasario 16, 1886- . Brooklyn, N.Y.
[etc.] Daily. Title varies; Wieni-
bė Lietuwniku, 1886-1889; Vienybe
Lietuvniku, 1890-1892; Vienybė Lietuvninkų, 1893-1919; Vienybė, Jan.1,
1920- . CtPAM(1897-1906) ICBM(1903
-1906) IU(1918-1924) OKentU([1959-
1965])

1254. VILNIAUS ŽINIOS. Nr.1-1175;
gruodis 1904-kovas 1909. Vilnius,
P. Vileišis, 1904-09. Daily.
CtTMF(1906) OKentU(1905, v.1, no.1-
61, 63-245, 250-299; 1906, v.2, no.
8-24,68-91,260; 1907, v.3, no.49-52,
64-79,109,113-117,120,122-124,127-
131,133-137,139,141,144-146,148,152,
154,158,160-162,164-165, 167-168,
173-175,179,181,186,188,191,192,196,
199,200,203,206,211,213,216,220,222,
223,226,229; 1908, v.4, no.2,3,12-
14,17,19,23,24,28,36,38-41,43,48,50-
54,56,60,62,63,72,79,84-86,92-96,98,
100,101,104,108-111,113,114,119,123-
128,130,132,133,135,138,142,144-146,
148-151,153,155,157,159,160,162,163,
167,170-172,178,180,185,187-190,192-
198,201-206,208,210,212,213,216,218,
219,223-225,228,234,236,240,242,246,
249-253,261-265,267,269,271,273,276-
278,281,285,286,288,293; 1909, v.5,
no.1-4,7,12,13,18,20,22-24,26,28-30,
33,35-37,40,43; on microfilm)

IV.2. PERIODICALS

1255. AIDAI: mėnesinis kultūros žurnalas. München, Ger.; Kennebunkport, Me.; Brooklyn, N.Y., 1945- . Monthly. In United States published by Franciscan Fathers; since Oct. 1949 in Kennebunkport, Me., and since Oct. 1952 in Brooklyn, N.Y. See serials consulted.

1256. AIDAS. Kovo 1911-vasaris 1912. Waterbury, Conn., 1911-12. Monthly. MeKPF(1911-1912)

1257. AIDAS LIETUVOS DARBININKŲ gyvenimo. Metai 1, no.1-3. (Serija 2) Zürich, 1899. BM(P.P. 3554. nba.(2.))

1258. AKADEMIKAS. Gruodis 1932-birželis 1940. Kaunas, Neo-Lithuania korp., 1932-40. Biweekly. CtTMF(1935-1939)

1259. AMERIKOS LIETUVIS. Worchester, Mass., 1907. 57.92.Am355 PU(no.1-5,7-14)

1260. APSZWIETA; literatūros ir mokslo mėnesinis laikrasztis. nr.1-15. Tilžė, Lietuvių mokslo draugystė Amerikoje, 1892-93. Monthly. BM(1-150 ICCC(1-15) OKentu(v.2, no.7-8)

1261. APŽVALGA. Nr.1-75; lapkričio 10, 1945-lapkričio 9, 1946. Kirchheim Teck, Ger., 1945-46. CtPAM(1946, no.23-24,26-75) OKentU (1945-1946, no.6-75; no.23-75 are on microfilm)

1262. ATEITIS; katalikiškojo jaunimo žurnalas. Nr.1- ; vasaris 1911- . Kaunas; München, Ger.; Tübingen, Ger.; Schwäbische Gmünde, Ger.; Brooklyn, N.Y. illus., ports. Monthly except July and August. See serials consulted.

1263. AUŠRA; lietuviškas katalikiškas laikraštis lietuviams rytiečiams šviesti. Nr.1-152; spalio 6, 1911-rugsėjo 1915. Vilnius, biweekly. CtPAM(1911-1915)

1264. AUSZRA; laikrasztis iszleidžiamas Lietuvos miletoju. Metai 1-4, nr.1-40, 1883-1886. Tilžėje; Ragainėj, Alban und Kibelka; Otto v. Mauderode [etc.] 1883-86. 4 v. BM(P.P. 4741. ab.; 1-4) CtPAM(1883-1886) CtTMF(1883-1886) ICBM(1883, no.1-7)

1265. BALTIC BULLETIN. News of Lithuania, Latvia and Estonia. v.1, no.1-3; 1922-May 1923. New York,

N.Y., 1922-23. CSt-H(no.3) MH(no.1, 3)

1266. BALTIC REVIEW. v.1-3(no.1-12); March 1, 1944-May 15, 1946. New York, N.Y., Joint Baltic American Information Committee, 1944-46. 3 v. in 1. No more published. D731.B35 DLC CU CtY ICU ULA UPB

1267. --- v.1-2; Dec. 1945-May 1949. Stockholm, Sweden, Baltic Humanitarian Association, 1945-49. 2 v. illus., maps. Irregular. Supersedes Revue Baltique and superseded in Dec. 1953 by the Baltic Review" published in New York. N.Y. DK511.B25B32 DLC CL CLSU CSt-H CU CaBVaU CoU CtY DW ICU IEN IaU InU IU KyU MB MH MH-L MH-P MdBJ MiD MiU MnU MoS MoU NN NNA NNC NNHi(1) NStC NNUN NjP NjR(1) OCl PPiU PU TNJ TxDaM VU WU WaS

1268. --- No.1- ; Dec. 1953- . New York, N.Y., Committee for a free Estonia, Latvia and Lithuania. Supersedes The Baltic Review published in Stockholm 1945-1949. DK511. B25B19 CaAEU(1-3,5,7-8,10,12,15-16, 19-) AMAU AzU CLU(9-) CtY(1-) CU(4-) DLC IEN(1-) KPT(4-) MH MiDW NN(1-) MnU(1,5-) NIC(8-) NNC(1-) NjP NcU (1-) NjR(19-) OKentU(1961-1971) OU (1-) PU(1-) ViU(4-) WU(1-)

1269. BALTIJAS UNIJA. L'Union baltique. Bulletin. Riga [1933-1934] 2 v. illus., ports. English or French translations appear in parallel columns with the text in Lettish or Estonian. DK511.B25B34 DLC CtY ICU(1) NN MH(1) NjP

1270. BARAS; literatūros ir meno mėnesinis žurnalas. Kaunas, 1925. 10 no. 891.92.B232 PU ICCC(1-3)

1271. BENDRAS ŽYGIS. Nr.1-4; gruodžio 17, 1938-vasario 28, 1939. Klaipėda, 1938-39. 4 no. Semimonthly (irregular) Title varies: no.1, "Žygis". Publication suspended by the government. (*QYA)NN(1-4)

1272. BIRUTĖ; lietuvių tautos veidrodis. Savaitinis laikraštis skiriamas visiems lietuviams. Leidėjas: J. Vanagat. Metai 1-5, nr.1-39; rugsėjis 1909-rugsėjis 1913. Tilžė, 1909-13. 39 no. one no. every six weeks. Balt 7825.8 MH(1-[4],5) MeKPF(1909-1910)

1273. DABARTIS. Tilžė; Kaunas; Baltstogė, Ob-Ost, 1915-18. 440 no. Superseded by Nauja Gadynė. Zeta BB165-202DI CtY

1274. DAINAVA; literatūros ir dailės lapai. [Redagavo Faustas Kirša ir Balys Sruoga] 1. Knyga.[Published by "Vilkolakis," Kaunas] Tilžė, "Spaudos" spaustuvė, 1920. 118 p. 891.92C.D144 PU CtTMF ICCC InNd OCl

1275. DARBAS; kultūros ir visuomenės mokslų žurnalas. Nr.1-45; 1947-1960. Boston, Mass.; Brooklyn, N.Y., Lietuvių darbininkų draugija, 1947-60. 45 no. in 3 v. Quarterly. AP95.L5D37 PU(1-45) NN (26-45) OKentU(1948-1950, 1956, 1958-1960; v.2, no.1; v.3, no.2; v.4, no.3; v.10, no.1-4; v.12, no. 1-2; v.13, no.4; v.14, no.1)

1276. DARBININKAS; katalikiškosios minties laikraštis. Nr.1- ; rugsėjo 19, 1915- . Boston, Mass.; Brooklyn, N.Y. Twice a week. CtPAM(1915-) OKentU(1919-1920, 1940, 1943-1946, 1959, no.1-86)

1277. DARBININKŲ BALSAS. Paris; London, Lietuviškoji social-demokratiškoji partija, 1901-03. BM(P.P. 3554. ela.)(Metai 1, no.1-7; metai 2, no.1-2) OKentU(1903-1905; v.2, no.2; v.3, no.1-5,7; v.4, no.1,4)

1278. DIENOVIDIS; literatūros, meno ir kultūros žurnalas. Nr.1-19. Kaunas, Sakalas, 1938-40. 19 no. Monthly. ICCC(1938, no.1-8)

1279. DIRVA; Lithuanian quarterly publication. Shenandoah, Pa., 1898-1906. 9 v. Merged in 1903 with Žinyčia, Tilsit and was published as Dirva-Žinynas for Lithuania, and Dirva for United States. See serials consulted.

1280. DIRVA; tautinės minties savaitraštis. Nr.1- ; rugpiūtis, 1916- . Cleveland, Ohio. Weekly; twice a week. See serials consulted.

1281. DRAUGIJA; literatūros, mokslo ir politikos mėnesinis laikraštis. Nr.1-153; 1907-1923; Nauja serija.T.1, nr.1-10, sausis-spalis 1923. Kaunas, Šv. Kazimiero draugija; "Šviesos" spaustuvė, 1907-23. Suspended 1915-1919. See serials consulted.

1282. DRAUGIJA; Kauno arkivyskupijos organas. Kaunas, 1937-40. Biweekly. See serials consulted.

1283 EKONOMIKA; ekonomistų žurnalas. Kaunas, Ekonomistų draugija, 1935-40. 6 v. NN(1-)

1284. ELTA PRESS SERVIZIO D'INFORmazioni lituane. 1- ; 1954- . Roma. DLC([1]-)

1285. ELTA-PRESSEDIENST. Nr.1- ; Januar 20, 1953- . Reutlingen,Ger., Lithuanian Press Service. irregular. Also published in Lithuanian since 1945, Italian in Rome since 1954, and English in New York, N.Y., since 1956. DLC([1954]-) CtPAM([1954-1967]) NN(English ed. no.8-)

1286. GABIJA; neperiodinis literatūros žurnalas. Nr.1-5. Brooklyn, N.Y., Lietuvių spaudos centras Amerikoje, 1951-55. 5 no. in 1 v. illus. AP95.L5G3 DLC(1-4) ICCC(1-4) ICLJF(1-4) PU(1-5)

1287. GAISAI; meno ir literatūros žurnalas. Nr.1-9 10, 1930; nr.1-5, 1931. Kaunas, 1930-31. ICCC(1930, no.1-7; 1931, no.1-5)

1288. GARNYS; satyrinis lietuvių katalikų laikraštis. Kaunas, 1909-1910. ICBM(1910) MePKF(1910)

1289. GIMTASAI KRAŠTAS; kraštotyros organas. Šiauliai, Kraštotyros draugija; Lietuvos Mokslų akademija, 1934-44. illus. Irregular; quarterly. See serials consulted.

1290. GIMTOJI KALBA. Kaunas,1933-41. 9 v. 10 no.a year. See serials consulted.

1291. --- ; bendrinės kalbos laikraštis. Lietuvių kalbos draugijos organas. Nr.1-11; liepa/rugsėjis 1958-1968. Riverside, Ill., JAV LB Kultūros Fondas. Quarterly. See serials consulted.

1292. GINTARAS; neperiodinis literatūros žurnalas. 1-4 ; 1945-1948. Haffkrug, Ger.; Spakenberg, Ger., 1945-48. Irregular. CaOTP(1948, no.1) ICCC(1946, no.8-10; 1947, no.11; 1948, no.1) OKentU(1946, no. 6-10; 1947, no.11)

1293. GIRIOS AIDAS; miškininkystės žurnalas. 1- ; 1950- . Chicago, Ill., Lietuvos miškininkų sąjunga išeivijoje. ports. Semiannual (irregular) 99.8G44 DNAL([2]-) DLC([4] ICCC(1950-1955, 1956, no.14, 1957, no.15) NN[2]-) OKentU(1952)

1294. GYVENIMAS; mėnesinis žurnalas. Chicago, Ill., A. Žymantas, 1926-29. 4 v. Ceased publication with v.4, no.5; May, 1929. NN(v.1-3, no.3,9,11; v.4, no.1-5)

1295. Į LAISVĘ; lietuvių Fronto bičiulių politikos žurnalas. 1- ; 1941- . Kaunas; Los Angeles, Calif. Lietuvių Frontas. June 25, 1941-December 31, 1942 daily newspaper. Suspended by German occupational

authorities and 1943-1944 published
as underground irregular newspaper
in Marijampolė, Utena, Telšiai, etc.
In 1948 published 3 no. in Germany
and since December 1953 publication
continued in Detroit, Mich. and Los
Angeles, Calif. See serials consulted.

1296. JAUNALIETUVIŲ VADOVAS. Nr.1,
1936; nr.1-4, 1937. Kaunas, 1936-37.
Quarterly. ICCC(1937, no.4)

1297. JAUNIEJI; pradedančiųjų rašytojų almanachas. Knyga 1- ;
1948- . [Kaunas] VGLL. PG8713.J3
DLC

1298. JAUNOJI KARTA. Rugsėjo 15,
1928-birželio 8, 1940. Kaunas, Jaunosios Lietuvos sąjunga, 1928-40.
Monthly; since 1930 biweekly, and
since 1933 weekly. CtPAM(1937-1938)
ICBM(1035) OKentU(1938, no.26)

1299. JAUNOJI LIETUVA; literatūros
ir mokslo laikraštis. Metai 1-3,
no.4; kovas 1914-balandis 1916.
Chicago, Ill., 1914-16. Irregular.
CtTMF(1914-1916) ICCC(1916, no.1)
NN(1-3) OKentU(1914-Feb.,1915, v.1,
no.10-12; 1916, v.3, no.1-4)

1300. ---; tautinės minties žurnalas. Rugsėjo 1923-birželis 1940.
Kaunas, Neo-Lithuania korp.; Jaunosios Lietuvos sąjunga; Pažangos bendrovė, 1923-40. Irregular, 1923-29;
monthly, March 1929-1940. Suspended 1930-April 1935. Subtitle varies: 1929-1940, Tautinės minties
moksleivių žurnalas. CtPAM([1928-
1929]) CtTMF(1939-[1940])

1301. KALBA; bendrinės kalbos žurnalas. Kaunas, Sakalo bendrovė,
1930. 3 no. in 1 v. (208 p.) See
serials consulted.

1302. KARDAS; iliustruotas satyros, juokų ir kritikos žurnalas.
Metai 1-10; rugpiūtis 1913-lapkritys
1923. Worchester, Mass.; Waterbury,
Conn.; Boston, Mass.; Chicago, Ill.,
1913-23. 10 v. Supercedes "Šakė"
in April 1916. (*QYA)NN([1-10])

1303. KARO ARCHYVAS. Kaunas, Krašto apsaugos ministerija, Karo mokslo skyrius, 1925-39. 11 v. D552.
L5A5 DLC(1-2,11) ICCC(7) PU(2-4,
6-8)

1304. KARYS. Gegužės 22, 1919-lie-
pos 5, 1940. Kaunas, Krašto apsaugos ministerijos literatūros skyrius, 1919-40. CtPAM(1930-1933,
[1934-1935], 1936-[1940]) CtTMF(1936-
1939) ICCC([1934-1935], 1937, 1939-
1940]) OKentU(1944, no.27)

1305. ---; pasaulio lietuvių karių-veteranų mėnesinis žurnalas.
Metai 1- ; 1950- . Brooklyn, N.Y.
Ten numbers a year. See serials
consulted.

1306. KELEIVIS. Boston, 1905- .
Weekly. F71.L714 PU(35-36,41-42,44-
52; 1940-1957) NN(37-)

1307. KELEIVIS; Mažosios Lietuvos
lietuvių laikraštis. 1- ; 1954- .
Hannover, Kl.-litauischer Heimatver-
ein. DLC(1954-)

1308. KETVIRTAS TAUTOS ŽODIS.
Kaunas, 1933. Monthly. NN(v.1,no.
1-4)

1309. KNYGOS; bibliografijos ir
kritikos žurnalas. Nr.1-6. Kaunas,
1922-24. PU(1-6)

1310. KOMMUNIST. Vil'nius, 1946- .
illus., ports., maps. Monthly.
HX8.K565 DLC CaOTU CtY NcD ViU

1311. KOMUNARAS. no.1-14; gruodis 1921-vasaris 1923. [Moscow] Ros-
siiskaia kommunisticheskaia partiia.
TSentral'nyi komitet. Litovskaia
sektsiia, 1921-23. (*QYA)NN(1-12)

1312. KOMUNISTAS; Lietuvos komunistų partijos žurnalas. T.1- ;
1946- . Vilnius, Lietuvos KPCK laikraščių ir žurnalų leidykla. illus.,
ports. Monthly. HX8.K588 DLC(38-)
OKentU(1972)

1313. KOMUNISTAS; Lietuvos ir Baltarusijos komunistų partijos C.K. organas. Vilnius; Smolensk, 1918-20.
Folio HX8.K588 PU(no.1-41,43; Dec.20,
1918-April 6, 1919) BM(no.111,124,
125) DLC(38-)

1314. KOLUMBIJOS LIETUVIS. 1- ;
liepos 1, 1950- . Medellin, Columbia, Kolumbijos lietuvių katalikų komitetas. Irregular. CtTMF(no.1-9;
1950-1953) DLC(3-) ICCC(no.1-16;
1950-1956) OKentU(1953, no.8,9)

1315. KOVA; lietuvių socialistų
sąjungos savaitraštis. Philadelphia,
Pa., Lietuvių socialistų sąjunga,
1905-18. Weekly. CtPAM(1905-1907)
ICCC(1907) ICBM(1909-1911) WHi([1],
6-12; 1905-1917)

1316. KRISTAUS KARALIAUS LAIVAS.
1- ; 1920- . Chicago, Ill., Weekly.
CtTMF(1930-1931, 1942-1962) ICCC([
1922-1924],1926-1932,[1933-1940],1941-
1956-)

1317. KRIVULĖ; iliustruotas žurnalas. Metai 1-3, no.33/34; liepa 1923
gruodis 1925. Kaunas, K. Puida; Lie-

tuvos telegramų agentūra Elta,1923-
25. 4 v. Monthly. (*QYA)NN(yr2,
no.4-8,10; yr3, no.7) DLC([2-3])
PU(yr3, no.10)

1318. KULTŪRA; mėnesinis iliustruotas mokslo, visuomenės ir literatūros žurnalas. Šiauliai, Kultūros bendrovė, 1923-41. Monthly.
See serials consulted.

1319. KULTŪROS BARAI. Vilnius,
Kultūros ministerija, 1956- . Bimonthly, 1956-1957,1959; 5 nos. in
1958; monthly, 1960- . Title varies: 1956-1964, "Meno saviveikla".
Unclassified DLC(1966-) InU(1968-)
PU(1967-) OKentU(1967, no.5,8-11,
1969-1972)

1320. KUNIGŲ VIENYBĖS BIULETENIS.
Brooklyn, N.Y., 1940-51. Monthly,
1940-1944; irregular, 1945-1951.
Superseded by LUX Christi in 1951.
ICCC(1940, [1941-1944])

1321. KURYBA; literatūros žurnalas. Kaunas, 1943-44. 5 no.
57.92.K968 PU(1943, no.1; 1944, no.
1-4)

1322. LAIKAS. Lapkričio 1, 1948-
Avellaneda, Argentina, Avellanedos
Marijonai. Biweekly. CtTMF(1948-
1949, no.1-15; 1953, 1960-1965, no.
265-375) ICCC(1948, no.1-3; 1949,
no.1-4,6-12)

1323. LAIŠKAI LIETUVIAMS. Metai
1- ; 1950- . Chicago, Ill., Lithuanian Jesuit Fathers. 11 no. a
year. CtPAM(1950-) CtTMF(1950-)
ICLJF(1950-) ICCC(1950-) OKentU(1950-
1973)

1324. LAISVOJI MINTIS; mėnesinis
iliustruotas mokslo ir literatūros
laikraštis. Sausis 1910-gegužis
1915. Scranton, Pa., Laisvosios
minties bendrovė, 1910-15. 60 no.
Monthly. CtPAM(1910-1915) ICCC(1910-
1915) NN(1913-1915)

1325. LIAUDIES ŪKIS; mėnesinis žurnalas, Lietuvos TSR Valstybinės plano komisijos, Liaudies ūkio tarybos
ir Mokslo akademijos Ekonomikos instituto. Nr.1- ; 1958- . Vil'nius, Gosplan Litovskoi SSR. Monthly. Unclassified DLC(1961-) MH(
1961-) OKentU(1964, no.6; 1968, no.
5,11)

1326. LIEPSNOS; dvisavaitinis katalikių mergaičių iliustruotas laikraštis. Sausis 1937-birželis 1940.
Kaunas, Pavasarininkių mergaičių sąjunga, 1937-40. Biweekly. CtTMF
(1937-1939)

1327. LIETUVA; politikos žurnalas.

New York, N.Y., 1952-56. 8 no.
See serials consulted.

1328. LIETUVIS. Philadelphia, Pa.,
1901. Weekly. Ceased publication
Oct. 1901. NN(1901, no.1-6,8-10,12)

1329. --- Liepos 23, 1949-birželio
16, 1950. Memmingen, Ger., 1949-50.
69 no. Twice a week, Jul.23-Dec.23,
1949; weekly, Jan.5-June 16, 1950.
NN(no.1-69; negative microfilm)
OKentU(1949-1950)

1330. LIETUVIŲ DIENOS. Lithuanian
Days. Metai 1-. ; 1946- . Los Angeles, Clif., A.F. Skirius. illus.
Monthly except July and August. See
serials consulted.

1331. LIETUVOS DARBININKAS. Robotnik Litewski. Nr.1-3; 1896-1899.
Zürich [etc.] J. Brandt, 1896-99.
3 no. BM(P.P. 3554 emb.(2.); (no,3)

1332. LIETUVOS MOKYKLA: KATALIKIŠkosios krypties mėnesinis pedagogikos
žurnalas. Kaunas, Lietuvių katalikų
mokytojų sąjunga, 1918-40. Monthly.
See serials consulted.

1333. LIETUVOS PAJŪRIS. Montreal,
Que., Kanados Mažosios Lietuvos bičiulių draugijų centro valdyba, 1960-
72. 42 no. Irregular; quarterly.
Unclassified DLC(2-)

1334. LIETUVOS SPARNAI. Metai 1-6;
sausis 1935-birželis 1940. [Kaunas]
1935-40. 6 v. illus., diagrs.
Monthly. TL504.L5 DLC(1-4)

1335. LIETUVOS ŪKININKAS. Gruodžio
1, 1905-birželis 1915; gruodis 1918-
birželio 20, 1940. Vilnius; Kaunas,
Varpo bendrovė, 1905-40. Weekly.
BM(1-9, no.29; 1905-1914) CtPAM(1905-
1906) ICBM(1909) NN(1913-1915,[1921],
1922-1924,[1925,1926,[1927],1928-
1929,[1940] OKentU(1909, no.1-59;
1912, no.1-152; 1913, no.1-154; 1914,
no.1-75,79-197; 1915, no.1-87; on
microfilm)

1336. LIETUVOS ŪKIS; mėnesinis visuomenės ūkio ir finansų laikraštis.
Finansų ministerijos leidinys.
T.[1]-6, Metai [1]-7; gruodis 1921-
gruodis 1928. Kaunas, Valstybės
spaustuvė [etc., 1921-28] 6 v. in 2.
(75 no) HC337.L5A16 DLC CtPAM(1-75)
NN(1-67,69-75)

1337. LIETUVOS ŪKIS IR RINKA. Litauens Wirtschaft und Markt. Nr.1- .
10/11; sausis/kovas 1930-balandis/rugsėjis 1932. Kaunas, Spindulio bendrovė, 1930-32. 3 v. in 1. maps, tables, diagrams. Quarterly (irregular) Published by Centralinis statistikos biuras. In Lithuanian and Ger-

man. Supersedes Lietuvos ūkis and
Tautos ūkis. HC337.L5A162 DLC
CtTMF(1932, no.1-3) BM MH(no.1-8,
10 11) NN(1930-1932, no.1-9) NNC
(1931-1932, no.5-9) NjP

1338. LITAUEN. Nr.1-32; Mai 1916-
Februar 15, 1919. Bern; Lausanne,
Librairie Centrale des Nationalités
[etc.] 1916-19. Monthly. WU(yr1,
no.1-2,4-7; yr2, no.1,4,6-7,10-12;
yr3, no.1-9)

1339. LITERATŪRA IR MENAS. 1- ;
liepa 1946- . Vilnius, Lietuvos
TSR Rašytojų sąjunga. Weekly. See
serials consulted.

1340. LITHUANIA. v.1-6, no.6;
June 1916-October 1924. New York,
N.Y.; Chicago, Ill., 1916-24. 6 v.
Title varies: vol.1, no.1-7; vol.5-
6, no.3, as "Booster"; vol.1, no.8-
vol.4, as "Lithuanian Booster."
Suspended Sept. 1918-Dec.1919, and
Jan.1921-Nov. 1922. ICU([4]-[6])
IEG(6) NN([1-3]-6)

1341. LITHUANIA. ŠVIETIMO MINIS-
TERIJA. Švietimo ministerijos žinios. [News Bulletin of the Department of Education] Klaipėda, Ryto
bendrovė, 1931-33. 3 v. in 2.
ports., tables, forms. L466.L5A32
DLC

1342. LITHUANIA TODAY. 1- ;
1965- . [Vilnius, Mintis.] illus.
Translation of "Lietuva šiandien"
Issued by the Lithuanian Society
for Friendship and Cultural Rela-
tions with Foreign Countries.
DK511.L2L42173 DLC IaU IU MH(1-3)
NcD

1343. LITHUANIAN AMERICAN WEEK.
Chicago, Ill., 1941-42. Bi-weekly;
irregular. NN(Oct.15/Dec.24, 1941-
Jan.2/May 22, 1942) OKentU(1942,
v.11, no.20)

1344. LITHUANIAN BULLETIN. v.1-
9, no.7; April 15, 1943-July 1951.
New York, N.Y., Lithuanian National
Council; Lithuanian American Coun-
cil, 1943-51. DK511.L2A26 DLC(1-)
AU(1-) CLSU(1-) CSt-H([1]-) CU(1-)
CtPAM(1943-51) CtY(1-9) DCE(1-) FTS
(1-) FU([1-5],6-8) GU(1-) IaU(1-)
InU(1-) IU(1-9) IEN(1-6) MH(1-9)
MdBJ(1-) MnU(1-) MoS([2]-) NIC(1-9)
NBuU(1-) NN(1-) NNC(1-) NcD(1-) NjP
(1-) NjR(1-) OC1(1-) OC1W(1-) PPi
PPT(1-) WU(1-9) WaU(1-)

1345. LITHUANIAN CULTURAL INSTITU-
TE. Publications. Section I: Lithu
anian language and literature. Chi-
cago, Ill., 1942. 2 no. ports. map.
PG8503.L5 CU AzU(1-) DLC(1-2) InU(1)
MH(1-2) MdBE(1) MiU(1-2) NN(1-2)
NNC(1-2) NNU(1-2) NcD(1-2) NcU(1)

MH(1-2) MdBE(1) MiU(1-) NN(1-2) NNC
(1-20 NNU(1-2) NcD(1-2) NcU(1) OkU
OrU PU(1-2) RPB(1-2) WU(1-2)

1346. LITHUANIAN INFORMATION BU-
REAU, PHILADELPHIA. A plea for the
Lithuanians, a monthly review. [Phi-
ladelphia, Pa.] 1916-17. 11 no.
DK511.L2L5 DLC MH NN(2,8)

1347. LITHUANIAN INFORMATION SER-
VICE, BROOKLYN, N.Y. Bulletin. no.
1- ; 1940- . Brooklyn, N.Y.
CU([1-9]) DLC(1-2) MdBE(1-2) NN(1-)
VU(2)

1348. LITHUANIAN REVIEW. Philadelphia, Pa., Lithuanian Information Bureau, 1918-19. 3 no. (Lithuanian
Information Bureau, Philadelphia, Pa.)
A plea for the Lithuanians, no.12-15.
940.91.L71 PP NjP MH(1-3)

1349. LITHUANIAN SITUATION. V.1-
12 (no.1-148); Aug. 3, 1940-Dec.
1957. Washington, D.C. [Lithuanian
Legation] 1940-46. 5 v. in 3. Title
varies: July 1941-Nov. 1954, Current
News on the Lithuanian Situation.
Suspended Sept. 1940-May 1941.
DK511.L2L72 DLC(1-) AU(1-) CL([1]-)
CLSU(1-) CSt-H(1-) CU(1-) CoD(4-)
CtY(no.1-148) DCE(1-) FU([3-12]) ICN
(1-) ICU(1-) IEN(1-) IU(1-) IaU(1-)
InU(1-) KyLo(1-) MB(1-) MH(1-) MnU(
1-) NBC(4-) NBuG(1-) NIC([1]-) NN(1-)
NNHi(1-) NNQ([4]-) NjP(1-) NjR(1-)
OCU(3-) OC1(1-9) OC1W(1-) OrU(no.3-
148) PP(4-) PPiU([1-2]-) WU(1-24)
WaS(1-9, no.9) WaU(1-12)

1350. LITUANUS. V.1- ; 1954- .
Brooklyn, N.Y.; Chicago, Ill., Lithuanian Student Association; Lituanus Foundation Inc. Quarterly. See
serials consulted.

1351. LITVA SEGODNIA. 1- ; 1965- .
Vil'nius, Gintaras, Balt 8021.22 MH
(no.2; 1966-) CaAEU(no.5; 1968) DLC
(no.2; 1966-)

1352. LITWA; tygodnik ilustrovany
litewski w języku polskim. Wilno,
M. Davainis-Silvestraitis, 1908-15.
Monthly; biweekly; weekly (irregular) Balt 7825.50.25 MH(Rok 1908-
1915) MeKPF(1908-1912) NN([6-7])

1353. LITWA I RUŚ; miesięcznik poświęcony kulturze, dziejom, krajoznaw-
stwu i ludoznawstwu. Wilno, Zawadzki, 1912-13. 4 v. Monthly. See serials consulted.

1354. LUX CHRISTI; trimėnesinis kunigų biuletenis. 1- ; 1951- .
New Britain; Putnam, Conn., Kunigų
vienybė. Quarterly. See serials consulted.

1355. MARGUTIS; mėnesinis...žur-
nalas. Metai 1- ; 1928- . Chicago, Ill., A. Vanagaitis; Margutis
Publishing Co. Monthly. See serials consulted.

1356. THE MARIAN. 1- ; 1948- .
Chicago, Ill., Marian Fathers.
289.4MA ICLJF CtTMF(1949, 1952-1955,
1959-1962) OKentU(1950, no.7-10)

1357. METMENYS; jaunosios kartos
kultūros žurnalas. 1- ; 1959- .
[Chicago, Ill.] Santaros-Šviesos
federacija. See serials consulted.

1358. MINTIS. Nr.1-572; vasario
19, 1946-liepos 15, 1949. Memmingen,
Ger., 1946-49. 3 no. a week.
CtTMF(1947-1949) OKentU(1946-1949)

1359. MOKSLAS IR GYVENIMAS. 1- ;
1957- . Vilnius, Lietuvos TSR Politinių ir mokslinių žinių skleidimo draugija. Unclassified DLC(1962-)
OKentU(1960, no.9; 1963, no.6,11;
1964, no.2,3,7; 1965, no.9; 1966,
no.2,8; 1967, no.12; 1969, 1970,no.
2-12; 1971, no.1-3; 1972)

1360. MOKSLO DIENOS. Kaunas, Lietuvių mokytojų dr. J. Basanavičiaus
vardo sąjunga, 1937-40. CtPAM(1937-
1938)

1361. MOKYKLA IR GYVENIMAS. Šiauliai; Kaunas, 1920-40. Monthly.
Published by the Lietuvių mokytojų
profesinė sąjunga. ICCC(1920; 1921,
no.2-12; 1922, no.2-8; 1923-1924,no.
3-12; 1925, no.1,4; 1926-1932, no.1-
9; 1933, no.1-7)

1362. MŪSŲ GIRIOS; miškininkystės,
gamtos apsaugos ir medžioklės žurnalas. Nr.1-104; 1929-1940. nr.1-4;
1942. nr.1- ; 1957- . Kaunas; Vilnius, Lietuvos miškininkų sąjunga;
Lietuvos TSR miškų ūkio ir miško pramonės ministerija. 1940-1957, publication suspended by the Soviet and
German occupational authorities.
Vol. for 1957 called also no.108,
etc., continuing the volume numbering of the previous publication.
SD1.M8 DLC(1957-) ICLJF(1958, no.1-
4) OKentU(1960, no.1,3; 1962, no.6;
1963, no.10)

1363. MŪSŲ KELIAS. Dillingen, Ger.
Lietuvių sąjunga, 1945-49. Weekly
(irregular) Merged with Mintis in
1949 and became Lietuvis. CtTMF(
1945-1948) OKentU(1945-1949)

1364. MŪSŲ LAIKRAŠTIS. Kaunas,
Katalikų veikimo centras, 1928-40.
Weekly. CtTMF(1934-1940) OKentU(
1939, no.30,31,33,34,36,37,48; 1940,
no.3,6-8,10,20-22,24,27)

1365. MŪSŲ LIETUVA. 1- ; sausis
1948- . Sao Paulo, Brasil. Biweekly; weekly. CtTMF(1951, 1953)
ICCC(1948, no.1-3,11,17; 1950, no.60-
61,63,65-66,68,75-77,78) OKentU(1949,
no.46; 1971, no.38,39,41-52)

1366. MŪSŲ SENOVĖ; žurnalas Lietuvos istorijos medžiagai rinkti. Kaunas, Švietimo ministerijos leidinys,
1921-22; 1937-40. 10 v. Irregular.
See serials consulted.

1367. MŪSŲ SODAI. 1- ; birželis
1959- . Vilnius, Lietuvos sodininkystės draugija. Monthly. 80.M973
DNAL([1962]-) OKentU(1962, no.6,8;
1964, no.1-3,8)

1368. MŪSŲ SPARNAI. 1- ; 1950 .
Chicago, Ill., Lietuvių evangeliků
reformatų leidinys. DLC(1952) ICCC
(1953, no3-4; 1954, no.5; 1955, no.
8-9) OKentU(1953, no.3; 1961, no.11-
12; 1963, no.13-14; 1964, no.16;
1965, no.18-19; 1967, no.22; 1971,
no.30)

1369. MŪSŲ VILNIUS. Lapkritis 1928-
gruodis 1938. Kaunas, Vilniui vaduoti sąjunga. Monthly, 1928-1929;
3 no. a month, 1930-1934; biweekly,
1935-1938. ICCC(1930-1933,[1934-1938]
OKentU(1929, no.6; 1930, no.1; 1931,
no.2,11,13,16,18,24; 1932, no.2,14,
24-26, 29,33,34; 1938, no.21-22)

1370. MŪSŲ ŽINYNAS; karo mokslo ir
istorijos žurnalas. T.1-38; kovas
1921-gegužis 1940. Kaunas, Krašto
apsaugos ministerija, Karo mokslo
skyrius, 1921-40. 38 v. Quarterly,
1921-1928; monthly, 1929-1940. See
serials consulted.

1371. MUZIKOS ŽINIOS. 1- ; 1934-
Chicago, Ill., Amerikos lietuvių R.K.
Vargonininkų sąjunga. illus., music
notes as supplements. Quarterly.
ICCC([1935-1939], 1940,[1941-1949],
1950,[1951-1952], 1953-1954,[1955-
1956]) ICLJF(1934-) OKentU(1962, no.1;
1963, no.3-4; 1964, no.1; 1967, no.4;
1970, no.4; 1971, no.1,4)

1372. NAUJA DRAUGIJA; nedėlinis
laikraštis paszvenstas darbininkų
reikalams. Metai 1-2, nr.1-19; spalio 19, 1898-gegužės 19, 1899. Baltimore, Md., 1898-99. Weekly. NN
(1-2)

1373. NAUJA GADYNĖ; lietuwiszkas
darbininkiszkas laikrasztis. Metai
1-3; sausio 23, 1894-birželio 2, 1896.
Mt. Carmel, Pa.; Shenandoah, Pa.;
Scranton, Pa., 1894-96. Q 57.92.M223
PU(1894-1896)

1374. NAUJAS LAIKAS. New Era.

Nr.1-8; vasario 16-rugsėjis 1930.
Bellshill Mossend, Scotland, Lietu-
vių švietimo draugija, 1930. 8 no.
BM(P.P. 1186. td.)

1375. NAUJOJI AUŠRA; lietuvių kultūros žurnalas. Nr.1-13; gruodis
1947-lapkritys 1949. Chicago, Ill.,
1947-49. 13 no. Q 59.9192.N224 PU
(no.1-13) OKentU(1947, no.1; 1948,
no.2-9; 1949, no.2-7)

1376. NAUJOJI GADYNĖ; socializmo
teorijos, mokslo ir literatūros i-
liustruotas mėnesinis žurnalas. The
New Era. Metai 1-2; birželio 21,
1916-spalis 1917. Philadelphia, Pa.,
1916-17. (*QYA)NN(2, no.3-7,9-10;
March-Oct. 1917) OKentU(1916; 1917,
v.2, no.17)

1377. NAUJOJI ROMUVA; iliustruotas
savaitinis kultūros gyvenimo žurnalas. Metai 1-10; Kaunas, Naujosios
romuvos bičiulių draugija, 1931-40.
Weekly; monthly. See serials consulted.

1378. NAUJOJI VAIDILUTĖ; moterų in-
teligenčių mėnesinis žurnalas. Kaunas, 1921-40. Monthly. ICCC(1921-
1940, no.1-4)

1379. NEPRIKLAUSOMA LIETUVA; demokratinės minties Kanados lietuvių
savaitraštis. 1- ; rugpiūtis 1940-
Toronto, Ont.; Montreal, Que., Kanados lietuvių taryba; "Nepriklausoma
Lietuva" spaudos bendrovė. Weekly.
See serials consulted.

1380. DAS NEUE LITAUEN. Jahrg. 1-
2; Oktover 1917-Sept. 1918. Berlin,
1917-1918. 36 no. DK511.L26N4 DLC
(1,[2]) CSt-H([1-2]) CtY(2, no.18-19)

1381. NEWSLETTER FROM BEHIND THE
Iron Curtain; reports on communist
activities in Eastern Europe. Stockholm, Sweden, The Baltic Review,
1947-51. 5 v. Irregular, 1947;
weekly, 1948-1951. DK1.N4 DLC([1-
5]) CLSU(1-) CSt-H(1-) CaOOP(1-)
CaOOAg(no.103-) CtY([2]-) IEN(no.
51-) IaU(1-) IU(1-) MH([1-3]-) MdBJ
([1]-) NN(1-) NjP([2]-) OC1([1-2]-)
WaU([1-3])

1382. PASAULIO LIETUVIS; Pasaulio
lietuvių sąjungos laikraštis. Kaunas, 1937-40. 59 no. Bi-weekly.
ICCC(1937-1939, no.1-13,18,21,22;
1940, no.2-4,6,9)

1383. --- Pasaulio Lietuvių bendruomenės informacinis biuletenis.
Nr.1- ; lapkritis 1963- . Cleveland, Ohio. 10 no. a year. DK511.
L223P38 PU(1-) DLC(1-) OKentU(no.1-
53)

1384. PAVASARIS. Kaunas, 1912-40.
Biweekly. Suspended 1916-1917.
ICCC([1921-1933]-1934-1935)

1385. PAŽANGA; literatūros, mokslo,
politikos ir visuomenės mėnesinis
žurnalas. Metai 1-3; balandis 1915-
birželis 1917. Chicago, Ill.; Gi-
rardville, Pa.; Mahanoy City, Pa.,
1915-17. Monthly. ICBM(1916-1917)
ICCC(1915-1917) OKentU(1915, v.1, no.
3; 1916, v.2, no.1)

1386. ---; laisvosios minties,
mokslo ir kritikos mėnesinis žurnalas. Metai 1, no.1-8; vasaris-rugsė-
jis, 1934. Chicago, Ill., Pažanga
Publishing Co., [1934] Monthly.
(*QYA)NN(1-8) OKentU(1934, v.1, no.1)

1387. PĖDSAKAI; lietuvių kultūros
ir visuomenės žurnalas. Nr.1-4;
Fulda, Ger.; Würzburg, Ger., 1946-47.
4 no. Monthly. PG8501.P42 PU

1388. PERGALĖ; literatūros, meno ir
kritikos žurnalas. 1- ; 1942-Vil-
nius. illus., ports. Monthly. See
serials consulted.

1389. PIETŲ AMERIKOS ŽINIOS. Metai
1-7; birželis 1935-1941. Buenos
Aires, Argentina, 1935-41. Weekly.
Supersedes "Argentinos Žinios". Superseded by "Žinios" CtTMF(1940-1941)

1390. POLICIJA; Lietuvos policijos
mėnesinis laikraštis. Nr.1-148. Metai 1-9; regsėjis 1924-1932. Kaunas,
Piliečių apsaugos departamentas,
1924-32. 9 v. illus. Monthly.
HV7551.P6 DLC(no.1-40,43-148)

1391. PRAEITIS. Kaunas, Lietuvos
istorijos draugija, 1930-33. 2 v.
illus., maps. See serials consulted.

1392. PRO LITUANIA; Bulletins du
Bureau d'Information de Lituanie.
Paris; Lausanne, 1915-19. 5 v.
Monthly. Ceased publication with yr
5, no.1, 1919. CSt-H([1-4]) DLL(3-4)
ICBM(3) IU(1-2) MH(1, no.1,8-9; 2-4,
no.1-9,11-12; 5, no.1) MH-L([2]) NN
([2]) WU(1, no.8-10; 2-5, no.1)

1393. REVISTA BALTICA. Editors: A.
Trimakas, A. Berzins, and L. Vahter
1- ; 1957- . Buenos Aires, Argentina. Semiannual. DLC RPB(1-)

1394. REVUE BALTIQUE. New York,
N.Y., 1959-61. 6 no. in 1 v. DK511.
B25R415 DLC(1-6)

1395. REVUE BALTIQUE; organe de la
collaboration des États Baltes. Tallinn, 1940. 2 no. Edited by the Bureau for Estonian, Latvian, and Lithuanian Cooperation. Articles in

French, German, or English. Superseded in Dec. 1945 by the "Baltic Review" published in Stockholm. DK511.B25R42 DLC(1-2) NN(1) NNC(1) MH(1-2)

1396. RYGOS GARSAS. Metai 1-9; kovas 1909-liepa 1917. Riga, Šv. Kazimiero draugija, 1909-17. Weekly 1909; twice a week 1910-17. NN (1913-1914) OKentU(1915, v.7, no. 74-82, 84-122,124-127; 1916,v.8,no. 1-16,18-33,43-45,48-49,51-59,63-64, 75-76,82-85,89-96; 1917,v.9,no.10, 19-20,22-24)

1397. RUOMUVA. Nr.1-2. Kaunas, Ruomuvos draugija, 1921. 2 no. CtPAM(1921,no.1-2) ICLJF(1921,no.1)

1398. ŠALTINIS. Metai 1-6; Tilžėje, Rūta, 1905-10. 6 v. Bimonthly. (*QYA)NN(1-2)

1399. ---; iliustruotas Lietuvių krikščionių demokratų savaitraštis. Seinai, Laukaitis, Dvaranauskas, Narjauskas ir bendrovė, 1906-15. Weekly. AP95.L5S25 PU(v.1,no.1-19) CtPAM(1906-1912) CtTMF(19-6-1914) ICBM(1908) ICCC([1906-1908],1909, [1910],1911-1912) OKentU (1912-13)

1400. --- Metai 1-15; kovas 1926-birželis 1940. Marijampolė, Tėvai Marijonai, 1926-40. Weekly. CtTMF (1926-1927,1932-1940) ICCC([1926-1940,no.1-25]) NN(1926,1933-[1935])

1401. SANTARVĖ; rezistencinis visuomeninių ir kultūros reikalų žurnalas. London, Lietuvių Rezistencinė Santarvė, 1953-58. 42 no. Irregular. AP95.L5S26 PU(6-42) DLC (1953) OKentU(1953,no.3; 1954,no.36, 10; 1955,no.4-5; 1957,no.2; 1958, no.1)

1402. SAULĖTEKA; mėnesinis literatūros ir politikos laikraštis. Nr. 1-18; sausis 1900-sausio 15, 1902. Bitėnai, 1900-02. 18 no. AP95. L5S286 PU(1-17)Xerox copy 1971.

1403. SAVIVALDYBĖ; mėnesinis Lietuvos savivaldybių laikraštis. Metai 1-18; birželis 1923-liepa 1940. [Kaunas], Savivaldybių departamentas [etc.] 1923-40. illus., ports., diagrs. Monthly. Subtitle varies. See serials consulted.

1404. SĖJA; tautinės demokratinės minties laikraštis. 1- ; 1953- . Melrose Park, Ill., Varpininkų leidinių fondo valdyba. Monthly, bimonthly. CtPAM(1953-1968) DLC(1956-) ICLJF(1962-) OKentU(1954,no.2; 1957, no.1,8; 1958,no.1-2,5-7; 1959,no.1-5; 1960,no.2-3,5-6; 1961,no.1-5; 1962,

no.1-4; 1963,no.1-6; 1964,no.2-6; 1965,no.1-3; 1966,no.1-3; 1967,no.1-4; 1968,no.1-3; 1969,no.1,4)

1405. SKAITYMAI; literatūros ir kritikos žurnalas. Kaunas, Švietimo ministerijos leidinys, 1920-23. 24 no. in 4 v. Monthly. See serials consulted.

1406. SKAUTŲ AIDAS. Toronto, Ont., 1950- . CtPAM(1964-1967)

1407. SODYBA; paukštininkystės, sodininkystės, bitininkystės ir daržininkystės mėnesinis laikraštis. Metai 1-3; liepos 1928-gruodžio 1930. [Kaunas] 1928-30. 3 v. in 1. illus. Monthly. S16.L5S6 DLC(1,[2],3)

1408. SPORTAS. Metai 1-5, no.1. Vilnius, Lietuvos TSR Kūno kultūros ir sporto komitetas, 1952-56. 5 v. Monthly. Unclassified DLC(4-5,no.1)

1409. STUDENTŲ DIENOS. Kaunas, 1937-40. Biweekly. CtTMF(1937-1940)

1410. STUDENTŲ ŽODIS. Metai 1-11; Sausis 1933-birželis 1943. Thompson, Conn., 1933-43. 11 v. ICC(1933,no. 2-9; 1934-1937,no.1-3,5-10; 1938-1943,no.1-5) ICLJF(1933-June 1939) OKentU(1933,no.1-5,7-9; 1934,no.1-2, 5-6,9; 1935,no.1-2,4-10; 1936,no.2, 4-8,10; 1937,no.1,5-6,9,10; 1938,no. 1-7,9,10; 1939,no.1-4,7,10; 1940,no. 2-6,9,10; 1942, no.1-4,6-10; 1943, no.1-5,10)

1411. --- Nr.1-3. Uppsala, Sweden, 1946. 3 no. Superseded by "Šviesa". CtPAM(1946)

1412. STUDI BALTICI. 1-8,1931-1940; [New series] 1(9)- ; 1952- . [Roma] L.S. Olschki. (Academia toscana di scienze e lettere "La Colombaria", Studi, 2) See serials consulted.

1413. ŠVENTO PRANCIŠKAUS VARPELIS. Metai 1- ; rugpiūtis 1923-liepos 1940; 1942- . Kaunas; Kretinga; Brooklyn, N.Y., Franciscan Fathers. Monthly. CtPAM(1923-) OKentU(1944-1951,1953-1971)

1414. ŠVIESA; politikos, mokslo, meno ir literatūros trimėnesinis žurnalas. Metai 1- ; 1934- . Brooklyn, N.Y., Amerikos lietuvių darbininkų literatūros draugija. Quarterly. CtPAM(1957-) CtTMF(1939-1944) OKentU(1934-1938, 1952-1957, 1959-1971)

1415. ŠVIETIMO DARBAS; mėnesinis Svietimo ministerijos žurnalas. Kaunas, 1919-30. 12 v. Monthly. See serials consulted.

1416. ŠVYTURYS; politinis-visuomeninis ir literatūrinis iliustruotas žurnalas. 1- ; 1948- . Vilnius, [LKP CK Laikraščių ir žurnalų leidykla] illus., ports., music. Semimonthly. AP95.L5S95 DLC(7-) NN(10) OKentU(1957,no.7-10,13,17,18,22; 1958,no.1,8; 1960,no.1-7; 1962, no. 2,5; 1963,no.8-10; 1964,no.1-11,13-19,21,23; 1965,no.17,23; 1967; 1968, no.1-10,13-15,17-24; 1969,no.2-22; 1970,no.5-16,18-21,23,24; 1972)

1417. SZVIESA; laikrasztis Žemaicziu ir Lietuvos mylėtoju iszleidžiamas. Rėdytas ir iszduotas Ernesto Veyerio. Tilžėje, 1887-88, 1890. BM(1887-1888, 1890) Not published in 1889.

1418. TALKA. Kaunas, Lietuvos Kooperacinių bendrovių sąjunga; Lietuvos Kooperatyvų taryba, 1919-41. Monthly; semimonthly. CtPAM(1938-1940) NN(no.256-267,270-279,282, 284-310;[1928-1932]) OKentU(1940, no.15)

1419. TARPININKAS. Mediator. v. 1-3,no.10; spalis 1928-liepa 1930. So. Boston, Mass., Lithuanian Chamber of Commerce, 1928-30. 3 v. Monthly; weekly. NN([1]-[3])

1420. TARYBINĖ MOKYKLA; Lietuvos TSR Švietimo ministerijos organas. 1- ; 1945- . Vilnius, Lietuvos TSR Švietimo ministerija. 370.5T175 PU(1958,1959,no.3-12; 1960-) DLC ([1955]-) OKentU(1961,no.1,6,8; 1963,no.12; 1971,no.3-4; 1972)

1421. TAUTOS MOKYKLA. Kaunas, V. Augustauskas; Lietuvių mokytojų sąjunga, 1933-40. Biweekly. CtPAM (1935-1936) DLL ICCC(1937,no.12-13, 16-21,24; 1938,no.1,4-24; 1939-1940, no.1-2)

1422. TAUTOS PRAEITIS; istorijos ir gretimųjų sričių neperiodinis žurnalas. [... Lithuanian historical magazine] Chicago, Ill., Lietuvių istorijos draugija, 1959- . Irregular. Each volume is divided into four books. DK511.L2A276 DLC (1-) CaOTU(1-) InU([2]) MH(1-) NN (1-) OKentU(1959-1961) PU(1-)

1423. TAUTOS ŪKIS. Metai 1-11; sausis 1930-liepa 1940. Kaunas, Ekonominių studijų draugija, 1930-40. Monthly; weekly. CtPAM(1931-1939)

1424. ---; Volkswirtschaft. Beilage der wöchentlichen Wirtschaftszeitung Tautos ūkis. Nr.1-16; gegužės 31, 1938-rugpiūtis 1940. [Kaunas] Ekonominių studijų draugija,

1938-40. 16 no. Monthly (irregular) HC337.L5A36 DLC

1425. TAUTOS VILNIS; lietuvių Brazilijoj sąjungos "Vilnis" neperiodinis leidinys, nr.1. [Redaktorius Juozas Janilionis] Rio, Brazil, 1940. 96 p. illus. 970.3TV ICLJF

1426. TECHNIKA IR ŪKIS. La technique et l'économie. Metai 1-12. Kaunas, Lietuvos inžinierių draugija, 1929-40. 12 v. illus., maps, diagrs. 3-6 no. a year. 947.59.T226 WaU(1930,no.2) CU(1-9,30-)

1427. TECHNIKOS ŽODIS; technikos darbuotojų mėnesinis laikraštis. Metai 1- ; April 1951- . Chicago, Ill., Amerikos lietuvių inžinierių ir architektų sąjunga. Monthly; bimonthly. See serials consulted.

1428. TEISĖ; teisės mokslų ir praktikos žurnalas. Kaunas, Lietuvos teisininkų draugija, 1922-40. 52 no. Quarterly. ICBM(no.1-35; 1922-1936)

1429. TEISININKŲ ŽINIOS. Chicago, Ill., Lietuvių teisininkų draugija, 1952-58. 26 no. Irregular. DLC-L (1-) MH-L(1-)

1430. TĖVIŠKĖS AIDAS. Fulda, Ger., 1946-47. 20 no. Irregular. CtPAM (1946-1947) OKentU(no.17-18,20; 1946-1947)

1431. TĖVIŠKĖS GARSAS. Schweinfurt, Ger., Lietuvių tremtinių bendruomenės komitetas, 1945-48. 117 no. Weekly. OKentU(1945-1948)

1432. TĖVIŠKĖS ŽIBURIAI. Metai 1- ; gruodžio 24, 1949- . Toronto, Ont., Kanados lietuvių katalikų kultūros draugija. Weekly. DLC(3-) OKentU (1960,no.1-48; 1972)

1433. TĖVŲ KELIAS. Metai 1- ; 1949- . Caracas, Venezuela. Monthly. DLC(1957-) CtPAM(1949-1955) ICCC(1949-1951,no.1-8,10-11; 1953-1954,no.1,5-10; 1955,no.1-2; 1956,no. 1) OKentU(1951,v.3,no.9; 1952,v.4, no.9)

1434. TĖVŲ ŽEMĖ. 1- ; 1955- . London, Lietuvos atgimimo sąjudis, Anglijos vietininkija. 1 no. every three weeks. DLC(3-) ICC(1956)

1435. TĖVYNĖ. Metai 1- ; sausio 1, 1896-. Plymouth, Pa. [etc.] Susivienijimas lietuvių Amerikoje. Monthly; weekly. CtPAM(1917-1918) CtTMF(1896-1898) NN(1896-1918) OCl(1910)

1436. TĖVYNĖ KVIEČIA. Nr.1- ; 1957- . Vilnius, Grįžimo į tėvynę komitetas. DLC(1-)

1437. TĖVYNĖN; neperijodinis kultūros, meno ir literatūros žurnalas. Nr.1-4; vasaris 1946-vasaris 1947. Salzburg (Glasenbach), Ger., 1946-47. 4 nos. illus. Irregular. (*QYA)NN

1438. TĖVYNĖS BALSAS. Metai 1-11; birželis 1957-sausis 1967. Vilnius, Grįžimo į tėvynę ir kultūrinių ryšių su tautiečiais užsienyje komiteto Lietuvos iniciatyvinė grupė. 950 numbers published. Superseded in 1967 by Gimtasis kraštas. OKentU(1957,no.37; 1958,no.18,88; 1959,no.50; 1961,no.13-15,19-22,52, 54,98,100-102,104; 1962,no.5,7,10, 52; 1964,no.20; 1965,no.12,14,24, 34,36-42,44-50,52-56,59-67,69-71, 75-77,79-81,83-89,91,94-104; 1967, no.1)

1439. TĖVYNĖS MYLĖTOJŲ DRAUGIJA. Leidinys. [Publications of the "Tėvynės mylėtojų draugija"] Chicago, Ill., 1897-1925. 38 no. CtY(1-2, 13,15,21,24,26-27,37) DLC(21-23,25-27,31,37-38) MnU(31) NN(6,21-26,31, 35,37)

1440. TĖVYNĖS SARGAS; mėnesinis laikraštis paskirtas dvasiškam ir medžiagiškam lietuvių tautos sulaikymui par jos apšvietimą. Metai 1-9; sausis 1896-gegužis 1904. Tilžė. Monthly. See serials consulted.

1441. ---; politikos ir socialinių mokslų žurnalas. Nr.1- ; 1947-Reutlingen, Ger.; Chicago, Ill., Lietuvių krikščionių demokratų partija. Irregular. See serials consulted.

1442. TIESOS KELIAS; religijos bei doros mokslo ir visuomenės gyvenimo žurnalas. Kaunas, 1925-40. 186 no. Monthly. See serials consulted.

1443. TREMTINIŲ ŽINIOS. Wiesbaden, Ger., Aistia, 1946. 14 no. Weekly. OKentU(1-14)

1444. TRIMITAS. Metai 1-21; birželis 1920-birželis 1940. Kaunas, Lietuvos šaulių sąjunga, 1920-40. 21 v. illus. Weekly. See serials consulted.

1445. ŪKININKAS; lietuviszkas laikrasztis paskirtas reikalams ūkinikų. Metai 1-16, no.10; sausis 1890-lapkritys 1905. Ragnit; Tilsit, Martynas Jankus, 1890-1905. 16 v. Monthly. Superseded by Lietuvos ūkininkas published in Vilnius. BM(1890-1905) CtPAM(1893-1901) NN(1)

1446. UŽUOLANKA; lietuvių išeivijos, buities, dailės ir kultūros mėnesinis žurnalas. Chicago, Ill., 1955-61. 40 no. ICCC(1955, no.2; 1956, no.3,5-6) OKentU(1955. no.1,2; 1957, no.6-7)

1447. VADOVAS; mėnesinis katalikų laikraštis. T.1-19, nr.1-76; rugsėjis 1908-rugpiūtis 1914. Seinai, Laukaičio, Narjausko bendrovės spaustuvė, 1908-1914. 76 no. Monthly. CtPAM(v.1-13, 1908-1912) CtTMF(1908-1914) ICCC(no.1-28,34-35,41,43,45-76) ICLJF(no.53-76) OKentU(1909, v.3 no.10-12)

1448. VAIRAS; literatūros, dailės, mokslo ir politikos laikraštis. Vilnius, 1914-15. 2 v. Irregular. ICCC(1914, no.6,11,12,14,17-18;1915, no.1-16) ICLJF(1914, no.1-18) NN(1914-1915)

1449. ---; kultūros žurnalas. Kaunas, Pažangos bendrovė, 1929-40. Monthly. CtPAM(1936-1940, no.1-4) ICCC(1936, no.11; 1937, no.1)

1450. VAIVORYKŠTĖ; literatūros ir dailės kritikos žurnalas. Kovas 1913-balandis 1914. Vilnius, 1913-14. 5 no. Quarterly. CtPAM(1913, no.1-4; 1914, no.1) ICCC(1913, no.4; 1914, no.1)

1451. VALTIS; nedėlinis laikraštis. Nr.1- ; 1894- . Plymouth, Pa. ICCC(1894-1895) MeKPF(April 1894-April 1895) OKentU(1894, v.1, no.1, 4-5,7,9-14,16-22,24-26,28-35,37,44-48,5154-56; on microfilm)

1452. VARPAS; literatūros, politikos ir mokslo mėnesinis laikrasztis. Metai 1-17; sausis 1889-kovas 1906. Tilžėje, Ragainėje, 1889-1906. 17 v. Monthly. Merged in "Lietuvos ūkininkas" BM(P.P. 4741. c.(1889-1906)) 57.92.V436 PU(1889-1891, 1892,no.6-12; 1893-1905) NN(1889-1891; 1893, no.4,6-8,10-11; 1894-1895, no.11-1896, no.3,5-10; 1901, no.3,5-1905)

1453. ---; visuomenės ir politikos laikraštis. Tilžė, 1913-14. 3 no. (*Zan.-*Q96)NN(no.1-3; 1913-1914)

1454. --- politikos, mokslo ir kultūros mėnesinis laikraštis. Kaunas, Varpo bendrovė, 1920-40. Monthly. (irregular) 57.92.V436 PU(1920, no.1-5; 1921, no.3; 1922-1924, no.1-7) NN(1920, no.1-9; 1921, no.1-6)

1455. ---; neperiodinis žurnalas. Nr.1- ; 1953- . Brooklyn, N.Y., Varpininkų leidinių fondas. Irregular.57.92.V438 PU(1-) DLC(1-) NN(1-) OKentU(1953, no.1; 1963, no.5; 1965, no.6)

1456. VIENYBĖ. Vilnius; Kaunas,
Šv. Kazimiero draugija; Lietuvos katalikų sąjunga, 1907-33. Weekly.
Supersedes Nedėldienio skaitymas.
AP95.L5V54 PU CtPAM(1908-1012, 1914)
ICCC(1909, no.1-27,29-50,52-53; 1910
no.1-9,11,14,16,18-35, 37,46,48-49;
1911, no.1-5,7-14,16-18,20,22-25,27,
43-45; 1912,no.1-5,7-52; 1914,no.1-
3,6-7,9-13,15-29)

1457. VILNIAUS RYTOJUS; lietuvių
visuomenės politikos ir literatūros
laikraštis. Vilnius, Laikinasis
Vilniaus lietuvių komitetas, 1928-
37. Weekly; 2 no. a week. CtTMF
(1930-1932, 1934-1937)

1458. VILTIS. Hope. A folklore
and Lithuanistica magazine. San
Diego, Calif..; [etc.] F.V. Beliajus, 1942- . Quarterly. DLC([7]-)
ICCC(1949, no.1) InU(5-) NN(15-)
OrU(8-) OKentU(1956, no.12; 1957,
no.1; 1961, no.3-4) WaS(v.25,no.1-
27)

1459. VISUOMENĖ. Vilnius, Alina
Ona Paulauskytė, 1910-11. 20 no.
Monthly. CtTMF(1910, no.5-12)

1460. VYTIS. The Knight. V.1-6,
1915-1918; New Series v.1-15, 1919-
1933; 1934-35; v.22, 1936- . Chicago, Ill., Lietuvos Vyčiai, 1915- .
Semimonthly. In English and Lithuanian. CtPAM(1915-) ICCC([1915-1930,
1936-1940], 1941-) ICBM(1921-1922)
ICJ(1-[6]; ns.v.[1]-4,8) ICLJF(3-
9;1921-1927) ICN[3]-6; ns.v.1-2,5-
7) NN(ns.v.5,[6],7,12,[13]-)

1461. ŽEMĖS ŪKIS; žemės ūkio mokslo žurnalas. Kaunas, Žemės ūkio ministerija; Žemės ūkio rūmai, 1925-44.
11 v. Frequency varies. 20.Z42 DNAL
(m.12,no.149-172; 1937) CtPAM(1927-31)

1462. ---; Lietuvos TSR žemės ūkio
produktų ministerijos... žurnalas.
1- ; 1956- . Vilnius. Monthly.
Supersedes Lietuvos kolūkistas; title
varies: Socialinis žemės ūkis.
20.Sol DNAL DLC(1957, no.2,12; 1958,
no.3-12; 1961-1963; 1964, no.1-)
OKentU(1963, no.12; 1964,no.5-7;
1970, no.8)

1463. ŽEMĖTVARKA IR MELIORACIJA.
Kaunas, Lietuvos matininkų ir kultūrtechnikų sąjunga, 1926-40. Quarterly; bimonthly. TC801.Z4 DLC(1930-
1940) DNAL

1464. ŽIBURIAI. Augsburg, Ger.,
1945-49. 261 no. Weekly. On Nov.3,
1949 merged with Aidai. CtPAM(no.1-
110) ICLJF(1945-1949) OKentU(1945-49)

1465. ŽIDINYS; literatūros, mokslo
visuomenės ir akademinio gyvenimo

mėnesinis žurnalas. Kaunas, Studentų ateitininkų sąjunga, 1924-40.
Monthly. 57.92.Z67 PU(25-31,no.1-4)
CtPAM(1924-1940,no.1-4) CtTMF(1925-
1940,no.1-4) ICCC(1924-1940,no.1-4)

1466. ŽINGSNIAI; kultūros žurnalas.
Flensburg, Ger.; Dedelsdorf, Ger.;
Seedorf b. Zeven, Ger., 1946-48.
15 no. ICBM(nr.9-15; 1947-1948)
OKentU(1946, no.4-5; 1947, no.10-11;
1948, no.13-14)

1467. ŽVAIGŽDĖ. Brooklyn, N.Y.;
Shenandoah, Pa., Philadelphia, Pa.,
1901-44. Published by Rev. V. Varna-
giris till 1903 and since by Rev. A.
Milukas. Weekly, 1901-1923; monthly,
1923-1926; quarterly, 1927-1944.
ICCC(1923, no.12; 1924, no.6,8-10,12;
1925, no.9-11; 1926-1929, no1,4; 1930
no.1-2,4; 1931-1937, no 1-3; 1938-
1943, no.1-2) OKentU(1931, no.1; 1933
no.2; 1935, no.1; 1936, no.1)

1468. ŽYGIO KARYS. Lithuania. East
Prussia, 1944. 2 no. OKentU(1-2)

IV.3. ANNUALS AND OTHER PUBLICATIONS

1469. AMERICAN LITHUANIAN ENGINEERS
AND ARCHITECTS OF NEW YORK. Metraš-
tis. [Yearbook] 1- ; 1951- . New
York, N.Y. (*QYA)NN(1951) DLC(1951)

1470. DAILĖ; tapyba, skulptūra,
grafika, taikomoji dailė. [Fine arts,
painting, sculpture, graphic art and
applied art] Kaunas, VGLL. illus.,
ports. Annual. N9.6D3 DLC(1960-)
MH(1961-) PU(1963-)

1471. GUBOS; literatūros almanachas.
[..... Literary almanac] Kaunas, 1927.
179 p. plates, ports. Only vol.1
published. 891.928G8 CtTMF NN

1472. KANADOS LIETUVIŲ DIENA. Metraštis. [Canadian Lithuanian Day; a
yearbook] 1- ; 1953- . [Toronto,
Ont.] illus., ports. Flo35.L5K3 DLC
CaBVaU CaOTU

1473. KRIVULĖ. Redagavo Albertas
Puskepalaitis. Detmold, Ger., Mažosios Lietuvos Taryba, 1948. 1 v.
Lithuanian and German. No more published. Q 947.5.K895 PU

1474. LIETUVIŲ STUDENTŲ SĄJUNGA.
Metraštis. [A yearbook] Chicago,
Ill., 1966. DLC(1966)

1475. LITERATŪRA; lietuvių literatūros, meno ir mokslo metraštis. [A
yearbook of Lithuanian literature,
art and science. Edited by Martynas

Gudelis et al.] Kn.1- ; 1950- .
Chicago, Ill., Lietuvių literatūros
draugija. illus. Balt 9601.258.5
MH(1950-) PU(1950-)

1476. LITERATŪROS IR MENO METRAŠ-
TIS. [The yearbook of literature
and arts] 1- ; 1959- . Vilnius,
VGLL. illus., ports. Annual.
AY1039.L5L57 DLC CtPAM(1959) CU(
1965-) CaAEU(1963, 1966-) ICU(1961-)
IEN(1962,1964) IU(1959-) InU(1966-
1967) MH(1959-) NNC(1966-) PU(1959-)

1477. LITERATŪROS LANKAI; neperiodinis poezijos, prozos ir kritikos
žodis. Buenos Aires, Argentina,
1952-59. 8 no. AP95.L5L5 DLC(4-8)
PU

1478. LITHUANIAN SSR. VALSTYBINĖ
ARCHITEKTŪROS PAMINKLŲ APSAUGOS INS-
PEKCIJA. Metraštis. 1- ; 1958- .
Vilnius. illus., facsims., plans.
Annual. Summaries in Russian. NA9.
L5 DLC(1-) MH PU

1479. MUZIKA IR TEATRAS; almanachas. 1- ; 1962- . Vilnius, VGLL.
illus., ports, music. ML21.M96 DLC
(1963-) MH(1962-) PU(1962-1963,1969-)

1480. PISMO ZBIOROWE WILEŃSKIE NA
rok 1859. Wilno, Druk. T. Glücksberga, 1859. 1 v. 491.922C.P674
PU

1481. PLUNKSNA IR ŽODIS; Plunksnos
klubo almanachas. [... a collection
of articles and literary works]
Sidney, Australia, Sydnėjaus lietuvių plunksnos klubas, 1966. 257 p.
891.92C.P744 PU CaAEU

1482. PRIEDAS PRIE ŪKININKĄ. [Sup-
plement to "Ūkininkas"] Tilžė, 1893-
95. BM(P.P. 4741.d.; 1893, no.1-6,
8-12; 1894, no.1-12; 1895, no.1-4)

1483. ŠIAULIŲ METRAŠTIS; informacinė knyga, 1930-1933 metams. [A
Yearbook of information about Šiau-
liai] Redaktorius F. Bugailiškis.
Šiauliai, Šiaulių kraštotyros draugija, 1930-1933. 4 v. in 1.
947.52.Si12 PU

1484. SOVETSKAIA LITVA; almanakh.
1- ; 1954- . Kaunas, Vil'nius,
Gos. izd-vo khudozh. lit-ry Litovs-
koi SSR. PG8771.R1S6 DLC(2-) CU(9-)
CtY(8-) IU(2,7) MH(2-) NN(2-)
NNC(2-) CaOTU(microfiche)

1485. STUDENTŲ VARPAS. [Schwein-
furt, Ger., Lietuvių tremtinių studentų Varpininkų sąjungos leidinys,
1948] 40 p. illus. LA853.L48S7
DLC

1486. TREMTIES METAI; lietuvių rašytojų metraštis,1947. [The years
in exile; a yearbook of Lithuanian
authors] Tübingen, Ger., Patria,
1947. 607 p. PG8713.T721 InNd CtY
CaAEU CaOTP CtTMF DLC MiD NN PU

IV.4. PUBLICATIONS OF THE UNIVERSI-
TIES, INSTITUTIONS AND
LEARNED SOCIETIES

1487. ACTA BALTICA. v.1- ; 1960/
61- . Königstein im Taunus, Ger.,
Institutum Balticum. See serials
consulted.

1488. ACTA BALTICO-SLAVICA. 1- ;
1964- . Białystok, Białostockie
Towarzystwo Naukowe. illus. Annual
See serials consulted.

1488. ACTA HISTORICA LITHUANICA.
1- ; 1967- . Vilnius, Mintis. At
head of title: Lietuvos TSR Mokslų
akademija. Istorijos institutas.
DK511.L2A16 ICU(1-) DLC

1490. ACTA PARASITOLOGICA LITHUA-
NICA. 1- ; 1958- . Vilnius, Is-
sued by Parazitologijos laboratorija
of the Lietuvos TSR Mokslų akademija.
Text in Lithuanian and Russian. Sum-
maries in English. QL757.A117 DLC
CLSU-H(1-) IaAS(2-) MH-Z(1-) NIC(1-)
NNM(1-) NbU(1-) PU(1-)

1491. ARCHIVUM PHILOLOGICUM. Commentationes ordinis philologorum
Universitatis Vitauti Magni. Ed.
Pr. Skardžius. Kn.1-8. Kaunas,Hu-
manitarinių mokslų fakultetas, 1930-
39. 8 v. illus. Irregular. Contains articles on Baltic linguistics
in French, German, or Lithuanian.
See serials consulted.

1492. ARCHYVINIAI DOKUMENTAI. Vilnius, VPMLL,1961- . facsims. (Faktai kaltina). At head of title: Lietuvos TSR Mokslų akademija. DK511.
L2A23 DLC(4-5) CU(4-) MH(3)

1493. ATENEUM WILEŃSKIE; czasopismo naukowe, poświęcone badaniom
przeszłości ziem Wielkiego Księstwa
Litewskiego. Wilno, Towarzystwo
Przyjaciół Nauk, 1923-39. 14 v.
illus., plates, maps, tables. Quarterly. See serials consulted.

1494. ATHENAEUM; kalbos, literatūros, istorijos ir geografijos žurnalas. Kaunas, Teologijos-filosofijos
fakultetas, 1930-38. 9 v. See serials consulted.

1495. BALTIC AND SCANDINAVIAN countries. Toruń; Leyden [etc.], Baltic Institute, 1935-39. 5 v. See serials consulted.

1496. BALTICA. Mezhdunarodnyi ezhegodnik po voprosam chetverticheskoi geologii, dinamiki i morfologii beregov, morskoi geologii i neotektoniki Baltiiskogo moria. 1- ; 1963- . Vilnius. illus. At head of title: Akademiia nauk Litovskoi SSR. Otdelenie geografii. Sovetskaia sektsiia INKVA. Summaries in Russian, English, and French language. QE260.B25 DLC CaAEU(1-4) ICU PU(3-)

1497. BALTICOSLAVICA. Wilno, Instytut Naukowo-Badawczy Europy Wschodniej, 1933-38. 3 v. (Its Bulletin) Irregular. See serials consulted.

1498. BALTISTICA. 1- ; 1965- . Vilnius, Mintis. Annual. An annual consisting of two parts issued at intervals of six month. Text in Lituanian, English, French, German, Latvian, and Russian with summaries in one or two of these languages. See serials consulted.

1499. BIBLIOGRAFIJOS ŽINIOS. Kaunas, 1928-44. 16 v. illus. Bimonthly. See serials consulted.

1500. COMMENTATIONES BALTICAE. Bd.1- ; L953- . Bonn, Ger., Baltisches Forschungsinstitut. illus., maps. Annual. See serials consulted.

1501. DOTNUVA, LITHUANIA. LIETUVOS ŽEMDIRBYSTĖS INSTITUTAS. Darbai. [Works of the Institute for the Lithuanian agriculture] Redakcinė komisija: J. Montvilaitė ir kiti. 1- ; 1954- . Dotnuva. At head of title: Lietuvos TSR. Žemės ūkio ministerija. Lietuvos žemdirbystės mokslinis institutas. Summaries in Russian. vol.1-2; 1954-1955 issued by the Žemdirbystės ir dirvožemio institutas of Lietuvos TSR Mokslų akademija. S16.L5D6 DLC(4-) DNAL(1-) CU(1-) NN(1-2)

1502. ERANUS; Commentationes Societatis philosophicae lithuanae. Kaunas, Humanitariniu mokslų fakultetas, 1930-38. 4 v. in 2. Irregular. B8.L5E7 CU(1-4) BM(1-) ICCC(1) ICU(1-3) MH(2) MoU(1-2) NN(1-3)

1503. GEOGRAFICHESKOE OBSHCHESTVO. SEVERO-ZAPADNYI OTDEL. Zapiski. Sanktpeterburg, 1911-13. 4 v. See serials consulted.

1504. GEOGRAFINIS METRAŠTIS. 1- ;

1958- . Vilnius. See serials consulted.

1505. IŠ MOKSLŲ ISTORIJOS LIETUVOJE. [About the history of sciences in Lithuania] 1- ; 1960- . Vilnius, VPMLL, Irregular. At head of title: Lietuvos TSR Mokslų akademija. Prezidiumas. Gamtos mokslų ir technikos istorijos komisija. Editor: V. Petrauskas et al. AZ718. L717 DLC CU CaAEU(1) CLU CtPAM(1) ICU NN PU(1-)

1506. KALBOS KULTŪRA. 1- ; 1961- Kaunas, Mintis. At head of title: Lietuvos TSR Mokslų akademija. Lietuvių kalbos ir literatūros institutas. PG8501.K34 PU(2-) CLU(1-) CU(2-) CaAEU(15) ICU(1-) MH(1-) NNC OkentU(1962, no.2,6,8,10-13)

1507. KAUNAS. LIETUVOS HIDROTECHNIKOS IR MELIORACIJOS MOKSLINIO TYRIMO INSTITUTAS. Darbai. [Works of the Lithuanian Research Institute of Hydraulic Engineering] 1- ; 195 - . Kaunas. TC7.K3 DLC(3-) NN

1508. KAUNAS. LIETUVOS VETERINARIJOS AKADEMIJA. Darbai. Trudy. 1- ; 1952- . Kaunas. illus., ports tables. SF604.K3 DLC(6-) BM

1509. KAUNAS. LIETUVOS ŽEMĖS ŪKIO AKADEMIJA. Moksliniai darbai. Nauchnye trudy. 1- ; 1953- . Kaunas. illus., diagrs. Text in Lithuanian or Russian with summary in the other language. Title varies. S13.K118 DLC(7-)

1510. --- --- Žemės ūkio akademijos metraštis. [Annals of the Academy of Agriculture] Kaunas, 1926-40. 13 v. illus., plates, plans, tables,diagrs. Annual. See serials consulted.

1511. KAUNAS. POLITECHNIKOS INSTITUTAS. Darbai. Trudy. 1- ; 1949- . Kaunas. illus., diagrs. Irregular. Vol.1(1949) published by Techniniai fakultetai. The continuation of the publication (vol.2 (1953) is by the Politechnikos institutas. TA7.K3 DLC(9) MCM(3-)

1512. KAUNAS. UNIVERSITETAS. BIBLIOTEKA. Leidinys. [Publications] Kaunas, 1929-34. 2 v. Contents.-- Nr.1. Daukantas, Simanas. Darbay senuju Lituwiu.--Nr.2. Jablonskis, Konstantinas. Istorijos archyvas, tomas 1. (QYA)NN BN(1-2) ICBM(2)

1513. KAUNAS. UNIVERSITETAS. BOTANIKOS SODAS. Raštai. [Annals of the Botanical Garden...] Kaunas, 1931-39. 6 v. DNAL(1-3,5-)

MH(1-3) MH-G(5,7,9) PU(1-2)

1514. KAUNAS. UNIVERSITETAS. HU-
MANITARINIŲ MOKSLŲ FAKULTETAS. Darbai ir dienos. Acta et commentationes ordinid philologorum. Kaunas,
1930-40. 9 v. illus. See serials
consulted.

1515. --- Raštai. [Annals of the
Department of Arts and Science]
Kaunas, 1925-37. 21 v. illus.,
ports. Irregular. Vol.1-4, v.5,
no.2-3 have also title: Commentationes ordinis philologorum. Pl9.K3
DLC(1-2,4-8,10,21) CU(1-) CaAEU(5)
CtY ICU([3-5]-7,9-11,13,16,19) MH
(10-11) MoU([3]) NNC(1-[3],4) NN(1-
15) PU(1-2)

1516. KAUNAS. UNIVERSITETAS. MA-
TEMATIKOS-GAMTOS FAKULTETAS. Darbai.
Mémoires de la Faculté des sciences
de l'Université de Vytautas le Grand.
Kaunas, 1923-39. 13 v. See serials
consulted.

1517. --- Leidiniai. [Publications
of the Department of Mathematics and
Natural Sciences] Nr.1- ; 1922- .
Kaunas. T.1-5 of Darbai are also
its Leidinys nr.1-4,21. MH(no.18,
21-24,26; 1929-1931)

1518. KAUNAS. UNIVERSITETAS. TEI-
SIŲ FAKULTETAS. Darbai. Ouvrages
de la Faculté de droit de l'Université de Lithuanie. Kaunas, Valstybės spaustuvė, 1924-39. 10 v. See
serials consulted.

1519. --- Teisės mokslų biblioteka. [Law series] Kaunas, 1931-
38. 26 no. (QYA)NN(1-10,12,14-17,
19-23,25-26; 1924-1938) CU(2,8,10,
12,14,16) MH(2,8,10,12,14,16)

1520. KAUNAS. UNIVERSITETAS. TEO-
LOGIJOS-FILOSOFIJOS FAKULTETAS. Leidiniai. [Publications of the Department of Theology and Philosophy]
Kn.1- ; 1928- . Kaunas. MH(no.5-
6,8-13; 1930-1932) NN(no.5-6,8-22)

1521. --- Mistinės literatūros
studijos. [Studies of the mystical
literature] Kn.1- ; 1928- . Kaunas. CU(no.2-4; 1929-1930) MH(no.3-
4; 1930) NN(no.3-4; 1930)

1522. KAUNAS. VALSTYBINIS MEDICI-
NOS INSTITUTAS. Darbai. Trudy.
1- ; 195 - . Vilnius. Wl.KA92
DNLM(2-)

1523. KNYGŲ LENTYNA. Bookshelf.
Memmingen, Ger.; Danville, Ill.,
1948-66. 19 v. Irregular. Current
bibliography. Editor: A. Ružancovas.
See serials consulted.

1524. KOSMOS; gamtos ir šalinių
mokslų iliustruotas žurnalas. Kaunas, 1920-40. Monthly. See serials consulted.

1525. LIETUVIŲ KALBOTYROS KLAUSI-
MAI. T.1- ; 1957- . Vilnius,
VPMLL. See serials consulted.

1526. LIETUVIŲ KATALIKŲ MOKSLO A-
KADEMIJA, ROME. Metraštis. [Year-
book of the Lithuanian Catholic Academy of Science in Rome] 1- ; 1965-
Roma. See serials consulted.

1527. --- Suvažiavimo darbai.
[Proceedings of the Congresses of
the Lithuanian Catholic Academy of
Science in Rome] 1- ; 1957- . Roma. ports. See serials consulted.

1528. LIETUVIŲ KATALIKŲ MOKSLO
akademijos suvažiavimo darbai, 1933
ir 1936. [Proceedings of the Congresses of the Lithuanian Catholic
Academy of Science in Kaunas, 1933
and 1936] Redaktoriai: Juozas Eretas ir Antanas Salys. Kaunas, Lietuvių katalikų mokslo akademijos
leidinys, 1935-37. 2 v. O 60.L
ICCC(1-2)

1529. LIETUVIŲ MOKSLO DRAUGIJA.
Lietuvių mokslo draugijos leidinys.
[Publications of the Lithuanian
Scientific Society] Vilnius, Švytu-
rio bendrovė. Hvol2.L62 CtY(no.13-
17,19,21,23-24; 1919-1921)

1530. LIETUVIŲ TARYBINĖ LITERATŪ-
RA. 1- ; 1957- . Vilnius, VPMLL,
At head of title: Lietuvos TSR Moks-
lų akademija, Lietuvių kalbos ir
literatūros Institutas. PG8701.L513
DLC(1957-) CLU(1958-) CaAEU(1957-58)

1531. LIETUVIŲ TAUTA; Lietuvių
mokslo draugijos raštai. Vilnius,
Ruch'o spaustuvė, 1907-35. 5 v.
See serials consulted.

1532. LIETUVOS MIŠKŲ ŪKIO MOKSLI-
NIO TYRIMO INSTITUTAS. Darbai. [An-
nals of the Lithuanian Forestry Re-
search Institute] 1- ; 1956- .
Kaunas. SD1.L52 DLC(3-) CU(3-)
DNAL(4-) ICRL(6-)

1533. LIETUVOS PRAEITIS. T.1, sąs.
1-2. Kaunas, Lituanistikos institutas, Lietuvos istorijos skyrius,
1940-41. 2 v. DK511.L2A233 DLC NN

1534. LIETUVOS TSR ARCHITEKTŪROS
klausimai. 1- ; 1960- . Kaunas.
Irregular. See serials consulted.

1535. LIETUVOS TSR AUKŠTŲJŲ MOKY-
klų mokslo darbai: Bibliotekininkystės ir bibliografijos klausimai.

[... Librarianship and bibliography]
1- ; 1961- . Vilnius, Mintis. See
serials consulted.

1536. ---: Biologija. 1- ;1961-
Vilnius, VPMLL. DLC(2) CU(1-) CLU
(1-) DNLM(2-) MiEM(1-) MiU(1-6)
MnU-A(1-)

1537. ---; Chemija ir cheminė
technologija. Khimiia i khimiches-
kaia tekhnologiia. 1- ; 1961- .
Vilnius, VPMLL. illus. QD1.L73
DLC(1-) CLU(3,5-) CU(6-) ICRL(1-)

1538. ---: Ekonomika. 1- ; 1962-
[i.e.1960- .] Vilnius. Begins
with vol.2(1962) continuing numbering of subseries "Ekonomika" of Vilnius. Universitetas. Mokslo darbai. Unclassified DLC(2-) CLU(1-)
MH(1-) MoU(1-) KU(5-)

1539. ---: Elektrotechnika ir automatika. Elektrotekhnika i avto-
matika. 1- ; 1966- . Vilnius,
Mintis. illus. Text in Lithuanian
or Russian with summaries in the
other language. Supersedes in part
subtitle "Elektrotechnika ir mechanika". TK4.L54 DLC(1-) NN

1540. ---: Elektrotechnika ir mechanika. Elektrotekhnika i mekhanika. 1-4. Vilnius, 1962-65. 4 v.
Title varies: vol.1(1962), Lietuvos
TSR Aukštųjų mokyklų mokslo darbai:
Elektrotechnika. Text in Russian or
Lithuanian with summaries in the
other language. Superseded in 1966
by subtitles "Elektrotechnika ir automatika" and "Mechanika". Unclassified DLC(1-4) CU(3-4) MCM(2,4)

1541. ---: Filosofija. 1- ;1962-
Vilnius. Commences with vol.2(1962)
continuing numbering of subseries
"Filosofija" of Vilnius. Universitetas. Mokslo darbai. See serials
consulted.

1542. ---: Geografija ir geologija. Geografiia i geologiia. 1- ;
1962- . Vilnius, VPMLL. See serials consulted.

1543. ---: Istorija. Istoriia.
1- ; 1958- . Vilnius, VPMLL. See
serials consulted.

1544. ---: Kalbotyra. Iazykozna-
nie. 1- ; 1958- . Vilnius, VPMLL.
See serials consulted.

1545. ---: Literatūra. Literatura.
1- ; 1958- . Vilnius, VPMLL. Title varies: vol.1-2(1958-1960),"Literatūra" issued by Vilnius. Universitetas as its Mokslo darbai. Text
and summaries in Lithuanian and Rus-

sian. PG8701.L72 DLC(2-) CLU(2-)
CaAEU(1-) ICU(1-) KU(1-) MH(1-)
MiU(1-) NNC(10-) PSt(1-) PU(10-)
NjP(1969-)

1546. ---: Mechanika. Mekhanika.
1- ; 1962- . Vilnius, VPMLL. Only
single issue published in 1962. In
1963 merged with subtitle "Elektrotechnika" to form a subtitle "Elektrotechnika ir Mechanika". In 1966
resumes independent publication com-
mencing with vol.1. Unclassified
DLC(v.1;1962)

1547. ---: Medicina. Meditsina.
1- ; 1962- . Vilnius, VPMLL.
CLU(1-) DNLM(7-) ICRL(7-) MH TxHMC
(8-)

1548. ---: Menotyra. Iskusstvove-
denie. 1- ; 1967- . Vilnius.
NX6.L53 PU(1-2) DLC(1-) MH(1-)

1549. ---: Pedagogika ir psicholo-
gija. Pedagogika i psikhologiia.
1- ; 1962- . Vilnius, VPMLL.
L56.L72 CaAEU(1-) DLC(1-) DNLM(7-)
InU(1-7) MH(1-) WaU(9-)

1550. ---: Statyba ir architektūra. Stroitel'stvo i arkhitektura.
1- ; 1962- . Vilnius, VPMLL.
Irregular. Text in Russian or Lithuanian with summaries in the other
language. Unclassified DLC(1-5)

1551. ---: Teisė. Pravo. 1- ;
1960- . Vilnius, VPMLL. Annual.
Commences with vol.2, continuing
numbering of subseries "Ekonomika"
issued by Vilnius. Universitetas,
as its Mokslo darbai. Text in Lithuanian or Russian with summaries
in other language. CLU(2-) InU(2-)
IU(3-) KU(2-) MoU(2-) DLC(3-)

1552.. LIETUVOS TSR MOKSLŲ AKADE-
MIJA, VILNA. Darbai. Serija A.
[Publications of the Soviet Lithuanian Academy of Sciences. Series A:
Humanities and Social Sciences]
1- ; 1955- . Vilnius, VPMLL. See
serials consulted.

1553. --- --- Serija B. [Publica-
tions of the Soviet Lithuanian Academy of Sciences. Series B: Natural
and technical sciences] 1- ; 1955- .
Vilnius, VPMLL See serials consulted.

1554. --- --- Serija C. [Publica-
tions of the Soviet Lithuanian Academy of Sciences. Series C: Biology, agriculture and medicine] 1(21)- ;
1960- . Vilnius, VPMLL 3 no. a
year. Series B has been split in
two: B and C beginning with volume
21. Lithuanian or Russian with summaries in the other language. See

serials consulted.

1555. --- Žinynas. Vestnik. Kaunas, Valstybinė enciklopedijų, Žodynų ir mokslo literatūros leidykla, 1947-55. 12 v. ports. Superseded by the Academy's "Darbai". Serija A and B. AS262.V42 DLC PU(3-5,9)

1556. LIETUVOS TSR MOKSLŲ AKADEMIJA, VILNA. BIOLOGIJOS INSTITUTAS. Darbai. Trudy. [Publications of the Institute of Biology of the Academy of Sciences] Kaunas, 1951-59. 4 v. Irregular. QH301.L53 DLC(1-) CU(1-) DNAL(1-) MH(1-) NN(1-) PPAN (1-) PU(1-)

1557. LIETUVOS TSR MOKSLŲ AKADEMIJA, VILNA. BOTANIKOS INSTITUTAS. Straipsnių rinkinys. [Collected works of the Institute of Botany of the Soviet Lithuanian Academy of Sciences] 1- ; 1961- . Vilnius, VPMLL. illus., maps, tables. Title varies: Botanikos klausimai. Summaries in Russian. QK1.L72 DLC(1-) CLSU-H(1-) CU(1-) DNAL(1-) MH(1-) NIC(1-) NN(1-)

1558. LIETUVOS TSR MOKSLŲ AKADEMIJA, VILNA. CENTRINĖ BIBLIOTEKA. Bibliotekininkystė ir bibliografija. [Librarianship and bibliography] 1- ; 1961- . Vilnius, VPMLL. See serials consulted.

1559. LIETUVOS TSR MOKSLŲ AKADEMIJA, VILNA. EKONOMIKOS INSTITUTAS. Darbai. Trudy. [Publications of the Institute of Economics of the Soviet Lithuanian Academy of Sciences] 1- ; 1954- . Vilnius, VPMLL. See Serials consulted.

1560. LIETUVOS TSR MOKSLŲ AKADEMIJA, VILNA. FIZIKOS-TECHNIKOS INSTITUTAS. Darbai. [Publications of the Institute of Physics and Technology of the Soviet Lithuanian Academy of Sciences] Vilnius, VPMLL. 1955-56. 2 v. Text in Lithuanian or Russian with summaries in the other language. Q60.L5 DLC(1-) NN(1-2)

1561. LIETUVOS TSR MOKSLŲ AKADEMIJA, VILNA. FIZIKOS IR MATEMATIKOS INSTITUTAS. Publikacija. [Publications of the Institute of Physics and Mathematics of the Soviet Lithuanian Academy of Sciences] 1- ; 1958- . Vilnius, VPMLL. Q60.L495 DLC(1-) CU(1-) AzU(1-) IdU(1-) MiU (1-)

1562. LIETUVOS TSR MOKSLŲ AKADEMIJA, VILNA. GEOLOGIJOS IR GEOGRAFIJOS INSTITUTAS. Moksliniai pranešimai. [Scientific reports of the In-

stitute of Geology and geography of the Soviet Lithuanian Academy of Sciences] 1- ; 1955- . Vilnius, VPMLL. See serials consulted.

1563. LIETUVOS TSR MOKSLŲ AKADEMIJA, VILNA. ISTORIJOS INSTITUTAS. Darbai. [Publications of the Institute of History of the Soviet Lithuanian Academy of Sciences] 1- ; 1951- . Kaunas; Vilnius, VPMLL. See serials consulted.

1564. --- --- Iš lietuvių kultūros istorijos. [On Lithuanian cultural history] 1- ; 1958- . Vilnius, VPMLL. See serials consulted.

1565. LIETUVOS TSR MOKSLŲ AKADEMIJA, VILNA. LIETUVIŲ KALBOS IR LITERATŪROS INSTITUTAS. Darbai. [Proceedings of the Institute of Lithuanian language and literature of the Soviet Lithuanian Academy of Sciences] T.1- ; 1956- . [Vilnius] illus., ports. PG8503.L6 DLC(1-) BM CU(1-) CLU(1-) ICU(1-6) NN(1-)

1566. LIETUVOS TSR MOKSLŲ AKADEMIJA, VILNA. LIETUVIŲ LITERATŪROS INSTITUTAS. Darbai. [Proceedings of the Institute of Lithuanian literature of the Soviet Lithuanian Academy of Sciences] [Kaunas] [Valstybinė enciklopedijų, žodynų ir mokslo literatūros leidykla, 1947. Summaries in Russian. Apparently only one volume published and superseded by "Literatūra ir kalba". PG8701.L55 DLC NN PU

1567. LIETUVOS TSR ZOOLOGŲ KONFERENCIJA. Tezisy dokladov. 1- ; 19- . Vil'nius. At head of title: Akademiia nauk Litovskoi SSR. Institut zoologii i parazitologii. QL1.L725 DLC(2-)

1568. LITAUISCHE LITERARISCHE GESELLSCHAFT, TILSIT. Mitteilungen. Bd.1-6 (Heft 1-31). Heidelberg, C. Winter, 1883-1912. 6 v. See serials consulted.

1569. LITERATŪRA IR KALBA. [Literature and language] 1- ; 1956- . Vilnius, VGLL. See serials consulted.

1570. LITHUANIA. ŠVIETIMO MINISTERIJA. KNYGŲ LEIDIMO KOMISIJA. Leidinys. [Publications of the Lithuanian Ministry of Education] Kaunas, 1920-35. Bw91#30p. CtY(14,21,24, 30,50,55,139,147-148,152,158,344, 377,378,448)

1571. LITOVSKII FIZICHESKII SBORNIK. 1- ; 1961- . Vil'nius, Min-

tis. illus. Chiefly in Russian.
QCl.L73 DLC(1-) CLU(1-) CsT([8]-)
CU(1-) CaAEU([2]-) CaOTU(6-) CMthL
([2]-) CtY(2-) ICRL(1-) IU(1-) KU
(4-) MH([3]-) MCM(1-) MdBJ([4],6-)
MoKL(6-) NN(1-) NjP(1-) OCoB(1-)
RPB(1-) TOU(1-)

1572. LITOVSKII MATEMATICHESKII
SBORNIK. 1- ; 1961- . Vil'nius,
Mintis. QAl.L48 DLC(1-) CU(1-)
CaAEU(7-) CaOTU(1-) CPT(4-) CtY
ICRL ICU IU(1-) MH(1-) NNC(1-)
NcU(1-) NjP(1-) OU(7-) RPB(1-)

1573. LITUANISTIKOS DARBAI. Lithuanian studies. 1- ; 1966- .
Chicago, Ill., Lituanistikos institutas. See serials consulted.

1574. LITUANISTIKOS INSTITUTAS.
Lituanistikos instituto 1971 metų
suvažiavimo darbai. Proceedings of
the Institute of Lithuanian Studies,
1971. Ed. Thomas Remeikis. Chicago, Ill., 1971. 280 p. Summaries in English. 080R ICBM

1575. LOGOS; filosofijos laikraštis. [Logos; journal of Philosophy]
Redaguoja Pranas Dovydaitis. Kaunas, Lietuvos Universiteto Teologijos-filosofijos fakulteto Filosofijos skyrius, 1921-39. 30 v. B.8
L6L6 DLC([1]-18) BM(1-30) CtTMF(1921,
1923-1930,1935-1937) ICCC(1921-1928,
no.2; 1929-1930) ICLJF(1921,no.1-2;
1922,no.1-2) ICU([8]-14) MH(1-2,[3],
6,10-12) MoU(8-18) NN(1-16) NNC(1-
[8])

1576. MEDICINA; mėnesinis laikraštis. Kaunas, Lietuvos Universiteto
medicinos fakultetas, and Kauno Medicinos draugija, 1920-40. Monthly. CSt-L([6],9-[11,13,16-19])
CU-M([10,11,14-16]) CaQMM([6-8,11]-)
CtY(18) DI-GS(6-[22]) ICU-R([6-7]-
[14-15]) MBM([]7-20]-) MBU([14-20]-)
NNN(6-[8]-) PPC(6-)

1577. MOKSLAS IR TECHNIKA. 1- ;
1959- . Kaunas. Issued by Lietuvos TSR Ministrų tarybos Valstybinio mokslinio tyrimo darbų koodina-
vimo komitetas and other similar
organizations. T4.M574 DLC(1961-)
ICRL(1963-)

1578. MŪSŲ TAUTOSAKA. Kaunas, Humanitarinių mokslų fakultetas, 1930-
35. 10 v. See serials consulted.

1579. PINNEBERG, GER. BALTIC UNI-
VERSITY. Contributions. Hamburg-
Pinneberg, Ger., 1946-48. 67 no. in
3 v. See serials consulted.

1580. --- Problems and discussions.
Pinneberg, Ger., 1946-47. 2 no. in
1 v. A32P656p CtY BM(Ac. 2631/2.)

NNC PU TxU

1581. SENOVĖ. [Antiquity] Kaunas, Humanitarinių mokslų fakultetas, 1935-38. 4 v. See serials
consulted.

1582. SOTER; religijos mokslo
laikraštis. [Journal of Theological Sciences] Kaunas, Teologijos-
filosofijos fakultetas, 1924-38.
28 no. See serials consulted.

1583. TAUTA IR ŽODIS. Epe lituana; sumptibus Ordinis philologorum Universitatis lituaniensis edita. Kn.1-7; 1927-1931. Kaunas,
Humanitarinių mokslų fakulteto leidinys, 1927-31. 7 v. See serials
consulted.

1584. TAUTOSAKOS DARBAI. [Folk-
loristic studies] Kaunas, Lietuvių
tautosakos archyvas, 1935-40. 7 v.
Editor: Jonas Balys. In Lithuanian,
English, and German. Vol. 4, covers
folklore of Vilnius region; vol. 7,
covers folklore of Klaipėda (Memel)
region; vol. 5 is the anthology of
the Lithuanian folksongs with music
and instrumental music. See serials consulted.

1585. TECHNIKA. Édition periodique de la faculté technique à l'
Université lithuanienne de Vytautas
le Grand. Kaunas, Technikos fakultetas, 1924-40. 11 v. See serials
consulted.

1586. VILNA. GEOLOGIJOS INSTITU-
TAS. Trudy. Vyp. 1- ; 1965- .
Vil'nius, Mintis. Irregular. Sum-
maries in English and Lithuanian.
QE276.V53 DLC(1-) CLU(1-) CU(1-)
CaBVaU CaOTU(3-) DI-GS(1-) ICU(1-)
InU(3-) IU(1-) MoKL(1-) NNC(1-)
PU(2,4-)

1587. VILNA. MOKYKLŲ MOKSLINIO TY-
RIMO INSTITUTAS. Pedagogikos dar-
bai. [Proceedings of Research on
Education] 1- ; 1964- . Vilnius.
DLC(1-)

1588. VILNA. OBSERVATORIUM ASTRO-
NOMICZNE. METEOROLOGIA. Biuletyn.
Bulletin de l'Observatoire astrono-
mique de Wilno. II.: Météorologie.
no.1-14. Wilno, 1921-39. 4 v.
plates. Irregular. QC802.V5 DLC
(1-2,5-14) CU(1-4,7-) CaQMM(1-2)
ICU(1,[2]) IEN(1-) MH-BH(5-6,12-14)
MNS(1-) NN(4-9) NNC(1-2) OO(9-14)

1589. VILNA. UNIVERSITETAS. Biologija, geografija, geologija. 1- ;
1949- . Vilnius, VPMLL. (Its Mokslo darbai) This is a subseries of
the Vilniaus Valstybinis V. Kapsuko
vardo Universitetas Mokslo darbai.

Vols.1-2(1949-1954) are unnumbered
and have title: Seriia estestnenno-
matematicheskikh nauk. Taitle varies: vols.3-4(1955-57), Biologijos,
geologijos ir geografijos mokslų
serija. Unclassified DLC(3-)

1590. --- Ekonomika. 1- ; 1955-
. Vilnius. Irregular. This is
a subseries of Its Mokslo darbai.
Title varies: v.1(1955), Ekonomika;
vol.2(1957), Ekonomikos ir teisės
mokslų serija; vol.3(1958) Ekonomikos mokslų serija. H31.V5 DLC(2-3)
MH

1591. --- Filosofija. Vilnius,
VPMLL, 1960. (Its Mokslo darbai,
t.35) Only vol.1 ever published.
Superseded in 1962 by the Lietuvos
TSR Aukštyjų mokyklų mokslo darbai:
Filosofija. Unclassified DLC(1)

1592. --- Matematika. Fizika.
1- ; 1949- . Vilnius, VPMLL.
(Its Mokslo darbai) Irregular.
Text in Lithuanian or Russian with
summaries in the other language.
Title varies: vols.1-2(1949-1954)
are unnumbered and have title:
"seriia estestvenno-matematicheskikh
nauk"; vols.3-7(1955-1957), "Matematikos, fizikos ir chemijos mokslų
serija". Unclassified DLC(7-)
RPB(1-9)

1593. --- Medicinos mokslų serija.
[Medical sciences series] 1- ; 1
1952- . Vilnius, VPMLL. illus.,
ports., tables. (Its Mokslo darbai)
Irregular. Text in Lithuanian or
Russian with summaries in the other
language. Vol.1(1952) is issued by
the Medicinos fakultetas and is en-
titles "Darbai"; vols.2-4(1955-1958)
have title: Medicinos mokslų serija.
R108.V5 DLC(3-)

1594. --- Mokslo darbai. [Pro-
ceedings of the University of Vil-
nius] 1-36; 1949-1960. Vilnius,
VPMLL. L Soc.2690.25 MH(1-4,6-13,17,
20-21,23-36) RPB(8,11,16,25)

1595. VILNA. UNIVERSITETAS. AS-
TRONOMIJOS OBSERVATORIJA. Biuletenis. [Bulletin of the Observatory
of Astronomy] 1- ; 1960- . Vilnius. Text in Russian with summaries in English and Lithuanian.
Two issues in 1960. Since 1961 the
consecutive numbering begins with
the no.1. Unclassified DLC(1960,
no.1-2; 1961,no.1-) AzU(1-) CLU(1-)
CU(1-) CaOTU(1-) CtY(1-) IU(1-)
InU(1-13) LU(1-) NNC(6-7) NjP(1-)
ViU(1-)

1596. VILNA. UNIVERSITETAS. BIBLI-
OTEKA. Mokslinės bibliotekos metraštis. [Yearbook of the Research

Library of the University of Vil-
nius] 1- ; 1957- . Vilnius,
VPMLL. Z821.7.V5 DLC(1957-) CaAEU
(1958-1959) CaOONL(1957-) MH(1958-)
InU(1958 59,1961) PU(1957-)

1597. VILNA. VALSTYBINIS PEDAGO-
GINIS INSTITUTAS. Mokslo darbai.
[Annals of the State Teachers' Col-
lege in Vilnius] 1- ; 1955- .
Vilnius. Text in Lithuanian or
Russian with summaries in Lithuani-
an, English, German, or Russian.
AS262.V442 DLC(9-) MH(1955-)

1598. VILNA. ŽEMĖS ŪKIO EKONOMI-
KOS MOKSLINIO TYRIMO INSTITUTAS.
Darbai. Trudy. 1- ; 1965- .
Vilnius, Mintis. Text in Lithuanian or Russian with summaries in the
other language. Unclassified DLC
(1-) MH(1-)

1599. VILNIAUS HIDROMETEOROLOGINĖ
OBSERVATORIJA. Trudy. Vyp. 1- ;
1964- . Vil'nius, Mintis. illus.,
maps. QC851.V54 DLC(1-)

IV.5. ALMANACS

1600. KALENDORIUS, ARBA METSKAJT-
lus ukiszkasis nuog užgimima Wieszpaties 1847 metu... kuriame ira:
atsitikimaj garsesniejej. Szwentes
Rima-Katiliku senowes ir naujoses
gadines... Paraszitas par L. Iwiński.
Wilniuje, Kasztu J. Zawadzkia, 1847.
38 p. AY1039.L5K32 1970 PU(Xerox
copy)

1601. --- Wilniuje, Kasztu J. Zawadzkia, 1848. 35 p. AY1039.L5K321
1970 PU(Xerox copy)

1602. --- Wilniuje, Kasztu J. Zawadzkia, 1849. 43 p. AY1039.L5K323
1970 PU(Xerox copy)

1603. --- Wilniuje, Kasztu J. Zawadzkia, 1860. 67 p. AY1039.L5K333
1970 PU(Xerox copy)

1604. --- Wilniuje, Kasztu J. Zawadzkia, 1861. 55 p. Bonaparte
Collection No. 13437 ICN

1605. KARIO KALENDORIUS. [Warri-
or's almanac] Kaunas, Kariuomenės
Vyr. Štabas, Spaudos ir švietimo
skyrius, 1933-39. 6 v. illus., map.
U135.L5K3DLC

1606. LIETUVININKŲ KALENDORIUS.
[Almanac of Lithuanians of Lithuania
Minor] 1952- . München, Ger.
illus., ports. AY1039.L5L54 DLC PU

1607. "LIETUVOS" KALENDORIUS.
Chicago, Ill., 1907-16. (*QYA)NN
(1908,1910,1916)

1608. LIETUVOS TSR KATALIKŲ KALEN-
dorius. [Almanac of Catholics in
the Soviet Union] Kaunas. DLC(1959-)

1609. MIESTO DARBININKŲ KALENDO-
rius. [An almanac of the city
workers]; 1908. Riga, [1907]
(*QYA)NN1908)

1610. MŪSŲ KALENDORIUS. Redagavo
A. Merkelis. Dillingen a.d. Donau,
Ger., 1947-48. 2 v. 891.920.M925
PU

1611. PIENO LAŠO DRAUGIJA, KAUNAS.
Pieno lašo draugijos informacijų
kalendorius, 1928. [An almanac of
information of "Pieno Lašas" soci-
ety] Kaunas. (*QYA)NN(1928)

1612. RUSSKO-LITOVSKII MIESIATSE-
slov na 1868 (visokosnyi) god. Ru-
sishkai-letuvishkasis kalendorius
ant (pribuvimas) mietu. Vil'na,
1867. Xerox copy, 1970. 65 p.
AY1039.L5R8 1970 PU(Xerox copy)

1613. VILNIAUS AIDAS; kalendorius
1916 metams. Vilnius, 1915. 491.
922V713 PU

1614. VILNIAUS KALENDORIUS. "Lietuvos ūkininko" priedas. [Vilnius
almanac; a supplement to the periodical "Lietuvos Ūkininkas"] Vilnius; Kaunas, 1906-40. Suspended
1916-1917. Title varies: Lietuvos
ūkininko kalendorius; Didysis Lietuvos ūkininko kalendorius. BM(4-9;
1908-1914) ICBM(1911,1922,1925-1926,
1930-1931) NN(1922-1933,1935,1937-
1938) PU(1926,1928)

V. EARTH SCIENCES

V.1. GENERAL STUDIES, CONFEREN-
CES, ETC.

1615. BÜSCHING, Anton Friedrich.
Erdbeschreibung. Hamburg, C.E. Bohn,
1787-1816. 14 v. in 22. Partial
contents.-Th. 2. Ost- und West Preussen, Poland und Litauen. 910.B928
MH MdBJ NcD

1616. GUDELIS, Vytautas. Lietuvos
geografinės aplinkos raida geologi-
nėje praeityje. Erdgeschichtliche
Entwicklung des geographischen Mil-
ieus Litauens. In Basalykas, Alfonsas. Lietuvos TSR fizinė geografija.
Vilnius, 1958. v.1, p.42-100.

GB276.L5B3 DLC CU CaOTU CtPAM
CtTMF DI-GS NN NNC PU WaU

1617. HYDROLOGISCHE KONFERENZ DER
BALTISCHEN STAATEN. 2d, Tallinn,
1928. Berichte. Tallinn, 1928.
35 no. illus., maps, diagrs. Text
in German, French or Russian. Issued also under an earlier name of
the conference: Baltische hydrologi-
scge und hydrometrische Konferenz
or Conférence baltique d'hydrologie
et hydrométrie. GB651.H8 1928a DLC
DI-GS

1618. --- 3rd, Warsaw, 1930. Ra-
domska, Lucine, 1930. Pam. DI-GS

1619. --- 4th, Leningrad, 1933.
Otchet o rabotakh IV. Baltiiskoi gi-
drologicheskoi konferentsii. Leningrad, Gosudarstvennyi gidrologicheskii institut, 1934. 339 p. illus.,
plates, ports., diagrs. GB651.H8
1933b DLC DI-GS

1620. --- 5th, Helsinki, June 1936.
Rapport. Nr.1-5. Helsinki, 1936.
5 no. 701(500)H994b & 701(500)H994c
DI-GS(2,3)

1621. 6th, Berlin, 1938. Berichte
und Mitteilungen. Nr.1-19. Berlin,
Landesanstalt für Gewässerkunde und
Hauptnivellements, 1938-39. 19 no.
GB651.H8 1938c DLC DI-GS(2,5,12,19)

V.2. GEOGRAPHY

V.2.a. GENERAL STUDIES, TEXT-
BOOKS, ETC.

1622. BIELIUKAS, Kazys. Geografijos moksliniai-tiriamieji darbai Lietuvoje tarybiniais metais. [The geographical research in Lithuania during the Soviet period] In Geografinis metraštis (Vilnius), v.2, 1959
p.5-27. Summaries in German and
Russian. See serials consulted.

1623. --- Geographical research
work in Lithuania under Soviet power.
In LTSRMAGGICPXIX. Vilnius, 1960.
p. 11-15. GB3.I45 1960ac CU DLC
CaAEU CaMWU ICU NNC

1624. GREAT BRITAIN. NAVAL STAFF.
NAVAL INTELLIGENCE DIVISION. Lithu-
ania; geography. London, Naval Staff,
Intelligence Department, 1918. 22 p.
DK511.L2G786 CSt-H

1625. IVANAUSKAS, Antanas. Geografiia Litovskoi SSR dlia VIII kla-
sa. Kaunas, Shviesa, 1965. 149 p.

illus., maps. DK511.L2I19 DLC

1626. KLIMAS, Adolfas. Lietuvos geografija. [Lithuanian geography] 2. leidimas. Kaunas, Dirva, 1923. 72 p. 947.52.K682 1923 PU

1627. --- --- 3. pataisytas ir papildytas leidimas. Kaunas, Dirva, 1927. 121 p. 947.52.K683 PU

1628. KUPFFER, Karl Reinhold. Baltische Landeskunde. Riga, G.Löffler, 1911. xvi, 557 p. illus, tables, 6 fold. maps. DAS ICJ

1629. LIETUVOS TSR MOKSLŲ AKADEMIJA, VILNA. GEOLOGIJOS IR GEOGRAFIJOS INSTITUTAS. Collected papers for the XIX International Geographic Congress. Edited by V. Gudelis. Vilnius, 1960. 482 p. illus., maps. Text in English or Russian with summaries in Lithuanian. On cover and spine: Collectanea acta geographica Lituanica. GB3.I45 1960ac CU CaAEU CaMWU DLC ICU NNC

1630. ŠINKŪNAS, Peliksas. Lietuvos geografija. [Geography of Lithuania] Kaunas, Sakalo bendrovė, 1927. 275 p. illus., maps. 914.475 CtTMF BN CaAEU RP

1631. VIRELIŪNAS, Antanas. Krašto mokslo vadovėlis. [Geography of Lithuania; a textbook] Kaunas, 1931. 182 p. 914.47.V5 CtTMF

V.2.b. CARTOGRAPHY

1632. ANDRIUS, Juozas. Kunigaikščio Radvilo Lietuvos žemėlapis. [The map of Lithuania by Duke Radvila] In Aidai (Kennebunkport, Me.), no.10(44), 1952, p. 439-450. See serials consulted.

1633. --- 1613 metų Lietuvos žemėlapis. [The map of Lithuania from 1613] In Karo archyvas (Kaunas), v.8, 1937. See serials consulted.

1634. CHOMSKIS, Vaclovas. The cartographical expression of the territory of Lithuania; a historical review. In LTSRMAGGICPXIX. Vilnius, 1960. p. 21-31. GB3.I45 1960ac CU CaAEU CaMWU DLC ICU NNC

1635. --- Lietuvos kartografinio vaizdo XVII ir XVIII a. vystymosi klausimu. [On the cartographic change of the landscape in Lithuania during the seventeenth and eighteenth centuries] In Vilnius. Universitetas. Gamtos mokslų serija (Vilnius),

v.4, 1957. (Its Mokslo darbai) See serials consulted.

1636. --- Lietuvos territorijos geografinio pažinimo ir kartografavimo istorijos bruožai. [The historical outline of the geographical research and cartographical works on Lithuanian territory] In Basalykas, A. Lietuvos TSR fizinė geografija. Vilnius, 1958. v.1, p. 16-30. GB276.L5B3 DLC CU CaOTU CtPAM CtTMF DI-GS NN NNC PU WaU

1637. GUSTAITIS, Algirdas. Kunigaikščio M.K. Radvilo (Našlaitėlio) 1613 metų žemėlapis amžių perspektyvoje. [The map of Duke M.K. Radvila from 1613... Brooklyn, N.Y.,1970] 21 p. illus., maps. Offprint from "Karys" no.8-9, 1970. GA1077.L5G8 PU CaAEU

1638. JAKUBOWSKI, Jan. W sprawie mapy Tomasza Makowskiego (1613) In Przegląd Geograficzny (Warszawa), v.1, 1918-1919, p. 297-306. See serials consulted.

1639. KVIETKAUSKAS, V. Keturspalvis morfologinis žemėlapis. Chetyrekhtsvetnaia morfologicheskaia karta. [Coloured morphological map] In Geografinis metraštis (Vilnius), v.6-7, p.87-107. Summaries in German or Russian. See serials consulted.

1640. MERCZYNG, Henryk. Mapa Litwy z roku 1613 Ks. Radziwiłła Sierotki pod względem matematycznym i kartograficznym. In Towarzystwo Naukowe Warszawskie. Sprawozdania z posiedzeń (Warszawa), v.6, 1913. See serials consulted.

1641. MORITZ, Theodor August Eduard. Die Entwicklung des Kartenbildes der Nord- und Ostseeländer bis auf Mercator. Halle, C.A. Kaemmerer & Co., 1908. v,82 p. Inaug.-Diss. --University of Berlin. GA781.M8 DLC ICJ MiU MH PU

1642. PETRULIS, Juozas (1904-) Antanas Vydas and his cartographic works. In LTSRMAGGICPXIX. Vilnius, 1960. p. 39-46. GB3.I45 1960ac CU DLC CaAEU CaMWU ICU NNC

1643. REKLAITIS, Povilas Viktoras. Lietuvos senoji kartografija. [The ancient cartography of Lithuania] In Tautos praeitis (Chicago, Ill.), v.2, 1964, p.64-76. See serials consulted.

1644. --- Neues zur Litauenkarte des Fürsten Nikolaus Christoph Radvilas. In Zeitschrift für Ostfor-

schung (Marburg), v.15, no.1, 1966,
p. 56-59. See serials consulted.

1645. SPEKKE, Arnolds. The Baltic
Sea in ancient maps. [Translated
from the Latvian by A.J. Grisberg et
al.] Stockholm, M. Goppers, 1961.
iv,75 p. illus. GA951.S713 DLC
CaAEU PU

V.2.c. ATLASES AND MAPS

1646. ANDRIUS, Juozas, comp. Lietuvos žemėlapis. [Map of Lithuania]
So.Boston, Juozas Kapočius, 1956.
col. map. 72 x 103 cm. fol to 22 x
15 cm. Scale 1:500,000. Includes
two historical maps: Maximal area
inhabited by Baltic tribes in the
Bronze and the Iron Ages, prepared
by M. Gimbutas, and Lithuania in
the fifteenth century prepared by
A. Šapoka. Includes text which contains: "Main statistical data on Lithuania" by A. Bendorius; "The boundaries of Lithuania and its population" by K. Pakštas; "Hydrography"
by S. Kolupaila; and "Gazetteer" by
A. Salys. 47 p. G7050.A5 1956 DLC
CaOTP ICLJF PU

BROGA, L. Turistskaia kar-
ta Litovskoi SSR. Perevod s litovskogo iazyka. Vil'nius, 1963. See
entry no. 1114.

BROGA, L. and E. Danilevičius, comp. Lietuvos TSR turistinis
žemėlapis. Vilnius, 1963. See serials consulted. entry no. 1114.

1647. BUREAU D'INFORMATIONS DE LI-
TUANIE, LAUSANNE. Carte de la Lituanie... 4-e éd. corr. Berne, Kummer-
ly & Frey [1920] map 89 x 61 cm.
fold to 18 x 13 cm. Echelle
1:1,500,000. 2d ed. has entry under
Lithuanian Information Bureau, Lausanne. GA1077 1920 L3L776 ed.4
CSt-H CSt

1648. CHARTE VON RUSSISCH LITAUEN
welche die von Polen und Russland ab-
getretene Woiewodschaften Liefland,
Witepsk, Mscislaw, und einen Theil
der Woiewodschaften Polock und Minsk
enthält. Nürnberg, auf Kosten der
Homännischen Erben, 1775. Map 56 x
43 cm. Scale 15 Deutsche Meilen zu
1. Grad des Aequatoris, oder 100
russisch Werst auf 1. Grad. ICBM

1649. DIRVA, PUBLISHERS, MARIJAM-
POLĖ. Kauno miesto planas. [The
city plan of Kaunas] Marijampolė,
1922. 16 p., fold map. Scale
1:10,000. 947.52.D639 PU

1650. FRIEDERICHSEN, Richard. Li-
tauen-Lietuva, nach amtlichen Quellen bearbeitet von R. Friederichsen
und K.A. Oželis. 5. verb. Auf...
unter Mitarbeit von Hans Mortensen.
Hamburg, Friederichsen & Co., 1926.
Map 65 x 71 cm. fold to 22 1/2 cm.
Scale 1:750,000. G1935.L7 1926 ICU
CLU MH PU

1651. GRODNA. Vera designatio ur-
bis in Littavia Grodnae. [n.p., n.d]
Col. map 30 x 48 cm. ICBM

1652. JAKUBOWSKI, Jan. Mapa Wielkiego Księstwa Litewskiego w połowie
XVI wieku. 1: Część północna. Kraków, Polska Akademia Umiejętności,
1928. 21 p. Scale 1:1,600,000.
In Atlas Historyczny Polski. Serja
B. BM(Ac. 750/121.) CU

1653. --- --- Another edition.
Warszawa, 1961. In Atlas Historyczny Polski. Seria B. Mapy przeglą-
dowe. G1951.S1A82 DLC CoU PU

1654. KVIKLYS, Bronius, ed. Lietuvos topografinis žemėlapis. [To-
pographical map of Lithuania] Chicago, Ill., Tėviškėlė, 1961. 1 v.
[126] leaves of maps. Scale
1:100,000. Q 912.475.K974 PU

1655. LIETUVOS KALNUOTUMO IR NUO-
takumo žemėlapis. [Topographical
map of Lithuania] Kaunas, Dirvos
bendrovės leidinys, 1937. Col. map
45 x 53 cm. Scale 1:800,000. ICBM

1656. LIETUVOS KELIŲ ŽEMĖLAPIS.
[Road map of Lithuania] Kaunas,
Lietuvos automobilių klubas, 1936.
Scale 1:500,000. DLC

1657. --- Braižė Br. Lazėnas. Kaunas, Spindulys, [n.d.] Scale
1:500,000. 59 x 74 cm. ICBM

1658. LIETUVOS ŽEMĖLAPIS. [Map of
Lithuania] Kaunas, Dirva, 1939.
49 x 56 cm. fold. to 17 x 12 cm.
Scale 1:800,000. G2Žem ICLJF

1659. LITHUANIA. Published by direction of the Lithuanian National
Council, U.S.A. Originally issued by
the Lithuanian Bureau of Information,
Lausanne, [1919?] Col. map. 66 x 97
cm. Scale 1:1,500,000. 7051.S500
1917 CaOTU ICBM

1660. LITHVANIA PER GERARDUM MER-
catorem. Cum privilegio. Amsterdam,
1609. Map 44 x 37 cm. Scale 10
Lithuanianmiles to one inch (10 mi-
liaria lithuanica communia) ICBM

1661. LITHUANIAN INFORMATION BUREAU
Lausanne. Carte de la Lituanie; éd.

par les soins soins du Bureau d'informations lituanien, Lausanne. 2. éd. corr. et augm, Berne, Kümmerly & Frey [1919?] Map 61 x 87 cm. Scale 1:1,500,000. 4th ed. has entry under "Bureau d'informations de Lituanie, Lausanne. D643.A7DP5L71 no.3 CSt-H MH

1662. MAGNI DUCATUS LITHUANIAE. Tabula, divisa tam in Palatinatus quam in subjacentes Castellanias. Per F. de Witt. Amstelodami, cum privilegiis potentiss. D.D. Ordinum Holl. Westfrisiaegs [n. d.] Col. map 43 x 52 cm. Scale 15 milliaria Germanica in uno gradu (2 1/4 inch), or 20 milliaria Gallica, sive Horae itineris in uno gradu, or 18 milliaria Lithuanica in uno gradu. ICBM

1663. MAGNI DUCATUS LITHUANIAE caeterumque regionum illi adiacentium extra descriptio... Principis Nicolai Christophori Radziwil...opera, cura et impensis facta ac in lucem edita. Amsterdami, Excudebat Guilhelmus Janssonius, 1613. Col. map 72 x 75 cm. Scale 30 milliaria magna, 35 milliaria mediocria, or 40 milliaria communia sive usitata to 6 3/4 inches. ICBM

1664. MATULIONIS, Povilas. Kalnuotumo ir nuotakumo Lietuvos ir jos pakraščių žemėlapis... iš naujo sustatytas 1919-1920 m. Berlin, S. Schropp'sche Lehrmittel-Handlung, 1922-23. Map Scale 1:630,000. ICBM

1665. A NEW AND ACCURATE MAP OF Europe collected from the best authorities, assisted by the most approv'd modern maps & charts. The whole being regulated and adjusted by astronomical observations. By Eman. Bowen. [London] E. Bowen, 1752. Map 35 x 41 cm. Scale 1 inch to 240 English miles. ICBM

1666. A NEW AND ACCURATE MAP OF Poland, Lithuania &c... Divided into its Palatinats, drawn from the best authorities, assisted by the most approv'd modern maps. The wholebeing regulated by astronomical observations by Eman'l Bowen, 1748. [London, 1748] Map 43 x 34 cm. Scale 32 common leagues of Poland to 2 inches, or 100 English miles to 2 inches. ICBM

1667. NOVISSIMA ET ACCURATISSIMA Magni Ducatus Lithuaniae in suos Palatinatus et Castellanias divisae. Delineatio cura et impensis Matthaei Seutteri [n.p., 1730] Map 58 x 50 cm. Scale 15 milliaria Germanica in uno gradu, or 20 milliaria Gallica

in uno gradu. ICBM

1668. OSTLAND. REICHSKOMMISSAR. Ostland-Atlas. Gesamtbearbeitung: Gottfried Müller, statistische Unterlagen: Jakob Jureviz, kartographische Arbeiten: Hermann Warren. Riga, 1942-43. [6], 60 [i.e. 62] fold. col. maps. (Its Strukturbericht über das Ostland, Bd.2) G2120.08 1942 DLC NNC

1669. LI PALATINATI DI MINSK, Mscislaw, Polock e Witebsk nella Lituania. Tratta dall'Atlante Polacco del Rizzi Zanoni. Venezia, Presso Antonio Zatta, 1781. Map 40 x 32 cm. Scale Miglia comuni di Germania, e di Polonia da 15, al grado, [or] miglia comuni d'Italia da 60 al grado. ICBM

1670. PHILIP, George and Son, Ltd. Timber and mercantile map of the Baltic with index. London, 1925. Col. map 156 x 110 cm. Scale 1:950,000; Equatorial scale 1:2,000,000. Shows forest areas, tariff zones, shipping districts, steamship routes with distances between ports, mail routes with duration of passage, etc. Index: 15 p. G2046.K1P5 1925 DLC

1671. POLEN, LITAUEN UND KURLAND im Jahr 1774, [1793, 1796] [Berlin 1820] 3 maps 55 x50 cm. fold. to 28 x 22 cm. From the Thomas Carlyle Papers purchased at Sotheby's June 14, 1932, item 199. Used by Frederick the Great. Ms. vault, Section 12, Drawer 3 CtY

1672. POTENTISSIMO BORUSSORUM REGI Friderico Wilhelmo... hancce Lithuaniam Borussicam in qua loco colonijs Salisburg. ad incolendum regio nuta concessa chorographice exhibentur. Cartographer I.F. Betaen Feb. 1733. Noribergae, Homanniani Heredes, 1735. Map 68 x 58. Scale 900 rhein. Fuss to 2- inches, or 15 milliarium communi in uno gradu. Includes: Plan von der in Lithauen neu angelegten Stadt Gumbinnen. ICBM

1673. REGNI POLONIAE MAGNIQUE DUCAtus Lithuaniae nova et exacta tabula ad mentem Starovoleij descripta à Iohanne Bapt. Homanno. Norimbergae, I.B. HOMANN [1712] Map 56x49. Scale 30 milliaria Germanica to 2 3/4 inches, or 40 milliaria Polonica to 2 3/4 inches. ICBM

1674. ROYAUME DE POLOGNE, GD. DUche de Lithuanie et Royaume de Prusse. Paris, Chez Bourgoin Graveur [n.d.] Map 45 x 36. Scale Lieues communes de France de 25 au degré, or lieues d'Allemagne et de Pologne du 18-e siecle. ICBM

1675. ŠLAPELIS, Skaistutis. Lietuvos žemėlapis. [Map of Lithuania. Tübingen, Ger.] Patria [n.d.] Map. 30 x 64 cm. fold. to 22 x 16 cm. Scale 1:1,000,000. As appendix to Ivinskis, Zenonas. Lietuvos sienų klausimu. G2Žem ICLJF ICBM

1676. TABULA NOVA TOTIUS REGNI Poloniae, in quo sunt Ducatus et Provinciae Prussia... Ducatus Lithuania, Ukraina, & c...cum suis Palatinatibus et confinijs. Authore N. Sansonio Abbevillensij, geographus Regis Galliae. Amsterdami, Apud Nicolaum Vischer, [1690?] Map 56 x42 cm. Scale 120 mille passus geometrici to 2 7/8 inches, or 40 milliaria communia sive usita to 2 7/8 inches. ICBM

1677. TALEIKIS, A. Lietuvos kelių žemėlapis su atstumais. [Road map of Lithuania] Kaunas, J. Taleikis, 1929. Map 73 x 85 cm. fold. to 25 x 11 cm. Scale 1:500,000. 947.59.T14L WaU DLC

1678. VILNA LITVANIAE METROPOLIS. Reproduction of a sixteenth century engraving. Map 27 x 38. ICBM

1679. VIRELIŪNAS, Antanas. Lietuva. [Map of Lithuania] 4th ed. Kaunas, Spaudos fondas, 1937. Map 162 x 150 cm. Scale 1:300,000. ICBM

1680. DIE VERBREITUNG DER DEUTSCEN in Litauen auf Grund der amtlichen litauischen Volkszählung vom 17. September 1923. [n.p.] 1935. 914.75 Map no.2 WaU

V.3. PHYSICAL GEOGRAPHY

V.3.a. GENERAL STUDIES, TEXT-BOOKS, ETC.

1681. BASALYKAS, Alfonsas. Lietuvos TSR fizinė geografija. [Physical geography of Lithuania] Vilnius, VPMLL, 1958-65. 2 v. illus., maps. Bibliography: v.1, p.467-478. At head of title: Lietuvos TSR Mokslų akademija. Geologijos ir geografijos institutas. GB276.L5B3 DLC CU CtPAM CtTMF CaOTU DI-GS NN NNC PU WaU

1682. KRAUS, E. Über tektonischen Gegenwartsbewegungen in Ostseegebiet. In Hydrologische Konferenz der baltischen Staaten. 4th, Leningrad,

1933. Otchet... 49 p. GB651.H8 1933b DLC DI-GS IaAS

1683. LIETUVOS TSR DIRVOŽEMIAI. [The soil of the Lithuanian SSR. Redakcinė kolegija: V.Ruokis, et al.] Vilnius, Mintis, 1965. 300 p. illus. fold. maps. S599.R92L5 DLC CU PU

1684. PAKUCKAS, Česlovas. Lietuvos žemės paviršiaus susidarymas ir upių atsiradimas. [The formation of the earth-crust and the origin of the rivers in Lithuania] In Židinys (Kaunas), no.5-6, 1934, p.497-505. See serials consulted.

1685. SROKOWSKI, Stanisław. Zarys geografii fizicznej ziem polsko-litewsko-ruskich. Kijów, Wydawn. Rady Okręgowej, 1918. xvii, 161 p. illus. maps GB276.P6S6 DLC MH PU

1686. TARVYDAS, Stasys. Lietuvos TSR fizinė-geografinė apžvalga. [An outline of physical geography of Soviet Lithuania] Vilnius, VPMLL, 1958. 76 p. illus., maps. (Pažinkime Lietuvą). GB276.L5T3 DLC

1687. --- Lietuvos TSR fizinio geografinio rajonavimo klausimu. [On the question of physico-geographical zoning of Soviet Lithuania] In LTSRMAGGIMP, v.1, 1955, p.17-32. map. See serials consulted.

1688. --- The physico-geographical zoning of the Lithuanian SSR. In LTSRMAGGICPXIX. Vilnius, 1960. p. 53-57. GB3.I45 1960ac CU CaAEU DLC ICU NNC CaMWU

1689. WOŁŁOSOWICZ, Stanisław. Litwa i Białoruś. Chęść 1: Budowa fizyczno-geograficzna. Warszawa, Zakłady Drukarskie Tow. "Rozwój", 1920. 107 p. illus., fold. map. At head of title: Polskie Towarzystwo Krajoznawcze. Q 947.52.W835 PU KU NN

1690. WOODS, Ethel G. (Skeat) The Baltic region; a study in physical and human geography. London, Methuen [1932] xv, 436 p. illus., maps, diagrs., fold. tables. Bibliography: p. 407-413. Lithuania: p. 389-406. GB171.W6 DLC CaAEU ICJ MiU NN OCl OU PPT PU

V.3.b. GEOMORPHOLOGY

1691. BASALYKAS, Alfonsas. Development of the valley-river network in Lithuania in late- and post-glacial times. In LTSRMAGGICPXIX. Vilnius, 1960. p. 83-89.

GB3.I45 1960ac CU CaAEU CaMWU DLC
ICU NNC

1692. --- Geomorfologinė Nemuno
upyno slėnių Lietuvos TSR ribose
charakteristika. [The geomorphological characteristic of the valleys
of the Nemunas river-basin in Lithu-
ania] In LTSRMAGGIMP, v.1, 1955,
p. 48-73. See serials consulted.

1693. --- Landšaftinių tyrimų
klausimu Lietuvoje. [On the question of exploration of the landsca-
pes in Lithuania] In Geografinis
metraštis (Vilnius), v.2, 1959, p.
115-133. Summaries in German or
Russian. See serials consulted.

1694. --- Lietuvos paviršiaus reljefas. Oberflächengestaltung Litauens. In Basalykas, A. Lietuvos TSR
fizinė geografija. Vilnius, 1958.
v.1, p. 101-166. GB276.L5L52 DLC
CU CtPAM CtTMF CaOTU DI-GS NN NNC
PU WaU

1695. --- Lietuvos TSR pietryčių
smėlėtoji lyguma; geomorfologinė apžvalga. [A geomorphological outline of the sandy plains in South-
Eastern Lithuania] In Vilna. Universitetas. Biologijos, geologijos
ir geografijos serija (Vilnius),
v.3, 1955, p. 65-118. (Its Mokslo
darbai) See serials consulted.

1696. --- Lietuvos TSR reljefo
morfogenezės klausimu. [On the question of morphogenesis of the Lithuanian relief] In LTSRMAGGIMP,
v.9, 1959, p. 57-86. map. Summaries
in German and Russian. See serials
consulted.

1697. --- Lietuvos teritorijos ge-
omorfologinių tyrimų istorija. [The
history of the geomorphological research of the Lithuanian territory]
In Geografinis metraštis (Vilnius),
v.2, 1959, p. 53-84. illus. Summaries in German and Russian. See serials consulted.

1698. --- Main features of the glacial morphology of Lithuania. In
LTSRMAGGICPXIX. Vilnius, 1960. p.
95-99. GB3.I45 1960ac CU CaAEU CaMWU
DLC ICU NNC

1699. --- Main features of the history of the geomorphological investigations on the territory of Lithuania. In LTSRMAGGICPXIX. Vilnius,
1960. p. 62-69. GB3.I45 1960ac CU
CaAEU CaMWU DLC ICU NNC

1700. --- Nemuno deltos žemuma; fi-
zinio-geografinio rajono apybraiža.
[The physico-geographical outline of

the delta of Nemunas River] In Geografinis metraštis (Vilnius), v.4,
1961, p. 5-44. illus., map. Summaries in German and Russian. See
serials consulted.

1701. --- Pakraštiniai ledyniniai
dariniai ir kai kurios pastabos Lietuvos TSR teritorijos deglaciacijos
klausimu. Kraevye lednikovye obrazovaniia i nekatorye zametki po voprosu deglatsiatsii territorii Litovskoi SSR. Summary in Russian.
In LTSRMAGGIMP, v.14, 1964, sąs.1,
p. 67-96. map. See serials consulted.

1702. --- Vilniaus miesto ir jo
apylinkių geomorfologiniai bruožai.
[The geomorphological characteristic of the City of Vilnius and its
environments] In LTSRMAGGIMP, v.1,
1955, p. 33-47. See serials consulted.

1703. BASALYKAS, Alfonsas and J.
Petrauskaitė. Kai kurie paskutini-
niojo apledėjimo nepaliestos Medininkų aukštumos fiziniai-geografi-
niai ypatumai. [Some physico-geographical features of the plateau of
Medininkai which was untouched by
the last glacial period] In Vilna.
Universitetas. Biologijos, geografijos ir geologijos mokslų serija
(Vilnius), v.4, 1957, p. 107-123.
illus., map. (Its Mokslo darbai)
See serials consulted.

1704. ČEPULYTĖ, Valerija. Lietuvos geomorfologiniai rajonai ir jų
geologinė raida. [The geomorphological districts of Lithuania and
their geological development] In
LTSRMAGGIMP, v.6, 1958, p. 23-53.
map. See serials consulted.

1705. --- Lietuvos žemės pavir-
šius. [The surface of the Lithuanian landscape] Vilnius, VPMLL,1957.
102 p. illus., maps. (Pažinkime
Lietuvą) GB276.L5C4 DLC ICBM

1706. DALINKEVIČIUS, Juozas. Lietuvos ir jos pakraščių pagrindinis
(podiliuvinis) reljefas. [The relief
of Lithuania and its adjoining areas]
In Kosmos (Kaunas), v.10, 1930, p.
145-154. See serials consulted.

1707. GAIGALAS, Algirdas and Česlovas Kudaba. Geologo-geomorfologi-
cheskoe stroenie rel'efa v raione
mezhdurechiia rek Neris i Shviantoii.
Geologic-geomorphologic set up of
the relief in the region between the
Neris and Šventoji Rivers. In
LTSRMAD. Serija B, v.2(57), 1969,
p. 179-187. Summaries in English
and Lithuanian. See serials con-

sulted.

1708. GAIGALAS, Algirdas and S. Vaitiekūnas. Sviaz pleistotsenovogo lednikovogo osadkoobrazovaniia s kharakterom podstilaiushchei poverkhnosti na territorii Litovskoi SSR. The relationship between glacial sedimentation of Pleistocene and the nature of surface foundation in the territory of Lithuanian SSR. In LTSRMAD. Serija B, v.1(56), 1969, p. 191-206. Summaries in English and Lithuanian. See serials consulted.

1709. GARMUS, Paulius. Lietuvos dirvožemis. [The soil of Lithuanian territory] In Basalykas, A. Lietuvos TSR fizinė geografija. Vilnius, 1958. v.1, p. 294-330. GB276.L5L52 v.1 CU CtPAM CtY DLC MH NN NNC OKentU

1710. GARUNKŠTIS, Aleksas. Dėl glacigeninių rininio (latakinio) tipo formų kilmės ir išsidėstymo Lietuvos TSR teritorijoje. [On the origin of types of the glacigenic channel lakes and their distribution in Lithuania] In LTSRMAD. Serija B, v.2, 1956, p. 73-88. map, tables. Summary in Russian. See serials consulted.

1711. JURGAITIS, Algirdas and A. Mikalauskas. Litologicheskaia kharakteristika otlozhenii fliuvioglatsial'noi terrasy Garūnai. Lithological characteristics of the outwash terrace sediments in Garūnai. In LTSRMAD. Serija B, v.2(57), 1969, p. 163-178. Summaries in English and Lithuanian. See serials consulted.

1712. KLIMAVIČIENĖ, O. Kazlų Rūdos ir Eičių limnoglacialinių smėlynų sąrangos litologijos ir morfologijos bruožai. Cherty stroeniia, litologii i morfologii Kazlu-Rudtskikh i Eichiaitskikh ozerolednikovykh peschanykh massivov. Summaries in German and Russian. In Geografinis metraštis (Vilnius), v.6-7,1963-1964, p. 129-143. illus., map. See serials consulted.

1713. KONDRACKI, Jerzy. Z morfogenezy doliny dolnego Niemna. In Przegląd Geograficzny (Warszawa), v.21, zesz.1-2, 1947, p. 11-36. Summary in French. See serials consulted.

1714. KONDRATIENĖ, O. Interglacial and interstadial deposits of Lithuania. In LTSRMAGGICPXXI. Vilnius, 1960. p. 205-[213] QE1.L4483 DLC CU DI-GS ICU MH-Z NNC

1715. MICAS, Liudas. Geomorfologiniai Vilnios baseino bruožai. [The geomorphologic features of the Vilnia River basin] In LTSRMAGGIMP, v.1, 1955, p. 74-83. Summary in Russian. See serials consulted.

1716. --- Nemuno žemupio slėnio morphologinės sąrangos klausimu. [On the question of the morphologic composition of the Nemunas River delta valley] In LTSRMAGGIMP, v. 14, sąs. 1, 1962, p. 203-216. graphs. See serials consulted.

1717. --- Nemuno slėnio struktūra Merkinės-Prienų ruože. [The structure of the Nemunas River valley in the Merkinė-Prienai district] In LTSRMAGGIMP, v. 10, fasc. 2, 1959, p. 27-45. illus. Summary in German and Russian. See serials consulted.

1718. --- Nemuno slėnio struktūra Prienų-Pažaislio ruože. [The structure of the Nemunas River valley in the Prienai-Pažaislis district] In LTSRMAGGIMP, v.9, 1959, p. 99-116. illus., map. Summaries in German and Russian. See serials consulted.

1719. --- Paskutiniojo apledėjimo ribos klausimu Vilnios baseine. [On the question of the boundary of the last glaciation in the Vilnia River basin] In LTSRMAGGIMP, v.9, 1959, 87-98. map. Summaries in German and Russian. See serials consulted.

1720. --- Vilnios baseino geomorfologiniai bruožai. [A geomorphological outline of the Vilnia River basin] In LTSRMAGGIMP, v.1, 1955, p. 74-83. See serials consulted.

1721. --- Vilnios slėnio raidos pagrindinės fazės. [The basic phases of the development of the Vilnia River Valley] In LTSRMAGGIMP, v.6, 1958, p.91-104. illus. See serials consulted.

1722. MIKAILA, V. Lietuvos stambesniųjų limnoglacialinių baseinų nuosėdos ir jų ryšiai su paskutiniuoju ledynu. [The deposits of the larger limnoglacial basins of Lithuania and their relation to the latest glacial period] In LTSRMAGGIMP, v.7, 1958, p. 5-17. map. Summaries in English and Russian. See serials consulted.

1723. --- Lietuvos TSR stambesniųjų limnoglacialinių baseinų struktūra ir litologinė charakteristika. [The structure and lithological characteristic of the limnoglacial basins in Lithuania] In LTSRMAGGIP,

v.10, fasc. 2, 1959, p. 249-277.
illus. Summaries in German and Russian. See serials consulted.

1724. --- Stambesniųjų pietų ir vidurio Lietuvos TSR limnoglacialinių baseinų išplitimo, struktūros ir trukmės klausimu. [On the question of extension, structure and time of the larger limnoglacial basins in Southern and Central Lithuania] In LTSRMAD. Serija B, v. 4(12), 1957, p. 95-107. map. Summary in Russian. See serials consulted.

1725. MIKALAUSKAS, A. Morfologiia, stroenie i genezis rel'efa Sredne-Litovskoi nizmennosti (3. k voprosu o degradatsii Niavezhskoi lednikovoi lopasti i razvitii gidrograficheskoi seti. Morphology, structure and genesis of the middle-Lithuanian plain relief...] In LTSRMAD. Serija B, v.2(57), 1969, p. 231-241. Summaries in English and Lithuanian. See serials consulted.

1726. MORTENSEN, Hans. Über eine Endmoräne im nordwestlichen Litauen. In Jahrbuch der Preussischen Geologischen Landesanstalt zu Berlin, v. 42, 1923, p. 621-625. QE269.A19P3 v.42 DLC CU CaOOG CtY DI-GS ICJ ICU IaU KU MBN MdBJ NN NNA NNM OClW OU PPAN

1727. OKOŁOWICZ, Wincenty. Geomorfologia okolic środkowej Wilii. Warszawa, Państwowe Wydawnictwo Naukowe, 1956. 68 p. illus. (Polska Akademia Nauk. Instytut Geografii. Prace Geograficzne, nr.6) G23.P615 no.6 DLC DI-GS IEN MnU NN NcD WaU

1728. PAKUCKAS, Česlovas. Galinių morenų kryptis rytinės Lietuvos aukštumose ir tų aukštumų kilmė. [The direction of the terminal moraine in the highlands of eastern Lithuania and their origin] In Kosmos(Kaunas), v.17, 1936, p. 323-334. See serials consulted.

1729. --- Pietinės Lietuvos glacialmorfologiniai bruožai. [The glacio-morphological features of Southern Lithuania] In Kosmos (Kaunas), v.19, 1938, p. 321-333. See serials consulted.

1730. --- Pietinės Lietuvos reljefo glacialiniai elementai. [The glacial elements of the relief in Southern Lithuania] In Kosmos (Kaunas), v.15, no.7-12, 1934, p. 185-200. See serials consulted.

1731. RAČINSKAS, A. Dabartiniai geomorfologiniai procesai rytų Lietuvos upių slėniuose. [The present geomorphological processes in the valleys of the rivers in Eastern Lithuania] In Geografinis metraštis (Vilnius), v.2, 1959, p. 339-362. illus. Summaries in German and Russian. See serials consulted.

1732. --- Kai kurie rytų Lietuvos aukštumų dirvožemio erozijos dėsningumai. [Some erosion patterns of the soil in the highlands of Eastern Lithuania] In LTSRMAD. Serija B, v.3(15), 1958, p. 215-226. illus. See serials consulted.

1733. --- Sezoninis šlaitų erozijos ritmas Rytų Lietuvos aukštumose. [The seasonal rhythm of erosion of the slopes in the highlands of Eastern Lithuania] In LTSRMAGGMP, v.10, fasc. 2, 1959, p. 5-26. illus. Summaries in German and Russian. See serials consulted.

1734. RYDZEWSKI, Bronisław. Fizjografja województwa Wileńskiego. In Wilno i ziemia wileńska (Wilno), v.1, 1930, p. 51-71. See serials consulted.

1735. --- Studia nad dyluwium doliny Niemna. In Towarzystwo Przyjaciół Nauk w Wilnie. Wydział II: Matematycznych i Przyrodniczych. Prace. (Wilno), v.3, 1927, p. 131-167. Summary in French. See serials consulted.

1736. SIEMIRADZKI, Józef. Beitrag zur Kenntnis des nördlichen Diluvium auf der polnisch-litauischen Ebene. In Austria. Geologische Bundesanstalt (Wien), v.39, no.3-4, 1889, p. 451-62. QE226.A165 DI-GS DLC CoDGS FU ICJ ICU MiU MB LU OrU OU PPAN TxU

1737. --- Przyczynek do znajomości napływów dyluwjalnych na polsko-litewskiej równinie. In Kosmos (Lwów), v.14, 1888. See serials consulted.

1738. VILIAMAS, Vladas. Sėlių aukštumų morfologiniai bruožai. [The morphological features of the highlands of Sėliai; a region in North Eastern Lithuania] In Kosmos (Kaunas) v.20, no.1-3, 1939, p. 35-54. See serials consulted.

1739. WOŁŁOSOWICZ, Stanisław. O grzedach morenowych ziemi Narockiej i granicy młodszego zlodowacenia w dorzeczu Wiliji. In Warsaw. Instytut Geologiczny. Sprawozdania, v.2, no.1-2, 1923, p. 77-95. Part of the text also in German or French. See serials consulted.

1740. Okolice Wilna pod względem ewolucyjno-morfologicznym. Wilno, J. Zawadzki, 1917. 23 p. 947.52. W835.2 PU

1741. --- Utwory dyluwjalne na południowo-zachodnim krańcu lądolodu Wilejskiego. In Warsaw. Instytut Geologiczny. Posiedzenia Naukowe, v.3, 1925. See serials consulted.

V.3.c. CLIMATOLOGY

1742. GERMANY. REICHSAMT FÜR WETTERDIENST. Klima des Ostlandes. Zugleich Nachtrag zu: Reichskommissar für Ostland. Strukturbericht über das Ostland, T.1: Ostland in Zahlen. Berlin, 1944- . 2 v. charts (part. col.) diagrs., tables. QC989.R5B35 DLC

1743. GORCZYŃSKI, Władysław. O podziałach klimatycznych Europy. In Przegląd geograficzny (Warszawa), v.14, 1934, p. 41-98. Summary in French. See serials consulted.

1744. GRICIŪTĖ, Angėlė. K voprosu o klimaticheskom raionirovanii Litovskoi SSR. [By A. Griciūtė, K. Kaušyla, B. Styra, and V. Ščemeliovas] In LTSRMAD. Serija B, v.4, 1957, p. 133-141. See serials consulted.

1745. --- Lietuvos TSR klimato gydomosios savybės. Terapevticheskie svoistva klimata Litovskii SSR. In Geografinis metraštis (Vilnius), v. 5, 1962, p. 171-291. tables. See serials consulted.

1746. GRICIŪTĖ, Angėlė and Balys Styra. Lietuvos klimato tyrimai ir ateities perspektyvos. [Research of the Lithuanian climate and plans for the future] In Geografinis metraštis (Vilnius), v.1, 1958, p. 23-32. See serials consulted.

1747. KAUŠYLA, Kęstutis. A short historical review of the climatic investigations in Lithuania. In LTSRMAGGICPXXIX. Vilnius, 1960. p. 209-213. GB3.I45 1960ac CU CaAEU CaMWU DLC ICU NNC

1748. --- The climatic regions of Lithuania. In LTSRMAGGICPXIX. Vilnius, 1960. p. 219-224. GB.3I45 1960ac CU CaAEU CaMWU ICU NNC

1749. --- K voprosu o raspredelenii krainykh dat zamorozkov na territorii Litovskoi SSR. In LTSRMAGGIMP, v.3, 1956, p. 62-67.

See serials consulted.

1750. --- Kai kurios oro temperatūros ypatybės metų eigoje ir terminiai sezonai. [Some peculiarities of weather temperature in Lithuania during the year] In LTSRMAGGIMP, v.5, 1957, p.129-135. See serials consulted.

1751. --- Lietuvos klimatas. [The climate of Lithuania] Vilnius, Valstybinė politinės ir mokslinės literatūros leidykla, 1959. 69 p. illus. (Pažinkime Lietuvą) QC989.I4K3 DLC

1752. LIETUVOS KLIMATAS. Visuomeniniais pagrindais redagavo Č. Garbaliauskas ir V. Ščemeliovas. [The climate of Lithuania] Vilnius, Mintis, 1966. 168 p. illus., maps. QC989.I4L5 DLC NN PU

1753. OLŠAUSKAS, Steponas Raimundas. Krituliai, oro temperatūra ir saulėtumas Lietuvoje. [Precipitation, weather temperature and sunny days in Lithuania] In Žemės ūkis (Kaunas), no.7-8, 1940. See serials consulted.

1754. --- Maksimalus liūčių intensyvumas Lietuvos TSR teritorijoje. [The maximal intensity of the rain in Lithuania] In LTSRMAGGIMP, v.5, 1957, p. 153-157. See serials consulted.

1755. --- O vetrovom rezhime nad territoriei Litovskoi SSR po dannym samopistsev vetra. In LTSRMAGGIMP, v.3, 1956, p. 9-10. See serials consulted.

1756. --- Veroiatnost' skorosti vetra po gradatsiiam dlia razlichnykh napravlenii na territorii Litovskoi SSR. In LTSRMAGGIMP, v.3, 1956, p. 109-110. See serials consulted.

1757. PAKŠTAS, Kazys. Le climat de la Lithuanie. Klaipėda, "Lithuania" 1926. 137 p. illus., tables, diagrs., fold. col. chart. Thesis—Fribourg. At head of title: Ministère de l'agriculture. Bibliography: p. 111-115. QC989.I4P35 DLC BM MH PU

1758. --- Lietuvos klimatas. [The climate of Lithuania] Klaipėda, "Lithuania" 1926. 124 p. illus., charts, tables, diagrs, fold. col. chart. Thesis—Université de Fribourg. Bibliography: p. 99-106. QC989.I4P3 1926 DLC CtTMF

1759. STYRA, Balys. Kai kurios

dinaminės Lietuvos TSR klimato charakteristikos. [Some dynamic characteristics of the climate in Li-
thuania] B. Styra, Č. Garbaliauskas
ir A. Buzas. In LTSRMAGGIMP, v.7,
1958, p. 19-73. See serials consulted.

1760. --- Lietuvos klimatas. [The
climate of Lithuania] In Lietuvos
TSR fizinė geografija. Vilnius,
1958. v.1, p. 167-205. GB276.L5B3
CU CaOTU CtPAM CtTMF CLD CI-GS NN
NNC PU WaU

1761. ŠTYRA, Balys and Česlovas
Garbaliauskas. Sumarinė saulės ir
dangaus skliauto radiacija Lietuvos TSR teritorijoje. [The total
radiation from the sun and the universe in Lithuania] In LTSRMAGGIMP,
v.2, 1955, p. 73-86. illus. See
serials consulted.

V.3.d. HYDROGRAPHY
V.3.d.1. GENERAL STUDIES

1762. BASALYKAS, Alfonsas, Kazys
Bieliukas and Eduardas Červinskas.
Vidaus vandenys. [Lithuania's in-
land waters] In Lietuvos TSR fi-
zinė georafija. By Basalykas,
Alfonsas. Vilnius, 1958. v.1, p.
206-293. GB276.L5B3 DLC CaOTU CU
CtPAM CtTMF DI-GS NN NNC PU WaU

1763. KOLUPAILA, Steponas. Hidrografija. [Hydrography] In
Lietuvių enciklopedija, Boston,
Mass., 1968. v.15, p. 26-42. For
holdings see entry no. 216.

1764. --- Materiaux de la part de
la Lithuanie concernant le bilan
hydrologique de la Baltique. In
Hydrologische Konferenz der baltischen Staaten. 5th, Helsinki,
1936. 701(500)H994b & 701(500)
H994c DI-GS LSC

1765. NAUCHNAIA KONFERENTSIIA PO
izucheniiu vodoemov Pribaltiki.
6th, Vilna, 1958. Tezisy dokladov.
[Proceedings. Board of editors: A.
Gediminas, I. Maniukas and B. Bar-
džius] Vil'nius, 1958. 120 p. At
head of title: Akademiia nauk Litovskoi SSR. Institut biologgi.
QH98.N3 1958c CtY CU DLC

1766. STUCKENBERG, Johann Christian. Hydrographie des Russischen
Reiches oder geographisch-statis-
tische Beschreibung seiner floss-
und schiffbaren Flüsse und Seen,
seiner Küsten, inneren Meeren, Hafen und Anfahrten. Vol. 1: Das

baltische Bassin. Sanktpeterburg,
1844-49. 6 v. BM

1767. VILNA. GEOLOGIJOS INSTITU-
TAS. Voprosy spetsial'noi gidrolo-
gii IUzhnoi Pribaltiki. Vil'nius,
Mintis, 1968. 162 p. graphs, ta-
bles. (Its Trudy, vyp. 6) At head
of title: Ministerstvo geologii
SSSR. Institut geologii (Vil'nius)
Summaries in English and Lithuanian.
QE276.V53 vyp.6 DLC DI-GS CaOTU

V.3.d.2. BALTIC SEA AND CURONIAN
BAY (KURŠIU MARĖS)

1768. ČERVINSKAS, Eduardas. Kai
kurie Kuršiu mariu vandens lygio
kitimo ypatumai. [Some peculiarities of the water level changes of
the Curonian Bay] In LTSRMAD.
Serija B, v.3(11), 1957, p. 109-119.
illus. See serials consulted.

1769. --- Vandens apykaitos tarp
Kuršiu mariu ir Baltijos jūros
klausimu. [On the question of the
exchange of water between Curonian
Bay and the Baltic Sea] In Geografinis metraštis (Vilnius), v.2, 1959.
p. 221-272. Summary in German and
Russian. See serials consulted.

1770. GASIŪNAS, Ipolitas. Baltijos jūros prie Lietuvos TSR kran-
tu kompleksiniai tyrinėjimai. 6:Dug-
no gyvūnija ir jos ryšys su Kuršiu
Mariomis. [The research of the Baltic Sea along the Lithuanian coast]
In LTSRMAD. Serija C, v.3(26), 1961,
p. 129-143. See serials consulted.

1771. GUDELIS, Vytautas. Baltijos
jūra; fizinė geografinė apybraiža.
[The Baltic Sea; a phisico-geogra-
phic outline] Vilnius, VPMLL, 1960.
84, [4] p. illus., maps. GC571.G8
DLC PU

1772. --- Dabartinės Kuršiu Mariu
nuosėdos ir jų litologinė charakteristika. [Recent deposits of the
firth of the Curonian Bay and its lithological characteristics] In
LTSRMAGGIMP, v.8, 1958, p. 25-52.
map., tables. See serials consulted.

1773. --- Keletas pastabų dėl go-
zos srauto seklios priekrantės jūros
paplūdimio sąlygomis. [Some remarks
on the dynamics of swash on the sand-
banks of the sea] In LTSRMAD. Serija B, v.4(12), 1957, p. 123-131.
graphs. Summary in Russian. Joint
authors of the article: S. Jankevi-
čiutė and E. Michaliūnaitė. See
serials consulted.

1774. --- Kuršių Marios, kaip se-
dimentogenetinė erdvė. [The Curonian Bay as a basin of sedimentation]
In LTSRMAGGIMP, v.1, 1955, p. 33-47.
See serials consulted.

1775. GUDELIS, Vytautas and E. Mi-
chaliūkaitė. Kuršių Nerijos dabartinių eolinių smėlių litologijos ir
eolodinaminės diferenciacijos klausimu. Zur Frage der Lithologie und
äolodynamischen Differenzierung der
gegenwärtigen Dünensande auf der
Kurischen Nehrung. In Geografinis
metraštis (Vilnius), v.2, 1959, p.
535-564. illus., map. Summaries in
German and Russian. See serials
consulted.

1776. GUDELIS, Vytautas and S.
Stakauskaitė. Pietrytinio Baltijos
pajūrio kranto zonos smėliai Šventosios uosto-Palvininkų ruože. [The
sands of the costal zone of the
Southeastern Baltic Sea between Šventoji harbour and Palvininkai] In
Geografinis metraštis (Vilnius),
v.2, 1959, p. 507-533. illus., map.
Summaries in German and Russian.
See serials consulted.

1777. LETTAU, Heinz. Freie Schwin-
gungen (Seiches) des Kurischen Haffes. In Physikalisch-ökonomische
Gesellschaft (Königsberg in Pr.),
v.67, no.3-4, 1952, p. 63-73. See
serials consulted.

1778. LIETUVOS TSR MOKSLŲ AKADEMI-
JA, VILNA. BIOLOGIJOS INSTITUTAS.
Kurshiu mares. Itogi kompleksnogo
issledovaniia. [Glav. redaktor K.
Jankevičius] Vil'nius, 1959. 545
p. illus., maps. QH92.L47 DLC

1779. PAKŠTAS, Kazys. Baltijos
jūra. [The Baltic Sea] Klaipėda,
Jūros dienos komiteto leidinys,1934.
83 p. illus., diagrs., maps. Bibliography: p. 81-82. 947.522.P178.2
PU CtTMF CtY ICBM

1780. PRATJE, O. Die Sedimente
des Kurischen Haffes. In Fortschritte der Geologie und Paläontologie
(Berlin), v.10, no.30, 1931, p.1-
141. See serials consulted.

V.3.d.3. RIVERS

1781. BASALYKAS, Alfonsas. Lietuvos upės. [Rivers of Lithuania]
Vilnius, VPMLL, 1956, 132 p. illus.
maps. (Pažinkime Lietuvą) GB1333.
L5B3 DLC PU

1782. --- Lietuvos upių dinaminių

faziu interpretavimo klausimu. [On
the question of interpretation of
the dynamic phases of the Lithuanian
rivers] In LTSRMAD. Serija B, v.3,
1958, p. 203-213. map. See serials
consulted.

1783. --- Nemuno deltos žemuma.
[The Nemunas River delta valley] In
Geografinis metraštis (Vilnius), v.4
1961, p. 5-44. illus., map. Summaries in German and Russian. See
serials consulted.

1784. --- Nemuno upės paleodinami-
nės fazės Alytaus-Kauno atkarpoje ir
kai kurie neotektoninio aktyvumo
klausimai. [The paleodynamic phases
of the Nemunas River in the section
Alytus-Kaunas and some neotectonic
activity] In LTSRMAD. Serija B,
v.4, 1956, p. 55-68. illus. Summa-
mary in Russian. See serials consulted.

1785. DAGYS, Jonas. Apaščios
upės mažieji viksvynai. [Small
areas of sedges along the Apaščia River] In KUBS. Raštai, v.4,
1936. See serials consulted.

1786. --- Apaščios upės pievos.
Die Wiesen des Flusses Apaščia. In
KUMGFD, v.7, 1933, p. 80-217.Summa-
ry in German. See serials consulted.

1787. GERMANY. HEER. GENERALSTAB.
Militärgeographische Angaben über
das Stromgebiet der Memel und der
benachbarten Küstenflüsse. [Riga]
Mil. Geo-Gruppe b. Währmachtbefehls-
haber Ostland, 1943. 1 leaf, 10
fold. col. maps (in portfolio)
G2117.M37G4 1943 DLC

1788. KOLUPAILA, Steponas. Įdomus
Nemuno praeities dokumentas. [An in-
teresting document about the past of
the Nemunas River] In Soter(Kaun-
nas), no. 28, 1939, p.90-111. See
serials consulted.

1789. --- Lietuvos hidrografija.
[Hydrography of Lithuania] In Tech-
nika (Kaunas), no.1, 1924. 58 p.
See serials consulted.

1790. --- Medžiaga monografijai
apie Nėrį; 100 metų nuo K. Tiškevi-
čiaus ekspedicijos Nerimi. [Some
information for the monograph of the
Neris river...] In Aidai (Brooklyn,
N.Y.), 1957, no.7, p.307-313; no.10,
p.416-469. See serials consulted.

1791. --- Narutis ir Nėris. [Ri-
vers: Narutis ir Nėris] In Kosmos
(Kaunas), no.1-3, 1940, p.49-64. See
serials consulted.

1792. --- Nemunas. [Nemunas River] 2. ed. Chicago, Ill., Lietuvių katalikų spaudos draugija, 1950. 257 p. illus., map. DK511.L2K68 DLC CaAEU CaOONL CtPAM CtTMF MiD MH OC1 PU

1793. --- Nemuno tyrinėjimų istorijos bruožai. [A history in outline of research about the Nemunas River] In Židinys (Kaunas), no.7,1934 p. 51-65. See serials consulted.

1794. --- Nevėžis; hidrografinė studija. [Nevėžis river; a hydrographic study] Kaunas, Kosmos, 1936. 127 p. 947.52.K835 PU

1795. --- Le Niémen, étude hydrologique. In Revue de Géographie Alpine (Grenoble, Fr.), v.25, no.2, 1937, p.381-409. DC611.A553R4 1937 DLC CU CaQMM CtY ICU MH MiU NN NNC

1796. --- Ökar Memel verklingen? In Terra (Helsingfors), no.2, 1933. 45 p. See serials consulted.

1797. --- Žemaičių upė-Dubysa. [The Samogitian river Dubysa] In Ateitis (Brooklyn, N.Y.), no.6(18), 1950, p.3-4. See serials consulted.

1798. KONFERENCIJA NEMUNO ŽEMUPIO sutvarkymo ir apsaugos klausimais. Vilna, 1960. Nemuno žemupio sutvarkymo klausimai; konferencijos...darbai. [On the question of the regulation of the lower Nemunas river; proceedings of the conference. Redakcinė kolegija: A. Basalykas et al.] Vilnius, VPMLL, 1961. 177 p. illus. maps., diagrs. At head of title: Gamtos apsaugos komisija prie Lietuvos TSR Mokslų akademijos prezidiumo. Summaries in Russian. DK511. M42K6 DLC

1799. LASINSKAS, Mykolas. Stok reki Niamunas (Neman) Pod. red. T.L. Zolotareva. Kaunas, 1961. 196 p. fold. map., diagrs., tables. Bibliography: p.195-196. GB1333.L5L3 DLC

1800. LIETUVOS TSR MOKSLŲ AKADEMIJA, VILNA. ENERGETIKOS IR ELEKTROTECHNIKOS INSTITUTAS. Lietuvos upių kadastras. [The river system of Lithuania] Vilnius, VPMLL, 1959-62. 3 v. fold. maps (in pocket v.1)diagrs. At head of title, v.1: M. Lasinskas, J. Macevičius ir J. Jablonskis; v.2: M. Lasinskas, J. Burneika; v.3: J. Jablonskis, M. Lasinskas. supplements 1-5 included in v.3. Bibliography: v.3, p.637-[639]

1800a. --- Kadastriniai grafikai. Vilnius, VPMLL, 1962. 191 p. diagrs. Constitutes supplement no.6 to v.3

of the main work. GB1333.L5L5 DLC CU DS NN NNC

1801. MACEVIČIUS, Juozas. The investigation of Lithuanian rivers. In LTSRMAGGCPXIX, Vilnius, 1960. p. 355-360. GB3.I45 1960ac CU CaAEU CaMWU DLC ICU NNC

1802. PRUSSIA. WASSER-AUSSCHUSS. Memel-, Pregel- und Weichselstrom, ihre Stromgebiete und ihre wichtigsten Nebenflüsse. Eine hydrologische, wasserwirtschaftliche und wasserrechtliche Darstellung. Auf Grund des allerhöchsten Erlasses vom 28. Februar 1892 im Auftrage des preussischen Wasser-Ausschusses hrsg. von H. Keller. Berlin, D. Reimer (E. Vohsen) 1899. 4 v. diagrs, and atlas. GB732.P6 DLC

1803. SOVETOV, V. S. Voenno gidrologicheskii ocherk reki Nemana. Leningrad, 1932. 203 p. illus. GB772.L5S6 DLC

1804. VISKONTAS, K. O. Nemuno-Ventos vandens kelio geologinis tyrinėjimas. [The geologic survey of the waterways Nemunas-Venta] In Technika (Kaunas), nr.6, 1930, p.65-94. Summary in French. See serials consulted.

1805. ŽEMAITIS, Vincas. Šešupė ir jos upynas. [Šešupė and its river-basin] Chicago, Ill., 1958. 1 v. (unpaged) fold map. 552(575)Ze4s DI-GS

V.3.d.4. HYDROMETRIC RESEARCH OF LITHUANIAN RIVERS

1806. KOLUPAILA, Steponas. Die Bestimmung des Abflusses des Memelstromes-Nemunas 1812-1832. 14 p. In Hydrologische Konferenz der baltischen Staaten. 4th, Leningrad, 1933. Otchet.. Comte rendu. Leningrad, 1934. GB651.H8 1933b DLC IaAS DI-GS

1807. --- Flügelprüfanstalt bei Kaunas und derer Arbeitsmethoden. 5 p. In Hydrologische Konferenz der baltischen Staaten. 2nd, Tallin, 1928. Berichte. GB656.H8 DLC DI-GS

1808. --- Lietuvos hidrometriniai tyrinėjimai per penkerius metus, 1923-1927. [Hydrometric research in Lithuania during the five years 1923-1927] In Kosmos (Kaunas), no. 5-6, 1928, p. 1-32. See serials consulted.

1809. --- Lietuvos upių maksimalinis debitas. [The maximal discharge of Lithuanian rivers] 27 p. In Žemėtvarka ir melioracija (Kaunas), no.2, 1934. See serials consulted.

1810. --- Nemuno kilpa. [The Nemunas River loop] In Kosmos (Kaunas), 1929, p. 169-200. See serials consulted.

1811. --- Nemuno matavimai Smalininkuose 1811-1930 metais. [The measurements of the Nemunas River at Smalininkai] In Lithuania. Hidrometrinis biuras. Hidrometrinis metraštis. Kaunas, 1930. v.2, p.1-376. GB772.L8A2 DLC DI-GS

1812. --- Nemuno nuotakis per 121 metus 1812-1932. [The discharche of the Nemunas River in 121 years, 1812-1932] In Kosmos (Kaunas), 1932, no. 7-12, p. 317-323. See serials consulted.

1813. --- Nemuno paleidimas ties Kaunu ir potvyniai. [The spring runoff of the Nemunas River at Kaunas and its floods] In Kosmos(Kaunas), no.3, 1936, p. 44-48. See serials consulted.

1814. --- Nemuno užšalimai per 120 metų 1811-1930. [The freeze up of the Nemunas River during the 120 years period] In Kosmos (Kaunas), no.10-12, 1930, p. 299-305. See serials consulted.

1815. --- Sur le débit maximal des fleuves de la Lithuanie. 11 p. In Hydrologische Konferenz der baltischen Staaten. 5th, Helsinki, June 1936. Rapport 1B. Helsinki, 1936. 701(500)H994c DI-GS LSC

1816. --- Uchet stoka reki Nemana za 1812-1932 gody. In Hydrologische Konferenz der baltischen Staaten. 4th, Leningrad, 1933. Otchet... Comte rendu. Leningrad, 1934. GB651.H8 1933b DLC IaAS DI-GS

1817. --- Uspekhi gidrometricheskogo issledovaniia v Litovskoi respublike. In Vsesoiuznyi gidrologicheskii s"ezd (Leningrad), Trudy, 2nd 1928. Leningrad, 1929. p.133-135. GB651.V83 DLC

1818. LASINSKAS, Mykolas. Lietuvos TSR upių nuotėkio pasiskirstymas per metus. [The distribution of discharge of the Lithuanian rivers during the year] In Lietuvos TSR Mokslų akademija, Vilna. Energetikos ir elektrotechnikos institutas. Mokslinės-techninės konferencijos darbai žemės ūkio elektrifikavimo ir kaimo hidroelektrinių projektavimo, statybos bei eksploatavimo klausimais. Vilnius, 1959. v.1, p.57-73. graphs. GB1333.L5L5 DLC

1819. LITHUANIA. HIDROMETRINIS BIURAS. Hidrometrinis metraštis. Jahrbuch des hydrometrischen Büros Litauens. T.1-3; 1925/27-1928/32. Kaunas, 1929-33. 3 v. GB772.L8A2 DLC DI-GS

1820. --- Die hydrometrischen Arbeiten in Litauen. Von S. Kolupaila. Kaunas, Valstybės spaustuvė, 1927. 32 p. illus., tables, diagrs. P(575)W28hk DI-GS

1821. --- Nemuno ties Kaunu 1877-1925 m. matavimai. [The measure ments of the Nemunas River at Kaunas 1877-1925] Kaunas, Valstybės spaustuvė, 1925. 192 p. plan, tables, diagrs. GB1333.L5A5 1925 DLC

1822. SILICH, M. V. Srednii godovoi stok rek Kaliningradskoi oblasti RSFSR i Litovskoi SSR. In LTSRMAGGIMP, v.3, 1956, p.78-95. See serials consulted.

1823. WRÓBLEWSKI, Witold. Stan wody na Niemnie pod Stołbcami, Grodnem i Kownem od 1877-1883. In Pamiętnik Fizjograficzny (Warszawa), v.2, 1883. See serials consulted.

V.3.e. LIMNOLOGY

V.3.e.1. GENERAL STUDIES

1824. EŽEROTYRA IR PELKĖTYRA. Ozerovedenie i bolotovedenie. Vilnius, VPMLL, 1963. 364 p. illus., map. (Lietuvos TSR Mokslų akademija, Vilna. Geologijos ir geografijos institutas. Moksliniai pranešimai, v.15) Summaries in German and Russian. QE1.L448 DLC CU CaOOGB CtY ICU InU MWHB NN PPAN WyU

1825. GARUNKŠTIS, Aleksas. Vandens srovių įtaka Lietuvos TSR ežerų atabrado formavimuisi. [The influence of the water currents on the formation of the sand-banks in the lakes of Lithuania] In LTSRMAD. Serija B, v.1(13), 1958, p. 73-89. See serials consulted.

1826. --- Vidurio Lietuvos limnoglacialinio baseino krantinių klausimu. [On the question of slopes in the limnoglacial basin of Central Lithuania] In LTSRMAD. Serija B, v.3 (26), 1961, p. 221-229. map. Summary in Russian. See serials consulted.

1827. KLIMKAITĖ, I. Hidrocheminė pietryčių Lietuvos ežerų klasifikacija. [The hydrochemical classification of the lakes in South Eastern Lithuania] In Geografinis metraštis (Vilnius), v.4, 1961, p. 337-368. See serials consulted.

V.3.e.2. LAKES

1828. BIELIUKAS, Kazys. Lietuvos TSR ežerai. [Lakes of the Lithuanian SSR] Vilnius, VPMLL, 1956. 52 p. illus., map. (Pažinkime Lietuvą). 914.75B473 PU

1829. BIELIUKAS, Kazys and Vaclovas Chomskis. Pagrindinės žinios apie ežero vandenų sąmaišą. [Basic information on the compound of the water in a lake] In Geografinis metraštis (Vilnius), v.2, 1959, p. 175-220. illus. Summaries in German and Russian. See serials consulted.

1830. BUNIKIS, A. Ilgio, Tausalo ir Plinkšių ežerų hidrocheminė charakteristika. [The hydrochemical characteristic of the lakes Ilgis, Tausalas, and Plinkšiai] In LTSRMAD. Seria B, v.3(19), 1959, p.203-219. graphs. Summary in Russian. See serials consulted.

1831. --- Platelių ežero hidrocheminis rėžimas. [The hydrochemical characteristics of the Plateliai lake] In LTSRMAD. Seria B, v.2(18), 1959, p.225-236. Summary in Russian. See serials consulted.

1832. GARUNKŠTIS, Aleksas. Rytų Lietuvos ežerų vystymosi dėsningumai. [The law of the development of the lakes in Eastern Lithuania] Vilnius, Universitetas, 1958. 1 v. Diss.-- University of Vilnius. Typescript.

1833. --- Vilkokšnio ežero raida vėlyvajame ledynmetyje ir poledynmečio pradžioje. [The development of the lake Vilkokšnis during the last glacial period and immediately after it] In LTSRMAGGIMP, v.9, 1959, p.117-135. illus., map. Summaries in German and Russian. See serials consulted.

1834. --- Zamechaniia po vostanovleniiu paleogidrologicheskogo rezhima nekotorykh ozer Litovskoi SSR. In Vsesoiuznyi gidrologicheskii s"ezd. 3rd, Leningrad, 1957. Trudy (Leningrad), v.4, 1959, p. 34-42. GB651.V83 DLC

1835. GARUNKŠTIS, Aleksas and A. Stanaitis. Dusios, Metelio ir Obelijos ežerų kilmės klausimu. [On the question of origin of the lakes Dusia, Metelis and Obelija] In LTSRMAGGIMP, v.10, no.2, 1959, p. 235-248. illus. See serials consulted.

1836. INGAUNIENĖ, A. (Šarauskaitė) Šventosios baseino kairiojo šono ežerai. [The lakes on the left bank of the Šventoji River] In Kosmos (Kaunas), no.7-12, 1940. See serials consulted.

1837. KLIMKAITĖ, I. Kai kurie duomenys apie Lietuvos TSR ežerų vandens dūjinį rėžimą. [Some data on the contents of gases of the Lithuanian lakes] In LTSRMAGGIMP,v.8, 1958, p. 107-119. See serials consulted.

1838. --- Kryžiuočių ežero hidrocheminis ir terminis rėžimas. [The hydrochemic and thermic features of the lake Kryžiuočiai] In LTSRMAGGIMP, v.10, no.2, 1959, p. 115-149. illus. Summaries in German and Russian. See serials consulted.

1839. --- Pietryčių Lietuvos ežerų priedugnio vandens sluoksnio cheminė charakteristika. [The chemical characteristics of the bottom layers of water in the lakes of South Eastern Lithuania] In Geografinis metraštis (Vilnius), v.4, 1961 p. 317-335. graphs, tables. Summaries in German and Russian. See serials consulted.

1840. KOLUPAILA, Steponas. Dzūkijos ežerų tyrinėjimas. [The research of the lakes in Dzūkija] In Lithuania. Hidrometrinis biuras. Hidrometrinis metraštis. Kaunas, 1929 v.1. GB772.L8A2 DLC DI-GS

1841. --- Lietuvos ežerai. [Lithuania's lakes] In Kosmos (Kaunas), v.9-12, 1932. See serials consulted.

1842. LIETUVOS TSR MOKSLŲ AKADEMIJA, VILNA. ZOOLOGIJOS IR PARAZITOLOGIJOS INSTITUTAS. Dūkšto ežerų hidrobiologiniai tyrimai. Gidrobiologicheskie issledovaniia Dukshtasskikh ozer. [B. Bagdžius, ats. redaktorius] Vilnius, Mintis, 1964. 146 p. illus. Lithuanian or Russian. Summaries in Russian or Lithuanian. QH98.L46 DLC CtY

1843. VSESOIUZNYI SIMPOZIUM PO OS-

novnym problemam presnovodnykh ozer.
Vil'na, 1970. Trudy. Vil'nius,1970.
3 v. Russian, Lithuanian or German.
GB1707.V75 1970 PU DI-GS

V.3.e.3. SWAMPS

1844. BRUNDZA, Kazys. Nekotorye
osobennosti stroeniia i razvitiia
melkikh bolot iugo-zapadnoi chasti
Litovskoi SSR. In LTSRMAD. Serija
B, v.4(16), 1958, p. 151-158. See
serials consulted.

1845. GRIGELYTĖ, M. Raistinės pa-
leofitocenozės Lietuvos TSR pelkėse.
Nizinnye lesnye paleofitotsenozy v
bolotakh Litvy. In Geografinis metraštis (Vilnius), v.6-7, p. 375-398.
diagrs., maps. Summaries in Russian
and German. See serials consulted.

1846. KUNSKAS, R. Poledynmečio
įvykių pėdsakai Nemuno slėnio pelkėse ties Merkine. Po sledam geogra-
ficheskikh sobytii golotsena v bolotakh doliny reki Nemunas pod gorodom
Merkine. In Geografinis metraštis
(Vilnius), v.6-7, 1963-64, p. 347-
374. illus. See serials consulted.

1847. PURVINAS, Erikas and A. Seibutis. Pagrindiniai pelkių rajonai
Lietuvos TSR teritorijoje. [The
principal districts of bogs in the
Lithuanian territory] In LTSRMAD.
Serija B, v.2(10), 1957, p. 127-
141. map. See serials consulted.

1848. SEIBUTIS, A. Lietuvos pel-
kės. Moore Litauens. In Basalykas,
A. Lietuvos TSR fizinė geografija.
Vilnius, 1958. v.1, p. 337-381.
GB276.L5B3 DLC CU CaOTU CtPAM CtTMF
DI-GS NN NNC PU WaU

1849. --- Rytų Lietuvos pelkių raidos bruožai. [An outline of the development of the bogs in Eastern Li-
thuania] In LTSRMAD. Serija B,
v.1, 1958, p. 55-72. Summary in
Russian. See serials consulted.

1850. ŠEPETA; aukštapelkio monografija... Monografiia verkhovnogo bo-
lota podgotovlennaia kollektivom
Sel'skokhoziaistvennoi akademii. Kaunas, 1940. xiv, 206 p. (Dotnuva.
Žemės ūkio akademija, Žemės ūkio
akademijos metraštis, t.13, sąs.4)
S13.D6 DLC CU DNAL IU NIC-A TxU

1851. SUDNIKAVIČIENĖ, F. AND A.
Seibutis. Medininkų-Eišiškių aukštumos pelkių pagrindiniai raidos
bruožai. [An outline of the principal developments of swamps in the

Medininkai-Eisiskiai Highlands] In
Geografinis metraštis (Vilnius), v.4
1961, p. 301-316. diagrs. Summaries
in German and Russian. See serials
consulted.

1852. ŽEMAITIS, Mečys. Kamanų
pelkės praeitis. [The past of the
Kamanos swamps] Kaunas, 1936. 82 p.
illus. (Dotnuva. Žemės ūkio akademija. Žemės ūkio akademijos metraštis, t.10, sąs.3-4) S13.D6 v.10 DLC
CU DNAL IU NIC-A PU TxU

V.3.e.4. BOGS

1853. GRIGELYTĖ, M. Švylingų durpių slūgsojimo ir paplitimo Lietuvos
TSR teritorijoj klausimu. [On the
question of the compression of peat
and its extent in the territory of
Lithuanian SSR] In LTSRMAGGIMP,v.10,
no.2, 1959, p. 215-233. Summaries in
German and Russian. See serials
consulted.

1854. PURĖNAS, Antanas. Lietuvos
TSR svarbesniųjų durpių rūšių charakteristika. [Characteristics of the
principal varieties of peat in Lithuania. By A. Purėnas, V. Ivanovas and
J. Vidmantas] In KPID, v.3, 1955,
p. 23-31. See serials consulted.

1855. PURVINAS, Erikas and M. Grigelytė. Lietuvos TSR šiaurės vakarų rajonų durpių rūšys ir jų slūgso-
jimas. [The varieties of peat and
its sinking in North Western Lithu-
ania] In LTSRMAGGIMP, v.6, 1958,
p. 143-172. illus. Summaries in
English and Russian. See serials
consulted.

1856. SEIBUTIS, A. General results of bog investigations in Lithuania. In LTSRMAGGICPXIX. Vilnius,
1960. p. 323-329. GB3.I45 1960ac
CU DLC CaAEU CaMWU ICU NNC

1857. SEIBUTIS, A. and F. Sudnikavičienė. K voprosu ob obrazovanii
podsapropelevnykh prosploev torfa v
bolotakh Litvy. In LTSRMAD. Serija B, v.1, 1959, p.79-93. See serials consulted.

1858. SIEMIRADZKI, Józef. Ein Beitrag zur Kenntnis der Torfmoore in
Litauen. In Dorpat. Naturforscher
Gesellschaft. Sitzungsberichte,
1884, v.7-8, p.174-177. See serials consulted.

1859. THOMSON, Paul William. Beiträge zur Stratigraphie der Moore
und zur Waldgeschichte süd-west Li-

tauens. In Geologiska föreningen. Förhandlingar (Stockholm), v.53, 1931, p.239-250. See serials consulted.

1860. VIDMANTAS, Jurgis. Kazlų Rūdos-Zapiškio komplekso durpių masės tyrimas. [The exploration of the peat-bog complex in the district of Kazlų Rūda-Zapiškis] In KPID, v.1, 1949. See serials consulted.

1861. --- Osnovnye raiony torfiannykh mestorozhdenii Litovskoi SSR. In Russia(1917-R.S.F.S.R.) Glavnoe upravlenie torfianogo fonda. Sbornik statei po izucheniiu torfianogo fonda (Moskva), 1957, Vyp.2, p.129-139. TN840.R9A28 DLC

1862. WEBER, Carl Albert. Über die Vegetation und Entstehung des Hochmoores von Aukštumai im Memeldelta. Berlin, P. Parey, 1902. vii, 252 p. illus., fold. maps, col. diagrs. 646(530)W38 DI-GS

V.4. ECONOMIC GEOGRAPHY

1863. AKADEMIIA NAUK SSR. INSTITUT GEOGRAFII. Sovetskaia Pribaltika; problemy ekonomicheskoi geografii. Otv. redaktor A.A. Mints i M.I. Rostovtsev. Moskva, Nauka, 1966. 275 p. illus., maps. HC243.A65 CaOTU

1864. ANDRÉE, Karl. Der Bernstein; das Bernsteinland und sein Leben. Stuttgart, Franckh, 1951. 95 p. illus. (Kosmos Bändchen) QE391. A5A48 DLC CU DI-GS NIC OrPR PPG PPULC PPAN

1865. --- Die Herkunft des Nordseebernsteins. In Forschungen und Fortschritte (Berlin), v.18, 1942, p.155-156. See serials consulted.

1866. BOCK, Friedrich Samuel. Versuch einer kurzen Naturgeschichte des preussischen Bernsteins und einer neuen wahrscheinlichen Erklärung seines Ursprungs. Königsberg in Pr., Bey J.D. Zeisens Wittwe und J.H. Hartungs Erben, 1767. 146 p. DI-GS ClSU IU MH

1867. DALINKEVIČIUS, Juozas. Lietuvos kreida. [Lithuania's chalk] In Kosmos (Kaunas), v.15, 1934, p. 233-293. See serials consulted.

1868. --- Lietuvos molių tyrinėjimai. Issledovaniia glin Litvy. In Technika (Kaunas), no.6, 1930, p.121-150. Summary in German. See serials

consulted.

1869. DAMUŠIS, Adolfas and Birutė Saldukienė. Lietuvos žemės turtai. [Natural resources of Lithuania] In Lietuva (New York, N.Y.), no.4, 1953 p. 100-117. See serials consulted.

1870. DOMAŠEVIČIUS, Adolfas. Biržų gipsas; žaliava chemijos pramonei. Birzhaiskii gips; syr'e dlia khimicheskoi promyshlennosti. In Technika ir ūkis (Kaunas), no.2(11), 1935, p. 43-55. See serials consulted.

1871. THE ECONOMICO-GEOGRAPHICAL essays on: Vilnius, Kaunas, Klaipėda, Šiauliai, etc. By various authors. In LTSRMAGGICPXIX. Vilnius, 1960. p. 393-436. GB3.I45 DLC CU CaAEU CaMWU ICU NNC

1872. JODELĖ, Pranas. Energijos komiteto žemės turtams tirti komisijos darbai kreidos atsargai aiškinti Jesios ir Marvos-Pyplių rajonuose. Raboty komissii po issledovaniiu bogatstv zemli Energeticheskogo komiteta po vyiasneniiu zapasov mela v raionakh Esia i Marva-Pipliai. In Technika ir ūkis (Kaunas), no.4(17), 1936, p. 118-123; no.1(18), 1937, p. 1-8. See serials consulted.

1873. KATINAS, Vladas. IAntar' i iantar'nosnye otlozheniia IUzhnoi Pribaltiki. Vil'nius, Mintis, 1971. 154 p. QE391.A5K38 PU

1874. LIETUVOS TSR MOKSLŲ AKADEMIJA, VILNA. GEOLOGIJOS IR GEOGRAFIJOS INSTITUTAS. Lietuvos TSR ekonominė geografija. [Economic geography of the Lithuanian SSR] Redagavo K. Meškauskas ir St. Tarvydas. Vilnius, Valstybinė politinės ir mokslinės literatūros leidykla, 1957. 401 p. illus., maps (part. fold.) HC337.L5L46 DLC CU CtPAM CtY MH NN NNC OKentU PU

1875. LITHUANIAN S.S.R. GEOLOGIJOS IR GELMIŲ APSAUGOS VALDYBA. GEOLOGINĖ PAIEŠKŲ-ŽVALGYBOS EKSPEDICIJA. Lietuvos TSR mineralinių žaliavų apžvalga. [A review of the mineral resources of Soviet Lithuania] Redaktorius V. Vonsavičius. Vilnius, Respublikinis mokslinės-techninės informacijos ir propagandos institutas, 1959- . TN86.L5A5 DLC

1876. MOLDENHAUER, Paul. Das Gold des Nordens. Ein Rückblick auf die Geschichte der Bernsteins. Danzig, C. Hinstorff, 1894. iv, 80 p. QE391.A5M6 DLC

1877. NARBUTAS, Vytautas. Kar-

stiniai reiškiniai ir gipsų paieškų
perspektyvos Biržų-Pasvalio rajone.
[The Karst phenomena and the possibilities of finding gypsym in the
Biržai-Pasvalys district] In
LTSRMAD. Serija B, v.2(12), 1957,
p. 77-93. illus. See serials consulted.

1878. NEFTEPOISKOVYE KRITERII
Pribaltiki i metody ikh izucheniia.
[Materialy seminara 24-25 marta
1966 g. Otv. red. K.A. Sakalauskas]
Vil'nius, Mintis, 1970. 199 p.
diagrs., maps. (Ministerstvo geo-
logii SSSR. Institut geologii
(Vil'nius). Trudy, vyp. 8)
QE276.N4 CaOTU

1879. ROSTOVTSEV, Mikhail Ivanovich. Soiuznye respubliki Pribaltiki; ekonomiko-geograficheskii o-
cherk. Posobie dlia uchitelei.
Moskva, Gos. uchebno-pedagog. izd-
vo Ministerstva prosveshcheniia
RSFSR, 1962. 217 p. illus., maps.
HC243.R6 CaOTU

1880. SAKALAUSKAS, K. Kharakteristika neftegazonosnosti IUgo-Zapadnoi
chasti Litvy. In LTSRMAD. Serija
B, v.2(29), 1962, p. 135-160. map.
See serials consulted.

1881. SIEMIRADZKI, Józef. Kri-
tische Bemerkungen über neue oder
wenig bekannte Amoniten vom braunen
Jura aus Popielany in Litauen. In
Neues Jahrbuch für Mineralogie,
Geologie und Paläntologie (Stutt-
gart, Ger.) v.1, 1890, p. 169-176.
See serials consulted.

1882. VILNA. GEOLOGIJOS INSTITU-
TAS. Geologiia i neftenosnost' pa-
leozoia IUzhnoi Pribaltiki. [Otv.
redaktor P.I. Suveizdis] Vil'nius,
Mintis, 1965. 187 p. illus., maps.
(Its Trudy, vyp. 1) At head of
title: Gosudarstvennyi geologiches-
kii komitet SSSR. Institut geologii
(Vil'nius) QE276.V53 vyp.1 DLC
DI-GS CaOTU

1883. --- Tektonika i neftegazo-
nosnost' IUgo-Zapadnoi Pribaltiki.
Vil'nius, Mintis, 1968. 193 p.
plans, tables. (Its Trudy, vyp.4)
Summaries in English and Lithuanian.
At head of title: Ministerstvo geo-
logii SSSR. Institut geologii
(Vil'nius) QE276.V53 vyp.4 DLC
CaOTU DI-GS

V.5. GEOLOGY

V.5.a. GENERAL STUDIES, CONGRESSES, AND TEXTBOOKS

1884. DALINKEVIČIUS, Juozas. Kratkii ocherk geologii Litovskoi SSR.
Pod obshchei red. I.A. Dalinkevi-
chiusa. Vil'nius, 1959. 78 p.
illus., fold. map. QE654.D3 DLC CU
DI-GS PU

1885. --- Lietuvos 1924-1925 m.
geologinių tyrinėjimų trumpa apžvalga. [A brief review of the geological research in Lithuania] In Kos-
mos(Kaunas), v.8, 1927, p. 84-96.
See serials consulted.

1886. --- Nauji bruožai apie šiaurės Lietuvos ir Kuršo geologiją ir
jų ryšiai su vidurine Lietuva.
[Novye cherty geologii Severnoi Litvy...] In Kosmos (Kaunas), v.9,
1928, p. 339-366. Summary in English. See serials consulted.

1887. GEDROITS, A. E. Geologi-
cheskie issledovaniia v guberniiakh
Vilenskoi, Grodnenskoi, Minskoi,
Volnyskoi i severnoi chasti TSarstva
Pol'skogo. In Materialy dlia geologii Rossii (Sanktpeterburg), v.17,
1895. QE1.M57 v.17 DLC

1888. GRIGELIS, Algimantas. O-
cherk geologicheskogo stroeniia i
razvitiia territorii Litovskoi SSR.
In Lietuvos geologijos klausimai
(Vilnius), 1963, p. 43-63. See
serials consulted.

1889. GUDELIS, Vytautas. An outline of the geological research work
in Lithuania. In LTSRMAGGICPXXI.
Vilnius, 1960. p.11-[22] Summaries
in Lithuanian and Russian. QE1.
L4483 DLC CU DI-GS ICU MH-Z NNC

1890. KAUNAS. UNIVERSITETAS.
GEOLOGIJOS KABINETAS. Spaudiniai.
Nauja serija, nr. 1-13. [Publica-
tions of the University of Lithuania,
Institute of Geology, Kaunas. New
Series] Kaunas, 1935-39.
G(575)K16p DI-GS

1891. KAVECKIS, Mykolas Stasys.
Geologijos kabineto 1931 metų tyrinėjimai. [The explorations in 1931
by the Department of Geology] In
KUMGFD, v.6, no.2, 1932, p. 141-180.
Summary in German. See serials consulted.

1892. --- Lietuvos geologijos pagrindai ir rementis gręžinių daviniais senesnių padarų geologinio
žemėlapio sudarymas. [The outline
of the Lithuanian geology...] In

KUMGFD, v.5, no.2, 1931, p. 585-671. Summary in German. See serials con-

1893. --- 1925 metų Lietuvos geologinės ekspedicijos darbų apyskaita. [A report on the explorations' of the Lithuanian geological expedition in 1925] In KUMGFD, v.4, 1928, p. 207-219. See serials consulted.

1894. --- 1927-1930 metų geologiniai tyrinėjimai...[The geological explorations in 1927-1930...] In KUMGFD, t.5, no.2, 1931, p.380-664. See serials consulted.

1895. --- 1928 metų geologinis rekognosciravimas Lietuvos šiaurės rytų rajone, pagrindinių kreidos sluoksnių Jurbarko rajone galutinas išaiškinimas ir Klaipėdos-Palangos rajone gintarinių sluogsnių ieškojimas. [The geological research in Lithuania, 1928] In KUMGFD, t.5, no.2, 1931, p. 413-459. Summary in German. See serials consulted.

1896. LIETUVOS GEOLOGIJA IR PROF. Mykolas Kaveckis. [Atsakingas redaktorius A. Grigelis] Vilnius, Mintis, 1969. 172 p. QE276.L5 PU

1897. LIETUVOS TSR MOKSLŲ AKADEMIJA, VILNA. GEOLOGIJOS IR GEOGRAFIJOS INSTITUTAS. Collected papers for the XXI session of the International Geological Congress. Edited by V. Gudelis. Vilnius, 1960. 445 p. illus., ports., maps. English and Russian; summaries in Lithuanian. QE1.L4483 DLC CU DI-GS ICU MH-Z NNC

1898. --- Voprosy geologii Litvy. Pod red. A.A. Grigelisa i V.N. Karataiute-Talimaa. Vil'nius, 1963. 623 p. illus., port., maps, diagrs. profiles, tables. Russian or Lithuanian; summaries in English, Lithuanian, and Russian. QE276.L54 DLC CaBVaU MH NN NNC WU

1899. LINČIUS, Augustinas and Vytautas Narbutas. Geologinės praeities pėdsakai Lietuvos kraštovaizdyje. Vilnius, [Mintis], 1969. 128 p. illus. (Lietuvos gamta, 1) QE276.L56 DLC PU

1900. OSCHMIAN, Jacob. Aperçu général sur la géologie de la Lithuanie. Paris, Les Presses modernes, 1931. 83 p. Thèse—University of Paris. CtY

1901. RÜGER, Ludwig. Die baltischen Länder; Estland, Lettland und Litauen. Heidelberg, Ger., C. Winters, 1934. 79 p. illus., map,

tables. (Handbuch der regionalen Geologie, Bd.4, Abt.4) QE26.H3 DLC CaOOG DI-GS FU ICU IaU OO

1902. TOMAŠAUSKAS, Marijonas. Geologinės ekspedicijos 1924 m. darbų prirengiamoji apyskaita. [The preliminary report of the geological expedition of 1924] In KUMGFD, v.3, 1926, p. 5-20. See serials consulted.

V.5.b. SPECIAL STUDIES

1903. BRINKMANN, Roland. Der ostpreussisch-litauische Dogger und Unteroxford. In Physikalisch-ökonomische Gesellschaft, Königsberg in Pr. Schriften... v.65, no.2, 1927, p. 49-96. See serials consulted.

1904. DALINKEVIČIUS, Juozas. Devono stratigrafija ir apatinio karbono transgresijos žymės Lietuvoje. [The stratigraphy of devonian deposits and lower carboniferous transgression in Lithuania] In KUMGFD, v.13, no.4, 1939, p. [9]-51. fold. graphs., fold. maps. See serials consulted.

1905. --- Lietuvos devonas ir jo ryšiai su Latvijos devonu. [The devonian deposits in Lithuania and their relation to those of Latvia] In KUMGFD, v.6, no.2, 1932, p. [89]-137. map. See serials consulted.

1906. --- The main features of the tectonic development of the Southern Baltic countries. In LTSRMAGGICPXXI. Vilnius, 1960. p. 137-[158] QE1. L4483 DLC CU DI-GS ICU NH-Z NNC

1907. --- On the problem of the lower cretaceous deposits in Lithuania. In LTSRMAGGICPXXI. Vilnius, 1960. p. 341-350. QE1.L4483 DLC CU DI-GS ICU MH-Z NNC

1908. --- Osnovnye cherty tektoniki i tektonicheskogo razvitiia IUzhnoi Pribaltiki. Hauptsächliche Linien der Tektonik und der tektonischen Etwicklung des Südbaltikums. In LTSRMAGGIMP, v.12, 1960, p. 205-[220] See serials consulted.

1909. --- Vilniaus geologinis profilis ir apatinio paleozojo klausimas Lietuvoje. [The profile of Vilnius and the question of the lower paleozoic deposits in Lithuania] In Kosmos (Kaunas), v.21, no.1-3, 1940, p. 65-98. Summary in German. See serials consulted.

1910. GAIGALAS, Algirdas and A. Klimašauskas. Vidurio Lietuvos skirtingo amžiaus dugninių morėnų mineraloginė bei petrografinė sudėtis ir kai kurie pleistoceno paleografijos klausimai. Mineralogo-petrograficheskii sostav raznovo zrastnykh dannykh moren srednie Litvy. In Geografinis metraštis (Vilnius), v.6-7, 1963-1964. See serials consulted.

1911. GUDELIS, Vytautas. Lietuvos TSR Baltijos pajūrio geologinės raidos vėlyvajame glaciale ir postglaciale (holocene) pagrindiniai etapai. [The Main stages of the Baltic Sea coast evolution in Lithuania during the late- and the post-glacial periods] In Vilna. Universitetas. Mokslo darbai, v.3, 1955, p. 119-139. See serials consulted.

1912. GUDELIS, Vytautas and V. Klimavičienė. Apie Lietuvos pleistoceno moreninių priemolių radioaktyvumą ir jo panaudojimą stratigrafijos bei geochronologijos tikslams. [On the radioactivity of the Lithuanian pleistocene morainic light clays...] In LTSRMAD. Serija B, v.2(18), 1959, p. 111-124. graphs. Summary in Russian. See serials consulted.

1913. --- and V. Mikaila. The largest glacio-lucustrine basins of Lithuania and their significance for geochronology and paleogeography of the late-glacial period. In LTSRMAGGICPXXI. Vilnius, 1960. p. 251-[282] QE1.L4483 DLC CU DI-GS ICU MH-Z NNC

1914. HUNDT, R. Beiträge zur Glazialgeologie Litauens und Südkurlands zwischen Illuxt, Dünaburg und Diswiaty-See. In Naturwissenschaftliche Wochenschrift (Jena), v.38, 1919, p. 545-549. See Serials consulted.

1915. IGNATAVIČIUS, Algimantas Konstantinas. Hydrogeological conditions of the quaternary deposits of the Lithuanian SSR. In LTSRMAGGICPXXI. Vilnius, 1960. p. 373-[389] QE1.L4483 DLC CU DI-GS ICU MH-Z NNC

1916. --- Lietuvos TSR pleistoceninių darinių sąrangos klausimu. [On the question of the structure of the Lithuanian pleistocene formations] In Geografinis metraštis (Vilnius), v.2, 1959, p. 435-460. illus. Summaries in German and Russian. See serials consulted.

1917. KAVECKIS, Mykolas Stasys. Šiaurės Lietuvos devono ir permės sluogsnių patikrinimas, Dubysos upės krantuose pagrindinių sluogsnių ieškojimas ir surinktų gręžinių medžiaga... [The Devon of Northern Lithuania...] In KUMGFD, v.5, no.2, 1931, p. 460-584. Summary in German. See serials consulted.

1918. KISNERIUS, J. Cretaceous deposits of Lithuania. In LTSRMAGGICPXXI. Vilnius, 1960. p. 117-[126] QE1.L4483 DLC CU DI-GS ICU MH-Z NNC

1919. --- Jurassic deposits of Lithuania. In LTSRMAGGICPXXI. Vilnius, 1960. p. 105-[116] QE1.L4483 DLC CU DI-GS ICU MH-Z NNC

1920. KRISHTAFOVICH, N. Stroenie lednikovykh obrazovanii na territorii Kovenskoi, Vilenskoi i Grodnenskoi gubernii. In Ezhegodnik po geologii i mineralogii Rossii (Warszawa), v.1, 1895. See serials consulted.

1921. MISSUNA, Anna. Über die Endmoränen von Weissrussland und Lithauen. In Deutsche geologische Gesellschaft, Berlin. Zeitschrift (Stuttgart), v.54, 1902, p. 284-301. See serials consulted.

1922. MORTENSEN, Hans. Beiträge zur Entwicklung der glazialen Morphologie Litauens. In Geologisches Archiv (Königsberg in Pr.), v.3, no. 1-2, 1924, p. 1-93. CU ICJ MdBJ NNM NjP OU PPAN

1923. NARBUTAS, Vytautas. The ancient Karst-phenomena in devonian deposits of North Lithuania. In LTSRMAGGCPXXI. Vilnius, 1960. p. 329-[340]. QE.L4483 DLC CU DI-GS ICU MH-Z NNC

1924. --- Kartiniai reiškiniai Lietuvoje. [Karst-phenomena in Lithuania] Vilnius, VPMLL, 1958. 65, [3] p. illus., map. (Pažinkime Lietuvą) GB608.55.N27 DLC

1925. PAKUCKAS, Česlovas. Vilniaus krašto pleistoceno klausimais. [On the question of the pleistocene in the region of Vilnius] In Kosmos (Kaunas), v.11, 1940, p. 98-106. See serials consulted.

1926. PAŠKEVIČIUS, Juozas. The silurian of Lithuania. In LTSRMAGGICPXXI. Vilnius, 1960. p. 65-[77] QE1.L4483 DLC CU DI-GS ICU MH-Z NNC

1927. RIMANTIENĖ, Rimutė (Jablonskytė). Kai kurie Lietuvos paleolito klausimai. [Some questions of paleolite in Lithuania] In

LTSRMAD. Serija A, v.l, p. 35-51. See serials consulted.

1928. --- Mezolit Litvy. In KSIIMK, v.42, 1952, 40-53. See serials consulted.

1929. --- Paleolit i mezolit Litvy. Vil'nius, Mintis, 1971. 202 p. GN776.L5R5 PU

1930. STRATIGRAFIIA NIZHNEGO PAleozoia Pribaltiki i korreliatsiia s drugimi regionami. [Sbornik statei. Otv. red. A.A. Grigialis] Vil'nius, Mintis, 1968. 318 p. diagrs. Summaries in English. QE654.S85 DLC CaOTU PU

1931. SOVESHCHANIE PO STRATIGRAfii i paleogeografii devona Pribaltiki, Vilna, 1962. Voprosy stratigrafii i paleogeografii devona Pribaltiki. Pod red. V.N. Karataiute-Talimaa i V.V. Narbutasa. Vil'nius, Mintis, 1964. 145 p. illus., maps. QE665.S56 1962 DLC NNC

1932. SOVESHCHANIE PO VOPROSAM neotektonicheskikh dvizhenii v Pribaltike, Tallinn, 1960. Materialy soveshchaniia. [Otv. red. G.A. Zhelnin] Tartu, 1960. 154 p. illus. profile. QE276.S63 160 DLC

1933. VAITIEKŪNAS, P. The history of the quaternary geology in Lithuania. In LTSRMAGGICPXXI. Vilnius, 1960. p. 159-[174] QE1.L4483 DLC CU DI-GS ICU MH-Z NNC

1934. --- Main features of the structure of quaternary (nathropogenic) deposits in Lithuania. In LTSRMAGGICPXXI, Vilnius, 1960. p. 185-[203] QE1.L4483 DLC CU DI-GS ICU MH-Z NNC

1935. VASILJEVAS, Viktoras. Drevnie kory vyvetrivaniia kristalicheskogo fundamenta IUzhnoi Pribaltiki. Vil'nius, Mintis, 1969. 173 p. illus., maps. (Ministerstvo geologii SSSR. Institut geologii (Vil'nius). Trudy, vyp. 7) QE451.B35V3 CaOTU

1936. VOPROSY GEOLOGII I PALEOGEOgrafii chetvertichnogo perioda Litvy. [Sbornik statei. Otv. red. M. V. Kabailene] Vil'nius, Mintis, 1967. 242 p. diagrs. (Ministerstvo geologii SSR. Institut geologii (Vil'nius). Trudy, vyp. 5) QE276.V53 vyp.5 DLC

V.5.c. PETROGRAPHY, PETROLOGY, ETC.

1937. GAIGALAS, Algirdas. Dzūkijos Ašmenos ir Gardino aukštumų galinių morenų bei keiminių kalvų petrografiniai bruožai. [The petrographical traits of the end moraines in Dzūkija, Ašmena and Gardinas districts] In LTSRMAGGIMP, v.9, 1959, p.5-22, diagrams. See serials consulted.

1938. --- Nemuno vidurupio mezopleistoceno morenų paleodulėjimo plutos klausimu. [On the question of the disintegration of the mesopleistocene moraines in the middle region of Nemunas river] In LTSRMAGGIMP, v.10, no.2, 1959, p.68-80. illus. See serials consulted.

1939. --- Petrographic examination of pleistocene moraines. In LTSRMAGGICPXXI. Vilnius, 1960. p. 227-234. QE1.L4483 DLC CU DI-GS ICU MH-Z NNC

1940. --- Rekonstruktsiia dvizheniia pleistotsenovykh lednikov na territorii Litovskoi SSR po petrograficheskim dannym izucheniia moren. In Lietuvos geologijos klausimai (Vilnius), p. 527-544. QE276.L54 DLC CaBVaU MH NN NNC WU

1941. JURGAITIS, Algirdas. Geneticheskie tipy i litologiia peschano-graviinykh otlozhenii Litovskoi SSR. [Otv. red. A. IUrgaitis] Vil'nius, Mintis, 1969. 172 p. illus., graphs, plans, tables. (Vilna. Geologijos institutas. Trudy, vyp.9) See serials consulted.

1942. VILNA. GEOLOGIJOS INSTITUTAS. Litologiia i geologiia poleznykh iskopaemykh IUzhnoi Pribaltiki. Vil'nius, Mintis, 1966. 359 p. illus., maps. (Its Trudy, vyp.3) At head of title: Ministerstvo geologii SSSR. Institut geologii (Vilnius) Summaries in German and Lithuanian. QE276.V53 vyp.3 DLC

V.5.d. EARTH MAGNETISM, GRAVITATION, ETC.

1943. BLINSTRUBAS, Stasys. The magnetic field of Lithuania. In LTSRMGGICPXXI. Vilnius, 1960. p. 419-[430] QE1.L4483 DLC CU DI-GS ICU MH-Z NNC

1944. BRAZDŽIŪNAS, Povilas. Magnetiniai Baltijos jūros Lietuvos pakraščio 1930 metų matavimai. Ergebnisse der magnetischen Messungen in der Ostsee im Jahre 1930 entlang der litauischen Küste. In KUMGFD, v.7, no.2, 1933, p.[277]-312. See serials consulted.

1945. RAŽINSKAS, A. Detalaus geoido tyrimo Lietuvos TSR teritorijoje perspektyvos. [Prospects of detailed investigation of Geoid-figure in the territory of Lithuania] In LTSRMAGGIMP, v.8, 1958, p.120-132. Summary in English and Russian. See serials consulted.

1946. --- Gravimetrinio atramos tinklo sudarymo ir išlyginimo klausimu. [On the question of the composition and counterpoising of gravimetrical basic network] In LTSRMAGGIMP, v.10, 1959, p.5-28. graphs. Summary in English and Russian. See serials consulted.

1947.--- Vertikalės nukripimas ir geoido unduliacija LTSR vakarinėje dalyje. Ukloneniia otvesa i unduliatsiia v zapadnoi chasti Litovskoi SSR. In LTSRMAD. Seria B, v.3, 1957, p.65-80. illus. See serials consulted.

1948. ŠLEŽEVIČIUS, Kazys. Gravimetriniai darbai 1934 m. ir svorio jėgos greitėjimas Lietuvoje. Gravimetricheskie raboty v 1934 g. i uskorenie sily tiazhesti v Litve. In KUMGFD, v.10, no.1, 1936, p.3-28. Summary in German. See serials consulted.

1949. ŠLEŽEVIČIUS, Kazys and Ignas Saldukas. Lietuvos magnetinė nuotrauka, padaryta 1936-1938 metais. Les mésures magnétques en Lithuanie, faits en 1936-1938. Vilnius, Vilniaus universitetas matematikos-gamtos fakultetas, 1941. 52 p. illus., fold. map.

1950. SALDUKAS, Ignas. Das Normalfeld und die Anomalien der erdmagnetischen Vertikalintensität im Ostseegebiet. In Deutsches hydrographisches Institut. Jahrbuch des Observatoriums Wingst, no.4, 1952, p.85-97. fold. graphs. QC830.W553 DLC

V.5.e. PALEONTOLOGY, PALEOBOTANY, AND AND PALEOZOOLOGY

1951. ALIKHOVA, Tat'iana Nikolaevna. Polevoi atlas kharakternykh kompleksov fauny otlozhenii ordovika i gotlandiia iuzhnoi chasti Litovskoi SSR. Moskva, Gos. nauch-tekh. izd-vo lit-ry po geologii i okhrane iedr,

1954. 96 p. illus. (Trudy Vsesoiuznogo nauchno-issledovatel'skogo geologicheskogo instituta) QE727. A55 DLC DI-GS

1952. BODEN, Karl. Die Fauna des unten Oxford von Popilany in Litauen. Jena, G. Fischer, 1911. 77, [17] p. illus., plates. (Geologische und paleontologische Abhandlungen. N.F., Bd.10, Hft.,2) Bibliography: p. 4-10. QE1.G492 Bd.10 DLC DI-GS ICJ

1953.DALINKEVIČIUS, Juozas. On the fossil fishes of the Lithuanian chalk. In KUMGFD, v.9, no.3, 1935, p. 245-305. See serials consulted.

1954. GRIGELIS, Algimantas. Micropaleontological investigations in Lithuania. In LTSRMAGGICPXXI. Vilnius, 1960. p. 317-[328] QE1. L4483 DLC CU DI-GS ICU MH-Z NNC

1955. KABAILIENĖ, M. Augalijos raida vėlyvajame ledynmetyje ir poledynmetyje Lietuvos ir pietinės Latvijos pajūrio zonoje. [The development of the flora in the late ice-age and post-ice-age in the seacoast region of Lithuania and Southern Latvia] In Geografinis metraštis (Vilnius), v.2, 1959, p. 477-505. See serials consulted.

1956. --- Lietuvos ir pietinės Latvijos Baltijos pajūrio raida vėlyvajame ledynmetyje ir poledinmetyje diatomijų floros tyrimų duomenimis. [The development of the Lithuanian and Southern Latvian Baltic Sea shore in the latest ice-age and after it, according to the research on the diatom algae] In LTSRMAGGIMP, v.10, no.2, 1959, p. 175-214. See serials consulted.

1957. PAKUCKAS, Česlovas. Papilės oksfordo ir kelojevo amonitų fauna. Die Ammoniten-Fauna des Oxford und Kellowey von Papilė. In KUMGFD, v.6, no.2, 1932, p. [1]-85, tables. Summary in German. See serials consulted.

1958. PALEONTOLOGIIA I STRATIGRAfiia Pribaltiki i Belorussii. Vil'nius, Institut geologii, 1966-71. 3 v. QE755.R9P282 PU(1,3)

1959. SIEMIRADZKI, Józef. O faunie kopalnej warstw brunatnego jura w Popielanach na Žmudzi. In Polska Akademia Umiejętności, Kraków. Wydział Matematyczno-Przyrodniczy. Pamiętnik, v.17, 1889, p. 114-127. See serials consulted.

V.6. IRRIGATION AND RECLAMATION

1960. LIETUVOS TSR MOKSLŲ AKADEMI-
JA, VILNA. MELIORACIJOS INSTITUTAS.
Artimiausi melioracijų uždaviniai.
[Future plans for the reclaiming of
land in Lithuanian SSR; collected
articles] Redagavo J. Čeičys ir K.
Ramanauskas. Vilnius, VPMLL, 1954.
138 p. TC978.L5L5 DLC

1961. KAUNAS. LIETUVOS HIDROTECH-
NIKOS IR MELIORACIJOS MOKSLINIO TYRI-
MO INSTITUTAS. Žemės ūkio meliorato-
riaus žinynas. [Handbook of the land
reclamation. Autorių kolektyvas: J.
Čeičys et al., redagavo K. Dabužins-
kas] Vilnius, VPMLL, 1960. 288 p.
illus., diagrs., tables. S621.K37
DLC

V.7. NATURAL HISTORY

V.7.a. GENERAL STUDIES

1962. BEITRÄGE ZUR NATUR- UND KUL-
turgeschichte Litauens und angrenzen-
der Gebiete. Hrsg. von E. Stechow.
München, Verlag der Wissenschaften,
1922-32. viii, 678 p. illus., plates, maps, diagrrs. (Abhandlungen
der matematisch-naturwissenschaftli-
chen Abteilung der Bayerischen Akademie der Wissenschaften. Suppl.Bd.)
Originally issued in 6 parts.
AS182.M8183 NjP CU CSt CaOTU CtY DLC
DNAL DI-GS ICJ IaAS IU MBN MH-Z MdBJ
MiU MnU NIC NN NNM OCU OClW PU TxU
WU WaU

1963. EICHWALD, Eduard Karl. Na-
turhistorische Skizze von Litauen,
Volynien, Podolien. Wilna, Auf Kosten des Verfassers, bei L. Voss, in
Leipzig, 1830. [6], 256 p. front.,
fold. map. QH162.E34 DLC PPAN DI-GS

1964. ISOKAS, Gediminas. Parkais
ir miškais; iš gamtininko bloknoto.
Vilnius, VPMLL, 1959. 150 p. illus.
QH178.L5I8 PU

1965. LIETUVOS GAMTA. [Nature in
Lithuania. Sudarytojas ir teksto
autorius R. Budrys. Dailininkas R.
Gibavičius] Vilnius, Mintis, 1966.
1 v. (chiefly illus.) QH46.L5 DLC
CtTPAM MH PU

1965a. --- [Priedas. Supplement]
Vilnius, Mintis, 1966. 103 p. Text
and list of illus. in Lithuanian,
Russian, Polish, English and German.
QH46.L5 DLC CtPAM MH PU

1966. MORKŪNAITĖ, Ž., comp. Tarybų Lietuvos gamta ir jos apsauga;
rekomenduojamos literatūros rodyklė.
[Nature in Soviet Lithuania and its
conservation; a list of recommended
works] Vilnius, 1966. 101 p. Summary in English. Z7164.N3M68 DLC

1967. NAUCHNAIA KONFERENTSIIA PO
zashchite rastenii. 2nd, Vilna,
1958. Tezisy dokladov. [Redaktor
A. Minkevichius et al.] Vil'nius,
1958. 83 p. At head of title: Akademiia nauk Litovskoi SSR. Institut
biologii, Litovskii nauchno-issledovatel'skii institut zemledeliia.
SB605.L5N3 1958c DLC CU

1968. RESPUBLIKINĖ KONFERENCIJA
gamtos apsaugos klausimais. 1st,
Vilna,1957. Gamta ir jos apsauga.
[Nature and its conservation] Redakcinė kolegija: A. Basalykas, V. Ber-
gas, T. Ivanauskas, K. Jankevičius,
A. Kvedaras, S. Maldžiūnaitė, A. Matulionis, V. Petrauskas. Vilnius,
VPMLL, 1958. 179, [4] p. illus.
At head of title: Lietuvos TSR Mokslų akademija. QH77.L5R4 1957 DLC NN

V.7.b. BOTANY

1969. BRUNDZA, Kazys. Nemuno už-
liejamų pievų augalija ir Lietuvos
TSR pievų augalijos tyrimų gairės.
[The flora of the meadows flooded by
the Nemunas River and the guidlines
for its research] In LTSRMABiID,
v.2, 1954, p. 10-45. See serials
consulted.

1970. GRYBAUSKAS, Kazys. Vaistingieji Lietuvos laukų augalai ir jų
pritaikymas. [The wild medicinal
plants of Lithuania and their uses]
Kaunas, S. Niemanto ir P. Šulaičio
leidinys, 1927-35. 2 pts. (Kaunas.
Universitetas. Matematikos-gamtos
fakulteto leidinys, nr.11) QK99.G88
ICU NN

1971. --- --- Kaunas, 1941. 128 p.
QK339.L5G73 PU

1972. GUDANAVIČIUS, Stasys. Vais-
tiniai augalai. [Medicinal plants]
Vilnius, VPMLL, 1969. 286 p. illus.
QK99.G87 DLC CU PPAN

1973. --- Vaistiniai-techniniai
[Medicinal-technical plants] Vil-
nius, VPMLL, 1956. 142 p. QK99.G88
DLC

1974. HRYNIEWIECKI, Bolesław. Ten-
tament florae Lithuaniae; matériaux
pour servir à l'étude de la Lithua-

nie. Warszawa, 1933. xvi, 367 p. illus., maps. (Archivum Nauk Biologicznych Towarzystwa Naukowego Warszawskiego , 4) Bibliography: p. 333-352. QH301.A7 DLC NN

1975. JUNDZIŁŁ, Stanisław Bonifacy. Opisanie roslin litewskich według układu Lineusza. Wilno, J. Zawadzki, 1811. 333 p. QK339.L5J8 DLC MH-A(1791 ed.)

1976. KAMANOS; geologiškai botaniška studija... [Kamanos; the geologic-botanical study...] Kaunas, 1936. xxii, 414 p. (Dotnuva. Žemės ūkio akademija. Žemės ūkio akademijos metraštis, v.10, no.3-4, 1936. Summary in German. See serials consulted.

1977. KUPFFER, Karl Reinhold. Grundzüge der Pflanzengeographie des ostbaltischen Gebietes. Riga, G.Löffler, 1925. 224 p. diagr., fold. map. QK321.K9 ICU IU NN

1978. LIETUVOS TSR MOKSLŲ AKADEMIJA, VILNA. BOTANIKOS INSTITUTAS. Lietuvos TSR flora. [Lithuania's flora] Ats. redaktorius A. Minkevičius. Vilnius, VPMLL, 1959-63. 3 v. illus., maps. Summaries in German and Russian; vol.1 has on title page: Lietuvos TSR Mokslų akademija. Biologijos institutas. QK339.L5L5 DLC CaAEU(3) CtPAM(1-3) DNAL MH NN(2) PU

1979. LUKAITIENĖ, Marija. Dekoratyviniai medžiai ir krūmai Lietuvos TSR parkuose ir sodybose. [Decorative shrubs and trees in the parks and farmsteads of Lithuania] In LTSRMABiID, v.1, 1951, p.125-151. See serials consulted.

1980. MAZELAITIS, Jonas, A. Gricius and V. Urbonas. Naujos Lietuvos TSR florai buožiagrybių (Basidiomycetes) rūšys. Novye dlia flory Litovskoi SSR vidy bazidial'nykh gribov. In LTSRMAD. Seria C, v.3, 1963, p.89-101. See serials consulted.

1981. MAZELAITIS, Jonas and Antanas Minkevičius. Valgomieji ir nuodingieji grybai. [Edible and poisonous mushrooms] Vilnius, VPMLL, 1957. 246 p. illus. At head of title: Lietuvos TSR Mokslų akademija. Biologijos institutas. QK608.L5M3 CU CtPAM DLC DNAL NIC

1982. MINKEVIČIUS, Antanas. Lietuvos TSR ežerų fitoplanktonas ir tolimesnės jo tyrimo perspektyvos. [The phytoplankton in the Lithuanian lakes and its future research] In Vilna. Universitetas. Biologijos, geografijos,geologijos mokslų serija, v.6,

1959, p.39-53. See serials consulted.

1983. --- Vadovas Lietuvos TSR miškų, pievų ir pelkių samanoms pažinti. [Guide of forests, meadows and peat-moss in Lithuania] Vilnius, VPMLL, 1955. 301 p. illus. QK544.L5M5 DLC CtPAM ICLJF

1984. MOWSZOWICZ, Jakub. Conspectus florae Vilnensis. Przegląd flory wileńskiej. Łódz, 1957-58. 2 v. (Łódzkie Towarzystwo Naukowe. Wydział III. Prace, nr.47, 51) QK322.M69 DLC NN(1) PU

1985. NATKEVIČAITĖ, Marija. Lietuvos TSR adventyvinė flora. [The adventive flora of Lithuania] In LTSRMABiID, v.1, 1951, p.77-124. See serials consulted.

1986. PIPINYS, J. Rytų Lietuvos didieji viksvynai. Krupnoosokovaia rastitel'nost' Vostochnoi Litvy. In LTSRMAD. Seria C, v.2, 1963, p.3-35. See serials consulted.

1987. --- Rytų Lietuvos mažieji viksvynai. Melkoosokovaia rastitel'-nost' Vostochnoi Litvy. In LTSRMAD. Seria C, v.3, 1963, p.3-24. See serials consulted.

1988. --- Rytų Lietuvos pievų ir žemapelkių augalija. [The vegetation of the meadows and the low-bogs in Eastern Lithuania] In LTSRMAD. Seria B, v.4(16), 1958, p.177-196. See serials consulted.

1989. RASTITEL'NOST' LUGOV I NIzinnykh bolot Litovskoi SSR. [Otv. red. K. Brundza] Vil'nius, Mintis, 1967. 162 p. illus., maps. QH541.5.P7R3 DLC

1990. REGEL, Konstantin. Bibliographia botanica lituana. In KUMGFD, v.7, 1932, p.5-28. See serials consulted.

1991. --- Fontes florae Lithuaniae I-VI. Lietuvos floros šaltiniai. In KUMGED, v.5, no.2, 1931, p.221-289; v.7, no.1, 1932, p.5-71; v.9, no.2, 1934, p.181-206; v.10, no.3, 1936, p.47-58; v.11, no.4, 1937, p. 299-315; v.12, no.2, 1939, p.5-24. See serials consulted.

1992. --- Medžiaga Lietuvos piktžolėms pažinti. I: Piktžolės Lietuvos laukuose. Beiträge zur Kenntnis der Unkräuter in Litauen. I: Die Unkräuter der Getreidefelder. In KUMGFD, v.13, no.3, 1939, p.[39]-92. See serials consulted.

1993. --- Šepetos durpyno ir Šimonių girios augmenija. [The vegetation of the bog of Šepeta and the forest of Šimoniai] In Kosmos (Kaunas), v.21, no.1-3, 1940. See serials consulted.

1994. REGEL, Konstantin and V. Šataitė. Le spectre phénologique d'une prairie en Lithuanie. In Acta phaenologica (The Hague), v.3, no.5, 1935, p. 66-75. CLSU CU CtY ICU IaAS MH-A MiU OCl OClW PPAN WU

1995. ŠIMKŪNAITĖ, E. Nemuno žemupio pievų vaistingieji augalai-pievų piktžolės. [The medicinal herbs of the lower Nemunas River meadows] In LTSRMABiID, v.2, 1954, p. 46-58. See serials consulted.

1996. SNARSKIS, Povilas. Vadovas Lietuvos augalams pažinti. [A guide to Lithuanian flora] Vilnius, 1954. 906 p. illus.

1997. --- --- [Another edition] Vilnius, Mintis, 1968. 581 p. illus. QE339.L5S55 PU

1998. --- Vadovas Lietuvos laukų piktžolėms pažinti. [A guide for identification of Lithuanian weeds] Vilnius, Mintis, 1968. 502 p. illus. DLC

V.7.c. ZOOLOGY

1999. ELISONAS, Jurgis. Mūsų šalies žinduoliai. [Mammals of our country] Kaunas, Švietimo ministerijos leidinys, 1932. 2 v. illus. 947.52.El45 PU NNCL

2000. --- Žinios apie vėbrą senovės Lietuvoje. [Information on the beaver in ancient Lithuania] In Kosmos (Kaunas), 1929, p. 388-399. See serials consulted.

2001. IVANAUSKAS, Tadas. Lietuvos paukščiai. [Birds of Lithuania] Vilnius, VPMLL, 1938-55. 3 v. plates. At head of title: Lietuvos TSR Mokslų akademija. Biologijos institutas. Vol.1 was published in Kaunas, 1938. QL690.L5I8 DLC CtPAM (2-3) ICLJF

2002. --- --- 2., papildytas ir pataisytas leidimas. [2nd ed.] Vilnius, VPMLL, 1957-59. 2 v. illus., plates (part. col.) maps. QL690.L5I82 DLC NN PPiU PU

2003. --- Paukščių žiedavimas Lietuvoje iki 1932 m. gruodžio mėn.

31 d. Baguage des oiseaux en Lithuanie jusq'au 31 décembre 1932. In KUMGFD, v.7, 1933, p. 317-361. See serials consulted.

2004. --- Paukščių žiedavimas Lietuvoje 1937 metais. Baguage des oiseaux en Lithuanie 1937. In KUMGFD v.13, 1939, p. [133]-160. See serials consulted.

2005. --- Vadovas Lietuvos žinduoliams pažinti. [A guide to mammals of Lithuania] Vilnius, VPMLL, 1964. 339 p. illus., (part. col.) maps. At head of title: Lietuvos TSR Mokslų akademija. Zoologijos ir parazitologijos institutas. QL728.L5I8 DLC DNAL MH NNM NN PPAN PPULC

2006. --- Žuvintas. [Lake Žuvintas] Vilnius, VPMLL, 1961. 46 p. illus. At head of title: Lietuvos TSR Mokslų akademijos zoologijos ir parazitologijos institutas. T. Ivanauskas, J. Muraška, T. Zubavičius. SB484. L5I9 DLC PU

2007. JAROCKI, Felix Paul von. Zubr; oder, Der litauische Auerochs. Hamburg, 1830. 23 p. MH

2008. KAKIES, Martin. Elche zwischen Meer und Memel. Berlin-Lichterfelde, H. Bermühler, [1936] 63 p. 56 plates on 28 leaves. QL737.U5K3 1936 DLC

2009. KAUNECKIENĖ, Justina. Kauno zoologijos sodas. [Zoological garden in Kaunas. Vilnius, VPMLL, 1960] 157 p. illus. QL77.K3K3 DLC

2010. KROTAS, Rostislavas. Lietuvos gėlavandenės žuvys. [The fresh water fishes of Lithuania] Vilnius, Mintis, 1971. 71 p. 14 leaves of illus. On verso of title page: Lietuvos TSR Mokslų akademija. Zoologijos ir parazitologijos institutas. QL633.L5K76 DLC

2011. KVARŠINAS-SAMARINAS, M. Stumbrų radiniai Lietuvoje ir jų rūšiavimo klausimas. Wiesentfunde in Litauen und Klassifizierungfrage. In KUMGFD, v.4, no.4, 1934, p. [489]-526. illus., tables. See serials consulted.

2012. LEŠINSKAS, Antanas. Vadovas Lietuvos vabzdžiams pažinti. [A guide to the insects of Lithuania] Vilnius, Mintis, 1967. 371 p. illus. QL482.L5L4 DLC

2013. LIETUVOS TSR MOKSLŲ AKADEMIJA, VILNA. BIOLOGIJOS INSTITUTAS. Lietuvos gėlųjų vandenų žuvys. [The fresh water fishes of Lithuania] Vil-

nius, VPMLL, 1956. 237 p. illus.
At head of title: Lietuvos TSR Mokslų akademija. Biologijos institutas: T. Ivanauskas et al. QL633.
L5L5 DLC CU CtY MH-Z NN NcD OkU

2014. MAČIONIS, A. Lietuvos gyvūnija. Tierwelt Litauens. In
Basalykas, Alfonsas. Lietuvos TSR
fizinė geografija. Vilnius, 1958.
v. 1, p. 418-441. GB276.L5B3 DLC
CU CaOTU CtPAM CtTMF DI-GS NN NNC
PU WaU

2015. PALIONIS, Alfonsas. Įdėlis
Lietuvos drugių faunai pažinti. [A
guide to the butterflies of Lithu-
ania] In KUMGFD, v.6, 1932, p. 1-
189. See serials consulted.

2016. PRIBALTISKAIA ORNITOLOGI-
CHESKAIA KONFERENTSIIA. Trudy.
1- konferentsiia; 1951- . Riga
[etc], Izd-vo Akademii nauk Latvi-
isloi SSR [etc] illus., maps.
QL671.P73 DLC(1954,1957,1960) CU
(1957) CaOTU(1960) MiU(1957)

2017. VAITKEVIČIUS, Antanas. Kamanų ir Tyrelio aukštapelkių ornitofauna. [The ornitofauna of the
swamps of Kamanos and Tyrelis] In
LTSRMAD. Serija C, v.3(29), 1962,
p. 135-149. map. See serials consulted.

2018. VALIUS, Mečys. Lietuvos
vandens ir pelkių paukščiai. [Wa-
ter and swamp birds of Lithuania.
Vilnius, VPMLL, 1960. 175 illus.
QL690.L5V3 DLC CU CtPAM PU

VI. THE PEOPLE

VI.1. GENERAL STUDIES, POPULATION, BOUNDARIES AND THE ETHNOGRAPHIC AND LINGUISTIC TERRITORIES

2019. AKIELEWICZ, Mikołaj. Rzut
oka na starożytność narodu litewskiego. Napisał Vytautas [pseud.]
Sanktpeterburg, Tip. F.S. Sushnis-
kago, 1885. 49 p. DK511.L8A7 WU PU

2020. BALTIISKAIA ETNOGRAFO-ANTRO-
pologicheskaia ekspeditsiia, 1952.
Materialy. In Akademiia nauk SSSR.
Institut etnografii(Moskva), N.S.
v.23, 1954. See serials consulted.

2021. BALTIISKII ETNOGRAFICHESKII
sbornik. [Otvetstvennye redaktory:
N.N. Cheboksarov i L.N. Tarent'eva]
Moskva, Izd-vo Akademii nauk SSR,
1956. 272 p. illus., maps. (Akade-

miia nauk SSSR. Institut etnografii.
Trudy. Moskva, 1956. Novaia seriia, t.32) See serials consulted.

2022. BORICHEVSKII, Ivan Petrovich. Sviedieniia o drevnikh litovtsakh. In ZMNP(Sanktpeterburg), Ch.
42, otd.2, 1844, p. 1-53. See
serials consulted.

2023. BRENNSOHN, Isidorus. Zur
Anthropologie der Litauer. Dorpat,
Druck von H. Laakmann's Buch und
Steindruckerei, 1883. 61 p. tables.
Inaug.Diss.--University of Dorpat.
GN585.R9B8 DLC DNLM CtY MB MiU NNC

2024. COON, Carlton Stevens. The
races of Europe. New York, N.Y.,
Macmillan, 1939. xvi, 739 p. illus.,
plates, tables, diagrs. GN575.C6
DLC CaAEU CaBVaU CaBViP CU KU-M MH
NcD OCl OClW OU OrU PP PPT TU

2025. DOGIEL, Maciej. Limites
regni Poloniae et Magni Ducatus Lituaniae ex originalibus et exemplis
authenticis descriti et in lucem
editi. Vilnae, Tip. Scholarum Pja-
rum, 1758. 131, 225 p. DK418.D65
DLC PU

2026. DOUBEK, Franciszek A. Die
litauisch-polnische Volkstumsgrenze.
In Jomsburg (Leipzig), v.2, 1938.
See serials consulted.

2027. ESSEN, Werner and Francizek
A. Doubek. Volks- und Sprachkarten
Mitteleuropas. 2: Litauen. In
Deutsches Archiv für Landes- und
Volksforschung (Leipzig), v.2, 1938.
See serials consulted.

2028. FORSTREUTER, Kurt Hermann.
Die Entwicklung der Grenze zwischen
Preussen und Litauen seit 1422. In
Altpreussische Forschungen (Königs-
berg in Pr.), v.18, no.1, 1941, p.
50-70. See serials consulted.

2029. FRÖLICH, Gustav. Beiträge
zur Volkskunde des preussischen Litauens. Insterburg in Pr., 1902.
18, vii p. (Beilage zum Programm d.
Kg. Gimnasiums zu Insterburg)
947.52F923 PU

2030. GALLOGLY, Inman Gray. Lithuanian territorial alterations, 1920-
1940. [Bloomington, Ind.], 1953.
102 p. Thesis (M.A.)--Indiana University. Typescript. DR29.G172 InU

2031. GORZUCHOWSKI, Stanisław.
Granica polsko-litewska w terenie.
Warszawa, 1928. 143 p. fold. maps.,
diagrs. Summary in French; Biblio-
graphy: p. [140]-143. DK418.5.L5G6
DLC PU CtY

2032. GROTELÜSCHEN, Wilhelm. Die Grenzen des Memelgebietes. _In_ Geographische Zeitschrift (Leipzig), v. 42, 1936, p. 281-292. maps. See serials consulted.

2033. HALECKI, Oskar. Poland's eastern frontiers. _In_ Journal of Central European Affairs (Boulder, Col.) v.1, 1941, p. 191-207, 325-338. See serials consulted.

2034. HAUSHOFER, Karl Ernst. Grenzen in ihrer geographischen und politischen Bedeutung. Berlin-Grüenwald, K. Vowinckel, 1927. xv, 350 p. illus., maps. JX4111.H3 DLC CSt-H CaAEU CtY ICN ICU LU MiU NN NcD OU OClW WU

2035. HOŁUBOWICZ, Włodzimierz. Granica osadnictwa słowian i litwinów na wileńszczyznie w czasach przed i wczesnohistorycznych. Wilno, Zakłady graficzne "Znicz", 1938. Offprint. 947.52H749 PU

2036. JAKUBOWSKI, Jan. Studya nad stosunkami narodowościowemi na Litwie przed Unią Lubelską. Warszawa, Nakładem Towarzystwa Naukowego Warszawskiego, 1912. 4, 104 p. (Prace Towarzystwa Naukowego Warszawskiego. Wydział II: Nauk Antropologicznych, Społecznych, Historyi i filozofii, nr.7) Summaries in Latin. DK511.L2J2 InU ICU NN NNC PU

2037. --- Tautybių santykiai Lietuvoje ligi Liublino unijos. [Relations of nationalities in Lithuania until the Lublin Union] Kaunas, 1921. 94 p. 947.5 Ji Ct TMF

2038. KARGE, Paul. Die Litauerfrage in Altpreussen in geschichtlicher Beleuchtung. Königsberg in Pr., B. Meyer, 1925. 100 p. DK511.L26K3 DLC ICU PU

2039. KLIMAS, Petras. Lietuva, jos gyventojai ir sienos. [Lithuania, its population and boundaries] Vilnius, M. Kuktos spaustuvė, 1917. 62 p. map. DK511.L713K651 InNd CtTMF ICBM ICLJF PU

2040. --- Lietuvos sienos rytuose. [The boundaries of Eastern Lithuania] _In_ Svietimo darbas (Kaunas), v.3, 1921. See serials consulted.

2041. --- La Lithuanie russe, considérations statistiques et ethnographiques par K. Verbelis [pseud.] Traduction d'Antoine Viscont. Genève, Édition Atar, [1918] 183 p. 2 fold. maps. DK511.L2K63 DLC CSt-H NN

2042. --- Russisch-Litauen; statistisch-ethnographische Betrachtungen. Von K. Werbelis [pseud.] Stuttgart, J. Schröder, 1916. vi, 108 p. DK511.L2K64 ICU CaAEU PU

2043. --- Les territoires de la Lituanie considerations ethnographiques et statistiques; le gouvernement de Vilna (Vilnius). Paris, 1919. 30 p. map. (Delegation de Lituanie à la Conference de la Paix. pt. V, 6-bis) D643.A7DP5L7 CSt-H DW NN PU

2044. --- ---; le gouvernement de Kovno (Kaunas) par P. Klimas. Paris, 1919. 18 p. DK511.K55K5 DLC CSt-H NN PU

2045. KOSTOMAROV, Nikolai Ivanovich. Litovskoe plemia i otnosheniia ego k russkoi istorii. _In_ Russkoe slovo (Sanktpeterburg) v.2, no.5, 1860, p. 4-100. AP50.R87 1860 DLC NN

2046. KROHNERT, Ernst Karl Gustav. Die deutsch-russische Grenze von Eydkuhnen bis Soldau. Lötzen, 1912. Bound with Behrendt, Kurt. Die Memelfrage. Würzburg, 1930. 914. 75B397 PU

2047. KUSHNER, Pavel Ivanovich (Knyshev). Etnicheskie territorii i etnicheskie granitsy. Moskva, Izd-vo Akademii nauk SSSR, 1951. 277 p. illus., maps (part. col., part. fold.) plans, tables. (Akademiia nauk SSR. Institut etnografii. Trudy. Novaia seriia, v.15) Part 2, p. 107-278 covers the ethnographic past of the South-Western Baltic region. GN.A2142 v.15 DLC MH-P PU

2048. LATVIJAS-LIETAVAS ROBEŽKOMISIJA. Latvijas-Lietavas robežas apraksts. [The description of the Latvian-Lithuanian boundaries] [Riga 1927] iv, 614, ii, iv p. and atlas of 111 maps. D651.L4A57 1927 DLC

2049. LITHUANIA. The boundaries of Lithuania. A memorandum to the State Department presented by the representative of Lithuania in America, April 1920. [Washington, D.C.] 1920. 1 v. DK511.L27A5 1920 DLC CLU WaU

2050. LITHUANIAN INFORMATION BUREAU. Des frontières lituano-allemandes et lituano-polonaises. [Paris, 1919?] [3] p. (Délégation de Lituanie à la Conférence de la Paix, [pt.] II, 1) D643.A7DP5L7 CSt-H

2051. ŁOWMIAŃSKI, Henryk. The ancient Prussians. Toruń, Poland; London, Eng., The Baltic Institute; J.B. Bergson, 1936. 109 p. (The Baltic pocket library) Translated from Polish: "Dzieje Prus Wschodnich". Bibliography: p. 107-109. DD336.L62 DLC CtY NN PU(microfilm 785)

2052. MACHLEJD, Jerzy. Mapa narodowościowa polskich kresów północnych i Litwy. [Warszawa, Gebethner i Wolff, 1922] 16 p. map. Slav 6254.22 MH

2053. MEYER, Percy. Rassen und Völker im europäischen Osten. III: Die Litauer. In Rasse (Leipzig), v.2, 1935, p. 345-352. See serials consulted.

2054. MORTENSEN, Gertrud (Heinrich). Beiträge zu den Nationalitäten- und Siedlungsverhältnissen in Preussisch-Litauen. Berlin, Memelland Verlag, 1927. 87 p. DK511.Z9 1927M CtY DLC PU

2055. MORTENSEN, Hans. Neues zur Frage der mittelalterlichen Nordgrenze der Litauer. Leipzig, 1933. In Zeitschrift für slavische Philologie (Leipzig), v.10, 1933, p. 273-305. See serials consulted.

2056. NATANSON-LESKI, Jan. Rozwój terytorialny Polski od czasów najdawniejszych do okresu przebudowy państwa w latach 1569-1772. [Wyd.1] Warszawa, Państwowe Wydawn. Naukowe, 1964. 167 p. fold. maps. Bibliography: p. 152-156. DK404.5. N3 DLC ICU MH NNC

2057. PAKŠTAS, Kazys. Baltijos respublikų politinė geografija. [The political geography of the Baltic Republics] Kaunas, 1929. 180 p. illus., maps. (Publicationes Instituti geografici Universitatis Lithuaniae, 1) 914.47.P3 CtTMF ICBM WaU

2058. --- Keletas samprotavimų apie Lietuvos ribas. [Several considerations about the boundaries of Lithuania] In Aidai (Kennebunkport, Me.), no.1-4, 1950, p. 8-14, 81-86, 123-129, 174-182. See serials consulted.

2059. --- Lietuvių tautos plotai ir gyventojai. [The Lithuanian national territories and their population] In Lietuvių enciklopedija. Boston, Mass., 1968. v.15, p. 430-450. See entry no. 216.

2060. --- Lietuvos ribų problema.

[The problem of the Lithuanian boundaries] Kaunas; Marijampolė, Dirva, 1939. 32 p. map. 914.5 ICBM

2061. --- Lietuvos valstybės plotai ir sienos. [The territories of the Lithuanian State and its boundaries] In Lietuvių enciklopedija. Boston, Mass., 1968. v.15, p. 450-464. See entry no. 216.

2062. --- National and state boundaries. In Lituanus (New York, N.Y.), v.5, no.3, Sept. 1959, p. 67-72. map. See serials consulted.

2063. --- The problem of Lithuanian boundaries. In Lithuanian Bulletin (New York, N.Y.), v.3, no. 1, 1945, p. 4-8; no.2, 1945, p. 4-8. See serials consulted.

2064. PODERNIA, Kazimierz. Obszar języka litewskiego w gubernii wileńskiej. Skreślił Anonim, [pseud.] Kraków, Nakł. Akademii Umiejętności, 1898. 72 p. Offprint. Also in Polska Akademia Umiejętności, Kraków. Komisja Antropologiczna. Materyały antropologiczno-archeologiczne i etnograficzne (Kraków), v.3, 1898. PG8693.V5P6 DLC and serials consulted.

2065. POGODIN, Aleksandr L'vovich. Drevnie litovtsy. Vil'no, Izd. "Litvy", 1920. 24 p. DK511.L22P6 DLC PU

2066. PRIOULT, A. Le peuple lithuanien. In Revue de psychologie des peuples (Le Havre), v.2, no.1, 1947, p. 23-45. See serials consulted.

2067. ROZWADOWSKI, Jan. Mapa językowego obszaru litewskiego. In Polska i Litwa w dziejowym stosunku. Warszawa, 1914. DK418.5.L5P6 DLC CU CSt-H BM

2068. SMETONA, Antanas. Lietuvos etnografinės ribos. [The ethnographic boundaries of Lithuania] In His Raštai. Kaunas, 1931. v.3, p. 42-54. 947.52Sm35.3 PU CtTMF

2069. STALŠANS, Karlis. Latviešu un Lietuviešu austrumu apgabalu likteni. [The fate of Latvian and Lithuanian eastern regions] Chicago, Ill., J. Škirmants, 1958. 456 p. illus., ports., maps., tables. Bibliography: p. 445-446. DK511. L17S78 ICU CtPAM CtY DLC-P4 NN PU

2070. TAUTAVIČIUS, Adolfas. Lietuvių ir jotvingių genčių gyventų plotų ribų klausimu. [On the question of boundaries of inhabited ter-

ritories by the Lithuanian and Yat-
wiag tribes] In LTSRMAD. Serija A.
v.2(21), 1966, p. 161-182. illus.
Summary in Russian. See serials
consulted.

VASMER, Max. Über die Ostgrenze der baltischen Stämme. In
His Beiträge zur historischen Völ
kerkunde Osteuropas. Berlin, 1932.
See entry no. 4246.

2071. VOLTER, Eduard Aleksandrovich. Spiski naselennykh miest Su-
vlakskoi gubernii kak material dlia
istoriko-etnograficheskoi geografii
kraia. Sanktpeterburg, Akademiia
nauk, 1901. 315 p. 947.52V885
PU NN

2072. WASILEWSKI, Leon. Litwa i
Białoruś; zarys historyczno-poli-
tyczny stosunków narodowościowych.
Warszawa; Kraków, J. Mortkowicz,
1925. vii, 251 p. DK511.L2W35 DLC
CSt-H CtY ICU MH NNC OCl PU WU

2073. ŽEMAITIS, Vincas. Lietuvių
etninių sienų klausimais. The study
of Lithuanian ethnic frontiers.
[Chicago, Ill.) Chicagos Lietuvių
literatūros draugijos leidinys,
1971. 106 p. 3 maps. Summary in
English. Bibliography: p. 101-
104. DK511.L22Z45 DLC

2074. --- Sienų klausimų srity
tarp Baltijos ir Juodųjų Jūrų. [A
study of the boundaries in the re-
gion between the Baltic and Black
Sea] V. Žemakis [pseud.] Chicago,
Ill., Author, 1960. 122 p. maps.
Summaries in English. D820.T4Z4
DLC CaOTU PU

2075. ŽILINSKAS, Jurgis. Les an-
cêtres lithuaniens à l'époque pré-
historique, protohistorique et historique. In KUMeFD, v.4, 1937, p.
481-555. DNLM

2076. --- Akmens periodo (mezoli-
thicum-neolithicum) žmogus Žemaiti-
joje ir Suvalkijoje. [Man in Samogitia and Suvalkija in the stone
age] Kaunas, V.D. Universiteto medicinos fakulteto leid., 1931. 36
p. 947.52.Z67.2 PU

2077. --- Lietuvių protėviai.
[The ancestors of Lithuanians] Kau-
nas, Spaudos Fondas, 1937. 143 p.
Bibliography: p. 136-143. 947.52.
Z67 PU CtY ICBM ICLJF

2078. ŽILIUS, Jonas. The boundaries of Lithuania [n.p.], 1920.
[20] p. 2 fold. maps (incl. front.)
D651.L5Z5 DLC CSt-H ICU ICN ICLJF
MeU MB OCl OrU TxU WyU

2079. --- Lietuvos rubežiai; isto-
riškai-etnografiška studija, surašyta
Lietuvos Misijos Amerikoje ir... Jono Žiliaus. [The boundaries of Li-
thuania] [n.p.] 1920. 20 p. fold.
col. map. D651.L5Z53 DLC CtY CtPAM
ICBM ICN PU

VI.2. LITHUANIANS AND THE NATIONAL
QUESTION

2080. BALKŪNAS, Jonas. Lietuvybės
silpnėjimo priežastys, ir kiti
straipsniai. [The causes of the
weakening of the Lithuanian national
consciousness and other articles]
New York, N.Y., "Amerikos" leidinys,
1950. 23 p. DK511.L22B3 DLC

BORCH, Nicolas, comte de.
Le principe des nationalités et la
question lithuanienne. Louvain, F.
Ceuterick, 1925. See entry no.3048.

2081. DAMBRAUSKAS, Aleksandras.
Lithuaniens et polonais; leurs rap-
ports dans le passé et dans present.
Par A. Jakštas [pseud.] Paris, Impr.
Chaix, 1913. 8 p. map. DK511.
L22D3 DLC MH PU

2082. GIRNIUS, Juozas. Tauta ir
tautinė ištikinybė. [Nation and national faithfulness. Chicago, Ill.,
1961] 320 p. (Į laisvę fondas lietuviškai kultūrai ugdyti. Leidinys,
nr.2) Bibliography: p.312-317.
DK511.L223G5 DLC CtY MH PU

2083. HERBAČIAUSKAS, Juozapas Albinas. Kur eini, lietuvi? [By] Juozapas Herbačevskis. [Lithuanians,
where are you going?] Vilnius, Autoriaus lėšomis, 1919. 16 p. 947.52.
H418.2 PU

2084. JURKŪNAS, Ignas. Kas tu esi
lietuvi? [Lithuanians, who are you?
By] Irvis Gedainis [pseud.] Klaipėda, Rytas, 1938. 166 p. 947.5.
J979.2 PU NN NNC

2085. KAVOLIS, Vytautas. Lietuviai, komunizmas ir tautinis charakteris. [Lithuanians, communism and
the national character] In Metmenys
(Chicago, Ill.), no.2, 1960, p.124-
140. See serials consulted.

2086. MANTAUTAS, Aleksandras, comp.
Neužmiršk Lietuvos. [By] Aleksand-
ras Marcinkevičius. [Do not forget
Lithuania] Kaunas, Narkevičius,
1927. 236 p. 914.75.M37 PPi CtTMF
OCl PU

2087. PAULIUKONIS, Vladas. Mūsų

bajorai ir lietuvystė. [Our noblemen and lithuanianism. By]Elžikonis [pseud.] Vilnius, M. Kuktos spaustuvė, 1907. 19 p. 947.5.P284 PU

2088. SHAMIS, Thomas. Lithuanians [Chicago, Ill., Printed by Park Press] 1940. 24 p. plates, ports. DK511.L2S48 DLC ICN NN

2089. ŠLIŪPAS, Jonas. Lietuviai! ar gerais keliais žengiame priekyn? Nuoširdus atsiliepimas į lietuvišką visuomenę. [Lithuanians! are we going in the right direction] Shenandoah, Pa., "Lietuvininkų Vienybė", 1907. 47 p. 947.5.S135.5 PU

2090. VANAGAITIS, Jonas. Lietuwininkų pustytojei senose gadynėsa ir szendiena; raštelis į brolius bei seseris dar neatsižadėjusius nuo lietuwystės. [Men working for the Lithuanian cause today and in the past] Bitėnai, Lithuania, 1901. 12 p. DK511.L2V34 1970 PU(Xerox copy 1970)

2091. YLA, Stasys, (1908-) Lietuva brangi; iškeliaujančiai sesei ir broliui. [My beloved Lithuania; to a parting sister and brother] Bielefeld, Ger., "Ventos" leidykla, 1950. 31 p. DK511.L223Y5 DLC ICLJF PU

2092. ŽADEIKIS, Povilas. Su Lietuva ar prie Lenkijos? Ekonominiai-politinis piešinys. [Are you for Lithuania or Poland?] New York, N.Y., 1921. 24 p. 947.5.Z13 PU CtPAM

VI.3. ARCHAEOLOGY

VI.3.a. GENERAL STUDIES, CONGRESSES, RESEARCH, ETC.

2093. AKADEMIIA NAUK SSSR. INSTITUT ARKHEOLOGII. Drevnosti Severo-Zapadnykh oblastei RSFSR v I. tysiacheletii n.e. Moskva, 1960. 451 p. illus. (Materialy i issledovaniia po arkheologii SSSR, 76) 913106. Ak12 no.76 PU DDO

2094. ARKHEOLOGICHESKII S"EZD. 9th, Vilna, 1893. Trudy Vilenskago otdieleniia Moskovskago predvaritel'-nago komiteta po ustroistvu v Vil'-nie IX Arkheologicheskago s"ezda. Vil'na, Tip. A.G. Syrkina, 1893. 3 v. fold. plates, fold. map. fold. plans. DK30.A75 1893 DLC KU

2095. ARKHEOLOGICHESKII S"EZD. 16th, Pskov, 1914. Baltische Studien zur Archäologie und Geschichte. Berlin, G. Reimer, 1914. 415 p. illus., map. 947.52.Ar47 PU NjP

2096. BARTNOWSKI, Władysław. Przegląd prac konserwacijnych na Górze Zamkowej w Wilnie w latach 1930-1936. In Ateneum Wileńskie (Wilno), v.13, no.1, 1938, p. 211-216. See serials consulted.

2097. BASANAVIČIUS, Jonas. Apie senovės Lietuvos pilis. [About the ancient Lithuanian castles] Tilžė, 1891. 55 p. 947.5.B4 CtTMF

2098. BŪTĖNAS, Petras. Lietuvių tautotyros žinių ir senienų rinkimo programa. [The program for the collection of folklore] Šiauliai, 1925 208 p. GN585.L5B8 PU CtTMF

2099. DĄBROWSKI, Jan. Zabytki metalowe epoki brązu między dolną Wisłą a Niemnem. Wrocław, Zakład Narodowy im. Ossolińskich, 1968. 231 p. 23 plates, maps. Summary in English. GN778.P7D15 ICU DLC

2100. DAUGIRDAS, Tadas. Wiadomość o wyrobach z kamienia gładzonego znalezionych na Żmujdzi i Litwie. Warszawa, Druk. J. Sikorskiego, 1890 [i.e. 1891] 20 p. illus. 947.52. D267 PU

2101. ENGEL, Carl. Typen ostpreussischer Hügelgräber. Bearb. von Rudolf Grenz. Mit einem Nachwort von W. La Baume. Neumünster, K. Wachholtz, 1962. 50 p., 35 plates. (Göttinger Schriften zur Vor- und Frühgeschichte, Bd.3) Q913. 4311.En33 PU DLC CU CtY ICU MH MoU NIC NN NNC WaU

2102. GAERTE, Wilhelm. Die Steinzeitliche Keramik Ostpreussens. Königsberg in Pr., Gräfe und Unzer, 1927. 90 p. 871.1.G113 PU BM

2103. GREWINGK, Constantin Caspar Andreas. Das Steinalter der Ostseeprovinzen Liv-, Est-, und Kurland und einiger angrenzenden Landstriche. Dorpat, Gedruckt bei E.J. Karow, 1865. 118 p. (Schriften der Gelehrten Estnischen Gesellschaft, nr. 4) GN776.R9G8 DLC

2104. --- Über heidnische Gräber Russisch Litauen und einiger benachbarter Gegenden. Dorpat, Druck von H. Lachmann, 1870. 241 p. illus., plates. (Verhandlungen der Gelehrten Estnischen Gesellschaft zu Dorpat, Bd.6, Hft.1-2) 913.475.G869 PU NNC

2105. GIMBUTAS, Marija (Alseikai-tė) A survey of the Bronze Age culture in the South Eastern Baltic area. In Światowit (Warszawa), v. 23, 1960. See serials consulted.

2106. KILIAN, L. Das Siedlungsgebiet der Balten in der älteren Bronzezeit. In Altpreussen; Vierteljahrsschrift für Vorgeschichte. (Königsberg in Pr.), v.3, pt.4, 1939 p. 107-114. MH

2107. KIRKOR, Adam Honory. Wucieczki archeologiczne po gubernji wileńskiej. In Biblioteka Warszawska, v.2, 1855, p. 433-452; v.3, 1855, p. 20-46; v.4, 1855, p. 237-257. See serials consulted.

2108. KONGRESS BALTISCHER ARCHÄOLOGEN. 2nd, Riga, 1930. Congressus secundus archaeologorum balticorum, Rigae, 19-23.VIII.1930. Rigae [Valstspapiru spiestuve] 1931. 494 p. illus., maps, plates, ports. Text chiefly in German. DK511.B29K6 DLC CS NN PU

2109. --- --- Katalog der Ausstellung zur Konferenz Baltischer Archäologen in Riga, 1930. Riga, 1930. 176 p. DK511.B29K6 1930z DLC PU

2110. KOSTRZEWSKI, Józef. Neolitische Depotfunde aus Polen und Litauen. In Prähistorische Zeitschrift (Leipzig), v.10, 1918, p. 157-160. See serials consulted.

2111. KRZYWICKI, Ludwik. Zhmudskie pil'kal'nisy. Sanktpeterburg, Tip. Glavnago Upravleniia Udielov, 1908. 83-129 p. illus. Ottisk iz Izviestii Imperatorskoi arkheologicheskoi kommissii, vyp.29. DK511.L2K78 CU NN

2112. KULIKAUSKAS, Pranas. Akmens amžius. [Stone Age] In His Lietuvos archeologijos bruožai. Vilnius, 1961. p. 34-86. illus., charts, plans, maps. GN845.L5K8 DLC CLU CU CaAEU CtY ICU IU KU MH PU

2113. --- Issledovanie arkheologicheskikh pamiatnikov Litvy. In KSIIMK, v.42, 1952, p. 92-107. See serials consulted.

2114. --- Kai kurie archeologiniai duomenys apie seniausiai Lietuvos istorijoje augintus javus. [Some archaeological data on the growing of grain on Lithuanian territory] In LTSRMAD. Serija A, no.1, 1955, p. 75-85. See serials consulted.

2115. --- Lietuvos archeologijos bruožai. [An outline of Lithuanian

archaeology. Redagavo: K. Jablonskis, P. Kulikauskas] Vilnius, VPMLL, 1961. 561 p. illus. GN845.L5K8 DLC CLU CU CaAEU CtY ICU IU KU MH PU

2116. --- Žalvario, arba bronzos amžius. [Bronze Age] In His Lietuvos archeologijos bruožai. Vilnius, 1961. p. 87-112. illus. GN845.L5K8 DLC CLU CU CaAEU CtY ICU IU KU MH PU

2117. KULIKAUSKIENĖ, Regina (Volkaitė) Lietuvos archeologiniai paminklai ir jų tyrinėjimai. [Archaeological monuments of Lithuania and their exploration] Vilnius, VPMLL, 1958. 181 p. illus. DK511.L21K8 DLC CLU CtPAM ICBM ICLJF IU MH NN OKentU PPiU PU

2118. --- Miniaturinių piliakalnių Lietuvoje klausimu. [On the question of small mounds in Lithuania] In LTSRMAIILKI, v.1, 1958, p. 125-137. See serials consulted.

2119. LIETUVOS ARCHEOLOGINIAI PAminklai; Lietuvos pajūrio I-VII a. kapinynai. [Archaeological monuments in Lithuania. Ed. by Adolfas Tautavičius] Vilnius, Mintis, 1968. 236 p. illus. GN824.L5L45 DLC CtY ICLJF ICU MH NjP

2120. LIETUVOS TSR MOKSLŲ AKADEMIJA, VILNA. ISTORIJOS INSTITUTAS. Archeologiniai ir etnografiniai tyrinėjimai Lietuvoje 1968 ir 1969. [Archaeological and etnographical research in Lithuania, 1968-1969. Atsakingieji redaktoriai: archeologija-Adolfas Tautavičius; etnografija-Antanas Daniliauskas] (Medžiaga konferencijai skirtai 1968 ir 1969 m. archeologinių ir etnografinių ekspedicijų rezultatams apsvarstyti. Vilnius, 1970 m. gegužės mėn. 14-15 d.) Vilnius, Mintis, 1970. 153 p. GN824.L5L52 PU

2121. --- 20 let; materialy k otchetnoi konferentsii arkheologicheskikh i etnograficheskikh ekspeditsii Instituta istorii Akademii nauk Litovskoi SSR 1948-1967 gg. Vil'nius, 13-15 maia 1968. Vil'nius, 1968. 143 p. GN824.L5L72 InU MH PU

2122. --- Materialy k otchetnoi konferentsii arkheologicheskikh i etnograficheskikh ekspeditsii 1964-1965 gg., Instituta istorii Akademii nauk Litovskoi SSR, Vil'nius, 17-18 marta 1966 g. [Otv. redaktora: A. Vishniauskaite, A. Tautavichius] Vil'nius, 1966. 45 p. GN824.L5L5 DLC IU

2123. NAVICKAITĖ, Ona (Kuncienė) Plokštinių kapinynų tyrinėjimai Lietuvoje, 1948-1958 m. [The excavations in 1948-1958 of the burial grounds in Lithuania] In LTSRMAIILKI, v.3, 1961, p.66-100. See serials consulted.

2124. NERMAN, Birger. Einige auf Gotland gefundene ostbaltische Gegenstände der jungeren Eizenzeit. In Tartu. Ulikool. Õpetatud Eesti selts. Toimetused (Verhandlungen der Gelehrten estnischen Gesellschaft), v.30, no.2, 1938, p.469-477. See serials consulted.

2125. --- Die Verbindungen zwischen Skandinavien und Ostbaltikum in der jüngeren Eisenzeit. In Acta archaeologica (København), v.4, 1929, p.237-252. See serials consulted.

2126. POKROVSKII, Fedor Vasil'evich. K issledovaniiu kurganov i gorodishch na vostochnoi okraine sovremennoi Litvy. In Arkheologicheskii s"ezd. 9th, Vilna, 1893. Trudy, v.2, 1897, p. 138-196. See serials consulted.

2127. --- Kurgany na granitse sovremennoi Litvy i Belorussii. In Arkheologicheskii s"ezd. 9th, Vilna, 1893. Trudy, v.1, 1895, p. 166-220. See serials consulted.

2128. PUZINAS, Jonas. Archeologiniai tyrinėjimai Lietuvoje XIX a. gale ir XX a. pradžioje. [The archaeologic discoveries in Lithuania towards the end of the nineteenth century and the begining of the twentieth century] In KUHMF. Senovė (Kaunas), v.1, 1935. 31 p. See serials consulted.

2129. --- Trečiosios Vilniaus pilies beieškant. [Looking for the third castle of Vilnius] In Metmenys (Chicago, Ill.), v.3, 1960, p. 164-171. See serials consulted.

2130. RADZIUKYNAS, Juozapas. Pilekalniai. [The mounds] Warszawa, Jurgio Pesio leidykla, 1909. 38 p. map. 913.R ICBM

2131. --- Suvalkų rėdybos pilekalniai su žemėlapiu. [The mounds of the Suvalkai district] Varšava, J. Pesys, 1909. 38 p. fold. map. 947.52.R115 PU CtTMF CtY

2132. ŠTURMS, Eduards. Die ältere Bronzezeit im Ostbaltikum. Berlin und Leipzig, W. de Gruyter & Co., 1936. viii, 155 p. 28 plates on 14 leaves., 6 maps. (Vorgeschichtliche Forschungen, Heft 10). Thesis-- University of Königsberg, 1927. CtY ICU MH MH-P MnU NN NNC NNM NjP

2133. --- Der Ursprung der kamm- und grübchenkeramischen Kulturen Osteuropas. In Commentationes Balticae (Bonn), v.3:7, 1957. 27 p. See serials consulted.

2134. SZUKIEWICZ, Wandalin. Narzędzia manienne gładzone w pow. Lidzkim i Trockim. Im Swiatowit (Warszawa), v.4, 1904, p.50-58. See serials consulted.

2135. --- Poszukiwanie archeologiczne w powiecie Lidzkim gubernji wileńskiej. Część 2. Kraków, Nakł. Akademii Umiejętności, 1910. 15 p. 947.52.Sz74.2 PU

2136. --- Poszukiwanie archeologiczne w powiatach Lidzkim i Trockim. In Swiatowit (Warszawa), v.3, 1901, p.3-29. See serials consulted.

2137. --- Skład chemiczny bronzów przedhistorycznych na Litwie. In Towarzystwo Przyjaciół Nauk w Wilnie. Rocznik (Wilno), v.5, 1914, p.28-37. See serials consulted.

2138. --- Strefy archeologiczne na Litwie. In Towarzystwo Przyjaciół Nauk w Wilnie. Rocznik (Wilno), v.6, 1918, p.5-16. See serials consulted.

2139. --- Szkice z archeologii przedhistorycznej Litwy. I:Epoka kamienna w gub. wileńskiej. Wilno, Księgarnia J. Zawadzkiego, 1901. 1 v. 947.52.Sz74 PU CtY

2140. TARASENKA, Petras. Gimtoji senovė. [Antiquities] Šiauliai, Kultūros bendrovės leidinys, [n.d.] 117 p. illus. 910.T ICBM

2141. --- Lietuvos archeologijos medžiaga. Materialien für litauische Archeologie. Kaunas, Švietimo ministerijos knygų leidimo komisijos leidinys, 1928. 358, xxxii p. Bibliography: p.[270]-311. DK511. L21T3 DLC CaAEU CtY ICBM PU

2142. --- Pėdos akmenyje; Lietuvos istoriniai akmenys. [Footprints in the stone; the historical stones of Lithuania] Vilnius, VPMLL, 1958. 81 p. illus., map. GN824.L5T3 DLC CtPAM ICBM NN PU

2143. --- Priešistorinė Lietuva; vadovas krašto praeities tyrimo darbams. [The guide for archaeologic work in Lithuania] Kaunas, Spaudos fondas,1927. 142 p. illus.

947.52.T172.2 PU MH

2144. TAUTAVIČIUS, Adolfas. Ankstyvasis geležies amžius. [The Early Iron Age] In His Lietuvos archeologijos bruožai. Vilnius, 1961. p.113 -[143] illus. GN845.L5K8 DLC CaAEU CLU CU CtY ICU IU KU MH PU

2145. --- Rytų Lietuvos pilkapiai. [The mounds of the Eastern Lithuania] In LTSRMAD. Seria A, v.1, 1955, p.87-97. See serials consulted.

2146. TISCHLER, Otto. Beiträge zur Kenntnis der Steinzeit in Ostpreussen und den angrenzenden Gebieten. In Physikalisch-Ökonomische Gesellschaft. Schriften(Königsberg in Pr.), v.23, 1882, p.17-40. See serials consulted.

2147. TYSZKIEWICZ, Eustachy. Badania archeologiczne nad zabytkami przedmiotów sztuki, rzemiosł i t.d. w dawnej Litwie i Rusi litewskiej. Wilno, J. Zawadzki, 1850. 96 p. 5 plates. 97.1.TI ICLJF

VI.3.b. ACCOUNTS OF ARCHAEOLOGICAL EXCAVATIONS

2148. BERNOTAITĖ, A. Rudnios (Varėnos rajono) akmens amžiaus stovyklos. [The camp sites of Stone Age in Rudnia] In LTSRMAIILKI, v.2, 1959, p.86-102. See serials consulted.

2149. BEZZENBERGER, Adalbert. Fundberichte; Hügelgrab bei Schlaszen, kr. Memel. In Altertumsgesellschaft Prussia. Sitzungsberichte (Königsberg in Pr.), v.21, 1900, p. 81-160. See serials consulted.

2150. --- Fundberichte; Hügelgrab bei Sorthenen, Kr. Fischhausen. In Altertumsgesellschaft Prussia. Sitzungsberichte (Königsberg in Pr.), v.23, pt.1, 1914, p.88-159. See serials consulted.

2151. --- Fundberichte; Hügelgräber in dem Förderdorfer Forst, Kr. Braunsberg. In Altertumsgesellschaft Prussia. Sitzungsberichte (Königsberg in Pr.), v.22, 1909, p. 1-194. See serials consulted.

2152. --- Das Graberfeld bei Schernen, Kr. Memel. In Altertumsgesellschaft Prussia. Sitzungsberichte (Königsberg in Pr.), v.17, 1892. p.141-168. See serials consulted.

2153. BŪTĖNIENĖ, E. Siraičių X-XII a. senkapis. [The burial grounds from the tenth-twelvth centuries in Siraičiai] In LTSRMAIILKI, v.2, 1959, p. 159-176. See serials consulted.

2154. DANILAITĖ, E. Archeologiniai tyrinėjimai Kiauleikiuose. [The archaeological research in Kiauleikiai] In LTSRMAIILKI, v.3, 1961, p. 101-124. See serials consulted.

2155. DAUGIRDAS, Tadas. Melžynkapas pod Jasnogórką. [Burial mound in Jasnogórka. By] T. Dowgird. In Pamiętnik Fizyjograficzny (Warszawa), 1887, p. 3-28. See serials consulted.

2156. --- Pamiątki z czasów przedhistorycznych na Żmujdzi; opis cmentarzyska i pilkalnia w Imbarach oraz robót dokonanych w roku 1885 i 1886. [By] T. Dowgird. Warszawa, Druk. J. Sikorskiego, 1889 [i.e. 1890] 11 p. 3 plates. Otbitka. 947.52.D267 PU; also in Pamiętnik Fizyjograficzny (Warszawa), v.9, 1889. See serials consulted.

2157. DAUGUDIS, V. Aukštadvario piliakalnio įtvirtinimai ir pastatai. [The fortifications and buildings of the mound of Aukštadvaris] In LTSRMAD. Serija A, no.1, 1962, p. 43-47. See serials consulted.

2158. --- Mazulonių piliakalnis. [The mound of Mazuloniai] In LTSRMAIILKI, v.3, 1961, p. 16-40. See serials consulted.

2159. ENGEL, Carl. Zwei spätheidnische Silberfunde aus alt-sudavischem Gebiete. In Altertumgesellschaft Prussia. Sitzungsberichte (Königsberg in Pr.), v.29, 1931, p. [68]-87. illus., maps. See serials consulted.

2160. GLEBOV, Ivan. Vilenskie zamki; verkhnii i nizhnii. In Vilenskii kalendar' (Vil'na) na god 1904, p. 292-336. See serials consulted.

2161. HOFFMANN, Joachim. Das Gräberfeld Linkuhnen, Kr. Niedrung, Ostpreussen, und die spätheidnische Kultur des Memelgebietes. In Altpreussen; Vierteljahrsschrift für Vorgeschichte... (Königsberg in Pr.), v.4, pt.3, 1939, p. 73-77. MH

2162. HOLUBOVIČIUS, Elena and Vladas Holubovičius. Gedimino kalno Vilniuje 1940 metų kasinėjimų pranešimas. [Report of the excavations in Vilna] Chicago, Ill., Vilniaus kraš-

to lietuvių sąjunga, 1956. 46 p.
illus. 913.5.Ho ICBM

2163. JANKEVIČIENĖ, Algė. Pabariụ pilkapiai. [The burial mounds
of Pabariai] In LTSRMAD, Serija A,
v.1(10), 1961, p. 37-48. See serials consulted.

2164. JANKUHN, H. Gürtelgarnituren der älteren römischen Keiserzeit. In Altertumsgesellschaft
Prussia. Sitzungsberichte (Königsberg in Pr.), v.30, pt.1, 1933, p.
166-201. See serials consulted.

2165. JASKANIS, Danuta. Cmentarzysko kurhanowe w miejscowości Krzywołka, pow. Suwałki. In Rocznuk
Białostocki (Białystok), v.4, 1963,
p. 279-308. See serials consulted.

2166. JASKANIS, Danuta and J. Jaskanis. Sprawozdanie z badań w
1957 roku na cmentarzysku kurhanowym
w miejscowości Osowa, pow. Suwałki.
In Wiadomości Archeologiczne (Warszawa), v.27, no.1, 1961, p. 27-49;
v.25, no.1-2, 1958, p. 75-98. See
serials consulted.

2167. JASKANIS, J. Wyniki badań
przeprowadzonych na cmentarzysku
kurhanowym w miejscowości Osowa,
pow. Suwałki w latach 1958-1959. In
Rocznik Białostocki (Białystok), v.1,
1961, p. 131-191. See serials consulted.

2168. --- --- w latach 1960-1961.
In Rocznik Białostocki (Białystok),
v.3, 1962, p. 233-297. See serials
consulted.

2169. JAWORSKI, Zygmunt. Wełny
tkanin z wczesnohistorycznych kurhanów L.S.R.R. In Slavia antiqua (Poznań), v.2, 1949-50, p. [486]-507.
diagrs. Summary in English. D147.
S5 DLC MH-P

2170. KEMKE, H. Hügelgräber im
nordwestlichen Samland. In Altertumsgesellschaft Prussia. Sitzungsberichte (Königsberg in Pr.), v.22,
1909, p. 384-423. See serials consulted.

2171. KLEBS, Hermann Erdmann Richard. Der Bernsteinschmuck der
Steinzeit von der Baggerei bei
Schwarzort und anderen Lokalitäten
Preussens. Königsberg in Pr., Königliche Physikalisch-Ökonomische
Gesellschaft, 1882. 75 p. (Beiträge zur Naturkunde Preussens...
Bd.5) GN799.A5K6 DLC BM(Ac.2337) PU

2172. KLEEMANN, O. Die Vorgeschichtlichen Funde bei Cranz und die

Siedlung von Wiskiauten. In Altertumsgesellschaft Prussia (Königsberg
in Pr.), v.33, 1939, p. 201-225. See
serials consulted.

2173. KRZYWICKI, Ludwik. Grodziska górno litewskie: I: Grodziśko w
Duksztach, II: Grodziśko w Warańcach. Warszawa, J. Cotty, 1914.
Offprint. Q 947.52.K949.2 PU; also
in Pamiętnik Fizyjograficzny (Warszawa), v.22, 1914. See serials
consulted.

2174. --- --- Grodziśko na górze
Ościkowej pod Rakiszkami. In Pamiętnik Fizyjograficzny (Warszawa), v.
24, 1917, p.1-6,17-42. illus.,
diagrs., plates. See serials consulted.

2175. --- Grodziśko Derbuckie na
Żmidzi. Warszawa, J. Cotty, 1931.
14 p. Offprint. 947.52.K949.3 PU;
also in Pamiętnik Fizyjograficzny
(Warszawa), v.21, 1913, p. 15-29.
See serials consulted.

2176. --- Pilkalnia pod wsią Petraszunami. In Towarzystwo Przyjaciół Nauk w Wilnie. Rocznik (Wilno)
See serials consulted.

2177. --- Pilkalnia w Gabryeliszkach. Warszawa, Uniwersytet Warszawski, 1931. 16 p. Offprint. 947.
52.K949.6 PU

2178. KULIKAUSKAS, Pranas. Kurmaicheskie arkhologicheskie pamiatniki i dannye ikh issledovaniia.
Vilnius, 1949. 10 p. Abstract of
diss(kandidat)--Institut istorii
Litvy Akademii nauk SSR. DK651.
K87K8 DLC

2179. --- Kurmaičiụ, Kretingos rajono plokštinio kapinyno tyrinėjimai.
[The excavations of the burial grounds at Kurmaičiai] In LTSRMAIID, v.1,
1951, p.315-365. See serials consulted.

2180.--- Naujai aptikta akmens-žalvario amžiụ gyvenvietė Palangoje.
[Recently disvovered camp site from
the Stone and Bronze Ages in Palanga]
In LTSRMAD. Serija A, v.2(7), 1959,
p.33-41. See serials consulted.

2181. --- Naujas archeologinis paminklas Užnemunėje (V-VI a. jotvingiụ senkapis Krištonyse, Lazdijụ rajone). [New archeological discovery in Užnemunė (the burial grounds
from 5th-6th centuries ...)] In
LTSRMAD. Seria A, v.1(6), 1959, p.
71-88. See serials consulted.

2182. --- Nauji radiniai Kurmaičiụ

kapinyne. [Recent archaeological discovery in the burial mound of Kurmaičiai] In LTSRMAD. Seria A, no.2, 1957, p. 141-151. See serials consulted.

2183. --- Nemenčinės piliakalnis. [The mound of Nemenčinė] In LTSRMAIILKI, v.1, 1958, p.20-43. See serials consulted.

2184. --- Raginėnų, Šeduvos rajono, archeologinių paminklų tyrinėjimai ir "Raginėnų kultūros" klausimas. [The exploration of archaeological monuments in Raginėnai and the question of the "Culture of Raginėnai"] In LTSRMAD. SeriaA, v.1 (4), 1958, p.65-89. illus. See serials consulted.

2185. --- Žalvario amžiaus pilkapiai Kurmaičiuose, Kretingos valsčiuje ir apskrityje. [The burial mound from the Bronze Age at Kurmaičiai] In Gimtasai kraštas(Šiauliai), v.31, 1943, p.32-52. See serials consulted.

2186. KULIKAUSKIENĖ,Regina (Volkaitė). Linksmučių kapinyno 1949 metų tyrinėjimų duomenys. [The excavation results of the burial mound of Linksmučiai] In LTSRMAIID, v.1, 1951, p.279-313. See serials consulted.

2187. --- Migonių, Jezno rajono, archeologiniai paminklai. [The archaeological discoveries in Migoniai district of Jeznas] In LTSRMAIILKI, v.1, 1958, p.44-64. See serials consulted.

2188. LABAUME, Wolfgang. Der Moorleichenfund von Drobnitz, Kreis Osterode, Ostpreussen. In Altpreussen; Vierteljahrsschrift für Vorgeschichte... (Königsberg in Pr.), v. 5, no.2, 1940, p.17-22. MH

2189. LINCKE, Barnim. Eine baltische Halsringform der Völkerwanderungszeit. Berlin, Berliner Zentraldruckerei, 1937. 62, [2] p. Inaug.-Diss--University of Berlin. 913.4311.L633 PU CtY NNC

2190. NAGEVIČIUS, Vladas. Das Gräberfeld von Prižmonti. In Kongress baltischer Archäologen, 2nd, Riga, 1930. [Proceedings] 1931, p.337-352. illus. DK511.B29K6 1930 DLC CS NN PU

2191. NAKAITĖ, Laimutė. Juodonių gyvenvietės, Rokiškio rajono, archeologinių tyrinėjimų duomenys. [The results of the archaeological excavations of the camp sites in Juodo-

niai] In LTSRMIILKI, v.2, 1959, p.138-150. See serials consulted.

2192. NAVICKAITĖ, Ona (Kuncienė). Balčininkėlių piliakalnis. [The mound of Balčininkėliai] In LTSRMIILKI, v.2, 1959, p.103-118. See serials consulted.

2193. --- Guogų-Piliuonos piliakalnis. [the mound of Guogai-Piliuona] In LTSRMAD. Seria A, v.1(6), 1959, p.89-101. See serials consulted.

2194. --- Prišmančių, Kretingos rajono, II.-IV. amžių plokštinio kapinyno tyrinėjimai. [The excavations of the burial grounds from the second to fourth centuries in Prišmančiai] In LTSRMAD. Seria A, v.2(7), 1959, p.43-56. See serials consulted.

2195. RIMANTIENĖ, Rimutė (Jablonskytė). Mezolitinė stovykla Puvočiuose, Merkinės valsčiaus, Alytaus aps. [The mezolitic camp site in Puvočiai] In Lietuvos praeitis (Kaunas), v.1, 1941, p.361-385. See serials consulted.

2196. --- Stoianki kamennogo veka v Eiguliai. In Pribaltiiskaia ob"edinennaia kompleksnaia ekspeditsiia. Trudy: Voprosy etnicheskoi istorii narodov Pribaltiki. Moskva, 1959. p.11-32. GN845.B3P7 DLC

2197. --- Vėlyvojo mezolito stovykla Lampėdžiuose. [The camp site of the late mezolite in Lampėdžiai] In LTSRMAD. Seria A, v.2, 1963, p.39-51. See serials consulted.

2198. --- Žemųjų Kaniukų IV.-I. tūkstantmečių prieš mūsų erą stovyklos. [The camp sites of Žemieji Kaniukai from 4,000-1,000 years B.C.] In LTSRMAD. Seria A, 1963, v.1, p.65-90. See serials consulted.

2199. SADAUSKAITĖ, I. XII.-XIII. amžių pirklio kapas Sargėnuose. [The merchant's grave from the twelfth and thirteenth centuries in Sargėnai] In LTSRMAD. Seria A, v.2(7), 1959, p.57-76. See serials consulted.

2200. SZUKIEWICZ, Wandalin. Cmentarzysko neolityczne w Łankiszkach pod Naczą. In Pamiętnik Fizjograficzny (Warszawa), v.23, 1916, p.1-12. See serials consulted.

2201. --- Kurhany ciałopalne w Pomusiu, pow. Troki. In Światowit, (Warszawa), v.2, 1900, p.3-18. See serials consulted.

2202. TARASENKA, Petras. Didžiųjų

Tyrulių paslaptys. [The secrets of Great Tyruliai. Iliustravo V. Jankauskas. Vilnius] VGLL, 1956. 284 p. illus. DK511.L21T29 DLC OKentU

2203. TAUTAVIČIUS, Adolfas. Archeologiniai kasinėjimai Vilniaus žemutinės pilies teritorijoje, 1957-1958 m. [Archaeological excavations in the area of the lower castle of Vilnius in 1957-1958] In LTSRMAD. Serija A, v.1(6), 1959, p. 115-1135. See serials consulted.

2204. --- ---, 1960 m. [Archaeological excavations in the area of the lower castle of Vilnius in 1960] In LTSRMAD. Serija A, v.2(11), 1961, p, 103-124. See serials consulted.

2205. --- Kapitoniškių piliakalniai. [The mounds of Kapitoniškiai] In LTSRMAD. Serija A, v.1, 1958, p. 95-109. See serials consulted.

2206. --- Šalčininkų rajono pilkapynų tyrinėjimai. [The exploration of the burial mounds in the district of Šalčininkai] In LTSRMAIILKI,v.1, 1958, p. 65-82. See serials consulted.

2207. TISCHLER, Otto. Ostpreussische Altertümer aus der grossen Gräberfelder nach Christi Geburt. Königsberg in Pr., W. Koch, 1902. 46, [60] p., 30 plates. DLC

2208. ZIEMLIŃSKA-ODOJOWA, W. Badania wykopaliskowe w 1959 roku na cmentarzysku kurhanowym w miejscowości Żywa Woda, pow. Suwałki. In Rocznik Białostocki (Białystok), v.1, 1961, p. 191-221. See serials consulted.

2209. ŽIOGAS, Juozapas. Archeologiški tyrinėjimai Gaidės apylinkėje. [Archaeological excavations in the district of Gaidė] In Tauta ir Žodis (Kaunas), v.1, no.3, 1923-1924, p. 313-333. See serials consulted.

VI.4. ANTROPOLOGY AND ETHNOLOGRAPHY

2210. ADOMAVIČIUS, Vladislovas. Zur Antropologie der litauischen Frau. Tübingen, 1949. 50 p. plates, illus. Thesis (M.D.)--University of Tübingen. Typescript. Ger. UT

2211. ARMON, Witold. Badania nad Litewską kulturą ludową w latach 1945-1965. In Etnografia Polska (Warszawa), v.12, 1965, p.452-475. See serials consulted.

2212. --- Wybrana bibliografia etnograficzna Litwy za lata 1945-1965. In Etnografia Polska (Warszawa), v.12, 1968, p.475-490. See serials consulted.

2213. AVIZHONIS, P. I. Boliezni glaz i sliepota sredi krest'ian-litovtsev Gruzdzevskoi i Ligumskoi volostei, Shavel'skago uiezda, Kovenskoi gubernii (po dannym pogolovnago osmotra). Dissertatsiia... P.I. Avizhonisa. Yurieff, Tipo-litografiia E. Bergmann, 1914. [4], 303 p. fold. tables, diagrs. Thesis--University of Yurieff(Tartu). Bibliography: p.[281]-303. 947.51(517) ICJ

2214. BARONAS, Jonas. K antropologii litovskago plemeni. [By] I.O. Baronas. In Russkii antropologicheskii zhurnal (Moskva), v.3, no.4, kn.12, 1902, p. 63-87. See serials consulted.

2215. BASANAVIČIUS, Jonas. Etnologiškos smulkmenos. [Lithuanian etnological details] Tilžė, Rašytojo kaštu, 1893. 32 p. RB572.B ICBM

2216. BAUDOUIN DE COURTENAY-EHRENKREUTZOWA, C. Kilka uwag i wiadomości o etnografii wojewóddztwa wileńskiego. In Vilna. Wojewódzki Komitet Regionalny. Wilno i ziemia wileńska. Wilno, 1939. p. 173-218. DK651.V4A57 DLC

2217. BEZZENBERGER, Adalbert. Bemerkungen zu Virchows Aufsatz: Die altpreussische Bevölkerung, namentlich Letten und Litauer. In Altertumsgesellschaft Prussia. Sitzungsberichte (Königsberg in Pr.), v.18, 1892-93, p. 1-8. See serials consulted.

2218. BUKANTAS, Dominikas. Iš Ežerėnų apylinkės lietuvių antropologijos. [On the anthopological research in the district of Ežerėnai] In Lietuvių tauta (Kaunas), v.1, 1907, p. 453-463. See serials consulted.

CAPPELLER, Carl. Leben und Gebräuche der alten preussischen Litauer. Holland, 1925. See entry no 1011.

2219. CHEBAKSAROV, N.N. Novye dannye po etnicheskoi antropologii Sovetskoi Pribaltiki. In Akademiia nauk SSSR. Institut etnografii. Trudy, v.23, 1954. See serials consulted.

2220. COLEMAN, Arthur Prudden. The Lithuanian-Whiterussian folk of

the upper Niemen. In Journal of
Central European Affairs (Boulder,
Col.), v.1, 1942, p. 399-416. See
serials consulted.

2221. DUKSZTA, Mieczysław. Étude
ethnographique sur l'ancien peuple
lithuanien. Genève, Athenaeum, 1917.
(Publication de l'Athenaeum, no.5)
BM(010007. ee.3.(2.)) NN

2222. EHRHARDT, Sophie. Zur Ras-
senkunde und Rassengeschichte der
baltischen Länder und Ostpreussens.
In Brackmann, Albert and Carl Engel.
Baltische Lande. Leipzig, 1939. v.1:
Ostbaltische Frühzeit, p. 86-166.
illus., map. DK511.B3B7 v.1 DLC

2223. FARMBOROUGH, Florence. Lithuania, a sturdy people and their
newwon freedom. In Peoples of all
nations. Ed. by J.A. Hammerton. London, 1922-24. v.5, p. 3343-3371.
illus., map. GN315.P4 DLC MH-P

2224. FISCHER, Adam Robert. A reconstruction of ancient Prussian
ethnography. In Baltic and Scandinavian countries (Gdynia), v.3, no.
3, 1937, p.441-449. See serials consulted.

2225. GAWEŁEK, Franciszek. Bibliografja ludoznawstwa litewskiego.
Wilno, 1914. 77 p. Offprint from
Rocznik Towarzystwa Przyjaciół Nauk
w Wilnie, v.5, 1914. MH-P WU

2226. GUMPŁOWICZ, Władysław. Die
ethnographischen Verhältnisse Litauens. In Polen (Wien), v.1, 1915, p.
269-270. See serials consulted.

2227. HERBURT, Jan z Fulsztyna.
Chronicon; seu, Rerum polonicarum
compendiosa descriptio. Königsberg
in Pr., L. König, 1615. 368 p.
Partial contents.--De moribus tartarorum, litvanorum et moscorum... Mi-
chalo Lituanus.--De diis samagitarum
caeterorumque sarmatarum... Jan Lasi-
cius. BM(590. g. 17.)

2228. HESCH, Michael. Letten, Litauer, Weissrussen; Beitrag zur Anthropologie des Ostbaltikums. Wien,
Rudolf Pösch Nachlass, 1933. 80 p.
illus., plates. CU CtY MnU NN

2229. HOFFMANN, Oskar Georg Adolf.
Volkstümliches aus dem preussischen
Litauen. In LLGM,v.6, 1898, p.1-10.
See serials consulted.

2230. IANCHUK, N. A. K voprosu ob
antropologicheskom tipie litovtsev.
In Obshchestvo liubitelei estestvoznaniia antropologii i etnografii,
Moscow. Antropologicheskii otdel.

Trudy (Moskva), v.2, 1890, p.201-
211. GN1.R85 DLC MH-P

2231. JURGELIŪNAS, Antanas and C.
Ravensberg. Verteilung der Blut-
gruppen bei dem litauischen Volk.
In Zeitschrift für Rassenphysiologie
(München), v.2, 1929, p. 39-41.
See serials consulted.

2232. KAPPSTEIN, Theodor. Die
Litauer; nach Bezzenbergers Studie
über den Werdegang des litauischen
Volkes. In Doegen, Wilhelm, ed.
Unter fremden Völkern. Berlin, 1925.
p.250-256. plate. GN4.D6 DLC MH-P

2233. KAUNAS. VYTAUTO DIDŽIOJO
KULTŪROS MUZIEJUS. ETNOGRAFIJOS
SKYRIUS. Etnografinė ir foto paroda V.D. Kultūros muziejuje Kaune,
1938. [Ethnographic and photo exibition in the museum of Vytautas the
Great in Kaunas] Kaunas, Matininkų
ir kulturtechnikų sąjunga, 1938.
25 p. 947.52.K163 PU

2234. LIETUVOS TSR MOKSLŲ AKADEMI-
JA, VILNA. ISTORIJOS INSTITUTAS.
Lietuvių etnografijos bruožai. [The
outline of Lithuanian ethnography.
Ed. by A. Vyšniauskaitė] Vilnius,
VPMLL, 1964. 680 p. illus., facsims,
maps. Summaries in German and Rus-
sian. HD725.7.L488 DLC CaAEU CtU
ICLJF ICU MH NN PU

2235. LINGIS, Juozas. The national character of Lithuanian people.
In Baltic Review (Stockholm), v.1,
no.1, 1945, p.3-13. See serials
consulted.

2236. MAŽIULIS, Antanas Juozas.
Lithuanian etnographical studies; a
survey of etnographical museums and
societies. In Lituanus (New York,
N.Y.), v.4, no.3, 1958, p.76-79.
See serials consulted.

2237. MILIUS, Vacius. Bibliogra-
fiia Litovskoi etnografii za 1947-
1964 gg. In Sovetskaia etnografiia
(Moskva), no.5, 1965, p.166-174.
See serials consulted.

2238. --- Etnografinių tyrinėjimų
apžvalga. [Ethnographical research
in Lithuania; an outline] In
LTSRMAII. Lietuvių etnografijos
bruožai. Vilnius, 1964. p.15-17.
facsims., fold map. HD725.7.L488
DLC CaAEU CtY ICLJF ICU MH NN PU

2239. MISZKIEWICZ, Brunon. Groby
z okresu brązu i wczesnego średnio-
wiecza: Peresopnica, Wolica Nowa,
Żwirble, Poszuszwie, Turów... crania
lithuanica, polonica et ruthenica.
Wrocław, Państwowe Wydaw. Naukowe,

1956. 90 p. illus. Polska Akademia Nauk. Zakład Antropologii. Materiały i Prace Antropologiczne, nr.
25) GN100.M57 DLC PU-Mu

2240. SAGAN, Lubomir. Materiały
osteologiczne z pilkalń żmudzkich.
In Wiadomości Archeologiczne (Warszawa), v.14, 1938, p. 176-188. plates, tables. Summary in German.
See serials consulted.

2241. SCOTTI, Pietro. Note di etnologia lituana. In L'Europa orientale (Roma), v.21, no.7-10, 1941,
p. 338-346. DR1.E8 v.21 DLC CtY IU
MH NN NNG

2242. TALKO-HRYNCEWICZ, Julian.
Charakterystyka fizyczna ludów Litwy i Rusi. Kraków, Nakładem Akademii Umiejętności, 1893. 122 p. tables. Osobne odbicie z tomu 17,
Zbioru Wiadomości do Antropologii
Krajowej, wydawanego staraniem Komisyi Antropologicznej Akademii Umiejętności w Krakowie. MH-P

2243. --- W kwestji badań oprawy
oka u Biało-Rusinów i Litwinów. In
Przegląd Antropologiczny (Poznań),
v.5, 1930, p. 8-11. Summary in
French. See serials consulted.

2244. TARAKANOVA, S. and L. Tarenteva. Nekotorye voprosy etnogeneza
narodov Pribaltiki. In Sovetskaia
etnografiia (Moskva), no.2, 1956, p.
3-17. See serials consulted.

2245. TRAUTVETTER, C. von. Ethnographisches über die Letten, die Littauer und die alten Preussen. In
Inland (Dorpat), no.39-41,47-48,50,
53, 1851; no.6-7, 1852. See serials
consulted.

2246. VIRCHOW, Rudolf. Die altpreussische Bevölkerung, namentlich
Letten und Litauer, sowie deren Häuser. In Zeitschrift für Ethnologie
(Berlin), v.23, 1891, p. 767-805.
See serials consulted.

2247. VIŠINSKIS, Povilas. Antropologicheskaia kharakteristika zhmudinov. In Mūsų tautosaka (Kaunas),
v.10, 1935, p. 124-178. See serials
consulted.

2248. VOL'TER, Eduard Aleksandrovich. O rezultatakh etnograficheskoi poezdke k prusskim litovtsam letom 1883 g. In Russkoe geograficheskoe obshchestvo. Izvestiia (Sanktpeterburg), v.21, no.2, 1885, p. 97-
113. See serials consulted.

2249. --- Obzor trudov po litovskoi etnografii, 1879-1890 gg. In

Zhivaia starina (Sanktpeterburg),
1890, p. 37-42,177-183. See serials
consulted.

2250. VYŠNIAUSKAITĖ, Angelė. Etnograficheskie issledovaniia v Litve
v 1940-1960 godakh. In Sovetskaia
etnografiia (Moskva), no.3, 1960, p.
134-138. See serials consulted.

2251. ŽILINSKAS, Jurgis. Lietuvių
kaukuolės dėžė. [The Lithuanian
scull] Kaunas, Varpo spaustuvė,
1927. 134 p. tables, diagrs. Bibliography: p. 131-134. GN103.L55Z5
CU NN

2252. ŽILINSKAS, Jurgis and J. Jurgutis. Crania lituanica. In KUMeFD,
v.5, no.3, 1939, p.303-462. CU CSt
DI-GS DNLM MH-P MoU NBM NNN PPC

2253. ŽILINSKAS, Jurgis and Romualdas Masalskis. Senojo geležies
periodo Lietuvos gyventojo kaukuolių
studija; kaukuolės dėžės evoliucija
ir rasinė priklausomybė. Une étude
sur les cranes des habitants de la
Lithuanie pendant l'ancienne époque
de fer... In KUMeFD, v.4, no.1-3,
1937, p.5-197. Summary in French.
CU CSt-L DI-GS DNLM MoU MH-P NBM PPC

VI.5. DEMOGRAPHY

2254. ARVYDAS, Felix. Das Memelland, ist es wirklich deutsches Land?
Die Anrechte Litauens im Spiegel der
Geschichte. Kaunas, Spaudos fondas,
1934. 52 p. DK511.L273A9 DLC CtY
PPULC PU

2255. CZEKANOWSKI, Jan. Stosunki
narodowościowo-wyznaniowe na Litwie
i Rusi, w świetle źródeł oficyalnych.
Lwów, Książka Polska, 1918. 113 p.
HB3118.6.C97 DLC CSt-H IU InU NN
NcU PU

2256. CONZE, Werner. Agrarverfassung und Bevölkerung in Litauen und
Weissrussland. Leipzig, S. Hirzel,
1940. 249 p. illus., maps (part.
fold) diagrs. (Deutschland und der
Osten; Quellen und Forschungen zur
Geschichte ihrer Beziehungen, 15)
HD719.W4C6 DLC CU CtY IaU ICU LU MH
NIC NcD NN NNC NbU NmU NjP RPB WaU

2257. ESSEN, Werner. Die ländlichen Siedlungen in Litauen, mit besonderer Berücksichtigung ihrer Bevölkerungsverhältnisse. [Leipzig]
R. Voigtländer, 1931. 133, iv p.
atlas of maps, diagrs. (Veröffentlichungen des Staatlich-sächsischen
Forschungsinstitutes für Völkerkunde

in Leipzig. 2. Reihe: Volkskunde,
Bd.1) DK511.L2E7 DLC CU ICU NIC
NNC PU

2258. FORSTREUTER, Kurt Hermann.
Die Anfänge der Sprachstatistik in
Preussen und ihr Ergebnis zur Litauerfrage. In Zeitschrift für Ostforschung (Marburg), v.2, no.3, 1953,
p. 329-352. See serials consulted.

2259. --- Die Entwicklung der Na-
tionalitätenverhältnisse auf der Kurischen Nehrung. In Altpreussische
Forschungen (Königsberg in Pr.),
v.8, no.1, 1931, p. 46-63. See serials consulted.

2260. GEOGRAFICHESKOE OBSHCHESTVO
SSSR. Geografiia naseleniia v SSSR;
osnovnye problemy. [Glav. redaktor
E.N. Pavlovskii] Leningrad, Nauka,
1964. 278 p. illus., maps.
HB3607.G35 CaAEU

2261. KREDEL, Otto. Die Nationa-
litätenverhältnisse im Wilnagebiet.
In Osteuropa (Königsberg in Pr.),
v.7, no.3, 1931, p. 207-222. See
serials consulted.

2262. MELEZIN, Abraham. Ze studjów nad demografją Wilna. Wilno,
Nakł. Tow. Przyjacoł Nauk; skł. gł.
w Księg. Św. Wojciecha, 1936. 1 v.
map. (Rozprawy i Materjały Wydziała 3., Towarzystwa Przyjaciół Nauk
w Wilnie, t.9, zesz.3) HB2278.V5M4
DLC NN

2263. MERKYS, Vytautas. Lietuvos
miestų gyventojų tautybės XIX a. pa-
baigoje--XX a. pradžioje klausimu.
[The nationalities of the urban population in Lithuania toward the end
of the nineteenth and the begining
of thetwentieth centuries] In
LTSRMAD. Serija A, v.2(5), 1958, p.
85098. See serials consulted.

2264. MOORA, Harri. O drevnei territorii nasseleniia baltiiskikh ple-
men. In Sovetskaia arkheologija
(Moskva), Novaia seriia, v.2, no.2,
1958, p. 9-33. See serials consulted.

MORTENSEN, Gertrud (Heinrich)
Beiträge zu den Nationalitäten- und
Siedlungsverhältnissen von Preussischen Litauen. Berlin, 1927. See
entry no. 2054.

2265. MORTENSEN, Hans. Landschaft
und Besiedlung Litauens in frühge-
schichtlicher Zeit. In Baltische
Lande edited by Albert Brackmann and
Carl Engel. Leipzig, 1939. p. 330-
349. illus., map. DK511.B3B7 v.1
DLC CtY

2266. MORZY, Józef. Kryzys demo-
graficzny na Litwie i Białorusi w
II. połowie XVII. wieku. Poznań,
1965. 403 p. (Uniwersytet im. A-
dama Mickiewicza w Poznaniu. Wydział Filozoficzno-Historyczny.
[Prace] seria Historia, nr.21) Summaries in German and Russian. Bibliography: p. [355]-386. HB3608.
6.M6 DLC CaBVaS CaOTU IU MH NNC PU
ViU WaU

2267. NAMSONAS, Andrivs. Die nationale Zusammensetzung der Einwoh-
nerschaft der baltischen Staaten.
In Acta Baltica (Königstein im Taunus), v.1, 1961, p.59-74. See serials consulted.

2268. OBSZAR JĘZYKA LITEWSKIEGO W
gub. wileńskiej. Skresił Anonim.
In Polska Akademia Umiejętności, Kraków. Materialy Antropologiczno- archeologiczne i etnograficzne, v.3,
pt.2, 1898, p.1-72. GN2.P582 v.3
DLC NNC PU

2269. PAKŠTAS, Kazys. The growth
and decline of small nations. In
Lituanus (New York, N.Y.), v.5, no.4,
1959, p.98-102. See serials consulted.

2270. RASCHKE-RASCHKES, Leo. Die
Bevölkerung Litauens nach ihrer nationalen Struktur, Berufsgliederung
und gesellschaftlichen Schichtung.
Charlottenburg, Gebr. Hoffmann,[1931
70 p. Inaug. Diss.--University of
Berlin. HB3608.6.R22 InU MH NNC PU

2271. REMEIKIS, Tomas. The impact
of industrialization on the ethnic
demography of the Baltic countries.
In Lituanus (Chicago, Ill.), v.13,
no.1, 1967. p.29-41. See serials
consulted.

2272. UNGERN-STERNBERG,Roderich,
Freiherr von. Die Bevölkerungsverhältnisse in Estland, Lettland, Litauen und Polen, eine demographisch-
statistische Studie. Berlin, R.
Schoetz, 1939. 126 p. illus., map.
(Veröffentlichungen aus dem Gebiete
des Volksgesundheitsdienstes. Bd.53,
Hft.1) HB3608.B3U5 DLC BM

2273. VILEIŠIS, Vincas. Tautiniai
santykiai Mažojoje Lietuvoje ligi
Didžiojo karo istorijos ir statistikos šviesoje. Die Nationalitäten-
verhältnisse in Klein-Litauen bis
zum Weltkriege in geschichtlicher
und statistischer Beleuchtung. Kaunas, Politinių ir socialinių mokslų
instituto leidinys, 1935. xvi, 271
p. 3 fold. maps. Bibliography: p.
xii-xvi. DK511.L22V5 DLC PU

2274. WIELHORSKI, Władysław. Stosunek ilościowy litwinów, białorusi-
nów i polaków w dziejach W. Ks. Litewskiego. In Alma Mater Vilnensis
(London), no.2, part 3, 1951, p. 31-
66. See serials consulted.

2275. ZUNDĖ, Pranas. Demographic
changes and structure in Lithuania.
In Lituanus (Chicago, Ill.), v.10,
no.3-4, 1964, p. 5-15. See serials
consulted.

VI.6. CENSUSES, THEIR INTERPRETATION AND VITAL STATISTICS

2276. BRENSZTEJN, Michał Eustachy.
Spisy ludności miasta Wilna za oku-
pacji niemieckiej od d. 1 listopada
1915 r. Warszawa, 1919. 27 p. fold.
sample. (Biblioteka Delegacji Rad
Polskich, Litwy i Białej Rusi)
947.52.B757.3 PU MH PPULC

2277. GEOGRAFICHESKOE OBSHCHESTVO
SSSR. SEVERO-ZAPADNYI OTDEL.
Vil'na perepisi 18 aprieliia 1875
goda, proizvedennoi pod rukovodstvom
... Geograficheskago obshchestva...
obrabot. N. Zinov'evym. Vil'na,
Tip. A.D. Syrkina, 1881. 77 p.
HA1449.V47G4 DLC CtY NN

2278. GERMANY. PUBLIKATIONSSTELLE
BERLIN-DAHLEM. Bevölkerungsstatis-
tik des litauischen Staates, mit besonderer Berücksichtigung der Deutschen, auf Grund der ersten litauischen Volkszählung vom 17.9.1923.
Berlin, 1935. 192 p.
HB3608.6.G4 DLC IaU MH NN

2279. --- Nachtrag. Berlin, 1940.
15 p. map, tables.
HB3608.6.G4 suppl. DLC NN

2280. GOSHKEVICH, I.I., ed. Vilenskaia guberniia; polnyi spisok naselennykh miest, so statisticheskimi
dannymi o kazdom poselenii. Vil'na,
Gub. tipografiia, 1905. 341 p.
JS6070.V5G6 DLC PU

2281. HORN, Erna. Die Bevölkerung
Litauens, dargestellt in ihrem nationalen Gefüge nach dem Stande von 1923
(Litauischer Staat) und 1919 bzw.
1921(Wilnagebiet). 1:1,000,000
40 x 33 cm. In Jomsburg (Leipzig),
v.5, no.2, 1941. See serials consulted.

2282. KAKLIAUSKAS, S. Naturalinis
gyventojų judėjimas Lietuvoje praeityje ir ateinančių 20 metų laikotarpyje. [The demographic change in
Lithuania in the past as well as in

the coming twenty years] Kaunas,
Vytauto Didžiojo Universiteto, Teisių fakulteto leidinys, 1936. 69 p.
diagrs, tables. (Kaunas. Universitetas. Teisių fakultetas. Teisės
ir ekonomijos studijos, t.1, kn.3)
Thesis--University of Lithuania.
947.52.K125 PU

KLIMAS, Petras. La Lituanie
russe, considérations statistiques
et ethnographiques... Genève, [1918]
See entry no. 2041.

2283. KÜHNAST, Ludwig, Reg. Rath.
Statistische Mittleilungen über Littauen und Mazuren. Nachrichten über
Grundbesitz, Viehstand, Bevölkerung
und offentliche Abgaben der Ortschaf-
ten nach ämtlichen Quellen mitgeteilt. Gumbinen in Pr., Selbstverlag, 1863. 3 v. BM

2284. LEAGUE OF NATIONS. The official vital statistics of the Scandinavian countries and the Baltic republics. Genève [Imp. Sonor] 1926.
107 p. forms, tables, maps. (Statistical handbooks series, no.6) At
head of title: C.H.428. League of
Nations. Health Organization.
HA1466.L4 1926 DLC ClU CSt-H CU CtY
IEN ICU LU NcU OrU PU RPB TxDaM ViU

2285. LITHUANIA. CENTRALINIS STA-
TISTIKOS BIURAS. Naturalinis gyventojų judėjimas Lietuvoje 1915-1922
m. [Demographic movement in Lithuania in 1915-1922] Kaunas [Valsty-
bės spaustuvė] 1923. 24 p. tables.
HB3608.6.A5 1923 DLC

2286. LITHUANIAN INFORMATION BU-
REAU. Déclation des Lituaniens re-
lative au recensement fait par les
autorités d'occupation Allemandes en
Lituanie en 1916. A Monsieur le
Bourgermestre Superior Allemand de
la ville de Vilna. [Paris, 1919?]
6 p. (Délégation de Lituanie à la
Conférence de la Paix, [pt.] V:4)
D643.A7.DP5L7 CSt-H

2287. --- Sur le prétendu recensement de Vilna en 1916. [Paris, 1919]
6 p. (Délégation de Lituanie à la
Conférence de la Paix, [pt.] V:3
CSt-H

2288. OCHMAŃSKI, Jerzy. Zaludnie-
nie Litwy w roku 1790. In Posen.
Uniwersytet. Seria Historia. Zeszyty Naukowe (Poznań), no.7, 1967,
p. [269]-279. See serials consulted.

2289. PAKŠTAS, Kazys. Changing population in Lithuania. In Lituanus
(Brooklyn, N.Y.), no.1(10) 1957,
p. 16-19. See serials consulted.

2290. --- Earliest statistics of nationalities and religions in the territories of Old Lithuania, 1861. In Commentaciones Balticae (Bonn), v. IV:V:6, 1958, p. 169-121. tables, maps. See serials consulted.

2291. RASTENIS, Vincas. Lithuania's population in Soviet statistics. In Baltic review (New York, N.Y.), no. 9, 1956, p. 17-28. See serials consulted.

2292. ROMER, Eugeniusz. Spis ludności na terenach administrowanych przez Zarząd Ziem Wschodnich(grudzień 1919). Statistics of languages of the provinces being under the Polish "Civil Administration of the Eastern Lands" (December 1919) [Lwów] Książka Polska T-wa Naucz. Szkół Wyższych, 1920. 49 p. fold. col. map, tables. (Prace Geograficzne, zesz.7) Polish, French, and English. HA1448.L5R6 DLC

2293. RUSSIA. TSENTRAL'NYI STATIS-TICHESKII KOMITET. Pervaia perepis' naseleniia Rossiiskoi Imperii 1897 goda. Sanktpeterburg, 1898-1905. Partial contents.--pt.4. Vilenskaia guberniia.--pt. 11.Grodnenskaia guberniia.--pt. 17. Kovenskaia guberniia.--pt.59. Suvalskaia guberniia. HA1431.I897 DLC(pt.59) NN(pts.1-3)

2294. RUSSIA (1923- U.S.S.R.) TSENTRAL'NOE STATISTICHESKOE UPRAV-LENIE. Itogi vsesoiuznoi perepisi naseleniia 1959 goda; Litovskaia SSR. Vil'nius, Gosstatizdat, Litovskoe otdelenie, 1963. 178 p. tables. Title page also in Lithuanian. HA1448.L5A615 DLC CaOHM CaOLU CaOTU CtY FU InU MH NN NNC NcD NcU NSyU NjP OrU PPiU PU WU WaU

2295. STIEDA, Eugen. Die Bevölkerung des Generalbezirks Litauen. In Ostland. Reichskommissar. Statistische Berichte für das Ostland (Riga), v.1, no.6, 1942, p.18-22. See serials consulted.

2296. ŚWIECHOWSKI, Marian. Das polnische Element in den litauischen Länden, mit besonderer Berücksichtigung des von dem Mittelmächten besetzten Gebietes. Bevölkerungsverhältnisse und Bodenbesitz, statistische Skizze nebst einer Karte und Tabellen im Texte. Krakau, Zentrales Verlagsbureau des Obersten Nationalen Komitees, 1918. 49 p. fold. map. tables. DK511.L2S83 DLC BM MH

2297. --- Population d'après les nationalités et la propriété foncière sur le territoire du grand duché de la Lithuanie. Cracovie, Bureau central d'édition du Comité Suprême

Polonaise, 1918. iv, 16, 17, [4] p. maps., tables. DK511.L26S8 DLC CSt-H

2298. --- Żywioł polski na ziemiach litewskich na szczególnem uwzględnieniem obszarów okupowanych przez mocarstwa centralne. Zakopane, Skład Gł. Księg. Podhalańska, 1917. 48 p. map. table. HB3118.6.S8 DLC MH PU

2299. TARULIS, Albert N. A heavy population loss in Lithuania. In Journal of Central European Affairs (Boulder, Colo.), v.21, no.4, 1962, p.452-464. See serials consulted.

2300. VOL'TER, Eduard Aleksandrovich. Die Zahl der Litauer im Gouvernement Wilna. In LLGM, v.5,1911, p.261-302. See serials consulted.

VI.7. LITHUANIANS ABROAD

VI.7.a. GENERAL WORKS

2301. BUDRECKIS, Algirdas. The Lithuanian World Youth Congress. In Baltic Review(New York, N.Y.), no. 32, 1966, p.56-62. See serials consulted.

2302. DRAUGIJA UŽSIENIO LIETUVIAMS REMTI. Pasaulio lietuviai. [The Lithuanians abroad. Edited by P. Ruseckas] Kaunas, 1935. 363 p. illus. DK511.L223D723 DLC CtPAM CtTMF ICCC PU

2303. GLIAUDYS, Jurgis. Simas. [By] Jurgis Gliauda [pseud.] Cleveland, Ohio, Viltis, 1971. 158 p. E183.8.G55 DLC

2304. Jakštas, Juozas. Lietuviai užsienyje. [Lithuanians abroad] In Lietuvių enciklopedija. Boston,Mass. 1968. v.15, p.414-429. For holdings see entry no.216.

2305. KRUPAVIČIUS, Mykolas. Lietuviškoji išeivija. [The Lithuanian emigrees. Castelnuovo Don Bosco] 1959. 140 p. DK511.L223K78 DLC CaAEU CtTMF ICCC MH PU

2306. PASAULIO LIETUVIŲ BENDRUOMENĖ. SEIMAS. Pasaulio lietuvių bendruomenės antrojo seimo darbai. [Proceedings of the second Congress of the World Lithuanian Community. Edited by A. Rinkūnas] Toronto, Ont., P.L.B. Valdyba, 1963. 114 p. illus. 325.2.P262 PU

2307. --- Pasaulio lietuvių bendruomenės seimo vadovas. [A guide to the Congress of the World Lithuanian Community. New York, N.Y., 1958] 64 p. illus., ports. DK511.L223P3 DLC

2308. PASAULIO LIETUVIŲ BENDRUOmenės keliu. [The World Lithuanian Community and its objectives. n.p.] Lietuvybės išlaikymo tarnybos leidinys [1950] 75 p. Includes: World Lithuanian Community's Charta and the draft of its charter. 970.4.PL ICLJF

2309. RAILA, Bronys. Iš paskendusio pasaulio. [Skraipsniai... kronikos, 1946-1958. Essays, etc.] Chicago, Ill., Srovė, 1962. 431 p. illus., ports. CE184.L7R35 CtY MH PU

2310. --- Laumių juosta. [A rainbow] London, Nida, 1966. 351 p. (Nidos knygų klubo leidinys, nr.61) E184.L7R3 DLC InU MnU NNC NBuU PU

2311. --- Tamsiausia prieš aušrą; straipsniai lietuvių politikos, visuomenės, idėjų klausimais, 1946-1958. [It is darkest before dawn; articles on the Lithuanian politics, society and thought, 1946-1958] Chicago, Ill., Srovė, 1960. 448 p. illus. DK511.L27R3 DLC CtY ICU MH NN PU

2312. --- Versmės ir verpetai. [Springs and whirlpools. Boston, Mass., 1970] 351 p. DK511.L22R32 PU

2313. RICHARD, Constantin. Litauen und Litauer; Beziehungen zwischen Muttervolk und Auslandlitauern. In Nation und Staat (Wien), v.9, no.4, 1936, p. 301-311. See serials consulted.

SIMUTIS, Anicetas, ed. Pasaulio lietuvių žinynas. New York, N.Y., [1958] See entry no. 232.

2314. TRUSKA, L. Emigracija iš Lietuvos 1868-1914 metais. [The emigration from Lithuania, 1868-1914] In LTSRMAD. Serija A, v.1(10), 1961, p. 71-85. See serials consulted.

2315. TUMAS, Juozas. Ten gera kur mūsų nėra. [The grass is always greener on the other side] Kaunas, S. Banaičio spaustuvė, 1912. 224 p. (Šv. Kazimiero draugijos leidinys, nr. 122) 891.92.T832T PU CtY CtTMF

2316. VILIAMAS, Vladas. Įsikūrimo galimybės užjūrio kraštuose; lietuvių

emigracijos ir kolonizacijos problemos. [The possibilities of settlement in the overseas countries; the problems of Lithuanian emigration and colonization. Nördlingen, Ger.] Sudavija, 1947. 112 p. illus., map HC59.V5 DLC ICCC

VI.7.b. DISPLACED PERSONS

2317. ALSEIKA, Vytautas. DP [Displaced persons] In Lietuvių enciklopedija. Boston, Mass., 1955. v.5, p. 147-158. For holdings see entry no. 216.

2318. BALTIC REFUGIES AND DISPLACed persons. Foreword by the Duchess of Atholl. London, Boreas Pub. Co., 1947. 40 p. D808.B3 DLC N NN

2319. BARĖNAS, Kazimieras. Tremtinio pergyvenimai keliaujant iš pavergtos Lietuvos, per įvairius kraštus, į laisvės šalį. [The experiences of an exile during his travels through many countries from occupied Lithuania to the country of freedom. By] K. Baras. Chicago, Ill., 1942. 80 p. 947.5.B232.2 PU ICLJF InNd

2320. BROEL-PLATERIS, Alexander Adam. Occupational adjustments of the Lithuanian refugee intelligentsia in Chicago. Chicago, Ill., 1955. 178 leaves. Thesis (M.A.)--University of Chicago. Typescript. F9999 ICU NN

2321. DIENOS BE TĖVYNĖS; Flensburgo lietuvių metraštis. [Days without a homeland... Rotatorinis leidimas. Leidėjas ir redaktorius A. Vaitkus. Flensburg, Ger.] 1946. 358 p. illus. PG8713.D5 PU ICLJF

2322. GAIDAMAVIČIUS, Pranas. Išblokštasis žmogus; benamio likimo perspektyvos. [A displased person; the destiny of a homeless man. Augsburg, Ger.] Venta [1951] 278 p. Bibliography: p. 275-278. D809.L5G3 DLC CaOONL NN OCl PU

2323. GUSTAITIS, Algirdas. Tarp Šveicarijos ir Danijos. [Between Switzerland and Denmark. Nördlingen, Ger.] 1946. 96 p. illus. DD42.G85 DLC PU

2324. KAASIK, N. The legal status of Baltic refugees. In Baltic review (Stockholm), v.1, 1945, p. 21-26. See serials consulted.

2325. KAPOČIUS, Feliksas. Lietuvių tremtinių bažnytinis-religinis gyvenimas vakarų Vokietijoje ir Austrijoje. [The religious life of Lithuanian displaced persons in West Germany and Austria] In Metraštis, 1950. Kennebunkport, Me., 1949. p. 175-184. CtPAM ICLJF

2326. KAVOLIS, Vytautas Martynas. Nužemintųjų generacija; egzilio pasaulėjautos eskizai. [An outline of feelings of an exile in relation to his environment] Cleveland, Ohio, Santara-Šviesa, 1968. 79 p. PG8737.K38 PU

2327. LIETUVIŲ MENO ANSAMBLIS "Dainava" 1945-1947. Frankfurt am Main, 1947. 15 p. illus. In Lithuanian and English. BM(7919. d. 44)

2328. MATEKŪNAS, Petras. Kufšteino lietuvių stovykla. [Lithuanian refugee camp in Kufstein. Brooklyn, N.Y.] Vaga [1956] 136 p. D809.A9M3 DLC PU

2329. NARKELIŪNAITĖ, Salomėja. DP Baltic Camp at Seedorf. Hamburg, UNRRA Team 295, 1948. 184 p. illus. D809.G3N3 PU ICCC ICLJF CtPAM

2330. PAŠILAITIS, Juozas. Hearken then judge; sidelights on Lithuanian DPs. Tübingen, Ger., Patria [1949?] 47 p. illus. D809.G3P32 DLC PU

2331. PLATERIS, Aleksandras. Beschäftigung- und Wirtschaftslage der litauischen Flüchtlinge in den Vereinigten Staaten. In Acta Baltica (Bonn), v.6, 1966, p. 181-206. See serials consulted.

2332. --- Occupational adjustment of professional refugees; a case study of Lithuanian professionals in the United States. In Lituanus (Chicago, Ill.), v.11, no.3-4, 1964, p. 27-44. See serials consulted.

2333. SABALIŪNAS, Leonas.Litauische Exilorganizationen und ihre Tätigkeit. In Acta Baltica (Bonn), v.6, 1966, p. 207-220. See serials consulted

2334. TREATMENT OF DISPLACED PERsons. In Lithuanian Bulletin (New York, N.Y.), v.5, no.1-2, 1947, p.1-36. See serials consulted.

VI.7.c. LITHUANIANS IN UNITED STATES

2335. A VISIT WITH LITHUANIAN GIRL guides. [Chicago, Ill., 1957] 24 p. illus. L 970.4.GG ICLJF

2336. AMBROSE, Aleksas. Chicagos

Lietuvių istorija, 1869-1959. [The history of Lithuanians in Chicago, 1869-1959. Chicago, Ill.] Amerikos lietuvių istorijos draugija, 1967. 664 p. illus., ports. F548.9.L5A65 DLC CtY ICU PU WU

2337. AMERIKOS LIETUVIŲ BALSAS. [The voice of the American Lithuanians. Detroito] vienkartinis leidinys penkmečio veiklos sukakčiai paminėti,1945-50. [Detroit, Mich., Amerikos lietuvių balso radio klubas] 1950. 30 p. illus. 970.4.LB ICLJF

2338. AMERIKOS LIETUVIŲ KATALIKŲ metraštis, 1916 m. Tvarkė ir redagavo P. Lapelis. [The yearbook of the American Catholic Lithuanians] Chicago, Ill., Lietuvių katalikų spaudos sekcija, 1915. 438 p. 937.75.Am35 PU

2339. AMERIKOS LIETUVIŲ MISIJA IR jos darbai. [The American Lithuanian Mission and its work.] Detroit, Mich., Petrikas, 1945. 32 p. L 970.4.LM ICLJF

2340. AMERIKOS LIETUVIŲ RYMO-KATALIKŲ KUNIGŲ VIENYBĖ. Metraštis,1941. [Yearbook, 1941. Redagavo Prel. Jonas Balkūnas. Brooklyn, N.Y., 1941] 101 p. illus. 325.2475.Am36.2 PU CaOONL ICLJF

2341. AMERIKOS LIETUVIŲ TAUTINĖ SĄJUNGA. BOSTONO SKYRIUS. Namai ir darbai. [Home and work. Leidinio bendradarbiai: Jonas Kasmauskas, Bruno Kalvaitis, Ignas Vilėniškis. Leidinėlio redaktorius: Stasys Santvaras. Boston, Mass.] 1954. 32 p. illus. E184.L7A69 DLC

2342. ASSOCIATION OF LITHUANIAN PATRIOTS. Tėvynės mylėtojų draugijos įstatai ir istorija. [The by-laws and history of the society "Tėvynės mylėtojų draugija"] Worchester, Mass. 1911. 62 p. HS2008.A72A5 PU

2343. ASSOCIATION OF LITHUANIAN STUDENTS IN U.S.A. Dienos tarp dangoraižių; studentijos sukaktuvinis leidinys. [Days among the skyscrapers; jubilee publication of the lithuanian student association. Edited by I. Čepėnaitė et al.] Chicago,Ill., 1957. 112 p. E184.L7A78 DLC

2344..BALTIMORĖS LIETUVIŲ TAUTIŠKO knygyno auksinis jubiliejus, 1908-1958. [The golden jubilee of the Lithuanian National Library in Baltimore] Baltimore, Md.,[1958] 1 v. (unpaged) L 020.BA ICLJF

2345. BANIŠAUSKAS, Antanas J.

Angliakasio atsiminimai. [Reminis-
cences of a miner. Long Island City, N.Y.] 1952. 208 p. illus.,
ports. E184.L7L3 DLC NN

2346. BARTUŠKA, Vincas. Les Lituaniens d'Amérique. Lausanne, Bureau
d'Information de Lituanie, 1918. 24
p. Offprint from "Pro Lituania,"
no.1-2, 1916. E184.L7B2 DLC CSt-H
DNW PPULC PU

2347. BIRŽIŠKA, Mykolas. Amerikos
lietuviai. [Lithuanians in America]
Kaunas ["Lithuania"] 1932. 79 p.
ports. Cb4yL7 CtY ICLJF

2348. CAVENDER, Frank W. American
Lithuanians in the Bridgeport community. [Bridgeport, Conn.] 1957. 12
p. (University of Bridgeport student
monograph; sponsored by the University of Bridgeport sociology society, no.10) NN

2349. ČEKIENĖ, Emilija. Kad ji bū-
tų gyva. [Tat she may live. Cleveland, Ohio] Viltis, 1971. 413 p.
illus., ports. E184.L7C4 DLC

2350. CHICAGOS LIETUVIŲ METRAŠTIS.
[Yearbooks of the Lithuanians of Chicago. Chicago, Ill.] Nemunas, 1955.
243 p. illus., ports. F548.9.L5C5
DLC IC KMK PU

2351. CICĖNAS, Jeronimas. Omahos
lietuviai. [The Lithuanians of Oma-
ha] Omaha, Neb., Omahos šimtmečio
minėjime lietuviams atstovauti komitetas, 1955. 278 p. illus. Summary in English. 325.C4850 MiD ICLJF

2352. CLEVELANDO LIETUVIŠKŲ DRAU-
gysčių istoriška peržvalga. [Histo-
rical review of Lithuanian societies
in Cleveland] Cleveland, Ohio, spauda "Dirvos", 1917. 114 p. illus.
F499.C6C666 DLC OCl ICLJF

2353. COULTER, Charles Wellsley.
The Lithuanians of Cleveland. Cleveland, Ohio, Cleveland Americaniza-
tion Committee, 1920. 24 p. illus.,
map. F499.C5C85 DLC CU CLU MB NN
OClW OU PPiU WaS

2354. ČUŽAUSKAS, Juozas J. Nuse-
kę antplūdžiai; Waukegan'o lietuvių
istorija; Šv. Baltramiejaus parapija. [Lithuanians in Waukegan] Waukegan, Ill., 1946. 120 p. illus.
289.5Ba ICLJF

2355. DARIAUS IR GIRĖNO GARBĖS PA-
minklo atidengimas 1935 liepos 28 d.
Marquette Parke, Chicagoj. [The dedication of the monument to Darius
and Girėnas] Chicago, Ill., Dariaus
ir Girėno paminklo fondas, 1935. 94 p

illus. 970.7DG ICLJF

2356. DOHERTY, Joseph F. Lithuanians. I: Their life and background
in America. II: Their history and
culture in the homeland. Edited by
Joseph Mayper. [New York, N.Y.,1921]
16 p. illus., map. (GLP p.v. 34,
nr.8)NN

2357. L'ÉMIGRATION LITUANIENNE AUX
États-Unis et la renaissance nationale. Lausanne, Bureau d'Information
de Lituanie, 1918. 32 p. DK511.
L2E53 CLU NN

2358. GEDVILAS, Zigmantas. Lietuvių Rymo katalikų labdarių sąjunga,
1914-1965. [The Lithuanian Roman
Catholic Welfare Association] Chicago, Ill., 1965. 72 p. E184.L7G4
PU

2359. GINEITIS, Kazys. Amerika
ir Amerikos lietuviai. [America and
American Lithuanians] Kaunas, Author,
1925. 325 p. illus., plates.
E184.L7G5 DLC ICCC ICLJF OCl PU RP

2360. GIRNIUS, Juozas. Idealas ir
laikas; žvilgsnis į dabarties ateiti-
ninkiją ir lietuviškąją išeiviją.
[A look at the Youth Organization
"Ateitininkai" of today and the Lithuanian exiles. Chicago, Ill.,
1966] 238 p. B68.G5 DLC MnU MH PU

2361. HUGHES, Elizabeth. Chicago
housing conditions, IX; the Lithuanians in the Fourth Ward. In American
Journal of Sociology (Chicago, Ill.),
v.20, 1914, p.289-312. See serials
consulted.

2362. ISTORIJA CHICAGOS LIETUVIŲ,
jų parapijų ir Kun. Kriaučiūno prova
su laikrasčiu "Lietuva" buvusi balandžio mėn. 1899. [A history of the
Lithuanians of Chicago] Chicago,Ill.
Spauda "Lietuvos", 1900. iv, 585,
iii p. illus., ports. F550.L7I8
ICU BM ICBM CtY

2363. JAKUBAUSKAS-JAKUBS, John.
Amerikos lietuvių sporto istorija.
[History of American Lithuanian sport.
Chicago, Ill., Author, 1966] 155 p.
illus. E184.L7J35 PU

2364. JONITIS, Peter Paul. The
accumulation of the Lithuanians of
Chester, Pennsylvania. Ann Arbor,
University Microfilms [1953] 536
leaves. Theses--University of Pennsylvania. Bibliography: leaves 525-
536. Microfilm AC-1 no. 4897.
DLC OrU PU

2365. JURGĖLA, Constantine Rudyard.
Lietuviai Amerikoje prieš masinę

imigraciją ir tautinį atgimimą. [By]
Kostas Jurgėla. [Lithuanians in
United States prior to the mass immi-
gration and national renaissance]
In LKMSD, v.5, 1964, p.453-[522]
Summary in English. See serials
consulted.

2366. --- --- Offprint from L.K.M.
akademija, Suvažiavimo darbai.
973.075.J978 PU

2367. KARPIUS, Kazys S. Amerikos
lietuvių veikla ir Lietuvos nepri-
klausomybė. [The American Lithuanian activities and the independence
of Lithuania] In Margutis (Chicago,
Ill.), 1952, no.7, p.11-19, no.8, p.
6-9, no.12, p.17-20; 1953, no.1, p.
9-10, no.2, p.8-9, no.3 p.7-9, no.4,
p.7-8. See serials consulted.

2368. KAŠKAITIS, Jonas. Iš atsiminimų. [Recollections. n.p.]
1958. 319 p. illus. (Amerikos lietuvių darbininkų literatūros draugijos leidinys, 64) CT1218.K35A3 1958
DLC CaOTP PU

2369. --- Kovos sūkuriai. [In the
whirlwinds of the battle] Vilnius,
VGLL, 1960. 314 p. illus.
CT1218.K35A3 1960 DLC

2370. KONČIUS, Joseph B. Atsiminimai iš BALFO veiklos 1944-1964. [The
recollections on the activities of
the United Lithuanian American Relief Fund, 1944-1964. Chicago, Ill.]
Draugo spaustuvė, 1966. 404 p. illus.
973.075.K873.2 PU ICLJF NN

2371. --- Lithuanians in the United States. In Catholic encyclopedia. New York, N.Y. [c1957] v.18,
suppl.2. BX841.C25 DLC CaAEU

2372. KUČAS, Antanas. Amerikos
lietuvių istorija. [History of American Lithuanians] Boston, Mass.,
Lietuvių enciklopedijos leidykla,
1971. 639 p. E184.L7K8 PU

2373. --- Amerikos lietuvių ryšiai
su tėvyne. Amerika-Litauer und ihre
Beziehungen zum Heimatland. In
LKMASD, v.5, 1964, p. 407-427. Summary in German. See serials consulted.

2374. ---, ed. Lietuvių Romos ka-
talikų susivienijimas Amerikoje.
[Alliance of the Lithuanian Roman
Catholics in America] Wilkes-Barre,
Pa., 1956. 370 p. ports.
HS1538.L53K8 DLC ICC PU

2375. KURAITIS, Dan. Atsiminimai.
[Recollections. Chicago, Ill.] Naujienų leidinys, 1953. 208 p. illus.

CT275.K892A3 DLC CaAEU CtTMF MH PU
WU

2376. LEVANDA, Juozas. Gyvenimo
saulėleidis, parašė ir išleido Juozas Levanda. [Recollections] Brooklyn, N.Y., 1941. 293 p. port.
(*QY)NN

2377. LIETUVIŲ KULTŪRINIS DARŽELIS.
Lithuanian Cultural Garden. Cleveland, Ohio [1963?] 63 p. illus.,
ports. 710.9771.L625 OCl

2378. LIETUVOS ATGIMIMO SĄJUDŽIO
įstatai. [Charter and by-laws of the
Lithuanian Revival movement. Chicago, Ill., 1965] 16 p. 970.4.LA ICLJF

2379. LITHUANIAN ALLIANCE OF AME-
rika. Constitution and by-laws.
New York, N.Y., 1940. 138 p. CtPAM

2380. --- Kas yra Susivienijimas
lietuvių Amerikoje. [What is the Lithuanian Alliance of America] New
York, N.Y., [n.d.] 47 p. HS2008.
L5A5 DLC

2381. --- Konstitucija Susivienijimo Amerikoje,sutaisyta pagal seimų
protokolus. [Charter of the Lithuanian Alliance of America] Shenandoah,
Pa., 1897. 40 p. HS2008.L53A51 1970
PU(Xerox copy, 1970)

2382. --- Susivienijimo lietuvių
Amerikoje auksinio jubiliejaus albumas. [An album of the golden jubilee
of the Lithuanian Alliance of Ameri-
ca] Redagavo ir tekstus parašė S.E.
Vitaitis. New York, N.Y., 1936. 303
p. illus., ports. E184.L7L5 CaOWtU
PU

2383. --- Susivienijimo lietuvių
Amerikoje istorija nuo 1886 ligi
1915 metų. [The history of Lithuanian Alliance of America, 1886-1915.
Edited by T. Astramskas] New York,
N.Y., Išleista S.L.A. lėšomis, "Tėvynės" spaustuvėje, 1916. 547 p.
tables., plates, ports. (Susivienijimas lietuvių Amerikoje. Leidinys,
nr.27) 973.075.L714 PU ICBM NN

2384. --- Susivienijimo lietuvių
Amerikoje 42-ras seimas, birželio 29,
1942, Pittsburgh, Pa. [The forty-
second Congress of the Lithuanian
Alliance of America] New York, N.Y.,
Tėvynės spauda, 1942. 250 p.
L 970.4.SL ICLJF

2385. LITHUANIAN CHAMBER OF COMMER-
CE OF ILLINOIS. Chicagos vadovas.
[Directory of Chicago] Chicago, Ill.
1952. 247 p. illus., ports., fold.
col. map. F548.18.L5 DLC PU

2386. LITHUANIAN COUNCIL OF CHICA-
GO. 50 Lietuvos Nepriklausomybės
atkūrimo ir 717 metų karalystės į-
steigimo minėjimas, 1251-1918-1968.
[Golden jubilee of the reestablishment of independence of Lithuania..]
Rengia Chicagos lietuvių taryba,
Civic Opera rūmuose, Chicagoje, 1968.
II.18. [Chicago, Ill., Chicagos lietuvių taryba, 1968] 64 p. illus.,
ports, facsims. E184.L7L77 CaAEU

2387. LITHUANIAN INFORMATION BU-
REAU. Les lituaniens d'Amérique.
[Paris, 1919?] 4 p. (Délégation de
Lituanie à la Conférence de la Paix.
[pt.], V:5) D643.A7DP5L7 CSt-H

2388. LITHUANIAN ROMAN CATHOLIC
FEDERATION OF AMERICA. Mūsų darbai;
Lietuvių Romos katalikų federacija,
1959-1961. [Our action; Lithuanian
Roman Catholic Federation, 1959-
1961. Brooklyn, N.Y.], 1961. 160
p. 973.075.L715 PU

2389. LITHUANIAN ROMAN CATHOLIC
PRIESTS' LEAGUE OF AMERICA. Amerikos lietuvių katalikų darbai. Catholic action of the Lithuanians of
America. [New York, N.Y.] 1943.
336 p. illus. BX1407.L5L5 DLC
ICCC ICLJF PU

MARGERIS, Algirdas. Amerikos lietuviai ir angliškųjų skolinių žodynas, 1872-1949. Chicago,
Ill., 1956. See entry no. 341.

2390. MICHELSONAS, Stasys. Lietu-
vių išeivija Amerikoje, 1868-1961.
[Lithuanian immigrants in the United
States, 1868-1961] South Boston,
Mass., Keleivis, 1961. xii, 499 p.
illus., ports. E184.L7M5 DLC CaAEU
CaOTP CtPAM CtY ICU MH NN PU

2391. MILUKAS, Antanas. Amerikos
lietuviai 19 šimtmetyje, 1868-1900.
[American Lithuanians in the nineteenth century, 1868-1900] Philadelphia, Pa., Pranaičių Julė, 1938-
42. 2 v. Vol. 1 has 348 p. facsims.
Publication of the material of vol.
2 was continued in "Žvaigždė", 1940-
1942 after the author's death. 973.
075.M649.4 PU ICCC(v.1) ICLJF(v.1)

2392. --- Amerikos lietuvių kronika, 1868-1893. [American Lithuanian
chronicle, 1868-1893] Philadelphia,
Pa., Žvaigždės spaustuvė, 1931. 272,
[10] p. 973.075.M649.5 PU ICC ICLJF

2393. --- Lietuviai Pennsylvanijo-
je; iš A. Miluko paskaitų. [Lithu-
anians in Pennsylvania] Philadelphia. Pa., Pranaičių Julės leidinys,
1936. 134 p. 973.075.M639.2 PU

2394. --- "Motinėlės" drugija. A.
Miluko paskaita. ["Motinėlės" soci-
ety] Philadelphia, Pa., Pranaičių
Julės leidinys, 1932. 34 p. 973.
075.M649.3 PU

2395. --- Pirmieji Amerikos lietuvių profesionalai ir kronika.
[Lithuanian professionals in the
United States] Iš A. Miluko paskaitų. Philadelphia, Pa., Pranaičių
Julės leidinys, 1929-31. 2 v.
973.075.M649.3 PU ICLJF

2396. --- Spaudos laisvė ir Amerikos lietuvių organizuotės sukaktuvės. [Freedom of the press and the
jubilee of American Lithuanian or-
ganizations] Philadelphia, Pa.,
1927. 468 p. 891.92.M649.3 PU ICCC

2397. --- --- 2d ed. Philadelphia,
Pa., 1929. 66,782 p. 891.92H.M649.3 PU

2398. MIZARA, Rojus. Žvilgsnis į
praeitį. [A glance into the past]
Vilnius, VPMLL, 1960. 333 p. illus.
PN4874.M55A3 DLC ICLJF PU

2399. NEW YORK. WORLD'S FAIR,
1939-1940. LITHUANIAN DAY COMMITTEE.
Lithuanian Day, New York World's
Fair, September 10, 1939. New York,
N.Y., 1939. 28 p. DK511.L2N4 PU MH

2400. NEW YORK. WORLD'S FAIR,
1964-1965. LITHUANIAN DAY. Lietuvių diena, 1964. [Lithuanian Day,
1964] Brooklyn, N.Y., 1964. 64 p.
E184.L7N4 PU

2401. PETKEVIČIENĖ, Leokadija. JAV
pažangiųjų lietuvių visuomeninė-kul-
tūrinė veikla, 1933-1940 m. [The
socio-cultural activities of the
progressive Lithuanians in the United States, 1933-1940] Vilnius,
Mintis, 1969. 175 p. ports. E184.
L7P4 DLC CaOTU CtY ICU NN PU

2402. PETRIKA, Antanas. Lietuvių
literatūros draugija ir pažangieji
Amerikos lietuviai. [Lithuanian literary society and the progressive
Lithuanians of the United States.
Brooklyn, N.Y., 1965] 363 p. (A-
merikos lietuvių darbininkų literatūros draugija. Leidinys, nr. 74)
PG9110.A225 DLC CaAEU NN

2403. PRŪSEIKA, Leonas. Atsiminimai ir dabartis. [Reminiscences and
the present time. Vilnius, VPMLL,
1960] 227 p. E184.L7P7 1960 DLC
CaAEU PU

2404. --- Publicistika. [Journa-
lism. Sudarė: S.J. Jokubka ir J.S.
Mažeika] Vilnius, Mintis, 1965.
334 p. E184.L7P75 DLC MH NN

2405. RĖKLAITIS, Antanas, ed. Lietuvių veteranų sąjungos Ramovės pirmasis dešimtmetis, 1950-1960. [The first decade of the Lithuanian Veteran's League "Ramovė". Antanas Rėklaitis, autorius-redaktorius. Čikagoje, Lietuvių veteranų sąjunga Ramovė, 1962] 353 p. illus., facsims., ports. DK511.L223R4 DLC CSt-H CaOTP CaOTU MH MnU NN NjP OClW PP PU

2406. ROUČEK, Joseph S. American Lithuanians. New York, N.Y., Lithuanian Alliance of America, 1940. 38 p. Bibliography: p. 35-38. E184.L7R67 DLC CaOWtU MH NNC PPiU PU

2407. --- Lithuanian Americans. In One America. 3d ed. Francis J. Brown and Joseph S. Rouček, eds. New York, N.Y., 1952, p. 190-198. E184.A1B87 1952 DLC

2408. --- Lithuanian immigrants in America. In American Journal of Sociology (Chicago, Ill.), v.41, no. 4, 1936, p. 447-453. See serials consulted.

2409. SAKALAS, Ignas. Lietuvos vyčiai Amerikoje; katalikiškojo jaunimo organizacijos penkiasdešimties metų veikimo žymesnieji bruožai. [Lithuanian knights in the United States; a Catholic Youth Organization] Čikagoje, Draugo spaustuvė, 1963. 160 p. illus., ports. HS2008.K53S3 DLC ICU ICLJF NN

2410. SAKALIENĖ, Sofija. Amerikos lietuvių Romos katalikių moterų sąjunga 25 metų veikimo šviesoje. [History of the American Lithuanian Roman Catholic women's association] Chicago, Ill., Draugo spaustuvė, 1939. 127 p. illus. 289.6.SA ICLJF

2411. SALIETIS, A.B. Po Amerikos dangum; laiškai iš JAV. [Under the sky of the United States...] Vilnius, Laikraščių ir žurnalų leidykla, 1963. 84 p. HN58.S3 DLC

2412. SELENIS, Robertas. Lithuanians in America; an historical sketch. In Lituanus (Chicago, Ill.), v.17, no.4, 1971, p. 44-58. See serials consulted.

2413. ŠIDLAUSKAS, Kazys. Amerikos lietuvių politika; John P. White studijos "Lithuanians and the Democratic Party" santrauka ir komentarai. [Lithuanians in American politics. Chicago, Ill.] Chicagos lietuvių literatūros draugija, 1966. 162 p. port. F348.9.L7S5 DLC PU WU

2414. ŠIMUTIS, Leonardas. Amerikos lietuvių taryba; 30 metų Lietuvos laisvės kovoje, 1940-1970. [Thirty years of struggle for Lithuania's independence by the Lithuanian American Council. Chicago, Ill., Amerikos lietuvių taryba] 1971. 499 p. illus. Lithuanian and English. E184.L7S56 DLC PU

SIRVAITIS, Casimir Peter. Religious folkways in Lithuania and their conservation among the Lithuanian immigrants in the United States. Washington, D.C., 1952. See entry no. 1049.

2415. SKIRIUS, Antanas F. Kalifornijos lietuvių almanachas. California Lithuanian almanac. [Los Angeles, Calif., Lithuanian Chamber of Commerce of Los Angeles, 1963] 133 p. F870.L755 DLC PU

2416. SUSITELKIMAS LIETUVIŲ AMERIkoje. Dalis 1. [Lithuanian societies in the United States] Chicago, Ill., "Lietuvos", 1905. (*QYA)NN (Dalis 1.)

2417. UNITED LITHUANIAN RELIEF FUND OF AMERICA. Bendrojo Amerikos lietuvių šalpos fondo pirmieji dešimt metų, 1944-1954. [Tenth anniversary of the United Lithuanian Relief Fund of America] Medžiagą surinko ir paruošė Antanas Sodaitis. Brooklyn, N.Y., 1954. 135 p. illus. ports. HV640.5.L5U55 DLC PU ICLJF KU NN

2418. --- Bendrojo Amerikos lietuvių šalpos fondo jubiliejinis seimas, 1944-1954. [The jubilee assembly of the United Lithuanian Relief Fund of America] Brooklyn, N.Y., 1954? 1 v. (unpaged) HV640.L5U54 DLC

2419. VITKAUSKAS, Arėjas. An immigrant's story. New York, N.Y., Philosophical, 1956. 192 p. Ct275.V85A3 DLC CaAEU KyU NN NcD OCl PP PU ViU

2420. WHITE, John P. Lithuanians and the Democratic Party: a case study of nationality politics in Chicago and Cook county. Chicago, Ill., The University of Chicago, 1953. vii, 263 leaves. Thesis--University of Chicago. JS9999 ICU

2421. WOLKOVICZ, William L. From Nemunas to the Assabet; a history of the Lithuanian-Americans of Hudson, Mass. Hudson, Mass., 1966. 1 v. (unpaged) 973.075.W834 PU

2422. ŽEMELIS, Henrikas, ed. Lie-

tuvių radio klubas, 1960] 1 v. (unpaged) L 970.4.ŽE ICLJF

2423. ŽILIS, Donna. Amerikos lietuvių Romos katalikių moterų sąjunga, 1914-1964. [American Lithuanian Roman Catholic Women's Association, 1914-1964. Chicago, Ill.,
1965] 248 p. illus. 289.6.ŽI
ICLJF

2424. ŽILIUS, Jonas. Lietuviai
Amerikoje. [Lithuanians in the U-
nited States. By Jr. Jonas, pseud.]
Plymouth, Pa., Spaustuvėj S.L.A.,
1899. 174 p. 973.075.Z67 PU BM
BM(10412. ee. 38.) ICBM ICCC WaS

VI.7.d. LITHUANIANS IN OTHER
COUNTRIES

2425. ANDRIUŠIS, Pulgis, ed.
Blezdingėlės prie Torrenso; lietuvių
įsikūrimas Pietų Australijoj, 1947-
1962. [... the settlement of Lithuanians in Southern Australia, 1947-
1962] Redagavo Pulgis Andriušis ir
Vladas Radzevičius. Sodus, Mich.,
J.J. Bachunas, 1962. 72 p. illus.
DU122.L5A6 DLC ICLJF PU

2426. ATOLAS; lietuvių kultūros
fondo Australijos valdybos metraštis.
[Atolas; a yearbook of the Australian Lithuanian Cultural Fund] Melbourne, Australia, Lietuvių kultūros fondo Australijos valdyba,
1954. 240 p. illus. 891.92c.At74
PU

2427. AUSTRALIJOS LIETUVIŲ METRAŠ-
tis. [A yearbook of the Australian
Lithuanians] Sidney, Australia,
[Mūsų pastogė] 1961. 291 p. illus.,
ports. DU122.L5A93 CaAEU ICLJF PU

2428. BARONAS, Kazys, ed. Lietu-
viai Hamiltone, 1948-1954 m. [Li-
thuanians in Hamilton, 1948-1954]
Spaudai paruošė Kazys Baronas ir
Stasys J. Dalius. [Hamilton, Ont.,
KLB Hamiltono apylinkės valdybos
leidinys, 1954] 201 p. illus.
F1059.5.H2B3 DLC CaOTP CaOTU ICBM
OrU PU

2429. BACHUNAS, Juozas J. Kelionė
į Pacifiko kraštus. [A journey to
the countries in the Pacific. Chicago, Ill., Amerikos lietuvių tautinė sąjunga, 1958] 94 p. illus.
DK511.L223B2 DLC PU

2430. BENDORIUS, Antanas and Kazys
Ališauskas. Sibiro lietuviai. [Li-
thuanians in Siberia] In Lietuvių
enciklopedija. Boston, Mass., 1962.

v.27, p. 358-364. For holdings see
entry no. 216.

2431. BRIZGYS, Jurgis, ed. Lietuviai Argentinoje. [Lithuanians in
Argentina. Leidėjai: Jurgis Brizgys ir Jonas Papečkys. Rosario,
Argentina] Rosario, Lietuvių bendruomenės leidinys, 1963. [80] p.
illus., ports. F3021.L7B7 DLC

2432. --- ---; Lietuvos laisvės
kovos metai, 1918-1968. [Lithuani-
ans in Argentina. Leidėjai: Jurgis
Brizgys ir Jonas Papečkys. Rosario,
Argentina] Rosario Lietuvių bendruomenės leidinys, 1968. 213 p.
illus. F3021.L7B7 1968 DLC

2433. CHARNEY, Daniel. A Litvak
in Polyn. [A Lithuanian in Poland.
New York. N.Y., Cyco-Bicher, c1955]
140 p. port. Y B C483A NB

2434. DAUGĖLA, JUOZAS. Lietuviai
Brazilijoje. [Lithuanians in Bra-
zil] Kaunas, 1933. 426 p. OCl

2435. DAUKANTAS, Teodoras. Pietų
Brazilija ir išeivybės perspektyvos.
[Southern Brazil and the immigration
possibilities] Kaunas, V.D. Universitetas, 1931. In KUMGFD, v.6, no.
4, 1931-32, p. 5-111. See serials
consulted.

2436. GORZUCHOWSKI, Stanisław.
Ludność litewska na kresach Państwa
Polskiego. Warszawa, Nakł. Insty-
tuta Badań i Praw Narodowościowych,
1929. 22 p. 947.52.G889.2 PU

2437. HUBATSCH, Walther. Masuren
und Preussisch-Litthauen in der Na-
tionalitätenpolitik Preussens, 1870-
1920. Marburg (Lahn), Ger., Elwert,
1966. 91 p., 2 maps (in pocket)
DD338.H8 DLC CaBVaS IEN NNC OrU ViU;
also in Zeitschrift für Ostforschung
(Marburg-Lahn, Ger.), Jg.14, 1965,
p. 641-670; Jg.15, 1966, p. 1-55.
See serials consulted.

KARGE, Paul. Die Litauer-
frage in Altpreussen in geschichtlicher Beleuchtung. Königsberg in
Pr., B. Meyer, 1925. 100 p. See
entry no. 2038.

2438. KENNAN, George. Siberia and
the exile system... New York, N.Y.,
The Century Co., 1891. 2 v. fronts.
illus. maps. DK755.K34 DLC CU DN DW
ICJ MH NN NjR MdBJ OCU OCl ColW OO OU
PPA PPL PU ViU WaU

2439. KUZMICKIS, Jonas. D. Brita-
nijos lietuviai ir Marijos šventė.
[Lithuanians in Great Britain and the
Marian year. Bradford, Yorkshire,

Bradfordo Lietuvių katalikų bendruomenė, 1954] 11 p. illus. BT646.K8
DLC

2440. LIETUVIAI ARGENTINOJE. [Li-
thuanians in the Republic of Argen-
tina] Rosario, Argentina, Lietuvių
bendruomenė, 1963. 1 v. (unpaged)
illus. 970.3.LA ICLJF CtTMF

2441. LIETUVIAI ŠVEICARIJOJE;
vienkartinis apžvalgos leidinys.
[Lithuanians in Switzerland... Leidėjai: Jurgis Gliaudys, Jonas Kalvaitis ir Adomas Kantautas] Yverdon,
Switzerland, [Lietuviškojo "Židinio"
komitetas] 1945. 46 p. illus.
Mimeographed. 970.3.LŠ ICLJF

2442. LIETUVININKAI; apie vakarų
Lietuvą ir jos gyventojus devynio-
liktajame amžiuje. [Lithuanians in
East Prussia. Red. komisija: K.
Korsakas (pirm.)] Vilnius, Vaga,
1970. 658 p. illus., facsims.
(Lituanistinė biblioteka)
DD339.L5 DLC PU

2443. LITHUANIANS IN CANADA. [By]
Pr. Gaida [and others] Ottawa, Ont.;
Toronto, Ont., printed by Lights
Printing and Pub. Co., 1967. xx,
370 p. illus., maps, ports. (Canada
ethnica, 5) Bibliography: p. [350]-
361. F1035.L5L5 DLC CaAEU CaBVaU
CaBVaS CaNSHD CaOLU CaOOP CaOTP
CaOTU CtPAM CtY MH MnU InND NjP OrU
PU ICU KU NbU

2444. MARTÍNEZ BERSETCHE, José
Pedro. Lituania mártir... Ed. es-
pecial en homenaje al 1er. Congreso
de lituanos en América del Sur, re-
alizado en Buenos Aires (Rep. Argentina) durante los días 2 al 5 de
diciembre de 1960. Montevideo,
Uruguay, 1960. 32 p. port.
DK511.L2M2 DLC

2445. MATULAITIS, Kazimieras Aloyzas. Londono lietuviai; jų kovos už
save ir bažnyčią ir jų visuomeniniai
darbai. [Lithuanians in London,
Eng.] Marijampolė, Marijonų vienuolijos leidinys, 1939. 210 p.
325.2475.M39 PU ICCC ICLJF

2446. MIKELIONIS, Juozas. Bena-
miai. [The homeless] Buenos Aires,
Aregntina, [1954] 215 p. illus.
DU122.L5M5 DLC PU

2447. MIZARA, Rojus. Argentina,
ir ten gyvenantieji lietuviai. [Li-
thuanians in Argentina] Brooklyn,
N.Y., Spauda "Laisvės", 1928. [191]
p. (Amerikos lietuvių darbininkų
literatūros draugijos leidinys, nr.
25) 970.3Mi ICLJF OCl OKentU

2448. THE MISERY OF THE LITHUANIAN
refugees in Russia. For the benefit
of the Lithuanian War Relief Fund.
Lausanne, "Pro Lituania" Editorial
offices [1916] 20 p. illus.
DK511.L26M5 WU

2449. MŪSŲ KELIAI. [Our activi-
ties] Roma [Kanados lietuvių katalikų moterų draugija] 1952. 108 p.
illus. 289.6MK ICLJF

2450. RÖMERIS, Mykolas. Litwini
w Prusiech Książęcych. Kraków, Nakł.
Świata Słowiańskiego, 1911. 52 p.
947.52.R663 PU

2451. SAVICKIS, Jurgis. Skandina-
vija. In Pirmasis Nepriklausomos
Lietuvos dešimtmetis. Kaunas; London, 1955. kn.1, p. 74-77.
DK511.L27P66 1955 CaAEU DLC ICLJF PU

2452. SKARDZIS, Vikentsii Iosifovich. Litoutsy u Sovetskai Belarusi.
Mensk, Vydavetstva Belaruskai akademii navuk, 1935. 122 p. tables,
plates. (*Q p.v. 429)NN

2453. SUŽIEDĖLIS, Simas. Petrapi-
lio lietuviai. [Lithuanians in Sankt-
peterburg] In Lietuvių enciklopedija. Boston, Mass., 1960. v.22, p.
365-374. For holdings see entry no.
216.

2454. --- Rygos lietuviai. [Lithu-
anians in Riga] In Lietuvių enciklopedija. Boston, Mass., 1961. v.
25, p. 267-276. For holdings see
entry no. 216.

2455. TETZNER, Franz Oskar. Die
Litauer in Ostpreussen. In Globus
(Braunschweig), v.68, 1895, p. 368-
371. See serials consulted.

2456. TREMTINIO KELIAIS. [The
life of an exile] Bologna, [Lux]
1947. 63 p. illus. 970.3.TK ICLJF

2457. TUMAS, Juozas. Su bėgliais
ir tremtiniais. [With refugees and
exiles] Vaižgantas [pseud.] Kaunas,
Spindulio bendrovės leidinys, 1929.
270 p. (Vaižganto raštai, t.16)
DK511.L223T8 DLC

2458. ULEVIČIUS, Pranas. Pietų
Amerikos lietuviai. [Lithuanians in
South America] Vilnius, VPMLL, 1960.
251 p. illus. F2239.L7U4 DLC PU

2459. URBŠIENĖ, Marija (Mašiotaitė)
1831 ir 1863 metų sukilimo emigracijos propaganda Prancūzijoje. [The
activities of exiles of the 1831 and
1863 revolutions in France] In Karo
archyvas (Kaunas), v.6, 1935, p. 7-
30. See serials consulted.

2460. UŽ ŠVIESIĄ ATEITĮ. [For a bright future] Montreal, Que., Lietuvių literatūros draugija, 1949. 48 p. 970.4.LL ICLJF

2461. VAIŠNORA, Juozas. Lietuviai misininkai Sibire. [Lithuanian missionaries in Siberia] In LKMASD, v. 7. 21 p. See serials consulted.

2462. VALBASYS, Linas. Pusė amžiaus tropikuose. [Half a century in the tropics] Vilnius, Vaga, 1966. 223 p. illus., ports. F2639.L5V3 DLC PU

2463. VOLTER, Eduard Aleksandrovich. Die Litauer im Kreise Slonim. In LLGM, 1899. See serials consulted.

2464. ZALENSAS, K. , ed. Toli nuo tėvynės. [Far away from the homeland] Vilnius, VPMLL, 1957. 218 p. illus. F2239.L7Z3 DLC

VI.7.e. LITHUANIAN RELIGIOUS ORDERS OUTSIDE LITHUANIA

2465. BURTON, Katherine (Kurz). The History of the Congregation of Sisters of St. Casimir (1907-1957). Milwaukee, Wis., Bruce Press, 1958. 178 p. BX4486.5.B85 PU ICCC

2466. DIEVO APVEIZDAI DĖKA; Šv. Pranciškaus seserų vienuolyno istorija 1922-1932. [The History of the convent of St. Francis] Pittsburgh, Pa., Šv. Pranciškaus seserys, 1932. 96 p. illus. 289.4PR ICLJF

2467. GABRIS, Paul. The past fifty years. [Chicago, Ill.) Marian Fathers, 1964. 119 p. illus. 243.1.M337Ga PU ICLJF MH

2468. GARŠVA, Pranas. Negęstanti šviesa; marijonų veikla Amerikoje. [Everlasting light; the activities of Marian Fathers in the United States] Chicago, Ill., 1964. 351 p. illus., ports. BX3782.Z5U6 DLC CtY ICLJF PU

2469. HISTORY OF THE MONASTERY IN Kennebunkport, Me. [Franciscan Fathers, n.d.] 32 p. 289.4.PR ICLJF

2470. KONČIUS, Joseph B. Šv. Kazimiero seserų kongregacija. [The Congregation of the Sisters of St. Casimir] Mount Carmel, Pa., 1932. xxii, 329 p. illus. BX4603.M6K6 DLC ICLJF NNC PU

2471. LITHUANIAN FRANCISCAN FATHERS, Brooklyn, N.Y. Fathers of the Commissariat of St. Casimir in the U.S.A.

[Brooklyn, N.Y., 1952] [52] p. illus. 289.4PR ICLJF

2472. MACIULIONIS, Joseph R. Sister Helen, the Lithuanian flower. New York, N.Y., J.F. Wagner; London, B. Herder [c1944] xii, 210 p. plates, ports. BX4705.H453M3 DLC PPCCH

2473. MATULAITIS, Kazimieras Aloyzas. Lietuvių vienuolijų įnašas mūsų išeivijai. Pars praestita religiosorum in vita formanda lituanorum in Statibus Unitis Americae Septentrionalis. In KLMASD, v.5, 1964, p. 429-[451] See serials consulted.

2474. NEKALTAI PRADĖTOSIOS ŠV. PANOS MARIJOS SESERŲ KONGREGACIJA. [The Congregation of the Sisters of the Immaculate Conception] Putnam, Conn., Vargdienių seserų gilda [1945] 56 p. illus. 289.4.NP ICLJF

2475. [PAX ET BONUS; the silver jubilee of the Lithuanian Franciscan Sisters, Mount Providence. Pittsburgh, Pa., 1947] 1 v. (unpaged) illus. 289.4PR ICLJF

2476. SUŽIEDĖLIS, Simas. Jėzaus Nukryžiuotojo Seserų Kongregacija. [Order of the Sisters of Crucified Jesus] Brockton, Mass., 1950. 303 p. illus. 4BX Cath. 416 DLC ICLJF MB NN OCl PU

VI.7.f. PARISHES OUTSIDE LITHUANIA

2477. ABELKIS, Povilas. Visų Šventųjų parapija Roselande, 1906-1956. [All Saints parish of Roseland, 1906-1956] Chicago, Ill., Draugas, 1956. 310 p. BX4603.C5A4 PU DLC ICHi DCU ICLJF

2478. BROOKLYN, N.Y. ST.GEORGE'S CHURCH. Atmintis jubiliejų, 1909-1914-1939, 30 metų nuo parapijos įsteigimo, 25 metai bažnyčios pastatymo. Šv. Jurgio bažnyčia, Brooklyn, N.Y., 1939. 1 v. (unpaged) illus., ports. BX4603.B8S57 DLC ICLJF NN

2479. CICERO, ILL. ST. ANTHONY'S PARISH. Auksinis jubiliejus; Šv. Antano parapija, Cicero, Ill., 1911-1961. [Golden jubilee; St. Anthony Parish. Į anglų kalbą tekstą vertė St. Gaučas, lietuviškas tekstas ir redakcija A. Barono. Chicago, Ill., 1961] 235 p. illus., ports. BX1418.C46C5 DLC ICLJF PU

2480. DIEVO APVAIZDOS PARAPIJA, 1900-1925. [The Providence of God, a Chicago Parish. Chicago, Ill.,

1925?] 80 p. illus. 289.5.DA
ICLJF

2481. ---, 1900-1950. [The Providence of God, a Chicago Parish.
Chicago, Ill., 1950?] 1 v. (unpaged)
illus. 289.5.DA ICLJF

2482. GARLIAUSKAS, Stasys, ed.
Šv. Antano lietuvių Romos-katalikų
parapija. Auksinio jubiliejaus su-
kaktuvinis leidinys, 1920-1970.
[Golden jubilee of Saint Anthony's
Lithuanian Roman Catholic Parish]
Detroit, Mich., [1971] 127 p.
BX4603.D43G3 PU

2483. GLIAUDYS, Jurgis. Šv. Kazi-
miero parapija Los Angeles mieste;
istoriniai bruožai, 1941-1966. [A
Historical outline of Saint Casimir
Parish, Los Angeles, Calif. By
Jurgis Gliauda, pseud.] Brooklyn,
N.Y., 1966. 231 p. illus., ports.
BX1418.L7G55 DLC ICLJF WH1 WU

2484. GOLDEN JUBILEE OF SAINT
Casimir Lithuanian Roman Catholic
Parish, Sioux City, Iowa, 1915-1965.
[Sioux City, Iowa, 1965] 217 p.
illus. 289.5.KA ICLJF

2485. KUČAS, Antanas. Shenandoah
lietuvių Šv. Jurgio parapija; dei-
mantiniam jubiliejui prisiminti,
1891-1966. [Diamond jubilee of St.
George Parish, Shenandoah, Pa.]
Brooklyn, N.Y., 1968. 316 p. illus.,
ports. Lithuanian and English.
BX4603.S7S3 DLC CaOONL PU WU

2486. --- Šv. Petro lietuvių para-
pija South Bostone. The history of
St. Peter's Lithuanian Parish, South
Boston, 1904-1954. Adapted from the
Lithuanian text by Albert J. Contons.
Boston, Mass., 1956. 303 p. illus.,
ports. BX4603.B7S53 DLC ICLJF PU

2487. LIETUVIU KATALIKŲ ŠV. JURGIO
parapija, Shenandoah, Pa., 1891-1941.
[Golden jubilee of St. George Parish,
Shenandoah, Pa.] Shenandoah, Pa.,
1942. 65 p. illus. 973.075.L626
PU ICLJF

2488. LIETUVIŲ TAUTINIŲ KAPINIŲ
50 metų sukaktis, 1911-1961. [Golden
jubilee of the Lithuanian National
Cemetery, 1911-1961] Willow Springs,
Ill., 1961. 1 v. (unpaged)
970.7.TK ICLJF

2489. LIETUVIŲ TAUTIŠKOS KAPINĖS,
1911-1936. [The Lithuanian National
Cemetery, 1911-1936] Chicago, Ill.,
1938. 52 p. illus. 970.7.TK
ICLJF

2490. LINKUS, Anicetas M., ed. Šv.

Kryžiaus lietuvių parapijos 50 metų
istoriniai bruožai. Golden jubilee
of Holy Cross Lithuanian Roman Catholic Parish, Chicago, Ill., 1904-
1954. [Chicago, Ill., 1954] 154 p.
illus., ports. BX4603.C5H6 DLC PU

2491. NEKALTO PRASIDĖJIMO BAŽNYČIA,
East St. Louis, Ill. [The Church of
the Immaculate Conception, East St.
Louis] East St. Louis, Ill., 1956.
128 p. illus. 289.5.NP ICLJF

2492. NEKALTO PRASIDĖJIMO PARAPIJA,
Chicago, Ill., 1914-1964. [The Pa-
rish of the Immaculate Conception,
Chicago, Ill., 1914-1964. Chicago,
Ill., 1964] 124 p. illus.
289.5.NP ICLJF

2493. PAMINKLINĖ MARIJOS KOPLYČIA
Nekalto Prasidėjimo vienuolyne, Putnam, Conn. [The Chapel of the Immaculate Conception in its Convent
at Putnam, Conn. Putnam, Conn., Immaculata, 1955? 32 p.] illus.,
ports. Lithuanian and English.
BX4500.6.Z9P8 DLC

2494. 50 METŲ PARAPIJOS GYVENIME;
Nekalto Prasidėjimo lietuvių parapijos istoriniai metmens. [Fifty years
of the Parish of the Immaculate Con-
ception] Cambridge, Mass., 1960.
100 p. illus. 289.5.NP ICLJF

2495. PITTSTON, PA. ST. MARY'S AS-
SUMPTION CHURCH. St. Mary's Assump-
tion Church, Pittston, Pennsylvania;
1863-1963, one hundred years. New
York, N.Y., Custombook, 1963. 1 v.
(unpaged) illus. BX4603.P56S2 DLC

2496. PRISIKĖLIMO PARAPIJOS TORONIE
leidinys, 1956. [The Resurrection
Parish, Toronto, Ont., 1956. Toronto, Ont.] 1956. 86 p. illus.
289.5.PR ICLJF

2497. PRISIKĖLIMO PARAPIJOS TORONTE
pirmasis dešimtmetis, 1953-1963.
[The first decade of the Parish of
the Resurrection in Toronto, 1953-
1963] Toronto, Ont., 1963. 184 p.
illus. 289.5.PR ICLJF

2498. PRISIKĖLIMO PARAPIJOS TORONTE,
1960 metų apžvalga. [A report for
1960 of the Parish of the Resurrection, Toronto] Toronto, Ont., 1961.
126 p. illus. 289.5.PR ICLJF

2499. RAILA, Stanislaus. Šv. Kazimiero parapijos auksinis jubiliejus,
1893-1943. [Golden jubilee of the
Parish of St. Casimir, 1893-1943.
Philadelphia, Pa., 1945] 140 p.
illus., ports. BX4603.P52S286 DLC PU

2500. ŠAUČIŪNAS, Jonas. Šv. Mari-

jos parapijos auksinio jubiliejaus
atsiminti. St. Mary's Annuncation
Lithuanian R.C. Parish golden jubilee remembrance, 1902-1952. Kingston, Pa., 1952. 125 p. BX4603.
K55S3 PU

2501. SOPULINGOSIOS DIEVO MOTINOS
lietuvių R. katalikų parapijos 40
metų sukaktis, 1916-1956. [The
fortieth anniversary of the Parish
of the Mother of Sorrow, 1916-1956.
Parašė Juozas Mėlynis. Kearny-
Harrison, N.J.] 1956. 120 p. illus. 289.5.SD ICLJF

2502. SUŽIEDĖLIS, Simas. Šv.
Pranciškaus lietuvių parapija. The
history of St. Francis' Lithuanian
Parish. Lawrence, Mass., 1953.
416 p. illus. English and Lithuanian. BX4603.L3S3 DLC CtPAM DCU
MB MH ICN NN NjP PU

2503. ŠV. JUOZAPO LIETUVIU PARAPI-
JA, Mahanoy City, Pa., 1888-1923.
[St. Joseph's Lithuanian Parish, Ma-
hanoy City, 1888-1923. Mahanoy City,
Pa., 1923] 27 p. illus. 289.5.JU
ICLJF

2504. ŠVENTO JUOZAPO LIETUVIŲ PA-
RAPIJOS, Waterbury, Conn., istorija
ir kiti įvairumai. [History of St.
Joseph's Lithuanian Parish, Waterbury, Conn. Brooklyn, N.Y., Garso
spaustuvė, 1919.] 48 p. illus.
289.5.Ju ICLJF

2505. ŠV. JUOZAPO PARAPIJA, Waterbury, Conn., 1894-1944. [Golden jubilee of the Parish of St. Joseph.
Waterbury, Conn., 1944?] 1 v. (unpaged) illus. 289.5.JU ICLJF

2506. ŠV. KAZIMIERO LIETUVIU BAŽ-
NYČIA, [Worcester, Mass.] 1894-1921.
[St. Casimir's Lithuanian Church,
1894-1921] Worcester, Mass., 1921.
55 p. illus. 289.5.KA ICLJF

2507. ŠV. KAZIMIERO LIETUVIŲ PARA-
PIJA, Amsterdam, N.Y., 1904-1954.
[Golden jubilee of St. Casimir Lithuanian Parish, Amsterdam, N.Y., 1904-
1954. n.p., 1954] 80 p. illus.
289.5.KA ICLJF

2508. ŠV. KAZIMIERO LIETUVIU PARA-
PIJA, Pittsburgh, Pa., 1893-1943.
[Golden jubilee of St. Casimir Lithuanian Parish, Pittsburgh, Pa.,
1893-1942. Pittsburgh, Pa., 1943]
104 p. illus. 289.5.KA ICLJF

2509. ŠV. KAZIMIERO LIETUVIŲ ROMOS
katalikų parapija; pirmojo dešimtmečio istorija. St. Casimir's Lithuanian Roman Catholic Parish, 1959-
1969. Edited by J. Gutauskas and

others] Delhi, Ont., [1970] 114 p.
BX4605.D43S33 PU

2510. ŠV. KAZIMIERO LIETUVIŲ PA-
RAPIJA, Sioux City, Iowa, 1916-1926.
[St. Casimir's Lithuanian Parish,
Sioux City, 1916-1926. Sioux City,
Iowa, 1926] 55 p. illus. 289.5.
KA ICLJF

2511. ŠVENTO KAZIMIERO PARAPIJOS,
Worcester, Mass., 50 metų sukaktuvės, 1894-1944. [Golden jubilee of
St. Casimir's Parish, Worcester,
1894-1944. Worcester, Mass., 1944]
111 p. illus. 289.5.KA ICLJF

2512. ŠV. KRYŽIAUS LIETUVIŲ PARA-
PIJOS [Čikagoje] 50 metų istoriniai
bruožai. [The history of the Holy
Cross Parish in Chicago... Redaktoriai Kazimieras Barkauskas ir Antanas Bendžiūnas. Chicago, Ill., Draugo spaustuvė] 1954. 154 p. illus.
289.5.ŠK ICLJF

2513. ŠV. KRYŽIAUS PARAPIAJA, DAY-
ton, Ohio, 1914-1964. [Holy Cross
Parish, Dayton, 1914-1964. Dayton,
Ohio, 1964?] 140 p. illus.
289.5.ŠK ICLJF

2514. ŠV. PRANCIŠKAUS LIETUVIŲ PA-
RAPIJA, East Chicago, Ind., 1913-
1963. [Golden jubilee of St. Francis
Lithuanian Parish, East Chicago,
1913-1963. Chicago, Ill., 1963] 54
p. illus. 289.5.PR ICLJF

2515. ŠV. PRANCIŠKAUS LIETUVIU PA-
RAPIJA [Lawrence, Mass.] 1903-1933.
[St. Francis' Lithuanian Parish,
Lawrence, Mass., 1903-1933. n.p.,
1933] 1 v. (unpaged) illus.
289.5.PR ICLJF

2516. [ŠV. VINCENTO PARAPIJA],
SPRINGFIELD, ILL., 1906-1956. [St.
Vincent's Parish, Springfield, Ill.,
1906-1956. n.p., 1956] 60 p.
illus. 289.5.VI ICLJF

2517. WESTFIELD, MASS., LIETUVIŲ
kolonijos istorija paminėjimui dešimts metų parapijos įsteigimo sukaktuvių, 1915-1925. [The Lithuanians
of Westfield, Mass., and the anniversary of the Parish, 1915-1925] So.
Boston, Darbininko spauda, 1925. 62
p. illus. 289.5.KA ICLJF

VII. THE STATE
VII.1. GENERAL STUDIES

2518. BARDACH, Juliusz. Studia z
ustroju i prawa Wielkiego Księstwa
Litewskiego XIV-XVII w. Warszawa,

Państwowe Wydawn. Naukowe, 1970.
401 p. AS262.B47A14 nr. 13 PU
CaOTU

2519. BATILLIAT, René. Origine
et développement des institutions
politiques en Lithuanie. Lille;
Paris, Mercure Universal, 1932.
268 p. fold. map Thèse--Université
de Paris, Faculté de droit.
JN6745.A2B3 CU BM CtY ICU MH NN NNC

2520. BIRŽIŠKA, Vaclovas. Provisional governments in Lithuanian
history. In Lituanus (Brooklyn,
N.Y.), v.8, no.1-2, 1962, p. 3-10.
See serials consulted.

2521. CZERMAK, Wiktor. Perlamen-
taryzm litewski przed unią lubelską.
In Polska Akademia Uniejętności,
Kraków. Sprawozdania z czynności i
posedzień, v.6, 1901, no.8, p. 10-
16. See serials consulted.

2522. DOVNAR-ZAPOL'SKII, Mitrofan
Viktorovich. Gosudarstvennoe khoziaistvo Velikago Kniazhestva Litovskago pri IAgellonakh. Kiev, Universitet, 1901. viii, 807 p.
DK511.L2D7 ICU BM IU NNC

2523. EHRENKREUTZ, Stefan, ed.
Księga pamiątkowa ku uczczeniu
czterechsetnej rocznicy wydania
pierwszego Statutu Litewskiego.
Wilno, Nakł. Tow. Przyjaciół Nauk;
skł. gł. w Księg. Św. Wojciecha,
1935. 362 p. facsims. (Rozprawy
Wydziału III Towarzystwa Przyjacól
Nauk w Wilnie, t.8) Contents.--
Kutrzeba, S. Charakter i wartość
unji polsko-litewskiej.--Adamus, J.
Państwo Litewskie w latach 1386-
1398-- Namysłowski, W. Pozasądowe
organy porzadku prawnego w krajach
południowo-słowiańskich i polsko-
litewskich.--Bossowski, F. Nowela
Justynjana 115.--Koranyi, K. O
niektórych postaniowieniach karnych
Statutu Litewskiego z r. 1529.--
Ptaszycki, S. Pierwsze wydanie
trzeciego Statutu Litewskiego i jego
przeróbki.--Łowmiański, H. Uwagi w
sprawie podłoża społecznego i gospo-
darczego unji jagiellońskiej.--Tau-
benschlag, R. Pozew w I. i II.
Statucie Litewskim.--Hejnosz, W.
Kilka uwag o "niewoli" w I. Statucie
Litewskim. DLC-L CU CtY InU MH NN
PU

2524. GRAHAM, Malbone Watson. New
governments of Eastern Europe. New
York, N.Y., H. Holt and Co., [c1927]
ix, 826 p. maps, fold diagrs.
D443.G56 DLC CaAEU CaBVaU CaOHM CaOKQ
CaOLU CaOOP CaOTU CaQMM CLU CSt CU
CtY CoU GU HU IaU InU ICN InNd IU MH
MnU NIC NN NjP NSyU NBuU NcD NcU OCl

OClW OrU PPiU PU RPB TxHU ViU

2525. HALECKI, Oskar. Litwa, Ruś
i Żmudź jako części składowe Wielkiego Księstwa Litewskiego. In Polska Akademia Umiejętności, Kraków.
Wydział Historyczno-Filozoficzny.
Rozprawy, v.59, 1916, p. 214-254.
See serials consulted.

2526. --- Wcielenie i wznowienie
państwa litewskiego przez Polskę,
1386-1401. In Przegląd Historyczny
(Warszawa), v.21, 1917-1918, p. 1-77.
See serials consulted.

2527. HELLMANN, Manfred. Zu den
Anfängen des litauischen Staates.
In Jahrbücher für Geschichte Osteuropas (Breslau, Ger.), v.4, no.2,
1956, p. 159-165. See serials consulted.

2528. IVINSKIS, Zenonas. Lietuvos
valstybingumo išplėtimas slavų erd-
vėje. [The expansion of the Lithuanian statehood into the Slavic ter-
ritories] In Tautos praeitis (Chicago, Ill.), v.1, no.4, 1960, p. 501-
520. See serials consulted.

2529. KAMIENECKI, Witold. Wpływy
zakonne na ustrój Litewski. In
Przegląd Historyczny (Warszawa), v.
5, 1925, p. 160-186. See serials
consulted.

2530. KOŚCIAŁKOWSKI, Stanisław.
Rzeczpospolita obojga narodów. In
Alma Mater Vilensis (Londyn), v.3,
1953, p. 68-99. See serials consulted.

2531. LAPPO, Ivan Ivanovich. Litovsko-russkoe gosudarstvo v sostavie Riechi-Pospolitoi. Praga, 1929.
p. 63-78. (Prague. Russkii svobod-
nyi universitet. Nauchnye trudy,
t.2) AS142.P942 t.2 DLC MH MiU NNC

2532. LEONTOVICH, Fedor Ivanovich.
Litovskie gospodari i tsentral'nye
organy upravleniia do i posle Liublinskoi unii. In IUridicheskiia zapiski (IAroslavl'. Demidovskii iuri-
dicheskii litsei), no.1, 1908, p.
11-60. NN MH-L

2533. LITHUANIA. UŽSIENIŲ REIKALŲ
MINISTERIJA. Formation de Gouvernement provisoire lithuanien. Mémoire
présenté aux représentants des puis-
sances de L'Entente en Suisse, en
décembre 1918. 11 p. (Délégation
de la Lithuanie à la Conférence de
la Paix. pt., IV: 4) Pam. D643.
A7DP5L7 CSt-H

2534. --- Lietuvos valstybės kūri-
mas ligi vyriausybei susidarius nuo

1915 ligi 1918 m. lapkričio měn. 11
d. [The genesis of the Lithuanian
state until the formation of the
Government from 1915 until 1918]
Vilnius, 1918. 23 p. 947.52.L715
PU

2535. LITOVSKO-RUSSKOE GOSUDARSTVO
i Pol'sha do Khmel'nichiny. In Akademiia nauk SSSR. Istoriko-arkheograficheskii institut. Trudy (Moskva), v.4, 1933, p. 143-180. DLC
CU NN

2536. LIUBAVSKII, Matvei Kuz'mich.
Ocherk istorii Litovsko-russkago
gosudarstva do Liublinskoi unii
vkliuchitel'no. S prilozheniem teksta khartii, vydanykh Velikomu
Kniazhestvu Litovskomu i ego oblas-
tiam. Moskva, Izd. Imp. Obshchestva
istorii i drevnostei rossiiskikh,
1910. 376, ii p. DK511.L23L5 DLC
CaAEU CaBVaU CaOLU CaOTU CaOWtU
CaQMM FU GU HU IaU InU InNd IEN MH
MnU NN NIC NNC NBuU NcD NcU NjP OCl
OClW OrU PU TxU WU

2537. --- ---. Izd. 2-oe. [Mosk-
va] Moskovskaia khudozhestvennaia
pechatiia, 1915. [4], 401, iii p.
947.5.L740 1915 IU CLU CtY KU

2538. --- ---. Moskva, Izd. Imp.
Obshchestva istorii i drevnostei
rossiiskikh, 1910; The Hague, Europe
Printing, 1966. 376, ii p. (Rus-
sian reprint series, no.14) DK511.
L23L5 1910b DLC CtY ICU IEN MH NjR
PPiU ScU

2539. ŁOWMIAŃSKI, Henryk. Studia
nad początkami społeczeństwa i pań-
stwa litewskiego. Wilno, Nakł.
Tow. Przyjaciół Nauk, 1931-32. 2 v.
(Towarzystwo Przyjaciół Nauk w Wil-
nie. Wydział III. Rozprawy, t.5-6)
DK511.L23L58 DLC CU CtY ICU KU MH
MiU NN NNC PU

2540. MAŠALAITIS, V. "Liaudies
vyriausybės" sudarymo kai kurios
aplinkybės. [Some particulars
about the formation of the "People's
Government" in Lithuania. By V.
Raistas, pseud.] In Lietuva (New
York, N.Y.), no.4, 1953, p. 166-169.
See serials consulted.

2541. PROCHASKA, Antoni. Nowsze
poglądy na ustrój wewnętrzny starej
Litwy. In Przegląd Historyczny
(Warszawa), v.15, no.1, 1912, p. 30-
54. See serials consulted.

2542. RHODE, Gotthold. Stände und
Königtum in Polen-Litauen und Böhmen-
Mähren. In Jahrbücher für Geschichte
Osteuropas (Breslau, Ger.), v.12, no.
2, 1964, p. 220-246. See serials

consulted.

2543. RUTENBERG, Gregor. Anerken-
nung des litauischen Staates. [Von]
G. Rutenbergas. In Zeitschrift für
ausländisches öffentliches Recht und
Völkerrecht (Berlin), 1929, p. 336-
364. See serials consulted.

2544. ŠAPOKA, Adolfas. Bajoriško-
ji demokratija. [The noblemen's de-
mocracy] In Lietuvos praeitis (Kaunas), v.1, no.2, 1941, p. 469-540.
See serials consulted.

2545. TIBAL, André. Problèmes
politiques contemporains de l'Europe
orientale. Conférence de M. le pro-
fesseur André Tibal, novembre 1928-
juin 1929. Paris, 1930. 1 v. (various pagings) At head of title:
Centre européen de la Dotation Carnegie pour la paix international.
342.4.T43 p IU PU

2546. VILEIŠIS, Jonas. Werdegang
und Selbstverwaltung Litauens. In
Zeitschrift für Kommunalwirtschaft
(Oldenburg, Ger.), v.23, no.13-14,
1933, p.515-523. See serials consul
sulted.

2547. WEDEL, Hasso von. Die Lage
der Diktatur in Litauen. In Preussische Jahrbücher (Berlin), v.224,
1931, p.297-302. See serials consulted.

VII.2. SYMBOLISM, COAT-OF-ARMS,
SEALS, ETC.

2548. DOBUŽINSKIS, Mstislav V.
Apie Vytauto ženklą. [Vytautas' in-
signia] In Praeitis (Kaunas), v.2,
1933, p.245-251. See serials consulted.

2549. --- Vytis; Didžiosios Lietuvos kunigaikštystės valstybinio erbo
istorinių varijantų bruožai, XIV-XVI
amž. [Vytis; the historical outline
of the state coat-of-arms of the
Grand Duchy of Lithuania] Kaunas,
Lietuvos istorijos draugija, 1933.
56 p. illus. 947.52.D654 PU CtY

2550. GUMOWSKI, Marian. Pieczęcie
książąt Litewskich. In Ateneum Wileński (Wilno), v.7, no.1-2, 1930,
p.684-725. See serials consulted.

2551. ILGŪNAS, Jonas. Vyčio kilmė.
[The origin of the coat-of-arms of
Lithuania] In Mūsų žinynas (Kaunas)
v.15, no.44, 1928, p.89-110. See
serials consulted.

137

2552. KARYS, Jonas.K. Lietuvių
tautiniai ženklai. [Lithuanian national insignias] In His Senovės
lietuvių pinigai. Putnam, Conn.,
1959. p. 192-236. CJ3028.L5K3 DLC
CtPAM CtTMF CaOONL PU

2553. VOSSBERG, Friedrich August.
Siegel des Mittelalters von Polen,
Litauen, Schlesien, Pommern und
Preussen. Berlin; Stargardt, 1854.
46 p. illus. BM(7709. k. 2.)

VII.3. GOVERNMENT

VII.3.a. EXECUTIVE GOVERNMENT

2554. GERUTIS, Albertas. Nepriklausomosios Lietuvos Ministrų kabinetai.
[The Council of the State of Independent Lithuania] In Lietuvių enciklopedija. Boston, Mass., 1968. v.15,
p.353-356. For holdings see entry
no.216.

2555. --- Die staatrechtliche Stel-
lung des Staatshauptes in Litauen,
Lettland und Estland. Kaunas, "Vil-
nius," 1934. 112 p. Inaug.-Diss.--
University of Bern, Switzerland.
FL6.G3846s 1934 CtY DLC ICRL

2556. LITHUANIAN INFORMATION BU-
REAU. La formation et la caractère
du Conseil d'État de Lituanie (Taryba) [Paris, 1919?] 7 p. (Délégation de Lituanie à la Conférence de
la Paix. [pt.], IV:2 D643.A7.DP5L7
CSt-H

2557. ŠIDLAUSKAS, Kazys. Lietuvos
prezidentų konstitucinės galios.
[The constitutionalpowers of the presidents of Lithuania] In Aidai (Kennebunkport, Me.), no.4(90), 1956,p.
145-156. See serials consulted.

2558. YČAS, Martynas. Lietuvos vyriausybės sudarymo etapai ir jos pirmieji žingsniai. [The stages of formation and the first steps of the government of Lithuania] In Pirmasis
Nepriklausomos Lietuvos dešimtmetis.
London, 1955. Kn,1, p. 78-127.
DK511.L27P66 1955 CaAEU DLC CLJF PU

VII.3.b. LEGISLATIVE GOVERNMENT. ITS
HISTORY AND LEGISLATION

2559. ANTROJI LIETUVOS VALSTYBĖS
konferencija. [Second conference of
the Lithuanian State] Kaunas, Šviesos spaustuvė, 1919. 72 p.

947.52.An89 PU

2560. CADZOW, John F. Material
germaine to Lithuania contained in
the stenographic reports of the first and second Dumas. In Lituanus
(Chicago, Ill.), v.17, no.2, 1971,
p.55-68. See serials consulted.

2561. DOVNAR'-ZAPOL'SKII, Mitrofan
Viktorovich. Spornye voprosy po istorii litovsko-russkago seima. In
ZMNP, Ch.337, no.10, 1901, p. 454-
498. See serials consulted.

2562. HALECKI, Oskar. Sejm obozo-
wy szlachty litewskiej pod Witebs-
kiem 1562 i jego petycja o unię z
Polską. In Przegląd Historyczny
(Warszawa), v.18, 1914, p. 320-352.
See serials consulted.

2563. ILOVAISKII, Dmitrii Ivanovich
Grodnenskii seim 1793 goda; posled-
nii seim Riechi-Pospolitoi. Moskva,
Tip. Katko, 1870. 350 p.
947.52.I185 PU BM(9476. f. 19.)

2564. JANULAITIS, Augustinas. Lietuvos bajorai ir jų seimeliai XIX a.
1795-1863. [The Lithuanian noblemen
and their diets in the nineteenth
century, 1795-1863] Kaunas, 1936.
xx, 629 p. (Kaunas. Universitetas.
Teisių fakultetas. Darbai, t.8, kn.
2) DK511.L25J354 1936 CaAEU CU
CtTMF DLC ICU NN NNC

2565. JUOZAPAVIČIUS, Antanas. Vivos voco! Sprawdzenia wyborcy do
4-tej Dumy. [By] Antoni Józefowicz.
[pseud.] Wilna, J. Zawadzki, 1913.
68 p. 947.52.J975 PU

2566. KALINKA, Walerian. Konstytucya trzeciego maja, kwiecień-czer-
wiec 1791. Lwów, Nakł. Księg. Gey-
fartha i Czajkowskiego, 1888. 115 p.
JN6753.K34 1791 DLC

2567. --- Sejm czteroletni. 2. wydanie. Lwów, Seyfarth, 1881. 2 v.
943.802K14s NcU

2568. --- --- Wyd. 4. W Krakowie,
Nakł. Księg. Społki Wydawniczej Pol-
skiej, 1895-1896. 5 v. DK434.K27
DLC CaAEU(1-2) MnU(2) NN(1-3) NNC

2569. --- Der vierjährige polnische Reichstag, 1788 bis 1791. Berlin, E.S. Mittler und Sohn, 1896-98.
2 v. DK434.K3 DLC ICU MH NN OCl PU
ViU

2570. KONCZYŃSKA, Wanda. Rejtan,
Korsak i Bohuszewicz na sejmie 1773
roku; materjały do monografji posła
nowogródzkiego. Wilno, 1935. 43 p.
DK434.8.R4K65 DLC NN

2571. KONFEDERACYA GENERALNA ORDI-
num regni, et Magni Ducatus Lithuanie, po niedoszlej Konwokacyey główney warszawskiey umowiona roku Pańskiego 1696 dnia 29. miesiąca sierpnia. [n.p., 1696] 24 p. DLC-L

2572. KONOPCZYŃSKI, Władysław.
Geneza liberum veto. In Przegląd
Historyczny (Warszawa), v.1, 1905.
See serials consulted.

2573. --- Liberum veto; étude sur
le développment du principe majori-
taire. Paris, Champion, 1930. 297
p. diagrs. (Institut d'études
slaves de l'Universitéde Paris.
Bibliotèque Polonaise, 2) JC273.K6
DLC CaAEU NN

2574. --- Sejm Grodzieński 1752
roku. Lwów, Drukarnia Ludowa, 1907.
118 p. Offprint from Kwartalnik
Historychny, v.20, 1907. DK432.5.K6
DLC MH NN

2575. KOWALEŃKO, Władysław. Geneza udziału stołecznego miasta Wilna w sejmach Rzeczypospolitej. In
Ateneum Wileńskie (Wilno), v.3, 1925-
1926, p.327-373; v.4, 1927, p.79-137.
See serials conseuled.

2576. LAPPO, Ivan Ivanovich. Iš
Vyriausiųjų Lietuvos suvažiavimų istorijos XVI amž. 1577 metų suvažiavimas Rytų Vilkaviškyje. Contribution à l'histoire des assemblées de
la Noblesse Lithuannienne au XVI
siècle. Réunion de Volkovysk de
1577. Kaunas, 1932. 43 p. (Kaunas.
Universitetas. Teisės mokslų biblioteka, nr. 16) BM(Ac. 1157. f/4.)
CU MH NN

2577. LEONAS, Petras. Lietuvių
atstovų t-ton Valstybės Dumon rinki-
mams pasibaigus. [After the election of Lithuanian candidates to the
fourth Duma (Parliament)] Kaunas,
1913. 36 p. 947.5.T4 CtTMF

2578. LEONTOVICH, Fedor Ivanovich.
Rada velikikh kniazei litovskih. In
Russia. Ministerstvo narodnogo prosveshcheniia. Zhurnal (Sanktpeterburg), Novaia seriia, Ch.11, 1907,
no9, p.122-178; no.10, p.273-331.
See serials consulted.

2579. LIUBAVSKII, Matvei Kuz'mich.
Litovsko-russkii seim; opyt po isto-
rii uchrezdeniia v sviazi s vnutren-
nim stroem i vniezhneiu zhizn'iu go-
sudarstva. Moskva, Izd. Imp. Ob-va
istorii i drevnostei rossiiskikh pri
Moskovskom universitetie, 1900. 2 v.
K.L7833 1900a OrU CaBVaU CaOTU CLU
CtY IU ICU KU MnU NIC NN NNC NjP PU
PPiU ViU

2580. --- Novye trudy po istorii
litovsko-russkago seima. In Russia.
Ministerstvo narodnago prosveshcheniia. Zhurnal (Sanktpeterburg),1903,
ch.335, no.2, p.379-393; ch.336, no.
3, p.121-167. See serials consulted.

2581. MAKSIMEIKO, Nikolai Alekseevich. Seimy litovsko-russkago gosudarstva do Liublinskoi unii 1569 g.
Kharkov, 1902. iv, 205 p.
947.5.M289 NNC BM(9455. ee. 14.)

2582. MALINOVSKII, Ioannikii Alekseevich. Rada velikago kniazhestva
Litovskago v sviazi s Boiarskoi Du-
moi drevnei Rossii. Tomsk, Tipo-lit.
Sibirsk. t-va pechatn. diela, 1903-
1912. 2 pts. JN6745.A71M2 DLC BM
NN(ch.2, vyp.2)

2583. --- Sbornik materialov otno-
siashchikhsia k istorii Panov- Rady
Velikago Kniazhestva Litovskago.
Tomsk, Tipo-litografiia P.I. Makushi-
na, 1901. iv, xx, 508 p.
JN6745.A71M2 DLC(ch.2) BM(9455.g.16)
NN(ch.2) NNC

2584. OCHMAN, Stefania. Sejmy lat
1615-1616. Wrocław, Zakład Narod.
im. Ossolińskich, 1970. 235 p. (Prace Wrocławskiego Towarzystwa Naukowego. Seria a, nr.141) AS262.W7 nr.
141 PU

2585. POLAND. KONFEDERACJA GENE-
RALNA, WARSZAWA, 1648. Confederacya
Generalna Omnivm Ordinvm Regni, et
Magni Dvcat: Lith. na Conwokacyey
główney Warszawskiey, uchwaloną roku
pańskiego M.D.C. XLVII, dnia 16. miesiąca lipca. W Krakowie, w druk.
wdowy A. Piotrkowczyka, 1648. 32 p.
J399.H85 DLC

2586. POLAND. KONFEDERACJA GENE-
RALNA, WARSAW, 1764. Confederacya
Generalna Omnivm Regni, et Magni Ducatus Lithvaniae na Konwokacyi głów-
nej Warszawskiej uchwaloną dnia siod-
mego miesiąca maja, ro[k]u Pańskiego
tysiącznego siedmsetnego sześćdzie-
siątego czwartego. W Warszawie, w
drukarni Rzeczypospolitey w Collegium
Xięży Scholarum Piarum [1764] 1 v.
(various pagings) Rare Book Room Osh
12+764P CtY DLC KU

2587. PTASZYCKI, Staniław. Konfederacja Warszawska roku 1573 w trzecim Statucie Litewskim. In Ehrenkreutz, Stefan, ed. Księga pamiątkowa ku uczczeniu czterechsetnej
rocznicy wydania pierwszego Statutu
Litewskiego... Wilno, 1935. p. 185-
213. DLC-L CU CtY InU MH NN PU

2588. RUSSIA. LAWS, STATUTES, ETC.
Cesorystés seimo įsteigimas; viršiau-

sias manifestas. [The manifest of
the founding of the Duma] Vilnius,
1905. 67 p. JN6556.A35 1971 PU

2589. SANCITA WIELKIEGO XIĘSTWA LI-
tewskiego, na Walnej Radzie Warszawskiej die 4 Februarii 1710 złożone y
postanowione. In Poland. Sejm. Po-
parcie Generalney Sandomirskiey Con-
federacyey... pt.2. 1710. 8 p.
BM(9475. g. 3.)

2590. ŠAPOKA, Adolfas. Atsakingieji Lietuvos politikos vadai reformų
seimo metu. [The responsible Lithuanian statesmen during the reforms
of the diet] In KUHMF. Senově, v.2,
1936, p. 61-173. See serials consulted.

2591. --- Die Sondertagungen der
litauischen Stände nach der Lubliner
Union von 1569. In Tartu. Ülikool.
Õpetatud eesti selts. Toimitused,
v.30, pt.2, 1938, p. 700-716. See
serials consulted.

2592. SMOLEŃSKI, Władysław. Konfederacja Targowicka. Kraków, skł. gł.
w Księg. G. Gebethnera, 1903. 463 p.
JN753 1793 S6 DLC CtY MH NN NNC

2593. --- Ostatni rok Sejmu Wielkiego. Wyd. 2. niezmienione. Kraków, Nakł. G. Gebethnera, 1897. 481
p. DK434.S63 1897 DLC MH NN

2594. SOBIESKI, Wacław. Pamiętny
Sejm 1606. Warszawa, Nakł. Gebethne-
ra i Wolffa, 1913. 111, 253 p.
JN6763.S6 DLC ICU MH NN OU

2595. SVFFRAGIA WOIEWODZTW Y ZIEM
Koronnych, y W. X. Litewskiego, zgod-
nie na Naiaśnieyszego Władysława Zyg-
munta, obranego króla... [Kraków,
Druk. A Piotrkowczyka, 1633] [30] p.
DLC-L

2596. SVFFRAGIA WOIEWODZTW Y ZIEM
Koronnych y W. X. Litewskiego. Zgod-
nie na Nayiaśnieyszego Augusta II.
obranego króla... [n.p.] 1697. 87 p.
DLC-L

2597. WĄSICKI, Jan. Konfederacja
Targowicka i ostatni Sejm Rzeczpospo-
litey 1793 roku. Poznań, Nakł. Poznańskiego Tow. Przyjaciół Nauk, 1952.
194 p. (Studia nad historią prawa
polskiego, t.21, zesz.2) Summary in
French. Bibliography: p. 166-169.
JN6753.W3 1793 DLC

2598. WEGNER, Leon. Dzieje dnia
3 i 5 Maja 1791. Poznań, Nakł. Tow.
Prszyjaciół Nauk , 1865. 409 p.
Oshl2.865w CtY

2599. --- Sejm Grodzieński ostatni,

1793. Poznań, Nakł. Tow. Przyjaciół Nauk, 1866. 352 p. DK434.W4
PU MH

2600. --- Tadeusz Rejtan na sejmie Warszawskim z roku 1773. Poznań, J.K. Żupański, 1873. 108 p.
DK434.8.R4W4 DLC

2601. WOLIŃSKI, Janusz, ed. Materiały do dziejów Sejmu Czterolet-
niego. Opracowali, przygotowali do
druku Janusz Woliński, Jerzy Michalski, Emanuel Rostworowski. Wrocław,
Zakład im. Ossolinskich, 1955- .
DK434.A2W6 DLC CaAEU(v.1)

2602. ZELESKI, Michał. Pamiętniki Michała Zaleskiego wojskiego
Wielkiego Księstwa Litewskiego,
posła na Sejm Czteroletni. Ze wstępem Bronisława Zaleskiego. Poznań,
1879. viii, xxv, 376 p. BM

VII.3.c. PARLIAMENTARY RECORDS

2603. LITHUANIA. SEIMAS. Seimo
stenogramos. [Stenographic records
of the Lithuanian parliament, 1922
23-1926 27] Kaunas, 1922-27. 6 v.
J400.L5H3 DLC CSt-H ICU(microfilm)
NN

2604. LITHUANIA. STEIGIAMASIS
SEIMAS. Steigiamojo seimo darbai...
[1920 m. gegužės měn. 15 d.-1922 m.
spalių měn. 6 d. Posėdžiai 1-257.
Parliamentary records of the Constituent diet. Sessions 1-257. Kaunas,
1920-22] 50 no. in 5 v. JN6745.
A3A2 1920-22 DLC ICU(microfilm)
PU(1-2,4,8,10-13,15,21)

2605. POLAND. WALNA RADA WARSZAW-
SKA. Diarjusz z roku 1710. Wydał
Ryszard Mienicki. Wilno, Nakł. Tow.
Przyjaciół Nauk; skł. gł. Księg. Św.
Wojciecha, 1928. xv, 416 p. (Źród-
ła i materiały Historyczne Wydawnic-
twa Wydziału III. Towarzystwa Przy-
jaciół Nauk w Wilnie, t.1) J399.
H87 DLC PU

2606. POLAND. SEJM, 1748. Dyar-
yusz sejmu r. 1748 wydał Władysław
Konopczyński. Warszawa, Nakładem
Towarzystwa Naukowego Warszawskiego,
sł. gł. w Księg. E. Wende, 1911.
xxvii, 401 p. (Wydawnictwa Towarzystwa Naukowego. Komisya Historyczna. Dyaryusze Sejmowe z wieku XVIII
1) (*QR)NN

2607. POLAND. SEJM, 1569. Dnev-
nik Liublinskogo seima 1569 goda;
soednienie Velikago Kniazhestva Litovskago s korolestvom Pol'skim. Pe-

revod s Pol'skago i pod redak. M.I.
Koialovicha. Sanktpeterburg, V. Go-
lovin, 1869. xvii, 786 p. facsims.
DK419.P67 CaOTU CtY IU InU KU NN PU

VII.3.d. CONSTITUTION, ITS HISTORY AND COMMENTARIES

2608. GIANNINI, Amedeo. La con-
stituzione lituana. [Roma] Istitu-
to romano editoriale, 1925. 42 p.
(Istituto per l'Europa orientale,
Rome. Publicazioni, ser.4, v.5)
GLP p.v. 80 NN

2609. GUSTAINIS, Valentinas.
L'Evolution du régime constitution-
nel en Lithuanie. In Revue Baltique
(Tallin) v.1, no.2, 1940. p. 176-
184. See serials consulted.

2610. LITHUANIA. CONSTITUTION.
Constitution de la Lithuanie. In
Kazlauskas, Bronius. L'entente bal-
tique. Paris, 1939. p. 291-315.
DK511.B3K3 1939 DLC CSt-H CtY NN

2611. --- Constitution de la Lithuanie; le 12 février 1938. Kaunas,
1938. 38 p. 342.4752.L939 PU

2612. --- Constitution de la république de Lithuanie. Kaunas,
1922. 16 p. GLP p.v. 53, no.1 NN
PU

2613. --- Constitution of the Republic of Lithuania. London, Lithuanian Information Bureau [Eyre &
Spottiswoode, 1924] 12 p. JN6745.A5
1924 DLC CSt-H IU PU

2614. --- The Constitution of the
Lithuanian Republic, August 6, 1922.
In Current History and Forum (New
York, N.Y.), v.17, 1922, p. 480-485.
D410.C8 DLC CLU CSt CSt-H CU CaBVaU
CaOH CaOKQ CaQMM CaOOP CaOTP CaOTU
CaBViP CaSSU CtY ICU KU MH MnU MiU
NIC NN NNC NjP OCl OU PU TU WaU

2615. --- Lietuvos valstybės konstitucija... Verfassung des litauischen Staates. In Rogge, A. Die
Verfassung des Memelgebietes. Berlin, 1928, p. 91-113. Lithuanian
and German. DK511.L273R7 CSt-H

2616. --- Lietuvos valstybės konstitucijos. Išrašai iš "Vyriausybės
žinių" 1922, 1928 ir 1938 metų [Con-
stitutions of the Lithuanian State.
Copied from "Vyriausybės žinios" of
1922, 1928, and 1938] Toronto,
"Žiburiai", 1952. 48 p. JN6745.
A13 1952 CaOTU DLC-L PU

2617. --- Loi constitutionelle de
l'État lithuaniene. [Berlin, Impr.
O. Eisner, 1922] 23 p. JN6745.A5
DLC NN PU

2618. --- Lois fondamentales de
la constitution provisoire de l'État
lituanien. [n.p., 1919] [3] p.
Authenticated by the delegation,
Paris Peace Conference, 1919.
D643.A7DP5L71 no.6 CSt-H

2619. MILLER, Artur. Nowa konstytucja Państwa litewskiego. Warszawa
Nakł. Księgarni F. Hoesicka, 1930.
39 p. JN6745.A3M5 DLC PU

2620. PARIS. PEACE CONFERENCE,
1919. LITHUANIA. Les principes de
la constitution provisoire de l'État
lituanien. [Paris, 1919?] 8 p.
D643.A7DP5L7 CSt-H

2621. RAČKAUSKAS, Konstantinas.
Lietuvos konstitucinės teisės klau-
simais. [On the questions of Lith-
uanian constitutional law] New
York, 1967. 178 p. JN6745.A3R3
DLC CaAEU PU

2622. ROBINSON, Jacob. Der litauische Staat und seine Verfassungsentwicklung. In Jahrbuch des öffentlichen Rechtes der Gegenwart
(Tübingen), v.16, 1928, p. 295-326.
Includes: the text of the Constitution of 1922 in German. See serials consulted.

2623. RÖMERIS, Mykolas. Dabartinės konstitucijos. Rinkinys. Kaunas, Vyt. Didž. Universitetas, Teisių fakulteto leidinys, 1932. 1 v.
(Teisės mokslų biblioteka, nr.10)
(*QYA)NN MH-L

2624. --- L'évolution constitutionelle de la Lithuanie. Bucarest,
Institut des arts, 1934. 19 p.
947.52.R663.5 PU

2625. --- Konstitucinės ir teismo
teisės pasieniuose. [On the constitutional law and judiciary] Kaunas,
1931. 193 p. (Kaunas. Universitetas. Teisių fakultetas. Darbai,
t.6, kn.1) 342.R663 PU

2626. --- Lietuvos konstitucinės
teisės paskaitos. [Lectures on the
Lithuanian constitutional law]
Kaunas, V.D. Universiteto Teisių fa-
kulteto leidinys, 1934-1935. 2 v.
(Teisės mokslų biblioteka, nr.20)
DLC-L NN

2627. --- Valstybė ir jos konsti-
tucinė teisė. [The state and its
constitutional law] Kaunas, V.D.
Universiteto Teisių fakulteto leidi-

nys, 1934-1935. 2 v. (Teisės mokslų biblioteka, nr.20) DLC-L NN

2628. --- Die Verfassungsreform
Litauens vom Jahre 1928. München;
Berlin [etc.] J. Schweitzer (A. Sel-
lier), 1930. 41 p. (Osteuropa-Institut in Breslau. Quellen und Studien. Abt. Recht, Neue Folge, Heft
7) JN6745.A3A5 1938 DLC ICU InU MH

2629. ROLNIK, Hirsch, ed. Die
baltischen Staaten; Litauen, Lettland und Estland und ihr Verfassungs-
recht. Leipzig, R. Noske, 1927. xi,
148 p. map (Abhandlungen des Instituts für politische Auslandskunde an
der Universität Leipzig, Heft 2)
JN6745.A3R64 DLC CSt-H CaOTU ICU MH
MnU NN NNC PU WU

2630. ROUZIER, A. La constitution
de la Lithuanie et le statut de Memel. [Toulouse] Faculté de droit,
1926. xv, 287 p. map. (Bibliothèque de l'Institut de législation
comparée de Toulouse. Série des
constitutions, iv) JF12.T6 v.4 DLC
CtY MH NN PU

VII.3.e. ADMINISTRATION OF JUSTICE
AND COURTS

2631. JANULAITIS, Augustinas. Sodžiaus teismas ir jo organizacija
Šiaulių ekonomijoje 18 amžiuje [Vil-
lage court and its organization in
the district of Šiauliai in the
eighteenth century] In Lietuvių
Tauta (Vilnius) v.2, 1919, p. 129-
131. See serials consulted.

2632. --- Vyriausiasis Lietuvos
Tribunolas XVII-XVIII amž. Jo atsiradimas ir reikšmė Lietuvos gyvenime.
[The Supreme Tribunal of Lithuania
in the sixteenth and eighteenth centuries. With the text of the statute of the Tribunal in Lithuanian,
White Russian and Polish, and of the
Konstytucja seymu walnego Warszawskiego...1578, in Polish] In KUTFD,
v.2, kn.4, 1928, p. 1-171. See
serials consulted.

2633. KRIVICKAS, Domas. Administra-
tion of justice; Lithuania. In
Gsovski, Vladimir. Government, law,
and courts in the Soviet Union and
Eastern Europe. London, 1959. v.1,
p. 628-633. JN6573.G89 CaAEU CSt-H
CU CaBVaU CaOKQL CtY CoU CLL DS
FTaSU GU ICU IaU IU MiD MiDW MnU NIC
NN NbU NcD-L NjR RPB WaU WaU-L

2634. LAPPO, Ivan Ivanovich. Iš
Vyriausiojo Lietuvos Tribunolo isto-

rijos. Contribution à l'histoire
du Tribunal Suprême de Lithuanie au
XVI sciècle. Kaunas, Spindulio
Spaustuvė, 1932. 27 p. (Teisès
Mokslų Biblioteka, no.14) Balt
7860.32.5 MH NN BM(Ac.1157.f/4.)

2635. LITHUANIA. LAWS, STATUTES,
ETC. Coaequatio jurium una cum
ordinatione judiciorum tribunali-
tiorum et repartitione locationeque
exercituum Magni Ducatus Lituaniae.
Wilno, 1699. 48 p. BM(5756. k. 2.
(3))

2636. --- Processus iudicarius;
czyli, sposób prawowania się w try-
bunale y wszystkich subselliach
Wiel. Xięs. Litewskiego, krótko ze-
brany a dla informacyi obywatelów
do druku podany. Wilno, Typ. J. K.
M. XX. Schl. Piarium, 1780. 299
p. 947.52L719.3 PU

2637. NAMYSŁOWSKI, W. Pozasądowe
organy porządku prawnego w krajach
południowo-słowiańskich i polsko-
litewskich. In Ehrenkreutz, Stefan,
ed. Księga pomiątkowa ku uczezeniu
czterechsetnej rocznicy wydania
pierwszego Statutu Litewskiego.
Wilno, 1935. (Towarzystwo Przy-
jaciól Nauk w Wilnie. Wydzial III.
Rozprawy, t.8) DLC-L CU CtY InU MH
NN PU

2638. RÖMERIS, Mykolas. Admini-
stracinis teismas. [Administrative
court] Kaunas, Valstybės spaustuvė,
1928. xii, 359 p. (Lietuvos Universiteto Teisių fakulteto darbai,
t.4, knyg. 2) CU ICU NN NNC

VII.4. LAWS, STATUTES, ETC.

VII.4.a. LEGAL HISTORY AND RESEARCH

2639. ADAMUS, Jan. Z zagadnień
prawa litewskiego. Lwów, 1926. 56
p. (Pamiętnik Historyczno-Prawny,
t.2, zesz. 3) DLC-L

2640. CZACKI, Tadeusz. O proiskhozhdenii zakonov, imievshikh silu
v Pol'shie i Litvie. In Viestnik
Evropy (Moskva), 1824, no.56, p.
120, 199, 272; no. 7-8, p. 21, 187,
261; no.9-10, p. 110. See serials
consulted.

2641. --- O litewskich, polskich
prawach, o ich duchu, źródłach,
związku i o rzeczach zawartych w
pierwszym Statucie dla Litwy 1529
roku wydanym. Warszawa, Druk. J.
C. G. Ragoczego, 1800-01. 2 v.

illus. P70.C99-800 CtY DLC-L MH-L
NN

2642. --- Poznań, W Nowej Księgarni, 1843-44. 2 v. illus. C998.1843
CSt

2643. --- --- Kraków, K.J. Turow-
ski, 1861. 2 v. DLC-L IU KU MH
MiU-L NNC-L PU

2644. DANIŁOWICZ, Ignancy. Historische Blick auf die litthauische
Gesetzgegung. In Dorpater Jahrbücher für Literatur, Statistik und Kunst
besonders Russlands, v.2, 1834, p.
289-296, 385-393, 481-491. See
serials consulted.

2645. IAKOVLIV, Andrii. Vplyvy
staroches'koho prava na pravo ukra-
ins'ke litovs'koi doby XV-XVI v.
Praha, Nakl. Ukr. Universitetu v
Prazi, 1929. 81 p. Summary in
French. K.I1154V7 CaOTU DLC MH
CaAEU

2646. JANULAITIS, Augustinas.
Lietuvos visuomenės ir teisės istorija. [The history of the Lithuanian law and society] Tilžė, Švietimo ministerijos Knygų leidimo
komisijos leidinys, 1920. 218 p.
Bibliography: p. [203]-210.
JN6745.A2J3 DLC CtTMF CtY ICJ PU

2647. --- Napoleono teisynas; jo
atsiradimas ir veikimas Prancūzijoje, išsiplėtimas svetur o ypatingai
Lietuvos Užnemunėje. [Napoleonic
law, its origin and application in
France, expansion abroad especially
in Southern Lithuania] Kaunas,
Varpo bendrovės spaustuvė, 1930.
viii, 204 p. (Kaunas. Universitetas. Teisių fakultetas. Darbai, t.
5, kn.6) See serials consulted.

2648. LEONTOVICH, Fedor Ivanovich.
Ocherki istorii litovsko-russkago
prava. Sanktpeterburg, 1894. xi,
393 p. BM(5756. d. 11.)

2649. MASIULIS, Boleslovas. At-
statytosios Lietuvos valstybės teisė. [The state law of independent
Lithuania] In Lietuvių enciklopedija. Boston, Mass., 1968. v.15, p.
80-90. For holdings see entry no.
216.

2650. MEYER, Alfred, ed. Das
Recht der besetzten Ostgebiete:
Estland, Lettland, Litauen, Weiss-
sruthenien und Ukraine. Hrsg. von
Alfred Meyer [et al.] München und
Berlin, C.H. Beck, 1943. 1 v.
looseleaf D802.A2M61 CSt-H DLC-L
CSt DS MnU

OKINSHEVICH, Leo. The law
of the Grand Duchy of Lithuania;
background and bibliography. New
York, N.Y., 1953. See entry no. 108.

2651. PICHETA, Vladimir Ivanovich.
Razrabotka istorii litovsko-belorus-
skogo prava XV-XVI vekov v istorio-
grafii. In His Belorussiia i Litva
v XV-XVI v. Moskva, 1961. p. 413-
455. DK507.65.P5 DLC ClU CSt CU
CaAEU NN NjP TU WaS

2652. PIEKOSIŃSKI, Franciszek
Ksawery, ed. Pomniki prawa litewskiego z XVI wieku. Kraków, 1900.
lxx, 568 p. facsims. (Polska Akademia Umiejętności, Kraków. Komisja
Prawnicza. Archivum, t.7) 349.475.
P596p 1900 KU; see also serials consulted.

2653. PLATERIS, Aleksandras. Co-
dification of the law in the Grand
Duchy of Lithuania. In Lituanus
(Chicago, Ill.), v.11, no.2, p. 28-
44. See serials consulted.

2654. PTASZYCKI, Stanisław. K
istorii litovskago prava poslie
Tret'iago Statuta. Sanktpeterburg,
V.S. Valasheva, 1893. 31 p. DLC-L;
also in Russia. Ministerstvo narodnogo prosveshcheniia. Zhurnal
(Sanktpeterburg), v.10, 1893, p.
489-515. See serials consulted.

2655. ROBINSON, Jacob. Lietuvos
įstatymai; sistematiška apžvalga.
[Laws of Lithuania; a systematic re-
view] Kaunas, Spaudos Fondas, 1940.
123 p. NNCL

2656. SWETSCHIN, A. Litauen;
Übersicht über die wesentliche Gesetzgebung im Jahre 1940. In Zeitschrift für osteuropäisches Recht
(Berlin), Neue Folge, v.6, 1939, p.
271; v.7, 1941, p. 371-378; v.8,
1942, p. 389-400. See serials
consulted.

2657. VLADIMIRSKII-BUDANOV, Mikhail Flegontovich. Niemetskoe pravo
v Pol'shie i Litvie. In Russia.
Ministerstvo narodnogo prosveshcheniia. Zhurnal (Snaktpeterburg),
1868, Ch. 139, p. 467-554, 720-806;
Ch. 140, p. 519-586, 772-833. See
serials consulted.

2658. --- Ocherki iz istorii litovsko-russkago prava. Kiev, Tip.
Imp. Universiteta Sv. Vladimira,
1889-1893. 3 v. DLC-L

2659. WITORT, Jan. Zarysy prawa
zwycajowego ludu litewskiego. Lwów,
Nakł. Tow. Ludoznawczego, 1898. 165
p. 947.52.W788 FU BM(5756. c. 15.)

VII.4.b. LIETUVOS STATUTAS-LITHUA-
NIAN CODE (GRAND DUCHY),
HISTORY AND COMMENTARIES

2660. ADAMUS, Jan. O wstępnych
aktach procesu litewskiego, do II.
Statutu. Garść notatek. Wilno,
1937. In Ateneum Wileńskie (Wilno),
v.12, 1937, p. 205-281. See serials consulted.

2661. BERSHADSKII, Sergei Aleksandrovich. Litovskii Statut i pol'-
skiia konstitutsii; istoriko-iuridi-
cheskoe izsledovanie. Sanktpeterburg, Tip. M. Stasiulevicha, 1893.
114 p. JN6745.A58B53 CSt-H DLC-L

EHRENKREUTZ, Stefan, ed.
Księga pamiątkowa ku uczczeniu
czterechsetnej rocznicy wydania
pierwszego Statutu Litewskiego.
Wilno, 1935. See entry no. 2523.

2662. --- Stan badań nad statuta-
mi litewskiemi. In Ateneum Wileńskie (Wilno), 1924, v.2, p. 289-349.
See serials consulted.

2663. --- Uwagi nad rozdziałem
VII-ym Statutu Litewskiego trzecie-
go. In Rocznik Prawniczy Wileński
(Wilno), v.1, 1925, p. 233-251.
See serials consulted.

2664. --- Zagadnienie wpływu prawa rzymskiego na statuty litewskie.
In Pamiętnik VI. powszechnego Zjazdu Historyków Polskich w Wilnie,
1935. Referaty (Lwów), v.1, 1935,
p. 189-196. See serials consulted.

2665. GERLACH, Jan. Stanowisko
duchownych wedle III Statutu Litewskiego. In Ateneum Wileńskie (Wilno), v.1, 1923, p. 205-225. See
serials consulted.

2666. LAPPO, Ivan Ivanovich. K voprosu o pervom izdanii litovskago
Statuta 1588 goda. Kaunas, Spindulys, 1928. 45 p. K/O.1/L316 WU

2667. LINDE, Samuel Bogumił. O
Statucie Litewskim, ruskim językiem
i drukiem wydanem, wiadomość. Warszawa, Nakł. Zawadzkiego i Węckiego,
1816. 218 p. 947.52.L643 PU ICBM
MH WU

2668. LITHUANIA. LAWS, STATUTES,
ETC. Didžiosios Lietuvos Kunigaikštijos 1529 metų statutas. [Statute
of the Grand Duchy of Lithuania of
the year 1529. Vertė Jonė Deveikė.
Vertimą spaudai parengė, įžangą ir
žodynėlį parašė bei bibliografiją
sudarė A. Plateris] Chicago, Ill.,

Algimanto Mackaus knygų leidimo fondas, 1971. 261 p. DK511.L23L53 PU

2669. --- Litovskii Statut v moskovskom perevodie-redaktsii [Edi-
ted by I.I. Lappo] IUr'ev, Tip. K.
Matisena, 1916. xxx, 395 p. (Russia. Arkheograficheskaia komissia.
Letopis' zaniatii, vyp.28)
DK511.L23L54 PU DLC IU MH-L

2670. --- Prawa z Statutu Wielkiego Xięstwa Litewskiego i Konstytucyi
... podlug alfabetu zebrane; a ile
w processa prawnw wchodzących o pre-
tensye wszelakie. Warszawa, M.
Gröll, 1783. 796 p. DLC-L BM

2671. --- Statut Litewski, drugiej
redakcyi, 1566. Statuta Magni Ducatus Lituaniae... E. Rutheno sermone
in latinum bona fide conversa. Statut Wielkiego Xięstwa Litewskiego,
którym się teras Woiewodztwa Kiiows-
kie, Wołyńskie y Bracząławskie sądzą.
Kraków, 1900. lxx, 568 p. (Polska
Akademija Umiejętności, Kraków. Komisja Prawnicza. Archivum, v.7)
DLC-L BM(Ac. 750/58.) MH

2672. --- Statut Velikogo Kniazhestva Litovskogo 1529 g. [Tr. and
comments by K.I. Jablonskis] Mensk,
Akademiia navuk BSSR, 1960. 253 p.
facsims. Osf80.960L CtY DLC-L CaB
CaBVaU CaOTU IEN IaU IU KU MH NN NcD
NcU NjP OrU PU RPB

2673. --- Statut Velikogo Kniazhestva Litovskogo 1566 goda. [Mosk-
va, 1855] 242 p. (Obshchestvo istorii i drevnostei rossiiskikh. Moskva. Vremennik. Materialy, kn.23)
NN

2674. --- Statut Velikogo Kniazh'-
stva Litovskogo 1588 goda. Novoe
izdanie [Moskva, Universitetskaia
Tip.] 1854. 24, 382 p. facsim.
DLC-L NN

2675. --- Statut Velykoho Kniaz'-
stva Lytovs'koho 1588 roku. W Krako-
ve, 1588. 618 p. illus. Microfiche
Tumba, International dokumentation
centre, 1963. 17 cards. CaOTU KU
WaU

2676. --- Statut Wielkiego Xięstw-
wa Litewskiego... naprzód... w roku
1588... trzeci raz z przyłożeniem
Constitucyi tak Koronie iako y W.X.
Litewskiego służących... tekstu sa-
mego Statutu niczym nieodmieniaiąc,
do druku podany. Trybunał Obywatelom Wielkiego Xięstwa Litewskiego
na Seymie Warszawskim dany roku
1581. [Comp. by S. Gałązka. Ed. by
J. Pistrowicz] Warszawa, 1648. 363,
60, 24 p. BM(5756. dd. 9.)

2677. --- Statut Wielkiego Xięstwa Litewskiego... czwarty raz... z przyłożeniem pod artykuły Constitucyi seymowych od seymy roku 1550 aż do seymu roku 1690... drukowany. Wilno, Drukarnia Akademiey Societatis Jesu, 1693-94. 421, 54, 10 p. Summerfield D413 KU MB(5756.k.2(1.)

2678. --- --- Teraz zaś piąty raz ... przedrukowany. Wilno, W Drukarni J.K.M. Akademickiej Societatis Jesu, 1744. 54, 30 p. DLC-L BM KU MH

2679. --- --- [Another edition] Wilno, W Drukarni J.K.M. Akademickiey Societatis Jesu, 1744 [i.e. 1780] 1 v. (various pagings) DLC-L

2680. --- --- ... w roku 1588... drugi raz w Wilnie, w roku 1619 z pokazaniem zgody i różnice Statutów Koronnych i W.X. Litewskiego. Trzeci raz za Nayjaśnieyszego Władysława IV. ... Wilno, Mci XX Akademij, 1786. Special Coll. E873 MH KU

2681. --- --- ... z dołączeniem treści Konstytucyi przyzwoitych. W Sanktpetersburgu, W Druk. Rządzącego Senatu, 1811. 2 v. Polish and Russian. 349.475.L713S 1811 KU DLC-L MH

2682. --- --- ... bez żadnej odmiany, podług wydania wileńskiego roku 1786, nakładem Wileńskiego Tow. Typograficznego przedrukowany. Wilno, A. Marcinkowski, 1819. 1 v. (various pagings) 349.475.L776 1819 InNd

2683. --- 1588 metų Lietuvos statutas. [Lithuanian Statute of 1588] Kaunas, Spindulio bendrovės spaustuvė, 1934-38. 2 v. in 3. facsims. (Švietimo ministerijos knygų leidimo komisijos leidinys, nr. 497) In Russian. Vol.1 contains investigation, vol. 2 text. Editor's and commentator's name J. Lappo. DLC-L BM(09456. g. 40.) CtY ICBM IU MH(t.1, ch.1-2) NN NNC WU

2684. MAKSIMEIKO, Nikolai Alekseevich. Istochniki ugolovnykh zakonov Litovskago Statuta. Kiev, Tip. Imp. Universiteta Sv. Vladimira, 1894. iv, 185 p. (Kiev. Universitet. Universitetskiia isviestiia. Ch.2) AS262.K7 v.34 DLC NN

2685. MALINOVSKII, Ioannikii Alekseevich. Uchenie o prestuplenii po Litovskomu Statutu. Kiev, Tip. Imp. Universiteta, 1895. 173 p. AS262.K7 v.35 DLC

2686. PICHETA, Vladimir Ivanovich. Izuchenie Litovskikh Statutov v no-

veishei istoriko-iuridicheskoi literature, 1918-1940 gg. In Akademiia nauk SSSR. Izvestiia. Seriia istorii i filosofii. Moskva, no.1, 1946, p. 31-42. See serials consulted.

2687. PTASZYCKI, Stanisław. K voprosu ob izdaniiakh i komentariakh Litovskago Statuta; istoriko-bibliograficheskaia spravka. Sanktpeterburg, Tip. S.A. Kornatovskago, 1893. 78 p. DLC-L

2688. TAUBENSCHLAG, Rafał. Wpływy rzymsko-bizantyńskie w drugim Statucie Litewskim. Lwów, Nakł. Tow. Naukowego, 1933. 36 p. (Studja nad Historją prawa Polskiego im. Oswalda Balzera, t.14, zesz.2) DLC NN BM(Ac. 764/9.)

VII.4.c. PRIVILEGES, CONSTITUTIONS, ETC.

2689. BALZER, Oswald Marian. Konstytucya Trzeciego Maja; reformy społeczne i polityczne, ustawy rządowe z r. 1791. 3. Wyd. Warszawa, Gebethner i Wolff [192?] 342.438.B219.K KU ICU MH NN

2690. BOGOSLAVSKII, Mikhail Mikhailovich. Prikazy Velikago Kniazhestva Smolenskago v Moskovskom gosudarstvie. Offprint from Zhurnal Ministerstva narodnago prosveshcheniia. Petrograd, 1906, no. 8. p. [220]-242. L451A55 DLC NN NNC

2691. CONSTYTUCYE WIELKIEGO XIĘStwa Litewskiego. In Lithuania. Laws, statutes, etc. Statut Wielkiego Xięstwa Litewskiego, naprzod... w roku 1588... teraz zaś piąty raz... przedrukowany. Wilno, 1744. DLC-L

2692. IASINSKII, Mikhail Nikitich. Ustavnyia zemskiia gramoty litovsko-russkago gosudarstva. Kiev, Universitetskaia Tip., 1889. vi, 207 p. table. (Kiev. Universitet. Universitetskaia izviestiia) DLC-L NNC

2693. JAKUBOWSKI, Jan. Zemskie privilegii Velikogo Kniazhestva Litovskogo. In ZMNP, v.70, ch.346, 1903, p. 238-278; ch.347, 1903, p. 245-303. See serials consulted.

2694. KACZMARCZYK, Zdzisław, ed. Konstytucje Grodzieńskie z r. 1793, dotyczące ustroju państwa wraz z ustawą "Miasta wolne Rzeczypospolitej". Poznań, 1949. 43 p. DK434.A2K3 PU NN

2695. KONSTYTUCYE WIELKIEGO XIĘS-

twa Litewskiego. In Lithuania.
Laws, statutes, etc. Statut Wielkiego Xięstwa Litewskiego. Wilno, 1744
[i.e. 1780] DLC-L

2696. LITHUANIA. LAWS, STATUTES,
ETC. Constitucie Wielkiego Xięstwa
Litewskiego anno M.DC.LXII. commissa-
rze do traktatów moskiewskich. [n.p.,
1662?] 28 p. Summerfield D415/23
KU

2697. --- Postanowienie generalne
stanów Wielkiego Xięstwa Litewski-
go na ziezdzie Walnym Woiewodztw y
Powiatów, Pospolytym Ruszeniem pod
Olkinikami uchwalone, roku 1700. Wilno, 1700. 33 p. BM(5756. dd. 3.)

2698. --- Trybunał obywatelom Wielkiego Xięstwa Litewskiego na seymie
Warszawskim dany roku tysiąc pięset
ośmdziesiątego pierwszego, prszedru-
kowany roku 1693. Wilno, Drukarnia
Akademickiey Societatis Jesu, 1693.
30 p. BM(5756. k. 2.(2))

2699. --- Tribunal obivateliam Velikogo Kniazhestva Litovskogo na sei-
me Varshavskom dani roku 1581. Moskva, 1857. 22 p. (Obshchestvo istorii i drevnostei rossiiskikh. Vreme-
nik, v.25. Materialy) (*QCB)NN

2700. POLAND. LAWS, STATUTES,ETC.
(INDEXES). Constitucye Koronne, y
Wielkiego Xięstwa Litewskiego od ro-
ku Pańskiego 1550 do roku 1683.
Przez Macieia Marcyna Ładowskiego
krótko zebrane. W Warszawie, w Druk.
Collegium Scholarum Piarum, 1685.
3, 926 p. DLC -L

2701. --- Inwentarz konstytucyi
Koronnych y W.X. Litewskiego od roku
1550 do roku 1683. Przez Macieia
Marcyna Ładowskiego. Lipsk, 1733.
9,[3], 676, [4] p. 349.438.P7621
DcD DLC-L MH

2702. POLAND. SEJM, 1611. Consti-
tucie W.X. Litewskiego, na seymie
Walnym Koronnym Warszawskim roku 1611
Kraków, A. Pietrkowczyk, 1611. 49,
[19], 19 p. Sammerfield E935/15 KU
BM

2703. POLAND. SEJM, 1661. Constytucye Wielkiego Xięstwa Litewskiego,
1661. [W Krakowie? 1661] 36 p.
DLC-L KU

2704. POLAND. SEJM, 1662. Subsidium reipublicae generalis contributions od stanów Koronnych, y Wielkiego Xięstwa Litewskiego na seymie Walnym Warszawskim extraordynarnym dnia
20. miesiąca lutego roku M.DC.LXII.
uchwalone. [Cracovie, Typis Schede-
lianis, 1676] 14 p.
Summerfield D415/24 KU

2705. POLAND. SEJM, 1717. Konstytucye Wielkiego Xięstwa Litewskiego. Warszawa. 1717. 22, [10], 30,
[31] p. Summerfield E935/14 KU

2706. POLAND. SEJM,1767-1768.
Konstytucye seymu extraordynaryinego
w Warszawie roku MDCCLXVII... przy
rozwiązaniu Konfederacyi Generalnych
Koronney y Wielkiego Xięstwa Litewskiego zakończonego, ex concensu ordinum totius Republicae ustanowione.
Warszawa, Drukarnia XX Scholarum Piarum, [1768?] 352, [7], 42, [2] p.
J399.A2 1768 DLC

2707. POLAND. SEJM, 1773-1775.
Konstytucye publiczne seymu Extraor-
dynaryinego Warszawskiego pod węzłem
Generalnej Konfederacyi oboyga naro-
dów, trwaiącego roku 1773... 1775.
Warszawa, Drukarnia XX Scholarum
Piarum, 1775. 2 v. in 1. illus.,
fold. tables. J399.A2 1775 DLC BM
MH NNC NjP

2708. POLAND. SEJM, 1776. Konstytucya seymu Ordynaryinego Warszawskiego roku MDCCLXXVI od dnia 26.
sierpnia aż do dnia 31 października.
Pod węzłem Konfederacyi Generalney
oboyga narodów agituiącego się. Warszawa, Drukarnia XX Scholarum Piarum,
1776. 73, [4] p. fold. table.
NNC-L

2709. PRZYWILEJ UNII WIELKIEGO XIĘ-
stwa Litewskiego z Koroną z dnia
1-go Julii, 1569. In Wójcicki, Kazimierz W., comp. Biblioteka Starożytna Pisarzy Polskich. Warszawa,
1843. v.6. BM(1338. f. 5.)

2710. --- --- Wyd. 2. Warszawa,
1854. BM(9475. bbb. 35.) NN

VII.4.d. COLLECTIONS OF LAWS

2711. BALTIC PROVINCES. LAWS, STA-
TUTES, ETC. Provinzialrecht der Ost-
seegouvernments. Sanktpeterburg,
Buchdr. der zweiten Abteilung Seiner
Kaiserlichen Majestät Kanzellei,
1845-64. 3 v. in 2. DLC-L

2712. --- Ukazatel' khronologiches-
kii i sistematicheskii zakonov dlia
Pribaltiiskikh gubernii s 1704 g. po
1888 g. Sostavlennyi Mikhailom Kha-
ruzinym. Revel', Pechatano v Est-
liandskoi gubernskoi tipografii,
1888. viii, 248 p. DLC-L

2713. KOŁUDZKI, Augustin. Promp-
tuarium legum et constitutionum Regni Poloniae ac Magni Ducatus Lithuaniae. Ad faciliorem indagationem,

publicamque utilitatem speciosum in ordinem reductum, concinnatum. Posnaniae, J.T. Keller, 1695. 4, 540, xvi p. BM

2714. LITHUANIA. LAWS, STATUTES, ETC. Lietuvos įstatymai. Sistematizuotas įstatymų, instrukcijų ir įsakymų rinkinys. [Laws of Lithuania; a systematic collection of laws... Comp. by A. Merkys, edited by A. Kriščiukaitis] Kaunas, A. Merkys & V. Petrulis, 1922-25. 2 v. Vol.2 has imprint: Klaipėda, Rytas, 1925. 340.ME ICLJF CtPAM CtTMF CtY DLC-L ICBM ICCC MH PPiU PU WaS

2715. --- Zakonodatel'nye akty Velikogo Kniazhestva Litovskogo XV-XVI vv. Sbornik materialov podgotovlen k pechati I.I. IAkovkinym. Leningrad, Leningradskoe otd-nie Gos. sotsial'-no-ekon. izd-va, 1936. xi, 152 p. (Dokumenty i materialy po istorii narodov SSSR) At head of title: Leningradskii gos. universitet. Istoricheskii fakultet. CLU CU DLC-L ICU MH MnU NNC NjP OrU PU WU

2716. --- Zbiór praw litewskich, od roku 1389 do roku 1529. Tudzież rozprawy seymowe o tychże prawach od roku 1544 do roku 1563. Wyd. przez A. T. Działyńskiego. Poznań, Drukarnia na Garbarach, 1841. iv, 542 p. illus., plates, facsims. P45.R78A2#841 CtY DLC-L ICU(microfilm) KU(Xerox copy) MH NjP PU

2717. POLAND. LAWS, STATUTES, ETC. Leges, statuta, constitutiones, privilegia Regni Poloniae, Magni Ducatus Lithuaniae, omniumque provinciarum, a commitiis Visliciae anno 1347 celebratis usque ad ultima regni comitia. Varsoviae, In typographia S.R.M. & Reipublicae colegij varsoviensis Scholarum Piarum, 1732-82. 8 v. vol.1, Latin; vol.2-8, Polish with the title: Prawa, Konstytucye y Przywileie Królewstwa Polskiego y Wielkiego Księstwa Litewskiego, y wszystkich prowincyi należnych, na Walnych Seymach Koronnych od seymu Wiślickiego roku Pańskiego 1347 aż do ostatniego seymu uchwalone. Beinecke Lib. P45.R9 732 CtY KU DLC-L(1-7) BM(25. e. 5-11.)

2718. --- Prawo polityczne i cywilne Korony Polskiey y Wielkiego Xięstwa Litewskiego; to jest, Nowy zbiór praw oboyga narodów od roku 1347 aż do teraźniejszych czasów [przez Antoniego Trębickiego ułożone] Warszawa, P. Dufour, 1789-91. 2 v. DLC-L (1)

2719. --- Volumina legum. Przedruk Zbioru praw staraniem XX Pijarów w Warszawie od roku 1732 do roku [1793]

wydanego. Petersburg, Nakł. J. Ohryzki, 1859-1952. 10 v. Vol 1-8 first published 1732-82 under title: Leges, statuta, constitutiones, privilegia Regni Poloniae, Magni Ducatus Lithuaniae, etc. Vol.1-6, edited by S. Konarski with the assistance of Andrzej Józef, Bp. of Kiev. Vol.9, issued by Komisja Prawnicza of Akademia Umiejętności with imprint: Kraków, Nakł. Akademii Umiejętności, 1889. Vol.10, edited by Z. Kaczmarczyk and issued as vol.11 of Wydawnictwa Żródłowe Komisji Historycznej of Poznańskie Towarzystwo Przyjaciół Nauk with imprint: Poznań, Nakł. Poznańskiego Towarzystwa Przyjaciół Nauk, 1952. DLC-L IU NN PU

2720. --- --- Inwentarz Voluminów Legum. Przedruk wyd. XX Piarów do tomów I-[VIII] Petersburg, Nakł. J. Ohryzki, 1860. 2 v. in 1. front. DLC-L IU NN PU

2721. --- Zbiór praw Polskich i Wielkiego Xsięstwa Litewskiego od roku 1347 seymu Wiślickiego aż do roku 1786, etc. W Krakowie, W Drukarni Akademickiey, 1813. 196 p. DLC-L BM(5760. ee. 1.)

2722. --- Kodeks Stanisława Augusta; zbiór dokumentów. Wydał Stanisław Borowski. Warszawa, Nakł. Tow. Prawniczego, 1938. xv, 348 p. Bibliography: p. 345-347. DLC-L

2723. ŠALKAUSKIS, Kazys, comp. Lietuvos novelos; veikiančiųjų 1935. II.16 d. Lietuvos įstatymų ir įsakymų, paskelbtų Vyriausybės žiniose, nr.1-476, rinkinys. [A collection of Lithuanian laws, valid on February 16, 1935, as promulgated in Official Gazette] Kaunas, Spaudos fondas, 1935. xxxiv, 813 p. 945.Š ICBM NNCL

2724. ZALASZOWSKI, Mikołaj. Jus Regni Poloniae, ex statutis et constitutionibus ejusdem Regni M.D. Lithuaniae collectum. Varsoviae, Reimpressum typis S.R.M.Collegij Societatis Jesu, 1741-42. 2 v. Bibliography: v.1, p. 14-20. DK414. A2Z34 PU DLC-L

2725. ZAMOJSKI, Andrzej. Sammlung gerichtlicher Gesetze für das Königreich Polen und Gross-Herzogthum Litauen: zufolge der Reichs-Konstitution des Jahres 1776 von Andreas Zamoyski ausgearbeitet und zusammen getragen und dem verssammelten Reichstage im Jahr 1778 übergegeben. Übersetzt von Gottfried Nikisch. Warshau; [etc.] Druck und Verlag M. Grölls, 1780. [12], xii, 306 p. table. Slav 5225.15F MH DLC-L

VII.4.e. CIVIL LAW AND CIVIL PROCEDURE

2726. BALTIC PROVINCES, LAWS, STA-
TUTES, ETC. Grazhdanskie zakony gubernii Pribaltiiskikh, s raz"iasneniiami. Sostavil V. Bukhovskii.
Riga, Pechatano v tip. "Astra",
1909. vii, 935 p. DLC-L

2727. --- Sammlung der in den Ostseeprovinzen geltenden Bestimmungen
des Civilprocesses. Nach der russischen Ausgabe des Svod dieistvuiush-
chikh v Pribaltiiskikh guberniiakh
zakonopolozhenii o grazhdanskom su-
doproizvodtstvie. Übersetzt, ver-
vollständigt und mit einem alphabe-
tischen Sachregister versehen von
Harald baron Loudon und Heinrich
baron Loudon. Riga, N. Kymmel,
1890. xv, 456 p. DLC-L

2728. --- Svod dieistvuiushchykh v
Pribaltiiskikh guberniiakh zakonopolozhenii o grazhdanskom sudoproiz-
vodtstvie s alfavitnym ukazatelem na
russkom i niemetskom iazykakh. Riga,
N. Kimmel', 1890. xv, 475 p. NN

2729. --- Svod grazhdanskikh uza-
konenii gubernii Pribaltiiskikh, s
prodolzheniem 1912-1914 gg. i s
raz"iasneniiami. Sostavil V. Bukhovskii. Riga, 1914. 2 v. DLC-L

2730. KOROWICKI, Aleksander. Proces cywilny litewski. Wilno, 1826.
313 p. K8435 PU

2731. LITHUANIA. LAWS, STATUTES,
ETC. Civiliniai įstatymai (X tomo,
1 dalis) [Civil laws as in force on
January 1, 1933] Civilinių įstatymų
tekstą su papildymais iki 1933.I.1.
bei Vyriausiojo tribunolo išspręstų
klausimų ištraukas nuo 1931 metų iki
1933 metų vasario mėn. sudarė V. Fin-
kelšteinas; rusų Senato sprendimų
ištraukas vertė J. Abramavičius.
Kaunas, "Literatūros" knygyno leidimas, 1933. 689 p. DLC-L MH

2732. MAČYS, Vladas. Civilinio
proceso paskaitos, surašytos Lietuvos Universiteto ord. prof. Vl. Ma-
čio. [Lectures on civil procedure]
Kaunas, Teisių fakulteto leidinys,
1924. 448 p. (Kaunas. Universitetas. Teisių fakultetas. Teisės
mokslų biblioteka, nr.4.)

VII.4.f. CRIMINAL LAW AND CRIMINAL PROCEDURE

2733. BALZER, Oswald Marian. Statuty Kazimierza Wielkiego; z rękopisu pośmiertnego wydali Z. Kaczmare-
zyk, M. Szaniecki, S. Weyman. Poznań, Nakł. Poznańskiego Towarzystwa
Przyjaciół Nauk, 1947. xxxciii, 527
p. (Studia nad historją prawa polskiego, 19) DK424.8.B19 CaAEU
DLC-L

2734. --- Studium nad tekstami ła-
cińskiemi objątku Wiślickiego statutów Kazimierza Wielkiego. In His
Statuty Kazimierza Wielkiego. Poznań, 1947. p. 15-238. DK424.8.B19
CaAEU DLC-L

2735. LITHUANIA. LAWS, STATUTES,
ETC. Baudžiamasis statutas. [1
leidimas. Criminal code] Kaunas,
"Literatūros" knygyno leidinys,
1930. 381, [3] p. School of Law
CtY

2736. --- Baudžiamasis statutas su
papildymais. 2-sis leidinys. [Cri-
minal code, 2d ed.] M. Kavolis ir S.
Bieliackinas. Kaunas, 1934. xix,
887 p. PU MH

2737. --- Baudžiamojo proceso įstatymas su komentarais, sudarytas iš
Rusijos Senato bei Lietuvos Vyriausiojo tribunolo sprendimų ir kitų
aiškinimų, liečiančių Didž. Lietuvos ir Klaipėdos krašto baudžiamojo
proceso teisę. Redagavo Martynas
Kavolis. Kaunas, "Literatūros"
knygyno leidimas, 1933. xxviii,
880 p. School of Law CtY PU-L

2738. --- Das litauische Strafpro-
zessgesetz; aus dem Litauischen ü-
bersetzt und hrsg. von G. Gronau.
Memel, [F.W. Krumpholz-Druck] 1934.
288, 56 p. DLC-L

2739. --- Kazimiero teisynas 1468.
Sudebnik Kazimira. [Spaudai parengė, įvadą ir paaiškinimus parašė J.
Jurginis. Ats. red. A. Tyla] Vilnius, Mintis, 1967. 34 p. (Lietuvos TSR Mokslų akademija, Vilna.
Istorijos institutas. Acta historica lituanica, 1) DK511.L23L52 PU MH

2740. --- Sudebnik korolia Kazimira IAgellovicha, dannyi Litvie 1468
goda fevr. 29. Pervyi, ili staryi,
Litovskii Statut 1529 g. In Russia.
Laws, statutes, etc. Sbornik pamiatnikov drevniago russkago prava.
[Compiled by I.A. Malinovskii] Ros-
tov na Donu, 1917. BM(5756. aa. 45.)

2741. MIKALAUSKAS, Antanas. Das Strafrecht der drei litauischen Statute von 1529, 1566 und 1588. Kaunas, J. Karvelis, 1938. 200 p. Thesis--University of Bern (Switzerland) 349.47.L17M58 NIC CtY DLC-L NNC PU

2742. WIRSCHUBSKI, Gregor. Das Strafrecht des litauischen Statuts. In Monatsschrift für Kriminalpsychologie und Strafrechtsreform (Heidelberg), v.25, 1934-1935, p. 557-573; v.26, p. 205-223. DLC-L

VII.4.g. DECISIONS OF THE SUPREME COURT AND THE STATE CHAMBER

2743. LITHUANIA. VALSTYBĖS TARYBA. Valstybės Tarybos nuomonės teisės klausimais, 1927-1937. [The opinions of the State Chamber on legal matters. Edited by J. Byla] Kaunas, Lietuvos teisininkų draugija, 1937. x, 190 p. K.712 PU DLC-L

2744. LITHUANIA. LAWS, STATUTES, ETC. Vyriausiojo tribunolo Suvalkijos įstatymų paaiškinimai (tėzės). Surinko, sistematizavo ir spaudai paruošė L. Veržbavičius ir S. Kiseniškis. [Opinions of the Supreme Tribunal concerning the laws of the region of Suvalkija] Kaunas "Literatūros" knygynas, 1932. 151 p. 349. 475.V6291 PU

2745. LITHUANIA. VYRIAUSIASIS TRIBUNOLAS. Vyriausiojo tribunolo baudžiamųjų kasacinių bylų sprendimai, pradedant 1933 metų rugsėjo mėn. 15 d. [Collection of decisions of the Supreme Court in criminal cases beginning from Sept. 15, 1933] Kaunas, Kooperatinė "Raidės" spaustuvė, 1933-34. 211 p. School of Law CtY

2746. --- Vyriausiojo Tribunolo baudžiamųjų kasacinių bylų sprendimų rinkinys su rodykle, 1924-1933. [Collection of decisions of the Supreme Court in criminal cases from 1924 to 1933. Edited by J. Byla] Kaunas, 1932-35. 2 v. DLC-L MH

2747. --- Vyriausiojo tribunolo praktika civilinių įstatymų (Xt. 1 d.) reikalu. [Decisions of the Supreme Court in civil cases] Kaunas, D. Gutmano leidinys, 1934. 303 p. DLC-L

2748. --- Vyriausiojo tribunolo visuotinių susirinkimų nutarimai, pra-

dedant 1933 m. rugsėjo mėn. 15 d. [Collection of decisions made in Plenary Sessions of the Supreme Court from Sept. 15, 1933] Kaunas, Kooperatinė "Raidės" spaustuvė, 1933-34. 107 p. School of Law CtY

VII.4.h. OFFICIAL GAZETTES

2749. KLAIPĖDOS KRAŠTO VALDŽIOS ŽINIOS. Amtsblatt des Memelgebietes. Klaipėda, 1920-1930. In Lithuanian and German. DLC-L

2750. LITHUANIA. LAWS, STATUTES, ETC. Lietuvos įstatymų raidynas: Vyriausybės žinių 1918-1932 m. rodyklė. [Index to Vyriausybės žinios, 1918-1932] Kaunas, 1935. 167 p. 947.52.L719.2 PU MH

2751. --- Vyriausybės žinios. [Official gazette] Vilnius; Kaunas, Ministrų kabinetas, 1918-40. 730 no. Number 1 issued at Vilnius; no. 1-37 have title: Laikinosios vyriausybės žinios. J7.L5 DLC(1918-1940, no. 1-730) NN(1937-1938, 1940)

2752. LITHUANIA. LAWS, STATUTES, ETC. (INDEXES) Vyriausybės žinių 1927-1929 metų rodyklė. [Index to Vyriausybės žinios, 1927-1929] Kaunas, Spindulio bendrovės spaustuvė, 1930. 46 p. DLC-L

2753. LITHUANIA. (TERRITORY UNDER GERMAN OCCUPATION 1915-1918) Verodnungsblatt der deutschen Verwaltung für Litauen. Paliepimų laiškas vokiečių valdžios Lietuvoje. no.1-9, [N.F.] no.1-15; 26 Oktover 1915-30. Juni, 1916. Tilsit; Kowno, [etc.] Verlag der deutschen Verwaltung für Litauen, 1915-16. 24 no. in 1 v. Irregular. German and Lithuanian in parallel columns. CSt-H MiU-L NN

2754. LITHUANIA. (TERRITORY UNDER GERMAN OCCUPATION 1941-1945). Generalkommissar in Kauen. Amtsblatt. Jahrgang 1-4; 1. Sept. 1941-1944. Kauen, Kauener Zeitung, 1941-44. 3 v. in 2. col. illus. Text in German and Lithuanian. CtY(1943-1944) DLC-L(1941-1944) MiU-L NN(1943-1944) NNC

2755. LITHUANIAN S.S.R. AUKŠČIAU- SIJI TARYBA. Žinios. [News, i.e. Official gazette of the Soviet Lithuanian Supreme Council] Vilnius, 1959- . Russian edition has title: Vedomosti Verkhovnogo soveta i Pravitel'stva Litovskoi SSR. DLC-L

2756. OSTLAND. LAWS, STATUTES, ETC.

Amtlicher Anzeiger des Reichskommissars für das Ostland. Aug. 25,
1943-Juni 14, 1944. Riga [Deutsche
Verlags- und Druckerei Gesellschaft
im Ostland] 1943-44. Irregular.
(BZAA-0823)NN NNC NcD

2757. --- Verordnungsblatt des
Reichskommissars für das Ostland.
30. Aug. 1941- 31. Aug. 1944. [Riga,
1941-44] 4 v. Title varies: Ver-
kündungsblatt. 349.47q085V DcD NN
CSt-H BM

VII.4.i. SPECIAL TOPICS AND LEGAL
COMMENTARIES

2758. ABRAMSON, A. Arbeitsrecht
in Litauen. In Zeitschrift für osteuropäisches Recht (Breslau), 1928.
p. 920-940. See serials consulted.

2759. ADAMUS, Jan. Zastaw w prawie litewskiem XV iXVI wieku. Lwów,
1925. 141 p. (Pamiętnik historyczno-prawny, t.1, zesz.7) DLC-L

2760. ALEKNAVIČIUS, T. Svetimša-
lių būklė Lietuvoje. [The legal
status of Aliens in Lithuania] In
Policija (Kaunas), no.4-6. p. 11-13;
21-24; 22-23. See serials consulted.

2761. ALSEIKA, Vytautas. Filmų
priežiūra Lietuvoje. [The censorship
of motion pictures in Lithuania]
Kaunas, V.D.U. Teisių fakulteto
leidinys, 1938. 72 p. (Teisės ir
ekonomijos studijos, t.2, kn.1.)
BM(AC. 1157. f/7.)

2762. BERSHADSKII, Sergei Aleksandrovich. O nasliedovanii v vymoro-
chnykh imushchestvakh po litovskomu
pravu. Sanktpeterburg, 1892. 44 p.
Caption title. Reprinted from,
Zhurnal Ministerstva narodnago prosvieshcheniia, v.284. 1892. no. 11.
DLC-L

2763. BÜCHLER, O. Bankanweisung
und Scheck in der russisch-litauischen Gerichtspraxis. In Zeitschrift
für das gesamte Handelsrecht und Konkursrecht (Stuttgart), 1933. p. 201-
220. See serials consulted.

2764. DĄBKOWSKI, Przemysław. Dobra
rodowe i nabyte w prawie litewskiem
od XIV do XVI wieku. Lwów, 1916.
117 p. (Studya nad historyą prawa
polskiego. Tom 6, zesz. 3)
BM(764/9.) CLU CtY-L DLC IU MH

2765. --- Stanowisko cudzoziemców
w prawie litewskiem w drugiej połowie XVI w XVI wieku (1447-1588). We

Lwówie, Nakł. Towarzystwa dla popierania nauki polskiej, 1912. 85
p. (Studia nad historya prawa polskiego, v.5, no.2) JX4270.L52D3
DLC BM(9476. cc. 10.) CtY

2766. DANIŁOWICZ, Ignancy. Kodex
Napoleona w porównaniu z prawami
polskiemi i litewskiemi; rozprawa,
opracowana w roku 1818. Z autogra-
fu wydał Alexander Kraushar. Warszawa, Księg. J. Fiszera, 1905.
177 p. Bibliography: p. 1-23. DLC

2767. HESSE, A. Das litauische
Grundbuchrecht nach dem Gesetz von
4. Dezember 1936. In Zeitschrift
für osteuropäisches Recht (Breslau,
Ger.), 1936/37. p. 619-630. See
serials consulted.

2768. --- Die privatrechtliche Gesetzgebung und Rechtssprechung im
Memelgebiet. In Zeitschrift für
ausländisches öffentliches Recht und
Völkerrecht (Berlin), 1932, p. 659-
675; 1936, p. 123-148. See serials
consulted.

2769. KAVOLIS, Martynas Arminas.
Das Eherecht in Litauen. In Zeitschrift für Ostrecht (Berlin), v.5,
no.1, 1931, p. 17-39. See serials
consulted.

2770. --- Des litauische Eherecht.
In Zeitschrift für osteuropäisches
Recht (Breslau), N.F., v.8, no.1-2,
1941, p. 53-74. See serials consulted.

2771. LAPPO, Ivan Ivanovich. Re-
kuperatornyi vladiel'cheskii isk v
litovskom pravie kontsa XVI stolietiia. Praga, 1933. 108 p.
HD701.L31 ICU

2772. LIETUVOS BANKAS. Lietuvos
bankas. [Bank of Lithuania. London,
Printed by Eyre and Spottiswoode,
1922] 23 p. Contents.--Law of the
Bank of Lithuania.--Bylaws of the
Bank of Lithuania.--Law of the mone-
tary unit. DH3135.7.L53 DLC CtY NN
NjP

2773. LITHUANIA. KARO MINISTERI-
JA. Karo baudžiamasis statutas.
[Military Criminal code. Comp. by]
J. Papečkis. Kaunas, 1922. 141,
viii p. DW

2774. LITHUANIA. LAWS, STATUTES,
ETC. Bendrasis sąskaitybos įstatymas (Įstatymų rinkinio VII t. 2 d.)
su paaiškinimais. [The general ac-
counting law... Translated by J.
Bobelis. Ed. J. Grabauskas] Kaunas, 1932. 196 p. MH-L

2775. --- Įstatymai apie valstybiní mokestį. [Public tax law] Kaunas, 1934. 29 p. MH

2776. --- Įstatymai darbo srityje Lietuvoj. [Labour laws in Lithuania] Kaunas, 1927. 128 p. DLC-L PU

2777. --- Lithuanie; loi sur la réforme agraire. Kaunas, Valstybės spaustuvė, 1927. 38 p. At head of title: Publication du Ministère de l'Agriculture. 947.59.L711L WaU

2778. --- Savivaldybių įstatymas. [Local government law] Kaunas, 1919. 80 p. 947.52L719.5 PU

2779. --- Teisiniai santykiai šeimoje. [Legal relations of the family] Santrauka veikiančiųjų šeimos teisės srityje įstatymų su Vyriausiojo Tribunolo paaiškinimais ir prašymų pavyzdžiais. Spaudai paruošė... L. Veržbavičius. Redagavo ir prakalbą parašė... Z. Toliušis. Kaunas, D. Gutman, 1932. 41 p. 349.475V6291 PU MH-L

2780. --- Veikiantieji Lietuvoje įstatymai darbo srityje. Žemės reformos įstatymas. [Labour laws in Lithuania and the Land reform act] Sutaisė V. Akėlaitis [ir] L. Volpertas. Kaunas, 1922. 134 p. 342. 475.L714 PU

2781. --- Zbiór praw y przywileiów miastu stołecznemu W. X. L. Wilnowi, nadanych na żądanie wielu miast koronnych, jako też Wielkiego Księstwa Litewskiego. Ułożony y wydany precz Piotra Dubińskiego. W. Wilnie, w Druk. J.K. Mci, 1788. 312 p. DLC-L NjP PU

2782. --- Žyminio mokesčio įstatymas su pakeitimais ir papildymais ir Vyriausiojo Tribunolo ir Rusų senato aiškinimais. [Stamp-duty law with amendments...] L. Veržbavičius [and] J. Rižis, [Comp.] J. Baltrušaitis [Ed.] Kaunas, 1935. 164 p. MH-L

2783. LIUTERMOZA, Martynas. Pramonės įstatymų leidimas ir darbininkų luomo padėtis Lietuvoje. [The legislation of industrial laws and the situation of workers in Lithuania] Kaunas, O. Esner, 1923. (Etingerys, J. Lietuvos pramonė, t.1) 970.6.ET ICLJF CtY CtTMF

2784. PRUNSKIS, Joseph. Comparative law, ecclesiastical and civil, in Lithuanian Concordat. A study with historical notes of the Concordat ratified on Dec. 10, 1927. Washington, Catholic University of America, 1945. viii, 161 p. (Canon law studies, no. 222) Thesis (J. C.

D.)--Catholic University of America. Bibliography: p. 135-144. BX1559. L5P85 DLC CtPAM CtY DCU NN PU ViU-L

2785. RAČKAUSKAS, Konstantinas. Das neue litauische Wechsel- und Scheckrecht. In Zeitschrift für osteuropäisches Recht (Breslau), 1938-39, p. 743-750. See serials consulted.

2786. ROBINSON, Jacob. Didžiosios Lietuvos piliečių užsieny sudarytų civilinių vedybų galia. [The legality of civil marriages concluded abroad by Lithuanian citizens] Detached from "Teisė" (Kaunas), 1933, no.20, p. 45-76. 947.53.B564.3 PU ICBM

2787. --- Lietuvos pilietybės teisių kolizijos. [Conflicts of citizens rights in Lithuania. By] Jokūbas Robinzonas. Kaunas, 1936. p. 45-76. 947.52.R564.3 PU

2788. --- Die litauische Staatsangehörigkeit. [By] Jakob Robinson. In Zeitschrift für Ostrecht (Berlin), 1928, p. 437-462. See serials consulted.

2789. RUSSIA. LAWS, STATUTES, ETC. 1855-1881 (ALEXANDER II) Najwyżej uchwalone przez jego Carską Mość dnia 19 lutego 1861 r. ustawy o włościanach, którzy wyszli z poddańczej zależności. Wilno, A.H. Kirkor, 1861. 947.52.R922 PU

2790. SCHWETSCHIN, A. Das Litauische Ehegesetz und das Matrikelgesetz vom 12.8.1940. In Zeitschrift für osteuropäisches Recht (Breslau), 1940-41, p. 279-302. See serials consulted.

2791. SIDZIKAUSKAS, Vaclovas. Lietuvos neutralumo įstatymas. [The Lithuanian Neutrality Law] In Mūsų žinynas (Kaunas), 1939, p. 222-229. See serials consulted.

2792. STRAVINSKAS, Petras. Užsienio akcinių bendrovių teisinė padėtis Lietuvoje. [The legal status of Foreign Companies in Lithuania] In Teisė (Kaunas), no.44, 1939, p. 383-394. ICBM

2793. VABALAS, Alfonsas. Les conflits de lois interprovinciaus dans le droit privé lituanien; exposé de droit comparé et de droit interprovincial en matière de mariage et de successions. Paris, Domat-Montchrestien, 1939. 165 p. maps. Thesis--University of Paris. Bibliography: p. 159-162. DLC-L CtY

2794. VALSONOKAS, Rudolfas. Lietuvos jūros teisė. [The Maritime Law of Lithuania] In Teisė (Kaunas), no.18, p.1-36. ICBM

2795. VERŽBAVIČIUS, Levas. Globa pagal Lietuvos statutus. [Guardianship according to the old Lithuanian Statutes] In Teisė (Kaunas), no.39, 1937 p.289-312. ICBM

2796. VILENSKAIA KOMISSIIA DLIA RAZBORA I IZDANIIA DREVNIKH AKTOV. Reviziia pushch i perekhodov zvierinykh v byvshem Velikom Kniazhestvie Litovskom, s prisovokupleniem gramot i privilegii na vkhody v pushchi i na zemli, sostavlennia Grigoriem Bagdavovichem Volovichem v 1559 godu, s pribavleniem drugoi aktovoi knigi, soderzhashchei v sebie privilegii, dannyia dvorianam i sviashchenikam Pinskago povieta, sostavlennoi v 1554 godu. Prigotovleny k pechati nachal-nikom TSentral'nago Arkhiva i ego pomoshchnikami Izdany Vilenskoiu Arkheograficheskoiu Kommissieiu. Vilna, v tip. Gubernskago pravleniia, 1867. v, 381 p. 947.59.V711r WaU DLC CSt-H CtY NN NNC PU

VII.5. ADMINISTRATION

VII.5.a. GENERAL STUDIES

2797. HONIK, Z. Urząd podwojewodziego w Wielkim Księstwie Litewskim, studium historyczne. Wilno [Kraj Spółka Drukarska] 1935. 39 p. (Wydawnictwa Towarzystwa Pomocy Naukowej im. E. i E. Wróblewskich) Osf80.935H CtY

2798. KOŚCIALKOWSKI, Stanisław. Z dziejów Komisji Skarbowej Litewskiej w początkach panowania Stanisława Augusta (1963-1780) In Ateneum Wileńskie (Wilno), v.2, 1924, p. 371-408. See serials consulted.

2799. LITHUANIA. MATŲ, SAIKŲ, SVARSTYKLIŲ IR PROBAVIMO RŪMAI. Vyriausiųjų matų, saikų ir svarstyklių rūmų penkerių 23.VIII.1919-23.VIII.1924 metų darbuotės apyskaita. [The five years report of the Agency of Weights and Measures] Kaunas [Valstybės spaustuvė] 1924. 46 p. tables. QC89.L5A45 DLC

2800. SCHULTZ, Georg Peter. Commentarius de marischalcis Regni Poloniae cum duplici mantissa de mareschalcis et cancellarijs M. Ducatus Lithuaniae ac Sereniss. Reginae, additis figuris sigillorum Lithuan. aeneis. Dantisci,

G.M. Knoch, 1743. 71 p. 947.52.Sch83 PU BM BN

2801. SENN, Alfred Erich. The formation of the Lithuanian Foreign Office, 1918-1921. In Slavonic and East European Review (Menasha, Wis.) v.21, no.3, 1962, p. 500-507. See serials consulted.

2802. STANKUS, Steponas. Ministerija. [Lithuania's Government Departments] In Lietuvių enciklopedija. Boston, Mass., 1959. v.18, p. 515-532. For holdings see entry no. 216.

VII.5.b. ADMINISTRATIVE BY-LAWS, INSTRUCTIONS, REGULATIONS, ETC.

2803. BURKEVIČIUS, Vilhelmas. Vyriausiojo notaro darbo praktika. [The work and procedures at the Land Title office] In Teisė (Kaunas),no. 14, p. 61-78. See serials consulted.

2804. LITHUANIA. KRAŠTO APSAUGOS MINISTERIJA. Internuotųjų stovyklų vidaus tvarkos taisyklės. Regulamin obozów dla internowanych. Kaunas, Kariuomenės štabas, Spaudos ir švietimo skyrius, 1939. 18 p. Lithuanian and Polish. D805.P7L53 1939a DLC(Photostat negative)

2805. LITHUANIA. LAWS, STATUTES, ETC. Muitinių įstatai. [Custom by-laws] Kaunas [Valstybės spaustuvė] 1924. 52 p. HJ6969.5.L5A5 1924 DLC

2806. LITHUANIA. PREKYBOS DEPARTAMENTAS. Prekybos departamento 1926-1927 metų aplinkraščių rinkinys. [Circular letters for 1926-1927 of the Department of Commerce] Kaunas, [F. Sokovskienė ir G. Lano spaustuvė] 1929. xxix, 291 p. incl. forms. (Prekybos departamento leidinys) DLC-L

2807. LITHUANIA. VIDAUS REIKALŲ MINISTERIJA. Medžioklės įstatymui vykdyti instrukcija. [Instructions for the application of game laws] Kaunas [K. Narkevičius ir V. Atkočiūnas] 1925. 8 p. SK543.L5A5 DLC

2808. LITHUANIA. VIDAUS REIKALŲ MINISTERIJA. ADMINISTRACIJOS DEPARTAMENTAS. Vidaus reikalų ministerijos administracijos departamento aplinkraščiai. [Administrative circular letters of the Ministry of the Interior] Kaunas, 1938. 535 p. forms. J400.L5R3 DLC

VII.5.c. POLICE AND SECURITY

2809. LITHUANIA. PILIEČIŲ APSAUGOS DEPARTAMENTAS. Geležinkelių policijos instrukcija. [The instructions for the Railway police] Kaunas, Valstybės spaustuvė, 1925. 32 p. HE1771.L5 DLC

2810. --- Instrukcija milicijos tarnautojams. [Instructions for the police employees] Kaunas [Valstybės spaustuvė] 1925. 60 p. U145.L8A5 1925 DLC

2811. --- Iš Lietuvos išsiųsti svetimšaliai 1918.II.16-1930.XII.31; 1931-1932; 1933-1934 metais. [The deported Aliens from Lithuania, 1918-1934] Kaunas, 1931-34. 3 pts. CtPAM

2812. --- Nusikaltimams kelti ir tirti vadovėlis. [A manual on lawsuits and investigation in criminal cases] Kaunas [Valstybės spaustuvė] 1925. 75 p. AV7762.6.A5 1925 DLC

2813. --- Vadovėlis policijai. [A handbook for police] Kaunas, K. Narkevičiaus ir V. Atkočiūno spaustuvė, 1926. 1 v. (various pagings) tables, forms. HV7355.6.A6 1926 DLC

2814. LITHUANIA. VIDAUS REIKALŲ MINISTERIJA. Vidaus reikalų ministerijos pasienio policijos instrukcijos. [Instructions for the border police...] Kaunas [Valstybės spaustuvė] 1924 32 p. HV7762.6.A5 DLC

2815. TOMAŠAUSKAS, Ignas, ed. Lietuvos policija, 1918-1928. [Lithuanian police, 1918-1928] Kaunas, V.R.M. Piliečių apsaugos departamento leidinys, 1930. 1 v. illus., ports. HV8227.6.A2T6 DLC

VII.5.d. POLITICAL PARTIES, THEIR PLATFORMS AND PRACTICAL POLITICS

2816. BIELINIS, Kipras and Stasys Michelsonas. Socialdemokratai Lietuvoje ir Jungtinėse Amerikos Valstybėse. [Socialdemocrats in Lithuania and the United States of America] In Lietuvių enciklopedija. Boston, Mass., 1963. v.28, p. 218-226. For holdings see entry no. 216.

BINKIS, Kazys. Antanas Smetona, 1874-1934, šešių dešimčių metų sukaktuvėms paminėti. Kaunas, 1934. 64 p. See entry no. 472.

2817. GABRYS, Juozas. Lietuvos valstiečių sąjunga. [Peasant Populist Union of Lithuania] In Naujoji romuva (Kaunas), no.13-14, 1937, p. 306-307. See serials consulted.

2818. GRIŠKŪNAITĖ, Emilija. Pozitsiia revoliutsionnykh sotsial-demokratov Litvy v periode vyborov i deiatel'nosti I. i II. Gosudarstvennykh Dum. In LTSRMAD. Serija A, v.1,1963, p. 165-182. See serials consulted.

2819. KAIRYS, Steponas. Socialinio sąjūdžio Lietuvoje išvakarės; Lietuvių sicialdemokratų partijos kūrimo ruoša... steigimas... programa, etc. [Before the dawn of the Lithuanian socialist movement; the preparations for the founding of the Socialdemocrat Party... its platform etc.] In His Lietuva budo. New York, N.Y., 1957. p.260-304. DK511.L25K13 CaAEU CtY DLC MH OC1 PU

2820. KAVOLIS, Vytautas Martynas, ed. Lietuviškasis liberalizmas. [Lithuanian liberalism. Chicago, Ill., Išleido Santaros-Šviesos federacija, 1959] 214 p. HM276.K26 DLC MH MiD OC1 PU

2821. KRUPAVIČIUS, Mykolas. Lietuvių politinės partijos. Parašė M. Keršys [pseud. Lithuanian political parties] Kaunas, [n.d.] 65 p. 947.5K948 PU

2822. --- Mūsų keliai (Leonas XIII ir mes). [Our road...] Kaunas, Šviesos, 1921. 38 p. (Lietuvių krikščionių demokratų partijos leidinys no.32) DK11.L713K9412 InNd PU

2823. KRUPAVIČIUS, Mykolas and Antanas Bendorius. Krikščionys demokratai. [The Christian Democrats] In Lietuvių enciklopedija. Boston, Mass. 1958. v.13, p.102-112. For holdings see entry no.216.

2824. L.S.D.P. [i.g. Lithuanian Social Democratic Party] for Lithuania's freedom. By S.A. Viktoras [pseud] London, 1955. 32 p. BM(08095. g. 8.)

2825. LIETUVIŠKOJI SOCIAL-DEMOKRATŲ partija. [The Lithuanian Social Democratic Party] In Lietuvos darbininkas (Zürich), 1900, no.3. BM(P.P. 3554/emb. (2.))

2826. LIETUVOS SOCIAL DEMOKRATŲ PARTIJA. Lietuvos socialdemokratų partijos dvyliktasis suvažiavimas. Kaune, 1925 metais balandžio 17-19 d. Kaunas, Raidės spaustuvė, 1925. 947.5.K948 PU

2827. LIETUVOS SOCIALISTŲ LIAUDI-ninkų demokratų partijos pamatiniai programos dėsniai ir organizacijos įstatai. [The platform of the People's Social Democratic Party] Kaunas, 1919. 7 p. Xerox copy, 1971. JN6745.A98L52 1971 PU

2828. LIETUVOS ŪKININKŲ PARTIJA. Lietuvos ūkininkų partijos programa. [The platform of the Lithuanian Farmers' Party] Kaunas, 1926. 25 p. 947.52.L6227 PU

2829. THE LITHUANIAN FARMERS PARty. In The Baltic Review (New York, N.Y.), no.10, 1957, p.63-68. See serials consulted.

2830. THE LITHUANIAN PEASANT Populist Union. In The Baltic Review (New York, N.Y.), no.10, 1957, p.51-56. See serials consulted.

2831. THE LITHUANIAN PEASANT UNION. In Baltic Review (New York, N.Y.), no.10, 1957, p.57-62. See serials consulted.

MERKELIS, Aleksandras. Antanas Smetona; jo visuomeninė, kultūrinė ir politinė veikla. New York, N.Y. 1964. 740 p. See entry no.608.

2832. MERKYS, Vytautas. Narodninkai ir pirmieji marksistai Lietuvoje. [Narodninkai (populists) and the first Marxists in Lithuania] Vilnius, Mintis, 1967. 160 p. illus., ports. HX315.65.A6M4 DLC NN PU

MYKOLAS ŠLEŽEVIČIUS. [Chicago, Ill., 1954] See entry no.627.

2833. OCHMAŃSKI, Jerzy. Polska socjalno-rewolucyjna partia "Proletariat", 1882-1886 i Litwini. In Roczniki Historyczne (Poznań), v.32, 1964, p.167-173. See serials consulted.

2834. PROGRAMAS LIETUVIŠKOS SOCIALdemokratiškos partijos. [The platform of the Lithuanian Social Democratic Party. n.p.] 1896. 17 p. BM(C. 115. a. 2.)

2835. RASTENIS, Vincas. Tautininkai. [The Nationalist Party] In Lietuvių enciklopedija. Boston, Mass. 1964. v.30, p.440-449. For holdings see entry no.216.

2836. SABALIŪNAS, Leonas. Lithuanian politics under stress: ideological and political developments before the Soviet occupation. In Lituanus (Chicago, Ill.), v.14, no.3, 1968, p.29-42. See serials consulted.

2837. --- Social-Democracy in Tsarist Lithuania, 1893-1904. In Slavic Review (Menasha, Wis.), v.31, no.2, 1972, p.[325]-342. See serials consulted.

2838. SMETONA, Antanas, Pres. Lithuania, 1874-1844. Tautos vado Antano Smetonos kalba, 1933 m. gruodžio mėn. 15 d. pasakyta visuotiname Lietuvos Tautininkų sąjungos suvažiavime. [The address by the President of Lithuania, Antanas Smetona to the Conference of the Federation of the Lithuanian Nationalist Party] Kaunas, "Savivaldybės" leidinys, 1934. 23 p. DK511.L27S54 DLC

2839. SOCJALDEMOKRACJA KRÓLEWSTWA POLSKIEGO I LITWY. SDPiL w rewolucji 1905 roku; zbiór publikacji.[Kolegium redakcyjne: T. Daniszewski, B. Krause, H. Mościcki. Wyd.1. Warszawa] Książka i Wiedza, 1955. 589 p. illus. DK438.S6 DLC CaOTU NcD NNC PU

2840. --- Sotsial-demokratiia Polshi i Litvy v revoliutsii 1905 g.; sbornik dokumentov. Perevod s pol'skogo Ch. Vol'skogo i M.Rymzha. Vstup. stat'ia A.M. Pankratovoi. Moskva, Izd-vo inostrannoi lit-ry, 1956. 789 p. At head of title: Otdel istorii partii TSK PORP. DK438. S617 DLC CaOTU IEN ICU MoU NcD NNC WU

2841. --- Socjaldemokracja Królestwa Polskiego i Litwy; materiały i dokumenty. Wydali H. Buczek i F. Tych. [Wyd. 1. Warszawa] Książka i Wiedza, 1957- . JN6769.A45S6 DLC PU(v.1, cz.2; 1962)

TERCIJONAS, Vincas. Dr. K. Grinius; gydytojas ir visuomenininkas. Kaunas, 1927. See entry no.673.

VII.5.e. ELECTIONS

2842. BULAVAS, Juozas. Rinkimai ir "tautos atstovavimas" buržuazinėje Lietuvoje. [Elections and "the representation of the people" in the bourgeoise Lithuania] Vilnius, VPMLL, 1956. 181 p. DK511.L27B8 DLC

2843. MAGGS, Peter B. Negative votes in Soviet elections. In Res Baltica. Leyden, 1968. p. 146-151. DK511.L18R4 DLC CaAEU CtY-L RP

2844. VENSTER, Steven. Bolshevik elections in Lithuania; terror and forgery to produce 99% majority. In Baltic Review (Stockholm), v.2, no.2, 1947-1949, p.52-60. See serials consulted.

VII.5.f. LOCAL GOVERNMENT

2845. LEONAS, Petras. Lietuvos savivaldybės; paskaitos. [Local government in Lithuania] Tilžė, "Ryto" (Pavlovskio) spaustuvė, 1923. 59 p. 947.52.L553 PU

LITHUANIA. LAWS, STATUTES, ETC. Savivaldybių įstatymas. Kaunas, 1919. See enry no. 2778.

2846. LITHUANIA. SAVIVALDYBIŲ DEPARTAMENTAS. Leidiniai. [Publications of the Department of Municipal Affairs] Marijampolė, 1925- . JS7.L5A3 DLC(no.2)

2847. --- Lietuvos savivaldybės 1918-1928. [Lithuanian local government in 1918-1928] Kaunas, "Savivaldybės" leidinys, 1928. 294 p. JS6131.52.A8 DLC OCl

2848. LIUBAVSKII, Matvei Kuz'mich. Oblastnoe dielenie i miestnoe upravlenie Litovsko-Russkago gosudarstva ko vremeni izdaniia pervago Litovskago Statuta; istoricheskie ocherki. Moskva, Univ. tip., 1892. viii, 884, c, vi p. fold. col. map. DLC-L CaBVaU CaOTU NN NNC NjP PU

2849. PUZINAS, Jonas. Iš mūsų savivaldybių praeities. [From the past of our local government] In Savivaldybė (Kaunas), 1928, no.5, p.10-15, 1929, no.6, p.10-20, no.7, p.9-16, no.8, p.11-20. Title varies. See serials consulted.

2850. SAVIVALDYBIŲ METRAŠTIS. [The yearbook of the Local Government] Kaunas, "Savivaldybės" redakcijos leidinys, 1935. xxxii, 143 p. JS6130.5.A1S32 DLC

2851. SONDECKIS, Jackus. Unternehmungen der Kommunalverwaltung in Litauen. In Zeitschrift für Kommunalwirtschaft (Oldenburg), v.23, no. 13-14, 1933, p.555-564. See serials consulted.

VII.6. ARMED FORCES

2852. ALIŠAUSKAS, Kazys. Lietuvos kariuomenė; istorinė apžvalga. [The Lithuanian Army; a historical rewiew] In Karys (Brooklyn, N.Y.), no.9,

1958, p.268-295. illus. See serials consulted.

2853. --- Lietuvos kariuomenė, 1918-1944. [Lithuanian military forces, 1918-1944] In Lietuvių enciklopedija. Boston, Mass., 1968. v. 15, p.93-121. For holdings see entry no. 216.

2854. BALTUŠIS-ŽEMAITIS, Feliksas. Karas su bolševikais Lietuvoje. [The war with Bolsheviks in Lithuania. Translated from Russian by V. S-tis] In Mūsų žinynas (Kaunas), v.17, no. 56, 1929, p.277-294. See serials consulted.

2855. BIRONTAS, Adolfas. Bermontininkams Lietuvą užpuolus; atsiminimai iš kovų už Lietuvos nepriklausomybę. [The invasion of Lithuania by the troops of Bermont...] Kaunas, "Žinijos" b-vės leidinys, 1934. 253 p. 947.52.B535 PPULC PU

2856. CHODKIEWICZ, Grzegorz. Articvli constitutionum bellicarum Magni Ducatus Lituaniae... In Republica, sive status regni Poloniae, Lituaniae Prussiae... Leiden, 1627. p. 309-317. DK405.R43 DLC BM(166. a.10.) CaBVaU NN

2857. DIRMANTAS, Stasys. Lietuvos kariuomenė po 1569 m. [Lithuanian army after 1569] Roma, 1967. [155]-233p. Atspaudas iš Žurnalo Tautos praeitis II t., 3-4 kn.) DK511. L24D55 PU

2858. --- Smolensko koridorius ir kas jame įvyko prieš 450 metų ties Orša. [The Smolensk Corridor and events on the river Orsha] Roma, 1965. 30 p., 16 tables. Offprint from: Tautos praeitis, t.2, kn.2, 1965, p.19-48. 947.5.D626 PU ICBM ICLJF DI

2859. DOBRAVOLSKAS, Jonas. Lietuviai kariai Didžiojo tėvynės karo frontuose. [Lithuanian warriors at the Frontline in the Great Patriotic War] Vilnius, Mintis, 1967. 186 p. plan. D764.D558 DLC CtY NN PU WaU

2860. IVINSKIS, Zenonas. Kariuomenės vaidmuo Lietuvos valstybę atstatant. [The role of military in restoring the State of Lithuania] In Židinys (Kaunas), v.22, no.7, 1935, p.31-40. illus. See serials consulted.

2861. JURGINIS, Juozas. Kauno įgulos kareivių sukilimas 1920 metais. [The revolt of the soldiers in Kaunas in 1920] Vilnius, 1955. 68 p. BM(9196. p. 41.)

2862. KAREIVIS LIETUVOS GYNĖJAS;
Lietuvos kareivio knyga. [The soldier, defender of Lithuania. Redagavo J.M. Laurinaitis] Kaunas, Vyriausio štabo karo mokslo valdybos
leidinys, 1926. 194 p. illus.
DK511.L27K25 InU PU

2863. KULIKAUSKIENĖ, Regina (Volkaitė) Lietuvos kario žirgas. [The
horse of Lithuanian soldier] Vilnius,
1971. 28 p. At head of title: Lietuvos TSR Mokslų akademija. Istorijos institutas. Acta historica lituanica, 7. DK511.L21K82 PU

2864. LÉONTIN, L. Les armées des
pays baltes; avec la preface du co-
lonel Jean Fabry. Paris, O. Zeluk,
1934. 93 p. illus. UA829.B18L57
CSt-H

2865. LITHUANIA. ARMY. Litovskii
ustav obshchevoiskovykh soedinenii.
Moskva, Voenizdat, 1939.
Slavic unclassified DLC

    LITHUANIA. KARO MINISTERIJA.
Karo baudžiamasis statutas. Kaunas,
1922. See entry no. 2773.

2866. LOEWE, Karl von. Military
service in early sixteenth-century
Lithuania: new interpretation and
its implications. In Slavic Review
(Menasha, Wis.), v.30, no.2, 1971,
pp. 249-256. See serials consulted.

2867. MATHIS, René. La Lithuanie
et ses décorations. In Les nouveaux
états européens et leurs décorations.
Nancy, 1929. UB430.M3 DLC CU

2868. --- Les nouveaux états européens et leurs décorations. Nancy,
Société d'impressions typographiques,
1929. xvi, 321 p. UB430.M3 DLC CU

2869. NATKEVIČIUS, Ladas. Lietuvos
kariuomenė. [Lithuanian armed forces]
New York, N.Y., Lietuvos atstatymo
bendrovė, 1919. 176 p. illus.
UA829.L8N3 DLC CtTMF ICCC ICBM ICJ
ICLJF NN NjP PCl PU

2870. OCHMAŃSKI, Jerzy. Organizacja obrony w Wielkiem Księstwie Litewskim przed napadami Tatarów krymskich
w XV-XVI wieku. In Studia i Materiały do Dziejów Wojskowości (Warszawa),
v.5, 1960, p. 349-398. See serials
consulted.

2871. PETRUŠAITIS, Petras, ed. Ne-
priklausomai Lietuvai. [For independent Lithuania] Čikaga, Lietuvos šaulių sąjungos tremtyje leidinys, 1965.
496 p. illus., facsims., ports.
UA777.P4 DLC CaOTP ICLJF MH PU

2872. POLAND. ARMIA. SZTAB GŁOW-
NY. Wojsko litewskie; opracował Oddział II Sztabu Generalnego. Warszawa, Wojskowy Instytut Naukowo-Wydawniczy, 1925. vii, 74 p. illus.,
fold. maps. UA829.L8P6 1925 DLC IU
CU NN PU

2873. RAULINAITIS, Zigmas. Aisčiai karinės istorijos šviesoje.
[A historical outline of the Baltic
people. Brooklyn, N.Y.] Karys,
1962. 64 p. Offprint from Karys,
no.6-10, 1961, with additions and
corrections. 970.5.RA ICLJF CtY

2874. --- Durbės mūšis, 1260 m.
liepos 13 dieną. [The battle of Durbė in 1260. Brooklyn, N.Y.] Karys,
1961. 96 p. illus. (Lietuvos Karinės istorijos raštai, nr.1) Offprint from Karys, 1961. DK511.Z9
1961 CtY CaOTP MH PU

2875. RAMOJUS, Vladas. Lenktynės
su šetonu. [The race against Satan.
Chicago, Ill.] Lietuviškos knygos
klubas [1956] 292 p. 970.5.Ra
ICLJF CtTMF

2876. RAŠTIKIS, Stasys. Kovose dėl
Lietuvos; kario atsiminimai. [In
battle for Lithuania; memoirs of a
soldier] Los Angeles, Lietuvių dienos, 1956-72. 3 v. DK511.L28R3 DLC
CSt-H CaAEU CtTMF ICLJF

2877. RUSECKAS, Petras. Lietuvos
kariuomenė. [Lithuanian armed for-
ces] Worcester, Mass., Spauda "Amerikos lietuvio," 1927. 44 p. illus.
947.52.R893.6 PU ICLJF

2878. --- Savanorių žygiai; nepriklausomybės karų atsiminimai. [Cam-
paigns of the volunteer army] Kaunas [Lietuvos kariuomenės kūrėjų savanorių sąjunga] 1937. 2 v. illus.
DK511.L27R85 DLC CtPAM CtTMF ICLJF
(1) OCl PU

2879. RUŽANCOVAS, Aleksandras.
Lietuvos kariuomenės dalys XVIII amžiuje. [Lithuanian army units in
the eighteenth century] In Karo archyvas (Kaunas), v.3, 1926, p. 299-
309. See serials consulted.

2880. SĄJUNGA GINKLUOTOMS KRAŠTO
PAJĖGOMS REMTI. Lietuvos kariuomenė. [The Army of Lithuania] Kaunas,
1938. 1 v. (chiefly illus.)
UA829.L8S3 DLC

2881. SCHMITTLEIN, Raymond. Lietuvos kariuomenė 1812 metais. [Lithu-
anian Army of 1812] Kaunas, Pribačis
[1937] 27 p. plates.
947.52.Sch55.2 PU

2882. ŠIPELIS, J. Artilerijos gyvenimo pirmas dešimtmetis. [First decade of the Artillery] In Mūsų Žinynas (Kaunas), v.15, no.45, 1928, p. 263-286. See serials consulted.

2883. SKORUPSKIS, Vladas. Karas už Lietuvos laisvę 1914-1934. [War for Freedom of Lithuania, 1914-1934] Kaunas, 1934. 187 p. illus., ports., maps. DK511.L27S52 DLC ICCC PU

2884. --- La résurretion d'un peuple, 1918-1927; souvenirs d'un témoin des événements militaires en Lithuanie. Paris-Limoges-Nancy, 1930. 148 p. illus., fold. map. DK511.L27S628 CaAEU BM CSt-H ICBM InU IaU MB MH MiU NN NjP PU

2885. ŚLIWIŃSKI, Artur. Jan Karol Chodkiewicz, hetman wielki litewski; z ilustracjami, mapą i planem bitwy pod Kircholmen. W. Warszawie [etc], Wydaw. M. Arcta, 1922. 170,[1] p. front., pl., ports., fold. plan. DK430.2.C5S55 DLC NN RP

2886. STEPONAITIS, Vytautas. Lietuviai rusų kariuomenėje. [Lithuanians in the Russian army] In Karo Archyvas (Kaunas), v.4, 1928, p. 131-136. See serials consulted.

2887. URBONAS, Simas. Kariūno atsiminimai. [Recollections of a cadet] Kaunas, Author, 1930-1931. 2 v. in 1. plates. NN

2888. VAIČELIŪNAS, Juozas. Tėvynės sargyboje; Lietuvos karininko-lakūno atsiminimai 1932-1941 m. [On guard for the fatherland...1932-1941] Sudbury, Ont., 1955. 230 p. illus. UA829.L8V3 DLC ICLJF MiD NN OCl PU

2889. VARIAKOJIS, Jonas. 4 pėstininkų Lietuvos Karaliaus Mindaugo pulkas. [The 4th regiment...; recollections] Brooklyn, New York, Karys, 1965. 120 p. illus., ports., maps, facsims. 947.5V424 PU

2890. ŽIBURKUS, Jonas. Žemaičių pulkas. [Samogitian (Žemaičių) batallion] Vilnius, Vaga, 1969. 324 p. illus., port. CaAEU OKentU

2891. ŽUKAITIS, Stepas. Panevėžio atvadavimas 1919 metais. [The liberation of Panevėžys, 1919] Kaunas, Vyr. štabo sp. ir šv. sk. leidinys, 1929. 34 p. illus. DK511.L26Z8 DLC

2892. ŽUKAS, Konstantinas. Žvilgsnis į praeitį. Žmogaus ir kario atsiminimai. Medžiaga istorikams. [A glance at the past. Memoirs of a man and a soldier. Historical material] Chicago, Ill., Terra, 1959. 477 p. DK511.L27Z8 DLC CaAEU ICLJF MH NN PU

VII.7. DIPLOMACY AND FOREIGN RELATIONS

VII.7.a. GENERAL STUDIES

2893. DUNDULIS, Bronius. Lietuvos užsienio politika XVI a. [Lithuanian foreign policy in the 16th century] Vilnius, Mintis, 1971. 306 p. DK511.L23D81 PU

2894. GERMANY. AUSWÄRTIGES AMT. Nazi-Soviet relations, 1939-1941; documents from archives of the German Foreign Office. Ed. by Raymond James Sontag and James Stuart Beddie. [Washington], Dept. of State, 1948. xxxvii, 362 p. (U.S. Dept. of State Publication 3023) Documents on Lithuania: p. 35, 38, 39, 76-78, 107, 112-118, 146-154, 165-171, 175-176, 192-194, 267-268. D754.R9G4 1948 DLC CaAEU NN

2895. JURKŪNAS, Ignas. Litauen genom tiderna. [Lithuania through the ages. By] Ignas Scheynius. In Baltiska Komittén. Ha de rätt att leva? Stockholm, 1943. p. 234-274. illus. DK511.B3B3 DLC DS NcD

2896. KIPARSKY, Valentin. Chronologie des relations slavobaltiques et slavofinnoises. In Revue des Études Slaves (Paris), v.24, 1948, p. 29-47. See serials consulted.

2897. KNIGA POSOL'SKAIA METRIKI Velikago Kniazhestva Litovskago, soderzhashchaia v sebie diplomaticheskiia snosheniia Litvy v gosudarstvovanie korolia Sigizmunda-Avgusta... izdana, po porucheniiu Imperatorskago obshchestva istorii i drevnostei rossiiskikh. Moskva, V Universitetskoi tipografii, 1843. 2 v. in 1. DK511.L23L55 CU KU

2898. KNIGA POSOL'SKAIA VELIKAGO Kniazhestva Litovskago, 1506. In Obolensky, Mikhail Andreevich. Sbornik Kniazia Obolenskago. Moskva, 1838. no.1 BM(9454. f. 1(1.)) DK3.02 DLC

2899. KONOPCZYŃSKI, Władysław. Udział Korony i Litwy w tworzeniu wspólnej polityki zagranicznej, 1569-1795. In PZHP w Wilnie, 1935. Pamiętnik, 6th. Referaty (Lwów), t.1, 1935, p. 78-81. See serials consulted.

2900. KRIVICKAS, Domas. Lietuvos užsienio politika, 1918-1940. [The Foreign Policy of Lithuania, 1918-1940] In Lietuvių enciklopedija. Boston, Mass., 1968. v.15, p. 344-352. For holdings see entry no. 216.

2901. LITHUANIAN INFORMATION BUREAU. Revendications. Paris, 1919. 4 p. (Délégation de Lituanie à la Conférance de la Paix. pt. III, 1-bis) D643.A7DP517 CSt-H PU

2902. MAČIULIS, Petras. Trys ultimatumai. [Three Ultimatums. Brooklyn, N.Y.] Darbininkas, 1962. 134 p. port. DK511.L27M2 DLC CaOTU CtY CtTMF ICLJF MH PU

2903. OSTEN-SACKEN, Paul. Von den livländisch-russischen Beziehungen während der Regierungszeit der Grossfürsten Witowt von Litauen, 1392-1430. Riga, 1908. Inaug.-Diss--University of Berlin. 947.5.Os78 PU MiU MH

2904. PARIS. PEACE CONFERENCE, 1919. LITHUANIAN DELEGATION. Material emanating from the Lithuanian delegation at the Paris Peace Conference. Balt 8295.10 MH

2905. PINON, Réné. La situation internationale de la République Lithuanienne. In Revue de sciences politiques (Paris), v.56, 1933, p. 481-490. See serials consulted.

2906. PIWARSKI, Kazimierz. Lithuanian participation in Poland's Baltic Policies, 1650-1700. In Baltic and Scandinavian Countries (Toruń), v.3, no.2, 1937, p. 219-226. See serials consulted.

2907. RÉGNAULT, Élias [Georges Soulanges Oliva]. La question européenne improprement appelée polonaise. Réponse aux objections présentées par MM. Pogodine, Schédo-Ferroti, parochine, Schnitzler, Solowiew, etc. contre le polonisme des provinces lithuano-ruthénes et contre le non-slavisme des moscovites. Paris, E. Dentu, 1863. xx, 228 p. DK437.R33 DLC

2908. ROBINSON, Jacob. Litauens aussenpolitische Probleme. In Zeitschrift für Politik (Berlin), v.18, no.8, 1929, p. 537-549. For holdings see serials consulted.

2909. ŠARMAITIS, Romas. Amerikos-Anglijos imperialistų intervencija Lietuvoje 1918-1920. [The intervention of Anglo-American imperialists in Lithuania, 1918-1920] Vilnius, Valstybinė politinės ir mokslinės

literatūros leidykla, 1955. 41 p. DK511.L26S28 DLC

2910. SHALKOVICH, Semen Vukolovich, ed. Sbornik statei raz"iasniaiush-chykh pol'skoe dielo po otnosheniiu k Zapadnoi Rossii. Vil'na, Tip. A. G. Syrkina, 1885-87. 2 v. 947.52. Sh74 PU ICLJF(1)

2911. STAKAUSKAS, Juozapas. Lietuva ir Vakarų Europa XIII-me amžiuje. [Lithuania and Western Europe in the thirteenth century] Kaunas, Švietimo ministerijos Knygų leidimo komisijos leidinys, 1934. 282 p. maps. Bibliography: p. 9-13. DK511.L23S78 DLC PU

2912. STRONG, Anna Louise. Lithuania's new way. London, Lawrence & Wishart [1941] DK511.L27S87 1941a DLC CaBvaU CU CtY IaU MH NN

2913. SURVEY OF INTERNATIONAL AFfairs, 1920-1923. London, Oxford University Press, 1920-23. Information related to Lithuania is in v.1, p. 248-261. D442.S8 DLC CaAEU

2914. TARULIS, Albert N. Unused springboard and insecure safety zone: a look at Soviet strategic arguments. In Baltic Review (New York, N.Y.), no.21, 1960, p. 42-57. See serials consulted.

2915. URBŠYS, Juozas. Aperçu de la politique étrangère de la Lithuanie. In Revue Baltique (Tallinn), v.1, no.1, 1940, p. 40-44. See serials consulted.

2916. VILEIŠIS, Petras. La Lithuanie et le problème de la sécurité internationale. Paris, Jouve et cie, 1937. 224 p. map. Bibliographie: p. 239-244. Thesis--University of Paris. DK511.L27V44 DLC BM CtY ICU MH NN NNC PU

2917. VYKINTAS, Stepas. Lithuania and the problems of Eastern Europe. In Lituanus (Brooklyn, N.Y.), no.4 (9), 1956, p. 14-18. See serials consulted.

2918. ZAUNIUS, Dovas. Du Lietuvos užsienio politikos dešimtmečiai. [Two decades of Lithuanian Foreign Policy] In Kemežys, V., ed. Lietuva, 1918-1938. Kaunas, 1939. p. 29-42. 947.52.L625 PU CtTMF ICLJF

VII.7.b. FOREIGN RELATIONS OF THE
BALTIC STATES

2919. BAADE, H. W. Die Bundesrepublik Deutschland und die baltischen Staaten. In Jahrbuch für internationales Recht (Kiel), v.7, no. 1, 1956, p. 34-68. See serials consulted.

BILMANIS, Alfreds. The Baltic states and the problem of the freedom of the Baltic Sea. Washington, D.C., 1943. See entry no. 763.

2920. ELKIN, Alexander. The Baltic States. In Survey of international affairs, 1939-1946. London, 1958, v.11, p. 52-58. Partial contents.--The Soviet-Lithuanian treaty. --The incorporation of the Baltic States in the Soviet Union. D442.S8 v.11 DLC CaOTP CtY-L DNAL FTS MiU-L IEN NNC NcU PEL

2921. GRAHAM, Malbone Watson. Security in the Baltic States. In Foreign Policy Reports (New York, N.Y.), v.7, 1932, p. 437-454. See serials consulted.

2922. KAELAS, Aleksander. Baltikum i Sovjetsfären. Stockholm, [Rabén & Sjögren] 1960. 32 p. (Världspolitikens deksfrågor, 1960, nr.9) DK511.B3K15 DLC PU

2923. KAJECKAS, Juozas. Some common misconceptions about the Baltic States. In Social Science (Winfield, Kansas), v.21, no.1, 1946, p. 39-46. See serials consulted.

2924. KARUS, G. Pribaltiiskie strany i podgotovka antisovetskoi voiny. Moskva, Gos. izd-vo, Otdel. voen. lit-ry, 1929. 62 p. DK511. B3K27 DLC NN

2925. KIRCHNER, Walther. The rise of the Baltic question. Newark, Delaware, University of Delaware Press, 1954. xi, 283 p. DL59.K5 DLC CaOTU NN PU

2926. --- --- Westport, Conn., Greenwood Press [1970] 283 p. map. DL59.K58 1970 CaAEU

2927. KONECZNY, Feliks. Walter von Plattenberg, landmistrz inflancki wobec Zkonu, Litwy i Moskwy, 1500-1525. Kraków, Nakł. Akademii Umiejętności, 1891. 947.52.P716.yK PU

2928. KRIVICKAS, Domas. Soviet efforts to justify Baltic annexation. In Lituanus (Chicago,Ill.), v.6, no. 2, 1960, p. 34-39. See serials consulted.

2929. LIGUE DES DROITS DES PEUPLES Les États Baltes; séance tenue à la Sorbonne le 31 mai 1948. Toulouse, 1948. 43 p. (Its Notes et documents, no.2) Includes: a speech by Mr. V. Sidzikauskas, p. 6-27. DK511.B3L5 DLC

2930. MEISSNER, Boris. Die Beziehungen zwischen der Sowjetunion und den baltischen Staaten von der deutsch-sowjetischen Interessenbegrenzung bis zum sowjetischen Ultimatum. In Zeitschrift für Ostforschung (Marburg), v.3, no.2, 1954, p. 161-179. See serials consulted.

2931. --- Die Grossmächte und die baltische Frage. In Osteuropa (Stuttgart), no.4, 1952, p. 241-250; no.5, 1952, p. 341-346. See serials consulted.

2932. --- Die Sowjetunion, die baltischen Staaten und das Völkerrecht. [Köln] Verlag für Politik und Wirtschaft [1956] 377 p. Bibliography: p. 318-348. JX1552.5. Z7R953 DLC CaAEU NN PU

2933. NATIONAL COUNCIL OF AMERICAN SOVIET FRIENDSHIP. The Baltic Soviet republics, based on [The Baltic riddle", by Gregory Meiksins. Introduction by Prof. Frederick L. Schuman. New York, N.Y., National Council of American-Soviet Friendship, 1944. 46 p. DK511.B3N25 1944a DLC DHEW CaQMM CSt-H NN PU

2934. NERMAN, Birger. Baltikum skall leva! Stockholm, Natur och Kultur [1956] 217 p. DK511.B3N37 DLC CaAEU CSt-H CU MnU NN NNC PU

2935. LA POLOGNE ET LA BALTIQUE; conférence données à la Biblioteque Polonaise de Paris par G. Pagés [et al.] Paris, Gebethner et Wolff, 1931. xii, 358 p. tables. (Problèmes politiques de la Pologne contemporaine, 1) NN

2936. PUSTA, Kaarel Robert. The Soviet Union and the Baltic States. New York, N.Y., J. Felsberg, [1942] x, 53 p. front. DK266.P8 DLC

2937. RAUCH, Georg von. Die baltischen Staaten und Sowjetrussland 1919-1939. In Europa-Archiv (Frankfurt, am M.), v.9, 1954, no.17, p. 6859-6868; no.20, p. 6965-6972; no. 22, p. 7087-7094. See serials consulted.

2938. RES BALTICA; a collection of essays in honour of the memory of Dr. Alfred Bilmanis. Edited by Adolfs Sprudzs and Armins Rusis.

Leyden, A.W. Sijthoff, 1968. 304 p. ports. DK511.L18R4 DLC CaAEU CtY-L RP

2939. RUTENBERG, Gregor. The Baltic States and the Soviet Union. In American Journal of International Law (Concord, N.H.), v.29, no.4, 1935, p. 598-615. See serials consulted.

2940. SCHNORF, Richard A. The Baltic States in U.S.-Soviet relations, 1939-1942. In Lituanus (Chicago, Ill.), v.12, no.1, 1966, p. 33-53. See serials consulted.

2941. SCHRAM, Stuart R. L'Union soviétique et les États Baltes. In Duroselle, Jean Baptiste. Les frontières européenes de L'U.R.S.S. Paris, 1957. p. [25]-166. map Bibliography: p. 334-341. DK67.D96 CaAEU CSt-H DLC IU MH NN

2942. SIDZIKAUSKAS, Vaclovas. Baltic States in the polycentric era. In Baltic Review (New York, N.Y.), no.27, 1964, p. 4-10. See serials consulted.

2943. --- The European Security Conference and the Baltic States. In Baltic Review (New York, N.Y.), no. 37, 1970, p. 3-6. See serials consulted.

2944. --- A review of Soviet policy toward the Baltic States. In Baltic Review (New York, N.Y.), no.8, 1956, p. 55-63. See serials consulted.

2945. --- The United Nations and the Baltic States. In Baltic Review (New York, N.Y.), no.25, 1962, p. 6-11. See serials consulted.

2946. SOBOLEVITCH, Elias. Les États Baltes et la Russie soviétique (relations internationales jusqu'en 1928. Paris Les Presses Universitaires de France [1930?] 265 p. Bibliography: p. 213-217. Thèse-- University of Paris. DL511.B3S57 DLC CSt-H CtY ICU MH NN

2947. SPEKKE, Arnolds. Some problems of the Baltic-Slavic relations in prehistoric and early historic times. Milwaukee, Wis., Marquette University, Slavic Institute, 1962. 16 p. (Marquette University. Slavic Institute. Papers, no.15) DK3. M295 no.15 DLC PU

2948. TARULIS, Albert N. Soviet policy toward the Baltic States, 1918-1940. [Notre Dame, Ind.] University of Notre Dame Press, 1959. xii, 276 p. maps. DK511.B3T28 DLC

CaAEU CaBVaU CaOTU CLU CSt CSt-H CU CtY GU InU IaU ICU MiU MnU MH NIC NNC NcU NjR NjP NcD OCl OrU PU ScU TxU WaU

2949 TURAUSKAS, Eduardas. Le sort des États Baltes. [Edité par les soins du Service d'information du comité supreme de liberation de la Lithuanie]. Reutlingen, Ger., 1954. 80 p. DK511.B3T8 DLC CaAEU

2950. VALTERS, Mikelis. Das Verbrechen gegen baltischen Staaten; Warnung an Europa und die Welt. [n.p.] Verlag Atlanta, 1962. 242 p. DK511.B3V3 DLC MH

2951. WEISS, Helmuth. Die baltischen Staaten; von den Moskauer Verträgen bis zur Eingliederung der baltischen Staaten in die Sowjetunion (1939-1940). In Die Sowjetisierung Ost-Mitteleuropas. Hrsg. von Ernst Birke [et al.] Frankfurt am M., 1959. V.1, p. 21-64. DR48.5.B52 DLC

VII.7.c. INTER-RELATIONS AMONG THE BALTIC STATES

2952. ANDERSON, Edgar. Toward the Baltic Entente; the initial phase. In Poska, Jüri G. Pro Baltica. Stockholm, 1965. p. 41-62. DK511. B25P6 DLC CaAEU CLU CU CtY InU ICU MiU-L NN PU

2953. --- Toward the Baltic Union; the initial phase [and] 1920-1934.. In Lituanus (Chicago, Ill.), v.12, 1966, p. 30-56; v.13, 1967, p.5-28; v.14, 1968, p. 17-39. See serials consulted.

2954. CONFÉRANCE DES ÉTATS BALTIQUES, Bulduri, Latvia, 1920. Minutes of the Baltic conference, held at Bulduri in Latvia in 1920. Washington, D.C., Latvian Legation, 1960. 105 p. All documents in French. DK511.B3C64 DLC CU ICU MH-L NN InU

2955. KAASIK, Nikolai. L'évolution de l'Union Baltique. Paris, Pedinet, 1934. 947.52.K112 PU NN; also in Revue général de droit international puvlic (Paris), yr41, p. 631-647. See serials consulted.

2956. KAZLAUSKAS, Bronius. L'Entente baltique... Paris, Imprimerie des Presses modernes, 1939. 327 p. fold. map. Thesis--University of Strasbourg. Bibliography: p. 317-321. DK511.B3K3 DLC CSt-H CtY NN

2957. PIIP, Ants. The evolution
of the idea of the union of the Baltic States. In Baltijas Unija (Riga)
Bulletin, no.2, 1934, p. 15-26. See
serials consulted.

2958. ROBINSON, Jacob. Baltiiskaia iuridicheskaia uniia. Kaunas,
Izd. Gutmana, 1937. 167 p. JX1552.
5.Z7L5 DLC

2959. SCHIEMANN, Paul. Über die
Aussichten des baltischen Staates.
In Preussische Jahrbücher (Berlin),
v.173, 1918, p. 305-319. See serials
consulted.

2960. ŠLIŪPAS, Jonas. Lietuvių-Lat-
vių respublika ir šiaurės tautų sąjunga. [Lithuanian-Lavian republic and
the Union of the Northern nations]
Stockholm, Svenska Andelsförlaget,
1918. 162 p. DK511.L2S86 DLC CtPAM
NN PU

2961. LE TRAITE D'ENTENTE ET DE
collaboration etre la Lettonie, l'Estonie et la Lithuanie. In Baltijas
Unija (Riga), Bulletin, no.2, 1934,
p. 59. See serials consulted.

2962. VILEIŠIS, Jonas. Unity of
the Baltic nations. In Revue Baltique (Tallinn), no.1, 1940, p. 78-83.
See serials consulted.

2963. VITOLS, Hugo. La mer Baltique et les états baltes. Paris,
Domat-Montchretien, 1935. 352 p.
Thèse--University of Paris. Bibliography: p. [341]-350. DK511.B3V56
1935a DLC CtY DNAL OOxM PU

VII.7.d. GERMANY

VII.7.d.1. FOREIGN AND GENERAL
RELATIONS

2964. ASKENAZY, Szymon. Przymierze
polsko-pruskie. Lwów, Nakł. Towarzystwa Wydawniczego, 1900. 257 p.
DK434.A8 CSt MiU MH WaU

2965 --- --- Wyd. 2. Warszawa,
Nakł. Gebethnera i Wolffa; [etc.]
1901. 257 p. DK434.A8 1901 DLC

2966. --- --- Wyd. 3., przejrzane
i dop. Warszawa, E. Wende i Spółka,
1918. 306 p. DK434.A83 1918 CtY
CaBVaU DLC InU KU MH MiD MiDW NN NcD

2967. COLLIANDER, Börje Erland.
Beziehungen zwischen Litauen und
Deutschland während der Okkupation
1915-1918. Åbo, Åbo Tidnings och

Tryckeri, 1935. 241 p. map.
DK511.L26C6 DLC ICU IEN NN PU

2968. DEGGELLER, Gerhard. Karl V.
und Polen-Litauen. Ein Beitrag zur
Frage der Ostpolitik des späten Kai-
sertums. Würzburg, K. Triltsch,
1939. 49 p. Inaug.-Diss.--Univer-
sity of Göttingen. DD180.D4 DLC MH

2969. FORSTREUTER, Kurt Hermann.
Deutschland und Litauen im Mittelal-
ter. Köln, Böhlau, 1962. 82 p.
(Studien zum Deutschtum im Osten,
Hft.1) DK511.L23F6 CaBVaU CaQMM
CaAEU CU CtY IaU ICU InND InU MH
MnU NIC NN NcD NNC NjR PU TxU

2970. GAIGALAT, Wilhelm. Die litauische Königswahl und die Beziehungen zwischen Deutschland und Litauen. Von Lituanus alter [pseud.]
In Germany and the European war,
1915-1921. v.13, no.3. 940.9108.
G317 v.13 no.3 TxU

2971. JURGĖLA, Constantinė Rudyard.
Lithuania in a twin Teutonic clutch;
a historical review of German-Lithu-
anian relations by C.R. Jurgėla, K.
Gečys and S. Sužiedėlis. New York,
N.Y., The Lithuanian American Infor-
mation Center, 1945. 112 p., 5 maps.
DK511.L2J75 DLC CaNSHD CaOTU CaSSU
CSt-H CtY IEN ICBM IaU IU InNd InU
KU MH MoU MU MnU MeU NIC NN NmU NcU
NNU-W NjR OrU PU RPB ScU VtU ViU WyU

2972. KRIVICKAS, DOMAS. Soviet-
German pact of 1939 and Lithuania.
Hamilton, Ont., Federation of Lithu-
anian-Canadians, Hamilton Branch,
1959. 14 p. map. DK511.L27K7 DLC
CaBVaU CaOTU

2973. LITHUANIA. UŽSIENIŲ REIKALŲ
MINISTERIJA. Documents diplomatiques.
Question de Memel...Kaunas,1923-1924.
2 v. At head of title: Republique
de Lithuanie. Ministère des affairs
étrangères. DK511.L273A5 1924 DLC
BM CLU CSt-H CtY KU MH NN NjP PU RPB

2974. PARIS. PEACE CONFERENCE,
1919. LITHUANIA. Lettre à la Conférence de la Paix concernant le point
de vue Lithuanien sur les prélimina-
res du traité de Paix avec l'Allemagne. Paris, 1919. 7 p. (Délégation de Lituanie a la Conférence de
la Paix, pt. III, 4) D643.A7DP5L7
CSt-H

2975. SCHAEDER, Hans Heinrich.
Deutsch- litauische Bündnispolitik
im Mittelalter. In Jomsburg (Leipzig), v.5, 1941. p.368-384. See
serials consulted.

2976. STUDIEN ZUM DEUTSCHTUM IM

Osten. Köln, Böhlau, 1962- . Issued by the Senatskommission für das Studium des Deutschtums im Osten an der Rheinischen Friedrich-Wilhelms Universität, Bonn. DD732.2.S78 DLC CaAEU IaU MH

2977. TIJŪNĖLIS, Juozas. La propagande Allemande contre la Lithuanie. Kaunas, Association pour l'ouest lithuanien, 1936. 48 p. 947.52.T446.FA PU

2978. --- Vokietijos propaganda prieš Lietuvą. [The German propaganda against Lithuania] Kaunas, Didžiosios ir Mažosios Lietuvos kultūrinio bendradarbiavimo sąjunga, 1935. 47 p. 947.52.T445 PU

VII.7.d.2. QUESTION OF KLAIPĖDA (MEMEL)·

2979. ALLIED POWERS (1919-) CONFERENCE OF AMBASSADORS. Memel Territory. Letter to the Secretary-General. Paris, Sept. 28, 1923. Chmbéry, Imp. réunies, 1923. 20 p. At head of title: League of Nations. Official noC.664.M.295. 1923. vii. JX1975.A2 1923.C.664.M.295.vii DLC OrU ViU

2980. ALLIED POWERS(1919-) TREATIES ETC. Convention between the British Empire, France, Italy, Japan and Lithuania respecting the Memel Territory and the Statute of the Memel Territory. Signed at Paris, May 8, 1924. London, H.M.S.O., 1924. 16 p. (Great Britain. Parliament. Papers by command. Cmd.2235) DK511.L273A6 1924 DLC CSt CU ICU MiU NN PP

2981. --- Convention et Disposition transitoire relatives à Memel, signées à Paris, le 8 mai 1924. Convention and Transitory provision concerning Memel, signed at Paris, May 8th, 1924. [Geneva, 1924] 13, 13 p. At head of title: Société des Nations ... League of Nations. French and English. DK511.L273A6 1924a DLC CLU CSt-H ICU LU NN OU OrU ViU

2982. --- Konvencija dėl Klaipėdos krašto. Konvention über das Memelgebiet. Statute of the Territory of Memel. Statut du territoire de Memel. Išleido Klaipėdos krašto direktorija. Klaipėda/Memel, F.W. Siebert Memeler Dampfboot, 1925. 83 p. Text in Finnish, German, English and French. DK511.L273A5 1925 CSt-H CSt PU

ARVYDAS, Felix. Das Memeland, ist es wirklich deutsches Land? Die Anrechte Litauens im Spiegel der Geschichte. Kaunas, 1934. See entry no.2254.

2983. BALTRAMAITIS, Casimir, V. Anglų periodinė spauda Klaipėdos klausimu. [A bibliography of articles on Klaipėda question published in English and American journals, 1920-1936] In Bibliografijos žinios (Kaunas), v.13, no.1(75), 1940, p. 21-23. See serials consulted.

2984. BEHRENT, Kurt. Die Memelfrage. Würzburg, 1930. 48 p. Inaug.-Diss.--University of Würzburg. 914.75B397 PU

2985. BÖGHOLM, Karl. Von Wilno bis Memel. Betrachtungen über die litauische Frage. 2. Auf. Danzig, Baltische Presse, 1928. 22 p. DK511.L2B6 InU PU

2986. DAUKŠA, Stasys. Le régime d'autonomie du territoire de Klaipėda; administration et organisation judiciaires. Paris, Recueil Sirey, 1936. 328 p. Thesis--University of Paris. JN6745.M4D3 DLC MH NN NNC PU

2987. DEBOEUF, Pierre. L'affaire de Memel. In Revue hebdomadaire (Paris), année 41, v.7, 1932, p.77-87. See serials consulted.

2988. DEU, Fred Hermann. Das Schicksal des deutschen Memelgebietes; seine wirtschaftliche und politische Entwicklung seit der revolution. Berlin, Verlag der Neuen Gesellschaft, 1927. 105 p. illus. 947.52.D487 PU MH NN

2989. DIDELOT, Jean François Octave. La Marine de l'aigle blanc. La Pologne et l'affaire de Mémel. Paris, 1924. 59 p. illus., maps. BM(9475. aa.41.) CSt MH NN

2990. FARERO, Stefan. Kłajpeda. In Sprawy obce (Warszawa), v.5, 1930, p.126-176. See serials consulted.

2991. FRIESECKE,Ernst. Das Memelgebiet; eine völkerrechtsgeschichtliche und politische Studie. Stuttgart, F. Enke, 1928. 76 p. (Tübinger Adhandlungen zum öffentlichen Recht... hft.13) 947.52.F913 PU

2992. GALVANAUSKAS, Ernestas. Kova dėl Klaipėdos. [The struggle for Klaipėda (Memel). Chicago, Ill., 1961] 26 p. Xerox copy, 1971, of clippings from Draugas (Chicago, Ill.) no.4-27,29, 1961. DK511.L273G3 1971 PU

2993. GIANNINI, Amedeo. La questione di Memel. Roma, Tip. Consorzio nazionale, 1935. 18 p. 947.52.G347 PU

2994. GLOGER, Kurt. Deutsches Memelland. [Berlin-Neutempelhof] E. Runge, 1935. 64 p. illus., maps. (Grenzkampfschriften, nr.14) DK511.L273G5 DLC IaU MH NN NNC

2995. GROSS, Leo. Der Memel-Fall. In Zeitschrift für Politik (Berlin), v.22, 1932, p. 518-532. See serials consulted.

2996. HALLIER, Joachim. Die Rechtslage des Memelgebiets; eine völker- und staatsrechtliche Untersuchung der Memelkonvention. Leipzig, R. Noske, 1933. viii, 232 p. (Frankfurter Abhandlungen zum modernen Völkerrecht ... Hft.39) DK511.L273H3 DLC

2997. HECKER, Hellmuth. Deutschland, Litauen und Memelland. In Jahrbuch der Albertus Universität zu Königsberg, v.4, 1955, p. 251. See serials consulted.

2998. HERMANN, Eduard. Die geschichtliche Rechte der Litauer auf Memel. In Völkerbund und Völkerrecht (Berlin), v.2, 1935-1936, p. 195- See serials consulted.

2999. HOPF, Hans. Auswirkungen des Verhältnisses Litauens zu seinen Nachbarn auf das Memelgebiet. Zur Vorgeschichte des deutsch-litauischen Staatsvertrages vom 22. März 1939. In Jahrbuch des Albertus Universität, v.12, 1962, p. 235-270. See serials consulted.

3000. IVINSKIS, Zenonas. Vokiečių literatūra Klaipėdos krašto klausimu. [German literature on the question of Klaipėda] In Bibliografijos žinios (Kaunas), no.1, 1933, p. 31-32. See serials consulted.

3001. JONAITIS, J.T. La propagande allemande contre la Lithuanie. Kaunas, Association pour l'Ouest Lithuanien [1936] 98 p. plates, maps, facsims. DD255.L5J6 DLC PU

3002. KALIJARVI, Thorsten. Die Entstehung und rechtliche Natur des Memelstatuts und seine praktische Auswirkung bis zum heutigen Tag. Aus dem Englischen übersetzt von Margarete Gärtner. Berlin, E. Ebering, 1937. 190 p. (Historische Studien, 3000) Bibliography: p. 184-190. CtY MB NNC OU PU

3003. --- The problem of Memel. In American Journal of International Law (Concord, N.H.), 1936, v.30, p. 204-215. See serials consulted.

3004. KOPP, Friedrich. Der Kampf um das Memel; ein Abriss einer politischen Geschichte. Berlin, Junker und Dünnhaupt, 1935. 66 p. illus. DK511.L273K6 DLC NN PU

3005. KOVO 20 DIENA; Mažosios Lietuvos prisiglaudimui paminėti. [The twentieth of March; a commemoration of the return of Lithuania Minor. Ed. by J. Šernas] Kaunas, 1921. 139 p. plates, ports. DK511.L27K6 DLC BM(S. c. 125.) CtTMF ICBM PU

3006. KOVOS KELIAIS; Klaipėdos Krašto prisijungimui prie Lietuvos 15-kos metų sukakčiai paminėti almanachas. [Through the path of struggles; an almanac to commemorate the fifteenth anniversary of the return of Lithuania Minor] Ed. by J. Vanagaitis. Klaipėda, 1938. 315 p. 891.92C.K848 PU

3007. L.R. The problem of Memel. In Bulletin of International News (London), v.11, no.26, 1935, p. 883-891. See serials consulted.

3008. LAWRENCE, Alexander. A memorandum on the Memel; treason trial in Kovno. London, 1935. iv, 65 p. map. DLC-L

3009. LEAGUE of NATIONS. Memel territory... Letter from the Conference of Ambassadors to the Secretary General September 28, 1923. Chambéry, Imp. reunies, 1923. 20 p. (C.664. M295. 1923) DK511.L273A6 1923 DLC CSt-H NN

3010. --- --- October 18th, 1923. [Genève] Imp. Kundig, 1923. 13 p. (C.678. M296. 1923.VII) DK511.L273A6 1923 DLC CSt-H NN

3011. --- The status of the Memel territory. [Geneva, 1924] 118 p. (C.159. M39. 1924.VII.) DK511.L273A6 1924b DLC CSt-H ICJ NN

3012. LEAGUE OF NATIONS. DELEGATION FROM LITHUANIA. The Memel problem. [With "Reply of the Lithuanian Government Delegation to the Questionnaire submitted by the Special Commission on the Memel problem] London [1922] 2 pts. map. BM(8093. cc. 33.)

3013. LEERS, Johann von. Memelland. München, Eher Nachf., 1932. 31 p. (Grossdeutsche Forderungen; Schriftenreihe zur Frage der nationalen Ansprüche des deutschen Volkes, Hft.1) DK511.L273L3 DLC CU CtY ICU MH NN NNC NcD PU WaU WU

3014. LENZ, Hellmuth. Deitsches

Schicksal an der Memel, die Wahrheit
über das Memel-land. München, J.F.
Lehmann, 1935. 79 p. illus., maps.
DK511.L273L4 DLC CU CSt-H ICMILC MH
MiU NN PU

3015. LITHUANIA. Memel territory.
[Memorandum from the Lithuanian Government to the Council of the League of Nations] Geneva, 1923. 24
l. At head of title: League of Nations. Official no.: C.727.M207.
1923 vii. NNUN-W

3016. LITHUANIA. MINISTRAS PIR-
MININKAS. Convention regulating the
status of the Memel Territory. Letter from Prime Minister and Minister for Foreign Affairs of Lithuania
Geneva, 1926. 18 leaves. At head
of title: League of Nations. Official no.: C.459.1926 vii. NNUN-W

3017. --- Territory of Memel. Pa-
ris, 1923. v.1. At head of title:
League of Nations. Official no.:
C.816.M.306. 1923 vii. NNUN-W

LITHUANIA. UŽSIENIŲ REIKALŲ
MINISTERIJA. Documents diplomatiques. Question de Memel... Kaunas,
1923-24. 2 v. See entry no. 2973.

3018. --- Territory of Memel. Geneva, 1924. 4 leaves. At head of
title: League of Nations. Official
no.: C.108. M31.1924.vii. NNUN-W

3019. LITHUANIAN INFORMATION BUREAU
Lithuania and the Klaipėda question.
Autonomy in relation to state sove-
reignty: review of present-day posi-
tion. London, 1934. 8 p.
BM(8093. h. 16.)

3020. --- The Lithuanian-Polish
dispute... London, Eyre and Spottiswoode, 1921-23. 3 v. DK511.L273L5
DLC CaOTU CaOKQ CtPAM CLU CSt-H ICU
IU ICJ MoU TU WaU

3021. --- The Memel convention.
Correspondence between the Conference
of Ambassadors and the Lithuanian Government, August 9th to September
21st, 1923. London, Eyre and Spottiswoode, 1923. 28 p. DK511.L273L5 DLC
MiU

3022. --- The Memel problem; with
a map of Lithuania and of the Memel
territory. London, Lithuanian information bureau, 1922?] 21 p. fold.
map. Appendix: p. 9-[22] contains
correspondence to and from the Council of Ambassadors, Paris.
DK511.L273L75 CSt-H ICJ MH MiU OClW
OU WaPS

3023. --- Le problème de Memel de-
vant la Conférence des Ambassadeurs.

Paris, Bureau d'information lithuanien, 1923. 37 p. map. DK511.L273
L57 DLC CSt-H MH-L PU

3024. --- The question of Memel.
Diplomatic and other documents from
the Versailles Peace Conference till
the reference of the question by the
Conference of Ambassadors to the
Council of the League of Nations
(1919-1923), including historical
sketches of the Memel region, and
other introductory statements...Lon-
don, Eyre and Spottiswoode, 1924.
189 p. map. At head of title: Lithuanian Ministry for Foreign Affairs.
Issued by the Lithuanian Information
Bureau (London) DK511.L273L6 DLC
CSt-H CtY CLU ICJ MH MiU NjP PPiU
RPB WaU

3025. LITHUANIAN NATIONAL COUNCIL.
Prusse Orientale. Declaration du
Conseil National des Lithuaniens sur
la propagande dans les régions li-
tuaniennes de la Prusse Orientale.
[Paris, 1919?] 3 p. (Délégation de
Lithuanie à la Conférence de la
Paix. [pt.] II:2) CSt-H

3026. --- [Revendications des lituaniens de la Prusse Orientale] à
son excellence Monsieur Georges Cle-
menceau, président de la Conférence
de la Paix et président du Conseil
des Ministres, Paris. [Paris, 1919]
5 p. (Délégation de Lithuanie à la
Conférence de la Paix. [pt.] III:3.
CSt-H

3027. LA LITHUANIE ET MEMEL. Editions de l'Europe Nouvelle. [Paris,
1922] [4], 11 p. map. Reprint
from L'Europe nouvelle, nov. 18,1922.
DK511.L273L5 InNd CSt-H MH PU

3028. MEUVRET, Jean. Le territoire de Memel et la politique européenne. Paris, Hartman, 1936. 86
p. map. (Centre d'etudes politique
étrangère. Section d'information.
Publication no.1) JX32.C42 no.1 DLC
NN NNC

3029. MISIŪNAS, Romualdas J. Versailles and Memel. In Lituanus (Chicago, Ill.), v.14, no.1, 1968, p.
65-93. See serials consulted.

3030. NÜSE, Karl Heinz. Litauen
und Memel. Berlin-Schönberg, A. Albrecht, 1932. 28 p. (Deutschland
und die Welt, 6) 947.52.N883 PU DLC
NN

3031. PAKŠTAS, Kazys. The problem of Lithuania Minor. Santa Moni-
ca, Calif., Author, 1946. 97 leaves.
maps. DD338.P3 DLC

3032. PREGEL, Reinhold. Die li-

tauische Willkürherrschaft im Memelgebiet. Berlin, Grenze und Ausland,
1934. 64 p. illus., map.
DK511.L273P92 CSt-H DLC CaOTU CU CtY
ICU IEN MH NN NNC NcD PU WU

3033. --- Memelfrage heute. Berlin, Volksbund für das Deutschtum
im Ausland, 1936. 31 p. (Kämpfen-
des Volk, Hft.2) DK511.L273P92 CSt
CSt-H NN PU

3034. --- Das Schicksal des Memelgebietes. Langensalza, 1935. 87 p.
DK511.L273P73 DLC NN PU

3035. SCHIERENBERG, Rolf. Die Me-
melfrage als Randstaatenproblem...
Berlin-Grünewald, K. Vowinckel,1925.
196 p. maps (part fold.)
DK511.L273S3 DLC CaAEU CU CtY ICU MH
NN NcD NNC PU

3036. STANIEWICZ, Witold. Sprawa
Kłajpedy. Wilno, Wydawn. Biura In-
formacyjnego, 1924. 33 p. 947.52.
St27 PU

3037. TOYNBEE, Veronica M. German-
Lithuanian relations, 1937-1939, and
the transfer of Memel to Germany,
March 1939. In Survey of International Affairs, 1938 (New York, N.Y.),
v.3, 1953, p. 357-390. See serials
consulted.

3038. VALSONOKAS, Rudolfas. Der
Fall Böttchers vor dem Haag. Memel,
Druck. "Rytas", 1932. 70 p.
947.52.V349 PU

3039. --- Klaipėdos problema. [The
problem of Klaipėda] Klaipėda, Ryto
b-vė, 1932. xv, 426 p. maps. Bibliography: p. 421-426.
DK511.L273V3 DLC ICCC KU OCl PU

3040. VOLDEMARAS, Augustinas. La
Lithuanie et ses problèmes. t.1:Li-
thuanie et Allemagne. Lille, Mercure universel [1933] 338 p. (Collection la Nouvelle Europe, 7) No
more published. DK511.L2V6 DLC CSt-H
CaOTU CtPAM ICLJF InU MH NN PU

3041. WASHINGTON JOURNAL. The Memel territory in distress... Washington, D.C., [1935] 19 p. From
"Memelland in Not" special edition.
947.5W317 CSt

3042. WENDENBURG, Walther and Hans
F. Lange. Die Memelfrage. Berlin,
G. Stilke, 1921. 61 p. 947.52.W4831
PU DLC NN

VII.7.e. POLAND

VII.7.e.1. FOREIGN AND GENERAL
RELATIONS

3043. ABRAHAM, Władysław. Polska
a chrzest Litwy. In Polska i Litwa
w dziejowym stosunku. Warszawa, 1914.
p. 1-36. DK418.5.L5P6 DLC BM CU
CSt-H

3044. ADAMUS, Jan. O prawno-pań-
stwowym stosunku Litwy do Polski.
In PZHP w Wilnie, 17-20 września
1935. Pamiętnik VI. Referaty (Lwów)
v.1, 1935, p. 174-180. See serials
consulted.

3045. BALZER, Oswald Marian. Nowsze poglądy na istotę prawno-pańswo-
wego stosunku Polski do Litwy w Jagiellońskim średniowieczu. In Towarzystwo Naukowe w Lwowie. Sprawozdania, v.1, 1921, p. 81-94. See
serials consulted.

3046. --- Tradycya dziejowa unii
polsko-litewskiej. Lwów; Warszawa,
Gubrynowicz i Syn, 1919. 24 p.
947.52.B2195 PU ICU MH NNC PPULC

3047. BOGATYŃSKI, Władysław. Stosunek Polski do Litwy w sprawie In-
flant (1560 r.) In Przegląd Historyczny (Warszawa), v.19, 1915,
p. 109-113. See serials consulted.

3048. BORCH, Nicolas. Le principe
des nationalités et la question lithuanienne. Louvain, F. Ceuterick,
1925. 189 p. Louvain. Université catholique. École des sciences
politiques et sociales. Collection.
DK511.L27B6 DLC BM CLU CU CSt CtY
CaOTU ICU IU MH MiU MnU NN NNC NjP
OClW PU PPULC WaU

3049. BUDECKI, Zdzisław. Stosunki polsko-litewskie po wojnie światowej, 1918-1928. Z przedmową Jul-
jana Makowskiego. Warszawa, Koło Naukowe Szkoły Nauk Politycznych, 1928.
93 p. DK418.5.L5B8 DLC CSt-H CtY PU
PPULC

CAMOGLIO, Costantino. La
questione lituana. Roma [1930] 143
p. See entry no. 870.

3050. DOWMUNT, M. Litwa z Polską.
[n.p., 1914] 27 p. NN

3051. EHRENKREUTZ, Stefan. Sepa-
ratyzm czy ciążenie Litwy ku Polsce
po Unii Lubelskiej. PZHP w Poznaniu
6-7 grudnia 1925. Referaty (Lwów),
v.1, 1925, p. 1-8. See serials consulted.

3052. GABRYS, Juozas. Lithuania and the autonomy of Poland. Paris, Lithuanian Information Bureau, 1915. 10 p. Reprint from British Review, Feb., 1915. 947.52.G113.2 PU ICBM NN

3053. GELEŽINIUS, Vytautas. Der litauisch-polnische Streit und die Möglichkeit seiner Lösung; Betrachtung eines objektiven Litauers. Aus dem Litauischen übersetzt. Kaunas, 1928. 61 p. DK418.5.L5G4 DLC MH WU

3054. GIERSZYŃSKI, Henryk. W kwestji polsko-litewskiej. Chicago, Ill., Zgoda, 1897. 18 p. NN

3055. GIERTYCH, Jędrzej. Sprawa litewska. Wilno, Nakł. autora, 1933. 30 p. 947.52.G535 PU

3056. GIRNIUS, Juozas. A glimpse into Polish-Lithuanian relations. In Lituanus (Brooklyn, N.Y.), no.3(12), 1957, p. 9-14. See serials consulted.

3057. GORZUCHOWSKI, Xavier. Les rapports politiques de la Pologne et de la Lithuanie. Paris, Les Presses modernes, 1927. 198 p. Thesis--University of Paris. 947.52.G692 PU CtY MH

3058. GRABIAŃSKI, Alexandre, ed. La Pologne et la Lithuanie. Paris, Section d'Études et de Publications Politiques du Comité National Polonaise, 1919. xxiv, 106 p. (Recueil des actes diplomatiques, traites et documents concernant la Pologne, t.3, fasc.1) DK402.B952 v.3 CSt-H CoU CtY ICLJF PU

3059. GROUPE PARLEMENTAIRE POLONO-FRANÇAIS, EN POLOGNE. Pologne et Lithuanie. Comité de rédaction Stanislas Thugutt [et al.] Varsovie, 1930. 167 p. (Its Recueil d'études, 3) BW89A.991R v.3 CtY DLC InU

3060. HALECKI, Oskar. Geschichte der Union Litauens mit Polen. Wien, M. Perles, 1919. 21 p. (Polens Grenzenprobleme, nr.3) DK511.L2H2 DLC BM(W.P. 6134-3.)

3061. HERBAČIAUSKAS, Juozapas Albinas. Litwa a Polska; rozważania na czasie. Wilno, Wyd. "Dzwonu Litwy," 1921. 28 p. 947.52.H418.2 PU

3062. JANOWSKI, Ludwik. Litwa i Polska. 2. wydanie. Lausanne, Imp. Hoirs Borgeaud, 1916. 30 p. (La Pologne et la guerre, 7) DK511.L2J33 1916 DLC BN NN WU

3063. JASTRZĘBIEC, M.R. Divide et impera; mysli niepolemiczne na tłe stosunków polsko-litewskich. Wilno, 1907. 24 p. 947.52.J315 PU

3064. KLIMAS, Petras. Les rapports des nations lithuanienne et polonaise; conférence fait le 23 mai 1927 au Centre Européen de la Dotation Carnegie, pour la paix internationale. Paris, Jouve & Cie.,1927. 23, [1] p. DK511.L2K6 DLC CtY InU MH NN PU

3065. KWESTYA LITEWSKA W PRASIE polskiej. Warszawa, 1905. 112 p. DK434.9.K86 CtY

3066. LEAGUE OF NATIONS. Questions raised by the Council in connection with freedom of communications and transit when considering the relations between Poland and Lithuania. Report of the Advisory and technical committee for communications and transit. [Geneva] 1930. 40 p. maps. At head of title: Geneva, September 5th, 1930. League of Nations. HE255.7.L47 1930 CIU CaOTU CaOWtU CSt-H CtY DLC IdU IU LU NcU NSyU OrU PU TxU WU

3067. LEAGUE OF NATIONS. SECRETARY GENERAL, 1919-1933 (Earl of Perth) Request by the Lithuanian Government referred by the Fourth to the Fifth Assembly: Reference of certain questions to the Permanent Court of International Justice for an advisory opinion. Memorandum. Geneva, 1924. 2 p. At head of title: Item 14 of the agenda of the Fifth Assembly. Official no.: A.11(1)1924.vii. Documents Division LN VII.1 v.1, no.13 OrU NNUN-W

3068. LE BIDEAU, Jean Louis Prosper Marie. Les relations lithuano-polonaises... [Oran, Ateliers L. Fouque, 1934] 169, vii, [2] p. maps. Thèse--Université d'Alger. DK511.L27L43 DLC CtY MH

3069. LESKOWIEC, Karol. Litwa a Polska. Londyn, Druk. Mildnera, 1941. 32 p. DK418.5.L5L4 DLC BM

3070. LEWANDOWSKI, Józef. Federalizm; Litwa i Bialoruś w polityce obozu Belwederskiego, XI.1918-IV.1920. [Wyd. 1] Warszawa, Państwowe Wydawn. Naukowe, 1962. 269 p. illus. DK440.L42 DLC CaOTU CoU CtY CSt-H InU IU KU MH NNC NcD PU WU

3071. LEWICKI, Anatol. Über das staatrechtliche Verhältnis Littauens zu Polen unter Jagiełło und Witold. In Altpreussische Monatsschrift (Königsberg in Pr.), N.F., v.31, 1894, p. 1-94. See serials consulted.

3072. LITHUANIA. Note adressée au gouvernement polonais par le gouvernement de Lithuanie [le 24 juillet 1919] Kaunas, 1919. 2 p. (Délégation de Lithuanie à la Conférence de la Paix. [pt.] VII:14) D643.A7DP5L7 CSt-H

3073. LITHUANIA. UŽSIENIŲ REIKALŲ MINISTERIJA. Documents diplomatiques. Conflit polono-lithuanien; question de Vilna, 1918-1924. Kaunas 1924. xx, 440 p. maps (part fold. col.) DK418.5.L5A5 DLC CLU CU CSt CSt-H CtY IaU ICU IEN KU MH MnU NN NNC NjP NSyU PU RPB WU WaU

3074. --- Lithuanie et Pologne. Notes de gouvernments lithuanien et polonais relatives au conflit lithuano-polonais. Kaunas, 1927. 26, 2 p. D651.L5A6 1927 DLC CU MH PU(Xerox copy) WaU

3075. LITHUANIAN INFORMATION BUREAU. Lituanie & Pologne. [Paris, 1919] 22 p. (Délégation de Lituanie à la Conférence de la Paix. [pt.] VII:1)

3076. ŁOSSOWSKI, Piotr. Stosunki polsko-litewskie w latach, 1918-1920. [Wyd. 1. Warszawa] Książka i Wiedza, 1966. 409 p. col. map. (Problemy dwudziestolecia, 1918-1939) DK418.5.L5L6 DLC CSt-H CaAEU CaBVaU CaOTU CtPAM CtY InU IU ICU KU MH MnU MU NcD NjP PU

3077. MACIEJOWSKI, Wacław Aleksander. Pierwotne dzieje Polski i Litwy zewnętrzne i wewnętrzne, z uwagą na ościenne kraje, a mianowicie na Ruś, Węgry, Czechy i Niemcy. Warszawa, Drukarnia Kommissyi Rządowej Sprawiedliwości, 1846. iv, 632 p. fold. map. DK420.M3 CU CoU CtY MH NNC

3078. MACKIEWICZ, Stanisław. Statut Litwy Środkowej. Wilno, Nakł. i druk. Ludwika Chomińskiego, 1922. 48 p. DK418.5.L7M15 InU PU

3079. MAKOWSKI, Juljan. Kwestja litewska, studjum prawne. Warszawa, Nakł. F. Hoesicka, 1929. 29 p. DK418.5.L5M3 DLC MH PU

3080. MALECZYŃSKA, Ewa. Polska wobec Czech i ziem litewsko-ruskich w okresie rozwoju ruchu husyckiego. In Polska Akademia Nauk. Instytut Historii. Historia Polski(Warszawa), v.1, no.1, 1960, p. 583-593. illus. DK414.P837 DLC

3081. MILOSZ, Oscar Vladislas. Les relations actuelles entre la Lithuanie et la Pologne; discours prononcé le 21 juin 1919, par M.O.W, Liubicz-

Milosz, a la salle de la Société de Géographie. Paris, Imp. Desmoineaux et Brisset, 1910. 23 p. D43.A7DP617.M662 CSt-H PU

3082. MIŠKINIS, P.A. Lietuvos ir Lenkijos santykių raida po II pasaulinio karo. [The development of relations between Lithuania and Poland after the World war II] In LTSRMAD. Serija A, v.1(32), 1970, p. 65-78. See serials consulted.

3083. MOŚCICKI, Henryk, ed. Unia Litwy z Polską; dokumenty i wspomnienia. Warszawa, Nakł. Gebethnera i Wolffa; [etc., 1919] 115, [1] p. DK418.5.L5M65 DLC BM(9745. aa. 40.) CtY InU MH ViU

3084. NA DRODZE DO ROZWIĄZANIA sprawy Litwy historycznej; etapy polskiej myśli politycznej... Kraków, Nakł. autora; Czionkami Drukarni Narodowej [1920] 37 p. (Problemy polskiej polityki wschodniej, 2) DK418.5.L5N3 DLC IU NN

3085. OCHMAŃSKI, Jerzy. Z dziejów współpracy politychno-kulturalnej polaków i litwinów w koncu XIX i początku XX wieku. In Rocznik Olsztyński (Olsztyn), v.4, 1964, p. 367-382. See serials consulted.

3086. ORZECHOWSKI, Stanisław Okszyc. Quincux; to jest, Wzór korony Polskiej na cynku wystawiony, przez Stanisława Orzechowskiego Okszyca... i za kolędę posłom koronnym do Warszawy na nowe lato roku... 1564 posłany. Wydanie Kazimierza Józefa Turowskiego. Kraków, Nakł. Wydawnictwa biblioteki polskiej, 1858. 113 p. diagr. JC381.07 1858 DLC CaAEU

3087. PAPÉE, Fryderyk. Polska i Litwa na przełomie wieków średnich. Kraków, Nakł. Akademii Umiejętności, 1904. 1v. map. DK418.5.L5P3 DLC BM(Ac. 750/67) CaOTU CtY MH NN PU

3088. PARIS. PEACE CONFERENCE, 1919. LITHUANIA. Lettre à la Conférence de la Paix concernant l'invasion du territoire lituanien par les troupes polonaises. Paris,1919. 4 p. (Délégation de Lituanie à la Conférence de la Paix. [pt.] VII:2) D643.A7DP5L7 CSt-H

3089. --- Lettre au Conseil Suprême des Alliés concernant les attaques polonaises contre les troupes lituaniennes. Paris, 1919. 3 p. (Délégation de Lituanie à la Conférence de la Paix. [pt.] VII:11) D643.A7DP5L7 CSt-H

3090. --- Lettre au président de la Conférence de la Paix, relative à la partipation des délégués lituaniens à la Commission des affaires polonaises à la Conférence de la Paix. Paris, 1919. 3 p. (Délégation de Lituanie à la Conférence de la Paix. [pt.] VII:5) D643.A7DP5L7 CSt-H

3091. --- Lettre au Conseil Suprême des Alliés relative aux relations lituano-polonaises. Paris, 1919. 7 p. (Délégation de Lituanie à la Conférence de la Paix. [pt.] VII:6) D643.A7DP5L7 CSt-H

3092. --- Lettre du 22 août exposant les agissements politiques de l'armée polonaise. Paris, 1919. 9 p. (Délégation de Lituanie à la Conférence de la Paix. [pt.] VII:17) D643.A7DP5L7 CSt-H

3093. --- Lettres au Conseil Suprême des Alliés concernant la violation de la ligne de démarcation entre les armées polonaises et lituaniennes par les troupes polonaises. Paris, 1919. 2 p. (Délégation de Lituanie à la Conférence de la Paix. [pt.] VII:12-13) D643.A7DP5L7 CSt-H

3094. --- Sur le transport de l'armée polonaise de Haller par la Lituanie et la formation d'un front unifié contre les Bolsheviks. Paris, 1919. 6 p. (Délégation de Lituanie à la Conférence de la Paix. [pt.] VII:4) D643.A7DP5L7 CSt-H

3095. PARIS. PEACE CONFERENCE, 1919. POLAND. Les relations entre la Pologne et les terres lithuaniennes et ruthènes avant les partages. Paris, 1919. 16 p. Slav 5912.20 MH

3096. PERNOT, Maurice. Les relations entre la Lithuanie et la Pologne. In Politique étrangère (Paris), v.3, no.3, 1938, p. 215-226. See serials consulted.

3097. POLAND. MINISTERSTWO SPRAW ZAGRANICZNYCH. Documents diplomatiques. Relations polono-lithuaniennes. Warszawa, 1928-29. 4 v. Partial contents.--v.1, Conférence de Koenigsberg. JX1555.7.P75d CLU CtY InU(1) NjP PU DLC MoU

3098. --- Documents diplomatiques concernant les relations polono-lithuaniennes. Varsovie, Imprimerie de l'État, 1920-21. 2 v. DK418.5.L5A3 DLC CaOTU CSt-H CtY InU(2) IU(1) MnU MoU NjP

3099. POLEN UND LITAUEN VON DER Dezemberrevolution des Völkerbundsrates bis September 1928. Danzig,

Danziger Zeitungsverlags-Gesellschaft, 1928. 16 p. DK440.P763 InU

3100. POLSKA I LITWA W DZIEJOWYM stosunku; praca zbiorowa. Warszawa, G. Gebethner, 1914. iv, 700 p. illus., map, facsim. Contents.-- Polska a chrzest Litwy, Władysław Abraham.--Kościół rzymsko-katolicki na Litwie, Jan Fijałek.--Mapa językowego obszaru litewskiego, Jan Rozwadowski.--Polacy a Litwini; język i literatura, Aleksander Brückner.-- Braterstwo szlachty polskiej z bojarstwem litewskim w Unii Horodelskiej, 1413 roku, Władysław Semkowicz.--Unia Polski z Litwą, Stanisław Kutrzeba. DK418.5.L5L6 DLC CU CSt-H InU KU MH NN PU

3101. ROZMOWA POLAKA Z LITWINEM, 1564. Wydał Józef Korzeniowski. W Krakowie, W Druk. C.K. Uniwersytetu Jagiellońskiego, 1890. viii, 91 p. (Polska Akademia Umiejętności. Biblioteka pisarzów polskich, 11) Ascribed to Augustyn Rotundus, pseud. i.e. Augustyn Mieleske. DK428.A2R68 NcU BM ICU NN PU

3102. ŠAPOKA, Adolfas. Lietuvių lenkų santykiai po Vytauto iki 1569 metų. [Lithuanian-Polish relations after Vytautas until 1569] In Naujoji romuva (Kaunas), no.38, 1931, p. 908-911. See serials consulted.

3103. --- Lithuania and Poland through the ages. In Lituanus (Brooklyn, N.Y.), no.5, 1955, p. 3-6. See serials consulted.

3104. --- Valstybiniai Lietuvos ir Lenkijos santykiai Jogailos laikais. [State relations between Lithuania and Poland during the reign of Jogaila] In His Jogaila. Kaunas, 1935. p. 185-266. 947.52.W797.yS PU OCl

3105. SENN, Alfred Erich. The Polish-Lithuanian war scare, 1927. In Journal of Central European Affairs (Boulder, Col.), v.21, no.3, 1961, p. [267]-284. See serials consulted.

3106. ŠLAŽAS, Paulius. Lietuva ir Lenkija, jų santykiai nuo seniausių iki šių dienų. [Lithuania and Poland; their relations from ancient to the present time] In Naujoji romuva (Kaunas), no.17, 1938, p. 400-402. See serials consulted.

3107. Šliūpas, Jonas. Litwini i Polacy. New York, N.Y., Nakł. i Drukiem Red. "Lietuviszkasis Balsas", 1887. 44 p. 947.5.Si35.4 PU

3108. SMETONA, Antanas. Lietuvių

santykiai su lenkais. [The Lithuanian-Polish relations] Kaunas, Spindulio b-vės spaustuvė, 1930. 312 p.
illus. (His Raštai, t.4) 081.S ICCC

3109. SMOLEŃSKI, Władysław. Sprawa stosunku Litwy do Polski na sejmie Wielkim. In His Pisma Historyczne. Warszawa, 1925. v.4, p. 60-
74. (*QR)NN

3110. STUDNICKI, Władysław. Współ-
czesne państwo litewskie i jego stosunek do polaków. Warszawa, Gebethner i Wolff, 1922. 107 p.
DK511.L27S89 DLC CtY ICBM ICU InU MH
NNC

3111. TOYNBEE, Veronica M. Relations between Poland and Lithuania,
1937-1939. In Survey of International Affairs, 1938. (New York, N.Y.),
v.3, 1953, p. 342-357. See serials
consulted.

3112. VOLDEMARAS, Augustinas. Lithuanie et Pologne. [Berlin, 1920?]
38 p. DK511.L27V5 DLC CSt-H PU

3113. --- Les relations russo-li-
thuaniennes. [Paris, Imp. Desmoineaux & Brisset, 1920] 32 p.
DK511.L27V6 DLC CSt-H PU

3114. WASILEWSKI, Leon. Stosunki
polsko-litewskie w dobie popowstaniowej. In Niepodległość (Warszawa),
v.1, 1929-1930, p. 30-59. See serials consulted.

3115. WIELHORSKI, Władysław. Pols-
ka a Litwa; stosunki wzajemne w bie-
gu dziejów. London, Polish Research
Centre, 1947. iv, 376 p.
DK418.5.5L5W5 DLC CSt-H CU CaBVaU
CaOTU CtY CoU InU KU MH NcD PU WaU

3116. WILKIEWICZ, Alina (Wawrzyń-
czykowa). Spory graniczne polsko-
litewskie w XV-XVII w. Wilno [Dru-
karnia Artystyczna "Grafika"] 1938.
[4], 93-200 p. Offprint from Wiadomości Studium Historii Prawa Litewskiego. DK418.W65e CLU; also in Vilna. Uniwersytet. Studium Historii
Prawa Litewskiego. Wiadomości, v.1,
1938, p. 93-200. See serials consulted.

3117. ZAJĄCZKOWSKI, Stanisław. W
sprawie badań nad dziejami stosunków
polsko-litewskich za Jagiellonów. In
Studia Historica. W 35-lecie pracy
naukowej Henryka Łowmiańskiego. Warszawa, 1958. p. 199-217. D6.S796
DLC CtY ICU MnU NIC NN

3118. ZE STOSUNKÓW LITEWSKO-POLS-
kich. Głosy litwinów... wydane staraniem J.K., etc. Warszawa, 1907.
231, iii p. A replay to "Kwestya

litewska w prasie polskiej." With
an inteoduction by L. Gira.
947.52.Z58 PU BM(8092. ee. 44.) MH

3119. ŽEMAITIS, Zigmas. O uniję
polsko-litewską; studjum ekonomicz-
ne i kulturalne. Z.Ž. Wilno, Wyd.
Echa Litwy, 1920. 64 p.
947.52.Z42.3 PU

3120. --- Próba pogodzenia Litwy
z Polską; notatki krytyczne. Z.Ž.
Kowno, 1921. 52 p. 947.52.Z42.2 PU

VII.7.e.2. QUESTION OF VILNIUS
(Vilna)

3121. ANYSAS, Martynas. Der litauisch-polnische Streit um das Wilnagebiet von seinen Anfängen bis zum
Gutachten des Ständigen Internationalen Gerichtshofs vom 15. Oktober
1931. Würzburg, 1934. v, 74 p.
Thesis--University of Hamburg.
Slav 6467.51.55 MH-L BM NN PPULC PU

3122. BALTRAMAITIS, Casimir V.
The Vilna controversy. In Bulletin
of bibliography and dramatic index
(Boston, Mass.), v.14, 1932, p. 195-
196. Z1007.B94 v.14 DLC NjP

3123. BARTEL, Paul. Cracow i Vilno. London, W.Hodge & Chilver [n.d.]
24 p. 914.38.B288 PU

3124. BARTUŠKA, Vincas. L'État
lituanien et le gouvernement de Suvalkai. Lausanne, Bureau d'Informations de Lituanie, 1918. 16 p. maps.
DK511.L2B3 DLC CSt-H DNW IU

3125. BIČIŪNAS, Vytautas Pranas.
Tiesa apie Vilnių. [The truth about
Vilnius] Kaunas, 1931. 72 p.

3126. BIRŽIŠKA, Mykolas. Na pos-
terunku wileńskim. Wilno, Wydawn.
"Głosu Litwy", 1920-22. 4 v.
947.5.B535.2 PU PPULC

3127. BIRŽIŠKA, Viktoras. Neužgijusios žaizdos; atsiminimai iš Vilniaus, 1920-1922 [Unhealed wounds;
recollections from Vilnius, 1920-
1922] Kaunas, Vilniui vaduoti sąjungos leidinys, 1936. 208 p.
947.52.B536 PU CtTMF PPULC

3128. BORKIEWICZ, Adam Józef. Wal-
ki z litwinami. In Borkiewicz, A.J.
Dzieje 1-go pułku piechoty legjonów,
1918-1920. Warszawa, 1929. Część
druga, Rozdział 10, p. 317-343.
illus. DK440.B65 DLC

3129. BORODZICZ, Józef. Kresy Wileńskie w niebezpieczeństwie. Wilno, Nakł. autora [192-] 52 p. illus., ports. 947.52.B648 PU

3130. BOUGOÜIN, Étienne. Pour un Locarno nord-oriental; le problème de Vilna. In La Revue des Vivants (Paris), no.6, 1928, p. 1134-1153. See serials consulted.

3131. BROCKELBANK, William John. The Vilna dispute. In American Journal of International Law (Concord, N.H.), v.20, 1926, p. 483-501. See serials consulted.

3132. CHKLAVER, Georges. Autour de Vilna. In Revue de droit international (Paris), v.2, 1928, p.224-250. Historical sketch of Lithuanian-Polish controversy about the Vilna territory. Several documents are quoted. See serials consulted.

3133. DELL, Robert Edward. The Geneva racket 1920-1939. London, Robert Dell [1941] 375 p. illus. Chapter IV: "Capitulation to Poland -Vilna," p. 37-47. JX1975.D48 DLC CaBVaU CaBViP CtY IaU MU NcD NcU NIC OCl OCU OO OU PBM PPD PR WA

3134. DU MORIEZ, Fernand. Wilno, la Lithuanie et la Pologne, la Bretagne et la France. Cette étude est suivie d'un postcriptum: Le véritable sens du Traité de Rapallo; les dangers qui menacent la Pologne - et la France; les alliances, nécessaires. Paris, Société Générale d'Imprimerie et d'Édition, 1922. 46 p. DK511.L27D89 CSt-H WU

GELEŽINIUS, Vytautas. Der litauisch-polnische Streit und die Möglichkeit seiner Lösung. Kaunas, 1928. See entry no. 3053.

3135. GERMANY. HEER. 10 ARMEE (1914-1919) SOLDATENRAT. Wilnas Auslieferung an die Polen; Denkschrift des zurückgetretenen Soldatenrats der 10. Armee. Stuttgart, 1919. 1 v. 947.52.G314 PU

GRABIAŃSKI, Alexandre. La Pologne et la Lithuanie; recueil des actes diplomatiques... Paris, 1919. See entry no. 3058.

3136. GRAPPIN, Henri. Pologne et Lithuanie. Paris, Imp. de Vaugirard, 1919. 23 p. D651.P7G6 DLC NN

3137. GRAUŽINIS, Casimir. La question de Vilna. Paris, Jouve & Cie, 1927. 206 p. fold maps. Thèse--Université de Paris. DL511.L27G7 1927 DLC CSt-H CtY DS IU MH MnU PU

3138. GRIESSINGER, Bruno. Die Wilnafrage; eine völkerrechtliche Studie. Würzburg, 1930. vii, 65 p. Thesis--University of Würzburg. 947.52.An98 PU CSt-H CtY DLC NN NNC

3139. HERBAČIAUSKAS, Juozapas Albinas. O Wilno i nie tylko o Wilno. [By] Józef Albin Herbaczewski. Wilno, Wydawn. "Mildy", 1922. 42 p. 947.52.H418 PU

3140. JONYNAS, Ignas. Vilniaus klausimas. [The question of Vilnius] In Lithuania. Centralinis statistikos biuras. Valstybės statistikos kalendorius 1937. Kaunas, 1937. p. 80-100. HA1448.L5A27 DLC BM DL MH NjP NN

KLIMAS, Petras. Les rapports des nations lithuanienne et polonaise. Paris, 1927. See entry no. 3064.

3141. KORWIN-MILEWSKI, Hipolit. Uwagi o konflikcie języków polskiego i litewskiego w dyacezji wileńskiej. Przekład z francuzkiego. Wilno, J. Zawadzki, 1913. Bound with Stosunki litewsko-polskie... 947.52.St.795 PU

3142. KRIVICKAS, Domas. Le question de Vilnius au point de vue du droit international. In Revue Baltique (Tallinn), v.1, no.2, June 1940, p. 193-202. See serials consulted.

3143. KUBILIUS, B. Diplomatinė kova dėl Vilniaus. [The diplomatic struggle for Vilnius] In Židinys (Kaunas), v.16, no.11, 1939, p. 524-545. See serials consulted.

3144. KUTRZEBA, Stanisław. La question de Wilno. Paris, A. Pedone, 1928. 21 p. DK511.L27K8 DLC PU

3145. LAPRADELLE, Albert Geouffre de. Consultations de MM. de Lapradelle, Louis Le Fur et André N. Mandelstam, concernant la force obligatoire de la décision de la Conférence des Ambassadeurs du 15 mars 1923. Paris, Jouve, 1928. 112 p. DK511.L27L3 DLC CSt-H CU CaOONL CtY ICJ ICU IaU InU IU MH MoU MH-L MnU NN NNC NbU NcU NcD NjP OClW OU PU TxU WaU

3146. --- The Vilna question; consultations of A. de Lapradelle, Louis De Fur, and André N. Mandelstam concerning the binding force of the decision of the Conference of Ambassadors of March 15, 1923; authorized translation from the original texts. London, Hazell, Watson & Viney, 1929.

91 p. DK511.L27L35 DLC CtY CoU IEN
ICN InNd KU MH MnU NN NB NIC NNC NjP
NjR NSyU NcU OCl OrU PP PU RPB ViU
VtU WU WaS WaU

3147. LEAGUE OF NATIONS. Différ-
rend entre la Lithuanie et la Pologne. Rapports de la Commission Mili-
taire de Contrôle dates des 24 décembre 1921, 12 février, 6, mars et
20 mars 1922... Dispute between Lithuania and Poland. [Nancy, Impr.
Berger-Levrault, 1922] [3], 3-28,
3-28 p. At head of title: Société
des Nations... League of Nations.
Official no.: C.329.M.183.1922.VII.
D651.L5A5 1922 DLC BM(Ac. 2290.)

3148. --- Différend entre la Pologne et la Lithuanie. Projet d'accord
préparé par Hymans... Dispute between
Lithuania and Poland. Draft agreement prepared by Mr. Hymans. [Genè-
ve, Imp. Jent, 1921] [3], 2-3, 2-3
p. At head of title: Genève, le 8
semtembre 1921. French and English
on opposite pages. Official no.:
C.317.A.59.1921. D651.L5A5 1921b
DLC

3149. --- Documents concerning the
dispute between Poland and Lithuania.
Geneva, League of Nations, Publishing
Service [1920] 3-155 p. (League of
Nations. Official Journal. Special
supplement, no.4) French and English
on opposite pages. JX1975.A32 no.4
DLC CaOTU MH

3150. --- Official journal; special
supplement, no. 4, 1920.
R341.61.L47o2os WaS

3151. LEAGUE OF NATIONS. ASSEMBLY.
SIXTH COMMITTEE. Question placed on
the agenda of the Fourth Assembly at
the request of the Lithuanian government. Report submitted to Assembly
by the Sixth Committee. [Geneva]
1923. 2 p. Official no.: A.104.1923.
VII. D651.L546 1923 DLC InU PU

3152. LEAGUE OF NATIONS. 2d ASSEM-
bly, 1921. Différend entre la Lithuanie et la Pologne. Résolution adop-
tée par l'Assemblée... 24 septembre
1921. [Genève, 1921] 1 leaf. Resolution no. 10. French and English.
Official no.: A.138.1921.
D651.L5A5 1921f DLC

3153. LEAGUE OF NATIONS. COUNCIL.
Conflit lithuano-polonais; correspondance échangée entre le Conseil de
la Société des Nations et le gouvernement lithuanien. Kaunas, 1922.
46 p. D651.L5A7 1922 DLC NN

3154. LEAGUE OF NATIONS. DELEGA-
TION FROM LITHUANIA. Les droits
de la Lithuanie sur Vilna et son
territoire. Mémoire présenté par la
Délégation lithuanienne à la Societé
des Nations. [n.p., 1921?] 18 p.
map. DK511.L27A5 1921a DLC CaOTU MH
PU

3155. --- The Lithuanian-Polish
dispute. Second Assembly of League
of Nations at Geneva, 1921. London,
Eyre and Spottiswoode, 1921. 101 p.
maps. At head of title: Lithuanian
Delegation. D651.L5L4 v.1 DLC CLU
CU CtY IEN IU MnU NN NNC NIC NmU NcU
NByU OCl PP PPi PU ViU WaS WyU

3156. LEAGUE OF NATIONS. DELEGA-
TION FROM POLAND. Mémoire sur la
Lithuanie et la volunté de ses habitants. Par E. Romer. Paris, 1919.
53 p. BM(08028. i. 27.) CSt-H

3157. --- O Wilno; memoriał Delegacji Polskiej przedłożony Konferen-
cji Brukselskiej. Lwów, 1921. 47p.
947.52.P194 PU

3158. LITHUANIA. Request of the
Lithuanian government under article
11 of the Covenant. Geneva, 1927.
17 leaves. At head of title: League
of Nations Official no.: C.525.M.183.
1927.VII. Letter dated October 15,
1927, protesting against the suppression of Lithuanian schools in Poland
and against Polish persecution of Lithuanian clergy. NNUN-W

3159. LITHUANIA (LITWA ŚRODKOWA,
1920-1922) SEJM. Sejm Wileński,
1922; przebieg posedzeń według sprawozdań stenograficznych w opracowaniu Kancelarji Sejmowej. Wilno, Wydawn. Księg. Józefa Zawadzkiego,1922.
1 v. (various pagings)
JS6130.59.V4A3 1922 CSt-H

3160. LITHUANIA (LITWA ŚRODKOWA,
1920-1922) GENERALNY KOMISARJAT WY-
BORCZY. Wybory do sejmu w Wilnie,
8 Stycznia 1922; oświetlenie akcji
wyborczej i jej wyników na podstawie
źródeł urzędowych, opracowane przez
Generalny Komisarjat Wyborczy. Wilno, 1922. 170 p. fold. maps, tables. JS6130.59.V4A32 1922 CSt-H

3161. LITHUANIA. DELEGATION TO THE
LEAGUE OF NATIONS. Différend entre
la Pologne et la Lithuanie. Lettre
de M. Galvanauskas. Dispute between
Poland and Lithuania. Genève, Impr.
Atar, 1921. 7, 7 p. D651.L5A5
1921d DLC BM CSt-H NN

3162. --- Exposé du conflit lithuano-polonais. Deuxième Assemblée de
la Société des Nations á Genève. Genève, Impr. Atar, 1921. 99 p. illus
fold. map. At head of title: Dele-

gation de Lithuanie. D651.L5A5
1921 DLC CLU CSt-H NjP

3163. LITHUANIA. MINISTRAS PIRMI-
NINKAS. Dispute between Lithuania
and Poland. Geneva, 1923. 7 leaves
At head of title: League of Nations.
Official no.: C.313.M151.1923.VII.
Letter dated Apr. 18, 1923, from the
Lithuanian Prime Minister referring
to the decision of the Conference
of Ambassadors giving Vilna to Poland. Includes note, dated Apr. 16,
1923, to the Conference of Ambassadors refusing to recognize the decision regarding Vilna. NNUN-W

3164. --- Request of the Lithuan-
nian government in virtue of article
11 of the Covenant. Letter from the
Lithuanian government dated October
24th, 1927. Geneva, 1927. 8 leaves.
At head of title: League of Nations.
Official no.: C.536.M199.1927.VII.
Letter from the Lithuanian Prime Minister giving a list of expelled Polish nationals together with their
petitions to the League of Nations
urging their return to Poland and
the reinstatement of their proper-
ties. NNUN-W

3165. LITHUANIA. TREATIES, ETC.,
1920-1926 (Stulginskis) Différend
polono-lithuanien. Genève, 1920.
10 leaves. At head of title: Société des Nations. Official no.:
20/4/458. Protocol of November 29,
1920, signed by the Lithuanian and
Polish representatives on the League
Commission of Control. French and
English. Includes declaration by
the Lithuanian representative urging
the evacuation of Zeligovski's troops.
NNUN-W

3166. LITHUANIA. UŽSIENIŲ REIKA-
LŲ MINISTERIJA. Conflit lithuano-
polonais. Correspondance échangée
entre les gouvernements lithuaniens
et polonais du 27 janvier au 8 avril
1922. Kaunas, 1922. 19 p.
D651.L5A6 1922 DLC CSt-H PU RPB

3167. --- Demande adressée à l'Assemblée par le Gouvernement lithuanien concernant: a) la résolution du
Conseil en date du 13 janvier 1922;
b) le renvoi de certaines questions
à la Cour Permanente de Justice Internationale en vue d'obtenir un ais
consultatif. Genève, 1923. [2] p.
At head of title: Société des Nations.
Official no.: A.7.1923.VII. Concerns
authority of the League of Nations
to intervene in Polish-Lithuanian
dispute. NNUN-W

--- Documents diplomatiques.
Conflit polono-lithuanien; question

de Vilna, 1918-1924. Kaunas, 1924.
See entry no. 3073.

3168. --- Le différend entre la Lithuanie et la Pologne; deux télégram-
mes, en date des 3 et 4 novembre
1920, émanant du Chargé d'Affaires
de Lithuanie à Londres. Genève,
1920. [5] leaves. At head of title:
Société des Nations. Official no.:
20/31/83. Appeal to the League of
Nations to enforce Poland's adheren-
ce to Council decisions. NNUN-W

3169. --- ---: Genève, 1921. 3,[3]
leaves. At head of title: Société
des Nations. Official no.: 21/68/30
Reply by the Lithuanian Foreign Minister to note from the League of
Nations (20/4/468) concerning the
proposal plebiscite in the Vilna region. NNUN-W

3170. --- ---: télégramme du chargé d'affairs de Lithuanie auprès du
gouvernement de la République Helvé-
tique, au sujet d'une concentration
de troupes polonaises contre la Lithuanie. Genève, 1921. [2] leaves.
At head of title: Société des Nations. Official no.: 21/68/49. NNUN-W

3171. --- ---: lettre, en date du
8 août 1922, transmettant pétition
du Comité Intérimaire Lithuanien de
Vilna. Dispute between Lithuania
and Poland; letter dated 8th August,
1922, transmitting petition from the
Provisional Lithuanian Committee of
Vilna. Genève, 1922. 4, 4 p. At
head of title: Société des Nations.
Official no.: A.20.1922.VII. NNUN-W

3172. --- Le différend entre la
Pologne et la Lithuanie: lettre en
date du 11 octobre 1920, émanant du
représentant de la Lithuanie à Paris. Londres, 1920. 3, 2 leaves.
At head of title: Société des Nations. Official no.: 20/4/335. Reports on the capture of Vilna by
Polish irregulars. NNUN-W

3173. --- ---: lettre en date du
2 novembre 1920, émanant du Chargé
d'Affaires de Lithuanie à Londres.
Genève, 1920. [5] leaves. At head
of title: Société des Nations. Official no.: 20/4/341. Includes Lithuanian note addressed to the Polish Government concerning exchange
of war prisoners, and telegram from
Kowno reporting air bombardment of
a church at Wilkomir. NNUN-W

3174. --- ---: letter from the Lithuanian Minister for Foreign Affairs,
together with the Secretary-General's
replay. Geneva, 1921. [12] leaves.
At head of title: League of Nations.

Official no.: C.514.M381.1921.VII.
Report of Poland's disregard for
the provisional demarcation line a-
greed upon, and violation of minority rights of Lithuanians in Poland.
NNUN-W

3175. --- ---: treatment of Lithuanians in Vilna. Geneva, 1921. [4]
leaves. At head of title: League of
Nations. Official no.: C.435.M.314.
1921.VII. Letter from the Lithuanian
Minister for Foreign Affairs requesting the League of Nations to pro-
tect the Lithuanian element in the
Vilna region under Polish occupation.
NNUN-W

3176. --- ---: reply of the Lithuanian government to the proposal of
the Council, dated September 20th...
Geneva, 1921. [3] leaves. At head
of title: League of Nations. Official no.: C.544.M.389.1921.VII.
Rejection of the draft agreement
proposed at the Brussels Conference.
NNUN-W

3177. --- ---: letter from the Minister for Foreign Affairs to the
President of the Council of the League. Geneva, 1921. [5] leaves. At
head of title: League of Nations.
Official no.: C.528.M.374.1921.VII.
Protest against the attempts made by
the Polish government to give legal
stability to the situation brought
about in Vilna by General Zeligows-
ki's action. NNUN-W

3178. --- ---: publication of documents. Letter from the Lithuanian
Chargé d'Affairs in Berne. Genève,
1922. 3 leaves. At head of title:
League of Nations. Official no.:
C.112.M.66.1922.VII. Letter, dated
Feb.4, 1922, replying to Poland's
protest (C.79.M28.1922.VII) against
the publication of the Lithuanian
Prime Minister's speech on the elections of Vilna. NNUN-W

3179. --- ---. Geneva, 1922. 3
leaves. At head of title: League of
Nations. Official no.: C.133.M.79.
1922.VII. Letter, dated March 1,
1922, from the Lithuanian Minister
of Foreign Affairs, replying to the
League Council's recommendation for
the establishment of diplomatic relations between Lithuania and Poland.
NNUN-W

3180. --- --- : proposed substitu-
tion of provisional line of demarcation for neutral forces. Letter from
the Lithuanian Minister for Foreign
Affairs. Geneva, 1922. 3 leaves.
At head of title: League of Nations.
Official no.: C.219.1922.VII. Con-

cerns Lithuania's reasons for not
assenting to neutral zones established by the League's Military Control
Commission. NNUN-W

3181. --- ---. Geneva, 1922. 4
leaves. At head of title: League of
Nations. Official no.: C.488.1922.
VII.Letter,dated July 17, 1922, from
the Lithuanian Delegation, replying
to Poland's allegations of violation
of the neutral zone by Lithuania.
NNUN-W

3182. --- ---. Geneva, 1922. 7
leaves. At head of title: League of
Nations. Official no.: C.597.1922.
VII. letter, dated Aug. 19, 1922,
from the Lithuanian Minister of Foreign Affairs protesting against ill-
treatment of the Lithuanian population in districts occupied by Poland
and requesting that a League Commission be sent to investigate conditions. Includes a memorandum addressed to the Lithuanian Republic by
delegates of the communes in the districts of Vilna and Grodno. NNUN-W

3183. --- Dispute between Lithuania and Poland in the territory of
Vilna. Geneva, 1922. 4 leaves. At
head of title: League of Nations.
Official no.: C.727.M.431.1922.VII.
Letter, dated Oct. 23, 1922 from the
Lithuanian Minister of Foreign Affairs
referring to Polish ill-treatment of
minorities. Includes petition addressed to the President of Lithuania by the delegates of the districts
of Vilna and Grodno. NNUN-W

3184. --- Dispute between Lithuania and Poland. Situation in the
neutral zone. Geneva, 1923. [1]
leaf. At head of title: League of
Nations. Official no.: C.34.1923.VII.
Letter, dated Jan. 12, 1923, from
the Lithuanian Minister of Foreign
Affairs, protesting against the Polish violation of the neutral zone
on Dec. 3, 1922. NNUN-W

3185. --- --- Polish prisoners at
Kovno. Geneva, 1923. [2] leaves.
At head of title: League of Nations.
Official no.: C.35.M.16.1923.VII.
Letter, dated Jan. 12, 1923, from
the Lithuanian Minister of Foreign
Affairs concerning the pardons gran-
ted to the Polish political priso-
ners. NNUN-W

3186. --- --- The neutral zone.
Geneva, 1923. 2 leaves. At head of
title: League of Nations. Official
no.: C.161.M.35.1923.VII. Telegram,
dated Feb. 10, 1923, from the Lithuanian Minister of Foreign Affairs,
refusing to accept the Council's re-

solution of Feb. 3, 1923, concerning the replacement of the neutral zone by a line of demarcation, and requesting that the matter be submitted to the Permanent Court of International Justice. NNUN-W

3187. --- Dispute between Poland and Lithuania:letter, dated 24th September 1920, from the Lithuanian Chargé d'Affaires, London. London, 1920. At head of title: League of Nations. Official no.: 20/4/258. Appeal for immediate intervention by the League to stop Polish aggression. NNUN-W

3188. --- ---:letter dated 27th September 1920, from the Lithuanian Chargé d'Affaires, London. London, 1920. [1] leaf. At head of title: League of Nations. Official no.: 20/4/269. Request for immediate con-vocation of the League of Nations Council, in accordance with articles 11 and 17 of the Covenant to consider the Polish invasion of Lithuania. NNUN-W

3189. --- ---: letter dated 1st October, 1920, from the Lithuanian Chargé d'Affaires, London. London, 1920. [3] leaves. At head of title: League of Nations. Official no.: 20/4/274. Includes telegram from the Soviet Foreign Commissioner, dated Sept. 28, 1920, regarding neutrality of Lithuanian territory. NNUN-W

3190. --- ---: letter, dated 2nd October 1920, from the Lithuanian Chargé d'Affaires, London. London, 1920. [1] leaf. At head of title: League of Nations. Official no.: 20/4/277. Reports unwillingness of Polish government to cease hostilities. NNUN-W

3191. --- ---: communication, dated 8th October, 1920, from the Lithuanian Chargé d'Affaires, London. London, 1920. [1] leaf. At head of title: League of Nations. Official no.: 20/4/295. Report on military action on the Polish-Lithuanian border. NNUN-W

3192. --- ---: communication, dated 8th October 1920, received from the Lithuanian Chargé d'Affaires, London. London, 1920. 2 leaves. Official no.: 20/4/296. At head of title: League of Nations. Official no.: 20/4/296. Protest against Polish military action in contravention of agreement sponsored by the League of Nations. NNUN-W

3193. --- ---:letter, dated 9th October 1920, from the Lithuanian Chargé d'Affaires, London. London, 1920. [2] leaves. At head of title: League of Nations. Official no.: 20/4/300. Includes copy of official telegrams received from Vilna reporting Polish military action near Vilna. NNUN-W

3194. --- ---: letter, dated 13th October 1920, from the Lithuanian Chargé d'Affaires, London. London, 1920. [1], 2 leaves. At head of title: League of Nations. Official no.: 20/4/324. Contains copy of official telegram from Kowno, dated October 11th 1920, including Polish proposal to resume direct negotiations. NNUN-W

3195. LITHUANIA. UŽSIENIŲ REIKALŲ MINISTERIJA. Financial arrangements for the settlement of the Polish-Lithuanian dispute. Correspondence between the Lithuanian Minister for Foreign Affairs and the Secretary-General of the League of Nations. Geneva, 1923. 6 leaves. At head of title: League of Nations. Official no.: C.188.M.111.1923.X. Allocation of expenses for the Military Commission appointed for the Polish-Lithuanian dispute. NNUN-W

3196. --- Incident de frontière polono-lithuanien. Polish-Lithuanian frontier incident. Geneva, 1925. [1], [1] leaves. At head of title: Société des Nations. Official no.: C.212.M.71.1925.VII. Telegram, dated Mar. 19, 1925, from the Lithuanian Minister of Foreign Affairs thanking the League of Nations for its intervention in the border incident (official no.: C.207.M.66.1925.VII.) NNUN-W

--- Lithuanie et Pologne. Notes de Gouvernement Lithuanien et Polonais relatives au conflit Lithuano-polonais. Kaunas, 1927. 26, 2 p. D651.L5A6 1927 DLC See entry no. 3074.

3197. --- Polish-Lithuanian dispute. Geneva, 1922. [1] leaf. At head of title: League of Nations. Official no.: C.193.M.107.1922.VII. Telegram from the Lithuanian Minister of Foreign Affairs, protesting against the annexation of Vilna, voted by the Diet of Warsaw on March 24th, 1922. NNUN-W

3198. --- Polish-Lithuanian incident. Geneva, 1925. [1] leaf. At head of title: League of Nations. Official no.: C.207.M.66.1925.VII. Telegram,dated March 17th, 1925, from the Lithuanian Minister of Foreign Affairs, protesting against a Polish incursion beyond the line of demarcation and requesting the League's intervention. NNUN-W

LITHUANIAN INFORMATION BUREAU The Lithuanian-Polish dispute... London, 1921-23. See entry no.3020.

3199. --- The Lithuanian-Polish dispute. Correspondence between the Council of the League of Nations and the Lithuanian government since the Second Assembly of the League of Nations 15th December, 1921-17th July 1922. London, Eyre and Spottis-woode, 1922. 65 p. DK511.L278 DLC IU ICU

3200. --- Il problema di Vilna. Genova, 1922. 38 p. 947.52.L717.3 PU

3201. --- Le problême de Vilna. Paris, Bureau d'information lithuanien, 1922. 32 p. maps. DK511.L27L53 DLC PU

3202. --- La vérité polonaise sur les lithuaniens par Lituanus. Lausanne, Bureau d'information de Lithuanie, 1917. 16 p. Pam. DK511.L2Ve CSt-H

3203. --- Vilna, capitale de la Lithuanie. Paris, 1919. 5 p. (Délégation de Lithuanie à la Conférence de la Paix. pt., V:2) D643.A7DP5L7 CSt-H

3204. --- The Vilna problem; with five maps. London, Lithuanian Information Bureau [1922] 24, 2 p. maps. DK511.L27L5 DLC CSt-H CtY In ICN ICBM MH MiU MnU NN NNC NjP OCl OU OClW PU WaU

3205. LITHUANIAN NATIONAL COUNCIL OF AMERICA. Lithuania against Poland; an appeal for justice, addressed to... the President of the United States, to the senators and representatives of the United States Congress, and to all American citizens. [Washington, D.C.] Executive Committee, Lithuanian National Council [1919] [3] p. D651.L5L5 DLC NN

3206. LITHUANIE ET RUTHENIE BLANCHE. Varsovie; Paris, Imp. Levé, 1919. 42 p. D643.A7 CSt-H BM(8092. g. 16.)

3207. MACKIEWICZ, Stanisław. Lwów i Wilno... London, Skład główny M.I. Kolin [1942] 30 p. DK441.M3 DLC NN

3208. MANDELSTAM, André N. et al. La décision de la Conférence des Ambassadeurs du 15 mars 1923; concer-

nant les frontières de la Pologne avec la Lithuanie. In Revue de droit international (Paris), v.2, 1928, p. 1075-1131. See serials consulted.

3209. MEMOIRE CONCERNANT DE LA SItuation des lithuaniennes du territoire de Vilna, presenté à la Assemblée de la Société des Nations. [n.p.] 1924. 947.52.M515 PU

3210. MERIGGI, Lea. Il conflitto lituano-polacco e la questione di Vilna. Milano, S. a. Istituto editoriale scientifico, 1930, 116 p. Bibliography: p. [114]-116. DK511.L27M4 DLC IU MH-L NN WaPS WaU

3211. MORESTHE, Georges. Vilna et le problème de l'est européen. Paris, Bossard, 1922. 129 p. DK651.V4M6 DLC CLU CU CSt-H CtY MnU NN OU PU

3212. NATKEVIČIUS, Ladas. Aspect politique et juridique du différend polono-lithuanien. Paris, E. Duchemin, L. Chauny & L. Quinsac, successeurs; Kaunas, Spaudos fondas, 1930. iv, 355, [2] p. maps. DK511.L2N3 DLC CU CLU CSt-H CaOTU CtY DCE IU KU MH MH-L NN PU WaU

3213. --- La ligne administrative polono-lithuanienne. In Revue générale de droit international public (Paris), v.38, 1931, p. 633-662. See serials consulted.

3214. NEWMAN, Edward William Polson. Poland and Vilna. In His Britain and the Baltic. London [1930] p. 123-146. DK511.B3N4 DLC CaAEU CSt-H CU MoU MWalB

NORUS, T. Lithuania's case for independence. Washington, D.C., 1918. See entry no. 5380.

3215. PAKŠTAS, Kazys. Vilniaus problema ir kaip ją spręsti. [The question of Vilnius and how to solve it] In Židinys (Kaunas), 1935, v.21, no.2, p. 129-139; no.3, p. 246-263. See serials consulted.

3216. PAWLIKOWSKI, Michał K. Sumienie Polski; rzecz o Wilnie i kraju wileńskim. Londyn, Nakł. Związku Ziem Północnowschodnich R.P., 1946. 44 p. illus. DK651.V4P3 DLC MH PU

3217. PETRĖNAS, Juozas. Mūsų Vilnius. [Our Vilnius] Kaunas, Lietuvos Šaulių sąjungos leidinys, 1924. 947.52.P445M PU

3218. POLAND. CENTRUM INFORMACJI I DOKUMENTACJI. The Polish territory occupied by the Lithuanians. [Paris, Angers, 1940] 12 numbered leaves. D821.P7A5 1940 DLC CSt-H CSt NjP

3219. POLAND. COMMISSION OF WORK PREPARATORY TO THE CONFERENCE OF PEACE. Droits de la Russie sur la Lithuanie et sur la Ruthénie-Blanche. Paris [Levé] 1919. 11 p. (BTZE p.v.)NN

3220. POLAND. MINISTERSTWO SPRAW ZAGRANICHNYCH. Dispute between Lithuania and Poland. [Geneva] 1921. 5 leaves. At head of title: League of Nations. Official no.: 21/68/89. Letter from the Polish Minister for Foreign Affairs, dated March 19th, 1921, declering Poland's readiness to submit to the Vilna plebiscite. NNUN-W

3221. --- ---: letter from the Polish Minister for Foreign Affairs, relating to the letter from the Lithuanian Minister for Foreign Affairs, dated 28th October, 1921 (document C.435.M.314), Geneva, 1921. [12] leaves. At head of title: League of Nations. Official no.: C.552.M.391. 1921.VII. Annexes: I: Memorandum regarding the facts set forth in the note sent on Oct. 28th, 1921, by M. Puryckis, Lithuanian Minister for foreign Affairs. II: Complaint by the Parents' Committee of the Polish College at Poniewież, Lithuania. NNUN-W

3222. --- --- Geneva, 1922. [2] leaves. At head of title: League of Nations. Telegram, dated March 20th, 1922, from the Polish Minister of Foreign Affairs, proposing replacement of the neutral zone by a provisional line of demarcation. NNUN-W

3223.--- --- Provisional line of demarcation in the neutral zone. Geneva, 1923. 2 leaves. At head of title: League of Nations. Official no.: C.171.M.96.1923.VII. Telegram, dated Feb. 21st, 1923, from the Polish Minister for foreign Affairs, denying Lithuania's allegations of Polish occupation of the neutral zone. NNUN-W

3224. --- The dispute between Poland and Lithuania. Geneva, 1922. [1] leaf. At head of title: League of Nations. Official no.: C.178.1922. VII. Telegram, dated Mar. 25th, 1922, refuting Lithuania's charges of Polish violation of the neutral zone. NNUN-W

--- Documents diplomatiques. Relations polono-lithuaniennes (1918-1939) Warszawa, 1928-29. See entry no. 3097.

--- Documents diplomatiques concernant les relations polono-lithuaniennes. Varsovie, 1920-21. See entry no. 3098.

3225. POLSKA RADA NARODOWA ZIEM BIAŁORUSKICH. Kresy litewsko-białoruskie Rzeczypospolitej Polskiej. Warszawa, [Druk J. Świętońskiego] 1919. 62 p. .Otbitka memorjału, złożonego Misjom Entente'y w Warszawie, przez P.R.N.Z.B. (*QO p.v. 90)NN

3226. PRAWA LITWY DO WILNA I Wileńszczyzny. Wilno, Wyd. "Dzwonu Litwy", 1921. 947.52.P898 PU

3227. ROSENBAUM, S. La question polono-lithuanienne. Paris, Imp. Desmoineaux & Brisset, 1919. 32 p. D651.L5R6 DLC IU NN

3228. ROZWADOWSKI, Jan Michał. My a Ruś i Litwa. Kraków, J. Czernecki, 1917. 28 p. 847.524.R8195 PU NN

3229. RUSECKAS, Petras. Kaip lenkinta Vilniaus kraštas. [Methods of polonization of the Vilnius region] Kaunas, Vilniui vaduoti sąjunga, 1930. 16 p. (Vilniui vaduoti sąjungos leidinys, nr.46) 370.31ŽE ICLJF

3230. RUTENBERG, Gregor. Die Entscheidung der Haager Weltgerichtshofes vom 15 Oktober, 1931 in den litauisch-polnischen Streitsachen. In Zeitschrift für Ostrecht (Berlin), v.7, 1933, p. 274-290. See serials consulted.

3231. --- Litauen, Russland und das Wilna problem. Eine Völkerrechtliche Darstellung. Breslau, J.U. Kern, 1929. 27 p. 947.52.R933 PU

3232. SAKAVIČIUS, Vladimiras. Gana tylėti; arba, Mūsų tautinio Vilniaus krašto veikimo skausmo balsas. [It is enough to be silent] Vilnius, 1934. 17 p. 947.52.Sa25 PU

3233. SCELLE, Georges. Le Conseil de la Société des Nations et le conflit lithuanien. In Revue politique et parlamentaire (Paris), v.134, no. 398, 1929, p. [69]-81. See serials consulted.

3234. --- La situation juridique de Vilna et de son territoire. In Revue général de droit international public (Paris), v.35, no.6, 1928, p. 730-780. See serials consulted.

3235. ŠEMIS, B. Vilniaus Golgota; okupuotosios Lietuvos lietuvių darbo ir kančių, 1919-1928 metų dienoraštis. [Diary of oppression in occupied Vilnius territory] Kaunas, Sąjungos Vilniui vaduoti leidinys,

1930. 658 p. illus. Author's real name Mykolas Biržiška. DK651.V4 S4 DLC OCl

3236. SENN, Alfred Erich. The great powers, Lithuania and the Vilna question 1920-1928. Leiden, E. J. Brill, 1966[1967], x, 242 p. (Studies in East European history, 11). DK511.L27.S42 DLC AzU CaBvaS CaBVaU CaOHM CaOLU CaOTU CaOWtU CU CSt-H CoU CtY FU GU HU IaU InNd InU IEN KU LU MH MU MnU NIC NN NNC NbU NBuU NcD NcU NjR NmU NvU NdU NjP OkU OrU OClW PPiU PU PP TU ScU WaU ViU WU

3237. SIDZIKAUSKAS, Vaclovas. Der litauisch-polnische Konflikt; die Wilnafrage. In Nord und Süd (Berlin), no.12, 1928, Jg.51, p. 1061-1072. See serials consulted.

3238. SMOGORZEWSKI, Kazimierz Maciej. Lwów and Wilno... London, Free Europe, [1944] 27 p. maps. (Free Europe pamphlet, no.9) DK418.5.R9S6 DLC CtY NNC NcD PU

3239. STRICTLY SECRET MEMORANDUM by the Vilna vaivode (governor) Bociański dated February 11, 1936, concerning the action of the general administrative authorities in respect of the Lithuanian minority in Poland, and proposed future measures in this regard. [Kaunas, Spaudos Fondas, 1940] 52 p. DLL

3240. STUDNICKI, Wacław Gizbert. Stosunek Wilna do legjonów; ... Wilno, 1928. 30 p. 947.52.St93.3 PU

3241. ŚWIECHOWSKI, Marian and St. Niekrasz. The Lithuanian problem. Two political maps with observations and tables of statistics. [Warszawa] Provisory Political committee of the Kowno Lands [1920?]. map. D651.L5S8 DLC NN

3242. --- O program w stosunku do ziem Litewsko-Białoruskich. Wilno, L. Chominski, 1920. 30 p. (*QO p.v.6, no.1)NN

3243. TEMPERLEY, Harold William Vazeille. The dispute between Lithuania and Poland. In His The second year of the League, London, [1922] p. 92-104. JX1975.T4 DLC BM InU

3244. TOWARZYSTWO STRAŻY KRESOWEJ, WARSZAWA. Poland and Lithuania; the question of Wilno. Warszawa, "Straż Kresowa", 1921. 37 p. tables, maps. (The Bibliotheque of "L'Est Polonais") (*GLP p.v.34 no.15)NN

3245. UNTULIS, Matas. Kodėl prarastas Vilnius? [Why was Vilnius taken?] Chicago, Ill., "Naujienų" bendrovė, 1931. 56 p. Bound with Vileišis, P. Lietuvių lenkų ginčas. 947.5.V713 PU

URBŠIENĖ, Marija. Sąrašas aktualių knygų ir rašinių apie Vilnių ir Vilniaus kraštą. Kaunas, 1939. See entry No. 121.

3246. URBŠYS, Juozas. Medžiaga Vilniaus ginčo diplomatinei istorijai. [Resources for the diplomatic history of Vilnius] Kaunas, Sakalo b-vė, 1932. p. 257-272. 947.52. Url4 PU

3247. VILEIŠIS, Petras. Le Conflit polono-lithuanien. Paris, [1921] 55 p. DK511.L2V45 DLC CSt-H ICBM BM(8094. ee. 49)

3248. --- Lietuvių-lenkų ginčas. [The Lithuanian-Polish conflict] Kaunas, 1922. 88 p. 947.5.V713 PU CtTMF

3249. VILNA. SEJM, 1922. Sejm Wileński 1922. Przebieg posedzeń według sprawozdań stenograficznych w opracowaniu kancelarji sejmowej. Wilno, 1922. 1 v. (various pagings) 947.52.V7135 PU MH

3250. VILNIAUS VADAVIMAS IR LIETUVIŲ politinio iždo programas Vilniui vaduoti. [The Lithuanian program for the liberation of Vilnius and its application] [n.p.], Lietuvių politinis iždas, 1930. 20 p. illus. 970.31.VV ICLJF

3251. WALIGÓRA, Bolesław Andrzej. Kaip Żeligowskis užėmė Vilnių. Iš lenkų kalbos išvertė Vilutis. Kaunas, Vyriausio štabo spaudos ir švietimo skyrius, 1931. 40 p. map, diag. Bound with Ruseckas, Petras. Kaip lenkinta Vilniaus kraštas, 1930. 947.5.R893.3PU CtTMF

3252. --- Walka o Wilno; Okupacja Litwy i Białorusi w 1918-1919 r. przez Rosję Sowiecką. Wilno, Wydaw. Zarządu Miejskiego; skł. gł. Księg. Św Wojciecha, 1938. 483 p.; illus., plans. (Biblioteczka Wileńska, nr. 9) DK 651.V4B47 no.9 DLC InU BM(09456. e. 14)

3253. WYPRAWA WILEŃSKA. In Borkiewicz, Adam Józef. Dzieje 1-go pułku piechoty legionów. Warszawa, 1929. Cręść druga, Rozdział I., p. 81-126. DK440.B65 DLC

3254. ŽEMAITIS, Zigmas. Vilnius Lietuvai ir Lietuva Vilniui; mūsų

kovos dėl Vilniaus esmė ir planas.
[Vilnius for Lithuania and vice versa...] Kaunas, [Vilniui Vaduati Sąjunga] 1928. 140 p. 947.52.Z42
PU CaOONL CILJF ICCC NN OCl

3255. ZDANKUS, Francis J. The
economic importance of Vilna to Lithuania and of Lithuania to Vilna.
69 p. maps (fold) tabs. Thesis
(M.A.)--University of Notre Dame,
1930. DK511.L713Z19e InNd

3256. ZULBERTI, Taulero. Lituania,
Vilna e memel. In Le opere e i
giorni (Genova), v. 13, luglio 1934,
p. 14-19. (*DO)NN

VII.7.e.3. DISCRIMINATION AGAINST
LITHUANIAN RIGHTS IN
THE VILNIUS REGION

3257. DIE LAGE DER KATHOLISCHEN
Litauer im Bistum Wilna und die
Ausschreitungen des Polonismus.
Denkschrift des katholischen Klerus
Litauens. Tilsit, Jagomast's Buch-
druckerei "Lituania", 1913. 145 p.
BX1559.L5L3 DLC MH

3258. LAIKINASIS VILNIAUS LIETUVIŲ
KOMITETAS. Bažnytinė padėtis Vilniaus krašte dokumentų šiesoje. [The
situation of the Church in the Vilnius region] Vilnius, Ruch spaustuvė, 1930. v, 47 p. 947.52.L144
PU

3259. PALMIERI, Aurelio. Le condizioni dei Lituani cattolici nella
diocesi di Vilna e gli eccessi del
panpolonismo. Memorandum de clero
cattolico lituano. Roma, Tip. E. de
Gregori, 1912. viii, 63 p.
BX2632.L5P3 DLC

3260. STOSUNKI LITEWSKO-POLSKIE W
djecezji wileńskiej i nadurzycie
partji wszechpolskiej... Wilno, J.
Zawadzki, 1913. 66 p. 947.52.St795
PU

3261. Ž., V. Mūsų kovos dėl kalbos Vilniaus krašto bažnyčiose. [Our
struggle for the Lithuanian language
in the Churches of the Diocese of
Vilnius (Vilna)] Kaunas, Vilniui
vaduoti sąjunga, 1932. 38 p. (Vilniui vaduoti sąjungos leidinys, nr.
49) 947.5.R993.3 PU

VII.7.f. FOREIGN RELATIONS WITH
RUSSIA

3262. BEMMANN, Rudolf. Russland
greift nach der Ostsee, die russischen Herrschaftsgelüste im Ostseeraum seit Peter dem Grossen. Gos-
lar, Ger., Blut- und Boden Verlag
[1939] 90 p. illus., maps.,
plates. DK511.B3B4 NNC

3263. BESTIALITY OF THE RUSSIAN
czardom toward Lithuania. Baltimore,
Md., The Lithuanian Society of
Sciences and Arts, 1891. 30 p.
DK511.L25B48 NSyU

3264. BIAŁOWIEJSKA, W. Stosunki
Litwy z Móskwą w pierwszej połowie
panowanie Aleksandra Jagiełłonezyka
1492-1499. In Ateneum Wileńskie
(Wilna), v.7, 1930, p. 59-110; p.
726-785. See serials consulted.

3265. ČIBIRAS, Kazimieras. Lituania y la URSS, la invasión soviética desde la perspective de un
quindenio, 1940-1955 [por] Casimiro
Verax [pseud.]. Medellín (Colombia),
Comité Católico Lituano, 1955. 62
p. DK511.L27C47 DLC

3266. GLIAUDYS, Jurgis. At the
Kremlin with Molotov. In Lituanus
(Chicago, Ill.), v.20, no.2, 1966,
p. 20-29. See serials consulted.

3267. JANULAITIS, Augustinas.
Lietuva ir dabartinė Rusija. [Lith-
uania and today's Russia] Kaunas,
1925. 45 p. DK511.L27J3 DLC

3268. KRIVICKAS, Domas. Formalities prelimary to aggression. Soviet and Nazi tactics against Lithuania and Austria. In Baltic Review
(New York, N.Y.), no.5, 1955, p. 5-
22. See serials consulted.

3269. KUTRZEBA, Stanisław. The
rights of Russia to Lithuania and
White-Ruthenia. Paris [Imp. M.
Flinikowski] 1919. 11, (1) p.
D651.L5K8 DLC CaOTU NN BM(8095. f. 33)

3270. LIESYTĖ, Julijona. Soviet-
Lithuanian relations, 1930-1939.
[Berkely, Calif., 1950]. v, 274
leaves. Thesis (M.A.)--University
of California. Bibliography: p.
269-274. 308t.L719 CU

3271. MIGLINAS, Simas. Lietuva
sovietinės agresijos dokumentuose.
[Lithuania's occupation in Soviet
documents. Memmingen Ger.] Tremtis [1958] 86 p. DK511.L27M5 DLC
NN

3272. NAVICKAS, Konstantinas.
TSRS vaidmuo, ginant Lietuvą nuo im-
perialistinės agresijos 1920-1940
metais. [The role of the USSR in

protecting Lithuania from imperial-
ist agressions from 1920-1940]
Vilnius, Mintis, 1966. 335 p.
DK511.L27N32 DLC CtY IU InU MH NN

3273. OTVIETY LITOVSKIKH POSLOV
Moskovskim dumnym boiaram, 1608-
1615. Moskva, 1838. 1 v. (Sbornik
Kniazia Obolenskago, nr. 10).
DK3.02 DLC BM(9454. f. 1(1))

3274. PARIS PEACE CONFERENCE,
1919. LITHUANIA. Lettre à la Con-
férence de la Paix concernant la
reconnaissance de l'amiral Koltchak.
Paris, 1919. 4 p. (Délégation de
Lituanie à la Conférence de la
Paix. pt., VII:8) D643.A7DP5L7
CSt-H

3275. RAČKAUSKAS, Konstantinas.
URSS et Lithuanie: aspects juridiques et politiques de leur relations. Paris, 1946. Thesis--Uni-
versity of Paris. Typescript.

3276. RUTENBERG, Gregor. Der
litauisch-russische Freundschafts-
und Neutralitäsvertrag und die
Wilnafrage im Lichte des Völkerrechts. In Zeitschrift für Völkerrecht (Breslau), v. 14, no.3, 1928,
p. 370-385. See serials consulted.

3277. STIKLIORIUS, Jonas Arvydas.
Inkorporacija; Lietuvos ir Sovietų
ankstesni santykiai, Sovietų ruoši-
masis Lietuvos inkorporavimui, so-
vietai Lietuvoje, etc. [Incorpora-
tion; Lithuanian-Soviet relations
and the preparatory work by the Soviets to incorporate Lithuania] In
Lietuvių enciklopedija. Boston,
Mass., 1956. v.8, p. 517-525.
For holdings see entry no. 216.

STRONG, Anna Louise. Lithuania's new way. London, [1941].
See entry no. 2912.

3278. UNITED STATES. DEPARTMENT
OF STATE. Russian series, no.1-5.
[Washington, D.C., Govt. Print. Off.,
1919]-20. 5 pamphlets. Partial contents.-No.5 Relations with Lithuania. 1920. DK266.A3U5 DLC CSt-H
PU

3279. VARDYS, Vytas Stanley, ed.
Lithuania under the Soviets; por-
trait of a nation, 1940-65. New
York, N.Y., Praeger, [1965]. ix, 299
p. illus. (Praeger publications in
Russian history and world communism,
no.162) DK511.L27V35 DLC CaBVaS
CaBVaU CaAEU CaOONL CaOTP CaOTU
CaOHM CaNBFU CaSSU CaSRU CaMWU CU
CSt CSt-H CtPAM CtY HU IaAS IC IaU
ICU IEN IU InNd InU KU LU MH MeU
MnU MoU MU NIC NN NNC NB NbU NBuU

NmU NcD NhU NjP NjR OCl OClW OkU
OrU PPi PPiU PP PPULC PU RPB TxHU
TxU TU ViU VtU WU WaU WyU

VII.7.g. FOREIGN RELATIONS WITH OTHER COUNTRIES

3280. BEBLAVÝ, Ján. Lietuvių
čekų santykiai Vytauto Didžiojo
laikais. [Czech-Lithuanian relations during the reign of Vytautas
the Great] Kaunas, 1930. 102 p.
facsims. (Vytauto Didžiojo Universiteto Evang. teol. fakulteto leidinys 2 nr.) DK511.L23B4 DLC
BM(ac. 1157. i.) ICU KU MH WaU

3281. IVINSKIS, Zenonas. Apaštalų Sosto santykiai amžių bėgyje,
iki XVIII amžiaus galo. [Lithuanian
relations with the Apostolic See
through the centuries...] In
LKMASD, v.4, 1961. p. 117-150.
Summary in English. See serials
consulted.

3282. JURGĖLA, Constantine R. Lithuania and the United States; the
establishment of state relations.
Fordham, N.Y., 1954. Thesis--Ford-
ham University. NNF

3283. KLIMAS, Petras. Ambrosio
Contarini. Venecijos ambasadorius
Lietuvoje, 1474-1477. [Ambrosio
Contarini, the Venetian ambassador
to Lithuania, 1474-1477] In Praeitis (Kaunas), v.2, 1933, p. 158-
182. See serials consulted.

3284. KRIVICKAS, Domas. Lietuvos-
Estijos byla Hagos Tribunole dėl
Panevėžio-Saldutiškio geležinkelio.
[The case between Lithuania and
Estonia regarding the railway,
Panevėžys-Saldutiškis, in the Court
of International Justice] In Teisė
(Kaunas), v.45-46, 1939, p. 1-12,
135-143. See serials consulted.

3285. LIMANOWSKI, Bolesław. Litwa
i Białoruś. In Krytyka (Kraków),
1912, v.9, p. 65-74. AP54.K8 t.5
DLC NN

3286. LUTOSŁOWSKI, Wincenty. Lithuania and White Ruthenia. Paris
[Imprimerie Levé] 1919. 36 p.
fold. map. D651.L5L8 DLC CSt-H NN

3287. MATULIS, Steponas. Lietuva
ir Apaštalų Sostas, 1795-1940. [Li-
thuania and the Holy See, 1795-1940]
In LKMASD, v.4, 1961, p. 153-174.
See serials consulted.

3288. NEWMAN, Edward William Polson. Britain and the Baltic. London, Methuen & Co. Ltd., 1930. xii, 275 p. 5 maps (1 fold.). DK511. B3N4 DLC CU CSt-H CaAEU CaBVaU CaOHM CaOTU CaQMM CtY DU DW FU IaU ICU IEN IdU InU KU MB MnU MoU NN NcD OkU OCU OCl OU PU WU

3289. PAKŠTAS, Kazys. Gudijos santykis su Lietuva. [Relations between White Russia and Lithuania] In Aidai (Brooklyn, N.Y.), v.3(89), 1956, p. 114-124; v.4(90), 1956, p. 174-182. map. See serials consulted.

3290. PLATERIS, Aleksandras. Teisiniai Livonijos ir Kuršo santykiai su Lietuva, XVI-XVII amžiais. Les relations juridiques de la Livonie et de la Courlande avec la Lithuanie, XVI-XVII siècles. Kaunas, 1938. vii, 267. p. (Teisės ir ekonomijos studijos. tom.2, kn.2.) With a summary in German. 947.52P692 PU BM(Ac. 1157. f/7.)

3291. SAUERVEINAS, Jurgis Julius Justus. A British Queen and a Lithuanian deputation. To Her Majesty Queen Victoria...[by] Girėnas [pseud.]. Leipzig, 1897. BM(11585. l. 22.)

3292. --- Anglijos Karalienė ir lietuwiszkas deputacijonas. [A British Queen and the Lithuanian deputation. By] G.S. [Memel, 1880?] BM(1865. c. 8.(82))

3293. SCHNORF, Richard A. The Baltic States in U.S.-Soviet relations; from Truman to Johnson. In Lituanus (Chicago, Ill.), v.14, no. 3, 1968, p. 43-60. See serials consulted.

3294. --- The Baltic States in U.S.-Soviet relations; the years of doubt, 1943-1946. In Lituanus (Chicago, Ill.), v.12, no.4, 1966, p. 56-75. See serials consulted.

3295. TARULIS, Albert N. American-Baltic Relations, 1918-1922; the struggle over recognition. Washington, D.C., Catholic University of America Press, 1965. xi, 386 p. Bibliography: p. 371-378. DK511.B3T26 DLC CaOTU DS ICU MH-L NjR NRU PU

3296. TRUMPA, Vincas. Liudvikas XIV ir Lietuva. [Louis XIV and Lithuania] In Naujoji romuva (Kaunas), v.40, 1938, p. 747-751. See serials consulted.

3297. WYCZAŃSKI, Andrzej. Francja

wobec państw jagiellońskich w latach 1515-1529; studium z dziejów francuskiej polityki zagranicznej epoki odrodzenia. Wrocław, Zakł. im. Ossolińskich, 1954. 193 p. (Prace Instytutu Historicznego Universytetu Warszawskiego, 6). DC57.W93 DLC

3298. ŽDAN, Michał. Stosunki litewsko-tatarskie za czasów Witolda Wielkiego Księcia Litwy. In Ateneum Wileńskie (Wilno), v.7, 1930, p. 529-601. See serials consulted.

VII.8. TREATIES

VII.8.a. PERSONAL AND LUBLIN UNIONS, THEIR HISTORY AND COMMENTARIES

3299. ALSEIKA Danielius, Lietuvos unija su Lenkija Jogailos ir Vytauto Didžiojo laikais. [Lithuania's union with Poland during the reign of Jogaila and Vytautas the Great] Vilnius, "Ruch" spaustuvė, 1927. 23 p. (Lietuvių mokslo draugijos leidinys). 947.52.A178.2 PU CtTMF PPULC

3300. BALZER, Oswald Marian. Unia horodelska. Odczyt wygłoszony na publicznem posiedzeniu Akademii Umiejętności dnia 3 maja 1913. In Rocznik Akad. Umiej. w Krakowie, 1912-1913, p. 146-177. See serials consulted.

3301. DOVNAR-ZAPOL'SKII, Mitrofan Viktorovich. Polsko-litovskaia uniia na seimakh do 1569 goda; istoricheskii ocherk. Moskva, Tip. G. Lissnera i A. Geshelia, 1897. 28 p. DK418.5.L5D6 DLC NN(1898 ed.)

3302. GABRYS, Juozas. Lietuvių-Lenkų unija. [The Lithuanian-Polish federation] Philadelphia, Pa., Žvaigždės sp., 1915. 67 p. 947.5.G113 PU ICBM ICLJF CtTMF OCl

3303. HALECKI, Oskar. Dzieje unii jagiellońskiej. Kraków, Akademia Umiejetności; skł. gł. w księg. G. Gebethnera, 1919-20. 2 v. DK425.H3 DLC ICU MH NN PU

--- Geschichte der Union Litauens mit Polen. Wien, 1919. See entry no.3060.

3304. --- Unia Lubelska; wykład habilitacyjny wygłoszony na Uniwersytecie Jagiellońskim 10 grudnia 1915 r. Kraków, "Czasu", 1916. 35p.

DK511.L2H3 WU

3305 INSTRUMENTUM PACIS INTER STA-
tus Confoederatos Regni Poloniae et
Magni Ducatus Litthuaniae... Leipzig, A.M. Hessin, 1717. 28, 10 p.
Latin and German. Q943.8DIn78 PU

3306. JAKUBOWSKI, Jan. Z zagadnień unii polsko-litewskiej. In
Przegląd Historychny (Warszawa), v.
22, 1919-1920, p. 136-155. See
serials consulted.

3307. KLACZKO, Julian. Anneksya
w dawnej Polsce; unia Polski z Litwą. Tłómaczył za zwoleniem autora
Karol Scipio. Z przedmową St. Tarnowskiego. Kraków, Spólka Wydawnicza Polska, 1901. 166 p.
DK426.K531 CtY CoU NN NNC

3308. --- Une annexion d'autrefois;
l'union de la Pologne et de la Lithuanie. Paris, Librarie du Luxem-
burg, 1869. 177 p. DK426.K6 DLC
DS MH

3309. KOIALOVICH, Mikhail Iosifo-
vich. Liublinskaia uniia ili pos-
liednee soedinenie Litovskogo Knia-
zhestva s Pol'skim Korolevstvom na
Liublinskom Seimie v 1569 godu.
Sanktpeterburg, Izd. Gaz. "Russkii
Invalid", 1863. 87 p. DK418.5L77K
CaAEU BM(9454. g. 26.)

3310. KUTRZEBA, Stanisław, ed.
Akta unji Polski z Litwą 1385-1791.
Wydali Stanisław Kutrzeba i Włady-
sław Semkowicz. Kraków, Gebethner i
Wolff, 1932. lvi, 570 p. Biblio-
graphy: p. xxxix-xli. DK418.5.L5K8
DLC BM CaBVaU CaOTU CSt CtY ICU IEN
InUKU MH MU NN NIC NNC NjP NjR PU

--- Charakter i wartość unji
polsko- litewskiej. In Ehrenkreutz,
Stefan, ed. Księga pamiątkowa...
Wilno, 1935. See entry no.2523.

3311. --- Charakter prawny związku
Litwy z Polską 1385-1569. In PZHP
w Wilnie. Pamiętnik VI. Referaty
(Lwów), v.1, 1935, p. 165-173. See
serials consulted.

3312. --- Unia Polski z Litwą. In
His Polska i Litwa w dziejowym sto-
sunku. Kraków, 1914. p. 447-658.
BM(9476. 1. 31.)

3313. --- Unia Polski z Litwą;
problem i metoda badania. Kraków,
Czas, 1911. 20 p. (*QO p.v.56, no.2)
NN

3314. ŁABUŃSKI, Józef Żerbiłło.
Unia Litwy z Polską, 1385-1569. Akty unii i przywilejów stanowych litewskich, przekład polski pierwszych

dołączył J. Żerbiłło Łabuński. Warszawa, Kronika Rodzinna [1913?]
247 p. DK418.5.L7Z58 InU MH

3315. LAPPO, Ivan Ivanovich. Liublinskaia uniia i Tretii Litovskii
Statut. In ZMNP. Novaia seriia,
chast' 69, 1917, p. 89-150. See
serials consulted.

3316. LEWICKI, Anatol. Nieco o
unii Litwy z Koroną. In Przegląd
Polski(Kraków), v.110, 1883, p. 235-
280. See serials consulted.

3317. ŁOWMIAŃSKI, Henryk. Wcielenie Litwy do Polski w 1386 roku.
In Ateneum Wileńskie (Wilno), v.12,
1937, p. 36-145. See serials consulted.

3318. MOSBACH, August. Początki
unii lubelskiej. Poznań, J.K. Żupański, 1872. 169 p. 943.8.M854
NNC BM(9456. f. 10.)

MOŚCICKI, Henryk, ed. Unia
Litwy z Polską; dokumenty i wspomnienia. Warszawa, [1919] See
entry no.3083.

3319. NOWICKI, Eustachy. Jak pow-
stała unja Polski z Litwą; w 350-let-
nią rocznicę unji lubelskiej. Warszawa, Arct, 1919. 11 p.
947.52.N864 PU

3320. PASZKIEWICZ, Henryk. O genezie i wartości Krewa. Warszawa,
Gebethner i Wolff, 1938. 356 p.tabl.
illus. DK511.L23P35 DLC CU KU MH NN
NNC PU

3321. PICHETA, Vladimir Ivanovich.
Litovsko-pol'skiia unii i otnoshenie
k nim litovsko-russkoi shliakhty. In
Sbornik statei posviashchennykh Va-
siliiu Osipovichu Kliucheskomu ego
uchenikami, druziami... Moskva, 1909.
p. 605-631. NN

3322. PROCHASKA, Antoni. Przyczyn-
ki krytyczne do dziejów unii. In
Polska Akademia Umiejętności, Kraków.
Wydział Historyczno-Filozoficzny.
Rozprawy, v.33, 1896, p. 55-122.
See serials consulted.

3323. --- Unie Kalmarska i Jagiel-
lońska. In Przegląd Polski (Kraków)
v.154, 1904, p. 193-212. See serials consulted.

3324. --- Z dziejów unii Jagiellońskiej. In Ateneum Wilenskie (Wilno),
v.4, 1927, p. 190-199. See serials
consulted.

Przywilej unii Wielkiego
Xięstwa Litewskiego z Koroną z dnia

1-go Julii, 1569. See entry no.
2709.

3325. ROSZKO, Stefan. Unja Polski z Litwą w 350-tę rocznicę Unji
Lubelskiej. Zamość, Z. Pomarański,
1919. 15 p. 947.52.R PU

3326. ŠAPOKA, Adolfas. Liublino
unija. [The Union of Lublin] In
Lietuvių enciklopedija. Boston, Mass.
1958. v.16, p. 330-338. For holdings
see entry no.216.

3327. SCHMITT, Henryk. Unja Litwy
z Koroną dokonana na Sejmie Lubels-
kim 1568-1569. Szkic dziejów. Lwów,
Author, 1869. 50 p. Reprint.
DK428.5.S35 PU; also in Mrówka(Lwów),
v.1, 1869. See serials consulted.

3328. SOPICKI, Stanisław. Unia Lubelska i jej znaczenie. Londyn, Polska Fundacja Kulturalna, 1969. 28p.
DK428.5.S76 CaOTU

3329. SYDOR, Mykola. Shiakh do Ho-
rodel's'koi unii, v svitli pol's'ko-
lytovs'ko-ukrains'kykh protivorich-
nostei. Miunkhen; Niu Iork, Vyd. av-
tora, 1951. xii, 155 p. DK508.7.S95
DLC CaSSU ICU IU InU

3330. VISKANTAS, Antanas. Wielki
książę litewski a Unja Horodelska.
In Ateneum Wileńskie (Wilno), v.7,
1930, p. 469-493. See serials consulted.

3331. ZAJĄCZKOWSKI, Stanisław.
Przymierze polsko-litewskie 1325 r.
In Kwartalnik Historyczny (Lwów),
w.40, 1926, p. 567-617. See serials
consulted.

3332. --- Wypadki lat 1382-1386 w
związku z genezą Unji. In PZHP w
Warszawie 28 listopada do 4 grudnia
1930. Pamiętnik V. Referaty (Lwów),
v.1, 1930, p. 345-354. See serials
consulted.

3333. --- Ze studjów nad dziejami
Unji polsko-litewskiej. In His Zagadnienia Historyczne. Lwów, 1936.
v.2, p. 177-229. (*QR)NN DLC
BM(Ac. 7215/92.)

3334. ŽEMAITIS, Vincas. Liublino
unijos sukakties paraštėje (santykiai
su mūsų kaimynais lenkais) 1569-1969.
[The Union of Lublin and Lithuanian-
Polish relations. Chicago, Ill.]
1970. 84 p. Reprint from "Naujienos" Dec., 1969. DK511.L2Z42 PU

VII.8.b. OTHER TREATIES

3335. AKADEMIIA NAUK SSSR. INSTI-
TUT ISTORII. Dukhovnye i dogovornye
gramoty velikikh i udel'nykh kniazei
XIV-XVI vv. [Podgotovil k pechati
L.V. Cherepnin] Moskva, Izd-vo Akademii nauk SSSR, 1950. 585 p. tables. DK70.A2A5 DLC
    ALLIED POWERS(1919-) TREATIES,
ETC. Convention between British Empire, France, Italy, Japan and Lithuania respecting the Memel Territory and the Statute of the Memel
Territory. London, 1924. See
entry no.2980.

3336. BANTYSH-KAMENSKII, Nikolai
Nikolaevich. Sobranie gosudarstvennykh gramot i dogovorov. Moskva,
Tip. N.S. Vsevolozhtskago, 1813-28.
5 v. facsims. (*QGO)NN

3337. CATHOLIC CHURCH. TREATIES,
ETC., 1922-1929 (PIUS XI) Il con-
cordato con la Lituania [di] Amedeo
Giannini. Roma,Anonima Romana editoriale, 1928. 23 p. (Publicazioni
dell'Istituto per l'Europa orientale,
Roma. Quarta serie: Leggi fondamen-
tali, 9) Balt 7879.28 MH CtY NN

3338. --- Konkordatas tarp Šven-
tojo Sosto ir Lietuvos valdžios.[The
Concordat between the Holy See and
Lithuania] Chicago, Ill., 1928. 16
p. 947.5.C284 PU

3339. CODEX DIPLOMATICUS REGNI PO-
logiae et Magni Ducatus Lithuaniae
in pacta, foedera, tractatus pacis...
nunc primum ex archivis publicis
eruta ac in lucem protracta exhibentur. Wyd. Maciej Dogiel. Wilno,
Tip. Regia, 1758-1764. v.1, 4-5 only
Vol.2-3 never published.
JX760.P6C6 DLC BM MH

3340. GERMANY. TREATIES, ETC.,
1919-1925 (EBERT). Handelsvertrag
zwischen den deutschen Reich und Litauischen Republik. Kaunas, 1924.
947.52.G316 PU

3341. GREAT BRITAIN. FOREIGN OF-
FICE. Agreement between his Majesty's government in the United Kingdom and the Lithuanian government
relating to trade and commerce. With
protocol, London, July 6, 1934, Cmd.
4648. London, H. M. S. O., 1934.
12 p. (Great Britain. Foreign Office. Lithuania (1934), no.1).
Gov. Doc. G.B. Foof. CaOTU

3342. --- Exchange of notes bet-
ween His Majesty's government in the
United Kingdom and in the Irish Free
State and the Lithuanian government

in regard to commercial relations as regulated by the exchange notes of May 6, 1922. London, November 28-December 10, 1929... London, H.M.S.O., 1930. 3 p. (Treaty series 1930, no.1) Papers by command. Cmd. 3462. JX636.1869 DLC CaBVaU CSt CtY ICU

3343. --- Notification extending to Canada as from the 18th September, 1928. The treaty between His Majesty and Lithuania for the extradiction of fugitive criminals. Signed at Kovno the 18th May, 1926. Ottawa, Ont., F.A. Acland, 1929. 10 p. (Canada. Treaties, etc. Treaties series, 1928, no.1) JX355.9A3 1928 no.11 DLC CtY MH

3344. GREAT BRITAIN. TREATIES, ETC., 1910-1936 (GEORGE V). Agreement between His Majesty's government in the United Kingdom and the Lithuanian government relating to trade and commerce, with portocol. [The agreement has not been ratified by His Majesty's government in the United Kingdom] London, H. M. S. O., 1934. 12 p. ([Foreign office] Lithuania no.1(1934)) HF1733.G8L8 1934 DLC CaBVaU CaOTU ICU OCl

3345. --- --- [Ratifications exchanged at London, August 2, 1934] London, H. M. S. O., 1934. 12 p. ([Foreign office] Treaty series, no. 20 (1934)) Parliament. Papers by command. Cmd. 4680. HF1733.G8L8 1934b DLC CaBVaU CtY ICU MH OCl

3346. --- Agreement between the British and Lithuanian governments respecting commercial relations. Signed May 6, 1922. London, H.M.S.O. 1922. 4 p. (Foreign office. Treaty series, 1922, no.9) Parliament. Papers by command. Cmd. 1711. JX636. A3 1922,no.9 DLC CSt-H CtY MnU

3347. --- Convention between His Majesty in respect of the United Kingdom and the President of Lithuania regarding legal proceedings in civil and commercial matters. Kovno, April 24, 1934. [The convention has not been ratified by His Majesty...] London, H. M. S. O., 1934. 21 p. ([Foreign office] Lithuania no.2 (1934)) Parliament. Papers by command. Cmd. 4693. JX637 1934 Apr.24 DLC CaBVaU ICU OCl

3348. --- --- [Ratifications exchanged at London on May 7, 1936]... London, H. M. S. O., 1936. 21 p. ([Foreign office] Treaty series, no. 14(1936)) Parliament. Papers by command. Cmd. 5197. 328.424.G798c OCl CtY DLC ICU

3349. --- Exchange notes between His Majesty's government in United Kingdom and the Lithuanian government respecting commercial relations between Tanganyika territory and Lithuania. Riga, December 15--Kovno, December 28, 1931... London, H.M.S.O. 1932. 3 p. ([Foreign office] Treaty series, no. 11(1932)) Parliament. Papers by command, Cmd. 4054. JX636 1892 DLC CaBVaU CtY ICU MH OCl

3350. --- Treaty between United Kingdom and Lithuania for the extradition of fugitive criminals. Signed at Kaunas, May 18, 1926. London, H.M.S.O., 1927. 8 p. ([Foreign office] Treaty series, 1927, no.15). Parliament. Papers by command. Cmd. 2897. JX4341.A5 1927 DLC CtY MH

3351. GRONSKII, Pavel Pavlovich. Instrumentum lithuanicae deditionis anno 1655. Kaunas, 1923. 16 p. DK511.L24G7 DLC; also in Tauta ir Žodis (Kaunas), no.2, 1923, p. 81-97. See serials consulted.

3352. KAASIK, Nikolai. Considerations juridiques sur les pactes Balto-Sovietiques. In Revue Baltique (Tallinn), no.1, 1940, p. 84-93. See serials consulted.

3353. KONOPCZYŃSKI, Władysław and K. Lepszy. Akta ugody kiejdańskiej 1655. In Ateneum Wileńskie (Wilno), v.10, 1910, p. 173-224. See serials consulted.

3354. LITHUANIA. TREATIES, ETC. Lietuvos sutartys su svetimomis valstybėmis. Recueil des traité conclus par la Lithuanie avec pays étrangers ... [Comp. by] Pranas Dailidė. Kaunas, [Ministère des affaires étrangères] 1930-39. 2 v. JX760.L52A3 DLC CLU(1) NN NNC PU WaU(1)

3355. LITHUANIA. TREATIES, ETC., 1920-1926 (Stulginskis) Convention et disposition transitoire relatives à Memel signées à Paris, le 8 mai 1924. Genève, 1924. 13, 13 p. Ozd844A167 1924 CtY

3356. --- Lietuvos taikos sutartis su Rusija. Mirnyi dogovor mezhdu Rossiei i Litvoi. Treaty signed at Moscow July 12, 1920. [n.p., 1920?] 11 p. Lithuanian and Russian texts on opposite pages. DK511.L27A 1920 CSt-H BM(S.N. 150/9.) PU

3357. LITHUANIA. TREATIES, ETC., 1926 (Grinius) Non-aggression treaty between the Lithuanian Republic and the Union of Soviet Socialist Republics. [n.p., 1926] 3 p. Typewritten carbon copy. At head of ti-

tle: Translation DK511.L27A 1927
CSt-H

3358. LITHUANIAN-WHITE-RUSSIAN SSR
(Feb. 1919-July 1919) The Congress
of Soviets of White-Russian SSR voted unification with the Lithuanian
SSR February 2, 1919; the Congress
of Soviets of Lithuanian SSR confir-
med unification February 18, 1919.
The United Lithuanian-White-Russian
SSR existed from February to July
1919. HD5047.6.L776 CSt-H

3359. MASER, Leo. Das Konkordat
zwischen dem Apostolischen Stuhle
und der Republik Litauen vom 27. September 1927 in rechtsvergleichender
Betrachtung. Lippstadt/Westf.,
Druck von C.J. Laumann, 1931. 39 p.
Thesis--University of Köln. Bibliography: p. v-viii. BR1050.L5M3 1931
DLC

3360. POLAND. MINISTERSTWO SPRAW
ZAGRANICZNYCH. Protocoles officiels
des Conférences polono-lithuaniennes
a Souwalki; aide memoire concernant
les négotiations de Souwalki depuis
le 30 septembre jusqu'à au 5 octobre
1920. Varsovie, 1921. 12 p.
DK418.5.L5A3 CSt-H NN NNC

3361. DER REICHS-RÄTHE... Beantwor-
tung... Revers der Waywoden und Stän-
den dess Grossherzogthumbs Littauen
von wegen der Huldigung... den Königen und Königreich Schweden... zu
leisten. In Sweden. Actorum et ges-
torum sueco-polonicorum semestrale.
Pt.1, 1657. BM(1315. c. 1.(8.))

3362. DIE REICHS-RÄTHE DESS GROS-
SHERZOGTHUMBS LITTAUEN... Francofurt,
1657. In Sweden. Appendix. History and politics. Actorum et gesto-
rum sueco-polonicarum semestrale;
das ist, Halb-Jährige Erzehl- und
Darstellung... in das Königreich Polen fürgenommen Feldzug vom Herbst,
dess 1655 biss Ostern 1656... Francofurt, 1657. Pt.1. BM(1315. c. .
(24 & 28.))

3363. RUZÉ, Robert. A propos des
nouveaux accords du Saint-Siège avec
Lithuanie. In Revue de droit inter-
national et de legislation comparée
(Bruxelles), v.10, 1929, p. 336-364.
See serials consulted.

3364. SABALIŪNAS, Leonas. The politics of the Lithuanian-Soviet non-
aggression treaty of 1926. In Lituanus (Brooklyn, N.Y.), v.7, no.4,
1961, p. 97-102. See serials consulted.

3365. UKRAINE. TREATIES, ETC.
Mirnyi dogovor mezhdu Ukrainoi i Lit-

voi. Kharkov, Shestaia sovetskaia
tip., 1921. 15 p. DK508.A2 1921
CSt-H

3366. UNITED STATES. TREATIES,
ETC., 1923-1929 (Coolidge) Agreement effected by exchange of notes
between the United States and Lithuania. According mutual unconditional most-favored-nation treatment
in customs matters. Signed December
23, 1925. Washington, D.C., G.O.P.,
1926. 3 p. (Treaty series, no.742)
Ratification by Lithuanian Seimas
notified to the government of United
States, July 10, 1926. JX235.9.A3
no.742 DLC CtY TxU

3367. --- Treaty between the United States and Lithuania. Arbitra-
tion. Signed at Washington, November 14, 1928. Washington, D.C.
G.P.O., 1930. [2], 2 p. (Treaty
series, no.809) JX235.9.A3 no.809
DLC CtY MH

3368. --- Treaty between the United States and Lithuania. Conciliation. Signed at Washington, November 14, 1928. Washington, D.C.,
G.P.O., 1930. [2], 3 p. (Treaties
series, no.810) JX235.9.A3 no.810
DLC CtY

3369. --- Treaty between the United States and Lithuania. Extradition. Signed at Kaunas, April 9,
1924. Washington, D.C., G.P.O.,
1924. 6 p. (Treaty series, no.699)
JX235.9.A3 no.699 DLC CSt CtY InU
TxU

3370. UNITED STATES. TREATIES,
ETC., 1933-1945 (FRANKLIN D. ROOSE-
VELT). Extradition. Supplementary
treaty between the United States of
America and Lithuania. Signed at
Washington, May 17, 1934. Washing-
ton, D.C., G.P.O., 1935. 1 p.l.,
2 p. (Treaty series, no.879)
JX235.9.A3 no.879 DLC CtY

3371. --- Liability for military
service and other acts of allegiance
of naturalized persons and persons
born with double nationality. Treaty between the United States of
America and Lithuania. Signed at
Kaunas, October 18, 1937. Washington, D.C., G.P.O., 1938. 4 p.
(Treaty series, no.936) JX235.A3
no.936 DLC CtY

3372. --- Parcel post agreement
between the United States of America
and Lithuania. Signed at Washington,
December 28, 1939, and at Kaunas,
December 4, 1939. Washington, D.C.,
G.P.O., 1940. 31 p. HE6471.A3
1939t DLC CtY ICU ICN MH OrU

3373. VISKANTAS, Antanas. Konkordat litewski wzestawieniu z konstytucja Panstwowa Litewska i konkordatem polskim. In Institut Naukowo Badawczy Europy Wschodniej w Wilnie, 1932. See serials consulted.

VII.9. THE STATE OF SOVIET LITHUANIA

VII.9.a. GENERAL WORKS

3374. ASSEMBLY OF CAPTIVE EUROPEAN NATIONS. A survey of recent developments in nine captive countries. V.1, Feb. 1956-Feb. 1957; v.2, Feb. 1957-Oct. 1957. New York, N.Y., ACEN sekretariat, 1956-1957. 2 v. DR48.5.A8 DLC CtPAP(v.1) PU

3375. BULLITT, William Christian. The great globe itself; a preface to World Affairs. New York, N.Y., C. Scribner's Sons, 1946. vii, 310 p. diagrams, map. DK273.B8 1947 DLC CaAEU

3376. DOMAŠEVIČIUS, Kęstutis. Tarybinio valstybingumo vystymasis Lietuvoje. [The development of the Soviet statehood in Lithuania. Vilniuje, Mintis, 1966]. 195 p. JN6745.A3D6 DLC CtY ICU IU InU MH NN

3377. GSOVSKI, Vladimir and K. Grzybowski, eds. Government, law and courts in the Soviet Union and Eastern Europe. New York, F.A. Praeger [c1959] 2 v. (xxxii, 2067 p.) Bibliography: "Lithuania" p. 1975-1976; Material pertaining to Lithuania is on pages 135-160, 628-633 and 1703-1724. JN6573.G89 CaAEU CSt-H CLL CU CaBVaU CaOKQL CtY CoU DLC-L DS GU ICU IaU MiD MiDW MnU NIC NN NbU NcD-L NjR PU RPB WaU

3378. LIETUVOS TSR MOKSLŲ AKADEMIJA, VILNA. EKONOMIKOS INSTITUTAS. Lietuvos TSR valstybės ir teisės istorijos klausimai. [Questions on the state and the law history of the Lithuanian SSR. Red. kol.: J. Bulavas (ats. red.) et al.] Vilnius, VPMLL, 1960. 176 p. (Lietuvos TSR Mokslų akademija, Vilna. Ekonomikos instituto teisės sektorius. Darbai, t.9) DLC-L MH

3379. MEDER, Walter. Das Staatsangehörigkeitsrecht der UdSSR und der baltischen Staaten. Frankfurt am Main, W. Metzner, 1950. 112 p. (Sammlung geltender Staatsangehörigkeitsgesetze, Bd.3) JX4270.R92M4 CaOTU BM(Ac. 2324. c.) DLC-L IaU PU

3380. VILNA. UNIVERSITETAS. TEISĖS MOKSLŲ FAKULTETAS. Tarybų Lietuvos valstybės ir teisės dvidešimtmetis. [The twentieth anniversary of the Soviet Lithuanian state and judiciary. Redakcinė kolegija J. Blieka et al.] Vilnius, VPMLL, 1960. 304 p. 947.52.V715 PU DLC-L MH

VII.9.b. SOVIET CONSTITUTIONS AND THEIR COMMENTARIES

3381. COLLINS, Henry Hill. The constitutions of the 16 constituent or Union Republics of the U.S.S.R. A comparative analysis. New York, N.Y., American Russian Institute, 1950. 17 v. 342.4703.C712 c TxDAM CSt-H ICU IEN MH NN NNC OU WaU-L

3382. KRIVICKAS, Domas. The evolution of the Soviet constitution imposed on Lithuania. In Baltic Review (New York, N.Y.), no.6, 1956, p. 41-62. See serials consulted.

3383. LITHUANIAN S.S.R. CONSTITUTION. Constitution (Fundamental law) of the Lithuanian Soviet Socialist Republic of August 25, 1940. As amended through April 7, 1948. New York, N.Y., American Russian Institute, 1950. 15 leaves. JN6745.A3 1950 HU CtY DLC-L LU MH NN NcU NjP PU ViU

3384. --- Konstitutsiia (osnovnoi zakon) S izmeneniiami i dopolneniiami, priniatymi na I., II. i IV. sessiiakh Verkhovnogo Soveta Litovskoi SSR tret'ego sozyva. Vil'nius, Gos. izd-vo polit. i nauch. lit-ry, 1954. 27 p. DLC

3385. --- Konstitutsiia (osnovnoi zakon) Litovskoi Sovetskoi Sotsialisticheskoi Respubliki. S izmeneniiami i dopolneniiami, priniatymi Verkhovnym Sovetom Litovskoi SSR do 9. sessii,5. sozyva vkliuchitel'no. Vil'nius, VPMLL, 1963. 27 p. JN6745.A3 1963 CSt-H CtY DLC

3386. --- Konstytucja (ustawa zasadnicza) Litewskiej Socjalistycznej Republiki Radzieckiej. Z uwzględnieniem zmian i uzupełnień uchwalonych przez I, II, i IV sesje Rady Najwyższej Litewskiej SRR trzeciej kadencji. Wilnius, Państwowe Wydawn. Literatury Politycznej i Naukowej, 1954. 27 p. DLC MH

3387. --- Lietuvos Tarybų Socialistinės Respublikos Konstitucija

185

(pagrindinis įstatymas) Su Lietuvos TSR Aukščiausiosios Tarybos 2. sušaukimo I, III, IV ir VI sesijose ir 3. sušaukimo I. sesijoje priimtais pakeitimais ir papildymais. [Constitution of the Lithuanian SSR...] Vilnius, VPMLL, 1951. 23 p. NjP DLC

3388. --- --- Su Lietuvos TSR Aukščiausiosios Tarybos priimtais pakeitimais ir papildymais iki 4. sušaukimo 8. sesijos imtinai. [Constitution of the Lithuanian SSR as amended and supplemented...] Vilnius, VPMLL, 1958. 23 p. DLC-L MH

3389. --- --- Su Lietuvos TSR Aukščiausiosios Tarybos priimtais pakeitimais ir papildymais iki 5. sušaukimo 7. sesijos imtinai. [Constitution of the Lithuanian SSR as amended and supplemented] Vilnius, VPMLL, 1962. 24 p. CtY DLC MH

3390. --- --- Su Lietuvos TSR Aukščiausiosios Tarybos priimtais pakeitimais iki 6. sušaukimo 6. sesijos imtinai. [Constitution of the Lithuanian SSR as amended and supplemented...] Vilnius, VPMLL, 1966. 24 p. JN6745.A3 1966 PU DLC

3391. SCHULTZ, Lothar. Die Verfassungsentwicklung der baltischen Statten seit 1940. Bonn, Baltisches Forschungsinstitut, 1959. 41 p. (Commentationes Balticae, VI/VII: 7) DK511.B3S37 PU MH See serials consulted.

VII.9.c. SOVIET EXECUTIVE GOVERNMENT AND ADMINISTRATION

3392. ANIČAS, Jonas and Sigita Noreikienė. Lietuvos reikalų komisariato veikla 1917-1918 metais. [The work of the Commissariat on Lithuanian affairs] Vilnius, VPMLL, 1959. 82 p. 947.5.An53 PU MH

3393. APYLINKIŲ IR GYVENIEČIŲ TArybų darbo klausimai. [On the question of the work of the Soviets of the districts...] Vilnius, Mintis, 1969. 191 p. JS6130.52.A8 DLC PU

3394. ČEPAS, A. Liaudies draugovininkai tvarkos sargyboje. [Peoples militia] Vilnius, VPMLL, 1964. 46 p. HV8226.L5C4 DLC

3395. GORŽANSKIS, Jokūbas. Reviziia predpriiatii mestnago khoziaistva; iz opyta raboty kontrol'no-

revizionnogo aparata Ministerstva finansov Litovskoi SSR. [By] I.I. Gozhanskis. Moskva, Gosfinizdat, 1961. 102 p. charts. HC337.L33A83 DLC MH CSt-H MiU NNC WaU WU

3396. INSTRUKCIJA LIETUVIŠKIEMS tikriniams vardams rusiškai transkribuoti. Instruktsiia po transkriptsii litovskikh sobstvennykh imen na russkii iazyk. [Sudaryt. K. Ulvidas] Vilnius, Lietuvos TSR Aukščiausiosios Tarybos Prezidiumas [1962]. 46 p. "Priedas prie Lietuvos TSR Aukščiausiosios Tarybos ir Vyriausybės Žinių, 1962, nr.15. DLC-L

3397. LIETUVOS TSR ADMINISTRACInis-teritorinis suskirstymas. [Lithuanian SSR administrative-territorial divisions] Vilnius, VPMLL, 1959. 1033 p. Issued by Lietuvos TSR Aukščiausios Tarybos Prezidiumo Organizacinis-informacinis skyrius. JS6130.5.A12L5 DLC PU

3398. LITHUANIAN S.S.R. Shtab grazhdanskoi oborony. Uchebno-metodicheskoe posobie dlia podgotovki naseleniia k grazhanskoi oborone... Vil'nius, Mintis, 1967. 175 p. forms. NA929.R9L56 DLC

3399. LITHUANIAN-WHITE RUSSIAN S.S.R. (1919-1920). LAWS, STATUTES, ETC. Dekret Soveta Narodnykh Komissarov Litovsko-Belorusskoi Sov. Sots. Respubliki o taryfnykh stavkakh rabotnikov sovetskikh, obshchestvennykh i torgovykh uchrezhdenii. Vilna, 1919. 22 p. HD5047.6.L776 CSt-H

3400. NEY, Gottlieb. Administrative Gliederung und Verwaltunsorgane der Sowjetisierten baltischen Staaten. In Acta Baltica (Königstein im Taunus), v.2, 1962, p. 9-34. See serials consulted.

3401. REMEIKIS, Thomas. The administration of power; the communist party and the Soviet government. In Vardys, V.S., ed. Lithuania under Soviets... 1965. p. 111-140. DK511.L27V35 DLC CSt CSt-H CU AzU IC MoU MU TU WaU PPi

VII.9.d. LEGISLATION AND PARLIAMENTARY RECORDS

3402. LITHUANIAN S.S.R. AUKŠČIAUSIOJI TARYBA. Lietuvos TSR Aukščiausiosios Tarybos stenogramos. [The stenographic record of the Su-

preme Soviet of the Lithuanian SSR]
Vilnius, VPMLL, 1957- . J400.
L5H45 DLC(1963-) MH(1959-) NNC

3403. --- Stenograficheskii otchet. Vil'nius, Gos. izd-vo polit.
i nauch. lit-ry Litovskoi SSR.
J400.L5H452 DLC NIC NNC(Sozyv 6.)
NcD ViU WU

3404. --- Torzhestvennaia, chet-
vertaia sessiia Verkhovnogo Soveta
Litovskoi SSR(5. sozyva) 21 iiulia
1960 g.; stenograficheskii otchet.
Vil'nius, Gos. izd-vo politiches-
koi i nauchnoi lit-ry Litovskoi
SSR, 1960. 139 p. JN6745.A3A5 InU
IEN OrU

3405. --- Vtoraia sessiia Verkhovnogo soveta Litovskoi SSR shestogo
sozyva) 27-28 dekabria 1963 g.;
stenograficheskii otchet. Vil'nius,
Mintis, 1964. 203 p. DK511.L27A3
1964 CaBVaU InU

3406. TARYBINĖS VALSTYBĖS IR TEI-
sės pagrindai. [An outline of Soviet state and law. Comp. by K.
Domaševičius et al.] Leista naudoti
vadovėliu respublikos ekonomikos,
žemės ūkio, politechnikos ir pedagogikos aukštosiose mokyklose. Vilnius, Mintis, 1967. 417 p. JN6515.
T35 1967 DLC

VII.9.e. JUDICIARY IN SOVIET
LITHUANIA

3407. BULAVAS, Juozas. Lietuvos
TSR teisingumo organizacija ir valdymas (1940-1967 m.) [Administra-
tion of justice in Lithuanian SSR
(1940-1967) Vilnius, 1968. 99 p.
tables. JN6745.A83B91 ICU

3408. ČERNIAUSKAS, Simonas. Lietuvos TSR draugiškųjų teismų nuostatai; praktinis komentaras. [Prac-
tical commentary on court rules in
labour discipline] Vilnius, Mintis,
1967. 133 p. DLC

3409. KAREV, Dmitrii Stepanovich.
Lietuvos TSR teismai. [The courts
of Soviet Lithuania] Vilnius,
VPMLL, 1960. 57 p. DLC-L

3410. KRIVICKAS, Domas. Laws and
courts in Soviet-occupied Lithuania.
In Baltic Review (New York, N.Y.),
no.19, 1960, p. 31-42. See serials
consulted.

3411. LIKAS, Albinas. Liaudies
teismų rinkimų tvarka. [The procedure of elections to the peoples

court] Vilnius, Mintis, 1965. 54 p.
DLC-L

3412. LITHUANIAN S.S.R. LAWS,
STATUTES, ETC. Lietuvos TSR draugiškųjų teismų nuostatai. Polozhenie o
tovaricheskikh sudakh Litovskoi SSR.
Vilnius, 1961. 31 p. DLC-L

3413. --- Lietuvos liaudies teismų rinkimų nuostatai... [Instructions
for election to the People's Courts
of Soviet Lithuania] Vilnius, Laikraščių ir žurnalų leidykla, 1957.
22 p. DLC-L

3414. --- Lietuvos TSR teismų,
santvarkos įstatymas, priimtas...
1960 m. birželio 8 d. [The Court law
of Soviet Lithuania...] Vilnius,
VPMLL, 1960. 20 p. DLC-L

3415. --- Polozhenie o vyborakh
narodnykh sudov Litovskoi SSR. Vil'-
nius, Gazetno-zhurnal'noe izd-vo,
1957. 23 p. DLC-L

VII.9.f. SOVIET LITHUANIAN LAWS,
STATUTES, ETC., AND
LEGAL COMMENTARIES

3416. APYLINKIŲ IR GYVENVIEČIŲ TA-
rybų darbo klausimai. [Laws governing workers in the communtities.
Leidinį sudarė A. Zallepuga. Vilnius, Mintis, 1969]. 191 p.
JS6130.52A8 PU DLC

3417. ČERNIAUSKAS, Simonas. Kaip
ginamos tarybinių piliečių civilinės
teisės. [Protection of people's
civil rights] Vilnius, Mintis, 1965.
47 p. DLC

3418. KRIVICKAS, Domas. Property
rights in Lithuanian Soviet Socialist Republic. In Federal bar news
(Washington, D.C.), v.2, no.10, 1955,
p. 311-313, 326.

3419. LITHUANIAN S.S.R. LAWS, STA-
TUTES, ETC. Butų buities klausimai;
nutarimų instrukcijų rinkinys. [Ques-
tions pertaining to housing problems.
Sudarė A. Varžgalys] Vilnius, VPMLL,
1961. 405 p. DLC-L

3420. --- Butų ūkis; įstatyminės
ir instruktyvinės medžiagos rinkinys
1955 m. gegužės 1 dienai. [A collection of the housing legislation.
Comp. by] V.T. Fateev. Vilnius, Lei-
tuvos Respublikinės profesinių sąjungų tarybos leidykla, 1955. 721 p.
forms. DLC-L

3421. --- Darbo įstatymų komenta-
ras. [A commentary on the Labour
Law. Knygą redagavo A. Mišutinas]
Vilnius, Mintis, 1970. 622 p. DLC

3422. --- Grazhdanskii kodeks Litovskoi Sovetskoi Sotsialisticheskoi
Respubliki. Vil'nius, Mintis, 1964.
404 p. JN6745.A35 1964 CSt-H DLC MH

3423. --- Grazhdanskii protsessu-
al'nyi kodeks Litovskoi Sovetskoi
Sotsialisticheskoi Respubliki. Vil'-
nius, Mintis, 1964. 370 p.
JN6745.A37 1964 CSt-H DLC MH NjP

3424. --- Khronologicheskoe sobranie zakonov Litovskoi SSR, ukazov
Prezidiuma Verkhovnogo Soveta i postanovlenii pravitel'stva Litovskoi
SSR. [Otvetstvennyi redaktor A.
Žirgulys] Vil'nius, Gos. izd-vo polit. i nauch. lit-ry, 1940/47-57.
3 v. DLC-L MH-L

3425. --- Kodeks o brake i sem'e
Litovskoi Sovetskoi Sotsialisticheskoi Respubliki. Vil'nius, Mintis,
1970. 116 p. KL715 PU

3426. --- Lietuvos TSR galiojančių
įstatymų normatyvinių aktų nuolati-
nė raidinė-dalykinė rodyklė. [Alpha-
betical subject index of statutory
rules governing work quotas] Vilnius, Lietuvos TSR Aukščiausiosios
Tarybos Presidiumo leidykla, 1967.
102 p. DLC-L

3427. --- Lietuvos TSR įstatymų,
Aukščiausiosios Tarybos Prezidiumo
įsakų ir Vyriausybės nutarimų chro-
nologinis rinkinys. [Chronological
collection of laws, edicts of Supreme Soviet, and Government decisions
of the Lithuanian SSR. Edited by
A. Žiurlys] Vilnius, VPMLL, 1956-58.
6 v. KL13 PU DLC-L(1-4) Ger.KIW
MH-L

3428. --- Lietuvos Tarybų Socialistinės Respublikos baudžiamasis kodeksas. [The criminal code of Soviet
Lithuania] Vilnius, VPMLL, 1961.
170 p. DLC-L MH

3429. --- Lietuvos Tarybų Socialistinės Respublikos baudžiamojo proceso kodeksas. [The code of criminal
procedure in Soviet Lithuania] Su
pakeitimais padarytais... Aukščiausiosios Tarybos Prezidiumo 1961 m.
liepos 5 d. ir rugsėjo 7 d. įsakais.
Vilnius, VPMLL, 291 p.
Lithuania 224 1961 CtY DLC-L MH

3430. --- --- Su pakeitimais pada-
rytais... Aukščiausiosios Tarybos
Presidiumo iki 1962 m. rugpiūčio ld.
Vilnius, VPMLL, 1962. 190 p.

343.475.L714.2 PU

3431. --- --- Su pakeitimais padarytais iki 1971 m. gegužės 1. d. ir
su pastraipsniui susistemintos medžiagos priedu. Vilnius, Mintis,
1971. 455 p. K.L716 PU

3432. --- Lietuvos Tarybų Socialistinės Respublikos civilinis kodeksas. [The civil code of Soviet Li-
thuania] Oficialus tekstas su pakeitimais ir papildymais 1968 m. sausio
1 d. ir su pastraipsniui susistemintos medžiagos priedu. Vilnius, Mintis, 1968. 602 p. DLC-L MH-L(1964
ed).

3433. --- --- Oficialus tekstas
su pakeitimais ir papildymais 1970
m. gruodžio 1 d. ir su pastraipsniui
susistemintos medžiagos priedu. Vilnius, Mintis, 1971. 474 p.
K.L715 PU

3434. --- Rinkimų į Lietuvos TSR
Aukščiausiąją Tarybą nuostatai. [In-
structions of election to the Supreme Council of Soviet Lithuania] Patvirtinta...1950 m. gruodžio 12 d. į-
saku su pakeitimais padarytais...ir
1963 m. sausio 2 d. įsakais. Vilnius, Laikraščių ir žurnalų leidykla,
1963. 30 p. DLC-L

3435. --- Rinkimų į Lietuvos TSR
rajonų, miestų, apylinkių ir gyvenviečių darbo žmonių deputatų tarybos
nuostatai... [Instructions of election to the district, town, and municipal councils...] patvirtinta...
1950 m. spalio mėn. 7 d. įsaku, su
pakeitimais padarytais... 1954 m.
gruodžio mėn. 20 d. ir gruodžio mėn.
28 d. įsakais. Vilnius, Laikraščių
ir žurnalų leidykla, 1956. 31 p.
DLC-L

3436. --- --- patvirtinti... su
pakeitimais... ir 1959 m. sausio 22
d. įsakais. Vilnius, Laikraščių ir
žurnalų leidykla, 1959. 32 p.
MH-L NNC-L

3437. --- Ugolovno-protsessual'nyi
kodeks Litovskoi Sovetskoi Sotsialisticheskoi Respubliki. Vil'nius, Gos.
izd-vo polit. i nauch. lit-ry, 1962.
336 p. DLC-L CSt-H

3438. --- --- S izmeneniiami vne-
sennymi ukazami Prezidiuma Verkhovnogo Soveta Litovskoi SSR ot 5 iiu-
liia i 7 sent. 1961 g. Vil'nius,
Gos. izd-vo polit. i nauch. lit-ry,
1961. 193 p. DLC-L CSt-H

3439. --- Ugolovnyi kodeks Litovskoi Sovetskoi Sotsialisticheskoi
Respubliki. S izmeneniiami na 1 apr.

1962 g. Vil'nius, Gos. izd-vo polit.
i nauch. lit-ry, 1962. 197 p.
DLC-L

3440. --- Zemel'nyi kodeks Litovskoi Sovetskoi Sotsialisticheskoi
Respubliki. Vil'nius, Mintis, 1971.
143 p.   K.L717 PU

3441. VAITIEKŪNAS, Vytautas. Sovietinis teisingumas; postalininių
sovietinių pagrindinių baudžiamųjų
įstatymų apžvalga. [Soviet justice;
review of the Soviet penal laws]
New York, N.Y., 1959. 76 p. Mimeographed.   DLC-L MH-L PU

VII.10. INTERNATIONAL LAW AND THE STATUS OF LITHUANIA

3442. BRAKAS, Martin. The Baltic
question in international law. In
Lituanus(Brooklyn, N.Y.), v.6, no.2,
1960, p. 90-95. See serials consulted.

3443. --- Lithuania's international status; some legal aspects. In
Baltic Review (New York, N.Y.), no.
37, 1970, p. 43-59. See serials
consulted.

3444. BRIGGS, Herbert W. Non-re-
cognition in the courts: the ships
of the Baltic Republics. In American Journal of International law
(Washington, D.C.), v.3, no.4, 1943,
p.585-596. See serials consulted.

3445. BÜCHLER, O. Das positive
internationale Privatrecht Litauens.
In Blätter für internationales Privatrecht (München), 1929, p.97-112.
See serials consulted.

3446. GINSBURGS, George. Nationality and state succession in Soviet
theory and practice. The experience
of the Baltic republics. In Res
Baltica. Leyden, 1968. p. 160-190.
DK511.L18R4 DLC CaAEU CtY-L RP

3447. --- Soviet views on the law
of state succession with regard to
treaties and acquired rights. The
case of Baltic republics. In Res
Baltica. Leyden, 1968. p. 191-229.
DK511.L18R4 DLC CaAEU CtY-L RP

3448. KRIVICKAS, Domas. The international status of Lithuania. In
Lituanus (Brooklyn, N.Y.), v.4, no.4,
1958, p. 99-104. See serials consulted.

3449. --- Lietuvos tarptautinis
status. [The international status of

Lithuania] In Varpas (Brooklyn, N.
Y.), no.3-4, 1958. See serials consulted.

3450. LOZORAITIS, Stasys. Some
juridical and moral aspects of the
occupation of Lithuania. In East
and West (London), v.2, no.7, 1956,
p. 29-37. See serials consulted.

3451. MAREK, Krystyna. The Baltic
States. In Her Identity and continuity of States in public international law. Genève, E. Droz, 1954,
p. 369-416. JX4053.M3 DLC-L CaAEU

MEISSNER, Boris. Die Sowjetunion, die baltischen Staaten und
das Völkerrecht. [1956] See entry
no.2932.

3452. RAČKAUSKAS, Konstantinas.
Power politics vs. international law.
In Baltic Review (New York, N.Y.),
no.14, 1958, p. 61-79. See serials
consulted.

3453. RAULINAITIS, Pranas Viktoras.
Lietuvių tautos suverenumas; istoriniai teisinė raida kovų už teisę ir
laisvę. [The sovereignty of the Lithuanian nation; an historical-legal
development of the struggle for freedom and rights. n.p.] 1952-[1954]
1 v. (various paging). DLC-L

3454. REPEČKA, Juozas. Der gegenwärtige völkerrechtliche Status der
baltischen Staaten; unter besonderer
Berücksichtigung der diplomatischen
Vorgeschichte der Eingliederung dieser Staaten in die Sowjet-union.
Göttingen, 1950. xii, 392 p. mimeographed. Thesis--University of Göttingen. JX1552.5.Z7R97 DLC NNC

3455. RIISMANDEL, Vaino J. The
continued legal existence of the Baltic States. In Baltic Review (New
York, N.Y.), no.12, 1957, p. 48-68.
See serials consulted.

3456. RUTENBERG, Gregor. Die baltischen Staaten und das Völkerrecht;
die Etstehungsprobleme Litauens, Lettlands und Estlands im Lichte des
Völkerrechts. Riga, G. Loeffler,
1928. xvi, 156 p. DK511.B3R78 DLC
CtY NN NNC NjP PU WU

--- Der litauisch-russische
Freundschafts- und Neutralitätsver-
trag und die Wilna-frage im Lichte
des Völkerrechts. In Zeitschrift
für Völkerrecht (Breslau), v.14, no.
3, 1928, p. 370-385; no.4, 1928, p.
548-558. See Serials consulted.

3457. SANDERS, Talivalds. Die Völkerrechtliche Stellung der baltischen

Staaten in den Jahren 1939-1948.
[Tübingen] 1949. 100 p. Typescript.
Thesis--University of Tübingen.
Ger. TU

3458. SELTER, Karl. Zur Rechtslage der baltischen Staaten. In Internationales Recht und Diplomatie (Hamburg), no.1-2, 1956, p. 33-51. See
serials consulted.

SIDZIKAUSKAS, Vaclovas. Lietuvos neutralumo įstatymas. [Lithu-
anian neutrality laws] In Mūsų Žinynas (Kaunas), 1939, p. 222-229.
See serials consulted.

3459. SINHA, S. Prakash. Self-de-
termination in international law and
its applicability to the Baltic people. In Res Baltica. Leyden, 1968.
p. 256-285. DK511.L18R4 DLC CaAEU
CtY-L RP

3460. VAITIEKŪNAS, Vytautas. The
continuity of Lithuania's statehood.
In Lituanus (Brooklyn, N.Y.), no.4
(13), 1957, p. 2-6. See serials consulted.

VIII. SOCIETY, SOCIAL STRUCTURE
AND CONDITIONS

VIII.1. GENERAL STUDIES

3461. DAUNORAS, Bronius. Duonos
beieškant. [Striving for daily bread]
Br. Dambaras [pseud. London] Nida,
[1954] 121 p. (Nidos knygų klubo
leidinys nr.2). DK511.L27D4 DLC
CtTMF PU

3462. DIRVELĖ, Eugenijus. Klasių
kova Lietuvoje. [The class struggle
in Lithuania, 1926] Vilnius, VPMLL,
1961. 193 p. facsims. DK511.L27D5
DLC PU

JANULAITIS, Augustinas. Lietuvos visuomenės ir teisės istorija.
[The history of the Lithuanian society and law] Tilžė, 1920. See
entry no.2646.

3463. ŁOWMIAŃSKI, Henryk. Z zagadnień spornych społeczeństwa litewskiego w XV wieku. In Przegląd Historyczny (Warszawa), v.40, 1950, p.
96-127. See serials consulted.

3464. MOORA, Harri. Vozniknovenie
klassovogo obshchestva v Pribaltike
po arkheologicheskim dannym. In
Sovetskaia Arkheologiia (Moskva), v.
17, 1953, p. 105-132. See serials
consulted.

3465. PAPLĖNAS, Jonas. Lietuvos
socialinės politikos bruožai. [The
outline of the Lithuanian social po-
licy] In Lietuva (New York, N.Y.),
no.1, 1952, p. 21-25. See serials
consulted.

VIII.2. FAMILY, MARRIAGE, AND
CHILDREN

3466. BRIZGYS, Vincentas. Negesin-
kime aukurų. [Retaining family tra-
ditions] Brooklyn, N.Y., Spaudė Tėvų Pranciškonų spaustuvė, 1958. 211
p. NN OCl

3467. ČIŽIŪNAS, Vaclovas. Šeima
tautinėje bendruomenėje. [Family in
the national community. n.p.]
P.L.B. Švietimo tarybos leidinys;
JAV Lietuvių Fondo lėšomis. 1971.
95 p. CtPAM ICLJF

3468. --- Tautinis auklėjimas šeimoje; trumpas tautinio auklėjimo vadovas lietuviškajai šeimai išeivijoje. [The ethnic education in the
family; a guide for the Lithuanian
family in exile] Memmingen, Ger.,
Vlikas, Lietuvybės išlaikymo tarnyba,
1953. 220 p. DK511.L223C58 CaAEU
DLC ICCC MiD PU

3469. JURGINIS, Juozas. Lietuvių
šeima XIII-XIV amžiais. [Lithuanian
family in thirteenth and fourteenth
centuries] LTSRMAIILKI, v.1, 1958,
p. 248-259. See serials consulted.

KAVOLIS, Martynas Arminas.
Das Eherecht in Litauen. In Zeitschrift für Ostrecht (Berlin), v.5, no.1,
1931, p. 17-39. See serials consulted.

--- Das litauische Eherecht.
In Zeitschrift für osteuropäisches
Recht (Breslau), N.F., v.8, no.1-2,
1941, p. 53-74. See serials consulted.

LITHUANIA. LAWS, STATUTES,
ETC. Teisiniai santykiai šeimoje...
Kaunas, 1932. See entry no. 2779.

3470. THE LITHUANIAN WOMAN. The
Lithuanian woman. [Editor Birutė
Novickis] Brooklyn, N.Y., Francis-
can Press, 1968. 197 p. Išleista
Lietuvių Moterų Klubų Federacijos.
HQ1665.65.L58 DLC PU

3471. NORUŠYTĖ, O. Dorinis auklėjimas lietuvių šeimoje. [Moral education in the Lithuanian family]
Kaunas, 1939. 92 p. 370.N2 CtTMF

SCHWETSCHIN, A. Das litauische Ehegesetz und das Matrikelgesetz vom 12.8.1940. In Zeitschrift für osteuropäisches Recht (Berlin), 1940-41, p. 279-302. See serials consulted.

VERŽBAVIČIUS, Levas. Globa pagal Lietuvos Statutus. [Social welfare and guardianship according to the Lithuanian Statutes] In Teisė (Kaunas), no.39, 1937, p. 298-312. See serials consulted.

3472. VOLTER, Eduard Aleksandrovich. Ob izuchenii semeinogo byta litovskozhemaitskogo naroda. In Pamiatnaia knizhka Kovenskoi gubernii na 1889 g. Kovno, 1888. p. 282-308. DK511. K55P32 DLC MH PU

VIII.3. NOBILITY, THEIR ORIGIN AND PRIVILEGES

3473. AVIŽONIS, Konstantinas. Bajorai valstybiniame Lietuvos gyvenime Vazų laikais. [Nobility in the public life of Lithuania during the reign of the Vasa dynasty] Kaunas, Lituanistikos institutas, Lietuvos istorijos skyrius, 1940. 592 p. Bibliography: p. 11-35. Summary in German. DK511.L24A83 CtY(positive photo copy) KU PPULC PU

--- Die Entstehung und Entwicklung des litauischen Adels bis zur litauisch-polnisch Union 1385. Berlin, 1932. See entry no. 710.

3474. BACKUS, Oswald Prentiss. Motives of West Russian nobles in deserting Lithuania for Moscow, 1377-1514. With maps drawn by George Frederick Jenks. Lawrence, Kan., University of Kansas Press, 1957. 174 p. maps. Bibliography: p. 155-163. DK100.B25 CaBVaU CtY CU CSt CLSU GU InU IU KU MH MiU MoU NN NNC NIC NcD NjR NbU OCl OClW OU PP PPiU PU RPB ScU TU WaU

3475. ---. Die Rechtsstellung der litauischen Bojaren 1387-1506. In Jahrbuch für Geschichte Osteuropas (Breslau), v.6, no.1, 1958, p. 1-32. See serials consulted.

3476. ČEGINSKAS, Kajetonas Julius. Die Polonisierung des litauischen Adels im XIX Jahrhundert. In Commentationes Balticae (Bonn),v. IV/V no.2, 1958, p. 19-42. See serials consulted.

DĄBKOWSKI, Przemysław. Dobra rodowe i nabyte w prawie litewskim

od XIV do XVI wieku. Lwów, 1916. See entry no.2764.

3477. ESSEN, Werner. Adel und Adelsdörfer in Litauen. In Gesellschaft für Geschichte und Altertumskunde. Riga. Sitzungsberichte, 1930-31. See serials consulted.

3478. GLOGER, Zygmunt. Szlachta okoliczna na żmujdzi. In Biblioteka Warszawska, v.4, 1877, p. 286-290. See serials consulted.

HALECKI, Oskar. Kwestje sporne w sprawie początków szlachty litewskiej. In Kwartalnik Historyczny (Lwów), v.30, 1916. See serials consulted.

3479. HELLMANN, Manfred. Der litauische Adel zur Zeit der Wasas. In Jomsburg (Leipzig), v.6, no.1-2, 1942, p. 141-143. See serials consulted.

JANULAITIS, Augustinas. Lietuvos bajorai ir jų seimeliai XIX amž. 1795-1863. See entry no.2564.

3480. KRASAUSKAITĖ, Marija Christina. Die litauischen Adelsprivilegien bis zum Ende des XV Jahrhunderts. Leipzig, R. Noske, 1927. vi, 72 p. Thesis--University of Zürich. CR4019.K85 UCL DLC PU

3481. SCHLINGENSIEPEN, Georg Herman. Der Strukturwandel des baltischen Adels in der Zeit vor dem ersten Weltkrieg. Marburg/Lahn, Johan Gottfried Herden Institut, 1959. 185 p. (Wissenschaftliche Beiträge und Landeskunde Ost-Mitteleuropas, no.41) CaBVaU CU DS ICU MH NNC NIC NcD NjP

PORAI-KOSHITS, Ivan Antonovich. Istoricheskii razkaz o litovskom dvorianstvie. Sanktpeterburg, 1858. See entry no.736.

SZYDŁOWSKI, Stefan, Graf von. Der polnische und litauische Hochadel. Budapest, 1944. See entry no.1054.

3482. TALKO-HRYNCEWICZ,Julian. Szlachta litewska. Studyum antropologiczno-etnologiczne. In Polska Akademia Umiejętności, Kraków. Komisja Antropologiczna. Matryały Antropologiczno-Archeologiczne i Etnograficzne, v.12, 1912. 111 p. See serials consulted.

VIII.4. PEASANTS, THEIR HISTORY AND
RELATIONS WITH OTHER
GROUPS

3483. BIELINIS, Jurgis. Istorisz-
ki pritikimai isz ukininkų gyvenimo
Lietuvoje; ju praeitė ir ateitė. Vilniuje, M. Jankus, 1899. 64 p. Photocopy on 33 leaves. 947.5.B47.4 PU

3484. DUNDULIS, Bronius. Valstiečių klausimas Lietuvoje 1812 metais.
[The peasants' problem in Lithuania,
1812] In LTSRMAII. Lietuvos valstiečiai XIX amžiuje. Vilnius, 1957.
p. 40-47. HD725.7.L5 DLC CaAEU CtPAM
CtY CU NN PU

IVINSKIS, Zenonas. Geschichte des Bauernstandes in Litauen.
Berlin, 1933. See entry no. 1017.

3485. --- Lietuvos valstiečių luomo susiformavimas ir raida. [The origin and development of Lithuanian
peasant] In Athenaeum (Kaunas), v.4,
no.4, 1933. 17 p. See serials consulted.

3486. JABLONSKIS, Konstantinas.
Archyvinės smulkmenos. [Archival
miscellanea] Contents.--1. Apie XVI
amžiaus ūkuninkų alaus apeigas.--2.
Nestojusių į 1567 m. kariuomenės
šaukimą, Kauno pavieto bajorų sąrašas.--3. Sokavičių dalybų sąrašas.--
4. Antstolių apkarpymas.--5. XVIII
amžiaus galo priesaikos formulė Pa-
girio ūkininkams.--6. Didž. kunigaikščio Kazimiero privilegija Žemaičių
žemėi.--7. Vytauto raštas keliems Medininkų bajorams.--8. Seniausieji
Deltuvos bažnyčios dokumentai.--9.
Keli XVI amžiaus aktai apie žmonių
ir vaikų teismą.--10. Žinutė apie
Motiejų Stryikauskį. In Praeitis
(Kaunas), v.2, 1933, p. 412-436. See
serials consulted.

3487. JANULAITIS, Augustinas. Valstiečiai ir 1831 metų revoliucija
Lietuvoje. [Peasants in the revolution of 1831] In Lietuvių tauta
(Kaunas), v.1, 1910, p. 469-494. See
serials consulted.

3488. JURGINIS, Juozas. Pasėdžiai
ir jų reikšmė Lietuvos valstiečių
feodalinių prievolių istorijoje.
[Free peasants and their importance
in connection with the peasants' feudal obligations in Lithuania] In
LTSRMAD. Serija A, v.2(5), 1958, p.
51-68. See serials consulted.

3489. --- Valstiečių bendruomenė
ir feodalinė tėvonija Lietuvoje XIII-
XIV amžiais. [The community of pea-

sants and the feudal patrimony in Lithuania in thirteenth and fourteenth
centuries] In LTSRMAD. Serija A,
v.1(2), 1957, p. 51-67. See serials
consulted.

3490. KATKUS, Mikalojus. Balanos
gadynė. [Age of the wooden torch]
In Mūsų tautosaka (Kaunas), v.4,
1931, p. 13-186. See serials consulted.

3491. KONECZNY, Feliks. Wiadomość
z roku 1447 o stanie ludu wiejskiego
w Polsce czy na Litwie. In Ateneum
Wileńskie (Wilno), v.6, 1929, p.8-15.
See serials consulted.

3492. LIETUVOS TSR MOKSLŲ AKADEMI-
JA, VILNA. ISTORIJOS INSTITUTAS.
Lietuvos valstiečiai XIX amžiuje.
[Lithuanian peasants in the nineteen-
th century] Redakcinė kolegija: K.
Jablonskis, J. Jurginis (atsak. re-
daktorius), J. Žiugžda. Vilnius,
VPMLL,1957. 270 p. HD725.7.L5 DLC
CaAEU CU CtY CtPAM PU

3493. --- Lietuvos valstiečių ir
miestelėnų ginčai su dvarų valdytojais; dokumentų rinkinys. [The dis-
putes of Lithuanian peasants and
town inhabitants with the estate ow-
ners; a collection of documents.
Comp. by K. Jablonskis] Vilnius,
VPMLL, 1959-61. 3 v. Documents in
Russian or Polish with translation
into Lithuanian. HD725.7.L53 DLC
CaAEU(2) CtPAM(1-2) CtY ICU MH MH-L
NN NNC PPiU PU WaU

LITHUANIA. European conference on rural life. Lithuania [Ge-
neva, 1939] See entry no.909.

3494. MILOVIDOV, Aleksandr Ivanovich. Ustroistvo obshchestvennogo
byta krest'ian Sievero-Zapadnago kraia pri graf. M.N. Murav'evie. Vil'-
na, Tip. Vilen. Sv.-Dukh. bratstva,
1902. 35 p. Z939.V5 DLC

3495. MOŚCICKI, Henryk. Sprawa
włościańska na Litwie w pierwszej
ćwierci XIX stulecia. Warszawa, Nakład Gebethnera i Wolffa, 1908. 38p.
BM(8275. g. 8.) NjP

3496. PICHETA, Vladimir Ivanovich.
Krest'iane tiaglye ve vtoroi polovine XVI veka v Velikom Kniazhestve
Litovskom. In Akademiia nauk USRS,
Kiev. Filolohichnyi viddil. Zbirnyk, nr. 76 (IUvileinyi zbirnyk na
poshanu... M.S. Hrushevs'koho, v.1,
1928, p. 169-175) AS262.A72532 DLC
NN

3497. POKHYLEVYCH, Dmytro Leonidovych. Krest'iane slugi v Litve i

Zapadnoi Belorussii v XVI-XVII vv.
In Lvov. Universytet. Naukovi Zapysky, vyp. 5, 1955. See serials
consulted.

3498. --- Krest'iane Belorussii i
Litvy v XVI-XVIII vv. [L'vov] Izd-
vo L'vovskogo universiteta, 1957.
174 p. map. HD719.L68P6 DLC CU
CLU InU MH NNC

3499. --- Krest'iane Belorussii i
Litvy vo vtoroi polovine XVIII v.
Vil'nius, 1966. 215 p. HD719.
L68P62 DLC PU

3500. SEL'SKIE POSELENIIA PRIBAL-
tiki XIII-XX vv. [Sbornik statei.
Otv. red. V.A. Aleksandrov] Moskva,
Nauka, 1971. 251 p. HD719.B28S43
PU

3501. VANSEVIČIUS, Stasys. Lietuvos valstiečių teisinė padėtis buržuazijos valdymo metais, 1919-1940.
[Legal status of Lithuanian peasants,
1919-1940] Vilnius, Mintis, 1968.
146 p.

3502. --- Lietuvos valstiečių teisinė padėtis po 1861 m. reformos
įvykdymo. [The legal status of the
Lithuanian peasants after the abolishment of serfdom in 1861] In
LTSRMAII. Lietuvos valstiečiai XIX
amžiuje. Vilnius, 1957. p. 213-
226. HD725.7.L5 DLC CaAEU CU CtPAM
CtY NN PU

VIII.5. PEASANT MOVEMENTS AND UPRISINGS

3503. JABLONSKIS, Konstantinas.
Valstiečių judėjimas Lietuvoje XIX
a. pirmoje pusėje ir valstiečių
siekimų reiškėjas Jonas Goštautas.
The peasants' movement in Lithuania
in the first part of the nineteenth
century and their spokesman Jonas
Goštautas] In LTSRMAII. Lietuvos
valstiečiai XIX amžiuje. Vilnius,
1957. p. 48-69. HD725.7.L5 DLC
CaAEU CU CtPAM CtY NN PU

3504. JANULAITIS, Augustinas. Iš
istorijos; Kaimiečių kovos su po-
nais. [Peasants' struggle with the
landowners] Sutaisė Varguolių Bičiuliai. Plymouth, Pa., Spauda
"Vienybės lietuvininkų", 1905. 63 p.
(Tėvynės mylėtojų draugystė. [Lei-
dinys] no.13) D8.J33 DLC

3505. --- Valstiečių sukilimas
XVIII amžiuje Lietuvoje. [The insurrection of the peasants in the
eighteenth century in Lithuania]

3506. KULA, W. and J. Leskiew-
czowa. Žródła do dziejów powstania
chlopów Szawelskich w 1769 roku.
In Teki Archywalne (Warszawa), v.5,
1957, p. 228-333. See serials consulted.

3507. MERKYS, Vytautas. Lietuvos
valstiečių ir žemės ūkio darbininkų
judėjimas 1901-1904 metais. [The
movement of the Lithuanian peasants
and farm labour in 1901-1904] Vilnius, VPMLL, 1959. 52 p. HD725.7M4
PU

3508. --- Valstiečių judėjimas
Lietuvoje XIX a. pabaigoje. [The
revolutionary movement of the Lithu-
anian peasants at the end of the
nineteenth century] In LTSRMAII.
Lietuvos valstiečiai XIX amžiuje.
Vilnius, 1957. p. 240-[271].
HD725.7.L5 DLC CaAEU CU CtPAM CtY
NN PU

3509. MULEVIČIUS, Leonas. Klasių
kovos paaštrėjimas Lietuvos kaime
Krymo karo metu, 1853-1856 m. [The
augmenting class struggle in Lithuania during the Crimean War, 1853-
1856] In LTSRMAII. Lietuvos valstiečiai XIX amžiuje. Vilnius,
1957. p. 70-82. HD725.7.L5 DLC
CaAEU CU CtPAM CtY NN PU

3510. --- Laisvųjų žmonių kova
dėl žemės Lietuvoje 1864-1882 metais. [The struggle for land of
the free peasants in Lithuania during the years 1864-1882] In
LTSRMAD. Serija A. no.2, 1962, p.
59-83. See serials consulted.

3511. NEUPOKOJEVAS, V. Valstiečių judijimas Lietuvoje panaikinus
baudžiavą, 1861-1862 m. [The peasants' movement in Lithuania after
the abolishment of serfdom in 1861-
1862] In LTSRMAII. Lietuvos valstiečiai XIX amžiuje. Vilnius,
1957, p. 105-133. HD725.7.L5 DLC
CaAEU CU CtPAM CtY NN PU

3512. ŽIUGZDA, Juozas. Lietuvos
kaimo darbo žmonių kova dėl žemės
buržuazijos viešpatavimo metais.
[The struggle for agricultural land
by the farm workers in Lithuania...]
Vilnius, VPMLL, 1952. 125 p.
HD725.7.Z5 DLC

VIII.6. LAND TENURE

3513. BALČIŪNAS, Valerionas. Lietuvos kaimų žemės tvarkymas istorijos, ūkio ir statistikos šviesoje.
[Land tenure in the villages of Li-

thuania from the viewpoint of history, economy, and statistics] Kaunas, Žemės reformos valdybos leidinys, 1938. 196 p. illus., maps. Bibliography: p. 193-196. HD725.7. B3 DLC PPULC PU

CHEREPNIN, Lev Vladimirovich. Russkie feodal'nye arkhivy XIV-XV. vekov. Moskva, 1948-51. See entry no. 4632.

CONZE, Werner. Agraverfassung und Bevölkerung in Litauen und Weissrussland. Leipzig, 1940. See entry no. 2256.

3514. DUNDULIENĖ, Pranė. Zemledelie v dofeodal'noi Litve. In Akademiia Nauk SSSR. Institut Etnografii. Kratkie Soobshcheniia (Moskva), v. 12, 1950, p. 74-82. See serials consulted.

3515. --- Zemledelie v Litvie v epokhu feodalizma. In Baltiiskii Etnograficheskii Sbornik. Moskva, 1956. p. 3-47. (Akademiia Nauk SSR. Institut Etnografii Trudy. Novaia Seriia, tom 32) GN2.A2142 DLC CaOONM ICMILC MnU NIC OU

3516. GRINIUS, Kazys. Teisingas žemės valdymas Lietuvoje. [Just land tenure in Lithuania] Tilžėjė, 1906. 24 p. Reprint from "Varpas" 947.52G447 PU

3517. IVINSKIS Zenonas. Kaimas Lietuvos praeityje. [The village in Ancient Lithuania] In Lietuvių enciklopedija. Boston, Mass., 1957, v.10, p. 228-233. For holdings see entry no. 216.

3518. JURGUTIS, Vytautas. Valstiečių kiemas... Le cour paysanne dans le droit rural Lituanien. Kaunas, 1939. vii, 227 p. (Kaunas. Universitetas. Teisų Fakultetas. Darbai, t.10, kn.1.) Summary in French. DLC-L

3519. KAIMAS, JO ŽEMĖS TVARKYMAS ir kaimo bendruomenė. [The village and the rural communities. By J. Gimbutas, V. Balčiūnas and A. Mažiulis] In Lietuvių enciklopedija. Boston, Mass., 1957, v.10, p. 233-241. For holdings see entry no. 216.

3520. KAMIENIECKI, Witołd. Rozwój własności na Litwie w dobie przed I Statutem. In Polska Akademia Umiejetności, Kraków. Wydział Historyczno-Filosoficzny. Rozprawy, v.32(57), 1914, p. 94-195. See serials consulted.

3521. KASPERCZAK, Stanisław. Roz-

wój gospodarki folwarcznej na Litwie i Bialorusi do połowy XVI wieku. Poznań, 1965, 408 p. (Universytet im. Adama Mickiewicza w Poznaniu. Wydział Filozoficzno-Historyczny. [Prace] Seria Historia, nr.19) Bibliography: p.[368]-393. HD725.7.K37 DLC CaOTU MH

3522. KLIMAS, Petras. Lietuvos žemės valdymo istorija iki lenkmečių. [History of land ownership in Lithuania] Vilnius, "Švyturio" spaustuvė, 1919. 65 p. (Lietuvių mokslo draugijos leidinys, 42) HD725.7.K6 DLC BM(09055. f. 21) InNd PU

3523. KREST'IANSKOE ZEMLEVLADENIE Kovenskoi gubernii. In Vilenskii Vremennik (Vilna), v.3, 1909. See serials consulted.

3524. LEONTOVICH, Fedor Ivanovich. Panskii dvor v litovsko-russkom gosudarstve. In Warsaw. Universytet. Izviestiia, v.5, 1895. See serials consulted.

3525. LIETUVOS TSR MOKSLŲ AKADEMIJA, VILNA. CENTRINĖ BIBLIOTEKA. Feodalinių žemės valdų Lietuvoje inventorių aprašymas. [The description of the inventories of the feudal land tenure in Lithuania. Comp. by V. Abramavičius. Ed. by A. Ivaškevičius] Vilnius, 1963. 557 p. facsims. HD725.7.L48 DLC CU CtY ICU MH NN PU

3526. LIETUVOS TSR MOKSLŲ AKADEMIJA, VILNA. ISTORIJOS INSTITUTAS. Lietuvos inventoriai XVII amžiuje; dokumentų rinkinys. [Lithuanian manorial inventories of the seventeenth century; a collection of documents. Comp. by K. Jablonskis and M. Jučas] Vilnius, VPMLL, 1962. 461 p. Documents are in Polish or Russian. HD725.7.L49 DLC CaAEU CU MH NN NjP PU WaU

3527. LIETUVOS TSR ŽEMĖS KADASTRAS. [An official register of quantity of land in Lithuania. Ats. redaktorius V. Mališauskas] Vilnius, Mintis, 1970, 352 p. HD719.L68L53 PU

3528. PICHETA, Vladimir Ivanovich. IUrydychnae stanovishcha viaskovaha nasel'nitstva no pryvatnaulas'nitskikh zemliakh k chasu vydan'nia Litouskaha statutu 1529 h. [By] Uladzimer Picheta. Mensk, 1928. 57 p. Adbitak z "Zapisak Addzelu humanitarnykh navuk" 1928, kn.3, t.2. Instytut belaruskae kul'tury. K.P583 PU

3529. POKHYLEVYCH, Dmytro Leonidovych. Zemleustroistvo i pozemel'nyi katastr v Belorussii, Litve i Ukraine v XVI-XVII vv. In Akademiia Nauk SSSR. Institut Istorii. Materialy po istorii zemledeliia SSSR. Sbornik. l. Moskva, 1952, p. 322-410. See serials consulted.

3530. RIMKA, Albinas. Dėl žemės klausimo Lietuvoje, 1-ji laida. [On the question of land tenure in Lithuania] Voronežas, Lietuvių spaustuvė, 1918. 55 p. 947.63R464.3 PU MH(Photoreproduction)

3531. SRUOGIENĖ, Vanda (Daugirdaitė). Žemaičių bajorų ūkis pirmoj pusėj XIX šimtmečio. [Noblemen's estates in Žemaitija (Samogitia) in the first part of the nineteenth century] In Senovė (Kaunas), no.4, 1938, p. 25-132. See serials consulted.

3532. STRAZDŪNAITĖ, R. Agrariniai santykiai Užnemunėje 1795-1864 m. [The agrarian relations in Suvalkija, 1795-1864] In LTSRMAII. Lietuvos valstiečiai XIX amžiuje. Vilnius, 1957, p. 201-212. HD725.7.L5 DLC CaAEU CU CtPAM CtY NN PU

3533. VLADIMIRSKII-BUDANOV, Mikhail Flegontovich. Formy krest'ianskago zemlevladeniia v litovsko-russkom gosudarstvie XVI v. In Kievskii Sbornik v pomoshch postradavshim ot neurozhaia (Kiev), 1892, p. 357-386. (*QDA)NN BM

VIII.7. SERFDOM AND SLAVERY

3534. BASANAVIČIUS, Jonas. Baudžiava Lietuvoje. [Serfdom in Lithuania] Vilnius, m. Kuktos spauda, 1907. 50 p. 947.5B3 CtTMF ICCC

3535. JABLONSKIS, Konstantinas. Apie vergus Didžiojoje Lietuvos Kunigaikštijoje XVI amžiaus pradžioje. [About slaves in Grand Duchy of Lithuania at the beginning of the sixteenth century] In Praeitis (Kaunas), v.1, 1930, p. 304-317. See serials consulted.

3536. --- Belaisviai kaimynai Lietuvoje. [The war prisoners in Lithuania] In Praeitis (Kaunas), v.1, 1930, p. 166-213. See serials consulted.

3537. JANULAITIS, Augustinas. Baudžiava Lietuvoje. Parašė Žmogus [psued. Serfdom in Lithuania...] Chicago, Ill., Spauda "Lietuvos", 1901. 76 p. port. (Tėvynės mylėto-

jų draugystė. [Leidinys] no.6) HT807.J35 DLC ICCC PU

3538. --- Baudžiavų panaikinimo sumanymai Lietuvoje... [Plans for the abolishment of serfdom in Lithuania, 1817-1819] Kaunas, Valstybės spaustuvė, 1929. 109 p. (Kaunas Universitetas. Teisių fakultetas. Darbai. T.5, kn.4) HT815.L5J3 PU CaAEU CU ICU MoU NN NNC

3539. JUČAS, Mečislovas. Baudžiavos irimas Lietuvoje. [Disintegration of slavery in Lithuania] Vilnius, Mintis, 1972. 317 p. HD725.7J8 PU

3540. JURGINIS, Juozas. Baudžiava Lietuvoje XIX amžiaus pirmoje pusėje. [Serfdom in Lithuania in the first part of the nineteenth century] In LTSRMAII. Lietuvos valstiečiai XIX amžiuje. Vilnius, 1957, p. 7-39. HD725.7.Ld DLC CaAEU CtPAM CtY CU NN PU

3541. --- Baudžiavos įsigalėjimas Lietuvoje. [The establishment of serfdom in Lithuania] Vilnius, VPMLL, 1962. 342 p. At head of title: Lietuvos TSR Mokslų akademija. Istorijos institutas. Summary in Russian. Bibliography: p. 317-329. HD725.7.J8 DLC CU CaAEU CtPAM CtY ICU NN PU

3542. --- Valstiečiai "veldamai" Lietuvoje XV-XVI amžiuje. [Serves in XV-XVI centuries in Lithuania] In LTSRMAD. Serija A, t.1(4), 1958, p. 113-127. See serials consulted.

3543. OWYSWOBODZENIU WŁOŚCIAN NA Litwie. Poznań, (Printed in Berlin), 1863. BM(8093. aaa. 41(4.))

3544. RUSECKAS, Petras, ed. Baudžiava; atsiminimai, padavimai, legendos. [Serfdom; recollections and legends] Kaunas, Author, 1936. 336 p. illus. HT807.R86 DLC CtTMF CtY ICLJF PU

RUSSIA. LAWS, STATUTES, ETC. Najwyżej uchwalone przez jego cesarską mość dnia 19 lutego 1861 r., ustawy o włościanach... Wilno, 1861. See entry no. 2789.

3545. RUSSIA. LAWS, STATUTES, ETC. 1855-1881 (ALEXANDRA II). Polozhenie 19 fevralia 1861 goda o krest'-ianakh, vyshedshikh iz kriepostnoi zavisimosti... Moskva, Izdanie istorikofilosofskago fakulteta Moskovskikh vysshikh zhenskikh kursov, 1916. vi, 410 p. DLC-L

3546. SEMENOV, Nikolai Petrovich.

Osvobozhdenie krest'ian v tsarstvo-
vanie Imperatora Aleksandra II;
khronika deiatel'nosti Komisii po
krest'ianskomu dielu. Sanktpeterburg, Izd. M.E. Komarova, 1889-
1892. 3 v. in 4. DK222.S5 DLC

3547. TRINKA, Vladas. Kai valgė
ponų duoną,iš baudžiavos gadynės
Lygumų valsčiuje. [From the age of
serfdom in the municipality of Ly-
gumai] In Gimtasai kraštas (Šiauliai), no.3-4, 1940. See serials
consulted.

3548. ZALESKI, Bronisław. Pomy-
sły do ostatecznego uregulowania
kwestyi włościańskiej. [By] "Litwin" [pseud.] Poznan, 1860.
BM(8094. f. 27.)

VIII.8. LABOUR AND LABOURING CLASSES

ABRAMSON, A. Arbeitsrecht
in Litauen. In Zeitschrift für
osteuropäisches Recht (Breslau),
1928, p. 920-940. See serials consulted.

3549. BALEVIČIUS, Zigmas. Darbininkų padėtis buržuazinėje Lietuvoje. [The labour conditions in Li-
thuania] Vilnius, VPMLL, 1960. 22
p. HD8535.7.B3 DLC OCU OKentU

3550. BIELINIS, Kipras. The labour problem in Lithuania. [Wash-
ington, D.C., 1953] 35 l. (Mid-
European Studies Centre. Research
documents, no.163) Typescript.
Microfilm DR-5 no.163 DLC MnU

BUČAS, Jonas. Darbo atlygi-
nimo minimumo įstatymais nustatymo
esmė ir prasmė. In Ekonomika (Kaunas), no.2, 1935. See serials consulted.

3551. ČEPULIENĖ, Stefa. Profsą-
junginis judėjimas Lietuvoje, 1919-
1926 m. [Trade-union movement in
Lithuania, 1919-1926] Vilnius,
Mintis, 1964. 119 p. illus., facsims. HD6735.65.C4 DLC CtY NN

3552. ČERNIAUSKAS, Simonas. Prof-
sąjunginis judėjimo vystymasis Lietuvoje, 1927-1940 metais. [The development of the trade unions in
Lithuania, 1927-1940] Vilnius,
Mintis, 1966. 60 p. HD6735.65.
L5C4 DLC

3553. GAIGALAITĖ, Aldona. Darbininkų judėjimo pakilimas Lietuvoje
1929-1934 metais. [The rise of the
labour movement in Lithuania during

1929-1934 period. Edited by J.
Žiugžda] Vilnius, VPMLL, 1957. 168
p. At head of title: Lietuvos TSR
Mokslų akademija. Istorijos insti-
tutas. HD8535.7.G3 MH CU CtY DLC
InU NN OKentU

3554. GRIŠKŪNAITĖ, Emilija. Darbininkų judėjimas Lietuvoje 1895-
1914 m. [The labour movement in
Lithuania 1895-1914] Vilnius, Mintis, 1971. 307 p. HD8535.7.G7 PU

LITHUANIA. LAWS, STATUTES,
ETC. Įstatymai darbo srityje Lie-
tuvoj. [Compiled by V. Akelaitis]
Kaunas, 1927. See entry no. 2776.

--- Veikiantieji Lietuvoj
įstatymai darbo srityje. Kaunas,
1922. See entry no. 2780.

LIUTERMOZA, Martynas. Pramonės įstatymų leidimas ir darbininkų luomo padėtis Lietuvoje. Kaunas,
1923. See entry no. 2783.

3555. MATULEVIČIUS, Jurgis. Miestų ir apskritai pramonijos darbininkų klausimas. [The problems of
city and industrial workers] Kaunas, 1909. 20 p. 330M1 CtTMF

3556. MERKYS, Vytautas. Vilniaus
darbininkų streikai 1895-1900 metais. [The strike of Vilnius' wor-
workers in 1895-1900] In LTSRMAD.
Serija A, v.1(6), 1959, p. 169-191.
See serials consulted.

3557. PAPLĖNAS, Jonas. Die Lohn-
politik in Litauen. Bonn, Ger.,
1948. 223 l. tables. Thesis--
University of Bonn. Typescript.
Ger.BU

3558. RAMANAUSKAS, Bonifacas. Die
soziale Gerechtigkeit in Arbeitsrecht der litauischen Republik.
Tübingen, 1945. Thesis--University
of Tübingen. Typescript. Ger.TU

3559. ŽEMECKAS, Kazys. Die Verhältnisse der Landarbeiter in Litauen. Tübingen, Ger., 1947.
Thesis--University of Tübingen.
Typescript. Ger.TU

VIII.9. URBAN COMMUNITIES, GUILDS,

CRAFTSMEN AND THEIR

PRIVILEGES

3560. DAUGUDIS, Vytautas. Stak-
liškių lobis. [Treasures of Stak-
liškiai] Vilnius, Mintis, 1968. 41
p. illus. (Acta historica lituani-

ca, 2) Summary in Russian.
DK511.L21D3 InU MH PU WaU

3561. IPPEL, A. Wilnaer Zunftbü-
cher. In Das Litauen-Buch. Eine
Auslese aus der Zeitung der 10. Armee. Wilna, 1918. p. 265-274.
DK511.L2L3 CaBVaU InU NN PU

3562. JABLONSKIS, Konstantinas.
Dėl 1408 metų Vytauto privilegijos
Kauno miestui tikrumo. [On the dispute of Vytautas privileges for Kaunas in 1408] In Praeitis (Kaunas),
v.1, 1930, p. 329-339. See serials
consulted.

3563. JALOVECKAS, R. Lietuvos miestų kūrimosi veiksniai. [The factors
of development of towns in Lithuania]
In Lietuvos TSR architektūros klausimai (Vilnius), v.1, 1960, p. 236-
244. See serials consulted.

3564. JAWORSKI, Iwo. Studja nad
ustrojem miast na prawie niemieckim
w Wielkiem Księstwie Litewskim w dobie Jgiellońskiej. In Rocznik
Prawniczy Wileński (Wilno), v.5,
1931, p. 297-352. See serials consulted.

3565. KRIŠČIUKAITIS, Kazys. Urbanizmas ir Lietuva. [The urbanism
and Lithuania] In Aidai (Brooklyn,
N.Y.) no.1(116), 1959, p. 1-9. See
serials consulted.

      LIETUVOS TSR MOKSLŲ AKADEMI-
JA, VILNA. ISTORIJOS INSTITUTAS.
Lietuvos valstiečių ir miestelėnų
ginčai su dvarų valdytojais. Vilnius,
1959-61. See entry no.3493.

3566. ŁOWMIAŃSKA, Maria. W sprawie
składu narodowościowego cechów Wileńskich. In Ateneum Wileńske(Wilno),
v.7, 1930, p. 346-350. See serials
consulted.

3567. ŁOWMIAŃSKI, Henryk. "Wchody"
miast litewskich. In Ateneum Wileńskie (Wilno), v.1, 1923, p. 398-466;
v.2, 1924, p. 1-30. See serials
consulted.

3568. MERKYS, Vytautas. Vilniaus
amatininkų cechų skaičiaus dinamika
XIX amžiuje. [The expansion of the
artisan guilds in Vilnius in the 19th
century] In LTSRMAD. Serija A,
v.1(10), 1961, p. 49-70. See serials
consulted.

3569. --- Vilniaus cechų amatininkų skaičius ir jų kilmė 1795-1893
metais. [The number and origin of
artisan guilds in Vilnius in, 1795-
1893] In LTSRMAD. Seria A, v.2(11)
1961. p.145-168. See serials consulted.

3570. MIŠKINIS, Antanas. Privile-
gijuotos Lietuvos gyvenvietės ir jų
tinklo vystymasis XIII-XVIII a. [The
elite and its development through
the 13-18th. centuries in Lithuania]
In LTSRAMMD: statyba ir architektūra, v.3, no.3, 1963, p. 123-146.
See serials consulted.

3571. NEZABITAUSKIS, Liudvikas.
Darbininkai, specialistai ir amati-
ninkai. [Workers, specialists and
artisans] In Gimtasai kraštas
(Šiauliai), no.1(9), 1936, p. 37-43.
See serials consulted.

3572. OCHMAŃSKI, Jerzy. W kwestii
agrarnego charakteru miast Wielkiego
Księstwa Litewskiego w XVI wieku. In
Studia Historica. 35-lecie pracy
naukowej Henryka Łowmiańskiego. Warszawa, 1958. p. 279-294. D6.S796
DLC CtY ICU NIC NN NNC MnU

3573. PUZINAS, Jonas. XIV-XV amžiaus Lietuvos miestai ir Magdeburgo
teisė. [The Lithuanian cities of
the fourteenth-sixteenth centuries
and their Magdeburg rights] In Savivaldybė (Kaunas), no.8, 1929, p.
10-16. See serials consulted.

3574. TALKO-HRYNCEWICZ, Julian.
Mieszkańcy Wilna z drugiej połowy
XVI i początków XVII stulecia. In
Polska Akademia Umiejętności, Kraków.
Komisja Antropologiczna. Dział II:
Materiały Antropologiczno-Archeolo-
giczne i Etnograficzne, v.9, 1907,
p.87-138. See serials consulted.

3575. TAUTAVIČIUS, Adolfas. Iš XIV
amžiaus Vilniaus gyventojų buities.
[The way of life in Vilnius in the
fourteenth century] In LTSRMAIILKI,
v.1, 1958, p.94-103. See serials
consulted.

3576. VILNA. LAWS, STATUTES, ETC.
Zbiór praw i przywilejów miastu sto-
łecznemu W.K.L. Wilnowi nadanych.
Na żądanie wielu miast Koronnych,
jako też Wielkiego Księstwa Litews-
kiego ułożony y wydany przez Piotra
Dubińskiego Burmistrza Wileńskiego.
Wilno, Drukarnia J.K. Mci przy Akade-
mii, 1788. 312 p. 947.52.V7132 PU
DLC NjP

3577. ŽILĖNAS, Vincas. Dailidės
ir jų darbo įrankiai. [Carpenters
of Lithuania and their working tools]
In LTSRMAIILKI, v.1, 1958, p.185-
188. illus. See serials consulted.

VIII.10. ETHNIC GROUPS

3578. BASANAVIČIUS, Jonas. Lenkai Lietuvoje. [Poles in Lithuania. Tr. from Russian by V. Gintautas] Chicago, Ill., Lietuvos spaustuvėj, 1903. 41 p. 947.5.B272.2 PU CtTMF InNd OCl PPULC PU

3579. BERSHADSKII, Sergei Aleksandrovich, comp. Dokumenty i registry k istorii litovskikh evreev iz aktovykh knig: Metriki Litovskoi, Vilenskago Tsentral'nago Arkhiva i niekotorykh pechatnykh izdanii. Sanktpeterburg, A.E. Syrkin, 1882. 2 v. DS135.L8D66 ICU BM(4515. e. 1.)

3580. --- Litovskie evrei; istoriia ikh iuridicheskago i obshchestvennago polozheniia v Litvie ot Vitovta do Liublinskoi unii. 1388-1569 g. Sanktpeterburg, Tip. M.M. Stasiulevicha, 1883. vii, 431 p. DS135.L5B45 DLC NN

3581. BILDER AUS DER GESCHICHTE des evangelischen Deutschen in Litauen. Salzgitter-Lebenstadt, Heimatstimme, [1965] 144 p. illus. DK511.L22B5 PU

3582. COHEN, Israel. Vilna. Philadelphia, Pa., The Jewish Publication Society of America, 1704-1943. xxiii, 531 p. plates, ports., map, plan, facsim. (Jewish communities series) History of Jews in Vilna. Bibligraphy: p. 517-519. DS135.R93V5 DLC CU CaOTU MB MH MiU NN NNC NcD NjP NcU OClW OrCS PU RPB ViU

3583. COMITÉ DES POLONAIS EXILÉS DE LA LITHUANIE. Minorités en Lithuanie. La situation de la minorité polonaise en Lithuanie. Genève, 1924. 1 p.l., 8 numb. leaves. At head of title: Société des nations. Official no.C265. 1924.I Mimeographed. NNUN-W

3584. --- --- Genève, 1925. 33 leaves. Official no.: C.304.1925.I. NNUN-W

3585. --- --- Genève, 1925. 6 leaves Mimeographed. Official no.: C.492. 1925.I. NNUN-W

3586. --- Observations et documens suplémentaires à la requéte au 1 juin 1924 des représentants de la minorité polonaise en Lithuanie. Réplique aux déclarations du représentation de la Lithuanie, M. Dovas Zaunius, faites à la séance du Conseil de la Société des Nations du 10 juin 1925. 19 p. DK511.L27C73 CSt-H

3587. COUNCIL OF MAIN DISTRICTS OF LITHUANIA. Pinkas ha-medinah... Oblastnoi pinkos Vaada glavnykh evreiskikh obshchin Litvy. Sobranie postanovlenii i reshenii Vaada (seima) ot 1623 do 1761 g. Pechatano s rukopisnoi kopii, khraniashcheisia v g. Grodnie, s dopolneniiami i variantami po spiskam gorodov Bresta i Vil'ny. Text s russkim perevodom d-ra I.I. Tuvima, pod redaktsiei, s predisloviem i primiechaniiami S.M. Dubnova. Sanktpeterburg, 1909-12. 2 v. DS135.L5C6 DLC CtY

3588. --- --- [Berlin, "Ajanoth," 1925] xxxi, 358 p. Bg20qR78+909ℓo CtY

3589. --- --- [Supplement... Jerusalem, 1934-35] 100 p. DS135.L5C62 supp. DLC

3590. CRONBACH, Abraham. Social action in Jewish Lithuania. In Hebrew Union College annual (Cincinati, Ohio), v.23, no.2, 1950-1951, p.593-616. See serials consulted.

3591. CZACKI, Tadeusz. Razprawa o żydach i karaitach. Kraków, Nakł. Wydawn. Biblioteki Polskiej, 1860. 178 p. CtY MH NN

DĄBKOWSKI, Przemysław. Stonowisko cudzoziemców w prawie litewskiem w drugiej polowie XV i w XVI wieku... Lwowie, 1912. See entry no.2765.

3592. DWORZECKI, Mark. Yerushalayim de'Lita in kamf un unkum. The Lithuanian Jerusalem in fight and death] Paris, L'Union Populaire Juive en France, 1948. 515 p. illus., ports. 940.5.D993L NB

3593. FAJNHAUZ, Dawid. Ludność żydowska na Litwie i Białorusi a powstanie styczniowe. In Żydowski Instytut Historyczny, Warsaw. Biuletyn, v.10, no.37, 1961, p. 3-34. See serials consulted.

3594. GOMER, Abba. Beiträge zur Kultur-und Socialgeschichte des litauischen Judentums im 17. und 18. Jahrhundert. Bochum, F.W. Fretlöh, 1930. x, 67 p. maps. Thesis--University of Köln. DS135.L5G63 CaAEU PU

3595. HANNOVER, Nathan Nata. Abyss of despair (Yeven Metzulah). The famous 17th. century chronicle depicting Jewish life in Russia and Poland during the Chmielnicki massacres of 1648-49. Tr. by Abraham J. Mesch... New York, N.Y., Bloch Pub.Co., 1950. xv, 128 p. illus. ports, map.

DS135.P6H32 DLC MH NN NNJ PPDrop TxU

3596. HEBERLE, Rudolf. Die Deutschen in Litauen. Stuttgart, Ausland und Heimat Verlags-Aktiengesellschaft 1927. ix, 159 p. illus., map. (Schriften des deutschen Auslandinstituts, Stuttgart. A. Kulturhistorische Reihe, Bd.19) Bibliography: p. 155-159. DK511.L2H35 DLC CU CSt-H CaAEU CtY MH NIC NN PU

3597. HEIMATGRUSS. Jahrbuch der Deutschen aus Litauen für 1957- . Saltzgitter-Lebenstadt, Landmannschaft der Litauendeutschen. Articles on life in Lithuania. MH(1965-)

3598. HELLMANN, Manfred. Die Deutschen in Litauen. Kitzingen am Main, Holzner-Verlag, 1951. 26 p. illus. (Der Göttinger Arbeitskreis; Schriftenreihe, Heft 15) DK511.L22H44 DLC MH PU

3599. INSTYTUT BADAŃ SPRAW NARODOŚCIOWYCH, WARSAW. Les cartes de l'établissement de la population polonaise et lithuanienne sur le territoire de la République Lithuanienne et... Varsovie, Institut pour l'études des questions minoritaires, 1929. 2 maps. Map room NN

JAKUBOWSKI, Jan. Studya nad stosunkami narodowściowemi na Litwie przed Unią Lubelską. Warszawa, 1912. See entry no.2036.

3600. JANULAITIS, Augustinas. Žydai Lietuvoje; bruožai iš Lietuvos visuomenės istorijos XIV-XIX amžiaus. [Jews in Lithuania] Kaunas, Autorius, 1923. 174 p. 947.52.J269.5 PU BM(20013. cc. 6.)

3601. KOWALSKI, Tadeusz. Karaimische tekste im dialect von Troki. Kraków, Polska Akad. Umiejętnosci, 1929. lxxix, 311 p. 494.57.Ka148K PU NN

3602. KRUPAVIČIUS, Mykolas. Lietuviai-naikinamu žydu gelbėtojai. [Lithuanians, the savers of the persecuted Jews] In Tėviškės žiburiai (Toronto, Ont.), no. 6-10, 1962. See serials consulted.

3603. KRYCZYŃSKI, Stanisław. Tatarzy litewscy; [Lithuania's Tatars] Warszawa [Wyd. Rady Centralnej Związku Kulturalno-Oświatowego Tatarów Rzeczypospolitej Polskiej] 1938. xvi, 318 p. (Rocznik Tatarski, t.3) DK412.R55 DLC CtY NN OCl

3604. KRYCZYŃSKI, Leon Najman, Mirza. Tatarzy litewscy w wojsku polskiem w powstaniu 1831 roku. In Rocz-

nik Tatarski (Warszawa), v.1, 1932, p. 113-151. See serials consulted.

3605. KUSSMAN, Leon. Litvishe geshtaltn; dartsaylungen. [Lithuanian configurations; stories] Warszawa, Brzoza, 1936. 180 p. PJ5129.K8L5 DLC

3606. LANDMANNSCHAFT DER LITAUENDEUTSCHEN IM BUNDESGEBIET. Litauen und seine deutsche Volksgruppe (litauendeutsche Studien) Würzburg, Holzner [1957] 87 p. "Vorträge, die auf der Zweiten Kulturtagung der Landmannschaft der Litauendeutschen am 10. bis 12. Februar 1956 in der Ostdeutschen Akademie, Lüneburg, gehalten wurden". 947.5.L237.2 PU CSt-H DLC LU MH NcD WU

3607. --- Litauen und seine Deutschen. Würzburg, Holzner, 1955. xii, 125 p. (Beihefte zum Jahrbuch der Albertus-Universität, Königsberg in Pr., 13) DK511.L22L3 DLC InU LU MH MoU NNC NcD PPiU

3608. --- Litauendeutsche Studien; Beiträge zur Ostfrage. Hrsg. von Johannes Strauch. Würzburg, Holzner, 1958. 93 p. "Vorträge, die auf der Dritten Kulturtagung der Landsmannschaft der Litauendeutschen am 19. bis 20. April 1958 in Essen-Werden, gehalten wurden. DK511.L22L32 DLC NN NcD PU WU

3609. LANGER, Gottfried. Die Rechtsformen der nationalen Organisationen der Deutschen in Baltischen Staaten. München, 1928. 22 p. Offprint. 947.52.L265 PU

3610. LIPMANAS, D.M. Le-toldot ha-Ychudim be-Lita-Zamut, 1400-1915. [The history of Jews in Lithuania, 1400-1915] Kaunas [1934] 81 p. DS135.L5L48 DLC

3611. LITAUEN UND SEINE DEUTSCHEN. Beiträge zur litauischen Geschichte sowie über die deutsche Volksgruppe in Vergangenheit und Gegenwart. Würzburg, Holzner, 1955. xii, 125 p.

3613. --- Minorités en Lithuanie. Genève, 1925. 6 leaves. At head of title: Société de Nations. Official no.: C.744.1925.I. Mimeographed. "Memorandum présentant les observations du Gouvernement lithuanien au sujet des diverses plaintes concernant la situation des minorités de race, de langue et de religion en Lithuanie" NNUN-W

3614. --- Minorities in Lithuania. Situation of the Polish minority in Lithuania. Geneva, 1925. 16 p. At head of title: League of Nations. Official no.: C.149.1925.I. Memorandum submited to the Council of the League of Nations by the Lithuanian government. Final text issued in the League of Nations Official Journal, 1925, p. 587-606. NNUN-W

3615. LITHUANIA. MINISTERIJA ŽYDŲ REIKALAMS. Di tsaytvaylike takones far di valn in di kehiles. [Rules for the local elections] Kaunas, 1919. 27 p. DLC

3616. --- Takanot ha-behirot le va'ade ha-kehilet. [Kaunas, 1921] 19 p. NNUN-W

3617. --- Takones far di valn in di vaaday ha-kehiles. [Kaunas] 1921. 24 p. NNUN-W

3618. LITHUANIA. UŽSIENIŲ REIKA-LŲ MINISTERIJA. Minorities in Lithuania. Letter from the Lithuanian minister for foreign affairs, dated July 28th, 1923. Geneva, 1923. 2 leaves. At head of title: League of Nntions. Official no.:C516.1923.I. NNUN-W

3619. MACIEJOWSKI, Wacław Aleksander. Żydzi w Polsce, na Rusi i Litwie. Warszawa, Druk. K. Kowalewskiego, 1878. viii, 151 p. MH OCH

3620. MALISZEWSKI, Edward. Polacy i polskośc na Litwie i Rusi. Warszawa, Tłocznia W. Lazarskiego, 1916. 37 p. DK511.L22M3 CSt-H PU

3621. MEYER, Percy. Ostland-Litauen. Ein Beitrag zur deutschen Diasporakunde. Riga, Jonck & Poliewsky, 1926. 57 p. DK511.L2M46 DLC PU

3622. MÜLLER, August. Die preussische Kolonisation in Nordpolen und Litauen, 1795-1807. Berlin, K. Curtius, 1928. 204 p. (Studien zur Geschichte der Wirtschaft und Geisteskultur, Bd.4) DK415.5.M9 ICU CaAEU NN PU

3623. NADEL, Beniamin. O stosunku Żydów na Wileńszczyźnie do powstania styczniowego. In Żydowski Instytut Historyczny, Warsaw. Biuletyn, v.7, no.28, 1958, p. 39-63; 113-114. See serials consulted.

3624. RABINOWITSCH, Wolf Zeev. Lithuanian hasidism from its beginnings to the present day. London, Valentine Mitchell, 1970. xiii, 263 p. illus. facsims., geneal. tables, map. Bibliography: p. 248-255. BM198.R2913 DLC CSt MH

3625. ROSENBERG, Leo. Die Juden in Litauen; Geschichte, Bevölkerung und Wirtschaft, politische Forderungen. Berlin; München, Neue jüdische Monatshefte, 1918. 48 p. DS135.L5R6 DLC BM(4516. e. 44.) OCH PPDrop

3626. RÓŻYCKI, Jerzy. Polacy na Litwie. Warszawa, Nakł. Tow. opieki kulturalnej nad polakami zamieszkanemi zagranicą im. A. Mickiewicza, 1929. 18 p. DK511.L22R6 DLC PU

3627. SACHS, Abraham Simchah. Worlds that passed. Philadelphia, Pa., Jewish Publishing Society of America [c1928] v, 289 p. 914.75.Sa14 WyU DLC PU

3628. SAGEL, Walter. Der Deutsche in Litauen. Langens, J. Beltz, 1935. 82 p. (Der Deutsche im Auslände, 3) 947.52.PAM16Sa16 PU

3629. SCHALL, J. Historyja żydów w Polsce, na Litwie, Russi... Lwów, Nakł. Wydawnictwa "Polska Niepodległa", 1934. viii, 320 p. plates, ports. MH NN

3630. SHATZKY, Jacob. Kultur-Geshichte fun der Haskole in Lite. (Historia de la cultura del iluminismo en Lituania) Buenos Aires, 1950. 231 p. Bibliography: p. 204-210. DK511.L25S5 CLU DLC

3631. STURM, Walter. Das Deutschtum in Litauen. Berlin, Schutzbund-Verlag, 1930. 16 p. 947.52.St97 PU NN

3632. --- Lebensfragen des Deutschtums in Litauen. In Volk und Rasse (München), v.3, 1928, p. 158-164. GN1.V6 DLC CU DNLM ICU MH MH-P NN NjP

3633. SZYSZMAN, A. Osadnictwo karaimskie i tatarskie na ziemiach W. Księstwa Litewskiego. Wilno, 1933. 10 p. Offprint from "Mys'l Karaimska", zesz.10. 947.52.Sz95 1933 PU ICBM

3634. TALKO-HRYNCEWICZ, Julian. Karaimi i Karaici litewscy. In Polska Akademia Umiejętności, Kraków, Komisja Antropologiczna. Dział II: Materiały Antropologiczno-Archeologiczne i Etnograficzne, v.7, 1904, p. 44-100. See serials consulted.

3635. --- Muślimowie, czyli tak zwani Tatarzy litewscy. Kraków, Nakł. Księgarni Geograficznej "Orbis" 1924. 126 p. illus. (Bibljoteczka geograficzna "Orbis" Polska, Ziemia i Człowiek. Serja 3., t.7) DK511.L22T3 DLC CU

3636. VILNA (GENERAL-GOVERNORSHIP)

Tainaia dokladnaia zapiska Vilenskago Gubernatora o polozhenii evreev
v Rossii. Zheneva, Tip. Bunda, 1904.
73 p. At head of title: Vseobshchii
evr. rabochii soiuz v Litvie, Pol'-
shie i Rossii. DS135.R9V5 DLC CtY
CSt-H

3637. VOROBEICHIC, Moïse. Rehov
ha-Yehudim be-Wilnah. Ein Ghetto im
Osten (Wilna); 65 Bilder von M.Voro-
beichic, eingeleitet von S. Chaseur.
[Herausgeber Emil Schaeffer] Zürich;
Leipzig, Orell Füssli Verlag [cl931]
7, 6 p., 64 plates on 32 leaves.
DS135.R93V58 DLC CtY FU PU

3638. WAGNER, Gustav. Die Deutschen in Litauen; ihre kulturellen
und wirtschaftlichen Gemeinschaften
zwischen den beiden Weltkriegen.
Marburg/Lahn, Herder Institut, 1959.
ix, 312 p. illus. (Wissenschaftliche Beiträge zur Geschichte und Landeskunde Ost-Mitteleuropas, nr.44)
Inaug.-Diss.--University of Königsberg in Pr., 1943. DK511.L22W3
CaOWtU CSt-H CaOTU CtY ICU MH MiU
MnU NNC NIC NcD NjP

3639. WIELHORSKI, Władysław. Byt
ludności polskiej w państwie litewskiem w świetle dochodzeń jej praw
przed Liga Narodów. Wilno, Wileńskie Biuro Informacyjne, 1925. xxiv,
184 p. (Materjały do sprawy litewskiej, t.2) DK418.5.L5W64 CSt-H IEN
MH-L PU

3640. YAHADUT LITA. Lithuanian
Jewry. [Tel-Aviv, 1950] 3 v.
illus., ports., maps, facsims.
DS135.L5Y3 DLC

VIII.11. NATIONAL MEDICINE, SOCIAL
INSURANCE AND HEALTH
SERVICES

3641. AKELAITIS, Vincas. Sociali-
nė apsauga Lietuvoje. [Social insurance in Lithuania] In Kemežys, V.,
ed. Lietuva 1918-1938. Kaunas,1938.
p. 339-354. 947.52.L625 PU ICLJF
CtTMF

3642. BASANAVIČIUS, Jonas. Mede-
ga mūsų tautiszkai vaistininkystėi.
[Information for our national phar-
maceutical services] Shenandoah,Pa.,
Dirva, 1898. 32 p. Reprint from
Dirva. 491.92.B292 PU

3643. GAVĖNAS, Petras. Inspection
des viandes et des produits alimen-
taires d'origine animale en Lithuanie, contrôle légal, seglementation.
Toulouse, 1931. 110 p. Thèse--École

veterinaire, Toulouse. Fr.TEV.

3644. JASAITIS, Domas. Sveikatos
draudimas ir socialinis saugumas.
Gesundheitsversicherung und soziale
Sicherheit. In LKMAM, v.2, 1966,
p. 209-264. See serials consulted.

3645. LIETUVOS DANTŲ GYDYTOJŲ KON-
gresas, Kaunas, 1938. Darbai. [Pro-
ceedings] Kaunas, 1939. 235 p.
illus. Summaries in German.
W3.LI431 DNLM

3646. LIETUVOS GYDYTOJŲ SUVAŽIAVI-
mas. 3d. Kaunas, 1924. Trečiasis
Lietuvos gydytojų suvažiavimas, spalių mėn. 2-4 d. 1924 m. Kaunas,
1926. 245 p. illus. W3.LI434 DNLM

3647. LIETUVOS GYDYTOJŲ KONGRESAS.
Darbai. [Proceedings] Redaktorius
V. Vaičiūnas. Kaunas, Lietuvos gy-
dytojų sąjungos centro valdybos lei-
dinys, 1937. 393 p. illus.
R106.L5 1937 DLC

3648. LITHUANIA. SVEIKATOS DEPAR-
TAMENTAS. Egzaminų programa medicinos felčerio teisėms įgyti. [Exami-
nation program for medical assis-
tants] Kaunas, 1924. 39 p.
R804.L5A58 DLC

3649. --- Viešosios sveikatos apžvalga 1928-38 m. [Review of the
public health, 1928-1938] Kaunas,
Spindulio b-vė, 1928-38. 4 v.
RA299.L5A3 DLC CtPAM(1936)

3650. LITHUANIA. UŽSIENIŲ REIKALŲ
MINISTERIJA. Le typhus en Lithuanie:
lettre en date du 10 mai 1921, émanant de M. Sidzikauskas, chargé d'-
affaires de la Lithuanie à Berne.
Genève, 1921. 5, 5 p. At head of
title: Société des Nations. Official no.: C.56.M.27.1921 IV. Includes appeals by the Lithuanian
Health Department and the Governing
Body of the Lithuanian Red Cross.
NNuN-W

3651. MANČINSKAS, Česlovas. Socialinis draudimas Lietuvoje ir kova dėl jo 1919-1940 metais. [So-
cial insurance in Lithuania, 1919-
1940] Vilnius, Mintis, 1971. 217
p. HD7197.7.M3 PU

3652. MATULIONIS, Balys. Sveikatos apsauga; okupaciniai 1940-1944
metai. Kurortai. [Health service
and resorts during the occupation,
1940-1944] In Lietuvių enciklopedija. Boston, Mass., v.15, 1968, p.
126-129. For holdings see entry no.
216.

3653. PAPLĖNAS, Jonas. Darbo ap-

sauga ir socialinis aprūpinimas.
[Labour laws and social security]
In Lietuvių enciklopedija. Boston,
Mass., v.15, 1968, p. 255-266. For
holdings see entry no. 216.

3654. PETKEVIČAITĖ, Gabrielė.
Materialy po narodnoi meditsine litovtsev. In Zhivaia Starina (Sanktpeterburg), v.12, 1911. See serials
consulted.

3655. REFORM OF SOCIAL INSURANCE
in Lithuania (Klaipėda). In International labour office. Geneva.
Industrial and labour information,
v.63, no.5, 1937, p. 140-141. See
serials consulted.

3656. SCHUCH, Ernst von. Die Entwicklung des Sozialversicherungs-
rechts im Memelgebiet. Dresden,
Dittert, 1938. vi, 70 p. Thesis--
University of Leipzig. Ger.LU

3657. SLONIMSKIS, S. Materialy
po istorii meditsiny v Litve. In
Tauta ir žodis (Kaunas), v.5, 1928,
p. 511-561. See serials consulted.

3658. TERCIJONAS, Vincas. Sveikatos apsauga; nepriklausomieji
1918-1940 metai. [Health service
during the years of independence
1918-1940] In Lietuvių enciklopedija, Boston, Mass., v.15, 1968, p.
122-126. For holdings see entry
no. 216.

3659. VENCLAUSKAS, Henry. Alko-
holizmus in Litauen. München,
1952. 25 leaves. Thesis--Univer-
sity of Munich. W4.M96 1952 DAFM

3660. VIRKUTIS, Simanas. Gesundheitswesen in Litauen. In Zeitschrift für Kommunalwirtschaft (Oldenburg), v.23, no.13-14, 1933, p.
541-548. See serials consulted.

3661. ŽUKAITIS, Mathews C. Daktaras namuose. [Folk medicine]
Knygelė talpinanti savyje 292 viso-
kių vaistažolių 50 receptų ir kiti
naudingi pamokinimai. Rochester,
N.Y., M. Žukaitis, 1919. v, 58 p.
illus. PG8788.Z8 DLC

VIII.12. RECREATION, GAMES AND
OLYMPIC GAMES

3662. DINEIKA, Karolis. Fizinis
auklėjimas. [Physical education]
In Kemėžys, V., ed. Lietuva 1918-
1938. p. 305-310. 947.52.L625 PU
CtTMF ICLJF

3663. --- Žaisk; žaidimų vadovas
tėvams, mokytojams, skautų ir kitų jaunimo organizacijų vadams...
[Handbook of games for parents,
teachers, etc.] Kaunas, 1934.
463 p. illus. 793.D ICCC

3664. GRIGONIS, Matas. Žaidimų
vainikas; savybės vakarėliams ir
gegužinėms nupintas. [Wreath of
games...] [Kaunas] "Svyturio B-
vės leidinys [1918]. 73 p.
GV1688.L5G7 PU ICLJF

3665. --- 200 Žaidimų. [Two hundred games] Seinai, Laukaičio,
1911. 144 p. OCl

3666. --- 200 žaidimų kambaryje
ir tyrame ore su dainomis, melodi-
jomis, paveikslėliais ir fantų pa-
vadinimais. [Two hundred games in
and out-doors...] Seinai, Šv.
Kazimero D-ja, 1914. 164 p. illus.
796G ICBM

3667. GUSTAITIS, Algirdas. Lie-
tuva-Europos nugalėtoja. [Lithu-
ania, champion of Europe] [Los
Angeles, Lietuvių Dienos, 1961].
37 p. illus. XL970.7GU ICLJF
CaAEU NN

3668. JUŠKEVIČIUS, J. Kai ku-
prinė ilsisi; žaidimai ir varžybos
jauniesiems turistams. [...games
and competitive games for young
people] Vilnius, Mintis, 1964.
183 p. G504.J8 DLC

3669. KAZAKEVIČIUS, Vytautas.
Sportininko žinynas. [Sportsman's
manual] Vilnius, Valstybinė politinės ir mokslinės literatūros
leidykla, 1960. 282 p. GV648.
L5K3 DLC

3670. KLUSIS, J. Pedagoginiai
žaidimai; skiriami pradžios ir vi-
durinių mokyklų mokytojams. [Games
for the Primary and Junior High
Schools] Biržai, Biržų spaustuvė,
1928. 112 p. 793K ICCC

3671. LIETUVOS TAUTINĖ OLIMPIJADA.
1st, Kaunas, 1938. Pirmoji Lietuvos tautinė olimpijada. The first
Lithuanian national olympiad. Redagavo V. Kemežys. Foto montažai
Ged. Orento. [Kaunas, Kūno kulturos rūmų leidinys], 1938. 67 p.
illus., ports. GV648.L5L53 1938
DLC CtPAM ICBM ICLJF NN NNC PU

3672. MANTVILA, Bagdonas and Karolis Dineika, comp. Skautiški
žaidimai. [Games for boy scouts.
Chicago, Ill.] Mūsų Vytis, [1954].
119 p. 790.MA ICLJF

3673. SAGYS, Liūdas, ed. Šokiai
ir žaidimai...[Dances and games]
Pittsburgh, Pa., Išl. Šv. Pranciškaus seserys, 1956. illus. 1 v.
793.31S ICCC

3674. ŠOLIŪNAS, Jonas, ed. Krep-
šinio išvyka Australijon. [Lithu-
anian basketball team journey to
Australia] Chicago, Ill., J.J.
Bachunas, 1966. 153 p. GV855.S65
PU

3675. SPALIUKŲ RATUKAI; šokiai ir
žaidimai. [Collection of dances
and games] Vilnius, VGLL, 1963-64.
2 v. illus., music. GV1799.S65
DLC

3676. SPORTAS TARYBŲ LIETUVOJE;
apybraižų rinkinys. [The sport in
Soviet Lithuania] Vilnius, VPMLL,
1955. 124 p. illus. L790ST ICLJF

3677. STEPONAITIS, Vytautas. Lietuvių liaudies žaidimai ir programos. [Lithuanian folk games and
recreation] Vilnius, VPMLL, 1956.
177 p. illus. GV118.L5S7 DLC
CtPAM IU MiD NN PPiU

3678. ŠULAITIS, Edvardas, ed. Lietuviškasis krepšinis...[Lithuanian
basketball] Chicago, Ill., 1957.
56 p. GV885.S84 DLC PU

3679. --- Lietuvių sporto dešimt-
metis Š. Amerikoje, 1949-1959.
[Tenth anniversary of Lithuanian
sport in North America, 1949-1959]
Chicago, Ill., 1959. 60 p. illus.
E184.L7S8 DLC ICLJF PU

VIII.13. RESORTS, PARKS, AND SPAS

3680. FONBERG, Ignacy. O druski-
nickiej mineralnej wodzie. In Wizerunki i Roztrząsania Naukowe
(Wilna), v.11, 1835, p. 1-60. See
serials consulted.

3681. GRICIŪTĖ, Angėlė. The climate of the resorts of the Lithuanian SSR. In LTSRMAGGICPXIX. Vilnius, 1960. p. 231-235. GB3.I45
1960ac CU CaAEU CaMWU ICU DLC NNC

3682. JUŠĖNAITĖ, J. Druskininkai.
[The Town of Druskininkai. By J.
Jušėnaitė and Ar. Medonis] Vilnius,
VPMLL, 1956. 109 p. (chiefly illus.)
RA887.L5J8 DLC ICBM ICLJF

3683. --- Kurort Druskininkai. [2.
ispr. i dop. izd.] Vil'nius, Gos.
izd-vo polit. i nauch. lit-ry, 1962.
92 p. illus., map. RA887.L5J82

1962 DLC ICBM

3684. KAVECKIS, Mykolas Stasys.
Apie Lietuvos mineralinius vandenis,
jų būtį ir perspektyvas. [On mineral springs in Lithuania, their
status and future] In Medicina
(Kaunas) v.10, no.6, 1929, p. 387-
398. Summary in German. See
serials consulted.

3685. KIAULEIKIS, Leonas. Palan-
ga. [The Town of Palanga] Vilnius,
VPMLL, 1961. 119 p. illus. DK651.
P105K5 1961 DLC ICBM NN

3686. KIRSNYS, Vytautas. Biršto-
nas. [The resort of Birštonas]
Vilnius, Mintis, 1966. 46 p.
DK651.B525K5 1966 DLC

3687. --- Likėnų kurortas. [The
resort of Likėnai] Vilnius, Mintis,
1967. 60 p. illus. RA887.L5K56
DLC MH

3688. KONDRATAS, Alfonsas. Gi-
drologicheskie usloviia formirova-
niia Likenaiskikh mineral'nykh vod.
In LTSRMAGGIMP, v.8, 1958, p. 133-
148. maps, tables. See serials
consulted.

3689. --- Pietų Lietuvos minera-
linės versmės. [The mineral springs
of Southern Lithuania] In Geografinis metraštis (Vilnius), v.1, 1958,
p. 329-352. Summaries in English
and Russian. See serials consulted.

3690. KONDRATAS, Alfonsas. The
spa of Druskininkai. Vilnius, Gintaras, 1969. 86 p. map. 914.K ICBM

3691. KRIVICKAS, S. Palanga. [The
resort of Palanga] Vilnius, Mintis,
1970. 62 p. illus. RA887.L5K7 DLC

3692. PALANGOS JŪROS MAUDYKLĖS.
Lietuvos gydymo ir poilsio vasaros
kurortas. [The Sea resort of Palanga...] Palanga, Kurorto inspekcija,
1929. 24 p. illus., maps. Text in
English, French, German and Russian.
947.59.P172 WaS

3693. TAURAS, Antanas. Lietuvos
TSR parkai. [Parks of the Lithuanian SSR] Leista naudoti mokymo prie-
mone Respublikos aukštosiose mokyklose. Vilnius, Mintis, 1966. 157 p.
illus., plans. Summaries in English
and Russian. SB484.L5T3 DLC CtPAM
PU

VIII.14. ASSOCIATIONS AND SOCIETIES

VIII.14.a. ASSOCIATIONS, SOCIETIES, AND FRATERNITIES

3694. ALIŠAUSKAS, Kazys. Lietuvos šaulių sąjunga. [The national guard of Lithuania] In Lietuvių enciklopedija. Boston, Mass., 1963. v.29, p. 375-383. For holdings see entry no. 216.

3695. BROSZAT, Martin. Die memelländischen Organisationen und der Nationalsozialismus. 1933-1939. In Vierteljahrshefte für Zeitgeschichte(Stuttgart), v.5, no.3, 1957. p. 273-278. See serials consulted.

3696. DAMBRAUSKAS, P. Žiburys; švietimo bei labdaros draugija. [The Light; educational and charitable society] In Lietuvių enciklopedija. Boston, Mass., 1966. v. 35, p. 271-281. For holdings see entry no. 216.

3697. DOTNUVA, LITHUANIA. JAUNŲJŲ ŪKININKŲ RATELIS. Dotnuvos dvaro Jaunųjų ūkininkų ratelis 1930-1932. [The Young farmers' club at Dotnuva, Lithuania, 1930-1932] Dotnuva, Dotnuvos dvaro Jaunųjų ūkininkų ratelio Patariamosios tarybos leidinys, 1932. 46 p. illus. Summary in English. 20.D74 DNAL

3698. FRATERNITAS LITHUANICA. Fraternitas Lithuanica; 1908-1958. [Redaktorius B. Matulionis] Putnam, Conn., [Immaculate Press], 1958. 398 p. illus., ports. R96.L5F7 DLC CaOTP ICLJF NN PU

3699. IDĖJA IR DARBAS; Lietuvos šaulių žodis broliams amerikiečiams. [The message to American brethren from the Lithuanian national guard. Kaunas, Lietuvos šaulių sąjunga, 1921] 84 p. illus. 970.4.ID ICLJF

3700. IVINSKIS, Zenonas. Ateitininkai 40 metų perspektyvoje. [A-teitininkai" during the forty years] In Ateitis (Kaunas), no.2, 1951. See serials consulted.

3701. KVIKLYS, Bronius, comp. Akademinė skautija 1924-1954 metais; trisdešimties metų gyvenimo, veiklos ir darbų apžvalga. [Lithuanian Student Scout Association, 1924-1954; a review of its activities...] Chicago, Ill., Akademinis skautų sąjudis, 1954. 236 p. illus. HS3313. B7L5 DLC ICLJF ICCC PU

3702. LEIMONAS, Juozas. Ateitininkai kovoje dėl Lietuvos Nepriklausomybės. ["Ateitininkai" in the fight for Lithuanian independence] In Ateitis (Kaunas), no.2-3, 1928, p. 82-83. See serials consulted.

3703. --- Pavasario sąjungos istoriniai bruožai. [The history of the "Pavasaris" Association] Kaunas, Pavasario sąjunga, 1931. 48 p. illus. L 289.5.LE ICLJF

3704. LIETUVIŲ DRAUGIJA NUKENTĖJUSIEMS DĖL KARO ŠELPTI. Trumpa "Lietuvių draugijos nukentėjusiems dėl karo šelpti" veikimo apyskaita nuo pradžios veikimo ligi 1915 metų balandžio mėnesio 8 dienos. ["Lietuvių draugija nukentėjusiems dėl karo šelpti"; a review of its activities. Vilnius, 1915] 6 p. DK511.L26L52 PU

3705. LIETUVIŲ STUDENTŲ TAUTININKŲ KORPORACIJA NEO-LITHUANIA. Lietuvių studentų tautininkų korporacija Neo-Lithuania, 1922-1964; kamieno žodis, pasaulėžiūra, istoriniai bruožai, atžalos. [Lithuanian National Student Fraternity of Neo-Lithuania, 1922-1964; its history, activities, etc. Ats. red. A. Diržys. Chicago, Ill., 1965] 327 p. illus., ports. LA853.L48L47 DLC PU

3706. LIETUVOS RAUDONASIS KRYŽIUS, 1922 metais; Vyriausios valdybos apyskaita. [The Lithuanian Red Cross 1922... report] Kaunas, 1923. 25 p. L 970.4.RK ICLJF

3707. LIETUVOS ŠAULIŲ SĄJUNGA. Šaulių sąjungos įstatymai ir statutas. [The Charter and By-Laws of the Lithuanian National Guard] Kaunas, 1936. 80 p. 330.Š2 CtTMF

3708. LIETUVOS VAIKAS. [Lithuanian Society for childrens' care] 1924-1934. Kaunas, 1934. 96 p. 947.5.L15 CtTMF

3709. MATUSAS, Jonas. Šaulių sąjungos istorija. [History of Šaulių sąjunga, a National Home Guard] Kaunas, Šaulių sąjungos leidinys, 1939. xii, 325 p. Bibliography: p. xi-xii. DK511.L2A25 DLC CtPAM PU

3710. --- --- [2d ed.] Sidney, Australia, Mintis, 1966. 277 p. DK511.L2M43 CaAEU

3711. PALTAROKAS, Kazimieras. Labdarybės tvarkymas kitur ir Lietuvoje. [The charitable work abroad and in Lithuania] Kaunas, 1920. 22 p. 330.PI CtTMF

3712. "PAVASARIO" MERGAIČIŲ SĄJUN-
GOS CENTRO VALDYBA. Veiklioji pa-
vasarininkė. [The active member of
the "Pavasaris" Association] Kaunas, 1939. 400 p. ("Pavasario"
mergaičių sąjungos leidinys, nr.2)
369.P ICCC

　　　　　PIENO LAŠO DRAUGIJA, KAUNAS.
Pieno lašo draugijos informacijų
kalendorius, 1928. See entry no.
1611.

3713. ŠALKAUSKIS, Stasys. Ateitininkų ideologija. [The ideology of
"Ateitininkai". 2. perredaguotas
leidimas] Putnam, Conn., P.M. Juras
[1954] 334 p. HS1537.A84S3 1954
DLC CaOONL CtTMF ICCC MH OCl PU

3714. ŠARSZCZEWSKA, Alina. Société Lithuanienne et des territoires Biélorusses et Ruthènes à Paris,
In Acta Baltico-Slavica (Baiałystok),
v.6, 1969. p. 76-102. See serials
consulted.

3715. STATUTS DE LA SOCIÉTÉ LITHU-
anienne et des terres Russiennes.
[Paris, 1832] In Polish and French.
BM(9475. bbb. 34)

3716. TRIMITAS; 1939 m. birželio
mėn. 24 d., nr. 25(966): Šaulių sąjungos dvidešimtmečio numeris.
[The twentieth anniversary of the
National Home Guard] Kaunas, 1939.
p. 577-624. Q 947.5.T734 PU; also
in Trimitas (Kaunas), no.25(966),
1939, p. 577-624. See serials consulted.

3717. V. D. UNIVERSITETO STUDENTŲ
ATEITININKŲ SĄJUNGA. Savu-keliu,
1922-1932. [The history of "Ateitininkai" 1922-1932] Kaunas, 1932.
144 p. illus. 369.V ICCC

3718. VAITKUS, Mykolas. Ateiti-
ninkijos genezė. [The genesis of
"Ateitininkai"] In Tėvynės sargas
(Reutlingen), no.4 1948, p. 249-254.
See serials consulted.

3719. VYTAUTO DIŽIOJO KOMITETAS.
Vytauto Didžiojo komiteto atliktų
darbų apžvalginis biuletenis, nr. 1.
[A report of the achievements of the
Committee of Vytautas the Great]
Kaunas, 1932. 30 p. 970.4.VD
ICLJF

3720. YLA, Stasys (1908-). Ateitininkų vadovas. [A guide for "Ateitininkai". Putnam, Conn., Ateitininkų federacija, 1960] 478 p.
illus. BX2347.8.S8Y55 DLC CtTMF
ICCC PU

VIII.14.b. FREEMASONS

3721. MAŁACHOWSKI-LEMPICKI, Stanisław. Wolnomularstwo na ziemiach
dawnego Wielkiego Księstwa Litewskiego, 1776-1822. Wilno, 1930.
viii, 212 p. (Towarzystwo Przyjaciół Nauk w Wilnie. Wydział III.
Rozprawy, v.4, zesz.1) HS627.6.
A5M3 DLC NN PU See also serials
consulted.

3722 PIGOŃ, Stanisław. Kampanja
przeciw masońska w Wilnie 1817 roku.
In Ateneum Wileńskie (Wilno), 1931-
1932, p. 143-159. See serials consulted.

3723. ZAHORSKI, Władysław. Przyczynek do dziejów Wileńskiej loży
masońskiej. Gorliwy Litwin, [pseud.]
In Litwa i Ruś (Wilno), no.3, 1912,
p. 145-161. See serials consulted.

VIII.14.c. SECRET AND SUBVERSIVE
ASSOCIATIONS

3724. BALYS, Jonas. Über die Ge-
heimbünde in Litauen. In Acta ethnologica (København), 1937. p. 131-
132. See serials consulted.

3725. BARANAUSKAS, B. Geležinis
vilkas; [dokumentų rinkinys. Collection of documents] Vilnius, Mintis,
1965. 140 p. facsims. (Archyviniai dokumentai, 7. rinkinys. Faktai kaltina.) DK511.L2A23 v.7 DLC
MH

3726. BIRŽIŠKA, Mykolas. Filoma-
tai, filaretai, filadelfistai.
Kaunas, 1939. 15 p. Reprint from
Lietuviškoji enciklopedija (Kaunas),
v.8, fasc. 2. For holdings see
entry no. 217.

3727. BUDRYS, Jonas. Kontržvalgy-
ba Lietuvoje. [Counterintelligence
in Lithuania] Brooklyn, N.Y., Darbininkas, 1967. 224 p. illus.,
port. DK511.L27B78 DLC CaAEU PU

3728. BURHARDT, Stefan, ed.
P.O.W. na ziemiach W. X. Litewskiego,
1919-1934; skice i wspomnienia.
Wilno, Wydawn. Wileńsko-Nowogródz-
kiego Okręgu Związku Peowiaków, 1934.
87 p. illus., ports. 947.52.B917
PU

3729. FAJNHAUZ, Dawid. Ruch konspiracyjny na Litwie i Białorusi,
1846-1848. [Wyd. 1.] Warszawa,

Państwowe Wydawn. Naukowe, 1965.
401 p. facsims. DK511.L25F3 DLC
CLU CaBVaU CaOTU CtY ICU InU KU MH
NN NNC NcD NjP NSyU PU WaU WU

LAWRENCE, Alexander. A
memorandum on the Memel; treason
trial in Kowno. See entry no. 3008.

3730. LITHUANIAN INFORMATION BUR-
EAU. La haute trahison de 44 polonais. Lausanne, 1917. 20 p.
947.52.L717.4 PU

3731. MOŚCICKI, Henryk. Młodzierz
litewska i dekabriści. In Biblioteka Warszawska. v.70, no.1, 1910, p.
474-505. See serials consulted.

3732. ---, ed. Promieniści; Filo-
maci-Filareci. Wyd. 2., poprawione
i uzupełnione. Warszawa [etc.] Nakł.
Gebethnera i Wolffa; [etc., 1919]
173, [3] p. DK435.M86 DLC CtY MH NN
OCl PU

3733. --- Z filareckiego świata;
zbiór wspomnień z lat 1816-1824.
Warszawa, Bibljoteka Polska, 1924.
372 p. front., plates, ports.
DK435.M87 DLC MH NN OCl PU

3734. NEUMANN, Ernst, defendant.
Dr. Neumann's von Sass' bei kitų bylos kaltinamasis aktas. [The bill of
indictment of Dr. Neumann von Sass
and the others] Kaunas, Spindulio
bendrovės spaustuvė, 1934. 528 p.
947.52.N394 PU

3735. PAPEČKYS, Juozas. P.O.W.
Lietuvoje. ["Polska organizacja Wojskowa" in Lithuania. By J. Rainys,
pseud.] Kaunas, Spaudos fondas,1936.
vii, 184 p. illus., fold. col. map,
facsims. 947.52.P198 PU

3736. PIGOŃ, Stanisław. Głosy z
przed wieku. Szkice z dziejów procesu filareckiego. Wilno, Wydawn.
Księg. Stow. Naucz. Pol., 1924. x,
236 p. ports, plate, plan.
Slav 6830.10 MH BM(9475. aa. 42.)

3737. POLSKA AKADEMIA UMIEJĘTNOŚCI,
Kraków. Archiwum Filomatów, 1815-
1821. Wyd. J. Czubek, S. Szpotański
i S. Pietraszkiewiczówna. Kraków,
1913-22. 3 v. BM(Ac. 1156. cz.3.)
NN(cz.2-3)

3738. PREGEL, Reinhold. Die War-
heit über den Prozess... Berlin, Verlag Grenze und Ausland [1935] 24 p.
illus. DK511.L27P92 CSt-H PPG PU

3739. ŠALČIUS, Matas. Lenkų samoks-
las Lietuvoje. [The Polish conspiracy in Lithuania] Chicago, Ill., Tėvynės mylėtojų draugija, 1921. viii,

94 p. illus. 947.5.L743LS PU CtTMF
ICBM ICLJF OCl

3740. ŠNIUKŠTA, Petras. Lenkų karo organizacijos veikimas Lietuvoje.
[Activities of Polish Military Organization in Lithuania] In Policija
(Kaunas), t.[2] 1925, no.2, p. 4-14;
no.3, p. 6-12; no.4, p. 7-11. See
serials consulted.

3741. TOWARZYSTWO FILOMATÓW.
Wybor pism folomatów. Konspiracje
studenckie w Wilnie 1817-1823. Wyd.
2., zmienione. Wrocław, Zkład Narodowy im. Ossolińskikh [1959] ccix,
483 p. (Biblioteka Narodowa. Seria
I, nr.77) LF4425.V58T63 1959 DLC
CtY ICU MiU NcD

3742. TWARDOWSKI, Józef. Process
filaretów w Wilnie. Dokumenta urzędowe z "Teki" rektora Twardowskiego.
Zebrał wydał i życiorysem Twardowskiego poprzedził Dr. Szeliga [pseud] ...
In Archivum do Dziejów Literatury i
Oświaty w Polsce (Kraków), v.6, 1890,
p. 170-332. See serials consulted.

3743. VORONKOV, I.A. Pol'skie tai-
nye obshchestva v Litve i Belorussi
v kontse XVIII i pervom tridtsatile-
tii XIX v. In Istoricheskie Zapiski (Moskva), v.60, 1957, p. 285-303.
See serials consulted.

3744. WASILEWSKI, Zygmunt. Promieniści, Filareci i Zorzanie. Dokumenty urzędowe dotyczące towarzystw taj-
nych na Litwie, 1822-27. W Krakowie,
1896. 132 p. DK435. W28 PU ICBM

VIII.15. SOVIET LITHUANIAN SOCIETY

3745. AKADEMIIA NAUK SSSR. INSTI-
TUT ETNOGRAFII. Sem'ia i semeinyi
byt kolkhoznikov Pribaltiki... Moskva, 1962. 158 p. (Its Trudy, novaia seriia, t.77) 572.06.AK13 n.s.
no.77 PU CLU CSt-H CtY DLC DNAL NN
NNC

3746. GEČYS, Kazys and William F.
Walsh. Shadow and substance; the
words and deeds of communism. New
York, N.Y., Institute of Contemporary Russian Studies, Fordham University [1965] vii, 232 p. illus.
IC599.R9G39 DLC CaAEU

3747. GEČYS, Kazys. Two worlds by
Casimir C. Gecys. New York, N.Y.,
Institute of Contemporary Russian
Studies, Fordham University, 1964.
xiv, 414 p. A study of Soviet Con-
stitution and civil rights.
JC599.R9G29 CaAEU DLC

3748. KUUSIK, Mall. Lebens- und Arbeitsbedingungen der Frau im sowjetisierten Baltikum. In Acta Baltica (Königstein im Taunus), v.4, 1964, p. 128-141. See serials consulted.

3749. NEY, Gottlieb. Das Gesundheitswesen in den baltischen Sowjetrepubliken. In Acta Baltica (Königstein im Taunus), v.4, 1964, p. 184-231. See serials consulted.

3750. PENKAUSKAS, B. Sveikatos apsauga Tarybų Lietuvoje. [Health care in Soviet Lithuania] Vilnius, VPMLL, 1950. 29 p. RA412.5.I5P4 DLC

3751. REMEIKIS, Tomas. Natur und Prozess der Verstädterung in Litauen. In Acta Baltica (Königstein im Taunus), 1967, p. 263-288. See serials consulted.

3752. SIDZIKAUSKAS, Vaclovas. Soviet colonialism; social and cultural aspects. In Lituanus (Brooklyn, N.Y.) v.4, no.3, 1958, p. 66-73. See serials consulted.

3753. VALTERS, Nikolaus. Soziale Veränderungen in den baltischen Sowjetrepubliken. In Acta Baltica (Königstein im Taunus), v.4, 1964, p.9-35. See serials consulted.

3754. VYŠNIAUSKAITĖ, Angelė. Lietuvių kolūkiečių šeimos struktūra ir organizacija. [The structure and organization of Lithuanian collective farmers' family] In LTSRMAD. Serija A, v.2(3), 1957, p. 123-140. See serials consulted.

IX. ECONOMY

IX.1. GENERAL STUDIES

3755. AMERBIURAS, Kaunas. Amerbiuro informacija lietuviams užsieniečiams. [Information for the Lithuanians living abroad] Red. V. Mačys. Kaunas, 1935. 63 p. (Amerbiuro leidinys, nr.4) HC337.L5A7 DLC PU

3756. AUDĖNAS, Juozas. The economic life of historic and modern Lithuania up to 1940. In Lithuanian Days (Los Angeles, Calif.), Oct.1958, p. 22-23; Nov. 1958, p. 20-22. See serials consulted.

CENTRAL EUROPEAN REVIEW. Special Lithuanian number... a detailed account of Lithuanian cultural and economic life. London, 1927. See entry no. 1012.

CHICAGO. UNIVERSITY. DIVISION OF THE SOCIAL SCIENCES. Lithuania in the last 30 years. New Haven, Conn., 1955. See entry no.821.

3757. COMMISSION FOR STUDY OF THE ECONOMIC RECONSTRUCTION OF LITHUANIA. Darbai [Proceedings] Boston, Mass., 1951-55. 11 v. HC337.L5C6 DLC PU

DAUNORAS, Bronius. Duonos beieškant. [London, 1954] See entry no. 3461.

3758. ECONOMIC REPORT; the Baltics. In East Europe (New York, N.Y.),1954, no.3(Oct.), p. 3-15; no.11(Nov.), p. 31-45. See serials consulted.

EICHHOLZ, Alvin Conrad. The Baltic states: Estonia, Latvia, and Lithuania. [Washington, D.C., 1928] See entry no. 771.

3759. L'ÉTAT ECONOMIQUE DE LA LITHUANIE. Lausanne, Pub. par les soins du Bureau d'information de Lituanie, 1919. 56 p. Extrait de Pro Lituania. HC337.L5E8 DLC CSt-H DW IU NNC

3760. GREAT BRITAIN. DEPARTMENT OF OVERSEAS TRADE. Economic conditions in Lithuania. Report. London, H.M.S.O., 1924- . Irregular. HC337.L5G5 DLC CLU CU CSt IEN IU NNC OCl OrU TxU

3761. GRUODIS, Domas, ed. Lietuvos eksporteriai, 1930. Litauens Export und Exporteure. Lithuanian exports & exporters. Kaunas, Vilniaus spaustuvė, [1930] 151 p. fold. map. HF3629.L5G7 CU DLC PU RPB

3762. GUSTAINIS, Valentinas. Die Grundlagen der litauischen Volkswirtschaft. In Zeitschrift für Kommunalwirtschaft (Oldenburg), v.23, no. 13-14, 1933, p.533-541. See serials consulted.

3763. IŠLAISVINTOS LIETUVOS ŪKIS. [Soviet Lithuanian economy. n.p.] K.Ū.A. tarnybos planavimo komisijos leidinys, 1949- . HC337.L5I75 DLC CaOTP PU

IVINSKIS, Zenonas. Geschichte des Bauernstandes in Litauen. Berlin, 1933. See entry no.1017.

3764. --- Senosios Lietuvos ūkis. [The economy of ancient Lithuania] In Vairas (Kaunas), no.7, 1934, p. 287-301. See serials consulted.

3765. JAKULIS, J. La Lithuanie restaurée; problèmes économiques, monétaires et financiers. Louvain, R. Fonteyn, 1932. 219 p. (Bibliothèque

de l'Ecole des sciences commercia-
les de l'Université de Louvain)
Bibliography: p. 213-215. HC337.
L5J3 DLC CLU CU CtY ICU KU MH MnU
MiU NN NNC WU WaU

3766. JUNGFER, Victor. Westliche
Wirtschaftsbeziehungen zu Litauen
bis zum Ausgang der Deutschen Hanse.
In Litauen und seine Deutschen
(Würzburg), 1955, p. 1-24.
DK511.L22L3 DLC CaAEU ICU IU IEN MH
NIC NN NcD PU

3767. KIEBELER, Alwin. Die wirtschaftliche Lage Litauens vor und
nach dem Weltkriege. Gelnhausen,
Kalbfleisch, 1934. 203 p. tables,
fold. map. Bibliography: p.1-11.
Thesis--University of Frankfurt a.M.
DK511.L27K5 CLU

3768. KNAAKE, Emil. Die wirtschaftlichen Zustände Ostpreussens und Litauens am Anfang dieses Jahrhunderts.
In LLGM, v.3, 1888, p. 1-93. See
serials consulted.

3769. KOCZY, Leon. Handel Litwy
przed połową XVII wieku In PZHP w
Wilnie. Pamiętnik VI. Referaty, v.
1, 1935, p. 272-278. See serials
consulted.

3770. KRIKŠČIŪNAS, Jonas. Trijų
didžiausių ūkinių organizacijų 15
metų darbo sukaktį minint. [Celeb-
rating the 15th anniversary of the
three largest farm organizations]
In Vairas (Kaunas), no.11, 1938,
p. 656-664. See serials consulted.

3771. KRIVICKAS, Domas. Economic
achievements of the Lithuanian State. In Baltic Review (New York, N.
Y.), no.13, 1958, p. 8-28. See
serials consulted.

3772. KRÜGER, Karl and Kurt Steu-
ernthal. Wirtschaftsgeschichtliche
Grundlagen Litauens vor 1940. Berlin, Volk und Reich Verlag, 1944.
76 p. (Zur Wirtschaftsgeographie
des Deutschen Ostens; politisch-und
wirtschaftsgeographische Untersuchungen und Darstellungen. Bd.19).
HC337.L5K7 DLC IU MH NN

3773. KUBILIUS, Antanas K. Lietuvos ūkio perspektyvos. [The future
of Lithuanian economy] Kaunas, Autoriaus leidinys, 1930. 281, [4] p.
tables. 947.59.K95L WaU

3774. KUNCIENĖ, Ona (Navickaitė).
Seniausios (X-XIII amžių) svorio ma-
tų sistemos Lietuvoje klausimu. [The
Lithuanian weight system of the tenth
to thirteenth centuries] In LTSRMAD.
Serija A, v.2(21), 1966, p.143-159.

illus., table. Summary in Russian.
See serials consulted.

3775. --- Vakarų Europos importas
Lietuvoje IX-XII amžiais. [Imports
from Western Europe to Lithuania in
9th-12th centuries] In LTSRMAD.
Seria A, v.3(22), 1966, p.85-103.
illus. Summary in Russian. See
Serials consulted.

3776. KUR LIETUVOS ATEITIS? LIETU-
vos vandenų galybė. [Where is the
Lithuanian future; Lithuanian hydro-
power] Kaunas, Galybės b-vė, 1923.
28 p. illus., plans. 970.6.GA
ICLJF

3777. KVIETKELIS, N. Išsilaisvinu-
sios Lietuvos ūkio atstatymas. [The
reestablishment of economy in libera-
ted Lithuania] Melbourne, Tėviškės
aidai, 1962. 31 p. 970.6KV ICLJF
CaOONL

3778. LEHNICH, Oswald. Währung und
Wirtschaft in Polen, Litauen, Lettland und Estland. Berlin, R.L. Pra-
ger, 1923. xii, 356 p. fold.diagrs.,
tables. Bibliography: p. [349]-356.
HG3942.L4 DLC BM(08229. c. 25.) CSt-H
ICU IU MH NN PU

3779. LIPČIUS, Mikalojus. L'économie nationale de la Lithuanie et
son développement. In Revue économique internationale (Paris), v.24,
1932, p. 123-146. See serials consulted.

3780. LITHUANIA. FINANSŲ DEPARTA-
MENTAS. Informations économiques de
Lithuanie; publiées par le Département des finances, Ministère des finances. Année 1-2; 1932-1933. Kaunas [1932-33] 1 v. tables, diagrs.
Semimonthly. HC337.L5A34 DLC(1932,
no.1-24; 1933, no.2) NN

3781. --- Wirtschaftliche Informa-
tionen des Finanzdepartements der Re-
publik Litauen. no. 1-63; 1930-1933.
Kaunas. Monthly. Also published in
French since 1932. HC337.L5A33 DLC
BM(S.C. 110.) NN(1-4)

3782. LITHUANIA. FINANSŲ MINISTE-
RIJA. Economic and financial situa-
tion of Lithuania in 1924. Kaunas,
Valstybės spaustuvė, 1925. 53 p.
HC337.L5A3 DLC(1924) CLU CtY CSt-H
(1924) NN NjP

3783. --- Économie et coopération
de Lithuanie; étude statistique.
Kaunas [Valstybės spaustuvė, 1924?]
40 p. illus. CtY NN

3784. --- Economy and cooperation
of Lithuania. Statistical study.

Kaunas [Valstybės spaustuvė, 1924?]
36 p. incl. illus., tables. HC337.
L5A6 1924 DLC CLU CSt-H CtY MnU NN
OrU

3785. LITHUANIA. PREKYBOS PRA-
MONĖS IR AMATŲ RŪMAI, KAUNAS. Lie-
tuvos importas ir importeriai...
Lithuanian imports & importers.
Kaunas, J. Leibenzonas, 1930. 268
p. tables, illus. (*TLE)NN

3786. --- Lietuvos importeriai,
eksporteriai ir pramonininkai; a-
dresų ir informacijos knyga. [Li-
thuanian importers, exporters and
manufacturers; trade directory. Sudarė ir išleido I.**Leibensonas**] Kaunas, 1938. 260 p. Lithuanian, German, English and French. HF3635.7.
L49 DLC MH

3787. --- Lietuvos ūkio paskutinis
dešimtmetis. [Ten years of Lithuanian economy, 1928-1938] Kaunas,
1938. 24 p. 330.9475.L714 PU

3788. --- Ten years of Lithuanian
economy. Kaunas, 1938. 167 p.
incl. tables, plates, diagrs. At
head of title: "Report of the Chamber of Commerce, Industry and Crafts!'
HC337.L5T3 DLC CU CSt-H CtY CoU FU
ICU ICLJF MH MiD NIC NN NNC NBuU NjP
OCl OClW PSt PPiU PU WU WaU

3789. --- Zehn Jahre litauischer
Wirtschaft. Kaunas, 1938. 172 p.
HC337.L5L52 DLC CSt-H PU WU

3790. LITHUANIA. UŽSIENIŲ REIKALŲ
MINISTERIJA. Situation économique
et financière de la Lithuanie au dé-
but de l'année 1922, Kaunas, Ministère des Affaires Étrangères, 1923.
63 p. HC337.L5A32 DLC CSt-H CtY InU
KU MH NN PU

3791. LITHUANIAN INFORMATION BUR-
EAU. Economic and financial condition of the Lithuanian Republic at
the beginning of 1922. London [1922?]
vi, 57 p. HC337.L5L5 DLC CSt-H MH-BA
NN

3792. --- L'état économique de la
Lituanie. [By Juozas Purickis]
Lausanne, 1919. 56 p. 957.52.L717.2
PU ICBM

3793. --- Die Volkswirtschaft in
Litauen. Lausanne, 1919. 52 p.
947.52.L717 PU

3794. LITHUANIAN TRADE DIRECTORY;
exports, imports, industry. Adress-
buch der Exporteure, Importeure und
der Industrie Litauens. Indicateur
d'exportateurs, d'importateurs et
d'industries de la Lithuanie. Kau-

nas, D. Gruodis, 1937. HF3635.7.L5
DLC NN OCl OrU

3795. LITVA ZA POLVEKA NOVOI EPO-
KHI. [Glav. red. K. Meshkauskas]
Vil'nius, Mintis, 1967. 448 p. with
diagrs. and maps, 19 leaves of illus.
and maps. HC337.L52L57 DLC CaBVaU
CaOTU CtY ICU InU MH NIC NcD NcU NjP
NSyU PPiU PU TU ViU VtU WaU

3796. LOSCH, Otto K. F. Litauen,
eine wirtschaftsgeographische Dar-
stellung. Königsberg in Pr.; Kaunas,
Juniores-Verlag, 1932. 114,[6] p.
Thesis--University of Königsberg.
HC337.L5L6 CU MnU

3797. MAČIUIKA, Benediktas Vytenis.
Lietuvos ūkio įsijungimas į Sovietų
Sąjungos ūkį. [The incorporation of
the Lithuanian economy into the Soviet Union economy] In Varpas
(Brooklyn, N.Y.), no.3-4, 1958, p.
87-99. See serials consulted.

3798. MAČYS, Vytautas Stasys. Litauens Wirtschaftsstruktur und ihre
Veränderungstendenz. In Revue Baltique (Tallinn), v.1, no.1, 1940, p.
105-114. See serials consulted.

3799. MAIMINAS, Jefremas. Teorijos ir tikrovė; buržuazinių ekonomi-
nų teorijų ir programų Lietuvoje
kritika, 1919-1940 m. [Theories and
Reality; the criticism of bourgeois
economic theories and programmes in
Lithuania, 1919-1940] Vilnius,
VPMLL, 1960. 231 p. HC337.L5M28
DLC PU

3800. MALOWIST, Marian. The Baltic and the Black Sea in Medieval
Trade. In Baltic and Scandinavian
Countries (Gdynia), no.5, January
1937, p. 36. See serials consulted.

3801. MATULAITIS, Stasys. 1863
metai Lietuvoj. Dalis pirmoji; so-
cial-ekonominis Lietuvos stovis prieš
    sukilimą. [The one thousand
eight hundred and sixty-third year
in Lithuania. First part: the so-
cio-economic situation in Lithuania
before the insurrection] Minsk,
1938. 276 p. map. (Baltarusijos
Mokslų Akademija. Lietuvių sektorius) DK511.L25M3 DLC PU

3802. MEŠKAUSKIENĖ, Malvina.
Ekonominė Lietuvos padėtis pirmojo
pasaulinio karo išvakarėse, 1900-
1913 m. [The economic position of
Lithuania on the eve of the World
War I] In LTSRMAEID, v.14, no.2,
1963, p. 106. Summary in Russian.
See serials consulted.

3803. MORAVSKIS, Alfonsas. Eko-

nomicheskoe polozhenie Litvy i Belo-
russii. A. IU. Moravskii. Moskva,
Redaktsionno-izdatel'skii Otdel V.
S.M.KH., 19- . 30 p. HC337.L5L831
CSt-H NN

3804. --- Gosudarstvennoe edinstvo
i nezavisimost' vsei Litvy-osnova
eia ekonomicheskago razvitiia i u-
reguliruvaniia vnieshnikh matrial'-
nykh otnoshenii. A. IU Moravskii.
Riga, 1923. 85 p. HC337.L5M6 DLC
CSt-H NN

3805. --- Lyginamoji pabaltės
valstybių visuomenės ūkių apžvalga.
[The comparative review of the na-
tional economies of the Baltic
States] Kaunas, Vytauto Didžiojo
Universiteto Teisių Fakulteto Lei-
dinys, 1931. 24 p. Balt. 7825.43
(VI.6) MH

3806. MOREIN, Icik. Wirtschaft
und Kultur der baltischen Staaten
Lettland, Estland, Litauen. Riga,
Verlag "Livonia", 1934. 120 p.
incl. tables. DK511.B28M6 DLC CLU
CSt-H InU NN

3807. MULEVIČIUS, Leonas. Nekotorye voprosy genezisa kapitalizma
v Litve. Vil'nius, 1968. 130 p.
Summary in German. HC337.L5M8 DLC
InU

3808. NEUMANN, Rudolf. Die Wirt-
schaftsentwicklung der baltischen
Staaten nach Eingliederung in die
Sowjetunion. In Zeitschrift für
Ostforschung (Marburg/Lahn), v.3,
no.2, 1954, p. 180-188. See serials
consulted.

3809. PASHUTO, Vladimir Teodorovich. Khoziaistvo i tekhnika srednevekovoi Litvy. In Voprosy istorii
(Moskva), no.8, 1947, p. 74-81. See
serials consulted.

3810. RAUD, Villibald. The Baltic
States as a British market in the
past and future. London, The Women's Printing Society, 1943? 31 p.
HF3508.B3R3 DLC CtY NN

3811. --- The smaller nations in
the world's economic life. London,
P.S. King and Staples, Ltd., 1943
36 p. tables. HC240.R27 DLC CtY
NN NNC

3812. RIMKA, Albinas. Lietuvos
visuomenės ūkio bruožai ligi Liublino unijos. [The outline of the
Lithuanian economies until the u-
nion of Lublin] Kaunas, 1925. 131
p. (Kaunas, Universitetas. Teisių
fakultetas. Darbai, v.1, kn.3)
Bibliography: p. 56-59. 947.52.

R464.2 PU DLC NN NNC

3813. ROMAS, Ilija. Die wirtschaftliche struktur der baltischen
Staaten und die Idee einer Zollu-
nion. Klaipėda, Rytas, 1934. 206
p. tables. Thesis--University of
Basel. HC243.R57 CaOTU NN PU

3814. ROMER, Eugeniusz. Beiträge
zur Litauens Wirtschaftgeschichte.
München, Kastner & Lossen, 1897.
iv, 188 p. Thesis--University of
München. HD1536.L77R7 ICU

3815. RUTKOWSKI, Jan. Medieval
agrarian society in its prime; Po-
land, Lithuania and Hungary. In
The Cambridge Economic History of
Europe. Cambridge, 1941-47. v.1,
p. [398]-417. HC240.C3 DLC CaBVa
CaViPR CaBVaU CU CoDU DCU DDO DAU
IdPI IdU ICJ IaU MH MtBC MtBuM MtU
MU MeB NIC NN NcD OCl OClW OOxM OU
ODW Or OrU OrMonO OrP OrPR OrCS
OrSaW PU ViU ViU-L Wa WaS WaSp
WaTC WaWW

3816. ŠALČIUS, Petras. "Auszros"
ir "Szwiesos" ekonomika. [Economics
during the era of Auszra and Szwie-
sa] Kaunas, VDU. Teisių fakultetas, 1932. 35 p. (Kaunas, Universitetas. Teisių fakultetas. Darbai, tom. 6, kn.9) See serials
consulted.

3817. SIMUTIS, Anicetas. The
economic reconstruction of Lithuania
after 1918. New York, Columbia
University Press, 1942. xiii, 148
p. incl. illus.(map), tables, diagrs.
Bibliography: p. [135]-138. HC337.
L5S5 1942 DLC CLU CU CSt CSt-H
CaOTU CaSSU CtPAM CtTMF CoU FU ICU
IEN IU IaU InU MH MoU NN NcU NjP NcD
OCl OClW OU PP PBm PU PHC ViU WaU WU

3818. STARZYŃSKI, Stefan. Litwa;
Zarys stosunków gospodarczych. Warszawa, Przemysł i Handel., 1928.
xliii, 122 p. map, tables. HC337.
L5S75 1928 DLC ICU MH NN PU

3819. STÖHR, Felix. Die Wirt-
schaft der Republik Litauen in er-
sten Jahrzehnt ihres Bestehens
(1918-1928). Erlangen, Druck der
Buch-und Akzidenzdruckerei Hofer &
Limmert, 1930. viii, 104 p. tables.
Thesis-- University of Erlangen.
HC337.L5S871 CSt-H InU MH NN NNC

STRAVINSKAS, Petras. Užienio akcinių bendrovių teisinė padėtis Lietuvoje. In Teisė, 1939.
See entry no. 2792.

3820. TENNENBAUM, Henryk. Les
liens economiques entre la Pologne,

la Lithuanie et les provinces ruthènes. Paris, Imp. C. Courment,
1919. 11 p. tables. (Commission
Polonaise des Travaux Préparatoire
au Congrès de la Paix. Publications.) D643.A7DP5P71 no.12 CSt-H
DLC NN

3821. UNITED STATES. OFFICE OF
THE COMMISSIONER FOR THE BALTIC
PROVINCES OF RUSSIA. Lithuanian
economic report. [Riga] 1920. 44
leaves. 150.1.L71 DNAL

3822. URBŠIENĖ, Marija (Mašiotaitė). Vokiečių okupacijos ūkis Lietuvoje. [The economic policy of
the German occupational forces in
Lithuania] In Karo archyvas (Kaunas), v.9-11, 1039, p. 176. See
serials consulted.

3823. VITKŪNAS, A. Imperializmo
požymių pasireiškimas buržuazinės
Lietuvos ekonomikoje. [The appearance of imperialistic characteristics in the Lithuanian bourgeoise
economy] In LTSRMAD. Serija A,
v.1(6), 1959, p. 25-43. See
serials consulted.

3824. DIE VOLKSWIRTSCHAFT IN LI-
TAUEN aus "Litauen". Lausanne,
Informationsbureau, 1919. 52 p.
fold. map. D643.A7DP6L7V921 CSt-H

WALLROTH, Erich. Die bal-
tischen Provinzen und Litauen.
Lübeck, 1915. 59 p. map. See
entry no. 810.

WALTER, Eginhard. Das Bal-
tikum in Zahlen: Estland, Lettland,
Litauen, Memelgebiet. Königsberg in
Pr., 1937. See entry no. 414.

3825. WAWRZYŃCZYK, Alina. Studia
z dziejów handlu Polski z Wielkim
Księstwem Litewskim i Rosją w XVI
wieku. [Warszawa] Państwowe Wy-
dawn. Naukowe [1956] 127 p. illus.
At head of title: Polska Akademia
Nauk. Instytut Historii. HF3638.
P6W3 DLC CaOTU CtY ICU InU MH MiDW
NN NNC PU

3826. ŽILINSKAS, Vladas. Independent Lithuania's economic progress.
In Baltic Review (Stockholm) v.1,
no.4-5, 1946, p. 175-178. See
serials consulted.

3827. ŽIUGŽDA, Robertas. Litovskaia SSR; kratkii istoriko-ekonomi-
cheskii ocherk. Pod obshchei red.
IU. I. Zhiugzhda. Moskva, Gos, izd-
vo polit. lit-ry, 1957. 182 p.
illus., maps. DK511.L2Z5 DLC CSt-H
KU MH NN NcD NjR NSyU WU

IX.2. AGRICULTURE

IX.2.a. AGRICULTURE, ITS HISTORY
AND ECONOMIC STUDIES

3828. ALEKSA, Jonas. Lietuvos
šios dienos žemės ūkis ir jo ateitis.
[The agriculture in Lithuania today
and its future] Kaunas, Lietuvos
žemės ūkio draugijos leidinys, 1924.
75 p. 947.52.A126 PU

3829. AUDĖNAS, Juozas. Animal
farming in Lithuania. In Baltic Review (New York, N.Y.), no.14, 1958,
p. 33-38. See serials consulted.

BALČIŪNAS, Valerijonas. Lietuvos kaimų žemės tvarkymas istorijos, ūkio ir statistikos šviesoje.
Kaunas, 1938. See entry no. 3513.

3830. BUTKYS, Adolph Sergius. The
development of export in an infant
agrarian economy: Lithuania between
1918 and 1940. Philadelphia, Pa.,
1965. xxx, 313 leaves. illus.,
maps. Thesis--University of Pennsylvania. Microfilm; Ann Arbor,
Mich., University microfilms, 1965.
HF3635.7.B88 CaOHM PU

3831. DAUPARAS, Juozas. Žemės
ūkio švietimas; studija. [Education
in agriculture] Chicago, Ill.,
1966. 287 p. Bibliography: p. 279-
281. S531.D29 DLC CaAEU ICN ICU IEN
DNAL OkS PU

3832. DUNDULIENĖ, Pranė. Žemdir-
bystė Lietuvoje nuo seniausių laikų
iki 1917 metų. [Agriculture in Lithuania from the most ancient times
until 1917] Ats. redaktorius: A.
Bendžius. Vilnius, VPMLL, 1963.
274 p. illus., fold. maps. (Lietuvos TSR Aukštųjų mokyklų mokslo darbai: Istorija, 5) Bibliography:
p. 243-250. Summary in Russian.
DK511.L2L4233 no.5 DLC CLU CtPAM ICU
InU KU MH PU

3833. DYBOWSKI, Tomasz. Gospodar-
stwo postępowe w Litwie, Wilno, J.
Zawadzki, 1850. 146 p. 947.52.D983
PU

3834. GINEITIS, Kazys. Lithuanian
quality products... A record of remarkable agricultural progress.
[London, Author, 1938] 52 leaves,
tables, ports. 33.31.G43 DNAL CtY NN

3835. KASPERCZAK, Stanisław. Rozwój gospodarki folwarcznej na Litwie
i Białorusi do połowy XVI wieku.
Poznań, 1965. See entry no. 3521.

3836. KRIKŠČIŪNAS, Jurgis. Agriculture in Lithuania. Kaunas, The Lithuanian Chamber of Agriculture, 1938. 155 p. plates. Translated from Lithuanian by Viktoras Kamantauskas. S469.L8K9 ICU CU DNAL ICBM NN

3837. --- Lietuvos žemės ūkis 1918-1938. [Agriculture of Lithuania in 1918-1938] In Kemežys, Vincas, ed. Lietuva 1918-1938. Kaunas, 1938. p. 111-138. 947.52. L625 PU CtTMF ICLJF ICCA

3838. --- Die litauische Landwirtschaft. Kaunas, Žemės ūkio rūmai, 1933. 304 p. illus., diagrs., fold. col. map. HD726.7.K92 CaAEU DNAL ICJ ICLJF NN PU

3839. KRIKŠČIŪNAS, Jurgis and Dietrich Gaul. Die Flachswirtschaft Litauens. Kaunas, Linas, 1941. 36 p. illus. Ger.KIW

3840. KUNCAITIS, Justinas. Versuche einer Monographie des Pferdes von Litauen. Kaunas, 1939. 92 p. Thesis--University of Bern. Uzfm.18B45 1939 CtY

3841. LANGE, Walter. Über die Agrargesetzgebung der baltischen Randstaaten. Leipzig, 1930. 100 p. Thesis--University of Leipzig. ICRL

3842. LITHUANIA. ŽEMĖS ŪKIO MINISTERIJA. Metraštis 1918-1924 m. m. [Yearbook of the Ministry of Agriculture, 1918-1924] Kaunas, Valstybės spaustuvė, 1927. 615 p. illus., tables, diagr. S242.L35A5 1924 DLC DNAL

3843. --- Metraštis, 1918-1938. [Yearbook of the Ministry of Agriculture, 1918-1938] Kaunas, Spindulio b-vė, 1938. 414 p. tables, map. S242.L35A5 1938 DLC CtTMF DNAL

3844. LITHUANIA. ŽEMĖS ŪKIO RŪMAI. Die Milchwirtschaft in Litauen. Kaunas, Varpas, 1930. 16 p. Ger.KIW

3845. MAČIUIKA, Benediktas Vytenis. Lithuanian agriculture; structure and output. In Lituanus (Brooklyn, N.Y.), v.7, no.1, 1961, p. 6-12. See serials consulted.

3846. MANELIS, Vitas. Agriculture in independent Lithuania, its progress and problems. In Lituanus (Brooklyn, N.Y.), no.5, 1955, p. 16-18. See serials consulted.

MUSTEIKIS, Antanas, ed. Lietuvos žemės ūkis ir statistika.

[Lithuania's agriculture and statistics] Dillingen, Ger., 1948. See entry no. 399.

3847. OBERLÄNDER, Theodor. Die landwirtschaftlichen Grundlagen des Landes Litauen. In Berichte über Landwirtschaft (Hamburg), neue Folge, v.13, no.1, 1930, p. 1-65. See serials consulted.

3848. OCHMAŃSKI, Jerzy. Renta feudalna i gospodarstwo dworskie w dobrach biskupstwa Wileńskiego od końca XIV do połowy XVI wieka. In Posen. Uniwersytet. Seria Historia. Zeszyty Naukowe, v.5, 1961, p. 37-94. See serials consulted.

3849. --- Rolnictwo na Litwie feudalnej w świetle nowszych badań. In Kwartalnik Historii Kultury Materialnej (Warszawa), no.3, 1961, p. 819-826.

3850. PALTAROKAS, Jonas. Žemės ūkis. [Agriculture] In Lietuvių enciklopedija. Boston, Mass., 1968. v.15, p. 180-192. For holdings see entry no. 216.

3851. POKHYLEVYCH, Dmytro Leonidovych. Dvizhenie feodal'noi renty v Velikom Kniazhestve Litovskom v XV-XVI vv. In Istoricheskie zapiski (Moskva), v.31, 1950, p. 191-221. See serials consulted.

3852. --- Perevod gosudarstvennykh krest'ian Velikogo Kniazhestva Litovskogo s otrabotochnoi renty na denezhnuiu v XVII v. In Istoricheskie zapiski (Moskva), v.36, 1951, p. 144-168. See serials consulted.

3853. --- Perevod gosudarstvennykh krest'ian Litvy i Belorussi v seredine XVIII v. s denezhnoi renty na otrabotochnuiu. In Istoricheskie zapiski (Moskva), v.39, 1952, p. 121-158. See serials consulted.

3854. ŠALČIUS, Petras. Žemės ūkio organizacijos Lietuvoje iki 1915 m. [The agricultural organizations in Lithuania until 1915] Kaunas, Vytauto Didžiojo Universitetas, 1937. iv, 277 p. (Kaunas. Universitetas. Teisių fakultetas. Darbai, v.9, kn.1) 947.52.Sa33 PU CU NN NNC

3855. SKALWEIT, Bruno. Die Landwirtschaft in den litauischen Gouvernements, ihre Grundlagen und Leistungen. Königsberg in Pr., 1918. vii, 219 p. maps. (Schriften des Instituts für ostdeutsche Wirtschaft in Königsberg, Heft 3) HD1995.L5S5 DLC ICJ PU NN

3856. STANIEWICZ, Witold. Rzut oka na rozwój dziejów agrarnych na ziemiach litewskich. In Ateneum Wileńskie (Wilno), v.2, 1924, p.103-121. See serials consulted.

3857. VALIUŠKIS, Antanas. Die Zucht und Haltung des Rindviehs sowie Milcherzeugung in Litauen. Hannover, Böcker, 1950. Inaug.-Diss--Veterinary School of Hanover. ArW2119 NIC

3858. VAZALINSKAS, Alfonsas. Der Fortschritt in der landwirtschaftlichen Erzeugung Litauens zwischen den beiden Weltkriegen und sein Einfluss auf den Export. Bonn, 1948. viii, 185 leaves. graphs, plates, xvi tables, map. Inaug.-Diss--Agricultural College in Bonn. Typescript. Ger. BU

3859. VERBICKAS, Antanas. Entwicklung und Aufbau der litauischen Pferdezucht. Giessen, 1947. 130 p. illus., plates, tables, map. Inaug.-Diss--Agricultural College in Giessen. Typescript. 636.1082.V583 PU

3860. WIECZOREK, Władysław. Z dziejów ustroju rolnego Wielkiego Księstwa Litewskiego w XVIII w. Poznań, 1929. 119 p. (Prace Komisji Historycznej Poznańskiego Towarzystwa Przyjaciół Nauk, t.6) HD1995.65W5 DLC PU

3861. VITKŪNAS, A. Žemės ūkio gamybos padėtis buržuazinėje Lietuvoje [The state of the farm pruduction in Lithuania] In LTSRMAD. Serija A, v.1(6), 1959, p. 3-24. See serials consulted.

3862. ŽABKO-POTOPOWICZ, Antoni. Praca najemna i najemnik w rolnictwie w Wielkim Księstwie Litewskim w wieku osiemnastym na tle ewolucji stosunków w rolnictwie. Warszawa, 1929. 245 p. Summary in French. 30.9Zi DNAL

3863. ZWECK, Albert. Der landwirtschaftliche Betrieb im Litauen. In His Litauen. Stuttgart, 1900. p. 196-216. illus. (Ostpreussen. Land und Volkskunde, Theil 5) DK511.L2Z97 DLC MB MH MiU OCl PU

IX.2.b. AGRARIAN REFORM

3864. BALSEVIČIUS, Kazimieras H. Die litauische Agrarreform und der landwirtschaftliche Fortschritt Litauens bis zum Jahre 1940. Hohenheim, Ger., 1947. v, 103 leaves. graphs, illus., map. Thesis-- Agricultural College in Hohenheim. Typescript. Ger.HoLI

3865. BROEDRICH, Silvio. Die Agrarreform in Litauen. In Sering, Max, ed. Die Agrarischen Umwälzungen im ausserrussischen Osteuropa. Berlin, 1930. p. [128]-153. HD581.S48 CaAEU CU DNAL NN NBC ViU

3866. ČINIKAS, Antanas. La réforme agraire en Lithuanie. Nancy-Saint-Nicolas-de-Cort, Imp. V. Idoux, 1937. 128 p. Thèse--Université de Nancy. Fr.NaU

3867. DIETZE, Constantin von. Stolypinische Agrarreform und Feldgemeinschaft. Leipzig, B.G. Teubner, 1920. viii, 89 p. (Osteuropa-Institut, Breslau. Quellen und Studien. Abt. 1, Hft.3) CU CSt-H DNAL IU ICU NN ViU

3868. ELSBERGAS, Stasys. Lietuvos žemės reforma. [The agrarian reform in Lithuania] Kaunas, 1936. 71 p. (Kaunas. Universitetas. Teisių fakultetas. Teisės ir ekonomijos studijos, t.1, kn.4) HD725.7.E55 PU

3869. --- Žemės reforma Lietuvoje. [The agrarian reform in Lithuania] Detached from "Židinys" v.31, no.2, 1940, p. 193-206. 947.52.NC78 PU

3870. GARMIZA, Vladim Vladimirovich. Podgotovka zemskoi reformy 1864 godu. Moskva, Izd-vo Moskovskogo universiteta, 1957. 263 p. Bibliography: p. 254-261. HD715.G32 DLC CU CaBVaU CaAEU CtY ICU IaU IEN InU MH MCM NN NcU OU OkU OrU RPB TU ViU WaU

3871. INTERNATIONAL INSTITUTE OF AGRICULTURE. The agrarian reform. Rome, Printing Office of the International Institute of Agriculture, 1930- vol.1, covers Austria, Finland, Latvia, Lithuania and Poland. HD585.I DNAL DS ICU NN WU

3872. KARP, Benedict von. Die Landwirtschaft Litauens. In Osteuropa (Stuttgart), v.8, no.6, 1958, p. 416-421. See serials consulted.

3873. KEYSERLINGK, Klaus von. Die Etwicklung der Agrarverhältnisse in Litauen und die litauische Agrarreform. [n.p., 1935] iv, 279 leaves. Inaug.-Diss.--University of Jena. Ger.JeU

3874. LEONAS, Petras. Po povodu agrarnoi reformy v Litve vkliuchaia i Suvalkskuiu guberniiu. Sanktpeterburg, Tip. N.N. Klobukova, 1907. 20 p. HD725.7.I4 DLC

LITHUANIA. LAWS, STATUTES, ETC. Lithuanie; loi sur la réforme agraire. Kaunas, 1927. See entry no. 2777.

3875. LITHUANIA. ŽEMĖS ŪKIO DE-PARTAMENTAS. Lietuvos žemės ūkis ir žemės reforma. [The agriculture of Lithuania and agrarian reform] Kaunas, Valstybės spaustuvė, 1922. 57, [2] p. tables. HD725.7.A4 1922 DLC

3876. MAČYS, Vladas. Socialinis teisių mokslo tikslas ir mūsų žemės reformos įstatymas. [Social goal of legal science and the law of agrarian reform] In KUTFD, v.1, kn. 2, 1924, p. 20-48. See serials consulted.

3877. OCHMAŃSKI, Jerzy. La grande réforme agraire en Lituanie et en Ruthénie Blanche au XVI-e ciecle. In Ergon (Warszawa), v.2, 1960, p. 327-342. See serials consulted.

3878. PAULIUKONIS, Pranas. Mykolas Krupavičius and Lithuanian land reform. In Lituanus (Chicago, Ill), v.16, no.4, 1970, p. 31-46. See serials consulted.

3879. PICHETA, Vladimir Ivanovich. Agrarnaia reforma Sigizmunda-Avgusta v litovsko-russkom gosudarstve. Moskva, Izd-vo Akademii nauk SSSR, 1958. 545 p. At head of title: Akademiia nauk SSSR. Institut slavianovedeniia. HD725.7.P52 DLC CaBVaU CaQMM CaOTU CtPAM CtY IEN ICBM MnU NN PU WU

3880. REGEL, Konstantin. Agrarverfassung als Landschaftsmerkmal in Litauen und Weissruthenien. In Zeitschrift für Erdkunde (Frankfurt am Main), v.11, no.3-4, 1943, p. 169-179. See serials consulted.

3881. ULASHCHIK, Nikolai Nikolaevich. Predposylki krest'ianskoi reformy 1861 g. v Litvie i Zapadnoi Belorussii. Moskva, Nauka, 1965. 479 p. (Akademiia nauk SSSR. Institut istorii) DK511.L2U3 CaAEU CaOHM CaBVaS CaOTU CaSRU CaBVaU FU ICU IEN MnU NcD PPiU PU ViU WaU WU

IX.3. FORESTRY.

3882. BRINCKEN, Juljusz. Mémoire descriptif sur la forêt impériale de Białowieża, en Lithuanie... Varsovie, N. Glücksberg, 1828. [8], 127 p., front., plates, fold. map. DK511.B5B8 DLC PU PPULC

3883. BROWN, John Croumbie. Forests and forestry in Poland, Lithuania, the Ukraine and the Baltic Provinces of Russia, with notices regarding the export of timber from Memel, Danzig and Riga. Edinburgh, Oliver, 1885. viii, 276 p. SD207.B88 DLC PU WaS

3884. BRUNDZA, Kazys. Lietuvos miškų istorijos pradmens. [The history of Lithuanian forests] In Mūsų girios (Kaunas), v.6, 1934. See serials consulted.

3885. HEDEMANN, Otto. Dawne puszczy i wody. Wilno, Skład główny Księgarni Św. Wojciecha, 1934. xii, 187 p. fold map. 947.52.H358 PU

3886. JANKAUSKAS, Mykolas. Miškų ūkio organizavimas kolūkiuose. [The organization of the forest industry on the collective farms] Vilnius, VPMLL, 1959. 211 p. SD391.J3 DLC

3887. LIETUVOS TSR MIŠKAI. [The forests of Soviet Lithuania. Ed. by] L. Kairiūkštis. Vilnius, VPMLL,1962. 365 p. illus. CtPAM

3888. LIETUVOS TSR MIŠKŲ ŪKIS. [The forest industry in the Lithuanian SSR] Ats. red. L. Kairiūkštis. Vilnius, Mintis, 1968. 220 p. maps. Summaries in English, German and Russian. SD217.L5L5 PU CtPAM DLC

3889. LITHUANIA. MIŠKŲ DEPARTAMENTAS. Miškų departamento metraštis, 1918-1938 m. Annuaire du Département des forêts, 1918-1938. Kaunas, Miškų departamento leidinys, 1940. viii, 127 p. illus., tables, diagrs. SD217.L8A5 1938 DLC DNAL

3890. LITHUANIA. ŽEMĖS ŪKIO MINISTERIJA. Revue économique des forêts lithuaniennes. Economie forestière pendant cinq ans 1919-1923. Kaunas, 1926. 13 p. 99.66L71 DNAL

3891. MATUSAS, Jonas. Lietuvos miškų gaminiai ir jų transportas iki XVI amžiaus pabaigos. [Lithuania's forest industry and its transport up to the late 16th century] In Mūsų girios (Kaunas), 1943. See serials consulted.

3892. O'HARA, Valentine J. The Lithuanian forest. In Review of Reviews (London), 1922, v.65, no.389, p.461-469. BM(8095. gg. 11(2.)) DLC(1-[87]) See serials consulted.

3893. RAUKTYS, Juozas. Miškų ūkis. [Forest industry] In Lietuvių enciklopedija. Boston, Mass., 1968. v.15, p. 192-202. For holdings see entry no. 216.

3894. RUKUIŽA, Antanas. Lietuvos miškai ir jų likimas. [The forests of Lithuania and their fate] Chicago, Ill., 1963. 58 p. illus., ports, map. (Lietuvos miškininkų sąjungos išeivijoje leidinys, 2) Lithuanian or English. SD121.A75 no.2 DLC CtTMF PU

3895. SČESNULEVIČIUS, Kazimieras, ed. Lietuvos girių milžinai. Lietuvos miškų departamento 30 metų nuo įkūrimo sukakčiai paminėti leidinys. [Thirtieth anniversary of the Department of Forestry] Chicago, Ill., Lietuvos miškininkų sąjunga, 1950. 117 p. illus., ports. SD327.L75S3 DLC CtTMF PU

3896. --- Tarp Varėnos ir Valkininko; straipsnių rinkinys. [Between Varėna and Valkininkai; collected articles] Chicago, Ill., 1953. DK511.L2S46 DLC PU

3897. --- Vartis. Chicago, Ill., Author, 1953-54. 2 pts in 1. 634.9.Sce96 PU

3898. SKĖRYS, Antanas. Lietuvos miškai ir jų ūkis. [Forests of Lithuania and their industry] In LKMAM, v.4, 1968, p. [163]-303; v.5, 1970, p. [415]-[546] Summary in French. See serials consulted.

IX.4. HUNTING, APIARIES, ETC.

3899. BALIŃSKI, Michał. O myśliwstwie Wielkich Xiążąt Litewskich w Rudnikach. In His Historia miasta Wilna. Wilno, 1937. v.2, p. 66-69. 947.52.B197.3 PU ICLJF(2) PPULC

3900. BUTKEVIČIUS, Izidorius. Medžioklė. [Hunting] In LTSRMAII. Lietuvių etnografijos bruožai. Vilnius, 1964. p. 126-[136] illus. HD725.7.L488 DLC CaAEU CtY ICLJF ICU MH NN PU

3901. GUKOVSKII, Konstantin Pavlovich. Pchelovodstvo v Kovenskoi gubernii. In Pamiatnaia knizhka Kovenskoi gubernii. Kovno, 1897. DK511.K55P32 DLC MH NN

3902. JANKAUSKAS, Mykolas, ed. Medžiotojo vadovas. [Hunter's handbook] Vilnius, VPMLL, 1957. 299 p. illus. SK223.L5J3 DLC NN

3903. MATUSAS, Jonas. Medžioklė pas mus senovėje. [Hunting in the old days] In Mūsų girios (Kaunas), liepos 1943. See serials consulted.

3904. MAŽIULIS, Antanas Juozas. Pasartiškių medžioklės būdai. [The hunting habits in Pasartiškiai] In Gimtasai kraštas (Šiauliai), no. 3-4, 1940, p. 229-242. See serials consulted.

3905. MEDŽIOKLĖ SENOJE LIETUVOJE, rusų okupacijos metu ir Nepriklausomoje Lietuvoje. [Hunting in Old Lithuania during the Russian occupation and in Independent Lithuania. By Zenonas Ivinskis, A. Rukuiža, and A. Mažiulis] In Lietuvių enciklopedija. Boston, Mass., 1959. v.18, p. 113-122. For holdings see entry no. 216.

3906. PAULĖKIENĖ, E. Bitininkystės reikšmė feodalinės Lietuvos ūkyje. [The importance of apiculture in Lithuania's feudal system] In LTSRMAIILKI, v.4, 1964, p. 97-108. See serials consulted.

IX.5. FISHING INDUSTRY

3907. GARGASAS, Petras. Lietuvos TSR jūrinė žvejyba ir jos materialinė-techninė bazė. [Salt water fishing in Soviet Lithuania] Vilnius, Mintis, 1965. 132 p. SH284.R9G3 DLC NN

3908. --- Lietuvos TSR žuvies pramonės išvystymas. [The development of the Soviet Lithuanian fishing industry] In LTSRMAD. Serija A, v.2(11), 1961, p. 31-49. See serials consulted.

3909. --- Lietuvos TSR žuvies pramonės pagrindiniai fondai ir jų struktūra. [Osnovnye fondy rybnoi promyshlennosti Litovskoi SSR i ikh struktura] In LTSRMAD. Serija A, v.1, 1963, p. 27-47. See serials consulted.

3910. MAŽEIKA, Povilas. Lietuvos žvejyba. [The fishing industry of Lithuania] In Lietuva (New York, N.Y.), no.4, 1953, p. 156-163. See serials consulted.

3911. MOSEVICH, N.A. AND I.L. Maniukas. Issledovanie nekotorykh ozer Litovskoi SSR i perspektivy ikh rybokhoziaistvennogo ispol'zovaniia. In LTSRMAD. Serija B, v.2(5), 1956, p. 105-125. See serials consulted.

3912. VOLAKIS, R. Žuvininkystė. [Fishing] Vilnius, Mintis, 1967. 239 p. illus. SH91.V64 DLC

IX.6. INDUSTRY

3913. BRENSZTEJN, Michał Eustachy. Zarys dziejów ludwisarstwa na ziemiach byłego Wielkiego Księstwa Litewskiego. Wilno, Księgarnia Stowarzyszenia Nauczycielstwa Polskiego, 1924. 226 p. illus., plates. Bibliography: p. 157-193. 947.52.B757 PU PPULC NN NNC

3914. CENTRALINĖ LIETUVOS PIENO PERDIRBIMO BENDROVIŲ SĄJUNGA "PIENOCENTRAS", 1927-1936. [The Federation of Dairy Co-operative Societies of Lithuania "Pienocentras"] Kaunas, 1937. 180 p. CtPAM

3915. EKONOMINIŲ STUDIJŲ DRAUGIJA, KAUNAS. Mūrinės statybos ugdymo planas; projektas. [The project to expand the use of bricks for building purposes. Prepared and edited by V. Juodeika and V. Švipas] Kaunas, F.M. kainų tvarkytojo įstaigos leidinys, 1938. 122 p. TH1201.E4 DLC

GREAT BRITAIN. DEPT. OF OVERSEAS TRADE. Economic conditions in Lithuania... Report... London, 1924- See entry no. 3760.

3916. GRUODIS, Domas. Lietuvos pramonė ir jos gamyba. [Lithuanian industry and its production] Kaunas, 1930. 200 p. illus., ports. 947.52.G925 PU

3917. IVINSKIS, Zenonas. Pramonė senoje Lietuvoje. [Industry in Old Lithuania] In Lietuvių enciklopedija. Boston, Mass., 1961, v.23, p. 405-409. For holdings see entry no. 216.

3918. JANKEVIČIUS, Juozas. Kainoraščiai statybos darbams... [Price lists in the building industry] Kaunas, Kelio tarnybos leidinys, 1924. 209 p. illus. HB235.L5J3 DLC

3919. KAIRYS, Steponas. Lietuvos pramonė. [Lithuanian industry] In His Lietuva budo. New York, N.Y., 1957. p. 197-215. DK511.L25K3 DLC CaAEU CtY MH OCl PU

3920. LAUCEVIČIUS, E. Popierius Lietuvoje XV-XVIII a.; atlasas. [The paper industry in Lithuania from the 15th to the 18th centuries, and atlas] Vilnius, Mintis, 1967. 284 p. atlas, illus., maps. Summaries in English and Russian. Z237.L38 CaOTU CtPAM CtY NN PU

3921. LIETUVOS PRAMONĖ. Iliustruotas leidinys. Tomas 1. [Lithuanian industry. Edited by J. Etingerys

and M. Liutermoza] Kaunas, O. Olsner, 1923. viii, 161 p. illus. Only vol.1 published. Nc95.R78+923e CtY CtTMF

3922. ŁOWMIAŃSKI, Henryk. Papiernie wileńskie XVI v. In Ateneum Wileńskie (Vilna), v.2, no.7-8, 1924, p.408-422. See serials consulted.

3923. MATUSAS, Jonas. Dzūkijos Kapčiamiestis Lietuvos ir jos pramonės istorinėje perspektyvoje. [The role of Kapčiamiestis of the region Dzukija in the economy of Lithuania] In Aidai (Brooklyn, N.Y.), no.10 (135), 1960, p. 431-436. See serials consulted.

3924. --- Mūrinė statyba pas senovės lietuvius. [Brick construction by the ancient Lithuanians] In Ateitis (Kaunas), no.24, 1943. See serials consulted.

3925. --- Stiklas Lietuvos senovėje. [Glass in old Lithuania] In Tautos praeitis (Chicago, Ill.), v.4, 1962, p. 595-604. See serials consulted.

3926. MAŽEIKA, Povilas. Die neuere Entwicklung der Industrie Litauens. In Acta Baltica (Königstein im Taunus), 1970, p. 177-227 See serials consulted.

3927. MEDŽIAGA PASKAITAI APIE MŪSŲ krašto pramonę. [Data for the lecture on Lithuanian industry] Kaunas, Savajai pramonei propaguoti komitetas, 1934. 32 p. illus. L 970.6.PR ICLJF

3928. MERKYS, Vytautas. Razvitie promyshlennosti i formirovanie proletariata Litvy v XIX v. Vil'nius, Mintis, 1969. 447 p. Bibliography: p. 426-[441] HC337.L5M37 DLC ICU MH

3929. SCHÖNEMANN, Adolf. Die Industrialisierung Litauens. In Osteuropa (Königsberg in Pr.), v.18, 1938, p. 348-357. See serials consulted.

3930. STANKUS, J. Geležinių įrankių gamybos technologija IX-XIII amžiuje. [The technology of tool manufacturing in Lithuania in the 9th-13th centuries] In LTSRMAD. Serija A, v.1(32), 1970, p. 113-134. Summaries in English and Russian. See serials consulted.

3931. TOWARZYSTWO PRZEMYSŁOWCÓW KRÓLEWSTWA POLSKIEGO, WARSAW. Wytwórczość przemysłowa na Litwie, Białej Rusi i Rusi. [Comp. by] Zygmunt Miduch. Warszawa, S. Orgelbrand, 1917.

146 p. Offprint from Ekonomisty.
HC331.T65 1917 DLC KU

3932. VASYS, Antanas. Popieriaus
pramonė Nepriklausomoje Lietuvoje.
[The paper industry in independent
Lithuania] In Lietuvių enciklopedija. Boston, Mass., 1961. v.23, p.
285-288. For holdings see entry no.
216.

3933. VISKANTA, Jonas D. Lietuvos
pramonės duomenys. [Data on Lithuania's industry] In Lietuva (New
York, N.Y.), no.6, April-June, 1954,
p. 134-137. See serials consulted.

IX.7. COMMUNICATION AND TRANSPORT

3934. BERNOTIENĖ, S. Valstiečių
sausumos susisiekimas. [The means
and ways of transportation on the
land by Lithuanian peasants] In
LTSRMAII. Lietuvių etnografijos
bruožai. Vilnius, 1964. p. 417-
[436] illus., map. HD725.7.L488
DLC CaAEU CtY ICLJF ICU MH NN PU

3935. LES CHEMINS DE FER DE L'ÉTAT
lithuanien de 1927 à 1931. In International Railway Union. Bulletin
(Paris), 1933. v.9, p. 156-162.
HE1001.I65 DLC

3936. CONTAG, Max and Fritz Simon.
Königsbergs Grossschiffahrtswege nach
Litauen, der Ukraine und Polen...
Königsberg in Pr., Hartungsche Buch-
dr., [1918?] 51 p. Q947.52.C681
PU DLC

3937. DAUKANTAS, Teodoras. Klaipėdos uostas. [The port of Klaipė-
da] Kaunas, Švietimo skyrius, 1930.
46 p. tables, diagrs. HE557.L8K63
CU PU

3938. FORSTREUTER, Kurt Hermann.
Die Memel als Handelsstrasse Preussens nach Osten. Königsberg in Pr.,
Gräfe ud Unzer, 1931. 108 p.
4D307DLC-P4 NN NcD

3939. GALVANAUSKAS, Gediminas.
Klaipėdos uosto užnugarys. [The hin-
terland of the port of Klaipėda] In
Naujoji romuva (Kaunas), no.1-2,
1938, p. 47-49. See serials consulted.

3940. GIMBUTAS, Marija. Gintaro
keliai priešistoriniais laikais. [Pre-
historic ruotes of amber. By M. Gim-
butienė] In Aidai (Kennebunkport,
Me),no.6(62), 1953, p. 249-253.
See serials consulted.

3941. GINTNERIS, Antanas, ed. Nuo
krivulės iki raketos; Lietuvos paš-
tininkų atsiminimai. [... recollections of the Lithuanian postmen]
Chicago, Ill., 1966. 538 p.
NE2065.6.G5 PU

3942. HAGUE. PERMANENT COURT OF
INTERNATIONAL JUSTICE. Affaire du
chemin de fer Panevėžys-Saldutiškis
(Exceptions préliminaires)... The
Panevėžys-Saldutiškis railway case
(Preliminary objections. Leyden,
A.W. Sijthoff [1938] 8, 8 p. (Its
[Publications] Sér. A/B, Arrêts,
donnances et avis consultatifs, fasc.
no.75) French and English on opposi-
te pages. Order of June 30th, 1938.
341.1.H123 Ser.A/B no.75 MnU

3943. --- --- Leyden, A.W. Sijthoff [1939] 59, 59 p. (Its [Publi-
cations] Sér. A/B, Arrêts, ordonnances et avis consultatifs, fasc. no.
76) French and English on opposite
pages. Judgment of February 28th,
1939. JX1971.5.A6 Ser. A/B no.76
NNCE MnU

3944. --- --- Order of June 30th,
1938. Judgment of February 28th,
1939. (Series A/B, fasc. no. 75 and
76)... Leyden, A.W. Sijthoff [1939]
756 p. (Its [Publications] Ser. C.
Pleadings, oral statements and documents... no.86) Added title page in
French. French and English on opposite pages. JX1971.5.A6 Ser.C no.86
NNCE MnU CaAEU

3945. --- Railway traffic between
Lithuania and Poland. Advisory opinion of October 15th, 1931. (Series
A/B, fasc. no.42) Leyden, A.W. Sijthoff, 1932. 477 (i.e. 616) p. (Its
Ser.C. Pleadings, oral statements
and documents no.54) JX1970.A3 Ser.
3, no.54 DLC CaAAU CSt-H ICN NCU OrU
WaU

3946. --- Trafic ferroviaire entre
la Lithuanie et la Pologne (section
de ligne Landwarów-Kaisiadorys)...
Railway traffic between Lithuania
and Poland (Railway sector Landwarów-
Kaišiadorys) Leyden, Société d'éditions A.W. Sijthoff [1931] p. [105]-
123, 108-123. (Its [Publications]
Sér. A/B, Arrêts, ordonnances et avis
consultatifs, fasc. no.42) Advisory
opinion of October 15th, 1931, 22nd
session. French and English on opposite pages. JX1971.5.A6 Ser. A/B,
no.42 NNCE MnU PU

3947. JAHN, Louis. Memel als Hafen und Handelsstadt, 1913-1922. Jena, G. Fischer, 1926. 141 p. tables,
maps. (Schriften des Instituts für
ostdeutsche Wirtschaft an der Univer-

sität Königsberg... Hft.13, 3,Reihe,
Oststaatenkunde, Hft.1) HC289.M4J3
DLC ICJ NN PU

3948. KOLUPAILA, Steponas. Vandens ūkis. [The water resources and
its use] In Lietuva (New York, N.Y.)
no.3, 1953, p. 8-14. See serials
consulted.

3949. LITERSKIS, Vladas. Der Memeler Hafen unter litauischer Verwaltung (1923-1938). In Commentationes Balticae (Bonn), v.4-5, 1958, p.
89-113. See serials consulted.

3950. LITHUANIA. GELEŽINKELIŲ VAL-
DYBA. Données principales concernant le compte rendu annuel des opérations des chemins de fer de l'État
Lithuanien. Pagrindiniai statisti-
niai duomenys iš Lietuvos geležinkelių ... apyskaitos, 1919-1938. Kaunas, 1925-1939. HE3139.5.A24 DLC
NN(1919-1938)

3951. --- Geležinkelių įstatymas ir
jam vykdyti taisyklės (paskelbta;
įstatymas V.Ž., nd. n.634, taisyklės
V.Ž., nd. n.583). Veikia nuo 1939 m.
liepos mėn. 1 d. [Railroad law...
Kaune] Ekonominės direkcijos leidinys, 1939. xvi, 144 p. 4 forms (3
fold.) HE3139.5.A5 1939 DLC

3952. --- Geležinkelių valdybos
darbuotės apyskaita, 1919-1923. [A
work report of the railway management]
Kaunas, Valstybės spaustuvė, 1925.
114 p. tables, fold, diagrs.
HE3139.5.A5 1923 DLC NN NjP

3953. --- Lietuvos geležinkelių
atstumų lentelės. [Tables of Lithuania's railroad distances] Tarifo
6. dalis. Veikia nuo 1931 m. rugpiūčio mėn. 1 d. Kaunas, Ekonominės direkcijos leidinys, 1931. 89 p. tables. HE3139.5.A5 DLC

3954. --- Lietuvos geležinkelių
pirmasis dešimtmetis. [The first
decade of the Lithuanian railway]
Kaunas, 1929. 88 p. plates.
HE3139.5.A5 1929 DLC

3955. LITHUANIA. PAŠTŲ TELEGRAFŲ
IR TELEFONŲ VALDYBA. Lietuvos pašto,
telegrafo ir telefono įstaigų, agen-
tūrų ir punktų sąrašas. [The list
of offices, agencies and service
points of the Lithuanian Post, Tele-
graph and Telephones] Kaunas, 1935.
HE7065.6.A3 DLC MH

3956. --- Lietuvos telefono abonentų sąrašas. [Telephone directory;
annual] Kaunas. HE9275.7A6 DLC
(1922, 1924, 1925, 1936)

3957. --- Pašto taisyklės. [The
rules of the Post Office] Kaunas,
Valstybės spaustuvė, 1923. 123, 40,
iii p. forms. HE7065.6.A4 1923 DLC

3958. Sąrašas valstybių ir vietų į
kurias gali būti priimami mažo svorio siuntiniai. [The list of countries to which the parcel post is ac-
cepted] Kaunas, 1924. 100 p.
HE7065.6.A52 DLC MH

3959.--- Telegrafo tarifas užsie-
niui. [Telegraph rates to foreign
countries] Kaunas, Akc. "Spindulio"
b-vės spaustuvė, 1929. 50 p.
HE7065.7.A25 1929 DLC

3960. LITHUANIA. SISISIEKIMO MI-
NISTERIJA. Lietuvos geležinkelių...
darbuotės apyskaita. Compte rendu
annuel des opérations des chemins de
fer de l'Etat Lithuanien puor l'exer-
cice, 1929/23- . Kaunas, 1927-1929.
3 v. tables, diagrs. HE3139.5.A3
DLC (1924, 1925, 1928) NN NjP

3961. --- Susisiekimo ministerijos
1937 metų metraštis. [The yearbook
of the Ministry of Communications]
Kaunas, 1938. 411 p. incl. tables,
ports., diagrs. French summary: p.
84-96. HE70.6.A5 1937 DLC

3962. LITHUANIA. UŽSIENIŲ REIKALŲ
MINISTERIJA. Lietuvių-lenkų byla dėl
tranzito Nemuno upynu ir Kaišedorių-
Lentvaravo geležinkelio ruožu. [Li-
thuanian-Polish lawsuit in regard to
the transit on the river basin Nemunas and the Kaišedorių-Lentvaravo
railway line] Kaunas, Užsienių Reikalų Ministerija, 1931, 2 v.
947.52.L715.5 PU

3963. MEMEL (TERRITORY) HANDELSKAM-
MER. Bericht über Handel und Schif-
fahrt im Memelgebiet für das Jahr
1920- . Erstattet von der Handelskammer, Memel. Memel, 1921-
HF328.M4A3 DLC NN(1922-1923)

3964. --- Statistik des Schiffsver-
kehrs über See und Binnen-Schiffahrt
im Hafen zu Memel. [Memel, 1923]- .
Annual. (TRD)NN(1922-1923)

3965. MEMEL (TERRITORY) UOSTO DIREK-
CIJA. Klaipėdos uosto direkcijos...
metinė apyskaita. [Annual report of
the Klaipėda harbour board...] Klaipėda, 1928-38. 947.52.M513 PU(v.1,
1928; v.2, 1930) NN(128-1938)

3966. PYRAGIUS, Jonas, ed. Paukščių keliais; pirmiesiems civilinės
aviacijos žingsniams Lietuvoje paminėti. [To commemorate the first steps
of the Lithuanian civil aviation]
Kaunas, Lietuvos aero klubo leidinys,

1933. 117 p. illus. TL526.L7P9
DLC

3967. REMEIKA, Jonas. Der Handel
auf der Memel vom Anfang des 14
Jahrhunderts bis 1430. In Tauta ir
Žodis (Kaunas), v.5, 1928, p. 386-
438. See serials consulted.

3968. SADOWSKI, Jan Nepomucen. Die
Handelsstrasse der Griechen und Rö-
mer durch das Flussgebiet der Oder,
Weichsel, des Dniepr und Niemen an
die Gestade des Baltischen Meeres.
Jena, H. Castenoble, 1877. liii,
210 p. maps. HF388.S3 DLC PU

3969. SCHÖNEMANN, Adolf. Die litauischen Binnenwasserstrassen. In
Osteuropa-Markt (Königsberg in Pr.),
v.16, 1936, p. 602-607. See serials
consulted.

3970. ŠIMOLIŪNAS, Jonas. Klaipėdos uostas. [The harbour of Klaipė-
da] In Technika (Kaunas), no.10,
1939, p. 1-96. See serials consulted.

3971. ŠLIŽYS, Balys. Klaipėdos
uostas. [Port of Klaipėda] In Naujoji romuva (Kaunas), no.1-2, 1938,
p. 29-30. See serials consulted.

3972. SOCHACZEWER, Ludwig. Memel
der Hafen von Litauen. [n.p.] Vor-
wärts, 1918. 78 p. map, plan.
947.52.Sol25 PU

3973. SPEKKE, Arnolds. The ancient
amber routes and the geographical
discovery of the Eastern Baltic.
Stockholm, M. Goppers, 1957. xiii,
120 p. maps. NK6000.S653 DLC CLU
CU CaBVaU CtY CaAEU KyU MH NN NNC
NIC NjR NjP OClW PU TxU WaU

3974. VALSONOKAS, Rudolfas. Der
Memeler Hafen und die litauische Ver-
kehrspolitik. Memel, Druck "Rytas,"
1933. 63 p. 947.52.V349 PU

3975. WYSŁOUCH, Seweryn. Posługi
komunikacyjne w miastach W.Ks. Litewskiego na prawie Magdeburskiem do
połowy XVI w. Wilno, Nakł. Institutu Naukowo-Badawczego Europy Wschodniej. Sekcja Historyczna. [Wydaw-
nictwa] nr.2) HE255.6.W9 DLC BM CU
MH PU

IX.8. FOREIGN AND DOMESTIC TRADE

3976. ALEKSANDROWICH, S. Miastecz-
ka Białorusi i Litwy jako ośrodki
handlu w XVI i pierwszej połowie XVII
wieku. In Rocznik Białostocki (Białystok), v.1, 1961, p.63-130. See
serials consulted.

3977. ANTONIEWICZ, Jerzy. Ślady
handlu słowian z baltami we wczesnym
średniowieczu. In Rocznik Olsztyński (Olsztyn), v.3, 1960, p. 9-20.
See serials consulted.

3978. ÅSTRÖM, Sven Erik. From
cloth to iron; the Anglo-Baltic tra-
des in the late seventeenth century.
Helsingfors, 1963. tables. (Socie-
tas scientiarum Fennica. Commentationes humanarum litterarum, 33:1,
etc.) HF3508.B3A37 CaOTU

3979. BENNINGHOVEN, Friedrich. Ri-
gas Entstehung und der frühhansische
Kaufmann. Hamburg, A.F. Velmede,
1961. 168 p. (Nord- und osteuropäische Geschichtsstudien, Bd.3) Bibliography: p. 9-15. ICU MH NIC NN
NNC

3980. DĄBROWSKI, Jan. Baltische
Handelspolitik Polens und Litauens
im XIV-XVI Jahrh. In Baltijas vēsturnieku konference. 1st., Riga,
1937. Runas un referāti. Riga, 1938.
German or French. DK511.B25.B35 1937
DLC CSmH NNC PPULC PU

3981. FINDLAY, James Arbuckle. The
Baltic exchange, being a short history of the Baltic mercantile and
shipping exchange from the days of
the old coffee house, 1744-1927, compiled and written by J.A. Findley,
secretary of the exchange. London,
[Printed by the Witherley & Co.] 1927.
55 p. front., plates, ports., facsims.
EcF.F4945B CaOTU

3982. GAZEŁ, Antoni. Foreign and
local trade of the Baltic countries.
Toruń, The Baltic Institute; London,
J.S. Bergson, 1936. 54 p. (The Bal-
tic pocket library) HF3499.B3G3 DLC
NN

3983. IVINSKIS, Zenonas. Lietuvos
prekyba su Prūsais. [Trade between
Lithuania and Prussia] Kaunas, 1934.
pt.1. (Kaunas. Universitetas. Teo-
logijos Filosofijos fakultetas. Leidinys, kn.19). BM(Ac. 1157. g/5.)

3984. JABLONSKIS, Konstantinas.
Prekinių-piniginių santykių plitimas
ir baudžiavinės reformos XVI amžiaus
antroje pusėje. [Expansion of goods-
money relationship and reforms of
serfdom in the late sixteenth centu-
ry] In LTSRMAII. Lietuvos Istorija
v.1, 1957, p. 179-194. DK511.L2L4235
v.1 DLC CU CaAEU CtY InU MH

3985. JACOB, Georg. Der nordisch-
baltische Handel der Araber im Mit-

telalter. Amsterdam, Meridian Pub.,
1966. 152 p. illus. HF406.J3 1966
CaOTU

3986. JUČAS, Mečislovas. Prekyba
Lietuvos kaime XVIII a. Torgovlia v
litovskoi derevne v XVIII v. In
LTSRMAIILKI, v.4, 1964, p. 109-122.
See serials consulted.

3987. KAŽDANAS, Vladimir Mikhailo-
vicz. Prekybiniai Lietuvos ir Tary-
bų Sąjungos santykiai iki 1940 metų.
[Lithuania's trade relations with
Soviet Union until 1940] Vilnius,
Mintis, 1967. 55 p. HF3635.7.K35
DLC PU

3988. KERSTEIN, Edith. Die Entwicklung der deutsch-litauischen Wirtschaftsbeziehungen im ersten Jahrzehnt seit Bestehen des Berücksichtigung seiner wirtschaftlichen Struktur. Duren, Spezial-Dissertations
Buchdruckerei, 1934. 121 p. plates. Thesis--Frankfurt am Main.
HF3568.L5K41 CSt-H CtY PU

3989. KHOROSHKEVICH, Anna Leonidov-
na. Torgovlia Velikogo Novgoroda s
Pribaltikoi i Zapadnoi Evropoi v XIV-
XV vekakh. Moskva, Izd-vo Akademii
nauk SSSR, 1963. 363 p. illus.
HF3625.K47 DLC CaAEU

3990. KIVIKOVSKI, Ella. Studien zu
Birkas Handel im östlichen Ostseegebiet. In Acta archeologica (Køben-
havnhavn), v.8, 1937, p. 229-250.
See serials consulted.

LITHUANIA. LAWS, STATUTES,
ETC. Bendrasis sąskaitybos įstatymas,
(Įstatymų rinkinio, t.7, dal.2) su
paaiškinimais. Kaunas, 1932. See
entry no. 2774.

3991. NERMAN, Birger. Der Handel
Gotlands mit dem Gebiet am Kurischen
Haff in 11. Jahrhundert. In Prussia;
Zeitschrift für Heimatkunde und Heimatschutz (Königsberg in Pr.), v.29, 1931,
p. [160]-173. illus. See serials
consulted.

3992. POLIESSKII, Rafail. System
der Handelverträge der baltischen
Randstaaten (Estland, Lettland und Litauen) mit besonderer Berücksichtigung
des völkerrechtlichen Inhalts. Riga,
1926. 104 p. (Bibliothek des baltischen Ostdienst-Verlages für Wirtschaft
und Recht, no.17) HF1721.P6 DLC CSt-H
CaAEU InU NN

3993. RIMKA, Albinas. Lietuvos prekybos santykiai ligi unijos su lenkais.
[Lithuania's trade relations with Poland before the Union] In KUTFD, v.2,
no.3, 1925, p. 23-86. See serials con-

sulted.

3994. ROBINSON, Nehemiah. Zehn
Jahre litauischer Aussenhandel 1919-
1928. In Weltwirtschaftliches Archiv
Chronik und Archivalien (Jena), v.30,
1929, p. 166-186. See serials consulted.

3995. RYBARSKI, Roman. Handel i
polityka handlowa Polski v XVI stole-
ciu. Warszawa, Państwowe Wydawn. Naukowe, 1958. 2 v. illus. Reprint
of 1928-1929 edition. HF3637.R9 DLC
CtY InU MH MiDW NIC NN NNC

3996. SOOM, Arnold. Der baltische
Getreidehandel im Brill 17. Jahrhundert. Stockholm, Almquist & Wiksell,
1961. 350 p. HD9045.B19S72 CaAEU
ICU NN

3997. STANKUS, Steponas. Lietuvos
prekyba vokiečių okupacijos metu.
[The Lithuania's trade during the German occupation] In Dirva (Cleveland,
Ohio), v.32, 1958. See serials consulted.

3998. STANKUS, Steponas and Antanas
Jasys. Prekyba; nepriklausomieji ir
okupaciniai laikai. [Trade; the periods of independent and occupied Li-
thuania] In Lietuvių enciklopedija.
Boston, Mass., 1968. v.15, p. 214-
218. For holdings see entry no. 216.

3999. ŠTURMS, Eduards. Der ostbaltische Bernsteinhandel in der vorchristlichen Zeit. In Commentationes
Balticae (Bonn), v.1, 1953 [i.e. 1954]
p. 167-205. See serials consulted.

4000. TIBAL, André. L'évolution du
commerce extérieur de la Lithuanie.
In Revue économique international
(Paris), no.26, 1934, p. 101-126. See
serials consulted.

4001. VALIŪNAS, Juozas Kęstutis.
Die deutsch-litauischen Aussenhandels-
beziehungen während der Unabhängig-
keit der litauischen Republik (1918-
1940) unter besonderer Berücksichtigung der Theorie der Komparativen
Kosten. [Tübingen, 1948] ii, 109
leaves. xxv tables. Inaug.-Diss.--
University of Tübingen. Typescript.
Ger.TU

4002. VERNADSKY, George. The Baltic
commerce of the West Russian and Lithuanian cities during the Middle
Ages. In Baltic and Scandinavian
countries (Toruń), v.3, 1937, p. 399-
409. map. See serials consulted.

IX.9. FINANCE

4003. BANDTKIE, Jerzy Samuel. Zakończenie o monetach polskich i litewskich, z dołączoną tablicą ewaluacyi monet polskich i litewskich z wyrażeniem wartości na monete podług stopy 1766 r. Detached from the author's Dzieje narodu polskiego. Wyd. 3. Wrocław, 1835. 947.52.B223.2 PU

BÜCHLER, O. Bankanweisung und Scheck in der russisch-litauischen Gerichtspraxis. In Zeitschrift für die gesamte Handelsrecht und Konkursrecht (Stuttgart), 1933, p. 201-220. See serials consulted.

4004. CESEVIČIUS, Domas. Das Finanzsystem Litauens. Bonn, L. Roerscheid, 1934. 112 p. (Kölner Studien, neue Folge, 3) Inaug Diss-- University of Köln. HJ1214.L8C3 CLU CU CtU DS IU MH NN PU

EICHHOLZ, Alvin C. The Baltic States: Estonia, Latvia and Lithuania. A short review of resources, industry, finance, and trade. [Washington, D.C.] 1928. See entry no.771.

4005. GARTMAN, V.G. Pol'skiia i litovskiia starinnye monety, 1056-1295; ikh tsiena i stepen' riedkosti. Syzran', 1901. 154 p. 947.52.G198 PU BM

4006. GUMOWSKI, Marian. Mennica wileńska w XVI i XVII wieku. Warszawa, E. Wende, 1921. vi, 200 p., 18 plates. CJ3028.L5G8 DLC CtY NN PU

4007. --- Numizmatyka litewska wieków średnich. In Wiadomości Numizmatyczno-Archeologiczne (Kraków), v. 9, 1920, p.55-106; v.9, 1921, p.1-27. CJ9.W5 DLC NNAN

JAKULIS, J. La Lithuanie restaurée. Louvain, 1932. See entry no.3765.

4008. KARDAKOFF, N. Katalog der Geldscheine von Russland und der Baltischen Staaten, 1769-1950. Berlin, 1953. xxx, 444 p. illus. German and Russian. HG1077.K35 DLC NN PU

4009. KARYS, Jonas K. Amber and furs; means of exchange in ancient Lithuania. In Lituanus (Brooklyn, N.Y.), v.5, no.3, 1959, p. 73-77. See serials consulted.

4010. --- Nepriklausomos Lietuvos pinigai: ostrublis, ostmarkė... istorija ir numizmatika. [The money of Independent Lithuania; history and numismatics] New York, N.Y., [Aukselis] 1953. 255 p. 160 illus. Summary in English. HG1080.L5K3 DLC CaAEU CaOONL CtTMF ICBM ICCC NN PU

4011. --- Senovės lietuvių pinigai, istorija ir numizmatika. [Ancient Lithuanian coins, history and numismatics] Putnam, Conn., "Aukselis", 1959. 396 p. illus. CJ3028.L5K3 DLC CaOONL ICBM CtPAM CtTMF PU

4012. KIRKOR, Adam Honory. Monetnoe dielo v Litvie. In Russkii istoricheskii sbornik. Moskva, 1839. Vyp.2. See serials consulted.

LEHNICH, Oswald. Währung und Wirtschaft in Polen, Litauen... Berlin, 1923. See entry no. 3778.

4013. LIETUVOS BANKAS. Apyskaita. [Annual report of Lietuvos bankas] Metai 1-17; 1923-1939. Kaunas. Annual. HG3129.L44A3 DLC(4-7; 1926-1929) NN(1926-1933)

4014. --- Balance sheet. 1927-1939. Kaunas, 1928-40. 13 v. Annual. MH-BA(1927-1939)

4015. --- Bulletin. no.1-19; Feb. 1931-Feb.1940. Semiannual. HG3135.7.L5 DLC IU(1-) MH-BA(1-) NIC-A(1-12,14-) NN(1-) NNC(1-) NjP (1-)

--- Lietuvos bankas. [London, 1922] See entry no. 2772.

4016. --- Lietuvos banko biuletenis. Kaunas, 1928-40. 13 v. illus. charts. Quarterly. HG3135.7.L5 DLC (1-10) NN(1-) NjP(no.7-48 in 3 v.)

4017. --- Pirmasis dešimtmetis, 1922-1932. [The first decade, 1922-1932] Kaunas, 1932. 74 p. illus., ports. HG3135.7.L55 DLC IU MH MnU NN NNC NjP

4018. --- Statement of the condition of Bank of Lithuania. Kaunas, 1927-40. Semimonthly. Ngh95R78L62e CtY(1927-1940)

4019. LITHUANIA. FINANSŲ DEPARTAMENTAS. Lietuvos valstybės... metų pajamos ir išlaidos... Receipts and expenditures of the Republic of Lithuania for the year... Kaunas, 19 . HJ55.5.C2 DLC(1933, 1935-1936, 1938) NN NjP

4020. LITHUANIA. FINANSŲ MINISTERIJA. Lietuvos Ministerių kabineto priimtasai Lietuvos valstybės 1925-metams biudžeto projektas. [Lithuania's State budget as approved by the

State Council for the year 1925- .
Kaunas. 19 .] HJ55.5.B15 DLC CtPAM
(1925-1927) NjP(1925)

4021. --- Lietuvos valstybės 1928-
1931 m biudžetai ir jų palyginimas.
[The budgets of the Lithuanian State
for the years 1928-1931 and the
comparison to each other] Kaunas,
1932. 76 leaves. tables. Mimeographed. NJ1215.A3 1932q NjP CtPAM

4022. --- Lietuvos valstybės 1932
m. biudžetas su payginamaisiais daviniais. Das litauische Staatsbud-
get für 1932. Kaunas, Valstybės
spaustuvė, 1932. 138 p. CtPAM

4023. --- Lietuvos valstybės 1933-
1938 metų biudžetai su palyginamai-
siais daviniais. [The Lithuanian
State budget for 1933-1938] Kaunas,
Valstybės spaustuvė, 1933-38.
CtPAM

4024. --- 1926 metų biudžeto pro-
jekto aiškinamasai raštas. [The explanatory paper of the projected budget for 1926. Kaunas] Valstybės
spaustuvė [1926] 124 p. CtPAM

4025. LITHUANIA. KOMMISSYJA SKARBU.
Wywody prawa o cłach Wielkiego Xięstwa Litewskiego na których ułożenie
instruktarza do exakcyi celnych fun-
dować się powinno. Wilno, 1766.
1 v. (unpaged) BM(5758. b. 17.)

4026. LITHUANIA. LAWS, STATUTES,
ETC. 1929 m. biudžetas; valstybės
biudžeto 1929 metams įstatymas ir
I-III dalys. [Lithuania's budget
for the year 1929] Kaunas, Valstybės spaustuvė, 1929. 45, 23, 7 p.
CtPAM

--- Žyminio mokesčio įstatymas... Kaunas, 1935. 164 p. See
entry no. 2782.

4027. MORAVSKIS, Alfonsas. Lietuvos finansai. [Lithuania's finances]
Kaunas, Valstybės spaustuvė, 1925.
2 v. (Ekonominių mokslų biblioteka,
kn.1-3) BM(Ac. 1157. f.) BN(2) PU

4028. PALIOKAS, Balys. Die Finan-
zen der Selbstverwaltungskörper Litauens einst und jetzt. Jena, 1937.
79 p. Inaug.-Diss.--University of
Jena. HJ1214.L5P16 CSt-H DLC PU

4029. PLATBĀRZDIS, Aleksandrs. Die
Münzen und das Papiergeld Estlands,
Lettlands, Litauens. [3. Aufl.]
Stockholm, 1953. ii, 192 leaves.
HG1080.2.P54 DLC CtY PU

4030. POKROVSKIS, Mykalojus. Valstybinis tiesioginių mokesčių tvarky-

mas Lietuvoje. [Direct taxes in Li-
thuania] In Lietuvos ūkis (Kaunas),
no.11, 1926, p.333-337; no.3-4, 1927,
p. 73-77, 109-113. See serials consulted.

4031. PRŪSAS, Adomas. Bankai ir
kreditas Lietuvoje iki 1915 metų.
[Banks and credit in Lithuania until
1915] Kaunas, 1926. 76 p.
947.52.P955 PU

RAČKAUSKAS, Konstantinas. Das
neue litauische Wechsel- und Scheck-
Recht. Breslau, 1938. See entry no.
2785.

4032. RAČKUS, Alexander Michaels.
Cyclopedia of Lithuanian numismatics.
Žinynas apie Lietuvos numizmatiką.
Chicago, Ill., Balzekas Museum of
Lithuanian Culture, 1965. 344 p.
illus., col. plates. Mimeographed.
Bibliography: p. 329-344. 737.5R
ICBM CJ3028.L5R3 PU

4033. --- Lietuvos pinigai Vytauto
Didžiojo gadynėje; medžiaga Lietuvos
tautinei numizmatikai. [Money of Lithuania during the reign of Vytautas
the Great. n.p.] 1930. 41 leaves.
illus. CJ3028f.L7R2 ICU

4035. Robinson, Nehemiah. Die Fi-
nanzwirtschaft Litauens als eines
neuen Staates. Prag, 1928. 122 p.
Inaug.-Diss.--University of Jena.
947.52.R563 PU CSt-H CtY DLC MH MiU

4036. RIMKA, Albinas. Lito pirmasis dešimtmetis. [The first decade
of Litas] In Tautos ūkis (Kaunas),
no.10, 1932, p. 269-271. See serials
consulted.

4037. ŠABŪNAS, Leonas. Didžiosios
Lietuvos Kunigaikštijos iždo tribunolas, 1613-1764. [The treasury tribunal of the Grand Duchy of Lithuania,
1613-1764] Kaunas, 1936. 99 p.
(Kaunas. Universitetas. Teisių fakultetas. Teisės ir ekonomijos studijos, t.1, kn.2) Thesis--University
of Lithuania. 947.62.Sa13 PU

4038. SRUOGA, Kazimieras. Die No-
tenemission der Republik Litauen.
Kaunas, Spindulio b-vė, 1930. 128 p.
fold. diagr. Thesis--University of
Bern. Bibliography: p. 126-128.
HG1080.L5S8 1930 DLC CtY NN PU

4039. --- Die Wirtschaft der Republik Litauen und ihre notenemission.
Kaunas, Verlag der deutschen Buchhandlung, 1930. 128 p. diagrs.
HG1080.L5S8 1930a DLC MnU NN PU

4040. VERIGA-DAREVSKIS, Antanas Ignas. Dvaro padūmės mokestis Užnemu-

nėje. [Land taxes in Suvalkija (Užnemunė)] Kaunas, 1932. 12 p. (Kaunas. Universitetas. Teisių fakultetas. Darbai, t.6, kn.7) DLC-L
CU ICU MoU NN NNC

4041. --- Lietuvos mokesčiai XV-
XVI amž. [The taxation system of
the fifteenth and sixteenth centuries
in Lithuania] Kaunas, Valstybės
spaustuvė, 1929. 52 p. (Kaunas.
Universitetas. Teisių fakultetas.
Darbai, t.5, kn.5) 947.52.V634 PU CU
ICU MH NN NNC

4042. ŽILĖNAS, Alfonsas. Buržuazinės mokesčių politikos klasinė esmė
ir mokesčių sistemos raidos Lietuvoje, 1919-1939 m., bruožai. [The
essence of the fiscal policy in Lithuania, 1919-1939] Vilnius, VPMLL,
1963. 80, [3] p. (Lietuvos TSR Mokslų akademijos ekonomikos institutas.
Darbai, t.14, sąs.1) HJ2809.L5Z5 DLC

4043. ŽYDŲ LIAUDIES BANKŲ LIETUVO-
JE SĄJUNGA. Di idishe hantverker in
Lite in tsifern. [The Jewish-worker's
bank organization in Lithuania. Kau-
nas] 1938. xv, 80 p. HD8535.7.Z9
DLC

IX.10. COOPERATIVES AND COOPERATIVE
MOVEMENT

4044. AUDĖNAS, Juozas. The cooperative movement. In Lituanus (Brooklyn, N.Y.), v.5, no.1, 1959, p. 13-
17. See serials consulted.

4045. BUBLYS, Vladas. Die genossen-
schaftliche Organization der Erzeugung und des Absatzes milchwirtschaft-
licher Produkte in Litauen. [Bonn]
1947. 118 leaves. graphs, tables,
map. Thesis--Agricultural College in
Bonn. Typescript. Ger.BU Ger.KIW

4046. CENTRALINĖ APDRAUDIMO SĄJUN-
GA "KOOPERACIJA". Apyskaita. [An-
nual report] 1- ; 1930- . Kaunas,
1931- . (*QYA)NN(1930)

4047. LA COOPÉRATION AGRICOLE EN
Lithuanie. In Revue internationale
d'agriculture (Rome), v.24, no.10,
1933, p. 415-430. See serials consulted.

4048. KAUNAS. LIETUVOS ŽEMĖS ŪKIO
AKADEMIJA. Lietuvos kooperacijos
teismas Žemės Ūkio Akademijos (Dotnuva), 1929 m., kovo mėn. 18 d. [Trial
of Lithuanian cooperative movement at
the Academy of Agriculture in Dotnu-
va] Kaunas, 1930. 69 p.
HD3517.6.K37 DLC

4049. KAUNO VARTOTOJŲ BENDROVĖ
"PARAMA". Apyskaita, 1930. [Annual
report of "Parama" Cooperative for
1930] Kaunas, 1931. 1 v. (*QYA)NN

4050. KEMĖŠIS, Fabian S. Cooperation among the Lithuanians in the
United States of America. Washington, D.C., 1924. 86 p. Bibliography: p. 83-85. Thesis--Catholic University of America, Washington, D.C.
HD3446.Z5L5 1924 DLC CSt CtY ICU ICJ
InNd ICLJF LU MiU NN NbU NdU NcU OU
OClW PPiU PU TxU WU

4051. KOOPERACIJOS SĄJUNGA "SPAUDOS
FONDAS". Apyskaita, 1930. [Annual
report of "Spaudos Fondas" Cooperative, 1930. Kaunas]1931. (*QYA)NN

4052. LIETŪKIS, 1923-1933. [Agri-
cultural Cooperative "Lietūkis", 1923-
1933] Kaunas, 1933. 112 p.
947.5.L13 CtTMF

4053. LIETUVOS KOOPERATYVŲ KONGRE-
SAS. Lietuvos kooperatyvų kongresai,
1-5 kooperatyvų kongresų rezoliucijos.
[Congresses of Lithuanian cooperative
movement; resolutions of the 1-5 con-
gresses] Kaunas, Lietuvos kooperatyvų taryba, 1939. 134 p. ports.,
diagrs. HD3517.6.A28 DLC

4054. LIETUVOS RESPUBLIKINĖ VARTO-
TOJŲ KOOPERATYVŲ SĄJUNGA. Tarybų
Lietuvos vartotojų kooperacijos dvidešimtmetis. [The twentieth anniversary of Soviet Lithuanian consumer coo-
peratives] Vilnius, Respublikinės
mokslinės-techninės informacijos ir
propagandos institutas, 1961. 1 v.
(chiefly illus.) HD3357.6.A4L5 DLC

4055. LIETUVOS ŽEMĖS ŪKIO KOOPERA-
TYVŲ SĄJUNGA. Apyskaita. [Annual
report] Kaunas, 1931. (*QYA)NN

4056. LITHUANIA. KREDITO ĮSTAIGŲ
IR KOOPERATYVŲ INSPEKCIJA. Lietuvos
kooperacija... Coopération de Lithuanie, 1927-1938. Kaunas, 1929-39.
5 v. Annual. (*SIO)NN

4057. ŠALČIUS, Petras. Das Genos-
senschaftswesen in Litauen von seinem
Beginn bis zur Gegenwart. [Tr. by
Victor Jungfer] Kauen, Lietuvos kooperatyvų taryba, 1938. 48 p.
324.9475.Sa33GJ PU IEN

4058. --- Kooperacija; kooperacijos
paskaitų kursas. [Lectures on coope-
ratives] Kaunas, VDU Teisių fakulteto leidinys, 1931. xii, 358 p. incl.
tables. (Kaunas. Universitetas. Teisių fakultetas. Ekonominių mokslų
biblioteka, nr.7) (*QYA)NN

4059. --- Kooperacija Lietuvoje;

bendra apžvalga iki 1937. [the co-operatives in Lithuania; general review until 1937] Kaunas, Kooperatyvų tarybos leidinys, 1937. 947.52.Sa33.2 PU

4060. --- Kooperatyvų įstatymai [Laws on cooperatives] In KUTFD, v.1, kn.4-5, 1924, p. 182-197. DLC-L CU NN NNC

4061. ŠAPYRO, B. Lietuvos vartotojų kooperacija Lenino keliu. [Lithuanian consumer cooperatives the Lenin way] Vilnius, Laikraščių ir žurnalų leidykla, 1961. 34 p. HD3357.6.S3 DLC

4062. TRIMAKAS, Antanas. Lithuanian cooperative movement in freedom and slavery. In Baltic Review (New York, N.Y.), no.11, 1957, p. 35-47. See serials consulted.

4063. --- Le movement coopératif en Lithuanie. Lille, Imp. G. Sautai, 1929. 446 p. (Publications de l'Ecole des sciences sociales et politiques de Lille) DLC-L DLL NN

IX.11. THE ECONOMY OF SOVIET LITHUANIA

IX.11.a. GENERAL STUDIES AND ECONOMIC PLANNING

4064. AUDĖNAS, Juozas. Seven fat years to come? The Soviet Union's seven-year economic plan. In Baltic Review (New York, N.Y.), no.17, 1959, p. 49-58. See serials consulted.

4065. BARKAUSKIENĖ, Z. Judėjimas už komunistinį darbą Lietuvos TSR pramonėje, 1958-1965. [The movement for development of working habits in the Communistic way in Soviet Lithuanian industry] Vilnius, Mintis, 1969. 175 p. HC337.L5B36 DLC

4066. BERKMANAS, Efroim Kalmanovich and Paulius Kiuberis. Ekonomika Litovskoi SSR. Moskva, "Ekonomika", 1967. 56 p. (Soiuznye respubliki v novoi piatiletke, 1966-1970 gg.) HC337.L5B4 DLC CaOTU CtY InU MH NIC NcD NcU NNC PPiU TU ViU

4067. BOETTCHER, Erik. Gedanken zur Sowjetisierung der Wirtschaft Litauens. In Litauen und seine Deutschen. Würzburg, 1955. See entry no. 3607.

4068. BUČAS, Jonas. TSRS liaudies ūkio planavimas. [Planning of Soviet economy] Vilnius, Mintis, 1967. 375 p. HC336.23.B9 DLC

4069. DAUKŠA, Antanas. TSRS valstybinis biudžetas. [The state budget of the USSR] Vilnius, Mintis, 1967. 412 p. HJ2129.D29 DLC

4070. DROBNYS, Aleksandras. Litovskaia SSR; rasskaz o semiletkie. Moskva, Proftekhizdat, 1961. 80 p. illus. (Molodezhi o semiletke) HC337.L5D7 DLC CSt-H InU MH NNC

4071. EKONOMICHESKIE SVIAZI PRIBALtiki s Rossiei; sbornik statei. [A.K. Biron, otv. red.] Rīgā, Zinātne, 1968. 284 p. HC243.E5 CaOTU

4072. ITSIKZON, M.R. Litovskaia SSR; lektsiia prochitanaia v Vil'nusskoi Vysshei partiinoi shkole. Moskva, VPSh, 1960. 63 p. HC337.L5I8 DLC CaOTU IaU IU MH NIC NNC TxU WU

4073. JABLONSKIS, Algimantas. Tarybų Lietuvos ekonomika ir jos ryšiai [The Soviet Lithuanian economy and its ties] Vilnius, Mintis, 1968. 215 p. illus. Summary in Russian. Bibliography: p. 209-215. HC337.L5J26 DLC InU MH MoU PU

4074. KIUBERIS, Paulius. Lietuvos TSR visuomeninis produktas ir nacionalinės pajamos. [The national gross product and the national income of the Lithuanian SSR] Vilnius, VPMLL, 1963. 90 p. HC337.L53I55 DLC CtY

4075. KONFERENTSIIA EKONOMIKO-GEOgrafov Pribaltiiskikh respublik po voprosam razmeshcheniia promyshlennosti i razvitiia gorodov. Vilna, 1962. Trudy konferentsii po voprosam razmeshcheniia promyshlennosti... Vil'nius, 1963. 200 p. illus., maps. HC58.K6 1962r DLC CtY

4076. KUTT, Aleksander. Reflections on Baltic economies under Soviet management. In Baltic Review (New York, N.Y.), no.35, 1968, p. 18-26. See serials consulted.

4077. LIETUVOS TSR MOKSLŲ AKADEMIJA, VILNA. EKONOMIKOS INSTITUTAS. 20 metų Tarybų Lietuvos liaudies ūkiui. [Twenty years of Soviet Lithuanian economy] Vilnius, VPMLL, 1960. 315 p. illus., tables. HC337.L5I44 DLC CtY MH OKent

4078. LITHUANIAN SSR. CENTRINĖ STATISTIKOS VALDYBA. Lietuvos TSR liaudies ūkis; statistinių duomenų rinkinys.[Soviet Lithuanian economy] Vilnius, Valstybinė statistikos leidykla, Lietuvos skyrius, 1957. 222 p. Annual. DLC(1957,1961-1962, 1965) PU

4079. LITHUANIAN SSR. LIAUDIES ŪKIO TARYBA. Semiletka promyshlennosti Sovnarkhoza Litovskoi SSR. Vilnius, TSentr. biuro tekh. informatsii 1959. 151 p. illus. HC337.L5A62 DLC MH

4080. MEŠKAUSKAS, Kazys. Tarybų Lietuvos liaudies ūkis šeštajame penkmetyje. [Soviet Lithuanian economy in the sixth five-year plan] Vilnius, VPMLL, 1957. 109 p. fold. map. HC337.L5M4 DLC

4081. MEZHOTRASLEVYE ISSLEDOVANIIA v ekonomicheskikh raionakh. Opyt raboty po Pribaltiiskim ekonomicheskim raionu. [Sbornik statei. Otv. red. L.E.Mints] Moskva, Nauka, 1967. 381 p. diagrs., tables. HD5797.B3T7 CaOTU

4082. NAUCHNOE SOVESHCHANIE PO problemam perspektivnogo razvitiia proizvoditel'nykh sil v Pribaltiiskikh soiuznykh respublikakh, Tallinn, 1968. Reziume dokladov. Tallinn, 1968. 153 p. HC243.N38 DLC

4083. NEY, Gottlieb. Sozialistische Industrialisierung und ihre Auswirkungen im Sowjetischen Baltikum. In Acta Baltica (Königsberg im Taunus), v.2, 1962, p. 129-145. See serials consulted.

4084. PRIBALTIISKII EKONOMICHESKII raion. [Otv. red. A.B. Margolin] Moskva, Nauka, 1970. 308 p. maps. Rasvitie i razmeshchenie proizvoditel'nykh sil SSSR) HC243.P94 DLC CaAEU CaOTU PU

4085. REMEIKIS, Tomas. Berücksichtigung der nationalen und verwaltungsmässigen Interessen der Unionsrepublik im Rahmen des zentralistischen Sowjetsystems, dargestellt am Beispiel Litauens. In Acta Baltica (Königstein im Taunus), 1970, p. 121-156. See serials consulted.

4086. TARULIS, Albertas. Lietuvos ūkio katastrofos pradžia. [The beginning of the catastrophy of the Lithuanian economy] In Lietuvių archyvas. Kaunas, 1942. v.2, p. 99-153. DK511.L27L47 v.2 DLC PU

4087. UUSTALU, Evald. Soviet reforms reactionary in character as proven by the development in the Baltic States. In International Peasant Union. Bulletin (Washington, D.C.), 1958, p. 17-20. See serials consulted.

4088. VARDYS, Vytas Stanley. Soviet social engineering in Lithuania; an appraisal. In His Lithuania under the Soviets... New York, N.Y., [1965] p. 237-259. DK511.L27V35 DLC CSt CU CSt-H IC MoU MWalB MU PPiU TU WaU

4089. ZUNDĖ, Pranas. Lithuania's economy; introduction of the Soviet pattern. In Vardys, V.S., ed. Lithuania under the Soviets... New York, N.Y., 1965. p. 141-169. DK511.L27V35 DLC AzU CSt CSt-H CU IC MoU MWalB MU PPi TU WaU

IX.11.b. INDUSTRY AND ITS DEVELOPMENT

4090. AUŠTREVIČIUS, Albinas and R. Razauskas. Pramonės normuotojo žinynas. [Handbook of industrial standards] Vilnius, Mintis, 1965. 273 p. illus. T60.P7A8 DLC

4091. BANAITIS, Walter C. Die Industrialisierung Sowjetlitauens. In Acta Baltica (Königstein im Taunus), v.2, 1962, p. 176-261. See serials consulted.

4092. BERKMANAS, Efroim Kalmanovich. Nekotorye voprosy perspektivnogo razvitiia promyshlennosti stroitel'nykh materialov Litovskoi SSR. In LTSRMAEID, v.4, 1957, p. 142-190. See serials consulted.

4093. BIJŪNAS, B. Darbo apmokėjimas pramonėje, statyboje, transporte, ryšių sistemoje ir už pakrovimo-iškrovimo darbus. [General salary and wages scale in industry, construction transport... Sudarė: B. Bijūnas, N. Gemskis ir G. Soročkinas] Vilnius, VPMLL, 1962. 387 p. HD5047.6.B5 DLC

4094. ČIUPLINSKAS, Algis. Tak rabotaet ob"edinenie "SIGMA" [By] A.B. Chuplinskas. Moskva, Ekonomika, 1967. HD70.R9C58 1967 ViU CaAEU

4095. GARGASAS, Petras. Lietuvos TSR maisto pramonės gamybos specializavimas. [The specialization in the meat industry of the Soviet Lithuania] In LTSRMAEID, v.10, 1961, p. 101-134. See serials consulted.

4096. GELEŽINIS, Martynas. Die Wirtschaft im Baltikum und Sowjetlitauen. In Europäische Osten (München), no.2, 1955, p. 79- . See serials consulted.

4097. IANKOIT', Genrikh Ivanovich. Obshchestvennyi kontrol' za zhilishchno-bytovym stroitel'stvom. [Moskva] Profizdat, 1964. 78 p. (Bibliotechka profsoiuznogo aktivista, 6(78)) HD7345.6.A3I2 1964 CaBVaU DLC NcD ViU

4098. INDRIŪNAS, Juozas. Lietuvos TSR lengvosios pramonės išvystymas ir perspektyvos. [The development and the future of the light industry in the Soviet Lithuania] In KPID, v.12, 1959, p. 63-68. See serials consulted.

4099. ISPOL'ZOVANIE OSNOVNYKH PRO-izvodstvennykh fondov v promyshlen-nosti Litovskoi SSR. [Sbornik sta-tei. Red. kollegiia: E. Berkmanas (otv. red.) i dr.] Vil'nius, 1968. 302 p. HD70.L5I75 DLC

4100. JANUŠKEVIČIUS, A. Baldų pra-monės išvystymas Tarybų Lietuvoje. [The development of the furniture in-dustry in the Soviet Lithuania] In LTSRMAD. Serija A, v.1(10), 1961, p. 3-18. See serials consulted.

4101. KADŽIULIS, M. Kai kurie spe-cializavimo ir kooperavimo klausimai Lietuvos TSR elektronikos ir prietai-sų gamybos pramonėje. [Some problems on the specialization and cooperation of the Lithuanian SSR electronics and intrument industry] In LTSRMAEID, v.10, 1961, p. 135-162. See serials consulted.

4102. KIUBERIS, Paulius. Promysh-lennost' Sovetskoi Litvy. [Perevod s litovskogo] Vil'nius, TSentr. biuro tekh. informatsii, 1959. 29 p. illus. HC337.L5K5 DLC IU

4103. KRIAUČIŪNAS, Jonas. Tarybų Lietuvos statybinių medžiagų pramo-nės vystymo klausimu. [The develop-ment of the building material indus-try in Soviet Lithuania] In Vilna. Universitetas. Ekonomikos ir teisės mokslų serija, v.4, 1959, p. 105-112. See serials consulted.

4104. LIAUDIES KONTROLIERIAI ŽYGYJE. [The people's investigators on the march] Vilnius, Mintis, 1965. 147 p. HC337.L53A85 DLC

4105. LIETUVOS TSR MAŠINŲ IR PRIE-taisų gamybos pramonės darbuotojų e-konominė konferencija, Vilna, 1962. Gamybos rezervai Lietuvos TSR maši-nų ir prietaisų pramonėje; ekonomi-nės konferencijos, įvykusios Vilniu-je 1962 m. gegužės 23-24 d., medžia-ga. [The production reserves of the industry of machinary and instruments in the Soviet Lithuania; proceedings of the economic conference held in Vilnius, May 23-24, 1962] Vilnius, 1962. 135 p. tables. At head of title: Lietuvos TSR LOT Mašinų ir prietaisų gamybos valdyba. Lietuvos TSR Mokslų akademija. Ekonomikos institutas. Lietuvos RMTD Tarybos technikos namai. HD9705.R93L54 DLC

4106. LIETUVOS TSR MOKSLŲ AKADEMI-JA, VILNA. EKONOMIKOS INSTITUTAS. Darbo našumas ir produkcijos savikai-na pramonėje. [Labour productivity and cost price in the industry] Vil-nius, VPMLL, 1960. 175 p. diagrs, tables. (Its Darbai, t.8) HD7o.L5L49 DLC MH

4107. --- Darbo našumas Lietuvos TSR pramonės įmonėse. [Productivity of the Lithuanian SSR industry. Ed. by P. Gargasas] Vilnius, VPMLL, 1962. 244 p. illus. (Its Darbai, t.12) HC337.L53L38 DLC MH

4108. --- Lietuvos TSR pramonės specializavimas ir kooperavimas. [The specialization and cooperation of in-dustry in Soviet Lithuania. Ats. red. V. Januškevičius] Vilnius, VPMLL, 1961. 161 p. tables (Its Darbai, t.10) Lithuanian or Russian with summaries in the other language. HC337.L5L445 DLC IU MH

4109. --- Pramonės ekonomikos klau-simai. [Problems of industrial eco-nomics. P. Gargasas, editor-in-chief] Vilnius, VPMLL, 1957. 190 p. (Its Darbai, t.4) HC337.L5L45 DLC

4110. --- Pramonės įmonių rentabi-lumo kėlimas. [An atempt to increase the productivity in the industry. Ats. red. P. Gargasas] Vilnius, VPMLL, 1958. 148 p. diagrs, tables. (Its Darbai, t.6) Lithuanian or Rus-sian. HD70.L5L5 DLC

4111. LITHUANIAN SSR. LIAUDIES ŪKIO TARYBA. Baldai. [Furniture. Kaunas, Lietuvos TSR liaudies ūkio ta-rybos Centrinis techninės informaci-jos biuras, 1959] 1 v. illus. Li-thuanian or Russian. NK2577.L5 DLC MH

4112. --- Razvitie pishchevoi pro-myshlennosti Litovskoi SSR, 1940-1965 gg. Vil'nius, TSentr. biuro tekh. informatsii, 1959. 48 p. illus. HD9015.L52A4 DLC MH

4113. LITHUANIAN SSR. VALSTYBINIS STATYBOS IR ARCHITEKTŪROS REIKALŲ KO-MITETAS. Preiskurant tsen stoimosti 1. kvadratnogo metra zhiloi ploshcha-di po Litovskoi SSR... Vil'nius, 1959. 51 p. HD9715.R93L52 DLC

4114. --- Sbornik edinichnykh ras-tsenok na stroitelnye raboty po Li-tovskoi SSR... Vil'nius, TSentr. biu-ro tekh. informatsii i propagandy, 19 . tables. TA183.L5 DLC

4115. --- Visuotinis statybos ir statybinio remonto darbų bei darbi-ninkų profesijų tarifinis-kvalifika-

cinis žinynas (VTKŽ) [Handbook of
job description in the building tra-
de] Vilnius, Centrinis techninės informacijos ir propagandos biuras,
1961. 154 p. HD8039.B92L64 DLC

4116. MANIUŠIS, Juozas. Industry
of Soviet Lithuania on the path of
technical progress. I.A. Maniushis.
Washington, D.C.,U.S. Joint Publications Research Service, 1962. 73
p. illus. (JPRS: 12043) Translation of a portion of Promyshlennost'
Sovetskoi Litvy na puti tekhnicheskogo progressa. HC337.L5M29 NSyU

4117. --- Promyshlennost' Sovetskoi Litvy na puti tekhnicheskogo
progressa. I.A. Maniushis. Vil'-
nius, Gos. izd-vo polit. i nauch.
lit-ry Litovskoi SSR, 1960. 120 p.
illus. HC337.L5M3 DLC

4118. --- Razvitie stroitel'stva
i ego material'no-tekhnicheskoi ba-
zy v Litovskoi SSR. I.A. Maniushis.
Vil'nius, Gospolitnauchizdat, 1963.
239 p. illus., maps, diagrs., tables. HD9715.R93L56 DLC CaOTU ICU

4119. --- Tarybų Lietuvos pramonės
kilimas. [The progress of Soviet
Lithuanian industry] Vilnius, VPMLL,
1958. 110 p. illus. 338.9475.M3lt
IU NN OKentU

4120. MEŠKAUSKAS, Kazys. Lietuvos
TSR tekstilės pramonės vietinės ža-
liavų bazės išplėtimo galimybės.
[The possibilities of expanding the
supply of local raw materials for the
Soviet Lithuanian textile industry]
In LTSRMAEID, v.4, 1957, p. 51-81.
See serials consulted.

4121. --- Tarybų Lietuvos industri-
alizavimas. [The industrialization
of the Soviet Lithuania] Vilnius,
VPMLL, 1960. 261 p. maps, tables.
HC337.L5M39 DLC CU CtY IU MH NN

4122. NAIDUŠKEVIČIUS, R. Lietuvos
TSR mašinų gamybos pramonės išvystymas. [The development of the machine
industry in Soviet Lithuania] In
LTSRMAD. Serija A, v.2(11), 1961,
p. 3-14. See serials consulted.

4123. ORGANIZATSIIA PROIZVODSTVEN-
nykh ob"edinenii v legkoi promyshlennosti Litovskoi SSR. Vil'nius,
1968. 226 p. diagrs. HD70.L507
DLC ICU PU

4124. RAGALEVIČIUS, J. Lietuvos
TSR rajoninės pramonės išsivystymo
klausimai. [The development of the
regional industry in Lithuanian SSR]
In LTSRMAEID, v.4, 1957, p. 82-111.
See serials consulted.

4125. TARVYDAS, Stasys and Vincas
Brazauskas. Rytų Lietuvos gamybinių
jėgų išvystimo perspektyvos. [The
possibilities to develop the industrial power in the Eastern Lithuania]
In LTSRMGGIMP, v.9, 1959, p. 137-
165. See serials consulted.

4126. TARVYDAS, Stasys and M. Gu-
donytė. Economic-geographical division of the Lithuanian SSR into districts. In LTSRMAGGI. Straipsnių
rinkinys... Vilnius, 1960, p. 437-
441. See serials consulted.

4127. VILNIAUS MIESTO EKONOMINĖ
konferencija statybos klausimais,
1962. Ekonomika stroitel'stva v g.
Vil'nius; materialy ekonomicheskoi
konferentsii. [Otv. red. E. Berkma-
nas] Vil'nius, Gos. izd-vo polit. i
nauch. lit-ry, 1963. 118 p. tables.
HD9715.R93V56 1962 DLC MH

4128. VITKEVIČIUS, Povilas. Razvi-
tie elektro- i radiosviazi v Litve.
Vil'nius, Mintis, 1972. 268 p.
TK5101.V56 PU

4129. ZUNDĖ, Pranas. Maskvos pra-
moninė politika pavergtoje Lietuvoje. [Moscow's industrial policy in
occupied Lithuania] In Varpas
(Brooklyn, N.Y.), no.5, 1963, p.88-
103. See serials consulted.

4130. --- Soviet industrial policy
in Lithuania. In Lituanus (Brooklyn, N.Y.), v.9, no.2, 1963, p. 35-
42. See serials consulted.

IX.11.c. COLLECTIVE FARMING; ITS
ECONOMIC, TECHNICAL, AND
SOCIAL DEVELOPMENT

4131. AUDĖNAS, Juozas. Agriculture
in Bolshevik occupied Lithuania. In
International Peasant Union. Bulletin (Washington, D.C.), v.3, no.9-10,
1952, p. 21-26. See serials consuted.

4132. --- Der Fluch des Kollektivs.
In Europäische Osten (München), v.4,
no.7, 1958, p. 410-417. See serials
consulted.

4133. --- Kolchozų krizė okupuotoj
Lietuvoj. [The collective farm crisis in occupied Lithuania] In Lietuva (New York, N.Y.), no.8, 1956, p.
41-52; 94. See serials consulted.

4134. BARŠAUSKAS, Juozas. Lietuviškos kolūkiečio sodybos architektūra. [The architecture of the Lithuanian collective farm] Vilnius,

VPMLL, 1956. 231 p. illus., maps, diagrs., plans, tables. Bibliography: p. 228-230. NA8206.B3 DLC

4135. DIČIUS, P. Tarybinė žemės reforma Lietuvoje 1940-1941 metais. [Soviet agrarian reform in Lithuania 1940-1941] In LTSRMAD. Serija A, 1(4), 1958, p. 19-30. See serials consulted.

4136. DROMANTAS, I.I. Progress report by Director of the Lithuanian Scientific Research Institute of Mechanization and Electrification of Agriculture. In USSR Industrial development, no.72. (JPRS:43,995) Jan.12, 1968, p. 26-28. DLC

4137. EFREMENKO, A. Sel'skoe khoziaistvo Litovskoi SSR v 1953-1958 gg. In LTRSMAD. Serija A, v.2, 1963, p. 153-183. tables. See serials consulted.

4138. GREGORAUSKAS, Marijonas. Tarybų Lietuvos žemės ūkis, 1940-1960. [Soviet Lithuanian agriculture, 1940-1960] Vilnius, VPMLL, 1960. 462 p. tables. HD1995.65.G7 DLC CtPAM PU

4139. GURKLYS, Balys. Kolūkių gamybiniai fondai ir jų naudojimo gerinimas. [The resources of the collective farms and the improvement of their utilization] Vilnius, Mintis, 1968. 92 p. maps. Bibliography: p. 92-[93] HD1492.R921L55 DLC

4140. KAPITKOVSKIS, S. Pensijos ir pašalpos kiolūkiečiams. [Pensions and grants for the collective farmer] Vilnius, Mintis, 1966. 106 p. DLC

4141. KAULAKIS, Leonas. Lietuvos TSR kolūkių elektrifikacija. [The extension of electric power for the collective farms in Soviet Lithuania. Pranešimas VIII Lietuvos TSR Mokslų akademijos sesijoje] In LTSRMA. Žinynas, v.6, 1950, p. 60-70. See serials consulted.

4142. KAUNAS. LIETUVOS ŽEMĖS ŪKIO AKADEMIJA. Žemės ūkio gamybos procesų mechanizacija ir elektrifikacija; straipsnių rinkinys. [The mechaniztion and electrification of the processes in agricultural production. Redaktorius S. Simatonis] Kaunas, Lietuvos žemės ir miškų ūkio mokslinės draugijos leidinys, 1960. 85 p. illus., diagrs. S675.K37 DLC

4143. KRIVICKAS, Domas. Land and peasant; Lithuania. In Gsovski, V., ed. Government, law, and courts in the Soviet Union and Eastern Europe. London, 1959. v.2, p. 1703-1724.

JN6573.G89 CaAEU CSt-H CU CaBVaU CoU CaOKQL CLL CtY DS FTaSU GU ICU IaU IU MiD MiDW MnU NIC NN NbU NcD-L NjR RPB WaU-L

4144. --- Results of five years' collective farming and so-called collective farms democracy. In Highlights of current legislation and activities in Mid-Europe (Washington, D.C.), v.5, no.1, 1957, p. 9-26. See serials consulted.

4145. KRUTULYTĖ, R. Žemės ūkio kolektivizacija Tarybų Lietuvoje. [The collectivization of the agriculture in Soviet Lithuania] In LTSRAMMD: Istorija, v.3, 1962, p. 5-23. See serials consulted.

4146. LIETUVOS TSR MOKSLŲ AKADEMIJA, VILNA. EKONOMIKOS INSTITUTAS. Kolūkių ekonomikos stiprinimo ir vystymo pagrindiniai klausimai; Dotnuvos MTS zonos kolūkių medžiagos pagrindu. [Basic problems of the development and strengthening of the economy in collective farming; based on available data from Dotnuvos MTS collective farms' district. K. Meškauskas (vyr. redaktorius)] Vilnius, VPMLL, 1957. 253 p. map, diagrs. (Its Darbai, t.3) HD1491.L5L5 DLC

4147. --- Lietuvos TSR žemės ūkio mechanizavimo ir elektrifikavimo klausimai. [Problems of mechanization and electrification of Soviet Lithuanian agriculture. Ed. by J. Pričinauskas] Vilnius, VPMLL, 1958. 131 p. tables. (Its Darbai, t.5) TK4018.L45 DLC CU MH

4148. --- Tarybų Lietuvos žemės ūkio specializavimas ir išdėstymas. [The zoning and specialization of the Soviet Lithuanian agriculture] Vilnius, VPMLL, 1959. 156 p. (Its Darbai, t.7) HC337.L5L45 DLC CU MH

4149. --- Žemės ūkio ekonomikos klausimai. [Problems of agricultural economics. Editor-in-chief J. Bulavas] Vilnius, VPMLL, 1956. 138 p. (Its Darbai, t.2) HD1995.65.L5 DLC CU MH

4150. LIETUVOS TSR ŽEMĖS ŪKIO TOLESnio išvystymo klausimai. [Problems of the future development of Soviet Lithuanian agriculture. Redakcinė komisija: Vyr. redaktorius V. Lašas, nariai: J. Kriščiūnas ir kiti] Vilnius, VPMLL, 1954. 370 p. At head of title: Lietuvos TSR Mokslų akademija. Lithuanian or Russian. S469.L5L5

4151. LITHUANIAN SSR. ŽEMĖS ŪKIO MINISTERIJA. Meropriiatiia po raz-

vitiiu sel'skokhoziaistvennogo proiz-
vodstva (vostochnaia zona Litvy)
Vil'nius, Gos. izd-vo polit. i nauch.
lit-ry, 1960. 191 p. illus.
S469.L5A55 DLC

4152. PADVAISKAS, Edmund R. Agriculture under Soviet control. In
Lituanus (Brooklyn, N.Y.), v.4, no.4,
p. 109-112. See serials consulted.

4153. PAURAZAS, Petras. Statybos
darbų organizavimas Lietuvos TSR
kolūkiuose. The organization of
construction on the collective farms
of Soviet Lithuania] Vilnius, VPMLL,
1962. 71 p. diagrs. (Lietuvos TSR
Mokslų akademija. Ekonomikos institutas. Darbai, t.11, sąs.4) Summary in Russian. HD9715.L52P3 DLC
MH; see also serials consulted.

4154. PETERSEN, Hans. Die sowjetische Agrarpolitik in den baltischen
Staaten, 1940-1952. In Osteuropa
(Stuttgart), v3, no.3, 1953, p. 191-
196. See serials consulted.

4155. POŠKUS, B. Savikainos ma-
žinimas kolūkiuose. [The means of
reducing cost price of production in
the collective farms] Vilnius,
VPMLL, 1961. 106 p. illus.
S567.P63 DLC DNAL

4156. PRAPUOLENIS, Leonas. Be-
triebsschema eines litauischen Kol-
chos. In Ostprobleme (Bad Nauheim),
v.4, no.33, 1952, p. 1119-1123. Tr.
from "News from behind the Iron Curtain", June, 1952. See serials consulted.

4157. RESPUBLIKINĖ MOKSLINĖ-TECHNI-
NĖ KONFERENCIJA ŽEMĖS ŪKIO ELEKTRIFI-
KAVIMO KLAUSIMU. Vilna, 1962. Že-
mės ūkio elekrifikavimo klausimai...
[The problems of extension of elec-
tric power into the rural areas]
Vilnius, 1963. 81 p. TK4018.R4 DLC

4158. ŠUSTAVIČIUS, Kazys. Kolūkių
ir tarybinių ūkių gamybiniai fondai
ir būdai geriau jiems naudoti. [Re-
sources of Collective and State
Farms and improved methods for using
them] Vilnius, VPMLL, 1960. 43 p.
tables. HD1492.L5S8 DLC

4159. VAZALINSKAS, Vytautas. LTSR
žemės ūkis 1946-1950 m. laikotarpyje.
[The agriculture of Soviet Lithuania,
1946-1950] In LTSRMA. Žinynas, v.1,
1947, p. 140-159. See serials consulted.

4160. VENCKŪNAS, Vytautas. Darbo
našumo kėlimas tarybiniuose ūkiuose.
[Efforts to increase productivity on
the state farms] Vilnius, VPMLL,

1961. 77 p. illus. S471.R92L5 DLC

4161. VITKŪNIENĖ, A. Galvijininin-
kystės produkcijos savikainos maži-
nimo galimybės Lietuvos TSR tarybiniuose ūkiuose. [The means of reducing the cost of beef production on
the state farms in Soviet Lithuania]
Vilnius, VPMLL, 1962. 70 p. diagrs.
(Lietuvos TSR Mokslų akademija, Vilna. Ekonomikos institutas. Darbai,
t.11, sąs.3) Summary in Russian.
See serials consulted.

4162. ŽEMĖS ŪKIO MECHANIZAVIMO KLAU-
simai. [On the question of mechanization in agriculture] Vilnius,
VPMLL, 1960. 223 p. illus.
S760.L3Z4 DLC

4163. ŽEMĖS ŪKIO ELEKTRIFIKAVIMAS.
[The extension of electric power into
rural areas. Knygą sudarė L. Kaulakis ir kiti] Vilnius, VPMLL, 1961.
541 p. TK4018.Z4 DLC

4164. ZUNDĖ, Pranas. The collectivization of Lithuanian agriculture,
1940-1952. In Lituanus (Chicago,
Ill), v.9, no.3, 1963, p. 82-88. See
serials consulted.

4165. --- Die Kollektivierung der
Landwirtschaft Sowjetlitauens. In
Acta Baltica (Königstein im Taunus),
v.2, 1962, p. 93-106. See serials
consulted.

4166. --- Die Landwirtschaft Sowjetlitauens. Marburg/Lahn, 1962. 155
p. tables (part. fold.) (Wissenschaftliche Beiträge zur Geschichte
und Landeskunde Ost-Mitteleuropas,
Nr.58) Bibliography: p. 89-105.
338.1o9475Z95L NcD CU ICU MH NNC PU

4167. --- The private plot and the
socialized sector of Lithuanian agriculture. In Lituanus (Brooklyn, N.Y.)
v.8, no.3, 1962, p. 65-70. See serials consulted.

4168. --- Valstiečių atlyginimas
okupuotoje Lietuvoje. [Peasant's
wages in occupied Lithuania] In Aidai (Brooklyn, N.Y.), no.2(147),1962,
p. 61-64. See serials consulted.

4169. --- Sodybinio sklypo reikšmė kolūkiečiui. [The importance of
private plot to the collective far-
mer] In Aidai (Brooklyn, N.Y.),
no.5(150), 1962, p. 202-207. See serials consulted.

229

IX.11.d. LABOUR RESOURCES, THEIR
UNIONS, INCOME, RIGHTS
AND DUTIES

4170. BALEVIČIUS, Zigmas. Darbininkų ir tarnautojų teisės ir parei-
gos. [Rights and duties of workers
and employees] Vilnius, VPMLL, 1958.
258 p. DLC-L MH-L

BIJŪNAS, B. Darbo apmokėjimas pramonėje, statyboje, transporte... See entry no. 4093.

4171. ČERNIAUSKAS, Simonas. Darbininkų ir tarnautojų moralinis ir
materialinis paskatinimas. [Moral
and material incentives for workers
and employees in industry] Vilnius,
VPMLL, 1962. 44 p. HF5549.5.I5C4
DLC

4172. --- Deiatel'nost' profsoiu-
zov Sovetskoi Litvy po ustanovleniiu
norm v oblasti trudovykh otnoshenii;
nauchno-metodicheskoe posobie. Vil'-
nius, Akademiia nauk Litovskoi SSR,
Otdel filosofii, prava i sotsiologii
pri institute istorii, 1971. 76 p.
HD6735.65.C44 PU

4173. DANILIAUSKAS, Antanas. Šiaurės rytų Lietuvos pramonės darbininkų materialinė kultūra. [The material culture of the industrial workers in Northeastern Lithuania]
Vilnius, 1970. 190 p. DK511.L212D3
PU

4174. EKONOMICHESKAIA KONFERENTSIIA
rabotnikov promyshlennosti goroda
Vil'niusa. Vilna, 1961. Proizvoditel'nost' truda i sebestoimost' pro-
duktsii... Vil'nius, Gos. izd-vo polit. i nauch. lit-ry Litovskoi SSR,
1961. 142 p. tables. HD70.R9E36
1961 DLC MH

4175. LIETUVOS RESPUBLIKINĖ PROFE-
SINIŲ SĄJUNGŲ TARYBA. Lietuvos TSR
profesinės sąjungos. Professional'-
nye soiuzy Litovskoi SSR. Statisti-
nis rinkinys. Vilnius, 1967. 49 p.
HD6735.65.A35 DLC

LIETUVOS TSR MOKSLŲ AKADEMI-
JA, VILNA. EKONOMIKOS INSTITUTAS.
Darbo našumas ir produkcijos savikai-
na pramonėje. Vilnius, 1960. See
entry no. 4106.

4176. PAŽĮSTAMI VEIDAI [Familiar
faces] Vilnius, VPMLL, 1962. 193 p.
HD8535.7.P3 DLC

4177. ŠADŽIUS, H. Vilniaus pramonės darbininkų kultūrinio-techninio
lygio kilimas socializmo statybos
laikotarpiu, 1944-1953. [The rising

of the cultural and technical level
of the industrial workers in Vilnius]
In LTSRMAIILKI, v.4, 1964, p. 48-78.
See serials consulted.

4178. STIMBURYS, Juozas. Sociali-
nis aprūpinimas Tarybų Lietuvoje.
[Social security in Soviet Lithuania]
Vilnius, VPMLL, 1950. 68 p.
HD7035.6.S8 DLC

4179. TRUDOVYE RESURSY PRIBALTIIS-
kikh sovetskikh respublik. [Avtora-
mi otdel'nykh glav iavliaiutsia: V.
E. Kaufman i dr. Redkollegiia: V.V.
Gulin i dr.] Riga, Zinātne, 1967.
147 p. fold. map. HD5797.B3T7 DLC
CaAEU CaOTU CtY NcD NjP ViU

4180. VAITIEKŪNAS, Vytautas. The
labor system in occupied Lithuania.
In Baltic Review (New York, N.Y.),
no.4, 1955, p. 18-24. See serials
consulted.

X. HISTORY

X.1. BIBLIOGRAPHIES

4181. ADOMONIENĖ, O., ed. Lietuvos
TSR istorijos bibliografija, 1940-
1965. [Bibliography of the Soviet
Lithuanian history, 1940-1965. Sudarė:). Adomonienė, V. Milius, A. Tau-
tavičius] Vilnius, 1969. 708 p.
Z2537.A6 DLC PU WaU

4182. --- 1863 m. sukilimo Lietuvoje bibliografija. [Bibliography of
the revolt of 1863] In Bibliotekininkystė ir bibliografija (Vilnius),
v.2, 1963, p. 305-318. See serials
consulted.

BALTRAMAITIS, Casimir V. Lithuanian affairs; ... New York, N.Y.,
1945. See entry no. 188.

4183. BARBASHEV, ALEKSANDR Ippolitovich, ed. Lietopisnye istochniki
dlia istorii Litvy v srednie veka.
Sanktpeterburg, Izdanie redaktsii zhur-
nala "Bibliografa", 1888. 29 p.
891.7.B232 NNC BM(9008. 1. (2.))

4184. CHOJNACY, Jadwiga. Materiały
do bibliografi bitwy pod Grunwaldem.
In Rocznik Olsztyński (Olsztyn), v.
3, 1960, p. 324-349. See serials
consulted.

4185. FORSTREUTER, Kurt. Das Preussische Staatsarchiv in Königsberg;
ein geschichtlicher Rückblick mit einer Übersicht über seine Bestände.
Göttingen, Vandenhoeck und Ruprecht,

1956. 114 p. illus. (Veröffentlichungen der Niedersächsischen Archiv-
verwaltung, Hft.3) CD1259.K6F6 WU
CtY InU MH NIC NN NNC NcD

4186. GĄSIOROWSKI, Janusz Tadeusz.
Bibliografja druków dotyczących
powstania styczniowego, 1863-1865.
Warszawa, Wojskowy Instytut Naukowo-
Wydawniczy, 1923. 394 p.
Z2526.G24 DLC IU NN CU

4187. GORBACHEVSKII, Nikita Ivanovich. Katalog drevnim aktovym knigam gubernii Vilenskoi, Grodnenskoi,
Minskoi i Kovenskoi, takzhe knigam
nekotorykh sudov gubernii Mogilevs-
koi i Smolenskoi, khraniashchimsia
nyne v TSentral'nom arkhive v Vil'-
nie. Vil'na, Tip. A.I. Zaka, 1872.
xxvi, 10, 861 p. tables.
BM(8094. i. l.) NN

4188. --- Kratkiia tablitsy neob-
khodimyia dlia istorii khronologii
voobshche... i v chastnosti dlia razbora drevnikh aktov i gramot Zapadnago Kraia Rossii i TSarstva Pol'skago. Vil'na, Tip. Gub. pravleniia,
1867. 49 p. tables. Be3015 CtY NN

4189. IVINSKIS, Zenonas. Vytautas
Didysis istorinėje literatūroje ir
jo periodo bibliografija. [Vytautas
the Great in the literature of history and the bibliography] In Athenaeum (Kaunas), v.1, no.2, 1930, p.
190-212; v.2, no.1, 1931, p. 89-141.
See serials consulted.

4190. LIETUVOS TSR ISTORIJA. Ano-
tuota rekomenduojamos literatūros rodyklė, 1944-1956. [Soviet Lithuanian
history] Vilnius, VPMLL, 1957. 76
p. CtPAM

4191. PETKEVIČIŪTĖ, D. Rankraščiai apie 1863 m. sukilimą Lietuvoje. Bibliografinė rodyklė. [Manu-
scripts about the Revolution of 1863
in Lithuania; a bibliography] In
LTSRMACBBB, v.2, 1963, p. 213-303.
See serials consulted.

4192. Širvydas, Vytautas and Česlovas Grincevičius. Naujausioji istorinė literatūra. [The most recent
historical literature] In Tautos
praeitis (Chicago, Ill.), v.1, no.3,
1961, p. 477-486; v.1, no.4, 1962,
p. 638-644. See serials consulted.

        Szameitat, Max. Bibliogra-
phie des Memellandes. Würzburg,
1957. See entry no. 119.

4193. URBŠIENĖ, Marija.(Mašiotaitė) Klaipėdos krašto istorijos paraštėje, 1900-1930. [Brief notes on
the history of Klaipėda Territory,

1900-1930] Kaunas, Sakalo b-vė,
1934.. 75 p. Bibliography: p. 51-
75. Z2537.U7 DLC-L PU

4194. UŽPURVIS, J., comp. Lietu-
vių tautos istorijos šaltiniai.
[Sources of Lithuania's history]
Klaipėda, 1938- . BM(9454. aa. 21.)

4195. WERMKE, Ernst. Bibliographie
der Geschichte von Ost- und Westpreussen. Königsberg in Pr., Gräfe und
Unzer, 1932-33. xv, 1098. Z2244.P9W4
DLC CtY PU

4196. --- --- Neudruck der Ausgabe
1933 mit ergänzendem Nachtrag. Aalen,
Scientia Verlag, 1962. xv, 1098, 21
p. 943.I.B.W498.2 PU CaAEU CSt ICN
InU MiDW MoSW MoU NIC NjR WU

4197. --- --- Für die Jahre 1930-
1938. Aalen, Scientia Verlag, 1964.
xi, 511 p. CLU CtY DLC FU IaU ICN
MoSW NIC NjR NNU WU

4198. --- --- Für die Jahre 1939-
1942 nebst Nachträgen zu den früheren
Jahren. Königsberg in Pr., Gräfe und
Unzer, 1944. 158 p.

4199. --- --- Für die Jahre 1939-
1951. Nebst Nachtrag aus den früheren Jahren. Marburg/Lahn, J.G. Herder Institut, 1953. 294 p. (Wissenschaftliche Beiträge zur Geschichte un
und Landeskunde Ost-Mitteleuropas,
11) 943.I.B.W498 PU

4200. --- --- Für die Jahre 1952-
1956, nebst Nachträgen aus früheren
Jahren.. Marburg/Lahn, J.G. Herder
Institut, 1958. x, 254 p. (Wissenschaftliche Beiträge zur Geschichte
und Landeskunde Ost-Mitteleuropas,
37) 943.I.B.W498.3 PU

4201. --- --- Für die Jahre 1957-
1961, nebst Nachträgen aus früheren
Jahren. Marburg/Lahn, J.G. Herder
Institut, 1963. xii, 377 p. (Wissenschaftliche Beiträge zur Geschichte und Landeskunde Ost-Mitteleuropas,
64) CLU MH MnU NcD NjP NNC

X.2. PREHISTORY

4202. ÅBERG, Nils Fritiof. Ostpreussen in der Völkerwanderungszeit.
Uppsala, Akademiska bokhandeln [1919]
viii, 175 p. illus., 8 fold. maps.
DD491.044A5 DLC CaOTU

4203. BAYE, Joseph, Baron de. Comp-
te-rendu des traveaux du neuvième
Congrès russe d'archéologie, 1893,
précédé d'une étude historique sur la

Lithuanie et Vilna. Paris, Nilsson,
1894. 136 p. illus., plates.
DK30.B38 DLC CtY MB MiU PU

4204. BŪGA, Kazimieras. Aisčių
praeitis vietų vardų šviesoje. [The
prehistory the Aisčiai (Balts) from
the point of view of the place-na-
mes] In His Rinktiniai raštai.
Vilnius, 1961. v.3, p. 728-742.
PG8509.B8 v.3 DLC CaAEU CU CtPAM
CtTMF ICU ICLJF IEN MH NN NjP PPiU
PU TxU

4205. --- Kalbų mokslas bei mūsų
senovė. [Linguistics and our pre-
history] In Draugija (Kaunas), v.20,
1913, p. 80-98. Also in His Rinktiniai raštai. Vilnius, 1958. v.1, p.
401-418. See serials consulted and
PG8509.B8 v.1 DLC CaAEU CU CtPAM
CtTMF ICU ICLJF IEN MH NN NjP PPiU
PU TxU

4206. --- Lietuvių įsikūrimas šių
dienų Lietuvoje. [The settling of
Lithuanians in present-day Lithuania]
In His Rinktiniai raštai. Vilnius,
1961. v.3, p. 551-583. PG8509.B8
v.3 CaAEU CU CtPAM CtTMF DLC ICU
ICLJF IEN MH NN NjP PPiU PU TxU

--- Lietuvių kalbos žodynas:
įvadas. Kaunas, 1924. See entry
no. 355.

4207. --- ŠIS-TAS IŠ LIETUVIŲ IR
indoeuropiečių senovės. [From Lithuanian and Indo-european Prehisto-
ry] In His Rinktiniai raštai. Vilnius, 1961. v.3, p. 584-599.
PG8509.B8 v.3 DLC CaAEU CU CtPAM
CtTMF IEN ICU MH NN NjP PPiU PU TxU

4208. --- Die Vorgeschichte der
aistischen (baltischen) Stämme im
Lichte der Ortsnamenforschung. In
Streitberg Festgabe (Leipzig), 1924,
p. 22-36. ViU; and in His Rinktiniai
raštai. Vilnius, 1961. v.3, p. 728-
742. See entry no. 4204.

4209. ENGEL, Carl. Ostbaltische
Frühzeit. Mit Beiträgen von Leonis
Arbusow u.a. Leipzig, S. Hirzel,
1939. x, 498 p. illus., maps.
(Deutsche Land, Bd.1) DK511.B3B7
DLC NNC OU MH

4210. FEUEREISEN, Arnold. Die
baltische vorgeschichtliche Forschungen und Prof. Dr. Max Ebert. Riga,
1930. 5 p. (Sonderdruck aus der
Baltischen Monatsschrift, Jg.61,
Hft.1) Mu Pam PU

4211. GABRYS, Juozas. Parenté des
langues hittite en lituanienne et la
préhistoire. Genève, Librairie de
l'université, Georg [1944] 288 p.
illus., maps.

GN741.G3 DLC CLU CU CaOTU ICU NN NNC
NjP PU

4212. GIMBUTAS, Marija (Alseikai-
tė) The Balts. New York, N.Y.,
Praeger, 1963. 286 p. illus., maps.
(Ancient people and places) GN824.
GN824.B25G5 DLC CaAEU CtPAM PU

4213. --- Die Bestattung in Litau-
en in der vorgeschichtlichen Zeit.
Tübingen, In Kommission bei J.C.B.
Mohr, 1946. 250 p. illus., plates,
fold. maps. Thesis--University of
Tübingen. GN796.L5G5 1946 DLC AzU
CoU CtY IU InU IEN MH MiU NN NNC PU
WU

4214. --- Bronze-Age cultures in
Central and Eastern Europe. The Hague, Mouton, 1965. 681 p. illus.,
maps. GN777.G5 DLC CaAEU PU

4215. --- Lietuvos proistorė.
[Prehistory of Lithuania] In Lietuvių enciklopedija. Boston, Mass.,
1968. v.15, p. 269-291. For holdings see sentry no. 216.

4216. --- The prehistory of Eastern Europe. Edited by Hugh Hencken.
Cambridge, Mass., Peabody Museum,
1956. ix, 241 p. illus., plates,
maps. (Harvard University. American School of Prehistoric Research.
Bulletin no.20) DR20.G5 DLC CaAEU
ICLJF MH NN

4217. --- Rytprūsių ir vakarų Lie-
tuvos priešistorinės kultūros apžval-
ga. [A survey of prehistory of East
Prussia and Western Lithuania] In
Lithuanian Research Institute, New
York, N.Y. Mažoji Lietuva, 1958,
p. 11-121. DK511.L2L715 DLC CLU
CaAEU

4218. GRIGAT, Fritz. Aus grauer
Vorzeit; Prähistorisches aus dem
Mauerseegebiet. Langensalza, J.
Beltz, 1927. 112 p. fold. map.
(Heimatforschung aus Ost-Preussens
Mauerseegebiet, t.1) 913.4311.G876a
TxU MH-P

4219. GROSS, Hugo. Auf den ältesten Spuren des Menschen in Altpreussen. In Altertumsgesellschaft Prussia. Sitzungsberichte (Königsberg
in Pr.), v.32, no.1, 1938, p. 84-139.
See serials consulted.

4220. --- Renntierjäger-Kultur Ostpreussens. In Prähistorische Zeitschrift (Berlin), v.30-31, 1940, p.
39-67. See serials consulted.

4221. GUREVICH, F.D. Drevnie pamiatniki IUgo-Vostochnoi Pribaltiki
i zadachi ikh izucheniia. In KSIIMK,
v.42, 1952, p. 13-23. See serials

consulted.

4222. --- K istorii drevnikh Prussov v 1. tysiacheletii n.e. In KSIIMK, v.70, 1957, p. 40-48. illus. See serials consulted.

4223. HEYM, W. Eine baltische Siedlung der frühen Eisenzeit am Kleinen See bei Kl. Stärkenau (Westpreussen) In Mannus (Würzburg), v. 29, 1937, p. 3-52. See serials consulted.

4224. HOFFMANN, Joachim. Die spätheidnische Kultur des Memellandes. Königsberg in Pr., Ost-Europa, 1941. x, 189 p. illus. DD491.M4H6 DLC CtY

4225. JANKUHN, H. Zur Besiedlung des Samlandes in der ältere römischen Kaiserzeit. In Altertumsgesellschaft Prussia (Königsberg in Pr.), v.30, no.1, 1933, p. 202-226. See serials consulted.

4226. KILIAN, Lothar. Haffküstenkultur und Ursprung der Balten. Bonn, Habelt, 1955. 320 p. illus., maps. DK511.B29K5 DLC MH NN PU

4227. KULIKAUSKAS, Pranas. Giminés santvarkos irimo laikotarpis (I-IV a.) [The period of disintegration of the family order] In His Lietuvos archeologijos bruožai. Vilnius, 1961. p. 144-[269] illus., plans, maps. GN845.L5K8 DLC CaAEU

4228. --- Nekotorye dannye o pervonachal'nom zaselenii territorii Litvy... In Akademiia nauk SSSR. Institut etnografii. Trudy (Moskva), v.23, 1954, p. 36-46. See serials consulted.

4229. --- Seniausieji Kuršių Neringos gyventojai. [The ancient inhabitants of the Curonian Sand Dunes] In LTSRMAIILKI, v.2, 1959, p. 72-85. See serials consulted.

4230. MAKARENKO, Nikolai Emel'ianovich. Zabytki przedhistoryczne gub. Kowienskiej. In Kwartalnik Litewski (Sanktpeterburg), v.2, 1910, p. 103-112. See serials consulted.

4231. MATTHEWS, William Kleesmann. Medieval Baltic tribes. In American Slavic and East European Review (Menasha, Wis.), v.8, no.2, 1949, p. 126-136. See serials consulted.

4232. NARBUTT, Teodor. Wiadomość historyczna o Liszkowie niegdyś Nowogródku Nadniemnowym czyli Nauenpille. In His Pomniejsze pisma historyczne. Wilno, 1856. p. 21-31.

DK511.L2N27 CU ICLJF MH PU

4233. OCHMAŃSKI, Jerzy. Weneckie początki Litwy. In Acta Baltico-Slavica (Białystock), v.3, 1966, p. 151-158. See serials consulted.

4234. OZOLS, Jekabs. Die baltische Steinkistengräberkultur. Berlin, De Gruyter, 1969. xix, 135, 84 p. illus., maps. (Vorgeschichtliche Forschungen, Bd.16) Bibliography: p. 117-124. DK511.B29 O9 DLC

4235. --- Vorgeschichtliche Forschung in den baltischen Staaten nach 1945. In Zeitschrift für Ostforschung (Marburg), v.9, 1960, p. 377-386. See serials consulted.

4236. PUZINAS, Jonas. Aisčiai istorinių šaltinių šviesoje. [The Balts in the light of the historical sources] In Aidai (Augsburg, Ger.), no.12, 1948, p. 97-103. See serials consulted.

4237. --- Naujausių proistorinių tyrinéjimų duomenys, 1918-1938. [Results of the most recent prehistoric research, 1918-1938] Kaunas, 1938. 131 p. 56 plates, 4 fold. maps. Reprinted from "Senové" v.4. 913.475.P998 PU BM(Ac. 1157. e/5.) DSI

4238. --- Proistoré apie lietuvių protévynę. [Prehistory of the forefatherland of Lithuanians] In Lietuva (New York, N.Y.), no.2, 1952, p. 149-154, ill. See serials consulted.

4239. --- In search of the origins of the Lithuanian people. In Lituanus (Brooklyn, N.Y.), no.1(1o), 1957, p. 7-11. See serials consulted.

--- Vorgeschichtsforschung und Nationalbewusstsein in Litauen. See entry no.984.

4240. RIMANTIENÉ, Rimuté (Jablonskyté). O drevneishikh kulturnykh oblastiakh na territorii Litvy. In Sovetskaia Etnografiia (Moskva), no. 3, 1955, p. 3-19. See serials consulted.

4241. ROSSIUS, K. O. Die sogenannten Pfahlbauten Ostpreussens. In Prähistorische Zeitschrift (Berlin), v.24, 1933, p. 22-95. See serials consulted.

4242. SAKS, Edgar V. Aestii, an analysis of an ancient European civilization. Heidelberg [Verlag "Voitleja"] 1960. 300 p. maps.

(Studies in the Ur-European history) Bibliography: p. 7-11. DK511.E53S3 DLC CtY IaU MiU MH NIC NNC PU

4243. SCHMIDT, EVGENII A. Baltiiskaia kul'tura v verkhov'iakh Dnepra vo vtoroi polovinie 1-go tysiacheletiia. In Acta Baltico-Slavica (Białystok), v.6, 1969, p. 129-144. illus. See serials consulted.

4244. SENN, Alfred. Bestrebungen auf dem Gebiete der Urgeschichte in Litauen. In Wiener prähistorische Zeitschrift (Wien), Jahrg. 11, 1922, p. 101-103. See serials consulted.

4245. TAUTAVIČIUS, Adolfas. Klasinės visuomenės formavimosi laikotarpis, V-VIII a. [The period of the development of class society in the fifth to the eighth centuries] In Kulikauskas, Pranas. Lietuvos archeologijos bruožai. Vilnius, 1961. p. 269-359. illus., charts, map. GN845.L5K8 DLC CaAEU

4246. VASMER, Max. Über die Ostgrenze der baltischen Stämme. In Beiträge zur historischen Völkerkunde Osteuropas. Berlin, 1932. p. 637-666. (Akademie der Wissenschaft, Berlin. Philosophisch-historische Klasse. Sitzungsberichte) See serials consulted.

X.3. GENERAL STUDIES OF THE HISTORY OF THE BALTIC COUNTRIES

4247. BABRIS, Peter J. Baltic youth under communism. Arlington Heights, Ill., Research Publishers, 1967. vi, 351 p. Bibliography: p. 340-346. HQ799.B3B3 PU CaAEU DLC

4248. THE BALTIC AND CAUCASIAN STATES. Boston, Mass.; and New York, N.Y., Houghton Mifflin Company. 1923. xx, 269 p. maps [The nations of today, [10]) DK46. B3 DLC CaAEU CaOLU CaBVaU Ca BViP CoDU CoU CSt CtY CU IEN ICU IU MiU NB NN NNC NBuU NbU OCl OO OkU OrP PPiU PU-W PPULC RPB TxDaM TxU ViU WU

4249. BALTIJAS VĒSTURNIEKU KONFERENCE, 1st, Riga, 1937. Runas un referāti. Rīgā [Latvijas Vēstures Instituta Izdevums] 1938. 588 p. port., plates, maps, diagrs. At head of title: Pirma Baltijas Vēsturnieku konference, Rīgā, 16.-

20.VIII. 1937. DK511.B25B35 DLC CSmH NNC PPULC PU

4250. BERGER, Paul C. La tragédie balte. In Écrits de Paris (Paris), 1953, p. 92-99. See serials consulted.

4251. BIRKE, Ernst, ed. Die Sowjetisierung Ost-Mitteleuropas: Untersuchungen zu ihrem Ablauf in den einzelnen Ländern. Im Auftrage des Johann Gottfried Herder-Forschungsrates hrsg. von E. Birke und R. Neumann unter Mitwirking von Eugen Lamberg. Frankfurt am Main, A. Metzner, 1959- . DR48.5.B52 DLC CaAEU(v.1) CU CtY CSt-H CaBVaU DS DeU FU LNHT LU ICU InU InNd MH MiU MnU NN NIC NNC NNCFR NNU NbU NjP PPiU PP RPB TxHR TxU WaU

4252. ČEGINSKAS, Ebba. Die baltische Frage in den Grossmächteverhandlungen, 1939. In Commentationes Balticae (Bonn), v.12-13, 1967, p. 31-73. See serials consulted.

4253. CHAMBON, Henry de. La tragédie des nations baltiques. Paris, Éditions de la Revue parlementaire [1946] 226 p. D754.B35C5 DLC CU CSt ICLJF InU NN PU

ELKIN, Alexander. The Baltic States. In Survey of International Affairs (London; New York, N.Y.), v.11, 1958, p. 42-58. See serials consulted.

4254. FARR, Philip. Soviet Russia and the Baltic republics. [London, Russia today Society, 1944] 52 p. illus. DK511.B3F3 DLC

4255. FORSTEN, Georgii Basil'-evich. Akty i pis'ma k istorii Baltiiskago voprosa v XVI i XVII stolietiiakh. Sanktpeterburg, Tip. I.N. Skorokhodova, 1889-1893. 2 v. DK511.B3F6 DLC PU

4256. FÜNFZIG JAHRE RUSSISCHER Verwaltung in den Baltischen Provinzen. Leipzig, Duncher & Humbolt, 1883. 297 p. DK511.B3F9 ICU

4257. GAILLARD, Gaston. L'Allemagne et le Baltikum. Paris, Champelot, 1919. 278 p. illus., maps. D523.G25 DLC CSt-H IU CtY NN NcU NjP

4258. GESSEN, Sergei IAkovlevich. Okrainnye gosudarstva; Pol'sha, Finliandiia, Estoniia, Latviia i Litva. Leningrad, Rabochee izdatel'stvo Priboi, 1926. 150 p. DK440. G392 CSt-H

4259. GIANNINI, Amedeo. L'equilibrio del Baltico. Firense, La Nuova Italia, 1940. 94 p. D965. G45 DLC MH NcD

4260. GIERE, Werner. Die ostbaltischen Staaten Litauen, Lettland, Estland (1928-1936). In Geographisches Jahrbuch 1936. Berlin, 1937, v.51, 358-418. G1.G4 v.51 DLC

4261. HAUPT, Werner. Baltikum, 1941; die Geschichte eines ungelösten Problems. Neckargemünd, K. Vowinckel, 1963. 200 p. 11 maps. (Die Wehrmacht im Kampf, Bd.37) D757.W37 Bd.37 DLC CSt-H CU NcD PU

4262. HERLING, Albert K. The Soviet slave Empire. New York, N.Y., Wilfred Funk [c1951] xi, 230 p. HV8888.H4 DLC CU CaAEU ICU MB MH NN ViU

4263. HEYKING, Al'fons Al'fonsovich. The Baltic minorities. In Grotins Society, London. Problems of peace and war... London, 1922, v.7, p. 119-132. JX31.G7 v.7 DLC MiU

4264. --- Bolshevism and pusillanimity. The Baltic problem. London, P.S. King and Son, 1919. 46 p. DK265.H4 DLC ICJ NN NjP

4265. HURWICZ, Elias. Der neue Osten; Wandlungen und Aussichten. Berlin, E.S. Mittler & Sohn, 1927. viii, 201 p. DK46.H967 CSt-H NN

4266. IVINSKIS, Zenonas. Die baltische Frage im 17. Jahrhundert. Köln, Böhlau Verlag, 1970, p. 119-140. Offprint from: Der Ostseeraum im Blickfeld der deutschen Geschichte. D178.I87 PU

4267. --- Pabaltijo istorijos problemos. [The problems of Baltic history] In Židinys (Kaunas), no. 10, 1937, p. [610]-634. See serials consulted.

4268. JACKSON, John Hampden. The Baltic. Oxford, Claredon Press, 1940. 32 p. illus., maps. (Oxford pamphlets on world affairs, no. 27) DK511.B3J3 DLC

4269. JAKŠTAS, Juozas. Das Baltikum in der Kreuzzugsbewegung des Jahrhunderts. In Commentationes Balticae (Bonn), v.6-7, 1959, p. 139-183. See serials consulted.

KAJECKAS, Juozas. Some common misconceptions about the Baltic States, In Social science

(Winfield, Kan.) v.21, no.1, 1946, p. 39-46. See serials consulted.

4270. KALNINŠ, Brūno. De baltiska staternas frihetskamp. Stockholm, Tidens Förlag [1950] 320 p. map. Bibliography: p.307-319. DK511.B3K25 DLC CaAEU CU MH NN NNC PU

4271. KIPARSKY, Valentin. The earliest contacts of the Russians with the Finns and Balts. In Oxford Slavonic Papers (Oxford), v.3, 1952, p. 67-79. See serials consulted.

4272. LEAGUE FOR THE LIBERATION OF the peoples of the USSR. Captive nations of the USSR. Munich, 1963. 112 p. plate, maps. DK33.L4 CaOWtU DLC InU NNC

4273. LEVINE, Isaac Don. The resurrected nations; short histories of the peoples freed by the Great War and statements of their national claims. New York, N.Y., Frederick A. Stokes, c1919. viii, 309 p. maps. D445.L5 DLC CaAEU CaMWU NB NN NdFA WaS

4274. LIEVEN, Wilhelm. Russlands Zerfall und die Erneuerung des Baltikums. Berlin, K. Curtius [1919] 31 p. DK265.L44 DLC

4275. MATTEWS, William Kleesmann. Nationality and language in the East Baltic area. In American Slavic and East European Review (Menasha, Wis.), May 1947, p. 62-78. See serials consulted.

4276. MEIKSINS, Gregory. The Baltic riddle; Finland, Estonia, Latvia, Lithuania - key points of European peace. New York, N.Y., L. B. Fischer [1943] 271 p. illus., diagrs., maps. Bibliography: p. 259-261. DK511.B3M36 DLC CU NN OCl OLaK OCU OO OU PP PPD PSc PU

4277. --- The Baltic Soviet Republics. Based on "The Baltic riddle" by Gregory Meiksins. Introduction by Prof. Frederick L. Schuman. New York, N.Y., National Council of American-Soviet Friendship, 1944. 46 p. Condensed version. (GLP p.v. 145) NN

4278. MEUVRET, Jean. Histoire des pays baltiques: Lituanie, Lettonie, Estonie, Finlande. Paris, A. Colin, 1934. 203 p. illus., maps. (Collection Armand Colin, no.168) DK511.B3M45 DLC NN

4279. MILOSZ, Czesław. Die baltischen Völker. In Der Monat (Berlin), v.4, no.41, 1952, p. 451-466. See serials consulted.

4280. --- The lesson of the Baltics. In His The captive mind. New York, N.Y., 1953, p. [223]-251. DK411.M5 DLC FTaSU MB MiU NcU NcD NN OO OClW OOxM PV PBm PSt PPT PHC TU TxU

4281. MOLTKE, Kai. De baltiske folks frihedskamp. Skive, Frit forlag [1948] 234 p. DK511. B3M63 DLC CSt-H

4282. MONTFORT, Henry de. Les nouveaux états de la Baltique. Paris, A. Pedone, 1933. 320 p. illus., map. (Le droit international et l'actualité) Bbiliography: p. [309]-315. DK511.B3M65 DLC NN

4283. MORTENSEN, Gertrud. Beiträge zur Kenntnis des nordöstlichen Mitteleuropa um 1400. In Zeitschrift für Ostforschung (Marburg), v.9, no.2/3, 1960, p. 333-361. See serials consulted.

4284. NEWMAN, Edward William Polson. The Baltic: yesterday and today. In His Britain and the Baltic. London [1930] p. 1-26. DK511.B3N4 DLC CaAEU CSt-H CU MoU MWalB

4285. NEY, Gottlieb. Das Baltikum gehört zum West. In Acta Baltica (Königstein im Taunus), v.3, 1963, p. 9-34. See serials consulted.

4286. --- Lebensraum und Schiksalswandlungen der Völder des Baltikums. In Acta Baltica (Königstein im Taunus), v.1, 1961, p. 9-58. See serials consulted.

4287. OERTZEN, Friedrich Wilhelm von. Baltenland; eine Geschichte der Deutschen Sendung in Baltikum. München, F. Bruckmann [1939] 337 p. maps. DK511.B3 029 Ca AEU MN NN

4288. OLBERG, Paul. Rysslands nya imperialism, de små nationernas drama i diktaturstaten. Med förord av Zeth Höglund. [Stockholm] Bogförlaget Natur och kultur [1940] 231 p. illus., maps. MH NN

4289. --- Tragedin balticum. Annektionen av de fria republikerna Estland, Lettland och Litauen. Baltic tragedy... 3. upplagan. Stockholm, Natur och kultur, 1941. 102 p. DK511.B304 DLC MH MnU NN

4290. --- Die Tragödie des Baltikums; die Annexion der freien Republiken Estland, Lettland und Litauen. Zürich, Europa Verlag, 1941. 87 p. DK511.B30416 DLC CSt-H IaU OCl PU

4291. PAKŠTAS, Kazys. The Baltoscandian confederation. [Chicago, Ill.] Lithuanian cultural institute, 1942. 27 p. illus. DK511. B3P17 CLU CSt-H DLC CU CtY ICU MH MiU NIC NNC PU

4292. PICK, Frederick Walter. The Baltic Nations; Estonia, Latvia and Lithuania. London, Boreas Publishing Co. [1945]. 172 p. maps. Bibliography: p. 155-165. DK511. B3P5 DLC CaAEU CU CtY CaOTP GU NN NjR OCl OCU PPTU PU

4293. POSKA, Jüri G., ed. Pro Baltica. Mélanges dédiés à Kaarel R. Pusta. [Stockholm] 1965. 244 p. illus. "Publication du Comité des amis de K.R. Pusta" DK511.B25P6 DLC CLU CU CaAEU CtY ICU InU MiU-L NN PU

4294. PRIBALTIISKIM SOVETSKIM RESpublikam tridtsat' let. Materialy k nauch. konferentsii in-tov istorii Akademii nauk Litov., Latv. i ESSR, 20-21 okt. 1970 g. [Red. kollegiia: G. Shadzhius (otv. red.) i dr.] Vil'nius, 1970. 105 p. At head of title: Akademiia nauk Litovskoi SSR. Institut istorii. DK511.B3P73 DLC PU

4295. LES PROBLÈMES DE LA BALTIQUE par K.R. Pusta, von Loesch, W. Kamieniecki [et autres]. Paris, Publications de la Conciliation internationale [1934] viii, 206 p. ([Conciliation internationale] Bulletin, no.8-9) JX1907.C75 1934 no. 8-9 DLC PU ViU-L

4296. RAUCH, Georg von. Geschichte der baltischen Staaten. Stuttgart, W. Kohlhammer Verlag, 1970. 224 p. DK511.B3R34 DLC CaAEU PU

4297. REDDAWAY, William Fiddian. Problems of the Baltic. Cambridge, The University Press, 1940. 120 p. illus., map. DK511.B3R37 DLC CaAEU CU NN NNC NcD OCl OCU OO OU PHC PPTU PU ViU

4298. RICHTER, Alexander von. Geschichte der dem russischen Kaiserthum einverleibten deutschen Ostseeprovinzen bis zur Zeit ihrer Vereinigung mit demselben. Th. 2: Die Ostseelande als Provinzen fremder Reiche, 1162-1721. Riga, N. Kymmel, 1859. 3 v. in 1.

947.52R418 PU NN

4299. ROTHELFS, Hans. The Baltic Provinces. Some historic aspects and perspectives. In Journal of Central European Affairs (Boulder, Col.), v.4, 1944, p. 117-146. See serials consulted.

RUTENBERG, Gregor. Die baltischen Staaten und das Völkerrecht. Riga, 1928. See entry no. 3456.

4300. RUTTER, Owen. The new Baltic states and their future; an account of Lithuania, Latvia and Estonia, by Owen Rutter. London; Boston, Mass.; New York, N.Y., Methuen & Co.; Houghton Mifflin Co., 1926. xi, 274 p. illus., maps, plates, ports. Bibliography: p. 265-270. DK511.B3R85 DLC CLU CSt CU CSt-H CaAEU CaOHM CaOLU CaQMM CaSRU CaOTU CoU CtY ICU IaU ICN IU MH MnU NN NIC NNC NcU NSyU OCl OClW PPiU PU RPB TxU WaS WU

4301. --- Towards the Baltic; Per aspera ad astra; The happy people; Down the Nemunas. In Lithuania Minor. In His The new Baltic States and their future. London [1925] p. 1-97. See entry no. 4406.

4302. SAMARIN, IUrii Fedorovich. Iuri Samarins Anklage gegen die Ostseeprovinzen Russlands. Übersetzung aus dem Russischen. Eingeleitet und commentiert von Julius Eckardt. Leipzig, F.A. Brockhaus, 1869. xx, 269 p. DK511.B3S2 DLC NcD

4303. SCHWABE, Arvid. Baltic States. In The Fate of East Central Europe. Istvan Kertész, ed. Notre Dame, Ind., University of Notre Dame Press, 1956, p. 103-128. D376.U6K4 DLC

4304. SENN, Alfred Erick. The Sovietization of the Baltic States. In American Academy of Political and Social Science (Philadelphia, Pa.), Annals, v.317, 1958, p. 123-129. See serials consulted.

4305. SERAPHIM, Ernst. Die baltischen Provinzen in der zweiten Hälfte des 19. Jahrhunderts. In Deutsche Monatsschrift für Russland (Reval), yr 1, v.2, 1912, p. 577-595. (*QCA)NN

4306. SIDZIKAUSKAS, Vaclovas. Fiftieth anniversary of the Baltic States. In Baltic Review (New York, N.Y.), no.35, 1968, p. 3-17. See serials consulted.

4307. SMOGORZEWSKI, K. M. The Russification of the Baltic States. In World Affairs (London), v.4, no. 4, 1950, p. 468-481. See serials consulted.

4308. SOBIESKI, Wacław. Der Kampf um die Ostsee von den ältesten Zeiten bis zur Gegenwart. Leipzig, Markert & Petters, 1933. vi, 269 p. At head of title: Schriften des Baltischen Instituts. Bibliographie: p. [242]-253. DD491.045S67K NRU ICU MB MH NN

4309. DIE SOWJETUNION UND DIE Baltischen Staaten. [Berlin, Deutsche Informationsstelle, 1942] 75 p. facsims. DK511.B3S7 DLC CaAEU

4310. SPEKKE, Arnolds. The Baltic case in the light of history. In Baltic Review (New York, N.Y.), no.35, 1968, p. 27-38. See serials consulted.

4311. STANKA, Vladimir Benediktovich. Sud'by narodov Rossii; Bielorussiia. Ukraina. Litva. Latviia. Estoniia. Armeniia. Gruziniia. Azerbaidzhan. Finliandiia. Pol'sha. [Vladimir B. Stankevich] Berlin, I.P. Ladyzhnikov, 1921. 373 p. illus. DK33.S8 DLC CaAEU NN PU

4312. SWETTENHAM, John Alexander. The tragedy of the Baltic States; a report compiled from official documents and eyewitnesses' reports. New York, N.Y., Praeger [1954] xi, 216 p. map. (Praeger publications in Russian history and world communism, 15) DK511.B3S9 1954 DLC CaAEU PU

4313. TORNIUS, Valerian Hugo. Die Tragödie der Baltischen Provinzen, von Germanicus [pseud.] Leipzig, Schulze & Co., 1915. 30 p. (Kriegs-Zeitfragen, Hft.6) DK511. B3T55 DLC NN

4314. TOWNSEND, Mary Evelyn. The Baltic states. [New York, N.Y.] The Institute of International Education, 1921. 30 p. (International relations clubs, syllabus no.10) DK511.B3T6 DLC CLU CU In IU MnU NN NBuU NcD OCl OCU PBm PPT PPiU TxDaM

4315. LA TRAGÉDIE DES ÉTATS BALTES; peuples opprimés. [By Stasys Bačkis] Paris, Monde nouveau [1952] 81 p. Bibliographie: p. 77-81. D802.B3T7 DLC CtPAM PU

4316. TRUMPA, Vincas. Some aspects of the Baltic area problem.

In Lituanus (Brooklyn, N.Y.), v.4,
no.1, 1958. p. 11-15. See serials
consulted.

4317. VIZULIS, I. The diplomacy
of the Allied Powers toward the
Baltic states, 1942-1954. In Baltic Review (New York, N.Y.), no.35,
1968, p. 49-61. See serials consulted.

4318. WITHDRAWAL OF GERMAN FORCES
from the Baltic Provinces. July 3-
December 16, 1939. In Gt. Brit.
Foreign Office. Documents on British foreign policy, 1919-1939.
London, H.M.S.O., 1949, 1st series,
v.3. DA566.7.A18 DLC

4319. WITTRAM, Reinhard. Baltische Geschichte; die Ostseelande:
Livland, Estland, Kurland, 1180-
1918. Erläuterung von Heinrich
Laakmann. München, R. Oldenbourg,
1954. 323 p. maps. (Geschichte
der Völker und Staaten) DK511.
B3W52 DLC

4320. --- Drei Generationen;
Deutschland, Livland, Russland,
1830-1914. Göttingen Deuerlich,
1949. 360 p. plates, ports.
CS887.V57 1949 DLC CaAEU CU MH NIC
NN NNC NcD

X.4. GENERAL STUDIES OF LITHUANIAN
HISTORY

4321. ANTONOVICH, Vladimir Bonifat'evich. Istoriia Velikogo Knia-
zievstva Litovskogo vod naidavnei-
shikh chasov azh' do upadku udiel'-
noi sistemy v Litovskoi Rusi. V.
Antonovicha i D. Ilovaiskogo. Ter-
nopol, I. Pavlovskii, 1887. 207 p.
(Ruska istorichna biblioteka, t.6)
DK508A2R87 t.6 CtY (Photocopy positive) BM

4322. --- Monografii po istorii
Zapadnoi i IUgozapadnoi Rossii.
Kiev, Tip. E. IA. Fedorova, 1885- .
DK511.L2A7 DLC CtY MH(v.1) PU WU
WaU(has microfiche v.1)

4323. --- Ocherk istorii Velikogo
Kniazhestva Litovskogo do poloviny
XV stoletiia. Vyp. 1. Kiev, Uni-
versitetskaia Tip., 1878. ii, 156
p. 947.52.An89 PU MH NN
BM(9455. de. 19.)

4234. BALIŃSKI, Michał. Studia
historyczne. Wilno, 1856. vi, 367
p. DK511.L2B32 PU

4325. --- Wielkie Księstwo Litew-

skie. In His Starożytna Polska.
Warszawa, 1886. v.4. DK420.B34
t.4 DLC PU

4326. BANDTKIE, Jerzy Samuel.
Historisch-kritische Analecten zur
Erläuterung der Geschichte des Os-
tens von Europa. Breslau, Goso-
horsky, 1802. xii, 308 p.
BM(1436. b. 8.)

4327. BATIUSHKOV, Peomei Nikolaevich, ed. Bielorussiia i Litva.
Istoricheskiia sud'by Sieverozapad-
nago kraia. Sanktpeterburg, Tip.
"Obshchestvennaia tovarichestva
pol'za", 1890. xxiv, 376, 183 p.
illus., map, ports. Bibliography:
p. 1-38. DK507.B333 CSt-H CaBVaU
ICU InU IU MH NN NNC BM(9456. g. 10.)

4328. BELIAEV, Ivan Dmitrievich.
Ocherk istorii Severo-Zapadnago
kraia Rossii. Vil'na, Tip. A.D.
Syrkina, 1867. 121 p. 947.7.B410 IU

4329. BIELSKI, Jan. Widok królewstwa Polskiego ze wszystkiemi
woiewodztwami, Xięstwy y ziemiami.
.. [Poznań] W Drukarni J. K. Mci
Collegium Soc. Jesu, 1763. [16],
301 p. 947.52.B478 PU

4330. BIRŽIŠKA, Vaclovas. Praei-
ties pabiros; rinkinys straipsnių
iš Lietuvos praeities. [From the
past; a collection of articles from
Lithuania's past] Brooklyn, N.Y.,
Karys, 1960. 352 p. illus.
DK511.L2B52 DLC CaAEU CaOTU CtY
CtTMF MH NN PU

4331. BRIANTSEV, Pavel Dmitrievich. Istoriia Litovskago gosudarstva s drevnieishikh vremen.
Vil'na, Tip. A. G. Syrkina, 1889.
xii, 659 p. DK511.L2B68 DLC CU InU
KU NN PU

4332. --- Ocherk drevnei Litvy i
Zapadnoi Rossii. Izd. 2-oe. Vil'-
na, A. G. Syrkina, 1896. 150 p.
Balt 7848.96 MH

4333. BROHM, Karl Friedrich
August. Geschichte von Polen und
Litauen seit der Entstehung dieser
Reiche bis auf die neuesten Zeiten.
.. Posen, 1810-11. 2 v. in 1.
tables. Ra943.8.B861 NSyU MH

4334. BRÜCKNER, Alexander. Starożytna Litwa; ludy i bogi. Szkice
historyczne i mitologiczne. Warszawa, Nakł. Księgarni Naukowej,
1904. iv, 166 p. DK511.L21P78 CU
ICU ICLJF InU MH PPULC PU

4335. CATHOLIC CHURCH. CANONS,
DECRETALS, ETC. Decretales summorum

Pontificum pro regno Poloniae et constitutiones synodorum provincialium et diaecesanarum regni ejusdem ad summan collectae... Edited by Edward Likowski and Z. Chodyński. Poznaniae, J. Leitgeber, 1882-89. 3 v. DLC

4336. CURIEUSER GESCHICHTS-CA-LENDER ... des Königreichs Polen und Grosshertzogthumbs Litthauen von Anno 1500 bis 1697. Leipzig, 1697. 125 p. illus. 232.9.H67e IU BM(1436. c. 32) MH NcD

4337. CZACKI, Tadeusz. Dzieła, zebrane i wydane przez Edwarda Raczyńskiego. Poznań, W Nowej Księgarni, 1843-45. 3 v. in 2, plates, tables. 947.52.C998.2 PU

4338. DAUKANTAS, Simanas. Budą senowęs-lėtuwiu kalnienu ir žemajtiu. Plymouth, Pa., 1892. vi, 216 p. 947.52.D269 PU CtPAM CtTMF ICCC MH MB

4339. --- Būdą senovės lietuvių, kalnėnų ir žemaičių išrašė Jokūbas Laukys [pseud.] Kaunas, Sakalas, 1935. 947.52.D269 PU

4340. --- --- Redagavo ir žodynėlį pridėjo J. Talmantas. [Viršelio aplanką piešė Viktoras Petravičius. Atspausta foto offsetu, pakartojant 3. laidą. A history of ancient Lithuanians, Samogitians, etc.] Čikagoje, Vytautas Saulius, 1954. xxxi, 359 p. port. DK511. L23D36 1954 DLC CtPAM CtY CaOTU ICCC MB MH OCl PU

4341. ---Darbay senuju Lituwiu yr Zemaycziu, 1822. Spaudai paruošė Vaclovas ir Mykolas Biržiškai. [A history of ancient Lithuanians, etc.] Kaunas, Spindulio spaustuvė, 1929. 213 p. facsims. DK511.L24D3 DLC CU ICU OCl PU

4342. --- Lietuvos istorija nū seniausių gadynių iki Gediminui, D.L. K. [Lithuanian history from the ancient times until the reign of Gediminas, Grand Duke of Lithuania] Plymouth, Pa., Kasztu ir spaustuvėje J. Paukszczio, 1893-97. 2 v. in 1., port. DK511.L23D37 DLC CtTMF ICBM ICCC(1-2) ICLJF KU MB MH NIC OCl OKentU PU RP WaS BM(9456. e.5.)

4343. --- Pasakojimai apie veikalus Lietuvių tautos senovėje. [A description of ancient Lithuanian deeds] Iszleista per J. Kauniszkį, Bitėnai, 1893-[1899] 2 pts. in 1 v. 240 p. 947.5.D28p PPi CtTMF OCl PU

4344. --- Rinktiniai raštai. [Selected works. Comp. by M. Lukšienė] Kaunas, VGLL, 1955. 479 p. port., facsims. DK511.L2D3 DLC CaAEU CtPAM CLU ICCC InU NN PU

4345. DLUGOSZ, Jan. Historia Polonica. Lipsiae, Svmptibus I.L. Gleditschii, 1711-12. 2 v. DK419. D58 DLC CU MH MiU NN NjP

4346. --- Opera omnia [Dzieła wszystkie] cura Alexandri Przezdziecki edita. [Cracoviae, e typographia ephemeridum, 1863-87] 14 v. Latin and Polish. Includes his Historia Polonica. DK425.3.D62 1863 CaAEU CaBVaU ICU MH NN

4347. EHRET, Joseph. Litauen in Vergangenheit, Gegenwart und Zukunft. Bern, A. Francke, 1919. 492 p. illus., maps, plates, ports. DK511.L2E33 CSt-H CtY CU ICU KU

4348. --- La Lituanie passé, présent, avenir. Genève, Edition Atar, 1919. 480 p. illus., col. front., plates, ports., fold. maps. DK511. L2E333 CSt-H CU CaAEU ICBM InU InW MH PU

--- FAJNHAUS, David. Ruch konspiracyjny na Litwie i Białorusi, 1846-1848. Warszawa, 1965. See entry no. 3729.

--- FORSTREUTER, Kurt. Deutschland und Litauen im Mittelalter. Köln, 1962. See etnry no. 2969.

4349. GERUTIS, Albertas. Lithuania 700 years. Edited by Dr. Albertas Gerutis. Translated by Algirdas Budreckis. Inrod. by Raphael Sealey. 2d rev. ed. New York, N.Y., Manyland Books [1969] xiv, 458 p. illus., map, ports. Bibliography: p. 433-448. DK511.L2G5 DLC CaBVaU CaBVaS CaAEU CaOLU CaOTY CaOTU CoU CtY CtPAM ICBM IaU InND InU IEN MH MU MWalB NIC NcU NhU NbU NjP NSyU NcD OCl OClW PPiU PU RPB TxU VtU WaU WU

4350. GRUSHEVSKII, Aleksandr Sergieevich. Ocherk istorii Turovo-Pinskago kniazhestva... [Kiev, Tip. Imp. Universiteta, 1901-1903] 3 v. in 1., fold. maps. DK511.L2G8 ICU

4351. GUAGNINO, Alessandro. Chorographia totius Poloniae, Lithuaniae... Basileae, 1585. In Pistorius, Johann. Polonicae historiae corpus... Basileae, 1585. Tomus 1. BM(1485. dd. 2.) NN

4352. --- Kronika Sarmacyey Europ-

skiey, w którey się zamyka królews-
two Polskie ze wszystkiemi Panstwy,
Xięstwy, y Prowincyami swemi: tudzież też Wielkie Xięstwo Lithewskie,
Ruskie... Moskiewskie, y część Tatarów przez Paszkowskiego... z lacin-
skiego na polskie przełożona. Kraków, M. Lob, 1611. 9 pts.
BM(9475. g. 4.)

4353. --- --- [Another edition]
Kraków, Nakł. Wydawn. Biblioteki
Polskiej, 1860. iv, 375 p. 947.52.
G932 PU

4354. --- Rerum Polonicarum tomi
tres: quorum primus omnium Poloniae
regum... tum principum Lituaniae,
chronologicam recensionem, ac singu-
lorum res gestas complectitur.
Francofurti, Excudebat Ioann. Wech-
selus, impensis Sigis. Feyerabendij,
1584. 3 v. in 1. DK414.A2G9 ICU NN

4355. --- --- [Another edition]
Warszawa, 1768. 714 p. (Zbiór
dziejopisów polskich, t.4) DK414.
Z39 v.4 ICU

4356. --- Sarmatiae europeae descriptio, quae regnum Poloniae, Lituaniam, Samogitiam, Russiam, Mas-
coviam, Prussiam, Pomeraniam, Livoniam et Moschoviae, Tartatiaeque
partem complectitur, Alexandri
Gwagnini Veronensis... conscriptae.
Cracoviae, M. Wierzbięta, 1578. 6
pts. illus. (*KB 1578)NN
BM(152. h. 1.)

4357. --- --- Cum supplementi loco ea quae gesta sunt superiori anno. Spirae, Apvd Bernardvm Albinvm
1581. 119 leaves. 947.52.0932.2
PU BM(798. cc. 9.)

HALECKI, Oskar. Geschichte
der Union Litauens mit Polen. Wien,
1919. See entry no. 3060.

4358. HARTKNOCH, Christoph. De
repvblica polonica libri dvo, qvo-
rvm... posterior autem jus publicum
reipuplicae polonicae, lituanicae
provinciarumque... Edito tertia al-
tero tanto fere auctior. Lipsiae,
Impensis Martini Hellervordii, 1698.
[16], 884, 115, [53] p. DK419.H3
1698 DLC ICU PU

4359. HAUTEVILLE, de, pseud. [i.g.
Gaspard de Tende]. Polnischer Staat;
oder, Eigentliche Beschreibung des
Königreichs Polen, und des Grossher-
zogthums Lithauen. Cologne, Peter
Marteau, 1697. 172 p.
BM(10290. bbb. 37.)

4360. HRUSHEVS'KYI, Mykhailo. Is-
toryia Ukrainy-Rusy. U Lvovi, Nakl.

Naukovoho t-va im. Shevchenka,
1898-1931. 9 v. fold. col. maps.
(Zbirnyk istorychno-filosofichnoi
sektsii Nauk, tov. im. Shevchenka,
t. 1-4; 6-8; 12-13) DK508.7.H68 DLC

4361. --- --- New York, N.Y., Kny-
hospilka, 1954-58. 10 v. in 11.
maps, ports. Facsimile reproduction of Kiev; Lvov, 1907-1936 ed.
DK508.H683 DLC CaAEU NN

4362. HUSLYSTYI, Kost' H. Ukraina pid lytovs'kym panuvanniam u
zakhoplennia ii Polsheiu, z XIV st.
po 1569. Kyiv, Vydavnytstvo Akademii nauk URSR, 1939. 194 p. illus.,
facsims, ports. (Narysy istorii
Ukrainy, vyp. 2) (*QGA)NN

4363. JABLONOWSKI, Horst. West-
russland zwischen Wilna und Moskau.
Die politische Stellung und die po-
litischen Tendenzen der russischen
Bevölkerung des Grossfürstentums
Litauen im 15. Jahrh. Leiden, E.
J. Brill, 1955. 167 p. fold. map.
(Studien zur Geschichte Osteuropas,
2) DK511.L23J3 DLC AZU CLU CU
CaAEU CaBVaS CaBVaU CaOHM CaQMM
CaOTU CoU CtY FU GU HU ICU IaU InU
IEN MH NIC NN NNC NcD NcU NjP NjR
OCl OkU OrU PPiU PU RPB TxHU TxU TU

JAROSZEWICZ, Jozéf. Obraz
Litwy pod względem jęj cywilizacji,
od czasów najdawniejszych do końca
wieku XVIII. Wilno, 1844-1845.
See entry no. 1020.

4364. JASIENICA, Paweł, pseud.
Polska Jagiellonów [Wyd. 1. Warsza-
wa] Państwowy Instytut Wydawniczy
[1963] 451 p. illus., ports.
DK425.J3 DLC ICU MiU MiD MH NN
CaAEU CaOTU

4365. JEZIERSKI, Edmund. Litwa z
Koroną... Warszawa, Nakł. Kasy
Przezorności i Pomocy Warszawskich
Pomocników Księgarskich, 1919. 226
p. DK511.L23J4 DLC CSt CU KU NN
NcD PU

4366. JOLLI, J.G. Histoire de Pologne, et du Grand Duché de Lithuanie,
depuis la fondation de la monarchie
jusques à present. Où l'on voit une
relation fidèle dece qui s'est passé
à la dernière élection. Amsterdam,
Daniel Pain, 1698. [16] 457 [14] p.
CLU

4367. --- Histoire des rois et du
royaume de Pologne et du grand Duché
de Lithuanie depuis la fondation de
la monarchie jusques à présent. Ou
l'on voit une relation fidèle de ce
qui s'est passé à la dernière élection. Amsterdam, D. Pain, 1699. 2 v.

Rare DK414.J75 1699 NIC DLC NN

4368. KATSEL', I.A. Istoria Litvy. Kovno, 1921. maps.
DK511.L2K34 DLC

4369. KLEIN, Boris Samuilovich. Naideno v arkhive. Minsk, "Belarus' 1968. 192 p. illus. DK507.5.K55 DLC CaAEU CaBVaU CtY ICU InU MH NNC NcD NcU NjP PPiU ViU MU

4370. KLIMAS, Petras. Lietuvių senobės bruožai. [Prehistory of Lithuania] Vilnius, "Žaibo" spaustuvėje, 1919. 169 p. (Lietuvių mokslo draugijos leidinys, 31) DK511.L23K53 DLC CtTMF PU

4371. KOIALOVICH, Mikhail Iosifovich. Chteniia po istorii Zapadnoi Rossii. Izd. 4. Sanktpeterburg [Tip. A.S. Suvorina] 1884. 341 p. fold. map. First ed. published under title: Lektsii po istorii Zapadnoi Rossii. Moskva, 1864. 947.7.K82l 1884 IU CaBVaS CaOTU ICU NNC NjR PU

4372. KOJAŁOWICZ, Wojciech Wijuk. Historiae lituanae pars prior; de rebus lituanorum ante susceptam christianam religionam conjunctionamque Magni Lituaniae Ducatus cum regno Poloniae libri novem. (Historiae lituanae a conjunctione. Magni Ducatus cum Regno Poloniae ad unionem eorum dominiorum libri octo) Antverpiae; Dantisci, Sumptibus G. Försteri, 1650-69. 2 v. 947.52.K827.2 PU BM(149. b. 10,11.) NjP

4373. KOŁANKOWSKI, Ludwik. Dzieje Wielkiego Księstwa Litewskiego za Jagiellonów. Warszawa, Skład główny: Kasa im. Mianowskiego, 1930- . Available only v.1 covering the period of 1377-1499. DK511.L2K65 DLC CU CtY FU ICU InU KU MH NN NNC OrU PU WaU

4374. --- Polska Jagiellonów; dzieje polityczne. Lwów, Skł. gł. w Księg. Gubrinowicza, 1936. 374 p. illus., ports. map. Bibliography: p. [337]-348. DK425.K6 DLC NN PU

4375. KONECZNY, Feliks. Dzieje Polski za Jagiellonów. Kraków, Nakładem Krak. Towarzystwa Oświaty Ludowej, 1903. 358 p. tables. CDU CtY DLC MH NN NNC

4376. KOTZEBUE, August Friedrich Ferdinand von. Switrigail; ein Beytrag zu den Geschichten von Litauen, Russland, Polen und Preussen. Leipzig, 1820. vi, 170 p. 947.52.Sv35.yK PU BM(9454. bb. 9.) MH

4377. KUKOL'NIK, Pavel Vasil'evich. Istoricheskiia zametki o Litvie. Vil'na, V tipografii A.K. Kirkora, 1864. 245 p. DK511.L2K8 DLC PU

4378. LAPPO, Ivan Ivanovich. Zapadnaia Rossia i eia soedinenie s Pol'sheiu v ikh istoricheskom proshlom; istoricheskie ocherki. Praga, Isd-vo "Plamia", 1924. 225 p. Bibliography: p. 211-225. DK434.9.L3 DLC CtY ICU InU IU NIC NN NjP NcD PU RPB TxU

4379. LELEWEL, Joachim. Dzieje Litwy i Rusi aż do unji z Polską w Lublinie 1569 zawartej. Wydanie drugie przejrzane i poprawione. Poznań, Nakładem i drukiem W. Stefańskiego, 1844. 202 p. DK414.L52 DLC CtY IU KU MoU ScU

4380. --- --- [Another edition] Poznań, Nakł. Księg. J.K. Żupańskiego, 1863. viii, 492 p. facsims. DK511.L2L47 ICU

4381. --- --- Opracował Jerzy Ochmański. Wstemp poprzedził Henryk Łowmiański. Warszawa, 1969. (His Dzieła... t.10) DK511.L23L44 1969 PU

4382. --- Histoire de la Lithuanie et de la Ruthénie jusqu'a leur union définitive avec la Pologne, conclue à Lublin en 1569. Tr. par E. Rykaczewski. Paris et Leipzig, A. Franck, 1861. xci, 228 p. maps. DK511.L2L5 DLC CU ICU KU MH MdBP MiU OkU PU

4383. LIETUVOS TSR MOKSLŲ AKADEMIJA, VILNA. 40 metų. [Forty years) Vilnius, VPMLL, 1958. 330 p. illus. DK511.L27L493 DLC PU

4384. LIMANOWSKI, Bolesław. Historya Litwy pokrótce opowiedziana. Nakładem Towarzystwa Litewskiego "Żelmuo" w Paryżu. Chicago, Ill., Drukiem i czcionkami "Zgody", organu Związku Narodowego Polskiego w Stanach Zjednoczonych Północnej Ameryki, 1895. 61 p. ports. 947.5.L629 MnU

4385. Litauen und seine Deutschen. Würzburg, 1955. See entry no. 3607.

4386. LIUBAVSKII, Matvei Kuz'mich. Lietuvos istorija ligi Liublino unijos. 1. dalis. Iš rusų kalbos vertė J. Sondeckis. [Lithuanian history until Lublin Union] Vilnius, Švyturio spaustuvė, 1920. (Lietuvių mokslo draugijos leidinys) 947.5.L743LS PU ICCC

--- Ocherk istorii litovsko-russkago gosudarstva... Moskva, 1910. See entry no. 2536-2538.

4387. ŁOWMIAŃSKI, Henryk. Uwagi o genezie państwa litewskiego. In Przegląd Historyczny (Warszawa), v.52, 1961, p. 127-146. See serials consulted.

4388. MACIEJ Z MIECHOWA. Descriptio sarmatiarum Asianae, Europianae ... [Cracoviae] 1521. 1 reel. Microfilm (negative). The original in the British Museum. Film 1627. 01.606 1521 NjP

4389. --- Traktat o dvukh sarmatiiakh. Vvedenie, perevod i kommentarii S.A. Anniiskogo. Moskva, Akademiia nauk SSSR, 1936. x, 268 p. facsims. (Izvestiia inostrantsev o narodakh SSSR) NN NjP

4390. MAUCLÈRE, Jean. O paiz do cavalleiro branco; ensaio de historia do povo lithuano. Traducção de Vina Centi. São Paulo-Brasil, Empreza graphica da "Revista dos tribunaes", 1932. 175 p. plates. DK511.L2MC DLC CSt-H CLU CU MiU PU WaU

4391. --- Le pays du chevalier blanc; essai d'histoire du peuple lithuanien. Paris, Édition Spes, 1930. 270 p. plates, port. DK511.L2M447 CSt-H CU CaOTU CoU CtY ICBM InNd MiU PU WaS

--- Sous le ciel pâle de Lithuanie. Paris [1926] See entry no. 1086.

4392. MIKŠYS, Liudas. Iš istorijos ūkanų ateina Lietuva. [From nebulous history, Lithuania emerges] Chicago, Ill., Draugas, 1967. 699 p. DK511.L22M53 PU CaAEU ICBM

4393. MORAWSKI, Kazimierz. Czasy Zygmuntowskie na tle prądów Odrodzenia. [Opracował i wstepem zaopatrzył Janusz Tazbir. Wyd. 1. Warszawa] Panstwowy Instytut Wydawniczy [1965] 180 p. illus., facsims., ports. Based on edition of: Warszawa, Instytut Wydawniczy "Biblioteka Polska", 1922. DK428.M65 1965 DLC CaAEU ICU MiDW MH MU NN OCl

4394. NADWIŚLAK, Szymon. Dwanaście Opowiadań z dziejów Polski, Litwy i Rusi... Wydanie nowe. Gródek, 1904. 354 p. BM(012590. ccc. 29.)

4395. NARBUTT, Teodor. Dzieje narodu litewskiego w krótkości zebrane. Wilno, Nakł. R. Rafałowicza, 1847. vii, 244 p. geneal. tables. DK511.L2H37 CtY IU MH PU BM(9476. g. 21.)

4396. --- Dzieje starożytne narodu

litewskiego. Wilno, Malinowski, 1835-1841. 9 v. illus., plates, (part. fold.) maps, tables, plan. DK511.L2N372 CtY CoU ICLJF KU MH PU BM(9475. d. 4.)

4397. --- T. Narbutta pomniejsze pisma historyczne, szczególnie do historyi Litwy odnoszące się. Wilno, T. Glücksberg, 1856. 300 p. illus. DK511.L2N27 CU ICLJF MH PU BM(9475. d.)

4398. OBST, Jan. Litwa w świetle prawdy historycznej. Wilno, Nakładem Księgarni W. i K. Mikulskich, 1922. 80 p. DK511.L2012 CaAEU PU

4399. OCHMAŃSKI, Jerzy. Historia Litwy. Wrocław, Zakład Narodowy im. Ossolińskich, 1967. 346 p. illus, maps (part. fold.), ports. Bibliography: p. 295-[314]. DK511.L2024 DLC CaAEU CaBVaU CaOTU CtPAM CSt CtY ICU InNd InU IU KU MH NIC NN NBuU NcD NUC NjP PU WU

4400. PASHUTO, Vladimir Terent'evich. Lietuvos valstybės susidarymas. Vilnius, 1971. 424 p. maps. At head of title: V. Pašuta. DK511.L23P316 DLC PU

4401. --- Obrazovanie Litovskogo gosudarstva. Moskva, Izd-vo Akademii nauk SSSR, 1959. 530 p. 2 fold. maps. At head of title: Akademiia nauk SSSR. Institut istorii. Bibliography: p. 427-[464]. DK511.L23P26 CLU CaQMM CaOTU CtY CoU ICU InU IU KU NNC NcD NcU NjP PU RPB TxU

4402. PASZKIEWICZ, Henryk. Jagiellonowie a Moskwa. Tom 1: Litwa a Moskwa w XIII i XIV wieku. Warszawa, 1933. 454 p. DK425.P3 DLC ICBM InU KU MH NN NNC NjP PPiU PU

4403. --- The making of a Russian nation. [Chicago, Ill.] H. Regnery [1963] 509 p. maps. Bibliography: p. 416-485. DK71.P29 1963a DLC CaAEU CaOTIM CLU DS IU MH MiU NN NNC NjP WU

4404. --- The origin of Russia. London, Allen & Unwin [1954] xii, 556 p. 2 fold. maps, geneal. tables. Bibliography: p. 470-519. DK511.P3 1954 DLC CaAEU NcD PU

4405. PICHETA, Vladimir Ivanovich. Belorussiia i Litva 15-16 vv.; issledovaniia po istorii sotsial'no-ekonomicheskogo, politicheskogo i kul'turnogo razvitiia. Moskva, Izd-vo Akademii nauk SSSR, 1961. 814 p. DK507.65.P5 DLC CaAEU CaQMM CaOTU CLU CU CSt CtPAM CtY FU GU HU

ICU IEU IaU InND IU MH MnU MU NIC
NN NcD NcU NNC NjR NSyU OrU PPiU
PU TxU VtU ViU WaU TU WU

--- Istoriia Litovskogo gosudarstva do Liublinskoi unii.
See entry no. 4478.

4406. PRESNIAKOV, Aleksandr Ev-
gen'evich. Lektsii po russkoi is-
torii. Moskva, Gos. sotsial'no-
ekonom. Izd-vo, 1938-1939. 2 v.
Contents.--T.1. vyp.1. Kievskaia
Rus'.--T.2. Vyp.1. Zapadnaia Rus'
i litovsko-russkoe gosudarstvo.
DK40.P7 DLC AzU CaBVaU CaOLU CaSSU
CtY CoU FU GU HU IaU InU IEN InNd
IU KU MoU MWalB NN NcU NBuU NmU
NjR OrU PU TU ViU WU

4407. --- --- Moskva, Gos. sotsial'no-ekon. izd-vo, 1938-39.
[The Hague, Europe Printing, 1966]
2 v. in 1. (Russian reprint series,
25) DK40.P93 1966 CaAEU CaOTU
CaOTY IEN ICU KU NcD ScU

4408. --- Zapadnaia Rus' i litovsko-russkoe gosudarstvo. In His
Lektsii po russkoi istorii. Moskva,
1939. v.2, vyp.1. See entry no.
4406 and 4407.

--- Respublica; sive, Status Regni Poloniae, Lituaniae,
Prussiae, etc. Diversorum autorum.
Lugduni Batavorum, ex officina Elzeviriana, 1627. See entry no.
798.

4409. RHODE, Gotthold. Die Ostgrenze Polens... Bd. 1. Im Mittelalter bis zum Jahre 1401. Köln,
Böhlau-Verlag, 1955. xvi, 457 p.
maps, tables. (Ostmitteleuropa in
Vergangenheit und Gegenwart no.2)
DK418.R5 DLC CaAEU PU

RÖMERIS, Mykolas. Stosunki
etnograficzno-kulturalne na Litwie.
Kraków, 1905. See entry no. 1045.

4410. SALVATORI, Guiseppe. I Lituani di ieri e di oggi... Bologna,
L. Coppelli [1932] [5]-189 p.,
plates. DK511.L2S3 CU CtPAM MH PU

4411. ŠAPOKA, Adolfas. Lietuva
iki Vytauto [Lithuania until Vytau-
tas] In Šležas, Paulius, ed. Vytautas Didysis. Kaunas, 1930. p.
xv-xxiv. DK511.L23S48 DLC CtTMF PU

4412. SAPUNOV, Aleksei Parfenovich, comp. Kratkii ocherk bor'by
Moskovskago gosudarstva s Litvoiu i
Pol'sheiu v XIV-XVII v. Vitebsk,
1885. p. 3-76. (In His Vitebskaia
starina, t.4, ch.1.) NN

4413. SCHLÖZER, August Ludwig von.
Geschichte von Lithauen als einem
eigenen Grossfürstenthum bis zum
Jahre 1569. Halle, Gebauer, 1785.
BM; also In Baumgarten, Siegmund J.
Fortsetzung der Algemeine Welthis-
torie. Halle, 1785, v.50, p. 1-300.
DK511.B3S34 CaAEU MH NN WU

4414. SHCHEBALSKII, Piotr Karlo-
vich. Razskazy o Zapadnoi Rusi.
2. izd. Moskva, Tipografiia Bakh-
meteva, 1866. 139, iv p.
L970.2Sč ICLJF

4415. SKIRMUNTT, Konstancija.
Nad Niemnem i nad Baltykiem w zaraniu dziejów. Warszawa, Gebethner
i Wolff [1897]-1919. 3 v. fold.
map. DK511.L23S46 DLC KU OCl PU
BM(9475. b. 52.)

4416. ŠLIŪPAS, Jonas. Lietuvių
tauta senovėje ir šiandien. [Li-
thuanian nation in the past and
present. By.] John Szlupas. Plymouth, Pa., Spauda ir kaštai
"Vienybės Lietuvninku", 1904-1905.
2 v. illus., maps. DK511.L2S863
DLC CtPAM CtTMF CtY ICBM ICLJF MH
NN PU WaS

4417. SPOŁECZNOŚĆ AKADEMICKA UNI-
WERSYTETU STEFANA BATOREGO NA OB-
CZYŹNIE. Dzieje ziem Wielkiego
Księstwa Litewskiego; cykł wykładów.
Londyn, 1953. 398 p. illus.,
ports., fold. map. (Alma Mater
Vilnensis, zesz. 3) LF4425.V55A4
vol.3 DLC CaOTU ICU PU WaU

4418. STANG, Christian Schwei-
gaard. Die westrussische Kanzlei-
sprache des Grossfürstentums Litau-
en. Oslo, Det Norske Videnskaps
Akademie, 1935. 166 p. facsims.
(Norske Videnskaps Akademie i Oslo.
Historisk-Filosofisk Klasse.
Skrifter, no. 2) AS283.057 1935
no.2 DLC CaAEU ICU NIC NN NCC NNU
PU WU

4419. VISCONT, Antoine. La Lituanie et la guerre; 9 planches
hors-texte et 2 cartes. Genève,
Edition "Atar", 1917. 206 p.
illus., ports., 2 fold. maps.
DK511.L2V5 DLC CSt-H ICU ICLJF IU
MB NN NNC NcD PU WU

VOLDEMARAS, Augustinas. La
Lithuanie et ses problèmes. Lille
[1933]. See entry no. 3040.

4420. WASILEWSKI, Leon. Kresy
wschodnie; Litwa i Białoruś, Pod-
lasie i Chelmszczyzna, Galicya
wschodnia, Ukraina. Warszawa, Tow.
Wydawnicze w Warszawie, 1917. 4 v.
in 1. 947.52.V284.3 PU MH

4421. --- Litwa i Białoruś; przeszłość; terasniejszość; tendencje rozwojowe. Kraków, Książka, 1912. 361 p. DK511.L2W32 CaAEU CaOTU CtY ICU IU MH NN NNC NjP PU WU

--- Litwa i Białoruś; zarys historyczno-polityczny stosunków narodowościowych. Warszawa, 1925. See entry no. 2072.

4422. --- Die Ostprovinzen des alten Polenreichs (Lithauen und Weissruthenien, die Landschaft Chełm-Ostgalizien-die Ukraina). Karkau, Zentral Verlagsbureau des Polnischen Obersten National-komitees, 1916. 364 p. diagrs. D651.P7W318 CSt-H DLC ICU KU MH NN

X.5. MINOR WORKS, OUTLINES, ETC.

4423. ADAMUS, Jan. O tytule panującego i państwa litewskiego parę spostrzeżeń. In Kwartalnik Historychny (Lwów), v.44, no.1, 1933, p. 313-332. See serials consulted.

4424. AGARAS, A. Lengvutė lietuvos istorija. [A short history of Lithuania] 1910. A. Maciejauskas. Ryga, išleido A. Maciejauskas, 1910. 88 p. illus. Reverse side: Lithuania (History). T947.5.A261 CaOTP

4425. AVIŽONIS, Konstantinas. Pastabos dėl "naujoviško V.T. Pašuto's Lietuvos valstybės pradžios aiškinimo". [Remarks about V.T. Pashuto's new interpretation of the beginning of the Lithuanian state] In Lituanistikos darbai (Chicago, Ill.), v.1, 1966, p. 89-93. See serials consulted.

BALTISCHE GESELLSCHAFT IN DEUTSCHLAND. Die baltischen Völker in ihrer europäischen Verpflichtung. Hannover-Döhren, 1958. See entry no. 760.

4426. BANDTKIE, Jerzy Samuel. Bieglyi vzgliad na istoriiu Litvy. In Viestnik Evropy (Sanktpeterburg), no.3-4, 1826, p. 191-213. See serials consulted.

4427. BAUMGARTEN, N. de. Polotzk et la Lithuanie, une page d'histoire. In Orientalia Christiana periodica (Roma), v.2, 1936, p. 223-253. See serials consulted.

4428. BERWINSKI, Teofil. Einige Betrachtungen über die ältesten Zustände Litauens und deren Umgestaltung im 13-ten und 14-ten Jahrhun-

dert. Trzemeczno, gedrukt bei Olawaski, 1857. 21 p. 947.Z80 NNC MH

4429. BOHDANOWICZ, Arslane. Un aperçu historique des relations entre la Horde d'or, la Pologne et la Lithuanie de 1242-1440. In Revue internationale d'histoire politique et constitutionelle, 1955, p. 186-200. See serials consulted.

4430. BRENSZTEJN. Michał Eustachy. Wystawa historyczna "Polska i Litwa" w łączności dziejowej (do roku 1863) w Wilnie we wrześniu 1935. Wilno, 1936. 16 p. (Wydawnictwa Bibljoteki Uniwersyteckiej w Wilnie, nr. 10) DK402.B7 DLC CtY

4431. A BRIEF HISTORICAL SKETCH of Lithuania. Kaunas, Bako ir Manklenės Spaustuvė [1920] 16 p. Issued also in French. DK511.L2B7 DLC

4432. BRÜCKNER, Alexander. Beiträge zur ältesten Geschichte der Slaven und Litauer. In Archiv für slavische Philologie (Berlin), v. 21, 1899, p. 10-27. See serials consulted.

4433. BŪGA, Kazimieras. Lietuvių įsikūrimas šių dienų Lietuvoje. [The settling of Lithuanians in the present territory of Lithuania] In Tauta ir žodis (Kaunas) no.1-2, 1923. See serials consulted.

4434. CHASE, Thomas George. Significance of Ruthenian and Muscovite elements in Lithuanian history. New York, N.Y., Lithuanian bulletin, 1944. 29 p. DK511.L22C48 InU CaOTU CSt-H ICBM ICLJF MH NIC PU

4435. DELLE TURBOLENZE DI POLONIA perpetuate dai p.o. Gezuiti; opera di un nunzio della Dieta, trasportata dalla lingua pollaca Venezia, Basil Graziozi, 1767. cxii, 78 p. Bound with Delle filiazioni gezuitiche... Lettera... 947.52.D383 PU MiU

4436. ESSEN, Werner. Litauen, ein europäisches Erschütterungsgebiet. In Osteuropa (Königsberg in Pr.), v.11, 1936, p. 248-259. See serials consulted.

4437. GABRYS, Juozas. La nation lituanienne; son état sous la domination russe et allemande, par Jerzy Gabrys. Paris, L. Maretheux, 1911. 24 p. DK511.L2G3 CaBVaU CaOTU MH NN

4438. GRAHAM, Malbone Watson.

The Lithuanian renaissance. In His
New governments of Eastern Europe.
New York, N.Y., 1927, p. 350-372.
D443.G56 DLC CLU CU CSt CSt-H CaAEU
CaBVaU CaOOP CaOTU GU IaU ICN InU
MH MnU NjP NSyU NcD NcU NIC NN OCl
OClW PPiU PU RPB ViU

4439. GREAT BRITAIN FOREIGN OF-
FICE. HISTORICAL SECTION. Russian,
Poland, Lithuania and White Russia.
London, H.M.S.O., 1920. 144 p.
incl. tables. (Handbooks, no.44;
Peace handbooks, v. VIII, no. 2)
DK507.G7 DLC CU CSt-H CaBVaU CaOTP
CaOTU CtY MH NN NNC NcD MnU OCl
OrU RPB TxU NjP

4440. GUAGNINO, Alessandro. Samogitia... In Respublica, sive
status regni Poloniae, Lituaniae,
Prussiae... Leiden, 1627. DK405.
R43 DLC CaBVaU BM NN

4441. GUSTAINIS, Valentinas.
Lithuania; the first twenty years.
In Slavonic and East European Review (London), v.17, no.51, 1939,
p. 606-617. See serials consulted.

4442. HALECKI, Oskar. Litwa,
Ruś i Żmudź, jako części składowe
Wielkiego Księstwa Litewskiego.
Kraków, Nakł. Akademii Umiejetności,
1916. 43 p. DK418.5.L7H18 InU

4443. HELLMANN, Manfred. Die geschichtliche Bedeutung des Grossfürstentums Litauen. In Saeculum
(Freiburg; München), v.9, no.1,
1958, p. 87-112. See serials consulted.

4444. --- Grundzüge der Geschichte
Litauens und des litauischen Volkes.
Darmstadt, Wissenschaftliche Buch-
gesellschaft, 1966. 179 p. 2 maps.
(Grundzüge, Bd.5) DK511.L2H37 DLC
CaAEU CSt CaOTU CtPAM InNd NIC InU
MH MnU NcU MU NNC NjP PU TxU WaU

4445. BERBERSTEIN, Sigismund. De
Lithuania, 1549. In Pistorius, Johann, of Nidda. Polonicae historiae corpus, 1582. BM(1485. dd. 2.)

4446. HERTMANOWICZ, Joseph John.
A brief historical sketch on Lithu-
ania. Chicago, Ill., Lithuanian
National League of America, 1943.
48 p. illus., ports., map.
DK511.L2H39 DLC ICBM IU NN

4447. --- Historical outlines on
Lithuania; part I. The republic of
Lithuania; part II. Ancient Lithu-
ania... Chicago, Ill., The Edgar A.
Russell Company, 1921. 43 p.
illus., fold. map. DK511.L2H4 DLC
ICBM ICN ICU NN NBuU OO BM

4448. HRUSHEVS'KYI, A. S. Ocherk
istorii Turovo-Pin'skago Kniazhestva
v sostave Litovsko-russkago gosudarstva XIV do XVI v. In Kiev. Universitet. Universitetskiia Izvestiia, 1902. See serials consulted.

4449. HRYSZKIEWICZ, Wincenty.
Rola ziem białoruskich w unjach
polsko-litewskich. In PZHP w Wilnie 17-20 września 1935. Referaty
(Lwów), v.1, 1935, p. 181-188. See
serials consulted.

4450. IN THE NAME OF THE LITHU-
anian people. Wolfberg, "Perkūnas",
1945. 71 p. D809.L515 DLC NSyU PU

4451. IR EIKIM LIETUVOS KELIU.
Trumpos paskaitos iš Lietuvos istorijos. [History of Lithuania]
Kaunas, Vyr. Komitetas Nepriklausomybės atgijimo 10 metų sukaktuvėms
ruošti, 1928. 78 p. 947.5 V ICBM

4452. IVINSKIS, Zenonas. Lietuvos istorija naujų šaltinių ir po-
karinių tyrinėjimų šviesoje. [His-
tory of Lithuania according to the
new sources and the research after
the Second World War] Rome, L.K.M.
Akademija, 1964. 78 p. 947.5.Iv54.4
PU

4453. --- --- In LKMASD, v.5,
1964, p. 523-600. See serials consulted.

4454. --- Lietuvos istorija ro-
mantizmo metu ir dabar. [The history of Lithuania at the time of
romanticism and at present] In
LKMASD, v.3, 1940, p. 320-341. See
serials consulted.

4455. --- Senovės lietuvių valstybės vaidmuo Europos istorijoje.
[Lithuania's role in European his-
tory] In Židinys (Kaunas), no.5-6,
1936. p. 507-516. See serials
consulted.

JAKUBOWSKI, Jan. Studya
nad stosunkami narodowościowemi na
Litwie przed Unią Lubelską. Warszawa, 1912. See entry no. 2036.

4456. JAROSZEWICZ, Józef. O
stanie Litwy do przyjęcia wiary
chrześcijańskiej. In Znicz (Wilno),
v.1, 1834. See serials consulted.

4457. KAMIENIECKI, Witold. Geneza państwa litewskiego. In
Przegląd Historyczny (Warszawa),
v.19, 1915, p. 1-52. See serials
consulted.

4458. --- --- Warszawa, Skł. gł.
w Księg. W. Jakowickiego, 1915.

52 p. Odbitka z "Przeglądu Historycznego". DK511.L23K3 DLC PU

4459. --- Państwo litewskie. Warszawa, Drukarnia Polska (Straszewiczów), 1918. 13 p. (Wolni z wolnymi, równi z rownymi. Nr.2) 947.52.K129.3 PU NN

KLIMAS, Petras. Ghillebért de Lannoy in medieval Lithuania. New York, N.Y., 1945. See entry no. 1170.

4460. KRAEMER, Ernst. Geschichte Litauens in Einzeldarstellungen. Memel, Verlag der "Sandara" Buchhandlung, 1933. 64 p. map. 947.52.K852 PU

4461. LANDSBERGIS, Gabrielius. Lenkai ir lietuviai nuo 1228 iki 1430 m. Parašė pagal lenkiškus istorikus Žemkalnis [pseud. A history of the Polish and Lithuanian people from Polish historical sources written by Žemkalnis] Chicago, Ill., Spauda "Lietuvos", 1899. 64 p. (Tévynės mylėtojų draugijos leidinys, no. 2) 947.5.L238 PU ICLJF

4462. --- Polacy i Litwini od r. 1228 do 1430; krytyczny rzut oka według polskich historików. Wilno, Druck M. Kuchty, 1907. 75 p. 947.52.L239 PU

4463. LAURINAITIS, Vincas. S. Daukanto jaunatvės kūryba; arba S. Daukanto "Darbay senuju Lituwiu yr Zemaycziu"1822 m. ir to veikalo reikšmė. [The early works of S. Daukantas...] In KUHMF. Darbai ir Dienos, v.5, 1936. See serials consulted.

4464. LECHEM, G. Divre yeme Lita. [History of Lithuania] Kaunas, 1922-1923. 56 p. DK511.L2L4 DLC

4465. LETTRES D'UN ÉTUDIANT LITHUANIEN. [Paris] E. Dentu, 1861. 32 p. (GLP p.v. 64, no.5)NN

4466. LIMANOWSKI, Bolesław. Dzieje Litwy. Warszawa, Kraków Towarzystwo Wydawnicze w Warszawie, 1917. 2, 68 p. DK511.L2L43 DLC MH NN NNC PU

4467. LIUBAVSKII, Matvei Kuz'mich. Litovitsy v proshlom i nastoiashchem. Petrograd, Tip. Zadruga, 1917. 91 p. (Svoboda i bratstvo narodov, no. 21) Cyr.4.DK857 DLC

4468. MAČIULIS, Jonas. Apsakymai apie Lietuvos praeiga. [Narrations of Lithuanians' duties] Parašė

Stanyslovas Zanavykas [pseud.] 1886. Tilžė, Kasztu Lietuvos mylėtojų spausdinta pas O. Mauderodės, 1891. 186 p. Xerox copy, 1971. PG511.L2M3 1971 PU

4469. MAŠIOTAS, Pranas. Apie Lietuvos senovę. [On Lithuania's past] Voronežas, Lietuvių spaustuvė, 1917. 43 p. 945 Ma ICBM

4470. NOVOE IZVESTIE O LITVE I Moskovitakh. (K istorii vtoroi osady Smolenska v 1513 godu) [The original title of this document is: New Zeyttung auf Litten rund von den Moskowitter] [ed. by] J[an] Riabinin. In Moskow Universitet. Obshchestvo Istorii i Drevnostei Rossiiskikh. Chteniia, v.218, 1906, p. 1-7. See serials consulted.

4471. OCHMAŃSKI, Jerzy. Uwagi o litewskim państwie wczesnofeudalnym. In Roczniki Historyczne (Poznań), v.27, 1961, p. 143-160. See serials consulted.

4472. OSTROWSKI, Radosław. Fragments from the history of Byelorussia (to 1700). Material for historical research and study of the subject. London, Byelorussian Central Council, 1961. 102 p. illus., maps. DK511.W5.086 NIC CSt CSt-H ICU MiU

PAKŠTAS, Kazys. Lithuania and World War II. Chicago, Ill., 1947. See entry no. 923.

4473. PALMIERI, Aurelio F. Catholic Lithuania. In Catholic World (New York, N.Y.), v.107, 1918, p. 591-604. See serials consulted.

4474. PANUCEVIČ, Vacłau. Žamojdź i Litva, roznyja krainy i narody. Chicago, 1953-1954. 382 p. illus., maps. DK511.L2P2 ICU ICBM MH

4475. PASHUTO, Vladimir Teodorovich. O vozniknovenii Litovskogo gosudarstva. In Akademiia Nauk SSSR. Izvestiia. Seriia istorii i filosofii (Moskva), v.9, no.1, 1952. p. 29-49. See serials consulted.

4476. --- Protiv nekotorykh burzhuaznykh kontseptsi obrazovaniia Litovskogo gosudarstva. In Voprosy Istorii. Moskva, no. 8, 1958, p. 40-62. See serials consulted.

4477. PAULIUKONIS, Pranas. Tautos istorijos mokymas. [The teaching of Lithuanian history] Čikaga, Pedagoginis lituanistikos institutas, 1963. 68 l. D16.2.P3 DLC

4478. PICHETA, Vladimir Ivanovich. Istoriia Litovskogo gosudarstva do Liublinskoi unii. Vil'na, 1921. 947.52.P584 PU

4479. POBŁOCKI, Leon von. Kritische Beiträge zur ältesten geschichte Litauens. Königsberg in Pr., A. Rosbach'sche Buchdruckerei [1879]. 41 p. Thesis--University of Königsberg. Bibliography: p. 3-16. DK511.L23P7 CLU PU

4480. RASTENIS, Vincas. Lithuania in 1958. In Lituanus (Brooklyn, N.Y.), v.4, no.2, 1958, p. 34-37. See serials consulted.

4481. ŠALČIUS, Matas. Paskaita iš Lietuvos istorijos. [A lecture on Lithuanian history] Chicago, Ill., Tėvynės Mylėtojų d-ja, 1918. 96 p. tables. DK511.L2S4 CtY DLC CtTMF ICBM MH

4482. SCHÄDER, Hildegard. Altlitauen zwischen West und Ost. [Berlin] Selbstverlag der Publikationsstelle, [1942?] 20 p. DK511.L23S38 InU LU NbU

4483. SERAFINAS, H., ed. Vytauto Didžiojo mirties 500 metų sukaktuvėms paminėti albumas. [The album commemorating the 500th anniversary of the death of Vytautas the Great] Kaunas, Spindulio spaustuvė, 1933. 474 p. illus. XL970.9SE ICLJF CtPAM

4484. ŠIRVYDAS, Joseph Otto. Attilos siaubimas lietuvių kraštais. [The hordes of Attila through the Lithuanian countries] Cleveland, Ohio, Spauda ir lėšos "Dirvos", 1919. 205 [3] p. illus. D141.S5 DLC CtY IaU ICJ OCl WaS

4485. SKIRMUNTT, Konstancja. Dzieje Litwy opowiedziane w zarysie. Kraków, W Księg. G. Gebethnera i Spółki, 1886. vii, 151 p. 947.5.Sk3d IU CtY

4486. --- Histoire de la Lithuanie. Traduite du polonais par L. Żoładż. Paris, 1901. 67 p. (Association des anciens élèves de l'école polonais. Procès verbal de l'assemblée générale. Bulletin, no. 151) Balt 7849.01 MH BM(Ac. 2617.)

4487. --- Trumpai išpasakota Lietuvos istorija. [Brief Lithuanian history] Pajauta [pseud.] Vilnius, J. Zawadzkis, 1912. 167 p. illus., ports., 3 fold. maps. DK511.L2S55

CtY PU

4488. --- Zarys dziejów litewskich. Helena-Pajauta [pseud.] Wyd. nowe popr. Warszawa, W. Makowski, 1901. 143 p. ports., 3 fold. maps. 947.52.Sk35.3 PU

4489. SLIZIEŃ, A. Litwa do Unii Lubelskiej. Przez autora Poglądu na literaturę polską. Poznań, J.K. Żupański, 1878. 57 p. DK511.L23S5 DLC KU PU BM(9456. f. 2.)

4490. SPULER, Berthold. Mittelalterliche Grenzen in Osteuropa. I: Die Grenze des Grossfürstentums Litauen im Südosten gegen Türken und Tartaren. In Jahrbücher für Geschichte Osteuropas (Breslau), v.6, no. 2-4, 1941, p. 152-270. See serials consulted.

4491. SRUOGIENĖ, Vanda (Daugirdaitė), ed. Lietuvos istorijos vaizdai ir raštai. [The views from Lithuanian history and historiography] Kaunas, Sakalas, 1939. 1 v. illus. DK511.L2S69 DLC

4492. STOROST, Georg. Litauische Geschichte von den ältesten Zeiten bis zur Gegenwart. Tilsit, Pawlowski, 1921. x, 152 p. DK511. L2S82 DLC IU NN PU

4493. STOROST, Wilhelm. Litauen in Vergangenheit und Gegenwart. By Vidūnas, W. St. [pseud.] Tilsit, Buchdr. Lituania, 1916. 132 p., plates. 947.52.St78 PU ICBM IU NIC

4494. --- La Lithuanie dans le passé et dans le présent; traduction et notes d'Antoine Viscont. Genève, Atar, [1918] 158 p. plates, ports., 2 fold. maps. DK511.L2S8 DLC CSt-H KU MH PU WU

4495. --- Litwa w swej pszeszłości i teraźniejszości. [By] Vidūnas [pseud.] Wilno, Glos Litwy, 1919. 60 p. (*QO p.m.21, no.10) NN

4496. STRONG, Anna Louise. The new Lithuania. New York, N.Y., Workers Library Publishers, [1941]. 63 p. DK511.L27S927 CSt-H DLC HU ICU MH MnU NIC WaU WU WyU

4497. STUKALICH, V. K. Bielorussiia i Litva. Ocherki iz istorii gorodov v Bielorussii. Vitebsk, Gubernskaia tipografiia, 1894. 62 p. DK507.S7 CU NN PU

4498. SUŽIEDĖLIS, Simas. Lithuania from medieval to modern times: a historical outline. In Vardys, Vytas Stanley, ed. Lithuania under

the Soviets, New York, N.Y., 1965,
p. 3-19. DK511.L27V35 DLC AzU CSt
CSt-H CU IC MoU MWalB MU PPi TU WaU

4499. THURSTON, Theodore S. Li-
thuanian history, philology and
grammar. 1st ed. By Theodore S.
Thurston, with the assistance of
Corine Coulson. Chicago, Ill.
Printed by Peoples Printing Co.,
1941. 39 p. illus. (map).
DK511.L2T5 DLC ICBM IEN

4500. VALIUKAS, Leonard. Lithuania: land and heroes... Hollywood,
Calif., "Lithuanian Days" Publishers, 1962. 88 p. illus., ports.,
maps. DK511.L27V3 DLC CaAEU CoU
CtY IaU InNd MH NSyU PP PU WU

VIJEIKIS, Vladas. Lietuva,
mano tėvų žemė. Chicago, Ill.
430 p. See entry no. 841.

VILNA. (GOVERNMENT) GUBERN-
SKII STATISTICHESKII KOMITET. Cherty iz istorii i zhizni litovskago
naroda. Vil'na, 1854. See entry
no. 950.

4501. WEJTKO, Władysław. Samoobro-
na Litwy i Białorusi; szkic historyczny. Wilno, Nakł. Związku Organizacyi
Wojskowych w Wilnie, 1930.
947.52.W439 PU

4502. ZAJĄCZKOWSKI, Stanisław Franciszek. Dzieje Litwy pogańskiej do
roku 1386. Lwów, Zakład Narodowy im.
Ossolińskich, 1930. 77 p. illus.,
plates, ports. Bibliography: p.
[73]-77. 947.5.Z13d 1930 KU CtY PU

4503. ZANAVYKAS, Stanislovas, pseud.
Apsakymai apie Lietuvos praeiga.
[History of Lithuania] Tilžė, O.V.
Mauderode, 1903. 190 p. 947.5.Z27
PPi OCl

4504. ZEILLER, Martin. Newe Be-
schreibung dess Königreichs Polen und
Gross-Herzogthumbs Lithauen... Ulm,
Balthasar Kühnen, 1647. 223, [20] p.
Bell Collection 1650Ze MnU NcU

4505. --- --- [Another edition]
Ulm, B. Kuehnen, 1652. 223, 22 p.
DK405.Z46 ICU

4506. --- --- [Another edition]
Ulm, G. Wildeysen, 1657. [10], 220,
[22] p. 942.7.Z35m OCl MH

4507. ZUMERIS, Bronius. Tylinti
tauta; Lietuvos didybės ir tragikos
keliu. [The greatness and the tragedy of Lithuania] Melbourne, 1953.
84 p. DK511.L2Z8 DLC PU

X.6. TEXTBOOKS

4508. ALEKNA, Antanas. Lietuvos
istorija. [History of Lithuania]
Praplatintoji laida. Kaunas, Šv. Kazimiero draugija, 1919. 253 p. maps
(Šv. Kazimiero draugijos leidinys,
nr. 252) 947.5.A125l 1919 KU ICBM
ICU PU

4509. --- --- Kaunas, Šviesos
spaustuvė, 1920. 75 p. illus., map.
(Šv. Kazimiero draugijos leidinys,
nr. 292) DK511.L713A366 InNd CtTMF
ICCC ICBM

4510. --- --- Antroji praplatintoji laida. [2d enlarged ed.] Tilžėje, J. Reylenderio spaustuvė, 1923.
235 p. fold. maps. (Šv. Kazimiero
draugijos leidinys, nr. 357)
DK511.L2A62 DLC CtY ICCC InU OCl PU

4511. --- --- 6., trumpesnysis pataisytas leidimas. [6th ed.] Kaunas, Šv. Kazimiero draugija, 1934.
96 p. [Šv. Kazimiero draugijos leidinys, nr. 598) DK511.L2A62 DLC

4512. --- --- Perspausdinta iš ket-
virtos laidos. [Reprinted from the
4th ed.] Glasenbach, Ger., Tėvynė,
1946. 62 p. NN

4513. JONYNAS, Ignas. Lietuvių
tautos istorija; paskaitų užrašai.
[History of the Lithuanian nation]
Kaunas, 1928-29. 3 v. (Studentų humanitarų draugija. Spaudos komisijos
leidinys, nr. 32) DK511.L2J6 DLC
ICCC

4514. Jurgėla, Constantine Rudyard.
History of the Lithuanian nation.
Introd. by Clarence Augustus Manning.
New York, N.Y., Lithuanian kultural
Institut, Historical Reasearch Sec-
tion, 1948 [c1947] 544 p. ilus.,
ports., maps. Bibliography: p. 529-
544. DK511.L2J73 DLC CaAEU CaBVaU
CaMWU CaOKQ CaOTU CtPAM CtY CU CSt-H
GU ICU ICN InNd InU IEN IU IC In KU
MH MiU MU NB NIC NN NcU NNC NjP OCl
OkU OClW PP PPiU PU TxU WU

4515. JUSAITIS, Antanas. The History of the Lithuanian nation and its
present national aspirations. Tr.
from the Lithuanian. [Philadelphia,
Pa.] Lithuanian Catholic Truth Society, 1918. ix, 156 p. fold. facsim. Translated from Lithuanian as
published in a weekly magazine, "Žvaigždė" in 1917, Philadelphia, Pa. Lithuanian organizations in America:p.
152-153. Books and pamphlets published on behalf of independent Lithuania:
p. 153-156. For holdings see next
entry.

4516. --- --- 2d enl. ed. Phila-
delphia,Pa., Lithuanian Catholic
Truth Society, 1919. 202 p. DK511.
L2J8 DLC CLU CSt-H CU CtY CoU CaAEU
ICJ ICN ICBM IEN IdU ICU InNd IU KU
MB MiU MnU MoU NB NBuU NN NNC NcD
NcU NjP NjR NSyU OCl OClW OkU OrU
PPi PU TxU ViU WU WaS

4517. KONČIUS, Joseph B. History of Lithuania. [Chicago, Ill.] Lithuanian American Community of the
USA [1972] 142 p. DK511.L2K65 PU

4518. LIETUVOS TSR MOKSLŲ AKADEMI-
JA, VILNA. ISTORIJOS INSTITUTAS.
Lietuvos TSR istorija. [History of
Lithuania] Redakcinė kolegija: K.
Jablonskis, J. Jurginis, J. Žiugžda
(vyrriausias redaktorius) Vilnius,
VPMLL, 1957-65. 3 v. illus., ports,
maps. DK511.L2L4235 DLC CU CaAEU
CSt-H CtY ICU IU(2-3) In InU KU MH
NN NNC NjP OrU PU WaU

4519. --- Lietuvos TSR istorija
nuo seniausiŲ laikŲ iki 1957 metŲ.
[The history of Lithuania from an-
cient times up to 1957] Redakcinė
kolegija: K. Jablonskis [et al.]
J. Žiugžda (vyriaus. redaktorius).
Vilnius, VPMLL, 1958. 518 p. illus.
ports., maps, facsims. DK511.L2L4234
DLC CaOTU CtY ICU InU IU MH NN NNC
PU TxU WaU

4520. MAŠIOTAS, Pranas. Lietuvos
istorija. [History of Lithuania]
Chicago, Ill., Draugo spauda, 1915.
106 p. DK511.L23M3

4521. MATULAITIS, Stasys. LietuviŲ tautos istorija. [History of
the Lithuanian nation] Voronežas,
LietuviŲ spaustuvė, 1918.
947.52.M439 PU

4522. --- --- Kaunas, Švyturio ben-
drovės leidinys, 1923. 260 p.
DK511.L2M24 DLC BM(09456. ee. 58.)
CtPAM CtTMF ICBM KU OCl

4523. PAPARONIS, pseud. Lietuvos
istorija. [History of Lithuania]
Seinai, Laukaičio spaustuvė, 1910.
140 p. illus., map. 945.P ICBM

4524. PIASECKAITĖ, Marija (Šlapelienė). Lietuvos istorija. [Histo-
ry of Lithuania] Vilnius, 1908. 79
p. 945.Pi ICBM

4525. PRANAS, pseud. Lietuvos istorija pradedamosioms mokykloms.
History of Lithuania for the elementary schools] Chicago, Ill., Draugas, 1915. 105 p. 945.Pr. ICBM

4526. --- --- Kaunas, 1922. 92 p.
945.Pr. ICBM

4527. --- --- [Another edition]
Chicago, Ill., Draugas, 1927. 95 p.

4528. ŠAPOKA, Adolfas, ed. Lietuvos istorija. [History of Lithuania]
Kaunas, Švietimo ministerija, 1936.
xvi, 688 p. illus., ports., facsims,
maps. (Švietimo ministerijos knygŲ
leidimo komisijos leidinys, nr. 479)
Bibliography: p. 677-686. DK511.L2S44
DLC CaOONL CtPAM CtY ICBM ICCC OCl
PPi PU

4529. --- --- [3rd ed. Fellbach,
Ger.] Patria [1950] xxviii, 697 p.
illus., ports., maps. Bibliography:
p. 685-694. DK511.L2S44 1950 DLC
ICBM PU

4530. ŠLEŽAS, Paulius and Ignas Malinauskas. Lietuvos istorija; vadovėlis. [History of Lithuania; a
textbook] Kaunas, Sakalo bendrovė,
1934. 118 p. illus. DK511.L2S54
DLC CtTMF PU

4531. SRUOGIENĖ, Vanda (Daugirdaitė) Lietuvos istorija. [History of
Lithuania] Kaunas, Skalo bendrovė,
1935. 207 p. illus. DK511.L2S68
DLC

4532. --- --- Vadovėlis gimnazijoms.
Kaunas, Sakalas, 1935. 184 p. illus.
945.5.S ICBM

4533. --- --- [Another edition]
[Chicago, Ill.] Terra [1953] 203 p.
illus. DK511.L2S68 1953 DLC ICBM

4534. --- --- ; Lietuva amžiŲ sū-
kury. [History of Lithuania...]
Chicago, Ill., Tėvynės mylėtojŲ draugija, 1956. 947 p. illus., ports.,
maps. Bibliography: p. 941-947.
DK511.L2S7 DLC CaOONL CtPAM CtY ICU
KU MH NN

4535. --- --- 6., laida. [6th ed.]
Chicago, Ill., Terra, 1966. 409 p.
illus., tables, maps. DK511.L2S7
1966 DLC CSt CaAEU CaOTP CaOTU MiD
NjP PU

4536. YČAS, Jonas. Lietuvos isto-
rija; paskaitŲ užrašai. [History of
Lithuania; notes of the lectures]
Kaunas, 1928-29. 2 v. DK511.L2Y25
DLC ICCC

X.7. HISTORIOGRAPHY, CRITICISM
AND REVIEWS

4537. ADAMUS, Jan. Najnówsza literatura o akcie krewskim. In Vilna.
Uniwersytet. Wiadomości Studium Historii Prawa Litewskiego (Wilno), v.1,

1938, p. 273-317. See serials consulted.

4538. BAGDANAVIČIUS, Vytautas Jonas. Sovietinė Lietuvos istoriografija. [The Soviet Lithuanian historiography] In Tautos praeitis (Chicago, Ill.), v.1, no.1, 1959, p. 3-24. See serials consulted.

BARBASHEV, Aleksandr Ippolitovich, ed. Lietopisnye istochniki dlia istorii Litvy... Sanktpeterburg, 1888. See entry no. 4183.

4539. BARYCZOWA, M. Augustyn Rotundus Mieleski, wójt wileński, pierwszy historyk i apologeta Litwy. In Ateneum Wilenskie (Wilno), v.10, 1935, p. 71-96; v.11, 1936, p. 117-172. See serials consulted.

4540. CHODYNICKI, Kazimierz. Przegląd badań nad dziejami Litwy w ostatnim dziesięcioleciu, 1920-1930. In Kwartalnik Historyczny (Lwów), v.44, 1930, p. 273-300. See serials consulted.

4541. DUNDULIS, Bronius. A historiographic survey of Lithuanian-Polish relations. In Lituanus (Chicago, Ill.), v.17, no.4, 1971, p. 5-34. See serials consulted.

4542. GIDŽIŪNAS, Viktoras. Lietuva Romos lenkų istorinio instituto darbuose. [Lithuania as interpreted in the works of the Polish Institute of History in Rome] In Aidai (Brooklyn, N.Y.), nr.2, 1964, p. 91-94. See serials consulted.

4543. HALECKI, Oskar. Przegląd badań nad dziejami Litwy 1385-1569. In PZHP w Wilnie 17-20 września 1935. Pamiętnik VI. Referaty (Lwów), v.1, 1935, p. 22-25. See serials consulted.

IVINSKIS, Zenonas. Lietuvos istorija naujų šaltinių ir pokario tyrinėjimų šviesoje. In LKMASD, v.5, 1964, p. 523-[600] See serials consulted.

4544. --- M.K. Lubauskio mokslo darbai Lietuvos istorijos srityje. [Works on Lithuanian history by M.K. Liubauskis] In Židinys (Kaunas), v.9, 1933, p. 164-171. See serials consulted.

4545. JAKŠTAS, Juozas. Russian historiography on the origin of the Lithuanian state; some critical remarks on V.T. Pashuto's study. In Lituanus (Chicago, Ill.), v.11, no.4, 1965, p. 25-46. See Serials consulted.

4546. --- Žvilgsnis į Mažosios Lietuvos istoriografiją. [The historiography on Lithuania Minor] In LKMAM, v.4, 1968, p. 1-49. Summary in English. See serials consulted.

4547. JUČAS, Mečislovas. Lietuvių karo su kryžiuočiais istoriografija. [The historiography of Lithuanian wars with the Teutonic Order] In Lietuvių karas su kryžiuočiais. Vilnius, 1964. p. 5-49. DK511.L23L45 DLC CtY MH

4548. --- Lietuvos metraščiai. [Chronicles of Lithuania] Vilnius, Vaga, 1968. 185 p. illus., maps. DK511.L2J72 InU CtY ICU MH

4549. --- Naujausi Lenkijos liaudies respublikos istorikų darbai apie Lietuvos Didžiąją Kunigaikštystę. [The most recent works of the historians of Polish People's Republic about the Grand Duchy of Lithuania] In LTSRMAD. Serija A, v.2(7), 1959, p. 71-90. See serials consulted.

4550. --- Rusų istorikai apie Lietuvos Didžiąją Kunigaikštystę. [Russian historians about the Grand Duchy of Lithuania] In LTSRMAD. Serija A, v.2(9), 1960, p. 67-77. See serials consulted.

4551. LAURINAITIS, Vincas. S. Daukanto "Darbay senuju Lituwiu yr Zemaycziu" 1822 m. ir to veikalo reikšmė. [The work of S. Daukantas about ancient Lithuanians and Žemaičiai (Samogitians) and its significance] In KUHMF. Darbai ir dienos, no.5, 1936. See serials consulted.

4552. OCHMAŃSKI, Jerzy. Dzieje Litwy w pracach współczesnych historyków polskich. In Rocznik Białostocki (Białystok), v.2, 1961, p. 451-458. See serials consulted.

4553. --- Historiografia rewolucji 1905 roku w Litwie. In Towarzystwo Naukowe w Toruniu. Wydział Nauk Historycznych, Prawniczych i Społecznych. Zapiski Historyczne (Toruń), v.33, 1968, no.4, p. [99]-109. See serials consulted.

4554. --- Lituanistyka w Polsce do 1965 r. [Poznań, 1968] 32 p. Offprint from Roczniki Historyczne, t.34. DK511.L2 025 PU

4555. --- Problematyka badań dziejów Litwy feudalnej we współczesnej historiografii litewskiej, 1945-1959. In Kwartalnik Historyczny (Lwów), no.5, 1960, p. 1160-1180. See serials consulted.

4556. PASHUTO, Vladimir Terent'evich.

Trudy pol'skogo akademika G. Lov-
mian'skogo po istorii Litvy, Rusi i
slavianstva. In Voprosy istorii (
(Moskva), no.10, 1959, p. 107-120.
See serials consulted.

4557. POBLOCKI, Leon von. Kriti-
sche Beiträge zur ältesten Geschichte Litauens. In Altpreussische Monatsschrift (Königsberg in Pr.),
v.17, 1880, p. 33-73. See serials
consulted.

4558. PUZINAS, Jonas. Žvilgsnis
į Jerzy Ochmański'o Lietuvos praeities tyrinėjimus. In Aidai (Brooklyn, N.Y.), no.4, 1969, p. 160-168.
See serials consulted.

4559. ŠAPOKA, Adolfas. Istoriškoji čekų literatūra ryšy su mūsų krašto istorija. [The Czech literature
related to the Lithuanian history]
In Praeitis (Kaunas), v.2, 1933, p.
350-374. See serials consulted.

4560. SENN, Alfred. A contribution to Lithuanian historiography.
In Studi Baltici (Roma), ns, v.1(9),
1952, p. 107-120. See serials consulted.

4561. TRUMPA, Vincas. Lietuvos
istorikų darbai. [The works of Lithuanian historians] In Aidai (Brooklyn, N.Y.), no. 6(131), 1960, p. 258-
263. See serials consulted.

4562. --- The work of Lithuanian
historians. In Lituanus (Brooklyn,
N.Y.), v.6, no.2, 1960, p. 75-79.
See serials consulted.

4563. JAJĄCZKOWSKI, Stanisław. Die
Geschichte Litauens bis 1386 in der
polnischen Geschichtsschreibung der
letzten zwanzig Jahre. In Jahrbücher
für Geschichte Europas (Breslau),
v.4, 1939, p. 136-148. See serials
consulted.

4564. --- The historical sciences
in Lithuania. In Baltic and Scandinavian Countries (Gdynia), v.4, 1938,
p. 239-246. See serials consulted.

4565. --- Litewski ruch naukowy w
zakresie historii. In Kwartalnik
Historyczny (Lwów), 1935, p. 301-339.
See serials consulted.

4566. --- Przegląd badań nad dziejami Litwy do 1385 r. In PZHP w Wilnie 17-20 września, 1935. Pamiętnik
VI. Referaty (Lwów), v.1, 1935, p.
3-21. See serials consulted.

X.8. SOURCES

X.8.a. CHRONICLES

4567. ARKHANGELOGORODSKII LETOPI-
SETS. Ustiuzhskii letopisnyi svod.
Red. K.N. Serbinnoi. Moskva; Leningrad, Izd-vo Akademii nauk SSSR,1950.
127 p. DK70.A8 DLC CaBVaU CoU

4568. BOHOMOLEC, F. Zbiór dziejopisów polskich. Warszawa, 1764-68.
4 v. Partial contents.--v.2. Stryjkowski, Maciej. Kronika polska, litewska, żmudzka... aż do dzisiejsze-
go roku 1582.--v.4. Guagnino, Alessandro. Sarmatiae europeae descriptio... BM(9475. f. 1.)

4569. BUNGE, Friedrich Georg von,
ed. Liv-, Esth-, und Curländisches
Urkundenbuch nebst Regesten. Revel;
Riga; Moskau, Kluge und Ströhm; J.
Deubner, 1853-1914. 15 v.
DK511.B25B8 DLC KU MH NN

4570. --- Aalen, Scientia, 1967- .
17 v. Reprint; Originally published
Revel, Kluge und Ströhm, 1853-1914.
PU

4571. DANIŁOWICZ, Ignacy, ed. La-
topisiec Litwy i kronika ruska. Z rękopisu sławiańskiego przepisane, wy-
pisane z Wremennika sofiyskiego po-
mnożone, przypisami i objaśnieniami
opatrzone, staraniem i pracą Ignace-
go Daniłowicza w jedno zebrane, do-
konczone i przedrukowane. Wilno, A.
Marcinowski, 1827. 528 p.
BM(9455. bbb. 12.)

4572. DAVID, Lucas G. Preussische
Chronik... mit Beifügung historischer
und etymologischer Anmerkungen. Hrsg.
von Ernst Henning. Königsberg in Pr.,
1812-17. 8 v. in 4. DD377.D3 DLC
CSt PU

4573. GRUNAU, Simonis. Preussische
Chronik. Hrsg. von M. Perlbach, R.
Philippi, P. Wagner. Leipzig, Dun-
cker & Humbolt, 1876-96. 3 v. (Die
Preussischen Geschichtsschreiber des
XVI und XVII Jahrhunderts, Bd. 1-3)
DD491.041P7 MdBJ OCl MH CU

4574. HENRICUS LETTUS, 13th cent.
The chronicle of Henry of Livonia.
A translation with introduction and
notes by James A. Brundage. Madison,
Wis., University of Wisconsin Press,
1961. vii, 262 p. DK511.L3H51 CaAEU
CtY DLC InU ICU MH MnU NNC NjP NjR
WU

4575. --- Henrici chronico Lyvo-
niae. Ex recensione W. Arndt in usum

scholarum ex Monumentis Germaniae Historicis recudi fecit G.H. Pertz. Hannoverae, Impensis bibliopolii Hahniani, 1874. xxiv, 223 p. (Scriptores Rerum Germanicarum) DK511.L3H51 CaAEU NN

4576. --- [Another edition] Reval, Druck von J.H. Gressel, 1867. 366 p. DLC PU

4577. --- Livländische Chronik von Heinrich von Lettland. Neu übersetzt von Albert Bauer. Würzburg, Holzner, 1959. xxxvi,354 p. DLC511.L3H4 DLC ClU ICU InU NN PU TxHR

4578. HERMANNUS DE WARTBERGE. Chronicon Livoniae. In Scriptores Rerum Prussicarum. Leipzig, 1863; Frankfurt am Main, 1965. v.2, p. [9]-178. DD491.041S43 CaAEU CSt CU CtPAM

4579. HILDEBRAND, Hermann. Die Chronik Henricus con Lettland. Berlin, E.S. Mittler und Sohn, 1865. 55 p. Inaug.-Diss.--University of Göttingen. DK511.L3H5 DLC CtY IU MH

4580. HOENEKE, Bartholomäus. Die jüngere livländische Reimchronik des Bartholomäus Hoeneke, 1315-1348. Leipzig, Duncker & Humblot, 1872. liv, 37 p. DK511.L3H65 DLC

4581. JABLONSKIS, Konstantinas, ed. Istorijos archyvas. Tomas 1. [The sources of Lithuanian history] Kaunas, Lietuvos Universiteto biblioteka, 1934. 679, 131 p. (Kaunas. Universitetas. Biblioteka. Leidinys, nr.2) (QYA)NN ICBM

4582. KHRONIKA BYKHOVTSA. [Predislovie, kommentarii i perevod N. N. Ulashchika. Otv. redaktor M. N Tikhomirov] Moskva, Nauka, 1966. 152 p. illus., facsims. (Pamiatniki srednevekovoi istorii TSentral'noi i Vostochnoi Evropy) DK511. L36K7 DLC CU CaAEU CaOHM CaOTU CtY ICU IEN InU InNd MH NNC NcD NcU NjP NSyU PU

4583. LIETOPIS' VELIKIKH KNIAZEI Litovskikh. Prigotovil k izd. A. N. Popov. Sanktpeterburg, Tip. Imp. Akademii nauk, 1854. 32 p. Otdiel'nye ottiski iz 1-oi knigi Uchenykh zapisok, izdavaemykh vtorym otdieleniem Imp. Akademii nauk. DK511.L23L65 InU

4584. LIETOPISETS VELIKOHO KNIAZHESTVA Litov"skoho i Zomoit"skoho. Pavodae s'pisku hr. Rachynskaho peradruk z XVII t. Polnogo sobraniia russkikh lietopisei. Vyd. V. Lastoskaha... Belaruskaha TSentru u Litve. Kouna, F. Sakalauskai i G. Lanz, 1925. 947.52.L619 PU

4585. LIETUVOS METRAŠTIS; Bychovco kronika. [Vertė, įvadą ir paaiškinimus parašė Rimantas Jasas] Vilnius, Vaga, 1971. 395 p. (Lituanistinė biblioteka) Bibliography: p. 345-[354]. DK511.L23L49 PU

4586. LIETUVOS TSR MOKSLŲ AKADEMIJA, VILNA. ISTORIJOS IR TEISĖS INSTITUTAS. Lietuvos TSR istorijos šaltiniai. [Sources of Lithuanian history] Redakcinė kolegija: K. Jablonskis et al. Vilnius, VPMLL, 1955-61. 4 v. DK511.L2L72 CaAEU DLC CSt-H CtY ICU InU MH NN PU

4587. LIVLÄNDISCHE REIMCHRONIK. Livländische Reimchronik. Hrsg. von Franz Pfeiffer. Stuttgart, Gedrücked auf Kosten des Literarischen Vereins, 1844. 332 p. (Literarischer Verein in Stuttgart. Bibliothek, Bd.7:II) DK511.L3L78 CaAEU DLC MB MiU NN NcD NjP OCU OCl OU PBm PU

4588. --- --- Mit Anmerkungen versehen von L. Meyer. Reval, F. Kluge, 1848. 947.52.L767GM PU

4589. --- Ditleb's von Alnpeke Livländische Reimchronik, enthaltend der riterlichen Meister vnd Bruder zu Lieflant Geschicht; nach dem Bergmannschen Drucke mit den Ergänzungen und dem abweichenden Lesearten der Heidelberger Handschrift neu bearb. und hrsg. In Scriptores Rerum Livonicarum. Riga und Leipzig, 1853. Bd. 1, p.[489]-827. "Einleitung, Paraphrase, Glossar und Erläuterungen von C.E. Napiersky, Text, Orts- und Personenregister von Th. Kallmeyer." - Winkelmann, Bibl. Livoniae historica. DK511.L3S4 DLC

4590. --- --- Hrsg. von Leo Meyer. Padeborn, F. Schöning, 1876. 947.52.L767 PU NN

4591. --- --- Mit Anmerkungen, Namenverzeichnis und Glossar hrsg. von Leo Meyer. Hildersheim, G. Olms, 1963. 416 p. "Reprografischer Nachdruck der Ausgabe Padeborn 1876" DK511.L3L5 1876a MU CaOTU

4592. MACIEJOWSKI, Wacław Aleksander. Roczniki i kroniki polskie i litewskie najdawniejsze. Warszawa, S. Orgelbrand, 1850. 281 p. maps. DK414.A2M3 CU MH WU

4593. MOSKOVSKII LETOPISNYI SVOD kontsa XV. veka. Izd. M.N. Tikhomirov. Moskva, Izd-vo Akademii nauk SSSR, 1949. 463 p. (Russia. Arkheograficheskaia komissiia. Polnoe sobranie russikikh letopisei, t.25) DK70.A53 DLC CaAEU

4594. NOVGORODSKAIA LETOPIS'. Novgorodskaia pervaia letopis' starshego i mladshego izvodov. [Pod red. A.N. Nasorova] Moskva, Izd-vo Akademii nauk SSSR, 1950. 640 p. 10 facsims. DK511.N7N62 DLC

4595. PETRUS OF DUSBURG. Chronicon Prussiae, in quo ordinis teutonici origo, nec non res ab ejusdem ordinis magistris ab an. 1226 usque ad an. 1326 in Prussia gestae exponetur... Auctore et collectore Chr. Hartknoch. Francofurti et Lipsiae, Sumptibus M. Hallervordii, 1679. 12 p.l., 484, [31], 456, [45] p. map. DD375.P4 DLC CtY MdBJ PU

4596. --- Chronicon terrae Prussiae. Hrsg. von Max Toeppen. In Scriptores rerum prussicarum. Leipzig, 1861. v.1, p. 3-269, 816-817. DD491.041S4 DLC CaAEU CtY NN

4597. POLLAKÓWNA, Marzena. Kronika Piotra z Dusburga. Wrocław, 1968. 229 p. DD491.046P64 PU

4598. POMNIKI DZIEJOWE POLSKI. t. 1-6; ser.2, t.1- . Kraków, Nakł. Polskiej Akademii Umiejętności, 1864-93. 6 v. (Polska Akademia Umiejętności w Krakowie. Komisja Historyczna. Wydawnictwa, nr.84, etc.) On added title pages: Monumenta poloniae historica. The work consists of chronicles in original languages with translation into Polish. Each volume has an index with entries related to Lithuania. DK402.P65 DLC CU CaAEU MdBJ MH

4599. PSKOVSKAIA LETOPIS'. Pskovskie letopisi. Prigotovlil k pechati A.N. Nasonov. Vyp.1-2. Moskva, Izd-vo Akademii nauk SSSR, 1941-55. 2 v. DK511.P8P8 DLC CaAEU ICBM NN

4600. PTASZYCKI, Stanisław. Kodeks Olszewski Chomińskich Wielkiego Księstwa Litewskiego i Żmudzkiego Kronika. Podług rękopisu z roku 1550. Wilno, 1907. viii, 49, 19 p. BM(9455. ee. 33.)

4601. --- --- Warszawa, 1932. x, 55 p. facsims. NN

4602. RADZIWIŁŁ CHRONICLE. Radzivillovskaia letopis'. Sanktpeterburg, Izd. Imp. Obshchestva liubitelei drevnei pis'mennosti, 1902. 2 v. (Numernyia izdaniia, no. 118) BM

4603. RIMBERT, Saint, Abp of Hamburg and Bremen. Anskar, the apostle of the North, 801-865. Translated from the Vita Anscarii by Bishop Rimbert, his fellow missionary and successor. By Charles H. Robinson. [London] The Society for the Propagation of the Gospel in Foreign Parts, 1921. 139 p. Bibliography: p. 22-24. BX4700. A59R5 DLC CtY NN OU

4604. RUSSIA. ARKHEOGRAFICHESKAIA KOMISSIIA. Polnoe sobranie russkikh lietopisei. T.17: Zapadnorusskie lietopisi. [Ed. by Stanisław L. Ptaszycki and A.A. Shakhmatov] Sanktpeterburg, 1907. xiv, 648 p. DK70.A53 v.17 DLC PU

4605. SARNICKI, Stanisław. Annales; seu, De origine et rebus gestis Polonorum et Lithuanorum libri VIII. Cracoviae, M. Szarffenberger, 1587. 410 p. Bw77A-587S CtY MH NNC NN

4606. SCRIPTORES RERUM LIVONICARUM. Sammlung der wichtigsten Chroniken und Geschichtsdenkmäle von Liv-, Esth- und Kurland. Riga und Leipzig, E. Frantzen's Verlags-Comptoir, 1848-53. 2 v. Vol. 1 has information on Lithuania. DK511.L3S4 DLC NNC OCl

4607. SCRIPTORES RERUM POLONICARUM. Cracoviae, Sumptibus Academiae Literarum; apud bibliopolam Societatis Librariae Polonicae, 1872-1917. 22 v. (Polska Akademia Umiejętności, Kraków. Komisja Historyczna. Wydawnictwa, t.2-22) DK402.S4 DLC CU(3-6, 10-11, 13-14, 16-20, 22) MH NN NNC

4608. SCRIPTORES RERUM PRUSSICARUM. Die Geschichtsquellen der preussischen Vorzeit bis zum Untergang der Ordenherrschaft. Hrsg. von Theodor Hirsch [et al.] Leipzig, Hirzel, 1861-74. 5 v. illus., facsims. Vol.1 includes Wulfstans Reisebericht which has some information about Lithuanians from the ninth century and also Chronicon of Petri de Dusburg. DD491.041S4 DLC CtY PU

4609. --- --- Frankfurt am Main, Minerva, 1965. 6 v. illus. Reprint; originally published: Leipzig, Hirzel, 1861-74. 5 v. DD491. 041S43 CaAEU CaOTU CU CSt CtPAM DLC

4610. SLOVO O POLKU IGOREVE. Slovo o polku Igoreve. Pod. red. V.P. Adrianovoi-Peretts. Moskva, Izd-vo Akademii nauk SSSR, 1950. 483 p. plates, maps. (Akademiia nauk SSSR.

Literaturnye pamiatniki) PG3300.S6
1950 DLC

4611. STRYJKOWSKI, Maciej. Kronika, polska, litewska, żmódzka i
wszystkiej rusi M. S.-wydanie nowe
będące dokładnem powtórzeniem wydania pierwotnego królewieckiego z
roku 1582 popzedzone wiadomością o
życiu i pismach, przez M. Malinow-
skiego, oraz rozprawą o latopiscakh
ruskich przez Daniłowicza, pomno-
żone przedrukiem dzieł pomniejszych
według pierwotnych wydań. Warszawa,
Nakład G.L. Glücksberga, 1846. 2 v.
DK414.S87 DLC CU CaOTU KU MH NN PU
WU CaAEU(1582, ed.)

4612. TIKHOMIROV, Mikhail Nikolaevich. Istochnikovedeniie istorii
SSSR; uchebnoe posobie. S drevnikh
vremen do kontsa XVIII v, vyp.l.
Moskva, Izd-vo sotsial'no-ekon.
lit-ry, 1962. Vol.1 includes Lithuanian chronicles and Bychovca chronicle. DK38.T5 DLC CaAEU

4613. --- Novogrodskaia kharak-
teinaia letopis'. Moskva, Nauka,
1964. 344 p. PG3300.L5A2 1964
CaAEU

4614. TROITSKAIA LETOPIS'; Troitskaia letopis'; rekonstruktsiia teksta. [Ed. M.D. Priselkov] Moskva,
Izd-vo Akademii nauk SSSR, 1950.
512 p. DK70.T7 DLC CaAEU NN

4615. WIGAND DE MARBURG. Chronicon; seu, Annales Wigandi Marburgen-
sis, equitis et fratris ordinis teutonici. Primum ediderunt Joannes
Voigt et E.C. Raczyński. Posnaniae
[W Księgarni Nowej] 1842. xii, 377
p. Latin and Polish on opposite
pages. 942.9.W638c OCl

4616. --- Cronica nova Prutenica,
1293-1394. In Scriptores rerum
Prussicarum. Leipzig. v.2, 1863,
p. 429-662 and v.4, 1870, p. 1-8.
DD491.041S4 DLC CtY NN PU

X.8.b. COLLECTIONS OF DOCUMENTS,
INDEXES TO DOCUMENTS,
AND THEIR DESCRIPTION

4617. ACTA BORUSSICA. Denkmäler
der preussischen Staatsvervaltung im
18. Jahrhundert. Hrsg. von der
Königlichen Akademie der Wissenschaften. Berlin, Parey, 1892-1936.
38 v. DD397.A18 CaAEU (Microfische)
DLC

4618. ACTA BORUSSICA, ECCLESIASTICA.

civilia, literaria; oder Sorgfätige
Sammlung allerhand zur Geschichte
des Landes Preussen gehörige Nach-
richten, Uhrkunden, Schriften und
Dokumenten. Königsberg in Pr., C.
G. Eckart, 1730. 6 v. in l. Rare
Book Collection DC7.Ac816.731a
PU(2)

4619. ACTA PRUSSICA; Abhandlungen
zur Geschichte Ost- und Westpreussens. Würzburg, Holzner Verlag,
1968. 357 p. port. (Beihäfte zum
Jahrbuch der Albertus Universität,
Königsberg in Pr.,29) DD491.045A18
CaAEU

4620. ACTA TOMICIANA: epistolae,
legationes, responsa, res gestae
serenissimi principis Sigismundi I.
per Stanislaum Gorski collectae.
Posnaniae, Sumptibus Bibliothecae
Kornicensis, 1852- . Vol. 35 published in 1968 and still continued.
DK428.A2 DLC CaBVaU CU CoU IaU InU
ICU MiU NcD OU

4621. ADAMUS BREMENSIS, 11th cent.
Adam's von Bremen Hamburgische Kirchengeschichte. Nach der Ausg. der
Monumenta Germaniae übersetzt von
J.C.M. Laurent. Berlin, W. Besser,
1850. 232 p. (Die Geschichtschreiber der deutschen Vorzeit. 11 Jahrhundert, Bd.7) ICU IU MH MiU OClW
PPULC

4622. --- --- Nach der Ausgabe der
Monumenta Germaniae übersetzt von
J.C.M. Laurent. Mit einem Vorworte
von J.M. Lappenberg. 2. Aufl. neu
bearbeitet von W. Wattenbuch. Leipzig, Dyksche Buchhandlung, 1893.
xiv, 262 p. (Die Geschichtschreiber
der deutschen Vorzeit. 11 Jahrhundert, Bd.6 (Bd.44)) DD3.G39 Bd.44
OCU CtY ICN MH OU TxU WU CaAEU(1888
ed.)

4623. --- --- Dritte Auglage, herausgegeben von Bernhard Schmeidler.
Hannover und Leipzig, Hahnsche Buchhandlung, 1917. lxvii, 353 p.
(Scriptores rerum germanicarum in
usum scholarum ex Monumentis Germaniae historicis separatim editi)
CU CtY CoCC MH NN NCN OCl OClW ODW
OrU OU PBm PPLT PPULC UPB UU

4624. --- History of the Arch-
bishop of Hamburg-Bremen. Translated by Francis J. Tschan. New York,
N.Y., Columbia University Press,
1959. xxxiv, 253 p. (Records of
civilization; sources and studies,
no.53) Bibliography: p. 230-238.
BR854.A313 1959 DLC AU CBPac CLSU
CSt CU CaAEU CtY CtY-D FMU FTaSU FU
IaU IEN InU ICU IU LU MB MH MiU MnU
MoU MtU NIC NN NNC NbU NcD NjPT NjR

NoU NRU OCl OCU OkU OO OU PAtM PPWe
RPB TU TxDaM TxU ViU

4625. AKTY, OTNOSIASHCHIESIA K IS-
torii IUzhnoi i Zapadnoi Rossii.
Sanktpeterburg, 1862-92. 15 v. in
13. Issued by Arkheograficheskaia
kommissiia. DK3.A68 DLC CLU CaBVaU
ICU CaOTU(microfiche) WU WaU

4626. AKTY, OTNOSIASHCHIESIA K IS-
torii Zapadnoi Rossii, sobrannye i
izdannye Arkheograficheskoiu kommissieiu. Sanktpeterburg, Tip. Eduarda
Pratsa, 1846-53. 5 v. Vol.1 contains information about Lithuania.
DK3.A13 DLC CtY ICU IU NN WU(Microfilm)

4627. AKTY, OTNOSIASHCHIESIA K IS-
torii Zapadnoi Rosii, sobrannye i
izdannye Arkheograficheskoiu komis-
sieiu. Sanktpeterburg, Tip. Eduarda
Pratsa, 1846-53. [The Hague, Mouton, 1970] 5 v. (Slavistic printings, 261, etc.) DK3.A69 1970 PU
(1-3, 5) CaOTU

4628. ARKHEOGRAFICHESKII SBORNIK
DOKUMENTOV, otnosiashchikhsia k istorii Sievero-Zapadnoi Rusi. Vil'-
na, Vilenskaia komissiia dlia razbora drevnikh aktov, 1867-1904. 14
v. in 9. Index: vols.1-13; 1867-
1902. 1 v. DK511.L21A7 DLC(1-14)
CLU(1-13) CSt-H(1-14) MH(1-12, 14)
MH-L(1-14) NN(1-14) RPB CU CtY ICN
ICU(9-10) IU(1,4-6,14) NNC PU(1-14)

BANTYSH-KAMENSKII, Nikolai
Nikolaevich. Sobranie gosudarstvennykh gramot id dogovorov. Moskva, 1813-28. See entry no. 3336.

4629. CATHOLIC CHURCH. LEGATES,
NUNCIOS, ETC., POLAND. Alberti
Bolognetti, nuntii apostolici in
Polonia, epistolae et acta, 1581-
1585. Cracoviae, Sumptibus Academiae polonae litterarum et scientiarum, 1923-50. 3 v. 943.8.D PU

4630. --- I.A. Caligarii, nuntii
apostolici in Polonia, epistolae et
acta, 1578-1581. Edidit Ludovicus
Boratyński. Cracoviae, Sumptibus
Academiae litterarum Cracoviensis,
1915. 920 p. (Monumenta Poloniae
Vaticana, 4) 947.52.C285 PU

4631. CATHOLIC CHURCH. POPE,
1740-1758 (BENEDICTUS XIV). Bulla-
rium in quo continentur epistolae et
constitutiones pro regno Poloniae et
M. Ducatu Lithuaniae... editae...
per A. Szylarski et al. Leopoli,
1760. 406 p. BM(5016. aaa. 4.)

4632. CHEREPNIN, Lev Vladimirovich.
Russkie feodal'nye arkhyvy XIV-XV vv.

Moskva, Izd-vo Akademii SSSR, 1948-
51. 2 v. DK3.C5 DLC CaBVaU NN OrU

4633. CHODKIEWICZ, Jan Karol.
Korrespondencya Jana Karola Chod-
kievicza, poprzedzone opisem z
rękopisów z archivum Radiziwiłłow-
skiego... Opracował i opisał Wł.
Chomętowski. Warszawa, J. Jaworski,
1875. 193 p. NN PU

4634. CODEX DIPLOMATICUS LITHUA-
niae. E. codicibus manuscriptis in
archivo secreto Regiomontano asser-
vatis, edidit Eduardus Raczyński.
Vratislaviae, Sumptibus Sigismundi
Schletter, 1845. xv, 391 p. Includes material for the year 1253-
1433 relating to Poland, Lithuania,
Teutonic Knights, and the Church.
BM(1314. k. 4.) NN

4635. CODEX DIPLOMATICUS POLONIAE
quo continentur privilegia Regnum
Poloniae, Magnorum Ducatum Lithua-
niae, bullae Pontificum... ab anti-
quissimis inde temporibus usque ad
annum 1506. Editus studio et opera
Leonis Rzyszczewskiwiski et Antonii
Muczkowski. Varsoviae, Typis S.
Strąbski, 1847-87. 4 v. in 6.
DK402.C64 DLC(1-3) BM IU(v.2, pt.2)
KU(1-3) MnU(1-4) NN(1-4)

CODEX DIPLOMATICUS REGNI PO-
loniae et Magni Ducatus Lithuaniae.
Wilno, 1758-64. See entry no. 3339.

4636. CODEX DIPLOMATICUS WARMIEN-
sis; oder, Regesten und Urkunden zur
Geschichte Ermlands. Gesammelt und
in Namen des Historischen Vereins
für Ermland hrsg. von Carl Peter
Wölky. Minz, Braunsberg, 1860-1935.
4 v. Ger.6905.102(1,2,5,9) MH

4637. CODEX EPISTOLARIS VITOLDI
Magni Ducis Lithuaniae, 1376-1430.
Collectus opera Antonii Prochaska.
Cracoviae, 1882. cxvi, 1113 p.
(Polska Akademia Umiejętności, Kra-
ków. Komisja Historyczna. Wydaw-
nictwa. Ser.1: Monumenta medii aevi
historica res gestas Poloniae il-
lustrantia, t.6) DK402.P63 DLC CU
MB MdBJ MH

4638. CZARTORYSKI, Adam Jerzy.
Memoires of Prince Adam Czartoryski
and his correspondence with Alexander I. With documents relative to
the prince's negotiations with Pitt,
Fox, and Brougham and on account of
his conversations with Lord Pamer-
ston and other English statesmen in
London in 1832. Ed. by Adam Gielgud.
2nd ed. London, Remington & Co.,
1888. 2 v. fronts (ports).
DK435.5.C8 1888 DLC CtY CoU NBuU NN
NjP NSyU NcD PP PPL PU

4639. --- --- New York, N.Y.,
Arno Press, 1971. 2 v. in 1. (The
Eastern Europe collection) Reprint
of the 1888 ed. DK435.5.C83A4 1971
CaAEU

4640. CZARTORYSKI, Władysław.
Pamiętnik, 1860-1864; protokoly posiedzeń Biura Hotelu Lambert, cz.
1:2 Entrevues politiques. Opracował Henryk Wereszycki. Wyd. 1.
Warszawa, Państwowe Wydawn. Naukowe, 1960. 400 p. DK437.C82 DLC
MiDW WaU

4641. DANIŁOWICZ, Ignacy. Skar-
biec diplomatów papieżskich, cesar-
skich, królewskich, książęcych...
Wydał Jan Sidorowicz. Wilno, A.H.
Kirkor i sp., 1860-62. 2 v. in 1.
DK511.L23D3 DLC CtY ICU KU MH(1) NN
PU ViU

4642. DEMBIŃSKI, Bronisław, ed.
Documents relatifs à l'histoire du
deuxième et troisième partage de la
Pologne. Léopol, Société de propa-
gation des travaux scientifiques,
1902. lxxi, 565 p. DK434.A2D4 DLC
CaAEU NN CU CtY ICU InU KU OU RPB
ViU

4643. --- Zródła do dziejów drugiego i trzeciego rozbioru Polski.
t.1: Polityka Rossyi i Prus wobec
Polski od początków Sejmu czterolet-
niego do ogłoszenia Konstytucyi
trzeciego Maja, 1788-1791. Lwów,
1902. lxxi, 565 p. 943.8D.D393 PU

4644. DOVNAR-ZAPOL'SKII, Mitrofan
Viktorovich, comp. Akty litovsko-
russkago gosudarstva. Moskva, Tip.
A. I. Mamontova, 1890-97. 2 v.
DK511.L2D58 DLC(2) CU NN NNC(2)

4645. DZIAŁYŃSKI, Adam Tytus.
Zródłopisma do dziejów Unii Korony
Polskiej i Wielkiego Księstwa Li-
tewskiego. Poznań, Czcionkami L.
Merzbacha, 1856-61. 2 v. J399.H287
CaOTU BM(1-2, pt.1) ICBM MH(2, pt.1)

4646. GAIGALAITĖ, Aldona, comp.
Lietuvos TSR istorijos chrestomati-
ja. [Reader of Lithuanian TSR his-
tory.] Sudarė. A. Gaigalaitė, E.
Griškūnaitė ir J. Jurginis] Kaunas,
Šviesa, 1964. 209 p. DK511.L2G38
DLC

4647. GERMANY. AUSWÄRTIGES AMT.
Documents on German foreign policy,
1918-1945, from the Archives of the
German Foreign Ministry. Washington, D.C., G.P.O., 1949- . ([Uni-
ted States] Department of State.
Publications, 32777) Ser. D (1937-
1945) v.5 and v.8 have documents
related to Lithuania. JX691.A45 DLC

4648. German Foreign Ministry Archives, 1867-1920. London. Ann
Arbor, Mich. 1956- . Microfilm
copy of a series of reels made at
Whaddon Hall, England by the University of Michigan. Faculty Research Project no. 1005. Partial
contents.--Reel 25-27. Die Zukunft
der Baltischen Provinzen: Litauen,
1916-1917. CD1261.G373 reel 25,26,
27 CSt-H MiU

--- Nazi-Soviet relations,
1939-1941; documents from the archives of the German Foreign Office.
[Washington, D.C.] 1948. See entry
no. 2894.

4649. GRAHAM, Melbone W. Select
documents on new governments of
Eastern Europe: Lithuania. In His
New governments of Eastern Europe.
New York, N.Y., 1927. p. 706-749.
D443.G56 DLC CLU CU CSt CSt-H CaAEU
IC TU

4650. GRAMOTY VELIKIKH KNIAZEI LI-
tovskikh s 1390 po 1569 god. Sobr.
i izd. pod red. Vladimira Antonovicha i Konstantina Kozlovskogo.
Kiev, 1868. ix, 163 p. (Kiev.
Universitet. Universitetskiia izviestiia) See serials consulted.

GUAGNINO, Alessandro. Sarmatiae europeae descriptio, quae
regnum Poloniae, Lituaniam, Samogitiam, Russiam, Moscoviam, Prussiam,
Pomeraniam, Livoniam, et Moschoviae
Tartariaeque partem complectitur.
Cracoviae, 1578. See entry no. 4356.

4651. HANSISCHES URKUNDENBUCH.
Hrsg. von Verein für hansische Ge-
shichte. Halle; Leipzig, 1876-1938.
Information on Lithuania in v.8, p.
715; v.10, p. 518, 544; v.11, p. 121,
142, 401 and 436. DD801.H18H7 DLC PU

4652. JABLONSKIS, Konstantinas,
ed. XVI amžiaus Lietuvos inventoriai. [Manorial inventories in Lithuania in the sixteenth century]
Kaunas, Vytauto Didžiojo Universitetas, 1934. xii, 680 columns, 131 p.
(Kaunas. Universitetas. Biblioteka.
Leidinys, nr.2) DK511.L23J3 CU ICU
NN PU

KNIGA POSOL'SKAIA VELIKAGO
Kniazhestva Litovskogo. In Obolensky, M. A. Sbornik..., no. 1. See
entry no. 2898.

4653. KOMISSIIA DLIA RAZBORA DREV-
NIKH AKTOV, Kiev. Pamiatniki. Izd.
2. Kiev, Tip. Val'nera, 1846-[1848]
4 v. plates, facsims. DK508.A2K66
DLC ICU(1-2)

KUTRZEBA, Stanisław, ed.
Akta unji Polski z Litwą, 1385-1791.
Kraków, 1932. See entry no. 3310.

4654. LIETUVIŲ ARCHYVAS; bolševizmo metai. [Lithuanian archives; the
years of Bolshevism] Vilnius, Studijų biuras, 1942-43. 4 v. illus.,
ports. DK511.L27L47 DLC PU

4655. LIETUVIŲ ARCHYVAS; bolševiz-
mo metai. [Paruošė J. Prunskis]
Brooklyn, N.Y., 1952. 436 p. Con-
densed version of the 1st ed.
DK511.L27L48 DLC CaAEU CaOTU CtY
ICBM IU NN

4656. LITES AC RES GESTAE INTER
Polonos Ordinemque cruciferorum.
Editio secunda. Posnaniae, Sumptibus Bibliothecae Kornicensis, 1890-
1935. 3 v. Vols. 2 and 3 contain
information related to Lithuania.
DK402.L7 DLC MH NN

4657. LITHUANIA. LAWS, STATUTES,
ETC. Akty litovskoi metriki. So-
branye F.I. Leontovichem. Tom 1,
Vyp.1 (1413-1498), Vyp.2(1499-1507).
Varshava, Varshavskii Universitet,
1896-97. 2 v. F947.5.L554a 1896
KU CtY DLC

4658. --- Litovskaia metriki.
Peterburg, 1903-15. 4 v. (Russkaia
istoricheskaia biblioteka, t.20,27,
30,33) DK3.R8 v.20 etc. DLC
BM(20,27,30) NN

MALINOVSKII, Ioannikii
Alekseevich. Sbornik materialov
otnosiashchikhsia k istorii Panov-
Rady Velikogo Kniazhestva Litovskogo. Tomsk, 1901. See entry no.
2583.

MICHALONIS LITUANUS. Apie
totorių, lietuvių ir maskvėnų papročius. De moribus tartarorum, lituanorum et moschorum. Vilnius, 1966.
See entry no. 839.

4659. MONUMENTA MEDII AEVI HISTO-
rica res gestas Poloniae illustrantia. t.1- . Cracoviae, Sumptibus
Academiae litterarum Cracoviensis,
1874-1927. 19 v. (Editionum Collegii historici Academiae litterarum Cracoviensis, nr.4-5, 8-9, 13,
22,24,33,46,52,55,59,62)
DK402.M7 DLC CtPAM (1-16)

4660. MONUMENTA POLONIAE VATICANA.
t.1- . Cracoviae, Sumptibus Academiae polonicae litterarum et scientiarum, 1913-51. 8 v. (Editionum
Collegii historici Akademiae poloniae litterarum et scientiarum, nr.
71-74, 82, etc.) BX1564.A2M7 DLC PU

4661. MONUMENTA REFORMATIONIS PO-
lonicae et lithuanicae. Zbiór pom-
ników reformacyi kościoła polskiego
i litewskiego... Staraniem Synodu
Jednoty Ewangelicko-Reformowanej
Litewskiej. Wilno, 1911-15. 3 v.
illus., facsims. BR420.P7M6 DLC
BM(20012. g. 41.) CU MH

4662. MUKHANOV, Pavel Aleksandrovich, comp. Sbornik Mukhanova.
Moskva [v Universitetskoi tip.]
1836. iii, ix, 262, xxx p. fold.
plates, facsim. Introduction in
Russian; text in Russian or in the
16th century official language of
Lithuania. DK3.M92 1836 DLC ICU
MH NN

4663. --- --- Izd. 2., dop.
Sanktpeterburg, Tip. Ed. Pratsa,
1866. 1 v. fold. tables, facsim. NN

4664. OBITUM JOANNIS III., scis-
sionem, pacificationem, Lituanicos,
tractatus cum Porta Othomanica et
alia acta usque ad annum 1701 ex-
clusive continens. Brunsbergae;
Vratislaviae, 1711. 15, 946, 8 p.
In Załuski, Andrzej Chryzostom.
Epistolarum historico-familiarum,
t.2. BM(149. g. 9)

4665. OBOLENSKII, Mikhail Andreevich. Sbornik Kniazia Obolenskago.
Moskva, 1838-59. 20 no. Consists
of historical documents relating to
Russia, Poland and Lithuania, 1506-
1766. DK3.O2 DLC BM(9454. f. 1.
(1.))

4666. PASZKIEWICZ, Henryk, ed.
Regesta Lithuaniae ab origine usque
ad Magni Ducatus cum Regno Poloniae
unionem. Recensuit Henricus Paszkiewicz. Varsoviae, Soc. Mianow-
skiane, 1930. xxiii, 183 p. (Studia seminarii historiae orient.
Univ. Vars. cura O. Halecki edita,
nr.1) 943.8.W265 v.1 NNC
BM(9455. k. 24.) PU

4667. PERLBACK, Max. Urkunden
des rigaschen Capitel-Archives in
der fürstlich-czartoryskischen Bibliothek zu Krakau. In Gesellschaft
für Geschichte und Altertumskunde,
Riga. Mitteilungen aud der livländischen Geschichte (Riga), v.13,
1881. See serials consulted.

POLAND. SEJM 1569. Dnevnik
liublinskago seima 1569 goda. Sanktpeterburg, 1869. See entry no. 2607.

4668. PREUSSISCHE REGESTEN BIS ZUM
Ausgang des 13. Jahrhunderts. Hrsg.
von Max Perlbach. In Altpreussische
Monatsschrift (Königsberg in Pr.),

v.11, 1874, p. 1-32,97-128,326-348, 385-432,546-572,609-624; v.12, 1875, p. 1-26,97-144,193-216,319-344,385-428,577-645. See serials consulted.

4669. PROCHASKA, Antoni, ed. Materiały archiwalne wyjęte głównie z Metriki Litewskiej od 1348 do 1607 roku. Lwów, J.S. Dunin-Borkowski, 1890. viii, 212 p. BM(9475. g. 7.) MH PU

PRZYWILEJ UNII WIELKIEGO Xięstwa Litewskiego z Koroną z dnia 1-go Julii, 1569. Warszawa, 1843. See entry no. 2709.

4670. PTAŠNIK, Jan, ed. Acta camerae apostolicae. Edidit Joannes Ptaŝnik. Cracoviae, Sumptibus Academiae litterarum, 1913. 2 v. (Monumenta Poloniae Vaticana, t.1-2) 947.52.P962 PU NN

4671. --- Analecta vaticana, 1202-1308. Edidit Joannes Ptaŝnik. Cracoviae, Sumptibus Academiae litterarum, 1914. 1 v. (Monumenta Poloniae Vaticana, t.3) 947.52.P962 PU NN

4672. RELATIONES STATUS DIOCESIUM in Magno Ducatu Lituaniae. Pluribus adlaborantibus in unum redegit Paulus Rabikauskas. Romae, Adademiae Lituane catholicae scientiarum, 1971- . maps. (Fontes historiae Lituaniae, no.1, etc.) Contents.--v.1. Dioeceses Vilnensis et Samogitiae. BX1559.L7R38 CaAEU

4673. RUSSIA. ARKHEOGRAFICHESKAIA KOMISSIIA. Dokumenty obiasniaiushchye istoriiu Zapadno-Russkago kraia i ego otnosheniia k Rossii i k Pol'shie. Documents servant à éclairir l'histoire des provinces occidentales de la Russie ainsi que leurs rapports avec la Russie et la Pologne. [Sobral i sostavil M. Koialovich] Sanktpeterburg, Tip. E. Pratsa, 1865. cciii, 658 p. maps. Original documents in Russian or Polish with parallel translation into French. DK3.R72 DLC CLU NN PU

4674. --- Russisch-livländische Urkunden. [Russko-livonskie akty] Gesammelt von K.E. Napiersky. Sanktpeterburg, Buchdr. der Kaiserlichen Akademie der Wissenschaften, 1868. xxiii, 162 [i.e. 462] p. German, Latin or Russian. DK3.A133 DLC PU

4675. RUSSIA. MINISTERSTVO INOSTRANNYKH DIEL. Documents diplomatiques secrets russes 1914-1917, d'après les archives du Ministère des affairs étrangères à Pétrograd. Tr. du russe par J. Polonsky.

Paris, Payot, 1928. 331 p. (Collection de mémoires, études et documents pour servir à l'histoire de la guerre mondiale) D505.R887 Carnegie endow. Intern. Peace Library.

4676. RUSSIA MINISTERSTVO IUSTITSII. MOSKOVSKII ARKHIV. Dokumenty Moskovskago arkhiva Ministerstva iustitsii. Moskva, Tovarichestvo tipografii A.I. Mamontova, 1897. xxiii, 569 p. Ceased publication with vol. 1. Documents extracted from "Lietuvos Metrika". 947.R922d WaU NN

4677. --- Knigi Litovskoi Metriki. In Opisanie dokumentov i bumag khraniashchikhsia v Moskovskom arkhive Ministerstva iustitsii. Sanktpeterburg, 1915. v.21 (xxviii, 352 p.) BM(11906. i. 1.) NN

4678. RUSSKOE ISTORICHESKOE OBSHCHESTVO, LENINGRAD. Pamiatniki diplomaticheskikh snoshenii Moskovskogo gosudarstva s pol'sko-litovskim gosudarstvom. [Edited by G.F. Karpov and S.A. Bielokurov (v.4-5)] Moskva, 1882-1913. 5 v. (Its Sbornik, t.35,59,71,137,142) Period covered: 1487 until 1615. DK3.R9 v.35, etc. DLC RPB(59)

4679. --- Sbornik russkogo imperatorskogo istoricheskogo obshchestva. Sanktpeterburg, 1867-1916. 148 v. Information related to Lithuania is in vols. 128,133 and 139. DK3.R9 DLC NN RPB(59)

4680. SIENKIEWICZ, Jan Karol. Recueil de documents historiques relatifs à la Russie et la Pologne. Paris, Pagnere, 1854. 654 p. PU

4681. SOBRANIE DREVNIKH GRAMOT I aktov gorodov Minskoi gubernii pravoslavnykh monastyrei, tserkvei i po raznym predmetam. Zbiór dawnych dyplomatów i aktów miast Mińskiej gubernii, prawosławnych monasterów, cerkwi i w różnych sprawach. Minsk, Gubernskaia tipografiia, 1848. xlviii, 402 p. DK511.M3S6 CU NN

4682. SOBRANIE DREVNIKH GRAMOT I aktov gorodov: Vil'ny, Kovna, Trok, pravoslavnykh monast

4682. SOBRANIE DREVNIKH GRAMOT I Aktov gorodov: Vil'ny, Kovna, Trok, pravoslavnykh monastyrei, tservei, i po raznym predmetam. S. prilozheniem trekh litografirovannykh risunkov. Vil'na, Tip. A. Martsinovskago, 1843. 2 v. illus., fold. plan, fold. facsims. DK511.L2S6 DLC CU CtY KU NN NNC

SOCJALDEMOKRACJA KRÓLEWSTWA

Polskiego i Litwy. SDKPiL w rewolucji 1905 roku. [Warszawa] 1955.
589 p. See entry no. 2839.

--- Sotsial-demokratiia
Pol'shi i Litvy v revoliutsii 1905
g. Moskva, 1956. 789 p. See entry
no. 2840.

4683. THEINER, Augustin, ed. Ve-
tera monumenta Poloniae et Lithuaniae gentiumque finitimarum historiam illustrantia maximam partem
nondum edita ex tabulariis vaticanis
deprompta collecta ac serie chrono-
logica disposita. Romae, Typis
vaticanis, 1860-64. 4 v. DK402.T4
DLC CLU(positive microfilm) CU(positive microfilm) IaU InNd InU MiU MH
NN NNJ PPPD PU

4684. VILENSKAIA ARKHEOLOGICHES-
KAIA KOMISSIIA. Sobranie gosudarstvennykh i chastnykh aktov, ka-
saiushchikhsia istorii Litvy i soe-
dinennykh s nei vladienii, ot 1387
do 1710 goda. Chast' 1. Zbiór dyplomatów rządowych i aktów priwat-
nych posługujących do rozjaśnienia
dziejów Litwy i złączonych z nią
krajów. Pod red. Mavrikiia Krupo-
vicha. Vil'no, Tip. O. Zavadzkago,
1858. viii, 163 p. Only part one
published. Includes legislation of
Lithuania and Poland. Text in
Russian, Polish and Latin.
DK511.L2V47 DLC BM KU MH

4685. VILENSKAIA KOMISSIIA DLIA
RAZBORA I IZDANIIA DREVNIKH AKTOV.
Akty. Vil'na, 1865-1915. 39 v.
illus., fold. plans, maps. In Polish
Russian of Latin with Polish translation. DK511.L2A28 DLC(12-20,22-23,
29-37) CLU CU CSt-H CtY(2,4,9-11,21-
23,29) ICU(2-5,8-13,15-16,21-23)
KU(3-9,11-39) MH(1-37) NN NNC(6-9,11,
17-18,20,28-29) NjP(4-8,17,27,36) WaS

4686. --- --- [Microfiche edition]
Vil'na, 1865-1915. Tumba, Sweden,
International Documentation Centre,
196-. Microfiche 799 cards
947.65.V71a IU InU NjR WU WaU

4687. --- Alfavitnyi ukazatel' k
2-5 tomam aktov (1867-1871) Vil'na,
Tip. Gub. pravleniia, 1872. 165 p.
DK511.L2A28 indexes DLC CSt-H PU

4688. --- Ordinatsiia korolevskikh
pushch v liesnichestvakh byvshago Velikago Kniazhestva Litovskago. Sos-
tavilli Piotr Dolmat Isaikovskii i
Khr. Bielozor po instruktsii korolia
Vladislava IV., 1641. Vil'na, Tip.
Shtaba Vilenskago voennago okruga,
1871. xviii, 325 p. 947.52.Or24 PU
CSt-H NN

4689. --- Pistsovaia kniga Grodnens-

koi ekonomii s pribavleniami izdan-
naia Vilenskoiu kommissieiu dlia razbora drevnikh aktov. Vil'na, Tip.
A.G. Syrkina, 1881-82. 2 v.
947.52.V7125 PU CSt-H NN(1)

4690. --- Pistsovaia kniga Pinskago i Kletskago Kniazhestv, sostavlennaia Pinskim Starostoiu Stanislavom
Khval'chevskim v 1552-1555 gg. Vil'-
na, A.G. Syrkin, 1884. 714 p.
WE945 CtY CSt-H NN NNC

4691. --- Reviziia Kobrinskoi ekonomii sostavlennaia v 1563 godu ko-
rolevskim revisorom Dimitriem Sapie-
goiu, s prisovokupleniem aktov Bras-
lavskago Zemskago Suda, otnosiashchikhsia k Kabrinskoi Arkhimandrii.
Vil'na, A.G. Syrkin, 1876. 387 p.
943.V7195 NNC CSt-H

--- Reviziia pushch i perekhodov zvierinykh v byvshem Velikom
Kniazhestvie Litovskom... sostavlennaia Grigoriem Bogdanovichem Volovichem v 1559 godu. Vil'na, 1867.
See entry no. 2796.

4692. --- Sbornik dokumentov, kasa-
iushchikhsia administrativnago ustroistva Sievero-Zapadnago kraia pri
Imperatritsie Ekaterinie II., 1792-
1796. Vil'na, Russkii Pochin, 1903.
lxxxviii, 350 p. illus. DK168.V54
DLC CSt-H KU WaU

4693. VILNA. TSENTRAL'NYI ARKHIV.
Katalog drevnim aktovym knigam gubernii: Vilenskoi, Grodnenskoi... Vil'-
na, 1872. Cyr. 4K12 DLC CtY; see also
entry no. 4187.

4694. --- Opis' dokumentov Vilenskago Tsentral'nago arkhiva drevnikh
aktovykh knig. Vil'na, Tip. D. i Kh.
IAlovtsev, 1901-13. 10 v. in 2.
Contents.--Vyp. 1-5. Akty Rossienskago zemskago suda za 1575-1600 gody.--
Vyp. 6,9. Akty Volkomirskago suda za
1596-1624 gody.--Vyp.7. Akty Upitskago zemskago suda za 1585-1587 gody.
Akty Rossienskago podkomorskago suda
za 1595-1655 gody.--Vyp. 8. Akty
Upitskago zemskago suda za 1584-1615
gg.--Vyp. 10. Akty Bretskago grods-
kago suda za 1575-1715 gody.
KR3039.V5 DLC CLU CSt-H NN PU

4695. VILNA (Diocese) Kodeks dyplo-
matyczny katedry i diecezji wileńskiej. Wydali Jan Fijałek i Władysław Semkowicz. W Krakowie, Nakł. Polskiej Akademji Umiejętności; Skład
główny w księg. Gebethnera i Wolffa,
1932-39. v. illus. (Wydawnictwa
Komisji Historycznej Polskiej Akademji Umiejętności, nr. 81, etc.) Documents mostly in Latin. BX1568.V5A5
DLC CtY MH NNC PU

4696. VILNA (General-Governorship) ARKHIV. Opisanie diel, khraniash-chikhsia v arkhivie Vilenskago gene-ral-gubernatorstva. Sostavil Andrei Engel' pri sodieistvii K.P. Gomoli-tskago. Vil'na, 1869-70. 2 v. inl. (vi p., 984 columns, xxxiii p.) DK511.L24V5 DLC

4697. VOIGT, Johannes, ed. Codex diplomaticus prussicus. Urkunden-Sammlung zur älteren Geschichte Preussens aus dem königl. Geheimen Archiv zu Königsberg in Pr., nebst Regesten. Königsberg in Pr., Gebr. Bornträger, 1836-61. 6 v. DD491.041V7 DLC

4698. --- --- Neudruck der Ausg. 1836-61. Osnabrück, Zeller, 1965. DD491.041V72 1965 CaOTU PU

4699. WAPOWSKI, Bernard. Dzieje Korony Polskiej i Wielkiego Księstwa Litewskiego od roku 1380 do 1535... ze swieżo odkrytego społecznego rę-kopismu, z języka łacinskiego na oj-czysty przetłom., przypisami objas-nił, poczet rzeczny i osób dodał, Mikołaj Malinowski. Wilno, T. Glückberg, 1847-48. 3 v. DK425.W34 CtY BM MH

4700. ZAŁUSKI, Andrzej Chryzostom. Epistolarum historico-familiarum... Andreae Chrysostomi in Załuskie Zału-ski. Brunsbergae, Typis Mandatus Academiae, 1709-11. 4 v. ICBM BM

X.8.c. COMMENTARIES AND INTERPRETA-TIONS OF SOURCE MATERIAL

4701. ADAMUS, Jan. Wydawnictwa źródeł do historii Litwy. In PZHP w Wilnie 17-20 września 1935 r. Pa-miętnik VI. Referaty (Lwów), v.1, 1935, p. 439-449. See serials con-sulted.

4702. BATŪRA, R. Lietuvos metraš-čių legendinės dalies ir M. Stryj-kovskio "Kronikos" istoriškumo klau-simu. [On the historical values of the legendary parts of Lithuanian chronicles and as well as M. Stryj-kovski's chronicle] In LTSRMAD. Serija A, v.2(21), 1966, p. 265-283. illus. Summary in Russian. See se-rials consulted.

4703. BAUER, Helmut. Peter von Dusburg und die Geschichtsschreibung des Deutschen Ordens in 14. Jahrhun-dert in Preussen. Berlin, Verlag dr. E. Ebering, 1935. 104 p. (His-torische Studien... Hft.272) Vaduz, Lichtenstein, Krauss reprint, 1965.

DD491.046P45 1965 PU NcD

4704. BEREZHKOV, Nikolai Georgie-vich. Litovskaia metrika kak isto-richeskii istochnik. Moskva, Izd-vo Akademii nauk SSSR, 1946. 175 p. At head of title: Akademiia nauk SSSR. Institut Istorii. Contents. --Ch.1. O pervonachal'nom sostave knig Litovskoi metriki do 1522 goda. 175 p. DK511.L23B4 CLU CU CtY ICU InNd InU IU KU MH NIC NN NcU NNC PU WaS WU

4705. CHODYNICKI, Kazimierz. Ze studjów nad dziejopisarstwem rusko-litewskim. (Tak zwany Rękopis Rau-dański) In Ateneum Wileńskie (Wil-na), v.3, 1925-26. p. 387-401. See serials consulted.

4706. DANIŁOWICZ, Ignacy. Über die litauischen Chroniken. Aus dem Jour-nal des Ministeriums der Volks-Auf-klärung mit Abkürzungen übersetzt von F. Löwe. In Beiträge zur Kennt-niss des russischen Reiches... (Sankt-peterburg), v.10, 1844, p. 227-267. See serials consulted.

4707. --- Wiadomość o właściwych litewskich latopiscach. In Stryjkows-ki, Maciej. Kronika polska, litews-ka i Żmudzka... Warszawa, 1846. v.1, p. 31-63. DK414.S87 DLC CU MH(1528 ed.) BM(1314. h. 18.)

4708. GEDIMINAS, Grand Duke of Li-thuania. Letters of Gediminas and the commentary by Paulius Rabikauskas. In Lithuanus (Chicago, Ill.), v.14, no.4, 1969, p. 4-54. See serials consulted.

4709. GIRGENSOHN, Joseph. Kriti-sche Untersuchung über das VII. Buch der Historia Polonica des Długosz. Göttingen, Universitäts-Buchdruckerei von E.A. Huth, 1873. vi, 95, p. Thesis--University of Göttingen. DK419.D6G5 DLC BM

4710. HERDA, Reinhold. Quaestiones de fontibus, quibus Dlugoszius usus sit in componenda Historia Polonica in disputationem adhibito libro deci-mo. Vratislaviae, typis Leopoldi Freund, 1865. 2 p.l., 52 p. Thesis --University of Breslau. DK419.D6H3 DLC MH

4711. ISTOCHNIKOVEDCHESKIE PROBLE-my istorii narodov Pribaltiki. [Red. kollegiia: IA.P. Krastyn' i dr.] Ri-ga, Zinātne, 1970. 484 p. DK511.B3.I73 PU

4712. IVINSKIS, Zenonas. Eiliuoti-nė Livonijos kronika ir jos autentiš-kumas. [Reimchronik and its authenticity] In Židinys (Kaunas), no.10, 1936, p. 289-302. See serials consulted.

4713. JAKUBOWSKI, Jan. Kroniki litewskie. In Towarzystwo Przyjaciół Nauk w Wilnie. Rocznik (Wilno), v.3, 1909, p. 68-76. See serials consulted.

4714. JANKOWSKA, Jadwyga. O tak zwanej Metryce Litewskiej w zasobie Archivum Głównego akt dawnych w Warszawie. In Archeion (Warszawa), v.32, 1960, p. 31-56, 195,197-198. See serials consulted.

4715. JUČAS, Mečislovas. Lietuvos didžiųjų kunigaikščių metraštis. [The chronicle of the Grand Dukes of Lithuania] In LTSRMAD. Serija A, v.2(3), 1957, p. 111-120. See serials consulted.

4716. --- Russkie letopisi XIV-XV vv. kak istochnik po istorii Litvy. In LTSRMAD. Serija A, v.2(5), 1958, p. 69-83. See serials consulted.

4717. LITHUANIA. METRIKA, WILNO. Starinnyia opisi Litovskoi metriki. Sanktpeterburg, 1903. 194 p. (Russia. Arkheograficheskaia Komissiia. Lietopis' zaniatii. Vyp.11, otd.2) (*QCB)NN

4718. Lohmeyer, Karl Heinrich. Wigand von Marburg. In Allgemeine Deutsche Biographie. Bd. 20, 1884, p. 293-294. CT1053.A5 DLC AU CaAEU CaBVaU CoU CoDU CU DSI DNO ICJ MdBJ MdBP MeB NBC NjP OClW OO OrPR OU OrU PBm PU PPULC ViU TU WaU

4719. MATUSAS, Jonas. Albertas Vijukas-Kojalavičius kaip Lietuvos istorininkas. [Kojałowicz, Wojciech Albert Wijuk as Lithuanian historian] In Praeitis (Kaunas), v.1, 1930, p. 318-329. See serials consulted.

4720. PERFETSKII, EVGENII IUl'evich. História polonica Jana Długosza a nemecké letopisectvo. Bratislava, Filozofická fakulta, 1940. 211 p. (Spisy Filozofickej fakulty Slovenskej Univerzity v Bratislave, 28) Summary in German. DK419.D6P4 DLC

4721. --- História polonica Jana Długosza a ruské letopisectví. V Praze, "Orbis", Tiskem státní tiskárny, 1932. 120 p. (Práce slovenského ústavu v Praze. Svazek 7) Summary in French. Bw81.44 CtY NN

4722. PERLBACH, MAX. Die jüngere livländische Reimchronik. In Alt-

preussische Monatsschrift (Königsberg in Pr.), v.9, 1872, p. 472-475. See serials consulted.

4723. --- Königsberger Correspondenzen aus der Zeit Werners von Orseln. In Altpreussische Monatsschrift (Königsberg in Pr.), Bd.10, 1873, p. 79-84. See serials consulted.

4724. --- Der Übersetzer des Wigands von Marburg. In Altpreussische Monatsschrift (Königsberg in Pr.), Bd.32, 1895, p. 410-429. See serials consulted.

4725. POGODIN, Mikhail Petrovich. Nestor, eine historisch-kritische Untersuchung über den Anfang der russischen Chroniken. Uebersetzt unter Revision und Erweiterung des Verfassers von F. Löwe. Angehängt ist: Danilowitsch über die Litauischen Chroniken, aus dem Journal des Ministeriums der Voksaufklärung, 1840, November, mit Abkürzungen, übersetzt von F. Löwe. Sanktpeterburg, gedruckt bei der Kaiserlichen Akademie der Wissenschaften, 1844. viii, 261 p. Rare DK3.B42 v.10 NIC CU

4726. PROCHASKA, Antoni. Długosz a cronica conflictus o grunwaldzkiej bitwie. In Kwartalnik Historyczny (Lwów), 1910, p. 407-421. See serials consulted.

4727. --- Latopis litewski; rozbiór krytyczny. Lwów, Gł. Skł. w Księg. G.Gebethnera, 1890. ii, 58 p. DK511.L23P72 DLC MH PU

4728. --- Z powodu wydawnictwa latopisów litewskich. In Przegląd Historyczny (Warszawa), v.12, 1910, p. 115-125. See serials consulted.

4729. PTASZYCKI, Stanisław. Opisanie knig i aktov Litovskoi Metriki. Sanktpeterburg, Tip. Pravitel'stvuiushchago Senata, 1887. viii, 278 p. 947.52.P957 PU KU NN BM(11918. s.12.)

4730. --- Sumariusz i inwentarze Metryki Litewskiej. In Archeion (Warszawa), v.8, 1930, p. 31-44. See serials consulted.

4731. ŠALŪGA, R. Bychovco kronika (Bykhovco chronicle). In LTSRMAD. Serija A, v.1(6), 1959, p. 149-154. See serials consulted.

4732. SHAKHMATOV, Aleksei Aleksandrovich. An account of the text of the Novgorod chronicle. Translated from Russian.... In Novgorod Chronicle. The chronicle of Novgorod, 1016-1471. London, 1914. p. xxxvii-xli.

DA20.R91 3d ser. v.25 RPB MB NN

4733. --- Obozrenie russkikh letopis'nykh svodov XIV-XV v. Moskva;
Leningrad, Izd-vo Akademii nauk SSSR.
1938. 372 p. diagr. DK39.S5 DLC
CaAEU

4734. SMOŁKA, Stanisław. Najdawniejsze pomniki dziejopisarstwa rus-
ko-litewskiego. Rozbiór krytyczny.
In Polska Akademia Umiejętności, Kraków. Wydział Filologiczny. Pamiętnik Akademji Umiejętności w Krakowie.
Wydziały: Filologiczny i Historyczno-
Filosoficzny, t.8, 1890, p. 1-55.
AS142.K865 DLC CaOTU MH

4735. SZARANIEWICZ, Izydor. O la-
topisach i kronikakh ruskikh XV i
XVI wieku a zwłaszcza o latopisie
"Velikoho Kniazhstva Litovskoho i
Žomoitskoho". In Polska Akademia
Umiejętności, Kraków. Wydział Historyczno-Filozoficzny. Rozprawy,
v.15, 1882, p. 65. See serials consulted.

4736. TIKHOMIROV, Ivan Aleksandrovich. O sostavie zapadno-russkikh,
tak nazyvaemykh litovskikh lietopisei. In ZMNP, v.335, 1901, p. 1-37,
70-120. See serials consulted.

4737. YČAS, Jonas. Simone Grunau
XVI amžiaus kronisto reikalu. [On
the question of Simone Grunau...]
In Švietimo darbas (Kaunas), no.3-6,
1922, p. 189-251. See serials consulted.

X.9. HISTORY BY PERIOD

X.9.a. EARLY HISTORY TO 1236

4738. KULIKAUSKIENĖ, Regina (Volkaitė) Ankstyvojo feodalizmo laikotarpis (IX-XII a.) [The early feudal period (IX-XII cent.)] In Kulikauskas, P. Lietuvos archeologijos
bruožai. Vilnius, 1961. p. 360-
[519]. illus. GN845.L5K8 DLC CaAEU

4739. --- Lietuviai IX-XII amžiais.
[Lithuanians in the ninth to the
twelfth century] Vilnius, Mintis,
1970. 294 p. illus. DK511.L21K813
DLC CaAEU PU

4740. --- Material'naia kul'tura
nasel'eniia Litvy 9-12 v. po dannym
issledovanii pogrebal'nykh pamiatnikov; pozdnii zheleznyi vek. Vil'-
nius, 1950. 19 p. DK511.L21K82 DLC

4741. PAPÉE, Fryderyk. Początki

Litwy. In Kwartalnik Historyczny
(Lwów), v.47, no.3-4, 1927, p. 465-
476. See serials consulted.

4742. PASZKIEWICZ, Henryk. Litwa
przed Mendogiem. In PZHP w Warszawie. Pamiętnik V. Referaty (Warszawa), v.1, 1930, p. 246-258. See serials consulted.

4743. VARAKAUSKAS, R. Vokiečių fe-
odalų agresija į rytinį Pabaltijį ir
lietuvių kova su jais XIII amžiuje
pirmajame ketvirtyje. [German agression into the Eastern Baltic territory and the Lithuanian struggle
against them during the first quarter of the thirteenth century] In
Vilna. Valstybinis pedagoginis institutas. Mokslo darbai, v.3, 1957,
p.5-31. See serials consulted.

4744. WINKLER DE KĘTRZYŃSKI, Wojciech Jan. O powołaniu Krzyżaków
przez Ks. Konrada. In Polska Akademia Umiejętności, Kraków. Wydział
Historyczno-Filozoficzny. Rozprawy,
1903. See serials consulted.

X.9.b. MINDAUGAS AND OTHER
DUKES, 1236-1316

4745. ANTONOVICH, Vladimir Bonifa-
t'evich. Litva i Rus' do nachala
XIV stoletiia. In His Monografii po
istorii Zapadnoi i IUgo-Zapadnoi Rossii. Kiev, 1885. v.1, p. 7-36.
DK511.L2A7 t.1 DLC CtY MH PU WaU WU

4746. BACKUS, Oswald Prentiss.
The problem of unity in the Polish-
Lithuanian state. In Slavic Review
(Menasha, Wis.), v.22, no.3, 1963, p.
411-455. See serials consulted.

4747. BATŪRA, R. Ar kovojo Lietuva su totoriais-mongolais Batu ant-
puolio į Europą metu? [Did Lithuania
fight the tatars and mongols during
the Batu invasion into Europe?] In
LTSRMAD. Serija A, v.3(22), 1966,
p. 185-199. illus. Summary in Russian. See serials consulted.

4748. --- XIII a. Lietuvos sostinės klausimu. [On the question of
the capital of Lithuania in the
thirteenth century] In LTSRMAD.
Serija A, v.1(20), 1966, p. 141-165.
map. Summary in Russian. See serials consulted.

4749. BERZINŠ, J. Kur notika Sau-
les kauja 1236 gada. [Where the
Battle of Saule of 1236 took place]
In Latvia. Izglitibas ministerija.
Menešraksts (Riga), no.1, Jan. 1935,

p. 1-17. L466.L3A3 DLC

4750. DUKSZTA, Mieczysław von. Le royaume de Lithuanie au XIII siècle et l'Ordre Teutonique, Prusiens actuels. Genève, "Athenaeum", 1917. 12 leaves. ports. (Publication de l'Athenaeum, no.7) DK511.L2D86 ICU BM(010007. ee. 3.(3.)) NN

4751. FORSTREUTER, Kurt Hermann. Fragen der Mission in Preussen von 1245 bis 1260. In Zeitschrift für Ostforschung (Marburg/Lahn), v.9, no.2-3, 1960, p. 250-268. See serials consulted.

4752. HALECKI, Oskar. Przyczynki genealogiczne do dziejów układu Krewskiego. In Miesięcznik Heraldyczny (Warszawa), v.14, 1935, p. 97-111. See serials consulted.

4753. HELLMANN, Manfred. Der Deutsche Orden und die Königskrönung des Mindaugas. In Zeitschrift für Ostforschung (Marburg/Lahn), v.3, no.3, 1954, p. 387-396. See serials consulted.

4754. IVINSKIS, ZENONAS. Durbės kautynės 1260 m. ir jų politinis vaidmuo. [The Battle of Durbė of 1260 and its political significance] Kaunas, Kariuomenės štabas. Spaudos ir švietimo skyrius, 1937. 114 p. 947.52.Iv54 PU; also in Karo archivas (Kaunas), v.8-9, 1937-1938, p. 1-114. See serials consulted.

4755. --- Mindaugas und die Žemaiten; das politische Verhältnis des ersten Litauerkönigs zu seinen Westgebieten (Žemaiten). In Tartu. Ülikool. Õpetatud eesti selts. Toimitused, v.30, pt.2, 1938. p. 930-958. See serials consulted.

4756. --- Mindaugas und seine Krone. In Zeitschrift für Ostforschung (Marburg/Lahn), v.3, no.3, 1954, p. 360-386. See serials consulted.

4757. --- Pirmasis Lietuvos karalius Mindaugas ir jo palikimas. [Mindaugas the first King of Lithuania and his legacy] In LKMAM, v.1, 1965, p. 53-116. See serials consulted.

4758. --- Saulės-Šiaulių kautynės 1236 metais ir jų reikšmė. [The Battle of Saulė-Šiauliai in 1236 and its significance] Kaunas, Kariuomenės štabas, Švietimo skyriaus leidinys, 1936. 50 p. Bibliography: p. 46-50. DK511.L2319 DLC CaAEU: also in Karo archyvas (Kaunas), v.7, 1936, p. 5-50.

4759. JONYNAS, Ignas. Kautynės netoli Saulės. [The Battle of Saulė] In Lietuvos aidas (Kaunas), no. 444-450, 1936. See serials consulted.

4760. --- Les peuplades lithuaniennes jusqu'au XIVe siècle. In Baltijas Vēsturnieku konference, 1st, Riga, 1937. Runas un referāti (Riga), 1938, p. 46-61. DK511. DK511.B25B35 DLC CSmH NNC PPULC PU

4761. JURGINIS, Juozas. Užkariautojai veržiasi i Pabaltiją. [The conquerors thrust on the Baltic Countries] In Lietuvių karas su kryžiuočiais. Vilnius, 1964. p. 50-78. illus. DK511.L23L45 DLC CaAEU CtY MH

4762. KEUSSLER, Friedrich von. Der Ausgang der ersten russischen Herrschaft in den gegenwärtigen Ostseeprovinzen im XIII Jahrhundert. Sanktpeterburg, 1897. 119 p. (Jahresbericht der St. Annen-Schule...) 947.52.K519 PU

4763. KRUMBHOLTZ, Robert. Samaiten und der Deutsche Orden bis zum Frieden am Melno-See. In Altpreussische Monatsschrift (Königsberg in Pr.), v.26, 1889, p. 193-258, 461-484; v.27, 1890, p. 1-74, 193-227. See serials consulted.

4764. ŁATKOWSKI, Juliusz. Mendog król litewski. In Polska Akademia Umiejętności, Kraków. Wydział Filozoficzno-historyczny. Rozprawy, v.3(28), no.2, 1892, p. 300-453. See serials consulted.

4765. MALECZYŃSKI, Karol. Sprawa chrztu i apostazji Mendoga w swietle krytyki dokumentów. In PZHP w Wilnie 17-22 września, 1935. Pamiętnik VI. Referaty (Lwów), v.1, 1935, p. 559-561.

4766. --- W sprawie autentyczności dokumentów Mendoga z lat 1253-1261. In Ateneum Wileńskie (Wilno), v.11, 1936, p. 1-60. See serials consulted.

4767. PUZYNA, Józef Edward. W sprawie pierwszych walk Litwinów z Tatarami o Ruś w latach 1238-1243. In Przegląd Historyczno-Wojskowy. Poland (1918-1939) Sztab generalny. Biuro Historyczne (Warszawa), v.9, no.3, 1937. D25.P6 DLC

4768. SKIRMUNTT, Konstancja. Mindaugas, Lietuvos karalius. [Mindaugas, the King of Lithuania] Kaunas, Banaičio, 1907. 120 p. 947.5.L M663.yS.LE PU CtTMF OCl

4769. --- Mindog król Litwy. In Nad Niemnem i nad Bałtykiem w zaraniu dziejów. Kraków, 1900. pt.3, 190, ii p. DK511.L23S46 DLC BM(9475. b. 52.)

STAKAUSKAS, Juozapas. Lietuva ir vakarų Europa XIII amžiuje. Kaunas, 1934. See entry no. 2911.

4770. STEPONAITIS, Antanas. Mindaugas ir vakarai. Vokiečių militarinių ordinų veikla ir Mindaugo santykiai su Roma. [Mindaugas and the West; the activities of the Teutonic Knights and the relations of Mindaugas with Rome] Kaunas, 1937. 98 p. DK511.L23S79 DLC IU MiD NN PU CtTMF

4771. SUŽIEDELIS, Simas. Kautynės ties Šiauliais, 1236. [The Battle of Šiauliai, 1236] Kaunas, 1936. 41 p. Bibliography: p. 39-41. DK511.L23S8 DLC; also in Athenaeum (Kaunas), v.6, 1935.

4772. TOTORAITIS, Jonas. Die Litauer unter dem König Mindowe bis 1263. Fribourg, 1905. 160 p. Thesis (Ph.D.)--University of Fribourg (Switzerland). 947.52.T645.2 PU MH NNC

4773. --- Mindaugas Lietuvos karalius. [Mindaugas, the King of Lithuania] Marijampolė, Marijonų spaustuvė, 1932. 124 p. (Marijonų kongregacijos leidinys) DK511.L2T65 DLC ICCC

4774. VARAKAUSKAS, R. Ledo mūšis ties Karūzu, 1270. ["Ledo" battlefield, 1270] In LTSRAMMD; Istorija (Vilna), v.4, 1962, p. 147-156. See serials consulted.

4775. --- Lietuvių kova su vokiškaisiais agresoriais Mindaugo valdymo laikotarpiu, 1236-1263. [Lithuanian struggle against Teutonic agressors during the reign of Mindaugas, 1236-1263] In Vilna. Valstybinis pedagoginis institutas. Mokslo darbai, v.4, 1958, p. 111-141. See serials consulted.

4776. VOL'TER, Eduard Aleksandrovich. Gorod Mendovga ili gdie iskat Letoviju XIII veka. In Akademiia nauk, Petrograd. Otdielenie Russkogo iazyka i slovesnosti. Izviestiia, v.14, no3, 1910, p. 95-102. See serials consulted.

4777. WINKLER DE KĘTRZYŃSKI, Wojciech Jan. Najdawniejsza stolica litewska. In Kwartalnik Historyczny (Lwów), v.21, 1907, p. 604-611. map. See serials consulted.

4778. --- O dokumentach Mendoga króla litewskiego 1263... In Polska Akademija Umiejętności, Kraków. Wydział Filozoficzny. Rozprawy, v.50, ser. II, no.25, 1907, p. 180-222. map. See serials consulted.

4779. WŁODARSKI, Bronisław. Rywalizacja o ziemie pruskie w połowie XIII wieku. In Towarzystwo Naukow w Toruniu. Roszniki (Toruń), 1958, p. 1-76. See serials consulted.

4780. ZAJĄCZKOWSKI, Stanisław. Studya nad dziejami Żmudzi wieku XIII... In Towarzystwo Naukowe we Lwowie. Wydział II. Historyczno-Filozoficzny. Archiwum, v.3, no. 2, 1925, p. 110. See serials consulted.

4781. ŽIUGŽDA, Juozas. Bor'ba litovskogo naroda s nemetskimi rytsariami v 13-14 vekakh. In Istoricheskii zhurnal (Moskva), v.15, no.8-9, 1943, p.[27]-33. See serials consulted.

X.9.c. GEDIMINAS AND OTHER DUKES, 1316-1345

4782. CHODYNICKI, Kazimierz. Książę litewski na Kujawach v w. XIV. Poznań, Nakł. Poznanskiego Towarzystwa Przyjaciół Nauk, 1933. 10 p. Offprint. 947.52.C458 PU

4783. CHUBATYI, Mykola. Derzhavno-pravne stanovyshche ukrains'kykh zemel' lytovs'koi derzhavy pid kinets' XIV v. In Naukove Tovarystv-Imeni Shevchenka. Zapysky (L'viv), v.144-145, 1926, p. 1-108. AS142.I45 DLC

4784. FILEVICH, Ivan Porfir'evich. Bor'ba Pol'shi i Litvy-Rusi za Galitsko-Vladimirskoe nasliedie. Sanktpeterburg, Tip. V.S. Balasheva, 1890. x, 233 p. DK421.3.F4 WU DLC MH NN

4785. FORSTREUTER, Kurt Hermann. Die Bekehrung Gediminas und der Deutsche Orden. In Altpreussische Forschungen (Königsberg in Pr.), v.5, 1928, p. 239-261. See serials consulted.

4786. --- Zur Geschichte des Christburger Friedens von 1249. In Zeitschrift für Ostforschung (Magburg), v.12, no.2, 1962, p. 295-302. See serials consulted.

4787. GEDIMINAS, Grand Duke of Lithuania. Gedimino laiškai.

[Letters of Gediminas. Ed. by V. Pašuta and I. Štal] Vilnius, Mintis, 1966. 197, [4]p. At head of title: Lietuvos TSR Mokslų akademija. Istorijos institutas. Text of letters in Latin, with Lithuanian and Russian translations. DK511.L23G4 DLC CaNSHD CaOHM CtPAM CtY IEN InNd InU IU NIC NN NcD NcU NjP PU

4788. HECHT, Kurt. Die Schlacht bei Rudau, 1370. Osterode, 1914. 67 p. Thesis--University of Königsberg in Pr. 947.52.H357 PU

4789. KUCZYŃSKI, Stefan Maria. Antymoskiewska inicjatywa Litwy w drugiej polowie XIV wieku. Warszawa, 1926. 30 p. Offprint from: miesięcznika "Polityka Narodów". 947.52K9535 PU

4790. LOHMEYER, Karl Heinrich. Die Littauerschlacht bei Rudau im Samland 1370, ihre gleichzeitige und ihre spätere Darstellung. Ein Vortrag... Königsberg in Pr., n.d. 15 p. (Geschichte. Nordeuropa. Nr.4) Ra940.G38 no.4 NSyU

4791. --- --- Berlin, 1870. Offprint. 947.52.L834 PU

4792. PASHUTO, Vladimir Terent'evich. Poslaniia Gedimina. [Podgotovili V.T. Pashuto i I.V. Shtal'] Vil'nius, Mintis, 1966. 197 p. Text in Russian, Lithuanian and Latin. DK511.L23P38 TU

4793. PASZKIEWICZ, Henryk. Ze studjów nad polityką polską litewską i krzyżacką Bolesława-Jerzego, ostatniego księcia Rusi halicko-włodzimierskiej. In Ateneum Wileśkie (Wilno), 1924, v.2, p. 31-67. See serials consulted.

4794. --- Stosunki Kryżaków z Giedyminen i Łokietkiem. In Kwartalnik Historychny (Lwów), v.10, 1896, p. 1-66. See serials consulted.

4795. PUZYNA, Jósef Edward. Kim był i jak się naprawdę nazywał Pukuwer ojciec Gedymina? In Ateneum Wilenskie (Wilno), v.10, 1935, p. 1-43. See serials consulted.

4796. SEMKOWICZ, Władysław. Hanul, namiestnik wileński, 1382-1387. In Ateneum Wileńskie (Wilno), v.7, 1930, p. 1-20. See serials consulted.

4797. SPLIET, Herbert. Die Briefe Gedimins; ein Beitrag zu der Geschichte der Stadt Riga. Sin-

sheim, Beckersche Buchdrückerei, 1953. 32 p. DK511.L28G38 DLC PU

4798. STADNICKI, Kazmierz. Koryjat Gedyminowicz i Koryjatowicze. In Polska Akademia Umiejętności, Kraków. Wydział Historyczno-Filozoficzny. Rozprawy i Sparawozdania z Posiedzeń. v.7, 1877, p. 1-146. See serials consulted.

4799. THOMAS, Alfred. Litauen nach den Wegeberichten im Ausgange des 14. Jahrhunderts. Tilsit, 1885. 16 p. (Program d. köngl. Realgymnasium, nr.21) 947.52.T362 PU MH

4800. VASIL'EVSKII, Vasilii Grigorevich. Obrashchenie Gedimina v katolichestvo. In ZMNP, v.159, no. 2, 1872, p. 135-169. See serials consulted.

4801. ZAJĄCZKOWSKI, Stanisław. Przyczyńki do hipotezy o pochodzeniu dynasty Giedymina ze Żmudzi. In Ateneum Wileńskie (Wilno), v.4, 1927, p. 392-451. See serials consulted.

4802. --- W sprawie zajęcia Podlasia przez Giedymina. In Ateneum Wileńskie (Wilno), v.6, 1929, p. 1-7. See serials consulted.

4803. --- Żmudź w początkach Unji polsko-litewskiej. In PZHP w Warszawie 28 listopada do 4 grudnia 1930. Pamiętnik V. Referaty (Lwów), v.1, 1930, p. 337-344. See serials consulted.

X.9.d. ALGIRDAS, KĘSTUTIS, AND JOGAILA, 1345-1392

4804. ADAMUS, Jan. Paśtwo Litewskie w latach 1386-1398. In Ehrenkreutz, Stefan, ed. Księga pamiątkowa... Wilno, 1935, p. 15-79. CU CtY DLC BM InU MH NN PU

4805. BALZER, Oswald, Marian. Istota prawna zależności książąt litewsko-ruskich w dobie 1385-1398. In Towarzystwo Naukowe we Lwowie. Sprawozdania (Lwów), v.1, 1921, p. 196-204. See serials consulted.

4806. DĄBROWSKI, Jan, ed. Korona i Litwa od chrztu Jagiełły do Warny, 1386-1444... Kraków, Nakł. Krakowskiej Spółki Wydawniczej, 1923. 32 p. (Teksty zródłowe do nauki historii w szkole średniej,24) 947.52.D114 PU

4807. GOŁĘBIOWSKI, Łukasz.
Dzieje Polski za Władysława Jagieł-
ły i Władysława III-go. [Warszawa,
Druk S. Orgelbranda, 1846-48] 3 v.
DK524.G6 DLC MH

4808. IVINSKIS, Zenonas. Jogaila
valstybininkas ir žmogus. [Jogaila
as statesman...] In Šapoka, Adolfas. Jogaila. Kaunas, 1935, p.
311-328. 947.52.W797.yS PU OCl

4809. JANULAITIS, Augustinas.
Kęstutis Marienburgo pilyje ir pa-
bėgimas iš ten 1361. [Kęstutis in
the castle of Marienburg and his
flight from there in 1361] In
Praeitis (Kaunas), v.1, 1930, p.
64-93. See serials consulted.

4810. KONECZNY, Feliks. Jagiełło
i Witold. Część pierwsza: Podczas
uniji Krewskiej, 1382-1392. Lwów,
1893. 212 p. BM(9456. dd. 29.);
also in Przewodnik Naukowy i Literacki. t.20, 1892, p. 1-14;97-
113;193-208;289-301;483-494;577-
591;673-690;769-780;865-898;961-983,
1057-1096. AP54.P823 v.20 DLC MH

4811. KOSMAN, Marcelin. Władysław
Jagiełło. [Warszawa] Książka i
Wiedza [1968]. 293 p. DK426.K67 PU

4812. KRÜGER, H. Ein Brief des
Litauerfürsten Olgerd [Algirdas] an
den Patriarchen von Konstantinopel.
In LLGM, v.5, 1907, p. 358-381.
See serials consulted.

4813. KUČINSKAS, Antanas. Kęstučio kovos su vokiečių ordenu. [Wars
of Kęstutis with the Teutonic Order]
In Athenaeum (Kaunas), v.4, 1933, p.
120. See serials consulted.

4814. --- Kęstutis lietuvių tautos gynėjas. [Kęstutis the protec-
tor of the Lithuanian nation] Kaunas, Sakalas, 1938. 228 p.
947.52.K953 PU CtTMF

4815. KUCZYŃSKI, Stefan Maria. O
pragramie pierwszych Jagiellonów,
tzw. idei Jagiellóńskiej i rzekomej
agreśji Polskiej na wschód w XV w.
In His studia z dziejów Europy
wschodniej... Warszawa, 1965, p.
[181]-188. DK420.K8 DLC CaAEU PU

4816. --- Sine wody; rzecz o wy-
prawie Olgierdowej 1362 r. In His
studia z dziejów Europy wschodniej.
.. Warszawa, 1965. p. [135]-180.
DK420.K8 DLC CaAEU PU

4817. --- Władysław Jagiełło,
1350-1434. [Wyd. 1. Warszawa] Wydawn, Ministerstwa Obrony Narodowej
[1971] 177 p. illus.

DK426.K83 CaOTU PU

4818. LIPKIN, Maksim. Keistut i
Biruta; litovskaia byl' iz XIV veka.
Sanktpeterburg, 1890, p. 739- .
(Viestnik Evropy, April 1890)
AP50.V5 t.24 DLC CSt-H CU CtY ICU
MH NN NNC

4819. MIERŻYŃSKI, Antoni. Das
Eid des Kęstutis im Jahre 1361. In
Altertumsgesellschaft Prussia.
Sitzungsberichte (Königsberg in
Pr.), v.18, 1892-93. See serials
consulted.

4820. PASZKIEWICZ, Henryk. Jagiełło w przededniu Unii polsko-
litewskiej w oświetleniu nowych
źródeł. In Teki Historyczne (London), v.4, no.4, 1950, p. 187-197.
See serials consulted.

4821. --- W sprawie inkorporacji
Litwy do Polski, w 80-ch latach XIV
w. Z powodu pracy prof. dr H. Łowmiańskiego "Wcielenie Litwy do Polski w 1386 roku". Warszawa, Gebethner i Wolff, 1938.
947.52.P365.4 PU

4822. PROCHASKA, Antoni. Król
Władysław Jagiełło. Kraków Akade-
mia Umiejętności, Nakłd. Fundus zu
Nestora Bucewicza, 1908. 2 v.
DK426.P7 DLC CaBVaU CaOTU CSt IU
InU KU NN PU

4823. --- Upadek Kiejstuta. In
Kwartalnik Historychny (Lwów), v.23,
1909. See serials consulted.

4824. ŠAPOKA, Adolfas, ed. Jogaila [Jagiełło]. Paražė J. Jakštas
[et al]. Kaunas, 1935. 333 p.
947.52W797.yS PU ICCC OCl

4825. SMOLKA, Stanisław. Kiejstut
i Jagiełło. In Polska Akademia
Umiejętnosci, Kraków. Wydział Historyczno-Filozoficzny. Pamiętnik
Akademii Umiejętności w Krakowie.
Wydziały (Kraków), v.7, 1889, p.
79-155. See serials consulted.

4826. SUŽIDELIS, Simas. Lietuva
ir Gediminaičiai sėdant Jogailai į
didžiojo Kunigaikščio sostą. [Li-
thuania and the descendants of Gediminas at the time of Jogaila becoming a Grand Duke] In Šapoka,
Adolfas, ed. Jogaila. Kaunas,
1935. 947.52.W797.yS PU OCl

4827. SZAJNOCHA, Karol. Jadwiga i
Jagiełło 1374-1413. Opowiadanie
historyczne. Wstempem opatrzył
Stefan M. Kuczyński. Warszawa,
Państwowy Instytut Wydawniczy, 1969.
4 v. in 2, illus. Other editions

published in Lwów, 1855-1856; 1854-
1869; 1877. DK426.S95 MU CaAEU CtY
ICU MH NN PU

X.9.e. VYTAUTAS, THE GREAT,
1392-1430

4828. AKADEMIJA POLIGŁOTYCZNA KU
czci Wielkiego Księcia Litwy Alek-
sandra-Witolda Kiejstutowicza urzą-
zona w 500-letnią rocznicę jego
zgonu (1430-1930), przez alumnów
Wyszszego Seminarium duchownego w
Pińsku. Pińsk, Seminarjum duchowne,
1930. 72 p. 947.52.F995yLo PU

4829. BARBASHEV, Aleksandr Ippolitovich. Vitovt i ego politika do
Griunval'denskoi bitvy 1410 g.
Sanktpeterburg, Tip. I.N. Skorokhodova, 1885. xvi, 165 p. (Zapiski
Istoriko-filologicheskago fakul'-
teta Sanktpeterburgskago Universiteta, Tom.15) DK511.L23B3 DLC CLU
CU IU ICLJF OrU WU

4830. --- Vitovt. Posliedniia
dvadtsat' liet kniazheniia, 1410-
1430. Sanktpeterburg, Tip. I.N.
Skorokhodova, 1891. viii, 340 p.
(Ocherki litovsko-russkoi istorii.
16 veka.) 947.52.B295.yB PU

4831. BAYSEN, Hans von. Witold-
Grossfürst von Lithauen. Altona,
Bey der Verlagsgesellschaft, 1796-
97. 2 v. illus. ViU

4832. BECH, Stanislaus F. Paulus
Vladimiri and his doctrine concerning international law and politics.
The Hague, Mouton, 1965. 2 v.,
illus. English and Latin. Bibliography: v.2, p. 1203-1237.
JX2060.P3B4 DLC CaAEU

4833. BUJACK, Georg. Das deutsche
Orden und Herzog Witold von Litauen;
historische Abhandlung. Königsberg
in Pr., 1869. [n.p.] (Bericht über
das Altstädtische Gymnasium zu
Königsberg in Preussen)

4834. DUCKIEWICA, Władysław. Witold Wielki Książę Litewski, w 500-
letnią rocznicę śmierci 1430-1930.
W Jarosławiu, Odbito w Polskiej
Drukarni Spółdzielczej, 1932. 139
p. DK511.L28W82 NIC

4835. DUNDULIS, Bronius. Impera-
toriaus arbitro B. Makros misija
Žemaičių sienų reikalu. [The mission of the Emperor's envoy B.
Makros in the dispute of the Samogitian borders] In VUMD, v.20,
1958, p. 127-149. See serials

consulted.

4836. --- Lietuvių kova dėl Žemaitijos ir Užnemunės XV amžiuje.
[The struggles of Lithuanians for
Žemaitija (Samogitia) and the
southern parts of it in the fifteenth century] Vilnius, VPMLL,
1960. 316 p., illus.
DK511.L23D8 DLC CtY CtPAM ICU PU

4837. --- Lietuvos kova prieš
kryžiuočius Konstanco bažnytiniame
susirinkime, 1414-1418 m. [Lithu-
ania's struggle against the Teutonic Order in the Council of Constance, 1414-1418] In Vilna. Universitetas. Istorijos-filologijos
mokslų serija. Vilnius, 1958. v.
4, p. 5-25. (Mokslo darbai, t.18)
See serials consulted.

4838. EISMANN, Friedrich W. Wy-
tautas. Geschichten und Geschichte
aus Litauens Vergangenheit. Breslau, Priebatsch, 1918. iv, 88 p.
947.52.Ei84 PU DLC

4839. GIDŽIŪNAS, Viktoras. Že-
maičių byla Konstancos susirinkime.
[The Samogitian case before the
Council of Constance, 1414-1418]
In Lituanistikos darbai (Chicago,
Ill.), v.2, 1969, p. 5-34. Biblio-
graphy: p. 28-31. Summary in Eng-
lish. See serials consulted.

4840. GOYSKI, Maryan. Wzajemme
stosunki Polski, Litwy i Zakonu w
latach 1399-1404. Kraków, 1906.
66 p. BM(09008. g. 12. (4.)); also
in Przewodnik Kaukowy i Literacki
(Lwów), v.34, 1906, p. 207-225;305-
322;398-413;501-518. AP54.P823
v.34 DLC MH

4841. HALECKI, Oskar. Witold.
In PZHP w Warszawe 28 listopada do
4 grudnia 1930 r. Pamiętnik V.
Referaty (Lwów), v.1, 1930, p. 153-
168. Protokoly (Lwów), v.2, 1931,
p. 361-375. See serials consulted.

4842. HEINL, Karl. Fürst Witold
von Litauen in seinem Verhältnis
zum Deutschen Orden in Preussen
wärend der Zeit seines Kampfes um
litauisches Erbe: 1382-1401. Berlin, E. Ebering, 1925. 200 p.
(Historische Studien, Heft 165)
Issued also as: Thesis--University
of Berlin. DK511.L23H47 1925 DLC
CtY IEN IdU IU KU MH NIC NN NcD
NSyU NcU OU PU WU

4843. IVINSKIS, Zenonas. Lietuvos vakarų sienos bei Klaipėdos
klausimas Vytauto laikais. [The
western boundaries of Lithuania and
the question on Klaipėda during the

time of Vytautas] In Naujoji romuva (Kaunas), no.120-121, 1933. See
serials consulted.

4844. --- Vytautas didysis Lietuvos Kunigaikštis, 1392-1430. [Vy-
tautas Grand Duke of Lithuania,
1392-1430] In Lietuvių enciklopedija. Boston, Mass., 1966, v.34, p.
373-390. For holdings see entry
no. 216.

4845. --- Vytauto didžiojo veiki-
mas iki 1392. [The activities of
Vytautas the Great until 1392] In
Sležas, P., ed. Vytautas Didysis.
Kaunas, 1930. p. 1-44.
DK511.L23S48 DLC CtTMF PU

4846. --- Vytauto Didžiojo darbai katalikų bažnyčiai Lietuvoje.
[The support of the Catholic Church
in Lithuania by Vytautas the Great]
Kaunas, 1930. 26 p. 947.5.Il CtTMF

4847. JABLONSKIS, Konstantinas.
Nauji Vytauto laikotarpio aktai.
[Newly found acts (documents) from
the period of Vytautas] In Praei-
tis (Kaunas) v.2, 1933, p. 375-411.
See serials consulted.

4848. JANULAITIS, Augustinas.
Žemaičiai ir bažnytinis seimas Kon-
stancijoj, 1414-1418 m. [Žemaičiai
(Samogitia) and the Church-Council
of Constance, 1414-1418] Kaunas
[Varpas], 1932. 63 p. Reprint
from Praeitis (Kaunas) v.2, p. 1-63.
See serials consulted.

4849. JUČAS, Mečislovas. Telkia-
mos jėgos galutinai sunaikinti or-
diną (1380-1409). [The concentration of troops for the final destruction of the Teutonic Order,
1380-1409] In Lietuvių karas su
kryžiuočiais. Vilnius, 1964, p.
232-265. DK511.L23L45 DLC CaAEU
CtY MH

4850. KARPAVIČIUS, Kazimieras S.
Vytautas Didysis; Lietuvos istorijos peržvalga ir apysakos bei padavimai apie tą mūsų karžygį. [Vy-
tautas the Great....] Cleveland,
Ohio, Dirva, 1930. 2 v. in 1.
illus. 947.5K CaOTP ICCC ICLJF PU

4851. KOCHANOWSKI, Jan Korwin.
Witold, Wielki Książę Litewski.
Studyum historyczne. Lwów, Gubrinowicz i Schmidt, 1900. 207 p.
947.52.V995.yK PU BM(010790. f. 18.)

4852. KOLANKOWSKI, Liudwik. Kwestja litewskiej korony. In Ateneum
Wileńskie (Wilno), v.5, 1928, p.
186-187. See serials consulted.

4853. --- O Litewską koronę. In
Kwartalnik Historyczny (Lemberg),
v. 40, 1926, p. 386-399. See
serials consulted.

4854. KONČIUS, Joseph B. Vytautas the Great; Grand Duke of Lithuania. Miami, Fla., The Franklin
Press, Inc., 1964. 211 p. illus.,
map. Bibliography: p. 195-206.
DK511.L2K8 CaAEU CaOONL CaOTU CtPAM
ICBM KU NN NNC

4855. KONECZNY, Feliks. Vitol-
diana. In Ateneum Wileńskie (Wilno), 1930, p. 494-504. See
serials consulted.

4856. KORCHINSKII, Ivan. Vitovt
Velikii, supremus Lithuaniae dux;
bieglyi obzor zhizni ego i dieiatel'nosti... Kaunas, Spindulys,
1930. 96 p. 947.52.V995.yKo PU

4857. KOSMAN, Marcel. Wielki
książę Witold. [Warszawa] Książka
i Wiedza, 1967. 279 p. illus.
DK511.L23K65 PU CaOTU

4858. KRASIŃSKI, Henryk. Le
célèbre Vitold, Grand Duc de Lithuanie, précédé de notions sur la Sa-
mogitie. Paris, Guiraudet et Jo-
naust, 1834. 36 p. BN(Mp.2979 &
Mp.2980)

4859. KRASZEWSKI, Józef Ignacy.
Litwa za Witolda, opowiadanie his-
toryczne. Wilno, 1850.
BM(12590. h. 14.)

4860. KRAUJELIS, Petras. Vytautas Didysis, Lietuvos didis kunigaikštis, Čekijos karalius, Lenkijos karūnos globėjas, Rygos arkivyskupijos protektorius ir Rusų
žemių valdovas. P. Vieštautas
[pseud. Vytautas the Great, Grand
Duke of Lithuania, King of Czekoslovakia...] Vilnius, [Ruch" spaustuvė, 1930. 20 p. 947.52.K8685.2
PU

KRUMBHOLTZ, Robert. Samaiten und der Deutsche Orden bis
Frieden am Melno-See, 1422. Königsberg in Pr., 1890. See entry no.
4763.

4861. LAPPO, Ivan Ivanovich. Istorinė Vytauto reikšmė. [The historical significance of Vytautas]
In Praeitis (Kaunas), v.2, 1933, p.
1-71. See serials consulted.

4862. LEWICKI, Anatol. Kiedy Witold został Wielkim Księciem Litwy?
In Kwartalnik Historyczny (Lwów),
v.8, 1894, p. 424-436. See
serials consulted.

4863. ŁOWMIAŃSKI, Henryk. Witold Wielki Księżę litewski. Wilno, Wydaw. Komitetu Obchodu Pięćsetnej Rocznicy Zgonu Wielkiego Księcia Witolda. 1930. 121 p. Bibliography: p. 118-121. DK511.L23L6 DLC MH PU

4864. MALECZYŃSKA, Ewa. Unia Polski z Litwą i walka z agresją Zakonu Krzyżackiego (1385-1422). In Polska Akademia Nauk. Instytut Historii. Historia Polski. Warszawa, v.1, 1960, p. 562-583. illus., plan. DK414.P837 DLC

4865. MORELOWSKI, Marian. Korona i hełm znalezione w Sandomierzu a sprawa korony Witolda i grobowców dynastycznych w Wilnie. In Ateneum Wileńskie (Wilno), v.7, 1930, p. 602-683. See serials consulted.

4866. NORKUS, Jonas. Vytautas, Didysis Lietuvos Kunigaikštis; istorijos skaitymai jo mirčiai, sukakus 500 metų, paminėti. [Vytautas, Grand Duke of Lithuania...] Kaunas, Spaudos fondas [n.d.], 57 p. illus. L970.2No ICLJF

4867. OSTEN-SACKEN, Paul von der. Livländisch-Russische Beziehungen während der Regierungszeit des Grossfürsten Witowt von Litauen (1392-1430). In Gesellsch. für Geschichte und Altertumskunde der Ostseeprovinzen Russlands. Mitteilungen (Riga), v.20, 1910, p. 169-294. See serials consulted.

4868. PENKAUSKAS, Pranas. Vytautas Didysis ir jo Čekijos politika Venceliui mirus. [Vytautas the Great and his policy toward the Czechs after the death of Vencelaus] In Židinys (Kaunas), 1930, v.11, no. 4, p. 334-347; no.5-6, p. 444-459. See serials consulted.

4869. PFITZNER, Jósef. Grossfürst Witold von Litauen als Staatsmann. Brün, R.M. Rohner, 1930. xiii, 239 p. (Schriften der Philosophischen Fakultät der Deutschen Universität in Prag, 6) Bibliography: p. 225-239. DK511.L23P4 CU CtY KU MH NN NNC NjP PU WaU

4870. PROCHASKA, Antoni. Dzieje Witołda Wiełkiego Księcia Litwy. Wilno, A. Rutkowski, 1914. 420 p. DK511.L23P7 DLC KU MH NjP NN PU

4871. --- Ostatnie lata Witolda. Studyum z dziejów intrygi dyplomatycznej. Warszawa, Gebethner i Wolff, 1882. 346, xxxii p. DK511.L23P76 CaOTU CoU ICLJF MB PU

4872. --- Zjazd monarchów w Lucku.

In Przewodnik Nauk. i Literacki (Lwów), v.2, no.1, 1874, p. 187-201; 270-288;376-389;450-456;no.2, 57-74. See serials consulted.

4873. --- Znaczenie niedoszłej koronacji Witolda. In Ateneum Wileńskie (Wilno) v.1, 1923, p. 337-351. See serials consulted.

4874. ŠAPOKA, Adolfas. Vytauto vieta mūsų istorijoje. [The place of Vytautas in our history] In Šležas, Paulius, ed. Vytautas Didysis. Kaunas, 1930. p. 267-293. DK511.L23S48 DLC CtTMF PU

4875. SARNES, Anton. Witold und Polen in den Jahren 1427-1431. Zur Kritik des II. Buches der Historia Poloniae des Johannes Dlugosz. In Altpreussische Monatschrift (Königsberg in Pr.), v.30, 1893, p. 101-206. See serials consulted.

4876. SEMKOWICZ, Władysław. Braterstwo szlachty polskiej z bojarstwem litewskim w unii Horodelskiej 1413 roku. In Polska i Litwa w dziejowym stosunku. Warszawa, 1914. p. 393-446. DK418.5.L5P6 DLC CU CSt-H BM

4877. --- Nieznane nadania Witolda dla osób prywatnych. In Ateneum Wileńskie (Wilno), v.7, 1930, p. 845-857. See serials consulted.

4878. --- Przywileje Witolda dla Moniwida, starosty Wileńskiego i testament jego syna Jana Moniwidowicza. In Ateneum Wileńskie (Wilno), v.1, 1923, p. 253-264. See serials consulted.

4879. ŠLEŽAS, Paulius. Ko bėgo Kęstučio sūnus iš Lietuvos? [Why did the son of Kęstutis flee Lithuania?] In Židinys (Kaunas), v.15, no.12, 1932, p. 449-457. See serials consulted.

4880. ---, ed. Vytautas Didysis, 1350-1430. [Vytautas the Great, 1350-1430] Kaunas, Sakalo bendrovės leidinys, 1930. xxiv, 300 p. front. (ports.) fold. map. Bibliography: p. [xi]-xiv. DK511.L23S48 DLC CtTMF ICCC ICBM PU

4881. --- Vytauto Didžiojo kovos dėl Žemaičių ir Klaipėdos. [The struggle of Vytautas the Great for Žemaičiai and Lithuania Minor] In Naujoji romuva (Kaunas), no.18, 1932, p. 409-412. See serials consulted.

4882. --- Vytauto konfliktas su Lenkija dėl karūnacijos. [The conflict of Vytautas with Poland on account of his coronation] In His Vytautas Didysis, 1350-1430. Kaunas, 1930. p. 205-234. DK511.L23S48 DLC CtTMF ICCC ICBM PU

4883. --- Vytauto santykiai su Lenkija. [Vytautas the Great, relations with Poland] In His Vytautas Didysis, 1350-1430. Kaunas, 1930. p. 141-204. DK511.L23S48 DLC CtTMF ICCC ICBM PU

4884. SUŽIEDĖLIS, Simas. Vytautas Didysis ir jo žygiai. [Vytautas the Great and his campaigns] Kaunas, Sakalo bendrovės leidinys, 1935. 175 p. 947.5L.V995.yS PU CtTMF ICCC

4885. --- Vytautas Didysis ir Lietuvos christianizacija. [Vytautas the Great and the christianizing of Lithuania] In Tiesos kelias (Kaunas), no.7-8, 1930, p. 442-483. See serials consulted.

4886. --- Vytauto ekonominė politika. [The economic policy of Vytautas] In Šležas, P. ed. Vytautas Didysis, 1350-1430. Kaunas, 1930. p. 235-252. DK511.L23S48 DLC CtTMF ICCC ICBM PU

4887. --- Vytauto galybės laikai. [The years of Vytautas' might] In Šležas, P. ed. Vytautas Didysis, 1350-1430. Kaunas, 1930. p. 125-140. DK511.L23S48 DLC CtTMF ICCC ICBM PU

4888. --- Vytauto vaidmuo Lietuvos christianizacijoje. [The role of Vytautas in christianizing Lithuania] In Šležas, P., ed. Vytautas Didysis. Kaunas, 1930. p. 91-124. DK511.L23S48 DLC CtTMF ICCC ICBM PU

4889. SZYMAŃSKI, Roman. Die Wahlen der Grossfürsten von Litauen und das Wahlgesetz seit 1386 bis in Mitte des XV. Jahrhunderts. Posen, L. Merzbach [1870] 36 p. Thesis--University of Leipzig. Ger.LU

4890. TOTORAITIS, Jonas. Vytautas katalikas. [Vytautas as a catholic] Marijampolė, Marijonų spaustuvė, 1930. 54 p. illus. 289.2To ICLJF CtTMF

4891. VASILIAUSKAS, Antanas. Vytauto Didžijo diplomatika. [The diplomacy of Vytautas the Great] In Senovė (Kaunas), no.2, 1935, 39 p. See serials consulted.

4892. YČAS, Jonas. Vytautas ir Žemaičiai. [Vytautas the Great and Žemaičiai (Samogitia)] In Praeitis (Kaunas), v.2, 1933, p. 87-93. See serials consulted.

4893. ZAJĄCZKOWSKI, Stanisław. Witold Wielki Książę litewski. In Ateneum Wileńskie (Wilno), v.7, 1930, p. 455-468. See serials consulted.

X.9.e.1. THE BATTLE OF TANNENBERG

4894. BISKUP, Marian. Z badań nad Wielką Wojną z Zakonem Krzyżackim. In Kwartalnik Historyczny (Lwów), v.66, no.3, 1959, p. 671-685. See serials consulted.

4895. CRONICA CONFLICTUS WLADISLAI regis Poloniae cum cruciferis anno Christi 1410. Z rękopisu Biblioteki Kórnickiej wydał Zygmunt Celichowski. Poznań, Nakł. Biblioteki Kórnickiej, 1911. 31 p. facsims. DK426.C7 CaOTU DLC CSt ICU

4896. DĄBROWSKI, Jan. Grunwald. In Małopilskie Studia Historyczne (Kraków), v.3, no.1-2, 1960, p. 5-13. See serials consulted.

4897. DŁUGOSZ, Jan. Griunval'dskaia bitva. Izd. podgotovili G.A. Stratanovskii i dr. Leningrad, Izdvo Akademii nauk SSSR, Leningradskoe otdelenie, 1962. 211 p. illus. (Akademiia nauk SSSR. Literaturnye pamiatniki) DK426.D517 DLC CaAEU

4898. EKDAHL, S. Die Flucht der Litauer in der Schlacht bei Tannenberg. In Zeitschrift für Ostforschung (Marburg/Lahn), v.12, no.1, 1963. See serials consulted.

4899. EVANS, Geoffrey Charles. Tannenberg, 1410:1914. London, Hamilton, 1970. x, 182 p. 15 plates, maps, ports. D552.T3E93 CaOTU

4900. GRABOWSKI, Ignacy. Grunwald. Warszawa, S. Orgelbrand, 1910. vii, 163 p. NN

4901. HEVEKER, Karl. Die Schlacht bei Tannenberg. Berlin, 1906. Thesis--University of Berlin. CtY MiU MH PU

4902. IVINSKIS, Zenonas. Žemaičių klausimas ir Žalgirio kautynės. [The problem of Samogitia and the battle of Tannenberg] In Aidai (Brooklyn, N.Y.), nr.7, 1960, p. 278-281; no.8, 1960, p. 323-328. See serials consulted.

4903. JAKŠTAS, Juozas. The Battle of Tannenberg, 1410. In Baltic Review (New York, N.Y.), no.20, 1960, p. 18-37. See serials consulted.

4904. --- Dlugošas apie Žalgirio

mūšį; Vytautas ir lietuviai kroni-kininko akimis. [Dlugosz about the Battle of Tannenberg] In Tautos praeitis (Chicago, Ill.), v.1, no.2, 1960, p. 165-182. See serials consulted.

4905. --- Dlugosz about the Battle of Tannenberg. In Lituanus (Brooklyn, N.Y.), v.8, no.3, 1962, p. 71-84. See serials consulted.

4906. JASLAW Z BRATKOWA. Grunwald; album jubileuszowy, szkic historyczny. Poznań, Rzepecki, 1910. 344 p. plates. 970.5JA ICLJF

4907. JOANNES VISLICIENSIS. Wojna Pruska (Bellum Prutenum) W przekładzie K. Mecherzyńskiego. Wstępem opatrzył i wydał W. Kłosowski. Kraków, 1910. 23 p. BM(09008.c.5.)

4908. JUČAS, Mečyslovas. Žalgirio mūšis. [The Battle of Tannenberg] Vilnius,VPMLL, 1959. 65 p. 947.5J ICCC

4909. --- 2. pataisytas leidimas. [2d ed.] Vilnius, VPMLL, 1960. 74 p. illus., maps. DD491.0475J8 1960 DLC ICU PU

4910. JURGĖLA, Constantine Rudyard. Tannenberg (Ėglija-Grünwald) 15 July 1410. New York, N.Y., Lithuanian Veterans Assoc. "Ramovė", 1961. 104 p. illus., maps. CR765.J8 DLC CaAEU ICLJF NvU PU

4911. --- 1410.VII.15 d. mūšis Eglijos girioje. [The Battle of Tannenberg, 1410] In Karys (Brooklyn, N.Y.), no.6, 1960, p. 162-200. See serials consulted.

4912. KOCZY, Leon. Grunwald; dzień chwały polskiego oręża. London; Glasgow, Nakł. Tow. Społecznego-Oświatowego, 1960. 40 p. 943.8.K815 PU DLC InU

4913. KOPCZEWSKI, Jan St., ed. Grunwald, 550 lat chwały. Wyd.1, uzupełnione przez Mateusz Siuchiński. Warszawa, Państwowe Zakłady Wydawn. Szkolnych, 1960. 389 p. illus. DK426.K65 DLC CtY MiDU NN NNC InU PU CU

4914. KROLLMANN, Christian Anton Christoph. Die Schlacht bei Tannenberg; ihre Ursachen und ihre Folgen. Königsberg in Pr. Deutschherrenverlag, 1910. 32 p. DLC

4915. KUCZYŃSKI, Stefan Maria. Grunwald. Warszawa, Arkady, 1960. 57 p. illus. DK436.K79 DLC IU ViU WU

4916. --- Grunwaldzkie pole. In His Studia z dziejów Europy wschodniej... Warszawa, 1965. p. [189]-202. DK420.K8 DLC CaAEU PU

4917. --- Informacje tzw. latopisu Bychovca o "Wielkiej Wojnie" lat 1409-1411; uwagi krytyczne. In His Studia s dziejów Europy wschodniej... Warszawa, 1965. p. [203]-219. DK420.K8 DLC CaAEU PU

4918. --- Wielka Wojna z Zakonem Krzyżackim w latach 1409-1411. Warszawa, Wydawn. Ministerstwa Obrony Narodowej, 1955. 551 p. tables, map. DK426.K8 DLC CtY NIC

4919. --- --- Wyd. 2. Warszawa, Wyd. Min. Obrony Narod., 1960. 622 p. tables, map. DK426.K8 1960 DLC CU CtY ICU IU MiD MiU NN NNC PPULC PU WU

4920. MAJEWSKI, W. Kilka uwag o bitwie pod Grunwaldem. In Zapiski Historyczne (Toruń), v.25, no.2, p. 9-33. See serials consulted.

4921. OEHLER, Max. Der Krieg zwischen dem Deutschen Orden und Polen-Litauen, 1409-1411. Elbing, Wernich's Buchdr., 1910. iv, 112 p. maps. Slav 5439.52 MH BM(09008. cc. 10.(4.) NbU (Microfilm) ICLJF

4922. PIERADZKA, Krystyna. Bitwa grunwaldzka w obcych relacjach kronikarskich prusskich, śląskich i zachodnio-europejskich. In Małopolskie Studia Historyczne (Kraków), 1960, p. 51-65. See serials consulted.

4923. SRUOGIENĖ, Vanda (Daugirdaitė) The Battle of Günwald-Tannenberg. In Lituanus (Brooklyn, N.Y.), v.6, no.3, 1960, p. 121-123. See serials consulted.

4924. THUNERT, Franz. Der grosse Krieg zwischen Polen und Deutschen Orden, 1410 bis 1. Februar 1411. Beilage: die Quellen zur Schlacht bei Tannenberg. Danzig, A.W. Kafemann, 1886. 70, [3] p. CR4765.T45 PU

4925. URBONAS, Oskaras. 1410 metų karas su kryžiuočiais ir Žalgirio mūšis; Žalgirio pergalės 550 metų sukakči paminėti. [The 550 y years anniversary of the Battle of Tannenberg, 1410] [Brooklyn, N.Y.] Karys, 1960. 94 p. illus., maps. Bibliography: p. 92. DK426.U7 DLC CaAEU MH PU

X.9.f. THE JOGAILA DYNASTY, 1430-1572

4926. ALBERTRANDY, Jan Chrzciciel. Panowanie Kazimierza Jagiellończyka, króla polskiego i W. Księcia Litewskiego; wyjęte z rękopismów Jana Albertrandego... Wydał Żegota Onacewicz. Warszawa, Nakładem A. Brzeziny, 1826-27. 2 v. port. DK511.L223A5 1826 DLC ICU IU

4927. BARVINS'KYI, Bohdan. Zhihimont Keistutovych Velykyi Kniaz litovs'ko russ'kyi, 1432-1440. Zhovka, Autor, 1905. xiv, 169 p.

4928. --- Zygmunt Kiejstutowicz Książę Starodubski. In Przewodnik Naukowy i Literacki (Lwów), v.34, 1906, p. 41-53,138-152. See serials consulted.

4929. BOGUCKA, Maria. Kazimierz Jagiellończyk. [Warszawa, Książka i Wiedza, 1970] 298 p. DK427.B6 PU

4930. CHODYNICKI, Kazimierz. Geneza i rozwój podania o zabójstwie Zygmunta Kiejstutowicza. In Ateneum Wileńskie (Wilno), v.5, no.15, 1928, p. 79-103. See serials consulted.

4931. CONTONS, Albert J. St. Casimir; 500 anniversary of his birth, 1458-October 3rd-1958. Boston, Mass, Knights of Lithuania [1958] 48 p. illus. BX4700.K3C6 DLC

4932. DĄBROWSKI, Jan. L'année 1444. Cracoviae, Académie polonaise des sciences et des lettres, 1952. 45 p. (Bulletin international de l'Académie polonaise des sciences et des lettres. Classe de philologie; Classe d'histoire et de philosophie. No. supplémentaire, 6) DK426.5.D3 DLC InU NN

4933. DEVEIKĖ, Jonė. The Lithuanian diarchies. In Slavonic and East European Review (Menasha, Wis.), v. 28, 1949-1950, p. [392]-405. See serials consulted.

4934. DNEVNIK LITOVSKIKH POSLOV, 1556. Moskva, 1838. In Obolenskii, Mikhail Andreevich. Sbornik Kniazia Obolenskago, no.5. DK3.02 DLC BM

4935. DONNERT, Erich. Der livländische Ordensritterstaat und Russland; die livländische Krieg und die baltische Frage in der europäischen Politik, 1558-1583. Berlin, Rütten & Loening, 1963. 320 p. Bibliography: p. 299-310. DK511.L36D6 DLC CaAEU CLU ICU MH NIC NN NNC PU ViU WaU

4936. DUNDULIS, Bronius. Lietuvos kova dėl valstybinio savarankiškumo XV amžiuje. [The Lithuanian struggle for independent statehood in the fifteenth century] Vilnius, Mintis, 1968. 312 p. illus., maps. DK511.L23D82 DLC CtY ICBM MH NjP

4937. FINKEL, Ludwik Michael. Elekcya Zygmunta I; sprawy dynastyi Jagiellońskiej i unii polsko-litewskiej. Kraków, Akademia Umiejętności, 1910. viii, 296 p. Bibliography: p. [281]-288. DK428.F6 DLC CLU CtY ICU ICBM InU IU KU NNC NcD PU WU

4938. FLORIDI, Ulisse Alessio. San Casimiro e la Lithuania. [Roma, Civiltà Cattolica, 1959] 11 p. Estratto da la Civiltà Cattolica, del 7 marco 1959. LB1.KAZ ICLJF

4939. GOŁĘBIOWSKI, Eugeniusz. Zygmunt August; żywot ostatniego z Jagiellonów. [Wyd.1. Warszawa] Czytelnik, 1962. 428 p. DK428.5.G6 DLC MH MiDW PU

4940. GÓRSKI, Konstanty. Wojny Litwy z Wielkim Księstwem Moskiewskiem za Zygmuntów. In Niwa Polska (Warszawa), v.20, 1891, p. 237-240, 255-258,273-276. NN

4941. HALECKI, Oskar. Die Beziehungen der Habsburger zum litauischen Hochadel im Zeitalter der Jagellonen. In Vienna. Institut für österreichische Geschichtsforschung. Mitteilungen, v.36, 1915, p. 595-660. See serials consulted.

4942. --- Ostatnie lata Świdrygiełły i sprawa wolyńska za Kazimierza Jagiellończyka. Kraków, Nakł. Akademii Umiejętności; Skład główny w Księg. Gebetnera, 1915. vi, 315 p. fold. map. DK511.L23H36 DLC CaBVaU CtY KU MH NN NNC NjP PU

4943. --- Problems of the new monarchy: Jagiełło and Witold, 1400-1434. In Cambridge history of Poland. Cambridge, 1950. Chapter 11. DK414.C3 DLC CU MH MiU NN NBuC NcD NcU NRU OCl OCU OU PPL PSt PP PU TxU

4944. IVINSKIS, Zenonas. Šv. Kazimieras. [Saint Casimir] 1458-1484. New York, N.Y., 1955. 222 p. illus. ports, facsim. Summary in English. Bibliography: p. 185-198. BX4700.K3I8 DLC CaAEU CtTMF MiD NN OCl PU

4945. JASAS, Rimantas. Karas su Livonijos ordinu XIII a. viduryje. Voina s livonskim Ordenom v seredine XIII v. In Lietuvių karas su kryžiuočiais. Vilnius, 1964. p.120-

184. illus., map. DK511.L23L45
DLC CaAEU CtY MH

4946. JASNOWSKI, Józef. Mikołaj
Czarny Radziwiłł, 1515-1565, kanc-
lerz i marszałek ziemski Wielkiego
Księstwa Litewskiego, wojewoda Wileński. Warszawa, Tow. Naukowe,
1939. viii, 447 p. (Rozprawy Historyczne Towarzystwa Naukowego we
Warszawie, t.22) Dl.R8 DLC CU CtY
ICU NN

4947. KARPOV, Gennadii Feodorovich.
Istoriia bor'by Moskovskago gosudar-
stva s pol'sko-litovskim, 1462-1508.
Moskva, Katkov, 1867. 2 v.
DK101.K DLC BM(9454. h. 7.) NN

4948. KOLANKOWSKI, Ludwik. Jagiellonowie i unija. In PZHP w Wilnie
17-20 września 1935 r. Pamiętnik VI.
Protokoly (Lwów), v.2, 1935, p. 263-
292. See serials consulted.

4949. --- Zygmunt August, Wielki
Książę Litwy do roku 1548. Lwów,
Nakł. Tow. dla Popierania Nauki Pol-
skiej, 1913. 418 p. tables, maps.
(Towarzystwo Naukowe we Lwowie.
Dział 1: Historyczno-Filologiczny.
Archivum Naukowe, t.7, zesz.1)
AS142.L38 v.7 DLC ICU MH NN PU

4950. KONECZNY, Feliks. Geneza
uroszczeń Iwana III do Rusi Litewskiej. In Ateneum Wileńskie (Wilno),
v.3, 1925-1926, p. 193-264. See serials consulted.

4951. --- Litwa a Moskva w latach,
1449-1492. Wilno, 1929. (Towarzystwo Przyjaciół Nauk w Wilnie. Wydział III. Rozprawy, t.2)
947.52.K838 PU MiU NN

4952. KOPYSTIAŃSKI, A. Książę Michał Zygmuntowicz. In Kwartalnik
Historyczny (Lwów), v.20, 1906, p.
74-165. See serials consulted.

4953. KUCZYŃSKI, Stefan Maria.
Ziemie Czernihowsko-Siewerskie pod
rządami Litwy. Warszawa, Z zasiłku
Funduszu Kultury Narodowej, 1936.
412 p. tables, map. (Pratsi Ukra-
ins'koho naukovoho institutu, t.33)
DK508.7.K83 CaOTU CaQMM InU IU KU
NN NNC

4954. LAPIŃSKI, Aleksander. Zyg-
munt Stary a Kościół Prawosławny.
Warszawa, Nakł. Towarzystwa Naukowe-
go Warszawskiego, 1937. xi, 206 p.
(Rosprawy Historyczne Towarzystwa
Naukowego Warszawskiego, t.19, zesz.
1) Bibliography: p. [iii]-xi.
Dl.R8 t.19 zesz.1 DLC NNC

4955. LEWICKI, Anatol. Powstanie

Świdrygiełły. In Polska Akademia
Umiejętności, Kraków. Wydział Historyczno-Filozoficzny. Rozprawy, t.29,
1892, p. 128-516. See serials consulted.

4956. MATUSAS, Jonas. Švitrigaila,
Lietuvos Didysis Kunigaikštis. [Švi-
trigaila, Grand Duke of Lithuania]
Kaunas, 1938. xiv, 238 p. maps.
Bibliography: p. [xi]-xiv. Summary
in French. 947.52.Sv35.yM PU

4957. OBOLENSKII, Mikhail Andreevich, comp. Pis'mo grafa litovskago,
Radvila, o pobiedie, oderzhanoi pri
Ulie, 1564 goda, genvaria 26-go. In
His Inostrannye sochineniia i akty...
t.2. Moskva, Universitetskaia tipografiia, 1847-48. DK111.O DLC

4958. PAPÉE, Fryderyk. Aleksander
Jagiellończyk. Kraków, Polska Aka-
demia Umiejętności, 1949. 120 p.
DK427.7.P3 DLC CU MiDW MH NN PU

4959. --- Aleksandrowa instalacja
na Litwie. In Kwartalnik Historyczny (Lwów), v.51, 1937, p. 189-201.
See serials consulted.

4960. --- Jan Olbracht. Kraków,
Skł. gł. w Księg. Gebethnera i Wolffa, 1936. 256 p. ports., fold. map,
facsim. DK427.5.P3 DLC CtY NNC NN

4961. --- Studya i szkice z czasów
Kazimierza Jagiellończyka. Warszawa,
Gebethner i Wolff, 1907. 327 p.
tables. DK427.P3 DLC MH NN

4962. PAWIŃSKI, Adolf. Młode lata
Zygmunta Starego. Warszawa, Gebethner i Wolff, 1893. 291, v p.
facsims. (*QR)NN MH

4963. PENKAUSKAS, Pranas. Bazelio
susirinkimas ir Lietuvos sosto reika-
las Vytautui mirus. [The Council of
Basel and the case of the Lithuanian
Crown after the death of Vytautas the
Great] In Tiesos kelias (Kaunas),
v.2, 1926, no.7-8, p.33-48, no.9, p.
77-83. See serials consulted.

4964. POCIECHA, Władysław. Królo-
wa Bona, 1494-1557; czasy, ludzie,
odrodzenia. Poznań, Państwowe Zakłady Wydawnictw Szkolnych, 1949-58.
4 v. illus., ports. Material on
Lithuania in vol.3. DK428.P6 DLC CU
CtY MH NN NNC OU PU

4965. SIGISMUND II., Augustus, King
of Poland. Listy originalne Zygmunta Augusta do Mikołaja Radziwiłła,
Czarnego, Wojewody Wileńskiego... Z
autentyków spisane i wydane przez
S.A. Lachowicza. Wilno, Glücksberg,
1842. viii, 323 p. (Pamiętniki do

dziejów Polski) BM(1436. h. 2.)

CtPAM PU

4966. SPULER, Bertold. Die Golde-
ne Horde; die Mongolen in Russland,
1223-1502. Leipzig, O. Harrassowitz,
1943. xvi, 556 p. maps.
DS22.7.S6 DLC

4967. SUŽIEDĖLIS, Simas. Livonijos prijungimas prie Lietuvos. [The
annexation of Livonia to Lithuania]
In Athenaeum (Kaunas), v.4, no.4,
1933. 18 p. See serials consulted.

4968. --- Šventas Kazimieras. [
[Saint Casimir] [Kirchheim-Teck,
Ger., Šv.Sosto delegatūra lietuviams]
1947. 32 p. Bl.KAZ ICLJF

4969. Šv. KAZIMIERAS, LIETUVOS KA-
ralaitis. [Saint Casimir, the Prince
of Lithuania] [Chicago, Ill., Drau-
gas] 1915. 38 p. Bl.KAZ ICLJF

4970. TSERETELI, Elena Filimonov-
na. Elena Ioannovna, Velikaia kia-
ginia litovskaia, koroleva pol'skaia. Biograficheskii ocherk v sviazi s istoriei togo vremeni. Sanktpeterburg, Tip. I.N. Skorokhodova,
1898. ii, 356 p. DK511.L23T7 DLC
MoU

4971. WOJCIECHOWSKI, Zygmunt.
Zygmunt Stary, 1506-1548. Warszawa
[S. Arct] 1946. 394 p. (Bibliote-
ka wiedzy o Polsce, t.1) DK428.W65
DLC CU MH NN OU PU

4972. ZAKRZEWSKI, Stanisław. W
pięćsetną rocznicę; Bitwa nad Święt-
tą, inaczej pod Wiłkomierzem, dnia
1 września 1435 r. In PZHP w Wilnie
17-20 września 1935 r. Pamiętnik VI.
Referaty (Lwów), v.1, 1935, p. 551-
558. See serials consulted.

4973. ZIVIER, Ezechiel. Die zwei
letzten Jagiellonen, 1506-1572. In
His Neuere Geschichte Polens. Gotha,
1915. Bd.1. 809 p. DK414.Z6 DLC
NN PU

X.9.g. TEUTONIC KNIGHTS AND THE
WARS WITH LITHUANIA, 12th-
15th CENTURIES

4974. ANYSAS, Martynas. Senprūsių
(Pruthenorum gentes) kovos dėl laisvės su Vokiečių riterių ordinu nuo
1230 iki 1283 metų. [Campaigns of
Prussians against the Teutonic Kni-
ghtly Order for their freedom from
1230 until 1283] Chicago, Ill.,
Mažosios Lietuvos lietuvių draugija,
1968. 329 p. illus. Summary in
English. DD336.A8 DLC CaAEU CaOTU

4975. ARVYDAS, Felix. Der litauische Nationalheld der Natanger Mon-
te, Führer des grossen Aufstandes
gegen den Kreuzritterorden, Memel,
Druck "Lituania", 1934. 32 p. MH

4976. BENNINGHOVEN, Friedrich.
Der Orden der Schwertbrüder. Köln;
Graz, Böhlau, 1965. xvi, 525 p.
illus., maps. (Ostmitteleuropa in
Vergangenheit und Gegenwart, 9)
CR5738.B4 DLC PU

4977. BEUMANN, Helmut, ed. Heiden-
mission und Kreuzzugsgedanke in der
deutschen Ostpolitik des Mittelalters. Darmstadt, Wissenschaftliche
Buchgesellschaft, 1963. xii, 485 p.
(Wege der Forschung, Bd.7) CSt DDO
ICU MH NN NIC NjPT NjR NNC

4978. BIRŽIŠKA, Vaclovas. Kryžiuočių keliai į Lietuvą XIV amžiuje; keliai į Žemaičius. [The roads of the
Teutonic Order to Lithuania in XIV
century and to Žemaitija (Samogitia)]
In Praeitis (Kaunas), v.1, 1930,
p.1-63. See serials consulted.

4979. BISKUP, Marian. Trzynasto-
letnia wojna z Zakonem Krzyżackim
1454-1466. Warszawa, Wydawn. Ministerstwa Obrony Narodowej, 1967. 822
p. illus., plans. Summaries in German and Russian. Bibliography: p.
742-760. DK427.B5 DLC PU

4980. BOLDT, Friedrich. Der Deutsche Orden und Litauen, 1370-1386.
Königsberg in Pr., A. Rosbachische
Buchdrukerei, 1873. 119 p. Thesis--
University of Göttingen. Reprint
from Altpreussischer Monatsschrift,
v.10. DD491.053B6 DLC IaU NIC

4981. DOUBEK, Franciszek A. Skar-
ga Żmudzinów i odpowiedz Zakonu niemieckiego z roku 1416. In Ateneum
Wilenskie (Wilno), v.7, 1930, p. 873-
892. See serials consulted.

4982. DUNDULIS, Bronius. Lietuvos
sąjunga su husitais kovoje prieš vokiečius. (The union between Lithuania and the Hussites in the struggle against the Germans] In VUMD.
(Vilnius), v.13, 1957, p. 59-83. See
serials consulted.

4983. --- Žemaičių sukilimas prieš
teutoniškuosius pavergėjus, 1401-
1409. [The insurrection of Žemaičiai
(Samogitians) against the Teutonic
subjugators, 1401-1409] In Vilna.
Universitetas. Istorijos-filologijos
mokslų serija, v.2, 1955, p. 118-145.
(Its Mokslo darbai, t.6) See Serials
consulted.

4984. ECKERT, W. Die kurische Landschaft Ceclis; Untersuchungen des Kampfes um Südkurland zwischen dem Deutschen Orden und Litauen. In Altpreussische Forschungen (Königsberg in Pr), v.20, 1943, p. 6-84. See serials consulted.

4985. GEČYS, Kazys. Seven centuries of Lithuanian resistance to Teutonic agression. In Jurgėla, C.R. Lithuania in a twin Teutonic cluch. New York, N.Y., 1945. p. 35-76. DK511.L2J75 DLC CSt-H CtY IU MoU MU NN NNU-W ViU

4986. GERSDORF, Harro. Der Deutsche Orden im Zeitalter der polnisch-litauischen Union: die Amtszeit des Hochmeisters Konrad Zöller von Rotenstein, 1382-1390. Marburg/Lahn, 1957. 354 p. illus. (Wissenschaftliche Beiträge zur Geschichte und Landeskunde Ost-Mitteleuropa, hrsg. von Johann Gottfried Herder Institut, 29) Thesis--University of Göttingen. 929.713.G328 PU CaBVaU ICU IEN MH MnU NIC NcD NNC NjP NN

4987. GIDŽIŪNAS, Viktoras. Vokiečių ordino politika ir jos priešai Pabalty. [The Teutonic Knights and their Baltic enemies] In Karys (Brooklyn, N.Y.), no.3, 1965, p. 65-73. See serials consulted.

4988. GRATSIANSKII, Nikolai Pavlovich. Bor'ba slavian i narodov Pribaltiki s nemetskoi agressiei v srednie veka. Moskva, Gos. ucheb.-pedagog. izd-vo, 1943. 63 p. illus, map. D147.G7 DLC

4989. HEIN, Max. Die Verleihung Litauens an den Deutschen Orden durch Kaiser Ludwig von de Bayern im Jahre 1337. In Altpreussische Forschungen (Königsberg in Pr.), v.19, no.1, 1942, p. 36-54. See serials consulted.

4990. IVINSKIS, Zenonas. Kovos bruožai dėl Žemaičių ir jų sienų. [The outline of the struggle for Žemaitija (Samogitia) and its boundaries] In Athenaeum (Kaunas), v.6, 1935, p. 54-117. See serials consulted.

4991. --- Vokiečių ordinas ir Lietuva. [The Teutonic order and Lithuania] In Naujoji aušra (Chicago, Ill.), no.4-5, 1949. See serials consulted.

4992. JAKŠTAS, Juozas. Vokiečių ordinas ir Lietuva Vytenio ir Gedimino metu. [The Teutonic Knights and Lithuania during the reign of Vytenis and Gediminas] In Senovė (Kau-

nas), v.1-2, 1935-1936, p. 125-155. See serials consulted.

4993. KOCZY, Leon. The Baltic policy of the Teutonic Order. Toruń, The Baltic Institute, 1936. 122 p. (The Baltic pocket library) DD491.O475K62 DLC CtY NN

4994. --- Polityka baltycka Zakonu Krzyżackiego; rozprawa z pracy zbiorowej... Toruń, 1936. iv, 73 p. (Instytut Baltycki. Serja: Balticum. Poszczególne rozprawy) NN

4995. KROLLMANN, Christian Anton Christoph. Der Deutsche Orden in Preussen. Elbing, Preussenverlag, 1935. 77 p. (Preussenführer, 4) DD491.O47K68 DLC MH NN

4996. --- The Teutonic Order in Prussia... with assistance from Sir Raymond Beazley. Tr. by Ernst Horstmann. Elbing, Preussenverlag [1938] 73 p. (Prussian guides, 4) DD491.O47.K682 DLC MH OCU PSC

4997. LIETUVIŲ KARAS SU KRYŽIUOčiais. [The Lithuanian war against the Teutonic Knights. Ed. by J. Jurginis] Vilnius, Mintis, 1964. 354 p. illus. Bibliography: p. 327-[333] DK511.L23L45 DLC CaAEU CtY MH

4998. ŁOWMIAŃSKI, Henryk. Agresja Zakonu Krzyżackiego na Litwę w wiekach XII-XV. In Przegląd Historyczny (Warszawa), v.45, 1954, p. 338-371,543-545,561-562. See serials consulted.

4999. MASCHKE, Erich. Der Deutsche Orden und die Preussen; Bekehrung und Unterwerfung in der preussisch-baltischen Mission des XIII Jahrhunderts. Berlin, 1928; Vaduz, Lichtenstein, Krauss reprint, 1965. xii, 100 p. (Historische Studien. Hft.176) DD491.O484M37 1928a CaOTU GU NIC NcD NjP

5000. --- Polen und die Berufung des Deutschen Ordens nach Preussen. Danzig, Danziger Verlagsgesellschaft, 1934. 84 p. (Ostland-Forschungen, 4) (*EAA)NN MH

5001. MURAWSKI, Klaus Eberhard. Zwischen Tannenberg und Thorn; die Geschichte des Deutschen Ordens unter dem Hochmeister Konrad von Erlichshausen, 1441-1449. Göttingen, Musterschmidt, 1953. 482 p. DD491.O554M8 DLC PU

5002. OEHLER, Max. Geschichte des Deutschen Ritterordens. Elbing, E. Wernichs Buchdrukerei, 1908-12. 2 v. illus., maps. GR4765.O3 DLC NN

5003. PAKARKLIS, Povilas. Kryžiuočių valstybės santvarkos bruožai.
[Sketches of the Teutonic Knights'
state organization] Kaunas, Valstybinė enciklopedijų, žodynų ir mokslo literatūros leidykla, 1948. 267
p. At head of title: Lietuvos TSR
Mokslų akademija. Istorijos Institutas. Bibliography: p. 200-202.
GR4765.P3 DLC PU(positive photocopy)

5004. --- Popiežių bulės kryžiuo-
čiams. [Special Bulls from the Pope
to the Teutonic Knights. Chicago,
Ill.] Chicagos lietuvių literatūros
draugija, 1961. 70 p. Excerpt from
the author's Kryžiuočių valstybės
santvarkos bruožai. Vilnius, 1948.
929.713P172.2 PU ICBM PPULC

5005. PASHUTO, Vladimir Terent'e-
vich. Bor'ba prusskogo naroda za
nezavisimost' do kontsa XIII veka.
In Istoria SSSR (Moskva), no.6, 1958,
p. 54-81. See serials consulted.

5006. ROGALSKI, Leon. Dzieje
Krzyżaków przez ich stosunki z Polską, Litwą i Prussami, poprzedzone
rysem dziejów wojen krzyżowych, czer-
pane z najlepszych źródeł. Warszawa, S. Orgelbrand, 1846. 2 v.
illus. 947.52.R632 PU ICLJF

5007. TEUTONIC KNIGHTS. Berichte
der Generalprokuratoren der Deutschen
Ordens an der Kurie. Göttingen,
Vanderhoeck & Ruprecht, 1960-61. 2
v. IaU ICU MH NIC NNC NjP NcD

5008. --- Regesta historico-diplo-
matica ordinis S. Mariae Theutonico-
rum, 1198-1525. Bearb. unter Mitwirkung zahlreicher anderer von Erich
Joachim. Hrsg. von Walther Hubatsch.
Göttingen, Vandenhoeck & Ruprecht,
1948- . CR4759.T53 DLC PU

5009. TUMLER, Marian. Der Deutsche
Orden im Werden, Wachsen und Wirken
bis 1400 mit einem Abriss der Geschichte des Ordens von 1400 bis zur
neuesten Zeit. Wien, Panorama, 1955.
746 p. illus., col. plate, maps.
DCU

5010. VENATOR, Johann Caspar. Historischer Bericht von den marianisch-
teutschen Ritter-Orden, wo und wie
derselbe entsprungen, von seiner Zeit
... Nürnberg, Gedruckt bey A. Knor-
zen, 1680. 15, 508, [42] p. plates.
GR4765.V4 DLC PU

5011. WAGNER, Karl. Vokiečių or-
dino pilys Kauno apylinkėje. Die
Burgen des deutschen Orden in der
Umgebung Kauens. In Naujoji romuva
(Kaunas), no.107, 1933, p. 65. See

serials consulted.

5012. WEISE, Erich. Der Heide-
kampf des Deutschen Ordens. In Zeitschrift für Ostforschung (Marburg),
no.3, 1963, p. 420-473; no.4, p. 622-
672. See serials consulted.

5013. WŁODARSKI, Bronisław. Między Polską, Litwą a Zakonem Krzyżackim. In Towarzystwo Naukowe w Toruniu. Wydział Nauk Historycznych,
Prawniczych i Społecznych. Zapiski
Historyczne, v.16, 1950, p. 5-21.
See serials consulted.

5014. ZAJĄCZKOWSKI, Stanisław.
Rise and fall of the Teutonic Order
in Prussia. Toruń, The Baltic Institute, 1935. 97 p. (The Baltic pocket library) DD491.047Z3 DLC CU

5015. --- Studja nad procesami Polski i Litwy z Zakonem Krzyżackim w
latach, 1420-1423. In Ateneum Wileńskie (Wilno), v.12, 1937, p. 282-
403. See serials consulted.

5016. --- Zaborczość Krzyżaków w
XIV wieku. In PZHP w Warszawie 28
listopada do 4 grudnia 1930 r. Pamiętnik V. Protokoly (Lwów), v.2,
1931, p. 212-216. See serials consulted.

X.9.h. LITHUANIAN-POLISH COMMON-
WEALTH, 1569-1795.

X.9.h.1. GENERAL STUDIES

5017. ALMQUIST, Helge Knut Hjalmar.
Sverige och Ryssland, 1595-1611. Tvis-
ten om Estland, förbundet mot Polen
de ryska gränslandens eröfring och den
stora dynastiska planen... Uppsala,
Almquist & Wiksells boktryckeri, 1907.
xxxv, 273 p. DK658.4.A6 DLC CtY IU
NcU PPULC PU

5018. AVIŽONIS, Konstantinas. Bajorų viešpatavimo laikai, 1572-1795.
[The noblemen's rule, 1572-1795] In
Lietuvių enciklopedija. Boston, Mass,
1968. v.15, p. 305-325. For holdings
see entry no.216.

BACKUS, Oswald Prentiss. Motive of West Russian nobles in deserting Lithuania for Moscow. Lawrence,
Kans., 1957. See entry no. 3474.

5019. CODELLO, Aleksander. Konfederacja wojskowa na Litwie w latach,
1659-1663. In Studia i Materjały do
Historii Wojskowości (Warszawa), v.
6, no.1, 1960, p. 20-46. See serials

consulted.

5020. --- Litwa wobec wojny z Tur-cją, 1672-1676 r. In Studia i Mater-jały do Historii Wojskowości (Warsza-wa), v.14, no.1, 1968, p. [136]-159. See serials consulted.

5021. CZUBEK, Jan. Pisma polity-czne z czasów rokoszu Żebrydowskie-go, 1606-1608. Kraków, Nakł. Akad. Umiejętności, 1916-1918. 3 v. illus. music. DK430.C9 DLC CU MH NN NNC OU

5022. DE-PULE, Mikhail Fedorovich. Stanislav-Avgust Poniatovskii v Grodnie i Litva v 1794-1797 godakh. Izd. 2. Sanktpeterburg, Tip. Maiko-va, 1871. ii, iv, 255 p. DK433.D4 DLC ICU NN WaU BM(9454. g. 9.)

5023. DRUZHCHYTS, V.D. Palazhen-ne Litouska-Belaruskai dziarzhavy pas'lia Liublinskai vunii. In Minsk. Universitet. Pratsy, no.6-7, 1925, p. 216-253. See serials consulted.

5024. EVLASHEVSKII, Fedor. Dnev-nik novgorodskago podsudka, 1564-1604 goda. In Kievskaia starina (Kiev), 1886, p. 124-160. See se-rials consulted.

5025. HALECKI, Oskar. Przyłącze-nie Podlasia, Wołynia i Kijowszczyz-ny do Korony w roku, 1569. Kraków, Nakładem Akademii Umiejętności, Skład Główny w Księgarni G. Gebethnera, 1915. 245 p. DK428.5.H3 DLC MH NN PU

5026. --- Les relations entre la Pologne et les terres lithuaniennes et ruthénes avant les partages. Pa-ris, Imp. C. Courmont, 1919. 16 p. (Commission Polonaise des travaux préparatoires au Congrés de la Paix. Publications) D651.P7A2 DLC CSt-H NN

5027. HELLMANN, Manfred. Die preussische Herschaft Tauroggen in Litauen, 1690-1793. Berlin-Dahlem, Ahnenerbe-Stiftung, 1940. 80 p. fold. maps. Bibliography: p. 79-80. Thesis--University of Königsberg. DK511.T33H4 1940 DLC CU CtY IU NN NcD

5028. JACOBY, Jörg. Boguslaus Ra-dziwill, der Staathalter des Grossen Kurfürsten in Ostpreussen. Marburg/Lahn, 1959. 310 p. illus. (Wissen-schaftliche Beiträge zur Geschichte und Landeskunde Ost-Mitteleuropas, nr.40) Bibliography: p. 299-310. DD391.R13J17 CaAEU DS ICU MH MnU NIC NNC NcU NjP PU

5029. JAKŠTAS, Juozas. How firm

was the Polish-Lithuanian federation? In Slavic Review (Menasha, Wis.), v.2, no.3, 1963, p. 442-449. See se-rials consulted.

5030. JANULAITIS, Augustinas. Lie-tuvos istorija XVII-XVIII a.; paskai-tų užrašai. [History of Lithuania, seventeenth and eighteenth centuries; lectures] Kaunas, 1928-29. 4 v. (Studentų Humanitarų spaudos komisi-jos leidiniai, 31,34,37-38) DK511.L24J3 DLC ICCC

5031. JAROCHOWSKI, Kazimierz. Dzieje panowania Augusta II od wstą-pienia Karola XII na ziemię Polską aż do elekcyi Stanisława Leszczyńs-kiego, 1702-1704. Posen, 1874. xxi, 644 p. NN

5032. JASIENICA, Pawel. pseud. Rzeczpospolita obojga narodów. [Wyd. 1. Warszawa] Państwowy Instytut Wydawniczy [1967] 2 v. illus. DK429.J3 NSyU CaAEU DLC

5033. KALINKA, Walerian. Ostatnie lata panowania Stanisława Augusta; dokumenta do historyi drugiego i trzeciego podziału. Poznań, J.K. Żu-pański, 1868. cclxxx, 401 p. (Pa-miętniki z ośiemnastego wieku, t.10) DK401.P2 t.10 DLC

5034. --- --- Wyd. 2. Kraków, Nakł. Księg. Spółki Wydawniczej Polskiej, 1891. 2 v. in 1. (His Dzieła, t.1-2) DK433.K14 1891 NIC

5035. KAPLAN, Herbert Harold. The first partition of Poland. New York, N.Y., Columbia University Press, 1962. 215 p. illus. DK434.K33 DLC CaAEU PU

5036. --- The forst partition of the Polish-Lithuanian Commonwealth, 1762-1773. New York, N.Y., 1960. x, 382 leaves. Thesis-- Columbia University. Typescript. D378.&CWO. K146 NNC

5037. KONOPCZYŃSKI, Władysław. Ge-neza i ustanowienie Rady Nieustającej. Kraków, G. Gebethner, 1917. x, 432 p. JN6762.Z7K6 DLC CU CaAEU CtY MH NN NNC

5038. --- Konfederacja Barska, wy-bór tekstów. Kraków, Nakładem Kra-kowskiej Spółki Wydawniczej, 1928. xlvi, 215 p. (Bibljoteka Narodowa) F554.K83 MiD

5039. --- --- [Another edition] Warszawa, Wydawn. Kasy im. Mianows-kiego-Instytutu Popierania Nauki, 1936-38. 2 v. DK434.K6 DLC NN

5040. KOSTOMAROV, Nikolai Ivanovich. Poslednie gody Riechi-Pospolitoi; istoricheskaia monografiia. Izd. 2. Sanktpeterburg, Tip. F. Sukhinskago, 1870. 870, vi p. DK433.K8 DLC

5041. --- --- Izd. 3. Sanktpeterburg, Stasiulevich, 1886. 2 v. in 1. 947.5.K846 PU ICLJF

5042. KRASIŃSKI, Henryk. Sketch of the union of the Grand Duchy of Lithuania with Poland. London, 1842. 60 p. 308.Z25 v.11 NNC

5043. KRASIŃSKI, Jan Andrzej. Pols-Polska, czyli opisanie topograficzno-polityczne Polski w wieku XVI, oraz materyały do panowania Henryka Walezyusza przetłumaczone z łacinskiego, zebrane i objaśnione przez Stanisława Budzińskiego. Warszawa, Druk S. Strabskiego, 1852. 250 p. DK425.K89 ICU

5044. KRAUSHAR, Aleksander. Książę Repin a Polska w pierwszem czteroleciu panowania Stanisława Augusta, 1764-1768. Wyd. 2., przejrzane i poprawione. Kraków, G. Gebethner, 1897-98. 2 v. in 1. port. DK433.K7 DLC CU ICU MH NN NNC PU

5045. KRECHETNIKOV, Mikhail Nikitich. Dnevnyia zapiski o dvizhenii dieistviiakh voisk russkikh v Pol'shie v 1792 godu, nakhodiashchikhsia pod nachal'stvom generala Krechetnikova. Moskva, 1863. 104 p. tables. (Chteniia v Imp. Obshchestvie istorii i drevnostei rossiiskikh, t.47) See serials consulted.

5046. KRECHETNIKOV, Petr Nikitich. Radom i Bar, 1767-1768. Dziennik wojennych działań... z rosyjskiego originalu przełożył K. Stolnikowich-Chełmski. Poznań, 1874. x, 251 p. (Pamiętniki z ośmnastego wieku, t.14) BM(10795. df.)

5047. LAPPO, Ivan Ivanovich. Lietuva ir Lenkija po 1569 m. Liublino unijos. [Lithuania and Poland after Union of Lublin in 1569] Kaunas, Vytauto Didžiojo Universiteto, Teisių fakulteto leidinys, 1932. 172 p. (Teisės mokslų biblioteka, 12) DK511.L24L27 DLC ICCC MH NN PU

5048. --- Velikoe Kniazhestvo Litovskoe vo vtoroi polovinie XVI stolietiia. Litovsko-russkii poviet i ego seimik. IUr'ev, Tip. K. Mattisena, 1911. xiii, 624, 191 p. Originally intended as vol.2 of the author's Velikoe Kniazhestvo Litovskoe za vremia ot zakliucheniia Liublinskoi unii do smerti Stefana Batoriia, 1569-1586. DK511.L23L3 CLU CU

CSt KU MH MoU NN PU

5049. --- Velikoe Kniazhestvo Litovskoe za vremia ot zakliucheniia Liublinskoi unii do smerti Stefana Batoriia, 1569-1586; opyt izsliedovaniia politicheskago i obshchestvennago stroia. Sanktpeterburg, Tip. I.N. Skorokhodova, 1901-11. 2 v. Vol.2 published as independent work under title: Velikoe Kniazhestvo Litovskoe vo vtoroi polovinie XVI stolietiia; and is Ottisk iz "Uchenykh zapisok Imperatorskago IUr'evskago universiteta (with imprint: IUr'ev, Tip. K. Mattisena)" DK511.L24L3 DLC CLU CSt(2) CU CtY IU InU NIC(1) NbU(1) MH NN OrU WU

5050. LEPSZY, Kazimierz. Rzeczpospolita Polska w dobie sejmu inkwizycyjnego, 1589-1592. Kraków, Nakładem Polskiej Akademii Umiejętności, 1939. 428 p. DK430.L4 DLC CaAEU MH NN NNC

5051. LORD, Robert Howard. The second partition of Poland; a study in diplomatic history. Cambridge, Harvard University Press, 1915. xxx, 586 p. Bibliography: p. [557]-572. DK434.L7 DLC NN

5052. LOSSKY, Andrew. Louis XIV, William III, and the Baltic crisis of 1683. Berkeley, Calif., University of California Press, 1954. xi,73 p. fold. map. (University of California publications in history, v.49) Bibliography: p. 47-66. E173.C15 v.49 CU

5053. MACKIEWICZ, Stanisław. Diariusz moskiewskiej wojny w Wielkim Xięstwie Litewskim będącej 1659-1660. In Pomniki Dziejów Polski w XVII w. Wrocław, 1840. Tom 1, p. 162-208. BM(9476. e. 13.)

5054. MEDEKSZA, Stefan Franciszek. Stefana Franciszka z Prószcza Medekszy, sekretarza Jana Kazimierza, sędziego ziemskiego kowieńskiego, Księga pamiętnicza wydarzeń zaszłych na Litwie 1654-1668. Wyd. Władysław Seredyński. Kraków, Nakładem Akademii Umiejętności w Krakowie, 1875. xxv, 526 p. (Scriptores rerum Polonicarum, t.3) DK402.S4 v.3 DLC ICU MH PU

5055. MOŚCICKI, Henryk. Dzieje porozbiorowe Litwy i Rusi. Wilno, Nakł. Kurjera Litewskiego, 1913-14. 476, 64 p. illus., ports. No more published. Contents.--T.1. 1772-1800, zesz. 1-15.--T.2. 1800-1806, zesz. 16-17. DK511.L24M6 DLC(1) BM(1) ICU(1) InU(1) MH(1-2; zesz.1-17)

5056. NARBUTT, Justyn. Dzieje wewnętrzne narodu litewskiego za cza-

sów Jana Sobieskiego i Augusta II,
królów panujących w Polsce. Wyd. 2.
Wilno, W Drukarni A. Dworca, 1843.
2 v. Balt 7896.24 MH BM(9475.a.16.)

5057. NIEMCEWICZ, Julian Ursyn.
Dzieje panowania Zygmunta III, króla
Polskiego, Wielkiego Księcia Litewskiego. Warszawa, Drukiem Zawadzkiego i Węckiego, 1819. 3 v. illus.,
ports., facsim. DK430.N6 InU

5058. --- --- [Another edition]
Wrocław, Z. Schletter, 1836. 3 v.
illus., ports., facsim. DK430.N5
DLC MH

5059. --- --- [Another edition]
Kraków, Nakł. Wydawnictwa Biblioteki
Polskiej, 1860. 3 v. in 1. MnU NN
NNC

5060. OBSERVATIONS SUR LES DÉCLA-
rations des cours de Vienna, de Pe-
tersbourg et de Berlin au sujet du
démembrement de la Pologne. Nouv.
éd. augmentée de notes historiques
et politiques. Londres, 1773. 46
p. 947.52.Ob73 PU

5061. PETER I, the GREAT, EMPEROR
OF RUSSIA. Sacrae Czareae Majesta-
tis declaratio, quo jure, et qua
intentione exercitum suum in Polo-
niam introduxerit, serenissimae Po-
loniarum Reipublicae, et toti christianorum orbi ostensa et exhibita.
[Potock?] 1705. [6] p.
JN5276.M89 1730 CaAEU

5062. PALIŃSKI, Tadeusz von. Das
polnische Interregnum von 1572-1573
und die Königswahl Heinrichs von Va-
lois. Bonn, Druck von C. Georgi,
1861. Thesis--University of Heidelberg. DK428.7.P64 DLC CU MiU

5063. PIWARSKI, Kazimierz. Kwes-
tia Bałtycka na Litwie w drugiej połowie XVII w. In PZHP w Wilnie 17-
20 września 1935 r. Pamiętnik VI.
Referaty (Lwów), v.1, 1935, p. 105-
111. See serials consulted.

5064. --- Opozycja litewska pod
koniec XVII wieku. In PZHP w Warszawie 28 listopada do 4 grudnia
1930 r. Pamiętnik V. Referaty
(Lwów), v.1, 1930, p. 259-277. See
serials consulted.

5065. POWIDAJ, Ludwik. Wojna domo-
wa Sapiehów z szlachtą litewską w os-
tatnich latach XVII i na początku
XVIII wieku. Szkic historyczny. In
Przegląd Polski (Kraków), yr 7, v.1,
1872, p. 68-88,211-231. See serials
consulted.

5066. PROCHASKA, Antoni. Dwa ob-

jasnienia do dziejów Litwy. In Kwartalnik Historyczny (Lwów), 1906, p.
64-73. See serials consulted.

5067. --- Dwie koronacye. In Przegląd Historyczny (Warszawa), v.1, 1905,
p. 184-208. See serials consulted.

5068. RADZIWIŁŁ, Albrycht Stanisław.
Memoriale rerum gestarum in Polonia
a morte Sigismundi tertii inchoatum
et continuatum, 1653-1655. [Edited
by] K. Avižonis. In Lietuvos praeitis (Kaunas), v.1, no.1, 1940, p.
211-292. See serials consulted.

5069. --- Memoriale rerum gestarum
in Polonia, 1632-1656. Oprac. Adam
Przyboś i Roman Żelewski. v.1- .
Wrocław, 1968- . DK430.3.R3 PU

5070. --- Pamiętniki Albrychta Stanisława Ks. Radziwiłła, kanclerza
wielkiego litewskiego, 1632-1653. Wydane z rękopismu przed E. Raczyńskiego. Poznań, 1839. 2 v. BM(10790.
d. 13.)

5071. RADZIWIŁŁ, Karol Stanisław.
Korespondencya Księcia Karola Stanis-
ława Radziwiłła... 1744-1790. Wydał
Cz. Jankowski. Kraków, 1898. 315 p.
BM(010910. b. 22.)

5072. RADZIWIŁŁ, Krzysztof II.
Sprawy wojenne i polityczne Księcia
Krzysztofa Radziwiłła, hetmana wiel-
kiego Księcia Litewskiego, 1621-1632.
Paryż, A. Martinet, 1859. xvi, 713 p.
DK430.2.R12 CaAEU NN

5073. RUDAWSKI, Laurentius Ioannes.
Historiarum Poloniae ab excessu Wladislai IV ad pacem Olivensem; seu,
Annales regente Ioanne Casimiro ab
anno 1648 usque ad annum 1660. Varsoviae et Lipsiae, Sumptibus Mizler-
ianis, 1755. [14], 516, [30] p.
ICBM

5074. ŠAPOKA, Adolfas. Jonušas
Radvila ir Švedija. [Jonušas Radvila and Sweden] In Židinys (Kaunas),
v.30, no.8-9, p. 214-229. See serials
consulted.

5075. --- Leonas Sapiega kaip Lietuvos politikas. [Leonard Sapieha
as a stateman of Lithuania] In Židinys (Kaunas), v.18, no.10, 1933,
p. 274-284. See serials consulted.

5076. --- Lietuva ir Lenkija po
1569 metų Liublino Unijos; jų valstybių santykių bruožai. [Lithuania
and Poland after the Lublin Union of
1569...] Kaunas, Spindulio b-vės
spaustuvė, 1938. xx, 394 p. (Švietimo ministerijos knygų leidimo komisijos leidinys, nr.494) Summary

279

in German. Bibliography: p. [xiii]-
xx. DK418.5.L5Se DLC CtTMF BM(9476.
aa. 17.)

5077. ŠLIŪPAS, Jonas. Gadynė šlek-
tos viešpatavimo Lietuvoje, 1569-
1795 m. ir Lietuviškasis Statutas
Zigmanto I. [By] John Szlupas.
[The rule of nobility in Lithuania,
1569-1795, and the Lithuanian Statute] Chicago, Ill., Turtu ir
spauda "Lietuvos", 1909. 2 v. in 1.
(552 p.) DK511.L24S9 DLC CaOTP CtTMF
ICBM MH MiD NN NjP PPi PU RP WaS

        SLIWIŃSKI, Artur. Jan Karol
Chodkiewicz, hetman wielki litewski.
Warszawa, 1932. See entry no. 2885.

5078. SUŁKOWSKI, Józef. Szczegu-
ły historyczne tyczące się wojny
polsko-rosyjskiej na Litwie 1792 r.
według tłumaczenia Ireny Bulicz Tru-
chimowej, przedmową... Stefan Tru-
chimi. Poznań, Fiszer i Majewski,
1923. 140 p. 914.5S ICBM NN

5079. SZELĄGOWSKI, Adam. Walka o
Bałtyk, 1544-1621. Lemberg, B. Po-
loniecki, 1904. xi, 399 p. NN

5080. --- --- Wyd. 2., przejrzane
i uzupełnione. Lwów; Poznań, Wydawnictwo Polskie, 1921. 324 p. front.
U 943.8.S997 NNUN MH OCl

5081. TRACHEVSKII, Aleksandr Semenovich. Pol'skoe bezkorolevie po
prekrashchenii dinastii IAgellonov;
istoricheskoe izsledovanie. Moskva, Izd. K. Soldatenkova, 1869.
1 v. DK428.7.T7 DLC CtY MH PU

5082. TRUMPA, Vincas. The disin-
tegration of the Polish-Lithuanian
Commonwealth. In Lituanus (Chicago,
Ill.), v.10, no.2, 1964, p. 24-32.
See serials consulted.

5083. TYSZKOWSKI, Kazimierz. Od-
głosy rokoszowe na Litwie. In Ateneum Wileńskie (Wilno), v.1, 1923,
p. 39-57. See serials consulted.

5084. URBONAS, Oskaras. Didžiojo
Šiaurės Karo frontas Lietuvoje.
[The front of the Great Northern
War in Lithuania] [Brooklyn, N.Y.]
Karys, 1963-64. 2 v. illus., maps,
plans, ports. (Lietuvos karinės is-
torijos raštai, nr.3) Revised off-
print from Karys, 1958 and 1961.
DK511.L24U74 1963 CaAEU ICBM ICLJF

5085. WALEWSKI, Antoni. Geschichte der Hl. Ligue und Leopold I., vom
Umschwung im Gleichgewichtssystem
des Westens durch den swedisch-pol-
nisch-österreichischen Krieg...1657-
1700. Krakau, Universitäts-Buchdru-

ckerei, 1857-61. 3 v. in 2. On Lithuania: Theil 2, Abt.1, p. 337-349.
DB67.W17 CaAEU

5086. WOLANSKI, Adam. Wojna polsko-rosyjska 1792 r. Tadeusz Soplica [pseud.] Kraków, Nakł. Księgarni D.E. Friedleina, 1906. 1 v.
fold. map, tables. NN

5087. --- --- Kampanja litewska.
Tadeusz Soplica [pseud.] Poznań,
K. Rzepecki, 1922. 2 v. illus.,
maps, plates, ports. DK434.W63 DLC
PU

5088. WOLIŃSKI, Janusz. Z dziejów
wojny i polityki w dobie Jana Sobieskiego. Redaktor Marian Anusiewicz.
Warszawa [Wydawn. Ministerstwa Obrony Narodowej] 1960. 202 p. illus.
DK431.W6 DLC CU MiDW MiU WU

X.9.h.2. INSURRECTION OF 1794

5089. BIRŽIŠKA, Mykolas. Lietuvos
sukilimas 1794 metais. [The insurrec-
tion of 1794 in Lithuania] Vilnius,
Bajevskio spaustuvė, 1919. 31 p.
(Lietuvių mokslo draugijos leidinys)
DK511.L24B62 CaAEU CtTMF PPULC PU

5090. DUBIECKI, Marian. Karol Pro-
zor obożny wielki, Wielkiego Księstw-
wa Litewskiego. Przyczynek do dziejów powstania kościuszkowskiego.
Monografia opracowana na podstawie
nowych źródeł archywalnych. Kraków,
Druk "Czasu",1897. 335 p. port.
DK435.5.P7D8 DLC MH NN

5091. GIESZYŃSKI, Henryk. Krótki
pogląd na powstanie kościuszkowskie.
Paryż, A. Reill, 1884. 28 p. NN

5092. KON, Pinchas. A yidishe stim
tsum oyfshtand 1794 in Vilna. [Wilno,
1933] 23 p. DK511.V4K6 DLC

5093. KORZON, Tadeusz. Kościuszko;
biografia z dokumentów wysnuta...
Kraków, Nakł. Museum Narodowego w
Rapperswylu, 1894. 691, viii p.
illus., ports, maps. DK434.8.K8K6
DLC ICLJF NN

5094. MOŚCICKI, Henryk. Generał
Jasiński i powstanie kościuszkowskie.
Warszawa [1917] 435 p. facsims.,
illus., plan, ports. DK434.8.J3M58
PU ICLJF NN

5095. POLAND. RADA ZASTĘPCZA TYM-
CZASOWA. Akty powstania Kościuszki.
Ed. by Szymon Askenazy i Wt. Dzwon-
kowski. Kraków, Nakł. Akademji Umiejętności; Skł. gł. w Księg. G. Gebeth-

nera, 1918-55. 3 v. J399.H24 DLC
CaAEU ICU NN WaU

5096. SKAŁKOWSKI, Adam. Z dziejów
insurekcji 1794 r. Warszawa, Gebethner i Wolff [1926] 248 p.
DK434.S55 DLC CtPAM

5097. ŚLIWIŃSKI, Artur. Powstanie
kościuszkowskie. Wyd. 2. Warszawa,
M. Arct, 1920. 192 p. front., plates, ports. DK434.8.K8S6 1920 DLC
ICU MH NN OCl

5098. TRĘBICKI, Antoni. Pamiętnik
o rewolucji 1794 roku. Wyd. A. Skałkowski. In Kwartalnik Historyczny
(Lwów), 1931, p. 267-328. See serials consulted.

5099. ŻYTKOWICZ, Leonid. Litwa i
Korona w roku 1794. In Ateneum Wileńskie (Wilno), v.12, 1937, p. 515-
566. See serials consulted.

5100. --- Stosunki skarbowe W. Ks.
Litewskiego w dobie insurekcji koś-
ciuszkowskiej. In Ateneum Wileńskie
(Wilno), v.10, 1935, p. 97-160. See
serials consulted.

X.9.i. LITHUANIA UNDER RUSSIAN
RULE, 1795-1915

X.9.i.1. GENERAL STUDIES

ALEKNA, Antanas. Žemaičių
vyskupas Motiejus Valančius. Klaipėda, 1922. See entry no. 455.

5101. AUS LITAUEN. Die letzten Ta-
ge der Russenherrschaft in Wilno. In
Polen (Wien), v.2, 1916, p. 186-189.
See serials consulted.

5102. BAGDANAVIČUS, Vytautas, ed.
Kovos metai dėl savosios spaudos.
[Lithuania's fight for a free press]
Chicago, Ill., Lietuvių bendruomenės
Čikagos apyg. leidinys [1957] 365 p.
Contents.--Svarbiausieji spaudos drau-
dimo tarpsniai, Vyt. Bagdanavičius.
--Bendroji rusinimo politika, K.J.
Avižonis.--Spaudos draudimas be tei-
sinio pagrindo, Vac. Biržiška.--Lie-
tuvių tautos atgimimi pradmenys, K.
J. Čeginskas.--Lietuviškojo raidyno
draudimas, J. Matusas.--Nuo raidžių
draudimo iki kalbos naikinimo, J.
Sangaila.--Pastangos draudimui nu-
galėti, Vac. Biržiška.--Knygų platinimo organizacijos ir knygnešiai, V.
Sruogienė.--Amerikos lietuvių knygos,
Vyt. Širvydas.-- Amerikiniai lietuvių laikraščiai, J. Prunskis.--Drau-
džiamojo laikotarpio grožinė litera-

tūra, D. Lipčiūtė-Augienė.--Rusiškos
raidės talkininkai, Vac. Biržiška.
PN5278.L5B3 DLC CaOONL CaAEU CaOTU
CtTMF ICCC ICLJF MH NN OCl PU

5103. BIRŽIŠKA, Vaclovas. Kražių
gimnazistų byla 1840-1841. [The
court case for the High School students of Kražiai in 1840-1841] In
Mūsų senovė (Kaunas), no.2, 1921, p.
105-106. See serials consulted.

5104. CZAPLICKI, Ferdynand Władys-
ław. Moskiewskie na Litwie rządy,
1863-1869. Dalszy niejako ciąg Czar-
nej Księgi przez autora "Powieści o
Horożanie". Kraków, Nakładem J.
Siedleckiego, 1869. xii, 375 p.
DK511.L25C99 InU BM(8094. g. 13.)
CaOTU CtY MH PU

5105. FAJNHAUZ, Dawid. Rok 1846
na ziemiach Litwy i Białorusi Zachod-
nej. In Przegląd Historyczny (Warszawa), v.48, 1957, p. 683-706. See
serials consulted.

5106. GIEEYSZTOR, Jakób Kazimierz.
Litwa przed rokiem 1863. [By] Lit-
win [pseud.] Lwów, Nakł. Drukarni
Ludowej, 1888. 42 p. 947.52.G798 PU

5107. GRIŠKŪNAITĖ, Emilija. Kassy
bor'by rabochikh Litvy v 1888-1897
gg. In LTSRMAD. Serija A, no.1,
1960, p. p. 87-100. See serials
consulted.

5108. --- Lietuva reakcijos metais,
1907-1910. In LTSRMAII. Lietuvos TSR
istorija. Vilnius, 1963. v.2, p.
356-374. illus. DK511.L2L4235 v.2
DLC CaAEU CU CtY InU MH

5109. --- Naujas revoliucinio judėjimo pakilimas, 1910-1914 m. Usile-
nie revoliutsionnogo dvizheniia v
1910-1914 gg. In LTSRMAII. Lietuvos
TSR istorija. Vilnius, 1963. v.2,
p. 374-404. illus. DK511.L2L4235
v.2 DLC CaAEU CU CtY InU MH

5110. IKSAS, pseud. Lietuvos respublikos istorija; nuo 1905 m. revoliucijos iki šių dienų. [The history of the Lithuanian Republic...]
So.Boston, Mass., Keleivio spauda,
1921. 96 p. fold. col. map.
947.5.I CaOTP CtY MH

5111. KAREIVIS, José. La Lithuanie sous la domination russe, 1795-
1915. Lausanne, Librairie centrale
des nationalités, 1917. 31 p.
DK511.L2K18 CSt-H CaBVaS MH PU

5112. KIRKOR, Adam Honory. V pamiat' prebyvaniia Gosudaria Imperatora Aleksandra II. v Vil'nie 6 i 7
sentiabria 1858 g.; istoriko-statis-

ticheskie ocherki goroda Vil'na.
Vil'no, Izd. Vilenskoi arkheolog.
komissii, 1858. 128 p. map.
DK651.V4K5 DLC

5113. KUKIEL, Marian. Próby pows-
tańcze po trzecim rozbiorze, 1795-
1797... Kraków i Warszawa, Druk
W.L. Anczyca i Spółki, 1912. xvii,
513 p. port. (Monografie w zakresie dziejów nowożytnych, t.19)
DK435.K83 DLC MH NN

5114. LIETUVIS, A., pseud. Augis
darbininkų judėjimo Lietuvoje. [The
worker's unrest in Lithuania] Plymouth, Pa., 1900. 58 p. BM(4034.
aa. 25.)

5115. MATROSOV, Evgenii Nikolaevich. Polozhenie litovskago naroda
v Russkom gosudarstvie; sotsiologi-
cheskii ocherk. V Shamokinie, Pa.,
Izdanie Litovskago literaturnago obshchestva v Soed. Shtat. Siev. Ameriki, 1896. 128 p. Author's pseud,
Count Leliva at head of the title.
DK511.L2M23 DLC CtTMF KU MH NN

5116. MILLER, Antoni. Pierwsza
porozbiorowa konspiracja litewska;
spisek Ks. Ciecierskiego, preora dominikanów wileńskich, 1796-1797;
studjum historyczne. [Kraków] Nakł.
OO Dominikanów w Krakowie [1936]
174 p. DK511.L25M55 PU

5117. MOŚCICKI, Henryk. Projekty
połączenia Litwy z Królewstwem Polskiem w okresie 1813-1830 r. In His
Pod berłem carów. Warszawa, 1924.
p. 77-102. DK434.9.M6 DLC MH NN OCl
PU

5118. --- Tajny materjał gen.-gu-
bernatora Trockiego o Litwie, 1899 r.
In His Pod berłem carów. Warszawa,
1924. p. [232]-242. DK434.9.M6 DLC
MH NN OCl PU

5119. ŻYTKOWICZ, Leonid. Rządy Re-
pina na Litwie w latach 1794-1797.
Wilno, Nakł. Tow. Przyjaciół Nauk;
Skł. gł. w Księg. Św. Wojciecha,
1938. 464 p. illus. (Rozprawy Wydziału III Towarzystwa Przyjaciół Nauk w Wilnie, t.10) DK435.Z92 DLC CU
ICU MiU NN PU

X.9.i.2. NAPOLEONIC WAR OF 1812

5120. DUNDULIS, Bronius. Napoléon
et Lithuanie en 1812. Paris, Presses
universitaires de France, 1940. 344
p. (Bibliothèque d'histoire contemporaine) Bibliographie: p. 315-334.
Thèse--Université de Paris.

DK511.L24D8 DLC CU CLU CaOWtU CaQMM
CoU CtY FTaSU FU ICU IaU ICN InNd
InU ICBM IU KU LU MH MoU NN NIC NNC
NcU NcD NjP NjR NcGW PU WU

5121. IWASZKIEWICZ, Janusz. Litwa
w roku 1812. Kraków, Druk W.L. Anczyca, 1912. 439 p. (Monografie w
zakresie dziejów nowożytnych, t.9)
DK511.L24I9 DLC CaOTU MH NN

5122. --- Rejestracja i indemniza-
cja strat wojennych na Litwie po roku 1812. In Poland. Rada Główna
Opiekuńcza. Wydział rejestracji
strat wojennych. Likwidacja skut-
ków wojny w dziedzinie stosunków
prawnych. Warszawa, 1917. v.2.
BM(08285. k. 45/2.)

5123. KUDRINSKII, F.A. Vil'na v
1812 godu. Vil'na, Izd. Uprav. Vilenskago Uchebnago Okruga, 1912. iv,
153 p. illus. DC235.5.V5K8 DLC I
ICLJF

5124. RUŽANCOVAS, Aleksandras. Iš
Kauno miesto valdybos archyvo 1812-
1813 metų bylų. [From the archives
of the City Council of Kaunas of 1812-
1813] In Karo archyvas (Kaunas),
v.4, 1928, p. 98-108. See serials
consulted.

5125. SCHMITTLEIN, Raymond, comp.
Avec Napoléon en Lituanie. Kaunas,
Pribačio leidinys, 1937. 88 p. pla-
tes. 947.52.Sch55 PU NN NNC

5126. --- Une district lituanienne
sous l'occupation Française 1812.
In Senovė (Kaunas), v.2, 1936, p.
215-272. See serials consulted.

5127. TATISIDIEV, IUrii Vladimirovich. Vil'na i litovskiia gubernii
v 1811-1813 gg.; sbornik dokumentov
arkhiva upravleniia Vilenskago, Ko-
venskago i Grodnenskago General-Gubernatora. Vil'na, Gubernskaia tipografiia, 1913. 355 p. illus.,
ports., plates, facsims, fold. col.
map. 947.5.T187v 1913 KU CSt-H

5128. VOENSKII, Konstantin Adamo-
vich. Litva i zapadnye gubernii. In
His Akty, dokumenty i materialy dlia
politicheskoi i bytovoi istorii 1812
goda. Sanktpeterburg, 1909. 1 v.
(Russkoe istoricheskoe obshchestvo.
Sbornik, t.128) BM(9456. k. 16.)

5129. --- Vil'na v 1812 godu. Iz
vospominanii grafa Gogendorfa, byvshago General-Gubernatora Velikago
Kniazhestva Litovskago. [Sanktpeter-
burg, Tip. Sel'skago viestnika, 1912]
38 p. CSt-H

X.9.1.3. INSURRECTION OF 1831

5130. BEM, Józef. O powstaniu narodowym w Polsce. Redaktor M. Anusiewicz. Warszawa, Wyd. Ministerstwa Obrony Narodowej, 1956. 215 p. illus. (Prace Komisji Wojskowo-Historicznej Min. Obr. Nar., Serja B, 3) InU MH MiDW NN NNC

5131. BENTLEY, J.A. Belgium and Poland in international relations, 1830-1831. Gravenhage, Mouton, 1960. 298 p. maps. Bibliography: p. 13-18. DH652.D4 DLC CaAEU CtY MH NNC NNC-L

5132. BERG, Nikolai Vasil'evich. Zapiski... o pol'skikh zagovorakh i vozstaniiakh 1831-1862. Izdanie "Russkago Arkhiva". Moskva, Tip. Gracheva, 1873. 383, 68 p. DK437. B4 DLC NN

5133. --- Zapiski o polskich spiskach i powstaniach. Przekład z rosyjskiego. Warszawa, A.T. Jezierskiego, 1906. 1 v. DK437.B49 CaAEU

5134. BIELIŃSKI, Kazimierz. Powstanie listopadowe w Wilnie i na Wileńszczyźnie. Wilno, Nakł. Dziennika Urzędowego Kuratorjum Okr. Szk., 1934. 52 p. (Bibljoteczka Poradni Dydaktyczno-Wychowawczej przy Kuratorjum Okręgu Szkolnego Wileńskiego, nr.3) DK511.L25B5 DLC CtY

5135. BRONIKOWSKI, Ksawery, ed. Pamiętniki Polskie. [Wyd.2.] Przemyśl, A. Kaczurba, 1883-84. 2 v. in 1. DK435.B76 DLC MH NN

5136. CHŁAPOWSKI, Dezydery. Lettre sur les événements militaires en Pologne et en Lithuanie. Berlin, 1832. 45 p. (Geschichte. Polen, no.3) 943.8.G38 no.3 NSyU MH

5137. --- Pamiętniki... Poznań, Nakł. Synów, 1899. 2 v. in 1. port. Contents.--Część 1. Wojny napoleonskie, 1806-1813.--Część 2. Wojna roku 1830-1831. MH NN

5138. CUKIERMAN, Liza. Die polenfreundliche Bewegung in Frankreich im Jahre 1830-1831. Warszawa, Druk J. Keltera, 1926. 81 p. Thesis--University of Zürich. Bibliography: p. i-[vi] CtY ICU IU WU

5139. DEMBIŃSKI, Henryk. Mein Feldzug nach und in Lithauen und mein Rückzug von Kurschany nach Warschau. Leipzig, Verlag der Dyk'schen Buchhandlung, 1832. 10, 206 p. map. DK436.D36 InU IaU MH PU

5140. --- Mémoires sur la campagne de Lithuanie. Strassburg, Heitz, 1832. xxxvi, 343 p. fold. map, facsim. A portion of the work first appeared under title: "Mein Feldzug nach und in Litauen". Leipzig, 1832. DK436.D37 DLC MH MiU WaU

5141. --- Pamiętniki o powstaniu w Polsce r. 1830-31. Wyd. 2. Kraków, Druk Czas, 1877. 2 v. in 1. DK436.2.D37A3 ICU

5142. DOMEIKO, Ignacio. Pamiętniki, 1831-1838. Z autografów wydał Józef Tretiak. Kraków Nakł. Akademii Umiejętności; Skł. Gł. w Księg. G. Gebethnera, 1908. vii, 226 p. (Źrodła do dziejów Polski porozbiorowych, 5) PG7158.D59Z52 DLC

5143. DUTKIEWICZ, Józef. Austrja wobec powstania listopadowego. Kraków, Gebethner i Wolff, 1933. 161 p. (Polskie Towarzystwo Historyczne. Oddział Krakowski. Prace nr.10). 943.8.P7581 no.10 NNC CtY MnU NN WaU

5144. --- Francja a Polska w 1831 r. Łódź, 1950. 185 p. (Łódzkie Towaarzystwo Naukowe. Wyd. II. Prace, nr.4) DC59.8.P7D8 DLC CaBVaU CoU ICU IU LU ML NN OU

5145. --- Wybór źródeł powstania listopadowego. Wrosław, Zakład Narodowy im. Ossolinskich, 1957. lviii, 268 p. DK436.D8 DLC CaBVaU ICU InU IU MH MiDW MnU NN NNC OU ViU

5146. HANDELSMAN, Marceli. Anglia a Polska, 1814-1864. Warszawa, E. Wende, 1917. 114 p. DK434.9.H35 DLC MH MiD NN

5147. HIRSCHBERG, Aleksander, ed. Bibliografja powstania narudu polskiego z roku 1830-1831... [Lwów] T. Rayski, 1882. p. 561-698. (*QO p.v.81.no.4)NN

5148. HOFFMAN, Jadwyga. Legia litewsko-wołyńska 1831 r. In Rocznik Wołyński (Równe), v.2, 1931, p. 213-241. See serials consulted.

5149. HORDYŃSKI, Józef. History of the Polish revolution and the events of the campaign. Boston, Mass., Carter and Hendee, 1832. xvi, 406 p. plans. DK436.H8 1832 DLC CU MeB MiU MWA NIC NjR NWM PPAmP PPLas PNortHi PKsL PU WaU

5150. --- --- 2nd ed. Boston, Mass., Printed for subscribers, 1833. xii, [5]-428 p. plans. DK436.H8 1833 DLC CU CtY AU ICU MdBJ NN NNC NcD NjP OCl OO OU PPA PPLas PU TU ViU NdFA

5151. --- --- 3rd. ed. Boston, Mass., Printed for subscribers, 1833. xii, [5]-428 p. plans. DK436.H8 1833a DLC NN

5152. --- --- 4th ed. Boston, Mass., Printed for subscribers, 1933. xii, 435 p. ports, maps. 943.8.H78 NdFA PU

5153. JANOWSKI, Jan Nepomucen. Les derniers moments de la révolution de la Pologne en 1831. Paris, Roret, etc., 1833. iv, 110 p. DK436.J34 DLC BN

5154. JANULAITIS, Augustinas. Valstiečiai ir 1831 metų revoliucija Lietuvoje. [Peasants and the revolution of 1831 in Lithuania] In Lietuvių tauta (Vilnius), v.4, 1910, 29 p. See serials consulted.

5155. KIRŠINAS, Vincas. Generolo Gelgaudo žygis į Lietuvą ir jo įvertinimas. [The campaign of General Gelgaudas into Lithuania and its evaluation] In Karo archyvas (Kaunas), v.6, 1935, p. 31-46. See serials consulted.

5156. LESLIE, R. F. Polish politics and the revolution of November 1830. [London] University of London, Athlone Press, 1956. xii, 307 p. maps. (University historical studies, 3) DK436.L545 DLC CLU CU CaAEU CaBVaU CtY ICU KU LU MB MH MdBJ MnU NN NNC NIC NcD NjR OCl OU PPiU TxU VtU WaU

5157. LIMANOWSKI, Bolesław. Szermierze wolności; Emilija Platerówna, Jan Szaniecki, Józef Zaliwski. Kraków, Książka [1911] [8], 285 p. ports. (*QR)NN

5158. LISTY GOŃCZE W SPRAWIE powstańców z r. 1831, pochodzących z Litwy. Pod. Stefan Pomarański. In Ateneum Wileńskie (Wilno), v.3, 1936, p. 146-157. See serials consulted.

5159. MACIŪNAS, Vincas. 1831 metų sukilimo emigrantų lietuviškieji spaudiniai. [The Lithuanian publications in exile by the participants of the insurrection of 1831] In Mūsų senovė (Kaunas), v. 2, no.3, 1938, p. 462-471. See serials consulted.

5160. MELOCH, Maksymilian. Sprawa włościańska w powstaniu listopadowym. Warszawa, Gebethner i Wolff, 1939. 175 p. NN DLC

5161. MIELŻYŃSKI, Maciej. Wyprawa na Litwę w 1830-31 r. Opowiedziana według zapisków. Kraków,

Czas, 1908. 68 p. 947.52.M5798 PU

5162. MOŚCICKI, Henryk, ed. Powstanie 1831 roku na Litwie; wspomnienia uczestników. Wilno, J. Zawadzki, 1931. xvii, 174 p. ports. DK436.M68 DLC CU CtY MH PU

5163. PAWŁOWSKI, Bronisław, ed. Źródła do dziejów wojny polsko-rosyjskiej 1830-1831 r. Warszawa, Wojskowe Biuro Historyczne, 1931-35. 4 v. fold. map, tables. DK436.P35 DLC MH

5164. PIETKIEWICZ, Michał. La Lithuanie et sa dernière insurrection. Bruxelles, H. Dumont, 1832. 318 p. fold. map. DK511.L25P4 DLC CtY PU WU

5165. LES POLONAIS, LES LITHUAniens et les Russiens célébrant en France les premiers anniversaires de leur révolution nationale du 29 novembre 1830 et du 25 mars 1831. Paris, H. Bossange, 1832. 68 p. DK436.3.P65 CoU BM MH

5166. PRĄDZIŃSKI, Ignacy. Pamiętnik historyczny i wojskowy o wojnie rosyjskiej w roku 1831. Kraków, K. Grendyszyński, 1894. iv, 292 p. MH

5167. --- Pamiętniki generała Prądzińskiego. Opracował Bronisław Gembarzewski. Kraków, Księg. Spółki Wydawniczej Polskiej, 1909. 4 v. DK436.P7 DLC NN

5168. PUZYREVSKII, Aleksandr Kazimirovich. Der polnisch-russische Krieg, 1831. Wien, Kreisel & Gröger, 1892-93. 3 v. maps, plans. DK436.P9 DLC MiU NN

5169. --- Polsko-russkaia voina 1831 g. Sanktpeterburg, Tip. Shtaba voisk gvardii, 1886. iv, xiii, 446, ccxvii p. tables and atlas. (Nikolaevskaia Akademiia general'-nago shtaba) DK436.P85 DLC

5170. RABINOWICZÓWNA, Sara. Wilno w powstaniu roku 1830-1831. Wilno, Wydawnictwo Magistratu m. Wilna, 1932. 158 p. (Bibljoteczka Wileńska, nr.4) DK651.V4R33 CtY KU NN NNC PU

5171. RUŽANCOVAS, Aleksandras. Iš 1831 metų sukilimo Kaune. [The insurrection of 1831 in Kaunas] In Karo archyvas (Kaunas), v.7, 1936, p. 73-99. See serials consulted.

5172. SLIESORIŪNAS, F. 1830-1831 m. sukilėlių valdžia Lietuvoje. [The government of the insurgents in Lithuania, 1830-1831] In LTSRMAD Serija A, v.1(20), 1966, p. 59-87.

Summary in Russian. See serials
consulted.

5173. ŚLIWIŃSKI, Artur. Powstanie listopadowe. Wyd. 5. Warszawa, M. Arct, 1920. 195 p.
DK436.S55 1920 DLC MH RP NN(1911 ed.)

5174. SOKOLNICKI, Michał. Les
origines de l'émigration polonaise
en France, 1831-1832. Paris, F.
Alcan, 1910. x, 239 p. Also
thesis--University of Bern, Switzerland. DK436.S68 NIC ICJ ICU
IaU InU IU MB MH NN

5175. --- Wojna polsko-rosyjska
w roku 1831. Poznań, K. Repecki,
1919. 364 p. illus., map, plates.
(*QR)NN

5176. SOKOŁOWSKI, August. Dzieje powstania listopadowego, 1830-
1831 r. Wiedeń, Nakł. F. Bondego,
1908. iv, 315 p. illus., plates,
ports., facsims. DK436.S585 DLC
CU CaAEU CtY MH NN

5177. SPAZIER, Richard Otto von.
Geschichte des Aufstandes des
polnischen Volkes in den Jahren
1830-1831. Altenburg, Literatur-
Comtoir, 1832. 3 v. tables.
DK436.S7 DLC ICU MH

5178. --- 2. Aufl. Stuttgart, Fr.
Brodhag, 1834. 3 v. NN

5179. STEPONAITIS, Vytautas.
Bartolomiejaus veikimas 1831 metais Lietuvoje. [The activities of
Bartolomiejus during the insurrection of 1831 in Lithuania] In
Karo archyvas (Kaunas), v.6, 1935,
p. 57-75. See serials consulted.

5180. STRASZEWICZ, Józef. I
polacchi della rivoluzione del 29.
novembre 1830. Capolago, Italy,
Tip. librari elvetica, 18333-34.
2 v. 947.52.St82 PU

5181. TOKARZ, Wacław. Wojna polsko-rosyjska 1830-1831. Warszawa,
Wojskowy Instytut Naukowo-Wydawniczy, 1930. xxxii, 635 p. and
atlas. Bibliography: p. xxi-xxxii.
DK436.T6 DLC CSt-H ICN IU NN PU

5182. WROTNOWSKI, Feliks. Historja powstania w roku 1831 na
Wołyniu, Podoliu, Ukrainie, Żmudzi
i Litwie. Lipsk, F.A. Brockhaus,
1875. 2 v. in 1. (Biblioteka
Piszrzy polskich, t.71-72)
947.52.W945 PU CaOTU MH NN

5183. --- Pamiętniki o powstaniu
Litwy i ziem ruskich 1831. Paryż,
W. Druk. A. Pinard, 1833- . Vol.
3 never published. Partial con-

tents.--v.1, pt.1. Ogulny rys powstania Litwy.--v.2. Zbiór pamiętników o powstaniu Litwy. Slav
5722.1 MH(v.1, pt.1, v.2,4-5)

5184. ---, comp. Zbiór pamiętników o powstaniu Litwy w r. 1831.
Paryż, W Księgarni Polskieg, 1835.
xii, 368 p. (His Pamiętniki o
powstaniu Litwy, t.2) DK511.L25W7
DLC ICU MH NN

5185. Z., A. .Wojna na Litwie w
roku 1831. Kraków, Skł. gł. w
Księg. Gebethnera, 1913.
947.52.Z12 PU

X.9.i.4. INSURRECTION OF 1863.

5186. AKADEMIIA NAUK SSSR. INSTI-
TUT SLAVIANOVEDENIIA. Revoliutsion-
noe dvizhenie v russkoi armii i vosstanie 1863 g. [By] V.A. Diakov
[and] I.S. Miller. Moskva, 1964.
446 p. DK437.D5 DLC BM(X. 639/76.)

5187. --- Revoliutsionnyi pod'em
v Litve i Belorussii v 1861-1862 gg.
Revoliucinis pakilimas Lietuvoje ir
Baltarusijoje 1861-1862 m. Moskva,
Nauka, 1964. lxix, 703 p. illus.,
facsims., ports. (Vosstanie 1863
goda; materialy i dokumenty) In
Russian; part of documents in Po-
lish. DK511.L25A67 DLC CSt CaBVaS
CaBVaU CaNSHD CaOTU CtY CoU ICU IEN
IaU InNd InU IU MH MnU MU NIC NN
NNC NcD NjP OrU PU ViU WU WaU

5188. --- Vosstanie v Litve i
Belorussii, 1863-1864 gg. Sukilimas Lietuvoje ir Baltarusijoje,
1863-1864 m. Moskva, Nauka, 1965.
iii, 583 p. illus., ports. (Vosstanie 1863 goda; materialy i dokumenty) In Russian; part of documents in Polish. DK511.L25A68 DLC
CaAEU CaBVaU CaNBFU CaOLU CaOTU CtY
CoU FU GU HU IaU ICU InNd ICU MH
MnU MU NIC NN NNC NcD NcU NjP OkU
OKentU OrU PPiU ViU

5189. ALEKNA, Antanas. Vyskupas
Motiejus Valančius ir 1863 metai.
[Bishop Motiejus Valančius and the
year of insurrection of 1863] In
Mūsų senovė (Kaunas), 1921, no.1,
p. 22-33; no.2, p. 38-53. See
serials consulted.

5190. AWEJDE, Oskar. K istorii
pol'skogo vosstaniia 1863 g. In
Krasnyi arkhiv (Moskva), v.57,
1933, p. 100-139. See serials
Consulted.

5191. --- Pokazaniia i zapiski o
pol'skom vosstanii 1863 goda...

Moskva, 1961. xvii, 662 p.
DK437.A9 DLC PU

5192. BERG, Nikolai Vasil'evich.
Zapiski o powstaniu polskim 1863 i
1864 roku i poprzedzającej powstanie epoce demonstracyi od 1856
roku. Z rosyjskiego oryginału...
dosłownie przełożył K.J. Kraków,
Spółka Wydawnicza Polska, 1898-
1899. 3 v. DK437.B427 DLC MH NN
OU

5193. BIČKAUSKAS, Leonas Nikifor-
as. 1863 metų sukilimas Lietuvoje.
[Insurrection of 1863 in Lithuania]
Vilnius, VPMLL, 1958. 350 p.
illus. DK511.L25B58 InU CaAEU
CtPAM CtY ICU ICBM NN PU

5194. BRIANTSEV, Pavel Dmitrievich. Pol'skii miatezh 1863 g.
Vil'na, Tip. A.G. Syrkina, 1892.
viii, 263 p. DK437.B73 DLC

5195. CEDERBAUM, Henryk. Powstanie styczniowe; wyroki audytoryatu
polowego z lat 1863, 1864, 1865 i
1866. Warszawa, Gebethner i Wolff,
1917. viii, 439 p. DK437.C5 DLC
MH NN

5196. COLEMAN, Arthur Prudden.
The Polish insurrection of 1863 in
the light of New York editorial
opinion. Williamsport, Pa., The
Bayard Press, [1934] [10], 131 p.
diagr. (Slavonic series) DK437.C6
DLC CU CoU InU NIC NN NcU OCl TxU
TU

5197. CWIEK, Zbigniew. Przywódcy
powstania styczniowego; sześć syl-
wetek. [Wyd. 1. Warszawa] Wiedza
Powszechna, 1955. 273 p. illus.,
ports, facsims. DK436.5.AlC9 InU
MH MiDW NN

5198. DĄBROWSKI, Józef. Powsta-
nie styczniowe, 1863-1864. Wyd. 2.
[By] Grabiec [pseud.] Warszawa;
Kraków, Wydaw. J. Mortkowicza, 1921.
217 p. DK437.D12 1921 DLC InU MH
NN NNC(1912, ed.)

5199. --- Rok 1863. [By] J. Grabiec [pseud.] Poznań, Nakł. Zdzisła-
wa Rzepeckiego, 1913. 464 p.
illus., ports, fold. map.
943.803.D114 KyU IU KU NN WU

5200. FAJNHAUZ, Dawid. Niektóre
zagadnienia powstania styczniowego
na Kowieńszczyznie. In Kwartalnik
Historyczny (Lwów), v.69, 1962, p.
835-851. See serials consulted.

5201. --- Niemcy a powstanie
styczniowe na Litwie i Białorusi.
In Przegląd Historyczny (Warszawa),

5202. --- 1863 metų sukilimas ir
Vakarų Europos visuomenė. [By] D.
Fainhauzas. [The insurrection of
1863 and Western European society]
In LTSRMAII. Lietuvos valstiečiai
XIX amžiuje. Vilnius, 1957, p.
176-200. See serials consulted.

5203. FELDMAN, Józef. Bismarck
a powstanie styczniowe. In His
Bismarck a Polska. Kraków, 1947.
p.[152]-235. Summary in English.
DD218.2.F45 1947 DLC CaAEU CU MH
MnU

5204. GENZELIS, B. 1863-1864 metų sukilimo Lietuvoje veikėjų pa-
saulėžiūros klausimu. K voprosu o
mirovozzrenii deiatelei vosstaniia
1863-1864 gg. v Litve. In LTSRAMMD:
Filosofija (Vilnius), v.4, 1964, p.
113-130. See serials consulted.

5205. GILLER, Agaton. Historya
powstania narodu polskiego w 1861-
1864 roku. Tomów IV. Paryż,
Księgarnia Luksemburgska; Druk Bra-
ci Rouge Cunon i Fresné, 1867-71.
4 v. BM(9476. c. 27.)

5206. GREAT BRITAIN. FOREIGN
OFFICE. Confidential correspondence
of the British Government respecting
insurrection in Poland, 1863. Edited by Tytus Filipowicz. Paris, H.
Le Soudier, 1914. xxxv, 16, 453 p.
DK437.G7 1863 DLC NN

5207. JAKŠTAS, Juozas. The 1863
revolt in Soviet historiography.
In Lituanua (Chicago, Ill.), v.9,
no.4, 1963, p. 145-148. See
serials consulted.

5208. JANOWSKI, Józef Kajetan.
Pamiętniki o powstaniu styczniowem.
Lwów, Komitet Jubileuszowy Obchodu
50 i 60 Rocznicy Powstania 1863 r.,
1923-25. 2 v. port. Slav 5769.1
MH MiU NN

5209. JANULAITIS, Augustinas.
1863-1864 metų sukilimas Lietuvoje.
[The insurrection of 1863-1864 in
Lithuania] Kaunas, Krašto apsaugos
ministerijos Literatūros skyriaus
leidinys, 1921. 44 p. Offprint
from Mūsų žinynas vol.1.
947.5.J269 PU XtTMF

5210. JURGĖLA, Constantine Rudyard. Lietuvos sukilimas, 1862-
1864 metais... [The insurrection of
1862-1864 in Lithuania. By.] Kostas R. Jurgėla. [Boston, Mass.]
Lietuvių enciklopedijos leidykla
[1970] 720 p. illus., facsims.,
ports. DK511.L25J82 PU CaAEU

5211. KARBOWSKI, Władysław. Lud-

wik Narbutt. Grodno, Wyd. 76
Lidzkiego P.P. im. Ludwika Narbutta,
1935. 250 p. illus., ports., maps,
geneal. tables. Bibliography: p.
[221-223] DK436.5.N37K35 DLC
BM(010795. l. 17.) NN

5212. KATKOV, Mikhail Nikiforo-
vich. 1863 god; sobranie statei po
pol'skomu voprosu pomieshchavshikh-
sia v Moskovskikh viedomostiakh,
Russkom viestnikie i Sovremennoi
Lietopisi. Moskva, v univ. tip.,
1887. 3 v. DK437.K26 DLC NN

5213. KORDOWICZ, Wiktor. Konstanty Kalinowski. Rewolucyja de-
mokracja polska w powstaniu stycz-
niowym na Litwie i Białorusi.
Warszawa, Ludowa Spółdz. Wydawnicza, 1955. 304 p. illus.
DK436.5.K35K6 DLC IU NN PU

5214. KORNILOV, Ivan Petrovich.
Pamiati grafa M.N. Murav'eva: k
istorii Vilenskago uchebnago okruga
za 1863-1868 gg. Sanktpeterburg,
Tip. V.V. Komarova, 1898. iii,
240 p. LA853.L6K8 ICU PU(microfilm)

5215. --- Russkoe delo v Sievero-
Zapadnom kraie. Materialy dlia istorii Vilenskago uchebnago okruga,
preimushchestvenno v Murrav'evs-
kuiu epokhu. Sanktpeterburg, Tip.
A.P. Lopukhina, 1901. xxii, 420,
vii p. BM(8311. gg. 19.) CtY NN
PU(Xerox copy, 1970)

5216. --- --- Izd. 2., prov. i
dop. Sanktpeterburg, [Tip. A.S.
Subarina] 1908. Vyp.1.
DK511.L251 1908 vyp.1 NcU

5217. KOWALSKI, Józef. Die rus-
sische revolutionäre Demokratie und
der polnische Aufstand 1863. [Ins
Deutsche übertragen von Regina
Klinger, Hildegard Zimmermann und
Felix Heinrich Gentzen. 1. Aufl.]
Berlin, Rüter & Loening, [1954,
c1953] 225 p. DK437.K765 DLC
CaAEU MH

5218. KUBICKI, Paweł, ed. Bo-
jownicy-kapłani za sprawę Kościoła
i Ojczyzny w latach 1861-1915. Materjały z urzędowych świadectw
władz rosyjskich, archiwów konsy-
storskich, zakonnych i prywatnych.
Sandomierz, Nakład Autora, 1933-
1939. 3 v. Part 2 is about Lithuania and White Russia. BX1566.K8
DLC MH

5219. LAZUTKA, Stanislav Antonovich. Revoliutsionnaia situatsiia
v Litve, 1859-1862 gg. Moskva,
Vysshaia shkola, 1961. 259 p.
Bibliography: p. 250-[258].

DK511.L25L3 DLC CSt-H InU IU KU MH
NN NNC WaU WU

5220. LESLIE, R. F. Reform and
insurrection in Russian Poland,
1856-1865. [London] Athlone
Press, 1963. 272 p. (University
of London historical studies, 13)
DK437.L48 DLC CaAEU

5221. LEWAK, Adam, ed. Polska
działalność dyplomatyczna w roku
1863-1864. Warszawa, Skład Główny
Gebethner i Wolff, 1937. 1 v.
illus., ports. JX760.P6A53 DLC NN

5222. LIASKOVSKII, Aleksandr Ivanovich. Litva i Bielorussiia v vosstanii 1863 g., po novym arkhivnym
materialam. [Berlin, Arzamas] 1939.
189 p. DK511.L2L5 DLC CaQMM CLU KU
CSt-H InNd MH MU NIC NNC NcD OkU PU
WaU WU

5223. LIMANOWSKI, Bolesław. Historja 1863-1864 r. Wyd. 2., przerobione. Lwów, Towarzystwo Nakładowe,
1909. viii, 516 p. port.
943.8.L6283 NNC MH NN NIC RP

5224. MAKSIMAITIENĖ, Ona. Lietuvos sukilėlių kovos 1863-1864 m.
[Combats of the Lithuanian insurgents
of 1863-1864] Vilnius, Mintis, 1969.
293 p. illus., port., map.
DK511.L25M26 DLC CtY NN NjP PPiU PU

5225. MILOVIDOV, Aleksandr Ivanovich. Perechen' stolknovenii russkikh voisk s pol'skimi powstantsami
v kompaniiu 1863-1864 gg... Vil'na,
Gub. tip., 1915. 38 p.
947.52.M638 PU

5226. MOŚCICKI, Henryk. Rządy Mu-
rawjewa na Litwie w świetle jego
listów, pamiętników i raportów pouf-
nych. In His Pod berłem carów. Warszawa, Bibl. Pol., 1924. p. 121-231.
DK439.9.M6 DLC MH NN OCl

5227. MOSOLOV, Aleksandr Nikolaevich. Vilenskie ocherki, 1863-1865
gg. (Murav'evskoe vremia) Sanktpeterburg, Tip. A. S. Suvorina, 1898.
vii, 253, iv p. port. DK651.V4M63
DLC CtY MH NN

5228. MURAV'EV, Mikhail Nikolaevich.
Der Diktator von Wilna. Memoiren
des Grafen M.N. Murawjew. Aus dem
Russischen. Mit einer biographi-
schen Einleitung. Leipzig, Demcker
& Humblot, 1883. lii, 202 p.
(*QW)NN MH MnU PPG

5229. --- Pamiętniki "Wieszatela,"
rządy hr. Michała Nikołajewicza Mu-
rawiewa na Litwie, 1863-1865. Według oryginału rosyjskiego streścił i
wstępem poprzedził Władysław Dębowski.

Kijów, W. Karpiński, 1917. 46 p.
DK437.M87 DLC MH

5230. --- --- Tłumaczenie z ori-
ginału rosyjskiego przez J. Cz. z
przedmową St. Tarnowskiego. [Rzym?]
Biblioteka Białego Orła, 1945. 148
p. illus., ports. 943.803.M934p2p
1945 KU CaBVaU CSt-H

5231. --- Pis'ma M.N. Murav'eva k
A.A. Zelenomu (1863-1864) Soobshchil
N.I. Shatilov. Predislovie i redak-
tsiia V.I. Semevskago. In Golos
minuvshago (Moskva), v.1, no.9,
1913, p. 240-264; no.10, 181-207;
no.12, 253-267; v.2, no.11, 1914,
p. 212-234. DK1.G6 DLC CSt-H CU ICU
ICN MH NN NNC OCl CaAEU(1-11 on
microfiche)

5232. MURA'EVSKII MUZEI. Arkhiv-
nye materialy Murav'evskago muzeia,
otnosiashchiesia k pol'skomu voz-
staniiu 1863-1864 gg. v predielakh
Sievero-Zapadnago kraia. Vil'na,
Gub. tip., 1913. illus., facsims.,
ports. (Vilenskii vremennik, kn.6)
DK511.L25M8 DLC NN

5233. --- Illiustrovannyi katalog
muzeia grafa M.N. Murav'eva v g.
Vil'nie; sostavil V.G. Nikol'skii.
Sanktpeterburg, T-vo R. Golika i A.
Vil'borga, 1904. 124 p.
947.52.V713K PU NN

5234. --- Sbornik dokumentov Mu-
zeia grafa M.N. Murav'eva. Sosta-
vil A. Lieletskii. Vil'na, Izd.
Ob-va revnitelei russkago istori-
cheskago prosvieshcheniia v pamiat'
Imperatora Aleksandra III. Vil'na,
Tip. Russkii pochin, 1906. 1 v.
DK511.L25M85 DLC ICU(Microfilm)

5235. PAMIATI GRAFA MIKHAILA NIKO-
laevicha Murav'eva; ko dniu otkry-
tiia emy pamiatnika v g. Vil'nie, 8
noiabria 1898 g. Vil'na, Izd. Vilenskago Uiezdnago kom-ta popechi-
tel'stva o narodnoi trezvosti,
1898. 53 p. port. DK188.6.M97P18
InU

5236. PANTELEEV, Longin Fedorovich. Vospominaniia proshlogo,
1863-1864. Vstu. stat'ia, podgotovka teksta i primechaniia S.A. Rei-
sera. Moskva, Gos. izd-vo khudozh.
lit-ry, 1958. 847 p. illus. (Seria literaturnykh memuarov)
DK32.7.P35 DLC CIU CU CSt-H CaAEU
ICU IEN InU MiU NIC NN NcD NNC OCl
RPB

5237. POWSZECHNY ZJAZD HISTORYKÓW
Polskich, 9th Warsaw, 1963. Powstanie styczniowe 1863. Redaktor,
Stefan Kieniewicz. Warszawa, Polskie Towarzystwo Naukowe, 1963.

186 p. (Its Referaty). DK401.P8943
1963 CSt-H DLC ICU MiU NN NNC OU
RPB WU

5238. PRZYBOROWSKI, Walery.
Dzieje 1863 roku... Kraków, Nakł.
W.L. Anczyca i Spółki, 1897-1919.
5 v. DK437.P8 DLC MH

5239. RATCH, Vasilii Fedorovich.
La Russie lithuanienne. Jusqu'à la
chute de la Pologne. Materiaux
pour servir à l'histoire de l'insurrection de 1863. Faisant suite
à l'ouvrage du même auteur "La
question polonaise dans la Russie
occidentale". Traduit du russe.
Paris, Librairie A. Laine, 1869.
vii, 404 p. DK511.L2R234 MiU BM

5240. --- Sviedieniia o pol'skom
miatezhie 1863 g. v Sievero-Zapadnoi Rossii. Vil'na, Tip. Gubernskago pravleniia, 1867-1898. 2 v.
plan. DK437.R DLC NN

5241. RÉGNAULT, Élias [Georges
Soulanges Oliva]. Mourawieff et
les archives du Tzarisme. Paris,
E. Dentu, 1863. 93 p. Documents
and list of 398 persons sentenced
by Murav'ev in Lithuania. BM

5242. REVUNENKOV, Vladimir Geor-
gievich. Pol'skoe vosstanie 1863
goda i evropeiskaia diplomatiia.
Leningrad, 1957. 357 p. At head
of title: Leningradskii gosudarstv.
universitet. DK437.R4 DLC

5243. SAWICKI-STELLA, Jan.
Szkice z powstania 1863 roku. Na-
kreślone przez Pułkownika Strusia
[pseud.] Kraków, Nakł. Wydawnictwa
"Nowej reformy", 1889. xi, 323 p.
(*QR)NN BM(9475. bbb. 18.)

5244. SCHALLHAMMER, R. Der pol-
nisch-litauische Aufstand von 1863,
sein Verlauf und die Verhandlungen
der europäischen Grossmächte. In
Litauen und seine Deutschen, Würzburg, 1955. p. 25-48. DK511.L22L3
DLC CaAEU IEN ICU IU MH NIC NN NcD
PU

5245. SIDOROV, A. A. Pol'skoe
vozstanie 1863 goda. Istoricheskii
ocherk. Sanktpeterburg, N.P. Kar-
basnikov, 1903. 256 p. illus.
DK437.S DLC

5246. ŠLEŽAS, Paulius. Muraviovo
veikimas Lietuvoje. [The Muraviov's
governing in Lithuania, 1863-1865]
In Athenaeum (Kaunas), v.4, 1933,
p. 40. See serials consulted.

5247. ŚLIWIŃSKI, Artur. Powstanie styczniowe. Wyd.2. Warszawa,
M. Arct, 1921. 245 p. DK437.S55

1921 DLC CSt-H(1945 ed.) MH NNC
(1938 ed.) OCl

5248. SMIRNOV, Anatolii Filipo-
vich. Manifestatsionnoe dvizhenie
v Belorussii i Litve 1861 g. In
Akademiia nauk SSSR. Institut istorii. Revolutsionnaia situatsiia v
Rossii v 1859-1861 gg. Moskva,
1960, p. 400-480. DK219.8.A32 DLC

5249. --- Vosstanie 1863 goda v
Litve i Belorussii. Moskva, Izd-
vo Akademii nauk SSSR, 1963. 390
p. DK511.L25S55 DLC CaBVaU CaOTU
CU CSt CSt-H CtY GU IaU ICU InNd
InU IU LU MH MnU MoU MWalB NN NNC
NIC NjP NcD OrU OKentU PU RPB TU
WaU WU

5250. SOKOŁOWSKI, August. Dzieje
powstania styczniowego, 1863-1864.
Berlin-Wiedeń, B. Harza [1910] 344
p. illus., 12 mounted col. pl.,
ports, facsims. DK437.S6 DLC CaAEU
NNC

5251. STEPONAITIS, Vytautas. Medžiaga 1863-64 m. sukilimo istorijai. [Material on the insurrection
of 1863-1864] In Karo archyvas
(Kaunas), v.2, 1925, p. 62-155.
See serials consulted.

5252. STUDNICKI, Wacław Gizbert,
ed. Wilenskie źródła archiwalne;
Rok 1863 wyroki śmierci. Wilno, L.
Chomiński, 1923. lxxiv columns,
122 p. 947.52.St93.2 PU

5253. TRUMPA, Vincas. The 1863
revolt in Lithuania. In Lituanus
(Chicago, Ill.), v.9, no.4, 1963,
p. 115-122. See serials consulted.

5254. TSYLOV, Nikolai Ivanovich.
Sigizmund Sierakovskii i ego kazn',
predshestvovavshimi pol'skimi mani-
festatsiiami v Vil'nie v 1861-1863
godakh. Iz diel Vil'enskoi slie-
dstvennoi kommissii po politiches-
kim dielam. Vil'na, v Tip. Gub.
pravleniia, 1867. iv, 60 p.
DK436.5.S5T7 DLC NN

5255. ---, comp. and ed. Sbornik
rasporiazhenii grafa Mikhaila Niko-
laevicha Murav'eva po usmireniiu
pol'skago miatezha v Sievero-Zapad-
nykh guberniakh, 1863-1864. Sostavil N. TSylov. Vil'na [Tip. A.
Kirkora] 1866. iv, 383 p.
DK437.T83 DLC

5256. TUMASONIS, Petras. Kator-
gon! Atsitikimas Muravjovo lai-
kuose. [By] P. Brandukas [pseud.]
[Banishment to forced labour camps
in Siberia, 1863-1864] Chicago,
Ill., "Katalikas", 1907. 18 p.

891.92.B224V PU

5257. VOSSTANIE 1863 goda; materialy i dokumenty. 1963- .
Kyiv, Vyd-vo Akademii nauk Ukrains'-
koi RSR. 947.08.V9713 IEN

5258. WERESZYCKI, Henryk. Aus-
trja a powstanie styczniowe. Lwów,
Wydawnictwo Zakładu Narodowego im.
Ossolińskich, 1930. 312 p. Sum-
mary in French. DK437.W4 DLC CtY
MiU MH MnU

5259. WRÓBLEWSKA, Ewelina, comp.
Rok 1863; wyjątki z dzieł i pamięt-
ników. Dokumenty. Odezwy. Wilno,
Wydawn. Księgarni Stow. Nauczyciel.
Polskiego, 1923. 257 p. plates.
DK437.W7 DLC MH OCl NN(1916, ed.)

5260. ZIELIŃSKI, Stanisław. Bitwy i potyczki w roku 1863-1864.
Kraków, Rapperschwyl-Museum Narodo-
we Polskie, 1913. 559 p. maps.
BM(Ac. 8950/3.)

5261. ZIENKIEWICZ-LELIVA, Kazimierz. Wspomnienia powstańca 1863
roku; do druku przygotował i wstępem opatrzył kpt. Stefan Pomarański. Warszawa, Wojskowy Instytut
Naukowo-Wydawniczy, 1932. xxx, 340
p. illus., port. DK437.Z5 DLC

5262. ŽIUGŽDA, Juozas. Antanas
Mackevičius. 1863-1864 metų sukilimo reikšmė lietuvių tautos istorijoje. [Antanas Mackevičius and
the significance of insurrection of
1863-1864 in Lithuania] Vilnius,
Mintis, 1971. 203 p. port. At
head of title: Lietuvos TSR Mokslų
akademija. Istorijos institutas.
DK511.L28M349 DLC PU

5263. --- Valstiečių sukilimas
Lietuvoje 1863 metais. [The peasants' insurrection of 1863 in Lith-
uania] In LTSRMAII. Lietuvos valstiečiai XIX amžiuje, 1957. p. 134-
175. See serials consulted.

X.9.1.5. MASSACRE OF KRAŽIAI
of 1893

5264. KRAŽIAI, Lithuania. Kražių
skerdynės ir kražiškių byla Vilniuje. [The massacre of Kražiai...]
[n.p. n.d.] 61 p. 947.5.K5 CtTMF

5265. MARCINKEVIČIUS, Jonas.
Kražių skerdynės; istorinis romanas.
[The massacre of Kražiai; historical
novel] 2. leidimas. [Chicago, Ill.]
Nemunas [195-] 2 v. illus.
PG8721.M34K7 DLC CaAEU(v.2) NN PU

5266. NAŠLYS, Pseud. Keletas
žodžių apie nežmoniškus maskolių
darbus Kražiuose ir apie sudyjimą
kražiečių Vilniuje. [A few words
about the inhuman atrocities of the
Russians in Kražiai] Tilžė, išleista M. Nevskio, 1895. 15 p. CtPAM

5267. PROCES KROŻAN PRZED IZBĄ
Sądową Wileńską na podstawie aktów
sądowych i innych dokumentów. Kraków, Skł. Gł. w Księg. S.A. Krzy-
żanowskiego, 1896. 292 p. ports.,
map. Trial of Antoni Dobkiewicz,
Jan Margiewicz and other in the
Izba Sądową Wilenska, September 20-
29, 1894. DLC-L

5268. VĖBLAUSKAS, Petras. Kražių
skerdynės. [The massacre in Kra-
žiai] In Naujoji romuva (Kaunas),
v.3, 1933, p. 145-155. See serials
consulted.

5269. ŽILIUS, Jonas. Kražių
skerdynė ir jos pasekmės... Ž., Jonas. [pseud. The massacre of Kražiai and its consequences] Chicago,
Ill., Lietuva [1894]. 75 p.
947.5.Sk35.yZ PU ICBM ICLJF

X.9.i.6. INSURRECTION OF 1905 AND
THE GREAT ASSEMBLY
OF VILNIUS

5270. BIELINIS, Kipras. Penktie-
ji metai; revoliucinio sąjūdžio
slinktis ir padariniai. [The year
1905; the course of the revolutionary movement and its consequences]
New Yorkas, N.Y., Amerikos lietuvių socialdemokratų sąjungos Literatūros fondo lėšomis, 1959. 592
p. ports. DK511.L25B46 DLC CaAEU
CaOTU CtY MH OKentU PU

5271. DAINAUSKAS, Juozas. Prelude to independence; the Great
Conference of Vilnius, 1905. In
Lituanus (Chicago, Ill.), v.11, no.
4, 1965, p. 47-60. See serials
consulted.

5272. GABRYS, Juozas. Didysis
Vilniaus Seimas. [The Great Assembly of Vilnius] In Naujoji romuva
(Kaunas), 1937, no.1, p.15-16; no.
3, p. 55-58; no.7, p. 155-158; no.
12, p. 270-272. See serials consulted.

5273. GRIŠKŪNAITĖ, Emilija. Vol-
neniia v voiskakh garnizonov ras-
polozhennykh v Litve, v 1905-1907
gg. In LTSRMAD. Seria A, no.2,
1960, p. 119-132. See serials
consulted.

5274. --- Zabastovki rabochikh
Litvy v ianvare 1905 g. In LTSRMAD.
Serija A, no.2, 1961, p. 169-184.
See serials consulted.

5275. GUDELIS, Martynas. Lietuviai gynė savo miškus; 1905-6 m.
kovų vaizdai. [Lithuanians defended their forests; episodes from
the struggles of 1905-1906] Chicago, Ill., Lithuanian books [c1950]
302 p. DK511.L25G8 DLC CU IEN MiD
NN PU

5276. KLIMAITIS, Pranas. Didysis
Vilniaus seimas. [The Great Assembly of Vilnius] In Židinys (Kaunas)
v.13, 1931, no.1, p. 43-56; no.2,
p. 146-160; no.4, p. 365-376. See
serials consulted.

SOCJALDEMOKRACJA KRÓLEWSTWA
Polskiego i Litwy. SDKPiL w rewo-
lucji 1905 roku... [Warszawa] 1955.
See entry no. 2839.

--- Sotsial-demokratiia
Pol'shi i Litvy v revoliutsii 1905
g. Moskva, 1956. See entry no.
2840.

5277. STEPONAITIS, Vytautas. Iš
Kauno gubernatoriaus archyvo bylų.
[From the archives of the Governor
of Kaunas] Kaunas, Valstybės spau-
stuvė, 1928. 17 p. DK511.L25S7
DLC

5278. TYLA, Antanas. 1905 metų
revoliucija Lietuvos kaime. [The
revolution of 1905 in Lithuania]
Vilnius, Mintis, 1968. 268 p.
DK511.L25T9 PU CtY DLC MH OKentU

5279. ŽIUGŽDA, Juozas, ed. Revo-
liutsiia 1905-1907 gg. v Litve;
dokumenty i materialy. Redaktsionnaia kolegiia IU. I. Zhiugzhda [i
dr.] Vil'nius, Gos. izd-vo polit.
i nauchnoi lit-ry, 1961. 570 p.
DK511.L25Z5 DLC CLU CSt-H CaAEU
CaOHM CaOLU CtY IaU ICU InNd InU KU
LU MH MoU NIC NcU NNC NjP NbU NcD
OrU PPiU PU RPB WU WaU

X.9.i.7. RUSSIFICATION AND TOTAL
SUPPRESSION OF THE
LITHUANIAN PRESS

5280. AVIŽONIS, Konstantinas.
Bendroji rusinimo politika; rusinimo politikos istorinė raida ligi
1863 m. [The general policy of
russification in Lithuania until
1863] In Bagdanavičius, V.J. Kovos
metai dėl savosios spaudos. Chicago, Ill., 1957. p. [27]-65.

PN5278.L5B3 DLC CaAEU OCl

BAGDANAVICIUS, Vytautas, J. ed. Kovos metai dėl savosios spaudos. Chicago, Ill., 1957. See entry no. 5102.

5281. BIRŽIŠKA, Vaclovas, ed. Medžiaga lietuvių spaudos uždraudimo istorijai. [Materials for the history of total suppression of the Lithuanian press] Martyno Jankaus archyvas. In Tauta ir Žodis (Kaunas), v.4, 1926, p. 370-425. See serials consulted.

5282. --- Pastangos draudimui nugalėti. [Efforts to regain the freedom of the press] In Bagdanavičius, V.J. Kovos metai dėl savosios spaudos. Chicago, Ill., 1957. p. [167]-195. PN5278.L5B3 CaAEU OCl

5283. --- 50 metų spaudos laimėjimo sukaktį minint. [Fifty year anniversary of the reinstatement of the free press] In Aidai (Kennebunkport, Me.), 1954, no.4, p. 147-156; no.6, p. 251-262. See serials consulted.

5284. --- Spaudos draudimas be teisinio pagrindo. [The total suppression of the press without any legal reason] In Bagdanavičius, V.J. Kovos metai dėl savosios spaudos. Chicago, Ill., 1957. p. [67]-76. PN5278.L5B3 DLC CaAEU OCl

5285. ČEGINSKAS, Kajetonas Julius. Die Russifizierung und ihre Folgen in Litauen unter zaristischer Herrschaft. In Commentationes Balticae (Bonn), v.6-7, no.2, 1959, p. 85-138. See serials consulted.

5286. GRINIUS, Kazys. Varpo metų knygnešiai. [The book distribution through undercover network during the "Varpas" period] Kaunas, 1924. 31 p. 947.52.G1 CtTMF

5287. HUEPEDEN, J. von(Derthesen). Die Russifzierung der Ostseeprovinzen, von J. von Dorneth, pseud. Leipzig, Duncker & Humblot. 1887. 94 p. Microfilm Z-204 NN

5288. JAKAVIČIUS, Liudas. Atsiminimai iš spaudos draudimo laikų. [Reminiscences from the period of the total suppression of the Lithuanian press] Šiauliai, Jakavičiaus spaustuvė, 1939. 312 p. DK511.L28J32 PU

5289. KARVELIENĖ, Veronika (Bakšytė). Beitrag zur Geschichte des Kampfes um die Schulsprache in Litauen, mit besonderer Berücksichtigung der Zeit der grossen Reformen, 1855-1864; von Vera Bakšytė. Memel, Druck "Rytas", 1930. 120 p. 947.52.K149 PU

5290. LIETUVOS ŪKININKAS. 10 metų spaudos atgavimo paminėjimas. [Tenth anniversary of the reestablishment of the free press in Lithuania...] Surengė ir išleido "Lietuvos ūkininko" redakcija. Vilnius, J. Zawadzkis, 1914. 32 p. 491.922.L628 PU

5291. MAŠIOTAS, Pranas. Kai knygas draudė; įspūdžiai ir atsiminimai. [As the Lithuanian free press was totally suppressed; recollections] Kaunas, 1924. 115 p. 947.5.M375 PU

5292. MATUSAS, Jonas. Lietuvių rusinimas per pradžios mokyklas. La russification des Lithuaniens per l'enseignement primaire. Kaunas, 1937. 179, iv p. map. 397.475M439 PU

5293. --- Lotyniškojo raidyno draudimas. [The prohibition of the Latin alphabet in Lithuania] In Bagdanavičius, V.J. Kovos metai dėl savosios spaudos. Chicago, Ill., 1957. p. [113]-130. PN5278.L5B3 DLC CaAEU OCl

5294. PRAPUOLENIS, Bronius. Barbarizmas apsireiškiąs Rusų lietuviams spaudos per grafą Muravjevą, 1863-1904 m. [The barbarism in suppressing the free press by Russian authorities... By] Perkūnėlis [pseud.] Tilžė, 1910. 16 p. DK511.L25P73 1969 PU(Xerox copy 1969)

5295. RACKUS, Alexander Michaelis. Medžiaga knygnešių kronikai. [Materials for the history of the book distribution through the undercover network] In Draugas (Kaunas), 1929, p. 99-116. See serials consulted.

5296. RUSECKAS, Petras, ed. Knygnešys, 1864-1904. [The distribution of books through the undercover network in Lithuania] Kaunas, Spaudos fondas, 1926-1928. 2 v. illus., ports. 947.52.R893.3 PU CtTMF(v.1) CtY ICLJF(v.1) CDU OKentU OCl

5297. --- Spaudos draudimo gadynė. [The period of total suppression of the Lithuanian press] Kaunas, Spaudos fondas, 1929. 47 p. 947.5.R893.2 PU

5298. ŠALKAUSKIS, Kazys. Bylos
dėl spaudos lietuvių raidėmis.
[Court cases for using the Latin
alphabet in Lithuania] In Teisė
(Kaunas), 1935, no.31, p. 305-312;
no.32, p. 403-410. See serials
consulted.

5299. ŠALKAUSKIS, Stasys. Spaudos draudimo pamoka lietuvių tautai. [The suppression of the press;
a meaningfull lesson for the Lithuanian nation] In Židinys (Kaunas),
1929, p. 462-465. See serials consulted.

5300. SANGAILA, J. Nuo raidžių
draudimo iki kalbos naikinimo.
[From the suppression of the Latin
alphabet to the destruction of the
language] In Bagdanavičius, V.J.
Kovos metai dėl savosios spaudos.
Chicago, Ill., 1957. p. [131]-165.
PN5278.L5B3 DLC CaAEU OCl

5301. SRUOGIENĖ, Vanda (Daugirdaitė). Knygų platinimo organizacijos ir knygnešiai. [The organization of distribution of books
through the undercover network] In
Bagdanavičius, V.J. Kovos metai
dėl savosios spaudos. Chicago,
Ill., 1957. p. 197-237.
PN5278.L5B3 DLC CaAEU OCl

5302. STALŠANS, Karlis. Krievu
ekspansija un rusifikacija Baltija
laikmetu tecejuma. [The Russian
expansion and the russification of
the Baltic countries through time]
Chicago, Ill., 1966. 187 p.
947.5.St15.2 1966 PU

5303. SUŽIEDĖLIS, Simas. Lietuvių tautos kova dėl raidės. [The
struggle of the Lithuanian nation
to retain the Roman alphabet] In
LKMASD, v.6, 1969, p. 21-[41]
See serials consulted.

5304. ŽUKAS, Vladas. Iš lietuvių
spaudos draudimo istorijos. [From
the history of the total suppression of the Lithuanian press] In
Vilna. Universitetas. Biblioteka.
Mokslinės bibliotekos metraštis,
1957. Vilnius, 1958. p. 104-[107]
Z821.7.V5 DLC CaAEU CaOONL InU MH
NN PU

X.9.k. FIRST WORLD WAR AND GERMAN
OCCUPATION, 1915-1918.

X.9.k.1. GENERAL STUDIES

5305. ABRAMOWICZ, Ludwik ed. Litwa podczas wojny; zbiór dokumentów,
uchwał, odezw i t.p. Warszawa,
1918. 143 p. 947.52.Ab82.2 PU

5306. AN DEN GRENZEN RUSSLANDS;
elf Abhandlungen aus der Sammlung
"Der Weltkrieg": Der Krieg und die
Polen (Bachem). Das russische Volk
(Keyser). Die russische Kirche
(Merkle). Kurland (Brentano). Der
Weltkrieg und Litauen (Brunavietis).
Litauen und Bessarabien (Schemai-
tis). Die Ukraine (Kisky). Die
Russen in Lemberg (Van Gember).
Rumänien (Krauss). Bulgarien
(Krauss). Russland Serbiens Toten-
gräber (Gopcevic). Hrsg. vom Se-
kretariat sozialer Studentenarbeit.
München; Gladback, Volksvereisver-
lag, 1916. 253 p. CSt

5307. ASKENAZY, Szymon. Zamuro-
wana Litwa w czasie I. Wojny Światowej. In His Uwagi. Warszawa,
1924. p. 58-64. D651.P7A7 DLC CSt
CaBVaU CtY InU IU MH MiU MU NN NNC
NcD OU KU

5308. BACMEISTER, Walter. Das
Baltikum bei Deutschen Reich. In
Das grössere Deutschland (Dresden),
v.5, pt.1, p. 513-524. See serials
consulted.

5309. BARTUŠKA, Vincas. Observations du délégué du Conseil national lituanien à la suite de son voyage dans les régions de la Lituanie
occupée par l'armée allemande.
Lausanne, Bureau d'informations lituaniens, 1918. 12 p. DK511.L26B3
DLC CSt-H DNW NNC

5310. BASLER, Werner. Deutschlands Annexionspolitik in Polen und
in Baltikum, 1914-1918. Berlin,
Rütten & Loening, 1962. 457 p.
(Veröffentlichungen des Instituts
für Geschichte der Völker der UdSSR
an der Martin Luther University.
Halle-Wittenberg. Reihe B. Abhandlungen, Bd.3) DD228.8.B29 DLC CSt-H
CaAEU ICU MH MiU NN NNC PU

5311. BIELSKIS, Julius J. Delega-
tų kelionė Lietuvon, 1916 m. [The
journey of delegates to Lithuania,
1916] So. Boston, Mass., Spauda
"Darbininkas", 1916. 94 p. illus
DK511.L26B5 DLC CtTMF ICLJH OKentU

5312. BROEDRICH, Silvio. Das neue

Ostland. Charlottenburg, Ostland-
verlag [1915] [31] p. DK511.B3B86
CSt-H DLC-P4 CU

5313. BRUNAVIETIS, Kasimir. Der
Weltkrieg und Litauen. Berlin,
Sekretariat sozialer Studenten-
arbeit, 1916. 23 p. In An den
Grenzen Russlands. München; Glad-
bach, 1916. CSt

COLLIANDER, Börje Erland.
Die Beziehungen zwischen Litauen
und Deutschland wärent der Okkupation, 1915-1918. [Abo, 1935] See
entry no. 2967.

5314. DU PARQUET, Emmanuel Joseph
Marie. Der Drang nach Osten; l'a-
venture allemande en Lettonie.
Préface du général Niessel. Paris,
Charles-Lavauzelle, 1926. 346 p.
map. DK511.L26D8 IaU

5315. GABRYS, Juozas. "Justice"
allemande en Lituanie occupée. Par
C. Rivas [pseud.] Genève; Nancy
[1918] 91 p. D552.L5G3 DLC PU MH
NN

5316. --- La Lituanie sous le
joug allemand, 1915-1918; le plan
annexioniste allemand en Lituanie.
[Par] C. Rivas [pseud.] Lausanne,
Librarie centrale des nationalités,
1918. 700 p. DK511.L26G3 DLC CLU
CSt-H CtPAM InU InNd IU ICU NjP PU

5317. --- Ober-Ost; le plan
annexioniste allemand en Lituanie,
par C. Rivas [pseud.] Lausanne,
Bureau d'information de Lituanie,
1917. 15 p. Extrait de Pro Lithuania, no.1, 1917. D651.L5G5 DLC
CtY

5318. --- Occupation allemande en
Lituanie. [Par] C. Rivas [pseud.]
Genève-Nancy [1918] 116 p.
D552.L5G32 DLC ICBM WU

5319. --- La vie publique en Lituanie occupée par les allemands,
par C. Rivas [pseud.] Genève,
[1917] 27 p. DK511.L2G32 DLC WU

5320. --- Visées annexionistes
allemands sur la Lituanie. Par C.
Rivas. Lausanne, Librairie centrale des nationalités, 1918. 267
p. DK511.L26G33 DLC NN

5321. GERMANY. REICHSARCHIV.
Der Weltkrieg 1914 bis 1918. Bear-
beitet im Reichsarchiv. Berlin, E.
S. Mittler, 1925. D521.G4 DLC CaAEU

5322. GLASER, Stefan. Okupacja
niemiecka na Litwie w latach, 1915-
1918; stosunki prawne. Lwów, 1929.

iv, 191 p. (Wschód; Wydawnictwo do
dziejów i Kultury Ziem Wschodnych
Rzeczypospolitej Polskiej,2) Slav
5198.749(2) MH

5323. HOFFMANN, Max. Die Aufzeichnungen des General-Majors Max
Hoffmann. Hrsg. von Karl Friedrich
Nowak. Berlin, Verlag für Kulturpolitik, 1929. 2 v. illus., fold.
map. DD231.H6A3 1929 DLC CtY MA MU
OU

5324. --- --- 4.-6., Aufl. Berlin, Verlag für Kulturpolitik, 1930.
2 v. DD231.H72A4 1930 CaAEU

5325. --- War diaries and other
papers... tr. by Eric Sutton. London, M. Secker [1929] 2 v. fronts
(ports.) fold. maps. DD231.H6A33
DLC CtY MiU NN OCl PU

5326. JANKOWSKI, Czesław. Z dnia
na dzień; Warszawa-1914-1915-Wilno.
Wilno, K. Rutski; Skł. Gł. w Księg.
Gebethnera i Wolffa, 1923. 413 p.
D640.J33 DLC CSt-H

5327. KESSLER, Otto. Die Baltenländer und Litauen; Beiträge zur
Geschichte, Kultur und Volkswirtschaft unter Berücksichtigung der
deutschen Verwaltung. Berlin, Puttkammer & Mühlbrecht, 1916. vi, [7]
237 p. DK511.B3K4 DLC CU CSt-H ICJ
IaU InU IEN IU MH MnU NN NNC NbU PU

5328. KUDIRKA, Juozas. Karės bai-
senybės Lietuvoje; pergyventų va-
landų atsiminimai. [The atrocities
of the war in Lithuania] Chicago,
Ill., Draugo spauda, 1916. 55 p.
illus. 970.2.Ku ICLJF CtTMF

5329. DAS LAND OBER OST: DEUTSCHE
Arbeit in den Verwaltungsgebieten
Kurland, Litauen und Bialystok-Grod-
no. Hrsg. im Auftrage des Oberbe-
fehlshabers Ost, bearbeitet von der
Pressabteilung Ober Ost; [Kowno]
Pressabteilung Ober Ost. Stuttgart
und Berlin, Im Buchhandel bei der
Deutschen Verlags-Anstalt, 1917.
xi, 472 p. illus., plans, maps.
D650.T4L3 DLC CaAEU CSt-H CtPAM
DI-GS MH PU

5330. LINDE, Gerd. Die deutsche
Politik in Litauen im ersten Welt-
krieg. Wiesbaden, Harrassowitz,
1965. xiii, 265 p. (Schriften der
Arbeitsgemeinschaft für Osteuropa-
forschung der Universität Münster)
Bibliography: p. [230]-235.
DK511.L26L48 DLC CaBVaU CaOHM CaOKQ
CaOTU CaBVaS CU CSt-H CtY FU GU IaU
IEN InU InNd ICU IU MH MnU MoU MU
NIC NbU NcU NBuU NcD NjR NmU NjP NNC
OClW PPiU PU TxHU TxU WaU WU

5331. LITHUANIAN INFORMATION BU-
REAU. Articles exportes de Lituanie
par les Allemands pendant l'occupation. Paris, 1919. (Délégation de
Lituanie à la Conférence de la Paix,
pt., V:7) D643.A7DP5L7 CSt-H

5332. LITWA POCZAS WOJNY. Zbiór
dokumentów, uchwał, odezw i t.p.
Zebrał i do druku pszygotował L.A.
Warszawa [Wyd. Departamentu Spraw
Politycznych], 1918. 143 p.
DK511.L26L55 CU CSt-H NN

5333. LITWA ZA RZĄDÓW KS. IZEN-
BURGA. Preface signed S.J. Kraków, Nakł. Krakowskiego Oddziału
Zjednoczenia Narodowego, 1919. iv,
157 p. DK511.L26L5 WU MH PU

5334. MANN, Bernhard. Die balti-
schen Länder in der deutschen
Kriegszielpublizistik 1914-1918.
Tübingen, Mohr, 1965. vii, 161 p.
(Tübinger Studien zur Geschichte
und Politik, 19) Bibliography: p.
[146]-156. D633.M28 CaAEU CtY DLC
MiU NcD PU

5335. MICHAELIS, Paul L. Kurland
und Litauen in deutscher Hand. 4.
Aufl. Berlin-Steglitz, F. Würtz
[1918?] 196 p. illus., plates.
D552.C7M5 DLC CSt-H DW IaU ICU ICBM

5336. OCHMAŃSKI, Jerzy. Polityka
Niemiec wobec Litwy podchas pierwszej wojny światowej. In Posen.
Uniwersytet. Seria Historia.
Zeszyty Naukowe (Poznań), v.8,
1968, p. 177-188. See serials consulted.

5337. POSECK, Maximilian von.
Die deutsche Kavallerie 1915 in
Litauen und Kurland. Berlin, E.S.
Mittler, 1924. x, 235 p. ports.,
maps. 529.4.P6 DLC PU

5338. RAGANA, pseud. La Lithuanie
sous la Botte allemande. Le Régime
prussien en Lithuanie et les Déportations. Paris, Libraire centrale
des Nationalités, 1917. 20 p.
DK511.L26R3 DLC CaAEU

5339. ROHRBACH, Paul. Unser
Kriegsziel im Osten und die russische Revolution. Weimar, A. Duncker, 1917. 29 p. map (Kriegs- und
Friedensziele; Deutsche Flugschrif-
ten, Heft 1) D551.R6 DLC

5340. RUSECKAS, Petras, ed. Lietuva Didžiajame kare. [Lithuanie in
the First World War] Vilnius, Vilniaus žodis, 1939. 336 p.
947.5.R893 PU CtTMF CtPAM

5341. SCHEMAITIS, Georg. Litauen

und Bessarabien. Berlin, Sekretariat Sozialer Studentenarbeit,
1917. 24 p. In An den Grenzen
Russland. München-Gladbach, Volks-
vereins-Verlag, 1916. CSt

5342. ŠILIETIS, J., pseud. Vokiečių okupacija Lietuvoje 1915-1919
m., paveikslėliuose ir trumpuose
aprašymuose. [The German occupation in Lithuania, 1915-1919, related in pictures and short des-
criptions] Kaunas, 1922. iv, 190
p. chiefly illus. Real name:
Jaroslavas Rimkus (Rimkevičius).
DK511.L26S5 DLC CtPAM CtTMF CtY NN

5343. LES SOUFFRANCES DU PEUPLE
lituanien. Lausanne [Imprimerie
Réunies], 1917. 32 p. 4 plates,
map. DK511.L26S6 1917 DLC

5344. SRUOGA, Balys. Vokiškasis
siaubas. [The teutonic terror,
1915-1918] Jurgis Plieninis [pseud.]
Kaunas, 1934. 69 p. DK511.L2S73
1970 PU(Xerox copy) OKentU

5345. STRAŽAS, Abelis. Bor'ba
litovskogo naroda protiv germanskikh kolonizatorov i ikh posobnikov
v 1915-1919 gg. In Voprosy istorii
(Moskva), no.10, 1959, p. 45-59.
See serials consulted.

5346. --- Kolonial'nyi rezhim
germanskikh imperialistov v Litve v
gody Pervoi Mirovoi voiny. In Voprosy istorii (Moskva), no.12, 1958,
p. 67-85. See serials consulted.

5347. TIBAL, André. Allemagne et
la Baltique orientale de 1915 à
1919. Riga, 1932. 50 p.
DK511.B3T5 DLC CtY IEN NN

5348. URBŠIENĖ, Marija. Vokiečių
karo meto spauda ir Lietuva. [The
German war press and Lithuania]
Kaunas, Spaudos fondas, 1939. 127
p. DK511.L26U7 DLC PU

VISCONT, Antoine. La Li-
tuanie et la guerre. Genève, 1917.
See entry no. 4419.

5349. WALZ, Erhard. Reichslei-
tung und Heeresleitung in der Period
des Friedens von Brest-Litovsk;
der Konflikt über die Ostannexionen.
Düsseldorf, G.N. Nolte, 1936. iv,
47 p. illus., map. Thesis--Univer-
sity of Berlin. 947.52.R188 PU

5350. WHEELER-BENNETT, John W.
Brest-Litovsk, the forgotten peace,
March 1918. London, Macmillan,
1938. xx, 478 p. plates, ports.,
map. (Studies in modern history)
D614.B6W45 1938 DLC AU CaAEU ICU ICN

LU NN NcD OO FMU

WITHDRAWAL OF GERMAN FORCES
from the Baltic Provinces. London,
1949. See entry no. 4318.

X.9.k.2. ACTION TAKEN FOR REESTAB-
LISHMENT AS AN INDEPEN-
DENT LITHUANIAN STATE

5351. THE AMERICAN PRESS ON LITH-
uania's freedom. Brooklyn, N.Y.
Tautos Fondas, 1920. 96 p.
D651.L5M7 DLC ICLJF ICN

5352. BARTUŠKA, Vincas. Lietuvos
nepriklausomybės kryžiaus keliais.
[Difficult was the road towards the
independence of Lithuania] Klaipėdoje, Ryto b-vė, [1937] 391 p.
front., plates, ports. 947.52.B288
PU PPULC OCl OKentU WU

5353. --- Recueil de documents
concernant la journée lituanienne
accordée par sa Sainteté Benoit XV.
Lausanne, Bureau d'information Lituanien, 1918. 36 p. DK511.L2B3
OKentU ICBM

5353a. CADZOW, John F. The Lith-
uanian question in the third state
Duma. Kent, Ohio, 1972. 187
leaves. tables. Thesis--Kent
State University. DK511.L25C3x
OKentU

5354. CONVENTION OF THE LITHUANI-
ans of America. New York, 1918.
Laisvėn bežengiant; Amerikos lietuvių visuotinojo Seimo protokolas ir
paveiksluotas aprašymas. Tvarkė ir
išleido Paulius Mulevičius. [March-
ing towards the independence of Li-
thuania] Brooklyn, N.Y., 1918.
[Xerox copy, 1970] 79 p.
E184.L7C63 1970 PU(xerox) ICN(orig.)
NN(orig.)

5355. ECONOMIC BASIS FOR LITHUA-
nia's claim to independence. In
Lithuanian Information Bureau,
Washington, D.C. Lithuanian recognition advocated... Washington, D.C.
[1921] p. 28-34. DK511.L26L5 DLC

5356. GABRYS, Juozas. Mémoire
relatif à la reconstruction de la
Lithuanie indépendante. Lausanne,
1918. 19 p. BM(8092. g. 11.)

5357. --- Vers l'indépendance lituanienne. Faits, impressions, souvenirs, 1907-1920. [Par] C. Rivas
[pseud.] Lausanne, Librairie centrale des nationalités, 1920. 304 p.

DK511.L23G3 CU CSt-H ICJ IU NIC NN
MH PU WU

5358. GIBBONS, Herbert Adams.
Lithuania, the United States and
the League of Nations. In Lithuanian Information Bureau, Washington, D.C., Lithuanian recognition
advocated... Washington, D.C. [1921]
p. 35-50. DK511.L26L5 DLC

5359. IVINSKIS, Zenonas. Lietuvos padėtis 1917 metais ir Vasario
16 dienos akto genezė. [The state
of affairs of Lithuania in 1917 and
the genesis of the act of February
sixteenth] In Židinys (Kaunas), v.
27, no.5-6, 1938, p. 610-634. See
serials consulted.

5360. --- Lietuvos politinė būklė
1918 metų pradžioje ir Vasario 16-
tos dienos aktas. [The political
situation of Lithuania at the beginning of 1918 and the act of February sixteenth] In Židinys (Kaunas),
v.29, no.1-2, 1939, p. 35-42; 196-
211. See serials consulted.

JUSAITIS, Antanas. The history of the Lithuanian nation and
its present national aspirations.
[Philadelphia, Pa.] 1918. See
entry no. 4515.

5361. KAIRYS, Steponas. Nepriklausomybės akto išvakarėse. [On
the eve of the proclamation of the
independence of Lithuania] In
Kultūra (Siauliai), no.2, 1938. See
serials consulted.

5362. --- Tau, Lietuva. [For you,
Lithuania] Boston, Mass., Amerikos
lietuvių socialdemokratų sąjungos,
literatūros fondo rūpesčiu, 1964.
480 p. port. illus. DK511.L26K13
CaAEU CaOTU DLC MH OKentU

5363. KEMĖŠIS, Fabijonas. Amerikos lietuvių kova už Lietuvos laisvę. [The struggle of American Lithuanians for the freedom of Lithu-
ania] In Pirmasis nepriklausomos
Lietuvos dešimtmetis, 1918-1928.
London, 1955. v.1, p. 50-62.
DK511.L27P66 1955 kn.1 CaAEU DLC
ICLJF PU

5364. KLIMAS, Petras. Le dévelop-
ment de l'État Lituanien à partir de
l'année 1915 jusqu'à la formation du
gouvernement provisoire au mois de
novembre 1918, d'après des documents
officiels. Paris, Imp. J. Lang-
lois, 1919. lxiv, 277 p.
DK511.L2K6 DLC CSt-H DW NN NjP PU

5365. --- Lietuvos valstybės kūri-
mas 1915-1918 metais Vilniuje. [The

establishment of the Lithuanian
State in Vilnius, 1915-1918] In
Pirmasis Nepriklausomos Lietuvos
dešimtmetis, 1918-1928. London,
Eng., 1955. kn.1, p. 7-32.
DK511.L27P66 1955 kn.1 CaAEU DLC
ICLJF PU

5366. --- Der Werdegang des litauischen Staates von 1915 bis zur
Bildung der provisorischen Regierung im November 1918. Dargestellt
auf Grund amtlicher Dokumente.
Berlin, Pass & Garleb, 1919. xxxix,
247 p. Issued also in French under
the title: "Le développement de
l'État lituanien". Paris, 1919.
DK511.L26K62 DLC CU CSt-H ICBM PU WU

5367. LEAGUE OF ESTONIANS, LETTS,
LITHUANIANS AND UKRAINIANS OF AMERI-
CA. The Case of the New Republics
of Estonia, Latvia, Lithuania and
the Ukraine presented at the First
Congress of the League... New York,
N.Y... September, 1919. New York,
N.Y., 1919. 15 p. D651.B2I4 DLC
BM(8095. f. 41.) CSt-H NN OCl

5368. LEAGUE OF NATIONS. ASSEM-
BLY. SIXTH COMMITTEE. Admission
de nouveaux membres dans la Société des Nations. Lithuanie. Rapport présenté par la Sixième Commission à l'Assemblée. League of Nations. Admission of new members to
the League of Nations. Lithuania.
Report presented by the Sixth Commission to the Assembly. Genève,
Imp. Vollet, 1921. 3, 3-4, 3-4 p.
(A102. 1921-VII) JX1975.A43 DLC
CaOTU CSt-H

5369. LEAGUE OF NATIONS. SECRE-
TARY-GENERAL. Application of Lithu-
ania for admission to the League of
Nations. Geneva, 1920. 15 p.
(Docs. Assembl. 100. 20/48/100 20th
Nov. 1920) Pamph. H. Mod. CaOTU

5370. LEES, G.F. The claims of
Lithuania. In Contemporary Review
(London), v.112, 1917, p. 178-185.
See serials consulted.

5371. LITHUANIAN COUNCIL OF CHI-
CAGO. Memorandum on the independence
of Lithuania; resolution adopted at
a special meeting of the Lithuanian
council... Aug. 20th, 1920. n.p.,
1920. 15 p. 947.5.P191 v.1, no.4
OrU CtY MH

5372. LITHUANIAN INFORMATION BUR-
EAU. Lithuanian recognition advo-
cated by Hon. William G. McAdoo,
Dr. Herbert Adams Gibbons, Hon.
Walter M. Chandler. Washington,
D.C., Lithuanian Information Bureau
[1921] 3 p. leaves, 70 p., map.

Contents.--Letter of McAdoo, Cotton
and Franklin to Secretary of State
Colby.--Memorandum to Secretary of
State in behalf of recognition of
Lithuania from McAdoo, Cotton and
Franklin.--Notes extending recogni-
tion to Lithuania by Great Britain,
France, Finland, Latvia, Norway,
Poland, Sweden Argentina, Mexico,
Russia.--Letter of W.O. McAdoo to
Secretary of State Hughes.--Econo-
mic basis for Lithuania's claim to
independence.--Lithuania, The Uni-
ted States and the League of Na-
tions, by H.A. Gibbons.--Plea of
W.M. Chandler for recognition of
Lithuania, Latvia and Esthonia.
DK511.L26L5 DLC CLU CU CSt-H CtY
ICU ICN ICJ ICLJF IdU IEN In IU KU
MiU MH MnU MoU NN NNC NB NbU NjP OO
PU WaU

5373. LITHUANIAN NATIONAL COUNCIL.
Projet de reconstitution de la Lithuanie indépendente, élaboré par la
Délégation Permanente du Conseil National Suprême Lithuanien. Lausanne,
1918. 19 p. illus., maps.
DK511.L2L776 CSt-H MH

5374. LITHUANIAN NATIONAL COUNCIL
OF AMERICA. Independence for the
Lithuanian nation. Statement set-
ting forth the claim for independent
government and freedom in the terms
of peace of Lithuania; by the Lithu-
anian National Council in the United
States; presented by Mr. Lodge [pre-
pared by T. Norus] Washington, D.C.,
Gov. Print. Off., 1918. 60 p.
(U.S. 65th Congress, 3rd session.
Senate. Document 305) DK511.L2N6
DLC CSt-H CtPAM CtY ICN InU InNd IdU
IU LU MnU NjP RPB TxU

5375. --- Lithuania; facts suppor-
ting her claim for re-establishment
as an independent nation. [Comp. by
J.J. Bielskis] Washington, D.C.
[1918] 48 p. DK511.L2L7 DLC CLU
CSt CSt-H CU CtY DW ICN ICLJF IaU
ICU InU IU MH MiU NN NB NBuU OCl OO
OClWHi OCW OU OrU PU WyU

5376. LITHUANIAN SOCIETIES' ACTING
COMMITTEE OF GREATER NEW YORK. Lie-
tuvių demonstracija Didžiajame New
Yorke, liepos 4 d., 1918. [The Li-
thuanian demonstration in Greater
New York, July 4, 1918...] Išleido
Didžiojo New Yorko lietuvių draugijų
veikiantysis komitetas... redagavo
J.O. Širvydas, spaudon tvarkė ir su-
statė P. Mulevičius ir M. Milukas...
Brooklyn, N.Y., 1918. 64 p. illus.
F128.9.L7L7 DLC ICLJF NN

5377. LITUANIE ET LA PAIX DE VER-
sailles. Lausanne, Librairie centrale des nationalités, n.d. 22 p.

Extrait de la "Lituanie Indépendante" du 1-er septembre. DK511.L2Li CSt-H NN

5378. LOPATTO, John S. Lithuania; its desires and claims. In Journal of Race Development, v.8, 1917, p. 188-196. HT1501.J7 v.8 DLC

5379. MOLIS, Povilas, comp. The American press on Lithuania's freedom. Brooklyn, N.Y., Tautos fondas, 1920. 96 p. D651.L5M7 DLC ICN ICBM ICU NN

5380. MEMOIRE DES DÉLÉGUÉS LITHUA-niene à la Conférence Internationa-le des Ouvriere Chrétiens à Lucerne. Berne, 1919. 23 p. 947.52.M516 PU

5381. NORUS, T. Lithuania's case for independence, by T. Norus and J. Zilius; issued by Lithuanian Natio-nal Council in United States of Ame-rica. Washington, D.C., B.F. John-son, 1918. 96 p. diagrs., tables. Also issued as "U.S. 65th Congress. 3rd Session. Senate. Document 306" with title: Independence for the Li-thuanian nation. DK511.L2N7 DLC CLU CU CSt CSt-H CtY IaU ICN IdU InNd InU ICU IEN ICLJF LU MH MoU MnU NN NIC NB NBuU NNC NjP OCl OClW OKentU OrU TxDaM WaS WaU WU

5382. PAGE, Stanley W. The forma-tion of the Baltic States; a study of the effects of Great Power poli-tics upon the emergence of Lithuania, Latvia, and Estonia. Cambridge, Mass. Harvard University Press, 1959. ix, 193 p. (Harvard historical monogra-phs, 39) DK511.B3P28 DLC CaAEU CaQMM MH OCl PU

5383. PARIS PEACE CONFERENCE, 1919 LITHUANIA. Délégation de Lithuanie à la Conférence de la Paix. Paris, 1919. 6 pt. in 1 v. fold. maps. A collection mimeographed and prin-ted documents put together and arranged by the Lithuanian delegation. JX1392.P21P234 NNC

5384. PURICKIS, Juozas. Lietuvių veikimas Šveicarijoje Didžiojo Karo metu. [Lithuanians in Switzerland and their activities during the First World War] In Pirmasis Nepri-klausomos Lietuvos dešimtmetis, 1918-1928. London, 1955. Kn.1, p.63-73. DK511.L27P66 1955 kn.1 CaAEU DLC PU ICLJF

5385. PUZINAS, Jonas. Kelias į Lietuvos nepriklausomybės atstatymą. [The path of the re-establishment of independence for Lithuania] Brook-lyn, N.Y., Karys, 1968. 96 p. DK511.L25P8 PU OKentU

5386. LA QUESTION LITHUANIENNE; mé-moire présenté par la Délégation Li-thuanienne à la III-me Conférence des Nationalités, Lausanne, les 27-29 juin 1916. Lausanne, Bureau d'infor-mation de Lithuanie, 1916. 16 p. maps. 308.Z Box 79 NNC

5387. RIMKA, Albinas. Lietuvių tautos klausimas Europos karės metu. [The question of the Lithuanian na-tion during the First World War] New York, N.Y., Išleista S.L.A. lė-šomis "Tėvynės" spaustuvėje, 1915. 102 p. (Susivienijimo Lietuvių Ame-rikoje leidinys, nr.23) 947.5.R464 PU CtTMF ICLJF NN OKentU

5388. ROMER, Eugeniusz. Mémoire sur la Lithuanie et la volonté de ses habitants. Paris, Imp. Flini-kowski, 1919. 53 p. maps. D643.A7DP6P7R763 CSt-H BM

SENN, Alfred Erich. Garlawa; a study in emigré intrigue, 1915-1917. In Slavonic and East European Review (Menasha, Wis.), v.45, 1967, p. 411-425. See serials consulted.

5389. ŠLIŪPAS, Jonas. Lietuvos laisvė. [Freedom for Lithuania] Brooklyn, N.Y., Vienybės lietuvini-ninkų, 1917. 67 p. 947.5.Si35.5 PU

5390. SMETONA, Antanas. Die litau-ische Frage; Vortrag gehalten vor einer Versammlung deutscher Politiker im Hotel Adlon zu Berlin am 13. No-vember 1917. Als manuscript gedrückt. Berlin, Verlag Das Neue Litauen, 1917. 32 p. (Germany and the European War, 1915-1921, v.3, no.2) DK511.L2S6 CU CSt-H MH PU TxU WaS

5391. TUMAS, Juozas. Tiesiant ke-lią Lietuvos nepriklausomybėi, 1916-1917 m. [Paving the way for Lithua-nia's independence. By] Vaižgantas [pseud.] Vilnius, "Žaibo" spaustu-vė, 1919. 40 p. DK511.L26T8 DLC CaOONL ICBM ICLJF InNd PU

5392. YČAS, Martynas. Rusijos lie-tuvių pastangos kovose už Lietuvos nepriklausomybę. [Efforts of Lithu-anians in Russia in the struggle for Lithuania's independence] In Pirma-sis Nepriklausomos Lietuvos dešimt-metis, 1918-1928. London, 1955. kn.1, p. 33-49. DK511.L27P66 1955 kn.1 CaAEU ICLJF DLC PU

X.9.ℓ. REPUBLIC OF LITHUANIA,
1918-1940

X.9.ℓ.1. GENERAL STUDIES

5393. BALTRUŠAITIS, Juozas. Lietuvos laisvė ar Lietuvos žmonių laisvė... Philadelphia, Pa., "Kovos", 1918. 30 p. (Lietuvių socialdemokratų sąjungos Amerikoje leidinys, nr.34) OCl

BARTUŠKA, Vincas. L'État lituanien et le gouvernement de Suvalkai. Lausanne, 1918. See entry no. 3124.

BIRONTAS, Adolfas. Bermontininkams Lietuvą užpuolus. Kaunas, 1934. See entry no. 2855.

BIRŽIŠKA, Viktoras. Neužgijusios žaizdos; atsiminimai iš Vilniaus, 1920-1922 m. Kaunas, 1936. See entry no. 3127.

5394. BULOTA, Andrius. Nuo baltojo žirgo iki svastikos. Ot belogo konia do svastiki. Vilnius, VPMLL, 1962. 176 p. illus. DK511.L27B84 DLC MH

5395. CHAMBON, Henry de. La Lithuanie pendant la Conférence de la Paix (1919) d'après les documents tirés des archives d l'auteur, avec annexes et cartes. l. éd. Paris, V. Bresle, [c1931] ii, 181 p. 2 fold. maps. (Collection "La nouvelle Europe", 4) DK511.L27C3 CLU CSt CSt-H MH NN NNC PU GU ICU InU InNd

CHICAGO. UNIVERSITY. DIVISION OF THE SOCIAL SCIENCES. Lithuania in the last 30 years. New Haven, Conn., 1955. See entry no. 821.

5396. DAUDZVARDAS, Vincas. Vasario 16-ji; Lietuvos Nepriklausomybės 13-kos metų sukaktuvėms paminėti. [The 13th anniversary of the Lithuanian indepdence] Kaunas, Lietuvos šaulių sąjungos leidinys, 1931. 104 p. 947.5.D264 PU

5397. --- Vasario 16-ji; Lietuvos Nepriklausomybės 15-kos metų sukaktuvėms paminėti. [February sixteenth; fifteenth anniversary of Lithuania's independence] Kaunas, Lietuvos šaulių sąjungos leidinys, 1933. 158 p. illus. DK511.L27D42 DLC CtTMF PU

5398. DZIAŁALNOŚĆ KOMISJI EWAKUAcyjnej litewsko-rosyjskiej w Wilnie.

Wilno, Wydn. Głosu Litwy, 1920. 92 p. 947.52.D998 PU

5399. GRINIUS, Kazys. Lithuania in a post-war Europe as a free and independent state. New York, N.Y., Lithuanian bulletin, 1943. 30 p. D829.L5G7 DLC CaOTU MH NN NNC

5400. HANDELSMAN, Marceli. W piątym pulku legjonów; dwa miesiące ofensywy litewsko-białoruskiej. Zamość, Z. Pomarański i Spółka [1921] 96 p. Slav. 6467.41.60 MH NN

HARRISON, Ernest John, ed. Lithuania, 1928. London, 1928. See entry no. 826.

5401. --- Lithuania past and present. New York, N.Y., R.M. McBride & Company, 1922. 229 p. front., plates, fold. map. DK511.L25H3 1922a DLC AzU CLU CSt CU CaOTP CaOTU CtY CoU IaU ICBM ICJ ICN IEN In IdU InU MB MH MU NmU NIC NN NNC NjP OCl OClW OkU OKentU OO PPL RPB ScU SdU VtU WU WaU

5402. IVINSKIS, Zenonas. Das unabhängige Litauen (1918-1940). [Saarbrücken, "Die Stimme der Freiheit", 1969-70] Xerox copy (1971) of clipping from: Stimme der Freiheit. Saarbrücken, no.11-12, 1969; no.2-5, 1970. DK511.L27.I91 1971 PU

5403. JACOVSKIS, E. Uždangą nuplėšus... Gruodžio 17 d. fašistinis perversmas ir visiškas atstovavimo teisės likvidavimas Lietuvoje 1926-1940 metais. [The revolt of December 17, 1926...] Vilnius, VPMLL, 1959. 177 p. illus. DK511.L27J2 DLC

5404. JAKŠTAS, Juozas. Nepriklausomybės laikai. [The period of independence] In Lietuvių enciklopedija. Boston, Mass., 1968 m. v. 15, p. 338-344. For holdings see entry no. 216.

5405. KAPSUKAS, Vincas. Buržuazinė Lietuva. [Bourgeoise Lithuania. Redaktorius Br. Vaitkevičius] Vilnius, VPMLL, 1961. 181 p. illus. DK511.L27K33 DLC

5406. KATELBACH, Tadeusz. Za litewskim murem. Warszawa, Tow. Wydawn. "Rój", 1938. 379 p. 947.52.K156 PU MH

5407. KEMĖŽYS, Vincas, ed. Lietuva 1918-1938; leidinys 20 metų Lietuvos Nepriklausomybės sukakčiai paminėti. [Lithuania, 1918-1938; publication to commemorate the 20th anniversary of Lithuania's Independence] Kaunas, Spaudos fondas, 1938. 367 p. 947.52.L625 PU CtTMF ICCA ICCC ICLJF

5408. KERNIUS-KERNAUSKAS, Alfonsas. Gruodžio 17 diena. [The seventeenth day of December] Istorinės Lietuvai dienos trimečio sukaktuvėms paminėti. 2. laida. Kaunas, J.K., 1929. 142 p. illus., maps. 947.52.K454 PU

5409. KLEIST, Peter. Zwischen Hitler und Stalin, 1939-1945. Bonn, Athenäum-Verlag, 1950. 344 p. DK754.R9K6 DLC DS NN TxU

KLIMAS, Petras. Les territoires lituaniens, considérations ethnographiques et statistiques. Paris, 1919. See entry no. 2044.

5410. --- Istorinė Lietuvos valstybės apžvalga. [Historical review of the Lithuanian state] In Visa Lietuva. Kaunas, 1922. p. 119-145. HC337.L5A25 1922 DLC CSt-H CtPAM ICU PU

5411. LIETUVOS ŠAULIŲ SĄJUNGA. 1928 m. vasario 16; 10 metų Lietuvos Nepriklausomybės sukaktuvėm paminėti. [February 16th, 1928; the commemoration of the Lithuanian Independence. Ed. by A. Marcinkevičius] Kaunas, 1928. 288 p. illus. DK511.L27L485 DLC CtY CtTMF ICLJF

5412. --- 1930-Vytauto Didziojometų Vasario 16; Lietuvos Nepriklausomybės 12 metų sukaktuvėms paminėti. [February 16th, 1930, the year of Vytautas the Great, the commemoration of the 12th anniversary of Lithuanian independence. Ed. by A. Marcinkevičius. Illus. by K. Simonis] Kaunas, 1930. 106 p. illus., ports, map. DK511.L2L423 DLC CtY ICBM

5413. --- 1931 metai Lietuvoje. [The year 1931 in Lithuania. Kaunas] Lietuvos šaulių sąjunga [1931] 56 p. illus. LG2 TUK ICLJF

5414. LITHUANIAN NATIONAL COUNCIL OF AMERICA. Dešimts Nepriklausomos Lietuvos metų. [Tenth anniversary of an independent Lithuania] Chicago, Ill., Lietuvių tautinis komitetas [1928] 26 p. illus. 970.2.Dn ICLJF

5415. MACKEVIČIUS, Rapolas. Dvidešimt metų, 1918-1938. [Twentieth anniversary of an independent Lithuania, 1918-1938] Vilnius, 1938. 76 p. 947.5.M192 PU CtTMF

5416. MITKIEWICZ, Leon. Litwa i Polska pomiędzy dwoma wojnami światowemi. Lithuania and Poland between the two world wars. [Washington, D.C., Photoduplication Service, Library of Congress, 1956] ([Free Europe Committee] Mid-European Studies Center. [Research documents] no.336-336a) Microfilm 2551 no.336-336aDR DLC

5417. --- Wspomnienia kowieńskie; z przdmową M.K. Dziewanowskiego. London, "Veritas", 1968. 294 p. illus., ports. (Biblioteka Polska. Seriia Czerwona, t.71) DK511.L27M56 DLC CaOTU ICU MH NjP OKentU PU

5418. NAVICKAS, Konstantinas. Litva i Antanta, 1918-1920 gg. Vil'nius, Mintis, 1970. 139 p. DK511.L26N36 DLC

5419. NEWMAN, Edward William Polson. Lithuania and her troubles. In His Britain and the Baltic. London [1930] p. 102-122. DK511.B3N4 DLC CaAEU CSt-H CU MoU MWalB

5420. NIESSEL, Henri Albert. L'évacuation des pays baltiques par les Allemands. Paris, Charles-Lavauzelle & Cie, 1935. 272 p. illus., map, port. D651.B2N5 DLC ICU NN NcD

NORUS, T. and J. Žilius. Lithuania's case for independence. Washington, D.C., 1918. See entry no. 5381.

5421. PIRMASIS NEPRIKLAUSOMOS LIEtuvos dešimtmetis, 1918-1928. [The first decade of independent Lithuania, 1918-1928] J. Barkauskas [et al.] Kaunas, Vyriausias Lietuvos Nepriklausomybės 10 metų sukaktuvėms ruošti komitetas [1930] 404 p. DK511.L27P5 DLC CaAEU OCl PU

5422. --- Parašė: P. Klimas ir kiti. Pirmoji knyga. Antroji laida. [The first decade of Independent Lithuania, 1918-1928] London, Nida, 1955. 173 p. (Nidos knygų klubo leidinys, nr.7) DK511.L27P66 1955 kn.1 CaAEU DLC ICCC ICLJF PU

5423. PÓŁ WIEKU, 1917-1967; [almanach. Wybrał i przygotował do druku M. Liubecki] Vilnius, Mintis, 1967. 229 p. illus., facsims., ports. DK511.L27P27 DLC

5424. PURICKIS, Juozas. L'État lituanien et le Gouvernement de Gardinas (Grodno). Lausanne, Ed. par les soins du Bureau d'Information de Lituanie, en vente à la

Librairie des nationalités, 1918.
15 p. maps. DK511.L2P8 DLC CSt-H
IaU IU MH NNC PU

5425. --- Seimų laikai. [The
period of parliamentary government]
In Pirmasis Nepriklausomosios Lietuvos dešimtmetis. London, 1955.
v.1, p. 128-173. DK511.L27P66 1955
kn.1 CaAEU DLC ICLJF PU

5426. --- Les territoires lituaniens, considérations historiques,
ethnographiques et statistiques;
le gouvernement de Grodno (Gardinas) [Paris? 1919?] 18 p. fold.
map. DK511.L27P8 DLC CSt-H PU

RAŠTIKIS, Stasys. Kovose
dėl Lietuvos; kario atsiminimai.
[Los Angeles, Calif., Lietuvių dienos, 1956-72. See entry no. 2876.

5427. SABALIŪNAS, Leonas. Lithuania, 1939-1940; a nation in crisis. [New York, N.Y.] 1963
[c1966] vi, 320 leaves, tables.
Bibliography: leaves 292-320.
Thesis--Columbia University.
DK511.L27S3 ViU NNC

ŠARMAITIS, Romas. Amerikos-
Anglijos imperialistų intervencija
Lietuvoje, 1918-1920. Vilnius,
1955. See entry no. 2909.

5428. ŠARŪNAS, J. Gruodžio 17
dienos perversmas. [The revolt of
December 17th, 1926. n.p.] Lietuvos demokratijos draugai, 1927.
38 p. WB25333 CtY ICLJF

5429. SAURUSAITIS, Peter. Thirty
days in Lithuania 1919. [By] Rev.
Peter P. Saurusaitis, being an account of personal experiences and
observations encountered in a trip
extending from August 30, 1919 to
February 16, 1920. East St. Louis,
Ill., Call Printing Company, 1920.
20 p. DK511.L26S3 DLC CU ICN MiU
MB NN NNC OrU IU

5430. SCHUMMER, Eugenjusz M.
Nowa Litwa. Warszawa, F. Hoesick,
1930. 159 p. illus.
947.52.Sch87 PU OCl

5431. --- Pod znakiem pogoni.
Lwów; Warszawa, Książnica Atlas,
1935. 141 p. illus. Bibliography:
p. 140-141. DK511.L22S39 CaAEU PU

5432. SENN, Alfred Erich. Die
bolschewistische Politik in Litau-
en, 1917-1919. In Forschungen zur
osteuropäischen Geschichte, v.5,
1957, p. 93-118. DR.B45 v.5 DLC
CLU CU ICU InU IEN MH MiU NIC NjP
PU WU

5433. --- The emergence of mo-
dern Lithuania. New York, N.Y.,
Columbia University Press, 1959.
272 p. illus. (Studies of the
Russian Institute, Columbia Univer-
sity) Bibliography: p. 241-259.
DK511.L27S4 DLC CLU CSt CSt-H CU
CaBVaS CaBVaU CaOHM CaOTP CaOTU
CaSSU CtY FU GU IaU IC ICU IdU IEN
In InNd InU IU KU LU MH MiU MnU
MoU MU NB NBuU NIC NN NNC NbU NcD
NcU NdU NjP NSyU NvU OCl OClW OkU
OrU PP PPiU PU RPB TxU TU ViU VtU
WU WaU WyU

--- The great powers, Lithuania and the Vilna question, 1920-
1928. Leiden, 1966 [1967] See
entry no. 3236.

5434. --- The origins of Lithuanian independence after World War
I. In Baltic Review (New York, N.
Y.,), no.37, 1970, p. 7-33. See
serials consulted.

5435. --- Soviet views of Lithuanian independence. In Baltic Review (New York, N.Y.), no.19, 1960,
p. 11-22. See serials consulted.

5436. SHKLIAR, Evgeniia Nikiforovna. Bor'ba trudiashchikhsiia Litovsko-Belorusskoi SSR s inostrannymi
interventami i vnutrennei kontrrevoliutsiei, 1919-1920 gg. Minsk, Gos.
izd-vo BSSR, 1962. 176 p.
DK511.L27S5 CU CSt-H CaBVaS CaNBFU
CaOTU DLC ICU IaU InU IU MH NIC NN
NNC NcD WU

5437. SIDZIKAUSKAS, Vaclovas.
Litauens erste Unabhängigkeits-
Feier nach Wiedergewinnung seiner
Hauptstadt Vilnius; Beitrag zur Ge-
schichte der litauisch-polnischen
Beziehungen nach dem Weltkriege.
In Revue Baltique (Tallinn), Feb.
1940, p. 125-130. See serials
consulted.

5438. SMETONA, Antanas. Antano
Smetonos didžiosios mintys... [The
great thoughts of Antanas Smetona]
Kaunas, Pažangos b-vės leid., 1935-
37. 2 v. 081.S ICCC

5439. --- Pasakyta-parašyta,
1927-1934. [It is said and written]
Kaunas, Pažangos b-vė, 1935. 360
p. illus. 947.52.Sm35 PU ICCC
CtTMF

--- Tautos vado Antano Smetonos kalba. Kaunas, 1934. See
entry no. 2838.

5440. STUDNICKI, Władysław. Państwo kowieńskie; dzisiejszy stosunek litvinów do polaków. Wilno,

Nakład. Związku Obrony Woli ludności, 1922. 16 p. 947.52.St94.3 PU

5441. SUPREME LITHUANIAN COMMIT-
TEE OF LIBERATION. Living in freedom; a sketch of independent Lithuania's achievements. [Augsburg]
Lithuanian Information Service [1949]
95 p. illus. DK511.L2S823 DLC
NN(microfilm)

5442. TURCHI, Nicola. La Litua-
nia nella storia e nel presente.
Roma, Istituto per l'Europa orien-
tale, 1933. 229 p. illus., incl.
lxxxiv, tab. plates, 2 fold. maps.
(Publicazioni dell' "Istituto per
l'Europa orientale", Roma. 2. ser.:
Politica, storia, economica)
DK511.L2T76 DLC CtY KU MH NN PU WU
CSt-H

5443. --- Nella lituania indipen-
dante. Roma, Libraria di scieze e
lettere, 1921. 116 p. fold. map.
DK511.L2T8 DLC PU

VAIČELIŪNAS, Juozas. Tėvynės sargyboje; Lietuvos karininko-
lakūno atsiminimai, 1932-1941.
Sudbury, Ont., 1935. See entry
no. 2888.

5444. VANLANDE, René. Avec le
Général Niessel en Prussie et en
Lithuanie; la dernière defaite
allemande... Paris, Charles-Lavan-
zelle, 1921. 184 p. map.
947.5.V264 PU CSt-H CtY IaU InU BM
MH WU

5445. VARDYS, Vytas Stanley.
Independent Lithuania: a profile.
In His Lithuania under the Soviets.
New York, N.Y., 1965. p. 21-46.
DK511.L27V35 DLC CSt CSt-H CU AzU
IC MoU MU MWalB PPi TU WaU

5446. VYKINTAS, Stepas, ed. Litauens Werden und Schaffen. [Hrsg.
vom Obersten Komitee zur Feier des
20 jährigen Jubiläums Litauens.
Kaunas, 1938] 218 p. illus.
DK511.L2V9 DLC

5447. WHITE, John P. The revolution in Lithuania 1918-19. In
Soviet Studies (Oxford), v.23, no.2,
1971, p. 186-200. See serials
consulted.

5448. WILLIAMS, Anthony Richard.
Lithuania, 1938 and 1939; years of
crisis. [Charlottesville, Va.],
1969. v, 96 leaves. Thesis (M.A.)
--University of Virginia. Bibliography: leaves [87]-96. Typescript.
Thesis 3607 ViU

5449. ZERTHE, Bermanaitė(?).

L'indipendenza della Lituania dal
1918 al 1920. Firenze, Universita,
1965. 416 p. Thesis--University
of Florence. Typescript; a carbon
copy. The name of author poorly reproduced on the carbon copy title-
page. Bermanaitė is the author's
surname. DK511.L27Z4 WaU

X.9.ℓ.2. THE WAR OF INDEPENDENCE,
1918-1920

5450. ALIŠAUSKAS, Kazys. Kovos
dėl Lietuvos nepriklausomybės,
1918-1920. [The war of independence,
1918-1920] Redaktorius Pranas Čepėnas. v.1- . Čikaga, Lietuvių
Veteranų sąjunga "Ramovė", 1972-
DK511.L27A55 PU

BIRONTAS, Adolfas. Bermontininkams Lietuvą užpuolus. Kaunas,
1934. See entry no. 2855.

5451. BUTKUS, Stasys. Savanoris,
1918-1920; Lietuvos kariuomenės
kūrėjų savanorių knyga. [Volun-
teers of the Lithuanian Independence
Wars, 1918-1920] Kaunas, Lietuvos
Kariuomenės savanorių sąjungos Centro valdyba, 1929. xvi, 256 p.
illus., ports., facsim, plans.
947.52.B974 PU PPULC CtPAM CtTMF ICCC

5452. GOLTZ, Rüdiger von der. Als
politischer General im Osten (Finland und Baltikum) 1918 und 1919.
Leipzig, K.F. Koehler, 1936. 173 p.
illus., plates, maps, ports. Published in 1920 under the title:
Meine Sendung in Finland und Baltikum. DK459.G6 1936 DLC CtY ICU MH
NN NNC NcD PU(1920 & 1936 ed.)
CaAEU

5453. NAVAKAS, Jonas. Lietuvai
besikeliant; iš 1918-1919 metų
užrašu ir atsiminimų iš Lietuvos
vasaros-rytų partizanų veikimo.
[The rise of Lithuania; from recollections of the 1918-1919 actions of
the insurgents in South-East Lithu-
ania] Kaunas, Vairo spaustuvė,
1928. 947.52.M229 PU

5454. PETRUITIS, Jonas. Laisvę
ginant mūsų žygiai; atsiminimai.
[Our campaigns defending freedom]
2. laida. [Brooklyn, N.Y.] Vaga
[1952-53] 2 v. Published in 1935-
37 under the title: Mūsų žygiai.
DK511.L27P42 DLC CaAEU CtY ICLJF MH
MiD OCl

5455. RAMOJUS, Vladas. Kritusieji
už laisvę. [Those killed for free-
dom] [Chicago, Ill.] Lietuviškos

knygos klubas [1967] 182 p.
DK511.L274R3 DLC CaOTU

RAŠTIKIS, Stasys. Kovose
dėl Lietuvos; kario atsiminimai.
Los Angeles, 1956-72. See entry
no. 2876.

RUSECKAS, Petras, ed. Sa-
vanorių žygiai; nepriklausomybės
karų atsiminimai. Kaunas, 1937.
See entry no. 2878.

SKORUPSKIS, Vladas. Karas
už Lietuvos laisvę, 1914-1934.
Kaunas, 1934. See entry no. 2883.

--- La résurrection d'un
peuple, 1918-1927; souvenirs d'un
témoin des événements militaires
en Lithuanie. Paris-Limoges-Nancy,
1930. See entry no. 2884.

5456. STEPONAITIS, Vytautas. Pas-
kutinės operacijos bolševikų fronte.
[The last operations against the
Bolsheviks] In Mūsų žinynas (Kaunas), v.1, no.3, 1921. See serials
consulted.

5457. --- Šiaulių miesto gimnazi-
jos užpuolimas. [The attack on the
High School of Šiauliai by the re-
treating Germans] In Karo archyvas
(Kaunas), v.3, 1926, p. 83-89. See
serials consulted.

5458. STOSIŪNAS, Bronius. Žaslių
partizanai. [The partisans of
Žasliai] In Karo archyvas (Kaunas),
v.8, 1937, p. 277-281. See
serials consulted.

5459. ŠUKYS, Antanas. Du mediniai
ir trys geležiniai kryžiai; atsiminimai iš Lietuvos napriklausomybės
kovų, 1919-1921 metais. [Two wood-
en and three iron crosses; reminiscences from the War of Lithuanian
Independence, 1919-1921] [London]
Nida [1964] 376 p. port. (Nidos
knygų klubo leidinys, nr.49)
DK511.L27S92 DLC CaAEU CtTMF ICLJF
MH PU

5460. VASILIAUSKAS, Antanas. Nepriklausomybės karas. [The war of
independence] In Kemežys, V., ed.
Lietuva, 1918-1938. Kaunas, 1938.
p. 45-60. 947.52.L625 PU CtTMF
ICLJF

5461. VĖGELIS, J. Šiaurės grupės
veiksmai kare su bermontininkais.
[The military activities of the
Northern group in the campaigns a-
gainst Bermont's armies] In Karo
archyvas (Kaunas), v.2, 1925, p.
203-218. See serials consulted.

5462. VYČIO ŽENKLAS; vienkartinis
iliustruotas Lietuvos laisvės kovų
invalidų d-jos leidinys. Kaunas,
1938. 64 p. illus. XL970VŽ ICLJF

5463. ZARANKA, Bronius. Mano
atsiminimai iš Lietuvos karų. [My
recollections of the Lithuanian
wars] Kaunas, Valstybės spaustuvė,
1924. 174 p. WA11107 CtY ICLJF

5464. ŽEMAITIS, Antanas. Priešui
ir tėvynei; netolimų laikų užrašai.
[Recollections from the immediate
past] Kaunas, Lietuvos šaulių
sąjungos leidinys, 1931. 111 p.
970.5.ZE ICLJF CtPAM CtTMF

ŽUKAS, Konstantinas.
Žvilgsnis į praeitį. Chicago, Ill.,
1959. See entry no. 2892.

X.9.m. SECOND WORLD WAR, 1939-1945

X.9.m.1. INCORPORATION OF LITHUANIA
INTO THE SOVIET UNION,
1940-1941.

5465. AUDĖNAS, Juozas. Paskutinis posėdis; atsiminimai. [Recol-
lections of the last meeting] New
York, N.Y., Romuva, 1966. 277 p.
ports. DK511.L28A3 DLC CaAEU CaOTU

5466. BOESGAARD, Eimar. Vi
bjaerged' dog Livet; danske oejen-
vidners beretning om de baltiske
landes undergang. København, J.
Willes, 1941. 172 p. plates,
ports. 947.4.B672v IEN

5467. BRAZAITIS, Juozas. Pirmoji
sovietinė okupacija, 1940-1941.
[The first Soviet occupation, 1940-
1941] In Lietuvių enciklopedija.
Boston, Mass., 1968. v.15, p. 356-
370. For holdings see entry no. 216.

5468. BUDRECKIS, Algirdas. Soviet
occupation and annexation of the
Republic of Lithuania, June 15-
August 3, 1940. New York, N.Y.,
Amerikos lietuvių tautinė sąjunga,
I-sis skyrius, 1968. 31 p.
DK511.L27B83 PU DLC OKentU

CHAMBON, Henry de. La
tragédie des nations baltiques.
Paris, 1946. See entry no. 4253.

5469. CHASE, Thomas George. Li-
thunaia and Moscow. In Lithuanian
bulletin (New York, N.Y.), v.2, no.
6, 1944, p. 1-7. See serials
consulted.

5470. CIALDEA, Lilio. L'espansione russa nel Baltico. Milano, Istituto per gli studi di politica internazionale [1940] 106 p. illus., maps. DK511.B3C5 DLC ICU NNUN

5471. ČIBIRAS, Kazimieras. Europe o Genghis Khan? Lituania y la URSS por Casimiro Verax [pseud] Buenos Aires, 1945. 115 p. fold. map. DK511.L27C463 DLC

5472. --- Lituania entre fuego cruzado, ensayos sobre el destino de un pais. [Buenos Aires] A. Moly, 1944. 477 p. plates, ports., maps. Bibliography: p.475-477. D742.L5C5 DLC CSt-H CtPAM MH PU

--- Lituania y la URSS, la invasión soviética... Medellin (Colombia) 1955. See entry no. 3265.

5473. DAILIDĖ, Pranas. Raudonojo voro tinkle. [In the web of the red spider] In Margutis (Chicago, Ill.), no.6-12, 1949; no.1-7, 9-12, 1951. See serials consulted.

5474. DOCUMENTAL FACTS OF LITHUANIAN HISTORY. In Lithuanian days (Los Angeles, Calif.), June 1958, p. 20-22. Prepared by the Committee for a Free Lithuania and reprinted from the "Congressional record". Corrects errors and misleading statements in the Special Report no.9, "Communist take-over and occupation of Byelorussia" (U.S. Congress, House. Select Committee on Communist Aggression). See serials consulted.

5475. DULONG, Gustave. Comment la Lituanie devint und Républic Soviétique Socialiste. In Revue des deux mondes (Paris), April 1, 1955, p. 521-527. See serials consulted.

5476. GAIDŽIŪNAS, Balys. Vieneri metai ir viena savaitė. [One year and one week] Cleveland, Ohio, Dirva, 1950. 183 p. 947.5.G127 PU CaAEU ICLJF

5477. GAR, Josef. Azoy iz es geshen in Lite. [Thus it came to pass in Lithuania; Soviet rule, 1940-1941] [n.p.] 1965. 157 p. facsims. DK511.L27G3 DLC CtY MWalB NB

5478. GLUŠAUSKAS, Jurgis. Negirdėtas smurtas socializmo vardu. [Unbelievable violence in the name of socialism] In Lietuvių archyvas (Kaunas), v.3, 1942, p. 72-97. See serials consulted.

5479. HORRORS OF THE INVASION OF LITHUANIA. In New York Times; current history magazine. v.7, pt.2, 1918, p. 504-509. D501.N5 v.7 pt.2 DLC

5480. JURKŪNAS, Ignas. Raudonasis tvanas. [The red flood] New York, N.Y. [Talka], 1953. 327 p. DK511.L27J8 DLC CtY NN PP PU

5481. --- Den röda floden stiger. [By] Ignas Šeinius [pseud.] Stockholm, Bonnier [1941] 298 p. illus. 947.5.J979.3 PU DLC MH

5482. --- Den röda floden svämar över. [By] I. Scheinius [pseud.] Stockholm, Natur och kultur. [1945] 257 p. DK511.B3J8 DLC MH PU

5483. --- Den röda resan; med 37 illustrationer efter texten. Stockholm, Fahlcrantz & Gumaelius, 1943. 356 p. illus. Microfilm copy (positive) DK27.J87 DLC MH

5484. KAJECKAS, Juozas. The Communist take over of Lithuania. The following is an interview with the Honourable Joseph Kajeckas, Chargé d'Affaires a.j. at the Lithuanian Legation in Washington, D.C. Broadcast on WEAM August 14, 1960. 10 p. CLU Ref. pams.

5485. KIESERITZKY, H. von. Die Bolschewisierung Litauens, 1940/41; ein Tatsachenbericht. Berlin, F. Eher Nachf., 1945. 104 p. illus., ports., map. (Schriftenreihe des NSDAP. Gruppe IX. Bolschewismus, Bd.2) DK511.L27K5 DLC CSt-H NNC

5486. KRĖVĖ-MICKEVIČIUS, Vincas. Conversations with Molotov. In Lituanus (Chicago, Ill.), v.11, no. 2, 1965, p. 7-27. See serials consulted.

5487. --- Pasikalbėjimas su Molotovu. [Negotiation with Molotov] In Aidai (Kennebunkport, Me.), no. 3(59), 1953, p. 122-131. See serials consulted.

5488. --- Plain talk in Moscow. In East and West (London), no.5, 1955, p. 16-28. See Serials consulted.

KRIVICKAS, Domas. Formalities preliminary to aggression. In Baltic Review (New York, N.Y.), no. 5, 1955. See serials consulted.

--- Soviet efforts to justify the annexation. In Lituanus (Brooklyn, N.Y.), v.6, no.2, 1960, p. 34-39. See serials consulted.

--- Soviet-German pact of 1939 and Lithuania. Hamilton, Ont., 1959. See entry no. 2972.

5489. LIETUVA TIRONŲ PANČIUOSE. [Lithuania in the tyrant's shackles] T.1: Bolševikų okupacija. Jonas Audrūnas [pseud.] ir Petras Svyrius [pseud.] Cleveland, Ohio, Lietuvai vaduoti sąjunga, 1946. [i.e. 1947] [16], 311 p. illus., port. 947.5D.628 PU CtPAM ICLJF ICBM

LIETUVIŲ ARCHYVAS; bolševizmo metai. Vilnius, 1942-43. See entry no. 4654.

--- --- [Paruošė J. Prunskis] Brooklyn, N.Y., 1952. See entry no. 4655.

5490. LITHUANIA. PASIUNTINYBĖ. U. S. Lithuania's occupation by the Soviet Union. Washington, D.C., Lithuanian Legation, 1960. 28 p. DK511.L27A54 DLC CtY MH NIC NN

5491. LITHUANIAN COMMITTEE FOR the World's Fair, New York, 1964-65. Lithuania. Brooklyn, N.Y., Franciscan Press, 1964. [10] leaves, illus. CLU Ref pams.

LOZORAITIS, Stasys. Some juridical and moral aspects of the occupation of Lithuania. In East and West (London), v.2, no.7, 1956, p. 29-37. See serials consulted.

5492. MANTAS, Jurgis. Lietuva bolševikų okupacijoj. [Lithuania under Soviet occupation] Buenos Aires [Lietuvos Inf. Centras P. Amerikoje] 1948. 135 p. illus. 970.2.MA ICLJF

5493. MEISSNER, Boris. Die kommunistische Machtübernahme in den baltischen Staaten. In Vierteljahreshefte für Zeitgeschichte (Stuttgart), v.2, no.1, 1954, p. 95-114. For holdings see serials consulted.

5494. MIGLINAS, Simas. Lietuva sovietinės agresijos dokumentuose; dokumentai ir svarstymai. [Lithuania in the documents of Soviet aggression; documents and deliberations] Memmingen, Ger., "Tremtis" [1958] 86 p. DK511.L27M5 DLC NN

5495. NARBUTAS, Titas. Who is worse; Stalin or Hitler? by T. Angelaitis [pseud.] Chicago, Ill., 1960. 48 p. 947.5.N168W PU

NOREM, Owen Joseph Christoffer. Timeless Lithuania. Chi-cago, Ill., 1943. See entry no. 921.

5496. PAKŠTAS, Kazys. The Lithuanian situation. [Chicago, Ill.] Lithuanian Cultural Institute, 1941. 61 p. map. DK511.L27P3 DLC CLU CSt-H

5497. PETRUITIS, Jonas. Lithuania under the sickle and hammer. Cleveland, Ohio. The League for the Liberation of Lithuania [19-] 78 p. illus. D805.R9P4 DLC CtY MH MB NN NjP OrU PU

PRUNSKIS, Joseph. Lietuva bolševikų ir nacių vergijoje. See entry no. 5561.

5498. RAŠTIKIS, Stasys. Okupantų priespaudoje. [Under the Russian and German oppression] In His Kovose dėl Lietuvos. Los Angeles, Calif., 1957. v.2, p. 19-419. DK511.L28R3 v.2 DLC CaAEU CSt-H PU

5499. REI, August. Have the Baltic countries voluntarily renounced their freedom? An exposé based on authentic documentary evidence, by August Rei. [New York, 1944] cover title, 47 p. DK511.B3R375 DLC CSt-H CtY MH NN PU

5500. --- Have the small nations a right to freedom and independence? London, Boreas publishing co. ltd. [1946] 32 p. DK511.E6R4 DLC CtY NN

5501. --- Nazi-Soviet conspiracy and the Baltic States... London, Boreas publishing co. [1948] 61 p. DK511.B3R376 DLC CSt-H ICU MH Mi NN OU PU RPB TxU

5502. RÖMERIS, Mykolas. Lietuvos sovietizacija, 1940-1941 m. [Sovietization of Lithuania, 1940-1941. By] X. Y. [pseud.] Augsburgas, Lietuvos Teisininkų Tremtinių Draugija, 1949. 48 p. 947.5.R663 PU CaOONL CtTMF BM(8081. b. 69.)

5503. SABALIŪNAS, Leonas. Prelude to aggression. In Lituanus (Brooklyn, N.Y.), no.3(12), 1957, p. 2-8. See serials consulted.

ŠAGAMOGIENĖ, Salomėja. Lietuva nacių ir bolševikų vergijoje. Chicago, Ill., 1944. See entry no. 5568.

5504. ŠKIRPA, Kazys. Lietuvos nepriklausomybės praradimas. [The loss of the independence of Lithuania] In Margutis (Chicago, Ill.), no.12, 1954, p. 4-6; 1955, no.1, p. 3-5; no.2, 3-5; no.3, p.3-5; no.4, p.3-5; no.5, p.3-5; no.7-8, p.34-38. See serials consulted.

5505. SMETONA, Antanas. Lietuva
prieš mirštama pavojų; atsiminimai.
[Lithuania faces deadly danger; re-
collections] In Margutis (Chicago,
Ill.), 1954, no.7, p. 8-9, 14-15;
no.8, p. 3-4; no.9, p. 3-5; no.10,
p. 3-5; no.11, p. 3-5. See serials
consulted.

5506. ŠMULKŠTYS, Julius Joseph.
The annexation of Lithuania by Soviet Union, 1939-1940. Urbana, Ill.
[1955] iv, 86 leaves. Thesis--
University of Illinaois. Bibliography: p. 83-86. 947.5.Sm84a IU

5507. --- The incorporation of the
Baltic States by the Soviet Union.
In Lituanus (Chicago, Ill.), no.14,
no.2, 1968, p. 19-44. See serials
consulted.

STIKLIORIUS, Jonas Arvydas.
Inkorporacija; Lietuvos ir Sovietų
ankstesni santykiai. Boston, Mass.,
1956. See entry no. 3277.

STRONG, Anna Louise. Lithuania's new way. London [1941] See
entry no. 2912.

5508. TARYBŲ VALDŽIOS ATKŪRIMA LIE-
tuvoje 1940-1941 metais; dokumentų
rinkinys. [Re-establishment of So-
viet rule in Lithuania 1940-1941.
Board of editors: E. Jacovskis et
al.] Vilnius, Mintis, 1965. 345 p.
At head of title: Archyvų valdyba
prie LTSR Ministrų tarybos; Lietuvos
TSR Centrinis valstybinis archyvas.
Summary in English and Russian.
DK511.L27T19 CSt-H CaOU CtY DLC IU
PU MH

5509. U.S. CONGRESS. HOUSE. SE-
LECT COMMITTEE ON COMMUNIST AGGRES-
SION. Baltic States investigation.
[First interim report] Hearings before the Select Committee to investigate the incorporation of the Baltic States into the U.S.S.R.... Nov.
30-Dec. 11, 1953. Washington, D.C.,
Govt. Print. Off., 1954. 2 pts.
(xii, 1448 p.) illus., ports., fold.
maps. Pt.2 has title: "Communist aggression investigation. Fourth interim report". DK511.B3U52 DLC CtTMF
ICLJF

5510. U.S. CONGRESS. HOUSE. SE-
LECT COMMITTEE ON COMMUNIST AGGRES-
SION. Investigation of Communist
takeover and occupation of Poland,
Lithuania, and Slovakia. Sixth interim report of hearings before the
Subcommittee on Poland, Lithuania,
and Slovakia of the Select Committee
on Communist aggression, House of Representatives, Eighty-Third Congress,
Second Session under authority of

H. Res. 346 and H. Res. 438... Washington, D.C., Govt. Print. Off.,
1954. x, 214 p. DK441.U63 DLC CSt-
H CtY ICU InNd In KU NIC NNC PP PU

5511. --- Report of the Select Committee to investigate Communist aggression against Poland, Hungary,
Czekoslovakia, Bulgaria, Rumania, Lithuania, Latvia, Estonia, East Germany, Russia and non-Russian nations
of the U.S.S.R. Second interim report to the Select Committee on Communist aggression. House of Representatives, 83rd Congress, 2d Sess-
sion under authority of H. Res. 346
and H. Res. 438. Washington, D.C.,
Govt. Print. Off., 1954. DK273.U516
DLC PU-L

5512. --- Report of the Select Committee to Investigate Communist Aggression and the Forced Incorporation of the Baltic States into the
U.S.S.R. Third interim report...
Washington, D.C., Govt. Print. Off.,
1954. ix, 537 p. Caption title:
The Baltic States; a study of their
origin and national development,
their seizure and incorporation into
the U.S.S.R. DK511.B3U53 DLC ICLJF
PU

5513. --- Special report of the Select Committee on Communist Aggression... Washington, D.C., Govt.
Print. Off., 1954-55. 16 pts. illus.
(Special report no. 14. Communist
takeover and occupation of Lithuania)
DK266.A3U45 no.14 DLC CaAEU ICBM PU

5514. VAITIEKŪNAS, Vytautas. Ker-
steno komisijos darbų rezultatai.
[The results of investigation by the
Kersten Committee] In Lietuva (New
York, N.Y.), no.7, 1955, p.28-43,79.
See serials consulted.

5515. VARDYS, Vytas Stanley. Ag-
gression, Soviet style, 1939-1940.
In His Lithuania under the Soviets.
New York, N.Y., 1965. p. 47-58.
DK511.L27V35 DLC AzU CSt CSt-H CU IC
MoU MWalB MU PPi TU WaU

X.9.m.2. INSURRECTION OF 1941

5516. BUDRECKIS, Algirdas Martin.
The Lithuanian national revolt of
1941. [Boston, Mass.] Lithuanian
enciklopedia press [1968] xvi, 147
p. maps. D802.L5B76 DLC CaAEU
CaOTU CaOTP ICU IaU InNd InU MU NN
NSyU OrU PU VtU

5517. GAIGALAITĖ, Aldona. Buržu-
aziniai nacionalistai Hitlerinės

Vokietijos tarnyboje, 1939-1941.
[The bourgeoise nationalists in the
service for Hitler's Germany, 1939-
1941] In LTSRMAD. Serija A, no.2,
1960, p. 133-151. See serials consulted.

5518. IVINSKIS, Zenonas. The Lithuanian revolt against the Soviets
in 1941. In Lituanus (Chicago,
Ill.), v.12, no.2, 1966, p. 5-19.
See serials consulted.

5519. MAŽIULIS, Antanas Juozas.
1941 birželio sukilimas; Lietuva so-
vietinėj okupacijoj. [The insurrection of June, 1941; Lithuania under
Soviet occupation] In Lietuvių enciklopedija. Boston, Mass., 1963.
v.29, p. 166-179. For holdings see
entry no. 216.

5520. RIMKUS, Vytautas. Lietuvių
sukilimas Vilniuje 1941 m.; iš asme-
niškų prisiminimų. [The revolt in
Vilnius, 1941] London, 1969. 47 p.
Offprint from Europos lietuvis,1969.
DK511.L27R53 PU ICBM

X.9.m.3. GERMAN OCCUPATION AND GUER-
RILLA WARFARE, 1941-1944

5521. APYVALA, Stasys. Sakalai
broleliai; partizano užrašai. [Re-
collection of the partizan] Literatūrinis bendrautorius Romualdas Kašauskas. Vilnius, VGLL, 1961. 270
p. D802.L5A63 DLC

5522. BALBERYSZKI, M. Likwidacja
geta Wileńskiego... Łódz, 1946. 40
p. Judaica Bia95.B18 CtY

5523. BILEVIČIUS, Elijas. Nemunas
grįžta į savo vagą; atsiminimai.
[Recollections...] Vilnius, VPMLL,
1961. 192 p. port. 947.5.B493 PU
MH

5524. BINKIENĖ, Sofija, comp. Ir
be ginklo kariai. [Worriors without
the guns] Vilnius, Mintis, 1967.
295 p. illus., facsims, ports.
DK511.L27B48 DLC NjP

5525. BRAZAITIS, Juozas. Vokiečių
okupacija, 1941-1944. [German occupation, 1941-1944] In Lietuvių enciklopedija. Moston, Mass., 1968.
v.15, p. 371-380. For holdings see
entry no. 216.

5526. BULAVAS, Juozas. Vokiškųjų
fašistų okupacinis Lietuvos valdymas
1941-1944 m. [German occupational
rule of Lithuania, 1941-1944]
Vilnius, 1969. 294 p. At head of

title: Lietuvos TSR Mokslų akademija.
Ekonomikos Institutas. DK511.L27B79
PU DLC

5527. BULOTA, Jonas. Reportažai
iš požeminio Vilniaus. [Reports
from the underground of Vilnius] Vilnius, Mintis, 1965. 134 p. DK651.
V4B83 DLC CtY MH

5528. --- Vilniaus požemiuose.
[In the undergroud of Vilnius. By]
J. Bulota ir R. Šalūga. Vilnius,
VPMLL, 1960. 101 p. illus.
DK651.V4B85 DLC MH

5529. BUNKUS, A. Ekonomika Litvy
v period okkupatsii. In Gitlerovskaia okkupatsiia v Litve. Vil'nius,
1966. 1 v. D802.L5G5 DLC TU

5530. BUTKUS, Tadas, ed. Štai jų
tikrasis veidas. [Here is their
real face. Sudarė T. Butkus] Vilnius, VPMLL, 1963. 145 p.
D802.L5B8 DLC MH

5531. DALLIN, Alexander. German
rule in Russia, 1941-1945; a study
of occupation policies. New York,
N.Y., St. Martin's Press, 1957.
xx, 695 p. illus., maps.
D802.R8D3 DLC CSt CU CaAEU CtY DS
FTaSU FMU FU GEU IaAS IdU InU IU KU
KyU LU MB MH MiHM MiEM MiU MdBJ MsSM
MnU MoU NIC NN NNC NbU NcD NcU NjR
NRU ODW OClW OkU RPB ScU TxU TNJ TU
ViU WU

5532. DOCUMENTS ACCUSE. [Compiled
and commented by B. Baranauskas and
K. Jurkšėnas. Edited by E. Rozaus-
kas] Vilnius, Gintaras, 1970. 309
p. illus., map. D802.L5D613 CaOTU

5533. DRUNGA, Karolis. Antinaci-
nės rezistencijos organizacija.
[The anti-nazi resistance and its
organization] In Santarvė (London),
1954, no.4-5, p. 146-149, no.6,
p. 185-188. See serials consulted.

5534. GAIDŽIŪNAS, Balys. Pakeliui
į mirtį; vokiečių kalėjimuose. [On
the way to death; in German prisons]
Cleveland, Ohio, Spauda Dirvos, 1948.
231 p. 940.547.G127 PU MiD NN OCl
OKentU

5535. GITLEROVSKAIA OKKUPATSIIA V
Litve; sbornik statei. Vil'nius,
Mintis, 1966. 354 p. illus., fold.
col. map, plans, ports. D802.L5G5
DLC CaAEU CaBVaS CaBVaU CaNSHD CaOHM
CtY IaU InNd InU ICU IEN IU MH MnU
MU NIC NcD NcU NjP NSyU OrU PPiU TU
ViU WU WaU

5536. GRAŽIŪNAS, Albinas. Nacinė
Lietuvos okupacija. [Nazi occupation
of Lithuania] In Tėvynės sargas

(Chicago, Ill.), no.1, 1966, p. 50-76. See serials consulted.

5537. GRIGOLAITIS, Jonas Endrikis. Kalinio nr. 40627 išgyvenimai nacių koncentracijos stovyklose, 1941-1945. [... in German concentration camps] Dillingen, Ger., "Mūsų kelis" 1946. 238 p. 940.547.G873 PU ICLJF MiD NN OKentU

5538. GRINIUS, Jonas. Rezistencija prieš vokiečius Kauno universitete. [The resistance against Germans in the University of Kaunas] In Naujoji aušra (Chicago, Ill.), no.4, 1948. See serials consulted.

5539. GURECKAS, Algimantas Petras. The national resistance during the German occupation of Lithuania. In Lituanus (Brooklyn, N.Y.), v.8, no. 1-2, 1962, p. 23-28. See serials consulted.

5540. HARRISON, Ernst J. Lithuania's fight for freedom. New York, N.Y., Lithuanian American Information Center, 1952. 95 p. illus. D742.L5H3 1952 DLC CLU CSt CSt-H CU CaAEU CaOTU CtY CoU HU ICBM IdU IEU InNd IU MoU MnU NIC NN NNC NjP NjR NSyU OKentU PPD PBm PU TxU WU

5541. HITLERINĖ OKUPACIJA LIETUVOje. [Nazi occupation of Lithuania] Vilnius, VPMLL, 1961. 544 (i.e. 454) p. illus., maps, ports. D802.L5H5 DLC CtPAM NN

5542. IVINSKIS, Zenonas. Lithuania during the war; resistance against the Soviet and the Nazi occupants. In Vardys, V.S. Lithuania under the Soviets. New York, N.Y., 1965. p. 61-84, 264-265. DK511.L27V35 DLC CtY DS MH MiU PPULC PU

5543. JASAITIS, Domas. Nacionalsocialistinis komunistinis genocidas Lietuvoje. [The nationalsocialist and communist genocide in Lithuania] In LKMASD, v.6, 1969, p. [367]-424. See serials consulted.

5544. JERUSHALMI, Eliezer. Das jüdische Martyrerkind; nach Tagebuchaufzeichnungen aus Ghetto von Schaulen 1941-1944. [Übersetzung aus dem Hebräischen von Mirjam Singer. Zeichnungen Abram Ameraut] Darmstadt; Eberstadt, Oekumenische Marienschwesternschaft, 1960. 63 p. illus. MH WaU WU

5545. JOESTEN, Joachim. German rule in Ostland. In Foreign Affairs (New York, N.Y.), v.22, 1943, p. 143-147. See serials consulted.

5546. KADŽIULIS, A. Kaltina nužudytieji. [The murdered accuse. Reportažų iš teismo salės autoriai: A. Kadžiulis et al. Redaktorė G. Gustaitė ir L. Kokštienė] Vilnius, VPMLL, 1963. 206 p. illus.,facsims. D804.G4K24 DLC

5547. KRIVICKAS, Domas. Analogija Lietuvos-Austrijos bylose; Sovietų ir Nacių agresijos lygiagretumas. [The analogy in the Lithuanian and Austrian cases; the parallelism of the aggression by the Soviets and Nazis] In Lietuva (New York, N.Y.), no.5, 1954, p. 4-12. See serials consulted.

5548. KRUPAVIČIUS, Mykolas. Memorandumai hitlerinės okupacijos generaliniam komisarui Kaune. [The memorandums to the General Commissar of the Nazi occupational Government in Kaunas] In Tėvynės sargas (Chicago, Ill.), no.17-18, 1959, p. 87-95. See serials consulted.

5549. KUTKA, Petras. Girioj aidi šūviai; partizano atsiminimai. [Echoing shots in the forest; partizan's reminiscences] Vilnius, VGLL, 1958. 283 p. D802.L5K8 DLC CaOTP

5550. KVIKLYS, Bronius. Lietuvių kova su naciais, 1941-1944. [Lithuanian struggle against Nazis, 1941-1944] Memmingen, "Minties" leidinys, 1946. 48 p. illus. 947.5.K974 PU CtTMF ICCC ICLJF

5551. LAGAUSKIENĖ, Edita. Faktai kaltina; literatūros apžvalga. [The facts are accusing; a review of literature] Kaunas, 1961. 34 p. illus. Z6207.W8L3 DLC

5552. LIETUVOS TSR MOKSLŲ AKADEMIJA, VILNA. ARCHYVINIAMS DOKUMENTAMS SKELBTI REDAKCIJA. Archyviniai dokumentai apie nacionalistų antiliaudinę veiklą. [Archival documents about the nazi activities against the people. Comp. by B. Baranauskas and J. Vicas] Vilnius, VPMLL, 1961. 144 p. (Archyviniai dokumentai, 3. rinkinys) DK511.L27L494 v.3 DLC MH

5553. --- --- Vilnius, VPMLL, 1962. 199 p. (Archyviniai dokumentai, 5. rinkinys) DK511.L2A23 v.5 DLC MH

5554. --- Hitleriniai parašiutininkai. [Hitler's parashutists. Rinkinį sudarė B. Baranauskas] Vilnius, Mintis, 1966. 165 p. (Archyviniai dokumentai, 8. rinkinys) DK511. L27L72 InU MH

5555. --- Hitleriniai žudikai Kre-

tingoje. [Murderers in Kretinga.
Paruošė spaudai ir red. B. Bara-
nauskas] Vilnius, VPMLL, 1960. 157
p. (Archyviniai dokumentai, 1. rinkinys) Balt 8319.61.1 MH

5556. --- Hitlerininkų penktoji
kolona Lietuvoje. [Hitler's fifth
column in Lithuania. Rinkinį paruošė B. Baranauskas] Vilnius, VPMLL,
1961. 227 p. facsims. (Archyviniai
dokumentai, 4. rinkinys) DK511.L2A23
v.4 DLC MH

5557. MITING PREDSTAVITELEI LITOVS-
kogo naroda. Moscow, Apr. 1942.
Lietuvių tautos atstovų mitingas;
įvykęs Maskvoje 1942 m. balandžio
26 d. Atstovų kalbos, kreipimasis į
Lietuvių tautą, sveikinimas draugui
Stalinui. [Meeting of the representatives of the Lithuanian nation in
Moscow April 26, 1942...] Moskva,
LTSR Valstybinė leidykla, 1942. 53,
[2] p. D802.L3M5 DLC MH

5558. MONČIUKAS, Teofilius. Ru-
dininkų girios partizanai. [The
partizans of the Rudninkai forest.
Vilnius] VPMLL [1959] 340 p. illus.
D802.L5M6 DLC

5559. NAUJALIS, S. Pėdsakai ding-
sta miške. [Footprints disappearing
into the forest] Vilnius, VGLL,
1963. 261 p. CtPAM

OSTLAND. REICHSKOMMISSAR.
Auf Informationsfahrt im Ostland.
[Riga, 1944] See entry no. 1096.

5560. --- Lagebericht. Juli/Dez.
1941-44. Riga, Reichskommissariat,
1941-44. HC243.078 DLC

PAKŠTAS, Kazys. The Lithuanian situation. Chicago, Ill.,
1941. See entry no. 5496.

5561. PRUNSKIS, Joseph. Lietuva
bolševikų ir nacių vergijoje. [Li-
thuania in Soviet and Nazi slavery]
Chicago, Ill., Draugas, 1944. 51 p.
947.520.P15 CtTMF PU

5562. RAKŪNAS, Algirdas. Lietuvos
liaudies kova prieš hitlerinę oku-
paciją. [Lithuania's struggle
against Hitler's occupation] Vilnius,
Mintis, 1970. 192 p. D802.L5R3 PU

5563. RAŠTIKIS, Stasys. The relations between the Provisional Gover-
ment of Lithuania and the German
authorities, June 23-Aug. 15, 1941.
In Lituanus (Brooklyn, N.Y.), v.8,
no.1-2, 1962, p. 16-22. See serials
consulted.

5564. RIMKUS, Petras. Rūstusis pa-

vasaris. [A gloomy spring] Vilnius,
VPMLL, 1962. 115 p. ports.
D802.L5R48 DLC

5565. RUKŠĖNAS, Kazys. Į vergovę.
[To slavery] Vilnius, Mintis, 1966.
149 p. DK511.L27R85 CtY

5566. RUKŠĖNAS, Kazys and V. Sinkevičius. Litva pod vlast'iu gitle-
rovskikh palachei. [By] K. Ruksche-
nas and Sinkiavichius. In Gitlerovskaia okkupatsiia v Litve. Vil'nius,
1966. D802.L5G5 DLC TU

5567. S-is, J. Lietuvių kova
prieš SS legioną. [Lithuania's
struggle against formation of the SS
legion] In Tėvynės sargas (Reutlingen, Ger.), no.2-3, 1948, p. 107-124.
See serials consulted.

5568. ŠAGAMOGIENĖ, Salomėja. Lie-
tuviai nacių ir bolševikų vergijoje.
[Lithuanians under the yoke of the
Nazis and Bolsheviks. Spaudai pa-
ruošė S.Š. ir Juozas Prunskis]
Chicago, Ill., ALRK Federacijos,
Chicagos apskr. spaudos sekcija,
1944. 51 p. 947.5.Sal3 PU

5569. [Scattered numbers of Lithuanian undergraound newspapers, published between 1942-1944. n.p.,
1942-44. 111 pieces] D802.L5S25
DLC

5570. SENN, Alfred Erich. On the
state of Central Lithuania. In Jahrbücher für Geschichte Osteuropas
(Breslau), v.12, no.3, 1964, p. 366-
374. See serials consulted.

5571. SLAVĖNAS, Julius Paulius.
Nazi ideology and policy in the Bal-
tic States. In Lituanus (Chicago,
Ill.), v.11, no.1, 1965, p. 34-47.
See serials consulted.

5572. SRUOGA, Balys. Dievų miš-
kas; atsiminimai iš konclagerio.
[The Forest of Gods; memoirs from
the concentration camp] Vilnius,
VGLL, 1957. 493 p. illus. (His
Raštai, t.5) PG8721.S68 1957 v.5
DLC CaAEU ICU CaOTP ICLJF NN PU

5573. --- --- [Another edition]
Chicago, Ill., 1957. D805.G3S77 DLC
CtY MiD NN PU

5574. --- --- [Another edition]
Iliustracijos E. Jurėno. Vilnius,
VGLL, 1960. 536 p. illus.
D805.G3S77 1960 DLC OKentU

5575. ŠTARAS, Povilas, ed. Kareiviai be milinių. [Soldiers without
uniforms. Sudarė P. Štaras] Vilnius,
VGLL, 1963. 293 p. ports, facsims.

D802.L5S7 DLC

5576. --- Lietuvos partizanai...
[Lithuania's guerrillas...] Vilnius,
Mintis, 1967. 343 p. illus., fac-
sims., ports. 940.5486qS795L NcD
DLC PU WaU

5577. --- Partizaninis judėjimas
Lietuvoje Didžiojo Tėvynės karo metais. [Partizan activities in Lithuania during the Great Patriotic War,
1939-1945] Vilnius, Mintis, 1966.
334 p. illus. D802.L5S75 PU DLC NN

5578. STUPPERICH, Robert. Sied-
lungspläne im Gebiet des Oberbefehlshaber Ost während des Weltkrieges.
In Jomsburg (Leipzig), v.5, 1941,
p. 348-367. See serials consulted.

5579. SŪDUVIS, N.E., pseud. Ein
kleines Volk wird ausgelöscht, brau-
ne und rote Staatspolizei am werk;
die Tragödie Litauens. Zürich, Tho-
mas-Verlag, 1947. 99 p. (Politische
Schriftenreihe) DK511.L27S9 DLC
CSt-H ICLJF IEN InU MnU

5580. UŽDAVINYS, Vincas. Pirčiu-
pio kaimo tragedija. [The tragedy
of the Pirčiupis village] Vilnius,
VPMLL, 1958. 91 p. illus., ports.
D802.L5U9 1958 DLC OKentU

5581. VAIČELIŪNAS, Juozas. Antrasis pasaulinis karas. [The Second
World War] Sudbury, Ont., 1960.
350 p. illus. D743.V24 DLC MiD NN
OCl PU

5582. YLA, Stasys. A priest in
Stutthof; human experiences in the
world of the subhuman. Authorized
translation from the Lithuanian by
Manyland Books and by Nola M. Zobarskas. Introd. by Charles Angoff.
New York, N.Y., Manyland Books,
1971. D805.G3Y5513 PU

5583. --- Žmonės ir žvėrys Dievų
miške; kaceto pergyvenimai. [Men
and beasts in the forest of Gods;
experiences from the German concentration camp] Putnam, Conn., Immaculata Press, 1951. 555 p.
illus., ports., fold. maps.
D805.G3Y55 DLC CaOTP CtTMF ICLJF PU

5584. ŽEMELIS, Henrykas. Okupantų replėse. [In the squeeze of
the occupational forces] Memmingen,
Ger., Mintis, 1947. 178 p.
947.5.Z43 PU CtPAM CtTMF ICBM
NN(negative microfilm) OKentU

X.9.n. SOVIET LITHUANIA, 1945- .

X.9.n.1. TREATISES AND TEXTBOOKS

5585. BIMBA, Anthony. Klesti Nemuno kraštas: Lietuva, 1945-1967.
[The flourishing country; Lithuania,
1945-1967] [Brooklyn] 1967. 287
p. illus. (Amerikos lietuvių darbininkų literatūros leidinys, 78)
DK511.L274B5 DLC NjP OKentU

5586. --- Naujoji Lietuva; faktų
ir dokumentų šviesoje. [The new
Lithuania; in the light of facts
and documents] [Chicago] Lietuvos draugų komitetas, 1940. 200 p.
L970.2.Bi ICLJF OCl OKentU

5587. DROBNYS, Aleksandras. 20
let Sovetskoi Litvy, 1940-1960 gg.
Moskva, Znanie, 1960. 31 p. (Vsesoiuznoe obshchestvo po rasprostra-
neniiu politicheskikh i nauchnykh
znanii. Izdaniia. Seriia 1: Istoriia, 28) AS262.V833 ser.1, 1960,
no.28 DLC CSt-H IU MH

5588. JURGINIS, Juozas. Istoriia
Litovskoi SSR; uchebnik dlia sred-
nikh shkol. Kaunas, Gos. izd-vo
pedagog. lit-ry, 1958. 186 p.
illus., fold. maps. DK511.L2J84
InU CaOTU CtY NNC

5589. --- Lietuvos TSR istorija;
vadovėlis vidurinėms mokykloms.
[History of Soviet Lithuania; textbook for Jr. High School] Kaunas,
Valstybinė Pedagoginės Literatūros
leidykla, 1957. 173 p. illus.
DK511.L2J76 DLC CaAEU NN PU

5590. --- Lietuvos TSR istorijos
bruožai. [The outline of Soviet
Lithuanian history. Sudarė ir redagavo J. Jurginis] Kaunas, Šviesa,
1965. 140 p. DK511.L2J77 DLC

LIETUVOS TSR MOKSLŲ AKADEMI-
JA, VILNA. EKONOMIKOS INSTITUTAS.
Ketvirtis amžiaus socializmo keliu.
See entry no. 1029.

--- Lietuvos TSR istorija.
Vilnius, 1957-65. 3 v. See entry
no. 4518.

--- Lietuvos TSR istorija
nuo seniausių laikų iki 1957 metų.
Vilnius, 1958. See entry no. 4519.

5591. LIETUVOS TARYBŲ SOCIALISTI-
NĖS RESPUBLIKOS DEŠIMTMETIS. [The
tenth anniversary of the Lithuanian
SSR. Vilniuje] VPMLL, 1950. 112
p. illus. DK511.L27L49 DLC

5592. OBSHCHESTVO "ZNANIE" LITOV-
skoi SSR. 25 let Sovetskoi Litve.
Vil'nius, 1965. 54 p. DK511.L274.02
DLC

5593. VILNA. PARTIJOS ISTORIJOS
INSTITUTAS. Kovų keliais; lietuviškoji divizija. Didžiajame Tėvynės kare. Tarybų Lietuvos išvada-
vimas. [...Lithuanian army division
in the Great Patriotic War; the liberation of Soviet Lithuania. Sudarė E. Dirvelė ir S. Kancedikas.
Tekstas Eduardo Mieželaičio] Vilnius, Vaga, 1965. 1 v. (unpaged,
chiefly illus.) D764.6.L52 16th V5
DLC MH

ŽIUGŽDA, Robertas. Litov-
skaia SSR; kratkii istoriko-ekonomi-
cheskii ocherk. Moskva, 1957. See
entry no. 3827.

X.9.n.2. CAPTIVE LITHUANIA

5594. A VISIT TO SOVIET-OCCUPIED
Lithuania, by a Chicagoan. Chicago,
Ill., Lithuanian American Council,
1962. 101 p., illus., map.
DK511.L27V48 DLC CaAEU CaOTU CtY
ICBM IEN MH

5595. ČIBIRAS, Kazimieras. Diez
años de martirio; la ocupación soviética de Lituania desde la per-
spectiva de un decenio por Casimiro
Verax [pseud. Editado por Francisco
Ramanauskas bajo los auspicios del
pro Liberación de Lituania en Argen-
tina] Buenos Aires, 1950. 74 p.
illus. DK511.L27C46 DLC ICBM ICLJF

5596. COMMITTEE OF LIBERAL EXILES.
Behind the iron curtain. London,
Liberal International, 1951. 32 p.
(World Liberalism. Supplement
series, no.1) BM(P.P. 3558. inh.(2))

5597. DANIEL, Hawthorne. The or-
deal of the Captive Nations. In-
trod. by Harold R. Medina. Garden
City, N.Y., Doubleday, 1958. 316 p.
Bibliography: p.[300]-301.
DR48.5.D3 DLC CaBVaU CLSU CLU CtY CU
DS FTaSU FU GU IaAS ICU IaU IU KU LU
MB MH MiU MnU NcD NIC NcU NN NNC NjP
NjR OO OU OrCS OrStbM PP PSC PU RPB
TNJ TU TxU

5598. GAUTHEROT, G. Derrière le
rideau de fer. Paris, Hachette,
1946. 200 p. illus. map. "Le
Calvaire des Pays Baltes: en Lithuanie": p. 67-76. D843.G3 DLC CSt

5599. --- 2 éd., rev. et augm.
Paris, Hermes-France, 1947. 257 p.
map. NN

5600. GRIŠMANAUSKAS, Juozas. To-
limieji kvadratai. [Distant images]
New York, N.Y., 1952. 192 p. illus.
DK511.L27G78 DLC CaAEU PU

5601. KAJECKAS, Juozas. The
story of captive Lithuania; an in-
formal survey. [Washington, D.C.,
The Lithuanian Legation, 1964] 12
p. DK511.L27K3 NSyU CaOTP CSt-H
CLU ICBM PU

5602. KAŠKELIS, Juozas. Komuniz-
mas be kaukės. [Communism unmasked]
Montreal, Que., 1954. HX315.65.K3
DLC CaOTP

5603. MAČIUIKA, Benediktas Vytenis. The Baltic states under Soviet
Russia: a case study in sovietization. [Chicago, Ill.] 1963. 496
leaves. Thesis--University of Chicago. ICU

5604. MANNING, Clarence Augustus.
The forgotten republics. New York,
N.Y., Philosophical Library [1952]
264 p., illus. DK511.B3M3 DLC
CaAEU NN PU

5605. MATUSEVIČIUS, K. Russia's
westward drive; the destruction of
Lithuania Minor. In Baltic Review
(New York, N.Y.), v.2, no.1, 1947,
p. 46-54. See serials consulted.

5606. MIGLINAS, Simas. Pavergto-
ji Lietuva. [Captive Lithuania]
Memmingen, Ger., "Tremtis" [1957]
148 p. HC337.L5M5 DLC NN

5607. MUSTEIKIS, Antanas. The
Nationality problem in the Baltic
States under the Soviet Union.
New York, Free Europe Committee,
1954. 116 p. (Study no. 307) Un-
published. Microfilm 2551 DLC

5608 NEMICKAS, Bronius. Soviet
rule in Lithuania. In The Baltic
Review (New York, N.Y.), no.26,
1963, p. 13-16. See serials
consulted.

5609. PASAULIO LIETUVIŲ BENDRUO-
MENĖ. Lietuva okupacijoje. Pranešimai Pasaulio Lietuvių Bendruomenės Seimui apie okupuotos Lietuvos gyvenimo kaikurias sritis.
[Lithuania under occupation. Reports to the Congress of World Lithuanian Community on some aspects
of life in occupied Lithuania] New
York, N.Y., PLB Seimo organizacinis
komitetas, 1958. 128 leaves. Mimeographed. 970.2.Lo ICLJF CLD NN

5610. PERKINS, Jeanne. Sovietiz-
ing Lithuania. In Plain Talk (New
York, N.Y.), v.2, no.8, 1948, p. 46-

51. See serials consulted.

5611. RASTENIS, Vincas. One
year of Destalinization in Lithuania. In Lituanus (Brooklyn, N.Y.),
no.1(10) 1957, p. 2-6. See
serials consulted.

5612. --- The World's "most dramatic" election. In Baltic Review
(New York, N.Y.), no.17, 1959, p.
59-64. See serials consulted.

        REPEČKA, Juozas. Der ge-
genwärtige völkerrechtliche Status
der baltischen Staaten. Göttingen,
1950. See entry no. 3454.

5613. SOME ASPECTS OF THE SOVIET
Russian rule in occupied Lithuania.
June 15, 1940-June 15, 1950; ten
years of Lithuania's sufferings
under foreign tyranny. [Washington,
DLC., Lithuanian Legation, 1950]
45 leaves. D742.L5S6 DLC CSt-H

5614. VAITIEKŪNAS, Vytautas.
Antrosios sovietinės okupacijos
laikai. [The period of the second
Soviet occupation] In Lietuvių
enciklopedija. Boston, Mass.,
1968. v.15, p. 380-401. For
holdings see entry no. 216.

        --- The labour system in
occupied Lithuania. In Baltic Review (New York, N.Y.), no.4, 1955,
p. 18-24. See serials consulted.

        --- Sovietinis teisingumas.
New York, N.Y., 1959. See entry
no. 3441.

5615. --- A survey of develop-
ments in occupied Lithuania in 1961.
New York, N.Y., Committee for Free
Lithuania [1962] 63 p.
DK511.L27V28 DLC PU

5616. --- A survey of developments
in occupied Lithuania in 1962.
New York, N.Y., Committee for Free
Lithuania [1963] 71 p.
DK511.L27V28 DLC CaOTU CLU CSt-H
InU NN OKentU PU

5617. --- A survey of developments
in captive Lithuania in 1963-1964.
New York, N.Y., Committee for Free
Lithuania [1965?] 141 p. tables.
DK511.L27V28 DLC CaOTU ICU MH NNC
PP PU

5618. --- A survey of developments
in captive Lithuania in 1956-1968.
New York, N.Y., Committee for Free
Lithuania [1969] 160 p.
DK511.L27V3 DLC CaOTU MH OKentU PU

5619. VARDYS, Vytas Stanley. The

colonial nature of Soviet nationality policy. Offprint from International Review of History and Political Science (Meerut, India), v.1,
no.3, 1964. 19 p. 947.4.V423.2 PU

5620. --- How the Baltic Republics
fare in the Soviet Union. In Foreign Affairs (New York, N.Y.),
April 1966, p. 312-317. See
serials consulted.

        --- Lithuania under the So-
viets. New York, N.Y. [1965]. See
entry no. 3279.

5621. --- Recent Soviet policy
toward Lithuanian nationalism. In
Journal of Central European Affairs
(Boulder, Col.), v.23, no.3, 1963,
p. 313-332. See serials consulted.

5622. --- Soviet colonialism in
the Baltic States; a note on the
nature of modern colonialism. In
Lituanus (Chicago, Ill.), no.2,
1964, p. 5-23. See serials consulted.

5623. --- Soviet colonialism in
the Baltic States, 1940-1965. In
Baltic Review (New York, N.Y.), no.
29, 1965, p. 11-26. See serials
consulted.

5624. --- Soviet nationality policy as instrument of political socia-
lization. In Res Baltica, Leyden,
1968. p. 117-132. DK511.L18R4
DLC CaAEU CtY-L RP

5625. --- Soviet policy toward
Lithuanian nationalism. In Journal
of Central European Affairs (Boulder, Col.), v.23, no.3, 1963, p.
313-332. See serials consulted.

5626. --- Sovietinio kolonializmo
25 metai. [Twenty-five years of
Soviet colonialism] In Aidai
(Brooklyn, N.Y.), no.6(181), 1965,
p. 249-259. See serials consulted.

5627. THE VIOLATIONS OF HUMAN
rights in Soviet occupied Lithuania;
a report for 1971. Prepared by Lithuanian American Community, Inc.,
February 16, 1972. [Chicago, Ill.,
1972] 64 p. DK511.L274V55 PU

5628. ---; a report fro 1972.
Prepared by Lithuanian American Com-
munity, Inc., February 16, 1973.
[Chicago, Ill., 1973] 88 p.
DK511.L274V56 PU

X.9.o. COMMUNISM IN LITHUANIA

X.9.o.1. GENERAL STUDIES

5629. ANDREEV, A. M. Bor'ba litovskago naroda za Sovetskuiu vlast', 1918-1919 gg. [Moskva] Gos. izd-vo polit. lit-ry, 1954. 162 p. DK511.L26A7 DLC CaBVaS CaOTU InU NIC NNC NcD WU

5630. BOR'BA ZA SOVETSKUIU PRIBAL-tiku v Velikoi otechestvennoi voine, 1941-1945. [Avtorskii kollektiv: P.D. Grishchenko i dr. Sostaviteli: G.A. Gurin i dr.] Riga, Liesma, 1966-1967. 3 v. D764.7.B3B6 DLC CaAEU(2) IEN PU

5631. BOR'BA ZA SOVETSKUIU VLAST' v Litve v 1918-1920 gg.; sbornik dokumentov. [Sostaviteli: A. Gaigalaite i dr. Redaktsionnaia kollegiia: B. Vaitkevichius i dr.] Vil'nius, Mintis, 1967. 473 p. (Iz istorii Grazhdanskoi voiny v SSSR) Bibliography: p. 404-[406] DK511.L27B59 DLC CaAEU CaBVaU CaNBFU CaOHM CaOTU CtY HU ICU IEN InU InNd KU MH MU NIC NcD NcU NjP NSyU NBuU OKentU OrU PPiU PU RPB TU ViU WU WaU

5632. BOR'BA ZA SOVETSKUIU VLAST' v Pribaltike. [Redkollegiia: I.I. Mints i dr.] Moskva, Nauka, 1967. 627 p. illus., facsims., ports. Bibliography: p. [586]-607. Summary in English. DK511.B3B59 DLC CaAEU CaOTU IU MiDW MU PU

5633. BUTRIMIENĖ, A. Visuomeninių organizacijų vaidmuo išplėstinės komunizmo statybos laikotarpiu, remiantis Lietuvos TSR medžiaga. [The role of public organizations during the period of growth of communism in Lithuania] Vilnius, Valstybinė politinės ir mokslinės literatūros leidykla, 1963. 39 p. HX315.65.B8 DLC

5634. DIRBTI IR GYVENTI KOMUNISTIŠ kai; dokumnetai ir medžiaga apie judėjimą uš komunistinį darbą Tarybų Lietuvoje, 1958-1964. [... documents and sources related to the movement for the communistic work in Soviet Lithuania, 1958-1964. Ats. redaktorius S. Atamukas] Vilnius, Mintis, 1965. 331 p. illus., ports. HC337.L5D5 DLC

DIRVELĖ, Eugenijus. Klasių kova Lietuvoje. Vilnius, 1961. See entry no. 3462.

5635. GIRDŽIUS-KLAUSUTIS, Jonas. Raudonieji viduramžiai, tai yra dvi-

dešimtojo amžiaus vidurio raganų medžionės kronika. [Red Middle Ages; or, Witchhunt in the middle of the twentieth century] London [Santarvė] 1957. 301 p. HX237.G5 MiD OCl

5636. IDEOLOGINIS DARBAS KAIME. [The communistic work in the rural areas. Sudarė S. Šimkus] Vilnius, Mintis, 1966. 174 p. JN6745.A98K698 DLC

5637. JABLONSKIS, Konstantinas, ed. Lietuvos darbo žmonių kova dėl Tarybų valdžios, 1917-1919. [The struggle of the Lithuanian working class for the Soviet government in 1917-1919] Vilnius, 1958. 324 p. DLC

5638. JURGINIS, Juozas, ed. Už socialistinę Lietuvą. [Pro socialist Lithuania] Redakcinė kolegija: J. Jurginis, R. Šarmaitis, J. Žiugžda (Vyr. red.) Vilnius, VPMLL, 1960. 294 p. At head of title: Lietuvos TSR Mokslų akademija, Vilna. Istorijos institutas. Nx55R78 960J CtY CtPAM

5639. KAPLANAS, O. Jaunieji leninečiai; iš Lietuvos pionierių organizacijos. [The young Leninists; from the organization of the Lithuanian Pioneers] Vilnius, VPMLL, 1963. 69 p. illus., ports. HQ799.R92L54 DLC MH

5640. KAPSUKAS, Vincas. Pirmoji Lietuvos proletarinė revoliucija ir tarybų valdžia. [The first Lithuanian proletarian revolution and the Soviet Government] 2. leidimas. Vilnius, VPMLL, 1958. 233 p. illus. DK511.L26K28 1958 DLC ICBM OKentU PU

5641. --- Raštai. [Works of V. Kapsukas] Vilnius, VGLL, 1960-70. 9 v. illus. At head of title, v.1-8: Partijos istorijos institutas prie Lietuvos KP CK, Marksizmo-leninizmo instituto prie TSKP CK filialas. HX315.65K25 DLC CtPam(1) CtY IU NN(1-3, 5)

5642. LENINAS IR LIETUVA. [Lenin and Lithuania] Dokumentai apie V. Lenino ryšius su Lietuvos revoliucinio judėjimo dalyviais. Redakcinė komisija: S. Juonienė, R. Šarmaitis, B. Vaitkevičius. Vilnius, 1969. 229 p. DK254.I42L389 PU

5643. LENINIZMO PERGALĖ LIETUVOJE. [The victory of Leninism in Lithuania. Atsakingasis redaktorius M. Burokevičius] Vilnius, 1970. 375 p. DK511.L2I45 PU

5644. LIAUKONIS, Alvydas. F. Dzeržinskio revoliucinė veikla Lietuvoje. [F. Dzerzhinski as a revolutionary in Lithuania] Vilnius, VPMLL, 1961. 54 p. DK268.D9L45 DLC

5645. MASIŲ ORGANIZATORIAI; iš instruktorių grupių patyrimo. [The organizers of the masses...] Vilnius, VPMLL, 1957. 78 p. S469.L5M3 DLC MH

5646. NOREIKA, A. Į pagalbą komjaunimo aktyvistui. [Pro help for the Communist Youth organization activist] Vilnius, VPMLL, 1961. 94 p. HQ799.L5N6 DLC

5647. OCHMAŃSKI, Jerzy. Rewolucyjna działalność Feliksa Dzierżyńskiego na Litwie w końcu XIX wieku. Poznań [Uniwersytet im. Adama Mickiewicza] 1969. 113 p. illus., facsims., ports. (Poznań, Uniwersytet. Prace Wydziału Filosoficzno-Historycznego. Seria Historia, no. 28) Summary in Russian. DK268.D9.O44 CaOTU PU

5648. POLITINIS-MASINIS DARBAS; iš kaimiškųjų partinių organizacijų darbo patyrimo. [The political work; from the experience of work among the rural party organizations] Vilnius, VPMLL, 1963. 127 p. JN6598.K7P55 DLC

5649. POŽĖLA, Karolis. Raštai. [Works of K. Požėla. Sudarė ir spaudai paruošė J. Lebedys] Vilnius, Mintis, 1966. 478 p. illus., facsims., ports. HX315.65.A6P6 1966 DLC CtY MH PU

SHKLIAR, Evgeniia Nikiforovna. Bor'ba trudiashchykhsia Litovsko-Belorusskoi SSR s inostrannymi interventami i vnutrennei kontrrevoliutsiei, 1919-1920 gg. Minsk, 1962. See entry no. 5436.

5650. ŠILBAJORIS, Rimvydas Pranas. Stepchildren of communism. In Lituanus (Brooklyn, N.Y.), no.2(11), June 1957, p. 3-8. See serials consulted.

5651. ŠKLIARSKAITĖ, Feigė. V. Kapsuko kova prieš buržuazinę idealogiją Lietuvoje. [The struggle of V. Kapsukas against the bourgeois idealogy in Lithuania] Vilnius, VPMLL, 1962. 174 p. DK511.L28K34 DLC NN OKentU ViU

5652. UŽ SOCIALIZMO SUKŪRIMĄ LIEtuvoje. Mokslinės konferencijos medžiaga, 1968 m. gruodžio 26-27 d. [A conference for the development of socialism in Lithuania; materials. Red. kolegija: M. Burokevičius (ats.

red.) ir kiti] Vilnius, 1969. 660 p. illus. JN6745.A98K76 DLC MH

5653. VAITKEVIČIUS, Bronius. Socialistinė revoliucija Lietuvoje 1918-1919 metais. [The Socialist revolution in Lithuania, 1918-1919] Vilnius, Mintis, 1967. 696 p. fold. map, ports. DK511.L27V29 DLC CtY MH NjP PU

5654. VETRY REVOLIUTSII. Sbornik vospominanii o proletarskoi revoliutsii, 1918-1919 gg. v Litve. [Sost. P. Shtaras] Vil'nius, Mintis, 1968. 308 p. illus. At head of title: Institut istorii partii pri TSK KP Litvy. Filial Instituta marksizma-leninizma pri TSK KPSS. DK511.L26V4 DLC CaOTU ICU InNd InU MH NIC NNC NcD NjP ViU

5655. VILNA. PARTIJOS ISTORIJOS INSTITUTAS. Lietuvos komjaunimas; straipsnių rinkinys. [Lithuanian communist youth; collection of articles. Ed. by R. Maliukevičius] Vilnius, VPMLL, 1962. 562 p. illus. HQ799.L5V5 DLC IU MH

5656. --- Literatūra ir menas kovoje del komunizmo; dokumentų rinkinys. [Literature and art in the struggle for communism; a collection of documents. Sudarė J. Zinkus] Vilnius, VGLL, 1962. 476 p. MH

5657. --- Proletarinė revoliucija Lietuvoje; 1918-1919 metų revoliucinių įvykių Lietuvoje dalyvių atsiminimai. [Proletarian revolution in Lithuania; memoires of the participants of the 1918-1919 revolutionary activities in Lithuania. Vyr. red. B. Vaitkevičius] Vilnius, VPMLL, 1960. 526 p. illus., ports., fold. map. At head of title: Partijos istorijos institutas prie LKP CK, Marksizmo-leninizmo instituto prie TSKP CK filialas. DK511.L26V48 DLC PU

5658. --- Revoliucinis judėjimas Lietuvoje; straipsnių rinkinys. [Revolutionary activities in Lithuania; collected articles. Rinkinį sudarė A. Kolodnas] Vilnius, VPMLL, 1957. 915 p. illus., ports., maps. At head of title: Partijos istorijos institutas prie LKP CK, Marksizmo-leninizmo instituto prie TSKP CK filialas. DK511.L27V46 DLC CSt-H CtY IU InU MH PU

5659. --- 40 let proletarskoi revoliutsii v Litve; sbornik statei. [Sostavitel' A. Kolodnas] Vil'nius, Gos izd-vo polit. i nauch. lit-ry, 1959. 261 p. ports., fold. map. At head of title: Partijos istorijos

institutas prie LKP CK, Marksizmo-
leninizmo instituto prie TSKP KPSS.
DK511.L26V5 DLC CLU CU CSt-H MH NNC
RPB

5660. YLA, Stasys (1908-   ). Ko-
munizmas Lietuvoje. [Communism in
Lithuania. By Juozas Daulius.
pseud.] Kaunas, 1937. 259 p.
DK511.L27Y4 DLC CtTMF ICCC ICBM
ICLJF PU

5661. ZIMANAS, Genrikas. Lietuvių socialistinės nacijos susifor-
mavimo prielaidos ir sąlygos. [As-
sumptions and conditions for the
formation of a Lithuanian socialist
nation] Vilnius, VPMLL, 1963. 71
p. HX315.65.Z5 DLC CtY MH

X.9.o.2. HISTORY OF THE COMMUNIST
PARTY

5662. ALEKSA-ANGARIETIS, Zigmas.
LKP įsikūrimas ir proletarinė revo-
liucija Lietuvoje, 1918-1919 m.
[The founding of the Lithuanian Com-
munist Party and the proletarian re-
volution of 1918-1919 in Lithuania.
Ats. red. B. Vaitkevičius   Vilnius,
VPMLL, 1962. 147 p. port.
JN6745.A98K685 DLC MH OKentU PU

5663. --- Už liaudies veiksmų
vienybę. [For the unity of peoples'
action. Red. kolegija: M. Burokevičius (ats. red.) ir kiti] Vilnius, Mintis, 1968. 379 p. 5 leaves
of illus. JN6745.A98K686 DLC

5664. ATAMUKAS, Solomonas. Kom-
partiia Litvy v bor'be za Sovetskuiu vlast', 1935-1940 gg. Moskva,
Gos. izd-vo polit. lit-ry, 1961.
262 p. JN6745.A98K69 DLC CaBVaU
CSt-H CtY IaU IEN ICU InU IU MH NIC
NNC NcU NjP WU

5665. BERŽINSKAITĖ, Anatolija.
LKP veikla auklėjant Lietuvos darbo
žmones proletarinio internacionaliz-
mo dvasia (1927-1940). [The activity of the Lithuanian Communist
party in 1927-1940 educating the
Lithuanian working class in the
spirit of proletarian internation-
alism] Vilnius, VPMLL, 1962. 149
p. JN6745.A98K693 DLC MH

5666. KOMMUNIST (Vilnius). Voprosy istorii Kommunisticheskoi
Partii Litvy; sbornik statei v
pomoshch' izuchaiushchim istoriiu
KPSS. Vil'nius, Gos. izd-vo polit.
i nauch lit-ry Litovskoi SSR, 1961.
221 p. fold. maps. JN6745.A98K7
DLC

5667. LIETUVOS KOMUNISTŲ PARTIJA.
Lietuvos Komunistų partijos atsišaukimai. [The proclamations of
the Lithuanian communist party]
Vilnius, VPMLL, 1962-63. 4 v. facsims. At head of title: Partijos
istorijos institutas prie Lietuvos
KP CK, Marksizmo-leninizmo instituto prie TKSP CK filialas.
JN6745.A98K6 DLC CtY(1-2, 4) MH NN
PU

5668. LIETUVOS KOMUNISTŲ PARTIJA.
CENTRO KOMITETAS. Ataskaitinis
pranešimas Lietuvos Komunistų partijos XII suvažiavime. Baigiamasis
žodis Lietuvos Komunistų partijos
XII suvažiavime. Lietuvos Komunistų
partijos XX suvažiavimo rezoliucija
dėl LKP Centro Komiteto ataskaitinio
pranešimo, priimto 1960 m. kovo 3 d.
[The report of the Central Committee
of the Lithuanian Communist Party
to the 12th Congress. The closing
address and the resolution of the
Lithuanian Communist party in connection with the report of the Central Committee to the 12th Congress]
Vilnius, Laikraščių ir žurnalų leidykla, 1960. 109 p. JN6745.A98K62
DLC MH

5669. --- Bol'she sel'skokhoziaist-
vennykh produktov sotsialisticheskoi
rodine; materialy IX plenuma TSK KP
Litvy [Doklad A. Snechkusa] Vil'-
nius, Gazetno-khudozh. izd-vo,
1960. 83 p. 338.047Z v.41 NNC MH

5670. --- Nutarimai idealoginiais
klausimais; LKP Centro Komiteto
1962-1963 m. priimtų nutarimų ideo-
loginiais klausimais išdėstymai.
[The decisions in the ideological
field by the Central Committee of
the Lithuanian Communist Party during the years 1962-1963] Vilnius,
Laikraščių ir žurnalų leidykla,
1964. 76 p. JN6745.A98K63 DLC

5671. --- Otchetnyi doklad na XII
S"ezde Kommunisticheskoi partii Litvy... Vil'nius, Gazetno-khudozhest-
venoe izd-vo, 1960. 109 p.
335.4L625 NNC MH

5672. --- Otchetnyi doklad TSentral'nogo Komiteta KP Litvy 10
s"ezda partii. Postanovlenie 10
s"ezda KP Litvy. Vil'nius, Gazetno-
zhurnal'noe izd-vo, 1958. 102 p.
JN6745.A98K65 DLC MH WU

5673. LIETUVOS KOMUNISTŲ PARTIJA.
SUVAŽIAVIMAS. S"ezd Kommunisticheskoi partii Litvy. Vil'nius, Gospolitnauchizdat. JN6745.A98K55 DLC
(13th)

5674. --- 9th, Vilna, 1956. Nutarimas. [Resolution] Vilnius, Laikraščių ir žurnalų leidykla, 1956. 15 p. JN6745.A98K66 1956 DLC

5675. --- 13th, Vilna, 1961. Lietuvos Komunistų partijos XII suvažiavimas. [The Thirteenth Congress of the Lithuanian Communist Party] Vilnius, Valstybinė politinės ir mokslinės literatūros leidykla, 1961. 154 p. JN6745.A98K66 1961 DLC CSt-H

5676. --- 14th, Vilna, 1964. Lietuvos Komunistų partijos XIV suvažiavimas. [The Fourteenth Congress of the Lithuanian Communist Party] Vilnius, Laikraščių ir žurnalų leidykla, 1964. 105 p. JN6745.A98K66 1964 DLC MH

5677. --- 15th, Vilna, 1966. XV S"ezd Kommunisticheskoi partii Litvy. Vil'nius, Gazetno-zhurnal'noe izd-vo, 1966. 95 p. HC337.L5L5 NNC

5678. LKP ISTORIJOS KLAUSIMAI. Voprosy Litovskoi KP. 1961- . Vilnius, Mintis [etc.] At head of title: Lietuvos TSR Aukštųjų mokyklų mokslo darbai. Lithuanian and Russian with summaries in other languages. HX315.65.A6L5 DLC(2-) MH(1-) NNC

5679. LOPAEV, Safronii Semenovich. Lietuvos Komunistų partijos idėjinis ir organizacinis stiprėjimas, 1919-1924. [The ideological and organizational consolidation of the Lithuanian Communist party in 1919-1924] Vilnius, VPMLL, 1964. 108 p. JN6745.A98K72 DLC CSt NN

5680. NIUNKA, Vladas. Lietuvos Komunistų partijos kova už darbininkų ir valstiečių sąjungos stiprinimą pereinamuoju iš Kapitalizmo į socializmą laikotarpiu. [The struggle of the communist party for the strengthening of the Union between workers and peasants in the transitory period from capitalism to socialism] In Komunistas (Vilnius), no.3, 1955, p. 18-31. See serials consulted.

5681. OLEKAS, Pranas. LKP kova už socialistinį žemės ūkio pertvarkymą tarybų Lietuvoje. [The struggle of the Lithuanian Communist Party for agrarian reform in Soviet Lithuania] Vilnius, Mintis, 1966. 148 p. HD1995.65.04 DLC CtY MH

5682. REMELIENĖ, Antanina (Butkutė). Lietuvos komunistų partijos kova už tarybų valdžios įtvirtinimą respublikoje, 1940-1941 m. [The Lithuanian Communist Party in a

struggle for the establishment of Soviet government in Lithuania] Vilnius, VPMLL, 1958. 206 p. DK511.L27B8 PU IU MH OKentU

5683. REMEIKIS, Thomas. The Communist Party of Lithuania; a historical and political study. Urbana, Ill., 1964. 550 p. Thesis--University of Illinois. Microfilm copy. Positive no.64-2949. Ann Arbor, Mich. CLU(Microfilm)

5684. ŠTARAS, Povilas. Rol' KP Litvy v organizatsii i razvitii partizanskoi bor'by. In Gitlerovskaia okkupatsiia v Litve. Vil'nius, 1966. D802.L5G5 DLC CaAEU CaBVaS CaBVaU CaNSHD CtY IaU InNd InU ICU IEN IU MH MnU MU NIC NcD NcU NjP NSyU OrU PPiU TU WU WaU

5685. SUDAVIČIUS, Bronius. LKP kova už darbininkų klasės vienybę, 1934-1937 metais. [The struggle of the Lithuanian Communist Party in 1934-1937 for the unity of the working people] Vilnius, Valstybinė politinės ir mokslinės literatūros leidykla, 1961. 152 p. illus. JN6745.A98K75 DLC

5686. VILNA. LIETUVOS TSR VALSTYBINĖ RESPUBLIKINĖ BIBLIOTEKA. Lietuvos komunistų partijos ir 1918-1919 metų proletarinės revoliucijos Lietuvoje 40-sios metinės; bibliografinės ir metodinės medžiagos rinkinys. [The Lithuanian Communist Party and its revolution in 1918-1919; a bibliography. Sudarė E. Lagauskienė ir R. Martinaitienė. Red. St. Elsbergas ir St. Tomonis] Kaunas, 1958. 117 p. Balt 8180.15 MH

X.9.o.3. REVOLUTIONISTS; THEIR PER
SONAL NARRATIVES, ME
MOIRS AND REMINISCENCES

5687. ALEKSANDRAVIČIŪTĖ, L. Negaliu užmiršti. [I can't forget it. Literatūrinis bendraautorius E. Zeifas] Vilnius, Vaga, 1964. 299 p. ports. HX315.65A8A79 DLC CtY MH

5688. BANAITIS, Vladas. Už akmeninių sienų. [Behind the stone walls. Literatūrinis bendraautorius F. Vaišnoras] Vilnius, Vaga, 1969. 164 p. ports. HX315.65.B32 PU CtY

5689. BARANAUSKAS, B. Devyniolika metų pogrindyje. [Nineteen years in the underground] Vilnius, Vaga, 1965. 242 p. facsims., ports.

DK511.L27B34 DLC CtY IU MH

5690. BILEVIČIUS, Elijas. Neda-
rom proshedshye gody. [Kaunas,
1959] 277 p. illus. CT1218.B5A3
DLC

5691. BORIKAS, S. Krauju sutvir-
tinta draugystė; dokumentinė apybraiža. [Friendship strengthened
with blood; a documental outline]
Vilnius, Mintis, 1966. 78 p.
D811.B6815 DLC CtY NN

5692. BRIGMANAS, Viktoras. Ma-
čiau saulėtekį. [I saw the sun-
rise. Literatūriniai bendraautoriai
P. Kirienka ir E. Vaserdamas] Vilnius, Vaga, 1964. 244 p.
HX315.65.A8B7 DLC IEN PU

5693. BUDINAS, Domas. Vėtros
Žemaičiuose; atsiminimai. [Storm
over the Žemaitija (Samogitia); re-
collections] Vilnius, VPMLL, 1959.
266 p. illus. DK511.L27B77 DLC PU

5694. DIDŽIULIS, Karolis. Už
liaudies laimę; atsiminimai, laiškai,
kalbos. [For the peoples' happiness;
recollections, letters and speeches]
Vilnius, VPMLL, 1963. 357 p.
illus., ports. HX315.65.D5 DLC

5695. GAŠKA, Ignas. Kovų augin-
tiniai. [Trainees from the struggle for communism. Literatūrinis
bendraautorius F. Vaišnoras] Vilnius, Vaga, 1965. 201 p. illus.,
ports. HX315.65.A6G3 DLC CtY IEN
IU MH OKentU PU

5696. JACOVSKIS, E. Už grotų; iš
buržuazinės Lietuvos kalėjimo istorijos. [Behind the bars; from the
history of Lithuanian jails] Vilnius, Mintis, 1965. 418 p. illus.,
facsims, ports. HV9715.65.J2 DLC
CtY

5697. KAPLANAS, O. Deviatyi fort
obviniaet. [Perevod s litovskogo]
Snimki i fotoreproduktsii P. Kaplanasa. Khudozhnik V. Kalinauskas.
Vil'nius, Gos. izd-vo polit. i nauch.
lit-ry Litovskoi SSR, 1962. 57 p.
illus. D805.L85K3 DLC

5698. --- --- 3., dop. izd. Vil'-
nius, Mintis, 1964. 58 p. illus.
D805.L85K3 1964 DLC NNC

5699. --- --- [4. izd. Perevod s
litovskogo] Vil'nius, Mintis, 1966.
58 p. illus. Balt 8100.01 MH

5700. KONDRATAS, Z. IX fort.
[Perevod s litovskogo M. Shul'kina]
Vil'nius, Gos. izd-vo polit. i nauch.
lit-ry Litovskoi SSR, 1961. 54 p.

illus. D805.L85K67 DLC MH NN NNC

5701. KAROSAS, Jonas. Kalba Vilniaus akmenys; iš 1926-1931 m. atsiminimų. [The stones of Vilnius
are speaking; recollections from
1926-1931] Vilnius, VGLL, 1963.
327 p. ports. DK651.V4K3 DLC CtY
MH NN

5702. --- Mówią kamienie Wilna.
Przekł. z litewskiego Anny Lau-Gnia-
dowskiej. [Wyd.1. Warszawa] Książka i Wiedza, 1968. 365 p.
DK651.V4K36 DLC NjP MH

5703. KUČINSKAS, Domas. Mirtinin-
kų vienutėje. [In the death cell.
Literatūrinis bendraautoris P. Mar-
gevičius] Vilnius, Vaga, 1964.
261 p. illus., facsims., ports.
HV8964.L5K8 DLC IEN NNC

5704. MACEVIČIUS, K. Ilgai bran-
dintas grūdas. [The growth of communism in Lithuania] Vilnius, Vaga,
1964. 321 p. ports. DK511.L28M33A3
CtY CtPAM IEN MH OKentU

5705. MACIJAUSKAS, Jonas. Saulė
leidžias, saulė teka; atsiminimai.
[...; recollections. Literatūrinis
bendraautorius: P. Margevičius]
Vilnius, VGLL, 1961. 285 p. illus.
DK511.L28M3 DLC CtPAM

5706. OLEKAS, J. Neramios naktys.
[Disturbed nights. Literatūrinis
bendraautorius V. Černeckis] Vilnius, Vaga, 1964. 238 p. ports.
DK802.L5.04 DLC CaOTU CtY IEN MH

5707. PAPLAUSKAS, J. Negreit
išaušo diena. [The day didn't soon
come] Vilnius, VGLL, 1963. 212 p.
ports. CtPAM

5708. STIMBURYS, Juozas. Drugoi
zhizni u menia net; vospominaniia.
Vil'nius, Gos. izd-vo khud. lit-ry
Litovskoi SSR, 1961. 330 p. illus.,
ports. CT1215.L2S85A3 ICU MH NN NNC
NcD NjP

5709. VILNA. PARTIJOS ISTORIJOS
INSTITUTAS. Vil'niusskoe podpol'e;
vospominaniia uchastnikov revoliutsionnogo dvizheniia v Vil'niusskom
krae, 1920-1939 gg. Otv. red. R.
Maliukevičius. Vil'nius, Vaga,
1966. 394 p. illus., facsims.
HX315.65.A6V5 MH CaAEU CaBVaS CtY
DLC IEN NcD NcU NjP PU ViU

X.9.o.4. SECRET POLICE ACTIVITIES; GENOCIDE, DEPORTATIONS, AND THE FORCED LABOUR CAMPS

5710. ARMONAS, Barbara. Leave your tears in Moscow, by Barbara Armonas as told to A.L. Nasvytis. 1st ed.] Philadelphia, Pa., Lippincott, [1961] 222 p. illus. HV8959.R9A75 DLC CaAEU CaOTU CtPAM NSyU PU

5711. BARAS, K., pseud. Bolševizmo siaubas Lietuvoje. [Ką pasakoja persekiojimų ir teroro ištremtasis. Soviet terror in Lithuania] Chicago, Ill., A.L.R.K. federacijos leidinys, 1941. 64 p. DK511.L27B36 DLC CtTMF MH PPULC PU

5712. BIELINIS, Kipras. Teroro ir vergijos imperija Sovietų Rusija. [Soviet Russia the empire of terror and slavery] New York, N.Y., Išleista lietuvių socialdemokratų sąjungngos, literatūros fondo lėšomis, 1963. 309 p. illus., ports, maps. HV8964.R8B46 DLC CtY CtPAM ICU MH NN OCl PU

5713. CHMIELIAUSKAS, Anatolijus. Mirties kolona; prie Červenės nužudytiems atminti. [March towards death; to commemorate those massacred near Červenė. By] Antanas Tolis [pseud.] Chicago, Ill., Draugas, 1947. 252 p. 947.5.C457 PU ICLJF

5714. ČIBIRAS, Kazimieras. El imperio del genocidio; [las deportaciones y la esclavitud en el mundo soviético, por] Casimiro Verax [pseud. Medellin] Impresos internationales, 1954. 133 p. illus. HV8964.R8C5 DLC NBuU

5715. CONQUEST, Robert. The Soviet deportation of nationalities. London, Macmillan; New York, N.Y., St. Martin's Press, 1960. 203 p. illus. DK33.C6 DLC CaAEU CaBVaU ClU CLSU CSt CSt-H CU CtY CtY-L DS FU IaU ICU InU IEN MH MeWC MiU MnU MsSM NIC NN NNC-L NcGN NcD NcU NjP NjR NRU OCl OClW OCU OkU OU OOxM PBL RPB ScU TNJ TxU ViU WaU

5716. DOGELIS, Povilas. Kalėjimuose pas bolševikus. [In the Soviet prisons] Kaunas, 1930. 160 p. 947.5.D675 PU CtTMF OCl

5717. GERVYDAS, A., pseud. Už spygliuotų vielų. [Behind barbed wire] Chicago, Ill., Lietuvių katalikų spaudos draugija, 1950. 221 p. illus. (Leidinys, nr. 2) Author's real name: Antanas Kučas. D805.G3G47 DLC

CaAEU CaOONL CtTMF ICLJF MH OKentU PU

JASAITIS, Domas. Nationalsocialistinis ir komunistinis genocidas Lietuvoje. In Lietuvių katalikų mokslo akademija, Roma. Suvažiavimo darbai, v.6, 1969, p. [367]-424. See serials consulted.

5718. JURGAITIS, Kazys. Pokarinės deportacijos Lietuvoje. [The deportations after the Second World War in Lithuania] In Į Laisvę (Los Angeles, Calif.), no.31, 1963, p.24-29. See serials consulted.

5719. KAELAS, Aleksander. Human rights and genocide in the Baltic States. A statement submitted to the delegations to the United Nations General Assembly, September 1950. Stockholm, Estonian Information Bureau, 1950. iii, 57 p. IC599.B3K3 DLC CtY DGU DS NN PU

5720. KALME, Albert. Sovjets blodbåd i Baltikum i dokumentarisk belysning. Stockholm, Natur och Kultur [1946] 284 p. illus., ports. DK511.B3K2 DLC NN

5721. --- Total terror; an exposé of genocide in the Baltics. New York, N.Y., Appleton-Century-Crofts [1951] vii, 310 p. illus. DK511.B3K23 DLC CU DS MB MiU NN TxU ViU

5722. NARBUTAS, Titas. Išlikom gyvi; vaizdai iš bolševikų okupacijos. [We succeeded in staying alive... By] T. Angelaitis [pseud.] Putnam, Conn. Immaculata press, 1960. 188 p. 891.92.N168I PU DLC OCl OKentU WU

5723. PADAUBIETIS, J., pseud. Telšių kankiniai. [The martyrs of Telšiai] Pittsburgh, Pa., Lietuvių žinios, 1949. 99 p. illus. Author's real name: Kazys Mockus. D804.R9P25 DLC CaOONL CtTMF ICLJF OKentU PU

5724. PAKŠTAS, Kazys. Colonialism and genocide in Lithuania. In Lituanus (Brooklyn, N.Y.), v.6, no.3, 1960, p.98-103. See serials consulted.

5725. --- Genocido poveikis Lietuvos gyventojams. [The influence of genocide on Lithuania's population] In Draugas (Chicago, Ill.), May 7 and May 14, 1960. See serials consulted.

5726. PELĖKIS, K., pseud. Genocide; Lithuania's treefold tragedy. Edited by Rumšaitis [pseud. n.p.] "Venta", 1949. 286 p. illus., maps,

facsims. Bibliography: p. 279-281.
DK511.L27P4 DLC CaOTP ICBM ICU ICLJF
IU MH NSyU OCl OKentU PU

5727. PERANDI, Adolf. Another
crime; Soviet acts of genocide
against Baltic nations. In Baltic
Review (New York, N.Y.), no.2-3,
1954, p. 25-51. See serials consulted.

5728. PETRUITIS, Jonas. Kaip jie
mus sušaudė. [How they executed us]
3. leidimas. Bad-Salzuflen, Ger.,
Dröge & Eggert, 1952. 221 p.
D805.R9P38 DLC MiD MH OCl PU CaAEU

5729. PFEIL, Elizabeth. Hunger,
Hass und gute Hände; Erlebnisse und
Begegnungen jenseits der Memel. Göt-
tingen, Elchland Verlag, 1956. 48 p.
(Kleine Elchland Reihe, 1) DD901.
K8P5 DLC CSt-H NN NIC PU

5830. PRUNSKIS, Joseph. Fifteen
"liquidated" priests in Lithuania.
Chicago, Ill., 1943. 16 p. ports.
BX1559.L5P86 DLC CtTMF ICBM MH PU

5831. --- Sibiro ištremime ir bolševikų kalėjime. [In exile in Siberia and in the Soviet prisons. Chicago, Ill.] A. Gilienė [1944] 20 p.
ports. BX4690.L5P7 DLC CaOONL
CtTMF

5732. RASTENIS, Vincas. Lietuvos
jaunimo genocidas. [Genocide of
youth in Lithuania] In Lietuva (New
York, N.Y.), no.7, 1955, p. 50-52,79.
See serials consulted.

5733. RIMAŠAUSKAS, Jonas. A look
behind the Iron-Curtain; exhibit of
genocide in Lithuania. n.p., 1951.
52 p. illus. 950.5R ICBM

5734. RŪKIENĖ, Stefanija. Vergijos kryžkeliuose; Sibiro tremtinės
užrašai. [Memoirs of the lady ba-
nished to Siberia] [Cleveland, Ohio]
Viltis, 1968. 2 v. HV8959.R9R85 PU
CaOONL DLC

5735. RUPEJKO, Pranas. Progress
of the extermination of the Baltic
nations, 1940-1950. In Eastern Quarterly (London), v.5, no.1-2, 1952,
p. 33-40. See serials consulted.

5736. RUSSIA. (1923-) NARODNYI
KOMISARIAT VNUTRENNYKH DEL. 34 secret documents issued by the People's Commissariat's for Internal
Affairs and State security pertaining to mass arrests, exile and deportation to corrective labour camps
from Lithuania in 1941. New York,
N.Y., Public Library, 1947. 1 reel
of microfilm. Film 1905 PU NN

5737. ŠILDE, Ādolfs. Balten und
Deutsche in sowjetischen Gefangenla-
gern. In Baltische Gesellschaft in
Deutschland. Die baltischen Völker
in ihrer europäischen Verpflichtung.
Hannover-Döhren, 1958. p. 50-54.
DK511.B3B285 DLC PU

5738. --- The profits of slavery.
Baltic forced laborers and deportees
under Stalin and Khrushchev. Stock-
holm, Latvian National Foundation
in Scandinavia, 1958. 302 p.
HV8931.R9S58 CaAEU CLU CU CtY DLC DS
ICU IEN InU MB MH MiD MnU MiU MdBJ
NIC NN NNC NcU NRU NhU OU OCl RPB
TxU ViU

5739. LA SITUATION EN LITHUANIE.
In Revue parlementaire (Paris),
no.13, 1947, p. 97-98, no.14, 1948,
p. 6-8. Contents.--Situation économique.--Russification et bolshevisa-
tion.--Arrestations, déportations.--
La situation de l'église.--Le maquis.
HC10.R4 DLC MnU NN

5740. SLAVĖNAS, Julius Paulius.
Deportations. In Lituanus (Brooklyn,
N.Y.), v.6, no.2, 1960, p. 47-52.

5741. SŪDUVIS, N.E., pseud. Ein
kleines Volk wird ausgelöscht, brau-
ne und rote Staatspolizei am Werk;
die Tragödie Litauens. Zürich, Thomas Verlag, 1947. 99 p. (Politische
Sriftenreihe) DK511.L27S9 DLC CaAEU
CSt-H ICLJF IEN InU MnU

5742. SUPREME LITHUANIAN COMMITTEE
OF LIBERATION. Appeal to the United
Nations on Genocide. [Germany] Li-
thuanian Foreign Service [1951] 80
p. DK511.L27S94 DLC CLU CSt-H DLL
ICBM MH NNC OKentU

5743. --- Les martyrs de Lithuanie.
[Memmingen, Ger., 1954] 63 p.
D804.R9S85 DLC CaAEU MH NN PU

5744. TAUTVAIŠIENĖ, Hilda. The cemetery of Nations in the Siberian
tundra. London, Nida, 1968. 112 p.
D805.R9T37

5745 --- Tautų kapinynas Sibiro
tundroje. [The cemetery of Nations
in the Siberian tundra] New York,
N.Y., 1962. 135 p. illus., maps
"Bielinis, K. Papildymas": p. 107-
129. D805.R9T36 DLC CaOTP CtY MiD
NN OKentU PU

5746. UNITED STATES. CONGRESS.
HOUSE. COMMITTEE ON FOREIGN AFFAIRS.
Subcommittee on State Department Organization and Foreign Operations.
Attempted defection by Lithuanian
seaman Simas Kudirka. Hearings, Ni-
nety-first Congress, Second Session.

Washington, D.C., Govt. Print. Off., 1971. 247 p. ports.
JX4345.L7U58 CaAEU DLC

5747. --- Report on the hearings held by the Subcommittee on December 3, 7-9, 14, 18 and 29, 1970 pursuant to H.Res. 143. 91st Congress, Second Session. Washington, D.C., Govt. Print. Off., 1971. 10 p.
JX4345.L7U58 CaAEU DLC

5748. VAITIEKŪNAS, Vytautas. On the occasion of the 30th anniversary of the first mass deportation from the Soviet occupied Lithuania. In Lituanus (Chicago, Ill.), v.17, no.2, 1971, p. 5-26. See serials consulted.

5749. --- Sovietinis genocidas. [Soviet type genocide] In Lietuva (New York, N.Y.), no.6, 1954, p. 106-113. See serials consulted.

5750. VYTENIS, A. The Red Star. Fifty-two authentic photographs on Soviet atrocities in Lithuania. [n.p.] 1950. 1 v. (unpaged)
947.5.V998 PU

5751. WIELHORSKI, Władysław. Wspomnienia z przeżyć w niewoli sowieckiej. Londyn, Orbis [1965] 140 p. D805.R9W38 PU

X.9.o.5. RUSSIFICATION OF LITHUANIA

5752. BUKŠS, Mikelis. Die Russifizierung in der baltischen Ländern. München, Latgalischer Verlag, 1964. 203 p. (Das Latgalische Forschungsinstitut. Serie A: Abhandlungen) Bibliography: p. 11-16.
DK511.B295B8 DLC CU MH NN

5753. GERUTIS, Albertas. Gedanken zur sowjetischen Russifizierungspolitik im Baltikum. In Acta Baltica (Königstein in Taunus), v.5, 1965, p. 9-35. See serials consulted.

5754. RASTENIS, Vincas. The russification of non-Russian peoples in the Russian Empire: under the Czars and under the Soviets. In Lituanus (Brooklyn, N.Y.), v.5, no. 4, 1959, p. 103-107. See serials consulted.

5755. TAUTRIMAS, R., pseud. Rusifikacijos reiškiniai Lietuvoje. [The symptoms of russification in Lithuania] In Metmenys (Chicago, Ill.), no.14, p. 145-162. See serials consulted.

5756. VAITIEKŪNAS, Vytautas. Lie-

tuva atviro rusinimo kelyje. [Lithuania is openly exposed to russification] In I Laisvę (Los Angeles, Calif.), no.30(67), 1962, p. 1-10. See serials consulted.

X.9.o.6. THE CHURCH AND RELIGIOUS PERSECUTION IN SOVIET LITHUANIA

5757. BIELIŪNAS, Antanas. Lietuvos katalikų bažnyčia po bolševizmo jungu. [The Catholic Church in Lithuania under the yoke of communism] In Lietuvių archyvas. Kaunas, 1942. v.1, p. 66-73. DK511.L27L47 v.1 DLC PU

5758. BRIZGYS, Vincentas. Religious conditions in Lithuania under Soviet Russian occupation. [Chicago, Ill., Lithuanian Catholic Press, 1968] 40 p. BR937.L5B7 PU CaOONL MH OKentU PPULC

5759. COMMUNISM'S STRUGGLE WITH religion in Lithuania. In Lituanus (Brooklyn, N.Y.), v.9, no.1, 1963, p. 1-16. See serials consulted.

5760. DUBNAITIS, Evalds. Der Kampf gegen Religion und Geistlichkeit in den sowjetisierten baltischen Ländern: Estland, Lettland und Litauen. Königstein in Taunus, Institutum Balticum, 1966. 96 p. illus. BR1050.B32D8 CaOTU

5761. FREE EUROPE COMMITTEE. Religious persecution in the Baltic countries, 1940-1952. Edited by the Lithuanian, Latvian and Estonian sections. New York, N.Y., 1952. 26 p. BR937.B3F7 DLC

5762. GALTER, Albert. Libro rosso della Chiesa perseguitada, pubblicato sotto gli auspici della Commissione per la Chiesa perseguitata istituita dalle organizzazioni internazionali cattoliche. Milano, Ancora, 1956. 374 p. Translation of: "Le communisme et l'Eglise catholique" Bibliography: p. 361-366. NIC

5763. GELŽINIS, Martinas. Christenverfolgung in Litauen. Königstein-in Taunus, Ostpriesterhilfe [1957] 88 p. DCU MH-AH WU

5764. KLESMENT, Johannes. Sowjetische Kirchenpolitik in den besetzten Baltischen Staaten. In Acta Baltica (Königstein in Taunus), v.5, 1955, p. 112-126. See serials consulted.

5765. MAC EÓIN, Gary. The Commu-

nist war on religion. New York, N.Y.,
Devin-Adair, 1951. 264 p. "The
Baltic States": p. 170-187.
HX536.M28 DLC CtY-D MB MH NN NNJ
TxU ViU

5766. MUSTEIKIS, Antanas. Koeg-
zistencija ir religinė laisvė. [Co-
existance and religious freedom] In
LKMASD, v.6, 1969, p. [301]-316.
See serials consulted.

5767. NAMSONS, Andrivs. Die Lage
der katholischen Kirche in Sowjetli-
ttauen. In Acta Baltica (Königstein
in Taunus), v.1, 1961, p. 120-130.
See serials consulted.

5768. PAUKŠTELIS, T. "Freedom of
religion" Soviet style. In Lituanus
(Brooklyn, N.Y.), v.6, no.2, 1960,
p. 53-60. See serials consulted.

5769. --- Religion under Soviet
rule. In Lituanus (Brooklyn, N.Y.),
v.6, no.1, 1960, p. 2-7. See serials
consulted.

PRUNSKIS, Joseph. Fifteen
"liquideted" priests in Lithuania.
Chicago, Ill., 1943. See entry no.
5730.

5770. RAIŠUPIS, Matas. Dabarties
kankiniai; Lietuvos vyskupų, kunigų
ir tikinčiųjų kryžiaus kelias pirmoje ir antroje sovietų okupacijoje.
[Martyrs of today; ordeals of Lithuanian bishops, priests and parishio-
ners during the first and second Soviet occupation. Chicago, Ill., 1972.
436 p.] BX1559.L5R3 PU

5771. SAVASIS, Jonas, pseud. Kova prieš Dievą Lietuvoje. [Religi-
ous persecution in Lithuania. Putnam, Conn., Išleista P.M. Juro, 1963]
91 p. illus., ports. BL2747.3.S36
DLC CtTMF OKentU PU

5772. --- La lucha contra Dios en
Lituania; tr. del lituano por Antonio Trimakas. Mexico, Ascaola, 1964.
137 p. illus. 289.2.SA ICLJF

5773. --- Religious persecution in
Lithuania. In Baltic Review (New
York, N.Y.), no.31, 1966, p. 22-61;
no.32, 1966, p. 41-55. See serials
consulted.

5774. --- The war agaist God in
Lithuania. New York, N.Y., Manyland
Books [1966] 134 p. illus., map,
ports. BL2747.3.S3613 DLC CaOONL
CaOTU ICLJF MH OCl PPi PP PU

5775. TRAKIŠKIS, A. The situation
of the Church and religious practi-
ces in occupied Lithuania. New York,

N.Y., Lithuanian Bulletin, 1944.
36 p. BR937.L3T7 DLC CaOTU InNd MH
NIC NN NcD NNC OKentU PU

5776. VAITIEKŪNAS, Vytautas. Com-
munismo y religion; ilustrativo ejem-
plo de Lituania bajo la ocupación Soviética. In Revista Baltica (Buenos
Aires), 1957, p. 6-24. See serials
consulted.

5777. --- Genocide against the Roman Catholic Church in Lithuania.
In Baltic Review (New York, N.Y.),
no.2-3, 1954, p. 54-68. See serials
consulted.

5778. VIGNIERI, Vittorio. Soviet
policy toward religion in Lithuania;
the case of Roman Catholicism. In
Vardys, V.S., ed. Lithuania under
the Soviets. New York, N.Y., 1965.
p. 215-235. DK511.L27V35 DLC AzU
CSt CSt-H CU IC MoU MWalB MU PPi TU
WaU

5779. ŽYMANTAS, Stasys. The
Church and Soviet Communism; a Lithuanian example. In East and West
(London), no.1 1954, p. 34-41. See
serials consulted.

X.9.o.7. ATHEISM AND THE ANTI-RELI-
GIOUS PROGRAMS

5780. BARTNINKAS, Mindaugas. Laisvamanybė Lietuvoj. [The freethinking
(atheism) in Lithuania, 1924-1941]
Vilnius, VPMLL, 1964. 50, [2] p.
BL2765.L5B3 DLC

5781. BARZDAITIS, Juozas. Ateis-
mas Lietuvoje; trumpa istorinė apybraiža. [Atheism in Lithuania; a
short historical outline] Vilnius,
Mintis, 1967. 100 p. BL2747.3.B28
DLC

5782. ČEDAVIČIUS, Aleksas. Ateis-
tinis darbo žmonių auklėjimas. [A-
theistic education of working class]
Vilnius, Mintis, 1964. 93 p.
BL2747.3.C4 DLC

5783. ČIŽAS, Stasys, ed. Atverk
akis; ateistinio repertuaro rinkinys.
[Open your eyes; collection of atheistic works] Vilnius, Lietuvos TSR
Kultūros ministerijos liaudies meno
rūmai, 1962. 323 p. illus.
PG8713.C5 DLC

8784. DAGELIS, Alfonsas. Dvivei-
džiai. [Doublefaced] Vilnius, VPMLL,
1962. 167 p. facsims BX1775.L55D3
DLC

5785. JABLONSKIS, Algimantas. Kalba faktai; ateizmo vaizdinės priemonės. [Facts speak; the visual aids of atheism] [Vilnius, Mintis, 1965] 1 v. (chiefly illus.) BX1765.2.J25 DLC

5786. KAPSUKAS, Vincas. Veidmainių darbai. [Activities of the hypocrites. Ats. redaktorė V. Brazaitytė] Vilnius, VPMLL, 1961. 227 p. illus. BX1774.L55K3 DLC

5787. LIETUVOS TSR MOKSLŲ AKADEMIJA, VILNA. LIETUVIŲ LITERATŪROS INSTITUTAS. Lietuvių literatūra kovoje prieš klerikalizmą; literatūrinis rinkinys. [A bibliography of Lithuanian literature in the struggle against the church. Redagavo K. Korsakas. Vilnius] VGLL, 1951. 398 p. PG8713.L5 DLC PU

5788. MARKONIS, Stasys. Didžioji iliuzija. [The great illusion] Vilnius, VPMLL, 1963. 118 p. BX1775.L55M3 DLC CaOTP MH PU

5789. MINIUS, Jonas. Lietuva kryžių šešėliuose. [Lithuania in the shadows of the crosses. Laisvūnas, pseud.] Kaunas, Lietuvos laisvamanių etinės kultūros draugijos leidinys, 1936. 52 p. BR937.L3M5 DLC

5790. RAGAUSKAS, Jonas. Ite, missa est. 2. leidimas. Vilnius, VGLL, 1960. 518 p. BX1559.L5R3 1960 DLC CaOTP CtPAM NN OKentU PU

5791. --- Nenoriu dangaus. 2. leidimas. [I don't want heaven] Vilnius, VGLL, 1964. 419 p. BX1775.L55R3 DLC CtPAM

5792. VILNA. LIETUVOS TSR. VALSTYBINE RESPUBLIKINĖ BIBLIOTEKA. Biblioteka kovoje prieš religinius prietarus. [The library in the struggle against religious superstition. Rinkinį sudarė ir redagavo R. Kriaučiūnaitė ir P. Misevičienė. Ats. redaktorius P. Kizis] Kaunas, 1961. 79 p. illus. BL2780.K3 DLC MH

5793. VILNA. MOKYKLŲ MOKSLINIO TYRIMO INSTITUTAS. Mokinių ateistinio auklėjimo metodikos klausimai; straipsnių rinkinys. [On the question of the methods used for the students' atheistic education. Collection of articles. Sudarė: B. Bitinas] Kaunas, Valstybinė pedagoginės literatūros leidykla, 1962. 56 p. (Mokytojo bibliotekėlė] At head of title: LTSR Švietimo ministerija. Summary in Russian. BL2747.3.V5 DLC MH

5794. YLA, Stasys (1908-   ). Laisvamanybė Lietuvoje. [Atheism in

Lithuania. By] J. Daulius [pseud.] Kaunas, 1936. 56 p. BL2747.3.Y55 1936a PU(Xerox copy)

X.10. UNDERGROUND MOVEMENT AND RESISTANCE AGAINST THE INCORPORATION INTO THE SOVIET UNION

5795. AUDĖNAS, Juozas. Lietuvos partizanų kovos. [The combats of Lithuanian partisans] In Varpas (Brooklyn, N.Y.), no.5, 1963, p. 55-87. See serials consulted.

5796. BRAZAITIS, Juozas. Rezistencija Lietuvoje. [Guerrilla warfare in Lithuania] In Lietuva (New York, N.Y.), no.8, 1956, p. 1-11,93. See serials consulted.

5797. BURŽUAZINIŲ NACIONALISTŲ gaujų siautėjimas Dzūkijoje. [Guerrilla warfare in Dzūkija. Spaudai paruošė V. Ditkevičius, redagavo Z. Vasiliauskas] Vilnius, Mintis, 1964. 231 p. (Archyviniai dokumentai, 6 rinkinys) DK511.L2A23 vol.6 DLC MH

5798. DAUMANTAS, Juozas, pseud. Partizanai už geležinės uždangos. [Partisans behind the Iron Curtain] Chicago, Ill., Lietuvių katalikų spaudos draugija, 1950. 398 p. illus. (Lietuvių Katalikų Spaudos Draugija. Leidinys, nr. 5) Author's real name is Juozas Lukša. D802.L5D3 1950 DLC CtTMF ICBM ICLJF NB NN MH PU

5799. --- Partizanai. 2., papildytas leidimas. [Guerrillas. 2nd enlarged edition] [Chicago, Ill., 1962] 510 p. illus. (Į laisvę fondas lietuviškai kultūrai ugdyti. Leidinys nr. 3) D802.L5D3 1962 DLC CtY CtPAM ICBM PU

5800. DAUNYS, Stasys. The development of resistance and the national revolt against the Soviet regime in Lithuania in 1940-41. In Lituanus (Brooklyn, N.Y.), v.8, no.1-2, 1962, p. 11-16. See serials consulted.

IVINSKIS, Zenonas. Lithuania during the war; resistance against the Soviet and the Nazi occupants. See entry no. 5542.

5801. KAPAČINSKAS, Juozas. Siaubingos dienos; 1944-1950 metų atsiminimai. [The terrible days, 1944-

1950] Chicago, Ill., Lietuvių literatūros draugija, 1965. 273 p.
947.5.K147 PU ICLJF

5802. LIETUVOS TSR MOKSLŲ AKADE-
MIJA, VILNA. ARCHYVINIAMS DOKUMEN-
TAMS SKELBTI REDAKCIJA. Krūvinos
žudikų pėdos; nacionalistų anti-
liaudinė veikla pietinėje Žemaitijos
dalyje. [The movement in Žemaitija
of nationalists against the Communist regime. Sudarė R. Čepas. Red.
Z. Vasiliauskas. Vilnius, Mintis,
1968. 331 p. illus. (Its Archy-
vinai dokumentai, 9 rinkinys)
DK511.L2A23 v.9 OKentU Balt 8682.1
MH

5803. --- Žudikai bažnyčios prie-
globstyje. [Murderers in the Church
Sanctuary. Rinkinį paruošė B. Baranauskas ir G. Erslavaitė] Vilnius,
VPMLL, 1963. 254 p. illus., facsims. (Archyviniai dokumentai, 2.
rinkinys) DK511.L2A23 vol.2 DLC
CtPAM MH

5804. LUŠYS, Stasys. The emergence of United Lithuanian Resistance movement against occupants,
1940-1943. Lituanus (Chicago, Ill.)
v.9, no.4, 1963, p. 123-127. See
serials consulted.

5805. MUSTEIKIS, Antanas. Re-
sentment and resistance in Lithuania. New York, Free Europe Committee, 1954. 23 p. (Study no.
308) Microfilm 2551 DLC

5806. PIERCING THE IRON CURTAIN;
a westward mission of an envoy of
the Lithuanian Underground. In
Lithuanian Bulletin (New York, N.Y.),
v.6, no.5-7, 1948, p. 1-10. See
serials consulted.

5807. REMEIKIS, Thomas. The
armed struggle against the svieti-
zation of Lithuania after 1944. In
Lituanus (Brooklyn, N.Y.), v.8, no.
42, 1962, p. 29-40. See serials
consulted.

5808. SELECTED DOCUMENTARY MATERI-
al on the Lithuanian resistance
movement against totalitarianism,
1940-1960. In Lituanus (Brooklyn,
N.Y.), v.8, no.1-2, 1962, p. 41-64.
See serials consulted.

5809. SŪDUVIS, N. E., pseud.
Allein, ganz allein. Widerstand am
Baltischen Meer. [New Rochelle,
N.Y.] 1964. 134 p. 947.5.Su25.2 PU

5810. --- Vienų vieni, dvidešimt
penkerių metų rezistencijoje. [All
alone. Brooklyn, N.Y.] Spausdino
Pranciškonų spaustuvė, 1964. 424 p.

(Į laisvę fondas lietuviškai kultūrai ugdyti. Leidinys, nr. 5)
CtPAM OCl

5811. TAURAS, K. V., pseud.
Guerrilla warfare on the amber
coast. [New York] Voyages Press
[1962] 110 p. D802.L5T3 DLC CaAEU
CaOTU CtPAM MH NSyU PU

5812. VARDYS, Vytas Stanley. The
partisan movement in postwar Lithuania. In His Lithuania under the
Soviets. New York, N.Y., 1965, p.
85-108. See entry no. 3279.

5813. --- The partisan movement
in postwar Lithuania. In Slavic
Review (Menasha, Wis.), v.22, no.3,
1963, p. 409527. See serials consulted.

5814. VAŠTOKAS, Romas. Image of
the partisan. Lituanus (Chicago,
Ill.), v.12, no.4, 1966, p. 26-47.
See serials consulted.

5815. ŽYMANTAS, Stasys. Twenty
years of resistance. In Lituanus
(Brooklyn, N.Y.), v.6, no.2, 1960,
p. 40-46. See serials consulted.

X.11. LIBERATION ACTIVITIES OUTSIDE
LITHUANIA

5816. ASSEMBLY OF CAPTIVE EURO-
PEAN NATIONS. Assemblée des nations
captives d'Europe. 1.- , sess.;
[New York, N.Y.] (Its Publication
ANCE) DR1.A8444 CSt-H CoFS OrU

5817. --- Assembly of Captive
European Nations. 1st.- , sess.;
Sept. 20, 1954-Feb.11, 1955- .
New York, N.Y. (Its ACEN Publica-
tion) DR1.A8 DLC AzU CaBVa CaBVaU
CoCC CoDU CoU CoFS IdU IdPS MeB OCU
OrPR OrP OrU OrCS PPULC PV TxLT TU
UPB UU Wa WaS WaSp WaT

5818. --- Official report of de-
bates [of the] plenary meeting.
13th- ; Apr. 15, 1955- . New York,
N.Y., ACEN. DR1.A83 DLC CaBVaU CoD
CoU ICU IU MB MiU NN NIC OrP OrU
PBm PPULC PU ViU WaS

5819. --- Resolutions, Reports,...
1st-12th sessions, Sept. 20-Dec. 20,
1954. New York, N.Y., 1954. (Its
publications) DR1.A8 DLC CaAEU(4th-
7th sess.) CtPAM(8th sess.) NN PU UU

5820. --- A study of the anatomy
of Communist takeover, for the Subcommittee of the Committee on the

Judiciary, United States Senate. Washington, D.C., G.P.O., 1966, iii, 70, v p. At head of title: 89th Congress 2nd session. D817.A8 DLC MH-L

5821. AUDĖNAS, Juozas. The activities of the Supreme Committee for the Liberation of Lithuania. In Audėnas, Juozas, ed. Twenty years' struggle for the freedom of Lithuania. New York, N.Y., 1963. p. 40-92. DK511.L27T84 CaBVaU CaQMM CaOOP CaOTP InNd MH NN NNC OCl OClW OrU PP PPiU PU

5822. ---, ed. Twenty years' struggle for the freedom of Lithuania. New York, N.Y., Supreme Committee for the Liberation of Lithuania [Elta Information Service] 1963. 149 p. illus., ports., map. DK511.L27T84 CaBVaU CaOOP CaOTU CaQMM ICBM InNd MH NN NNC OKentU OCl OrU OClW PP PPiU PU

5823. --- Vyriausiasis Lietuvos Išlaisvinimo Komitetas. [The Supreme Committee for the Liberation of Lithuania] In Lietuvių enciklopedija. Boston, Mass., 1966. v.34, p. 283-290. For holdings see entry no. 216.

5824. BALKŪNAS, Jonas. Baltic exiles continue struggle for freedom. John Balkūnas. New York, N.Y., Ukrainian Quarterly, 1966. 7 p. Offprint from the Ukrainian Quarterly, v.22, no.2, 973.075B197 PU

5825. FORTIETH ANNIVERSARY OF INdependence proclamation of Lithuania. In U.S. Congressional record. Proceedings and debates of the 85th Congress, second session, February 13, 1958. Senate: p. 1-9; House of Representatives: p. 10-40. J11.R31 CaAEU DLC

5826. GRAHAM, Melbone W. The recognition of the Baltic States in the configuration of American diplomacy. In Poska, Jüri G., ed. Pro Baltica. Stockholm, 1965. p. 137-146. DK511.B25P6 DLC CaAEU CLU CU CtY ICU InU MiU-L NN PU

5827. IN THE NAME OF THE LITHUanian people. Wolfberg, Ger., Perkūnas, 1945. 72 p. illus. 947.5.P ICBM D809.L5 DLC NSyN PU

5828. LITHUANIAN AMERICAN INFORMATION CENTER, NEW YORK. An appeal to fellow Americans on behalf of the Baltic states by united organizations of Americans of Lithuanian, Latvian and Estonian descent. New York, N.Y., 1944. 54 p. illus., facsims.

D802.B3L5 DLC CaOTU CSt-H NN MH NIC PU

5829. --- --- Supplement... no.1- New York, N.Y., 1944- illus., facsims. Bibliography: no.1, p. 28-31. D802.B3L5 suppl. DLC CtY ICU PU

5830. LIULEVIČIUS, Vincentas. Išeivija Lietuvos atkūrimo darbe; rankraščio teisėmis. [The exiles in the activities for the independent Lithuania] Čikaga, Pedagoginis lituanistikos institutas, 1971. 66 p. illus. ICLJF

5831. ŠKIRPA, Kazys. Apie Lietuvių Aktyvistų Fronto veiklą. [About the action of the Lithuanian Activist Front] In Lituanistikos darbai. Čikaga, 1969. v.2, p. 77-123. See serials consulted.

5832. --- --- Detached from Lituanistikos darbai, v.2, 1969. DK511.S62 CaAEU

5833. SUPREME LITHUANIAN COMMITTEE OF LIBERATION. Memorandum on the restoration of Lithuania's independence. [n.p.] Lithuanian Executive Council, 1950. 93 p. fold. maps. Also published in French. DK511.L27S95 DLC CSt-H ICBM ICLJF InNd KU NNC OKentU(French ed.) PU

5834. TĖVYNEI. Lietuvos dienai Argentinoje, 1945 paremti. [n.p.] Išleido Lietuvai išlaisvinti centras Argentinoje [1945] 40 p. illus. 977 ICBM

5835. UNITED STATES CONGRESS. Freedom for Lithuania: "Lithuania's Independence Day in the Congress of the United States". Exerpts from proceedings of the United States Senate and House of Representatives. Washington, D.C., G.P.O., 1955. 75 p. DK511.L27U58 CSt-H MH

5836. --- Lithuania shall be free; exerpts from proceedings of the Senate of the United States and House of Representatives, February 16-19, 23,25-27; March 1, 8 and 16; April 8 and June 21, 1948. Washington, D.C., G.P.O., 1948. 38 p. DK511.L2Li CSt-H

5837. --- "Lithuania's Independence Day in the Congress of the United States". Excerpts from proceedings of the Senate of the United States and House of Representatives, Washington, D.C., G.P.O., 1953. 49 p. BM(8178. cc. 19.)

5838. VLIKO GRUPIŲ KOMISIJOS PRAnešimas tų grupių atstovų 1958 m.

gegužės 8 d. pasitarimui (New York,
N.Y.) apie pastangas įtraukti į
VLIKĄ bendram Lietuvos laisvinimo
darbui jame nedalyvaujančias grupes.
[The report of the Sub-Committee to
the Supreme Lithuanian Committee of
Liberation] Cleveland, Ohio, Viltis,
1958. 80 p. 947.5.V844 PU

5839. ZALATORIUS, Vytautas. Eastern European minorities and the U.S.
foreign policy during the Cold War;
a case study of Lithuanian activities. Chicago, Ill., 1961. 126
leaves. Thesis(M.A.)--University of
Chicago. F9999 ICU

X.12. LOCAL HISTORY

X.12.a. CITIES

X.12.a.1. KAUNAS

5840. BIČIŪNAS, Vytautas Pranas.
Kaunas, 1030-1930. Kaunas, Dirvos
b-vės leidinys, 1930. 256 p.
illus. DK651.K125B5 DLC ICCC OCl
PPULC PU

5841. DAUGIRDAS, Tadas. Kaunas
vokiečių okupacijoje. [Kaunas during the German occupation. Spaudai parengė M. Urbšienė] Kaunas,
Spindulio spaustuvė, 1937. 68 p.
Q947.52.D267.3 PU

5842. FORSTREUTER, Kurt Herman.
Kauen, eine deutsche Stadtgründung.
In Jomsburg (Leipzig), v.6, no.1-2,
1942, p. 18-37. See serials consulted.

5843. FROMAS, Aleksandras. Iš-
griovimas Kauno pilies, 1362 metais;
dramatas keturiuose apsireiškimuose.
[The distruction of Kaunas castle,
1362; drama in 4 acts] Plymouth,
Pa., 1906. 85 p. 891.92F3 CtTMF

5844. GULBINSKIENĖ, Aleksandra.
Kaunas, jo praeitis, dabartis ir
ateitis. [Kaunas, its past, present and future. By] A. Gulbinskienė, V. Černeckis, P. Kežinaitis.
Kaunas, VPMLL, 1960. 143 p. illus.
DK651.K125G8 DLC MH PU

5845. --- Kaunas. [By] A. Gulbin-
skiene, V. Chernetskis & P. Kezhi-
naitis. Vil'nius, Gos. izd-vo polit. i nauch. lit-ry Litovskoi SSR,
1962. 172 p. In Russian.
DK651.K125G87 DLC CoU CtY FMU ICU
InU IU MH MiU MiDW NIC NcD TxU

5846. KAUNAS; vardas, proistorė,
pilis ir meno paminklai. [Kaunas;
its name, prehistory, castle and
its art monuments. By A. Salys, J.
Puzinas, A. Kučas and P. Reklaitis]
In Lietuvių enciklopedija. Boston,
Mass., 1957. v.11, p. 201-224.
For holdings see entry no. 216.

5847. LITHUANIA. GELEŽINKELIŲ
VALDYBA. Kaunas. Ausgabe der Ver-
waltung der litauischen Eisenbahnen.
Kaunas, "Spindulio" bendrovės spau-
stuvė, 1930. 29 p. illus., map.
DK651.K125A5 1930a DLC PU

5848. --- Kaunas. Published by
the Lithuanian Department of Rail-
ways. Kaune, "Spindulio" b-vės
spaustuvė, 1930. 31 p. illus.,
diagr. map. DK651.K125A5 1930 DLC
CSt-H NcU PU

5849. LITHUANIAN SSR. CENTRINĖ
STATISTIKOS VALDYBA. VALSTYBĖS
STATISTIKOS KAUNO MIESTO INSPEKTŪRA.
Kauno ekonomika ir kultūra; statis-
tinių duomenų rinkinys. [Kaunas
economy and culture; statistics.
Sudarė F. Obelenis] Kaunas, Šviesa,
1968. 229 p. DK561.K125L5 PU

5850. NAUJAS ŽODIS. Naujas žodis
(Kaunas), special Kaunas City issue,
no.23-24, 1930. Q57.92N234 PU

5851. PILYPAITIS, Antanas. Kauno
rotušė. [City Hall of Kaunas]
Vilnius, VPMLL, 1961. 58 p. illus.,
map. diagr., plans. (Lietuvos TSR
Architektūros paminklai, 2) Summary
in Russian and English.
NA4435.L52K34 DLC CtPAM MH NN PU

5852. STEPONAITIS, Vytautas. Iš
Kauno gubernatoriaus archyvo bylos.
[From the archives of the governor
of Kaunas] In Karo archyvas (Kaunas), v.4, 1928, p. 228-242. See
serials consulted.

5853. TUMAS, Juozas. Steigiamajame Kaune 1920-21 m. [In develop-
ing Kaunas. By] Vaižgantas [pseud.]
Kaunas, Švyturio bendrovės Leidinys,
1922. 255 p. (Vaižganto raštai,
t. 3) DK651.K125T8 DLC CtTMF PU

X.12.a.2. VILNIUS

5854. AKTY KASAIUSHCHIESIA GORODA
VILNA. In Vilenskaia komissiia dlia
razbora i izdaniia drevnikh aktov.
Akty. Vil'na, 1893. T.20.
DK511.L2A28 t.20 DLC CIU CU CSt-H KU
MH NN NNC WaS WU

5855. BALIŃSKI, Michał. Historya miasta Wilna. Wilno, A. Marcinowskiego, 1836-37. 2 v. in 1. plates, ports., facsims., plans. 947.52.B197.3 PU PPULC ICLJF

5856. --- Opisanie statystyczne miasta Wilna. Wilno, J. Zawadzki, 1835. x, 207 p. tables. DK651.V4B2 ICU PPULC PU

5857. BANDROWSKI, Juliusz Kaden. Wyprawa wileńska. [Warszawa, 1919] 48 p. illus., map. DK440.B348 DLC

5858. BATIUSHKOV, Pompei Nikolaevich. Pamiatniki russkoi stariny v zapadnykh guberniiakh imperii izdavaemye po vysochaishemu povelieniiu. Sanktpeterburg, 1872. 1 v. Partial contents.--Vyp. 5. Vil'na. Slav 6467.41.45F MH

5859. BATŪRA, R. Vilniaus aukštutinė pilis. [The upper castle of Vilnius] Vilnius, Mintis, 1964. 40 p. illus. Text in English, German, Lithuanian, Polish and Russian. Balt 7832.6 MH NIC

5860. BERNATSKII, N. Sobytiia v Vil'nie vo vremia Otechestvennoi voiny. Vil'na, 1912. 947.52.B458 PU

5861. BULAKA, Mečys. Vilnius; senamiestis... [Vilnius: the old part of the City] Vilnius, VPMLL, 1958. [12] p. 24 plates(in portfolio). NC1200.V5B8 DLC PU

5862. BUŁHAK, Jan. Wilno. W Warszawie,Wydawn. J. Martkowicza, Nakł. Księg. Stowarzyszenia Nauczycielstwa Polskiego w Wilnie, 1924. 1 v. illus. DK651.V4B8 DLC MiD PU

5863. --- Wilno; 20 widoków z fotografji J. Bułhaka. Wilno, W. Borkowski, 1937. 1 v. (chiefly illus.) 947.52.B874.2 PU

5864. CICĖNAS, Jeronimas. Vilnius tarp audrų. [Vilnius between storms] Chicago, Ill., Terra [1953] 561 p. illus. DK651.V4C5 DLC CtTMF ICCC ICLJF MiD NN OCl PU

COHEN, Israel. Vilna. Philadelphia, Pa., 1704-1943. See entry no. 3582.

5865. FIJAŁEK, Jan. Opisy Wilna aż do połowy wieku XVII. In Ateneum Wileńskie (Wilno), v.1, no.3-4, 1923, p. 313-336; v.2, no.5-6, 1924, p. 122-158. See serials consulted.

5866. --- Teksty opisowe Wilna. In Ateneum Wileńskie (Wilno), v.1, no.3-4, 1923, p. 506-526. See

serials consulted.

5867. GAIŽUTIS, Vladas. Vilniaus reikšmė Lietuvai. [The importance of Vilnius to Lithuania] Kaunas, 1929. 84 p. 947.52.G1295 PU

5868. HOŁUBOWICZ Włodzimierz. Gdzie stał trzeci zamek Wilna zburzony przez Konrada Wallenroda w 1390 r. Wilno, Zakłady Graficzne "Znicz", 1939. 947.52.H749.2 PU

5869. JANOWSKI, Ludwik. W promieniach Wilna i Krzemieńca. Wilno, J. Zawadzki, 1923. xi, 71, 271 p. port. 947.52.J267 PU MH NN NNC

5870. JAWORSKI, Iwo. Zarys dziejów Wilna. Wilno, Wydawn. Magistratu Miasta Wilna, 1929. 30 p. 947.52.J329 PU

5871. JĘDRYCHOWSKA, Anna. Zygzakiem i po prostu. [Wyd.1. Warszawa]Czytelnik, 1965. 372 p. illus., facsims, ports. DK651.V4J43 DLC CU CtY MB

5872. JURGINIS, JUOZAS. Aušros Vartai. [The shrine of Aušros Vartai] Vilnius, VPMLL, 1960. 44 p. illus., ports, facsims. DK651.V4J78 DLC

5873. --- Reakcinis bažnytinių jurisdikcijų vaidmuo Vilniaus istorijoje. [Reactionary character of the church jurisdiction in the history of Vilnius] In LTSRMAIID, v. 1, 1951, p. 88-153. See serials consulted.

5874. --- Vilniaus miesto įkūrimo klausimu. [About the founding of the City of Vilnius] In LTSRMAD. Serija A, v.1(6), 1959, p. 103-113. See serials consulted.

5875. --- Vilniaus miesto istorija; nuo seniausių laikų iki Spalio revoliucijos. [History of the City of Vilnius from the ancient times to 1917. J. Jurginis et al.] Vilnius, Mintis, 1968. 394, [5] p. illus., facsims, fold. map. ports. Bibliography: p. 382-395.

5876. KIRKOR, Adam Honory. Groby wielkoksiążęce i królewskie w Wilnie. Wilno, 1882. 1 v. 947.5K28 PPi OCl

5877. --- Obrazki litewskie. Ze wspomnień tułacza Sobarri [pseud.] Poznań, Nakładem Tygodnika Wielkopolskiego, 1874. 215 p. (*QR)NN

5878. KLIMAS, Petras. Mūsų kovos dėl Vilniaus. 1. dalis: nuo Vil-

niaus įkūrimo ligi laikinosios vyriausybės sudarymo 1918 metais.
[Our struggle for Vilnius. Part 1:
from the founding of Vilnius until
the formation of the temporary
government in 1918] Kaunas, A. ir
P. Klimų, 1923. 102 p. illus.
BW93.W68.923k CDU CtY ICBM ICLJF PU

5879. KRASZEWSKI, Józef Ignacy.
Wilno od początków jego do roku
1750. Wilno, J. Zawadzki, 1840-
1842. 4 v. tables, ports., plates.
947.52.K858 PU BM ICLJF KU MH

5880. KRAUJELIS, Petras. Trijų
kryžių kalnas Vilniuje. [The hill
of three crosses in Vilnius. By]
Vieštautas, [pseud.] Vilnius,
Švyturio b-vė, 1923. 8 p.
970.31.VI ICLJF

5881. LAISVŪNAS, Petras. Laisvie-
ji Aušros Vartai. [The free Aušros
Vartai] Vilnius, Knygynas "Aukuras",
1940. 17 plates. 914.5L ICBM

LITHUANIA. LAWS, STATUTES,
ETC. Zbiór praw y przywileiów
miasta stołecznemu W.X.L. Wilnowi...
W Wilnie, 1788. See entry no. 2781.

5882. ŁOWMIAŃSKA, Maria. Wilno
przed najazdem moskiewskiem, 1655
roku. Wilno, Wydawn. Magistratu m.
Wilna; Skł. Gł. w Domu Książki Polskiej w Warszawie,1929. 198 p.
illus. (Bibljoteczka Wileńska, nr.
3) DK651.V4L6 DLC NNC PU

5883. MERKYS, Vytautas. Vilniaus
miesto gynybiniai įtvirtinimai 1503-
1805 metais. [The fortification of
Vilnius City in 1503-1805] In
LTSRMAIILKI, v.2, 1959, p. 193-213.
See serials consulted.

5884. MIKALAUSKAS, Bronius. Vilnius prieš lenkams jį pagrobiant.
[The City of Vilnius before occupation by Poland] Kaunas, Vilniui
vaduoti S-ga, 1930. 15 p.
970.31ŽE ICLJF

5885. MIKKOLA, Jooseppi Julius.
Finlandja a Wilno. In Ateneum Wilenskie (Wilno), v.8, 1931-1932,
p. 136-142. See serials consulted.

5886. MILOVIDOV, Aleksandr Ivanovich. Vilenskii khram-pamiatnik v
oznamenovanie 300-lietia tsarstvo-
vaniia doma Romanovykh i v pamiat'
kniazia K.K. Ostrozhskago. Izdanie
Vilenskago Sv.-Dukh. bratstva.
Vil'na, tip. A.G. Syrkina, 1913.
(*Q p.v. 280)NN

MORESTHE, Georges. Vilna
et le problème de l'est européen.

Paris, 1922. See entry no. 3211.

5887. MOŚCICKI, Henryk. Wilno i
Warszawa w "Dziadach" Mickiewicza;
... trzeciej części "Dziadów". Warszawa, Nakł. Gebethnera i Wolffa,
1908. 203 p. illus., ports.
PG7158.M5D925 CaOTU BM(11850. s. 13.)
NcD

5888. NAGÓRSKI, Teodor. Gospodar-
ka finansowa miasta Wilna z przedmową Mieczysława Gutkowskiego. Wilno,
Wydawn. Magistratu m. Wilna, 1929.
947.52.N135 PU

5889. NARBUTT, Teodor. Obwarowa-
nia miasta Wilna murem obronnym. In
His Pomniejsze Pisma Historyczne,
1856. DK511.L2N27 CU ICLJF MH PU

5890. P., M. O przyszłość miasta
Wilna i gubernji wileńskiej. Wilno,
Nakł. autora, 1918. 17 p. Offprint
from Nowiny Litewskie, 1918.
970.31MP ICLJF

5891. POLISH RESEARCH CENTER, LON-
DON. The story of Wilno. [London,
1942] 30 p. plates. DK651.V4P6
DLC MH

5892. PRUNSKIS, Joseph. Aušros
Vartai Vilniuje. [The shrine of Aušros Vartai in Vilnius] Chicago, Ill.,
1949. 40 p. illus. 970.31PR ICLJF

5893. PUZINAS, Jonas. Iš Vilniaus
pilių praeities. [From the past of
the castles of Vilnius] In Kūryba
(Kaunas), no.2, 1944, p. 80-88.
57.92K968 1944 PU

5894. --- Vilniaus proistorė.
[Prehistory of Vilnius] In Aidai
(Brooklyn, N.Y.), no.6(82), 1955,
p. 211-219. See serials consulted.

5895. REMER, Jerzy. Wilno. Poznań, Wydawnictwo Polskie [1934] 210
p. illus. ports. DK651.V4R4 DLC
CaOTU OCl PU

5896. ŠAPOKA, Adolfas. Senasis
Vilnius; Vilniaus miesto istorijos
bruožai iki XVIIa. pabaigos. [The
old Vilnius; an outline of its history until the end of the 17th Century. Brooklyn, N.Y., 1963] 332 p.
illus., map. Bibliography: p. 306-
318. DK651.V4S38 DLC CaOONL CaOTP
CLU CtTMF CtY ICLJF MH NN NjR PU

5897. --- Vilnius in the life of
Lithuania. Toronto, Ont., Lithuanian
association of the Vilnius region,
1962. 174 p. illus., map. Bibliography: p. 168-174. DK511.L2S24
CaAEU CaOONL CaOONL CaOTU DLC DS CtY
MH NcU NjR OKentU PU

5898. --- Vilnius Lietuvos gyvenime. [Vilnius in the life of Lithu-
ania] Toronto, Author, 1954. 96 p.
illus. Bibliography: p. 92-95.
DK651.V4S39 DLC CtY ICBM ICLJF MH PU

5899. SENN, Alfred Erich. Vilna
as the cultural centre of Lithuania
before 1861. In East European
Quarterly (Boulder, Col.), v.2,
1968, p. 139-146. See serials consulted.

5900. SOKOLOV, Nikodim. Ostrovo-
rotnaia ili Ostrobramskaia chudot-
vornaia ikona Bogoroditsy v gorodie
Vil'nie; istoricheskoe izsledovaniie.
Vil'na, [izd. avtora] 1883. 506 p.
illus. 970.31SO ICLJF

TATISIDIEV, IUrii Vladimirovich. Vilna i litovskiia gubernii
v 1811-1813 gg. See entry no. 5127.

5901. TUMAS, Juozas. Lenkų okupuotame Vilniuje 1919 m. [In Vilnius occupied by Poles. By] Vaižgantas [pseud.] Kaunas, Švyturio
bendrovės leidinys, 1922. 227 p.
(Vaižganto raštai, t.2)
DK651.V4T8 DLC CtTMF PU

5902. --- Vokiečių okupuotan Vilniun sugryžus, 1918 metais. [My
return to German-occupied Vilnius,
1918. By] Vaižgantas [pseud.]
Kaunas, Švyturio bendrovės leidinys,
1922. 224 p. (Vaižganto raštai,
t.1) DK651.V4T82 DLC CtTMF PU

5903. VILNA. LIETUVOS TSR VALSTY-
BINĖ RESPUBLIKINĖ BIBLIOTEKA. Tarybinis Vilnius; rekomenduojamos literatūros rodyklė. [Soviet Vilnius;
a list of recommended literature.
Sudarytojai: Ona Kriukelienė, et
al.] Vilnius, 1966. 156 p.
Balt 8641.2 MH

5904. VILNIAUS MIESTO GEOGRAFIJA;
mokymo priemonė. [Geography of the
City of Vilnius... Autorių Kolektyvas: S. Tarvydas et al. Redagavo
S. Tarvydas] Vilnius, Laikraščių
ir žurnalų leidykla, 1965. 85, [3]
p. illus., maps. DK651.V4v413 DLC

5905. VILNIUS; 1323-1923. Istori-
jos spžvalga. [Vilnius; 1323-1923;
a historical outline. Parašė K.
Binkis ir P. Tarulis...] Kaunas,
"Švyturio" bendrovės leidinys, 1923.
63 p. plans, plates. DK651.V4V45
DLC CtPAM CtTMF CtY ICLJF NN OKentU
PU RPB WaU

5906. VILNIUS IR VILNIAUS KRAŠTAS;
krašto pažinimo pradai. [Vilnius
and its environs; know your country]
Kaunas, 1932. 365 p. illus., ports.,

map. (Vilniui vaduoti sąjungos
Kauno ruožo geležinkeliečių skyriaus
leidinys nr. 1) DK511.V4V5 DLC
CtTMF PU

5907. VILNIUS LIETUVOS SOSTINĖ.
[Vilnius, the capital of Lithuania.
By A. Salys, A. Bendorius, J. Puzi-
nas, S. Sužiedelis, V. Kulbokienė,
A. Mažiulis and P. Reklaitis] In
Lietuvių enciklopedija. Boston,
Mass. 1966. v.34, p. 210-249.
For holdings see entry no. 216.

5908. WILNA (CITY). Ukazatel'
goroda Vil'ny; sostavlen po rasporiazheniiu glavnago nachal'nika
kraia, Vil'na, 1864. 1 v.
BM(10290. aa. 14.)

5909. WOŁŁOSOWICZ, Stanisław.
Ziemia Wileńska, Kraków, Orbis,
1925. 130 p. illus., fold. map.
Bibliography: p. 125-128.
DK511.L2W6 DLC PU

5910. ŻYTKOWICZ, Leonid. Zburzenie murów obronnych Wilna, 1799-
1805. Wilno, Wydawn. Magistratu
Miasta Wilna, 1933. 1 v. (Bibljoteczka Wileńska, 5) 947.52Z99.2 PU

X.12.a.3. OTHER CITIES

5911. ANYKŠČIAI. [Parengė Anykščių kraštotyrininkai. The Town of
Anykščiai. Vilnius, Mintis, 1971]
111 p. DK511.A58A5 PU

5912. BALIŃSKI, Michał. Wspom-
nienie jednego dnia wędrówki po
kraju, Krewo, starodawny zamek w
Litwie. In His Pisma historyczne...
Warszawa, 1843. v.4. (*QR)NN MH
WaU

5913. BASANAVIČIUS, Jonas. Iš
Palangos istorijos. [From the history of Palanga] Vilnius, "Vil-
niečio" leidinys, 1922. 52 p.
WB25337 CtY PPULC PU(Xerox copy,1971)

5914. BIRŽYS, Petras. Anykščiai.
[The Town of Anykščiai] Kaunas, Vl.
Dagilis, 1928. 74 p. illus.,
ports., map. (Lietuvos miestai ir
miesteliai, no. 3) DK511.L2B55 DLC
CtY PU

5915. --- Taujėnai. [Town of Taujėnai. By] Akiras [pseud.] Kaunas, V. Dagilis, 1928. 48 p.
(Lietuvos miestai ir miesteliai, no.
2) 947.52.B539.2 PU

5916. BITINAITĖ, Vilhelmina and
E. Trečiokas. Biržai. [Town of

Biržai] Vilnius, Mintis, 1971. 44
p., 16 leaves of illus.
DK651.B528B58 DLC

5917. BLAŽYS, A. Šiluvos istorija. [The history of Šiluva] Marijampolė, 1929. 54 p. 947.5.B619 PU

5918. BUŠACKIS, Brunonas. Istori-
nai Raseiniai. [The historical Ra-
seiniai] In Naujienos (Chicago,
Ill.), April 24, 1957. See serials
consulted.

5919. ČAPLIKAS, J. Kėdainiai.
[Town of Kėdainiai] Vilnius, VPMLL,
1963. 47 p. illus., facsims.
DK651.K25C3 DLC PU

5920. DAGELIS, Alfonsas. Pane-
vežys. [The City of Panevežys]
Vilnius, VPMLL, 1960. 38 p. illus.
MH

5921. --- --- [Another edition]
Vilnius, 1970. 78 p. DK651.P15D3
PU ICBM

5922. DIRŽINSKAITĖ, L. Šiauliai.
[The City of Šiauliai] Vilnius,
VPMLL, 1961. 76 p. illus., ports.
HC337.L52S5 DLC CaOTP OKentU PU

5923. DOVGIALLO, Dmitrii Ivanovich.
Nemenchin, miastechko Vil'enskoi gubernii; istoriko-statisticheskii
ocherk. Vil'na, 1908. 1 v.
947.52.D955 PU

5924. ERETAS, Juozas. Rėzos gim-
tinė Karvaičiai ir jų poėtai.
[Karvaičiai, the birthplace of
Rheza...] In Atheneum (Kaunas), v.
9, 1938, p. 153-186. See serials
consulted.

5925. GASIŪNAS, Vytautas. Rokiš-
kis...[Town of Rokiškis] Vilnius,
Mintis, 1967. [64] p. illus., map,
ports. DK651.R64G3 DLC NN

5926. GIDŽIŪNAS, Viktoras. Iš
Simno istorijos. This and that
about Simnas. In LKMAM, v.1, 1965,
p. 145-174. See serials consulted.

5927. GUMOWSKI, Marjan. Herby
miast litewskich. In Ateneum Wileńskie (Wilno), v.10, 1935, p. 256-
294. See serials consulted.

5928. GUTAUSKAS, Juozas. Sienieji
Lazdijų dokumentai. [The old docu-
ments of Lazdijai] In Mūsų senovė
(Kaunas), no.1, 1921, p. 88-102.
See serials consulted.

5929. HEDEMANN, Otto. Dzisna i
Druja, magdeburskie miasta. Wilno,
Towarzystwo Przyjaciół Nauk w Wil-

nie, 1934. 486 p. tables, illus.,
maps, plans. 947.52.H358.2 PU CtY
NN

5930. JANKUS, Lionginas. Šiluva;
prisiminimai. [Šiluva; recollec-
tions] Brooklyn, N.Y. [Pranciškonų
spaustuvė] 1966. 56 p. illus.
289.5ŠI ICLJF

5931. JODKOWSKI, Józef. Grodno;
okolice w znaniu dziejów Litwy.
Grodno [Zakłady L. Mejłachowicza]
1928. 9 p. illus., plan.
DK651.G7J6 DLC MH PU

5932. JONAITIS, M. Veliuonos ir
Vytauto Didžiojo praeitis. [The
history of Veliuona and Vytautas
the Great] Kaunas, K. Vaičiūnas,
1930. 24 p. 947.52.J693 PU

5933. JUCEWICZ, Ludwik Adam.
Szydłów. In His Wspomnienia Žmudzi.
Wilno, 1842. 491.922.J873 PU
BM(12342. f. 2.)

5934. KOLUPAILA, Steponas. Senasis ir naujasis Gardinas. [The
old and the new Gardinas] In Naujoji romuva (Kaunas), no.39, 1932.
See serials consulted.

5935. KOREVO, Anton Ksaver'evich.
Razvaliny Krevskago zamka. In
Pamiatnaia Knizhka Vilenskoi gubernii na 1861. Vilna, 1860. p. 59-
68. DK511.V4A32 1861 DLC

5936. LASTAS, V. Šiaulių miesto
istorinė-geografinė apžvalga. [The
historical-geographical review of
the City of Šiauliai] In LTSRAMMD:
Istorija, v.4, 1963. See serials
consulted.

5937. LIETUVOS TSR PAMINKLŲ APSAU-
GOS IR KRAŠTOTYROS DRAUGIJA. Die-
veniškės. Redakcinė komisija:
Vanda Barauskienė [et al.] Vilnius,
Vaga, 1968. 411 p. illus., maps.
Summary in Russian. D651.D5L5 DLC
PU ICU

5938. --- Eržvilkas. [Redakcinė
komisija: Antanas Balašaitis, Jonas
Kubilius, Stasys Skrodenis, Antanas
Stravinskas (pirmininkas)] Vilnius,
Mintis, 1970. 272 p. illus.,
music, 36 leaves of illus.
DK511.E36L5 PU DLC

5939. --- Merkinė. [Redakcinė
komisija: Jadvyga Kardelytė et al]
Vilnius, Vaga, 1970. 452 p.
DK651.M45L5 PU

5940. MASILIONIS, Juozas, ed.
Panevėžys; geografinės ir istorinės
žinios apie apylinkes ir miestą.

[Geographical and historical facts
about the environs and the City of
Panevėžys. Chicago, Ill.] Pane-
vėžiečių klubas [1963] 430 p.
illus., maps, posts. DK651.P15M3
DLC CaAEU CaOONL CtPAM CtTMF

5941. PETRULIS, Juozas (1904-).
Kaimo istorija ir būtovė; Rudikai,
Kupiškio valsčiaus. [History of
the country and its life; Rudikai in
the Municipality of Kupiškis] In
Gimtasai kraštas (Kaunas), no.1-2,
1941, p.2-15. See serials consulted.

5942. PUZINAS, Jonas. Šiaulių
miestas ir jo istorija. [The City
of Šiauliai and its history]
Šiauliai, Kraštotyros draugijos
leidinys, 1930. 1 v.
947.52.P998.2 PU

5943. RAGAŽINSKAS, Antanas. Žemaičių Kalvarijos aprašymas, ypatingai dievobaimingiems keleiviams
į tą stebuklingąją vietą, kun. Ra-
gaišio [pseud.] sudėtas. [The description of Žemaičių Kalvarija...]
Vilnius, "Vilniaus žinių" spaustuvė,
1906. 947.5.R126 PU

5944. REITELAITIS, Jonas. Gudelių
parapijos monografija. [The parish
of Gudeliai] In Lietuvių tauta
(Vilnius), v.2, no.2, 1919, p. 405-
431. See serials consulted.

5945. --- Kalvarija. District,
ville et paroisse de Kalvarija. In
LKMAM, v.3, 1967, p. 11-132; v.4,
1967, p. [369]-[511]. Summary in
French. See serials consulted.

5946. --- Leipalingio monografija.
[Leipalingis; a monograph] In Tauta
ir žodis (Kaunas), v.3, 1925, p.
253-275. See serials consulted.

5947. --- Liškiava; monografija.
[Liškiava; a monograph] In Mūsų
senovė (Kaunas), v. 2-3, 1921-1922.
See serials consulted.

5948. --- Veisiejai. [Town of
Veisiejai] In Tauta ir žodis (Kaunas), v.5, 1928, p. 248-307. See
serials consulted.

5949. RUGIS, Jonas. Švėkšnos
praeitis; vieno Žemaitijos miestelio
istorija. [The history of the Town
of Švėkšna] Chicago, Ill., author,
1950. 63 p. 947.5.R635 PU ICLJF

5950. RUŠKYS, Petras. Biržų pilis ir jos apylinkės. [The Castle
of Biržai and its environs] In
Mūsų senovė (Kaunas), v.1, 1921,
p. 148-171. See serials consulted.

5951. ŠAKENIS, Konstantinas. Va-
balninkas ir jo apylinkė praeityje,
iki Lietuvos Nepriklausomybės atgavimo. [Vabalninkas and its environs...] Kaunas, Lietuvos istorijos draugija, 1935. iv, 188 p.
illus., ports., fold. map. ("Praeities" biblioteka, 2)
DK651.V2S3 DLC PU

5952. ŠALŪGA, R. Kernavė. [The
Town of Kernavė] Vilnius, VPMLL,
1960. [30] p. (chiefly illus.)
DK651.K33S3 DLC ICBM NN

5953. ŠINKŪNAS, Peliksas. Kė-
dainių miesto istorija. [History
of the Town of Kėdainiai] Kaunas,
Author, 1928. iv, 100 p. illus.,
ports. DK651.K25S5 DLC PU

5954. SMOKOWSKI, Wincenty. Wspom-
nienie Trok w 1822. In Athenaeum
Wileńskie (Wilno), v.5, 1841, p.
157-181. See serials consulted.

5955. TOTORAITIS, Jonas. Žemaičių Kalvarija. [The Town of Žemaičių Kalvarija] Marijampolė, Marijonų spaustuvė, 1937. 73 p.
CtPAM CtTMF

5956. TYSZKIEWICZ, Eustachy.
Birže; przeszłość miasta. [The
Town of Biržai] Sanktpeterburg,
1869. 170 p. 947.52.T988 PU

5957. URBONAVIČIUS, Vytautas.
Rumšiškėnai XIV-XVI amžiais. [Rum-
šiškėnai in the 14th-16th centuries]
Vilnius, LTSRMAII, 1970, 81 p.
DK511.L21U7 PU

5958. VADEIKIS, Jonas. Šiluva.
[The Town of Šiluva] Vilnius, VPMLL,
1960. 49 p. BX1559.L5V25 DLC

5959. VEBLAITIS, Petras. Šiluvos
bažnyčia ir jos infulatai. [The
Church of Šiluva...] In Draugija
(Kaunas), 1940, no.1, p. 35-42; no.
2, p. 78-86. See serials consulted.

5960. VEBLAUSKAS, Petras. Zapyš-
kio senoji bažnyčia. [The old
church in Zapyškis] In Naujoji
romuva (Kaunas), no.22, 1932, p.
517-519. See serials consulted.

5961. VORONIN, Nikolai Nikolaevich.
Drevnee Grodno; po materialam arkheologicheskikh raskopok, 1932-1949 gg.
Moskva, Izd-vo Akademii nauk SSSR,
1954. 236 p. illus. (Materialy i
issledovaniia po arkheologii drev-
nerusskikh gorodov, tom 3. Materialy
i issledovaniia po arkheologii SSSR,
nr. 41) 913.06Ak12 no.41 PU-Mu ICBM

5962. YČAS, Jonas. Biržai, tvir-

tovė, miestas ir kunigaikštystė.
[Biržai; the castle, town and city]
Kaunas, Spindulio b-vės spaustuvė,
1931. xv, 191 p. 947.52.Y25 PU

5963. YLA, Stasys (1908-).
Šiluva žemaičių istorijoje. [Šiluva
in the history of žemaitija (Samogitia)] Boston, Mass., 1970. illus.
facsims., ports. (Krikščionis gyvenime, nr. 4) Bibliography: p. 268-
293. DK651.S499Y55 DLC(1-) OKentU
PU(1-)

5964. --- Vainikuotoji Šiluva.
[The crowned Šiluva] Putnam, Conn.,
Immaculata Press, 1957. 15 p.
947.5.Y3 CtTMF

5965. ŽILEVIČIUS, L. Birštonas.
[The resort of Birštonas] Vilnius,
VPMLL, 1958. 103 p. illus., map.
914.5Ž ICBM

X.12.b. REGIONS, DISTRICTS, ETC.

5966. AFANAS'EV, Dmitrii Fedorovich, ed. Kovenskaia guberniia.
Sanktpeterburg, Tip. T-va Obshchestvennaia pol'za, 1861. x, vii, 743
p. maps, plan, tables. (Materialy
dlia statistiki i geografii Rossii
sobrannye ofitserami General'nogo
shtaba, t. 11) (*QC)NN
BM(10291.g.)

5967. ALSEIKA, Danielius. Vilniaus krašto lietuvių gyvenimas
1919-1934 m. [The life of the lithuanians in the Vilnius district,
1919-1934] Vilnius, 1935. 180 p.
947.52.A178 PU

5968. BIRŽYS, Petras. Lietuvos
miestai ir miesteliai. [Lithuania's
cities and towns. By] Akiras
[pseud.] Kaunas, V. Atkočiūno
spaustuvė, 1931-34. 3 v. Contents.--1.Alytaus aps.--2.Biržų aps.
--3.Kėdainių aps. DK511.L2B55 DLC
(v.2-3) OCl(v.1)

5969. BOBROVSKII, Pavel Osipovich.
Grodnenskaia guberniia. Sanktpeterburg, v Tip. Departamenta general'-
nago shtaba, 1863. 2 v. fold. map,
fold. plans. (Materialy dlia geografii i statistiki Rossii, sobranye
ofitserami General'nago shtaba).
DK511.G7B DLC

5970. BUSZYŃSKI, Ignacy. Opisanie
Historyczno-Statystyczne powiatu
Rossieńskiego gubernji Kowieńskiej,
z dodaniem Listy poprawnej generalnych starostw Księstwa Żmujdzkiego
i Popisu szlachty żmujdzkiej 1528

roku. Wilno, Drukiem J. Zawadzkiego, 1874. 235 p. DK511.R35
DLC PU

5971. GUKOVSKII, Konstantin Pav-
lovich. Poneviezhskii uiezd.
Kovno, Gubernskoe pravlenie, 1898.
143 p. Ottisk iz Pamiatnoi knizhki
Kovenskoi gubernii na god 1898.
BM(010290. f. 49.) NN

5972. --- Vilkomirskii uiezd.
Kovno, Gubernskoe pravlenie, 1890.
54 p. Ottisk iz Pamiatnoi knizhki
Kovenskoi gubernii, 1891.
947.52.G955 PU

5973. HEDEMANN, Otto. Historja
powiatu Brasławskiego. Wilno,
Nakł. Sejmiku Brasławskiego, 1930.
xxxi, 483 p. illus., ports., maps.
Bibliography: p. xiii-xvii.
947.52.H358.3 PU

5974. JAKUBOWSKI, Jan. Opis
Księstwa Trockiego w r. 1387.
Przyczynek do badań nad ustrojem
Litwy przedchrześcijańskiej. In
Przegląd Historyczny (Warszawa),
v.5, 1907, p. 22-48. map. See
serials consulted.

5975. JANKOWSKI, Czesław. Powiat
Oszmiański; materjały do dziejów
ziemi i ludzi. Sanktpetersburg,
Księgarnia K. Greudyszyńskiego[etc.]
1896-1900. 4 pts. illus., ports.,
plates., maps, tables. BM(10291. c.)

5976. JANULAITIS, Augustinas.
Užnemunė po Prūsais (1795-1807).
Istorinis teisės ir politikos tyrinėjimas. [Užnemunė under the rule
of Prussia, 1795-1807; a historical
essay on law and politics] Kaunas,
1928. x, 404 p. fold. map.
(Lietuvos universiteto Teisių fakulteto darbai, IV t., kn.1) At head
of title: Transnemunie sous la
domination prussienne. Bibliography:
p. v-x. 947.52.J269.4 PU CU DLC-L
ICU NN NNC

5977. JUCEWICZ, Ludwig Adam.
Wspomnienia Żmudzi. Wilno, T.
Glücksberg, 1842. 3 v. 491.922.J873
PU BM(12352. f. 2.)

5978. JUŠKEVIČIUS, Adomas and J.
Maceika. Vilnius ir jo apylinkės.
[Vilnius and its immediate environs]
Vilnius, Lietuvių mokslo draugijos
leidinys, 1937. xi, 255 p.
947.52.J9841 PU CtTMF

5979. KONČIUS, Ignas and Viktoras
Ruokis. Palangos kraštas. [Dis-
trict of Palanga] Kaunas, Valstybės
spaustuvė, 1925. 255 p. illus.,
diagr., tables, 3 fold. plans.

DK651.P105K6 DLC PU

5980. KOREVO, Anton Ksaver'evich, ed. Vilenskaia guberniia. Sankt-peterburg, Tip, T-va obshchestven-naia pol'za, 1861. viii, 804 p. maps, plan. (Materialy dlia statis-tiki i geografii Rossii sobrannye ofitserami General'nogo shtaba, t. 3) BM(10291. g.) NN

5981. KRÓLIKOWSKI, Eugeniusz. Wileńszczyzna. Roma, Sitwa, 1946. 160 p. illus. 914.5K ICBM

KVIKLYS, Bronius. Mūsų Lietuva; krašto vietovių istoriniai, geografiniai, etnografiniai bruožai. [Boston, Mass., 1964-68] See entry no. 834.

5982. LAPPO, Ivan Ivanovich. Tverskoi uiezd v XVI stolietii. Ego naselenie i vidy semel'nago vladieniia. Moskva, 1894. 238 p. (Moscow. Universitet. Obshchestvo istorii i drevnostei rossiiskikh. Chteniia. Kn.4, ch.1, st.1) See serials consulted.

5983. LIETUVOS TSR PAMINKLŲ APSAU-GOS IR KRAŠTOTYROS DRAUGIJA. Gaidės ir Rimšės apylinkės. [The regions of Gaidė and Rimšė. Redakcinė komisija: Vanda Barauskienė et al.] Vilnius, Vaga, 1969. 421 p. DK511.G25L5 PU

5984. --- Ignalinos kraštas. [The country of Ignalina. Redakcinė komisija: K. Aleksynas et al.] Vil-nius, Vaga, 1966. 337 p. illus., music, map. Summary in Russian. DK511.I35L5 DLC CaAEU NN PU

5985. LIPNITSKII, I. Nekotorye dannye dlia izucheniia Kovenskoi gubernii v statisticheskom otnoshe-nii. Braki. In Pamiatnaia knizhka Kovenskoi gubernii na 1899 g. Kovna, 1898. p. 309-322. DK511.K55P32 DLC

5986. PANEMUNIŲ DZŪKAI. Redagavo Angelė Vyšniauskaitė. [Dzūkai of the Memel Valley] Vilnius, "Min-tis", 1970. 143 p. illus., maps. At head of title: Lietuvos TSR Mokslų akademijos Istorijos insti-tutas. Summary in Russian. DK511.M42P3 DLC PU

5987. PANEVĖŽYS, DISTRICT OF. Un district lituanien sous l'occupa-tion française 1812. In Senovė (Kaunas), no.2, 1936. 57 p. See serials consulted.

5988. PERKOWSKI, Józef. Senovės gadynės pėdsakai Telšių apskrity.

[The footprints of ancient ages in the Telšiai district] In Gimtasai kraštas (Šiauliai), no.2, 1934, p. 112-114; no.3, 1935, p. 160-163. See serials consulted.

5989. PRONSKUS, Juozas. Lietuvos Sahara; Kuršių užmaris. [The Lith-uanian Sahara; Curonian sand dunes] Klaipėda, Rytas, 1923. 51 p. 947.52.P945 PU

5990. SAPUNOV, Aleksei Parfenovich, comp. Materialy po istorii i geo-grafii Disnenskago i Vileiskago uiez-dov Vilenskoi gubernii. Izdanie A. Sapunova i Kn. V. Drutskago-Liubets-kago. Vitebsk, Gubernskaia tipo-li-tografiia, 1896. 262, 144 p. illus., plates, ports, maps (part. fold.), plans. DK511.V4S DLC

5991. SCHLICHT, Oscar. Die Kuri-sche Nehrung in Wort und Bild. Kö-nigsberg in Pr., Gräfe und Unzer, 1924. 127 p. 947.52.Sch35 PU

5992. --- --- 2. Auflage. Königs-berg in Pr., Gräfe und Unzer, 1927. 180 p. illus., maps. (Ostpreussi-sche Landeskunde in Einzeldarstel-lung) DD491.0695S36 1927 DLC

5993. STAUGAITIS, Justinas. Zana-vykai. [Sudovians] In Švietimo dar-bas (Kaunas), no.3-4, 1921, p. 66-105 See serials consulted.

5994. STUDIA I MATERIAŁY DO DZIE-jów Suwalsczyzny. Pod red. Jerzego Antoniewicza. Białystok, 1965. 681 p. illus., maps. (Białostockie Towarzystwo Naukowe. Prace, nr.4) AS262.B47A14 no.4 1965 DLC PU

5995. STUDNICKI, Władysław. Zie-mia Wileńska, jej stan gospodarczy i pożądany statut. Wilno, L. Chomiń-ki, 1922. 67 p. tables. DK511.V4S93 CSt-H MH

5996. SYLWESTROWICZ, Mieczysław Dowojna. Żmudz. In Słownik Geogra-ficzny... Warszawa, 1895. t.14, p. 795-807. DK403.S53 DLC (microfilm)

5997. TOTORAITIS, Jonas. Sūduvos Suvalkijos istorija. [History of Sūduva-Suvalkija] Kaunas, VDU Teolo-gijos-filosofijos fakulteto leidinys, 1938. iv, 702 p. fold. col. maps. DK511.L2T65 PU CtTMF DLC

5998. --- Zanavykų istorija. [His-tory of Sudovians] Marijampolė, Ma-rijonų vienuolijos leidinys, 1929. 104 p. 947.52.T645 PU

5999. TREČIAKAUSKAS, K. Prie Ig-nalinos ežerų. [At the lakes of Ignalina] Vilnius, VPMLL, 1963. [32] p. illus., map. DK511.I35T7 DLC

6000. ZAJĄCZKOWSKI, Stanisław. Studya nad dziejami Żmudzi wieku XIII. Lwów, Nakł. Tow. Naukowego, 1925. 110 p. map. (Archivum Tow. Naukowego we Lwowie. Dział II, t.3, zesz.2) DK511.L23Z21 ICU KU PU

6001. ZEITUNG DER 10. ARMEE. Zwischen Wilia und Düna; Rundschau aus Etappe und Front. Auslese aus einem Arbeitgebiet der Zeitung der 10. Armee. nr.1 bis 400. Wilna, 1918? 24 p. 947.52.Z37.3 PU

6002. Žemaitis, Vincas, ed. Pietinė Lietuva Grigaliaus Valavičiaus 1599 metų Lietuvos girių aprašyme. [Southern Lithuania as described by Grigalius Valavičius in his Lithuanian forests of 1599. Redagavo Vincas Žemaitis] Čikaga, 1964. 252 p. Lietuvos miškininkų sąjungos išeivijoje leidinys, nr.3) Balt 8575.58 MH

6003. --- Sūduvos praeitis; 4000 metų Sūduvai-Jotvai-Dainavai. Trumpa archeologinė, politiniai istorinė ir kalbinė šio krašto apybraiža su išvadomis ir 2 žemėlapiais. [Sūduva and its past; 4000 years of Sūduva-Jotva-Dainava] Chicago, Ill., Čikagos lietuvių literatūros draugija, 1964. 131 p. maps. Summary in English. Bibliography: p. 119-121. DK511.L23Z4 DLC CtY OKentU PU

X.12.c. TERRITORY OF MEMEL (KLAIPĖDOS KRAŠTAS)

X.12.c.1. GENERAL STUDIES

BALTRAMAITIS, Casimir V. Anglų periodinė spauda Klaipėdos klausimu. In Bibliografijos žinios (Kaunas), v.13, no.1(75), 1940, p. 21-23. See serials consulted.

6004. BENDORIUS, Antanas. Klaipėdos krašto geografiniai savumai. [The geographic characteristics of the Territory of Memel] In Naujoji romuva (Kaunas), no.1-2, 1938, p. 22-25. See serials consulted.

6005. BEZZENBERGER, Adalbert. Die Kurische Nehrung und ihre Bewohner. Stuttgart, 1889. 140 p. illus. (Forschungen zur deutschen Landes- und Volkskunde, Bd.3) G58.F73 v.3 no.4 NIC MH PPULC PU

6006. BIENAIMÉ, Georges. Les lituaniens et le territoire de Memel.

In La Pologne (Paris), année 13, no. 1, 1932, p. 119-123. See serials consulted.

6007. BITTENS, Artur. Heimatkunde des Kreises Memel. Ausgabe A. Memel, R. Schmidt, 1914. vii, 55 p. 947.52.B548 PU

6008. BOCHET, Lucien. Klaipėda-Memel, la porte et la ville. Paris, A. Colin [1938] 22 p. Extrait des Annales de géographie, Paris, 1938. 947.52.B628 PU; also in Annales de géographie (Paris), v.47, no.268, 1938, p. 373-392. See serials consulted.

BROSZAT, Martin. Die memelländische Organisationen und der Nationalsozialismus, 1933-1939. In Vierteljahreshefte für Zeitgeschichte (Stuttgart), v.5, no.3, 1957, p. 273-278. See serials consulted.

6009. BRUOŽIS, Ansas. Mažosios Lietuvos mokyklos ir lietuvių kova dėl gimtosios kalbos. [Schools of the Lithuania Minor and Lithuanian struggle for their native language] Kaunas, Didžiosios ir Mažosios Lietuvos kultūrinio bendradarbiavimo sąjungos; Finansų ministerijos leidinys, 1935. 94 p. port. Bibliography: p. [95-96] DD338.B7 DLC PPULC PU

6010. --- Vadovėlis po Klaipėdos kraštą ir Žemaičių bei Prūsų paribius. [A guide through the Lithuania Minor. By] A. Klaipėdiškis [pseud.] Klaipėda, Rytas, 1924. 88 p. 947.52.B835 PU

DEU, Fred Hermann. Das Schicksal des Deutschen Memelgebietes. Berlin, 1927. See entry no. 2988.

6011. ENGEL, Carl. Die Kultur des Memellandes in vorgeschichtlicher Zeit. Memel, Siebert, 1931. 67 p. InU

6012. --- --- [Another edition] Königsberg in Pr., Gräfe und Unzer, 1937. 947.52.En331 PU

6013. ENGELHARDT, Walter. Ein Memelbilderbuch mit einer Einführung von Ernst Wiechert. Berlin, Verlag, Grenze und Ausland, 1936. 95 p. illus., map. 947.52.En36 PU IU NN

6014. FORSTREUTER, Kurt. Memelland. Elbing, Preussenverlag [1939] 59 p. illus., maps. (Preussenführer, 8) DK511.L273F67 DLC MH NN PU

6015. GAIGALAITĖ, Aldona. Klaipėdos krašto užgrobimas 1939 metais.

[The Territory of Memel is seized by the Germans in 1939] In LTSRMAD. Serija A, v.2(7), 1959, p. 105-130. See serials consulted.

6016. GANSS, Johannes. Das Memelland. [Berlin, Deutscher Schutzbund-Verlag, 1929] 23 p. illus. (Taschenbuch des Grenz- und Auslanddeutschtums, Hft.16a) 947.52.G155.2 PU NN

6017. --- Die völkischen Verhältnisse des Memellandes. Berlin, Memelland-Verlag, 1925. 144 p. diagrs, map. DK511.L273G3 DLC MH-P PU

6018. GERULLIS, Georg. Muttersprache und Zweisprachigkeit in einem preussisch-litauischen Dorf. In Studi Baltici (Rome), v.2, 1932, p. 59-67. See serials consulted.

6019. GRIGAT, Christian. Unter russischer Knute im deutschen Gebiet nördlich der Memel. Tilsit, J. Reylaender & Sohn, 1916. 48 p. D551.G78 DLC

6020. HORN, Werner. Der Volkswille im Memelgebiet zur Frage von Sprache und Gesinnung in völkisch umstrittenen Gebieten. In Petermanns Mitteilungen (Gotha), no.4, 1938, p. [97]-104. See serials consulted.

6021. --- The will of the people in the Memel Territory; a contribution to the problems of language and nationality in borderline territories. Translated by Dr. Ruth Hoppe. Gotha, Justus Perthes, [nd] p. [97]-103. fold. maps, tables. 940.96.H78w OkU

6022. IVINSKIS, Zenonas. Mažosios Lietuvos lietuviai. [The Lithuanians of the Lithuania Minor] In Aidai (Kennebunkport, Me.), no.2, 1953, p. 57-62. See serials consulted.

6023. KARP, Franz Constantin von. Beiträge zur ältesten Geschichte des Memellandes und Preussisch Litauens. Memel, Druck "Rytas" 1934. 131 p. Bibliography: p. 129-131. (GLP p.v. 116)NN DLC

6024. KATSCHINSKI, Alfred. Das Schicksal des Memellandes; eine vergleichende und zusammenfassende Heimatgeschichte. Tilsit, Selbstverlag des Memelgaubundes, 1923. 51 p. 947.52.K158 PU

6025. --- --- 2., verb. Auflage. Breslau, H. Handel, 1935. 1 v. 947.52.K158 1935 PU

6026. KLAIPĖDA. [The city of Klaipėda. Comp. by Alg. Petraitis] Vil-

nius, Mintis, 1965. 117 p. illus. DK651.M29K55 DLC

6027. KREFTAS, Haraldas. Klaipėda. [The city of Klaipėda] Vilnius, Gintaras, 1969. 111 p. illus. 914.5K ICBM

6028. KURSCHAT, Heinrich Albert. Das Buch von Memelland; Heimatkunde eines deutschen Grenzlandes. Oldenburg, F.W. Siebert, 1968. 644 p. illus., facsims, maps, ports. DK511.L27K8 DLC

6029. LANGHAUS, P. Deutsche und Litauer im Memelgebiet. In Petermann's geographische Mitteilungen (Gotha), v.69, Jan.-Feb. 1921, p. 27. map. See serials consulted.

LAWRENCE, Alexander. A memorandum on the Memel; treason trial in Kovno. London, 1935. See entry no. 3008.

6030. LITHUANIAN RESEARCH INSTITUTe, New York. Mažoji Lietuva. [Lithuania Minor] New York, N.Y., 1958. 327 p. illus., maps. (Its Studia Lituanica, 1) DK511.L2L715 DLC CLU CaAEU CaOTU CtY CtTMF FU ICLJF ICU MH NN NSyU PU

6031. MANDELSTAM, André N. Memel-Klaipėda. In Esprit international (Paris), Jan. 1, 1936, p. 20-41. See serials consulted.

6032. MAUCLÈRE, Jean. Memel et son territoire. In Études (Paris), fév.5, 1935, p. 337-349. (*DM)NN

6033. MERKYS, Vytautas. Klaipėdos kraštas Prūsijos valdžioje. [The Territory of Memel under the rule of Prussia] In LTSRII. Lietuvos TSR istorija. Vilnius, 1963. v.2, p. 404-419. illus. DK511.L2L4235 v.2 DLC CU CaAEU CtY InU MH

6034. MEYER, Richard. Heimatkunde des Memelgebietes. Memel, R. Schmidt, 1922. xi, 116 p. 947.52.M579 PU

6035. --- Das Memelland. Kitzingen am Main, Holzner [1951] 26 p. illus., map. (Der Göttinger Arbeitskreis. Schriftenreihe, Hft., 12) DK511.L273M45 DLC NN PU

6036. NADOLNY, Erwin, ed. Bis an die Memel; Beiträge ostpreussischer Wissenschaftler der Jahrhundertfeiern von Memel (1252) - Zinten (1352) - Tilsit (1552) Leer/Ostfriesland, Rautenberg & Möckel, 1952. 47 p. (Schriften der Norddeutschen Akademie Lüneburg) 493.11.N12S PU InU MH NN

6037. NEU, Heinrich. Das Wappen von Memel; Entstehung und Geschichte eines ostdeutschen Wappenbilders. Bonn, Wissenschaftliches Archiv, 1958. 19 p. illus. CR614.M4N4 DLC PU

6038. OBERLÄNDER, Theodor. Nationalität und Volkswille im Memelgebiet. Greifswald, Bamberg, 1939. 14 p. (Greifswalder Universitätsreden, 50) 63.G873 no.50 PU ICU NN

6039. PAKARKLIS, Povilas. Mažoji Lietuva vokiečių mokslo šviesoje. [Lithuania Minor from the German point of view] Kaunas, 1935. 75 p. (Socialinių ir politinių mokslų institutas. Leidinys, nr.4) 947.52.P172 PU CtTMF

6040. --- Vokiečiai apie Mažąją Lietuvą. [What Germans say about Lithuania Minor?] Kaunas, Spindulys, 1935. (Socialinių ir politinių mokslų institutas. Leidinys, nr.5) 947.52.P172 PU

6041. PLIEG, Ernst Albrecht. Das Memelland, 1920-1939; Deutsche Autonomiebestrebungen im litauischen Gesamtstaat. Würzburg, Holzner, 1962. xii, 268 p. (Marburger Ostforschungen, Bd.19) DK511.L273P55 DLC CSt-H CLU CaBVaU CaOTU CaAEU CoU GU ICU InU IU MH MiU MdBJ NIC NN NcD NjR PU WU

PREGEL, Reinhold. Die litauische Willkürherrschaft im Memelgebiet. Berlin, Grenze und Ausland, 1934. See entry no. 3032.

--- Memelfrage heute. Berlin, 1936. See entry no. 3033.

6042. RUSECKAS, Petras. Rambyno tėvynėje; du vaizdeliai iš Prūsų Lietuvos. [Two historic sketches from Lithuania Minor] Kaunas, Švyturio bendrovė [1920] 64 p. 947.5.R893.2 PU ICBM CtTMF OCl

6043. SEMBRITZKI, Johannes Karl. Geschichte der königlich preussischen See- und Handelsstadt Memel. 2. Aufl. Memel, Siebert, 1926. 380 p. 947.52.Se531 PU DLC NN PU

6044. --- Geschichte des Kreises Heydekrug. Memel, Druck von F.W. Siebert, 1920. vi, 373 p. col. map, tables. PU

6045. --- Geschichte des Kreises Memel. Festgabe zur Andenken an die 34 jährige Verwaltung des Kreises durch Geheimen Reg. Rath. Cranz. Im Auftrage des Kreisausschusses verfasst von Johannes Sembritzki. Memel, F.W. Siebert, 1918. xii, 400 p. port.

947.52.Se53 PU DLC NN NjP

6046. --- Memel im 19. Jahrhundert. Memel, F.W. Siebert, 1902. 207 p. tables, plan. (*EKZ)NN

6047. SEMRAU, Arthur. Beiträge zur Topographie der Burg und der Stadt Memel im Mittelalter. Thorn, 1929. Detached from Mitteilungen des Copernicus-Vereins für Wissenschaft und Kunst zu Thorn, Hft.37, p. [89]-116. 947.52.Se55 PU

6048. SENN, Alfred Erich. Die Besetzung Memels im Januar 1923. In Forschungen zur osteuropäischen Geschichte, v.10, 1965, p. 334-352. Offprint. 947.5.Sa57.3 PU

6049. SIDZIKAUSKAS, Vaclovas. Klaipėdos krašto ūkis seniau ir dabar. [The economy of the Territory of Memel previously and at the present] Kaunas [Spindulio bendrovės spaustuvė] 1935. 19 p. (Socialinių ir politinių mokslų institutas. Leidinys, nr.2) 320.967.Si113 PU CtTMF

6050. ŠLEŽAS, Paulius. Klaipėdos miesto istorijos bruožai, 1252-1466. [The outline of history of the City of Klaipėda (Memel) 1252-1466] In Mūsų žinynas (Kaunas), v.26, 1933, p. 187-191. See serials consulted.

URBŠIENĖ, Marija (Mašiotaitė) Klaipėdos krašto istorijos paraštėje. See entry no. 4193.

VOLSONOKAS, Rudolfas. Klaipėdos problema. Klaipėda, 1932. See entry no. 3039.

6051. Willoweit, Gerhard. Die Wirtschaftsgeschichte des Memelgebiets. Marburg/Lahn, 1969. 2 v. (927 p.) illus., maps, plan. (Wissenschaftliche Beiträge für Geschichte und Landeskunde Ost-Mitteleuropas, nr.85) Bibliography: p. 699-726. DR10.W5 nr.85 DLC

6052. ZURKALOWSKI, Erich. Studien zur Geschichte der Stadt Memel und der Politik des deutschen Ordens. Königsberg in Pr., 1906. 51 p. 914.75.B397 PU

X.12.c.2. AUTONOMY, THE STATUTE, LAWS, STATUTES, ETC., AND THEIR INTERPRETATION

ALLIED POWERS (1919-) CONFERENCE OF AMBASSADORS. Memel Territory. Letter to the Secretary General. Paris, 1923. See entry no.2979.

ALLIED POWERS (1919-)
TREATIES, ETC. Convention between
the British Empire, France, Italy,
Japan and Lithuania respecting the
Memel Territory and the Statute of
the Memel Territory... London, 1924.
See entry no. 2980.

--- Convention et disposition transitoire relatives à Memel.
[Genève, 1924] See entry no. 2981.

--- Konvencija dėl Klaipėdos krašto. Konvention über das Memelgebiet. Statute of the Territory of Memel. Klaipėda, 1925. See
entry no. 2982.

6053. BÖTTCHER, Herbert. Die Kol-
lision des memelländischen Privatrechts mit dem litauischen Privatrecht. Leipzig, L. Seidel Nachf.,
1931. 87 p. Inaug.-Diss.--Univer-
sity of Leipzig. JX6223.L7B6 CLU
DLC PPULC PU

6054. BORCHERT, Hans. Die wesent-
lichen Grundrechte der Memelländer.
Leipzig, L. Seidel Nachf., 1931.
52 p. Inaug.-Diss.--University of
Leipzig. JN6745.M4B6 1931 DLC PU

6055. BORCHERT, Paul. Über die
Kompetenzabgrenzung zwischen dem Memelgebiet und Litauen auf dem Gebiete des Strafrechts in Gesetzgebung
und Gerichtsbarkeit. Leipzig, R.
Noske, 1933. 79 p. (Abhandlungen
des Instituts für Politik, ausländisches öffentliches Recht und Völkerrecht an der Universität Leipzig,
Hft.,32) DLC-L

6056. BULOTA, Vytautas. Klaipėdos
krašto teisinė santvarka. [The ju-
dicial organization of Territory of
Memel] In Lietuvių enciklopedija.
Boston, Mass., 1968. v.15, p. 76-
79. For holdings see entry no.216.

DAUKŠA, Stasys. Le régime
d'autonomie du territoire de Klaipėda... Paris, 1936. See entry
no. 2986.
FRIESECKE, Ernst. Das Memelgebiet; eine völkerrechtliche und
politische Studie. Stuttgart, 1928.
See entry no. 2991.

6057. HAGUE. PERMANENT COURT OF
INTERNATIONAL JUSTICE. Interpréta-
tion du Statut du territoire de Memel (exception preliminaire)... Interpretation of the Staute of the
Memel territory (preliminary objec-
tion) Leyden, A.W. Sijthhoff [1932]
24, 24 p. ([Publications], Sér.A/B,
Arrêts, ordonances et avis consultatifs, fasc. no.47) Paged in duplicate; French and English on opposite

pages. JX1971.A6 ser. A/B, no.47 DLC
CLU IEN ICU IU HU MnU NN NbU NcD NcU
PPiU TxDaM WaU

HALLIER, Joachim. Die
Rechtslage des Memelgebiets. Leipzig, 1933. See entry no. 2996.

6058. HÉliARD, Madeleine. Le statut international du territoire de
Memel. Troyes, Grand impr. de Troyes,
1932. 154 p. 947.52.H369 PU NN

6059. HESSE, A. Die Entwicklung
des Privatrechts im Memelgebiet. In
Zeitschrift für ausländisches öffentliches Recht und Völkerrecht (Berlin),
1927, p. 678-709. See serials consulted.

6060. --- Gerichtsverfassung und
Rechtsgang im Memelgebiet. In Ost-
recht (Berlin), 1927, p. 269-277.
See serials consulted.

6061. --- Der Zivilprozes im Memelgebiet. In Zeitschrift für Ostrecht
(Berlin), 1927, p. 734-743. See serials consulted.

6062. JANZ, Friedrich. Die Entstehung des Memelgebiets; zugleich
ein Beitrag zur Entstehungsgeschich-
te des Versailler Vertrags. Berlin-
Lichtenfelde, E. Runge, 1928. 136 p.
(Schriften zu Politik und öffentlichen Recht Mittel- und Osteuropas,
Bd.1) DK511.L273J3 DLC PU

KALIJARVI, Thorsten. Die
Entstehung und rechtliche Natur des
Memelstatuts. Berlin, 1937. See
entry no. 3002.

6063. --- The Memel statute; its
origin, legal nature, and observa-
tion to the present day. London,
R. Hale, 1937. vi, 256 p. Bibliography: p. 245-256. DK511.L273K2
CaAEU CtY DLC DS InU NN NNC OCl PU

6064. KAUFMANN, Erich. Die Okku-
pationskosten und die Militärrouten
des Memelgebiets. In Zeitschrift
für ausländisches öffentliches Recht
und Völkerrecht (Berlin), v.3, pt.1,
1932, p. 297-312. See serials consulted.

6065. LANGER, Gottfried. Die
Rechtsverhältnisse im autonomen Memelgebiet. In Akademie zur wissenschaftlichen Erforschung und zur
Pflege des Deutschtum. Deutsche Kultur im Leben der Völker (München),
1927, p. 389-408. See serials consulted.

6066. PETKEVIČIUS, Tadas. Klaipėdos statuto vykdymo priežiūra. [The

335

supervision of the execution of the Statute of Memel Territory) Kaunas, Spindulio bendrovės spaustuvė, 1932. 21 p. (Kaunas. Universitetas. Teisių fakultetas. Darbai, v.6, kn.14) See serials consulted.

6067. ROBINSON, Jacob. Klaipėdos krašto konvencijos komentaras. [Commentary of the Convention on the Memel territory] Kaunas, Spaudos fondas, 1934. 2 v. DK511.L273R56 DLC PU

6068. --- Kommentar der Konvention über das Memelgebiet vom 8. Mai, 1924. Kaunas, Spaudos fondas, 1934. 2 v. Bibliography: p. v.1, p. 1-23. DK511.L273R6 DLC CtY PU

6069. RÖMERIS, Mykolas. La jurisdiction dite "statuaire" en Lithuanie en ce qui concerne le territoire autonome de Memel. In Revue internationale française du droit des gens (Paris), 1936, p. 361-376. See serials consulted.

6070. --- Le système juridique des guaranties de souveraineté de la Lithuanie sur le territoire de Memel. In Revue général de droit international publique (Paris), 1936, p. 257-270. See serials consulted.

6071. ROGGE, Albrecht, ed. Die Verfassung des Memelgebiets; ein Kommentar zur Memelkonvention. Berlin, 1928. 493 p. tables. (Handbücher des Ausschusses für Minderheitenrecht) Bibliography: p. [xi]-xiv. DK511.L273R7 CaAEU IU MH NN PU ViU-L

ROUZIER, A. La constitution de Lithuanie et le Statut de Memel. [Toulouse] 1926. See entry no. 2630.

6072. SCHMIDT, Hans and Paul Adam. Der Civilprozess im Memelgebiet; allgemein verständlicher Wegweiser durch den memelländischen Zivilprozess nebst Mustern von Gerichtsbefehlen, Klagen und verschiedenen Anträgen... 1. Aufl. Memel, F.W. Krumpholz, 1935. 71 p. DLC-L

6073. SCHNEIDEREIT, Rudolf. Der Bruch der Verfassung des Memelgebiets durch Litauen. In Zeitschrift für Politik (Berlin), no.1, 1922, p. [1]-11. See serials consulted.

X.12.d. LITHUANIA MINOR AND EAST PRUSSIA

X.12.d.1. GENERAL STUDIES

CAPPELLER, Carl. Leben und Gebäude der alten preussischen Litauer. Aufzeichnungen aus dem Kreise Stallupönen. Holland in Pr., 1925] See entry no. 1010-1011.

6074. CASPAR, Erich Ludwig Eduard. Herman von Salza und die Gründung des Deutschordensstaates in Preussen. Tübingen, J.C.B. Mohr, 1924. viii, 107 p. DD491.0496C3 DLC CU-S CtY CaBVaU DDO IEN InU IU MH MiU NN OCU PPULC PU WaU

6075. CLASEN-SANDT, Käthe. Zur Baugeschichte der Memelburger Ragnit, Splittern und Tilsit. In Altertumsgesellschaft Prussia (Königsberg in Pr.), v.29, 1931. p. 196-222. plates, fold. plan. See serials consulted.

6076. ENGEL, Carl. Aus ostpreussischer Vorzeit. 2. völlig umgearb. und stark erweiterte Auflage der "Bevölkelicher Zeit". Königsberg in Pr., Gräfe und Unzer, 1935. vii, 156 p. GN814.P8E58 DLC

6077. --- Vorgeschichte der altpreussischen Stämme. Königsberg in Pr., Gräfe und Unzer, 1935- . plates, ports, maps. GN814.P8E6 DLC

6078. --- and W. La Baume. Kulturen und Völker der Frühzeit im Preussenlande. Königsberg in Pr., Gräfe und Unzer, 1937. 291 p. 947.52.En331 PU

6079. EWALD, Albert Ludwig. Die Eroberung Preussens durch die Deutschen. Halle, Buchhandel des Waisenhauses, 1872-86. 4 v. in 1. col. map. 947.52.Ewl2 PU BM(9386. bb. 37.(2.))

6080. FORSTREUTER, Kurt. Preussen und Russland im Mittelalter; die Entwicklung ihrer Beziehungen vom 13. bis 17. Jahrhundert. Königsberg in Pr.; Berlin, Ost-Europa Verlag, 1938. (Osteuropäische Forschungen. Neue Folge, Bd.25) DD363.F6 DLC PU

6081. --- Preussen und Russland von den Anfängen des Deutschen Ordens bis zu Peter dem Grossen. Göttingen, Musterschmidt [1955] 257 p. (Göttinger Bausteine zur Geschichtswissenschaft, Bd.23) DD363.F DDO MH

6082. --- Vom Ordenstaat zum Fürstentum; geistige und politische Wandlungen im Deutschordensstaate Preussen unter den Hochmeistern Friedrich und Albert, 1498-1525. Kitzingen am Main, Holzner [1953?] 151 p. CR4765.F6 DLC ICU ICN MH MnCS NIC NcD NjP PU TU

6083. FRICCIUS, Karl Friedrich. Zur Geschichte der Errichtung der Landwehr in Ost- und Westpreussen und in Litauen im Jahre 1813. Königsberg in Pr., W. Koch, 1863. 42 p. Ger. 263.01 MH

6084. GAERTE, Wilhelm. Urgeschichte von Ostpreussen. Königsberg in Pr., Gräfe und Unzer, 1929. viii, 406 p. illus., plates. 947.52.G116 PU CtY WU

6085. GERULLIS, Georg. De Prussicis Sambiensium locorum nominibus. Tilsis, Mauderodiana, 1912. 168 p. Inaug.-Diss.--University of Königsber in Pr. 929.4.G329 PU CtY MH NN

6086. HANOVER. NIEDERSÄCHSISCHE LANDESBIBLIOTHEK. Katalog des Schrifttums über den deutschen Osten. 1. Ostpreussen und Westpreussen. Stand vom 31.12.1957. Hannover, 1 1958. vi, 242 p. Z2244.E38H25 DLC ICU PU

6087. HARMJANZ, Heinrich. Ostpreussisch Bauern; Volkstum und Geschichte. Königsberg in Pr., Reichsnährstand Verlag, 1938. 129 p. illus., maps. HD659.P9H28 DLC CtY MH NN

6088. HAXTHAUSEN-ABBENBURG, August Freiherr von. Die ländliche Verfassung in den Provinzen Ost- und West-Preussen. Königsberg in Pr., Stettin, Gebrüder Bornträger, 1839-61. 2 v. NN CtY(1) MH(1)

6089. HENNENBERGER, Caspar. Kurtze und wahrhaftige Beschreibung des Landes zu Preussen. Königsberg in Pr., 1584. 1 v. maps. Positive photocopy. 947.52.H397 PU

6090. HOLLACK, Emil. Haben die Polen und Litauer eine historische Recht auf Ostpreussen? Beantwortet von einem Altpreussen durch Geburt und Abstammung. Königsberg in Pr., Ostpreussische Druckerei, 1919. 89 p. (Königsberg (Schloss), Ostdeutsche Heimatdienst. Blätter zur Heimatskunde) CSt-H NN

6091. HORN, Alexander. Die Verwaltung Ostpreussens seit der Säkularisation, 1525-1875. Beiträge zur deutschen Rechts-, Verfassungs- und Verwaltungsgeschichte. Königsberg in Pr., B. Teichert, 1890. xxiv,

653 p. Bibliography: p. [xviii]-xxiv. NN

6092. HUBATSCH, Walther. Eckpfeiler Europas. Probleme des Preussenlandes in geschichtlicher Sicht. Heidelberg, Quelle & Meyer, 1953. 141 p. MH

6093. JANKUS, Martynas. Trumpi nusidavimai Prūsų Lietuvos užrašyti M. Jankaus. [Some events in Lithuania Minor] Tilžėje, 1891. 15 p. DD491.043J35 1970 PU(xerox copy)

6094. KEIL, Adolf. Das Volksschulwesen im Königreich und Herzogtum Litthauen unter Friedrich Wilhelm I. Königsberg in Pr., Buchdruck. R. Leupold, 1886. p. [93]-137. 947.52.K267 PU

6095. KENKEL, Horst. Bauernlisten des Amts Tilsit aus der Zeit vor- und nach dem Grossen Pest von 1709-1710. Hamburg, 1968. 70 p. DD491.061K4 PU

6096. KIRRINNIS, Herbert. Geschichte der Friedrichsschule zu Gumbinen; ein Beitrag zur Kultur- und Bildungsgeschichte Ostpreussens. Würzburg, Holzner Verlag, 1963. 176 p. illus. (Göttinger Arbeitskreis, Bd. 26, Veröffentlichungen, nr. 283) DLC MiU NN NNC NcD

6097. KOTZEBUE, August Friedrich Ferdinand von. Preussens ältere Geschichte. Riga, Carl Johann Gottfried, 1808. 4 v. BM(1194. d. 28) ViU

6098. --- --- [Another edition] Hamburg, 1811. 4 v. NN NNC PU

6099. KROLLMANN, Christian Anton Christoph. Politische Geschichte des Deutschen Ordens in Preussen. Königsberg, in Pr., Gräfe und Unzer [c1932] viii, 205 p. plates, ports, map. (Ostpreussische Landeskunde in Einzeldarstellungen) DD491.047K7 DLC CtY MH MiU NN

6100. KUNTZE, August. Bilder aus dem Preussischen Littauen. Erinnerungsblätter, etc. Rostock, 1884. v, 74 p. Based on the manuscript by Schultz: "Einige Bemerkungen über die Nationalität der Litauer in Preussen 1832". BM(10107. bbb. 13.(5.))

6101. ŁOWMIAŃSKI, Henryk. Stosunki polsko-pruskie za pierwszych Piastów. In Przegląd Historyczny (Warszawa), v.41, 1950, p. 152-179. See serials consulted.

6102. LUCANUS, August Hermann.

Preussens uralter und heutiger Zustand. Lötzen, In Kommission bei Thomas Oppermann, 1901. 1 v. table. (Literarische Gesellschaft Masovia. Mitteilungen. Beilagen Hft.6-7, 26-27) Vol.1 issued in three parts with reproduction of original title page. Reprint of 1748 ed. NN

6103. MACHHOLZ, E. Kirchenbücher in den Kreisen Heydekrug, Labiau, Litauische Niederung, Memel, Stallupönen und Tilsit. In LLGM, v.5, 1907, p. 362-365. See serials consulted.

6104. MANTFORT, Henri de. La Prusse au temps des prussiens. Paris, Bibliothèque polonaise [1946] 92 p. illus., ports. DD336.M65 DLC CaAEU MH

6105. MORTENSEN, Hans. Die litauische Einwanderung nach Ostpreussen. In Altertumsgesellschaft Prussia. Sitzungsberichte (Königsberg in Pr.) v.30, 1933, p. 133-141. See serials consulted.

6106. PAKARKLIS, Povilas. Senasis prūsų teisynas. [The ancient Prussian law] Chicago, Ill., Chicagos lietuvių literatūros draugija, 1960. 31 p. Excerpt from the author's Kryžiuočių valstybės santvarkos bruožai. Vilnius, 1948. 929.713.P172.3 PU PPULC

6107. PENNERS, Theodor. Untersuchungen über die Herkunft der Stadtbewohner im Deutsch-Ordensland Preussen bis in die Zeit um 1400. Leipzig, S. Hirzel, 1942. viii, 184 p. maps. (Deutschland und der Osten: Quellen und Forschungen zur Geschichte ihrer Beziehungen, Bd.16) DD491.0475P4 DLC CU CtY ICU IU MH NN NNC NcD NjP OCU

6108. PERLBACH, Max. Die ältesten preussischen Urkunden. In Altpreussische Monatsschrift (Königsberg in Pr.), v.10, 1873, p. 609-649. See serials consulted.

6109. --- Die Geschichte des ältesten Grossgrundbesitzes im Deutschordenslande Preussen. In Altpreussische Monatsschrift (Königsberg in Pr.) v.39, 1902, p. 78-124. See serials consulted.

6110. --- Preussische Urkunden aus polnischen und englischen Archiven. In Altpreussische Monatsschrift (Königsberg in Pr.), v.18, 1881, p. 225-244. See serials consulted.

6111. --- Regesten der Stadt Königsberg 1256-1524. In Altpreussische Monatsschrift (Königsberg in Pr.), v.18, 1881, p. 1-39. See serials consulted.

6112. PERTSEV, V.N. Kul'tura i religiia drevnikh prussov. In Minsk. Universitet. Uchenye zapiski. Seriia istoricheskaia, vyp.16, 1953, p. 329-378. AS262.M522 DLC NNC

6113. --- Nachal'nye periody istorii drevnei Prussii (Genesis prusskoi narodnosti) In Minsk. Universitet. Uchenye zapiski. Seriia istoricheskaia, vyp.30, 1956, p. 109-122. AS262.M522 DLC NNC

6114. PREUSS, A.E., ed. Preussische Landes- und Volkskunde; oder, Beschreibung von Preussen. Königsberg in Pr., 1835. xx, 633. About Lithuania: p. 224-232. BM(10240. bbb. 4.)

6115. PRUSSIA. LAWS, STATUTES, ETC. Prūsijos valdžios gromatos, pagraudenimai ir apsakymai lietuviams valstiečiams. [Letters, appeals and proclamations of the Prussian Government to the Lithuanian peasants. Comp. by P. Pakarklis, ed. by K. Jablonskis] Vilnius, VPMLL, 1960. 664 p. At head of title: Lietuvos TSR Mokslų akademija. Istorijos institutas. DD339.P97 CaAEU DLC CtPAM CtY ICBM IEN MH NN NjP PU

6116. PRUTZ, Hans. Die Anfänge des Deutschen Ordens in Preussen und seine Beziehungen zum Heiligen Lande. In Altpreussische Monatsschrift (Königsberg in Pr.), N.F., v.15, 1878, p. 1-26. See serials consulted.

6117. RAUSCHNICK, Gottfried Peter. Bemerkungen eines Russen über Preussen und dessen Bewohner. Gesammelt auf einer im Jahre 1814 durch dieses Land unternommenen Reise. Mainz, F. Kupferberg, 1817. x, 398 p. About Lithuanians: p. 22-39. DD316.R3 DLC

6118. RIEMANN, Erhard. Volkskunde des Preussenlandes. Kitzingen am Main, Holzner, 1952. 36 p. (Der Göttinger Arbeitskreis. Schriftenreihe, Hft.19) DD491.045R5 DLC

6119. SAHM, Wilhelm. Geschichte der Pest in Ostpreussen. In Publikationen des Vereins für die Geschichte der Provinz Ost- und Westpreussen (Leipzig), 1905. viii, 184 p. BM(Ac. 7351/12.)

6120. SAUERVEINAS, Georg Julius Justus. Die littauische Frage einiger Zeitungen... Von Girēnas [pseud.] Keliū laikraszcziū Lietuwiszkasis klausymas su wokiszku bey lietuwiszku atsiliepimu. Sutaise Girēnas. Tilžēje, 1888. xxiv, 90 p. In German and Lithuanian. 947.52.Sa89 PU BM(8094. e. 34.) and (8092. de. 48.)

6121. SCHÜTZ, Caspar. Historia rervm Prvssicarvm. Wahrhafte und eigentliche Beschreibung der Lande Preussen... von den eltesten Königen an derselben Regierung und heidnischer Aufopfferung auch vom Vrsprung des Deutschen Ordens. [Leipzig] Typis et svmtibvs Grosianis, 1599. [14], 555 (i.e. 548), [11] leaves. Rare Books and Spec. Coll. CaOTU

6122. SKALWEIT, August Karl Friedrich. Die ostpreussische Domänenverwaltung unter Friedrich Wilhelm I. und das Rétablissement Litauens. Leipzig, Duncker & Humblot, 1906. x, 357 p. (Staats- und sozialwissenschaftliche Forschungen, Bd.25, Hft. 3) HB41.S7 v.25 DLC CSt CU IaU ICJ ICN ICU IEN MnU MH NIC NNC PU WU

6123. ŠLIŪPAS, Jonas. Mažoji arba prūsiškoji Lietuva 19-tame šimtmetyje. [Lithuania Minor or Prussian Lithuania in the nineteenth century] Chicago, Ill., "Laisvosios Minties" leidinys, 1910. 21 p. 947.5.V713 PU CtPAM CtTMF

6124. STOROST, Wilhelm. Gyvenimas Prūsų Lietuvos apie 1770 m. Kaip jį vaizdavo Kristijonas Donelaitis. [By] Vydūnas [pseud.] Kassel-Mattenberg, Mažosios Lietuvos tarybos spaudos komisija, 1948. 47 p. illus. 390.V ICBM

--- Sieben hundert Jahre deutsch-litauischer Beziehungen. Tilsit, 1932. See entry no. 1053.

6125. TERVEEN, Fritz. Gesamtstaat und Rétablissement; der Wiederaufbau des nördlichen Ostpreussens unter Friedrich Wilhelm I., 1714-1740. Göttingen, Musterschmidt, 1954. 234 p. maps, plans. (Göttinger Bausteine zur Geschichtswissenschaft, Bd.16) (Historische Kommission für Ost- und Westpreussische Landesforschung. Veröffentlichungen, nr.7) Bibliography: p. 201-208. JS5471.P8E37 DLC CaAEU CtY ICU NN PU

6126. --- Das Rétablissement König Friedrich Wilhelms I. in Preussisch Litauen von 1714-1740. In Zeitschrift für Ostforschung (Marburg/Lahn) v.1, no4, 1952, p. 500-515. See serials consulted.

6127. THALMANN, Waldemar. Stadtgeschichte Tilsits. Tilsit, O. v. Mauderode, 1938. 48 p. illus. WU

6128. THIENEMANN, Johannes. Rositten; drei Jahrzehnte auf der Kurischen Nehrung. 3., verb. und verm. Auflage. Neudamm, J. Neumann, 1927. 326 p. illus., maps, diagrs. DD9o1.R75T4 DLC

6129. --- 3., verb. und verm. Auflage. Neudamm, J. Neumann, 1930. iii, 332 p. 947.52.T347 PU

6130. TÖPPEN, Max Pollux, ed. Acten der Ständetage Preussens unter der Herrschaft des Deutschen Ordens. Leipzig, Duncker & Humblot, 1886. 5 v. DD491.046A2 DLC(5, no.2) IaU MH PU

6131.--- Historisch-komparative Geographie von Preussen. Gotha, J. Perthes, 1858. xii, 398 p., and atlas of 5 maps. DD310.T64 DLC NN PU

6132. ---Zur Geschichte der historischen Literatur Preussens im 16. Jahrhundert. In Altpreussische Monatsschrift (Königsberg in Pr.), v.5, 1868, p. 243-264. See serials consulted.

6133. TYMIENIECKI, Kazimierz. Misja Polska w Prusiech i sprowadzenie Krzyżaków. Toruń, Kasa im. Mianowskiego, 1935. 52 p. At head of title: Wydawnictwa Instytutu Bałtyckiego. Bibliography: p. 49-52. "Rozprawa z pracy zbiorowej: Dzieje Prus Wschodnich." (*QO p.v. 110)NN CtY

6134. VALANČIUS, Grigas. Lietuva ir Karaliaučiaus kraštas. [Lithuania and the region of Königsberg] Kirchheim-Teck, Ger., 1946. 93 p. fold. map. DD491.066V3 DLC CaOONL ICLJF PU

6135. VOIGT, Johannes. Geschichte Preussens von den ältesten Zeiten bis zum Untergange der Herrschaft des Deutschen Ordens. Königsberg in Pr., Bornträger, 1827-39. 9 v. 947.52.V873 PU CtY IaU ICU DLC(1-5, 7-9) MH MiU MdBJ(7) NN

6136. --- --- Reprint. Hildersheim, Olms, 1968. 9 v. DD377.V72 1968 CaOTU

6137. WEISE, Erich. Die alten Preussen. Elbing, 1934. 38 p. DD336.W45 DLC

6138. --- The ancient Prussians. Tr. by Else Deckner. Elbing, Preussenverlag, 1934. 39 p. illus., maps, facsims. (Prussian guides, 3) CtY MH OO PU

6139. --- Der Bauernaufstand in Preussen. Elbing, Preussenverlag,

1935. 69 p. illus., maps, facsims.
DD183.W4 DLC

6140. ---, ed. Die Staatsverträge
des Deutschen Ordens in Preussen im
15. Jahrhundert. Hrsg. im Auftrage
de Historischen Kommision für ost-
und westpreussische Landesforschung.
Königsberg in Pr., Im Kommissionsverlag Gräfe und Unzer, 1939-58. 3 v.
DD491.046W4 DLC CaAEU(1) CtY ICU MH
NN
    WERMKE, Ernst. Bibliogra-
phie der Geschichte von Ost- und
Westpreussen, 1931-1933. Königsberg
in Pr., 1933. See entry no. 4195.

    --- --- Neudruck der Ausgabe
1933 mit ergänzendem Nachtrag. Aalen,
1962. See entry no. 4196.

    --- ---, für die Jahre 1930-
1938. Aalen, 1964. See entry
no. 4197.

    --- ---, für die Jahre 1939-
1942. Königsberg in Pr., 1944. See
entry no. 4198.

    --- ---, für die Jahre 1939-
1951. Marburg/Lahn, 1953. See entry no. 4199.

    --- ---, für die Jahre 1952-
1956. Marburg/Lahn, 1958. See entry no. 4200.

    --- ---, für die Jahre 1957-
1961. Marburg/Lahn, 1963. See entry no. 4201.

6141. YČAS, Jonas. Mažosios Lietuvos praeitis, XIII-XX amžių bruožai. [The past of Lithuania Minor,
XIII-XX centuries; an outline] In
Kovo 20 diena, Mažosios Lietuvos
prisiglaudimui paminėti. Kaunas,
1921. p. 24-90. DK511.L27K6 DLC BM
CtTMF ICBM PU

6142. --- Prūsų žemės istorija.
[The history of ancient Prussia]
Kaunas, Studentų humanitarų draugijos spaudos komisijos leidinys,
1929. 79 p. Rankraščio teisėmis.
947.5.Y ICCC

6143. ŽOSTAUTAITĖ, P. Prūsijos
lietuvių valstiečių padėtis XVIII a.
antroje pusėje. [The conditions of
the Prussian Lithuanian peasants in
the second part of the eighteenth
century] In LTSRMAD. Serija A, v.
1(12), 1962, p. 91-113. See serials
consulted.

X.12.d.2. COLONIZATION OF LITHUA-
NIAN LANDS

6144. BARKOWSKI, O. Die Besiedlung des Hauptamtes Insterburg unter
Herzog Albrecht und Markgraf Georg
Friedrich von Ansbach, 1525-1603. In
Altertumsgesellschaft Prussia. Sitzungsberichte (Königsberg in Pr.),
v.28, 1928, p. 159-243; v.30, 1933,
p.3-131. See serials consulted.

6145. BEHEIM-SCHWARZBACH, Max.
Friedrich Wilhelm's I. Colonisations-
werk in Litauen, vornehmlich die
Salzburger Colonie. Königsberg in
Pr., Hartung, 1879. x, 423 p.
DD403.8.B419 NIC MH NSyU PPULC PU

6146. --- Hohenzollernsche Coloni-
sationen. Ein Beitrag zu der Geschichte des Preussischen Staates und
der Colonisation des östlichen Deutschlands. Leipzig, Duncker & Humblot, 1874. xviii, 637 p.
DD335.B4 DLC CtY NIC PPULC PU

6147. HARMJANZ, Heinrich. Volkskunde und Siedlungsgeschichte Altpreussens. Berlin, Juncker und
Dünnhaupt, 1936. 75 p. fold. map.
DD491.0431H3 DLC MH

6148. HOESE, Alexander and Hermann
Eichert. Die Salzburger; kurze Geschichte und namentliches Verzeichnis der im Jahre 1732 in Litauen
eingewanderten Salzburger. Gumbinnen, 1911. xii, 40 p. DD491.06H64
PU

6149. JAKŠTAS, Juozas. Mažosios
Lietuvos apgyvendinimas iki XVII amžiaus pabaigos. [The population of
Prussian Lithuania until the end of
the seventeenth century] Roma, 1970.
12, xx, 126 p. Offprint from L.K.M.
akademija. Metraštis, v. 5, 1970.
DD491.045J34 PU; also in LKMAM, v.5,
1970, p. 339-414. See serials consulted.

6150. KASISKE, Karl. Die Siedlungstätigkeit des Deutschen Ordens in
östlichen Preussen bis zum Jahre 1410.
Königsberg in Pr., Gräfe und Unzer,
1934. xi, 175 p. (Einzelschriften
der historischen Kommission)
CU CtY NN

6151. KENKEL, Horst. Französische
Schweizer und Réfugiés als Siedler
im nördlichen Ostpreussen (Litauen),
1710-1750. Unter Auswertung des
Nachlasses von Bernhard Haagen.
Hamburg, Selbstverlag des Vereins,
1970. 164 p. maps. (Sonderschrif-
ten des Vereins für Familienforschung
in Ost- und Westpreussen, 13)

340

Ger.11610.68(13) MH

6152. KÖTZSCHKE, Rudolf. Geschichte des ostdeutschen Kolonisation. Leipzig, Bibliographisches Institut [1937] 251 p. illus., plans, maps. Bibliography: p. 239-251. HD1516.G3K6 DLC CoFcS CtY MH NN NcD NCH WU

6153. --- Quellen zur Geschichte der ostdeutschen Kolonisation in 12 bis 14 Jahrhundert. Hrsg. von Rudolf Kötschke. Leipzig; Berlin, B.G. Teubner, 1912. vii, 142 p. (Quellensammlung zur deutschen Geschichte) HD659.W4K72 DLC BM CtY OCl OU

6154. KROLLMANN, Christian Anton Christoph. Die Besiedlung Ostpreussens durch den Deutschen Orden. In Vierteljahrschrift für Sozial- und Wirtschaftsgeschichte (Leipzig), v.21, 1928, p. 280-298. See serials consulted.

6155. KUCK, Johannes. Die Siedlungen im westlichen Nadrauen. Leipzig, Hoffmann, 85 p. Inaug.-Diss.-- University of Königsberg in Pr. DLC DSG CtY MH PU

6156. LOOKING EAST; Germany beyond the Vistula. [Berlin] Terramare Office, 1933. 81, [3] p. illus., front. DD491.045L6 DLC CtY ICU MH NcU ODW ViU

6157. ŁOWMIAŃSKI, Henryk. Polityka ludnościowa Zakonu Niemieckiego w Prusach i na Pomorzu. Gdańsk, Instytut Bałtycki, 1947. 72 p. (Prace Naukowo-Informacyjne. Seria Pomorze) DD491.0475L6 DLC NIC NNC

6158. MORTENSEN, Hans. Siedlungsgeographie des Samlandes. In Forschungen zur deutschen Landes- und Volkskunde (Leipzig), v.22, 1923. See serials consulted.

6159. MORTENSEN, Hans and Gertrud Mortensen. Die Besiedlung des nordöstlichen Ostpreussens bis zum Beginn des 17. Jahrhunderts. Leipzig, S. Hirzel, 1937-38. 2 v. fold. plan, diagrs., maps, facsims. (Deutschland und der Osten, 7-8) Bibliography: v.1, p. 207-212; v.2, p. 247-254. DD491.0431M6 DLC CtY IaU MH MiD NN NcD NdU NmU OU PSt WU

MÜLLER, August. Die preussische Kolonisation in Nordpolen und Litauen. Berlin, 1928. See entry no. 3622.

6160. OSTPREUSSISCHE LANDGESELLSCHAFT m.b.H. ZU KÖNIGSBERG IN PR. Zwanzig Jahre deutscher Siedlungsarbeit im Ostpreussen, 1906-1926; ein Überblick über die Tätigkeit der Ostpreussischen Landgesellschaft... gemeinnütziges, provinzielles Siedlungsunternehmen für die Provinz Ostpreussen. Königsberg in Pr., Gräfe und Unzer [1927] 134 p. illus. 2 fold. maps, 8 plans. HD1516.G3075 DLC DNAL NN

6161. RIEHL, Klaus. Die Siedlungstätigkeit des Deutschen Ordens in Preussen in der Zeit 1410-1466. In Altpreussische Forschungen (Königsberg in Pr.), v.14, 1937, p. 224-267. See serials consulted.

6162. ZAJĄCZKOWSKI, Stanisław. Podbój Prus i ich kolonizacja przez Krzyżaków. Toruń, Kasa im. Mianowskiego, 1935. iv, 57 p. map. DD491.0475Z3 DLC NN

X.12.e. YATWYAGS (SUDOVIANS)

6163. ANTONIEWICZ, Jerzy. The mysterious Sudovian people. In Archaeology (New York, N.Y.), v.11, 1958, p. 158-161. illus., map. See serials consulted.

6164. --- Odkrycie grobu rolnika jaćwieskiego z narzędziami produkcji z okresu rzymskiego. In Rocznik Białostocki (Białystok), v.3, 1962, p. 205-223. See serials consulted.

6165. --- The Sudovians. [Translated by Halina Modrzewska] Białystok, Białystok Scientific Society, 1962. 20 p., 24 plates. DK409.A63 CaAEU IU MH MiDW PU

6166. --- Wyniki dotychczasowych badań starożytnego osadnictwa jaćwieskiego w dorzeczu Czarnej Hańczy. In Wiadomości Archeologiczne (Warszawa), t.25, 1958, p. 1-19. See serials consulted.

6167. BIAŁOSTOCKIE TOWARZYSTWO NAUKOWE. Kompleksowa ekspedycja Jaćwieska. Materiały do dziejów ziemi sejneńskiej i praca zbiorowa pod red. Jerzego Antoniewicza. Białystok, 1963. 436 p. illus., maps. (Prace Białostockiego Towarzystwa Naukowego, nr.1) Summaries in English and Russian. DK511.S46B57 ICU MH PU

6168. --- --- Studia i materiały do dziejów Pojezierza Augustowskiego. Praca zbiorowa pod red. Jerzego Antoniewicza. Białystok, 1967. 796 p. illus., maps. (Prace Białostockiego Towarzystwa Naukowego, nr. 9) DK511.A88B57 ICU MH PU

6169. --- --- Studia i materiały do dziejów Suwalszczyzny; praca zbiorowa pod red. Jerzego Antoniewicza. Białystok, 1965. 681 p. (Prace Białostockiego Towarzystwa Naukowego, nr. 4) 943.8.B472 PU MH MiDW

6170. FALK, Knut Olaf. Kilka uwag w sprawie osadnictwa południowych puszcz pojaćwieskich od XV do XVII w. In Rocznik Białostocki (Białystok), v.1, 1961. See serials consulted.

6171. JAKIMOWICZ, Roman. Wschodnia granica osadnictwa mazowieckiego w X i XI wieku z Jaćwieżą i Russią i zasiąg kolonizacji mazowieckiej na wschodzie. In PZHP w Wilnie września 17-20, 1935. Pamiętnik VI. Referaty (Lwów), v.2, 1936, p. 246-250. See serials consulted.

6172. JASKANIS, DANUTA. Jaćwież; katalog opracowano w związku z wystawą "Jaćwież w swietle wykopalisk", czerwiec-lipiec, 1962. Białystok, 1962. 44 p. PU-Mu(Pam)

6173. KAMIŃSKI, Aleksander. Jaćwież; terytorium, ludność, stosunki gospodarcze i społeczne. [Wyd. 1.] Łodz, 1953 [i.e. 1954] 207 p. illus. (Łódzkie Towarzystwo Naukowe. Wydział II. Prace, nr.14) DK34.Y38K3 DLC ICU NN PU

6174. --- Materialy do bibliografii archeologicznej Jaćwieży od I. do XIII. wieka. In Materiały Starożytne (Warszawa), v.1, 1956, p. 193-271. CaOTU CU CtY MH-P NN NNM PU-Mu WU

6175. --- Z badań nad pograniczem polsko-rusko-jaćwieskim w rajonie rzeki Sliny. In Wiadomości Archeologiczne (Warszawa), v.23, 1956, p. 131-167. See serials consulted.

6176. NALEPA, Jerzy. Jaćwięgowie; jazwa i lokalizacja. Białystok,1964. 60 p. fold. map. (Prace Białostockiego Towarzystwa Naukowego, nr.2) DK421.2.N35 NmU ICU PU

6177. OTRĘBSKI, Jan Szczepan. Zagadnienie Galindów. In Studia Historica (Warszawa), 1958, p. 37-42. D6.S796 DLC CtY ICU MnU NN NIC NNC

6178. RAULINAITIS, Zigmantas. Galindai prieš Romą. [Galindai against Rome. Brooklyn, N.Y.] Karys, 1963. 80 p. illus. (Lietuvos karinės istorijos raštai, 4) Revised offprint from Karys, 1962. 970.5.RA ICLJF MH

6179. SEMBRITZKI, Johannes. Die Nord- und Westgebiete der Jadwinger

und deren Grenzen. In Altpreussische Monatsschrift (Königsberg in Pr.), v.28, 1891-1892, p. 76-89. See serials consulted.

6180. SJÖGREN, Anders Johann. Über die Wohnsitze und die Verhältnisse der Jatwägen; ein Beitrag zur Geschichte Osteuropas um die Mitte des XIII. Jahrhunderts. In Académie Impérial des sciences de St. Pétersburg. Mémoires, VI-e série, second partie, t.9, 1859, p. 161-356. See serials consulted.

6181. VOL'TER, Eduard Aleksandrovich. O iatviagakh; k kakomu antropologichesko-etnologicheskomu tipu prinadlezhali iatviagi. Sanktpeterburg, 1908. 1 v. Offprint from Ezhegodnik Russkago antropologicheskago obshchestva. Sanktpeterburg, 1908. 947.5.V887 PU

6182. ZAJĄCZKOWSKI, Stanisław. Kaip jotvingiai buvo vadinami viduriniais amžiais? [What was the name for the Yatwyags in the Middle Ages?] In Lietuvos praeitis (Kaunas), v.1, no.1, 1940, p. 57-76. See serials consulted.

6183. --- O nazwach ludu Jadzwingów. In Towarzystwo Naukowe w Toruniu. Wydział Nauk Historycznych, Prawniczych i Społecznych. Zapiski, v.18, 1952, p. 175-195. See serials consulted.

6184. --- Problem Jaćwieży w historiografii. In Towarzystwo Naukowe w Toruniu. Wydział Nauk Historycznych, Prawniczych i Społecznych. Zapiski, v.19, 1953, p. 7-56. See serials consulted.

6185. --- Problematyka dziejów Jadzwingów w historiografii. In Łódzkie Towarzystwo Naukowe. Sprawozdania z Czynności i Posiedzeń, v.6-9, 1951-1954, p. 47-55. See serials consulted.

X.13. PERSONAL NARRATIVES

6186. BAGDONAS, Juozas. Iš mūsų kovų ir žygių... [From our struggles ...] Kaunas, Autoriaus leidinys, 1930-31. 2 v. 947.5.B146 PU(1) PPULC

6187. BALČIŪNAS, Juozas. Dangus debesyse; autoriaus išgyvenimai, 1918-1919 metais. [... Author's experiences in 1918-1919. By] J. Švaistas [pseud.] London, Nida, 1967. 325 p. (Nidos knygų klubo leidinys, nr.63)

PG8721.B27 PU CaAEU

6188. BARTUŠKA, Vincas. Kelionė
Lietuvon Didžiosios karės metu.
[Journey to Lithuania during the
First World War] So. Boston, Mass.,
Spauda Darbininko, 1916. 85 p.
DK511.L26B28 DLC CtY CtTMF ICLJF
OKentU PPULC PU

6189. BIELINIS, Kipras. Dienojant;
spaudos draudimo laikų atsiminimai.
Priedai: Kauno gubernija prieš 100
metų. Kauno gubernija kapitalisti-
nio ūkio laikais. Kražių skerdynės
ir kiti. [At dawn; reminiscences
from the period of total suppression
of the Lithuanian press...] New
Yorkas, Amerikos lietuvių socialdemokratų sąjungos literatūros fondo
lėšomis, 1958. 464 p. illus., ports.
DK511.L25B45 DLC CaAEU CaOTU ICU MH
MiD NN OCl OKentU PU

6190. --- Gana to jundo. [It's
enough of that yoke] New Yorkas,
Išleista Kipro Bielinio ir Amerikos
lietuvių socialdemokratų sąjungos literatūros fondo lėšomis, 1971. 492 p.
DK511.L28B46 PU DLC

6191. BIRŽIŠKA, Mykolas. Dėl mūsų sostinės; iš Vilniaus darbo atsiminimų. [About our capital city;
reminiscences from the work in Vilnius. London] Nida [1960-62] 2 v.
(Nidos knygų klubo leidinys, no.31,
38) DK651.V4B49 DLC CaAEU CaOTU
CaOTP CtTMF CtY ICLJF ICCC MH PU

6192. --- M. Biržiškos anuo metu
Viekšniuose ir Šiauliuose; iš 1882-
1901 m. atsiminimų, pasakojimų ir
raštų. [The Biržiškos at that time
in Viekšniai and Šiauliai; memoirs
from the years, 1882-1901] Kaunas,
1938. xii, 378 p. illus., ports.
947.52.B537 PU BM(010795. 1. 24.)

6193. --- Vilniaus Golgota; okupuotosios Lietuvos lietuvių darbo ir
kančių 1919-1928 metų dienoraštis,
iš laikraščių surinktas. [The suf-
fering Vilnius... By] Šemis [pseud.]
Kaunas, Vilniui vaduoti sąjungos leidinys, 1930. 658 p. illus.
DK651.V4B5 DLC CtPAM CtTMF ICCC
PU(xerox copy of 1971)

6194. BORODZICZ, Józef. Pod wozem
i na wozie; pamiętniki... kilka lat
pracy na Litwie. Chrzanów, Author,
1911. 266 p. illus., ports.
947.52.B648 PU CaAEU InU NNC

6195. BUČYS, Pranciškus Petras.
Vysk. P.P. Bučio atsiminimai. [Me-
moirs of P.P. Bučys] Surašė Z. Ivinskis, redagavo J. Vaišnora. [Chica-
go, Ill.] Lietuviškos knygos klubas,

[1966] 2 v. illus., ports.
BX4705.B894A3 DLC ICLJF OKentU PU

6196. BUTKUS, Stasys. Vyrai Gedimino kalne.; pirmūno ir savanorio
atsiminimai. [Men on the hill of
Gediminas; recollections. Memmingen,
Ger., Aušra leidinys, 1957] 225 p.
947.5.B974 PU CtTMF ICLJF MiD NN
OKentU

6197. DIDŽIULIENĖ, Liudvika (Nit-
kaitė) Ką aš beatmenu. [This is
what I remember. By] Žmona [pseud.]
Redagavo J. Tumas. Kaunas, Spaudos
fondas, 1926. 179, iii p.
491.922.D566 PU

6198. DOGELIS, Povilas. Mano gyvenimo prisiminimai. [Memoirs from
my life] Kaunas, 1936. 272 p.
947.52.D676 PU CtTMF

6199. DOVYDĖNAS, Liudas. Mes val-
dysim pasaulį; atsiminimai. [We
shall rule the world; memoirs. Wood-
haven, N.Y., 1970] 2 v.
DK511.L27D65 PU

6200. ENSKAITIS, Pranas. Audra
eina; atsiminimų pynė iš praslinku-
sių skaudžių audros sūkuriuose pra-
leistų dienų. [The storm is continuing; recollections...] Hamilton,
Ont., Rūta, 1961. 146 p.
891.92.En78A PU

6201. GARMUS, Antanas. Nemuno pa-
krantėmis. [Along the Nemunas river]
Chicago, Ill., Nemunas, 1951. 136
p. R575.L4G3 DLC PU

6202. GIEYSZTOR, Jakób Kazimierz.
Pamiętniki Jakóba Gieysztora z lat
1857-1865, poprzedzone wspomnieniami
osobistemi prof. Tadeusza Korzona,
oraz opatrzone przedmową i przepisa-
mi. Wilno, "Kurjer Litewski", 1913.
2 v. ports. 947.52.G365 PU ICU NN

6203. --- --- [Another edition]
Wilno, Księgarnia Stowarz. Nauczy-
cielstwa Polskiego, 1921. 2 v.
Bibliography: v.2, p. [257]-326.
DK436.5.G5A3 DLC MnU NB

6204. GINTNERIS, Antanas, ed. Lietuva caro ir kaizerio naguose; atsiminimai iš I-mo pasaulinio karo laikų, 1914-1918 m. [Lithuania in the
shackles of the Czar and Kaiser...]
Čikaga, 1970. 508 p. DK511.L26G5 PU

6205. GRAŠIS, Vincas. Atsiminimai
iš bolševikų nelaisvės. [Recollec-
tions of the bolshevik captivity]
Marijampolė, Šaltinis, 1927. 48 p.
ICLJF

GRINIUS, Kazys. Atsiminimai

ir mintys. Tübingen, 1947-62. See entry no. 531.

6206. GUSTEDT, Ernst Carl Albert von. Aus Russisch Litauen, 1916-1917; Erinnerungen und Erwägungen. Halle a.S., W. Knapp, 1918. vi, 71 p. DK511.L26G982 CSt-H NbU

6207. HARTMANN, Fritz. Ob-Ost; friedliche Kriegsfahrt eines Zeitungsmannes. Hannover, Gebr. Jänecke, 1917. 103 p. 947.52.H259 PU

6208. JONAITIS, Jurgis F. Mano patyrimai Didžiojoj Karėj, 1918 ir 1919 metais. [My experiences during the First World War] Boston, Mass., Spauda Darbininko, 1920. 64 p. 947.5.D676 PU CtTMF OCl

6209. JONUŠKA, Vincas. Dienoraštis, 1915-1919. [Memoirs, 1915-1919. Ed. by V. Steponavičius] In Karo archyvas (Kaunas), v.7, 1936, p.226-299. See serials consulted.

6210. KAIRYS, Steponas. Lietuva budo. 1. Vaiko ir jaunystės atsiminimai. 2. Kas buvo Lietuva? [Lithuania awakening: 1. Memoirs of childhood. 2. What Lithuania was?] New York, Amerikos lietuvių socialdemokratų sąjungos literatūros fondo lėšomis, 1957. 416 p. DK511.L2K3 DLC CaAEU CtY MH OCl OKentU PU

6211. KAPLANAS, Ch. Kareivinėse neramu; iš atsiminimų, 1918-1927. [... Recollections from 1918-1927. Literatūrinis bendraautorius P. Kirijenka] Vilnius, VGLL, 1961. 402 p. ports. HX315.65.K22 DLC

6212. KAPSUKAS, Vincas. Caro kalėjimuose; užrašai ir atsiminimai V. Mickevičius-Kapsukas. [In the Czar's prisons...] Brooklyn, N.Y., "Laisvės" spauda, 1929. 320 p. (Amerikos lietuvių darbininkų literatūros draugijos leidinys, nr.27) HX315.65.A6K3 DLC CtTMF OKentU PU

6213. KRUPAVIČIUS, Mykolas. Atsiminimai. [Recollections. Chicago, Ill.] Lietuviškos knygos klubas [1972] 364 p. illus. DK511.L28K75 PU DLC

6214. LAVINSKAS, Frank. Angliakasio atsiminimai. [Memoirs of a miner] Long Island City, N.Y., 1952. 2 v. in 1. illus. E184.L7L3 DLC ICN NN PU

6215. MATULAITIS, Stasys. Atsiminimai ir kiti kūriniai. [Recollections and other works] Vilnius, VGLL, 1957. 404 p. ports., facsim. 891.92.M437A PU CtPAM

6216. MIŠKINIS, Jonas. Manoji Dzūkija; atsiminimai. [My Dzūkija; reminiscences] London, Nida, 1966. 192 p. 947.5.M684 PU CaAEU CaOTU OKentU

6217. MUSTEIKIS, Kazys. Prisiminimų fragmentai. [Fragments of reminiscences. London] Nida [1970] 126 p. port. (Nidos knygų klubo leidinys, nr.77) DK511.L28M83 DLC PU

6218. PAJAUJIS, Juozas. Fiftieth anniversary of the declaration of Lithuania's independence. In Lituanus (Chicago, Ill.), v.14, no.1, 1968. p.5-16. See serials consulted.

6219. PALECKIS, Justas. Žingsniai smėly; 1926 metai. [Paces in the sand; year 1926] Vilnius, Vaga, 1968. 342 p. DK511.L28P35A3 CtY CaAEU CtY OClW PU

6220. PASEK, Jan Chryzostom. Pamiętniki; z rękopisu wydał Jan Czubek. Kraków, Polska Akademia Umiejętności, 1929. xxxiv, 635 p. (Polska Akademia Umiejętności. Bibljoteka Pisażów Polskich, nr.81) DK431.2.P3A3 1929 DLC CaAEU MH NN WU

6221. PAWŁOWICZ, Eduard. Wspomnienia z nad Wilji i Niemna. Lwów, Dobrynowicz i Schmidt, 1822. 178 p. 947.22.P289 PU

6222. --- --- [Another edition] Lwów, 1881-1904. 178 p. BM(10291. bb. 17.)

6223. --- Z życia Litwina. Lwów, 1904. 19 p. BM(10601. de. 17.(5)

6224. PETRAUSKAS, Antanas. Praeities pabyros; atsiminimai iš pergyventų laikų, 1905-1914. [Miscellany from the past; reminiscences from 1905-1914] Chicago, Ill., Draugas, 1934. 192 p. DK511.L713P477 InNd ICLJF PU

6225. PIETARIS, Vincas. Iš mano atsiminimų. [My recollections. Spaudon prirengė J. Basanavičius] Chicago, Ill., Spauda Lietuvos, 1905. 301 p. port. 891.92.P618 PU CtTMF NN OCl

6226. POTOCKI, Leon. Pamiętniki pana Kamertona [pseud.] Przez L.P. Poznań, J.K. Żupański, 1869. 3 v. in 1. DK511.L2P86 ICU

6227. POŽELA, Vladas. Jaunystės atsiminimai. [Recollections from the past] Redagavo Pranas Čepėnas. [London, Nida] 1971. 335,iv p.

Išleido Amerikos lietuvių socialdemokratų sąjunga, literatūros fondas.
DK511.L28P69 PU

6228. PRANAITYTĖ, Julė. Laisvo-
sios Lietuvos aplankytų; atsiminimai. [By Pranaičių Julė. A visit
to free Lithuania...] Philadelphia,
Pa., Author, 1928. 356 p. illus.
LG2.PRA ICLJF CtTMF

6229. PUZYNA, Gabrjela. W Wilnie
i dworach litewskich. Pamiętnik z
lat 1815-1843. Wilno, Nakł. J. Zawadzkiego, 1928. xviii, 389 p.
illus., ports. 947.52.P999 PU CtY

6230. RACZYŃSKI, Edward. Wspomnienia wielkopolskie; to jest, Woje-
wództw: Poznańskiego, Kaliskiego i
Gnieznieńskiego przez... byłego posła
z pow. Poznańskiego na sejmach W.X.
Litewskiego, dziś deputatów z pow.
Śremskiego na sejmie W.K. Litewskiego. Poznań, Orędownik, 1842-1843.
2 v. illus., atlas. BM(1298.1.19.)

6231. RUCEVIČIUS, Antanas. Sunkiaisiais laikais. [During the difficult days] Kaunas Švyturys, 1920.
114 p. 947.5.R823 PU CtTMF

6232. SAVICKIS, Jurgis. Žemė dega.
[The earth in flames] Chicago, Ill.,
Terra [1956] 2 v. port.
PG8721.S26Z28 CaAEU CaOTU CtY DLC
ICLJF NN OCl PU

6233. SEMKOWICZ, Władysław. Wspomnienia z Litwy kowieńskiej. Kraków,
Author, 1930. 947.52.Se54 PU

6234. SKIPITIS, Rapolas. Nepriklausoma Lietuva; atsiminimai. [In-
dependent Lithuania; recollections]
Chicago, Ill., [Terra] 1967. 477 p.
illus., ports. DK511.L27S49 DLC
CaAEU CaOTU CtPam InNd NN OKentU PU
WU

6235. --- Nepriklausomą Lietuvą
statant; atsiminimai. [Building independent Lithuania; recollections.
Chicago, Ill.] Terra [1961] 440 p.
illus. DK511.L27S5 DLC CaAEU CaOTU
CSt CtPAM CtY ICLJF InNd MH NN PU
OKentU WU

6236. SKIRMUNTT, Konstancja.
Kartki krajowe (w dalszym ciągu kar-
tek politycznych) II. Reminiscen-
cya z prasy wileńskiej, 1906-1913.
Wilno, Druk J. Zawadzkiego, 1913.
111 p. 947.52.Sk35.4 PU

6237. SMETONA, Antanas. Atsiminimai. [Recollections] In Margutis
(Chicago, Ill.), 1955, v.28, no.7-8,
p. 3-8. See serials consulted.

6238. --- Raštai. [Works] Kaunas,
Pažangos bendrovė, 1930-31. 4 v.
Contents.--v.1.Vienybės gairėmis.--
v.2. Šviesos takais.--v.3. Atgimstant.
--v.4. Lietuvių santykiai su lenkais.
947.52.Sm35.3 PU ICCC CtTMF

6239. STANKA, Vladas. Vospominaniia, 1914-1919 gg. Vladimir B. Stan-
kevich. Berlin, I.P. Ladyzhnikov,
1920. 356 p. DK265.7.S83 DLC PU

6240. STEPONAITIS, Antanas. Tėvynėje ir pasauly; prisiminimai ir
apybraižos. [In the country and in
the world; reminiscences. Brooklyn, N.Y., 1962] 319 p.
DK511.L27S8 DLC ICLJF MH PU

6241. SZUMSKI, Stanisław. W wal-
kach i więzieniach; pamiętniki z
lat 1812-1848. Wilno, Nakładem i
Drukiem J. Zawadzkiego, 1931. vi,
216 p. plates., facsims. Bibliography: p. [185]-208. 943.8.Sz745 ICU
CaAEU

6242. USPENSKII, Aleksandr Aref'-
evich. Na voinie; Vostochnaia Prus-
siia-Litva, 1914-1915 gg. Vospominaniia. Kaunas, author, 1932. 226 p.
D551.U8 PU

6243. VAINEIKIENĖ, Stasė. Iš praeities kovų. [From the past strug-
gles] Kaunas, 1935-36. 3 v. in 1.
947.52.V194 PU

6244. VAITKUS, Mykolas. Baltijos
gražuolė, Liepoja; atsiminimai.
[Recollections on the beauty of Baltic, the City of Liepaja] London,
Nida, 1963. 332 p. (Nidos knygų
klubo leidinys, nr.42)
PG8721.V322Z5 DLC CtTMF OKentU PU

6245. --- Keturi ganytojai; atsiminimai. [Four pastors; reminiscen-
ces] Chicago, Ill., Lietuviškos
knygos klubas, 1960. 180 p.
BX1559.L5V27 DLC CtTMF OKentU PU

6246. --- Milžinų rungtynėse, 1940-
1944; atsiminimai, 8. tomas. [Con-
test of giants, 1940-1944; recollections. London] Nida [1972] 203 p.
PG8721.V322Z53 PU

6247. --- Mistiniame sode; kunigų
seminarija Kaune, 1903-1906. [Theo-
logical seminary in Kaunas, 1903-
1906. Putnam, Conn.] Immaculata
Press [1957] 207 p. BX920.K3V3 DLC
CaAEU CtTMF ICLJF MiD OCl OKentU PU

6248. --- Per giedrą ir audrą,
1909-1918; atsiminimai. [Through
the sunshine and the storm; remi-
niscences] London, Nida, 1964. 272
p. (Nidos knygų klubo leidinys, nr.

56)   891.92.V195P PU

6249. --- Šiaurės žvaigždė; atsiminimai, III. [The North Star; recol-
lections] London, Nida [1965] 297
p. (Nidos knygų klubo leidinys, nr.
53)   891.92.V195Si PU CaOTU

6250. --- Su Minija į Baltiją; atsiminimai, I. [On the river Minija
into the Baltic Sea; recollections]
London, Nida [1962] 210 p. (Nidos
knygų klubo leidinys, nr.41)
891.92.V195S PU CtTMF ICLJF RP

6251. VALEIKA, Matas. 25 metai
Vilniaus krašte. [25 years in the
region of Vilnius] Kaunas, Spaudos
fondas, 1934. 123 p. 947.52.V233 PU

6252. VEITAS, Matas Kiprijonas.
Atsiminimai iš 1863 metų. [Recollec-
tions from the insurrection of 1863]
In Mūsų senovė (Kaunas), v.2, no.1(6)
1937, p.62-77. See serials consulted.

6253. VIENUOLIS, A., pseud. Iš
mano atsiminimų. [My recollections]
Vilnius, VGLL, 1957. 317 p. illus.
PG8721.V5Z52 DLC PU

6254. YČAS, Martynas. Atsiminimai;
nepriklausomybės keliais. [Towards
independence; recollections] Kaunas,
1935-1936. 3 v. DK511.L26Y25 DLC
(v.3) CtTMF OLC PU

6255. ŽADEIKIS, Pranciškus. Didžiojo karo užrašai. [Recollections
from the First World War] Klaipėda,
Lietuvių spaustuvė "Lietuva", 1921-
1925. 2 v. in 1. 947.52.Z125 PU
ICBM ICLJF(v.1)

     ŽEMELIS, Henrikas. Okupantų
replėse. Memmingen, Ger., 1947.
See entry no. 5584.

6256. ŽUKAUSKAS, Bernardas. Pirmojo pasaulinio karo tremty; atsiminimų pluoštas. [In exile during the
First World War; recollections.
Chicago, Ill.] Lietuvių krikščio-
niškosios demokratijos studijų klubų leidinys, [1961] 136 p. illus.
947.5.Z92K PU CaOONL ICLJF MH
OKentU

6257. ZUMERIS, Bronius. Vilniaus
kraštas faktų ir atsiminimų šviesoje.
[The region of Vilnius; facts and
reminiscences] In LKMA, 1967. t.3,
p. [267]-[361] maps. See serials
consulted.

X.14. HISTORICAL NOVELS, POETRY AND DRAMA

6258. ANDREEV, A. Dovmont, kniaz'
pskovskii; istoricheskii roman XIII
veka. Moskva, Tip. N. Stepanova,
1835. 2 v. in 1. 491.922An26 PU

6259. BERNATOWICZ, Feliks. Pa-
jauta Lizdeikos duktė; arba Lietuva
XIV metašimty, istoriškas romanas.
[Pajauta Lizdeika's daughter; or
Lithuania in the fourteenth century
...] Sulietuvino Jonas Montvila.
Chicago, Ill., Spauda "Katalíko",
1911. 468 p. 891.85B458P.LM PU NN

6260. BITEL', Piatro Ivanovich.
Zamki i liudzi. Gistorychnaia
poema. Minsk, "Belarus'", 1968.
102 p. illus. PG2835.2.B5Z2 DLC

6261. BROOKE, Rupert. Lithuania;
a drama in one act. Cincinnati,
Ohio, S. Kidd, [c1915] 39 p.
(Stewart Kidd modern plays)
PR6003.R4L5 DLC CaOLU CaOTY CaOTU
CtY CLU GU ICU IEN IU KU KMK ICN MH
MiU MB MtU NN NNC NjP NSyU NB OCl
PPULC PPPlay PPM PPE PU RPB ScU TxU
TxDaM WU

6262. --- Lithuania: a play in one
act. London, Sidgwick & Jackson
[1935] vii, 38 p. 822.B7971 1935
IU CaSSU CaOTY KU MH NjP ScU

6263. BURACZEWSKA, Stanisława.
Lietuvos girios; XIII metašimčio
istorijos apysaka. [Lithuanian
forests; a historical novel. Vertė
A. Musteikis] Vilnius, Strazdas ir
Vėgėlė, 1913. Bound with Jokė M.
Pajudinkime... 491.922.J572.LK PU

6264. BUTLERIS, Vladas. Už ką?
[For what? Riga] Autoriaus leidinys, 1929-1930. 2 v. At head of
title: Serija romanų iš lietuvio
gyvenimo, 1863 metais į Sibirą iš-
tremto. 891.923B ICCC NN

6265. DAVIE, Donald. The forest
of Lithuania, a poem. [Hessle,
Yorkshire] Marvell Press [1959]
62 p. illus. Adapted from Pan Ta-
deusz, by Adam Mickiewicz.
PR6007.A667F6 DLC CLU CU CtY ICU MH
MNS MiDW NIC NN NNC NjP OCU TU ViU
WU

6266. DOBILAS, J., pseud. Bludas;
arba Lietuva buvusios Rusijos revoliucijos metu; romanas. [Lithuania
during Russian occupation; novel]
Tilžė, J. Dobilas, 1912. 428 p.
Author's real name is Julijonas
Lindė. PG8721.D6 DLC PU

6267. DRUCKI-LUBECKI, Hieronim.
Taip mirdavo lietuviai; 5 veiksmų
istoriška drama. [Thus died Lithuanians; drama] Laisvai vertė Petras Vaičiūnas. Kaunas, "Angos"
leidinys, 1924. 79 p.
891.92.Sa13L PU

6268. FROMAS, Aleksandras. Baisioji gadynė. [The terrible times.
Ed. by B. Prunskis] A. Fromas-
Gužutis. Vilnius, VGLL, 1955.
637 p. port. Bibliography; p. 633-
635. 891.92.F924B PU NN

6269. --- Vargdieniai; Apysaka iš
tikrų atsitikimų penktos ir šeštos
dešimties 19-tojo šimtmečio. [True
story from happenings in the middle
of the 19th century. By] A. Gužutis [pseud.] Plymouth, Pa.,
Spauda ir kaštai "Vienybės Lietuvninkų", 1906. 187 p.
891.92.F924V PU DLC OKentU

6270. HATZFELD, Adolf von. Der
Flug nach Moskau. Potsdam, Ritten
& Loening, 1942. 177 p.
DR592.E6H36 CSt-H CU

6271. KALUGIN, S. F. Svershanie
iazychestva v Vil'nie; dramatiches-
kiia stseny iz vremen Velikago
Kniazia Ol'gerda, 3-kh dietstviiakh
(Siuzhet zaimstvovan iz Pecherskoi
rukopisi v Pskovie) Vil'na, 1866.
Bound with: Otviet na adres...
947.52.Ot99 PU

6272. KARPIUS, Kazys S. Alpis,
Kęstučio išlaisvintojas; istorinė
apysaka. [Alpis, the rescuer of
Kęstutis; a historical story. By
Kazimieras Karpavičius] Cleveland,
Ohio, Dirva, 1942. 288 p.
891.92.K149A PU ICCC

6273. --- --- [Autoriaus pataisy-
ta 2. laida. Cleveland, Ohio]
Viltis, 1971. 227 p.
PG8749.K3A5 1971 PU

6274. KOBRIN, Leon. A Lithuanian
village, authorized translation
from the Yiddish, by Isaac Goldberg.
New York, N.Y., Brentano's [c1920]
x, 193 p. PZ3.K795Li DLC CtY ICU
MH NcU OClW OkU OrU RPB WaS

6275. KONDRATOWICZ, Ludwik. Mar-
gier; poemat z dziejów Litwy. W.
Syrokomla [pseud.] Wilno, R. Rafa-
lowicz, 1855. viii, 136 p.
491.922.K837.2 PU NN

6276. KRALIKAUSKAS, Juozas. Mindaugo nužudymas; premijuotas romanas. [The assassination of Mindaugas. Chicago, Ill.] Lietuviškos
knygos klubas [1964] 246 p.

PG8721.K65M5 DLC CaAEU CaOTU PU

6277. KRASZEWSKI, Józef Ignacy.
Kunigas; dzieje Litwy i Krzyżaków
w początkach XIV wieku. Z rycinami
M.A. Andriollego. Warszawa, M.
Arct, 1929. 249 p. 491.922.K868.2
PU

6278. --- --- [Another edition]
Łódz, W. Bąk [194-] 280 p.
PG7158.K75K8

6279. --- --- [Another edition].
Text przygotował... Stefan Lech
Swierzewski] Warszawa, Spółdzielczy
Instytut Wydawniczy, 1947. 232 p.
illus. (Powieści Polskie)
PG7158.K75K8 1947 WU

6280. --- --- [Another edition]
Warszawa, Ludowa Spółdzielnia Wy-
dawn. 1954. 230 p. illus.
PG7158.K88K9 CaAEU NjP

6281. --- --- [Another edition];
powieść z podań litewskich. Z ry-
sunkami M.E. Andriollego. [War-
szawa] Ludowa Spółdzielnia Wydawnicza, 1955. 230 p. illus.
PJ7158.K75K8 1955 DLC MH MiU NN

6282. --- Vitolio rauda. [Vito-
lis' song of lamentations] Poznań,
1882. 320 p. 800K14 CtTMF

6283. --- Vitolio rauda; giesmės
iš Lietuvos padavimų. [Vitolis'
song of lamentations] Iš lenkų
kalbos vertė Faustas Kirša. Kaunas, J.J. Staniškaitė, 1924. 149
p. 891.85.K868W.LK PU

6284. KRĖVĖ-MICKEVIČIUS, Vincas.
Mindaugo mirtis; drama. [Death of
Mindaugas; drama] Kaunas, Spaudos
fondas, 1935. 140 p.
PG8721.K7M52 PU CtTMF

6285. --- Šarūnas, Dainavos kunigaikštis; 4 dalių su įžanga dramatizuota apysaka. [Šarūnas, Grand
Duke of Dainava; dramatic play]
Vilnius, M. Kuktos spaustuvė, 1911.
891.92.K889Sa PU CtTMF OCl ICCC

6286. --- --- [Another edition]
Kaunas, 1923. (His Raštai, t.4-5)
891.92.K889Sa 1923 PU ICCC OCl

6287. --- --- 3. leidimas. Kaunas, Humanitrainių mokslų fakultetas, 1939. 891.923K ICBM

6288. --- --- [Another edition]
Vilnius, Vaga, 1966. 477 p.
PG8721.K7S2 1966 DLC NN PU

6289. --- Skirgaila. Mindaugo
mirtis. [Skirgaila. The death of

Mindaugas. Plays] Vilnius, Vaga,
1967. 212 p. PG8721.K7S54 1967
DLC

6290. KUKOL'NIK, Nestor Vasil'-
evich. Kniaz' Marger Pilonskii.
Razkaz TSvirkuna, Velikago Koniu-
shago Velikago Kniazhestva Litovskago. Istoricheskaia poviest' XIV
vieka. Sanktpeterburg, 1841. p.
1-44. (Russkaia besieda, 1841, v.
1) BM(12265. c. 15.) NN

6291. LAUCKNER, Rolf. Der letzte
Preusse; tragödie vom Untergang
eines Volkes, in vier Akten. Ber-
lin, Theaterverlag A. Langen, G.
Müller, 1937. 162 p.
PT2623.A83L4 1937 DLC NN

6292. --- Predigt in Litauen;
Drama. Berlin, E. Reiss, 1919. 144
p. 834.L3620p IU CSt CtY

6293. --- --- In Ausgewählte Bü-
nendichtungen. Emsdetten/Westf.,
1963. PT2623.A83A19 1963 DLC CLU CU
CtY IaU MiDW NcU NhD NB WU

6294. LAURINAITIS, Jonas Martynas.
Laisvės keliais; apysakos iš laisvės kovų. [Short stories from the
Wars of Independence] Kaunas, 1934.
223 p. 947.52.OL1 CtTMF

6295. LUKASZEWICZ, Joseph. Girys
i Biruta; poemat z dawnych czasów
litewskich. [1st ed.] Detroit,
Mich., Endurance Press, 1964. vi,
69 p. PG7399.L8G5 DLC InNd

MARCINKEVIČIUS, Jonas.
Kražių skerdynės; istorinis romanas.
Chicago, Ill., 195- . See entry no.
5265.

6296. --- Mindaugas; dviejų dalių
drama-poema. [Mindaugas; drama in
two acts] Vilnius, Vaga, 1968.
119 p. illus. PG8721.M35M5 DLC
CaOTU OClW OKentU PU

6297. MICKIEWICZ, Adam. Grażyna;
powieść litewska. London, M.I.
Kolin [1941] 51 p. PG7158.M5G7 DLC

6298. --- --- Wyd. 2, poprawione.
Wrocław, Zakład im. Ossolińskich,
1953. 88 p. MH

6299. --- Konrad Wallenrod.
Powieść historyczna z dziejów litewskich i pruskich. Sanktpeterburg,
Drukiem K. Kraya, 1828, viii, 88 p.
plates. PG7158.M5K6 DLC

6300. --- --- [Another ed.]
Lipsk, F.A. Brockhaus, 1878. 117 p.
PG7158.M5K6 1878 DLC NN

6301. --- Konrad Wallenrod, and
other writings... tr. by Jewell
Parish, Dorothea Prall Radin, George
Rapale Noyes, and other. Berkeley,
Calif., University of California
Press, 1925. ix, 209 p. (Univer-
sity of California syllabus series,
170) PG7158.M5Z34 1925 DLC NN

6302. --- Pan Tadeusz; czyli
ostatni zajazd na Litwie, historija
szlachecka z roku 1811 i 1812. We
dwunastu księgach, wierszem. Wyd.
Aleksandra Jełowickiego. Paryż
[Typ. A. Pinard] 1834. 2 v. in 1.
port. PG7158.M5P3 1834 DLC CaOTU
NN

6303. --- --- [Warszawa] Czytelnik, 1953. 426 p. illus.
PG7158.M5P3 1953 MiDW MB

6304. --- --- [Warszawa] Czytelnik, 1954. 417 p. port.
PG7158.M5P3 1954 DLC CU CtY KyU NN

6305. --- --- [Warszawa] Czytelnik, 1955. 473 p. front. (His
Dziela. Wydano w setną rocznicę
smierci poety, 4) Slav.7117.1.4(4)
MH

6306. --- Pan Tadeusz; or, The
Last Foray in Lithuania. Translated
by Watson Kirkconnell. With an introductory essay by William J. Rose
and notes by Harold B. Segel.
Toronto, Ont., 1962. 388 p.
PG7158.M5P312 DLC CaBVaU MiU

6307. --- --- New York, Polish
Institute of Arts and Sciences in
America, 1962. xix, 388 p.
PG7158.M5P312 1962a DLC CU CaAEU
CLSU CtY InU MH MiU MiDW NN NNC NcU
NjP OrU ViU

6308. --- Pan Tadeusz; oder, Der
letzte Eintritt in Litauen...
Berlin, Aufbau-Verlag, 1955. 602
p. DLC MH NN OCl PU

6309. --- Pan Tadeusz; oder Der
letzte Fehde in Litauen. Nachdruck
von Herman Buddensieg. München,
Eidosverlag, 1963. 381 p.
PG7158.M5P18G3B9 CaAEU

6310. --- Ponas Tadas. Vertė K.
Šakenis. Kaunas, Raidės spaustuvė,
1924. viii, 330 p.
491.922.M583.4.LS PU

6311. MILLER, Antoni Witold. Po-
wołanie; powieść osnuta na tle stosunków polsko-litewskiego kleru na
Litwie. Wilno, 1928. 242 p.
491.922.M513 PU

6312. MINTSLOV, Sergei Rudol'fovich. Liesnaia byl'; istoricheskii roman. [4. izd.] Riga, M. Didkovskii [192-] 333 p. Ed. 1-3, published in 2 parts under separate titles: "V liesach Litvy" and "Na Krestakh". 891.73.M66L ed. 4 CSt PU

6313. --- Litva; istoricheskiia poviesti. Sanktpeterburg, K.N. Kosobriukhov, 1911. 346 p. NN

6314. --- Pod shum dubov; istoricheskii roman. Berlin, Sibirskoe kn.-vo [n.d.] 234 p. 491.922.M665 PU

6315. MINTSLOVA, M. S. Po drevnie Litvie; potsvye nabroski. Sanktpeterburg, Tip. T-va tekhnich. shk., 1914. 80 p. 947.52.M665 PU

6316. NOREIKA, Jonas. Trys velniai; apysaka iš nepriklausomybės kovų su bolševikais. [Three devils; stories from the Wars of Independence] Hamilton, Ont., Rūta, [196-] 67 p. PG8721.M65T7 PU

6317. PETRAUSKAS, Antanas. Laisvės metu; apysaka iš paskutinių atsitikimų. [During the time of freedom] Seinai, Laukaičio spaustuvėje, 1908. 187 p. 891.92.P446L PU

6318. POTOCKI, Leon. Powieść z czasu mojego, czyli przygody litewskie. [London] 1854. ii, 315 p. BM(12588. aa. 5.)

6319. SCHEU, Werner. Birute. Roman aus Litauen. München, Damm Verlag [1966] 418 p. PT2680.E8B5 DLC InNd NN NjP OC1 PU WU

6320. SELMONS, Prancas. Testamentas; vaizdelis dviejų veiksnių iš gyvenimo Prūsų lietuvių. [Last will; two-act play of life of Lithuanians in Prussia] Tilžė, J. Vanagaitis, 1909. 35 p. 891.92Se47T PU

6321. SIENKIEWICZ, Henryk. Krzyżacy; powieść historyczna. Warszawa, Państwowy Instytut Wydawniczy, 1938. 2 v. PG7158.S4K9 CaAEU

6322. --- --- Wstępem opatrzył Julian Krzyżanowski. [Wyd. 20. Warszawa] Państwowy Instytut Wydawniczy [1965] 774 p. PG7158.S4K7 1965 DLC MU NIU

6323. SRUOGA, Balys. Giesmė apie Gediminą. [Song about Gediminas] Grafika Viktoro Petravičiaus. M. Dobužinskio viršelis ir iliustracijos. Kaunas, Sakalas, 1933. 61 p. 491.922.Sr85 PU

6324. --- --- Kaunas, Sakalas, 1938. 63 p. 891.921.S ICCC

6325. --- --- Chicago, Ill. [Terra] 1952. [32] p. illus. part. col. PG8721.S68G5 1952 CaOTU OC1 PU

6326. ŠUKYS, Jonas. Komunistas; 1919 metų kovų romanas. [Communist; novel on the War of 1919 in Lithuania] Kaunas, 1937. 265 p. 891.93.Š27 CtTMF

6327. SUŽIEDELIS, Juozas. Žalgiris; istorijos apysaka iš Vytauto Didžiojo laikų. [Žalgiris; a story from the time of Vytautas the Great] Pagal Chruščovo-Sokalnikovo romaną. .. [London] Nida [1954] 127 p. (Nidos knygų klubas, nr. 1) 891.93.S24 CtTMF DLC

6328. VENCKŪNIENĖ, Juzė (Povylaitytė). Ona, didžioji Lietuvos kunigaikštienė; istorinė drama, 6 veiksmai 12 paveikslų. [Ona, Grand Duchess of Lithuania; a historical drama in six acts] Kaunas, 1937. 93 p. PG8721.V39.05 PU CtTMF

XI. PHILOSOPHY

6329. BIRALO, Al'bert Afanas'evich. Filosofskaia i obshchestvennaia mysl' v Belorussii i Litve v kontse XVII-seredine XVIII v. Minsk, Izd-vo BGU, 1971. 179 p. B4757.B57 PU

6330. BUDRIKAS, Vincas J. Filosofijos straipsniai. [Essays on philosophy] Cleveland, Ohio, Spauda "Dirvos", 1920. 232 p. B798.L5B8 DLC OC1

6331. DŽIAVEČKA, E. Vydūno pasaulio struktūros koncepcija. [The Vydūnas' conception of the world structure] In LTSRMAD. Serija A. Vilnius, 1970. v.1(32), p. 55-63. See serials consulted.

6332. MACEINA, Antanas. Tautinis auklėjimas. [Nationalistic education] Kaunas, 1934. 293 p. 301.1M ICCC

6333. PLEČKAITIS, Romanas. The scholastic moral philosophy in Lithuania. In Lituanus (Chicago, Ill.), v.16, no.4, 1970, p. 21-29. See serials consulted.

6334. ŠALKAUSKIS, Stasys. Lietuvių tauta ir jos ugdymas. [The Lithuanian nation and its fostering]

Kaunas, Sakalo b-vė, 1933. 196 p.
Sp947.5.Sa34 PU CtTMF ICCC also
DK511.L212S32 1970 PU(Xerox copy)

--- Sur les confins de
deux mondes; essai... Genève, [1919]
See entry no. 1048.

6335. --- Visuomeninis auklėjimas;
epizodinis kursas, skaitytas L. U.
Teologijos-Filosofijos fakultete
1927 m. pavasario semestre. [Edu-
cation in social sciences; lectures
...] Kaunas, 1927. 199 p.
301.1.Š ICCC

6336. STOROST, Wilhelm. Likimo
kilmė. [Origin of destiny. By]
Vidūnas [pseud.] Tilžė, Rûta, 1908.
100 p. 891.92.St78L PU CtTMF MiD NN

6337. --- Mirtis ir kas toliau
[Death and what is after? By] Vidûnas [pseud.] Tilžė, 1907. 64 p.
891.93.V74 CtTMF

6338. --- Slaptinga žmogaus didî-
bė. [Mysterious greatness of men.
By] Vidūnas [pseud.] Tilžė,
1907. 64 p. 891.93.V74 CtTMF NN

6339. --- Tautos givata. [The
inner life of the nation. By] Vidûnas [pseud.] Tilžė, Rûta, 1920.
152 p. 891.93.V82 CtTMF

6340. --- Visatos sąranga. [Com-
position of the universe. By] Vidûnas [pseud.] Tilžė, Rûta, 1907.
32 p. 891.93.V74 CtTMF NN

6341. --- Žmonijos kelias. [The
way of mankind. By] Vidûnas
[pseud.] Tilžė, Rûta, 1908. 43 p.
891.93.V74 CtTMF NN

XII. RELIGION

XII.1. CATHOLIC CHURCH

XII.1.a. GENERAL STUDIES

6342. ANIČAS, Jonas. Katalikiš-
kasis klerikalizmas Lietuvoje 1940-
1944 metais. [Catholic clericalism
in Lithuania, 1940-1944] Vilnius,
Mintis, 1972. 253 p. BX1559.L5A5
PU

6343. --- Socialinis politinis
katalikų bažnyčios vaidmuo Lietuvoje 1945-1952 metais. [Social and
political influence of the Catholic
Church in Lithuania, 1945-1952]
Vilnius, 1971. 212 p. At head of

title: Lietuvos TSR Mokslų akademija. Filosofijos, teisės ir socio-
logijos skyrius prie Istorijos
instituto. Summary in Russian;
Bibliography: p. 101-[206].
BX1775.L55A64 DLC PU

6344. BASANAVIČIUS, Jonas. Apie
lenkų kalbą Lietuvos bažnyčiose;
lietuvių raštas, paduotas Jo Šven-
tenybei Pijui X. Popiežiui... De
lingua polonica in ecclesiis Lithuaniae. Kaunae, S. Banaičio spaustuvė, 1906. 75 p. BX1559.L5B3
DLC CtTMF ICU MH PU

6345. CHATKOWSKI, Władysław Longin. Dzieje zniweczenia Św. Unii
na Białorusi i Litwie w świetle pamiętników Siemaszki. W. Krakowie,
Spółka Wydawn. Polska, 1898. 205
p. port. BX4711.522.I6A324 CaOTU
PU

6346. CHODYNICKI, Kazimierz.
Kościół prawosławny a Rzecapospolita
Polska; zarys historyczny, 1370-1632.
Warszawa, Skład gł. Kasa im. Mia-
nowskiego, 1934. 632 p. Biblio-
graphy: p.[604]-618. BX750.P6C48
DLC CU CtY ICU IU InU MH NN NNC NjP
OU

6347. CZERMAK, Wiktor. Sprawa
równouprawnienia schizmatyków i ka-
tolików na Litwie, 1432-1553 r. In
Polska Akademia Umiejętności. Wydział Historyczno-Filozoficzny.
Rozprawy (Kraków), vol.44, 1903,
p. 348-405. See serials consulted.

6348. DERUGA, Aleksy. Piotr
Wielki a unici i unja Kościelna,
1700-1711. Wilno, 1936. 207 p.
BM(Ac. 1156. K/2.)

6349. DUKSZTA, Mieczysław von.
Grands héros de la Lithuanie païenne
et sanglantes expéditions chré-
tiennes au XIV siècle. Genève,
"Athenaeum", 1918. 17 leaves,
ports. (Publication de l'Athenaeum,
no. 13.)

6350. EINES VORNEHMEN ICTI GRÜND-
liche Nachricht von dem Zustand der
evangelischen Religion in Pohlen
und dem Gross-Hertzogthum Litthauen,
darinnen unumstösslich erwiesen
wird, dass der Dissidenten oeffent-
liches Religions-Exercitium auf die
Fundamental-Gesetze des Reichs ger-
gründet sey. Auch A. Lipski a Lipe
dagegen gemachte Schein-Gründe über
den Hauffen gestossen werden. Warsaw?, 1726. 24 p.
BM(1367. h. 22. (1.))

6351. GABRYS, Juozas. Mémoire
concernant la situation de l'Église

Catholique en Lithuanie présenté à
sa Sainteté Benoît XV. Lausanne,
1918. BM(3926.K.43)

6352. GAIGALAITĖ, Aldona. Bažnyčios vaidmuo Lietuvoje 1919-1940 m.
[The role of the Church in Lithuania, 1919-40] Vilnius, Mintis,
1967. 33 p. BX1775.L55G3 DLC MH
NN PU

6353. --- Klerikalizmas Lietuvoje,
1917-1940. [Clericalism in Lithuania, 1917-1940] Vilnius, Mintis,
1970. 312 p. BX1559.L5G32 PU

6354. GIANNINI, Amedeo. La con-
stituzione apostolica "Lituanorum
gente". Rome, Anonima romana editoriale, 1926. 8 p. (Istituto per
l'Europa orientale, Rome. Pubbli-
cazioni, ser. 4, v. 8) NN

6355. HALECKI, Oskar. The reli-
gious crisis in Poland and Lithu-
ania. In His From Florence to
Brest. Rome, 1958. p. 141-157.
BX323.H16 CaAEU CaBVaU CSt CtY DCU
ICU IU InU MH MiU NB NIC NN NNC NcU
NjR NcD OCl PU ScU TxDaM TxU ViU
WaU

6356. IVINSKIS, Zenonas. Kir-
chengesang in Litauen im XVI-XVII.
Jahrhundert. In Commentationes
Balticae (Bonn), v.1, 1954, p. 69-
106. See serials consulted.

6357. KAMIENIECKI, Witold. O-
graniczenie wyznaniowe w prawodaws-
twie litewskim w XV i XVI w. In
Przegląd Historychny (Warszawa), v.
13, 1911, p. 268-282. See serials
consulted.

6358. KATOLITSIZM V SSSR I SOVRE-
mennost' (Materialy nauchnoi konferentsii, sostoiavshei v g. Shau-
liai 17-18 dekabria 1969 g.) Vil'-
nius, 1971, 255 p. BX1765.2.K36 PU

6359. KIPRIANOVICH, G. IA. Istoricheskii ocherk pravoslavia,
katolichestva i unii v Bielorussii
i Litvie s drevnieishago do nastoiashchago vremeni. 2. znachitel'no
dop. izd. Vil'na [Tip. I. Bliumo-
vicha] 1899 xv, 288 p.
BR937.W6K6 ICU MH

6360. KOIALOVICH, Mikhail Iosifovich. Litovskaia tserkovnaia uniia.
Sanktpeterburg, Tip. N. Tikhmeneva,
1859-1861. 2 v. in 1. BX1559.L5K6
DLC PU

6361. KOT, Stanisław. Szymon Bud-
ny, der grösste Häretiker Litauens
im 16 Jahrhundert. In Wiener Archiv für Geschichte des Slaventums

und Osteuropas (Graz), v.2, 1956.
p. 63-118. See serials consulted.

6362. KRIKŠČIONYBĖ LIETUVOJE;
praetis, dabartis, ateitis.
[Christianity in Lithuania; past,
present and future] Kaunas, Šv.
Kazimiero dr-ja, 1938. viii, 263
p. (Šv. Kazimiero draugijos leidinys, nr. 726) BR937.L3K7 DLC PU

6363. KURCZEWSKI, Jan. Opowiada-
nia o dziejach chrześcjaństwa na
Litwie i Rusi. Cz.1: od chrztu
Litwy do końca XVI wieku. Wilno,
Druck J. Zawadzkiego, 1914. 234 p.
947.52K968.3 PU

6364. --- Święci biskupi i apostołowie Litwy i Rusi litewskiej,
Wilno, J. Zawadzki, 1913. 82 p.
947.52K968.2 PU

6365. LIETUVIŲ KATALIKŲ MOKSLO
AKADEMIJA, ROME. Istorinė krikščionių atsakomybė; V susažiavimo
darbai, 1961 m. rugsėjo mėn. 1-3d.
Chicagoje. Redagavo A. Liuima.
Roma, 1964. 647 p. port. [Lietu-
vių katalikų mokslo akademijos
leidinys, nr. 7) BX839.R4L72 t.5
CaAEU PU PPULC

6366. --- Lietuvių mokslinės problemos naujausių Katalikų Bažnyčios
direktyvų šviesoje: IV suvažiavimo
darbai, 1957 m. spalio mėn. 2-4 d.,
Romoje. Redagavo A. Liuima. [Lith-
uanian scientific problems in the
light of new directives from the
Catholic Church: Proceedings of the
4th Congress] Roma, 1961. xiii,
321 p. port. (Lietuvių katalikų
mokslo akademijos leidinys, nr. 6)
BX839.R6L5 1957 DLC ICCC

6367. MACEINA, Antanas. Didieji
dabarties klausimai; pasaulio seku-
liarizacija, evangelijų numitinimas,
evolicija ir religija. [The Big
Questions of Today: World Secular-
ization, Evolution and Religion.
Chicago, Ill., Krikščionis gyvenime,
1971] 327 p. BL51.M31 PU

6368. MAČIULIS, Vytautas. Das
religiöse und kirchliche Leben in
Litauen. In Acta Baltica (Königstein im Taunus), v.8, 1968, p. 9-
39. See serials consulted.

6369. MALYSHEVSKII, Ivan Ignat'-
evich. Zapadnaia Rus' v bor'bie za
vieru i narodnost'. Sanktpeterburg,
1897. 402 p. BR937.U4M26 InU

6370. --- --- Moskva, T-vo tipo-
lit. V. Chicherin, 1903-05. 2 v. in
1. BR936.M34 DLC

MASER, Leo. Das Konkordat zwischen dem Apostolischen Stuhle und der Republik Litauen. Lippstadt/Westf., 1931. See entry no. 3359.

6371. MATULEVIČIUS, Jurgis, Abp. Užrašai. [Memoirs. London, Tėvai Marijonai, 1953] 220 p. illus., ports. BX4705.M4295.A3 DLC CtTMF

6372. OCHMANSKI, Jerzy. Najdawniejsze przywileje Jagiełły i Witolda dla biskupstwa wileńskiego z lat 1387-1395. In Posen. Universytet. Seria Historia. Zeszyty Naukowe, no.5, 1961, p. 19-36. See serials consulted.

6373. --- Uprzywilejowanie gospodarcze kościoła katolickiego na Litwie w sredniowieczu. In Roczniki Dziejów Społecznych i Gospodarczych (Poznań), v.23, 1962, p. 89-108. See serials consulted.

6374. PAKARKLIS, Povilas. Ekonominė ir teisinė katalikų bažnyčios padėtis Lietuvoje, XV-XIX a. [The Economic and Legal Situation of the Catholic Church in Lithuania in the 15th and 16th centuries] Vilnius, VPMLL, 1956. 387 p. illus. BX1559.L5P27 DLC CtPAM PU

6375. --- Popiežiai-lietuvių tautos priešai. [The popes; enemies of the Lithuanian nation] Vilnius, VPMLL, 1948. 139 p. BX1559.L5P28 DLC NN

6376. PRAPUOLENIS, Kazimieras. L'église polonaise en Lithuanie, par l'abbé C. Propolanis. Tr. par J. Gabrys. 2., éd. Paris, Bureau d'information lithuanien, 1914. xxxvii, 170 p. BX1559.L5P8 DLC CSt-H MH NN PU

6377. --- Lenkų apaštalai Lietuvoje. [Apostolic work of Poles in Lithuania. Tr. by K. Vairas-Račkauskas (Patriotas, pseud.) from Polish title: Polskie-Apostolstwo w Litwie. With extensive explanatory notes by A. Jasiūnas. 2d ed.] New York, N.Y., "Tėvynės" spauda, 1938. 264 p. (Amerikos lietuvių spaudos draugijos leidinys) BX1559.L5P38 DLC CtTMF NN OCl

6378. --- Lenkų apaštalavimas Lietuvoje (historinis škicas 1387-1912), lenkiškai parašė kun. Kaz. Propolianis. Iš lenkų kalbos vertė Patriotas. [The apostolic work of Poles in Lithuania] New York, N.Y., "Tėvynės" Spauda, 1918. 264 p. (Amerikos lietuvių spaudos draugija. Leidinys, no. 2) BX1559.L5P83 DLC

CtTMF NN OCL OKentU WaU

6379. --- Polscy "apostołowie Litwy". [By] K. Propolianis. Wilno, "Litwa", 1911. 44 p. Balt 7901.01 MH

6380. --- Polskie apostolstwo w Litwie; szkic historyczny, 1387-1912. [By] K. Propolanis. Wilno, Druk M. Kuchty, 1913. xvi, 202 p. 947.52.P882 PU MH

PRUNSKIS, Joseph. Comparative law, ecclesiastical and civil in Lithuanian concordat... Washington, D.C., 1945. See entry no. 2784.

6381. SŁAWOCZYŃSKI, Salomon M. Giesmės tikėjimui katalikam priderančios, 1646. Fotografuotinis leidimas. [Hymns becoming the Catholic faith, 1646. A photographic edition Prepared by Jurgis Lebedys] Vilnius, VPMLL, 1958. 556 p. facsims. Original edition: Vilnae, Typis Academicic Soc. Jesu, 1646. 2 pts., 156 and 124 pages. BV357.C3S5 1646a DLC CU ICU IU ICLJF NN OKentU PU TxU

6382. ŠLEZAS, Paulius. Bažnyčios ir valstybės santykiai Žemaičių vyskupijoj Valančiaus laikais. [The relations between the Church and the State in the Diocese of Samogitia during the time of Valančius] In Židinys (Kaunas), no.7, 1938, p. 46-59. See serials consulted.

6383. STAKAUSKAS, Juozapas. Katalikybė ir Lietuvių tauta. [Catholicism and the Lithuanian nation] In Tiesos kelias (Kaunas), v.5, 1938, p. 265-272. See serials consulted.

6384. STOSUNKI KOŚCIELNE NA LITWIE. Kraków; Monachium, 1905. 104 p. BM(8094. e. 54.)

6385. TOTARAITIS, Jonas. Seinų vyskupijos vienuolynų naikinimas. [The closing down of monasteries in the Diocese of Seinai] In Tiesos kelias (Kaunas), yr 2, v.2, no.9, 1926, p. 84-95. See serials consulted.

6386. VALADKA, Mykolas. Už laisvą lietuvį. [The Free Lithuanian] Scranton, Pa., 1970. 409 p. BX1770.V28 DLC OKentU PU

6387. VALANČIUS, Motiejus. Pastabos pačiam sau. Iš lenkiškosios vyskupo Motiejaus rašliavos sulasė ir savo pastabų pridėliojo J. Tumas. [Remarks for myself. Tr. from

Polish and with notes by J. Tumas]
Klaipėdoje, Spaudė Akcinė "Ryto"
bendrovė, 1929. 190 p. illus.,
port. (Švietimo ministerijos knygų
leidimo komisijos leidinys, nr. 151)
BX890.V22 DLC CtTMF OCl PU

6388. VARDYS, Vytas Stanley. Catholicism in Lithuania. In Aspects
of religion in the Soviet Union,
1917-1967. Ed. by R.H. Marshall.
Chicago, Ill., 1971. [379]-403 p.
BX1559.L5V35 PU

6389. VĖBRA, Rimantas. Lietuvos
katalikų dvasininkija ir visuomeninis judėjimas (XIX a. antroji pusė).
[Catholic clergy in Lithuania and
their public and political activi-
ties] Vilnius, Mintis, 1968. 223
p. Summary in Russian. Bibliography: p. 210-]219]. BX1559.L5V4
DLC PU

6390. VISCONT, Antoine. La Lituanie religieuse. 23 planches
hors texte et 2 cartes. Paris, Éditions G. Grès & Cie; Genève, Édition
Atar [1918]. 350 p. illus., plates,
ports., 2 fold. maps. BR937.L3V5
DLC BM(04685. c. 11.) CSt-H CtY IaU
ICJ MH NN NNC NcD PU WU

XII.1.b. HISTORY OF THE CATHOLIC
CHURCH IN LITHUANIA

6391. ALEKNA, Antanas. Katalikų
bažnyčia Lietuvoje. [The Catholic
Church in Lithuania. Ed. by J.
Stakauskas] Kaunas, Šv. Kazimiero
D-ja, 1936. 154 p., 4 maps.
BX1559.L5A6 DLC ICLJF

6392. --- --- Xerox copy, 1970.
154 p. BX1559.L5A62 1970 PU

6393. ANDZIULYTĖ RUGINIENĖ, Marija. Žemaičių christianizacijos
pradžia. Die Angänge des Christen-
tums in Žemaiten. Kaunas, 1937.
145 p. BR1050.L5A5 PU

6394. BOUDOU, Adrien. Le Saint-
Siège et la Russie; leurs relations
diplomatiques au XIXᵉ sciècle.
Paris, Plon-Nourrit et Cie [1922] 1
v. DK67.3.B6 DLC CaBVaU CU CoW CtY
MH MB MU NIC NcGW NcD OO OCl OU
PPULC PU ViU WaSpG

6395. --- Stolica Swięta a Rosja.
Stosunki dyplomatyczne między niemi
w XIX stuleciu. Pszekład z francus-
kiego Zofji Skowrońskiej. Kraków,
Nakładem Wydawnictwa Księży Je-
zuitów, 1928. 2 v. Bibliography:
v.1, p. [592]-598; v.2, p. [662]-

667. NNC DLC-P4

6396. CHODYNICKI, Kazimierz.
Próby zaprowadzenia chrześcijaństwa
na Litwie przed r. 1386. In Przegląd Historychny (Warszawa), v.18,
1914, p. 215-319. See serials
consulted.

CONTONS, Albert J. St.
Casimir; 500th anniversary of his
birth, 1458-1958. Boston, Mass.
[1958] See entry no. 4931.

6397. DĄBROWSKA, Stanisława Ste-
fanja. Sekularyzacja dóbr duchownych na Litwie za rządów Mikołaja I.
In PZHP w Wilnie 17-20 wrzesnia
1935 r. Pamiętnik VI. Referaty
(Lwów) v.1, 1935, p. 58-67. See
serials consulted.

6398. DE APUD VARIAS NATIONES
ECCLESIAE CATHOLICAE CONDITIONE JURI-
DICA INQUISITIO: de ecclesia lithu-
ana. In Jus pontificium. Roma,
1929. p. [270]-280. See serials
consulted.

6399. FIJAŁEK, Jan. Kościól rzymsko-katolicki na Litwie. In Polska
i Litwa w dziejowym stosunku. Warszawa, 1914. DK418.5.L5P6 DLC CU
CSt-H InU KU MH NN PU

6400. --- Uchrześcijanienie Litwy przez Polskę i zachowanie w niej
języka ludu. In Kraków, Polska i
Litwa w dziejowym stosunku. Warszawa, 1914, p. 37-333. DK418.5.L5P6
DLC BM CU CSt-H InU KU MH NN PU

6401. GIDŽIŪNAS, Viktoras. The
introduction of Christianity into
Lithuania. In Lituanus (Brooklyn,
N.Y.), v.4, no.13, Dec. 1957, p. 6-
13. See serials consulted.

6402. --- Katalikų bažnyčia Lietuvoje; Didžiojoje Lietuvos Kunigaikštijoje. [The Catholic Church
in Lithuania; Grand Duchy of Lithu-
ania] In Lietuvių enciklopedija.
Boston, Mass., 1968. v.15, p. 131-
141. For holdings see entry no.
216.

6403. --- Krikščionybės įvedimas
Lietuvoje. [The introduction of
christianity in Lithuania] In Lux
Christi (Putnam, Conn.), no.3, 1964,
p. 37-52; no.1-2, 1965, p. 24-29.
See serials consulted.

6404. --- Pirmieji bandymai krikš-
tyti Žemaičius. Žemaičių krikšto
550 m. sukakties proga. Prima ten-
tamina Samogitas ad christianismum
convertendi. Occasione 550 anni-
versarii ab eorum conversione.

Brooklyn, N.Y., 1967. 16 p. Offprint from Karys (Brooklyn, N.Y.),
no.8(1435), Oct. 1967, p. 225-233.
DK511.L2G45 CaAEU See also serials
consulted.

6405. GIMBUTAS, Jurgis. Lietuvos
bažnyčių chronologija ir statistika.
[The chronology and statistics of
church erection in Lithuania. In
LKMAM, v.5, 1970, p. [215]-[259]
maps. See serials consulted.

6406. IVINSKIS, Zenonas. Aus den
entscheidenen Jahren der Restaura-
tion des Katholizismus in Litauen;
der Kampf um den Bischöfsstuhl von
Medininkai (Žemaiten), 1574-1576.
Heidelberg, 1967. Offprint from
Festschrift für Margarete Woltner
zum 70. Geburtstag. p. [91]-101.
BX1612.L5.I85 PU

6407. --- Krikščionybės kelias
Lietuvon. [The way of introducing
christianity into Lithuania] In
Tiesos kelias (Kaunas), no.5, 1938.
See serials consulted.

6408. --- Lietuvos bažnyčios kelių;
karaliaus Mindaugo krikšto 700 metų
ir Lietuvos bažnytinės provincijos
25 metų sukaktuvėms paminėti. [Li-
thuania after 700 years of Chri-
stianity] Brooklyn, N.Y., 1951.
30 p. Lithuanian and English.
947.5.Iv54.7 PU CtTMF

--- Šv. Kazimieras, 1458-
1484. New York, N.Y., 1955. See
entry no. 4944.

6409. --- Žemaičių religinė padėtis vysk. Jurgio Petkūno laikais.
[The state of religious life of Žemaičiai (Samogitians) during the
time of Bishop Jurgis Petkūnas] In
Aidai (Brooklyn, N.Y.), no.9(85),
1955, p. 377-381. See serials consulted.

6410. JAKŠTAS, Juozas. Pavėluo-
tas Lietuvos krikštas. [The de-
layed conversion of Lithuania to
christianity] In LKMASD, v.6,
1969, p. [173]-[188] See serials
consulted.

6411. --- Šis tas dėl atskiro
Žemaičių krikšto. [Why Samogitia
(Žemaičiai) was not baptized with
the rest of Lithuania in 1387] In
LKMAM, v.3, 1967, p. 1-[9]. Summary in English. See serials consulted.

6412. JARLATH, Perschek, O.S.F.
Sister. The persecution of Ca-
tholicism in Lithuania under the
Tsarist and Soviet regimes. Mil-

waukee, Wis., 1954. 266 p. Thesis
(M.A.)--Marquette University.
WMM

6413. JURGINIS, Juozas. The reasons for the belated dissemination
of christianity in the Baltics.
Moscow, Nauka, 1970. 11 p.
DK511.B295J85 PU

6414. DIE KIRCHLICHEN ZUSTÄNDE IM
Bistum Wilna. Lausanne, Librairie
Centrale des Nationalités, 1918.
Auszug aus "Litauen", no.2-7.
Slav 6467.41.30 MH

6415. KRASAUSKAS, Rapolas. Katalikų bažnyčia Lietuvoje 16.-17.
amžiuje; nuosmukio priežastys ir atgimimo veiksniai. Die katolische
Kirche in Litauen im XVI-XVII
Jahrhundert; die Ursachen des Ver-
falls und Faktoren des Aufschwungs.
In LKMASD, v.6, 1969, p. [189]-241.
Summary in German. See serials
consulted.

6416. KRASAUSKAS, Rapolas. Ka-
talikų bažnyčia Lietuvoje; carinės
Rusijos okupacijos laikais. [The
Catholic Church in Lithuania during
the occupation by Czarist Russia]
In Lietuvių, enciklopedija. Boston,
Mass., 1968. v.15, p. 141-146.
For holdings see entry no. 216.

6417. KURCZEWSKI, Jan. Stan koś-
ciolów parafjalnych w djecezji Wileńskiej po najściu nieprzyjaciel-
skiem, 1655-1661 r. In Litwa i Ruś
(Wilno), 1912, v.1, no.3, p. 162-
169; v.2, no.1, p. 59-63; v.3, no.1,
p. 54-59; v.3, no.3, p. 204-215; v.
4, no.2, p. 106-111. See serials
consulted.

6418. LAPPO, Ivan Ivanovich.
Bandymas pavesti lenkui Vilniaus
vyskupo katedra XVI amžiaus pabaigoje. [An attempt to assign a Pole
as a bishop to the Cathedral of Vilnius at the end of the 16th century]
In Praeitis (Kaunas), v.1, 1930, p.
94-138. See serials consulted.

6419. LITHUANIAN INFORMATION BUR-
EAU. La situation de l'église catholique en Lithuanie. Lausanne,
Pro Lituania. 1917. 14 p. Extrait
de "Pro Lituania", no.3, 1917.
947.52.L717.5 PU

6420. LITWA POD WZGLĘDEM PRZEŚLA-
dowania w niej rzymsko-katolickiego
kościoła szczególniej w dyacezyi Wileńskiej od roku 1863 do 1872. Wydanie Biblioteki Polskiej w Paryżu.
Poznań, Nakł. J.K. Żupańskiego,
1872. 107 p. 947.52.L738 PU

6421. NAVROTSKII, Aleksandr Aleksandrovich. Kreshchenie Litvy. Sanktpeterburg, 1902. 132 p. 891.71.N224K PU

6422. ORŁOWSKI, Michał. Mowa do ludu w Wilnie,na nieszporach w kościele XX Fanciszkanów miano przez X. Michała Orłowskiego... 1850 roku grudnia 7 dnia o nawróceniu się Litwy na katolicką wiarę. Wilno, Drukarnia A. Marcinowskiego, 1861. 47 p. Mgf91.Or5 CtY NN

6423. PURICKIS, Juozas. Die Glaubenspaltung in Litauen im XVI. Jahrhundert bis zur Ankunft der Jesuiten im Jahre 1569. Freiburg, Switzerland, Buchdr. Gebr. Frangiére, 1919. iv, 199 p. BR420.L5P8 DLC PU

6424. THE RACOVIAN CATECHISM. ENGLISH. The Racovian catechisme... of those Churches... in the kingdom of Poland, the Great Dukedom of Lithuania... Amsterdam, 1652. BM(E. 1320.)

6425. --- The Racovian catechism, with notes and illus.; translated from the Latin: to which is prefixed a sketch of the history of Unitarianism in Poland and the adjacent countries by Thomas Rees. London, Longman, Hurst, Rees, Orme, and Brown, 1818. xcii, 404 p. BT1480.A5E6 1818 DLC

6426. SEMKOWICZ, Władysław. Pierwsze przywileje fundacyjne Witolda dla kościoła na Żmudzi. In Kwartalnik Historyczny (Lwów), v.44, 1930, p. 348-355. See serials consulted.

6427. ŠLEŽAS, Paulius. Bandymai apkrikštyti Lietuvą Algirdo ir Kęstučio laikais. [The attempt to baptize Lithuania during the reign of Algirdas and Kęstutis] In Tiesos kelias (Kaunas), yr 8, no.12, 1932, p. 781-793. See serials consulted.

6428. VAIŠNORA, Juozas. Katalikų bažnyčia Lietuvoje; nepriklausomaisiais ir okupaciniais laikais. [The Catholic Church in Lithuania during the period of independence and occupation] In Lietuvių enciklopedija. Boston, Mass., 1968. v.15, p.146-151. For holdings see entry no.216.

6429. VALANČIUS, Motiejus. Maskoliams katalikus persekiojant. [The Russian persecution of catholics. Surinko ir paaiškino J. Tumas] Kaunas, Žinijos b-vė, 1929. 124 p. 491.922.V232 PU ICBM

6430. VĖBLAITIS, Petras. Kova su caro valdžia už Kęstaičių bažnyčią

[The struggle with the Czar's government for the church of Kęstaičiai] Kaunas, 1938. 114 p. 947.5.V494 PU

6431. YLA, Stasys, 1908- . Krikščionybės įvedimas Lietuvoje. [The introduction of christianity into Lithuania] Kaunas, 1938. 154 p. 947.5.Yl CtTMF

--- Šiluva žemaičių istorijoje. [Boston, Mass.] 1970. See entry no. 5963.

6432. ŽIUGŽDA, Juozas. Katalikų bažnyčios ekspansija į Pabaltį ir Rytų Europą. [The expansion of the Catholic Church into the Baltic area and East-Europe] Vilnius, VPMLL, 1962. 123 p. BX1765.2.Z5 DLC

X.1.c. RELIGIOUS ORDERS

6433. BORĄCZ, Sadok. Rys dziejów zakonu kanodziejskiego w Polsce. Lwów, Nakł. W. Manieckiego, 1861. 2 v. Extensive information on the Church organisation in Lithuania. MH

6434. BIČIŪNAS, Jonas. Apaštalų sosto ir jėzuitų ordino pirmieji bandymai jezuitus įkurdinti Lietuvoje. [The first attempts by the Holy See and Jesuit Order to establish jesuits in Lithuania] In Tautos praeitis (Roma), v.2, no.1, p. 33-42. See serials consulted.

6435. --- Pirmieji jėzuitai Lietuvoje. [The first jesuits in Lithuania] In Tautos praeitis (Roma), v 2, no.1, 1964, p. 37-41. See serials consulted.

6436. --- Pirmieji jėzuitai Vilniuje. [The first jesuits in Vilnius] Roma, 1965. 32 p. Offprint fom Tautos praeitis. 243.4.B475 PU; also in Tautos praeitis (Roma), v.2, no.2 1965, p. 49-80. See serials consulted.

6437. GIDŽIŪNAS, Viktoras. Augustinionai Lietuvoje. [The Augustinian Fathers in Lithuania] In LKMAM, v.4, 1968, p. [305]-320. See serials consulted.

6438. --- De Fratribus Minoribus in Lituania, usque ad definitivam introductionem Observantiae, 1245-1517. Romae, Sumptu proprio, 1950- . 243.1.G84G1 PU DLC CtTMF ICLJF

6439. --- De initiis Fratrum Minorum de Observantia in Lituania, 1468-

1600. Firenze, Typographia Collegii S. Bonaventurae, 1970. [60] p. In Archivum Franciscanum historicum (Firenze), v.63, 1970, p. [44]-103. See serials consulted.

6440. --- Legendariškieji Pranciškonų kankiniai Vilniuje. [The legendary Franciscan Fathers' martyrs in Vilnius] In Aidai (Brooklyn, N.Y.), no.3(69), 1954, p. 105-110, no.4(70), p. 175-180. See serials consulted.

6441. --- Lietuvos vienuolijų augimas ir jų sunaikinimas. [The expansion and destruction of the monasteries in Lithuania] In LKMAM, v.5, 1970, p. 262-290. See serials consulted.

6442. --- De missionibus Fratrum Minorum in Lituania (Saec. XIII et XIV) In Archivum Franciscanum historicum (Firenze), v.42, no.1-4, 1949, (pub. 1950), p. 3-36. See serials consulted.

6443. --- Pranciškonai observantai Lietuvoje XV ir XVI a. Fratres Minores de Observantia in Lituania, saec. XV. et XVI. In Aidai (Brooklyn, N.Y.), 1970, no.2, p. 71-77, no.3, p. 116-122. See serials consulted.

6444. --- Trečiasis Šv. Pranciškaus ordinas. [The Third Order of St. Francis] Brooklyn, N.Y., [Trečiojo ordino Šv. Kazimiero provincija] 1971. 286 p. BX3651.G52 PU CaAEU

6445. --- Vienuolijos Lietuvoje IX-XV amžiuje. [Monastic orders in Lithuania in 9th to 15th centuries] In KLMASD, v.6, 1969, p. [243]-275. See serials consulted.

6447. --- Vienuolijos Lietuvoje XIII-XVI amžiuje. [Monasteries in Lithuania in thirteenth to sixteenth centuries] Roma, 1967. 33 p. Offprint from Lietuvių katalikų mokslo akademija, Rome. Suvažiavimo darbai, v. 6. BX2676.L5G5 PU; see also serials consulted.

6448. --- Vienuolijos Lietuvoje XIII-XX amžiuje. [Monastic orders in Lithuania in thirteenth-twentieth centuries] Roma, 1970. 39 p. Offprint from Lietuvių katalikų mokslo akademija, Rome. Metraštis, v.5, 1970, p. [261]-299. BX2676.L5G51 PU; see also serials consulted.

6449. GIŽYCKI, Jan Marek Antoni. Bazylianie na Žmudzi. [By] J.M. Wołyniak [pseud.] In Przegląd Powszechny (Warszawa), v.31-32, 1891. See

serials consulted.

6450. --- Z przeszłości Karmelitów na Litwie i Rusi. [By] J.M. Wołyniak [pseud.] Z przedmową Franciszka Rawity Gawronskiego. Kraków, Nakł. OO Karmelitów na Piasku, 1918. 2 v. BX3245.L5G5 DLC PU

6451. --- Z przeszłości Zakonu Bazyliańskiego na Litwie i Rusi. [By] J.M. Wołyniak [pseud.] In Przewodnik Naukowy i Literacki (Lwów), v.32, 1904, p. 65-82,157-172,249-268,352-360,449-463. See serials consulted.

6452. JANULAITIS, Augustinas. Juodieji broliai Kražiuose. [The Black Brothers in Kražiai] In Praeitis (Kaunas), v.1, 1930, p. 214-303. See serials consulted.

6453. KANTAK, Kamil. Bernardyni polscy, 1453-[1932] Lwów, Nakł.. Prowincji Polskiej OO Bernardynów, 1933. 2 v. in 1. BX3057.K3 DLC PU

6454. LIETUVOS JĖZUITAI; praeitis ir dabartis. [Lithuanian Jesuit Fathers; their past and present. Putnam, Conn.] Tėvų jėzuitų leidinys [1957] 79 p. illus., ports., map. BX3706.2.L5 DLC CtTMF ICLJF PU

6455. LIUBOVICH, Nikolai Nikolaevich. K istorii iezuitov v litovsko-russkikh zemliakh v XVI v. In Warsaw. Uniwersytet. Izviestiia, 1888. See serials consulted.

6456. MARIJONŲ NEKALTAI PRADĖTOSIOS Šv. P. MARIJOS VIENUOLIJA Lietuvoje. [The Marian order in Lithuania] Marijampolė, Marijonų vienuolijos leidinys, 1929. 32 p. 243.1.M337M PU

6457. RABIKAUSKAS, Paulius. Iš Pašiaušės jėzuitų kolegijos metraščių. [From the chronicles of the Jesuit Father's College in Pašiaušė] In Tautos praeitis (Chicago, Ill.), v.1, no.3, 1961, p. 345-391. See serials consulted.

6458. ROSIAK, Stefan. Bonifratrzy w Wilnie, 1635-1843-1924; szkic z dziejów opieki społecznej w Wilnie. Wilno, Konwent Wileński OO Bonifratrów, 1928. 102, xxii p. 947.52.R737 PU

6459. ROSTOWSKI, Stanisław. Lituanicarum societatis Jesu historiarum libri decem, auctore Stanislao Rostowski, recognoscente Joanne Martinov... Parisiis, Apud Victorem Palmé, 1877. xv, 507 p. map. First ed. Vilnae, 1768. BX3745.L5R7 DLC ICBM PU

6460. RUŠKYS, Petras. Kretingos vienuolynas. [The monastery of Kretinga] In Tiesos kelias (Kaunas), v.2-3, 1928, p. 61-72,125-135. See serials consulted.

6461. SIDERAVIČIUS, Juozas. Pranciškonai Lietuvoje. [Franciscan Fathers in Lithuania] Vilnius, VPMLL, 1962. 103 p. BX3645.L5S5 DLC

6462. TOTORAITIS, Jonas. Marijampolės kunigų marijonų vienuolynas. [Marian Fathers' monastery in Marijampolė] Marijampolė, "Šešupės" knygyno spaustuvė, 1924. 65 p. 243.1.M337T PU CtTMF DLC OKentU

6463. --- Marijonų vienuolija nuo 1864 metų iki atgaivinimui. [The Marian order from 1864 until its revival] In Tiesos kelias (Kaunas), no.9-11, 1936. See serials consulted.

6464. ZALESKI, Stanisław. Jezuici w Polsce. Kraków, 1901-1907. 11 v. in 5. About Lithuania v.4, p. 59-107. MH

XII.1.d. PARISHES AND THEIR HISTORY

6465. BARTKUS, Feliksas. Prie Viešpaties daigyno: atsiminimų žiupsnys apie grynai lietuviškąją Seinų kunigų seminariją ir apie Vilkaviškio kunigų seminariją. [Recollections about the Theological Seminaries in Seinai and Vilkaviškis] Chicago, Ill., 1968. 96 p. BV4140.L5B32 PU

6466. BASANAVIČIUS, Jonas. Iš Seinų vyskupystės istorijos. [From the history of the diocese of Seinai] In Lietuvių tauta (Vilnius), v.1, 1910, p. 364-380. See serials consulted.

6467. HOLTZMANN, W. Die Gründung des Bistums Samaiten. In Zeitschrift für die Geschichte des Oberrheins (Heidelberg), v.32, 1917. p. 70-84. See serials consulted.

6468. IVINSKIS, Zenonas. Žemaičių (Medininkų vyskupijos įkūrimas (1417) ir jos reikšmė lietuvių tautai (1417-1967). [The founding of the Samogitian (Medininkų diocese, 1417...] Roma, Lietuvių katalikų mokslo akademija, 1972. 78 p. Offprint from Lietuvių katalikų mokslo akademija, Rome. Suvažiavimo darbai, v.7, 1972. BR1050.L5.I85 PU; see also serials consulted.

6469. KURCZEWSKI, Jan. Biskupstwo wileńskie od założenia aż do dni obecnych, zawierające dzieje i prace biskupów i duchowieństwa djecezji wileńskiej, oraz wykaz kościołów, klasztorów, szkół i zakładów dobroczynnych i społecznych. Wilno, Nakł. J. Zawadzkiego, 1912. 614 p. BX1559.V5K85 PU NN

6470. --- Kościół Zamkowy; czyli katedra Wileńska w jej dziejowym, liturgicznym, architektonicznym i ekonomicznym rozwoju. Wilno, J. Zawadzki, 1908-1916. 3 v. 947.52.K968 PU(v.1-2) ICLJF MH

6471. OCHMAŃSKI, Jerzy. Powstanie i rozwoj latyfundium biskupstwa wileńskiego, 1387-1550. Poznań, Zakład Prod. Skryptów Politechniki Warszawkiej, 1963. 223 p. maps, tables. (Poznań. Uniwersytet. Wydział Filozoficzno-Historycznego. Prace. Seria Historia, nr. 13) HD729.V.025 DLC CaOTU MH PU

RELATIONES STATUS DIOCESIUM in Magno Ducatu Lituaniae. Romae, 1971- . See entry no. 4672.

6472. SAWICKI, Jakub, ed. Concilia Poloniae; źródła i studia krytyczne. [T.2: Synody diecezji wileńskiej i ich statuty] Warszawa, Nakł. Tow. Naukowego Warszawskiego, 1948. xi, 145 p. 248.138.Sa99 t.2 PU DLC

6473. VALANČIUS, Motiejus. Biskupstwo żmudzkie... ze żmujdzkiego na język polski przełożył i niektóre przypisy historyczne dodał M. Hryszkiewicz. Karków, Gebethner, 1898. xiv, 247 p. 947.52.V232.2 PU BM(4695. dd. 26.)

6474. --- Žemajtiu Wiskupiste. [The diocese of Samogitia] Aprasze Motiejus Wolonczewskis. Wilniuj, Spaustuwieje Juozapo Zawadzki, 1848. 2 v. BR1050.L5V3 1970 PU(Xerox copy)

6475. --- Žemaiczių vyskupystė. [The diocese of Samogitia] Išleista kasztais kun. V. Matulaiczio. Shenandoah, Pa., Garso Amerikos lietuvių, 1897. 247 p. 947.5.V232 PU CtY OCl BM(4695. d. 49.)

6476. VILNA (DIOCESE). Informatio de bonis ecclesiasticis diaecesis Vilnensis non desolatis necue ruinatis contra informationes falsas Constantini Brzostowski, episcopi. [Halae] 1895. [30] p. 1638.598q NjP

--- Kodeks diplomatyczny katedry i diecezji wileńskiej. W Krakowie, 1932-1939. See entry no. 4695.

6477. --- Synody diecezji Wileń-skiej i ich statuty. Warszawa, 1948. xi, 145 p. In Sawicki, J. Concilia Poloniae. v.2.
BM(W.P. C. 769/1.)

XII.2. PROTESTANT CHURCH: GENERAL STUDIES AND HISTORY

6478. ADAMOWICZ, Adam Ferdinand A. Die evangelische-lutherische Kirche zu Wilna. Eine Chronik geschrieben ... von A.F.A. Übersetzung aus dem Polnischen. Wilna, 1855. 94 p.
BM(4695. d. 10.)

6479. AKTA, THO JEST SPRAWY ZBORU Krześciańskiego, Wileńskiego, które się poczęli R.P. 1557 miesiąca Decembra dnia 14. Ze sprawą kxiędza Simona z Prossowic, tego Zboru superintendenta, kaznodzieia Oświeconego Kxiążęcia pana Mikołaia Radziwiła, Woiewody Wileńskiego, etc. w Brześciu Litewskim 1559. Wilno, 1913. xii, 32 p. (Monumenta reformationis Polonicae et Lithuanicae. Ser. 10, zesz.1) BR420.P7M6 Ser.10 zesz.1 DLC CU MH BM(20012. g. 41.)

6480. ALLERUNTERTHÄNIGSTE SUPPLIque an Ihro Königliche Majestät und Republique von Pohlen, derer Dissidenten im König-Reich Pohlen, Gross-Fürstenthum Littauen und incorporirten Landen. [Warszawa?] 1725. 24 p. Supposed author: D. E. Jabłonski. BM(3925. e. 7.)

6481. BALLERSTEDT, Kurt. Die evangelisch-lutherische Kirche in Litauen im Kampf um ihre Freiheit. Leipzig, Centralvorstand d. Evang. Vereins d. Gustav-Adolf-Stiftung, 1928. 65 p. (Die evangel. Diaspora. Beihefte, nr. 16)
BM(4685. i. 27.)

6482. BARYCZ, Henryk, ed. Obraz historyczny kalwinizmu na Litwie, 1650-1696 r. In Reformacja w Polsce (Trzaska), v.4, 1926, p. 206-221. BR420.P7R4 DLC See serials consulted.

6483. BERTULEIT, Hans. Die Reformation unter den preussischen Litauern. Von Johann Bertoleit. Königsberg in Pr., Wichern-Buchhandlung, 1932-33. 2 v. (Synodal Kommission für ostpreussische Kirchengeschichte. Jahrbuch, 2-3)
DLC serial-4 PU

6484. BUŠACKIS, Brunonas. Martynas Mažvydas. Chicago, Ill., Lietuvos Evangelikų spaudos centras, 1963. 69 p. illus., facsims., maps. (Lietuvos Evangelikų spaudos centras. Leidinys, nr. 1)
BX8080.M36B8 DLC ICU

6485. BUSCH, Ernst H. von, ed. Materialien zur Geschichte und Statistik des Kirchen- und Schulwesens der evangelisch-lutherischen Gemeinden in Russland. Sanktpeterburg, Commissionsverlag von G. Haessel, 1862. xxvi, 696 p. 2 fold. col. maps. BX8027.B8 DLC

6486. CONSENSUS IN FIDE ET RELIgione Christiana inter Ecclesias Evangelicas... Poloniae, magnique Ducatus Lithuaniae et caeterarum... accesserunt... acta et conclusiones synodi generalis. Toruniensis, Heidelbergae Typis Voegelinianis, 1605. 88 p. BM(3925. aa. 5.(2))
NN

6487. FALKENHAHN, Viktor. Der Übersetzer der litauischen Bibel Johannes Bretke und seine Helfer; Beiträge zur Kultur- und Kirchengeschichte Altpreussens, von Viktor Falkenhahn. Königsberg in Pr. und Berlin, Ost-Europa-Verlag, 1941. xv, 487 p. illus., facsims, tables. (Schriften der Albertus-Universität. Geisteswissenschaftliche Reihe, Bd. 31) Bibliography: p. 470-477. BS264.F3 DLC CU CtY DCU MH NN NNUT PU

6488. GAIGALAT, Wilhelm. Die Evangelische Gemeinschaftsbewegung unter den preussischen Litauern... Königsberg in Pr., Ost-preussische Druckerei und Verlangsanstalt, 1904. 36 p. 947.52.G127.3 PU

6489. --- Die evangelische-lutherische Kirche in Litauen, ihre Kämpfe und Nöte im Zeitraum von 1925-1929... Memel, Kommissionverlag der "Sandora", 1929. 110 p. 947.52G127.4 PU

6490. GAILIUS, Valentinas. Zur Vorgeschichte und zur Geschichte des memelländischen Kirchenstreites ... Memel, Selbstverlag des Verfassers, 1924. 60 p. 947.52.G129 PU

6491. GERECHTSAME UND FREYHEITEN der Dissidenten in der Christlichen Religion, in der Krone Polen, und im Grossherzogthume Litthauen, aus den Privilegien, Reichstags-Constitutionen, Statuten des Grossherzogthums Litthauen, und verschiedenen andern ungezweifelten Urkunden gesammelt... [Warszawa?] 1772 150 p. BM(3926. f. 17.)

6492. GILBERT, Eleazar. Newes from Poland. Wherein declared the cruel practice of the Polish clergy against the Protestants, and in particular against the ministers of the City of Vilna... London. Printed by E. P. for N. Butler, 1641. 2 p.l. 32 p. British Tracts 1641 G373 CtY

6493. GUDAITIS, Kristupas. Tikybiniai ir kultūriniai ryšiai tarp Didž. bei Maž. Lietuvos evangelikų lietuvių. [Cultural and religious ties between evangelical Lithuanians in Lithuania Minor and Lithuania Proper] In Lietuvininkų Kalendorius, 1952. p. 41-47. AY1039.L5L54 DLC PU

6494. --- Lietuvos evangelikai. [Evangelics of Lithuania] Hamilton, Ont., Spaudos b-vė "Rūta", 1957. 434 p. ports. Bibliography: p. 215-409. BX4849.G9 DLC CtPAM ICN ICU PU

6495. --- Tauragės evangelikų liuteronų parapijos istorija. [The history of the evangelic-lutheran parish in Tauragė] In Tautos praeitis (Roma), v.2, no.3-4(7-8), 1967, p. 271-286. See serials consulted.

6496. HAAGEN, Bernhard. Burggraf Alexander zu Dohna und die Schweizerkirchen in Litauen. Zum 200 jährigen Gedächtniss der Entsehung der reformierten Gemeinden zu Judschen und Gumbinen 1713-1913. Berlin, Gselliusche Buchhandlung, 1913. 30 p. Offprint from Altertunsgesellschaft Insterburg. Insterburg, 1913. MH CtY

6497. HARTKNOCH, Christoph. Preussische Kirchen-Historie. Dantzig, Simon Bechenstein, 1696. 1098 p. maps. NjP PPeSchw

6498. HARTLEB, Kazimierz. Zagadnienie reformacji na ziemiach litewskich. Problemy postulaty. In PZHP w Wilnie 17-20 września 1935 r. Pamiętnik VI. Referaty (Lwów), v.1, 1935. p. 329-337. See serials consulted.

6499. HILFSKOMITEE DER EVANGELIschen Deutschen aus Litauen. Bilder aus der Geschichte der evangelischen Deutschen in Litauen. [Atzenhausen, 1964] 144 p. illus. BX8663.L5H5 DLC PU

6500. HŁASKO, Edward. Stosunek Jednoty Litewskiej do Arjan w świetle kanonów z wieku XVII. In Ateneum Wileńskie (Wilno), v.11, 1936, p. 283-290. See serials consulted.

6501. IVINSKIS, Zenonas. Die Entwicklung der Reformation in Litauen bis zum Erscheinen der Jesuiten. Berlin, 1967. 45 p. map. Offprint from Forschungen zur Osteuropäischen Geschichte. Berlin, 1967. Bd.12, p. 1-45. BR420.L5I93 PU; see also serials consulted.

6502. JABŁOŃSKI, Daniel Ernest. Historia concensus Sendomiriensis, inter Evangelicos Regni Poloniae, et M. D. Lithuaniae... Berolini, apud A. Haude, 1731. 263, 29 p. maps. BX4854.P7J2 ICU BM PU

6503. KAHLE, Wilhelm. Die Begegnung des baltischen Protestantismus mit der russische orthodoxen Kirche. Leiden, E.J. Brill, 1959. xvi, 295 p. 10 plates (Oekumenische Studien, 2) BX8027.K3 DLC CLU CU CaAEU CtY-D GU ICU InU KU MH-AH MiU MnU NN NIC NNC NcD NjP OrU OU RPB WU

6504. KOSSOWSKI, Aleksander. Stan dotychczasowych badań nad dziejami protestantyzmu na ziemiach Wielkiego Księstwa Litewskiego w XV-XVII w. In PZHP w Wilnie 17-20 września 1935 r. Pamiętnik VI. Referaty (Lwów), v.1, 1935, p. 338-343. See serials consulted.

6505. KOT, Stanisław. Ausbruch und Niedergang des Täufertums in Wilna, 1563-1566. In Archiv für Reformationsgeschichte (Berlin), v.49, 1959, p. 212-226. See serials consulted.

6506. --- La réforme dans le Grand-Duché de Lithuanie, facteur d'occidentalisation culturelle. In Brussels. Université libre. Institut de Philologie et d'histoire orientales et slaves. Annuaire, v.12, 1953, p. 201-261. See serials consulted.

6507. KRAINSKI, John de Kraino. A relation of the distressed state of the Church of Christ, professing the Protestant religion in the great dukedom of Lithvania, presented to the view of all compassionate Christians. London, n.p., 1661. 1 p.l., 6 p. (In Stuart tracts. Series 2, v.8) 942.06.Z2 v.8 MnU

6508. ŁUKASZEWICZ, Józef. Dzieje kościołów wyznania helweckiego w Litwie. Poznań, 1842-1843. 2 v. BM(1368. i. 12.)

6509. --- Geschichte der reformirten Kirchen in Litauen. Leipzig, Dykshe Buchhandlung, 1848-50. 2 v. in 1. BR937.L7L9 InU PU BM(1368. i. 27.)

MONUMENTA REFORMATIONIS POlonicae et Lithuanicae; Wilno, 1911-1915. See entry no. 4661.

6510. MOŚCICKI, Henryk. Szymon Konarski, w 85-tą rocznicę stracenia. Wilno, Nakł. Synodu Wileńskiego Ewangielicko-Reformowanego, 1924. 20 p. port. DK435.5.K6M6 DLC CU MH PU

6511. PFUHL, Karl Edward Georg. Überlick über den protestantischen Kirchenbau ir preussischen Litauen von der Reformation bis Beginn des 19 Jahrhunderts. Berlin, Technische Hochschule, 1922. 93 p. Thesis--Technische Hochschule, Berlin. PU

6512. RHESA, Ludwig Jedemin. Geschichte der litthauischen Bibel. Ein Beitrag zur Religionsgeschichte der nordischen Völker. Königsberg in Pr., Verlag Enslin, 1816. viii, 60 p. BM(03128. h. 38. (1.))

6513. --- Kurzgefasste Nachrichten von allen seit 1775 an den evangelischen Kirchen in Ostpreussen angestellten Predigern, als Fortsetzung der Arnoldtschen Presbyterologie... Königsberg in Pr., 1834. BM(4662. dd. 1. (1.))

6514. RHODE, Gotthold. Die Reformation in Osteuropa; ihre Stellung in der Weltgeschichte und ihre Darstellung in den Weltgeschichten. In Osteuropa (Stuttgart), v.7, no. 4, 1958, p. 481-500. See serials consulted.

6515. SAKS, Wincenty. Zbiory rękopiśmienne Synodu Ewangelickoreformowanego w Wilnie. In Reformacja w Polsce (Trzaska), v.5, no.17-18, 1928, p. 151-155. See serials consulted.

6516. SCHEIDEMANTEL, Heinrich Gottfried. Allgemeines Kirchen-Recht beyder evangelischen Confessionen in Polen und Litthauen... Warszawa, 1780. xix, 262 p. BM(5152. a. 48.)

6517. SCHMITTLEIN, Raymond. Facteurs politiques et sociaux dans l'Évangélisation de la Lituanie. In Festgabe Joseph Lortz. Glaube und Geschichte. Baden-Baden, 1958, v.2, p. 243-271. BR50.I8 v.2 DLC

6518. ŠEPETYS, Jonas. Reformacijos istorija Lietuvoje. [History of Reformation in Lithuania] Vilnius, 1922. 77 p. BM(4663. b. 16.)

6519. SOBIESKI, Wacław. Nienawiść wyznaniowa tłumów za rządów Zygmunta III. Warszawa, S. Demby, 1902. 199 p. (*QO)NN MH

6520. SPIS SYNODÓW I SESJI PROWINCJONALNYCH JEDNOTY LITEWSKIEJ 1611-1913. Wilno, 1913. vii, 62 p. (Monumenta Reformationis Polonicae et Lithuanicae. Ser. 6, z.1.) BR420.P7M6 DLC CU MH

6521. STASIEWSKI, Bernhard. Reformation und Gegenreformation in Polen; neue Forschungsergebnisse. Münster in Westfalen, Aschendorff [1960] 99 p. (Katholisches Leben und Kämpfen im Zeitalter der Glaubenspaltung, 18) DLC-P4 CSaT CSt IEG ICU NIC JnPT NNUT OU

6522. STUDNICKI, Wacław Gizbert. Kościół ewangelicko-reformowany w Wilnie; historja, organizcja... Wilno, Wydawn. Wileńskiego Synodu Ewangelicko-Reformowanego, 1935. 68 p. illus. (incl. plans.) BX9480.P7S8 DLC

6523. SUŽIEDELIS, Simas. Reformacijos nuoslūgis ir katalikų reakcija. [The ebb of reformation and the catholic reaction] In Židinys, v.28, no.11, 1938, p. 554-570. See serials consulted.

6524. --- Reformacijos sąjūdis Lietuvoje. [Reformation activities in Lithuania] In Židinys (Kaunas), v.28, no.8-9, 1938, p. 242-261. See serials consulted.

6525. SYNOD EWANGELICKO-REFORMOWANy w Wilnie. Katalog pokazu zabytków ze zbiorów Synodu ewang.-reformowanego w Wilnie; pamiątka zjazdu ewangelickiego w Wilnie, 1926. [Wilno, Druk "Lux"] 1926. 43, xxiv p. BX9480.P7S9 DLC BM(Ac. 1156. g.)

6526. WITTRAM, Reinhard, ed. Baltische Kirchengeschichte; Beiträge zur Geschichte der Missionierung und der Reformation, der evangelisch-lutherischen Landeskirchen und des Volkskirchentums in den baltischen Landen. Göttingen, Vandenhoeck & Ruprecht, 1956. 347 p. BR937.B3W5 DLC CaBVaU CLU CU CtY ICU ICN InU MH MoU NN NcD NjPT OU

6527. WOTSCHKE, Theodor. Georg Weigel; ein Beitrag zur Reformationsgeschichte Altpreussens und

Litauens. In Archiv für Reformationsgeschichte (Berlin), v.19, 1922, p. 22-47. See serials consulted.

6528. ZWOLSKI, B. Zburzenie zbioru ewangelicko-reformowanego w Wilnie w roku 1682. In Ateneum Wileńskie (Wilno), v.12, 1937, p. 482-514. See serials consulted.

XII.3. OTHER CHURCHES

6529. BANTYSH-Kamenskii, Nikolai Nikolaevich. Istoricheskoe izviestie o voznikshei v Pol'shie unii s pokazaniem nachala i vazhnieishykh, v prodolzhenie onoi chrez dva vieka, prikliuchenii... Moskva, v Sinodalnoi tipografii, 1805. 454 p.

6530. --- --- Vil'na, Tip. A. Syrkina, 1866. 387 p. BX1558.B3 DLC

6531. BOBROVSKII, Pavel Osipovich. Uprazdnenie Supral'skoi greko-unitskoi eparkii i voztanovlenie Vilenskoi metropolitskoi eparkii... Vil'na, Gub. tip., 1890. 58 p. BX1568.V5B6 DLC

6532. CAHN, Zvi. The rise of the Karaite sect; a new light on the Halakah and origin of Karaites. New York, N.Y., M. Tausner Publishing Co., [1937] 128 p. BM175.K3C3 DLC NcD OCl OCH PPLT PPULC

6533. CHARKIEWICZ, Walerian. Zmierzch unji kościelnej na Litwie i Białorusi. Słonim, Nakł. Grupy Ziemian, 1929. 158 p. ports. 947.52.C374 PU PPULC

6534. GIDŽIŪNAS, Viktoras. Scotism and scotists in Lithuania. Roma, 1968. v.4, [239]-248 p. Extractum de De doctrina Ioannis Duns Scoti. Acta Congressus Scotistici internationalis Oxonii et Edinburgi, 11-17 sept. 1966 celebrati, t.4. B734.S85 v.4 DLC MA-AH NN NNG

6535. --- Skotizmas ir skotistai Lietuvoje. Scotismus et scotistae in Lituania. Brooklyn, N.Y., Pranciškonų spaustuvė, 1966. 32 p. Offprint from Aidai (Brooklyn, N.Y.), no.2(187), 1966, p. 75-83. B765.J34G45 CaAEU ICLJF PPULC PU

6536. IOSIF, Metropolitan of Lithuania. Vilenskii pravoslavnyi nekropol'. Vil'na, Tip. I. Bliumovicha, 1892. vi, 422 p. maps. Balt 8411.55 MH

6537. --- Zapiski Iosifa Mitropolita Litovskago, izdannyia Imperat. Akademieiu nauk po zavieshchaniiu autora. Sanktpeterburg, tip. Imper. Akad. nauk, 1883. 3 v. facsim., fronts, plate. 970.9.IO ICLJF NN

6538. KAROL, Anatol. Karotki narys historyi pravaslaunae tsarkvy u Vialikim Kniastve Litouskim (Belaruskim) Peryiad XI-XVI stah. N'iu Bransvik, N. Dzh., 1957. 94 p. illus. Added t.p.: A short outline of Greek Orthodox church history in the Grand Principality of Lithuania (Bielorussia). BX730.W5K28 DLC NN

6539. LIKOWSKI, Edward. Dzieje kościoła unickiego na Litwe i Rusi w XVIII i XIX wieku... [1st ed.] Poznań, J. Leitgeber, 1880. xvi, 495 p. 936.L627 NNC DLC ICU MH

6540. --- --- Wyd. 2. Warszawa, Skł. Gł. w Księg. Gebethnera i Wolffa, 1906. 2 v. in 1. (Biblioteka Dzieł Chrześcijańskich) Bibliography: v.1, p. [ix]-xiv. BX4711.622.L5 1906 DLC IU NN PU

6541. --- Unja Brzeska w roku 1596. Poznań, Autor, 1896. Slav. 5490.2 MH

6542. --- --- Wyd. 2. przejrzane i poprawione. Warszawa, Skład Główny w Księgarni Gebethnera i Wolffa, 1907. xvii, 355. (Biblioteka dzieł chrześcijańskich) BX1520.R8L52 1907 DLC NN

6543. MISIŪNAS, Romualdas J. The orthodox church in the Lithuanian state, 1315-1377. In Lituanus (Chicago, Ill.), v.14, no.3, 1968, p. 5-28. See serials consulted.

6544. POLOVTSOV, Anatolii Viktorovich. Strazh' pravoslaviia v Litvie; pamiatki IUvenaliia arkhiepiskopa Litovskago i Vilenskago. Moskva, Universitetskaia tipografiia, 1904. 153 p. 289.8.PO ICLJF BM(4888. de. 8.)

6545. PRAVOSLAVIJA KAUNO GUBERNIJOJE. [The orthodox Church in Kaunas district] In Varpas (Tilžė), no.6, 1894. See serials consulted.

6546. SHIRKOV, Glegont. Vilenskii Sv.-Dukhov monastyr', istoricheskoe opisanie. Vil'na, Izd. Sv.-Dukh. monastyria, 1888. 373 p. Cyr.4.BX123 DLC ICLJF

XIII. CULTURE

XIII.1. GENERAL STUDIES

ALEKSA, Jonas. Lietuvių tautos likimo klausimu. Kaunas, 1925. See entry no. 1007.

6547. ANYSAS, Martynas and Valerija Anysienė. Žymios lietuvės moterys mitologijoje, padavimuose ir istorijoje. [Famous Lithuanian women in mythology, history, etc.] Medžiaga surinkta iš įvairių literatūrų: lietuvių, lenkų, rusų ir vokiečių. Toronto, Ont., Leidėjas Lietuvos skautų sąjungos Kanados rajonas, 1970. xvii, 287 p. illus. DK511.L28A13 DLC PU

6548. BALYS, Jonas. Lithuanian folklore... folk songs... mythology. In Funk and Wagnalls standard dictionary of folklore, mythology and legends. New York, N.Y., 1949-50. v.2, p. 627-634. GR35.F8 DLC CaAEU CaBVaU CaBViP CU CtY-M DNAL DNLM DSI ICU IcU KyU-N KyU MB MH MeB MdBP MiU MoU MtU NN NBuC OCl OClW OO OrU OCU OU PP PPL PSt PPT PU TxU TU ViU Wa WaS WaWW WaT

6549. BASANAVIČIUS, Jonas. Iš krikščionijos santykių su senovės lietuvių tikyba ir kultūra. [The relations of Christianity with the old Lithuanian religion and culture] Vilnius, M. Kuktos spaustuvė, 1913. 100 p. 947.52.B292 PU CtTMF

6550. BIRŽIŠKA, Mykolas. Iš mūsų kultūros ir literatūros istorijos. [From the history of our culture and literature] Kaunas, Vytauto Didžiojo Universiteto humanitarinių mokslų fakulteto leidinys, 1931-38. 2 v. No more published. Includes bibliography of works of Mykolas Biržiška comp. by Izidorius Kisinas: v.1, p. [3]-85; v.2, p. [1]-85. PG8703.B48 DLC CU ICU MH OCL(1) ICCC(1) PPULC(1) PU

6551. BOETTICHER, Adolf G. Die Bau- und Kunstdenkmäler der Provinz Ostpreussen. Heft V: Litauen. Heft VIII: Aus der Kulturgeschichte Ostpreussens. Königsberg in Pr., B. Teichert, 1895-98. NA1077.B6 DLC CtY MH OO PU

6552. CHODŹKO, Ignacy. Pisma. Wyd. nowe. Wilno, J. Zawadzki, 1880. Partial contents.--t.1-2. Obrazy litewskie.--t.3. Podania litewskie. PG7158.C54 1880 InU CaAEU(1-2) CtY MH MiU NNC

6553. DULAITIENĖ, Elvyra (Glemžaitė). Kupiškėnų senovė; etnografija ir tautosaka. [The antiquity of Kupiškis] Vilnius, VGLL, 1958. 470 p. illus., plates. Bibliography: p. 455-[462]. T914.75D CaOTP DLC ICCC ICLJF NN OU

6554. DUNN, Stephen Porter. Cultural processes in the Baltic area under Soviet rule. Berkeley, Calif., Institute of Intern. Studies [1966] vi, 92 p. (California. University. Institute of International studies. Research studies, no.11) Bibliography: p. 87-92. DK511.B29D8 1966 DLC CU DS FTaSU MH NhU TxU CSt WU

6555. ECKERT, Rainer. Forschungsunternehmen zur litauischen Sprache und Literatur in Vilnius; Stand vom September 1958. In Zeitschrift für Slavistik (Berlin), v.4, no.3, 1959, p. 418-423. See serials consulted.

6556. FORSTREUTER, Kurt Hermann. Deutsche Kulturpolitik im sogenannten Preussisch-Litauen. In Deutsche Hefte für Volks- und Kulturbodenforschung (Langensalza), v.3, 1933, p. 259-266. See serials consulted.

6557. GALAUNĖ, Paulius. Dailės ir kultūros baruose; straipsnių rinkinys. [On art and culture; collection of articles] Vilnius, Vaga, 1970. 312 p. N6995.L5G32 PU

6558. HORN, Alexander. Friedrich Tribukeits Chronik. Schilderung aus dem Leben der preussisch-litauischen Landbewohner des 18 and 19 Jahrhunderts. Insterburg, Selbstverlag, 1894. 47 p. BM(9004. k. 15. (8))

6559. IVINSKIS, Zenonas. Vatikano archyvas-aruodas lietuvių kultūros istorijai. [The archives of the Vatican; a source for the history of Lithuanian culture] In Aidai (Kennebunkport, Me.), no.3(29), 1950, p. 110-113. See serials consulted.

JUCEWICZ, Ludwik Adam. Litwa pod względem starożytnych zabytków, obyczajów i zwyczajów. Wilno, 1846. See entry no. 1021.

6560. JONYNAS, Ambraziejus. Klasių kovos atspindžiai lietuvių tautosakoje. [Reflections of the class struggle in the Lithuanian folklore] Vilnius, VPMLL, 1957. 31 p. 891.92.H.J739 PU

JUNGFER, Victor. Kulturbilder aus Litauen. Berlin, 1918.

See entry no. 1022.

6561. --- Litauen, Antlitz eines Volkes. Leipzig, Breitkopf & Härtel [1938] 324 p. plates. PG8703.J8 DLC CaAEU CSt-H CtY IEN ICBM NNC NN NjP NBuU OCl PPiU PU

6562. --- ---; Versuch einer Kultursoziologie. [2. Aufl.] Tübingen, Patria-Verlag [1948] 341 p. PG8703.J8 DLC CSt-H CaAEU CaQMM CtY CoU ICU IEN LU MH NN NNC NBuU NmU NjP PPiU PU

6563. JURGINIS, Juozas. Istorija ir poezija; kultūros istorijos etiudai. [History and poetry...] Vilnius, Vaga, 1969. 346 p. DK511.L212J82 PU CtY CaAEU DLC

6564. JURKŪNAS, Ignas. Litauisk kultur. Av Ignas Scheynius [pseud.] Stockholm, Svenska Andelsförlaget, 1917. 86 p. illus., plates. DK511.L22J95 CaAEU NNC PU

KESSLER, Otto. Die Baltenländer und Litauen. Beiträge zur Geschichte, Kultur und Volkswirtschaft unter Berücksichtigung der deutschen Verwaltung. Berlin, Puttkammer & Mühlbrecht, 1916. 237 p. See entry no. 5327.

6565. KRAŠTOTYRA; leidinys skirtas Tarybų valdžios atkūrimo Lietuvoje 25-mečiui. [A study of the country ... Vyr. redaktorius B. Vaitkevičius. Spaudai parengė: A. Balašaitis et al.] Vilnius, 1966. 236 p. illus., map, music, ports. At head of title: LTSR Paminklų apsaugos ir kraštotyros draugija. DK511.L27K65 DLC CaAEU

6566. LEPNER, Theodor. Der preusche Littauer; oder, Vorstellung der Nahmens-Herleitung, Kind-Tauffen, Hochzeit... und andere dergleichen Sachen der Littauer in Preussen; kürtzlich zusammen getragen... im Jahr... 1690. Danzig, J.H. Rüdiger, 1744. 152 p. illus. GR15.L77 Reel 241:8 CaAEU (Microfilm) PU ICN

6567. --- --- [Another edition. Tilsit, W. Sommerfeld, 1848] xvi, 127 p. With reproduction of original t.p. and frontispiece. Bonaparte Collection no. 13451 ICN

6568. LIETUVOS TSR KRAŠTOTYROS DRAUGIJA. Zervynos; kraštotyros bruožai. [Zervynos; a study of the environs of Zervynai. Vyr. redaktorius V. Milius. Vilnius, 1964] 240 p. illus., maps, music, ports. (Its Leidinys, nr. 10) Summaries in German and Russian.

DK651.Z46L5 DLC PU

6569. LIETUVOS TSR KULTŪROS DARbuotojų suvažiavimas. 1st, Vilna, 1969. Pirmasis Lietuvos TSR Kultūros darbuotojų suvažiavimas. [Conference of Lithuanian cultural activities personnel. Sudarė Eduardas Maurukas. Redagavo Petras Dabulevičius] Vilnius, Mintis, 1971. 248 p. DK511.L27L492 1969 PU

6570. LIETUVOS TSR MOKSLŲ AKADEMIJA, Vilna. Istorijos institutas. Iš lietuvių kultūros istorijos. [rom the Lithuanian history of culture. Vyr. redaktorius J. Žiugžda] Vilnius, VPMLL, 1958- illus. DK511.L212L5 DLC CtPAM(1-4) CtY ICU ICBM IU MH(1-3) NN NNC OClW OKentU PPiU WaU

6571. MACEINA, Antanas. Task of Baltic exiles. In Lituanus (Brooklyn, N.Y.), v.5, no.2, 1959, p. 34-40. See serials consulted.

6572. MIČIULIS, J. K. Cultural progress of Independent Lithuania. In Baltic Review (New York, N.Y.), no.13, 1958, p. 29-39. See serials consulted.

6573. MOSKOS, Ulyssa Alice. A comparison of Spanish and Lithuanian customs and legends. Urbana, University of Illinois, 1926. 84 leaves. Typescript. Thesis for the degree of B.A. in Spanish. 1926M85 IU

6574. TRUMPA, Vincas. Intelektualinis baikštumas Sovietijoje ir Lietuvoje. [Intellectual timidity in the Soviet Union and in Lithuania] In Metmenys (Chicago, Ill.), no.1, 1959, p. 92-107. See serials consulted.

6575. --- Literature and art in the snares of socialist realism. In Lituanus (Brooklyn, N.Y.), v.5, no.3, 1959, p. 80-83. See serials consulted.

6576. --- The problem of cultural heritage. In Lituanus (Brooklyn, N.Y.), v.7, no.3, 1961, p. 66-74. See serials consulted.

6577. --- Ties kultūrinio palikimo problema. [On the problem of cultural heritage] In Metmenys (Chicago, Ill.), no.3, 1960, p. 16-32. See serials consulted.

6578. VAITIEKŪNAS, Vytautas. Soviet cultural invasions. In Baltic Review (New York, N.Y.), no.9, 1956,

p. 58-67. See serials consulted.

6579. WASILEWSKI, Leon. Die nationalen und kulturellen Verhältnisse im osgenannten Westrussland... In Polen (Wien), yr 1, no.1, 1915, p. 5-45. See serials consulted.

WIELHORSKI, Władysław. Litwini, białorusini, i polacy w dziejach kultury Wielkiego Księstwa Litewskiego. London, 1951. See entry no. 1058.

XIII.2. PRIMITIVE RELIGION AND MYTHOLOGY

6580. BALYS, Jonas. Baum and Mensch im litauischen Volksglauben. In Deutsche Volkskunde (München), 1942, p. 171-177. See serials consulted.

6581. --- Dievai ir dvasios. [Gods and ghosts] In Lietuvių enciklopedija. Boston, Mass., 1968. v.15, p. 469-473. For holdings see entry no. 216.

6582. --- Dvasios ir žmonės; liaudies sakmės. [Ghosts and men; Lithuanian folk legends about the dead] Bloomington, Ind., Author, 1951. 126 p. (Lietuvių tautosakos lobynas, 1) GR203.L5B27 DLC CaAEU ICCC KU MH NN OC1 OOxM PPULC PU

6583. --- Donner und Teufel in den Volkserzälungen der baltischen und skandinavischen Völker. In Tautosakos darbai (Kaunas), v.6, 1939, p. 1-220, viii. Lithuanian and German. Bibliography: p. 7-9. See serials consulted.

6584. --- Griaustinis ir velnias Baltoskandijos kraštų tautosakoje. [The thunder and the devil in the folklore of the Balto-Scandian countries] In Tautosakos darbai (Kaunas), v.6, 1939, p. 1-220. See serials consulted.

6585. --- Lietuvių mitologiškos sakmės. Lithuanian mythological legends. London, Nida, 1956. 191 p. (Nidos knygų klubo leidinys, nr. 13) GR203.L5B313 DLC CaAEU CLU CaOTU CtTMF IEN ICU ICLJF ICCC InU IU MnU NIC OC1 PU

6586. --- Parallels and differences in Lithuanian and Latvian mythology. Eutin, Auseklis, 1953. 7 p. Offprint from Festschrift for

Kārlis Kundziņš, 1953, p. 5-11. 285.1.B219 PU

6587. --- Perkūnas lietuvių liaudies tikėjimuose. [Thunder in Lithuanian folk beliefs] In Tautosakos darbai (Kaunas), v.3, 1937, p. 149-238. Bibliography: p. 237-238. See serials consulted.

6588. --- Die Sagen von den litauischen Feen. In Die Nachbarn (Göttingen), v.1, 1948, p. 31-71. See serials consulted.

6589. --- Tautosaka apie dangų. [Lithuanian folklore of the Sky] Sodus, Mich., J.J. Bachunas, 1951. 24 p. Summary in English. GR203.L5B317 DLC CaAEU ICLJF IEN PU PPULC

6590. --- Tikėjimai. [Folk worship] In Lietuvių tautosakos skaitymai. [Tübingen, 1948] v.2, p. 5-96. GR203.L5B315 v.2 DLC

6591. BALYS, Jonas and Haralds Biezais. Baltische Mythologie. In Wörterbuch der Mythologie. Stuttgart, 1965. Lief. 7, p. 373-454. Editor: H.W. Haussig. BL945.B3 PU DLC CaOONL

6592. BASANAVIČIUS, Jonas. Iš gyvenimo vėlių bei velnių. [From the life of ghosts and devils] Chicago, Ill., Spauda "Lietuvos", 1903. lxxxiii, 386 p. GR203.L5B38 DLC CtTMF ICBM ICCC ICLJF InNd MiD NN NB OC1 OrP PU PPULC WaS

6593. BENDER, Joseph. Zur altpreussischen Mythologie und Sittengeschichte. In Altpreussische Monatsschrift (Königsberg in Pr.), v.2, 1865, p. 577-603, 694-717; v.4, 1867, p. 1-27, 97-135. See serials consulted.

6594. BERTULEIT, Hans. Das Religionswesen der alten Preussen mit litauisch-lettischen Paralellen. [Von] J. Bertoleit. Königsberg in Pr., Altertumsgesellschaft Prussia, 1924. 113 p. (Sitzungsberichte, Prussia, Bd. 25) MH-P

6595. BIEZAIS, Haralds. Die Religionsquellen der baltischen Völker und die Ergenbnisse der bisherigen Forschungen. Vorwort von C.M. Edsman. Uppsala, 1954. 64 p. GR1.G823 v.9 DLC CU DeU ICU INC InU MH MdBJ MnU MiU NIC NN NjPT OC1 Or OU PPULC PU

6596. BROSOW, August. Über Baumverehrung, Wald- und Feldkulte der litauischen Völkergruppe. Königs-

berg in Pr., Hartung, 1887. 35 p.
(Program - Altstädtisches Gymnasium
zu Königsberg i. Pr.) GR785.B79u
CLU PU WU

6597. BRÜCKNER, Alexander. Beiträge zur litauischen Mythologie.
In Archiv für slavische Philologie
(Berlin), v.9, 1886, p. 1-35. See
serials consulted.

6598. --- Litauische Götternamen.
In Archiv für slavische Philologie,
v.22, 1900, p. 569-571. See
serials consulted.

6599. --- Osteuropäische Götternamen. In Zeitschrift für vergleichende Sprachforschung (Berlin), v.50, 1922, p. 161-197. See
serials consulted.

--- Starożytna Litwa; ludy
i bogi. Warszawa, 1904. See entry
no. 4334.

6600. BŪGA, Kazimieras. Medžiaga
lietuvių, latvių ir prūsų mitologi-
jai. [Materials for Lithuanian,
Latvian and Prussian mythology]
Wilna, M. Kuktos spaustuvė, 1908-
1909. 2 pts. NN NB OCL PU; also
in His Rinktiniai raštai, v.1, 1958,
p. 143-188.

6601. BUJAK, Franciszek. Dwa
bóstwa prusko-litewskie "Kurche"i
"Okkopirnus". Lwów, Towarzystwo
ludoznawcze, 1924. 14 p. Offprint
Kwartalnik etnograficzy "Lud".
Serja 2, t.2, 1923.
(*QO p.v. 37 no.7)NN

6602. DUKSZTA, Mieczysław von.
Résumé de mythologie lithuanienne.
Travail primé au 11e concurs de
l'Academie des sciences à Genève.
[Genève, E. Pfeffer, 1914] 68
leaves. NN

6603. --- Résumé de mythologie
lithuanienne. [Genève, E. Pfeffer,
1918] 1 v. (Unpaged)
BM(12431. p. 14.)

6604. GAERTE, Wilhelm. Volks-
glaube und Brauchtum Ostpreussens;
Beiträge zur vergleichenden Volkskunde. Würzburg, Holzner, 1956.
128 p. (Marburger Ostforschungen,
Bd. 5) GR167.P7G3 DLC CLU CU ICU
InU MH NN NIC

6605. GIMBUTAS, Marija (Alseikai-
tė). The ancient religion of the
Balts; Prussians, Lithuanians and
Letts. In Lituanus (Brooklyn,N.Y.),
v.8, no.4, 1962, p. 97-109. See
serials consulted.

6606. --- Mūsų protėvių pažiūros
į mirtį ir sielą. [The opinions of
our forefathers on death and the
soul. Tübingen, "Patria", 1947]
21 p. Offprint from "Tremties metai" 1947. BL530.G491 InNd ICLJF
PU

6607. HANUŠ, Ignác Jan. Wissenschaft des slawischen mythus im
weitesten, den altpreussisch-lithau-
ischen Mythus mitumfassenden Sinne.
Nach Quellen bearb., sammt der Literatur der slawisch-preussisch-
lithauischen Archäologie und Mythologie. Lemberg, J. Millikowski,
1842. xx, 432 p. 285.H195 PU

6608. IVINSKIS, Zenonas. Medžių
kultas senovės lietuvių religijoje.
(Cultus arborum in antiqua religione lituanorum) In Soter (Kaunas),
no.27, 1938, p. 141-176; no.28, 1939,
p. 113-144. See serials consulted.

--- Senovės lietuvių religijos bibliografija. Kaunas, 1938.
156 p. See entry no. 95.

6609. JASKIEWICZ, Walter C. A
study in Lithuanian Mythology; Jan
Lasicki's treatise on the Samogitian Gods. Philadelphia, Pa., 1951.
525 leaves. Thesis--University of
Pennsylvania. 285.1.J.316 PU

6610. --- --- In Studi Baltici
(Firenze), v.1(9), 1952, p. 65-106.
See serials consulted.

6611. KRAUS, Friedrich S. Vampir-
glaube in Serbien und in Lithuania.
In Österreichische Gesellschaft für
Anthropologie, Ethnologie und Prähistorie. Mitteilungen. Wien,
1887, Bd. XVII [n.f., Bd. VII] p.
67-68. See serials consulted.

6612. KROLLMANN, Christian Anton
Christoph. Das Religionswesen der
alten Preussen. In Altpreussische
Forschungen (Königsberg in Pr.),
v.4, 1937, p. 5-19. See serials
consulted.

6613. LASICKI, Jan. Apie Žemaičių, kitų Sarmatų bei netikrų krikščionių dievus. De diis Samagitarum
caeterorumque Sarmatarum et falso-
rum christianorum. Nunc primum per
I. Iac. Grasserum. ... ex manuscripto authentico edite. Basileae,
apud Conradum Waldkirchium, 1615.
Vilnius, Vaga, 1969, 100 p. facsims. BL945.L3 1969 PU CaAEU DLC
OKentU

6614. --- De diis Samagitarum
libellus; hrsg. von W. Mannhardt,
mit Nachträgen von A. Bielenstein.

Riga, J. Bacmeister, 1868. 64 p.
945.52.L334 PU NIC NN

6615. MANNHARDT, Wilhelm. Letto-
preussische Götterlehre. Fortgeführt
und abgeschlossen von C. Bergholz
und A. Bauer. Riga, Lettische Literarische Gesellschaft, 1936. xiii,
647 p. (Magazin der Lettischen Literarischen Gesellschaft, Bd.21)
Comprehensive work containing sources on Baltic mythology and customs
and bibliographical footnotes.
BL945.M35 DLC InU NN PU(micro)

6616. MELETIUS, Joannes. De sacrificiis et idolatria veterum Livo-
num et Borussorum libellus. In Hor-
nerus, T. Livoniae historia...
Item, de sacrificiis et idolateria.
A reprint of the edition of 1562
which is published in Scriptores
rerum livonicarum... Riga und Leipzig, 1848. Lief.2. DK511.L3S4 DLC
NN

6617. MIERZYŃSKI, Antoni. Ian
Lasitski i ego sochineniie "De
diis Samagitarum". In Arkheologi-
chesheskii s"ezd. 3d., 1878. Trudy
See serials consulted.

6618. --- Jan Lasicki źródło do
mytologii litewskiej. In Towarzystwo Przyjaciół Nauk w Krakowie.
Rocznik, v.18, 1970, p. 1-102. See
serials consulted.

6619. --- O nadrovskom zhretsie
ognia, Krive. A.F. Merzhinski. In
Arkheologicheskii s"ezd. 9th Vilna,
1893. Trudy (Moskva), v.1, 1895,
p. 246-259. See serials consulted.

6620. --- Romove. In Arkheologicheskii s"ezd. 10th Riga, 1899.
Trudy (Moskva), 1899. See serials
consulted.

6621. ---, comp. Źródła do mito-
logji litewskiej. Warszawa, 1892-96.
2 v. Added title page: Mythologiae
lituanicae monumenta.
947.52.M583 v.2 PU

6622. MISEVIČIUS, Vytautas. Vienuolyno požemio vaiduokliai. [The
ghosts in the monastery] 2., pataisytas ir papildytas leidimas. Vilnius, VPMLL, 1961. 113 p.
BR136.L5M5 DLC

6623. OSTERMEYER, Gottfried. Gö-
tzendienst der Preussen. In Preussisches Archiv (Königsberg in Pr.),
1790, p. 179-188. See serials consulted.

6624. --- Kritischer Beytrag zur
altpreussischen Religionsgeschichte.

Marienwerder, 1775. 56 p.
BM(4503. bb. 2.)

6625. QUAEDAM AD LITHUANIAM PERTI-
nentia, ex fragmentis Michalonis Lituani. In Respublica; sive, status
regni Poloniae, Lituaniae, Prussiae
... Leiden, 1627. p. 366-402.
DK405.R43 DLC CaBVaU BM(166. a. 10.)
NN

6626. SCHROEDER, Leopold von. Der
Himmelsgott bei den Kelten, Litauern
und Letten. In His Arische Religio-
nen (Wien), 1923. 2. Aufl. v.1,
p. 524-554. BL660.S28 DLC

6627. SEALEY, Raphael. Velnias
lietuvių tautosakoje. [The devil in
Lithuanian folklore] In Lituanistikos darbai (Chicago, Ill.), v.1,
1966, p. 68-84. DK511.L2A264 v.1 DLC
CaAEU CaOTU FU ICU ICLJF MH NIC NN
PU WU

6628. ŠLIŪPAS, Jonas. Lietuvių,
Latvių bei Prūsų arba Baltų ir jų
prosenių mythologija. [The mytholo-
gy of the forefathers of Lithuanians,
Latvians and Prussians] Šiauliai,
Spaustuvė "Titnagas", [1932] MH

6629. ŠTURMS, Eduards. Die Alk-
stätten in Litauen. Hamburg, 1946.
36 p. (Contributions of Baltic University, 3) AS182.P5 no.3 DLC CU
CtY MH NNC NhD NNRI WU

6630. TARASENKA, Petras. Apeigi-
niai Lietuvos piliakalniai. [Cere-
monial mounds of Lithuania] In Židinys (Kaunas), v.11, 1934, p. 409-
418. See serials consulted.

6631. THOMAS, Heinz. Die slawische und baltische Religion verglei-
chend dargestellt. Bonn, Wohlau,
1934. 83 p. Thesis--University of
Bonn. 491.922.D713 PU

6632. TÖPPEN, Max Pollux. Geschichte des Heidentums in Preussen.
In Neue Preussische Provinzial-Blätter (Königsberg in Pr.), 3. Folge,
v.1, 1864. See serials consulted.

6633. --- Die letzten Spuren des
Heidentums in Preussen. In Neue
Preussische Provinzial-Blätter (Königsberg in Pr.), v.2, 1846, p. 210-
228,294-303,331-344. See serials
consulted.

6634. TOTORAITIS, Jonas. Senovės
liekanos ir lietuvių mitologiški at-
minimai. [Relics from the past and
mythological recollections of Lithu-
anians] In Lietuvių tauta (Vilnius),
v.1, 1910, p. 177-204. See serials
consulted.

6635. USENER, Hermann K. Litauische Götter. In His Götternamen, 2. Aufl., Bonn, F. Cohen, 1929. p. 79-122. BL473.U8 1929 DLC

6636. VALAITIS, Jonas. Senovės lietuvių dievai; mitologijos posmai. [Ancient Gods of Lithuanians; in verse. Chicago, Ill., 1970] 54 p. PG8721.V325S4 PU

6637. WOTSCHKE, Theodor. Jan Lasicki. In Zeitschrift für slavische Philologie (Leipzig), v2, 1925, p.77-104,442-471. See serials consulted.

XIII.3. ANCIENT FOLK CULTURE

XIII.3.a. GENERAL AND MISCELLANEOUS STUDIES

6638. AARNE, Antti Amatus. Leitfaden der vergleichenden Märchenforschung. Hamina, Finland, Suomalaisen tiedeakatemian kunstantama, 1913. iv, 86 p. In Folklore Fellows, Helsingfors. F F Communications (Helsingfors), no.13. See serials consulted.

6639. AMBAINIS, O. Skazki ob umnykh otvetakh v latyshskom i litovskom fol'klore. In Fol'klor baltskikh narodov. Riga, 1968. p. 187-218. GR203.L3F6 CaAEU CaOTU DLC ICU NjP PPiU PU WaU

6640. BAGDANAVIČIUS, Vytautas Jonas. Kultūrinės gelmės pasakose. [Cultural wellsprings of folktales] Chicago, Ill., Lietuviškos knygos klubas, 1969. 2 v. GR203.L5B25 OKentU ICBM

6641. BALMONT, Constantin. La Lithuanie et la chanson. Traduit du texte russe inédit par O.V. de L.-Milosz. In Mercure de France (Paris), v.211, 1929, p. 351-366.

6642. BALYS, Jonas. Folklore research in the Baltic countries, especially Lithuania, in the Soviet period. In Lituanistikos darbai (Chicago, Ill.), v.2, 1929, p.67-75. Bibliography: p. 73-75. See serials consulted.

6643. --- Klaipėdiškių lietuvių tautosaka. [Lithuanian folklore from the Klaipėda territory] In Tautosakos darbai. Kaunas, 1940. v.7, p. 165. See serials consulted.

6644. --- Lietuvių folkloristikos istorija. [History of scientific studies of the Lithuanian folklore] In

Lietuvių tautosakos skaitymai. Tübingen, Ger., 1948. p. 201-268. GR203.L5B315 DLC CoD ICLJF IEN MB MH MiD OCl PU PPULC

6645. --- Lietuvių liaudies pasaulėjauta tikėjimų ir papročių šviesoje. World conception in Lithuanian folklore. Chicago, Ill., Lithuanian Institute of Education, 1966. 120 p. GR203.L5B185 CaAEU CaOONL CaOTU MnU PU

6646. --- Lithuanian narrative folk songs; a description of types and a bibliography. Washington, D.C. 1954. 144 p. (A treasury of Lithuanian folklore, 4) MI3695.B3 DLC CaAEU CaOONL CtY FTaSU IEN KU MnU MB NIC NNC OKentU OOxM PP PPULC RPB

6647. --- Mažosios Lietuvos tautosakos bruožai. [An outline of the folklore of Lithuania Minor] In Lithuanian Research Institute, New York. Mažoji Lietuva. New York, N.Y., 1958. p. 217-255. DK511.L2L715 DLC CIU CaAEU

6648. --- Pasakojamoji tautosaka ir jos tyrinėjimai. [Narrative folklore and its research] In Tautosakos darbai (Kaunas), v.2, 1935, p. 255-295. See serials consulted.

6649. --- Vilniaus krašto lietuvių tautosaka. [Folklore of the Vilnius region] Spaudai paruošė J. Balys. Kaunas, Lietuvių tautosakos archyvo leidinys, 1938. xvii, 330 p. illus. (Tautosakos darbai, 4) GR203.V5B3 PU PPULC PSt and serials consulted.

6650. BARAUSKIENĖ, Vanda. Obshchie momenty v litovskikh i latyshskikh trudovykh pesniakh. In Fol'klor baltskikh narodov. Riga, 1968. p. 27-52. GR203.L3F6 CaAEU CaOTU DLC ICU NjP PPiU PU WaU

6651. --- Über litauische Volkslitteratur. In LLGM, no.2, 1887, p. 75-110. See serials consulted.

6652. BASANAVIČIUS, Jonas. Levas lietuvių pasakose ir dainose. [The lion in the Lithuanian tales and folk songs] Folkloriškai-archaiologiška studija. Kaunas, 1919. xliv, 235 p. BM(11859. c. 8.)

6653. BEZZENBERGER, Adalbert. Litauische Forschungen; Beiträge zur Kenntnis der Sprache und des Volkstums der Litauer. Göttingen, Peppmüller, 1882. viii, 206, 7 p. PG8713.B5 ICU CU CaAEU(Microfilm) ICN IU MH MdBJ NIC NN NNC NmU NcU OCl PPULC PU WU

6654. BRAZAITIS, Juozas. Lietuvių tautosaka. [Lithuanian folklore. By] J. Ambrazevičius. [n.p., n.d.] 73 p. Typescript. 398.A ICCC

6655. CHODŹKO, Ignacy. Obrazy litewskie. Wyd. Adama Zawadzkiego. Serya 2. Wilno, Nakł. i drukiem J. Zawadzkiego. 1843. 1 v. illus., music. PG7158.C44.02 CU

6656. --- --- Serya I-III. Lwów, Złoczów [etc.] Nakładem i Drukiem Księgarni W. Zukerhandla [etc.] 1889-99. 3 v. MH NN

6657. --- Pamiętniki Kwestarza. Wyd. 10. Odessa, J. Zawadzki, 1894. 248 p. illus. PG7158.C39P3 1894 DLC

6658. --- --- Wyd. 2. Warszawa, Gebethner i Wolff, 1901. 262 p. PG7158.C39P3 1901 OU

6659. --- --- [Another edition] Warszawa, Gebethner i Wolff, 1924. [114 p.] OCl

DAUKANTAS, Simanas. Rinktiniai raštai. Kaunas, 1955. See entry no. 4344.

6660. ELISONAS, Jurgis. Gamtos garsų pamėgdžiojimai lietuvių tautosakoje. [The imitation of nature's sounds in Lithuanian folklore] In Tautosakos darbai (Kaunas), v. 6, 1939. See serials consulted.

6661. --- Mūsų krašto fauna lietuvių tautosakoje. [The fauna of our country in the Lithuanian folklore] In Mūsų tautosaka (Kaunas), v.5, 1932. See serials consulted.

6662. --- Mūsų krašto ropliai lietuvių folkloro šviesoje. [The reptiles of our country in Lithuanian folklore] In Mūsų tautosaka (Kaunas), v.3, 1931, p. 81-181. See serials consulted.

6663. --- Vilkas tautosakoje. [The wolf in the folklore] In Mūsų tautosaka (Kaunas), v.2, 1930, p. 127-144. See serials consulted.

6664. FOL'KLOR BALTSKIKH NARODOV. Riga, Izdatel'stvo "Zinatne", 1968. 399 p. illus., facsims, map. At head of title: Institut iazyka i literatury Akademii nauk Latviiskoi SSR. Institut litovskogo iazyka i literatury Akademii nauk Litovskoi SSR. Articles related to Lithuania: p. 9-25, 27-67, 69-104, 177-278. GR203.L3F6 DLC CaAEU CaOTU ICU NjP PPiU PU WaU

6665. GRIGAS, Kazys. Tautosakos

rinkimas ekspedicijose. Sobiranie fol'klora v ekspeditsiiakh. In Literatūra ir kalba (Vilnius), v.9, 1968, p. 444-[460]. Summary in Russian. See serials consulted.

6666. JANULAITIS, Augustinas. Iš Lietuvos folkloro. [On Lithuanian folklore] In Tauta ir žodis (Kaunas), v.1, 1923, p. 333-343. See serials consulted.

6667. JONYNAS, Ambraziejus. Iz istorii issledovaniia litovsko-latyshskikh fol'klornykh sviazei. In Fol'klor baltskikh narodov. Riga, 1968. p. 9-25. GR203.L3F6 CaAEU DLC CaOTU ICU NjP PPiU PU WaU

6668. --- Der Kampf der Fronbauern gegen die Gutsherschaft im Spiegel der litauischen Märchen, Schwenke und Schwankmärchen. In Deutsches Jahrbuch für Volkskunde (Berlin), v.7, 1961, p. 205-214. See serials consulted.

6669. --- Lietuvių liaudies dainos. [Lithuanian folk songs] In LTSRMAIKLI. Lietuvių tautosaka. Vilnius, 1962. v.1, p. 9-34. GR203.L5L495 v.1 DLC CaAEU CaOTU CtPAM CtY ICU MH NN PU

6670. ---, ed. Pasakojamoji tautosaka. [Folk tales. By Amb. Jonynas, M. Vymerytė and A. Salčiūtė] In LTSRMAIKLI. Lietuvių tautosakos apybraiža. Vilnius, 1963. p. 308-[392]. GR203.L51497 DLC CaAEU CU CtY ICU MH NN

6671. JOVAIŠAS, Albinas. L. Rėzos literatūrinės-tautosakinės veiklos idėjiniai-meniniai bruožai. [The artistic traits of L. Rėza in his folklore-literary activities] In LTSRMAD. Serija A, v.2(11), 1961, p. 243-258. See serials consulted.

6672. JUNGFER, Victor. Litauen im Spiegel seiner Volksliteratur. In Landsmannschaft der Litauen Deutschen im Bundesgebiet. Litauische Studien. Würzburg [1958] p. 33-48. DK511.L22L32 DLC NcD NN WU

6673. KATKUS, Mikalojus. Raštai. [Works of Mikalojus Katkus] Vilnius, Vaga, 1965. lxxv, 630 p. illus., facsims, ports. Bibliography: p. 553-[562]. GR203.L5K3 DLC IU IEN MH PU

6674. KERBELYTĖ, Bronislava. K voprosu o repertuare litovskikh volshebnykh skazok. In Fol'klor baltskikh narodov. Riga, 1968. p. 177-185. GR203.L3F6 CaAEU CaOTU

DLC ICU NjP PPiU PU WaU

6675. --- Pasakojamoji tautosaka.
[The narrative folklore] In Literatūra ir kalba (Vilnius), v.6,
1962, p. 404-408. See serials consulted.

6676. KONČIUS, Ignas. Žemaičio
šnekos; etnografo atsiminimai. [A
Samogitian talks; the ethnographer's
recollections] London, Nida, 1961.
2 v. (Nidos knygų klubo leidinys,
nr. 33-34) 572.9475.K837 PU CtTMF
ICLJF DK511.L21.2K82 CaAEU

6677. KORSAKAS, Kostas. Berichte
über die Forklorforschung in Litau-
en. In Deutsches Jahrbuch für
Volkskunde (Berlin), v.6, 1960, p.
451-453. See serials consulted.

KRĖVĖ-MICKEVIČIUS, Vincas,
ed. Mūsų tautosaka. [Our folklore]
Kaunas, 1930-35. 10 v. in 5. See
entry no. 1578.

6678. LAUTENBACHS, Jēkabs. Ocherki iz istorii litovsko-latyshskogo
narodnogo tvorchestva. Parallel'nye
teksty i izsliedovaniia IA. Lauten-
bakha. [IUr'ev, 1896] xii, 221 p.
(Tartu. Ulikool. Uchenyia zapiski,
god 4, no.2, prilozheniia, st.2,
no.3, prilozheniia, st.2)
PG8709.L38 1896 CaAEU NN PU(ed.1915)

6679. LIAUDIES KŪRYBA. [Red.
komisija: A. Stravinskas (komisijos
pirmininkas) ir kiti] Vilnius,
"Mintis", 1969- . illus., music.
Title also in Russian and German:
Narodnoe tvorchestvo; Volksschaffen.
ML3681.L6L5 DLC(1-) CtPAM(1-)

6680. LIETUVIŲ TAUTOSAKA. [Lithu-
anian folklore. First edition]
1956. 158 p. ICBM MH PU

6681. --- --- 2. leidimas. [Ed.
D. Galnaitytė] Kaunas, Valstybinė
pedagoginės literatūros leidykla,
1957. 151 p. (Mokinio biblioteka)
GR203.L5L45 1957 DLC IU MH OKentU

6682. LIETUVOS TSR MOKSLŲ AKADE-
MIJA, VILNA. LIETUVIŲ KALBOS IR
LITERATŪROS INSTITUTAS. Dangus,
kunigai ir liaudis; antireliginė
lietuvių tautosaka. [Heaven,
priests and people: antireligious
Lithuanian folklore] Paruošė K.
Grigas ir S. Skrodenis. Vilnius,
VGLL, 1963. 361 p. GR203.L5L492
DLC MH NN OU

6683. --- Lietuvių tautosaka.
[Lithuanian folklore] Vilnius,
VPMLL, 1962-1968. 5 v. illus.,
music. Contents.--T.1. Dainos.--

T.2. Dainos, raudos.--T.3.Pasakós.
--T.4. Pasakos, sakmės, pasakojimai,
operacijos.--T.5. Smulkioji tauto-
saka, žaidimai ir šokiai.
GR203.L5L495 DLC CaAEU CaOTU CtPAM
CtY ICU MH NN OKentU(5) PU

6684. --- Lietuvių tautosakos
apybraiža. [Outline of Lithuanian
folklore. Ed. by K. Korsakas]
Vilnius, VPMLL, 1963. 473 p.
illus., facsims., music, ports.
GR203.L5L497 DLC CU CaAEU CtPAM
CtY ICU MH NN PU

6685. MOCKUS, Antanas. Lietuvių
folkloristikos istorinė apžvalga.
[The historical review of the research of Lithuanian folklore] In
LTSRMAIKLI. Lietuvių tautosakos
apybraiža. Vilnius, 1963. p. [19]-
[116]. GR203.L5L497 DLC CaAEU CU
CtY ICU MH NN

6686. SALVATORI, Guiseppe.
Storia, miti e canzone degli an-
tichi Lituani. In Nuova Antologia
(Firenze: Roma], v.65, 1930, p.
248-261. See serials consulted.

6687. SAUKA, Donatas. Tautosakos
savitumas ir vertė. [The peculiarities and value of the folklore]
Vilnius, Vaga, 1970. 458 p.
GR203.L5S25 DLC CaOTU PU

6688. SESELSKYTĖ, A. Iš Lietuvių
kalbos ir literatūros instituto
folkloristų mokslinės veiklos. Iz
nauchnoi deiatel'nosti fol'kloris-
tov Instituta litovskogo iazyka i
literatury. In Literatūra ir kalba
(Vilnius), v.9, 1968, p. 461-[477].
Summary in Russian. See serials
consulted.

6689. ŠEŠPLAUKIS, Alfonsas.
Goethe ir lietuvių liaudies kūryba.
[Goethe and Lithuanian folksongs]
In Židinys (Kaunas), v.23, 1936, p.
529-535. See serials consulted.

6690. VILMANTIENĖ, A. Prūsų Lietuvos tautosakos likimas. [The
fate of the folklore of Lithuania
Minor] In Vairas (Kaunas), no.2,
1937, p. 196-198. See serials consulted.

6691. VIŠČINIS, K. K voprosu o
zhanrovoi samostoiatel'nosti i
opredelennosti litovskikh narodnykh
anekdotov. In Fol'klor baltskikh
narodov. Riga, 1968. p. 219-226.
GR203.L3F6 CaAEU CaOTU DLC ICU NjP
PPiU PU WaU

XIII.3.b. FOLKLORE

XIII.3.b.1. BIBLIOGRAPHIES

6692. BALYS, Jonas. Lietuvių pasakojamosios tautosakos motyvų katalogas. Motif-index of Lithuanian narrative folklore. Kaunas, Lietuvių tautosakos archyvas, 1936. xxxvii, 295 p. (Tautosakos darbai, 2) GR203.L68T2 v.2 CLU CaAEU CU PU

--- Lithuanian narrative folksongs; a description of types and a bibliography. Washington, D.C., 1954. See entry no. 6646.

6693. LIETUVIŲ LITERATŪROS ISTOrija ir tautosaka; bibliografinė rodyklė, pagrindinė literatūra. [A bibliography on the history of Lithuanian literature and folklore. Sudarė P. Česnulevičiūtė et al. Vilnius] Vilniaus Universiteto Lietuvių literatūros katedra, 1967. 60 p. Z2537.L43 DLC MH

6694. GRIGAS, Kazys. Simano Daukanto lietuvių tautosakos rinkiniai ir leidiniai. [The collections and publications of Lithuanian folklore by Simonas Daukantas] In LTSRMAD. Serija A, v.1(4), 1958, p. 225-243. See serials consulted.

6695. KALVELIS, Leonas. Lietuviška tautosakos bibliografija. [Bibliography of Lithuanian folklore] In Tautosakos darbai. Kaunas, v.6, 1939, p. 353-384. See serials consulted.

6696. ŠNEIDERAITIENĖ, Magdalena. Lietuviška tautosakos bibliografija. [Bibliography of Lithuanian folklore] In Tautosakos darbai. Kaunas, v.1, 1935, p. 284-304; v.3, 1937, p. 332-362. See serials consulted.

6697. VIŠČINIS, K. Lietuvių tautosakos rankraštynas. Rukopisnye fondy litovskogo fol'klora. In Literatūra ir kalba. Vilnius, v.9, 1968, p. 430-[443]. See serials consulted.

XIII.3.b.2. GENERAL COLLECTIONS

6698. BALYS, Jonas, ed. Iš Mažosios Lietuvos tautosakos. [From the folklore of Lithuania Minor] Surinko J. Banaitis, J. Bruožis, D. Jagomastas, N. Jankutė, V. Vilman-

tienė ir Kt. Redaktorius J. Balys. Kaunas, 1937. 90 p. Offprint from Tautosakos darbai (Kaunas), v.3, 1937, p. 1-90. 491.922.B219 PU; see serials consulted.

6699. --- Lietuvių tautosakos skaitymai. [Readings in Lithuanian folklore. Tübingen] Patria [1948] 2 pts. in 1 v. GR203.L5B315 DLC CLU CtTMF CoD ICCC IEN ICLJF MB MH MiD NN OKentU PPULC PU

6700. BASANAVIČIUS, Jonas. Rinktiniai raštai. [Collection of works] Vilnius, Vaga, 1970. xxiv, 1034 p. illus. DK511.L2B33 PU DLC OKentU

6701. DAVAINIS-SILVESTRAVIČIUS, Mečislovas. Patarlės ir dainos surasze nuog žmoniu Mieczysław Sylvestrowicz Dowojna. [Folk sayings and songs] Tilžė, 1889. 30 p. 784.D8 CtTMF BM(12431. a. 41.)

6702. LESKIEN, August. Litauische Volkslieder und Märchen aus den preussischen und dem russischen Litauen, gesammelt von A. Leskien und F.K. Brugmann. Strassburg, K.J. Trübner, 1882. viii, 578 p. PG8696.L4 DLC CaOHM CaOTU CU CtY ICN MH MnU MdBP NN NNC NjP NIC NSyU OCl OClW PBm PU WU TxU

6703. LIETUVOS TSR MOKSLŲ AKADEMIJA, VILNA. LIETUVIŲ KALBOS IR LITERATŪROS INSTITUTAS. Lietuvių tautosaka užrašyta 1944-1956. [Lithuanian folklore collected in 1944-1956. Vyr. redaktorius K. Korsakas] Vilnius, VGLL, 1957. 534 p. ports. Includes unacc. melodies. PG8713.L48 DLC CaAEU CaOTP CU CtY ICCC ICLJF InU MH NN PU

6704. --- Lietuvių tautosakos rinktinė. [Selected Lithuanian folklore. Ats. redaktorius K. Korsakas, Paruošė Tautosakos sektoriaus kolektyvas: Amb. Jonynas et al. Dailininkas T. Kulakauskas. Vilnius] VGLL, 1954. 558 p. illus., ports. Includes unacc. melodies. GR203.L5L5 DLC BM CLU CU PU

6705. SCHLEICHER, August, ed. Litauische Märchen, Sprichwörte Rätsel und Lieder, gesammelt und übersezt von August Schleicher. Weimar, H. Böhlau, 1857. ix, 244 p. illus., music. PG8779.S341 CLU CU CaBVaU CaOTU ICU ICN MH MdBP MdBJ NIC NN NNC OCl OClW WU

6706. TREASURY OF LITHUANIAN Folklore. Lietuvių Tautosakos Lo-

bynas. Editor and publisher Jonas
Balys. Cleveland, Ohio, 1951-1959.
5 v. GR203.L5B27 DLC(3-) CLU CaAEU
CaOONL CtPAM(1,2) KU MH NN PU

6707. VALANČIUS, Motiejus. Paau-
gusių žmonių knygelė. [Readings
for the more mature] Tilžė, 1902,
104 p. PG8721.V327P29 1902 PU
CtTMF ICBM

6708. --- --- 3. laida. Kaunas,
Švyturys, 1920. 135 p.
891.92.V232Pa PU CtTMF

6709. --- --- Perredagavo, žo-
džius paaiškino ir įžangą parašė
A. Merkelis. Kaunas, 1930. 169 p.
BM(012591. aa. 56.)

XIII.3.b.3. NARRATIVE FOLKLORE

6710. BAGDANAVIČIUS, Vytautas
Jonas. Cultural wellsprings of
folktales. Translated from Lithuanian by Jeronimas Žemkalnis. New
York, N.Y., Manyland Books, 1970.
196 p. GR80B32 PU CaAEU

6711. BAJERČIUS, K. Iš pasakų
krašto. [From the land of tales]
Marijampolė, 1939. 102 p.
398.2.B5 CtTMF

6712. BALČIŪNAS, Juozas. Aukso
kirvis; rinktinės mūsų žmonių pasakos. [Golden axe; selected folk
stories] Parengė Juozas Švaistas
[pseud.] Chicago, Ill., 1952.
224 p. illus. "Panaudojau Jono
Basanavičiaus pasakų knygas": p. 7.
891.926.B183 PU PPULC OCl

6713. BALYS, Jonas. Istoriniai
padavimai... [Historical legends]
Chicago, Ill., Lietuvių Katalikų
spaudos draugija, 1949. 101 p.
illus. DK511.L713B219 InNd CtTMF
ICCC ICLJF MH PU

6714. --- Lietuvių liaudies baladės. [Lithuanian folk ballads]
In Židinys (Kaunas), 1938, v.28,
no. 8-9, p. 213-227; no.10, p. 379-
398. See serials consulted.

6715. ---, ed. Lietuvių liaudies
sakmės. Lithuanian folk legends.
Kaunas, A. S. Lituanistikos instituto Lietuvių tautosakos archyvas,
1940. xxvi, 424 p. (Lietuvių
tautosaka. Serija A: Sakmės) Summary in English. GR203.L5B312 DLC

6716. ---, comp. Lietuvių samo-
jus liaudies anekdotai. [Lithuani-
an wit...] Spaudai paruošė J. Balys. Kaunas, Sakalas, 1937. 255 p.

GR203.L5B2 InU

6717. --- Lietuviškos pasakos.
[Lithuanian tales] 2. leidimas.
[Chicago, Ill., Lietuvių knygos
klubas, 1951] 230 p. illus.
GR203.L5B3 1951 DLC CLU CaOONL
CaOTP CaOTU CtY ICCC ICBM ICLJF IEN
MiD NN OKentU PPULC PU

6718. ---, ed. Lithuanian historical legends. Istoriniai padavimai. [Chicago, Ill.] Lietuvių
katalikų spaudos draugija. [1949]
103 p., illus., port. (Lietuvių
katalikų spaudos draugija. Leidinys, nr. 1) GR203.L5B32 DLC CLU
MiD MH MnU PPULC

6719. --- Über die litauischen
Volksballaden. In Acta ethnologica
(Copenhagen), no.2-3, 1938, p. 73-
99. See serials consulted.

6720. --- Užburti lobiai; lietuvių liaudies sakmės. [Enchanted
treasures; Lithuanian folk legends.
London] Nida [1958] 95 p. (Nidos
knygų klubo leidinys, nr. 22)
GR203.L5B33 DLC CLU CtTMF IEN ICLJF
MiDW MtU OCl PU

6721. BASANAVIČIUS, Jonas. Lietuviškos pasakos. [Lithuanian
tales] Shenandoah, Pa., V.J. Stagaro spaustuvė, 1898-1902. 2 v.
GR203.L5B385 DLC CtTMF ICCC ICBM
ICU PPULC PU

6722. --- --- [Iš Jono Basanavičiaus rinkinių paruošė vaikams
Jonas Stukas] Vilnius, Vaga, 1969.
319 p. CaAEU

6723. --- Lietuviškos pasakos
yvairios. [Various Lithuanian
tales] Dalis 1-4. Chicago, Ill.
"Lietuva", 1903-11. 4 v.
PG8719.B3 DLC CtY CtTMF ICCC ICBM
IEN ICLJF IU MB MH NN OKentU OCl PU
RP WaS

6724. --- Rinktinės pasakos.
[Selected folk tales] Kaunas,
VGLL, 1948. 315 p. GR203.L5B39
DLC

6725. Becker, Friedrich, ed.
Litauische und Preussische Volks-
sagen nach zum Theil ungenutzten
Quellen poetisch bearbeitet und mit
erläuternden Anmerkungen versehen,
von F. Becker, C. Roose und J.G.
Thiele. Königsberg, in Pr., A.
Samter, 1847. vi, 146 p.
PT921.P9B3 1847 CaAEU

6726. BELIAJUS, Vytautas Finadar.
The evening song. Vakarinė daina.
A collection of Lithuanian legends

and fables. Los Angeles, Calif.,
Lithuanian Days [1954] 100 p.
illus. GR203.L5B4 CaAEU CLSU CaOTU
DLC InU MH MiD NN NRU OCl PPULC PU
WaS

6727. BOEHM, Maximilian. Lettisch-
litauische Volksmärchen, hrsg. von
M. Boehm und F. Specht. Jena, Die-
derichs, 1924. 333 p. front.
(Die Märchen der Weltliteratur)
Bibliography: p. 324-331.
GR203.L5B6 DLC CLU CU ICU MiU NN
OCl PPULC PBM WU

6728. BORUTA, Kazys. Dangus
griūva; arba mūsų pasakų išmintis
ir samojis visiems mažiems ir dideliems. [Collection of folk tales
for young and old] Vilnius, Vaga,
1965. 302 p. PG8721.B6D3 PU

6729. BŪGA, Kazimieras. Seinų
parapijos Dzūkų mislės. [The
riddles of the parish Seinai] In
Tauta ir žodis (Kaunas), v.1, 1923,
p. 315-316. See serials consulted.

6730. CAPPELLER, Carl. Litauische
Märchen und Geschichten... Berlin,
W. de Gruyter, 1924. viii, 168 p.
illus., plates. GR203.L68C17 CLU
ICU ICN PU CaOTU

6731. --- Noch zwölf Pasakos. In
Indogermanische Forschungen (Berlin)
v.35, 1915, p. 114-131. See serials consulted.

6732. --- Zwölf Pasakos aus dem
preussischen Südlitauen. In Indogermanische Forschungen (Berlin),
v.31, 1912-1913, p. 427-447. See
serials consulted.

6733. CHODŹKO, Ignacy. Podania
litewskie, serya 1-4... Wyd. nowe.
Wilno, Nakł. J. Zawadzkiego, 1881.
(His Pisma... t.3) 491.922.C458
PU CtY InU MH MiU NNC

6734. DAUKANTAS, Simanas. Pasakos massių, suraszitas 1835 metuose
apigardosi Kretiu, Palangos, Gunde-
nės. [Folk tales; collected in
1835 in the districts of Kretinga,
Palanga and Gundinė] Vilnius,
1932. 114 p. (Lietuvių tauta.
Vilnius, Prech'o spaustuvė, 1932.
Knyga 4, Sąs.3) DK.L2A245 Kn.4,
sąs.3 DLC

6735. --- Žemaičių pasakos. [Sa-
mogitian tales] Paruošė M. Matulis.
Redagavo Babrauskas. Iliustracijos
K. Žinonio. Kaunas, 1941. 207 p.
GR203.L5D3 1941 PU

6736. --- --- Illus. V. Banys.
Kaunas, VGLL [1947] 123 p. illus.

NN

6737. --- --- [Illus. by I. Na-
ginskaitė] Vilnius, VGLL, 1955.
132 p. illus. NN

6738. --- --- Dailininkas Vytautas Valius. Vilnius, Vaga, 1965.
157 p. col. illus. GR203.L5D3
1965 DLC CaOTP IEN

6739. DAVAINIS-SILVESTRAVIČIUS,
Mečislovas. Litovskiia legendy.
In Etnograficheskoe obozreniie
(Moskva), 1891. See serials con-
sulted.

6740. --- Podania zmujdzkie, zebrał i dosłownie spolszczył Mieczysław Dowojna Sylwestrowicz...
Warszawa, Skład Główny w Księgarni
M. Arcta, 1894. 2 v. (Bibljoteka
"Wisły", t. XII-XIII, wychodząca
pod redakcją i nakładem Jana Kar-
łowicza) GR203.L5S85 DLC

6741. DIDŽIULIS, Stanislovas
Feliksas. Senųjų kalbos. [Conver-
sations of the elderly people] In
Tauta ir žodis (Kaunas), v.4, 1926,
p. 509-517. See serials consulted.

6742. DOVYDAITIS, Jurgis. Lietuvių liaudies pasakos. [Lithu-
anian folk tales] Vilnius, VGLL,
1957. 351 p., music. GR203.L5D6
PU

6743. GIEDRAITIS, Antanas, ed.
Tėvų pasakos; iš lietuvių liaudies
pasakų lobyno parinko ir skaityti
paruošė. [Folk tales of our
fathers...] A. Giedrius [pseud.]
Iliustravo J. Kaminskas. [Memmin-
gen, Ger., PLB Vokietijos krašto
valdyba, 1951] 1 v. illus. (PLB
Vokietijos krašto valdybos knygų
leidyklos leidinys nr. 2)
GR203.L5G5 DLC ICCC NN OKentU PU

6744. GISEVIUS, Eduard Karl
Samuel. Der Kank-Stein; Sage von
Kallehnen an der Jura. In Neue
Preussische Provinzial-Blätter
(Königsberg in Pr.), v.7, 1849, p.
456-463; v.8, 1850, p. 469-471.
See serials consulted.

6745. --- Der Rombinus. In
Preussische Provinzial-Blätter
(Königsberg in Pr.), v.18, 1837, p.
3-32. See serials consulted.

6746. --- Sagen vom Gillander,
Wartulischken und Absteiner Schloss-
berg, gennant Abte; mit Lithographie
und Lageskizze. In Altertumsgesellschaft Prussia (Königsberg in Pr.),
v.46, 1890, p. 80-85. See
serials consulted.

6747. --- Volkssagen von den
Schlossagen im Juragebiet. In Neue
Provinzial-Blätter (Königsberg in
Pr.), Series 3, v.3, 1859, p. 37-53,
101-108; v.4, 1859, p. 169-214. See
serials consulted.

6478. GRIGAS, Kazys, comp. Menu
mislę keturgyslę. [Guessing a
riddle... Dailininkas K. Juodikaitis. Vilnius, Vaga, 1970] 199 p.
illus. PN6377.L5G7 PU

6749. --- Smulkioji tautosaka;
Patarlės ir priežodžiai, mislės,
garsų pamėgdžiojimai ir uškalbėji-
mai. [Proverbs, sayings, riddles,
mimicry and charms] In LTSRMALKLI.
Lietuvių tautosakos apybraiža.
Vilnius, 1963. p. 393-[433]
GR203.L5L497 DLC CaAEU CtY CU ICU
MH NN

6750. GRIGAS, Kazys, and Ambraziejus Jonynas. Lietuvių liaudies
patarlės ir priežodžiai. [Lithu-
anian proverbs and sayings] In
Their Patarlės priežodžiai. Vilnius, VGLL, 1958, p. 5-26.
PN6505.L5G7 DLC CaAEU CtPAM CtY IEN
ICLJF PU

6751. ---, eds. Patarlės ir
priežodžiai. [Proverbs and sayings]
Vilnius, VGLL, 1958. 477 p.
PN6505.L5G85 DLC CaAEU CtPAM CtY
ICCC ICLJF IEN NN PU

6752. GULBĖ, KARALIAUS PATI; lietuvių liaudies pasakos. [Lithuani-
an folk tales. Sudarė A. Liobytė.
Iliustracijos A. Makūnaitės] Vilnius, VGLL, 1963. 286 p.
891.92.G957 PU

6753. JANULAITIS, Augustinas.
Litauische Märchen; Laumė. In
LLGM, v.4, 1899, p. 516-527. See
serials consulted.

6754. JOKIMAITIENĖ, P. Lietuvių
liaudies baladės. [Lithuanian folk
ballads] In Literatūra ir kalba
(Vilnius), v.9, 1968, p. 297-350.
Summary in Russian: p. 351-[353].
See serials consulted.

6755. JUCEWICZ, Ludwik Adam.
Przysłowia ludu litewskiego. Wilno, Druk Marcinowskiego, 1840.
125 p. BM(1075. i. 18.)

6756. JURGELIONIS, Kleofas, comp.
Mislių knyga; lietuvių mislių rinkinys. [Book of riddles; a collection of Lithuanian riddles] Chicago, Ill., Spauda Naujienų [1913]
xiv, 162 p. PN6377.L5J8 DLC CtY
ICCC ICLJF OCl PU

6757. JURKSCHAT, Christoph, comp.
Litauische Märchen und Erzählungen.
Aus dem Volke gesammelt und in ver-
schiedenen Dialekten, besonders in
der Galbraster Mundart mitgeteilt.
Hrsg. von der Litauisch-littera-
riaschen Gesellschaft zu Tilsit.
Heidelberg, C. Winter, 1898. 144
p. Text in Lithuanian and German.
GR203.L68J9 v.1 CLU BM CaBVaU ICU
MH NIC NN PU NjP WU

6758. KAI MILŽINAI GYVENO; padavimai apie miestus, ežerus, kalnus,
akmenis. [Legends of towns, lakes,
mountains and stones. Paruošė
Bronislava Kerbelytė] Vilnius,
1969. 118 p. GR203.L5K3 PU

6759. KERBELYTĖ, Bronislava. Lietuvių liaudies padavimai. [Lithu-
anian folk legends] Vilnius, Vaga,
1970. 269 p. GR203.L5K47 PU

6760. KOROLEVA LEBED'; litovskie
narodnye skazki. [Sostavila A.
Liobitė. Ilius. A. Makūnaitė]
Vil'nius, 1962. 410 p.
GR203.L5K6 DLC CtY PU WU

6761. --- --- [Another edition]
Vil'nius, Vaga, 1965. 414 p.
illus. GR203.L5K6 DLC CaAEU NIC

6762. KRĖVĖ-MICKEVIČIUS, Vincas.
Aitvaras, liaudies padavimuose.
[House demons] Kaunas, Spindulio
b-vė, 1933. 156 p. (Kaunas.
Universitetas. Humanitarinių moks-
lų fakultetas. Leidinys.)
PG8721K74A5 1933 CU ICCC MH NN

6763. --- Apsakymai ir padavimai.
[Stories and legends] Vilnius,
VGLL, 1955. 278 p. 891.92.K889A PU

6764. --- Dainavos šalies senų
žmonių padavimai. [Legends of
ancient people in the country of
Dainava] 5. laida. Schweinfurt
[Išleido "Tėviškės" knygų leidykla]
1948. 221 p. PG8721.K7D2 1948
DLC CaOTP PU

6765. --- --- [Another edition.
Iliustravo S. Valiuvienė. Kaune]
VGLL, 1957. 252 p. illus.
PG8721.K7D2 1957 DLC CaAEU CaOTP
OKentU

6766. --- Mislės surinktos Alytaus, Niedzingės, Perlojos, Kabelių ir Merkynės parapijose.
[Riddles collected from the parishes
of Alytus, Niedzinga, Perloja, Ka-
beliai and Merkynė] In Tauta ir
žodis (Kaunas), v.5, 1928, p. 594-
628. See serials consulted.

6767. --- Patarlės ir priežodžiai.

[Proverbs and sayings] Kaunas, 1934-37. 3 v. 398.2.K3.4 CtTMF (v.1-2)

6768. --- Patarlės, priežodžiai ir išireiškimai. [Proverbs and sayings. Parts 1-3] In Tauta ir žodis (Kaunas), v.3, 1925, p. 375-389; v.5, 1928, p. 594-628. Part 4 In Darbai ir dienos, v.6, 1937, p. 213-354; v.7, 1938, p. 323-392. See serials consulted.

6769. --- Sparnuočiai liaudies padavimuose... [Birds in folklore. ..] Kaunas, Spindulys, 1933. 190 p. (Kaunas. Universitetas. Humanitarinų mokslų fakulteto komisija. Leidinys) GR203.L5M62 ICU ICCC NN

6770. LANGKUSCH, A. G. Litauische Sagen. In Altpreussische Monatsschrift (Königsberg in Pr.), v.15, 1878, p. 412-459. See serials consulted.

6771. LEBEDYS, Jurgis. Smulkioji lietuvių tautosaka XVII-XVIII a.; priežodžiai, patarlės, mįslės. [Lithuanian folklore recorded in the 17th-18th centuries; popular sayings, proverbs and riddles] Vilnius, VGLL, 1956. 630 p. illus. PN6505.L5L4 DLC CtPAM ICCC NN PPiU PU

6772. LITOVSKIE NARODNYE SKAZKI. Perevod s litovskogo K.D. Bal'monta. Riga, Shkola i zhizn' [1930-31] 112 p. PG2097 DLC PU

6773. --- [Perevod i obrabotka F. Shuravina i E. Shishovoi] Risunki A. Lapteva. Moskva, Gos. izd-vo detskoi lit-ry, 1953. 127 p. illus. PZ64.1.S4 WU

6774. --- Perevod s litovskogo F. Shuravina. Risunki A. Lapteva. Moskva, Detgiz, 1954. 176 p. illus. BM(12594. k. 22.) MH

6775. THE MARIAN. The first Marian reader; folktales, legends and short stories, translated from Lithuanian. Chicago, Lithuanian Catholic Press Society [1951] 96 p. illus. PZ1.M32Fi DLC CaAEU InNd NNC PU

6776. MAUCLÈRE, Jean. Contes lithuaniens. Illus. de Pierre Rousseau. Paris, F. Lanore, 1945. 154 p. GR203.L5M3 1945 DLC CU CaAEU CaOTU MH NcD NN PU

6777. MILOSZ, Oscar Vladislas. Contes et fabiaux de la vieille Lithuanie. Paris, G.O. Fourcade,

1930. 491.922.M639.5 PU WaU NNC

6778. --- --- [Another edition] Paris, Egloff [1946] 233 p. (Oeuvres complètes, 6) PQ2625.I558A1S58 v.6 CaAEU CtY IaU MH MiDW NIC NBuU NcD PU WaU

6779. --- Contes Lithuaniens de ma mère l'oye suivis de Daïnos les origines de la nation lithuanienne. Paris, N. Chiron, 1933. 107 p. illus. 491.922.M638 PU DLC

6780. --- --- [Another edition] Paris, Éditions André Silvaire, [1963] 232 p. (Oeuvres complètes, 9) PQ2625.I558A6 1963 DLC CaAEU CtY CU IEN InU MH MiDW MiU NN NNC NcD OLU OrU OU PU TxU WaU

6781. MINGIRDAS, Jonas, ed. Smulkioji tautosaka; patarlės... [Folklore; proverbs and sayings. Los Angeles, Calif., Spaudė Bonnie Press, 1958] 182 p. illus. PN6505L5M66 1958 CaAEU CaOTU

6782. MULEVIČIUS, Paul. Patarlės ir išminties grudeliai. [Proverbs. ..] Chicago, Ill., Draugas, 1917. 48 p. PN6095.L5M8 DLC PP

6783. NĖ VELNIO NEBIJAU; lietuvių liaudies pasakos. [I am not even afraid of the devil; Lithuanian folk tales. Iliustravo Rimt. Gibavičius. Paruošė A. Liobytė] Vilnius [Vaga] 1964. 175 p. illus. GR203.L5N4 DLC IEN OKent

6784. NEGIRDĖTOS NEREGĖTOS PASAKOS. [The unheard and untold tales. Sudarė B. Kerbelytė] Vilnius, VPMLL, 1961. 152 p. PZ70.L5N37 DLC

6785. NĖRIS, Salomėja, comp. Mūsų pasakos; spaudai paruošė S. Nėris. [Our folk tales] Vinjetas piešė K. Šimonis. Kaunas, Humanitarinų mokslų fakultetas, Tautosakos komisija, 1934. 160 p. illus. 398.B ICCC

6786. PLENZAT, Karl. Der Wundergarten: deutsche litauische und masurische Volksmärchen aus Ostpreussen... Berlin und Leipzig, Franz Schneider, 1922. 183 p. illus. MH

6787. --- --- 2. Aufl. Leipzig, H. Eichblatt, 1928. PN997.P7 1928 ICU

6788. PUIKŪNAS, Jonas, comp. Lietuvių smulkioji tautosaka: mįslės; minklių, mįslių šimtagyslių rinkinys-šiupinys. [Riddles, proverbs, etc.] Surinko ir užrašė Jonas

Mingirdas Puikūnas. [Los Angeles, Calif., Bonnie Press] 1971. 173 p. PN6377.L5P8 PU

6790. REMEIKA, Jonas. Ką kalneliai pasakoja. Padavimai iš Klaipėdos krašto piliakalnių praeities. [What are the hills saying; legends] Klaipėda, Sakalas, 1938. 93 p. illus. 398.2.R2 CtTMF ICCC

6791. ---, comp. Lietuvos pajūrio padavimai. [Legends from the sea shore of Lithuania. Memmingen, Ger.] Tremtis [1954] 111 p. GR203.L5R38 ICU CaOTP ICCC PU

6792. RUDOLPH, Margueritta. I am your misfortune; a Lithuanian folk tale retold. Illus. by Imero Gobbato. New York, N.Y., Seabury Press [1968] 1 v. illus. PZ8.1.R851 DLC WaS

6793. RUSSELL, Reaver J. Lithuanian tales from Illinois. In Southern folklore quarterly (Jacksonville, Fla.), v.14, no.3, 1950, p. 160-169. See serials consulted.

6794. SABALIAUSKAS, Adolfas. Pušaloto priežodžiai. [Proverbs from Pušalotas] In Tauta ir žodis (Kaunas), v.1, 1923, p. 316-322. See serials consulted.

6795. SCHEU, Hugo. Pasakos apie paukščius; žemaitische Tierfabeln; Text, Wörterverzeichnis und Übersetzung, hrsg. von Hugo Scheu und Alexander Kurschat. Heidelberg, C. Winter, 1913. 335 p. W384.751. Sch29p OCl ICU MnU MH NN NjP

6796. ŠLAPELIS, Jurgis. Mįslės surinktos Lazdūnų parapijoj. [Riddles collected from the parish of Lazdūnai] In Lietuvių tauta (Kaunas), v.3, 1925, p. 462-464. See serials consulted.

6797. ŠNAPŠTYS, Juozas. 62 sakmės (48 naujai surengtos). [Sixty-two folk tales. By] Margalis [pseud.] Kaunas, 1918. 56 p. PG8721.S59S4 PU

6798. SODAITIS, Juozas, comp. Karaliaus vainikas; legendos ir padavimai. [The king's wreath; legends. New York, N.Y.] Gabija [1958] 111 p. illus. 398.21.S CaOTP OCl PU

6799. DIE TANNE UND IHRE KINDER. Märchen aus Litauen. [Hrsg. von Edmund Danner. Übersetzung; Ernst Ehlers und der Herausgeber. Illustrationen von Herbert Bartholomäus. 3., veränderte Aufl. Berlin] Alt-

berliner Verlag [1965] 174 p. GR203.L5T3 DLC

6800. TETTAU, Wilhelm Johann Albert, Freiherr von, comp. Die Volkssagen Ostpreussens, Litthauens und Westpreussens, gesammelt von W.J.A. von Tettau und J.D.H. Temme. Berlin, Nicolai, 1837. xxvii, 286 p. PT919.P9T34 NIC CU CtY IU MH MdBP OCl

6801. TIJŪNAITIS, Stasys. Mįslės. [Riddles. Iliustravo A. Steponavičius] Vilnius, VGLL, 1958. 106 p. illus. 891.92C.T747 PU NN

6802. --- Mūsų pasakos. [Our folk tales. Iliustravo R. Ulbikaitė] Vilnius, VGLL, 1958. 360 p. illus. GR203.L5T5 PU

6803. TININIS, Juozas. Similes in Lithuanian folk proverbs. In Lituanus (Chicago, Ill.), v.17, no. 2, 1971, p. 48-54. See serials consulted.

6804. TRAUTMANN, Reinhold. Zwei zemaitische Erzählungen. In Akademie der Wissenschaften, Berlin. Sitzungsberichte. 1918, p. 797-804. See serials consulted.

6805. UŽBURTA KARALYSTĖ; lietuvių liaudies pasakos. [Enchanted kingdom; Lithuanian folk tales. Iliustravo V. Palaima] Vilnius, VGLL, 1957. 308 p. illus. GR203.L5U7 PU NN

6806. VAIČIULAITIS, Antanas. Auksinė kurpelė; pasakų rinktinė. [A collection of folk tales. Dailininkas V.K. Jonynas. Nördlingen, Ger.] Venta [1957] 244 p. illus. PG8721.V3A9 DLC CtY NN OCl PU

6807. VAIČKUS, Juozas and Kazys Būga. Sedos parapijos žemaičių patarlės. [The riddles of Samogitia in the parish of Seda] In Tauta ir žodis (Kaunas), v.1, 1923, p. 312-314. See serials consulted.

6808. VECKENSTEDT, Edmund. Mythai, pasakos ir legendos žiamaicziu. Surinkti ir iszleisti per D-ra Edm. Veckenstedta. Lietuviszkai iszguldė J. Szliupas, M.D. Plymouth, Pa., Kasztu ir spaustuvėje Juozo Paukszczio, 1897. 191 p. 389.V ICCC

6809. ---, comp. Die Mythen, Sagen und Legenden der Zamaiten (Litauer), gesammelt und hrsg. von E. Veckenstedt. Heidelberg, C. Winter, 1883. 2 v. in 1. GR203. L541 ClU ICN ICU MH MdBP NIC OCl

6810. VOL'TER, Eduard Aleksandrovich. Litovskiia legendy. In Etnograficheskoe obozrienie (Moskva),
v.2, no.3, 1890, p. 139-148. See
serials consulted.

6811. --- Romantische-sagenhafte
Motive des litauischen Volksliedes.
Von E. Wolter. In LLGM, v.4, 1894,
p. 64-49. See serials consulted.

6812. WICHERT, Ernst. Gesammelte
Werke. 8. Aufl. Dresden, C. Reissner, 1900-02. 6 v. (v.1-3, 16-
18) PT2558.A1 1902 DLC NcU

6813. --- Litauische Geschichten.
2. Aufl. Dresden und Leipzig, C.
Reissner, 1900-01. 2 v. (His Gesammelte Werke, v.16-17)
PT2558.L6 1900 DLC NcU

6814. --- --- 3. und 4., Aufl.
Dresden und Leipzig, C. Reissner,
1914. 2 v. 491.922.W633 PU DLC

6815. --- --- [Another edition]
Hrsg. von P. Wichert. Berlin-Char-
lottenburg, Volksverband der Bücher-
freunde Wegweiser-Verlag [1927]
472 p. illus., ports. PT2558.L6 CU

6816. --- --- Einmalige Ausg.
Hamburg, Deutsche Hausbücherei
[1934] 317 p. illus.
PT2558.L6 1934 DLC

6817. ZAHORSKI, Władysław. Lakštingala ir radasta, iš Vilniaus le-
gendų surinktų dr. Vlado Zahorskio
iš senų kronikų. [Legends from
the district of Vilnius. Vertė]
Jadvyga Juškytė. Kaunas, 1928. 39
p. 491.922.Z16.2 PU

6818. --- Vilniaus padavimai;
sekdamas d-ru Zahorskiu parašė P.
Vingis. [Legends from the district
of Vilnius] Kaunas, Aitra, 1931.
230 p. Original title: Podania i
legendy Wileńskie. 947.5.Zalv WaU

6819. ŽEKEVIČIUS, Jonas, ed.
Karžygiai; dzūkų pasakos ir porin-
gos. [The heroes; folk tales from
Dzūkija] Kaunas, 1935. 144 p.
illus. 398.Ž. ICCC

6820. --- Karžygiai; poringės ir
pasakos. Augsburg, Ger., Sudavoje,
1947. 148 p. PG8719.Z4 PU

6821. ZOBARSKAS, Stepas, comp.
and ed. Lithuanian folk tales.
Illus. by Ada Korsakaitė. [Brook-
lyn, N.Y.] G.J. Rickard [1959]
240 p. illus. Bibliography: p.
239-240. GR203.L5Z6 1959 CaAEU DLC
CU CtPAM CtY CSt CaOTU InU MH MnU
NB NIC NcU NjR NRU OC1 OO OOxM

XIII.3.b.4. FOLKSONGS

6823. AISTIS, Jonas, ed. Laisvės
kovų dainos. [Songs from the period of the Wars of Independence]
New York, N.Y., Lietuvos Nepriklausomybės fondas, 1962. 342 p.
illus. M1786.I4A4 DLC CaOTP PU

6824. BALYS, Jonas. Lietuvių
dainos Amerikoje; pasakojamosios
dainos ir baladės. Lithuanian
folksongs in America; narrative
folksongs and ballads. [Boston,
Mass.] Lietuvių enciklopedijos
leidykla [1958, i.e. 1959] xlii,
326 p. music. (Lietuvių tautosakos lobynas, 5) Melodies, tape
recordings transcribed by Vladas
Jakubėnas. M1668.7.B3L5 DLC CaAEU
CaOTP CaOTU CtPAM CtTMF CtY ICBM
IEN NNC OC1 PU

6825. --- Lithuanian folk songs
in the United States. In International Folk Music Council, London.
Journal, v.3, 1951, p. 67-70. See
serials consulted.

6826. --- --- [Phonodisc] New
York, Folkways Records P 1009,
1955. 2 s. 12 in. 331/3 rpm. micro-
groove. (Ethnic folkways library.
Monograph series) No.69-97-C InU-A
CU

6827. BARAUSKIENĖ, Vanda. Sisteminis lietuvių liaudies dainų tekstų katalogas. Sistematicheskii
katalog tekstov litovskikh narodnykh
pesen'. In Literatūra ir kalba.
Vilnius, v.9, 1968, p. 389-[407]
See serials consulted.

6828. BARTSCH, Christian. Dainų
balsai. Melodien litauischer
Volkslieder. Heidelberg, Ger., C.
Winter, 1886-89. 2 v. M1766.B29
DLC CU CtTMF CtPAM CtY ICN IEN InNd
MH MdBJ MiU MnU NN NNC NcU NjP OC1
PPULC PU

6829. --- --- [Reprint. Walluf
bei Wiesbaden] M. Sandig [1972]
2 v. in 1. Reprint of Heidelberg,
1886-89 ed. M1766.I4D3 CaOTU

6830. --- Totenklagen in der litauischen Volksdichtung. In Zeitschrift für vergleichende Literaturgeschichte.. v.1, 1889, p. 81-99.
PN851.S6 DLC

6831. --- Über das litauische
Volkslied, oder die "daina". Mit
zahlreichen Liedtexten. In Litauische Literarische Gesellschaft,
Tilsit. Mitteilungen, v.1, 1883,
p. 186-219. See serials consulted.

6832. BASANAVIČIUS, Jonas. Dajnos
isz Oszkabaliu. [Folk songs from
Ožkabaliai] In LLGM, v.1, 1880, p.
114-118. See serials consulted.

6833. --- Lietuvių raudos. [Lith-
uanian wails] In Lietuvių tauta
(Vilnius), v.4, 1926, p. 59-145.
See serials consulted.

6834. --- Ožkabalių dainos. [Folk
songs from Ožkabaliai] Shenandoah,
Pa., Stagaro spaustuvė, 1902. 2 v.
in 1. 891.920.B292 PU CtTMF ICCC
MiD PPULC

6835. --- Vilnius lietuvių dainose. [Vilnius in Lithuanian folk
songs] In Lietuvių tauta (Vilnius),
v.3, no.3, p. 583-652. See serials
consulted.

6836. --- Žiponas bei žiponė ir
auksingumas bei sidabringumas lie-
tuviškum dainun. [Lithuanian folk
songs and their musical qualities]
Tilžė, Otto Mauderode, 1885. [29]
p. OCl

6837. BERG, Nikolai Vasil'evich.
Litovskie pesni. Vil'no [Izd.
"Litvy", 1921] 17 p. PG8771.R3B4
DLC

6838. BIELINIS, Alfonsas. Lata-
kiškių dainos. [Songs from Lata-
kiškės, parish of Tverečius] In
Lietuvių tauta (Vilnius), v.4, no.2,
1928, p. 266-311. See serials consulted.

6839. BINKIS, Kazys, ed. Dainos;
žmonių poezijos antologija. [Folk
songs; the anthology of folk poetry]
Šiauliai, Kultūros bendrovė, 1922.
194 p. 891.922.B517 PU MiD PPULC

6840. BIRŽIŠKA, Mykolas. Dainos
keliais; vadovėliui bent kiek medžiagos. [An outline of the history of Lithuanian folk songs]
Vilnius, Švyturio bendrovės spaustuvė, 1921. 118 p. (Lietuvių
mokslo draugijos leidinys)
PG8709.B625 CaAEU BM(Ac. 1156. h/3.)
ICBM ICCC OCl PU

6841. --- Dainų atsiminimai iš
Lietuvos istorijos. [The history
of Lithuanian folksongs] Vilnius,
Švyturio spaustuvė, 1920. 142 p.
(Lietuvių mokslo draugijos leidi-
nys, 48) Bibliography: p. [114]-
142. PG8709.B46 DLC CaOONL CtTMF
InU InNd MH MiD OCl PPULC PU

6842. --- Dainų istorijos vadovėlis; 3 čias leidimas. [The history
of Lithuanian folk songs] Kaunas,
1925. 109 p. 784.4.B ICCC

6843. --- Dainų literatūros vadovėlis. 2-sis, naujai paruoštas
leidimas. Kaunas, Švyturio bendrovė, 1923. 101 p. (Svyturio
b-vės knygynas, nr. 23)
491.922.B536.2 PU CtY ICCC PPULC

6844. --- Lietuvių dainos; vidurinėms mokykloms vadovėlis.
[Lithuanian folksongs; text book]
Vilnius [Lietuvių mokslo draugija]
1916. 55 p. (Lietuvių mokslo
draugijos leidinys, 2)
PG8715.B5 DLC PU

6845. --- Lietuvių dainų literatūros istorija. [History of the
Lithuanian song literature] Vilnius, Žaibo spaustuvė, 1919. 118
p. (Lietuvių mokslo draugijos
leidinys, 36) PG8709.B62 CaAEU
CtTMF DLC ICLJF InU InNd MH(microfilm) PU

6846. BIRŽIŠKA, Vaclovas. Lie-
tuviškųjų dainų literatūros bibliografija. [A bibliography of Lithuanian folk songs] In Mūsų tautosaka (Kaunas), v.3, 1931, p. 187-229.
See serials consulted.

6847. BOHLEN, P. Sammlung litthauischer Volkslieder. In Neue
Preussische Provinzial-Blätter
(Königsberg in Pr.), v.10, 1865, p.
323-338; v.11, 1866, p. 88, 97-102,
240-251. See serials consulted.

6848. BOTSFORD, Florence Hudson
(Topping), comp. Botsford collec-
tion of folksongs with English
versions by American poets. New
York, N.Y., G. Schirmer, 1930-1933.
3 v. Includes (v.2, p. 126-136)
the Lithuanian National Anthem and
six folksongs. M1627.B72 1930 DLC
CaBVa CaBVaU CoD CoDU FU FTaSU KMK
MB MoK NN NcD OCl OClC ODW OO Or
OrAshs MonO OrU OEac OClND PPULC
PPWILP PWcT UPB

6849. BRAZYS, Teodoras. Lietuvių
liaudies daina vestuvėse. [The
Lithuanian folksong at the wedding]
In Tauta ir žodis (Kaunas), v.2,
1924, p. 190-238. See serials consulted.

6850. BRENSZTEJN, Michał Eustachy.
Dajny litewskie, zapisane przez
Adama Mickiewicza. [Lithuanian
folksongs, written down by Adam
Mickiewicz] Wilno, Nakł. Przyjaciół
Nauk, 1927. 25 p. At head of
title: M. Brensztejn i J. Otrębski.
PG8709.B7 DLC NN RPB

6851. BRZOZOWSKI, Karol M. Pieśni ludu nadniemenskiego z okolic
Aleksoty zebrał i przełożył K.M.

Brzozowski. Poznań, 1844. 129, 13 p. BM(11585. a. 12.) CtY

6852. BUDRIUS, Heindrik and E. Gisevius. Litthauischer Volksgesang. In Neue Preussische Provinzial-Blätter (Königsberg in Pr.), v.5, 1848, p. 59-75, 88-94, 344-359; v.6, 1849, p. 16-25, 190-205. See serials consulted.

6853. BŪGA, Kazimieras. Seinų parapijos dainos. [Songs from the parish of Seinai] In Tauta ir žodis (Kaunas), v.1, 1923, p. 144-153. See serials consulted.

6854. ČAPLIKAS, Juozas. Trakiečių dzūkų dainos. [Songs of dzūkai around Trakai. Užrašytos J. Šimtakojo, pseud.] Shenandoah, Pa., 1899. 82 p. 784.Ši CTMF

6855. ČIURLIONYTĖ, Jadvyga. Iz istorii litovskoi pesni. In Sovetskaia muzyka (Moskva), v.2, 1955, p. 69-77. See serials consulted.

6856. --- Lietuvių liaudies dainos; rinktinė. [Lithuanian folksongs; a selection] Vilnius, VGLL, 1955. 610 p. music. Text in Lithuanian and Russian. M1766.C66L5 DLC ICCC ICLJF NN PU

6857. ---, comp. Lietuvių liaudies melodijos. [Lithuanian folk melodies] Kaunas, Lietuvos tautosakos archyvo leidinys, 1938. vi, 310 p., 16 plates, music. (Tautosakos darbai, 5) Bibliography: p. 281-310 by Z. Slaviūnas. M1766.I4C62 DLC PP1U PU

6858. --- Litovskaia narodnaia pesnia. In Sovetskaia muzyka (Moskva), v.6, 1949, p. 60-64. See serials consulted.

6859. DABRILA, Justinas, ed. Vai lėkite dainos! [Oh, fly ye songs!] Vilkaviškis, 1938. 230 p. 784.V2 CtTMF

6860. --- --- Papildyta rinkinį išleido P.M. Juras. [5. leidimas] So. Boston, Darbininkas [1940] 220 p. PG8715.D3 1940a DLC CaOONL CtTMF PU

6861. DAINY; litovskie narodnye pesni. [Pereveli Aleksandr Prokof'-ev, Anatolii Chepurov i Georgii Gerasimov] Vil'nius, 1965. 210 p. illus. PG8715.D13 NIC NN NNC

6862. DAUKANTAS, Simanas. Dajnes Žiamajtiŭ pagal Žôdiu Dajninikŭ iszraszytas... [Songs of Samogitia. By] Simon Dowkont. Petropilie, 1846. 168 p. PG8715.D32 1970

PU(Xerox copy)

6863. DAVAINIS-SILVESTRAVIČIUS, Mečislovas. Zhmudskiia piesni iz Polangena. Zapisanye v iiunie 1893 g. Perevedeniia A. Pogodinym. Palongos žemaitiškos dainos. [By] M. Dowojna-Sylvestrovich. In Zhivaia starina (Sanktpeterburg), v.3, no.4, 1893, p. 519-531. See serials consulted.

6864. DEUTSCH, Leonhard. A treasury of the world's finest folk songs. New York, N.Y., Howell, Soskin [1942] 430 p. M1627.D45T7 DLC CaBVaU CaBViP CoU IdB IdU KyLx MtU NIC NcD NcRS OCl OClW OCU OO OOxM Or OrP OrU OrCS OU PPD PPCI PPE PPTU PSt PPL ViU WaI WaE Wa WaWW

6865. DOMEIKAITĖ, Antanina. Die litauischen Volkslieder in der deutschen literatur... Warupönen bei Schirwindt, Ostpr., 1928. 70 p. Thesis--University of München. Bibliography: p. 2-4. 831.04.D668 CSt CtY IU MH MiU NNC OCl PBm PU WaU

6866. DOVYDAITIS, Jurgis, comp. Dainos. [Songs] Kaunas, Spindulio spaustuvė, 1930. 386 p. (Kaunas. Universitetas. Humanitarinių mokslų fakultetas. Tautosakos komisijos leidinys) M1766.I4D6 CU MH NN OCl

6867. DRIZULE, R. Skhodnye obrazy i motivy sirottskikh svadebnykh pesen' v latyshskom i litovskom fol'klore. In Fol'klor baltskikh narodov. Riga, 1968. p. 69-104. GR203.L3F6 CaAEU CaOTU DLC ICU NjP PP1U PU WaU

6868. DRYSKIS, K., pseud. Dainelės. Surinktos ir išleistos per K. Dryskį. [pseud. Songs collected and published by K. Dryskis] Tilžėje, O.v. Mauderodės spaudinimu [1900] 16 p. 891.92.D849D PU

6869. ENGERT, Horst, tr. Aus litauischer Dichtung; deutsche Nachdichtungen. 2., vermehrte und veränderte Auflage. Kaunas; Leipzig, Ostverlag der Buchhandlung Pribačis, 1938. 112 p. illus. PG8772.G1E7 DLC CtY IEN MH NN NIC NNC PP1U PU

6870. GREGOR, Josef, ed. Europäische Lieder in den Ursprachen; im Auftrage der Deutschen UNESCO-Kommission; Hrsg. von Josef Gregor [et al.] Der zweite Band. Berlin, Verlag Merseburg, 1960. CaAEU InU MH MNS OrU

6871. HAGEN, Ernest August. Über das Wesen der litthauischen Volkslieder. In Neue Preussische Provinzial-

Blätter (Königsberg in Pr.), v.2, 1846, p. 261-294. See serials consulted.

6872. JABLONSKIS, Jonas. Zamietka po povodu izdaniia zhmudskikh piesen' iz Polangena. [By] I.O. IAblonskii. Sanktpeterburg, 1895. In Zhivaia starina (Sanktpeterburg), v.3-4, 1895, p. 467-469. See serials consulted.

6873. JANULAITIS, Augustinas. Malavėnų dainos. [Folk songs from Malavėnai district] In LLGM, v.4, no.23, 1898, p. 433-459,497-516; v.5, p. 270-298. See serials consulted.

6874. JOKIMAITIENĖ, Pranė. Dainuojamoji tautosaka. Pesennyi fol'klor. In Literatūra ir kalba (Vilnius), v.6, 1962, p. 396-403. See serials consulted.

6875. --- Lietuvių liaudies vaikų dainos. [The songs of Lithuanian children] Vilnius, Mintis, 1970. 265 p. PG8709.J63 PU

6876. --- Litovskie i latyshskie kolybel'nye pesni. In Fol'klor baltskikh narodov. Riga, 1968. p. 53-67. GR203.L3F6 CaAEU CaOTU DLC ICU NjP PPiU PU WaU

6877. JONYNAS, Ambraziejus. Dainuojamoji tautosaka. [Folk songs] In LTSRMAIKLI. Lietuvių tautosakos apybraiža. Vilnius, 1963. p. 119-241,253-277. GR203.L5I497 DLC CtY CU ICU CaAEU MH NN

6878. --- Vestuvinės dainos. Wedding songs] In LTSRMALKLI. Lietuvių tautosakos apybraiža. Vilnius, 1963. p. 163-187. GR203.L5I497 DLC CaAEU CtY CU ICU MH NN

6879. JORDAN, Wilhelm. Litauische Volkslieder und Sagen. Berlin, Springer Verlag, 1944. 104 p. MH NjP OCl BM(1462. h. 20.(3.))

JOVAIŠAS, Albinas. Liudvikas Rėza. Vilnius, 1969. See entry no. 555.

6880. JUCEWICZ, Ludwik Adam. Pieśni litewskie. Przekładania Ludwika z Pokiewia. Wilno, R. Daien, 1844. 106 p. BM(11585. c. 32.)

6881. JUNGFER, Viktor. Litauischer Liederschrein; Volkslieder in deutschen Übertragungen und Nachdichtungen, mit einer Einführung. Kaunas, Deutsche Buchhandlung, 1939. 123 p. PG8771.G3J9 CLU DLC IU PU

6882. --- --- [Another edition]

Tübingen, Patria [1948] 123 p. PG8713.J955LG InNd PU

6883. JUŠKA, Antanas. comp. & ed. Liètuviškos dájnos užrašýtos par Antáną Juškevičę, apigardoje Púšałačiu ir Velůnós iš žodžiu liètuviu dajninínku ir dajninínkiu. Litovskiia narodnyia piesni zapisannyia Antonom IUshkevichem. Kazan', Tip. Imperatorskago universiteta, 1880-82. 3 v. in 1. Text in Lithuanian only. "Pechatano po opredieleniiu Sovieta Imperatorskago universiteta. Kazan' 13 aprielia 1879 goda." Supplement to: Kazan, U.S.S.R. Universitet. Uchenye zapiski, 1880; 1881, mart-apriel'; 1882, mai-avgust. PG8715.I87 NSyU CtPAM CtY ICU NN OCl PU

6884. --- Lietuviškos dainos. [Another edition. Lithuanian folk songs] Vilnius, VGLL, 1954. 3 v. music (at end of each volume) Photographic reproduction of 1st ed. 1880-82. M1766.I4J77 DLC CaAEU CtY CtPAM ICLJF IEN NN OKentU PU

6885. --- Lietùviškos svotbìnes dájnos, užrašýtos par Antáną Juškévičę. Litovskiia svadebnyia narodnyia piesni, zapisannyia Antonom IUshkevichem i izdannyia Ivanom IUshkevichem. Sanktpeterburg, Tip. Imperatorskoi Akademii nauk, 1883. xxiv, 898 p. (Akademiia nauk, Sanktpeterburg. Sbornik Otdieleniia russkago iazyka i slovesnosti, t.35) PG8715.I873 NSyU MH NN NNC OCl PU

6886. ---,comp. Lietuviškos svodbinės dainos. [Lithuanian wedding songs] Užrašytos Antano Juško ir išleistos Jono Juškos. Vilnius, VGLL, 1955. 2 v. music. M1766.I4J8 DLC ICCC ICLJF MH NN OKentU PU

6887. --- Litovskiia narodnyia piesni. S perevodom na russkii iazyk I.A. Iushkevicha. Sanktpeterburg, A. Bazunova, 1867. 43 p. "Prilozhenie k 12-mu tomu Zapisok Imp. Akademii nauk, no.1" PG8546.I92 CLU MH NIC NNC

6888. KALVAITIS, Vilius. Prūsijos lietuvių dainos. [Lithuanian folk songs of Prussia] Tilžė, Atspaudė E. Jagomastas, 1905. 408 p. 3057.509 NjP CtTMF ICLJF OCl WaS

6889. --- Rūtų lapelei. 100 dainelių. [Leaves of the rue; one hundred Lithuanian songs] Surinko ir iszleido W. Kalwaitis. Tilžė, 1894. 128 p. BM(011586. de. 119.)

6890. KATZENELENBOGEN, Uriah, comp. and tr. Antologye fun Litvishe un

Letishe folks-lider. [Chicago, Ill. 1930] 427 p. PG8709.K28 DLC CaOTU MWalB NN OCl WU

6891. --- The daina; an anthology of Lithuanian and Latvian folk songs. Chicago, Ill., Lithuanian News Publ. Co., 1935. xii, 165 p. map. PG8709.K3 DLC CU CaMWU CaOTU CaBVaS CtY IC ICN ICU In MiU MnU NN NNC NB NcD NjP OCl PU PP RPB ViU

6892. KAZLAUSKIENĖ, B. Dainuoja- mosios lietuvių tautosakos tekstų klasifikavimo sistema. [The classi- fication system of the texts of Li- thuanian folk songs] In LTSRMAD. Serija A, v.2(7), 1959, p. 233-254. See serials consulted.

6893. --- Vestuvinių lietuvių liau- dies dainų klasifikavimas. [The classification of the Lithuanian wedding songs] In LTSRMAD. Serija A, 1967. v.1(23), p. 135-149. See serials consulted.

6894. KOLBERG, Oskar. Litwa. [Z rękopisów opracowali Czesław Kudzi- nowski i Danuta Pawlak. Warszawa] Ludowa Spółdzielnia Wydawnicza [1966] xxvi, 561 p. facsims., music. (His Dzieła wszystkie, t.53) Bibliogra- phy: p. 485-504, [525]-[529] ML3687.K64 DLC CaSSU CaAEU CtY CSt PU WU

6895. --- Piesni ludu litewskiego. Kraków, w Drukarni Uniwersytetu Ja- giellońskiego, 1879. 64 p. "Osob- ne odbicie ze Zbioru Wiadomości do Antropologji Kraj., t.3" OCl

6896. KONCĖ, A. Panevėžio ir Paystrės parapijų dainos. [Songs from the parishes of Panevėžys and Paystrė] In Tauta ir žodis (Kau- nas), v.4, 1926, p. 573-606. See serials consulted.

6897. KRASZEWSKI, Józef Ignacy. Lietuvių dainos. [Piesni z podań Litwy] Versta iš lenkų kalbos. [M. Biržiška išlygino vertimą ir papildė savo prierašais] Vilnius, 1921. 53 p. PG8703.K73 PU

6898. KRĖVĖ-MICKEVIČIUS, Vincas. Dainavos krašto liaudies dainos. [The folk songs of the Dainava district] Kaunas, 1921. 152 p. 891.93.K40 CtTMF; also in Tauta ir žodis (Kaunas), v.1, 1923, p. 157- 307; v.2, 1924, p. 263-437. See serials consulted.

6899. --- --- Kaunas, Humanitari- nių mokslų fakulteto leidinys, 1924. 298 p. (Tautos ir žodžio biblioteka, nr. 1.) PG98515.L72

PU ICCC ICU NN

6900. KRIŠTOPAITĖ, Danutė. Lie- tuvių liaudies karinės-istorinės dainos; feodalizmo epocha. [Lith- uanian war and historical folk songs, the feudal era] Vilnius, Vaga, 1965. 283, [3] p. PG8709.K7 DLC CaAEU CtY ICU OClW OKentU PU

6901. KRIVICKIENĖ, Gražina. Dainos; vieux chants lithuaniens. Fribourg en Brisgau, Erwin Burda [c1948] 160 p., 20 leaves illus., music. (Les documents de l'art lituanien) Folksongs from Liudvi- navas and environs. Music, tran- scribed by Adomas Germanavičius. Illustrated by Viktoras Petravičius. Foreword by Jonas Balys. Includes an article: Petravičius, les dai- nos et l'âme de la Lithuanie by Aleksis Rannit. M1766.L4K7 DLC CaOONL ICBM ICCC ICLJF InU OCl PU

6902. --- --- Priedas. Melodijos. Melodijas užrašė Adomas Germanavi- čius. Dainavo Gražina Krivickienė. [Supplement. Music transcribed by Adomas Germanavičius, sung by Gra- žina Krivickienė] Freiburgas, 1950. 20 leaves. PU

6903. ---, comp. Vilnius lietu- vių liaudies dainose. Vilnius in Lithuanian folksongs. Compiled and edited by Gražina Krivickienė-Gus- taitytė. Adaptation and glossary by Pr. Skardžius. Cover by Marija Žymantienė-Biržiškaitė. [Chicago, Ill., Draugo spaustuvė, 1970] 384 p. music. Introductory remarks in English: p. 28-33. Contents of songs in English: p. 34-67. PG8715.K74 PU CaOONL OKentU

6904. LANDSBERGIS, Algirdas and Clark Mills, eds. The green linden, selected Lithuanian folksongs. With a foreword by Robert Payne, an introd. by Marija Gimbutas and illus. by Viktoras Petravičius. [1st ed.] New York, N.Y., Voyages Press [1964] 137 p. illus. PG8771.E3L29 DLC AzU CaAEU CaOTP CaOTU InNd IEU MU NN NmU OrU PP PU RPB TxU TU WU

6905. LARISH, Hugo de. La tra- dition lithuanienne dans les chan- sons populaires. In Études tradi- tionnelles (Paris), v.44, 1939, p. 322-340. See serials consulted.

6906. LEONAS, Petras. Poetiškos dainų grožybės. [The poetical beauty of folk songs] In Draugija (Kaunas), nr. 37, 1910, p. 41-59. See serials consulted.

6907. LESKIEN, August. Eine litauische Totenklage; das Begräbnis
als Hochzeit. In Festschrift Ernst
Windisch zum siebzigsten Geburtstag
... dargebracht. Leipzig, 1914.
p. 5-7. PK2Z5W5 DLC CU CtY ICU IU
MH MiU NN NIC NRU NjP OCl OO PU

6908. --- Litauische Volkslieder
aus Wilkischken, gesammelt von A.
Leskien. In Archiv für Slavische
Philologie (Berlin), v.4, p. 591-
610. See serials consulted.

6909. LIETUVIŲ TĖVYNĖS DAINOS;
tautiečių naudai išleido "Birutė"
[Lithuanian folk songs] Tilžė, O.
v. Mauderodės spaustuvė, 1911, 65
p. PG8715.L57 PU ICCC

6910. LIETUVOS TSR MOKSLŲ AKADE-
MIJA, VILNA. LIETUVIŲ KALBOS IR
LITERATŪROS INSTITUTAS. Dainuoja-
mosios tautosakos klausimai.
[Questions on the folk songs. Ed.
by Amr. Jonynas. Board of editors:
K. Aleksynas, K. Grigas and L.
Sauka] Vilnius, Vaga, 1968. 511
p. (Literatūra ir kalba, 9)
PG8503.L6 v.9 DLC CaAEU CLU CtY
ICU InU IU KyU MH NN PU

6911. LÖBELL, R. Über litauische
Volkspoesie. Oppenheim am Rhein,
M. Treumüller, 1884. 29 p.
491.922.L826 PU

6912. MACEINA, Antanas. Das
Volkslied als Ausdruck der Volks-
seele; Geist und Charakter der
litauischen Dainos. Bonn, Baltisches Forschungsinstitut, 1955.
41 p. (Commentationes Balticae II:
3) PG8001.C6 v.3 DLC; see also
serials consulted.

6913. MACIUS, K. Prasmė ir
gražumas Lietuvos dainų. [The meaning and beauty of the Lithuanian
folk songs. By] Samogitia [pseud.]
In Žinyčia (Tilžė), no.1, 1900, p.
33-84. See serials consulted.

6914. MEULEN, Reinder van der.
Die Naturvergleiche in den Liedern
und Totenklagen der Litauer. Leiden, A.W. Sijthoff, 1907. xiv,
178 p. PG8694.M4 DLC CaAEU IaU ICU
MH MnU OCl PU WU ICLJF

6915. MORICI, Giuseppe, tr. Canti
popolari lituani. 2e ed. Roma,
1930. xvi, 248 p. (Poesia popolare
indo-europea, 2) 1st ed. Roma,
Anonima romana editoriale, 1925.
491.922.M827 PU MH NN

6916. NAST, Louis. Die Volkslieder der Litauer, inhaltlich und
musikalisch. Tilsit, O. v. Maude-

rode, 1893. 52 p. music.
GR203.L2N2 InU MH OCl PU

6917. NESSELMANN, Georg Heinrich
Ferdinand. Dainos; litauische
Volkslieder. Berlin, F. Dümmler,
1853. vii, 196 p. PG8771.G3N4
DLC CaOHM CU CtY ICN ICU MH MdBP MU
NN OCl OClW

6918. --- Littauische Volkslieder,
ges., kritisch bearb, und metrisch
übers. Berlin, F. Dümmler, 1853.
xiv, 368 p. music. PG8771.G3N4
NSyU BM(11585. k. 37.) CaOTU ICU
NIC OClW PU

6919. --- Zur Kritik des litauischen Volksliedes. In Neue Preussischen Provinzial-Blätter (Königsberg in Pr.), v.12, 1851, p. 177-
186. See serials consulted.

6920. NIEMI, Aukusti Robert and
Adolfas Sabaliauskas. Lietuvių
dainos giesmės šiaur-rytinėje Lietuvoje. A.R. Niemi ir kun. A. Sabaliausko surinktos. [Lithuanian
hymns and folksongs in Northeast
Lithuania] Riga, A.R. Niemi ir A.
Sabaliausko, 1911. xxiv, 363 p.
illus. OCl

6921. --- --- Helsinki, Suomalainen Tiedeakatemia, 1912. xxiv, 363
p. (Helsinki. Suomalainen Tiedeakatemia. Suomalaisen Tiedeakatemian toimituksia. Annales. Serja
B, nid. 6.) Q60.H53 DLC CSt CaOON
Ca CaOG CaQMM CtY MH MdBJ MnU NNC
NjP PPAN PU RPB

6922. NIEMI, Aukusti Robert.
Lietuvių liaudies dainų tyrinėjimai.
[Research in Lithuanian folk songs.
Tr. by] Adolfas Sabaliauskas. Kaunas, 1932. 318 p. (Mūsų tautosaka,
6) CU MH NN; see also serials consulted.

6923. --- Tuktkimuksia lietualais-
ten kansanlaulujen alalta. [Studies
in Lithuanian folk songs] In Suomalainen tiedeakatemia, Helsingfors.
Suomalaisen tiedeakatemian toimituksia. Annales Academicae scientiarum
fennicae. Ser. B., v. 12, no.1,
1913. xii, 327 p. See serials consulted.

6924. NIEMINEN, Eino Kalervo. Litauische Volkslieder aus dem handschriftlichen Nachlass Prof. J.J.
Mikkolas. Helsinki, 1949. 59 p.
(Annales Academiae Scientiarum Fennicae, Ser. B, v. 63, no.1) See
serials consulted.

6925. NORKUS, Jonas, comp.
Didžiojo Karo laikų lietuvių dainos.

[Lithuanian folk songs from the First World War] Kaunas, Vairo b-vės leidinys, 1927. 239 p. 784.8N ICCC

6926. PAKALNIŠKIS, Jonas. Klaipėdiškių dainos. [Songs from the territory of Klaipėda] Surinko Jons Pakalniškis. Išleido A. Bružis. Vilnius, M. Kuktos spaustuvė, 1908. 107, iii p. Hvc42+P17 CtY CtTMF

6927. PAUKSZTYS, Juozas, ed. Lietuviškos dainos iš visur surinktos. [Lithuanian songs... collected from everywhere] Plymouth, Pa., Kasztu ir spaustuvėje Juozo Paukszczio, 1893. 496 p. 891.92.CP284 PU CtTMF ICLJF MH

6928. PLENZAT, Karl. Der Liederschrein. 110 deutsche, litauische und masurische Volkslieder aus Ostpreussen mit Lautensatz von Heinrich Scherrer. Leipzig, F. Hofmeister, 1922. vi, 160 p. PT1204.P7 ICU DLC IU MH(1918 ed.) NN(1934 ed.)

6929. RHESA, Ludwig Jedemin. Abhandlung über die Litthauischen Volksgedichte. In His Dainos; oder littauische Volkslieder. Königsberg in Pr., 1825. Hvc42.R34 CtY IU MH NjP OCl

6930. ---, ed. and tr. Dainos; oder, Litthauische Volkslieder gesammelt, übersetzt und mit gegenüberstehendem Urtext herausgegeben von L.J. Rhesa. Nebst einer Abhandlung über die litthauischen Volksgedichte. Königsberg in Pr., Druck und Verlag der Hartungschen Hofbuchdrukkerei, 1825. 362, [8] p. Hvc42.R34 CtY IU MH NjP OCl

6931. --- --- Neue aufl. Durchgesehen, berichtigt und verbessert von Friedrich Kurschat. Berlin, T.C.F. Enslin, 1843. viii, 246 p. PG8771.G3R5 1843 DLC CaOHM ICN MH MdBJ NN

6932. --- Lietuvių liaudies dainos. [Lithuanian folk songs. Paruošė J. Jurginis ir B. Kmitas] Vilnius, VGLL, 1958-64. 2 v. GR8771.G3R47 1958 CaAEU DLC CtY PU

6933. --- Lietuvių liaudies dainų tyrinėjimas. [The research of Lithuanian folk songs] In His Lietuvių liaudies dainos. Vilnius, 1958. v.1, p. 327-363. GR8771.G3R47 v.1 1958 CaAEU CtY DLC PU

6934. --- Litewské národní pisně.

Z půwodniho gazika dle sebránj. L. J. Rhezy přeloženė a wydanė od F. L. Čelakowského (Připogena staroruská powėst: Potok Michajlo Iwanowič) W Praze, J.H. Pospissil, 1827. 132, 12 p. PG5038.C42M33 1827 ICU BM(11585. a. 54.(1.)) MH

6935. --- Liudo Rėzos dainos, pirmojo lietuviško dainyno 3. leidimas, 1 dalis. [Lithuanian folk songs collected by L. Rhesa. Paruošė M. Biržiška] Kaunas, VDU Humanitarinių mokslų fakulteto leidinys, 1935. 170 p. 891.92.CR 1935 PU

6936. --- Prutena, oder Preussische Volkslieder und andere vaterländische Dichtungen. Königsberg in Pr., H. Degen, 1809. 179 p. PT1205.P8R54 CU MH NjP OCl BM(11521. b. 21.)

6937. RŪTŲ VAINIKĖLIS; dainos surinktos Šešupės apylinkėse. [The little wreath of Rue. By] K. Lakšas. Seinai, Laukaičio spaustuvė, 1909. 92 p. 784.4R ICCC

6938. SAUKA, Leonardas. Apie vestuvinių dainų savitumus. [On the originality of the wedding songs] In Pergalė (Vilnius), no.1, 1958, p. 141-163. See serials consulted.

6939. --- Lietuvių vestuvinės dainos. Litovskie svadebnye pesni. In Literatūra ir kalba (Vilnius), v.9, 1968, p. 7-275. Bibliography: p. 278-[285]. See serials consulted.

6940. SCHERRER, Heinrich. Der Liederschrein; hundert und zehn deutsche, litauische und mazurische Volkslieder. Leipzig, Hoffmeister, 1918. vi, 160 p. plates, music. NjR

6941. SEEMANN, Erich. Deutschlitauische Volksliedbeziehungen. In Jahrbuch für Volksliedforschung (Berlin; Leipzig), v.8, 1951, p. 142-211. See serials consulted.

6942. SENKUS, Kazimieras. Die Formen der litauischen Volkslieder. Bonn, Baltisches Forschungsinstitut, 1957. 47 p. music. Offprint from Commentationes Balticae (Bonn), v. 3, no. 4, 1957. M13693.L5S4 PU See also serials consulted.

6943. ŠEŠPLAUKIS, Alfonsas. J.G. Herder und die Dainos. In Commentationes Balticae (Bonn), v.8-9(5), 1962, p. 1-47. See serials consulted.

6944. SLANČIAUSKAS, Motiejus. Šiauliškių vestuvių dainuškos talaluškos. [Wedding songs from the Šiauliai area] In Lietuvių tauta. (Vilnius) v.3, no.2, 1923, p. 411-450. See serials consulted.

6945. SLAVIŪNAS, Zenonas. A. Juškos "Svodbinės dainos". [Wedding songs] In Juška, Antanas. Lietuviškos svodbinės dainos užrašytos. .. Vilnius, 1955. v.1, p. 5-20. M1766.L4J8 DLC ICCC ICLJF MH NN PU

6946. SRUOGA, Balys. Apie lietuvių liaudies dainas. [Lithuanian folk songs] In His Raštai. Vilnius, 1957. v.6, p. 339-394. PG8721.S68 1957 DLC CaAEU ICU PU

6947. --- Dainavos krašto liaudies dainos. [Folk songs of Dainava district] In Tauta ir žodis (Kaunas), no.4, 1927, p. 513-562. See serials consulted.

6948. --- Dainų poetikos; etiudai. [A study of the poetics of the Lithuanian folk songs] Kaunas, Valstybės spaustuvė, 1927. x, 172 p. (Kaunas. Universitetas. Humanitarinių mokslų fakulteto leidinys) PG8709.S78 CU ICU NN OCl

6949. --- --- In His Raštai. Vilnius, 1957. v.6, p. 103-328. PG8721.S68 1957 v.6 DLC CaAEU ICU CU NN OCl

6950. --- Lietuvių dainų poetinės priemonės. [Poetical means of the Lithuanian folk songs] In Tauta ir žodis (Kaunas), v.3, 1925; p. 1-75; v.4, 1926, p. 187-231. See serials consulted.

6951. --- Lithuanian folk songs; Lithuanian folk song literature. In Folk-Lore (London), v.43, 1932, p. 301-324. See serials consulted.

6952. STANEVIČIUS, Simonas. Dainos Žemaičių. [Songs of Samogitia. A facsimile of the edition of 1829 together with a modern version of the text, commentary and notes. With the music of the songs] Vilnius, 1954. 220 p. 891.92.Cst27 PU CtPAM ICLJF BM(11588. pp. 33.)

6953. STANIEWICZ, Emerik. Spiewy ludu litewskiego. In Tygodnik Wileński (Wilno), v.9, 1820; v.10, 1821; v.11, 1822. See serials consulted.

6954. SURINKTOS DAINOS ISZ VISOS Lietuvos. [Lithuanian folk songs] So. Boston, Mass., išleista turtu P.P. Mikalucko [n.d.] 128 p.

784.8S ICCC CtTMF

6955. TARDEL, Hermann. Zum Problem der Entstehung und Wesenart des Volksliedes. Bremen, 1937. In Bremer Wissenschaftliche Gesellschaft. Festschrift zur Feier des zehnjährigen Bestehens der Bremer Wissenschaftlichen Gesellschaft. Abhandlungen und Vorträge, bd. 8-9, 1937, p. 223-256. AS182.B75 Jahrg. 8-9 DLC ICU NNC

6956. TETZNER, Franz Oskar, ed. Dainos; litauische Volksgesänge mit Einleitung, Abbildungen und Melodien, herausgegeben von F. und H. Tetzner. Leipzig, P. Reclam jun., [1897] 112 p. illus., music. List of author's works: p. [109]-112. PG8771.G3T2 CLU MB NN

6957. VASAITIS, J., ed. Leiskit į tėvynę; dainų rinkinys. [Let us back to our country; a collection of folk songs] Memmingen, Ger., Mintis, 1946. 272 p. PG8715.V35 PU CtTMF ICCC NN

6958. VIRELIŪNAS, Antanas. Kupiškėnų dainos. [Folk songs from Kupiškėnai] In Tauta ir žodis (Kaunas), v.3, 1925, p. 390-480 and v.4, 1926, p. 518-563. See serials consulted.

6959. VYŠNIAUSKAITĖ, Angėlė. Lietuvių šeimos tradicijos. [Customs of the Lithuanian family. Dailininkai: V. Jucys ir V. Kisarauskas] Vilnius, Mintis, 1967. 182 p. illus., music. At head of title: Lietuvos TSR Mokslų akademija. Istorijos institutas. DK511.L212V9 DLC CtPAM ICU InU MH NN PPiU PU

6960. ZABUTIENĖ, Juozapa. Zabutienės Juozapos dainos parapijos Vižanų, 1895. [Folk songs from the parish of Vižainis, 1895] Manuscript. 784.Z1 CtTMF

6961. ŽIUGŽDA, Juozas. Dainy; litovskie narodnye pesni. Perevod s litovskogo S. Mar. Moskva, Goslitizdat, 1944. 36 p. PG8771.R3Z56 DLC

XII.3.c. FOLK MUSIC, FOLK DANCES AND FOLK FESTIVALS

6962. BACEVIČIUS, Vytautas. Four Lithuanian dances. Op. 35. For piano [by] Vytautas Bacevičius. New York, N.Y., Paragon Music Publishers [1945] 22 p. [Paragon modern classic series, no. 1) Contents.--Klumpakojis (Wooden shoes) --Blezdingėlė (Swallows)--Noriu miego (I want to sleep)--Suktinis (Round dance) M31.B DLC OC1

6963. BALYS, Jonas. Lithuanian folk dances. In English Folk Dance and Song Society. Journal (London), v.2, 1935, p. 139-142. See serials consulted.

6964. BELIAJUS, Vytautas Finadar. Dance and be merry. Collected and described by Finadar Vytautas Beliajus. [Chicago, Ill.] C. F. Summy Co., 1940-1942. 2 v. diagrs. MTA50.B35D3 DLC CaBVa CaBVaU CoD CoU CoGrS CoDPS CoDU IdU MtBC OC1 OO OrCS OrP OrU OrPS OYesA OrSaW PPULC PU TxU TU UPB UU

6965. --- The dance of Lietuva; fifty-four circle and folk dances from Lithuania. Chicago, Ill., Summy, 1951. 96 p. illus., music. GV1688.L5B4 DLC CaAEU CaOTU InU IdPI MB MH NN OrU PPULC PU WaS

6966. --- Let's be merry; linksmi būkim. [Delaware, Ohio, Cooperative Recreation Service, 1951] 38 p. illus., music. M1766.L4B4 CLU-Phys. Ed. InU(1955 ed.)

6967. BOYD, Neva L. Lithuanian, Polish and Russian folk dances, with descriptions. Chicago, Ill., Recreation training school of Chicago, Ill. n.d., 7 pts. in 1 v. music. 613.741.L713 OrU OC1 PP PU WaS

6968. BRAZYS, Teodoras. Apie tautines lietuvių dainų gaidas; studija. [The study on the tunes of the Lithuanian folk songs] Tilžė, Švyturio spaustuvė, 1920. 43 p. illus., music. A784.475.B739 PU CtY ICBM

6969. --- Kai kurie lietuvių ir latvių dainų melodijų giminystės bruožai. [Some similar traits of the tunes of Lithuanian and Latvian songs] In Tauta ir žodis (Kaunas), v.5, 1928. p. 215-224. See serials consulted.

6970. --- Lietuvių tautinių dainų melodijos. [The melodies of Lithuanian folk songs] Kietaviškių parapijos apylinkėje, surinko ir surašė doc. kun. Teodoras Brazys. Tekstą redagavo prof. V. Krėvė-Mickevičius. [Kaunas] Humanitarinių mokslų fakulteto leidinys, 1927. 112, [3] p. music. PG8656.B8 ICU ICCC NN

6971. --- Die Singweisen der li-

tauischen Dainos. Stuttgart, J. Schrader, 1918. 46 p. music. ML3681.B82 NIC PPULC PU

6972. --- --- [Another edition] In Tauta ir žodis (Kaunas), v.4, 1926, p. 3-50. music. See serials consulted.

6973. ČETKAUSKAITĖ, Genovaitė. Lietuvių dainuojamosios tautosakos melodijos. [The melodies of Lithuanian folk songs. Edited by P. Jokimaitienė and L. Sauka] In LTSRMAIKLI. Lietuvių tautosakos apybraiža, Vilnius, 1963. p. 277-307. GR203.L51497 DLC CaAEU CU CtY ICU MH NN

ČIURLIONYTĖ, Jadvyga. Lietuvių liaudies dainos; rinktinė. Vilnius, 1955. See entry no. 6856.

6974. --- Lietuvių liaudies dainų melodikos bruožai. [An outline of the melodies of the Lithuanian folk songs] Vilnius, Vaga, 1969. 344 p. Bibliography: p. 324-[327] ML3681.L6C6 DLC CaAEU ICBM OKentU PU

---, comp. Lietuvių liaudies melodijos. Kaunas, 1938. See entry no. 6857.

6975. ČIŽAUSKAS, A. Dainų šventė. [Song festival] Vilnius, VPMLL, 1960. 142 p. illus. 791Č ICBM

6976. DAINŲ ŠVENTĖ, VILNA, 1955. Dainų šventė. [Song Festival, 1955. Teksto autorius P. Pukys. Dailininkas A. Kučas] Vilnius, VPMLL, 1957. 150 p. (chiefly illus.) ML37.L5D3 DLC CaOTP CtPAM IEN NN OKentU

6977. --- Dainų šventės šokiai ir žaidimai, 1955 m. [Song and Dance Festival, 1955] Respublikinės jubiliejinės dainų šventės repertuaras. [J. Lingys ir K. Poškaitis] Vilnius, VGLL, 1955. 303 p. illus. NN

6978. 25 dainos metai; nusipelnęs respublikos kolektyvas-Vilniaus valstybinio V. Kapsuko vardo universiteto akademinis choras. [Twenty-five years for the choir of the University of Vilnius... Leidinį sudarė: T. Ramanauskaitė-Pažusienė et al. Meninis redaktorius A. Jurėnas] Vilnius, Vaga, 1965. 71 p. illus., facsims., map, ports. ML302.8.V542U54 DLC CaOONL

6979. GOTTHOLD, T. A. Über die Kanklys und die Volksmelodien der Lithauer. In Neue Preussische Pro-

vinzial-Blätter (Königsberg in Pr.),
v.4, 1847, p. 242-256. See serials
consulted.

6980. JAKELAITIS, Vytautas. Lietuvos dainų šventės. [Lithuanian
song festivals] Vilnius, Mintis,
1970. 252 p. ML37.L5J3 PU

JUŠKA, Antanas. Lietuviš-
kos dainos. Vilnius, 1954. See
entry no. 6883-6884.

--- Lietuviškos svodbinės
dainos. Vilnius, 1955. See etnry
no. 6885-6886.

6981. --- Melodye ludowe litewskie, zebrane przez księdza Antoniego Juszkiewicza. Kraków, Wydawn.
Akademji Uniejętności, 1900. 1 v.
ports., facsims. 491.P22J984.4
PU BM CtY MB NN

KOLBERG, Oskar. Litwa.
[Warszawa, 1966] See entry no.
6894.

6982. LINGYS, Juozas. Dainų
šventės šokiai ir žaidimai. [Folk
dances and folk games at the song
and dance festival] Vilnius, VGLL,
1955. 306 p. illus.
793.31.L ICCC

6983. --- Dovanų šokis. Šalaba-
nas. [Gift dance. Šalabanas]
Vilnius, Lietuvos TSR Kultūros
ministerijos liaudies meno rūmai,
1964. 40 p. illus., music.
GV1688.L5L49 DLC

6984. --- Lietuvių liaudies šokiai. [Lithuanian folk dances]
Kaunas; Vilnius, VGLL, 1948-1959.
3 v. music. GV1688.L5L5 DLC
CaAEU(3) CaOTU(2) PU

6985. --- --- 2. laida. Chicago,
Ill., B. Pakštas ir J. Kreivėnas,
1954. GV1688.L5L5 1954 CaOTU PU

6986. --- Lietuvių liaudies
žaidimai. [Lithuanian folk games.
Kaunas] VGLL [1955] 197 p.
music., diagrs. GV1688.L5L52 DLC
ICBM ICCC ICLJF MH PU

6987. --- Litovskie narodnye
tantsy. 2-e dop., i perer. izd.
Pod red. Z. Slaviunasa. Vil'nius,
Gos. izd-vo polit. i nauch lit-ry
Litovskoi SSR, 1955. 308 p.
illus., col. plates. GV1688.L5L53
1955 PU NN

6988. --- O litovskikh narodnykh
tantsakh i khorovodakh. In His
Lietuvių liaudies šokiai. Vilnius,
1953. v.2, p. 5-40. GV1688.L5L5

v.2 DLC CaOTU PU

6989. --- Porelės, vestuvinis
liaudiškas šokis. [Porelės, wedding folk dance] Vilnius, Lietuvos TSR Kultūros ministerijos
liaudies meno rūmai, 1963 [i.e.,
1964] 50 p. illus.
GV1688.L5L54 DLC

6990. LITHUANIAN FOLK-DANCE
FESTIVAL, 3RD, CHICAGO, 1968.
Trečioji tautinių šokių šventė,
1968 m. liepos mėn. 7 d. [Pro-
grama. Redagavo Vytautas Radžius.
The third Lithuanian Folk-Dance
Festival in Chicago, Ill.] Chicago, Ill., Lietuvių bendruomenė,
1968. 112 p. illus. 184.L7L52
1968 PU ICBM OKentU

6991. LITHUANIAN FOLK SONGS AND
MUSIC. New York, N.Y. and Camden,
N.Y., 193- . 9 records in one
album. 10 in. 78 rps. Columbia
E 7025, E 7603, 1616035-F, 16038-F;
Victor 65116, 65123, 65128, 65130;
Odeon 26028. Music L713 NjP

6992. MORKŪNIENĖ, E. Lietuvių
liaudies choreografijos klasifikacija. The classification of Lithuanian folk choreography. In
LTSRMAD. Serija A, v.1(32), 1970,
p. 163-181. See serials consulted.

6993. --- Lietuvių liaudies
vestuvių choreografija XIX a. pabaigoje ir XX a. [The choreography of
Lithuanian folk-wedding customs at
the end of the nineteenth and in
the twentieth centuries] In
LTSRMAD. Serija A, v.1(32), 1970,
p. 183-198. See serials consulted.

6994. PALIULIS, Stasys. Lietuvių liaudies instrumentinė muzika.
Pučiamieji instrumentai. [Lithu-
anian folk music on woodwinds]
Vilnius, VGLL, 1959. 426 p.
illus., music. ML766.I4P24 DLC PU

6995. PETRUTIS, Petras, ed. Mūsų šokiai. [Our folk dances.
Chicago, Ill., Jungtinių Amerikos
Valstybių ir Kanados Lietuvių 1-
osios Tautinių šokių šventės komitetas, 1962] 261 p. illus.,
diagrs., music. GV1688.L5P4 DLC
CaAEU ICBM

6996. POŠKAITIS, Kazys, ed. Kas
rūtelę skynė; šokiai ir žaidimai.
[Who has gathered rue; folk dances.
Sudarė K. Poškaitis] Vilnius,
VGLL, 1961. 222 p. illus., music.
GV1688.L5P6 DLC

6997. PUTEIKIENĖ, Z. Sisteminis

lietuvių liaudies dainų melodijų katalogas. Sistematicheskii katalog melodii litovskikh narodnykh pesen'. In Literatūra ir kalba (Vilnius), v.9, 1968, p. 408-[429]. Summary in Russian. See serials consulted.

6998. RESPUBLIKINIAI LIAUDIES KŪRYBOS NAMAI. Lietuvių liaudies šokių ir žaidimų autorinis sąrašas. [An author list of works on Lithuanian folk dancing and games] Paruošė Lietuvos TSR Respublikinė choreografinė sekcija. Vilnius, 1957. 18 p. Z7514.D2R4 DLC

RHESA, Ludwig Jedemin, ed. and tr. Lietuvių liaudies dainos. Vilnius, 1958-64. See entry no. 6932.

6999. SABALIAUSKAS, Adolfas. Apie žiemių-rytiečių lietuvių tautinę muziką ir muzikos instrumentus. [On the North-East Lithuanian folk music and musical instruments] Vilnius, 1911. 15 p. 947.520.D4 CtTMF; also in Lietuvių tauta (Vilnius), v.2, no.1, 1911. See serials consulted.

7000. --- Lietuvių dainų ir giesmių gaidos. Mélodies des chansons populaires lithuaniennes. A. Sabaliauskas ir Aukusti Robert Niemi. Helsinkai, Suomių literatūros draugijos spaustuvė, 1916. xvi, 233 p. illus. music. M1766.L4S3 DLC PU

7001. --- Sutartinės ir mūsų muzikos įrankiai. [Harmony songs and our musical instruments. By Žalia Rūta, pseud.] In Dirva-Žinynas (Tilžė), v.4, 1904, p. 25-39. See serials consulted.

7002. SAUDARGIENĖ, Vlada R. Liaudies šokis Lietuvoje. [Folk dance in Lithuania. Minden in Westfalen, P.L.B. Vokietijos krašto valdyba, 1958] 140 p. GV1688.L5S3 PU

7003. SLAVIŪNAS, Zenonas. Lietuvių etnografinės muzikos bibliografija. [Bibliography of Lithuanian folk music] In Tautosakos darbai (Kaunas), v.5, 1938, p. 281-300. See serials consulted.

7004. --- Šokių ir žaidimų dainos. [Songs of dances and games] In LTSRMALKLI. Lietuvių tautosakos apybraiža. Vilnius, 1963. p. 241-253. GR203.L5L497 DLC CaAEU CU CtY ICU MH NN

7005. --- Sutartinės; daugiabal-

sės lietuvių liaudies dainos. Polyphonic Lithuanian folk songs] Vilnius, VGLL, 1958-59. 3 v. music. M1766.L4S6 DLC CtPAM(v.2,3) ICCC ICLJF PU

7006. --- Zur litauischen Vokalpolyponie. In Deutsches Jahrbuch für Volkskunde (Berlin), v.13, no.2, 1967, p. 223-243. See serials consulted.

7007. SUKTINIS; liaudies šokiai. [Folk dances] Vilnius, VGLL, 1959. 325 p. illus., music. GV1688.L5S9 DLC

7008. VECKENSTEDT, Edmund. La musique et la dansé dans les traditions des lithuaniens, des allemands et des greces... Paris, Au bureau de la traditions, etc., 1889. vii, 98 p. (Collection internationale de la tradition... v. 3) GR885.V3 v.3 DLC ICU

7009. ŽILEVICIUS, Juozas. Mažosios Lietuvos liaudies muzikos bruožai. [An outline of the folk music of Lithuania Minor] In Lithuanian Research Institute, New York, N.Y., Mažoji Lietuva. 1958. p. 259-282. DK511.L2L715 DLC CLU CaAEU

XIII.3.d. MANNERS AND CUSTOMS

7010. ALEKSA-ANGARIETIS, Zigmas. Šeimyniškas lietuvių gyvenimas Juškevičiaus dainose. [The Lithuanian family life in folk songs collected by Juškevičius] So. Boston, Mass., Spauda ir turtas "Keleivio", 1911. 118 p. 392.3.A126 PU

7011. AUGUSTAITIS, Dainė. Litauisches Brauchtum im Jahresverlauf vom Frühlingsanfang bis Herbstbeginn. In Die Welt der Slawen (Wiesbaden), v.12, no.4, 1967, p. 417-433. See serials consulted.

7012. BALDŽIUS, Juozas. Pirktinės vestuvės. [Contract-type marriage. By] J. Baldauskas. In Mūsų tautosaka (Kaunas), v.10, 1936. 123 p. See serials consulted.

7013. --- Vogtinės vestuvės. [Marriage by abduction] In KUHMF. Darbai ir dienos, v.9, 1940, p. 3-128. See serials consulted.

7014. BALYS, Jonas. Fastnachtbräuche in Litauen. In Schweizerisches Archiv für Volkskunde (Basel), v.45, no.1, 1948, p. 40-69. illus. See serials consulted.

7015. --- Gero ir pikto prado kova liaudies tradicijose. [The conflict of good and evil in folk traditions] Kaunas, Pažanga, 1938. 20 p. In Vairas (Kaunas), v.21, no. 11-12, 1937. See serials consulted.

7016. --- Kalėdų papročiai ir burtai. [Christmas customs and magic] In Mūsų tautosaka (Kaunas), v.1, 1930, p. 124-153. See serials consulted.

7017. --- Liaudies magija ir medicina. [Folk magic and folk medicine] Bloomington, Ind., Author, 1951. 94 p. (Lietuvių tautosakos lobynas, 2) GR203.L5B27 DLC CaAEU KU MH NN PPULC PU OOxM

7018. --- Litauische Hochzeitsbräuche. Hamburg [Baltic University] 1946. 78 p. (Contributions of Baltic University, 9) 392.5.B219 PU ICU CtY

7019. --- Litauische Volksbräuche; volkskundliche Skizzen. In Folkliv (Stockholm), v.12-13, 1948-49, p. 112-140. See serials consulted.

7020. --- Volkscharakter und Volksbräuche der Litauer. In Scholar (Heidelberg), no.1, 1947, p. 37-48. See serials consulted.

7021. BIRŽYS, Petras. Kaimo vestuvininkai. [The wedding in the village. By] Akiras. [pseud.] Kaunas, J. Balčiūnas, 1930. 27 p. 392A ICBM

7022. BURAČAS, Balys. Kupiškėnų vestuvės. [The wedding in the district of Kupiškis] In Tautosakos darbai (Kaunas), v.1, 1935, p. 195-278. See serials consulted.

7023. CALAND, W. Die vorchristlichen baltischen Totengebräuche. In Archiv für Religionswissenschaft (Freiburg in Br.), v.17, 1914, p. 476-512. See serials consulted.

7024. ČILVINAITĖ, Mariona. Vestuvės Upynos apylinkėje. [The wedding in the district of Upyna] In Gimtasai kraštas (Šiauliai), no.5-8, 1935, p. 238-242; p. 294-301, 371-378. See serials consulted.

7025. DARGIS, Alfonsas. Lietuvių vestuvių papročiai; tempera piešiniai. [Lithuanian wedding customs; paintings. Paaiškinamasis tekstas paimtas iš Baldausko. Göttingen, 1946] 1 v. illus. ND699.D37B3 DLC CtTMF ICBM OKentU PU

7026. DAUGIRDAS, Tadas. Pisanki, jajka malowane wielkanocne. T. Dow-

girdi i Zygmunt Wolski. In Wisła (Warszawa), v.4, 1890, p. 818-825.. See serials consulted.

7027. DEDELEV, A. Svatovstvo i svad'ba u litovtsev Sesikskoi volosti. Vilkomirskogo uiezda. In Pamiatnaia knizhka Kovenskoi gubernii na 1892 g. Kovna, 1891. p. 182-186. DK511.K55P32 DLC

7028. DOVYDAITIS, Jurgis. Vestuvių vaidinimai rytų Lietuvoje. [Wedding plays in East Lithuania] In Naujoji romuva (Kaunas), no.121, 1933, p. 398-399. See serials consulted.

7029. DUNDULIENĖ, Pranė. Rugiapiūtės pabaigtuvės Lietuvoje XIX-XX a. pradžioje. [The feast of the rye harvest in Lithuania in the nineteenth and the beginning of the twentieth centuries] In Vilna. Universitetas. Istorijos-filosofijos mokslų serija, v.5, 1958, p. 103-126. See serials consulted.

7030. ELISONAS, Jurgis. Burtai. [Witchcraft] In Tauta ir žodis (Kaunas), v.3, 1925, p. 341-363. See serials consulted.

7031. --- Kaimiečių pasveikinimų ir etiketo formos. [The forms of etiquette among the rural population] In Tautosakos darbai (Kaunas), v.1, 1935, p. 27-48. See serials consulted.

7032. GEISLER, V. Svadebnye obriady u litovtsev v Shadovskom prikhode Shavel'skogo uiezda. In Pamiatnaia knizhka Kovenskoi gubernii na 1899 g. Kovna, 1898. p. 90-104. DK511.K55P32 DLC

7033. GLEMŽAITĖ, Michalina. Kupiškėnų vestuvininkai. [Wedding customs of Kupiškis] Dotnuva, author, 1936. 16 p. 16 col. plates. 391.9475.G847.3 PU ICBM ICCC ICLJF OKentU

7034. HANUŠ, Ignác Jan. Über die alterthümliche Sitte der Angebinde bei Deutschen, Slaven und Litauern. Als ein Beitrag zur comparative deutsch-slavischen Archäologie entworfen von I.J. Hanuš. Prag, Druck von C. Bellmann, 1855. 42 p. GT3050.H3 DLC OCl

7035. HARTKNOCH, Christoph. Alt und neues Preussen; oder, Preussischen Historien... zwei Teile. Frankfurt; Königsberg, Druckts J. Andrae, 1684. 2 v. in 1. (668 p.) 4K2489 DLC ICU ICN MdBP PU

7036. JUŠKA, Antanas. Hochzeitbräuche der wielonischen Litauer, beschrieben im Jahre 1870 [von Anton IUshkevich] übers. im Jahre 1888 von Arved Petry, unter der Redaktion des Professors J. Baudoin de Courtenay. [Heidelberg, 1891] [2], 135-383 p. OCl

7037. ---, ed. Svodbinė rėda Veluonyčiu Lietuviu, surašyta par Antáną Juškevičę 1870 metuose. [Lithuanian wedding customs in the district of Veliuona] Kazan', Tip. Imperatorskogo universiteta, 1880. 120 p. (Kazan'. Universitet. Uchenye zapiski, ianvar'fevral'. Prilozheniia) 491.922.J984.2 PU CtTMF MH

7038. --- Wesele litewskie z okolic Wielony. [Translated by] Jan Karłowicz i Iz. Kopernicki. In Wisła (Warszawa), v.7, 1893, p. 443-493, 703-719; v.8, 1894, p. 114-131, 419-434. See serials consulted.

7039. KRĖVĖ-MICKEVIČIUS, Vincas. Dzūku vestuvės. [Wedding customs in Dzūkija] In Mūsu tautosaka (Kaunas), v.2, 1930, p. 17-93. See serials consulted.

7040. --- Krikštynu apeigos Dzūkijoje. [Baptizing customs in Dzukija] In Mūsu tautosaka (Kaunas), v.7, 1933, p. 30-46. See serials consulted.

7041. KULIKAUSKIENĖ, Regina (Volkaitė). Pogrebeniia s koniami u drevnikh litovtsev. In Sovetskaia arkheologiia (Moskva), v.16, 1953, p. 211-222. See serials consulted.

7042. LANGE, Erwin R. Sterben und Begräbnis im Volksglauben zwischen Weichsel und Memel. Würzburg, Holzner-Verlag, 1955. 176 p. (Beihefte zum Jahrbuch der Albertus-Universität, Königsberg in Pr., 15) GT3242.L3 DLC CSt PU

7043. LAUTENBACHS, Jėkabs. Litauische und lettische Verwünschungen und Flüchte. In Magazin der Lettisch-literarischen Gesellschaft (Riga), v.20, 1905, p. 31-55. See serials consulted.

LEPNER, Theodor. Der preusche Littauer; oder, Vorstellung der Nahmens-Herleitung, Kind-Tauffen ... Danzig, 1744. See entry no. 6566-6567.

7044. MANSIKKA, Viljo Johannes. Litauische Zaubersprüche. Helsinki, Suomalainen tiedeakatemia, 1929. 116 p. ([Folklore fellows] FF communications, no. 87) See serials consulted.

7045. MEŠKAUSKAS, Pranas. Volksbräuche; Niederkunft, Taufe, Hochzeit und Begräbnis der preuss. Litauer. Tilsit, "Lituania", 1936. 66 p. Thesis--University of Leipzig. 491.92.Sa33 PU CtY MH NNC

MICHALONIS LITUANUS. Apie totoriu, lietuviu ir maskvėnu papročius... Vilnius, 1966. See entry no. 839.

7046. MICKEVIČIUS, Juozas. Žemaičiu krikštynos. [Baptizing customs in Samogitia] In Tautosakos darbai (Kaunas), v.1, 1935, p. 86-111. See serials consulted.

7047. --- Žemaižiu vestuvės. [Wedding customs in Samogitia] In Mūsu tautosaka (Kaunas), no.8, 1933, p. 47-125. See serials consulted.

7048. MIŠKINIS, Jonas. Trys šimtai dzūku burtu ir prietaru. [Three hundred formulas of fortune telling and superstition in Dzūkija] In Tauta ir žodis (Kaunas), v.4, 1926, p. 463-475. See serials consulted.

7049. NEZABITAUSKIS, Liudvikas. Talkos žemaičiuose. [Collective assistance customs in Samogitia] In Tautosakos darbai (Kaunas), v.1, 1935, p. 112-127. See serials consulted.

7050. PETRULIS, Juozas (1904-). Rugiapiūtės papročiai. [Harvest customs] In Mūsu tautosaka (Kaunas), v.8, 1934, p. 87-135. See serials consulted.

7051. PIUS, Helen and Frank Zapolis. Lithuanian Christmas tree ornaments. [Chicago, Ill.] 1969. 12 p. illus. 392.P ICBM

7052. SENN, Alfred. Notes on religious folklore in Lithuania. In Slavic Studies, ed. by A. Kaun and E. J. Simmons. Ithaca, N.Y., Cornell University Press, 1943. p. 162-179. PG14.N6 DLC NIC

7053. ŠINKŪNAS, Peliksas. Lietuviškieji žavėtojai. [The Lithuanian charmers] In Mokykla ir gyvenimas (Kaunas), no.6(79), 1930, p. 293-301. See serials consulted.

7054. SVODBOS DAINOS. [Wedding songs] Chicago, Ill., 1916. 32 p. 784.S2 CtTMF

7055. TETZNER, Franz Oskar.
Feste und Spiele der Litauer. In
Globus (Hildburghausen; Brunswick),
v.73, 1898, p. 317-323. See
serials consulted.

7056. TYSZKIEWICZ, Eustachy.
Obrazy domowego pożycia na Litwie.
Pan Choraszcza. Wilno. 1842.
BM(1206 h. 14.)

7057. VOL'TER, Eduard Aleksandrovich. Zur Geschichte des litauisch-
en Hexenwesens. In LLGM, v.4, 1897,
p. 375-382. See serials consulted.

7058. VYŠNIAUSKAITĖ, Angėlė. Lai-
dotuvių papročiai Lietuvoje XIX-XX
a. pirmaisias dešimtmečiais. [The
burial customs in Lithuania in the
19th and the beginning of the 20th
centuries] In LTSRMAIILKI, v.3,
1961, p. 132-157. See serials
consulted.

--- Lietuvių šeimos tradicijos. Vilnius, 1967. See entry
no. 6959.

7059. --- Šeima ir visuomeninis gyvenimas. [Family and community] In
LTSRMAII. Lietuvių etnografijos
bruožai. Vilnius, 1964. p. 437-
[562] illus. HD725.7.L488 DLC CaAEU
CtY ICU ICLJF MH NN PU

7060. WITORT, Jan. Kucya na
Litwie. [Christmas Eve in Lithu-
ania] In Lud (Lwów), v.3, 1897,
p. 1-6. See serials consulted.

7061. WOYCKE, August, ed. Sitten-
und Charakterbilder aus Polen &
Lithauen, mit biographischen Notizen.
Berlin, 1862. 2 v. in 1.
914.75.W91 IU CtY NNC

7062. YLA, Stasys, 1908- .
Kūčios, prasmė, simboliai, maldos.
[Christmas Eve, its meaning and
religious customs] Putnam, Conn.,
Immaculata Press [n.d.] 20 p.
390.Y ICBM

7063. ŽEMAITIENĖ, Uršulė. Wedding customs of Suvalkiečiai. Suvalkiečių vestuvės. Redagavo Jonas
Balys. Cleveland, Ohio, 1953. 76,
[4] p. [A Treasure of Lithuanian
folklore, 3] GT2771.L8Z4 DLC CaAEU
ICCC OKentU

XIII.3.e. MATERIAL CULTURE

XII.3.e.1. NATIONAL COSTUMES, WEAV-
ING, ORNAMENTS, ETC.

7064. AUDINIAI. [Fabrics of the
folk art of weaving. Sudarė ir
paruošė J. Balčikonis, M. Glemžaitė et al. Vilnius] VGLL, 1957-
62. 2 v. (chiefly illus.) Lietuvių liaudies menas) Lithuanian
and Russian. NK8856.A9 DLC CaOTU
CtPAM CtY ICBM ICLJF IEN IU MB NN
PPiU PU

7065. BALČIKONIS, Juozas (1924-).
Audinių raštai. [The patterns of
the folk art of weaving] Vilnius,
VPMLL, 1961. 214 p. illus. Bi-
bliography: p. 214. NK8856.B3
DLC PU

7066. BRENSZTEJN, Michał Eustachy.
The peasant art of Lithuania. In
Holme, Chr. Peasant art in Russia.
New York, N.Y., 1912. p. 47-52 and
plates no. 518-550. NK975.H6 DLC
MiU NIC NN OCl OCU OU PP PPD PPL
PU-Mu TU NjP

7067. ČEPELYTĖ, Emilija. Ausk,
seselė, drobeles. [Let's weave
linen, sister] Vilnius, VGLL,
1960. 163 p. illus. 745.52.C338
PU

7068. ČILVINAITĖ, Marijona. Moterų išeiginiai ir dėvimieji drabužiai bei papuošalai Girdiškės
apylinkėje. [The Sunday best and
everyday dresses of women and their
jewellry in the district of Gir-
diškė] In Gimtasai kraštas (Šiauliai), no.4-5, 1935, p. 353-356.
See serials consulted.

7069. GLEMŽAITĖ, Mikalina. Lietuvių moterų tautinai drabužiai.
[The national costumes of the Lithuanian women] Kaunas, Moterų šaulių taryba, 1939. 28 p. illus.,
drawings (unpaged). 709.1.GL
ICLJF CtPAM CtTMF ICCC ICBM NNC
OKentU PU

7070. --- Lietuvių tautiniai drabužiai. [Lithuanian national cos-
tumes] Vilnius, VPMLL, 1955. 205
p. illus., col. plates.
GT1330.L5G55 DLC ICLJF CtY ICCC NN
PPiU PU

7071. --- Narodnoe priadenie i
tkachestvo litovtsev: po materialam
Kupishkskogo raiona Shiauliaiskoi
oblasti Litovskoi SSR. In Akademiia nauk SSR. Institut etnografii.
Kratkie soobshcheniia, v.15, 1952,

p. 39-51. See serials consulted.

7072. --- Verpimo ir audimo tradicijos Lietuvoje. [The traditions of spinning and weaving in Lithuania] In LTSRMAIILKI. Iš Lietuvių kultūros istorijos, v.1, 1958, p. 212-227. Summary in Russian p. 303-304. See serials consulted.

7073. JUOSTOS. [Sashes. Sudarė ir parengė A. Mikėnaitė, J. Balčikonis. Redakcinė komisija J. Kuzminskis, L. Vaineikytė, A. Venclova. Dailininkas V. Bačėnas] Vilnius, Vaga, 1969. xxiv, 195 p. chiefly illus., part. col. (Lietuvių liaudies menas) NK8856.J84 PU CaAEU DLC ICBM

7074. KLIKŪNAITĖ, Ona. Rankdarbai. [Knitting and crocheting] Vilnius, VPMLL, 1959. 275 p. illus., plates (part. col.) TT750.K63 DLC

7075. KULIKAUSKIENĖ, Regina (Volkaitė). Senovės lietuvių moterų galvos danga ir jos papuošalai. [The ancient Lithuanian head dress for women and its ornaments] In LTSRMAIILKI, v.2, 1959, p. 30-53. See serials consulted.

7076. LIETUVIŠKŲ JUOSTŲ RAŠTAI. [Patterns of Lithuanian woven sashes] Kaunas, Žiedas [1928] 40 plates (in portfolio) Preface signed by P. Galaunė. NK9256.L5 DLC

7077. MARGINIAI. KAUNAS, BENDROVĖ MARGINIAI [1936.] 87 samples of the national costumes' fabrics arranged by districts of Lithuania. CtPAM

7078. MASIONYTĖ, M. Drabužiai. [Attire] In LTSRMAII. Lietuvių etnografijos bruožai. Vilnius, 1964. p. 332-[385] illus. HD725.7.L488 DLC CaAEU CtY ICLJF ICU MH NN PU

7079. NIUNKIENĖ, G. (Tallat-Kelpšaitė). Audiniai ir jų gamyba. [Gewebe und ihre Anfertigung] In LTSRMAII. Lietuvių etnografijos bruožai. Vilnius, 1964. p. 286-[331] illus. HD725.7.L488 DLC CaAEU CtY ICLJF ICU MH NN PU

7080. --- Lietuvių liaudies audiniai. [The Lithuanian national weaving] In LTSRMAD. Serija A, v. 1(20), 1966, p. 107-120, illus. Summary in Russian. See serials consulted.

7081. REKLAITIS, Povilas Viktoras. Die graphischen Trachtdarstellungen der Litauer im 16. Jahrhundert. In Commentationes Balticae (Bonn), v.11-13, no.3, 1967. See serials consulted.

7082. SAUERVEINAS, Georg Julius Justus. Über littauisches Volksthum und littauische Volkstracht. Von Girėnas [pseud.] Tilsit, O. v. Mauderode, 1894. 48 p. plates. 447.5.C443u OCl MiD

7083. SENOVĖS LIETUVIŲ PAPUOŠALAI. [Lithuanian ornaments and decorations of the past. Sudarė ir paruošė: R. Kulikauskienė ir R. Rimantienė. Red. komisija J. Kuzminskis, L. Vaineikytė, A. Venclova] Vilnius, Vaga, 1958-1966. 2 v. illus. (Lietuvių liaudies menas) NK976.L5S4 DLC CaOTP CtPAM IEN OKentU PU

7084. TAMOŠAITIENĖ, Anastazija. Mūsų rankdarbiai. [Our handicrafts] Kaunas, "Naujosios Vaidilutės" leidinys, 1939. 56 p. illus. 745.5.T ICCC

7085. --- Namie austi drabužiai. [Hand-woven garments] Kaunas, Žemės ūkio rūmų leidinys, 1935. 60 p. 947.52.T155 PU

7086. --- Tapestries, weaving, knitting. [n.p.] Romuva, 1948. 4p. 13 mount. illus. NK3056.T15 CaOKQ CLSU PU

7087. TAMOŠAITIS, Antanas. Austiniai kilimai. [Woven rugs] Kaunas, Žemės ūkio rūmų leidinys, 1935. 81 p. illus. 745.52.T ICCC ICBM

7088. --- Lietuvių moterų tautiniai drabužiai. [The folk costumes of the Lithuanian women] Kaunas, Žemės ūkio rūmai, 1939. 206 p. 746T ICBM

7089. --- Sodžiaus pramonė; austiniai kilimai. [Rural industry; woven rugs] Kaunas, Žemės ūkio rūmai, 1935. 80 p. illus. 700Tl CtTMF

7090. --- Sodžiaus pramonė; staltiesės. [Rural industry; tablecloths] Kaunas, Žemės ūkio rūmai, 1935. 78 p. illus. 700T2 CtTMF

7091. TARVYDAS, Balys. Senovės gintarinių papuošalų rinkinys. [The collection of the ancient amber jewellery and adornments] In Gimtasai kraštas (Šiauliai), no.1(13), 1937, p. 46-56. See serials consulted.

7092. TAUTINIAI DRABUŽIAI IR JUOStų raštai. [The patterns of the national costumes and sashes. Tautinių drabužių aprašymą parašė Antanas Ta-

mošaitis. Juostų audimo instrukci-
jas parašė Nina Nenortienė. New
York, N.Y., 1965. 41 p.
GT1330.L5T38 PU

7093. TRINKA, Vladas. Prieškarinė
mergaitė sekmadienį. [The Sunday
dress of a girl before the First
World War] In Gimtasai kraštas(Šiauliai), no.2-4, 1936, p. 508-510.
See serials consulted.

7094. VIJEIKIS, Vladas. Lietuvių
tautinės puošmenos. [Lithuanian national jewellery and adornaments.
Chicago, Ill., J. Karvelis, 1957]
41 p. illus. NK1456.V55 DLC CaOTU
CtY OKentU

7095. VILNA. VALSTYBINIS DAILĖS
MUZIEJUS. Juostos; katalogas. [A
catalogue of sashes. Sudarė A. Mi-
kėnaitė. Spaudai parengė S. Jakštas]
Vilnius, 1967. 123 p. illus.
NK8856.V5 PU

7096. WAETZOLD, D. Zur Tracht der
Bewohner des Memelgebiets in der Eisenzeit. In Altertumsgesellschaft
Prussia (Königsberg in Prussia), v.3,
no.4, 1939, p. 116-120. See serials
consulted.

7097. Žirgulienė, Klementina. Mez-
giniai. [Knitting. Vilnius] VPMLL,
1958. 286 p. illus (part. col.)
NN

XIII.3.e.2. FOLK ART, WOOD CARVING,
CROSSES, ETC.

7098. BALTRUŠAITIS, Jurgis, 1903-.
Lithuanian folk art. Editor: T.J.
Vizgirda. 256 illus. [München, 1948]
80 p., 82 plates. (Lithuania, coun-
try and nation, 3) NK976.L5B3 DLC
CaAEU CaBVaU CtU CtY CtTMF CaOTU ICBM
IC ICLJF MH NIC NN NFQC Or OCIND
OKentU PPiU PPULC PU PU-FA UU WaS WyU

7099. BALYS, Jonas. Liaudies or-
namentai ir kryžių kilmė. [Folk ornaments and the origin of ornamental
crosses] In Margutis (Chicago, Ill.)
no.6-7, 1957. See serials consulted.

7100. BEZZENBERGER, Adalbert. Über
Grabkreutzformen. In LLGM, v.2,1887,
p. 34-79,629-633. See serials consulted.

7101. BRENSZTEJN, Michał Eustachy.
Krzyże i kapliczki żmudzkie; materjały do sztuki ludowej na Litwie. Kraków, Nakł. Akademii Umiejętności,
1906. 16 p. plates. 947.52.B757.2
PU PPULC

--- The peasant art of Lithuania. London, 1912. See entry
no. 7066.

7102. ČERBULĖNAS, Klemensas. Razvitie litovskogo narodnogo derevian-
nogo zodchestva i ego osnovnye cherty. In Akademiia nauk SSSR. Institut etnografii. Kratkie soobshcheniia, v.12, 1950, p. 62-73. See serials consulted.

7103. --- Tautinis elementas lietuvių kryžiuose. [National element
in the Lithuanian crosses] In Naujoji romuva (Kaunas), no.4-5, 1937, p.
87-92. See serials consulted.

7104. DANIŁOWICZ, Casimir de. La
lituanie artistique; pub. par les
soins du Bureau d'information de Lituanie. Lausanne, Librairie centrale des nationalités, 1919. 71 p.
illus., plates. Delegation propaganda: Lithuania miscellanea.
D643.A7DP6L7D186 CSt-H DLC-P4 DNW IU
MH NN OCl PU

7105. DAUZVARDIS, Josephine J.
Popular Lithuanian recipes. [2d rev.
ed.] Chicago, Ill., 1955. [i.e.
1958] 128 p. illus. TX725.D33 1958
DLC CU WaS

7106. DUNDULIENĖ, Pranė. Arimo į-
rankiai Lietuvoje feodalizmo laiko-
tarpy. [The ploughing implements in
Lithuania during the feudal period]
In Vilna. Universitetas. Istorijos-
filologijos mokslų serija. Vilnius,
1955. v.2. (Its Mokslo darbai).
See serials consulted.

7107. DYMOWSKI, Witold. Barwne
kufry chlopskie z okolic Wileńszczy-
ny i Polesia. Die vielfarbigen Bau-
ernkoffer auf dem Gebiete von Wilna
und in Polesien. Wilno, 1934. 64 p.
(Instytut Naukowo-Badawczy Europy
Wschodniej. Sekcija Etnologiczna.
Wydawnictwa, nr.1) NK2725.D9 DLC BM

7108. --- Sztuka ludowa Wileńszczyzny i Nowogródszczyzny. Wilno, Skład
Główny w Księgarni Šw. Wojciecha,
1935. 40 p. (Wilno. Kuratorjum O-
kręgu Szkolnego. Bibljoteczka Poradni Dydaktyczno-Wychowawczej. Serja
2., nr.4) Bibliography: p. 39-40.
NN

7109. FELDON, Victoria. Lithuanian folk art; an exhibition presented by the Museum and Laboratories
of Ethnic Arts and Technology at the
University of California, Los Angeles. UCLA Art Galleries. November
21, 1966-January 15, 1967. [Los Angeles, Calif., 1966] 1 v. plates.

NK976.L5F4 DLC ICU IaU MeU NNC NjP
NdU NcU PPiU PU TU TxDaM

7110. --- On American and Lithuanian folk art. In Lituanus (Chicago, Ill.), v.13, no.2, 1967, p. 65-
72. See serials consulted.

7111. GALAUNĖ, Paulius. L'art lithuanien; un recueil d'images avec
une introduction par P. Galaunė.
Editeur: John Kroon. Malmö, Malmö
ljustrycksanstalt [1934] 180 p.
(chiefly plates) 709.475.G132.2 PU
CtY CtTMF ICLJF InU NNC OKentU PU

7112. --- L'art populaire lithuanien. In L'Art Vivant (Paris), no.
82, 1928, p. 386-391. See serials
consulted.

7113. --- Lietuvių liaudies menas,
jo meninių formų plėtojimosi pagrindai. [Lithuanian folk art and its
development...] Kaunas, Lietuvos
Universiteto humanitarinių mokslų fakulteto leidinys, 1930. 301 p., 131
illus., 43 plates. Bibliography: p.
275-278. 700.G3 CtTMF ICCC NN

7114. --- --- 2. leidimas. Čikaga,
J. Karvelis, 1956. 301 p. illus.
Added title page: Lithuanian folk
art. Bibliography: p. 275-287.
NK976.L5G3 1956 DLC CaAEU CaOTP CaOTU
CU CtY ICCC NN OCl PU

7115. --- Litauens konst en över-
sikt i bilder med inledande text av
P. Galaunė och J. Vienožinskis. Ut-
givare John Kroon. Malmö, Malmö
ljustrycksanstalt [1931] 168 p.
illus. 947.52.G132.2 PU NN

7116. GIMBUTAS, Jurgis. Mažosios
Lietuvos krikštų formos. [Typical
forms of tomb monuments in Lithuania
Minor] In Lituanistikos darbai (Chicago, Ill.), v.1, 1966, p. 19-47.
illus. Summary in English. Bibliography: p. 41-42. See serials consulted.

7117. GIMBUTAS, Marija (Alseikaitė)
Ancient symbolism in Lithuanian folk
art. Philadelphia, Pa., American
Folklore Society, 1958. 148 p. illus.
(Memoirs of the American Folklore So-
ciety, 49) Bibliography: p. 139-148.
GR1.A5 v.49 DLC CaAEU CaOG CU CSt
CtY ICN IEN IaU NbU NcD NcU NN NNC
NmU NdFA NjP NjR OC PP PPiU PU TxU
ViU WaU

7118. --- Lietuvių liaudies meno
simbolių kilmės klausimu. [The origin of symbols of the Lithuanian
folk art] In Aidai (Brooklyn, N.Y.),
no.8(84), 1955, p. 310-315. See serials consulted.

7119. --- The origins of folk art.
In Lituanus (Brooklyn, N.Y.), v.7,
no.1, 1961, p. 13-17. See serials
consulted.

7120. GINET-PIŁSUDZKI, Bronisław.
Les croix lithuaniennes. Basel,
1916. 13 p. Offprint from Schweizerisches Archiv für Volkskunde (Basel), v.20, 1916, p. 246-258. See
serials consulted.

7121. GRINIUS, Jonas. Die Herkunft
der litauischen Kreuze. Bonn, Baltisches Forschungsinstitut, 1957.
45 p. illus. In Commentationes
Balticae (Bonn), III:2) See serials
consulted.

7122. --- Lietuvos kryžiai ir kop-
lytėlės. Les croix et les chapelles
lituaniennes. In LKMAM, v.5, 1970,
p. 1-182. See serials consulted.

7123. JAROŠEVIČIUS, Antanas. Lietuvių kryžiai. Croix lithuaniennes.
Surinko Antanas Jaroševičius. Įžangą parašė J. Basanavičius, vinjetes
iš tautinių motyvų sutaisė A. Žmuidzinavičius. Vilnius, 1912. 36 p.
illus. Text in Lithuanian and French
in parallel columns. DK511.L21B37
CtY CU ICCC NN PU WaU

7125. KALVAITIS, Vilius. Lietuvos
kanklės. [The Lithuanian kanklės]
Tilžė, V. Kalvaitis, 1895. 105 p. CtY

7126. KAUNAS. VYTAUTO DIDŽIOJO
KULTŪROS MUZIEJUS. M.K. ČIURLIONIES
GALERIJA. Lietuvių liaudies raiži-
nių katalogas. [The catalogue of
Lithuanian folk art; woodcarvings]
Sudarė P. Galaunė. Kaunas, 1927.
57 p. 708.9475.K164 PU

7127. KONČIUS, Ignas. Medžio dro-
žiniai gimtajam kraštui atsiminti.
[Woodcuts] Dorchester, Mass., L.J.
Končius, 1954. 223 p. (chiefly
illus.) NK9789.K6A47 DLC CtPAM CtTMF
ICBM ICLJF NcD PU

7128. --- Žemaičių kryžiai ir kop-
lytėlės. [The crosses and shrines
of Samogitia] Chicago, Ill., Tėviškėlė, 1965. 176 p. illus.
BX2320.K82 CaAEU CaOTU ICBM PU

7129. KRASZEWSKI, Józef Ignacy.
Sztuka u słowian, szczególnie w Pols-
ce i Litwie przedchrześcjańskiej.
Wilno, A.H. Kirkor, 1860. 391 p.
N6991.K7 DLC MH

7130. KURSCHAT, Alexander Theodor.
Haus- und Küchengerät im preussischen
Litauen. In LLGM, v.5, Hft.29, 1911,
p. 424-443. PG8503.L7 DLC CU CtY MH
MiU NjP

7131. LIETUVIŲ LIAUDIES MENAS.
[Lithuanian folk art. Sudarė ir paruošė J. Balčikonis, M. Glemžaitė et
al.] Vilnius, VGLL, 1956- . illus.,
plates. Contents.--Medžio dirbiniai,
1956-58, kn.1-2.--Audiniai, 1957-62,
kn.1-2.--Architektūra, 1957-65, kn.
1-2.--Senovės lietuvių papuošalai,
1958-66, kn.1-2.--Keramika, 1959.--
Skulptūra, 1963-65, kn.1-2.--Grafi-
ka, 1968.--Juostos, 1969.--Mažoji
architektūra, 1970- , kn.1- .
NK976.L5L5 DLC CtY IEN IU MB NN
PPiU OKentU

7132. LIETUVOS TSR LIAUDIES MENO
RŪMAI. Auksinės rankos; liaudies
dailės meistrai Tarybų Lietuvos
25-mečiui. [Masters of the Lithuanian national art. Sudarė: D. Bru-
sokienė, M. Žilevičienė, A. Valiuškevičiūtė. Atsakingasis redaktorius
S. Sverdiolas] Vilnius, 1965. 1 v.
illus. NK976.L5L2 DLC

     LIETUVOS TSR MOKSLŲ AKADEMI-
JA, VILNA. ISTORIJOS INSTITUTAS.
Lietuvių etnografijos bruožai. Vil-
nius, 1964. See entry no. 2234.

7133. LINGIS, Juozas. Arklas Baltų srityse. [The plow in the Baltic
area] In Lithuanian Research Institute, New York, N.Y. Mažoji Lietuva.
New York, N.Y., 1958. p. 123-149.
DK511.L2L715 DLC CLU CaAEU

7134. LITAUISK FOLKEKUNST; udstilling udlånt af Čiurlionis Museum i
Kaunas. April-Maj 1933. København,
1933. 24 p. plates. (Copenhagen.
Danske Kunstindustrimuseum)
947.52.C793 PU

7135. ŁOWMIAŃSKI, Henryk. Przyczynki do kwestji najstarszych ksz-
tałtów wsi litewskiej. In Ateneum
Wileńskie (Wilno), v.7, no.3-4,
1929, p. 293-336. See serials consulted.

7136. MALMÖ, SWEDEN. MUSEUM. Ut-
ställing av litauisk folkkonst från
Čiurlionis galleri i Kaunas; katalog
December 31, 1931. 23 p.
WA10223 CtY

7137. MAŽIULIS, Antanas Juozas.
Lietuviškasis kryžius ir jo kilmė.
[The Lithuanian wayside cross and
its origin] In Aidai (Kennebunkport,
Me.), no.2, 1951, p. 60-70. illus.
See serials consulted.

7138. --- Lietuvių gyvenos metmenys. [The outline of Lithuanian et-
nography] In Lituanistikos darbai
(Chicago, Ill.), v.1, 1966, p. 133-
149. See serials consulted.

7139. MILIUS, Vacius. Kaimo ama-
tai. Ländliche Handwerke. In
LTSRMAII. Lietuvių etnografijos
bruožai. Vilnius, 1964. p. 386-
[416] illus. HD725.7.L488 DLC
CaAEU CtY ICLJF ICU MH NN PU

7140. --- Maistas ir namų apyvokos
daiktai. [Nahrung und Hausgeräte]
In LTSRMAII. Lietuvių etnografijos
bruožai. Vilnius, 1964. p. 386-
[416] illus. HD725.7.L488 DLC CtY
CaAEU ICLJF ICU MH NN PU

7141. --- Pishcha i domashniaia
otvar' litovskikh krest'ian v XIX
i nachale XX v. In Baltiiskii etnograficheskii sbornik (Moskva), 1956,
p. 127-169. (Akademiia nauk SSSR.
Institut etnografii. Trudy. Novaia
seriia, t.32) See serials consulted.

7142. MULEVIČIENĖ, I. Puodų ženklai Lietuvos teritorijoje XII-XVI
amžiais. [The patterns on the pots
from the 12th-16th centuries in Li-
thuania] Summaries in English and
Russian. In LTSRMAD. Serija A,
v.1(32), 1970, p. 135-144. See serials consulted.

7143. NAGEVIČIUS, Vladas. Mūsų
pajūrio medžiaginė kultūra VIII-XIII
amž. Pryšmančių ir kitų vietų kasinėjimai. [Our material culture of
the 8th-13th centuries at the sea
coast; excavations at Pryšmančiai
and other places] In Senovė (Kaunas), no.1, 1935, p. 1-60,75-124.
See serials consulted.

7144. NAKAITĖ, Laimutė. Senovės
lietuvių sidabriniai papuošalai.
[The silver jewellery and adornaments
of the ancien Lithuanians] In
LTSRMAIILKI, v.2, 1959, p. 54-69.
See serials consulted.

7145. PARIS. MUSEÉ d'ETHNOGRAPHIE.
Guide de l'exposition d'art populaire baltique: Estonia, Lettonia, Lithuania. Paris, 1935. 1 v. (unpaged)
Museum PAM PU

7146. REKLAITIS, Povilas Viktoras.
Iconography of the Lithuanian peasant in Lithuania Minor. In Lituanus (Brooklyn, N.Y.), v.10, no.1,
1964, p. 61-71. See serials consulted.

7147. RIMANTIENĖ, Rimutė (Jablonskytė) Ankstyvojo geležies amžiaus
Lapainios puodžiai. [The ceramics
from Lapainiai of the early Iron
Age] In LTSRMAIILKI, v.3, 1961,
p.3-15. See serials consulted.

7148. RŪKŠTELĖ, Antanas. Lietuvių

tautodailė. [Lithuanian folk art]
Kaunas, Lietuvių tautodailės draugija, 1929. 103 p. illus.
947.52.R857 PU CtTMF ICCC NN OCl WaU

7149. SACHS, Curt. Die litauischen
Musikinstrumente in der Klg. Sam-
mlung für Deutsche Volkskunde zu
Berlin. In Internationales Archiv
für Etnographie (Berlin), v.23, no.
1, 1915, p. 1-7. GN1.I6 v.23 DLC
CU CtY DSG DSI-E ICU IU MH-P MnU NN
NNC NbU NjP OU PPAP TxU WaU

7150. SALVATORI, Giuseppe. L'arte
rustica e populare in Lituania.
Milano, Grandi Edizione Artistiche
[1925] 44 p. illus., plates.
Q947.52.Sa35.3 PU CaOTU WaU

7151. --- Rustic and popular art
in Lithuania. Milano, Gea [1925]
43, [5] p. illus., plates.
N7255.L5S3 DLC ICLJF IEN MH MoU NN
PP PU-Pe PPi ViU WaU

7152. ŠEIMININKĖS VADOVAS. 2.
leidimas. [A guide for the house-
wife. Autorių kolektyvas: VI. Lašas
et al. Sudarytoja E. Drąsutienė.]
Vilnius, VPMLL, 1959. 742 p.
illus. TX145.S52 1959 DLC

7153. SLAVIŪNAS, Zenonas. Lietuvių kanklės. [Lithuanian kanklės]
In Tautosakos darbai (Kaunas), v.
3, 1937, p. 244-320. See serials
consulted.

7154. SODŽIAUS MENAS. [Rustic
art. Redagavo Antanas Tamošaitis]
Kaunas, Žemės ūkio rūmai, 1931-39.
8 v. illus., plates. Contents.--
v.1. Rinktiniai audiniai.--v.2.
Prijuostės.--v.3. Liaudies meno
dirbinių raštai.--v.4. Juostos.--v.
5. Mezgimo-nėrimo raštai.--v.6.
Senoviškų rankdarbių raštai.
Q947.52.So13 PU CaOONL(1-2,4)
CtPAM(3) ICBM ICCC(1-6) NNC(1-4)

7155. STEPULIS, Pranas. Kanklės.
[Kanklės; a music instrument] Vilnius, VGLL, 1955. 225 p. illus.,
music, ports. ML509.S8 DLC CtPAM
PU

7156. VALGIŲ GAMINIMAS. [Lithu-
anian cookery. By E. Drąsutienė et
al.] Vilnius, VPMLL, 1956. 545,
[3] p. illus. TX725.V185 DLC CaOTP

7157. ŽILEVIČIUS, Juozas. Liaudies muzikos instrumentai. [Folk
music instruments in Lithuania] In
Lietuvių enciklopedija. Boston,
Mass., 1968. p. 487-493. For
holdings see entry 216.

7158. --- Native Lithuanian musical instruments. In Lituanus
(Brooklyn, N.Y.), no.1(10), 1957,
p. 12-15. See serials consulted.

7159. ZNAMIEROWSKA-PRÜFFEROWA,
Maria. Rybackie narzędzia kolne w
Polsce i w krajach sąsiednich.
Toruń, 1957. 325 p. illus., maps.
(Studia Societatis Scientiarum
Toruniensis, Toruń, Polonia. Sup-
plementum, 4) Summary in English
and Russian. Bibliography: p. 265-
274. SH458.Z58 DLC CLU DSI ICU NN

7160. --- Rybołówstwo jezior
Trockich. Die Fischerei auf den
Troker Seen; eine ethnographische
Skizze. Wilno, Nakładem Towarzys-
twa Przyjaciół Nauk w Wilnie, 1930.
105 p. illus., plates, tables.
(Towarzystwo Przyjaciół Nauk w
Wilnie. Wydział I. Rozprawy i
materjały, t.3, zesz. 2) See
serials consulted.

7161. --- Thrusting implements
for fishing in Poland and neighbor-
ing countries. Tr. from Polish by
J. Bachrach. Warsaw, Scientific
Publications Foreign Cooperation
Center of the Central Inst. for
Scientific, Technical and Economic
Information, 1966. 536 p. illus.,
maps. Bibliography: p. 412-430.
GN447.H29Z573 DLC CLSU CtY CoFS ICU
IU IaAS KMK NIC WaU

XIII.4. LANGUAGE

XIII.4.a. BIBLIOGRAPHIES AND GUIDES
           TO LITHUANIAN LANGUAGE

7162. BALČIKONIS, Juozas (1885-
1969) Jauniaus mokslo darbai. [Sci-
entific works of Jaunius] In Švietimo darbas (Kaunas), no.3, 1928.
See serials consulted.

7163. EIGMINAS, K. Lituanistinė
medžiaga naujausioje tarybinėje rusų
lingvistinėje literatūroje,1950-1957.
[Lithuanian studies in contemporary
Soviet Russian linguistic literature]
In Literatūra ir kalba.(Vilnius), v.3
p. 581-594. PG8503.L6 DLC CLU InU
IU KyU MH NN OClW PU

7164. HOOD, Gary A. A bibliography of works dealing with the relationship between Baltic and Slavic.
In Lituanus, v.13, no.2, 1967, p. 38-
46. See serials consulted.

7165. KUBICKA, Weronika. Bibliografia języka staroprusskiego. In Acta
Balto-Slavica, v.3, p. 257-311. See
serials consulted.

7166. --- Języki bałtyckie; bibliografia. [Baltic languages; bibliography. Łódz, 1967- . (Wydawn. Bibliograficzne Biblioteki Uniwersyteckiej, 10) Z7041.K8 CaOTU

7167. LIETUVOS TSR MOKSLŲ AKADEMIJA, VILNA. CENTRINĖ BIBLIOTEKA. Lietuvių kalbotyra, 1944-1960; [bibliografinė rodyklė. Lithuanian linguistics, 1940-1960; a bibliography. Sudarė: A. Bielinis ir E. Stanevičienė. Atsakingasis redaktorius: A. Ivaškevičius] Vilnius, Laikraščių ir žurnalų leidykla, 1963. 279 p. Z7044.L4L53 DLC CtY ICU MH PPiU PU

7168. --- Lietuvių kalbotyra, 1961-1964; [bibliografinė rodyklė. Lithuanian linguistics; a bibliography for 1961-1964. Sudarė: A. Bielinis ir E. Stanevičienė] Vilnius, 1965. 221 p. Z7044.6.L4L5 DLC CtY PU

7169. MERKELIS, Aleksandras. Jono Jablonskio bibliografija. [A bibliography of Jonas Jablonskis] In Archivum philologicum (Kaunas), v.2, 1931, p. 15-37. See serials consulted.

7170. OCHMAŃSKI, Jerzy. Lituanistyka w Polsce do 1965 roku. In Roczniki Historyczne (Poznań), v.34, 1968, p. 137-168. See serials consulted.

7171. PUPKIS, A. Lietuvių kalbos bendrinė tartis; bibliografinė rodyklė. [The standard pronunciation in Lithuanian] Vilnius, 1968. ii, 31 p. 3297.02 MH

XIII.4.b. INDO-EUROPEAN, PRUSSIAN AND BALTIC LANGUAGES

7172. ARNTZ, Helmut. Sprachliche Beziehungen zwischen Arisch und Balto-Slawisch. Heidelberg, C. Winter, 1933. xi, 63 p. (Indogermanische Bibliothek... 3 Abt. Untersuchungen. Bd. 13) P371.A7 DLC CaAEU CaBVaU IU MiU NN OU PPULC PBm PU ViU TxU

7173. BALTIC LINGUISTICS. Edited by Thomas F. Magner and William R. Schmalstieg. University Park, Pa., Pennsylvania State University Press, [1970] 177 p. PG8002.B3 PU CaAEU CaOTU OKentU

7174. BERNEKER, Erich Karl. Die preussische Sprache. Texte, Grammatik, etymologisches Wörterbuch. Strassburg, K.J. Trübner, 1896. x, 333 p. PG8202.B4 DLC CLU CU CtY InU MiU MnU MdBJ MH NcU NjP PPULC PU WU

7175. BEZZENBERGER, Adalbert. Über die Sprache der preussischen Letten. Göttingen Vandenhoeck & Ruprecht, 1888. 170 p. 491.93.B469 PU CU IU InU MH NN PPULC TxU WU

7176. BLESE, Ernest. Die Kuren und ihre sprachliche Stellung im Kreise der baltischen Volkstämme. In Kongress baltischer Archäologen, 2nd, Riga, 1930. Riga, 1931. DK511.B29K6 1930 DLC CS NN PU

7177. BOPP, Franz. Über die Sprache der alten Preussen in ihren verwandschaftlichen Beziehungen. Berlin, F. Dümmler, 1853. 55 p. 491.922.B643 PU ICU ICN MH

7178. BŪGA, Kazimieras. Aistiški studijai; tyrinėjimai lygintojo prūsų, latvių ir lietuvių kalbomoksljo srityje. I-oji dalis. Aistische studien; Beiträge zur vergleichenden Grammatik der preussischen, lettischen und litauischen Sprache. Peterburgas, Imp. Mokslų akademijos spaustuvė, 1908. xvi, 216 p. (Šv. Kazimiero draugijos išleidimas, no. 45) Title also in German. PG8018.B8 DLC CtPAM CtTMF CtY ICBM ICCC MnU NB PPULC PU

7179. --- Baltica v "praslavianskoi grammatike" G.A. Ilinskogo. In Archivum philologicum (Kaunas), v. 1, 1930, p. 37-68. See serials consulted; also in His Rinktiniai raštai, v.1, 1958, p. 581-607. PG8509.B8 v.1 DLC CU CaAEU CtPAM CtTMF ICLJF ICU IEN MH NN NjP PPiU PU TxU

7180. --- Baltiiskie (aistiiskie) etimologii. In Russkii filologichekii vestnik (Varshava), v.66, 1912. See serials consulted; also in His Rinktiniai raštai, v.1, 1958, p. 305-322. PG8509.B8 v.1 DLC CU CaAEU CtPAM CtTMF ICLJF ICU IEN MH NN NjP PPiU PU TxU

7181. --- Kann man Keltenspuren auf baltischem Gebiet nachweisen? In His Rinktiniai raštai. Vilnius, 1958. v.1, p. 496-530. PG8509.B8 v.1 DLC CU CaAEU CtPAM CtTMF ICLJF ICU IEN MH NN NjP PPiU PU TxU

7182. --- Slaviano-Baltiiskie etimologii. In Russkii filologicheskii vestnik (Varshava; Warszawa) v.67, 1912, p. 232-250; v.70, 1913, p. 10-108, 248-256; v.71, 1914,

p. 50-60, 464-471; v.72, 1914, p. 187-202; v.73, 1915, p. 335-343; v.75, 1916, p. 141-156. See serials consulted.

7183. CHATTERJI, Suniti Kumar. Balts and Aryans in their Indo-European background. [1st ed.] Simla, Indian Institute of Advanced Study, 1968. xx, 180 p. map, plates. PG8018.C5 DLC CaOTY CaOTU OKentU PU

7184. DUKSZTA, Mieczysław. Recherches ethnographiques concernant la langue primitive des peuples aryens et l'apparition des races baltico-slaves et autres en Europe. Genève, 1916. Publication de l' Athenaeum, no.1. BM(010007. ee. 3. (1.))

7185. DURIDANOV, Ivan. Thrakisch-dakische Studien. 1. Teil: Die thrakisch- und dakisch-baltischen Sprachbeziehungen. Sofia, Bulgarska akademiia na naukite, 1969. 103 p. 491.7.P.B197 t.13:2 PU

7186. ECKERT, Rainer. Baltistische Studien. Mit einem Geleitwort von Rudolf Fischer und einer Bibliographie von Rainer Eckert und Frido Mětšk. Berlin, Akademie-Verlag, 1971. 102 p. (Sitzungsberichte der Sächsischen Akademie der Wissenschaften zu Leipzig. Philologisch-Historische Klasse, Bd. 115, Heft 5) Bibliography: p. [75]-98. AS182.S213 Bd. 115, Heft 5 DLC

7187. ENDZELĪNS, Jānis. Altpreussische Grammatik. Riga, Verlag Latvju Gramata, 1944. 200 p. PG8204.E7 DLC CtY INU ICU NIC NN NjP OCl PU ViU

7188. --- Baltu kalbų garsai ir formos. [Sounds and forms of Baltic languages] Vilnius, VPMLL, 1957. 237 p. PG8021.E6 DLC NN OKentU PU

7189. --- Baltu valodu skanas un formas. [Sounds and forms of the Baltic languages] Riga, 1948. 260 p. PG8021.E59 PU

7190. --- Comparative phonology and morphology of the Baltic languages. Translated by William R. Schmalstieg and Benjamiņš Jēgers. The Hague, Mouton, 1971. 357 p. PG8021.E5913 PU

7191. --- Slaviano-baltiiskie etiudy. Khar'kov, Tip. M. Zil'berga, 1911. viii, 208 p. PG8015.E5 DLC CaAEU (microfiche 1962)

7192. FORTUNATOV, Filip Fedorovich. Udareniie v prusskom iazyke. In Russkii filologicheskii viestnik, (Warszawa), v.33, 1895. See serials consulted.

7193. FRAENKEL, Ernst. Analogische Umgestaltung und Volksethymologie besonders im Baltischen und Slavischen. In Zeitschrift für Slavische Philologie (Leipzig), v. 23, no.2, 1954, p. 334-353. See serials consulted.

7194. --- Beiträge zur baltischen Wortforschung. In Zeitschrift für vergleichende Sprachforschung (Berlin), v.69, 1948, p. 67-94. See serials consulted.

7195. --- Baltoslavica, Beiträge zur balto-slavischen Grammatik und Syntax, von Ernst Fraenkel... Göttingen, Vandenhoeck & Ruprecht, 1921. 84 p. PG8021.F7 DLC CaOTU CtY ICU MH NN NNC OcU PU ViU

7196. --- Der baltische Sprachstamm und sein Verhältnis zu den anderen indogermanischen Idiomen. In Scholar (Heidelberg), no.1, 1947, p. 26-36. See serials consulted.

7197. --- Die baltische Sprachwissenschaft in den Jahren 1938-1940. In Academia Scientiarum Fennicae. Annales (Helsinki), v.51, 1941. See serials consulted.

7197. --- Die baltischen Sprachen; ihre Beziehungen zu einander und zu den indogermanischen Schwesteridiomen als Einführung in die baltische Sprachwissenschaft. Heidelberg, C. Winter, 1950. 126 p. PG8008.F7 DLC CaAEU CaOTU CtY IaU IU ICU CU LU MH MB NIC NN NCC NRU NjP NCU OCU PU TxU ViU

7199. --- Baltisches und Slavisches. In Lingua Posnanensis (Poznań), v.2, 1950, p. 99-122. See serials consulted.

7200. --- Baltisches und Slavisches. In Zeitschrift für vergleichende Sprachforschung (Berlin), v.70, no.3-4, 1952, p. 129-152. See serials consulted.

7201. --- Baltu kalbos: jų tarpusavio santykiai ir santykiai su kitomis indoeuropiečių kalbomis. [Baltic languages and their reciprocal relations... Vertė S. Karaliūnas. Baltų kalbotyros įvadas] Vilnius, Mintis, 1969. 127 p. PG8008.F715 PU CaAEU

7202. --- Zum baltischen und slavische Philologie (Leipzig), v.20, 1943, p. 236-320. See serials consulted.

7203. GORNUNG, E. K diskussii o balto-slavianskom iazykovom i etnicheskom edinstve. In Voprosy iazykoznaniia (Moskva), no.4, 1958, p. 55-62. See serials consulted.

7204. HJELMSLEV, Louis. Études baltiques. Copenhague, Levin & Munksgaard, 1932. xi, 270 [2] p. Thesis--University of Copenhagen. PG8029.H64e CLU BM CaAEU CaBVaU CaOTU CTY ICU KU MiU MnU NNC NN NcU NjP NmU NbU PBm PU TxU WaU WU

7205. HOFMANN, Erich. Ausdrucksverstärkung, Untersuchungen zur etymologischen Verstärkung und zum Gebrauch der Steigerungsadverbia im balto-slavischen und in anderen indogermanischen Sprachen. Göttingen, Vandenhoeck & Ruprecht, 1930. viii, 156 p. (Ergänzungshefte zur Zeitschrift für vergleichende Sprachforschung auf dem Gebiete der indorgermanischen Sprachen. nr. 9) Bibliography: p. vi-viii. PG8067.H6 DLC OCU OU PBm PU NN ViU

7206. ILLICH-SVITYCH, Vladislav Markovich. Imennaia aktsentuatsiia v baltiiskom i slavianskom. Moskva, Akademiia nauk SSSR, Institut slavianovedeniia, 1963. 176 p. On Lithuanian language: p. 8-88. Bibliography: p. 166-172. PG8032.I4 DLC CaAEU CaOTU

7207. JACOBSSON, Gunnar. L'histoire d'un groupe de mots balto-slaves. Göteborg, Almquist & Wiksell, 1958. 121 p. (Acta Universitatis Gothoburgensis. Göteborgs universitets Årsskrift, v. 64, 1958, p. 8) Bibliography: p. 111-120. AS284.G6 vol.64, no.8 MiU CLU CLSU CtY DSI InU IU MH MNS NNC CaAEU CaOTU

7208. KELLER, Georg Siegmund. Das Asyndeton in den balto-slavischen Sprachen. Heidelberg, 1922. 107 p. (In Slavica; Beiträge zum Studium der Sprache, Literatur, Kultur, Volks- und Altertumskunde der Slaven, 4) PG13.S5 v.4 1922 ViU CaAEU CaBVaU CU CtY ICU MH MiU MnU NN NNC PU WaU

7209. KIPARSKY, Valentin Julius Alexander. Baltische Sprachen und Völker. In Brackmann, Albert and Carl Engel, eds. Baltische Lande. v. 1: Ostbaltische Frühzeit. Leipzig, 1939. p. 48-59. DK511.B3B7 v.1 DLC CtY ICU MH NN

7210. KLIMAS, Antanas. Baltic, Germanic, and Slavic. [Stockholm, Almquist & Wiksell, 1970] [263]-269 p. Offprint from Donum Balticum. PG8014K53 PU CaAEU DLC

7211. --- Balto-Slavic or Baltic and Slavic. In Lituanus (Chicago, Ill.), v.13, no.2, 1967, p. 5-37. See serials consulted.

7212. --- The importance of Lithuanian for Indo-European linguistics. In Lituanus (Chicago, Ill.), v.15, no.3, 1969, p. 10-24. See serials consulted.

7213. KRAHE, Hans. Vorgeschichtliche Sprachbeziehungen von den baltischen Ostseeländer zu den Gebieten um den Nordteil der Adria. Mainz, Verlag der Wissenschaften und Literatur, 1957. 21 p. PG8018.K73 CaOTU CtY CLU IU MH MiU NIC PU

7214. KURYŁOWICZ, Jerzy. L'accentuation des langues indo-européennes. [2nd edition] Wrocław, Zakład Narodowy Imienia Ossolińskich, 1958. 433 p. (Polska Akademia Nauk. Komitet Językoznawczy. Prace Językoznawcze, 17) PG597.K8 1958 DLC CaAEU CtY CLSU CoU DeU ICU LU MdBJ MoU MH MoSW NN NIC NNC NcD NcU NiP OU PU RPB TNJ TxU

7215. LESKIEN, August. Die Declination im Slavish-Litauischen und Germanischen, Leipzig, S. Hirzel, 1876. xxix, 158 p. illus. (Preisschriften gekrönt und hrsg. von der Fürstlich Jablonowski'schen Gesellschaft zu Leipzig. Nr.11 der historisch-nationalökonomischen Section) AS182.L3 no.19 DLC CaOTU CaQMM CSt CtY DCU ICU ICJ MH MnU NNC NcU NjP OClW PU ViU

7216. --- --- [Another edition] Leipzig, Zentral-Antiquariat der Deutschen Demokratischen Republik, 1963. xxv, 158 p. (Preisschriften gekrönt und hrsg. von der Fürstlich Jablonowski'schen Gesellschaft zu Leipzig. Nr.11 der Historisch-nationalökonomischen Section) Reprint: originally published Leipzig, S. Hirzel, 1876. P623.L48 NSyU CaBVaS CaAEU MiDW OU TxHR WaU

7217. LIDÉN, Ewald. Ein baltisch-slavisches Anlautgesetz. Göteborg, W. Zachrisson, 1899. (Göteborgs Högskolas Årsskrift, Bd. 5) 491.9.L617 PU

7218. LINDE, Samuel Bogumił. O języku dawnych Prusaków. Rozbiór dzieła Profesora Vatera... czytany na posiedzeniu publicznym Król. Towarzystwa Warszawskiego Przyjaciół Nauk dnia 26. listopada 1821. Warszawa, Drukiem XX. Piarów, 1822. 116 p. (Towarzystwo Królewskie Warszawskie Prszyjaciól Nauk. Rocznik, t.15) AS262.W29 T.15 DLC MH PU

7219. LUDWIG, Alfred. Der Infinitiv im Veda, mit einer Systematik des litauischen und slavischen Verbs. Prag, J.G. Calve, 1871. 159 p. PK291.L8 DLC CU CoU CtY ICU NNC NjP OCl TxU

7220. MATTHEWS, William Kleesmann. The interrelations of Baltic and Slavonic. In Slavonic and East European review (Menasha, Wis.), v.35, no.85, 1957, p. 409-427. See serials consulted.

7221. MAŽIULIS, Vytautas. Baltų ir kitų indoeuropiečių kalbų santykiai (deklinacija). [The relations of the Baltic and other Indo-European languages] Vilnius, 1970. 343 p. PG8018.M38 PU CaAEU

7222. --- Zametki k voprosu o drevneishikh otnosheniiakh baltiiskikh i slavianskikh iazykov. Vil'nius, Gos. izd-vo polit. i khudozh. lit-ry, 1958. 20 p. (Mezhdunarodnyi s"ezd slavistov. 4th Doklady) 491.9.M459 PU CaAEU NNC

7223. MITZKA, W. Altpreussisches. In Zeitschrift für Vergleichende Sprachforschung (Berlin), v.52, 1924, p. 129-147. See serials consulted.

7224. NEPOKUPNYI, Anatolii Pavlovich. Areal'nye aspekty balto-slavianskikh iazykovykh otnoshenii. Kiev, Naukova Dumka, 1964. 162 p. maps. PG8096.AlN4 DLC CaAEU CaOTU PU

7225. NESSELMANN, Georg Heinrich Ferdinand. Die Sprache der alten Preussen an ihren Überresten erläutert. Berlin, Reimer, 1845. xxxvi, 158 p. PR8208.N4 1845 MdBJ CU ICN KU NN PU

7226. --- Thesaurus linguae prussicae. Der preussische Vocabelvorrath... nebst Zugabe einer Sammlung urkundlich beglaubigter Localnamen. Berlin, F. Dümmler, 1873. vii, 222 p. PG8206.N5 DLC CtY ICU MB MaBJ NN NNC NjP OClW PU

7227. --- --- [Another edition] Wiesbaden, M. Sändig [1969] 222 p. Reprint: originally published Berlin; Bonn, F. Dümmler, 1873. PG8206.N46 1969 CaAEU CaOTU

7228. NIEDERMANN, Max. Balto-Slavica. Genève, E. Droz, 1956. 214 p. (Université de Neuchâtel. Recueil de travaux publiés par la Faculté des lettres, 27. fasc.) PG8703.N66 CaAEU CaBVaU CaBVaS ClU CSt CtY ICU IaU LU MH MoU MnU NIC NN NNC NcD NcU NjP NjR PU RPB WaU WU

7229. NIEMINEN, Eino Vilho Kalervo. Über einige Eigenschaften der baltischen Sprache, die sich in den ältesten baltischen Lehnwörtern der ostseefinnischen Sprachen abspiegelt. In Suomalainen tiedeakatemia, Helsingfors, Sitzungsberichte, 1956. Helsinki, 1957. p. 185-206. See serials consulted.

7230. --- Der urindogermanische Ausgang -ai. Helsinki, Druckerei der Finnischen Literaturgesellschaft, 1922. 185 p. Thesis--University of Helsinki. Bibliography: p. [180]-185. 891.8.565 NNC

7231. NONNENMACHER, Elizabeth. Die baltoslavischen Akzent- und Intonationsverhältnisse und ihr quantitativer Reflex im Slovakischen. Wiesbaden, O. Harrassowitz, 1961. vi, 196 p. (Bibliotheca slavica) 491.7.N734 PU CaBVaU CaOTU ClU CU CtY MH MiU MiDW NN NNC NcD NjP RPB WU

7232. OINAS, Felix J. Russian and Eastern Balto-Finnic linguistic contacts. 's-Gravenhage, Mouton, 1958. 12 p. Text in English, summary in Russian. Preprint [of] American contributions to the Fourth International Congress of Slavicists. Moscow, September 1958. PG44.039 NSyU

7233. OTRĘBSKI, Jan Szczepan. Slaviano-baltiiskoe iazykovoe edinstvo. In Voprosy iazykoznaniia, (Moskva), no.5, 1954, p. 27-42; no. 6, p. 28-46. See serials consulted.

7234. PETRUS OF DUSBURG. De lingua veterum Prussorum. In His Chronicon Prussiae... Francofurti et Lipsiae, Sumptibus M. Hallervordii, 1679. pt. 2, p. 78-108. DD491.046P4 DLC CtY MdBP

7235. POTT, August Friedrich. De borusso-lithuanicae tam in slavicis quam letticis linguis principatu commentatio. Halis Saxonum, In libraria Gebaueria, 1837-41. 2 v. 491.922.P852 PU ICN MH

7236. --- Etymologische Forschungen auf dem Gebiete der indogermanischen Sprachen, mit besonderem Bezug auf die Lautumwandlung im Sanskirt, Griechischen, Lateinischen, Littauischen und Gothischen. Lemgo, Meyersche Hof-Buchhandlung, 1833-36. 2 v. P721.P8 1833 DLC CaAEU

7237. --- --- 2. Aufl. in völlig neuer Umarbeitung. Lemgo, Meyer'sche Hof-Buchhandlung, 1859-76. 10 v. P721.P8 1859 DLC

7238. PRŪSŲ KALBOS PAMINKLAI. [Monuments of the Prussian language] Vilnius, Mintis, 1966. 251 p. facsims. Photographic reproduction of some old texts: Codex Neumannianus; Elbing dictionary.--Simon Grunau dictionary.--Catachismus in preüssnischer Sprach und dagegen das Deüdsche. PG8208.L72 CaAEU CaOTU CtPAM CtY DLC ICU MiU MH NN NcD NcU PPiU NjP RPB OClW PU

7239. SABALIAUSKAS, Algirdas. Baltų ir Pabaltijo suomių kalbų santykiai. [The relationship of Baltic and Finnish languages] In Lietuvių kalbotyros klausimai (Vilnius), v.6, 1963, p. 109-136. See serials consulted.

7240. --- Baltų kalbų tyrinėjimas Tarybinės santvarkos metais. [The research of Baltic languages during the Soviet period] In Baltistica (Vilnius), v.1, no.2, 1966, p. 201-205. See serials consulted.

7241. SANDBACH, Edmund. Die indogermanischen zweisilbigen schweren Basen und das baltische (litauische) Präteritum. Heidelberg, C. Winter, 1930. 95 p. (Indogermanische Bibliothek. 3. Abt.: Untersuchungen, Bd. 11) PG8597.S3 DLC BM CL CLU CSt CaAEU CaBVaS CaBVaU CaOHM CtY CU ICN ICU LU MnU MH NNC NjP NBuU OU PU TxU ViU WaU

7242. SCHERER, Philip. Germanic-Balto-Slavic etyma. Baltimore, Md., Linguistic Society of America [1941] 63 p. (Language dissertation no. 32) Thesis--Yale University, 1935. Bibliography: p. 59-60. PD582.S35 DLC PU CtY DSC OCU OU ViU

7243. SCHMALSTIEG, William Riegel. Baltic ei and depalatization. In Lingua (Haarlem, Netherlands), v.9, 1960, p. 258-266. See serials consulted.

7244. --- A note on certain Balto-Slavic accusatives. In Baltistica (Vilnius), v.3, no.1, 1967, p. 47-54. See serials consulted.

7245. --- The thematic vowel in Baltic. In Lingua (Haarlem, Netherlands), v.7, 1958, p. 428-432. See serials consulted.

7246. --- The vocalic distinctive features of primitive East Baltic. In Lituanistikos darbai (Chicago, Ill.), v.1, 1966, p. 85-88. See serials consulted.

7247. SCHMID, Wolfgang Paul. Studien zum baltischen und indogermanischen Verbum. Wiesbaden, O. Harrassowitz, 1963. 123 p. Bibliography: p. [106]-109. PG8061.S35 CaOTU CaAEU NcU PU

7248. SENN, Alfred. Slavic and Baltic linguistic relations. In Donum Balticum. To Professor Christian S. Stang on the occasion of his seventieth birthday 15 March 1970. Ed. by Velta Rūke-Draviņa. Stockholm, Almqvist & Wiksell, 1970. xiv, 598 p. illus. PG8002.D6 DLC PU CaAEU

7249. --- On the degree of kinship between Slavic and Baltic. In Slavonic and East European Review (Menasha, Wis.), v.20, 1941, p. 251-265. See serials consulted.

7250. --- The relationship of Baltic and Slavic. Offprint from Ancient indo-european dialects; proceedings of the Conference on Indo-european linguistics, held at the University of California, Los Angeles, April 25-27, 1963. Berkeley, Calif., 1966. p. 131-151. 491.9.Se57 PU

7251. SEREBRENNIKOV, B. A. O nekotorykh sledakh izcheznuvshego indoevropeiskogo iazyka v tsentre evropeiskoi chasti SSSR, blizkogo k baltiiskim iazykam. In LTSRMAD. Serija A, v.1(2), 1951, p. 69-72. See serials consulted.

7252. SPECHT, Franz. Baltische Sprachen. In Stand und Aufgaben der Sprachwissenschaft. Heidelberg, 1924. p. 622-648. P545.S7 DLC MB NN

7253. STANG, Christian Schweigaard. Das slavische und baltische Verbum. Oslo, J. Dybwad, 1942. 280 p. (Skrifter utgitt av det Norske videnskaps-akademi i Oslo. II. Historisk-filosof. klasse, nr. 1) AS283.O57 1942, no.1 DLC CaOTU

7254. --- --- [Another edition] Tumba, International Documentation Centre, [n.d.] 5 cards. Microfiche: originally published Oslo,

J. Dybwad, 1942. PG8061.S78 CaAEU

7255. --- Vergleichende Grammatic
der baltischen Sprachen. Oslo, Uni-
versitetsforlaget, 1966. viii,
483 p. (Scandinavian University
books) PG8018.S7 DLC CaAEU CaOTU
MCM MBuU PPULC PU

7256. STUDIA LINGUISTICA SLAVICA
baltica Canuto-Olavo Falk sexage-
nario a collegis amicis discipulis
oblata. Lund, 1966 [i.e. 1968]
ix, 399 p. PG14.F3 PU

7257. THOMSEN, Vilhelm Ludvig
Peter. Berøringer mellem de finske
og de baltiske (litavisk-lettiske)
sprog. En sproghistorisk undersø-
gelse af Vilh. Thomsen... Køben-
havn, B. Lunos, 1890. 308 p.
(Danske videnskabernes selskab
[Copenhagen] Selskab skrifter. 1.
Historisk og filosofish afdeling...
ser. 6, v.1, no.1) AS281.D222
Ser.6, v.1, no.1, DLC CLU IaU MH
NIC NN PU ViU

7258. --- Berührungen zwischen
den finnischen und den baltischen
(litauisch-lettischen Sprachen.
København, Gyldendalske Boghandel-
Nordisk Vorlag, 1931. (His Sam-
lede Afhandlinger, bd. 4)
408.T383 bd.4 PU

7259. TRAUTMANN, Reinhold. Die
altpreussischen Sprachdenkmäler;
Einleitung, Texter, Grammatik,
Wörterbuch. Göttingen, Vandenhoeck & Ruprecht, 1910. xxxii,
470 p. PG8202.T7 DLC CtY MB MiU
NN NjP OCU

7260. --- --- [Another edition]
Göttingen, Vandenhoeck & Ruprecht,
1970. Reprint: originally pub-
lished Göttingen, Vandenhoeck &
Ruprecht, 1910. PG8202.T77 CaAEU
CaOTU

7261. UHLENBECK, Christian
Cornelius. Die lexicalische Ur-
verwandtschaft des Baltoslavischen
und Germanischen. Leiden, Blanken-
berg & Co., 1890. xii, 51 p.
PG305.U4 DLC BM(12901. d. 33. (4))
PU

7262. VATER, Johann Severin.
Die Sprache der alten Preussen;
Einleitung. Braunschweig, Vieweg
& Sohn, 1821. xii, xxxviii, 181
p. 491.91.V45 PU ICN IU MB

7263. --- --- [Another edition]
Wiesbaden, Martin Sändig [1966]
xii, xxxviii, 181 p. Reprint:
originally published Braunschweig,
Vieweg & Sohn, 1821. PG8202.V3

1966 DLC CSt CaOTU NjR

7264. WIJK, Nicolaas van. Altpreussische Studien; Beiträge zur
baltischen und zur vergleichenden
indogermanischen Grammatik, von dr.
N. van Wijk. Haag, M. Nijhoff,
1918. xi, 150, xxxii p.
PG8204.W5 DLC CLSU ICU MH OCU PU
PBm ViU

7265. --- Die baltischen und
slavischen Akzent- und Intonations-
systeme; ein Beitrag zur Erforschung
der baltisch-slavischen Verwand-
schaftsverhältnisse. 2. Aufl.
's-Gravenhage, Mouton, 1958. 160
p. illus. (Janua linguarum, 5)
PG76.W5 1958 DLC CaAEU CaOTU NSyU
PU

7266. --- Een phonologiese parallel tussen Germans, Slavies en
Balties. Amsterdam, Noord-Hol-
landsche uitgevers-maatschappij,
1934. 35 p. AS244.A51 DLC OCl

7267. WITTE, Wilhelm. Baltische
Philologie; der Übersetzer S.
Waischnoras. Braunschweig, Ver-
vielfältigungsanstalt Hunold,
1931. vii, 207 leaves. Thesis--
University of Breslau.
Rvc 22W78 CtY NNC

XIII.4.c. HISTORY AND RESEARCH

7268. ALEKSANDROV, Aleksandr
Ivanovich. Litovskie etiudy. Vyp.
1: narodnaia etimologiia. Varshava, 1888, 1 v. 491.922.A126 PU

7269. AŠMANTAS, Andrius.
Jaunius-gramatikas. [Jaunius, the
grammarian] In Židinys (Kaunas),
v.28, no.10, 1938, p. 369-378. See
serials consulted.

7270. BARANAUSKAS, Antanas. Zamietki o litovskom iazykie i slovarie. I-VIII. [By] Antoni Baranowski. In Akademiia nauk, Sanktpeterburg. Otdelenie russkogo
iazyka i slavesnosti. Sbornik, v.
65, no.9, 1898, p. 1-80.
PG2013.A65 T.65 DLC MH NNC PU

7271. BASANAVIČIUS, Jonas. Prie
historijos musun rašybos. [History
of Lithuanian lexography] Tilžė,
Otto v. Mauderode, 1899. 17 p.
Hve 22+1B29 CtY

7272. --- Über die Sprachverwand-
schaft der alten Thraker und heutigen Litauer. Wilna [Ruch] 1925.
23 p. Bibliography: p. 21-23.

491.92.B29u PSt PPULC

7273. BEZZENBERGER, Adalbert.
Beiträge zur Geschichte der li-
tauischen Sprache auf Grund litau-
ischer Text des XVI. und des XVII.
Jahrhunderts. Göttingen, Pepp-
müller, 1877. xxxvii, 356 p. (Die
Litauische und Lettische Drucke
des 16. und 17. Jahrhunderts)
PG8525.B57 ICU ICN IEN MH McBJ MnU
NIC NN NNC NcU NjP OClW PPULC PBm
PU WU

--- Litauische Forschungen.
Göttingen, 1882. See entry no.
6653.

7274. BOHLEN, P. von. Über die
Verwandschaft zwischen der litauischen und sanskrit Sprache. In
Königliche deutsche Gesellschaft,
Königsberg. Historische und litterarische Abhandlungen (Königsberg in Pr.), v.1, 1830, p. 111-
140. AS182.K782 v.1 ICU DLC IEN
OCl OClW

7275. BORICHEVSKII, Ivan Petrovich. Izsliedovanie o proizkhozh-
denii, nazvanii i iazykie litovskago naroda. In ZMNP, v.56, no.2,
1847, p. 272-314. See serials
consulted.

7276. BRÜCKNER, Alexander. Das
Litauische und seine Verwandten.
In Streitberg, Wilhelm. Geschichte
der Indogermanischen. Sprachwis-
senschaft... T.2: Die Erforschung
der indogermanischen Sprachen. Bd.
3. Slavisch-Litauisch, Albanisch.
Strassburg, 1917. p. 80-107.
(Grundriss der indogermanischen
Sprach- und Altertumskunde, 2)
P541.S7 DLC CaAEU CLU ICU MH NN
OCU ViU

7277. --- Slavisch-Litauisch,
Albanisch. Strassburg, Karl J.
Trübner, 1917. [8], 154 p. (Grundriss der indogermanischen Sprach-
und Altertumskunde. I. Geschichte
der indogermanische Sprachwissenschaft, T.2 [Bd.] 3. F59ℓI.2 v.3
CtY OU WU

7278. BŪGA, Kazimieras. K voprosu o khronologii litovskikh zaims-
tvovanii s russkogo. In His Rinktiniai raštai, v.1, 1958, p. 339-
351. PG8509.B8 v.1 DLC CaAEU CU
CtPAM CtTMF ICLJF ICU IEN MH NN NjP
PPiU PU TxU

7279. --- Kalba ir senovė. [Lan-
guage and the past. 1 dalis] Kaunas, Švietimo ministerijos leidinys,
1922. PG8661.B9(S) ICU InU MH PPULC
PU; also in Švietimo darbas (Kau-

nas), 1920, no.11, p. 33-45, no.12,
p. 40-48; 1921, no. 1/2, p. 72-88,
no. 3/4, p. 41-58, no. 5/6, p. 12-
28, 141-152, no.7/8, p. 16-43, 124-
139, no.9/10, p. 21-37, 122-139,
no.11/12, p. 65-84, 121-133; 1922,
no.1/2, p. 22-31, 72-91, no.3/6,
p. 285-295, 416-426, no.6/9, p. 295-
311. See serials consulted.

7280. --- --- In His Rinktiniai
raštai, v.2, 1959, p. 7-328.
PG8509.B8 v.2 DLC CaAEU CU CtPAM
CtTMF ICU ICCC ICLJF IEN MH NN NjP
PPiU PU TxU

--- Kalbų mokslas bei mūsų
senovė. Kaunas, 1913. See entry
no. 4205.

7281. --- Die litauisch-weissrus-
sischen Beziechungen und ihr Alter.
In His Rinktiniai raštai, v.3, 1961,
p. 749-778. PG8509.B8 v.3 DLC
CaAEU CU CtPAM CtTMF ICLJF ICU IEN
MH NN NjP PPiU PU TxU Also in
Zeitschrift für slavische Philolo-
gie (Leipzig), v.1, 1925, p. 26-55.
See serials consulted.

7282. --- Lituanica. Sanktpeterburg, 1912. 49 p. In Akademiia
nauk, Peterburg. Otdeleniie russkago iazyka i slovesnosti. Izvestiia, v.17, no.1, 1912, p. 1-49. See
serials consulted.

7283. --- Rinktiniai raštai.
[Selected works. Sudarė Z. Zinkevičius. Redagavo V. Mažiulis]
Vilnius, VPMLL, 1958-61. 3 v.
illus., ports., maps, facsims.

7284. --- --- Rodyklės. [Indexes]
Vilnius, VPMLL, 1962. 397 p.
PG8509.B8 DLC CU CaAEU CtPAM CtTMF
IEN ICU ICLJF MH NB NN NBuU NjP
PPiU PU TxU

7285. --- Visų senieji lietuvių
santykiai su germanais. [The most
ancient relations of Lithuanians
with the Germanic tribes] In His
Rinktiniai raštai, v.2, 1959, p.
80-98. PG8509.B8 v.2 DLC CaAEU CU
CtPAM CtTMF ICLJF ICU IEN MH NN NjP
PPiU PU TxU

7286. BYTAUTAS, Romas. Šis tas
iš lietuvių kalbos filosofijos;
pavesta a. a. kun. Jauniaus pagar-
bai. [Article on philosophy of
Lithuanian language dedicated to
the late Rev. Jaunius] Kaunas,
Saliamono Banaičio spaustuvė, 1908.
31 p. Perspausta iš "Draugijos".
491.92.B10 CtTMF OCl PG8523.B9
1971 PU(Xerox copy, 1971)

7287. CHYLIŃSKI, Samuel Boguslaus.

An account of the translation of
the Bible into the Lithuanian
tongue... in the University of Ox-
ford, November 15, 1659. Oxford
Hen. Hall, 1659. 1 v. (unpaged)
Oxford, Printed by Hen. Hall,
Printer to the University, 1659.
C4280.Bd.w.160a DFo BM(1214. a. 5.)

7288. DAA, Ludvig Kristensen. Om
den litauiske folkestammes forhold
til den slavoniske. In Nytt magazin for natur videnskapene. Chris-
tiania, 1851. Bd.6, hft. 3-4, p.
[292]-424. Bonaparte Collection
no. 8992 ICN CaQMM CaOG CtY MH-Z
MdBJ NIC-A NN NNC PPAN DLC

7289. DABARTINĖ LIETUVIŲ KALBA;
straipsnių rinkinys. [The contemporary Lithuanian language... Redakcinė kolegija: J. Kazlauskas,
A. Laigonaitė, V. Urbutis] Vilnius, VPMLL, 1961. 279 p.
PG8524.D3 DLC CaOTU CtPAM MH
OKentU PU

7290. DAMBRIŪNAS, Leonardas. A
general characterization of the
Lithuanian language. In Lituanus
(Chicago, Ill.), v.10, no. 3/4,
1964, p. 16-26. See serials consulted.

7291. --- The problem of the norm
for standard Lithuanian. In Acta
Baltico-Slavica (Białystok), v.3,
1966, p. 43-49. See serials consulted.

7292. FORD, Gordon Buell. Three
articles on old Lithuanian etymology, phonology and syntax. (Chicago, Ill.) Northwestern University
[1968] 1 v. (unpaged) PG8509.F63
PU CSt ICN ICU PPULC

7293. FRAENKEL, Ernst. Apie
kalbininkus, tyrinėjusius lietuvių
kalbą. [About the linguists who
have made research on the Lithuanian language] In Aidai (Kennebunkport, Me.), no.9(35), 1950, p.
410-417. See serials consulted.

7294. --- Apie vokiečių mokslinin-
kus, tyrinėjusius lietuvių kalbą.
[About the German scientists who
made research on the Lithuanian
language] In Aidai (Schwäbische
Gmünde, Ger.), no.19, 1948, p. 410-
415. See serials consulted.

7295. --- Bedeutungsveränderungen
von Wörtern der heutigen litauisch-
en Schriftsprache. In Zeitschrift
für slavische Philologie (Leipzig), v.6, 1929, p. 85-104. See
serials consulted.

7296. GAILIŪNAS, Pranas. Lietuvių kalbos gramatinis nagrinėji-
mas; metodinis laiškas... [The
grammatical parsing of Lithuanian..
.] Kaunas, Valstybinė pedagoginės
literatūros leidykla, 1956. 74 p.
PG8519.G18 ICU CtY

7297. GEITLER, Leopold. Litauische Studien; Auswahl aus den
ältesten Denkmälern, dialectische
Beispiele, lexikalische und sprach-
wissenschaftliche Beiträge. Prag,
Mourek, 1875. 123 p. PG8535.G31
IU CtY ICN InU MH ICU NjP PBm PU WU

7298. --- Starobulharská fonologie
se stálým zřetelem k jazyku litevs-
kému. Praha, Nakladatel T. Mourek,
1873. vi, 132 p. PG628.G5 DLC
BM(12975. l. 8.)

7299. HATTALA, Martin. O abla-
tivě ve slovančině a litvančině.
V Praze, A. Renn, 1858. 65 p.
"Zvláštní otisk z Časopisu Musea
král. Českého r. 1857, II,
227-250 a IV, 564-580; r. 1858, III,
347-357 a IV, 519-533." Bonaparte
Collection no. 13435 ICN

7300. HERMANN, Eduard. Die litauische Gemeinsprache als Problem der
allgemeinen Sprachwissenschaft. In
Akademie der Wissenschaft, Göttingen. Philologisch-Historische
Klasse. Nachrichten (Göttingen),
no.1, 1929, p. 65-125. AS182.G823
DLC

7301. IŠ VAKARINĖS VIDURINĖS MO-
kyklos lietuvių kalbos ir literatūros mokytojų darbo patirties.
[From the experiences of Lithuanian
language and literature teachers in
the night classes of Junior High
School. Sudarė A. Gudonytė] Kaunas, Šviesa, 1967. 57 p. (Mokytojo bibliotekėlė) PG8519.I8 DLC

7302. IVINSKIS, Zenonas. Lietuvių kalba viešajame Lietuvos XI-XVII
amžiaus gyvenime. [Lithuanian language in the public life of the
11th-17th centuries in Lithuania]
In Aidai (Kennebunkport, Me.),
1953, p. 408-417. See serials
consulted.

7303. JABLONSKIS, Jonas. Raštai.
[Collected works] Redagavo J.
Balčikonis. Kaunas, Ryto bendrovė,
1932-36. 5 v. illus., ports.
(Švietimo ministerijos leidinys,
nr. 344, 377, 378, 448) PG8509.J3
DLC(3) CtY(1-4) CtTMF(1-2) ICCC(1-3)
MH(1,3-4) PU(1-5)

7304. --- Rinktiniai raštai.

[Selected works. Sudarė J. Palionis] Vilnius, VPMLL, 1957-59. 2 v. ports. PG5809.J33A6 1957 DLC CU CtY ICU MH NB NN OKentU PU

7305. JABLONSKIS, Konstantinas. Lietuviški žodžiai senosios Lietuvos raštinių kalboje. 1. dalis: Tekstai. [Lithuanian words in the public office language of the Lithuanian State] Kaunas, Lietuvos istorijos draugija, 1941. xv, 376 p. No more published. DK511.L212J3 PU

7306. --- --- [Another edition] Tumba Sweden, International Dokumentation Centre, 1966. 11 cards. Microfiche; originally published Kaunas, Lietuvos istorijos draugija, 1941. W67 MH

7307. JONIKAS, Peter. Gimtojo žodžio baruose; bendrinės kalbos patarimai ir paaiškinimai. [The native language; advice and explanation of standard Lithuanian] Čikaga [Terra] 1951. 167 p. PG8524.J6 DLC CtPAM CtTMF ICBM ICCC MiD OCU PU

7308. --- Bendrinė kalba. [The standard Lithuanian] In His Lietuvių kalbos istorija. Chicago, Ill., 1952. p. 159-193. PG8525.J6 DLC CaAEU CtY ICN CaOTP NN NNC PU

7309. --- Lietuvių bendrinės rašomosios kalbos idėja priešaušrio metu. [The idea of the written standard Lithuanian before the "Aušra" time (1883)] In Archivum philologicum (Kaunas), v.6, 1937, p. 36-73. See serials consulted.

7310. --- Lietuvių bendrinės rašomosios kalbos kūrimasis antroje XIX a. pusėje. [Development of the standard Lithuanian in the second half of the nineteenth century] Čikaga, Pedagoginis lituanistikos institutas, 1972. xi, 334 p. PG8525.J61 PU DLC

7311. --- Lietuvių kalba ir jos gaivinimas prieš "Aušrą". [Lithuanian language and its revival before "Aušra"] In Mūsų senovė (Kaunas), v.3, no.1, 1940, p. 1-53. See serials consulted.

7312. --- Lietuvių kalbos istorija. [History of the Lithuanian language. Chicago, Ill.] Terra [1952] 255 p. Summary in English. Bibliography: p. 221-230. PG8525.J6 DLC CaAEU CaOTP CtY ICN NN NNC OKentU PU

7313. --- Lietuvių kalbos raidos apžvalga. [An outline of the development of the Lithuanian language] Boston, Mass., 1969. 38 p. Offprint from Lietuvių enciklopedija. Boston, Mass., 1968. v.15. PG8524.J6 PU

7314. JORDAN, Karl August. Einige Worte über die litauische Sprache und Professor Schleicher. [Königsberg in Pr., E.J. Dalkowski, 1853] 6 p. Caption title: Aus den Neuen preussischen Provinzial-Blättern a.f., Bd.4, 1853, abgedrückt. 491.92.Sdh333 PU ICN

7315. KANTRIMAS, J. Lietuvių kalbos gyvatos raida Mažojoje Lietuvoje. [The development of the Lithuanian language in Lithuania Minor] In Aidai (Augsburg, Ger.), no.18, 1948, p. 368-373, 387-388. See serials consulted.

7316. KARŁOWICZ, Jan. O języku litewskim. In Polska Akademia Umiejętności, Kraków. Wydział Historyczno-Filozoficzny. Rozprawy i Sprawozdania z posiedzeń, v.2, 1875, p. 135-376. Bibliography: p. 331-362. See serials consulted.

7317. KAZLAUSKAS, Jonas and Algirdas Sabaliauskas. Izuchenie litovskogo iazyka v Litovskoi SSR. In Voprosy slavianskogo iazykoznaniia (Moskva), v.3, 1958, p. 166-169. See serials consulted.

7318. KLIMAS, Antanas. Lithuanian and Indo-European. In Lituanus (Brooklyn, N.Y.), no.4(13), 1957, p. 14-16. See serials consulted.

7319. --- Lithuanian and Sanskrit. In Lituanus (Brooklyn, N.Y.), v.5, no.3, 1959, p. 78-79. See serials consulted.

7320. --- Lithuanian and the Germanic languages. In Lituanus (Brooklyn, N.Y.), v.4, no.2, 1958, p. 41-46. See serials consulted.

7321. --- Lithuanian and the Slavic languages. In Lituanus (Brooklyn, N.Y.), v.5, no.1, 1959, p. 10-12. See serials consulted.

7322. KOCHUBINSKII, Aleksandr Aleksandrovich. Litovskii iazyk i nasha starina. Moskva, 1895. p. 92-108. (Imperatorskoe moskovskoe arkheologicheskoe obshchestvo. Trudy deviatago arkheologicheskago s"iezda v Vil'nie, 1893, t.1.) DK30.A75 1893 t.1 DLC CU MH NN NNC NjP OrU

7323. KURSCHAT, Friedrich. Bei-
träge zur Kunde der littauischen
Sprache... Eine ergänzende Beilage
zum Ruhig-Mielckeschen Wörterbuch.
Königsberg in Pr., 1843-49. 2 v.
PR8523.K8 1843 MdBJ ICU ICN NmU PU

7324. LEMCHENAS, Chackelis. Lietuvių kalbos įtaka Lietuvos žydų
tarmei. [The influence of Lithuanian language on the dialect of
Lithuanian Jews] Vilnius, 1970.
137 p. PJ5118.L45 PU

7325. LESKIEN, August. Aus Ar-
beiten litauischer Gelehrter über
ihre Sprache. In Indogermanische
Forschungen. Anzeiger (Strasbourg;
Berlin), v.13, 1902, p. 79-97.
See serials consulted.

7326. LIETUVIŲ KALBA TARYBINIAIS
metais. [The Lithuanian language
in the Soviet period. Ats. redaktorius V. Ambrazas. Vilnius,
Mintis, 1967] 193 p. PG8524.L5 PU
CaAEU CtY DLC MH WaU

LIETUVIŲ KALBOS LEKSIKOS
raida. Vilnius, 1966. See entry
no. 7850.

7327. LUKŠAITĖ, Ingė. Lietuvių
kalba reformaciniame judėjime XVII
a. [The Lithuanian language during
the Reformation. Vilnius, Mintis,
1970] 66 p. (Lietuvos TSR Mokslų
akademijos istorijos institutas.
Acta historica lituanica, 5) Summary in English and Russian.
PG8525.L8 DLC OKentU PU

7328. MACIŪNAS, Vincas. Lituanistinis sąjudis XIX a. pradžioje.
[The Lithuanian movement at the beginning of the nineteenth century]
Kaunas, Humanitarinių mokslų fakultetas, 1939. 344 p. (Darbai ir
dienos, 9) Thesis (Ph.D.)--Univer-
sity of Kaunas. P19.K3 DLC CU MoU
NN PU(Xerox)

7329. MATTHEWS, William K. The
affinities and structure of Lithuanian. In Slavonic and East European Review (London), v.35, no.84,
1956, p. 40-73. See serials consulted.

7330. --- Phonemes and phoneme
patterns in contemporary Russian and
Lithuanian. In Slavonic and East
European Review (London), v.36, no.
87, 1958, p. 317-339. See serials
consulted.

7331. MAŽIULIS, Vytautas. Die
litauische Sprachwissenschaft seit
1945. In Wissenschaftlicher Dienst
für Ost-Mitteleuropa (Marburg/

Lahn), v.9, no.8, 1959, p. 300-303.
See serials consulted.

7332. NIEDERMANN, Max. Gli inizi
della linguistica lituana. In Studi Baltici (Roma), v.1, 1931, p.
32-49. See serials consulted.

7333. OTRĘBSKI, Jan Szczepan.
Przyczynki słowiańsko-litewskie.
Wilno, Instytut Naukowo-Badawczy
Europy Wschodniej, 1930-1935. 2 v.
(Sekcja Filologiczna, nr.1, 4.)
Summary in French: v.1, p. [59]-66.
491.922.Ot73.2 PU BM NN NNC(v.1)
WU(v.1)

7334. PALIONIS, Jonas. Jonas
Jablonskis ir jo lietuvių kalbos
vadovėliai. [Jonas Jablonskis and
his textbooks of Lithuanian lan-
guage] In Jablonskis, Jonas. Rinktiniai raštai (Vilnius), 1957. v.
1, p. 7-56. PG8509.J33A6 1957 DLC
CU CtY ICU MH NB NN PU

7335. --- Jono Jablonskio kalbi-
niai taisymai. [Grammar corrections
of Jonas Jablonskis] In Jablonskis,
Jonas. Rinktiniai raštai. Vilnius,
1959, v.2, p. 5-54. PG8509.J33A6
1959 v.2 DLC CU CtY ICU MH NB NN PU

7336. --- Lietuvių kalbotyros
laimėjimai tarybinės santvarkos metais. [The successes of the Lithuanian philology during the Soviet
period] In LTSRAMMD: Kalbotyra,
v.1, 1958, p. [6]-20. See serials
consulted.

7337. --- Lietuvių literatūrinė
kalba XVI-XVII a. [The literary
Lithuanian language in the 16th-
17th centuries] Vilnius, Mintis,
1967. 333 p. PG8525.P3 DLC CaOTU
CtY ICU InNd ICBM MH NN NjP OKentU
PU

7338. --- Rusų kalbininkų indėlis
i lituanistiką. [The contributions
to the Lithuanian language studies
by the Russian linguists] Kaunas,
VPMLL, 1963. 73 p. illus.
3297.195 MH

7339. PETERSON, Mikhail Nikolae-
vich. Ocherk litovskogo iazyka.
Moskva, Izd-vo Akademii nauk SSSR,
1955. 158 p. PG8523.P4 DLC CU
CaAEU CaBVaU CaOTU CtY FU ICU KU MH
MnU NN NNC NcD NSyU PU WU

7340. PIKČILINGIS, Juozas. Lek-
sinė ir gramatinė sinonimika. [The
lexical and grammatical synonymy]
Kaunas, Šviesa, 1969. 140 p.
PG8665.P5 DLC CaAEU

7341. --- Žodžio aiškumas ir tik-

slumas. [Semantics of the word]
Vilnius, Mintis, 1965. 91 p.
PG8527.P5 DLC MH PU

7342. PIROČKINAS, Arnoldas. J.
Jablonskio seminaras. Mokymo priemonė studentams lituanistams. [Se-
minar about J. Jablonskis; a textbook for the students] Vilnius,
1970. 122 p. At head of title:
Vilniaus Valstybinis V. Kapsuko
Universitetas. Lietuvių kalbos
katedra. PG8517.J3P5 PU

7343. PUZINAS, Jonas. Kalbotyra
apie lietuvių protėvynę. [Linguis-
tic research on the Lithuanian
prehistory] In Lietuva (Chicago,
Ill.), no.1, 1952, p. 46-53, 96.
See serials consulted.

7344. RHESA, Ludwig Jedemin.
Philologisch-kritische Anmerkungen
zur litthauischen Bibel als Erläuterungen zu der bei der neuen Ausgabe veranstalteten Umarbeitung des
litthauischen Textes. Königsberg
in Pr., Verlag Enslin, 1816-24.
2 v. 491.92.R343 PU
BM(03128. h. 38.(2.))

7345. ROTHKIRCH, W. Litovsko-
iazycheskie ocherki istoricheskiia
izsliedovaniia Teobal'da [pseud.]
Vil'no, Tip. O. Zawadzkavo, 1890.
201 p. 491.922.R744 PU

7346. RUHIG, Philipp. Betrachtung der litauischen Sprache in
ihrem Ursprung, Wesen und Eigenschaften. Königsberg in Pr., Hartung, 1745. 88 p. 3297.8 MH
BM(12975. f. 6. (1.))

7347. RUKŠA, Antanas. "Diarium
Societatis Jesu ir lietuvių kalba
Vilniuje. ["Diarium Societatis
Jesu" and the Lithuanian language
in Vilnius] In Tautos praeitis
(Chicago, Ill.), v.1, no.3, 1961,
p. 409-423. See serials con-
sulted.

7348. SALOPIATA, Paul. Das
Verhältnis der Evangelien-Texte in
den ältesten katholisch-litauischen
Drucken. Göttingen, Vandenheock &
Ruprecht, 1929. 58 p. Thesis--
University of Königsberg.
BS2554.L78S18 DLC CtY MH MiU PU

7349. SCHMALSTIEG, William Riegel. Linguistic problems in translations with special reference to
the translation from Lithuanian
into English. In Lituanus (Chicago, Ill.), v.15, no.3, 1969, p.
5-9. See serials consulted.

7350. SENN, Alfred. Handbuch der
litauischen Sprache. Heidelberg, C.

Winter, 1957-66. 2 v. (Indoger-
manische Bibliothek. 1. Reihe:
Lehr- und Handbücher) PG8523.S4
DLC CLU CU CaAEU CaBVaS CaOTU
CaOWtU CtY FU GU HU ICU IEN ICN
InNd IU LU MH MnU MWalB MU NN NbU
NcD NIC NcU NNC NjP OClW OrU PPiU
PU ScU TxU WU WaU

7351. --- The historical develop-
ment of the Lithuanian vocabulary.
[n.p.] 1943. 24 p. Offprint from
Polish Institute of Arts and
Sciences in America. Bulletin
(New York, N.Y.), July, 1943.
PG8524.S4 CaBVaU; see also serials
consulted.

7352. --- The Lithuanian language,
a characterization. Chicago, Ill.,
Lithuanian Cultural Institute,
1942. 49 p. illus., maps, diagrs.
Bibliography: p. 45-49. PG8524.S4
DLC CaSSU CtY ICU In ICLJF ICBM MH
NN NcD OCl OrU PU RPm RPB ViU

7353. --- Prof. K. Būgos reikšmė
kalbų mokslui. [The importance of
Prof. K. Būga for linguistics] In
KUHMF. Raštai, v.1, 1925, p. 274-
293. See serials consulted.

7354. --- Standard Lithuanian in
the making. In Slavonic and East
European Review (London), v.22, no.
59, 1944, p. 102-116. See serials
consulted.

7355. SKARDŽIUS, Pranas.
Ankstyvesnė ir dabartinė lietuvių
bendrinės kalbos vartosena. [The
previous and present usage of the
Lithuanian standard language]
Cikaga, Pedagoginis Lituanistikos
Institutas, 1971. 80 p.
PG8524.S55 PU

7356. --- Lietuvių kalba, jos
sudarymas ir raida. [The Lithuanian language; its construction and
evolution. Tübingen, Ger., Patria,
1947] 28 p. PG8525.S6 DLC CaOONL
InNd PU

7357. --- Bendrinė kalba ir jos
vartojimas. [The standard language
and its usage] In Švietimo darbas
(Kaunas), v.9-10, 1927-28. See
serials consulted.

7358. --- Daukša pirmasis bendrinės kalbos kūrėjas Lietuvoje.
[Daukša, the pioneer of the standard Lithuanian language] In Archivum Philologicum (Kaunas), v.4, no.
1, 1933. See serials consulted.

7359. --- J. Jablonskis ir dabartinė lietuvių bendrinė kalba.
[J. Jablonskis and the present Lithuanian standard language] In

Archivum Philologicum (Kaunas), v.6, 1937, p. 12-35. See serials consulted.

7360. --- Kalbotyrinis darbas Lietuvoje. [The philological research in Lithuania] In Aidai (Brooklyn, N.Y.), no.3-4, 1962, p. 111-116, 156-162. See serials consulted.

7361. --- The Lithuanian language in the Indo-European family of languages. Lithuanian Bulletin (New York, N.Y.), v.5, no.9-11, 1947, p. 1-4; 3-4. See serials consulted.

7362. --- Die offizielle Urkundensprache des Litauischen Grossfürstentums als kulturgeschichtliche Quelle. In Baltijas Vēsturnicku konference, 1st, Riga, 1937. Runas un referāti. Riga, 1938. DK511.B25.B35 1937 DLC CSmH NNC PPULC PU

7363. --- Tarybinė kalbotyra Lietuvoje. [Philological research in Soviet Lithuania] In Aidai (Brooklyn, N.Y.) no.10 (115), 1958, p. 444-451. See serials consulted.

7364. --- Tarybinės kalbotyros teorija ir praktika. [The theory and practice of the Soviet philological research] In Aidai (Brooklyn, N.Y.), no.3(89), 1956, p. 128-133. See serials consulted.

7365. SPECHT, Franz. Das litauische Seminar an der Universität Halle. In Archivum philologicum (Kaunas), v.5, 1935, p. 36-53. See serials consulted.

7366. --- Weiteres zur Geschichte der pronominalen Flexion. In Zeitschrift für Vergleichende Sprachforschung (Göttingen), v.60, no. 3/4, 1933, p. 254-271. See serials consulted.

7367. --- Zur Geschichte der pronominalen Flexion im Indogermanischen und im Litauischen. In Zeitschrift für Vergleichende Sprachforschung (Göttingen), v.56, 1929, p. 264-275. See serials consulted.

STANG, Christian Schweigaard. Die westrussische Kanzleisprache des Grossfürstentums Litauen. Oslo, 1935. See entry no. 4418.

7368. SZEMERÉNYI, O. Sur l'unité linguistique balto-slave. In Études slaves et roumaines (Budapest), v.1, 1948, p. 65-85. See serials consulted.

7369. TETZNER, Franz Oskar. Das litauische Sprachgebiet. In Globus (Hildburghausen; Brunswick), v.71, 1897, p. 381-384. See serials consulted.

THURSTON, Theodore S. Lithuanian history, philology and grammar. Chicago, Ill., 1941. See entry no. 4499.

7370. ULVYDAS, Kazimieras. Daugiau dėmesio spaudos kalbos kultūrai. [More attention to the culture of the press language] In Kalbos kultūra (Vilnius), no.7, 1964, p. 8-21. See serials consulted.

7371. VILNA. RESPUBLIKINIS MOKYTOJŲ TOBULINIMOSI INSTITUTAS. Lietuvių kalbos ir literatūros mokymo klausimai. [The teaching of Lithuanian language and literature] Vilnius, Profleidykla, 1960. 91 p. illus. LB1577.L5V53 DLC

7372. VIRELŪNAS, Antanas. Mūsų kalbos ūgdymas. [The development of our language] Kaunas, 1925. 48 p. Offprint from Švietimo darbas. 491.92.V2 CtTMF

7373. VOELKEL, Maximillian J. A. Litauische Studien: die lettischen Sprachreste auf der Kurischen Nehrung. Tilsit, Druck von J. Reyländer, 1879. 32 p. PG8993.K8V6 CU MH PU

7374. VOSYLYTĖ, Bronč. J. Jablonskio vaidmuo lietuvių literatūrinės kalbos istorijoje. [The role of J. Jablonskis in the history of the Lithuanian literary language] In Literatūra ir kalba (Vilnius), v.1, 1956, p. 40-65. See serials consulted.

XIII.4.d. OLD TEXTS

7375. AKTAI IR DOKUMENTAI: Prūsų vyriausybės skelbimai lietuvių kalba; 1794 metu skelbimai ir 1812 metų atsišaukimai. [Acts and documents: the proclamations of the Prussian government in Lithuanian language; the proclamation of 1794 and the announcements and proclamations of 1812. Edited by Augustinas Janulaitis] In Praeitis (Kaunas), v.1, 1930, p. 347-365. See serials consulted.

7376. BARTNIKOWSKI, Piotr. Kielawiedis apwaykszcziajuńcziem paminkłu iżganitojaus musu Jezusa

Pona kielu jerozolimsku, Dieceziay
wileńskay, ant kalnu Werkowsku, pa
Wilnium ażudietu pa sergibu kunigu.
Iżdotas par kunigu Pietru Bartni-
kowsku... isz iżguldinima letuwiszka
par kunigu Henriku Balewiczu...
Wilniuy, Kasztu J. Zawadzkia, 1857.
72 p. Bonaparte Collection No.
13444 ICN

7377. BIBLE. MANUSCRIPTS, LITHU-
ANIAN. Biblia; tai est Wissas
Schwentas Raschtas, lietuwischkai
perguldytas per Jana Bretkuna, Lietuvos plebona Karaliaucziuje, 1590.
3 reels. Film 1436 PU

7378. BIBLE. LITHUANIAN. 1755.
QUANDT. Biblia, tai esti: Wissas
Szwentas Rásztas, Seno ir Naujo
Testamento pagal Wokiszką Pérstatt-
imą D. M. Luteraus... Lietuwiszkay
pérstattytas, ir antra kartą iszspáustas. [Translated, under the
supervision of Johann Jacob Quandt,
by J. Behrendt, Philipp Ruhig and
others; with a preface in German by
J. J. Quandt. A short preface in
Lithuanian is signed: A.F.S., R.R.,
i.e. A.F. Schimelpfennig. The
Psalter is based on Bretkun's ver-
sion] Karalauczuje, pas P.K. Kan-
teri, 1755. 1416, 364 p. Page for
the Prophets bears the date 1815.
BM(3061. c. 14.)

7379. BIBLE. LITHUANIAN. 1816.
RHESA. Biblia, tai esti: Wissas
Szwentas Rásztas Séno ir Naujo Testamento, su kiekwieno Pérskyrimo
trumpu Praneszimmu... trecżą kartą
iszspaustas. [Quandt's version revised by L. J. Rhesa and others.
With a Lithuanian translation of
Francke's preface to the Canstein
edition] Karalauczuje, 1816. xv,
1520, 384 p. No Lithuanian Bible
had been published since Quandt's
second edition in 1755. The title-
-Second edition of the bible of
1755. BM(3061. b. 18.) NN

7380. BIBLE. LITHUANIAN. 1824.
RHESA. Biblia, tai esti: Wissas
Szwentas Rásstas Séno ir Naujo Testamento, lietuwisskay pérstattytas
iss naujo pérweizdétas ir ketwirta
kartą issspáustas. Tilżeje, E.
Post, 1824. 1304. 334 p. The
version of 1816, further revised by
L.J. Rhesa, and issued by the
Königsberg Bible Society. Bonaparte Collection No. 13424 ICN

7381. BIBLE. LITHUANIAN. 1853.
RHESA. Bybelēs, tai esti: Wissas
Szwentas Rasstas Seno ir Naujo Testamento, lietuwisskay perstattytas,
iss naujo pérweizdētas ir penktą
kartą issspaustas. Frankfurte prie

upês Main, H.L. Broenner, 1853.
1024, 305 p. New Testament has
special t.p. A publication of the
British and Foreign Bible Society.
Rhesa's version of 1816, with
minor corrections. Inserted:
Apokrypa [from the Tilsit edition
of 1824] Bonaparte Collection No.
13425 ICN BM(3061. d. 16.)

7382. BIBLE. LITHUANIAN. 1865.
Bybelēs, tai esti: Wissas Szwentas
Rasztas Seno ir Naujo Testamento,
lietuwiszkay perstatytas, isz naujo
perweizdētas ir septintą kartą iszspaustas. Berline, Iszspaustas
prie Trowitsch, 1865. 892, 284 p.
BS263 1865 PU

7383. BIBLE. LITHUANIAN. 1908.
Biblija, tai esti visas Šventas
Raštas Senojo ir Naujo Testamento
i lietuviškąją kalbą perstatytas.
Išnaujo perveizdetas ir 9. kartą
atspaustas. [Bible. 9th rev.
edition] Berlyne, Atspausdinta
nuo Britiškosēs bei svetimyjų žemių Biblijų draugystės, 1908. 2 v.
in 1. BS263 1908 DLC

7384. BIBLE. LITHUANIAN. 1910.
Biblija, tai esti wissas šwentas
raštas... iš naujo perveizdatas ir
10. kartą atspausdintas. Berlyne,
...Biblijų draugystės, 1910. 2 v.
in 1. 214.67 1910 PU

7385. BIBLE. LITHUANIAN. 1910.
SKVIRECKAS. Šventasis Raštas
Senojo ir Naujojo Testamento, su
Vulgatos tekstu. Vertė ir komen-
torių pridėjo Juozapas Skvireckas.
Kaunas, Šv. Kazimiero dr-jos lei-
dinys, 1910-1937. 5 v. Complete
text of Old and New Testament in
Lithuanian with Latin Vulgata text
and comments. BS263 1910 DLC(5)

7386. BIBLE. LITHUANIAN. 1937.
SKVIRECKAS. Šventas Raštas Senojo
ir Naujojo Testamento, su Vulgatos
tekstu. Vertė ir komentorių pri-
dėjo Juozapas Skvireckas. Kaunas,
"Šviesos" spaustuvė, 1937. v.5
Šv. Raštas Naujo įstatymo.
BS263 1937 DLC

7387. BIBLE. N. T. GERMAN. 1727.
LUTHER. Das Neue Testament Unsers
Herrn Jesu Christi, und der Psalter
Davids, deutsch und litthauisch...
aufs neue übersetzet, mit jedes
Capitels kurtzen Summarien auch
beygefügten nöthigen Parallelen.
Königsberg, C.G. Eckart, 1727.
1046, [11], 260 p. Added t.p. in
Lithuanian. Der Psalter Davids has
special t.p., dated 1728, and
separate paging. The Lithuanian
version of the New Testament is

that of J. J. Quandt, made with the assistance of Philipp Ruhig. The Psalter is based on the version of Jan Bretkun. Bonaparte Collection No. 13476 ICN

7388. BIBLE. N. T. LITHUANIAN. 1591. J. BRETKŪNAS. Postilla; tatai esti, Trumpas ir prastas ischguldimas Euangeliu.. per Jana Bretkuna Lietuvos plebona. Karaliaucziuie, Jurgio Osterbergero, 1591. 2 v. BM(C37. f. 29.)

7389. --- ---. Xerox copy. Karaliaucziuie, Jurgio Osterbergero, 1591. 2 v. BV4254.L5B7 1972 PU (Xerox copy)

7390. BIBLE. N. T. LITHUANIA. [SAMOGITIAN DIALECT] 1816. Naujas istatimas Jezaus Christaus in Wieszpaties musu Lietuwiszku Lezuwiu iszgulditas par Jozapa Arnulpha Kunigaykszti Giedrayti, Wiskupa ziemayciu. [Translated from the Vulgate] Wilniuje, iszspaustas pas kunigus Missionierius, 1816. [12], 388 p. CBPX.L. 1816 CaQMM BM(466. a. 17.) ICN NN PPAmP

7391. BIBLE. N. T. LITHUANIAN. 1816. Naujas Testamentas musu pono bey Iszganytojo Jezaus Kristaus... [J.J. Quandt's version, revised by L.J. Rhesa and others] Karalauczuje, 1816. 384 p. BM(1410. b. 3.)

7392. BIBLE. N. T. LITHUANIAN. 1834. Naujas Testamentas Musû Iszganytojo Jezaus Kristaus. Tilzéje, E. Post, 1834. 556 p. "Psalmai Dowido": p. [447]-556. Bonaparte Collection No. 13479 ICN BM(1110. e. 5.)

7393. BIBLE. N. T. LITHUANIAN. 1853. Naujas Testamentas Mûsû Wieszpatiês ir Iszganytojo Jēzaus Kristaus, i Lietuwiszkaję kalbą iszwerstas. Frankfurte, H.L. Broenner, 1853. 305, 84 p. "Psalmai Dowido" has special t.p. and separate paging. Bonaparte Collection No. 13480 ICN BM(3061. d. 16.) CBPX.L. 1853 CaQMM

7394. BIBLE. N. T. LITHUANIAN. 1861. Naujas Testamentas mûsû Wiesspatiês ir Issganytojo Jēzaus Kristaus, i lietuwisskaję kalbą isswerstas. Berlynė, Trowitzsch, 1861. 394 p. Followed by "Psalmai Dowido" (108 p.) with special t.p. and separate paging. X8845.095 ICN

7395. BIBLE. N. T. LITHUANIAN. 1865. Naujas Testamentas mûsû Wiesspatiês ir Issganytojo Jēzaus Kristaus, i lietuwisskaję kalbą isswerstas. Berlynè, Trowitzsch,

1865. 390 p. Followed by "Psalmai Dowido" (102 p.) with special t.p. and separate paging. X8845.096 ICN BM(3061. d. 4.) MH(Balt 9640.75)

7396. BIBLE. N. T. LITHUANIAN. 1866. GIEDRAITIS. Naujas Testamentas Wieszpaties musu Jēzaus Kristaus, su didžiu dabojimu pérguldijtas, o ánt Garbês Diewui Traicej' Szwentoj' wienatijam, Lietuwos žmonéms ánt iszganitingos naudôs iszspáustas. Berlyné, Trowitzsch, 1866. 474 p. X88485.1 ICN CtY

7397. BIBLE. N. T. LITHUANIAN. 1874. RHESA. Naujas Testamentas mûsų Wieszpaties ir iszganytojo Jezaus Kristaus į lietuwiszkaję kalbą iszwerstas. Berliné, Trowitzsch ir jo sunaus, 1874. 394 p. BM(3068. de. 36.) NN

7398. BIBLE. N.T. LITHUANIAN. 1906. Sventas Raštas, arba Biblija Naujo Istatymo Lietuviškon kalbon išguldyta Juozapo Arnulpo Giedraičio. 2. kartu atspausta. Su komentorium, parengtu A. Staniukyno. Shenandoah, Pa., "Žvaigždės" spaustuvėje, 1906. 494 p. BS2163 1906 DLC NN

7399. BIBLE. N. T. LITHUANIAN. 1945. SKVIRECKAS. Naujasis Jezaus Kristaus mûsų Viešpaties Testamentas Vertė Juozapas Skvireckas. 2. pataisyta laida. Išleido P.M. Juras. So. Boston, Mass., "Darbininko" spauda, 1945. xix, 765 p. BS2163 1945 DLC CaOONL PU

7400. BIBLE. N. T. LITHUANIAN. 1947. SKVIRECKAS. Naujasis mûsų Viešpaties Jēzaus Kristaus Testamentas. [New Testament of our Lord Jesus Christ] Vertė Juozapas Skvireckas. 4. laida. Stuttgart, Ger. [Lux] 1947. xxiii, 620 p. BS2163 1947 DLC CaOONL NN PU

7401. BIBLE. N. T. LITHUANIAN. 1949. SKVIRECKAS. Šventasis Raštas Naujojo Testamento. [Holy Scripture of the New Testament] Vertė ir komentorių pridėjo Juozapas Jonas Skvireckas. Zams, Austria, Lux, 1949. 2 v. BS2163 1949 DLC

7402. BIBLE. N. T. LITHUANIAN. 1958. CHYLIŃSKI. Biblia litewska Chylińskiego: Nowy Testament. Wydali Czesław Kudzinowski [i] Jan Otrębski. Wstęp napisali Stanisław Kot, Jan Otrębski [i] Czesław Kudzinowski. Poznań, Zakład Narodowy im. Ossolińskich we Wrocławiu, 1958- BS2163 1948 CaAEU(3) DLC CU CaBVaU CtY CtPAM ICU MiU MH-AH

NIC WU

7403. BIBLE. N. T. EPISTLES AND GOSPELS, LITURGICAL. LITHUANIAN. (1579) 1966. VILENTAS. Baltramiejus Vilentas' Lithuanian translation of the Gospels and Epistles, 1579. Edited by Gordon B. Ford, Jr. Louisville, Ky., Pyramid Press [1966-] Includes: facsims of the 1579 Königsberg ed.; The Life and Works of Baltramiejus Vilentas (20 leaves included in v.1) BS2547.A4L5 1966 DLC PU

7404. BIBLE. N. T. EPISTLES AND GOSPELS, LITURGICAL. POLISH. 1858. Ewangelje polskie i żmudzkie na niedziele i wszystkie święta całego roku. Wilno, J. Zawadzki, 1858. 386 p. Bonaparte Collection no. 13481 ICN

7405. BIBLE. N. T. GOSPELS. LITHUANIAN. 1674. Ewangelie polskie y litewskie, tak niedzielne iako y wszystkich świąt, które w kościele katholickiem, według Rzymskiego porządku przez cały rok czytaią. Vilnae, Typis academicis, 1674. 219 p. Reproduced by microfilm-xerography, 1972. Lithuanian translation attributed to Jonas Jaknavičius. BS2565.A4L5 1972 PU

7406. BIBLE. O. T. LITHUANIAN. 1660. Pirma kniga Mayzёszaus wadynama Genesis. [Genesis, etc. Tr. by Jan Bretkun. Edited by Samuel Bogusław Chyliński] [London? 1660?] 176 p. A gragment containing only Genesis-Joshua xv. 63. BM(C. 51. b. 13.)

7407. BIBLE. O. T. LITHUANIAN. 1955. SKVIRECKAS. Šventasis Raštas Senojo Testamento. [Holy Scripture of the Old Testament] Vertė ir komentorių pridėjo Kauno Arkivyskupas Metropolitas Juozapas Jonas Skvireckas. 2. laida. Roma, 1955-58. 2 v. BS964.S92 DLC PU

7408. BIBLE. O. T. APOCRYPHA. LITHUANIAN. 1824. Apokrypa; arba, Knygos, pagal sswentą rasstą naudingay skaityti. [Tilžeje, 1824] p. 1104-1304. Extract from the Tilsit edition of 1824, which was published by the Königsberg Bible Society. Bound with Bible. Lithuanian. 1853. Rhesa. Bybelĕs. Frankfurte, 1853. Bonaparte Collection no. 13425 ICN

7409. BIBLE. O. T. PSALMS. LITHUANIAN. 1625. Psaltaras Dowido ing lietuvischkus szodzius pirmiausiei ischgulditas per Jona Bretkuna... bet nuo dabbar... per Jona Rheza... su pilnaste atnau-

gintas. Karaliautzoje Prussu, 1625. 512 p. Negative microfilm. Film 1437 PU

7410. BIBLE. O. T. PSALMS. LITHUANIAN. 1861. Psalmai Dowido. Berlynĕ, Trowitzsch, 1861. 108 p. Bound with Bible. N. T. Lithuanian. 1861. Naujas Testamentas. Berlin, 1861. X8845.095 ICN

7411. BIBLE. O. T. PSALMS. LITHUANIAN. 1865. Psalmai Dowido. Berlynĕ, Trowitzsch, 1865. 102 p. Bound with Bible. N. T. Lithuanian. 1865. Naujas Testamentas. Berlin, 1865. X8845.096 ICN BM MH

7412. BIBLE. O. T. PSALMS. LITHUANIAN. 1874. Psalmai Dowido. Berlinĕ, Trowitzsch ir jo sunus, 1874. 108 p. Bound with Bible. N. T. Lithuanian. 1874. Rhesa. Naujas Testamentas. Berlin, 1874. BM(3068. de. 36.) NN

7413. BIRŽIŠKA, Vaclovas. Nežinomieji senieji lietuviški tekstai. [Unknown old Lithuanian texts] Kaunas, 1931. 104 p. (Tauta ir žodis, v.7) PG8501.T3 DLC

7414. CATHOLIC CHURCH. LITURGY AND RITUAL. LITHUANIAN. Aktas ir poterej. Wilniuj, J. Blumowicz, 1862. 24 p. Bonaparte Collection no. 13421 ICN

7415. --- Garbie Diewa, knigiele jaunumenej pawesta. Wilniuj, Kasztu J. Zawadzkie, 1860. 280 p. Bonaparte Collection no. 13431 ICN

7416. --- Griesznikas priwerstas metawoties; arba, Kałba użkietejuse griesznika su Wieszpacziu Diewu... Kunegas Peliksas Werejka... isz- guldze. Wilniuje, Kasztu J. Zawadzkia, 1860. 48 p. Bonaparte Collection no. 13433 ICN

7417. --- Jezus Maria Juozapas szwętas. Knigiała ta ape tajemnicia septiniu sopulu yr linksmibiu Juozapa szwęta. Isz nauja spaustuwien paduota. Wilniuje, Kasztu A. Dworcziaus, 1853. 469 p. Bonaparte Collection no. 13438 ICN

7418. --- Rożanczius szwenczausios Maryjos Panos ir saldziausi warda Jesusa su rejkalingiasniomis małdomis... katalikuj isz nauja spaustuwien paduotas. Wilniuje, Kasztu S.L. Solca, 1861. 344 p. Bonaparte Collection no. 13467 ICN

7419. --- Senas auksa ałtorius; arba, Surynkimas iwayriu małdun ir giesmiun... Ysz nauja spaustuwien

paduotas. Wilniuje, Kasztu S.L.
Solca, 1861. 571 p. Bonaparte
Collection no. 13471 ICN

7420. --- Swejka Marija ir gyweni-
mas Panos szwencziausios. Wilniuje,
A. Syrkin, 1860. 31 p. Bonaparte
Collection no. 13473 ICN

7421. CATHOLIC CHURCH. LITURGY
AND RITUAL. Novenas. Lithuanian.
Nowenas pri Jezaus Kristaus, szwen-
cziausies Marijos Panos ir kitu
szwentu. Wilniuje, Kasztu J. Zawadzkie, 1857. 190 p. Bonaparte
Collection no. 13460 ICN

7422. CATHOLIC CHURCH. LITURGY
AND RITUAL. Stations of the cross.
Lithuanian. Kałwaria; arba Kialas
križius suopulu Jezusa Kristusa isz
namu Piłota ant kałna Kałwarios.
Wilniuj, Kasztu J. Zawadzkie, 1862.
48 p. Bonaparte Collection no.
13441 ICN

7423. DAUKŠA, Mikalojus. Prakalba; jo mirties... 350 metų sukakčiai
paminėti. [An address. Redagavo
Domas Velička. Iš lenkų kalbos
išvertė Aleksandras Dundulis] Chicago, Pedagoginis lituanistikos
institutas, 1963. 23 p. Bibliography: p. 20. BX1756.A2D3 1963
DLC CaOONL CaOTU PPULC PU

7424. FORD, Gordon Buell, comp.
Lithuanian texts of the sixteenth
and seventeenth centuries, with a
glossary, edited by Gordon B. Ford.
The Hague, Mouton, 1969. 43 p.
Label mounted on t.p.: Humanities
Press, New York. PG8713.F6 DLC AzU
CaAEU CaBVaS CaOTU CtY IaU NSyU
OClW PU WaU

7425. GAIGALAT, Wilhelm. Die
Wolfenbütteler litauische Postillen-
handschrift aus dem Jahre 1573.
Erster Teil: Einleitung und Lautlehre. Tilsit, Druck O. v. Mauderode, 1900. 57 p. Thesis--Uni-
versity of Königsberg. PG8541.G2
DLC CtY MH NN OCl NNC

7426. GERULLIS, Georg. Litauischer Erbeid von 1572. In Archiv
für slavische Philologie (Berlin),
1926, p. 293-308. See serials
consulted.

7427. --- Senieji lietuvių skaitymai. I. dalis: Tekstai su įva-
dais. [The ancient Lithuanian
textx] Kaunas, Lietuvos universiteto leidinys, 1927. x, 311 p.
Z2514.L6G4(S) CU CtTMF ICU MH(xerox
copy) NN NNC PU

7428. HOFFHEINZ, Waldemar, comp.
Giesmių balsai. Litauische Kirchen-
gesänge, gesammelt durch W. Hoff-
heinz. Tilsit; Heidelberg, Ger.,
Mauderode, 1894. 113 p. music.
M2132.L4H6 PU CU CtY MiU NN

7429. ISZGULDIMAS EVANGLIU PER
wisus mettus, surinktas dalimi isch
daugia pastillu, tai est isch pa-
stillas Nicolai Hemingy, Antony
Corvini, Johannis Spangenbergi...
295 leaves. Ms. in the Herzog
August Bibliothek, Wolfenbüttel
(MS Aug. 11.2) from 16th century
[1573] Microfilm. Film 2135
1 reel PU

7430. JUZUMOWICZ, Wincentas.
Szwentas Izidorius artojas. Knige-
le diel žinios ir naudos artoju
žemajtiszkaj. Wilniuje, Kasztu, J.
Zawadzkia, 1854. 80 p. Bonaparte
Collection no. 13474 ICN

7431. KANTYCHKAS; arba, Kniga
giesmiu, par Motieju Volonchevski
viskupa parveizieta ir ishnaue ish-
spausta. Vil'niui, 1865. p. 41-
708. In cyrillic characters. Copy
imperfect. BV510.L5K3 PU

7432. KANTYCZKOS ŽEMAYTISZKOS;
arba, Giedojmay Diewa garbingi.
Wilniuje, Drukarnici Diecezijos pri
Bažniczies Kunigu Missionoriu,
1837. 693, [9-] p. Without music;
tunes indicated by title. Imperfect: 1 or 2 leaves at end (of
index) wanting. X88485.461 ICN

7434. LEBEDYS, Jurgis and Jonas
Palionis. Seniausias lietuviškas
rankraštinis tekstas. [The oldest
Lithuanian manuscript] In LTSRAMMD:
Bibliotekininkystės ir bibliografijos klausimai (Vilnius), v.3, 1964,
p. 109-132. See serials consulted.

7435. LEDESMA, Diego de. Litovskii katekhisis M. Daukshi. Po iz-
daniiu 1595 goda vnov' perepecha-
tannyi i snabzhennyi ob"iasneniiami
E. Vol'terom. Sanktpeterburg [Tip.
Imp. akademii nauk] 1886. vii,
lxxxvi, 191 p. (Akademiia nauk
SSSR. Zapiski, t.53, prilozh. 3)
491.922.L496 MH NN

7436. --- Katechismus des Ledezma
und die litauischen Katechismen des
Daugsza und des Anonymus vom Jahre
1605, nach den Krakauer Originalen
und Wolters Neudruck interlinear
herausgegeben von Ernst Sitting.
Göttingen, Vandenhoeck & Ruprecht,
1929. viii, 163 p. (Ergänzungshefte zur Zeit für vergleichende
Sprachforschung, nr.6)
BX1966.P7L45 1929 DLC PBm CaAEU

7437. LITAUISCHE UND LETTISCHE
Drucke des 16. Jahrhunderts hrsg.

von Adalbert Bezzenberger. Göttingen, R. Peppmüller [etc.] 1874-84. 4 v. Contents.--Hft. 1. Der litauische Katachismus vom Jahre 1547.--Hft. 2. Der lettische Katechismus vom Jahre 1586. Das litauische Taufformular vom Jahre 1559. Anhang: Das (angeblich altpreussische) lettische Vaterunser des Simon Grunau.--Hft. 3. Bartholomäus Willen's litauische Übersetzung des Luther'schen Enchiridions und der Episteln und Evangelien... hrsg. von Fritz Bechtel.--Hft. 4. Szyrwid's Punkty kazan (Punktay sakimu) vom Jahre 1629... hrsg. von Richard Garbe. PG8002.L6 DLC CU CtY ICU MiU MdBJ MH MnU(1-2,4) NN NNC NcU NjP PBm PU OClW TxU

7438. LUTHER, Martin. Catechismus minor, germanico-polonico-lithuanico-latinus. Nunc tertium in his quatuor linguis editus. Der kleine Catechismus. Königsberg in Pr., 1700. BM(3905. b. 22.)

7439. --- The Lithuanian catechism of Baltramiejus Vilentas (1579). Edited by Gordon B. Ford, Jr. First edition. Louisville, Ky., Pyramid Press, 1964. [3], 77 [i.e. 149] p. Facsim. of the 1579 Königsberger edition. In Gothic type with Lithuanian transcription. BX8070.L727A2 1579a DLC IEN ICU MH MH-AH NjP NjPT

7440. --- --- 2. ed. Louisville, Ky., 1965. v, 75, 78 leaves. BX8070.L727A2 1579b DLC IEN ICN NcD PU

7441. --- --- 3d rev. ed. Louisville, Ky., Pyramid Press, 1966. xxv, 77 78 leaves. BX8070.L727A2 1579c DLC CaOTU NjP

7442. --- Pirmoji lietuviška knyga. [The first book in Lithuanian language. Redaktorius Jonas Kruopas, dailės redaktorius Mečislovas Bulaka] Kaunas, Valstybinė enciklopēdijų, žodynų ir mokslo literatūros leidykla [1947] xv, 182 p. facsims., music. In duplicate, in Gothic and Roman type. Translation of Kleiner Catechismus, translated and first published by Martynas Mažvydas under title: Catechismusa prasty szadei. At head of title: Lietuvos TSR Mokslų akademija, Vilna. Lietuvių kalbos institutas. BX8070.L727K7 DLC NN

7443. --- The old Lithuanian catechism of Martynas Mažvydas (1547). Edited and translated by Gordon B. Ford, Jr. Assen, Van Gorcum, 1971. xvi, 104 p. PG8525.L85 1971 PU CaOTU

7444. LUTHERAN CHURCH IN PRUSSIA. Liturgy and ritual. Lithuanian. Iss naujo pérweizdētos ir pagérintos giesmjů-knygos, kurrosa brangiáusos sénos ir naujos giesme surassytus Diewui ant garbés ir Prusů karalystéje ēsantiems lietuwninkams ant dussů issgánimo, podraug su maldů-knygomis. Karaláuczuje, Isssphaustos karalisskoje knyg-drukkawonéje Artungo [1751] 790 p. "Vorrede" signed: Joh. Jacob Quandt. "Naujos... maldů knygéle... lietuwoj' surassytos nůg m. Daniel Klein"; p. [617]-790. Bonaparte Collection no. 13432 ICN

7445. MAŽVYDAS, Martynas, comp. and tr. Die ältesten litauischen Sprachdenkmäler, bis zum Jahre 1570. Hrsg. von Georg Gerullis. Heidelberg, C. Winter, 1923. xxxx, 592 p. facsim., music. (Indogermanische Bibliothek. 5 Abt.: Baltische Bibliothek, Bd. 2) Compiler's name, Mosvid, at head of title. PG8701.M3 1570a DLC CLU CSt CaBVaU CaBVaS CaOHM CaOONL CU CtTMF ICN ICU KU MH MnU MiU NN NcD NcU NjP OrU OU PBm PU TxU WU WaU

7446. NAMU KRIŽIUS; arba, Kajp rejkie suditi yr misliti apej gierima ariełkas... Par Z.N. lenkiszkaj paraszitas. O dabarczio ant liežuwi lietuwiszka pardietas. Wilniuje, M. Orgelbrand, 1859. 86 p. "Prakalbieimas" signed: K. Dominikas Budrykas. Bonaparte Collection no. 13456 ICN

7447. NEPOS, Cornelius. Giwatas didiujů karwaidů senowês. Surasze łotiniszkay Kornelius Nepos. Iszguldę isz łotiniszkos i letuwiszką kalbą jaunuomenés naudon J. Dewinakis [pseud.] o apskelbę Ksaweras Kanapeckis. Petropilie, 1846. [Xerox copy, 1970] 250 p. PA6514.L5D3 1970 PU

7448. PATENTAS ROŽANCZIAWAS APREJZKUNS atpuskus yr priwilijus nuog staliczes apazstaliszkos arcebroctwaj rožancziaus s. dowenotus... [Wilno, A. Syrkin, 1861] 8 p. Bonaparte Collection no. 13462 ICN

7449. PRADŽIA PAMOKSLA DEL MAŽU weykialu... Katechizmas mažiasnis... del naudos surinkima Lietuwiszka. Königsberg in Pr., 1680. BM(c. 38b. 47.)

7450. PRASTA ALLE UZ AUKSA BRANGESne skarbinyczéle Diewo waiku, sawo skarbą danguje turrinczuju, kurroje yra randami kelli sswento rassto ludijimai su nabassnais giesmu atsidusaujimais... Tilžeje, 1847.

366 p. 241.L71 MnU

7451. PRZYAŁGOWSKI, Kazimierz. Naujes ałtorius, arba Surynkimas parsergieimu yr małdu pri spawiednes, kamunyjes szwętos, diel ligoniu ir myrsztanczlu... Wilniuje, Kasztu J. Zawadzkia, 1861. xx, 712 p. Bonaparte Collection no. 13457 ICN

7452. RACZKAUSKIS, Jeronimas. Bałsą Diewa pri żmogaus; arba, Apdumojimą gieradieiszcziu Wieszpaties Diewa. Wilniuje, Kasztu J. Zawadzkie, 1858. 128 p. Bonaparte Collection no. 13466 ICN

7453. --- Munką Wieszpaties Jezaus; arba, Diewabajmingus dumojimus apej munką Jezaus Kristaus diel kiekwienos dienos par isztisą gawienę. Wilniuje, Kasztu J. Zawadzkia, 1857. 200 p. Bonaparte Collection no. 13465 ICN

7454. --- Wadowas i dangu ir meditacijes diel penkiu dienu rekolekciju. Wilniuje, Kasztu J. Zawadzkia, 1857. 231 p. Bonaparte Collection no. 13464 ICN

7455. RUPEJKO, Józef. Jonas Iszmisłoczius, krominlnkas. Pirmu kartu isz lenkiszkos in lietuwiszką kałbą perstatitas per Juozupą Rupeiką... o dabar isz naujo perwejdetas ir spaustuwen paduotas per Jurą Warneli. Wilniuja, Spaustuweja A.H. Kirkora, 1860. 173 p. Bonaparte Collection no. 13439 ICN

7456. SCHMID, Christoph von. Genawejte; pasaka wiena tarp grażiausiu ir werksmingiausiu, apej jos wargus, rupesnius ir stebuklingus Diewa pariedimus, kajp giariems użmok giaru, o piktiems atiduoda piktu. Isz lenkiszka lieżuwia iszguldita par L. Iwiński. Wilniuje, 1858. 187 p. Xerox copy, 1970. PT2504.S88G415 1970 PU

7457. ŠIRVYDAS, Konstantinas. Szyrwid's Punkty kazań... vom Jahre 1629. Mit einer grammatischen Einleitung herausgegeben von R. Garbe. Göttingen, Vandenhoeck & Ruprecht, 1884. xlviii, 156 p. Slav 9325.5.IV BM

7458. --- Punktay sakimu, Punkty kazań Litauisch und Polnisch... Teil 1: 1629, Teil 2: 1644, von Konstantin Syrwid. Mit kurzer grammatischer Einleitung hrsg. von Franz Specht. Göttingen, Vandenhoeck & Ruprecht, 1929. 61, xii, 382, viii, 259 p. facsim. BX1756.S53P8 DLC ICU MiU MH MnU PU

7459. --- Punkty kazań od Adwentu aż do postu, litewskim językiem, z wytłumaczeniem na polskie przez K. Szyrwida. Wilno, Druk Academiey Societatis Jesu, 1629-44. 2 v. in 1. 491.922.S178.2 PU BM(4423. g. 38.)

SŁOWACZYŃSKI, Salomon M. Giesmės tikėjimui katalickam priderančios, 1646. Vilnius, 1958. See entry no. 6381.

7460. ŠRUBAUSKIS, Pranciškus, supposed compiler. Balsas szirdies pas Pona Diewa Szwęciausy, Maryja Panna yra Szwętus Danguy karalaujencius... nauiey su pazwaliimu wiresniuju dwasyszku iszduotas par viena kuniga Soc. J. Wilniuy, 1970. 272 p. Reproduced by microfilm-xerography, 1972. BV510.L5S7 1972 PU

7461. SZWĘSTAS GIESMES DIEL KRIKszcionu kataliku suraszitas ir iszspaustas su pridieimu giesmiu ir psalmes. Wilniuj, Kasztu J. Zawadzkia, 1861. 716 p. Bonaparte Collection no. 13475 ICN

7462. TATARĖ, Antanas. Pamoksłaj iszminties ir tejsibes, iszguldineti priliginimajs gałwocziu wisu amżiu deł Lietuwos wajkielu. Suwałkuase, 1851. 378 p. Reproduced by microfilm-xerography, 1972. PG8721.T37P32 1972 PU

7463. --- Tiesiauses kieles ing dangaus karaliste; deszymtis prysakimu Wieszpaties pagał pamoksłu Bażniczios szwentos katalikiszkos rymiszkos. Paraszytas metuase 1849 nog użgimimo Jezuso Chrystuso. Suwałkuose, 1853. xxi, 265 p. Reproduced by microfilm-xerography, 1972. PG8721.T37T5 1972 PU

7464. --- Żyburys rankoje duszios krykszczioniszkos kielaujenczios in amżyna i szczesliwa giwenima; taj ira, Trumpas iszguldymas moksłu wieros szwentos katalikiszkos. Suwałkuase, 1848. 378 p. Reproduced by microfilm-xerography, 1972. Imperfect: p. 158-159 wanting. PG8721.T37Z9 1972 PU

7465. TEWE MUSU, MAŁDA WIESZPAties Iszganytojaus. Antru kartu isspausta. Wilniuja, R.M. Romm, 1860. 16 p. Bonaparte Collection no. 13482 ICN

7466. VALANČIUS, Motiejus. Giwenimaj szwentuju Diewa. Tilžėj, 1868. 292 p. Xerox copy, 1970. PG8721.V327G5 1970 PU

7467. --- Istorije szwęta Senoje
istatima. Nu sutwierima pasaules
lig uzgimima Kristaus Wieszpaties.
Ketwirta karta iszspausta. Wilniuj,
Kasztu J. Zawadzkia, 1860. 94 p.
"Prokałba" (Preface) signed: Motiejus Wiskupas. Bonaparte Collection
no. 13436 ICN

7468. --- --- 3. iszdavimas.
Philadelphia, Pa., 1907. 181 p.
891.92.V232I PU

7469. --- Prade ir iszsiplietimas
kataliku tikieima. Wilniuje, 1864.
311 p. Xerox copy, 1970.
PG8721.V327P7 1970 PU

7470. --- Żine kajp rejk atlikti
spawiednę isz wisa amżiaus. Trete
karta iszspausta. Wilniuj, Spaustuwieje J. Zawadzkia, 1857. 36 p.
Bonaparte Collection no. 13485 ICN

7471. --- Żiwataj szwętuju, tu
kuriu wardajs żemajczej... wadin-
ties. Ejłu abeciełas suraszyti. 2.
karta iszspaustas. Wilniuj, 1863.
302 p. Klaipėda, 1881; Xerox copy
of 1863 ed., 1970. PG8721.V327Z5
1970 PU

7472. --- Żiwatas Jezaus Kristaus
Wieszpaties musu; arba, Istorije
Naujoje Istatima iszspausta. Wilniuj, Spaustuwiej A. Dworcziaus,
1853. 266 p. "Prakałba" (Preface)
signed: Motiejus Wołonczewskis,
Wiskupas. Bonaparte Collection no.
13486 ICN Xerox copy, 1970.
PG8727.V327Z92 1970 PU

7473. WOLFENBÜTTEL. HERZOG-AUGUST-
BIBLIOTHEK. MSS. (AUG.11.2). The
Wolfenbüttel Lithuanian Postile
manuscript of the 1573. Edited by
Gordon B. Ford, Jr. Louisville,
Ky., Pyramid Press, 1965-66. 3 v.
BS2547.W62 DLC CaOTU NcD

7474. WUJEK, Jakób. Daukšos Pos-
tilė; fotografinis leidimas. Kaunas, Lietuvos universiteto leidinys,
1926. 16, 6, 625, 7 p. illus.,
facsim. Jakób Wujek's "Postilla
catholicka", translated into Lithuanian by Mikalojus Daukša. 1st ed.
printed in Vilnius, 1599.
BX1756.W8P615 DLC CtPAM NN PU

7475. --- Postilla catholicka
IAkuba Vuika v litovskom perevodie
N. Daukshi. [Ed. by] E.A. Vol'ter.
Sanktpeterburg, Tip. Imperatorskoi
akademii nauk, 1904-17. 3 v.
491.922.W954.2 PU(1-2) BM(Ac.1124/38.)
KU(1-3) NN

XIII.4.e. PHONETICS, ACCENT AND
ACCENTUATION

7476. AKIELEWICZ, Mikołaj. Gra-
matyka języka litewskiego. Głosow-
nia. Poznań, Nakładem Biblioteki
Kórnickiej, 1890. xi, 204 p.
PG8540.A6 DLC CaAEU CaBVaU CU CtY
ICU MH NN OrP PU

7477. ALEKSANDRAVIČIUS, J. Kirtis ir priegaidė Kretingos tarmėje.
[Stress and intonation in the Kretinga dialect] In Lietuvių kalbotyros klausimai (Vilnius), v.1,
1957, p. 97-107. See serials consulted.

7478. AUGUSTAITIS, Dainė. Das
litauische Phonationssystem. München, O. Sagner, 1964. 155 p.
illus. (Slavistische Beiträge, Bd.
12) Bibliography: p. [1]-3.
Thesis--University of München.
PG8540.A85 DLC CaAEU CaBVaU CLU CU
CSt CoU CtY IaU ICN InNd MH NIC NN
NNC NcU NSyU PPiU PU WaU WU

7479. BABRAUSKAS, Benys. Kirčiavimo taisyklės; 99 lietuvių kalbos
kirčiavimo taisyklės. [99 rules of
accentuation in the Lithuanian lan-
guage] Kaunas, Sakalas, 1939. 45
p. PQ8544.B3 PU CtTMF ICCC

7480. BALAŠAITIS, Antanas. Lietuvių kalbos fonetikos terminai.
[The terminology of the phonetics
of the Lithuanian language] In
LTSRMAD. Serija A, v.1(10), 1961,
p. 183-206. See serials consulted.

7481. BUCH, Tamara. Die Akzen-
tuierung des Christian Donelaitis.
Wrocław, Zakład Narodowy Imenia
Ossolinskich, 1961. 147 p. (Pols-
ka Akademia Nauk. Komitet Językoz-
nawczy. Prace Językoznawcze, 25)
PG8721.D7B6 DLC CaAEU CtY InU NcU
NmU NjP PU

7482. BŪGA, Kazimieras. Fonetika
kontsa slova v litovskikh govorakh.
In His Rinktiniai raštai. Vilnius,
1958. p. 558-577. PG8509.B8 v.1
DLC CaAEU CU CtPAM CtTMF ICLJH ICU
IEN MH NN NjP PPiU PU TxU

7483. --- Kirčio ir priegaidės
mokslas. [Science on the stress
and intonation] In His Rinktiniai
raštai. Vilnius, 1959. v.3, p.
19-84. PG8509.B8 v.3 DLC CaAEU CU
CtPAM CtTMF ICLJF ICU IEN MH NN
NjP PPiU PU TxU

7484. --- Die Metatonie im Litauischen und Lettischen. In His
Rinktiniai raštai. Vilnius, 1959.

v.2, p. 386-483. PG8509.B8 v.2 DLC
CaAEU CU ICLJF ICU MH NN NjP PPiU
PU TxU

7485. --- O proiskhozhdenii litovskogo "ž". In His Rinktiniai
raštai. Vilnius, 1958. v.1, p.
273-291. PG8509.B8 v.1 DLC CaAEU
CU CtPAM CtTMF ICLJF ICU IEN MH NN
NjP PPiU PU TxU

7486. BŪTĖNAS, Petras. Lietuvių
kalbos akcentologijos vadovėlis
mokyklai ir gyvenimui. [A textbook of accentuation of the Lithuanian language for the school and
general use] Kaunas, Spindulio
b-vės spaustuvė, 1931. 215 p.
PG8544.B8 PU CtTMF ICCC

7487. EKBLOM, Richard. Manuel
phonétique de la langue lituanienne.
Stockholm, P.A. Norstedt, 1922.
71 p. (Archives d'études orientales, vol.19) PG8543.E5 CaBVaU
CtY HU ICU MnU NIC NNC NmU NjP OCl
RPB ViU WU

7488. --- Quantität und intonation im zentralen Hochlitauischen.
Uppsala, Lundsquistska bokhandeln
[1925] 155 p. diagrs. (Uppsala
universitets årskrift 1925, [bd.1])
(Filosofi, språkvetenskap och his-
toriska vetenskaper, 3 [no.4])
AS284.U68a 1925 CLU CU CSt CtY ICU
MH MnU NIC NNC NbU PPDrop PU WU

7489. --- Zur Entstehung und Entwicklung der slavobaltischen und
nordischen Akzentarten. Uppsala,
Almqvist & Wiksells, 1930. 63 p.
LaE3672Zur CaOTU CLSU

7490. --- Zur Physiologie der
Akzentuation langer Silben im Slavo-
Baltischen. Uppsala, Akademiska
bokhandeln, 1922. 39 p. (Skrif-
ten utg. af K. Humanistiska Ve-
tenskabssamfundet i Uppsala, bd.1)
68Up75 1922 PU CLSU

7491. FRAENKEL, Ernst. Zur Bedeutung der Nasalvokale bei Daukša.
In Tauta ir žodis (Kaunas), v.4,
1926, p. 63-66. See serials consulted.

7492. FRANCIS, John Melton. The
accentuation of the denominative
verbs in Lithuanian. Thesis--Har-
vard University, 1967. Typescript.
HU90.9153.5(2 cop.) MH

7493. GERULLIS, Georg. Gespannte
und geblähte Konsonanten. In Archivum philologicum (Kaunas), v.5,
1935, p. [14]-22. See serials
consulted.

7494. GOIDÁNICH, Pietro Gabriele.
L'origine e le forme della ditton-
gazione romanza. Le qualità d'ac-
cento in sillaba mediana nelle
lingue indoeuropee. Halle a.S., M.
Niemeyer, 1907. 218 p. (Beihefte
zur Zeitschrift für romanische
philologie, Hft. 5) PC92.G7 DLC
CaAEU FU GU IaU ICN InNd IEN ICU LU
MH MiU MB NIC NNC NcD NcU NBuU NjR
NmU OU PPTU PSC PU OrU RPB ViU
TxU WaU

7495. HERMANN, Eduard. Die Betonung des litauischen Verbums.
Göttingen, Vandenhoeck & Ruprecht,
1949. In Akademie der Wissenschafte,
Göttingen, Mitologish-historische
Klasse. Nachrichten, no.12, 1949.
p. 333-343. AS182.G823 DLC CLU

7496. --- Litauische Studien; eine
historische Untersuchung schwachbe-
tonter Wörter im Litauischen. Mit
einem Wort- und Sachverzeichnis von
Wolfgang Krause. Berlin, Weid-
mannsche Buchhandlung, 1926. xviii,
423 p. tables. (Abhandlungen der
Gesellschaft der Wissenschaften zu
Göttingen. Philologisch-historische
Klasse. n.F. Bd.10, no.1)
AS182.G812 n.F. Bd.19,no.1 DLC CLU
CU CaAEU CtY IC ICN ICU MB MH NN
NIC NNC NcU NjP RPB

7497. JAUNIUS, Kazimieras. In-
tonatsii glasnykh zvukov litovskago
iazyka. Kaunas, 1910. Offprint
from Pamiatnoi knizhki Kovenskoi
gubernii na god 1900.
BM(12976. r. 14.)

7498. KAMANTAUSKAS, Viktoras.
Trumpas lietuvių kalbos kirčio
mokslas. [The art of accentuation
of Lithuanian in brief] Kaunas,
Švyturio bendrovės leidinys, 1928-
29. 2 v. PG8544.K3 DLC CtTMF CtY

7499. KAZLAUSKAS, Jonas. Dėl
lietuvių kalbos vardažodžio kirčiavimo sistemos. [On the rules of
accentuation of the proper names in
Lithuanian] In LTSRAMMD: Kalbotyra
(Vilnius), v.7, 1963, p. 171-180.
See serials consulted.

7500. --- Fonologinė kirčio raidos baltų kalbose interpretacija.
[The interpretation of the phonological development of the stress in
the Baltic languages] In Baltistica (Vilnius), v.3, 1967, p. 13-23.
See serials consulted.

7501. --- O meste vozvratnoi mor-
femy i ee udarenie v litovskom
iazyke. In Baltistica (Vilnius), v.
1, 1966, p. 143-149. See serials
consulted.

7502. KURSCHAT, Friedrich. Laut- und Tonlehre der littauischen Sprache. Berlin, Th. Enslin, 1849. vii, 212 p. (His Beiträge zur Kunde der littauischen Sprache, Hft. 2.) BM(1332. a. 12.)

7503. LAIGONAITĖ, Adėlė. Dėl lietuvių kalbos kirčio ir priegaidės supratimo. [On the understanding of the stress and intonation in the Lithuanian language] In LTSRAMMD: Kalbotyra (Vilnius), nr.1, 1958, p. [71]-100. See serials consulted.

7504. --- Lietuvių kalbos kir- čiavimas. [The accentuation of the Lithuanian language] Kaunas, Šviesa, 1970. 108 p. PG8544.L31 PU CaAEU DLC

7505. --- Literatūrinės lietuvių kalbos kiržiavimas. [Accentuation of the Lithuanian literary language] Vilnius, VPML, 1959. 134 p. PG8544.L3 DLC CtY ICU PU

7506. LESKIEN, August. Der Ab- laut der Wurzelsilben im Litaui- schen. Leipzig, 1884. 192 p. (Sächsische Akademie der Wissen- schaften, Leipzig. Philologisch- historische Klasse. Abhandlungen, Bd.21, no.4, 1852, p. [263]-454) AS182.S211 Bd.21 no.4 DLC CLU CaBVaU FU ICU MH NIC NN NNC OClW ViU WU

7507. MIKALAUSKAITĖ, Elzbieta. Kirčio ir priegaidės kaita, arba metatonija, pietvakarių dzūkų tar- mėje. [Shifting of the stress and intonation of the dialect of South- western Dzukija] In Lietuvių kal- botyros klausimai (Vilnius), v.1, 1957, p. 85-95. See serials con- sulted.

7508. SAUSSURE, Ferdinand de. A propos de l'accentuation lithua- nienne. In Société de linguistique de Paris. Mémoires, v.8, 1894, p. 425-446. See serials consulted.

7509. SCHMALSTIEG, William Rie- gel. The Lithuanian vocalic system revisited. In Lituanus (Chicago, Ill.), v.15, no.3, 1969, p. 35-40. See serials consulted.

7510. SCHULTZE, Paul August Lud- wig. Der Ausklang der litauischen Sprache im Kirchspiel Pilluponen. Halle, a.S., 1932. 78 p. Thesis-- University of Halle. 491.92.Sch85 PU MH NNC

7511. SITTIG, Ernst. Litauisch. Bearbeitet von prof. dr. Ernst

Sittig. Berlin, Institut für Laut- forschung an der Universität Ber- lin, in Kommission bei O. Harrasso- witz, 1935. 2 v. (Lautbibliothek; Texte... nr.36-37) P215.L35 nr. 36-37 DLC PBm

7512. SKARDŽIUS, Pranas. Ben- drinės lietuvių kalbos kirčiavimas; teorija su praktiniais pavyzdžiais. [Accentuation of the standard Li- thuanian language] Kaunas, 1936. 95 p. 491.922.Sk14 PU CtTMF ICCC

7513. --- Daukšos akcentologija. Kaunas, V.D.U. Humanitarinių mokslų fakulteto leidinys, 1935. 311 p. (Kaunas. Universitetas. Humanita- rinių mokslų fakultetas. Raštai, v. 17) PG5383D.SK16 WU IDLJF PU(Xerox copy, 1971) See serials consulted.

7514. --- Dėl skolinių kirčiavimo lietuvių kalboj. [On the accentu- ation of loan-words in Lithuanian] In Švietimo darbas (Kaunas), v.9, 1928, p. 936-941. See serials consulted.

7515. --- Lietuvių kalbos kirčia- vimas. Accentuation of Lithuanian language. Chicago, Ill., Pedagogi- nis lituanistikos institutas, 1968. 117 p. PG8544.S5 DLC CaAEU CaOONL ICLJF ICU PU

7516. SPECHT, Franz. Betonung der litauischen Direktive auf -na und -pi. In Zeitschrift für ver- gleichende Sprachforschung (Göttin- gen), v.53, 1925, p. 90-93. See serials consulted.

7517. TORBIÖRNSSON, Tore. Litau- ische Akzentfragen. In Archivum philologicum (Kaunas), v.5, 1935, p. [66]-99. See serials consulted.

7518. --- Die litauischen Akzent- verschiebungen und der litauische Verbalakzent. Heidelberg, C. Win- ter, 1924. 54 p. (Slavica; Bei- träge zum Studium der Sprache, Li- teratur, Kultur, Volks- und Alter- tumskunde der Slaven, 9) PG8544.T6 CSt CU CaBVaU CtY ICU MnU NN NNC NcU PBm PPiU PU TxU WU

7519. --- Litauiska akcentfrågor. Die Akzentuierung der Ordinalzahlen im Slavo-baltischen. In Uppsala Universitets årsskrif, v.10, 1936, p. 1-30; 31-38. See serials con- sulted.

7520. VAITKEVIČIŪTĖ, Valerija. Fonetika. [Phonetics] In LTSRMALKLI. Lietuvių kalbos grama- tika. Vilnius, 1965. v.1, p. 43-

160. PG8533.L5 v.1 DLC CLU CSt
CaAEU CaBVaU CaOTU CtY ICU MH NN
NNC NBuU PU

7521. --- Die Intonationen der
Anregungssätze im Litauischen. In
Zeitschrift für Phonetik (Berlin),
v.20, no.4, 1967, p. 357-368. See
serials consulted.

7522. --- Lietuvių kalbos balsių
ir dvibalsių ilgumas arba kiekybė.
[The length and intonation of the
vowels and diphthongs in the Lithuanian language] In Lietuvių kalbotyros klausimai (Vilnius), v.3,
1960, p. 207-218. See serials
consulted.

7523. --- Lietuvių literatūrinės
kalbos balsinės ir dvibalsinės
fonemos. [The phoneme of the vowels and diphthongs in the Lithuanian literary language] In Lietuvių kalbotyros klausimai (Vilnius)
v.4, 1961, p. 19-47. See serials
consulted.

7524. VOELKEL, Maximillian J. A.
Der Tonwandel in der litauischen
Deklination. Tilsit, 1873. 32 p.
491.92.V853.3 PU MH

7525. WIEDEMANN, Oskar. Zu den
litauischen Auslautsgesetzen. In
Zeitschrift für vergleichende
Sprachforschung (Berlin), v.32,
1893, p. 109-122. See serials
consulted.

7526. WIJK, Nicolaas van. Kür-
zung und Metatonie im litauischen
Auslaut. In Zeitschrift für
slavische Philologie (Leipzig), v.
5, 1928, p. 1-17. See serials
consulted.

7527. WOOD, Frederic Turnbull.
The accentuation of nominal com-
pounds in Lithuanian. Baltimore,
Md., Waverly Press, inc. [1930]
90 p. Thesis--Princeton Univer-
sity, 1928. "Reprint of Language
Dissertation no. 7, published by
the Linguistic Society of America,
December 1930." Bibliography: p.
7-10. PG8544.W6 DLC CaBVaS CaNSHD
CaOLU CoU CtY GU IaU ICN ICU InNd
KU LU MH MnU MiU MoU MU NB NN NIC
NNC NbU NcD NcU NSyU NjP NjR OCl
OClW OkU OrU OO PPiU PU RPB TxDaM
TxHU TxU ViU VtU WU WaU

XIII.4.f. GRAMMAR

XIII.4.f.1. GENERAL STUDIES, TEXT
BOOKS AND EXERCISES

7528. AMBRAŠKA, Jurgis and Juozas
Žiugžda. Lietuvių kalbos gramatika.
I dalis: Fonetika ir morfologija.
[By] J. Ambraška and Juozas Žuigžda.
[6th ed. Chicago, Ill.] JAV LB
Kultūros fondas [1966] 181 p.
illus. Reprinted from the 1st edi-
tion: Kaunas, Sakalo bendrovė,
1937. PG8533.A49 1966 CaAEU DLC
OKentU

7529. BEZZENBERGER, Adalbert.
Zur zemaitischen Grammatik. In
Beiträge zur Kunde der indogermanischen Sprachen (Göttingen), v.10,
1886, p. 307-314. See serials
consulted.

7530. BŪGA, Kazimieras. Kalbos
dalykai; quaestiones grammaticae.
Kaunas, Benaičio spaustuvė, 1909.
65 p. 491.922.B866.4 PU CtTMF

7531. DAMBRIŪNAS, Leonardas. In-
troduction to modern Lithuanian [by]
Leonardas Dambriūnas, Antanas
Klimas [and] William R. Schmalstieg.
Brooklyn, N.Y., Franciscan Fathers
Press [c1966] viii, 471 p. illus.
PG835.D28 DLC CaAEU CaBVaS CaOTP
CaOTU CtPAM CtY CoU ICBM ICLJF ICU
IEN InNd LU MnU MH MU NB NbU NIC NN
NNC NBuU NcD NjP NSyU NvU OClW
OKentU PP PPi PU TxU

7532. DAMIJONAITIS, Juozapas.
Lietuvių kalbos gramatikos trumpas
vadovėlis mokykloms. [A short
Lithuanian grammar for the school]
Kaunas, Švyturio bendrovė, 1922.
125 p. Hvc24.D18 CtY ICBM WaS

7533. --- --- 2. leidimas. Kaunas; Vilnius, Švyturio bendrovės
leidinys, 1923. 166 p.
PG8535.D3 1923 DLC ICBM

7534. --- Trumpa lietuvių kalbos
gramatika. [A brief grammar of the
Lithuanian language] Kaunas, K.
Rutkausko knygynas, 1909. 90 p.
PG8535.D29 OKentU ICBM

7535. --- --- 2. leidimas. Kaunas A. Rutkausko knygynas, 1912.
116 p. 491.92.D ICBM

7536. --- --- 3. leidimas. Chicago, Ill., Draugas [1915] 119 p.
491.92.D184 PU ICBM ICLJF ICJ MBtS
OCl CtY ViU OKentU

7537. --- --- [Another edition]

Kaunas, Švyturio bendrovė, 1920.
491.92.D184 PU

7538. DEGUTIS, Jonas. Trumpa
pagelbinė gramatika lietuvių kalbos. [A short Lithuanian grammar]
Eitkūnai, A. Fraedorfas, n.d. 44[2]
p. Bound with Schiekopp, J. Litauische Elementargrammatik. Tilsit. 1901. 491.922.Sch33 PU

7539. DĖJUS, Titas and S. Ma-
ceikienė. Lietuvių kalbos grama-
tika; IV. klasei. 13. leidimas.
[A Lithuanian grammar...] Kaunas,
Šviesa, 1966. 89 p.
T491.925.D CaOTP

7540. ERHART, Adolf. Litevština.
Praha, Státní pedagog. nakl., 1956.
153 p. (Učební texty vysokých
škol) 3297.198F MH

7541. GRAMMATICA BREVIS LINGUAE
lituanicae; seu, Samogiticae, a
quodam Pio. Societatis Jesu sacer-
dote conscripta et typis mandata
Vilnae anno M.Dccxxxvii, nunc reper-
ta et iterum in lucem edita. Trumpas pamokimas kałbos lituwiszkos
arba żemaytyszkos... nuo nekurio
nobażna ysz draugistes Jezaus ku-
nyga lotinyszkay paraszitas yr
dabarcziu atrastas yr ysznauja
swietuy parôditas. [A short Lithuanian grammar. Edited by Simonas Stanevičius] Vilnae, Neumann, 1829. 57 p. 491.922.G757 PU

7542. JABLONSKIS, Jonas. Lietu-
viškosios kalbos gramatika; rašy-
tojams ir skaitytojams vadovėlis.
[Lithuanian grammar...] Tilžėje,
Otto v. Mauderode, 1901. 88 p.
At head of title: Petras Kriaušai-
tis. 491.922.J114.2 PU BM ICCC
ICLJF

7543. --- Lietuvių kalbos gramatika: etimologija. Pirmosioms
mūsų aukštesniosioms mokslo įstaigoms. [Lithuanian grammar... By]
Rygiškių Jono [pseud.] Vilnius,
Lietuvių mokslo d-ja, 1919. 237 p.
PG8531.K89 InNd ICCC ICBM MiD NN PU

7544. --- Lietuvių kalbos gramatika. Etimologija, vidurinėms mokslo įstaigoms. [Grammar of the Lithuanian language. Etymology, for
higher schools. Antrasis leidimas.
By] Rygiškių Jono [pseud.] Kaunas,
Vilnius, "Švyturio" bendrovės leidinys, 1922. 280 p. PG8533.J2
1922 DLC ICLJF ICCC NNC PU WaU

7545. --- --- [Another edition]
Kaunas, Vaiva, 1925. 103 p.
PG8535.J16 ICU

7546. JAUNIUS, Kazimieras. Gram-

matika litovskago iazyka; litovskii original i russkii perevod.
Petrograd, Tip. Imp. akademii nauk,
1916. 1 v. (various pagings)
port. Lithuanian and Russian.
"Spisok trudov IAvnisa i otzyvov o
nem": p. [xv]-xxii. PG8535.J3 DLC
CU(microfilm) MH NIC NN

7547. --- Lietuvių kalbos gramatika. [Grammar of the Lithuanian
language] Peterburgas, Mokslų akademijos spaustuvėje, 1911.
491.922.J324 PU

7548. KAI KURIE GRAMATIKOS IR
stilistikos klausimai; medžiaga mo-
kytojui. [Some grammatical and
stylistic questions. Sudarė B.
Dobrovolskis] Kaunas, Valstybinė
pedagoginės literatūros leidykla,
1963. 93 p. P8531.K3 DLC

7549. KAI KURIE LIETUVIŲ KALBOS
gramatikos klausimai; straipsnių
rinkinys. [Some problems of the
Lithuanian grammar; a collection of
articles] Vilnius, VPMLL, 1957.
188 p. PG8533.K2 DLC CaAEU MH PU
TxU

7550. KAZLAUSKAS, Jonas. Lietuvių kalbos istorinė gramatika;
kirčiavimas, daiktavardis, veiksma-
žodis. [A historic grammar of the
Lithuanian language] Vilnius, Mintis, 1968. 414 p. PG8531.K36 DLC
CtY ICBM MH NN PU

7551. KLEIN, Daniel. Grammatica
litvanica... primùm in lucem edita
à m. Daniele Klein... Regiomonti,
Typis & sumptibus J. Reusneri, 1653.
[28], 174 p. Bonaparte Collection
no. 13445 ICN

7552. --- Grammatica litvanica,
et Compendium litvanico-germanicum.
Vyr. redaktoriai: J. Balčikonis ir
B. Larinas. Vilnius, VPMLL, 1957]
654 p. PG8535.K55 DLC CU CSt CtY
ICN ICLJF ICU MH NN NcU OKentU PU

7553. KOTWICZ, Władysław. Grama-
tyka języka litewskiego w zarysie.
Wilno, 1940. 137 p. PG8535.K56
CSt CaBVaU CtY ICU MH NN NNC NjP

7554. KRAEMER, Ernst. Lehrbuch
der litauischen Sprache... 2. Auflage. Kaunas, 1938. 122 p.
Hvc24.K85 CtY BM(W.P. 12599.)

7555. KURSCHAT, Friedrich. Gram-
matik der littauischen Sprache...
Mit einer Karte des littauischen
Sprachgebiets und einer Abhandlung
über littauische Volkspoesie, nebst
Musikbeilage von 25 Dainosmelodien.
Halle, a.S., Verlag der Buchhandlung
des Waisenhauses, 1876. xxiv,

476 p. fold. map. illus.
PG8535.K8 DLC CLU CaOHM CaQMM CtY
ICU ICN IaU HU MH MiU MnU NN NNC
NIC NcU NjP NmU NCU OCl OClW PBm
PU TxU WU

7556. LESKIEN, August. Litauisches Lesebuch mit Grammatik und Wörterbuch. Heidelberg, C. Winter,
1919. xx, 312 p. (Indogermanische
Bibliothek. 1. Abt.: Sammlung in-
dogermanischer Lehr- und Handbücher. 1. Reihe: Grammatiken. 12. Pd.)
PG8537.L4 DLC CaAEU CaBVaU CaOHM
CaQMM CaOTU CtY FU ICN InNd ICU KU
LU MH MnU NIC NN NNC NcU NjP PU TxU
WaU WU CLU

7557. LIETUVOS TSR MOKSLŲ AKADE-
MIJA, VILNA. LIETUVIŲ KALBOS IR
LITERATŪROS INSTITUTAS. Lietuvių
kalbos gramatika. [Lithuanian
grammar. Edited by K. Ulvydas]
Vilnius, Mintis, 1965- .
PG8533.L5 v.1 DLC CaAEU CaBVaU
CaOTU CLU CtY CSt ICU MH NN NNC
NBuU

7558. MALINAUSKAS, Ignas and J.
Talmantas. Lietuvių kalbos gramatika pratimais. [Exercises in Lithuanian grammar] Kaunas, 1934.
pts. 2-4. 491.92.K684 PU CtPAM
ICLJF

7559. MEŠKAUSKAS, Pranas. Lietuvių rašomosios kalbos vadovėlis.
I-II Dalis. [A handbook of the
written Lithuanian language] Klaipėda, Spaustuvė "Lituania", 1926-
28. 2 v. 491.922.D935 PU ICCC
ICLJF

7560. MIELCKE, Christian Gottlieb.
Anfangs-Gründe einer littauischen
Sprach-Lehre. Königsberg in Pr.,
Verlag der Hartungschen Hofbuch-
drukerei, 1800. 208 p. MdBP MnU
NN NNU-W PBm PU

7561. MIEŽINIS, Mikolas. Lietu-
viszka gramatika. [Lithuanian gram-
mar] Tilžėje, 1886. 53 p.
BM(12901. d. 35/3.)

7562. ORVIDIENĖ, Emilija. Lietuvių kalbos vadovėlis. [Reader
of Lithuanian language] Vilnius,
Mintis, 1968. 519 p. PG8535.07
1968 DLC CtY ICU NIC NN NjP PU

7563. OSTERMEYER, Gottfried.
Neue littauische Grammatik.
Königsberg in Pr., G.L. Hartung,
1791. xxiv, 194 p. Bonaparte
Collection no. 13461 ICN OClW PU

7564. OTRĘBSKI, Jan Szczepan.
Gramatyka języka litewskiego. Warszawa, Państwowe Wydawnictwo Nau-

kowe, 1956- . v. Contents:--
T.1. Wiadomości wstępne. Nauka o
głoskach.--T.2. Nauka o budowie
wyrazów.--T.3. Nauka o formach.
PG8539.08 DLC CaAEU CaBVaS CaBVaU
CaOTU CU CSt CoU CtY HU ICU KU MH
MnU MoU MU NIC NN NNC NjP NBuU
NSyU NcD PPiU PU RPB TxU WaU WU

7565. PEDERSEN, Holger. Études
lituaniennes. København, Levin &
Munksgaard, 1933. 63 p. (K.
Danske videnskabernes selskab. His-
torisk-filologiske meddelelser.
XIX, 3) AS281.D214 v.19 no.3 DLC
CLU CSt CtY ICN ICU IEN MH MiU MoU
NNC NcU NjP PPAmP PU RPB TxU WaU WU

7566. PILKA, Dominikas. Lietuvių
kalbos gramatika, pritaikyta Ame-
rikos lietuviams. [Grammar of the
Lithuanian language, adapted for
American Lithuanians] So. Boston,
Mass., 1939. 143 p. PG8535.P5
DLC CU CaBVaU ICU MiD NN NjP OU
OKentU PP PU WU

7567. RUHIG, Paul Friedrich.
Anfangsgründe einer littauischen
Grammatick in ihrem natürlichen
Zusammenhänge. Königsberg in Pr.,
1747. 154 p. 3297.8 MH
BM(12975. f. 6. (2)); also Hvc24R85
CtY(1800 ed.) ICN(1800 ed.)

7568. RŪTELIONIENĖ, Petronėlė.
Gramatika praktikoj: lietuvių kalbos mokymasis. Grammatika v prak-
tike; samouchitel' litovskogo
iazyka. Kaunas, "Spindulio" b-vės
spaustuvė, 1929. 116 p.
422Ru ICLJF

7569. --- Kirčiuctoji praktikos
gramatika; aukštesniems pradžios
mokyklų skyriams ir žemesniosioms
gimnazijų klasėms. [The accentuated practical grammar of Lithuanian language] Kaunas, 1930. 132 p.
491.925R ICCC

7570. SAURUSAITIS, Peter. A
brief Lithuanian grammar or principal rules to learn the Lithuanian
language. [Waterbury, Conn., Author, c1910] 64 p., 12 folded unnumbered p. PG8535.S2 DLC CtY
DCU-H MH NN WaU

7571. SCHIEKOPP, Julius Erdmann.
Gramatyka litewska początkowa.
Przełożona z niemieckiego i opraco-
wana przez J. Januszkiewicza i A.
Maciejewskiego, et. Kraków, 1902.
104 p. 491.92.Sch29 PU
BM(12975. l. 29.)

7572. --- Litauische Elementar-
Grammatik. 2. Auflage, durchgesehen
von A. Kurschat. Tilsit, 1901-

1902. 2 pts. in 1 v. 148 p.
(Beilage zum Jahresbericht des Kgl.
Gymnasiums zu Tilsit. Programm nr.
16) 491.922.Sch33 PU CaBVaU CLSU
ICU MdBJ NjP

7573. --- Briefe über die Erfolge
einer Wissenschaftlichen Reise nach
Litauen. [Wien, 1852] 36 p.
table. "Aus dem Octoberhefte des
Jahrganges 1852 der Sitzungsberich-
te der philos.-histor. Classe der
Kais. Akademie der Wissenschaften.
PG8533.S34.1 CLU PU

7574. --- Handbuch der litauisch-
en Sprache von August Schleicher...
Prag, J.G. Calve, 1856-1857. 2 v.
in 1. Contents.--v.I.Grammatik.--
v.II. Lesebuch und glossar.
PG8531.S4 DLC CaOHM CaOTU CLU CtY
ICU IEN MH NN NSyU PU TxU WU

7575. --- Lituanica [Wien, K.K.
Hof- und Staatsdruckerei, 1853]
In Akademie der Wissenschaften,
Wien. Sitzungsberichte, v.11,
1853, p. 76-156. See serials con-
sulted.

7576. SEIDEL, August. Grammatik
der litauischen Sprache mit Wörter-
verzeichnissen und Lesestücken.
Wien, A. Hartleben [1915]. viii,
180 p. (Die Kunst der Polyglottie,
Theil 114) Biography: p. 4-8.
PG8535.S4 DLC CaOHM CtY DK ICN NIC
NN NcU OCl PBm PU ViU WU

7577. SEREISKIS, Benjaminas.
Lietuvių kalbos vadovėlis. Uchebnik litovskogo iazyka. Kaunas,
Valstybinė pedagoginės literatūros
leidykla, 1947. 345 p. (*QY)NN

7578. ŠESPLAUKIS, Alfonsas. Lietuvių kalbos gramatika; gramatika
ir sintaksė. 4. pataisytas leidimas. [Lithuanian grammar... Chicago, Ill.] J. Karvelis, 1966.
118 p. PG8535.S493 InNd CaAEU

7579. --- Pratiminė lietuvių
kalbos gramatika mokyklai ir namams.
[Exercises in Lithuanian grammar
for school and home. Eutin] Bendrija, 1954. 97 p. PG8535.S45 DLC
CaAEU MH NN NNC PU

7580. STARKUS, Jonas. Lietuvių
kalbos gramatika skiriama amerikiečiams. [Lithuanian grammar for
Americans] Thompson, Conn., Mari-
anapolio Kolegija, 1938. 208 p.
PG8531.St28 InNd ICCC ICLJF MH NN PU

7581. STOROST, Wilhelm. Einführ-
rung in die litauische Sprache.
Tilsit, Ruta-Verlag, 1919. 144 p.
PG8535.S7 DLC

7582. --- Vadovas lietuvių kalbai
pramokti. Litauischer Führer zur
Erlernung der Anfangsgründe der
litauischen Sprache. Tilžėje,
"Rūta", 1912. viii, 111 p. illus.
At head of title: Vydūnas.
PG8535.S75 DLC CaAEU CtY

7583. TANANEVIČIA, S. P. Trumpa
lietuvių kalbos gramatika. [Lithu-
anian grammar...] Dėl lietuviškų
mokyklų šiaurinėje Amerikoje. Pagal Stuobrį ir kitus parengė, S.P.
Tananevičia. Chicago, Ill., Sapuda
ir lešomis "Kataliko", 1909. 102
p. (*QYL p.v. 2 no.12) NN ICCC

7584. U.S. ARMY LANGUAGE SCHOOL,
MONTEREY, CALIF. Lithuanian; basic
course. Lithuanian text. Presidio
of Monterey, 1955- . v.
PG8535.U53 DLC

7585. --- Lithuanian; military
terminology. Exercises 1-10.
Presidio of Monterey, Calif., 1960.
90 p. PG8538.S6U5 DLC

7586. UNIVERSITAS LINGUARUM LIT-
vaniae in principali ducatus eius-
dem dialecto grammaticis legibus
circumscripta... anno a descriptione
universi orbis 1737 Vilnae typis
Collegii academici Soc. Jesu, denuo
edidit, indicem verborum adjecit,
Ioannes Rozwadowski. Cracoviae,
Sumptibus academiae litterarum,
1896. 87 p. PG8533.U52 1896 PU
CtY NN

7587. VOELKEL, Maximillian J. A.
Litauisches Elementarbuch. Heidelberg, C. Winter, 1879. viii, 111
p. PG8535.V85 CLU ICN NmU

7588. --- --- 2. neu bearb. und
verm. Aufl. Heidelberg, 1900. 12,
192 p. PG8535.V6 1900 CaBVaU CtY
MH MnU PU RPB WU

7589. --- --- 2. neu bearb. und
verm. Aufl. 3 Ausg. Heidelberg,
C. Winter, 1913. xii, 192 p.
PG8535.V6 1913 DLC BM ICU MB

7590. --- --- 2. neu bearb. und
verm. Aufl. 4. Abd. Heidelberg, C.
Winter, 1923. xii, 192 p.
PG8535.V6 1923 CoU CaOHM CaQMM GU
LU OClW NN PPiU PU

7591. WIEDEMANN, Oskar. Hand-
buch der litauischen Sprache.
Grammatik. Texte. Wörterbuch.
Strassburg, K.J. Trübner, 1897.
xvi, 353 p. PG8531.W63 CLU CaBVaU
GU ICU IEN InU MH MdBT MnU NIC NN
NjP NmU NbU PU TxU WU

7592. ŽIUGŽDA, Juozas. Lietuvių

kalbos gramatika. Vidurinėms mokykloms. [Lithuanian grammar] 3.
leidimas. Kaunas, Valstybinė pedagoginės literatūros leidykla,
1947. 2 v. in 1. Contents.--1
dalis. Fonetika ir morfologija.--
2 dalis. Sintaksė. (*QY)NN

7593. --- --- 7. leidimas. Kaunas, Valstybinė pedagoginės literatūros leidykla, 1954. 2 v.
(*QY)NN

7594. --- --- 8. leidimas. Kaunas, Valstybinė pedagoginės literatūros leidykla, 1955. 2 v.
PG8531.Z53 1955 DLC CaBVaU CtY ICU
MnU NcU NjP

7595. --- --- 9. leidimas. Kaunas, Valstybinė pedagoginės literatūros leidykla, 1956. 215 p.
891.925.Z69 NNC NcU OKentU

7596. --- --- 10. leidimas. Kaunas, Valstybinė pedagoginės literatūros leidykla, 1957. 2 v.
3297.112.2 MH ICLJF MiD NN

7597. --- --- 11. pataisytas leidimas. Kaunas, Valstybinė pedagoginės literatūros leidykla, 1958.
2 v. MiU MH NIC

7598. --- --- 14. leidimas. Kaunas, Valstybinė pedagoginės literatūros leidykla, 1961. 2 v. NN

7599. --- --- 16. leidimas. Kau-
nas, Šviesa, 1965. 2 v.
PG8531.Z82 1965 PPiU(v.2 is 17 ed.)
CaOTU PU(v.2 is 9th ed.)

7600. --- --- 17. leidimas. Kau-
nas, Šviesa, 1967. 2 v. illus.
Written by Juozas Žiugžda and Pranas
Gailiūnas. T491.925.Z CaOTP

7601. --- --- 18. leidimas. Kaunas, Šviesa, 1969. 227 p. Contents.--1 dalis. Fonetika ir morfologija. Written by Juozas Žiugžda and Pranas Gailiūnas.
PG8613.G13 1969 CaAEU

7602. ZUBATY, Josef. Zu Schlei-
cher's litauischen Studien. Prag,
Königl. böhm. Gesellschaft der
Wissenschaften in Prag, 1901. 29
p. In Česká společnost, Prague.
Třída filosoficko-historicko-filo-
logická. Věstnik (Sitzungsberichte)
1901. 063.7.CESP IU CaBVaU CtY DLC
DDo GU KU MdBJ MiU NN NNC OClW OrU
PPAmP PU

XIII.4.f.2. READERS, PRASE BOOKS
AND ORTHOGRAPHY

7603. AŠMYS, Mikelis. Eine ver-
kürzte Methode Toussaint-Lange-
scheidt. Litauisch, von Michael
Aschmies. Berlin-Schöneberg, Lan-
genscheidt, 1917. 171 p. (Metou-
la-Sprachführer) PG8539.A8 DLC
CSt OCl OClW

7604. BABRAUSKAS, Benys. Lietuvos keliu;skaitiniai lietuviškai
ištrėmimo mokyklai. [Lithuanian
reader for Lithuanians abroad]
Weilheim-Teck, Ger., Atžalynas,
1947. 2 v. in 1. PG8713.B119
InNd CaOONL CaOTP PU

7605. BARAVYKAS, Vaclovas. Lietuvių-anglų pasikalbėjimų knygelė.
2 pataisytas ir papildytas leidimas.
[Lithuanian phrase book] Vilnius,
VPMLL, 1961. 327 p. PE1129.S79B3
1961 DLC CtY MH PU

7606. BENDORIUS, Petras. Vaikų
žvaigždutė. [Children's reader]
Dalis I. Sutaisė mokytojas P. Bendorius. Chicago, Ill., Draugas,
1916. 2 v. illus. PG8537.B4 1916
ICJ PU

7607. BIRŽIŠKA, Mykolas. Rinktiniai mūsų senovės raštai;[Selections
from our older literature]; medžiaga lietuvių raštijos mokslui aukš-
tesniosiose mokyklose. Kaunas [Švie-
timo ministerijos leidinys] 1927.
254 p. illus. CtTMF MiD OCl PU

7608. BŪGA, Kazimieras. Dėl mūsų
rašybos. [On our orthography] In
His Rinktiniai raštai. Vilnius, 1948.
v.1, p. 384-400. PG8509.B8 DLC CU
CaAEU CtPAM CtMF ICU ICLJF IEN MH NB
NN NBuU(1-2) NjP PPiU PU TxU

7609. BUSILAS, Antanas. Rašybos
reformos klausimu. [Concerning reforms in orthography] Kaunas, Spaudos fondas, 1934. 39.
491.922.B964 PU

7610. ČEPAITIENĖ, Jadvyga. Lietuvių kalbos vadovėlis; mokyklų dėsto-
maja rusų kalba IX klasei. Uchebnik litovskogo iazyka dlia IX klassa
shkol s russkim iazykom obucheniia.
J. Čepaitienė, T. Dėjus [ir] S. Jankevičienė. [Šeštasis perdirbtas
leidimas] Kaunas, Šviesa, 1965.
125 p. CaAEU

7611. DABUŠIS, Stasys. Reformuo-
dami rašybą, pasilengvinkim raštą.
[Orthography reforms and suggested
simplifications] Kaunas, 1934. 31
p. Atspaudas iš "Ryto".

PG8545.D3 1971 PU

DAMBRIŪNAS, Leonardas.
Introduction to modern Lithuanian.
Brooklyn, N.Y. 471 p. See entry
no. 7531.

7612. --- Kalbos patarėjas. [A
language manual. By] L. Dambrauskas. Redagavo A. Salys ir Pr.
Skardžius. Kaunas, 1939. 141 p.
PG8645.D32 PU

7613. GAUČYS, Povilas and Viktoras Kamantauskas, comp. Chrestomatija prieš "Aušros" gadynės dainių, su J. Vaižganto prakalba.
[Anthology before "Aušros" period]
Kaunas, Biržų spaustuvė, 1924.
118 p. PG8715.G35 PU

7614. GIRA, Liūdas. Lietuvių
rašybos vadovėlis. Ketvirtasis
leidimas...[Manual of orthography..]
Kaunas; Vilnius, Švyturio Bendrovės
leidinys, 1924. 78 p. Hvc28.G44
CtY NN OKentU

7615. GRIGAS, Napalys. Lietuvių
kalbos rašybos žodynas mokykloms.
[The orthographic dictionary of the
Lithuanian language for schools.
Sudarė N. Grigas ir A. Lyberis]
Kaunas, Valstybinė pedagoginės li-
teratūros leidykla, 1956. 244 p.
PG8547.G7 DLC CtY MH NN OKentU
(1958 ed.)

7616. --- --- 3. pataisytas leidimas. Kaunas, 1966. 258 p.
PG8547.G7 1966 PU CtY

7617. HERMANN, Eduard. Litauisch-
deutsches Geschprächbüchlein. Kaunas, Sakalas, 1931. 157 p.
491.92.H427 PU CtTMF ICU

7618. JABLONSKIS, Jonas. Mūsų
rašyba. [Our orthography] Rygiškių,
Jonas [pseud.] Voronežas, Kultūros
ir švietimo sekcijos leidinys,
1917. 62 p. 491.922.J114.5 PU

7619. --- Rašomosios kalbos dalykai. [Some points concerning
written language] Rygiškių, Jonas
[pseud.] Vilnius, 1912. 41 p.
(Lietuvių Mokslo draugijos kalbininkų komisijos leidinys, nr.1)
491.922.J114.6 PU

7620. --- Rašybos dalykai. [Or-
thography] Vilnius, M. Kuktos
spaustuvė, 1915. 64 p.
491.922.J114 PU

7621. JACOBY, Rudolf. Litauische
Chrestomatie zur Schulgebrauch.
Mit dem 20 Jahresberichte des Gym-
nasiums in Memel. Leipzig, B.G.

Teubner, 1880. vi, 96 p. (*QT)NN

7622. JONYNIENĖ, Sofija. Lietuvos laukai. [Lithuanian fields]
Chicago, Ill., JAV LB Kultūros
fondas, 1959. 219 p. illus.
PG8537.J6 DLC CaAEU PU

7623. --- Tėvų šalis. [The
homeland] Chicago, Ill., JAV LB
Kultūros fondas, 1964. 360 p.
illus. 491.92.J739.2 PU CaAEU

7624. JUŠKA, Jonas. Kalbos
lėtuviszko lėžuvo ir lėtuviszkas
statraszimas arba ortograpija.
Jon's Juszka. [The orthography of
the Lithuanian language] Peterburge, Spaustuvėje mokslu akademijos, 1861. 56 p. 491.922.J984.3
PU

7625. JUZUMOWICZ, Tadeusz. Di-
desis elementorius ir katakismas
arba trumpas mokslas wieros kriksz-
czioniszkos paraszitas par kun.
Tadeusza Juzumowicze. [A Lithuanian catechism. The author's name
is Juzumas-Juzumavičius, Tadas]
Wilniuje, J. Zawadzkie, 1860. 64
p. Bonaparte Collection no.
13427 ICN

7626. KAMANTAUSKAS, Viktoras.
Kirčiuota lietuvių literatūros
chrestomatija aukštesniajai mokyklai. [An accentuated chrestomathy
of the Lithuanian language...]
Kaunas, Sakalo bendrovės leidinys,
1929. xv, 350 p. PG8537.K3 DLC
CtY CtTMF ICCC PU

7627. --- --- 2. leidimas. Kaunas, Sakalo bendrovės leidinys,
1932. iv, 351 p. PG8537.K3 DLC
CaBVaU CtTMF ICCC WU

7628. --- Lietuvių literatūros
chrestomatija: 1. Lyrika. [A
chrestomathy of Lithuanian literature; poetry] Kaunas, 1926. 75 p.
891.928.K1 CtTMF

7629. --- Trumpas prancūziškai
lietuviškas vadovėlis. [A concise
French-Lithuanian reader] Vilnius,
Patria [146] 54 p. PC2121.K3
InNd CtY

7630. KASHKEVICH, John Joseph.
English-Lithuanian self-instructor;
simplified grammar, exercises, key
and vocabularies, with proper pronunciation. Brooklyn, N.Y., Lithuanian daily "Laisvė", 1940. 252 p.
PG8535.K3 DLC CU NN OCl PU MBrigStJ

7631. KATINSKAITĖ-DOVEIKIENĖ,
Ona. Lietuviški-prancūziški pasikalbėjimai. Guide parlé lituanien-

français. Vilnius, VPMLL, 1959.
335 p. PC2121.K3 DLC
BM(12974. ccc. 6.)

7632. KLEIN, Daniel. Compendium
litvanico-germanicum; oder, Kurtze
und gantz deutliche Anfürung zur
littauischen Sprache wie man recht
Littauisch lesen, schreiben und re-
den sol. Königsberg in Pr., Gedruckt und verlegt durch Johann
Reusnern, 1654. 112 p. Bound with
His Grammatica litvanica. Königsberg, 1653. Bonaparte Collection
no. 13445 ICN

7633. KLIMAS, Petras. Skaitymų
knyga lietuvių kalbos pamokoms.
[Reader of the Lithuanian language]
Vilniuje, 1916. 288 p. (Lietuvių
mokslo draugijos leidinys)
491.922.K684 PU

7634. --- --- 2. išleidimas.
Tilžė [n.d.] 294 p. 891.928.K6
CtTMF

7635. --- --- 3. išleidimas.
Tilžė, O. v. Mauderode, 1918. 294
p. (Lietuvių mokslo draugijos leidinys) 891.92c.K684 PU

7636. --- Skaitymai lietuvių kalbos pamokoms. [Reader of the Lithuanian language] 5. išleidimas.
Kaunas, Švyturio bendrovės leidinys, 1922. 294 p. PG8537.K5 1922
DLC CtY

7637. --- --- 6. pataisytas leidimas. Kaunas, Šv. Kazimiero draugija, 1929. 382 p. PG8537.K5
1929 DLC CtTMF PU

7638. --- --- 7. pataisyta laida.
Sukirčiavo ir retesniuosius žodžius
paaiškino Stasys Dabušis. Kaunas,
Šv. Kazimiero draugija, 1932. 396
p. (Šv. Kazimiero draugijos leidinys, nr.547) KF.14535 MH

7639. KRECHINSKII, Ivan, tr.
Bukvars zhemaitishkai-rusishkasis.
Bukvar' zhmudsko-russkii, sostav-
lennyi po metodie V. Zolotova, pe-
revod I. Krechinskago. Kovnia,
Tip. Sh. Sokolovskago, 1865. 88 p.
Lithuanian text in Cyrilic charac-
ters. Hvc35.K87 CtY

7640. KURSCHAT, Alexander Theodor.
Litauisches Lesebuch. Tilsit, Reyländer, 1911-13. 3 v. in 1.
491.92.L964 PU BM NNC ViU

7641. LAIGONAITĖ, Adėlė. Lietu-
vių kalbos vadovėlis IX-XI klasei.
[Textbook of Lithuanian language.
By] Adėlė Laigonaitė, Juozas Pik-
čilingis, Adomas Šoblinskas [and]
Kazimieras Župerka. Kaunas, Šviesa,

1971. 330 p. PG8535.L3 PU

7642. LAMENTORIUS; arba, Pradžia
mokslo sudeta mažiems wajkeliems.
Wilniuja, A. Syrkin, 1860. 59 p.
Bonaparte Collection no. 13449 ICN

7643. LAUKIS, Joseph. Angliškos
kalbos vadovėlis tiems, kurie nori
trumpu laiku pramokti angliškai
susikalbėti kasdieniniuose reika-
luose. [Handbook of English language...] Sutaisė J. Laukis.
Chicago, Ill., Turtu ir spauda
"Lietuvos", 1911. 94 p. Imprint
covered by label of C.N. Caspar
Co., Milwaukee, Wis.
PE1129.S79L25 DLC CaBVaU NB NN

7644. --- Lithuanian self-instruction... with the assistance of Rev.
C.E. Edwards. For practical use
by travellers, tourists and those
who wish to learn Lithuanian.
Chicago, Ill., "Lietuva", 1908.
74 p. PG8539.L3 DLC CaBVaU ICBM
NN OCl PU

LESKIEN, August. Litau-
isches Lesebuch mit Grammatik und
Wörterbuch. Heidelberg, 1919.
See entry no. 7556.

LIETUVIŲ KALBOS RAŠYBOS ŽO-
dynas. Kaunas, 1948. See entry
no. 359.

7645. MAČKUS, Valteris. Lietuviš-
ki-vokiški pasikalbėjimai. Litauisch-deutsches Gesprächbüchlein.
2. ištaisytas ir papildytas leidimas. Vilnius, VPMLL, 1960. 510
p. PF3129.L5M3 DLC IEN
MH(1958 ed.) NNC

THE MARIAN. The first
Marian reader; folktales, legends...
Chicago, Ill., [1951] See entry
no. 6775.

7646. MOKSŁAS SKAYTIMA RASZTA
lietuwiszka dieł mažu wayku. Wil-
niuy, Kasztu Meumana ir Solca,
1860. 32 p. Bonaparte Collection
no. 13454 ICN

7647. --- [Another edition]
Wil-niuy, J. Blumowicz, 1862. 36
p. Bonaparte Collection no. 13455
ICN

7648. MURKA, Jonas. Lietuvių
kalbos vadovėlis... [A Lithuanian
language reader] Petrapilis, Lietuvių spaustuvė, 1917. 2 v.
491.922.M944 PU

7649. --- --- [Another edition]
Kaunas, Švyturio bendrovė, 1921.
2 v. Hvc24.M94 CtY ICCC

7650. --- --- 3. leidimas. Kaunas, Švyturio bendrovė, 1922-23. 3 v. Hvc24.M95 CtY

7651. --- Vaikų darbymečiui. 1. dalis. Knygos 1-jam pradžios mokyklos skyriui. 3. laida. [A reader for children...] Kaunas; Vilnius, 1921. 180 p. illus. PC8537.M9 1921 RPB

7652. NORKUS, Jonas. Lietuvių kalbos rašyba; rašybos vadovėlis su rašybos žodynėliu. [Orthography of the Lithuanian language] Kaune, Spaudos fondas, 1926. 84 p. Xerox copy, 1971. PG8545.N6 1971 PU

ORVIDIENĖ, Emilija. Lietuvių kalbos vadovėlis. Vilnius, 1968. See entry no. 7562.

7653. OTRĘBSKI, Jan Szczepan, ed. Teksty litewskie. [Wyd.1.] Warszawa, Państwowe Wydawn. Naukowe, 1957-59. 2 v. (Teksty do ćwiczeń językoznawczych, nr.2) PG8701.085 DLC CLU CtY ICU MH NIC NN NNC PPiU PU TxU

7654. PRADINIS MOKSLAS ANGLISZKOS kalbos, dėl lietuvių per Lietuvos Mylėtoją karta iszleistas. [The primer of English for Lithuanians] Bitėnai, M. Jankus, 134 p. PG8539.P7 CaBVaU

7655. PUPEIKIS, Stasys. Lietuvių kalbos vadovėlis. 2. pataisytas leidimas. Uchebnik litovskogo iazyka. Kaunas, Valstybinė pedagoginės literatūros leidykla, 1954. 262 p. 3297.36.5 MH BM(012977. f. 20.)

7656. RIMKA, Albinas. Skaitymo vadovėlis. 2. pataisyta ir papildyta laida. [A Lithuanian reader] Su P. Rusecko priedu: kariškio knyginėlis. [Kaunas, Lietuvos valstybės spaustuvė, 1920.] 35 p. Z2537.R55 1920 DLC

7657. RUSSKAIA GRAMOTA DLIA LItovtsev. Rusishkas mokslas del' letuvniku... dlia obucheniia russkoi gramotie v litovskikh shkolakh. Izd. 3. Vil'na, A.G. Syrkin, 1878. Lithuanian text in Russian alphabet. Sp.491.922.R927 PU

SCHLEICHER, August. Handbuch der Littauischen Sprache. Prag, 1856-1857. See entry no. 7574.

7658. SCHMALSTIEG, William Riegel and Antanas Klimas. Lithuanian reader for self-instruction.

Brooklyn, N.Y. Franciscan Fathers Press, 1967. 59 p. PG8537.S34 CaOTY CaAEU CaOTU InNd NcD PPiU PU

7659. SCHMALSTIEG, William Riegel, ed. Readings in old Prussian. University Park, Pa., State Univ. of Pa., 1965. iii, 21 leaves. Old Prussian text with German and English translations. PG8208.S3 DLC CtY MH NN NjP PPULC PU

7660. SENN, Alfred. Accented Lithuanian texts, with vocabulary. Philadelphia, Pa., Department of Slavic and Baltic Studies, 1951. 2 p.l., 50 l. 491.9286Se58a TxU CSt

7661. --- Kleine litauische Sprachlehre. Heidelberg, J. Groos, 1929. xi, 304 p. (Lehrbücher: Methode Gaspey-Otto-Sauer) PG8535.S47K CLU CSt CaBVaU CaQMM CtY ICU IaU MH NIC NNC OCU OClW PU TxU WU

7662. SEREISKIS, Benjaminas. Sistematicheskoe rukovodstvo k izucheniiu litovskogo iazyka. Kaunas, Spaudos fondas, 1929. 1 v. 491.92.Se68 1929 PU NNC

7663. ŠEŠPLAUKIS, Alfonsas. Ten, kur Nemunas banguoja. [Over there, where the waves of Nemunas are rolling] A. Tyruolis [pseud.] Cleveland, Ohio, Kultūros fondas, 1962, 216 p. illus. PG8537.S49 1962 CaAEU OCl

7664. ŠOPARA, Ignacas. Trumputis lietuviškai-rusiškas kalbamokslis. Parengė ir parašė kunigas Ignacas Šopara. Koroten'kaia litovsko-russkaia grammatika... Vilnius, M. Kuktos spaustuvė, 1906. 89 p. L422Šo ICLJF

7665. STAŠAITIENĖ, V. Russkolitovskii razgovornik. [Russian-lithuanian phrase book] Vilnius, VPMLL, 1961. 327 p. PG2121.S79 CaAEU CU MH MWalB WU

7666. TALMANTAS, Jurgis. Lietuvių kalbos vadovėlis; skaitimai, gramatika ir žodynas. Gramatikos dalykai išdėstyti lenkų kalba. [A handbook of the Lithuanian language] Kaunas, A. Ptašekas, 1940. 191 p. PG8535.T3 PU

7667. TANANEVIČIA, S. P. Vienatinis savo rūšies lietuviškai-angliškos kalbos; rankvedis bei žodynėlis lietuviškai-angliškas su fonetišku ištarimu ir kaip tapti Jungtinių Amerikos Valstybių piliečiu. [A unique Lithuanian-English phrase book; with phonetical pronunciation and how to become a U.S. citizen. Chicago, Ill., Spauda ir lešomis "Kataliko", 1909. 154, iv p. PE1129.S79.T3 DLC

7668. --- --- 2. leidimas. Chicago, Ill., Spauda ir lešomis "Kataliko", 1912. 236, iv p. (*QY)NN

7669. TWO-SPEED RECORD COURSE. Lithuanian. [Phonodisc] Modern Way 2-Speed Record Ali-1-4. [New York, Foreign Language Studies, c1959] 4 s. 7 in. 33 1/3 or 45 rpm. microgroove. Accompanied by two texts; one in English and one in Lithuanian. L 62-3 OCl

7670. UNITED STATES ARMY LANGUAGE SCHOOL, MONTEREY, CALIF. Lithuanian: basic course; lessons 1-103, dialogue cartoon guide. Presidio of Monterey, 1956. 154 p. illus. PG8539.U5 DLC

7671. --- Lithuanian: illustrated military situations. Presidio of Monterey, 1960- . v. illus. PG8539.U53 DLC

7672. --- Lithuanian: military film textbook, film teaching units 1-15, application phase. Presidio of Monterey, 1960. 228 p. illus. PG8519.U5 DLC

7673. --- Lithuanian basic course; military word list. English-Lithuanian and Lithuanian-English. Presidio of Monterey, 1961. 118 p. illus. PG8539.U52 1961 DLC MH

7674. VARIAKOJYTĖ INKENIENĖ, M. Lithuanian self-taught by the natural method with the English phonetic pronunciation. London, E. Marlborough & Co., Ltd. [1936] x, 146 p. PG8535.V3 DLC CLU CaAEU CaOTU CaOTP NN OCl OkU PP PU

7675. VASILIAUSKAS, Mečislovas. Rašyk taisyklingai. [Spelling book] 2. pataisytas leidimas. Kaunas, Dirva, 1927. 175 p. 491.92.Vl CtTMF

7676. VIKONIS, Pranas. Lietuvių kalbos pamokos skiriamos svetimtaučiams. Uroki litovskago iazyka. Kaunas, A. Ptašeko, 1921-22. 2 v. PG8535.V5 DLC BM(12976. pp. 29.)

VOELKEL, Maximillian J. A. Litauisches Elementarbuch. See entry no. 7587-7590.

7677. VOL'TER, Eduard Aleksandrovich. Litovskaia khrestomatiia.

Lietuviška chrestomatija. Sanktpeterburg, 1901-04. 2 v. in 1, facsims. PG8713.V6 DLC CtPAM MH PU NSyU

7678. ZHEMOITSKO-LITOVSKII BUKVAR'. Izdannyi po rasporiazheniiu... glavnago nachal'nika Sievero-Zapadnago kraia M.N. Murav'eva. Vil'no, Tip. A.K. Kirkora, 1864. 42 p. illus. Hvc35.Z42 CtY

XIII.4.f.3. MORPHOLOGY

7679. ALEKSANDROV, Aleksandr Ivanovich. Litauische Studien. I. Nominal-zusammensetzungen. Dorpat, 1888. ix, 124 p. Thesis--University of Dorpat (Tartu) PG8561.A53 ICU MH WU

7680. ALEKSYNAS, K. Veiksmažodžių samplaikos lietuvių liaudies dainose. Glagol'nye parnye sochetanniia v. litovskikh narodnykh pesniakh. In Literatūra ir Kalba (Vilnius), v. 9, 1968, p. 354-388. Bibliography: p. 385-386. See serials consulted.

7681. AMBRAZAS, Vytautas. Absoliutinis naudininkas su dalyviu XVI-XVII aa. lietuvių kalbos paminkluose. [The unconditional dative with participle in the written Lithuanian language of 16th and 17th centuries] In LTSRMAD. Serija A, 2(5), 1958, p. 147-164. Summary in Russian. See serials consulted.

7682. --- Dėl esamojo laiko neveikiamųjų dalyvių vartojimo. [On the usage of participles in the present tense of passive voice] In Lietuvių kalbotyros klausimai (Vilnius), v.4, 1961, p. 93-115. See serials consulted.

7683. --- Lietuvių kalbos dalyvių ir veiksmažodžių konstrukcijos su ir bei jų slaviški atitikmenys. [The construction of participles and verbs in Lithuanian language with ir and its slavic counterparts] In Baltistica (Vilnius), v.1, 1965, p. 53-65. See serials consulted.

7684. ARUMAA, Peeter. Untersuchungen zur Geschichte der litauischen Personalpronomina. [Tartu K. Mattiesens Buchdruckerei A.G.] 1933. 189 p. (Tartu. Ulikool. Acta et commentationes Universitatis tartuensis. B: Humaniora, 32, no.2) AS262.D62 B v.32 DLC CSt CtY CLU ICU MiU MnU NIC NNC PU RPB WU

424

7685. BALDAUF, Lucia. Der Gebrauch der Pronominalform des Ad-
jektivs im Litauischen. München,
O. Sagner, 1967. 104 p. (Slavistische Beiträge, Bd. 26) Bibliography: p. 94-102. Issued also as
thesis, München, 1965. PG8577.B3
1967 DLC AzU CaAEU CaBVaS CaOTU
CaOWtU IaU InNd MoU MU RPB WaU

7686. BRAUNER, S. Funktionen des
litauischen Verbalprefixes pa-.
Ein Beitrag zum Studium der Aspekt-
frage in Litauischen. [Leipzig,
1960] 136 p. Thesis--University
of Leipzig. Bibliography: p. 4-11.
NN(microfilm negative)

7687. BUCH, Tamara. Būtojo kar-
tinio laiko vartojimas lietuvių
literatūrinėje kalboje. [The usage
of the past tense in the Lithuanian
literary language. By] Tamara
Buchienė. In LTSRMAD. Serija A,
v.2(3), 1957, p. 219-228. See
serials consulted.

7688. BŪGA, Kazimieras. Priesagos -ūnas ir dvibalsio uo kilmė.
[The origin of the suffix -ūnas and
a diphthong uo] In His Rinktiniai
raštai. Vilnius, 1959. v.2, p.
331-376. PG8509.B8 DLC CU CaAEU
CtPAM CtTMF ICU ICLJF IEN MH NB NN
NBuU NjP PPiU PU TxU

7689. BŪTĖNAS, Petras. Lietuvių
kalbos prielinksnių mokslas. [Pre-
positions of the Lithuanian lan-
guage] Kaunas, Spindulio bendrovės
spaustuvė, 1930. 187 p.
3297.228 MH CtTMF ICCC

7690. --- Trumpas linksnių mokslas; praktiškam lietuvių kalbos
reikalui. [A concise grammar of
inflection...] Kaunas, 1929. 67
p. PG8575.B8 PU CtTMF ICCC

7691. ČAIKAUSKAS, M. Veiksma-
žodžiai lietuvių kalbos žodžių
junginiai su prielinksniu "iš".
[Verbs with the preposition "iš" as
a connecting word in the Lithuanian
language] In Vilna. Valstybinis
pedagoginis institutas. Mokslo
darbai, v.8, 1959, p. 31-48. See
serials consulted.

7692. DAMBRIŪNAS, Leonardas.
Lietuvių kalbos veiksmažodžių as-
pektai. [Verbal aspects in the
Lithuanian language] Boston, Mass.,
Lietuvių enciklopedijos leidykla
[1960] 160 p. PG8597.D3 DLC CaOTU
CtY ICLJF MH PU

7693. DUMAŠIŪTĖ, Zelma Mėta.
Apibendrintas esamasis laikas dabartinėje lietuvių literatūrinėje

kalboje. [The generalized present
tense in the contemporary literary
Lithuanian language] In LTSRMAD.
Serija A, v.1(10), 1961, p. 153-
166. See serials consulted.

7694. --- Perkeltinės reikšmės
vientisinio esamojo laiko vartojimas dabartinėje lietuvių literatūrinėje kalboje. [The use of the
figurative sense in the present
tense of the contemporary literary
Lithuanian language] In LTSRMAD.
Serija A, v.1(10), 1961, p. 139-
152. See serials consulted.

7695. --- Ypatinga kalbos veiksmažodžių (verba dicendi) reikšmė
ir jų vartojimas. [Special meaning
of the verbs (verba dicendi) and
their usage] In Vilna. Valstybinis pedagoginis institutas.
Mokslo darbai, v.1, 1961, p. 143-
157. See serials consulted.

7696. FORD, Gordon Buell, Jr.
The old Lithuanian catechism of
Baltramiejus Vilentas (1579). A
photological, morphological and
syntactical investigation. The
Hague, Mouton, 1969. 421 p., 74
p. of photos. (Slavistic printings
and reprintings, 71) BX8070.L77F67
CaOTU

7697. FRAENKEL, Ernst. Syntax
der litauischen Kasus. In Tauta
ir žodis (Kaunas), v.4, 1926, p.
126-186; v.5, 1928, p. 1-169. See
serials consulted.

7698. --- Syntax der litauischen
Postpositionen und Präpositionen.
Heidelberg, C. Winter, 1929. xi,
292 p. (Indogermanische Biblio-
thek. 1. Abt.: Sammlung indoger-
manischer Lehr- und Handbücher.
1. Reihe: Grammatiken, Bd. 19)
PG8605.F7 DLC CaAEU CaBVaS CaOHM
CaOTU CtY IEN ICU ICN LU MH MnU MoU
NIC NN NBuU NjP OU PU TxU WaU

7699. JABLONSKIS, Jonas. Links-
niai ir prielinksniai. [Cases and
prepositions. By] Rygiškių,
Jonas [pseud.] Kaunas, Valstybės
spaustuvė, 1928. 134 p.
PG8535.J3 MB CtTMF ICCC

7700. JANUSCHAS, Norbert. Das
litauische Adverb. [Berlin, Ernst
Reuter-Gesellschaft, 1962] 99 p.
Thesis--Free University of Berlin.
PG8577.J3 PU InU MH NIC

7701. KAZLAUSKAS, Jonas. Iš
optativo istorijos. [From the history about the optative] In
Lietuvių kalbotyros klausimai (Vilnius), v.4, 1961, p. 73-89. See

serials consulted.

7703. KLIMAS, Antanas. Primitive
Germanic -kuningaz and its spread.
Philadelphia, Pa., 1956. xi, 99
leaves. Thesis--University of
Pennsylvania. Bibliography: vii-xi.
431.2.K684 PU LU (microfilm)

7704. KNIŪKŠTA, O. Priesagos
-inis ir darybinės galūnės -is vartojimas sudurtiniuose būdvardžiuose.
[Suffix -inis and formant -is in
the compound adjectives] In
LTSRMAD. Serija A, v.1(32), 1970,
p. 199-[207]. See serials consulted.

7705. LABUTIS, Vitas. Dalelytės
ir jų vieta kalbos dalių tarpe.
Chastitsy i ikh mesto sredi chastei
rechi. In Literatūra ir kalba
(Vilnius), v.6, 1962, p. 354-370.
See serials consulted.

7706. LAIGONAITĖ, Adėlė and
Vincas Urbutis. Daiktavardis.
[The noun] In LTSRMALKLI. Lietu-
vių kalbos gramatika. Vilnius,
1965. v.1, 1965. p. 161-473.
PG8533.L5 v.1 DLC CSt CLU CaAEU

7707. --- Vietininkų reikšmė ir
vartosena dabartinėje lietuvių
kalboje. [The meaning and use of
locatives in the contemporary Lithuanian language] Vilnius,
VPMLL, 1957. 57 p. 491.92.L143 PU

7708. LESKIEN, August. Die Bildung der Nomina im Litauischen.
Leipzig, 1891. 468 p. (Sächsische
Akademie der Wissenschaften. Abhandlungen der philosophisch-histo-
rischen Classe, v.12, pt.3, 1852,
p. [151]-618) See serials consulted.

7709. LIETUVOS TSR MOKSLŲ AKADE-
MIJA, VILNA. LIETUVIŲ KALBOS IR
LITERATŪROS INSTITUTAS. Lietuvių
kalbos morfologinė sandara ir jos
raida. [The morphologic structure
of the Lithuanian language and its
development] Vilnius, Mintis,
1964. 255 p. (Lietuvių kalbotyros
klausimai, 7) PG8501.L5 v.7 DLC
CU CLU CtY ICU InU IU MH NN PU

7710. MAŽIULIS, Vytautas. Skait-
vardis. [The numerals] In
LTSRMALKLI. Lietuvių kalbos gramatika. 1965. p. 604-636.
PG8533.L5 v.1 DLC CLU CSt CaAEU

7711. MEULEN, Reinder van der.
Over een aardige Litouwse uitdruk-
king. In Mededelingen der Konink-
lijke Nederlandse Akademie van
Wetenschappen, Amsterdam. Afd.

Letterkunde, Nieuwe reeks, deel
21, no.8, 1958, p. 223-232.
AS244.A51 n.r., deel 21, no.8 DLC
CLU CtY ICU InU MH NNC

7712. MIKUTSKII, S. P. O filo-
logicheskom puteshestvii po Za-
padnym kraiam Rossii. Sanktpeterburg, V. Tip. Imperatorskoi akademii nauk, 1855-56. 4 pts in 1 v.
Binder's title: Mukudzka. Voyage
à l'Ouest de Russie. Otchety--
Imperatorskaia akademiia nauk.
2. otd. PG8561.M63 NIC

7713. NIEDERMANN, Max. Die
Benennung der Kartoffel im Litauischen und Lettischen. In Wörter
und Sachen (Heidelberg), v.8,
1923, p. 33-96. See serials consulted.

7714. --- Die Namen des Storches
im Litauischen. In Festgabe Adolf
Kaegi zum 30. September 1919.
Trauenfeld, 1919, p. 66-92.
408.F418 CLU CU CtY DCU ICU IaU IU
MH NIC NN NcD WU

7715. --- --- Sonderabdruck.
Frauefeld, Ruber, 1919. 26 p.
491.922.N553 PU

7716. PAULAUSKAS, Jonas. Veiksmažodžių priešdėlių funkcijos da-
bertinėje lietuvių literatūrinėje
kalboje. [The function of the
prefixes with verbs in the present
Lithuanian literary language] In
Literatūra ir kalba (Vilnius), v.
3, 1958, p. 303-453. See serials
consulted.

7717. PAULAUSKIENĖ, Aldona.
Veiksmažodžių gretinimas veiksmo
atžvilgiu (veikslinė koreliacija).
[The comparison of verbs from the
tense-aspects] In LTSRAMMD: Kalbotyra (Vilnius), v.10, 1964; v.13,
1965, p. 53-75. See serials consulted.

7718. --- Lietuvių kalbos veiksmažodžių veikslai; paskaita studentams neakivaizdininkams. [The
tense-aspects of verbs in Lithua-
nian] Vilnius, 1965. 22 p.
Balt 9606.27 MH

7719. RŪKE-DRAVIŅA, Velta. Di-
minutive bei Familiennamen im Litauischen und Lettischen. In
Scandoslavica (Copenhagen), v.2,
1956, p. 41-47. See serials consulted.

7720. SABALIAUSKAS, Algirdas.
Baltų kalbų žemės ūkio augalų pava-
dinimų kilmės klausimu. [On the
question of the origin of the names
of the agricultural plants in the

Baltic languages] In Literatūra ir kalba (Vilnius), v.3, 1958, p. 454-461. See serials consulted.

7721. SCHMALSTIEG, William Riegel, Jr. A descriptive study of the Lithuanian verbal system. In General Linguistics (Lexington, Ky.), v.3, no.3, 1958, p. 85-105. See serials consulted.

7722. --- The vocalism of the Lithuanian sigmatic future. In Slavic and East European Journal (Bloomington, Ind.), n.s., v.2(16), no.2, 1958, p. 120-129. PG38.U6A5 DLC CaAEU CtY IU NN NPV

7723. SENN, Alfred. Zu den litauischen Zahlwörtern für 11-19. Roma, Istituto per l'Europa orientale, 1936. [69]-84. Offprint from Studi Baltici. PG8534.S4 CaBVaU; also in Studi Baltici (Roma), v.5, 1935, p. [69]-84. See serials consulted.

7724. SKARDŽIUS, Pranas. Alte Wurzelnomina im Litauischen. In Indogermanische Forschungen, Zeitschrift für Indogermanistik und allgemeine Sprachwissenschaft (Berlin), v.62, 1956, p. 158-166. See serials consulted.

7725. --- Lietuvių kalbos daryba. Die Wortbildung im Litauischen. Vilnius, 1943. 768 p. At head of title: Lietuvos Mokslų akademija. Lietuvių kalbos institutas. Summary in German. PG8561.S55 DLC CtY ICU MH PU

7726. --- Pirties žodžio sąvoka ir kilmė. [The idea and the origin of the word "pirtis"] In Gimtasai kraštas (Šiauliai), v.2, 1934, p. 74-75. See serials consulted.

7727. SPECHT, Franz. Die Flexion der n-Stäume im Baltisch-Slavischen und Verwandtes. In Zeitschrift für vergleichende Sprachforschung (Göttingen), v.59, no.3-4, 1932, p. 213-298. See serials consulted.

7728. --- Lituanica; der instrumental Pluralis. In Zeitschrift für vergleichende Sprachforschung (Göttingen), v.60, no.3-4, 1933, p. 272-281. See serials consulted.

7729. STEGMANN VON PRITZWALD, Kurt. Das Attribut im Altlitauischen. Heidelberg, C. Winter, 1934. xi, 140 p. (Indogermanische bibliothek, hrsg. von H. Hirt und Streitberg. 3. abt.: Untersuchungen. 14. bd.) Bibliography: p.

135-140. PG8625.S7 DLC CLU CSt CaBVaS CaOTU CtY ICU IEN MH MnU ICN NIC NN NNC NBuU NcD NjP TxU WaU WU

7730. TANGL, Eberhard. Der accusativus und nominativus cum participio in altlitauischen. Weimar, H. Böhlaus Nachf., 1928. 54 p. 491.922.T713 PU MH

7731. VAITKEVIČIUTĖ, Valerija. Kai kurios skatinimo rūšys ir jų reiškimo būdai lietuvių kalboje. [Some varieties of prompting and encouraging in the Lithuanian language and the ways of application] In LTSRMAD. Serija A, v.1(16), 1964, p. 219-229. See serials consulted.

7732. --- Lietuvių literatūrinės kalbos prieveiksmių fonemų sudėtis. [The structure of the phoneme of adverbs in the Lithuanian literary language] In Lietuvių kalbotyros klausimai (Vilnius), v.1, 1957, p. 5-66. See serials consulted.

7733. VALECKIENĖ, Adėlė. Budvardis. [The adjective] In LTSRMAIKLI. Lietuvių kalbos gramatika. Vilnius, 1965. v.1, p. 474-603. PG8533.L5 v.1 DLC CLU CSt CaAEU

7734. --- Dabartinės lietuvių kalbos įvardžiuotinių būdvardžių vartojimas. [The use of definite adjectives in the present Lithuanian language] In Literatūra ir kalba (Vilnius), v.2, 1957, p. 159-328. See serials consulted.

7735. --- Dabartinės lietuvių literatūrinės kalbos būdvardžių laipsniai ir jų reikšmės. [The degrees of adjectives and their meaning in the present Lithuanian literary language] In Lietuvių kalbotyros klausimai (Vilnius), v.4, 1961, p. 49-66. See serials consulted.

7736. --- Įvardis. [The pronoun] In LTSRMAIKLI. Lietuvių kalbos gramatika. Vilnius, 1965. v.1, p. 637-721. PG8533.L5 v.1 DLC CLU CSt CaAEU

7737. WIEDEMANN, Oskar. Das litauische Präteritum. Ein Beitrag zur Verbalflexion der indogermanischen Sprachen. Strassburg, K.J. Trübner, 1891. xv, 230 p. PG3597.W63 CLU CaAEU CtY DLC ICU IU MH MnU MiU MdBJ NNC NjP PU ViU WU

7738. --- Das litauische Präteritum... Erster Teil: zum litauischen Vokalismus. Strassburg, J. K. Trübner, 1889. 52 p. Thesis-- University of Tartu. PG8595.W64 NIC DLC NNC ViU

7739. --- Zu einigen Dativ- und Lokativformen der litauischen i- und u- Deklination. In Zeitschrift für slavische Philologie (Leipzig), v.12, 1935, p. 240-251. See serials consulted.

7740. ZINKEVIČIUS, Zigmas. Lietuvių kalbos įvardžiuotinių būdvardžių istorijos bruožai. [The historical outline of the definite adjectives in the Lithuanian language] Vilnius, VPMLL, 1957. 129 p. tables. PG8583.Z4 CaBVaU InU MH NIC PU

XIII.4.f.4. SYNTAX

7741. BALKEVIČIUS, Jonas. Dabartinės lietuvių kalbos sintaksė. [Syntax of the present Lithuanian language] Vilnius, VPMLL, 1963. 479 p. PG8613.B3 DLC IEN OKentU PU

7742. DAMBRIŪNAS, Leonardas. Lietuvių kalbos sintaksė. [Syntax of the Lithuanian language] Tübingen, išleido tremtiniai, 1946. 98 p. 491.92.D183 PU

7743. --- --- 2. laida. Tübingen, Patria, 1947. 99 p. PG8613.D3 1947 DLC CaAEU CtY ICLJF OKentU

7744. --- --- 3. papildytoji laida. [Chicago, Ill.] Pedagoginis Lituanistikos institutas, 1963. 103 p. PG8613.D3 1963 PU CaAEU CaOONL CaOTU PPULC

7745. DURYS, Mykolas. Lietuvių kalbos sintaksė, vidurinei mokyklai. [The Syntax of the Lithuanian language for the Jr. High School] Kaunas, 1927, 100 p. 491.922.D935 PU

FRAENKEL, Ernst. Syntax der litauischen Kasus. Kaunas, 1928. See entry no. 7697.

--- Syntax der litauischen postpositionen und präpositionen. See entry no. 7698.

7746. GAILIŪNAS, Pranas. Lietuvių kalbos gramatika; 2 dalis. Sintaksė. [Grammar of the Lithuanian language; syntax. 2. patai-

sytas leidimas] Kaunas, Šviesa, 1969. 214 p. illus. PG8613 1969 CaAEU OClW

7747. --- --- 3. leidimas. Kaunas, Šviesa, 1971. 214 p. At head of title: P. Gailiūnas, J. Žiugžda. PG8535.G3 PU

7748. HERMANN, Eduard. Über die Entwicklung der litauischen Konjunktursätze. Jena, H. Pohle, 1912. 98 p. table. 491.922.H427 PU ICU MH NN NNC

7749. JABLONSKIS, Jonas. Lietuvių kalbos sintaksė. 1. dalis. [Syntax of the Lithuanian language. Part 1. By] Rygiškių Jonas [pseud.] Seinai, Laukaičio, Dvaranausko, Narjausko spaustuvėje, 1911. 104 p. 491.922.J114.7 PU CtTMF ICCC ICBM

7750. --- --- [Another edition] In His Rinktiniai raštai, v.1, 1957. PG8509.J33A6 1957 DLC CU CtY ICU MH NB NN PU

7751. JOPSON, N. B. The syntax of Lithuanian compared with that of Latin and Greek. In Slavonic and East European Review (London), v.24, no.63, 1946, p. 148-155. See serials consulted.

7752. KLIMAS, Petras. Lietuvių kalbos sintaksė. [Syntax of the Lithuanian language] Rygiškių Jono [pseud.] sintaksės turiniu naudodamasis parašė P. Klimas. Trečias pataisytasis leidimas. Kaunas, Švyturys, 1921. 60 p. PG8613.K65 InNd

7753. --- --- 4. leidimas. Kaunas, Švyturys, 1922. 51 p. Hvc26.K68 CtY PU

7754. --- --- 5. leidimas. Kaunas, Švyturio bendrovės leidinys, 1924. 51 p. PG8613.K6 1924 DLC

7755. --- --- 7. leidimas. Kaunas, Sakalo bendrovės leidinys, 1928. 51 p. PG8613.K6 1928 DLC

7756. KUZMICKIS, Zigmantas. Lietuvių kalbos sintaksė. [Lithuanian syntax] Vadovėlis vidurinėms ir aukštesniosioms mokykloms. Kaunas, Sakalo bendrovės leidinys, 1931. 169 p. PG8613.K83 PU ICLJF OCl

7757. MEŠKAUSKAS, Pranas. Lietuvių kalbos sintaksė; vadovėlis mokykloms ir rašto žmonėms. [Syntax of the Lithuanian language; a textbook for High Schools] Kaunas,

Šviesos spaustuvė, 1929. 108 p.
491.92.M56L WaU

7758. SCHWENTNER, Ernst. Die
Wortfolge im Litauischen. Heidel-
berg, Carl Winter, 1922. 33 p.
(Slavica; Beiträge zum Studium der
Sprache, Literatur, Kultur, Volks-
und Altertumskunde der Slaven, 5)
PG8621.S41 InU CaBVaS CaBVaU CaOTU
CtY ICU LU MnU NN NNC NcU NjP PU
TxU WU

        STEGMANN VON PRITZWALD, Kurt.
Das Attribut im Altlitauischen.
Heidelberg, 1934. See entry no.
7729.

XII.4.f.5. GRAMMATICAL USAGE BY
PARTICULAR AUTHORS

7759. ALEKSANDROV, Aleksandr
Ivanovich. Sprachliches aus dem
Nationaldichter Litauens Donali-
tius... Dorpat, Schnackenburg's
Buchdr., 1886. viii, 69 p.
Thesis--University of Tartu (Dor-
pat). PG8699.D775A5 ICU

        FORD, Gordon B., Jr. The
old Lithuanian catechism of Baltramiejus Vilentas (1579). Hague,
1969. See entry no. 7696.

7760. --- A phonological, morphological and syntactical investigation of the Old Lithuanian Catechism of Baltramiejus Vilentas
(1579). [n.p.] 1965. 2 v.
Thesis--Harvard University. MH

7761. FRAENKEL, Ernst. Sprachliche, besonders syntaktische Untersuchung des kalvinistischen Katechismus des Malcher Pietkiewicz
von 1598. Göttingen, Vandenhoeck
U Ruprecht, 1947. 140 p. (Ergan-
zungshefte zur Zeitschrift für
vergleichende Sprachforschung auf
dem Gebiet der indogermanischen
Sprache, nr. 14) CSt ICU ICN MH
MnU NIC NNC NjP OCU PU RPB

7762. JAUNIUS, Kazimieras. Apie
kun. A. Juškos dainų kalbą. [On
the language of folksongs of Rev.
A. Juška] In Lietuvių tauta (Vilnius, v.1, 1910, p. 549-562. See
serials consulted.

7763. JONIKAS, Petras. Kleino
gramatikų bendrinė kalba. [The
standard language of Klein's gram-
mar] In Archivum philologicum
(Kaunas), v.7, 1938, p. 57-72.
See serials consulted.

7764. KABELKA, Jonas. Kristijono Donelaičio raštų leksika.
[Lexicology of the works of Kristijonas Donelaitis] Vilnius, Mintis, 1964. 278 p. PG8721.D68Z7
CaAEU CaOTU DLC ICBM NN OKentU PU

7765. MASILIŪNAS, Kazimieras.
Antano Smetonos raštų žodynas; su
sintaksės ir stilistikos pavyzdžiais.
[Dictionary of the works of A.
Smetona] Kaunas, Švietimo Ministerija, 1934. 112 p. (Švietimo
m-jos knygų leidimo k-jos leidinys
nr.449) DK511.L28S6 DLC PU

        SKARDŽIUS, Pranas. Dauk-
šos akcentologija. Kaunas, 1935.
See entry no. 7513.

7766. STANG, Christian Schweigaard. Die Sprache des litauischen
Katechismus von Mažvydas. Oslo,
1929. 192 p. (In Norske Videnskaps-Akademi i Oslo, Historisk-
filosofisk Klasse. Skrifter.
1929. no.3) AS283.057 DLC CaOTU
CoU ICU IEN NIC PU

7767. VAŠKELIS, Bronius. The
language of Jurgis Baltrušaitis.
Philadelphia, Pa., 1964. viii,
348 leaves. Thesis--University of
Pennsylvania. PU

7768. VENGRIS, Antanas. Pagrindinės poetiškos kalbos savybės
Daukanto "Būde". [The basic
qualities of the poetical language
of Daukantas in his book "Būdą
senovės letuviu..."] In Židinys
(Kaunas), v.27, no.4, 1938, p.
448-459. See serials consulted.

XIII.4.g. STYLE, COMPOSITION, ETC.

7769. BŪGA, Kazimieras. Lietuvių kalbos žodžių iškraipytai var-
tojamų kalbos mokslo literatūroje,
sąrašas. Spisok litovskikh slov,
upotrebliaemykh v linvisticheskoi
literature v iskazhennom vide. In
His Rinktiniai raštai, v.2, 1959,
p. 695-725. PG8509.B8 DLC CU CaAEU
CtPAM CtTMF ICU ICLJF IEN MH NB NN
NBuU NjP PPiU PU TxU

7770. GIRDZIJAUSKAS, J. Lietuvių
eilėdara; silabinės-toninės sistemos susiformavimas. [Lithuanian
versification (structure of
verses)] Vilnius, Vaga, 1966. 280
p. music. Bibliography: p. 271-
[281]. PG8653.G5 DLC CaOTU CtY
InNd MH NN NjP PU

        KAI KURIE GRAMATIKOS IR

stilistikos klausimai. Kaunas, 1963.
See entry no. 7548.

KAMANTAUSKAS, Viktoras.
Trumpas kalbos netaisyklingumų ir
barbarizmų žodynėlis. Kaunas,
1928. See entry no. 327-328.

7771. PIKČILINGIS, Juozas. Lietuvių kalbos stilistika. [Stylis-
tics of the Lithuanian language]
Vadovėlis respublikos aukštųjų mokyklų lietuvių kalbos ir literatūros bei žurnalistikos specialybėms.
Vilnius, Mintis, 1971- .
PG8637.P5 PU(1-)

XIII.4.h. ONOMASTICS; PERSONAL, GEO-
GRAPHIC NAMES, ETC.

7772. BALČIKONIS, Juozas. Naz-
vaniia litovskikh naselennykh punk-
tov, obrazovannye ot nazvanii rek
i ozer. In Lingua Posnanensis
(Poznań), v.7, 1958 (1959), p. 240-
252. See serials consulted.

7773. BIRYLA, Mikola Vasil'evich
and Aleksandras Vanagas. Litous-
kiia elementy u belaruskai anamas-
tytsy. Mensk, Navuka i tekhnika,
1968. 100 p. PG2833.B55 PU

7774. BIRŽIŠKA, Mykolas. Apie
lietuviškus Vilniaus miesto gatvė-
vardžius. [On the Lithuanian names
of the streets in Vilnius] Kaunas,
1939. 29 p. (In Narbutas, Jonas
Vytautas. Vadovas po Vilnių)
Xerox copy, 1971 from Mūsų, Vilnius, no.23-24, 1938. DK651.V4B52
1971 PU

7775. BŪGA, Kazimieras. Aistiš-
kos kilmės Gudijos vietovardžiai.
[The place-names in White Russia
of Baltic origin] In His Rinktiniai
raštai. Vilnius, 1961. v.3, p.
518-550. PG8509.B8 DLC CU CaAEU
CtPAM CtTMF ICU ICLJF IEN MH NB NN
NjP PPiU PU TxU

7776. --- Apie lietuvių asmens
vardus. [On the Lithuanian person-
al names] In His Rinktiniai raštai.
Vilnius, 1958. v.1, p. 201-269.
PG8509.B8 DLC CU CaAEU CtPAM CtTMF
ICU ICLJF IEN MH NB NN NBuU NjP
PPiU PU TxU

7777. --- Apie senovės prūsų ir
lietuvių tikrinius vardus. [On
the Old-Prussian and Lithuanian
proper names] In His Rinktiniai
raštai. Vilnius, 1958. v.1, p.
419-428. PG8509.B8 DLC CU CaAEU
CtPAM CtTMF ICU ICLJF IEN MH NB

NBuU NjP PPiU PU TxU

7778. --- Upių vardų studijos ir
aisčių bei slavėnų senovė. [The
studies of the names of rivers and
the prehistory of the Balts and
Slavs] In His Rinktiniai raštai.
Vilnius, 1961. v.3, p. 493-530.
PG8509.B8 v.3 DLC CU CaAEU CtPAM
CtTMF ICU ICLJF IEN MH NB NN NjP
PPiU PU TxU

--- Die Vorgeschichte der
aistischen (baltischen) Stämme im
Lichte der Ortsnamenforschung. In
His Rinktiniai raštai. Vilnius,
1961. See entry no. 4208.

7779. DUMČIUS, Jonas. Antikiniai
vardai lietuvių liaudies kalboje.
[Ancient names in the Lithuanian
colloquial language] In Vilna.
Universitetas. Istorijos-filologijos mokslų serija. v.3, 1957, p.
171-185. (Its Mokslo darbai, v.13)
See serials consulted.

7780. --- Antikiniai
vardai lietuvių raštuose. [The
ancient names in the Lithuanian
writings] In Vilna. Universitetas.
Istorijos-filologijos mokslų serija,
v.4, 1958, p. 81-110. (Its Mokslo
darbai, v.18) See serials consulted.

FALK, Knut Olaf. Wody Wi-
gierskie i Hucianskie, Uppsala,
1941. See entry no. 416.

7781. --- Ze studiów nad sławiza-
cją litewskich nazw miejscowych i
osobowych. In Scandoslavica (Copenhagen), v.9, 1963, p. 87-103. See
serials consulted.

FENZLAU, Walter. Die deu-
tsche Formen der litauischen Orts-
und Personennamen des Memelgebiets.
Halle, a.S., 1936. See entry no,
417.

7782. --- Grundsätzliches zur Mund-
art- und Ortsnamenforschung des Memelgebiets. In Zeitschrift für deutsche Mundarten (Berlin), v.14, no.3,
1938, p. 139-145. See serials consulted.

GAUSE, Fritz. Neue Ortsnamen in Ostpreussen seit 1800. Königsberg in Pr., 1935. See entry
no. 418.

GERULLIS, Georg. Die alt-
preussischen Ortsnamen. Berlin, 1922.
See entry no. 419.

7783. JACOBY, Karl Rudolf. Litauische Pflanzennamen. In LLGM, v.2,
1881, p. 134-143. See serials consulted.

7784. JONIKAS, Petras. Asmenvardžiai ir vietovardžiai. [Per-
sonal and place names] In Lietuvių enciklopedija. Boston, Mass.,
1968. v.15, p. 555-571. See entry
no. 216.

7785. --- Mūsų pavardės ir jų
atsiradimas. [Our surnames and
their origin] Literatūra (Chicago,
Ill.), v.2, 1954, p. 109-146. See
serials consulted.

7786. --- Zu den litauischen
Ortsnamen. In Beiträge zur Namenforschung (Heidelberg), v.2, 1950,
p. 1-32. See serials consulted.

7787. JURKĖNAS, J. Lietuvių senųjų dvikamienių vardų morfologiniai tipai. [The morphological
types of the ancient Lithuanian
double-stem names] In LTSRAMMD:
Kalbotyra (Vilnius), nr.8, 1965,
p. 54-64. See serials consulted.

7788. KALVAITIS, Vilius. Lietu-
wiszkų wardų klėtelė. [The source
of Lithuanian names. By] Wilius
Kalwaitis. Tilžėje, O. v. Mauderode, 1910. vii, 117 p. ports.
Text in Lithuanian and German.
491.9233 ICJ PU OCl

7789. KARŁOWICZ, Jan. Czterysta
kilkadziesiąt nazwisk miejscowości
litewskich. In Pamiętnik Fizjograficzny (Warszawa), v.3, 1883, p.
500-511. Title also in French:
Quatre cents et quelques douzaines
de noms des entrees lithuanienes.
QE276.5.P3 DLC MH-P NNM

7790. KLIMAS, Antanas. Some
problems in Lithuanian onomastics;
a case study of the family names
(surnames). In Lituanus (Chicago,
Ill.), v.15, no.3, 1969, p. 41-50.
See serials consulted.

7791. KUZAVINIS, K. Lietuvos vardo kilmė. [The origin of the Lithuania name] In LTSRAMMD: Kalbotyra (Vilnius), v.10, 1964, p. 5-
18. See serials consulted.

7792. LESKIEN, August. Die litauische zweistämmigen Personennamen. In Indogermanische Forschungen, Zeitschrift für indogermanistik und allgemeine Sprachwissenschaft (Berlin), v.34, 1914, p. 296-
333. See serials consulted.

LIETUVOS TSR MOKSLŲ AKADE-
MIJA. VILNA. LIETUVIŲ KALBOS IR
LITERATŪROS INSTITUTAS. Lietuvos
TSR upių ir ežerų vardynas. Vil-
nius, 1963. See entry no. 420.

7793. MÜLLER, H. Über die Ört-
lichkeiten der "Wegeberichte" in-
nerhalb der heutigen Landesgrenze.
In Altpreussische Forschungen
(Königsberg in Pr.), 1927, p. 43-
65. See serials consulted.

7794. NESSELMANN, Georg Heinrich
Ferdinand. Über altpreussische
Ortsnamen. In Neue Preussische
Provinzial-Blätter (Königsberg in
Pr.), 1848, p. 4-18. See serials
consulted.

7795. OCHMAŃSKI, Jerzy. Noms
des lituaniennes au XIIIe siecle.
In Lingua Posnaniensis (Poznań),
v.9, 1963, p. 169-174. See serials
consulted.

7796. OTRĘBSKI, Jan Szczepan.
Beiträge zur baltisch-slavischen
Namenkunde. In Beiträge zur Namenforschung (Heidelberg), v.11, 1960,
p. 172-178; v.12, 1961, p. 39-44,
262-265; v.13, 1962, p. 148-149,
265-267; v.14, 1963, p. 193-197.
See serials consulted.

7797. --- La formation des noms
de lieux en lituanien. In Lingua
Posnaniensis (Poznań), v.2, 1950,
p. 4-43. See serials consulted.

7798. --- La formation des noms
physiographiques en lituanien. In
Lingua Posnaniensis (Poznań), v.1,
1949, p. 199-243. See serials consulted.

7799. --- Lietuva. [Lithuania]
In Beiträge zur Namenforschung
(Heidelberg), v.9, 1958, p. 116-118,
188. See serials consulted.

7800. --- Tiernamen als Gewässer-
namen in Litauen. In Beiträge zur
Namenforschung (Heidelberg), v.10,
1959, p. 24-27. See serials
consulted.

7801. PEARCE, Ruth (Lilienthal).
The Lithuanian months names. In
Studi Baltici (Firenze) n.s., v.1
(9), 1952, p. 121-162. See
serials consulted.

7802. --- Months names in Lithuanian and Lettish. Philadelphia,
Pa., 1949. 165 leaves. Thesis--
University of Pennsylvania. Typescript. 491.9.P312 PU

7803. PRINZ, Jürgen. Die Slavi-
sierung baltischer und die Balti-
sierung slavischer Ortsnamen im
Gebiet des ehemaligen Gouvernement
Suwałki; Versuch der Entwicklung
einer Theorie der Umsetzung von
Ortsnamen am praktischen Beispiel.

Wiesbaden, O. Harrassowitz, 1968. 32 p. fold. map. (Veröffentlichungen der Abteilung für slavische Sprachen und Literaturen des Ost-europa-Instituts (slavisches Seminar) an der Freien Universität Berlin, Bd.34) PG303.P7 CaOTU

7804. RUKAS, Anis. Asmenų, dievybių ir didvyrių vardynas. [The list of names of the deities, heroes, and personal names] [Chicago, Ill., 1964] 88 p. PG8662.R8 PU ICU

7805. SAFAREWICZ, Jan. Litewskie nazwy miejscowe na -iszki. In Onomastica (Wrocław), v.2, 1956, p. 15-64. See serials consulted.

7806. SALYS, Antanas. Apie mūsų vardus ir pavardes. [On our names and surnames] In Židinys (Kaunas), v.17, no.5-6, 1933, p. 484-488. See serials consulted.

7807. --- Mūsų lietuviškieji vardai. [Our Lithuanian names] In Gimtoji kalba (Kaunas), 1933, no.4, p. 49-51; no.5, p. 69-74; no.6-7, p. 86-96; no.8, p. 121-124. See serials consulted.

7808. SAURUSAITIS, Peter. List of Lithuanian family names. Shenandoah, Pa., Lithuanian Catholic Publishing Co., 1908. 30 p. CS2880.S3 DLC

7809. SAVUKYNAS, Bronius. Ežerų vardai. [Names of the lakes] In Lietuvių kalbotyros klausimai (Vilnius), v.3, 1960, p. 289-298; v.4, 1961, p. 219-226; v.5, 1962, p. 191-198; v.8, 1966, p. 183-194. (Covers only letters A-G) See serials consulted.

7810. --- Kilmininkiniai lietuvių vietovardžiai. [The possessive kind of Lithuanian place names] In Lietuvių kalbotyros klausimai (Vilnius), v.6, 1963, p. 235-246. See serials consulted.

7811. SCHLEICHER, August. Tomy imen chislitel'nykh, kolichestvennykh i poriadkovych v litvo-slavianskom i nemetskom iazykakh. Sanktpetersburg, Tip. Imperat. akad. nauk, 1866. 69 p. In Akademiia nauk SSSR. Zapiski (Sankt-peterburg), v.10, 1866, prilozh.2. See serials consulted.

SCHMITTLEIN, Raymond. Études sur la nationalité des Aestii. I.: Toponomie lituanienne. Bade, 1948. See entry no. 421.

7812. --- Les noms de lieux lituaniens dans la Deutsche Namen-kunde d'Adolf Bach. Revue internationale d'onomastique (Paris), v.9, no.2, June 1957, p. 119-131. See serials consulted.

7813. --- Sur quelques toponymes lituaniens. In Zeitschrift für Namenforschung, v.14, 1938, p. 233-248; v.15, 1939, p. 51-71, 152-179. G104.Z4 DLC CLU CU CtY ICU IU MH NN NNC NjP OCU TxU WU

7814. --- Voies et impasses de la toponymie lituanienne. In Revue internationale d'onomastique (Paris), v.10, no.2, 1958, p. 107-138. See serials consulted.

7815. SEMBRITZKI, Emil. Slawen-Spuren auf deutscher und litauisch-deutscher Orts- und Flurnamen. Berlin-Charlottenberg, W. Göritz [1929] 48 p. 432.5.Se52 MnU

7816. SENN, Alfred. Lithuanian surnames. In American Slavic and East European Review (Menasha, Wis.), v.4, no.8-9, 1945, p. 127-137. See serials consulted.

7817. SKARDŽIUS, Pranas. Dėl kai kurių mūsų tikrinių vardų aiškinimų. [On some interpretations of our proper names] In Aidai (Brooklyn, N.Y.), no.2, 1968, p. 74-77. See serials consulted.

7818. --- Lietuvių mitologiniai vardai. [Lithuanian mytological names] In Aidai (Brooklyn, N.Y.), no.5, 1954, p. 218-226. See serials consulted.

7819. --- Litauische zweistämmige Personennamen mit mant- und manta "bewegliche Habe". In Zeitschrift für Slavische Philologie (Leipzig), v.29, 1960, p. 146-150. See serials consulted.

7820. --- Mėnesių pavadinimai lietuvių kalboje. [The names of the months in the Lithuanian language] In Archivum philologicum (Kaunas), v.1, 1930, p. 103-113. See serials consulted.

7821. --- XVI AMŽIAUS LIETUVIŲ asmenvardžiai. [Lithuanian personal names of the sixteenth century] In Aidai (Brooklyn, N.Y.), no.1, 1954, p. 27-33. See serials consulted.

7822. --- Upių ir ežerų vardai. [Names of the lakes and rivers] In Gimtoji kalba (Riverside, Ill.), no.3-4, 1963, p. 3-5. See serials consulted.

TARVYDAS, Stasys. Lietuvos

vietovardžiai. Vilnius, 1958.
See entry no. 424.

7823. TETZNER, Franz Oskar. Die
Tolminkemischen Taufregister des
Christian Donelitius. In Alt-
preussische Monatsschrift (Königs-
berg in Pr.), v.33, 1896, p. 18-35.
See serials consulted.

7824. TOPOROV, Vladimir Nikolaevich. K voprosu o toponomiches-
kikh sootvetsviiakh na baltiiskikh
territoriiakh i k zapadu ot Visly.
In Baltistica (Vilnius), v.2, 1966,
p. 103-111. See serials consulted.

7825. --- O baltiiskikh sledakh
v toponimike russkikh territorii.
In Lietuvių kalbotyros klausimai
(Vilnius), v.2, 1959, p. 55-63.
See serials consulted.

7826. TOPOROV, V. N. and O. N.
Trubachev. Baltiiskaia gidronimiia
Verkhnego Podneproviia. In Lietuvių kalbotyros klausimai (Vilnius),
v.4, 1961, p. 195-217. See serials
consulted.

7827. --- Lingvisticheskii analiz
gidronimov verkhnego Podneproviia.
Moskva, Izd-vo Akademii nauk SSSR,
1962. 266 p. maps. PG303.T6 DLC
CaAEU PU

7828. TRAUTMANN, Reinhold. Die
altpreussischen Personennamen; ein
Beitrag zur baltischen Philologie.
Göttingen, Vandenhoeck & Ruprecht,
1925. vii, 204 p. PG8205.T7 DLC
CtY ICU MB NN OClW OCU OU PBm PU

7829. VADOPALAS, Antanas. Iš
kur galėjo kilti vardas Lietuva;
etimologijos tyrimas. [From where
could the name Lithuania be de-
rived; an etymological research]
Chicago, Ill., Sandaros leidinys,
1954. 23 p. PG8669.N3V3 DLC

   --- Vardai dumblynams ir
durpynams. Chicago, Ill., 1966.
See entry no. 429.

   VANAGAS, Aleksandras. Lietuvos TSR hidronimų daryba. Vilnius, 1970. See entry no. 427-428.

7830. --- Nauji duomenys iš topo-
nimikos. [New data from the topo-
nymy] In Lietuvių kalbotyros
klausimai (Vilnius), v.5, 1962, p.
185-190. See serials consulted.

7831. --- Raymond Schmittlein;
les noms d'eau de la Lithuanie. In
Baltistica (Vilnius), v.2, no.1,
1966, p. 97-102. See serials
consulted.

7832. VARDAI IR ŽODŽIAI. [Su-
darė Bronius Savukynas] Vilnius
[Mintis] 1971. 244 p. illus.
At head of title: LTSR Paminklų
apsaugos ir kraštotyros draugija.
Lietuvių kalbos sekcija.
PG8523.V37 PU

   VOL'TER, Eduard Aleksandrovich. Spiski naselennykh mest Su-
valkskoi gubernii. Sanktpeterburg,
1901. See entry no. 2071.

7833. ZIESEMER, Walther. Beo-
bachtungen zur Wortgeographie Ostpreussens. In Zeitschrift für
deutsche Mundarten (Berlin), v.18,
1923, p. 149-155. See serials consulted.

XIII.4.1. FOREIGN ELEMENTS IN THE
LITHUANIAN LANGUAGE

7834. ALMINAS, Kazys. Die Ger-
manismen des Litauischen. 1. Die
deutschen Lehnwörter im Litauischen.
Von K. Alminauskis. Kaunas, Šv.
Kazimiero draugijos knygynas [1934]
152 p. Thesis--University of Leipzig. Bibliography: p. [6]-10.
491.9224A166g TxU CtTMF CtY InU MH
NNC PU WU

7835. BOROWSKA, Nina. Wpływy
słowiańskie na litewską terminolo-
giękościelną na podstawie Dictionarium Szyrwida. In Studia z Filologii Polskiej i Słowiańskiej. Warszawa, 1957. v.2, p. [320]-365.
PG6001.S8 v.2 DLC CaAEU CSt ClU IU
NN

7836. BRÜCKNER, Alexander. Die
slavischen Fremdwörter im Litauischen. In His Litu-slavische Studien, Theil 1. Weimar, H. Böhlau,
1877. xiv, 207 p. PG8664.S6B7
DLC CaBVaU CaOHM CU CTU ICN ICU InU
MH NIC NN NcU NjP NSyU PPULC PBm
PU WU

7837. GERULLIS, Georg. Die Herkunft der slavischen Lehnwörter im
Preussisch-Litauischen. In Indogermanische Forschungen, Zeitschrift
für indogermanische Sprach- und
Altertumskunde (Berlin), v.42, 1924,
p. 183-185. See serials consulted.

7838. OTRĘBSKI, Jan Szczepan. Les
mots d'origine commune des langues
slaves et baltiques. In Lingua
Posnaniensis (Poznań), v.1, 1949,
p. 121-151. See serials consulted.

7839. PRELLWITZ, Walther. Die

deutschen Lehnwörter im Preussischen, und Lautlehre der deutschen Lehnwörter im Litauischen. Göttingen, Vandenhoeck & Ruprecht, 1891. 64 p. (Die deutschen Bestandteile in den lettischen Sprachen, ein Beitrag zur Kenntnis der deutschen Volkssprache, Heft 1.) PG8664.G3P74 NSyU ICU NN PU WU

7840. SCHMALSTIEG, William Riegel. Criteria for the determination of Slavic borrowings in Lithuanian. Ann Arbor, Mich., University Microfilms [1956] xxv, 123 leaves. (University microfilms. Publication no. 17, 273) Thesis--University of Pennsylvania. Film 1503 LU PPiU PU(typescript)

7841. SKARDŽIUS, Pranas. Die slavischen Lehnwörter im Altlitauischen. Kaunas, 1931. 252 p. Thesis--University of Leipzig. PG8664.S6S5 1931 DLC CLU(photocopy) CtY MH MiU MnU NNC NjP PU

7842. WESTFAL, Stanisław. Uwagi o zapożyczonych słów polskich w języku litewskim. In Towarzystwo Naukowe w Warszawie. Wydział I. Sprawozdanie z posiedzeń. Warszawa, v.25, 1933, p. 75-95. See serials consulted.

XIII.4.k. DICTIONARIES AND LEXICOGRAPHY

BARANAUSKAS, Antanas. Zamietki o litovskom iazykie i slovarie. Sanktpeterburg, 1898. See entry no. 7270.

7843. BENDER, Harold Herman. On the Lithuanian word-stock; Indo-European material. In Studies in honor of Maurice Bloomfield, professor of Sanskrit and comparative philology in the Johns Hopkins University, Baltimore, Maryland, by a group of his pupils. New Haven, Yale University Press, 1920. p. [19]-34. PJ26.B6 DLC OCl

7844. ELISONAS, Jurgis. Lietuvių sodiečių technikos žodyno mėginimas. [An attempt to devise a technical dictionary for the Lithuanian peasant] In Archyvum philologicum (Kaunas), v.3, 1932, p. 125-167. See serials consulted.

7845. FRAENKEL, Ernst. Zum litauischen Wortschatz und zur litauischen Phraseologie. In Indogermanische Forschungen (Berlin), v.47, 1929, p. 334-349. See

serials consulted.

7846. KAŠARAUSKIS, Ambraziejus. Rzecz o litewskich słownikach i ogólny pogląd na kraje litewskie. Wilno, 1862. p. 133-212. Detached from Pismo Zbiorowe Wileńskie, 1862. 491.922.K149 PU BM

7847. KRUOPAS, Jonas. Simano Daukanto leksikografiniai darbai. [The lexicographic works of Simanas Daukantas] In Lietuvių kalbotyros klausimai (Vilnius), no.4, 1961, p. 301-316. See serials consulted.

7848. LARIN, Boris Aleksandrovich. Kratkii istoricheskii obzor litovskoi leksikografii. In Leksikograficheskii sbornik (Moskva), v.2, 1957. p. [119]-144. See serials consulted.

7849. LIETUVIŲ KALBOS LEKSIKOS RAIDA. [The lexical development of the Lithuanian language] Vilnius, Mintis, 1966. 239 p. (Lietuvių kalbotyros klausimai, 8) At head of title: Lietuvos TSR Mokslų akademija, Vilna. Lietuvių kalbos ir literatūros Institutos. PG8501.L5 v.8 DLC CaOTU CU CLU CtY ICU InU IU MH NN PU WaU

7850. ŁOWMIAŃSKI, Henryk. Uwagi o wpływach słowiańskich na litewską terminologię kościelną. In Studia z filologii polskiej i słowiańskiej. Warszawa, 1947. v. 2, p. [366]-372. See serials consulted.

7851. LYBERIS, Antanas and Kazimieras Ulvydas. Lietuvių literatūrinės kalbos leksikos praturtėjimas tarybinės santvarkos metais. [The enrichment of the vocabulary of the Lithuanian literary language during the Soviet period] In Literatūra ir kalba (Vilnius), v.3, 1958, p. 31-110. See serials consulted.

7852. NIEDERMANN, Max. Quelques dictionnaires lituaniennes. Roma, 1936-40. p. [75]-82; 1-14. In Studi Baltici (Firenze), v.6, 1936-37, p. [75]-82; v.7, 1938-40, p. 1-14. See serials consulted.

7853. PAKALKA, Kazys. Dėl K. Širvydo "Dictionarium trium linguarum" lenkiškos dalies šaltinio. [On the sources of the Polish part of the Dictionarium trium linguarum of K. Širvydas. In LTSRMAD. Serija A, no.1, 1960, p. 229-233. See serials consulted.

7854. --- Iš K. Širvydo "Dictio-

narium trium linguarum" by K. Šir-
vydas] In Lietuvių kalbotyros
klausimai (Vilnius), v.3, 1960, p.
277-286. See serials consulted.

7855. --- K. Širvydo "Dictiona-
rium trium linguarum" naujadarai.
[New words in K. Širvydas' "Dic-
tionarium trium linguarum"] In
Lietuvių kalbotyros klausimai
(Vilnius), v.4, 1961, p. 281-300.
See serials consulted.

7856. PIROČKINAS, Arnoldas. Jono
Jablonskio leksiniai taisymai.
Apybraiža. [Description of lexi-
cography corrections by Jonas
Jablonskis] Kaunas, Sviesa, 1970.
96 p. PG8517.J2P5 DLC PU

7857. SABALIAUSKAS, Algirdas.
Lietuvių kalbos leksikos raida.
[The development of Lithuanian
lexicology] In Lietuvių kalbotyros klausimai (Vilnius), v.8, 1966,
p. 5-140. See serials consulted.

7858. SALYS, Antanas. Lietuvių
kalbos žodynai. [Dictionaries of
the Lithuanian language] In Lietuvių enciklopedija (Boston, Mass.),
1966. p. 400-413, illus. See
entry no. 216.

7859. --- The russianization of
the Lithuanian vocabulary under the
Soviets. In Lituanus (Chicago,
Ill.), v.13, no.2, 1967, p. 47-62.
See serials consulted.

SENN, Alfred. The historical development of the Lithuanian
vocabulary. In Polish Institute of
Arts and Sciences in America, New
York City. Bulletin, v.1, no.4,
1943, p. 946-969. See serials
consulted.

SKARDŽIUS, Pranas. Lietu-
vių kalbos vadovas. [Bielefeld]
1950. See entry no. 362.

7860. TOLUTIENĖ, Birutė. Antanas
Juška leksikografas. [Antanas
Juška, a lexicographer] In Literatura ir kalba (Vilnius), v.5, 1961,
p. 87-377. See serials consulted.

XIII.4.ℓ. DIALECTOLOGY: DIALECTS,
PROVINCIALISMS, ETC.

7861. ARUMAA, Peeter. Litauische
mundartliche Texte aus der Wilnaer
Gegend, mit grammatischen Anmerkungen. Dorpat, Drukerei "Postimees",
1930. 75 p. illus., map. (Tartu.
Ulikool. Acta et commentationes

Universitatis tartuensis. B: Humaniora, 23, no.3) AS262.D62 B
v.23, no.3 CSt CtY CLU DLC ICU MnU
NIC NNC NjP PPULC PU RPB WU

7862. BARANAUSKAS, Antanas. Li-
tauische Mundarten. [By] A. Bara-
nowski. Hrsg. von Franz Specht.
Leipzig, Koehler, 1920-1922. xv,
467 p. (Texte aus dem H. Weberschen
Nachlass, herausgegeben von Dr.
Franx Specht.) At head of title:
Sächsische Forschungsinstitute in
Leipzig, Forschungsinstut für Indo-
germanistik. Hvc33.B23 CtY CaBVaU
CLSU ICU InU MH MiU NNC NNU NjP
PPULC PBm PU WU

7863. BARANAUSKAS, A. and Hugo
Ernst Barthold Weber. Ostlitaui-
ische Texte mit Einleitungen und
Anmerkungen hrsg. von A. Baranowski
und H. Weber. Hft. 1. Weimar,
1882. xxxv, 23 p. PG8693.A6B3
ICU CaQMM CU MiU MdBJ NNU NjP PPULC
PU WU ICN ICRL

7864. BECKER, Johann. Die Sprache
der Kurischen Fischer in Perwelk
auf der Kurischen Nehrung. Göttingen, Huth, 1904. 25 p. Thesis--
University of Berlin. 491.9.F493 PU

7865. BEZZENBERGER, Adalbert.
Litauische und lettische mundartliche
Texte. I. In Zeitschrift für vergleichende Sprachforschung (Berlin), v.51, 1923, p. 63-66. See
serials consulted.

7866. --- Zur litauischen Dialekt-
forschung. In Beiträge zur Kunde
der indogermanischen Sprachen
(Göttingen), v.8, 1884, p. 98-142;
v.9, 1885, p. 253-293; v.20, 1894,
p. 105-110. See serials consulted.

7867. BROCH, Olaf. Zum Litaui-
ischen südlich von Wilna. In Norsk
tidskrift for sprogvidenskap
(Oslo), v.19, 1959, p. 1-71. See
serials consulted.

7868. BRUGMANN, Friedrich Karl.
Zur Grammatik der godlewischen
Mundart. In Leskien, August und K.
Brugmann, comp. Litauische Volks-
lieder. Strassburg, 1882, p. 277-
329. PG8696.L4 DLC CaOHM CaOTU CU
ICN MnU NIC NN NNC NSyU OCl TxU

7869. BUTĖNAS, Petras. Aukš-
taičių tarmės okuojančiosios paš-
nektės sienos. [The boundaries of
the High Lithuanian dialect which
uses "o" instead of "a"] In Archivum philologicum (Kaunas), v.3,
1932, p. 168-193. See serials
consulted.

7870. DORITSCH, Alexander. Beiträge zur litauischen Dialektologie. Heidelberg, C. Winter, 1912. ccxl, 136 p. (Mitteilungen der litauischen literarischen Gesellschaft, Hft. 31) PG8688.D7 InU NN PU

7871. FRAENKEL, Ernst. Beiträge zur litauischen Textkritik und Mundartenkunde. In Zeitschrift für Slavische Philologie (Leipzig), v.3, 1926, p. 68-86. See serials consulted.

7872. --- Calchi semantici e sintattici dallo Slavo nei Lituano del territorio di Vilna. In Studi Baltici (Rome), v.4, 1934/35, p. 25-44. See serials consulted.

7873. --- Der Stand der Erforschung des im Wilnagebiete gesprochenen Litauischen. In Balticoslavica (Wilno), v.2, 1936, p. 14-107. See serials consulted.

7874. --- Untersuchungen zur litauischen Dialektologie. In Tauta ir žodis (Kaunas), v.4, 1926, p. 57-66. See serials consulted.

7875. --- Zum Dialekt von Buividze. In Zeitschrift für vergleichende Sprachforschung (Berlin), v.54, 1927, p. 293-294. See serials consulted.

7876. --- Zur Behandlung der slavischen Lehnwörter im ostlitauischen Dialekte von Twerecz (Tverečius). In Indogermanische Forschungen. Zeitschrift für Indogermanistik und Sprachwissenschaft (Berlin), v.53, 1935, p. 123-134. See serials consulted.

7877. GAUTHIOT, Robert. Le parler de Buividze; essai de description d'un dialects lituanien oriental, par R. Gauthiot. Paris, E. Bouillon, 1903, 113 p. (Bibliothèque de L'École des hautes études... Sciences historiques et philologiques, 146. facs.) Bibliographie: p. 5-7. PQ139.P21b no. 146 CU CLU DLC ICU ICN KU LU MH MnU NIC NNC NcU NjP OrU PU TxDaM TxU WaU

7878. GEITLER, Leopold. Beiträge zur litauischen Dialektologie. Wien, Gerold, 1885. 70 p. PG8688.G27b CLU NjP; also in Akademie der Wissenschaften. Philosophisch-Historische Klasse. Sitzungsberichte, Bd. 108, 1884. p. 339-406. See serials consulted.

7879. GERULLIS, Georg. Litauische Dialekstudien. Leipzig, Markert & Petters, 1930. iv, 110 p. illus. (Staatlich Forschungsinstitut in Leipzig. Forschungsinstitut für Indogermanistik. Slavische Abteilung. Slavisch-baltische Quellen und Forschungen, Heft 5.) PG8688.G38(s) CtY CU ICU MnU NNC NcD NN NjP PU WU

7880. --- Zur Sprache der Sudauer-Jatwinger. In Festschrift Adalbert Bezzenberger zum 14. April 1921... Göttingen, 1921. p. 44-51. NN CU CtY DLC-P4 IU MH NIC NNU NRU NcD NcU OCl OU PU TxU

7881. GERULLIS, G. and Christian Stang. Lietuvių žvejų tarmė prūsuose. [The dialect of the Lithuanian fishermen in Prussia] Kaunas, Švietimo ministerijos Knygų leidimo komisijos leidinys, 1933. xvi, 105 p. (Lietuvių kalbos tarmės, v.1) Half-title: Das Fischer-Litauisch in Preussen. PG8688.G42 PU CtTMF OCl

7882. GIRDENIS, A. and Zigmas Zinkevičius. Dėl lietuvių kalbos tarmių klasifikacijos. [On the classification of the Lithuanian dialects] In LTSRAMMD: Kalbotyra (Vilnius), v.14, 1966, p. 139-147. map. See serials consulted.

7883. GRINAVECKIENĖ, Elena. Kai kurios lietuvių kalbos tarmių ypatybės. Nekotorye osobennosti govorov litovskogo iazyka na osnove materialov sobrannykh dialektologicheskimi ekspeditsiiami v 1961 godu. In Lietuvių kalbotyros klausimai (Vilnius), v.5, 1962, p. 147-169. See serials consulted.

7884. --- Mituvos upyno tarmės fonetika. [The phonetics of the dialect of Mituva River basin] In Lietuvių kalbotyros klausimai (Vilnius), v.1, 1957, p. 119-180. See serials consulted.

7885. --- Tarmių medžiagos rinkimas lietuvių kalbos atlasui. [The collection of data for the atlas of Lithuanian dialects] In Lietuvių kalbotyros klausimai (Vilnius), v. 3, 1960, p. 191-206. See serials consulted.

7886. GRINAVECKIS, Vladas. Dzūkavimas ir jo kilmė. [The dialect of Dzūkija and its origin] In Vilnius. Valstybinis pedagoginis institutas. Mokslo darbai, v.8, 1959, p. 91-95. See serials consulted.

7887. --- Keli lietuvių kalbos

tarmių fonetinių ypatybių istorijos klausimai. [Some historical questions on the phonetic peculiarities of the dialects of the Lithuanian language] In LTSRAMMD: Kalbotyra (Vilnius), v.3, 1961, p. 115-125. See serials consulted.

7888. --- Kirčio atitraukimas ir nukėlimas lietuvių kalbos tarmėse. [Shifting of the accent's position in the dialects of Lithuanian language] In Lietuvių kalbotyros klausimai (Vilnius), v.4, 1961, p. 117-134. See serials consulted.

7889. --- Prevrashchenie diftongicheskikh sochetanii il, im, in, ir, ul, um, un, ur, & iel, iem, ien, ier, uol, uom, uon, uor v govorakh litovskogo iazyka. In Acta Baltico-Slavica (Białystok), v.3, 1966, p. 65-68. See serials consulted.

7890. --- Priebalsių j, v, n išnykimas, pridėjimas ir įterpimas žemaičių tarmėse. [The disappearance, addition and insertion of consonants j v n in the Samogitian dialects] In Acta Baltico-Slavica (Białystok), v.3, 1967, p. 161-169. See serials consulted.

7891. --- Šiaurės vakarų dūnininkų tarmių fonetinės ypatybės ir jų raida. [The phonetic characteristic of the North-West "dūnininkai" dialects and its development] In Vilna. Valstybinis pedagoginis institutas. Mokslo darbai, v.9, 1963, p. 41-110. See serials consulted.

7892. --- Šiaurės vakarų dūnininkų tarmių kirtis. [The stress of the dialects "dūnininkai" in the North-West] In Lietuvių kalbotyros klausimai (Vilnius), v.1, 1957, p. 109-118. See serials consulted.

7893. --- Žemaičių tarmių vokalizmo susiformavimas. [The formation of a system of vowels in the Samogitian dialects] In LTSRAMMD: Kalbotyra (Vilnius), v.6, 1963. p. 37-64. See serials consulted.

7894. --- Žemaičių tarmių žodžio galo dėsnių susiformavimas. [The formation of laws for the ending of words in the Samogitian dialect] In LTSRAMMD: Kalbotyra (Vilnius), v.9, 1963, p. 74-97. See serials consulted.

7895. --- Žemaičių tarmių žodžio pradžios vokalizmo dėsnių susiformavimas. [The formation of vocal rules for the beginning of words in the Samogitian dialects] In

LTSRAMMD: Kalbotyra (Vilnius), v.9, 1963, p. 62-73. See serials consulted.

7896. HERMANN, Eduard. Einteilung der litauischen Mundarten. In Akademie der Wissenschaften, Göttingen. Philologisch-Historische Klasse. Nachrichten, no.4, 1948, p. 137-139. See serials consulted.

7897. JABLONSKIS, Jonas. Po povodu prilozheniia k otchetu A.L. Pogodina v ego poiezdkie v Kovenskuiu guberniiu. [By] I. IAblonskii. In Zhivaia starina (Sanktpeterburg) v.1, 1896, p. 123-130. See serials consulted.

7898. JACOBY, Karl Rudolf. Beitrag zur Kunde des litauischen Memeler Dialekts. In LLGM, v.1, 1880, p. 61-82. See serials consulted.

7899. JAŠINSKAITĖ, I. Kirtis, priegaidė ir jų poveikis vokalizmui Biržų tarmėje. [Stress, intonation and their influence on use of vowels in Biržai district] In Lietuvių kalbos klausimai (Vilnius), v.1, 1957, p. 189-195. See serials consulted.

7900. JAUNIUS, Kazimieras. Dialektologicheskiia osobennosti litovskago iazyka v Rossienskom uiezdie. Kovno, 1892. p. 110-145. Detached from Pamiatnaia knizhka Kovenskoi gubernii na 1893 god. 491.922.J324.2 PU

7901. --- Ukmergės, Kauno, Raseinių, Zarasų ir Panevėžio apskričių tarmių aprašai. [The description of the dialects in the districts of Ukmergė, Kaunas...] In Pamiatnaiia knizhka Kovenskoi gubernii na god 1891-93, 1895, 1898-1899. See serials consulted.

7902. JONIKAS, Petras. Pagramantis] Kaunas, Švietimo ministerijos leidinys, 1939. 93 p. 491.42.J737 PU

7903. JURGELIONIS, Kleopas. Panemunėlio tarmės fonetika. [Phonetics of the Panemunėlis dialect] Chicago, Ill., 1911. Hvc22.ℓJ97 Pamph. CtY

7904. KARDELYTĖ, Jadvyga. Liepiamosios nuosakos dvejopos formos ir jų vartojimas rytų Lietuvos tarmėse. [The dual forms of the imperative mood and their usage in the dialects of Eastern Lithuania] In Lietuvių kalbos klausimai (Vilnius), v.1, 1957, p. 181-188. See serials consulted.

7905. KINDURIS, M. K. Litovskii govor v belorusskom okruzhenii; govor der. Mal'kovka v BSSR; avtoreferat dissertatsii. Leningrad, 1956. 22 p. Thesis--University of Leningrad. LSOC.3983.151 MH

7906. KONCEVIČIUS, Jonas. Wörter und Redensarten in Schadowscher Mundart. In LLGM, v.1, 1881, p. 222-238. See serials consulted.

7907. LARIN, Boris Aleksandrovich. Materialy po litovskoi dialektologii. In IAzyk i literatura (Leningrad), v.1, 1926, p. 93-170. See serials consulted.

7908. LIETUVIŲ KALBOS TARMĖS. Chrestomatija. Vilnius, Mintis, 1970. 513 p. At head of title: Lietuvos TSR Mokslų akademija. Lietuvių kalbos ir literatūros institutas. By E. Grinaveckienė and others. Summary in Russian and German. PG8687.A3L5 DLC PU

7909. LIETUVOS TSR MOKSLŲ AKADEMIJA, VILNA. LIETUVIŲ KALBOS IR LITERATŪROS INSTITUTAS. Lietuvių kalbos atlaso medžiagos rinkimo programa. 2. leidimas. [The program of collecting materials for linguistic atlas of the Lithuanian language. Ats. redaktorius J. Senkus. Kaune] VPMLL, 1956. 118 p. PG8687.A1L5 DLC MH

7910. OTRĘBSKI, Jan Szczepan. Wschodniolitewskie narzecze twereckie. Wydane z zasiłku Funduszu Kultury Narodowej. Kraków, Nakł. Polskiej Akademji Umiejętności, 1932-34. 3 v. Contents.--v.1. Gramatyka.1934.--v.2 Teksty i słowni.--v.3. Zapożyczenia słowiańskie. 1932. PG8688.089 CaAEU(3) CaOTU CtY CoU(1,3) ICU (1,3) MH(1,3) NNC(1,3) NBuU(1,3) PU WU(1)

7911. PORZEZIŃSKI, Wiktor. Zametki po dialektologii litovskago iazyka: I. Dialekticheskiia granitsy v russkoi Litvie, II. K fonetikie vostochno-litovskago narechiia... In Akademiia nauk SSSR. Otdielenie russkago iazyka i slovesnosti. Izviestiia (Sanktpeterburg), v.1, no.3, 1896, p. 467-492. See serials consulted.

7912. ROKAITĖ, B. Kai kurie nauji žemaičių dounininkų tarmių fonetikos dalykai. [Some new phonetic points on the Šamogitian dialect of "dounininkai"] In Lietuvių

kalbotiros klausimai (Vilnius), v. 4, 1961, p. 141-155. See serials consulted.

7913. SALYS, Antanas. Kelios pastabos tarmių istorijai. [A few remarks on the history of dialects] In Archivum philologicum (Kaunas), v.4, 1933, p. 21-34. See serials consulted.

7914. --- Lietuvių kalbos tarmės. [Dialects of the Lithuanian language] Tübingen, Ger., 1946. 3, 67 p. map. Mimeographed. 1st ed. Kaunas, 1935. 87 p. PG8688.S3 1946 PU ICCC NN

7915. --- Die žemaitischen Mundarten. Geschichte des žemaitischen Sprachgebietes. Kaunas, 1930. 146 p. map. Thesis--University of Leipzig. Reprinted from "Tauta ir žodis", v.6, 1930, p. 173-314. PG8501.T3 v.6 DLC CaOTU CtY MH NNC PU

7916. SEDELSKYTĖ, O. Debeikių tarmės daiktavardžių linksniavimas. [The declension of the nouns in the Debeikiai dialect] In LTSRMAD. Serija A, v.1(4), 1958, p. 195-208. See serials consulted.

7917. SENKUS, Juozas. Daiktavardžių linksniavimas kapsų ir zanavykų tarmėse bruožai. [The outline of the declension of nouns in the dialects of Kapsai and Zanavykai] In LTSRMAD. Serija A, v.2 (9), 1960, p. 157-170. See serials consulted.

7918. --- Daiktavardžių priebalsinio kamieno linksniavimo kapsų ir zanavykų tarmėse. [The declension of the nouns of consonant stems in the dialects of Kapsai and Zanavykai] In LTSRMAD. Serija A, v.7, 1959, p. 167-174. See serials consulted.

7919. --- Kai kurie lazūnų tarmės ypatumai. [Some features of the Lazūnai dialect] In LTSRMAD. Serija A, v.1(4), 1958, p. 183-194. See serials consulted.

7920. --- Kai kurios kapsų ir zanavykų tarmių veiksmažodžio ypatybės. [Some peculiarities of the verb in the Kapsai and Zanavykai dialects] In LTSRMAD. Serija A, v.2(5), 1958, p. 127-145. See serials consulted.

7921. --- Kapsų-zanavykų tarmių būdvardžio ir skaitvardžio kaitybos bruožai. [The outline of the inflection of the adjective and

438

numerals in the dialects of Kapsai-
Zanavykai] In Lietuvių kalbotyros
klausimai (Vilnius), v.3, 1960, p.
133-158. See serials consulted.

7922. --- Kapsų-zanavykų tarmių
įvardžai. [The characteristic of
the pronoun of the dialect Kapsai-
Zanavykai] In LTSRMAD. Serija A,
v.2(13), 1962, p. 205-216. See
serials consulted.

7923. --- Pirmosios lietuviškos
knygos tarmė. [The dialect of the
first Lithuanian book] In Lietuvių
kalbotyros klausimai (Vilnius), v.1,
1957, p. 67-83. See serials consulted.

7924. SENN, Alfred. Einiges aus
der Sprache der Amerika-Litauer.
In Studi Baltici (Firenze), v.2,
1932, p. 35-58. See serials consulted.

7925. --- Lithuanian dialectology.
Menasha, Wis., Banta Pub. [1945]
57 p. fold. map. (Supplement to the
American Slavic and East European
Review, 1) Bibliography: p. 1-8.
PG8688.S4 1945 PU CtY IaU ICBM MnU
NN NNC

7926. --- --- [Another edition.
New York, N.Y., Johnson Reprint
Corp., 1966] 57 p. maps. (Sup-
plements to the American Slavic and
East European Review, no.1) Reprint:
originally published Menasha, Wis.,
Banta Pub., [1945] PG8688.S4 1945a
PU CSt ICU MWalB NIC NjP

7927. SHAKHMATOV, Aleksei Aleksandrovich. Spoly, iskonnye sosiedi
slavian. In Zhivaia starina (Sanktpeterburg), v.20, 1911, p. [21]-26.
See serials consulted.

7928. SITTIG, Ernst, ed. Litauische Dialekte, bearbeitet unter
der Leitung von Ernst Sittig. Berlin, Preussische Staatsbibliothek,
1928-31. 5 pts. (Lautbibliothek;
phonetische Platten und Umschriften
hrsg. von der Lautabteilung der
Preussischen Staatsbibliothek Hft.
30-34) P215.L35 no.30-34 DLC

7929. SOKOLOV, Nikolai Nikolaevich. Iz poiezdki v Litvu. In
Etnograficheskoe obozrienie (Moskva),
v.14, no.2, 1902, p. 21-30. See
serials consulted.

7930. STANG, Christian Schwei-
gaard. Die litauische Mundart von
Zasėčiai im Gebiet von Wilna. In
Norsk tidskrift for sprogvidenskap
(Oslo), v.18, 1958, p. 171-201.
See serials consulted.

7931. ZINKEVIČIUS, Zigmas. Lie-
tuvių dialektologija; lyginamoji
tarmių fonetika ir morfologija.
[Lithuanian dialectology] Vilnius,
Mintis, 1966. 541 p. 75 maps.
PG8688.Z66 DLC CaAEU CaOTU CoU CtY
ICU MH NjP PU

7932. --- Lietuvių kalbos tarmės.
[Lithuanian dialects] Kaunas,
Šviesa, 1968. 88 p. illus., maps.
CtPAM

XIII.5. LITERATURE

XIII.5.a. BIBLIOGRAPHIES

7933. BIRŽIŠKA, Mykolas. Mūsų
raštų istorija 1547 m. - 1904 m.
[Tilsit] Švyturio [1920] 112 p.
Z2537.B6 InU CtTMF ICCC PU

7934. BUFIENĖ, Teklė. Tarybinė
lietuvių literatūra; teminiai rekomenduojamosios literatūros sąrašai.
[Soviet Lithuanian literatur; a list
of recommended literature] Vilnius,
Mintis, 1966. 165 p. (Skaitykime
grožinę literatūrą) Z2537.B94 DLC

7935. FREIDHEIMAS, Peisachas.
Litovskaia literatura; rekomendatel'nyi ukazatel' proizvedenii Litovskikh pisatelei imeiushchikhsia
v perevode na russkii iazyk. Moskva, 1955. 66 p. Z2537.F7 DLC PU

7936. GROŽINĖ LITERATŪRA; katalogas: literatūra, dailė muzika,
1940-1960. [Belles-Lettres; catalogue: literature, arts, music,
1940-1960. Paruošė A. Bačienė et
al. Redagovo I. Jurevičiūtė]
Vilnius, VGLL, 1961. 476 p.
Z2537.G7 DLC CaAEU CaOONL MH PU WU

7937. JUREVIČIŪTĖ, I. Vaikų
literatūra; bibliografija, 1940-
1964. [Childrens' literature; bibliography, 1940-1964] Vilnius,
Vaga, 1965. 398 p. Z1037.8L5J8
DLC CaAEU PU

LANKUTIS, Jonas. E. Mieželaičio kūrinių ir literatūros apie
jo kūrybą bibliografija. See
entry no. 137.

LEBEDIENĖ, Elena. Kristi-
jono Donelaičio bibliografija.
Vilnius, 1964. See entry no. 138.

LIETUVIŲ LITERATŪROS ISTO-
rija ir tautosaka; bibliografinė
rodyklė, pagrindinė literatūra.
Vilnius, 1967. See entry no. 6693.

7938. LIETUVOS TSR MOKSLŲ AKADEMI-
JA, VILNA. LIETUVIŲ KALBOS IR LI-
TERATŪROS INSTITUTAS. Lietuvių
literatūriniai ryšiai, 1944-1959;
bibliografinė rodyklė. [Lithu-
anian literary relations, 1944-
1959, a bibliography. Sudarė E.
Stanevičienė] Vilnius, VPMLL, 1960.
42 p. Z2537.L49 DLC MH PU

7939. --- Tarybinė lietuvių literatūra ir kritika, 1945-1955; bibliografija. [Soviet Lithuanian literature and criticism, 1945-1955;
a bibliography. Paruošė S. Stanevičienė. Redagavo A. Šešelgis] Vilnius, 1957. 232 p. Z2537.L5 DLC
CLU CU CaAEU CtY ICU IU InU MH NN
NNC PU

7940. --- Tarybinė lietuvių literatūra ir kritika, 1956-1960;
bibliografinė rodyklė. [Soviet
Lithuanian literature and criticism,
1956-1960; a bibliography. Sudarė
E. Stanevičienė] Vilnius, 1961.
325 p. Z2537.L5 PU CLU CU CaAEU
DLC ICU IU InU MH NN

7941. --- Tarybinė lietuvių literatūra ir kritika, 1961-1965;
bibliografija. [Soviet Lithuanian
literature and criticism, 1961-1965;
a bibliography. Paruošė S. Stanevi-
čienė] Vilnius, 1967. 333 p.
Z2514.L6L742 ICU CaOTU CtY MH NNC
NjP PU

7942. --- Tarybinis lietuvių literatūros mokslas ir kritika apie
literatūrinį palikimą, 1944-1958;
bibliografinė rodyklė. [A study of
Soviet Lithuanian literature and a
criticism of the literary heritage,
1944-1958; a bibliography. Paruošė
E. Stanevičienė] Vilnius, VPMLL,
1959. 148 p. Z2537.L515 DLC CU
CaAEU MH PU

7943. LYROVIENĖ, Sulamita and
Viktoras Lyrovas. Lietuvių grožinė
literatūra TSRS tautų kalbomis;
vertimų bibliografija 1940-1965.
[Lithuanian belles lettres in languages of the people of the Soviet
Union; bibliography of translations
during 1940-1965] Vilnius, Vaga,
1968. 734 p. Z2537.L9 PU CaAEU
CaOTU CtY MH

MERKELIS, Aleksandras.
Vaižgantika. In Bibliografijos
žinios (Kaunas), v.4, 1931. See
serials consulted.

7944. MOSCOW. PUBLICHNAIA BIB-
LIOTEKA. Litovskaia literatura;
rekomendatel'nyi ukazatel'... imeiushchikhsia v perevode na russkii
iazyk. P.A. Freidgeimas i S.B. To-

monis. Moskva, 1955. 66 p.
Balt 7830.955 MH

7945. REINHOLD, Heinrich. Litera-
turbericht für 1903-1906, nebst Nachträgen. In LLGM, v.5, no.5, Hft.29,
1907, p. 483-529. See serials consulted.

7946. RUŽANCOVAS, Aleksandras.
Lietuviškoji literatūra tremtyje;
1945-1949 metų bibliografija. [Li-
thuanian literature in exile; bibliography for 1945-1949] In Knygų
lentyna (Danville, Ind.), no.3-10,
1952; no.1-12, 1953. Total 172
entries. See serials consulted.

7947. VAIČIULAITIS, Antanas. American writers in Lithuania. In Books
Abroad (Norman, Okla.), v.17, no.4,
1943, p. 334-337. See serials consulted.

7948. VILNA. JUBILIEJINĖ KRISTI-
JONO DONELAIČIO PARODA, 1964. Kristijonas Donelaitis, 1714-1964; parodos katalogas. [Kristijonas Donelaitis, 1714-1964; exibition catalogue. Sudarė P. Mikelinskaitė et al.]
Vilnius, 1964. 101 p. illus., facsims., ports. PG8721.D7Z9 DLC CLU
CaOONL ICU MH PPULC PU

VILNA. LIETUVOS TSR VALSTY-
BINĖ RESPUBLIKINĖ BIBLIOTEKA. Antanas Vienuolis, 1882-1957; rekomenduojamosios literatūros rodyklė.
Kaunas, 1960. See entry no. 142.

--- Eduardas Mieželaitis;
rekomenduojamosios literatūros rodyklė. Kaunas, 1962. See entry
no. 143.

--- Jovaras; rekomenduojamosios literatūros rodyklė. Vilnius,
1964. See entry no. 144.

--- Liudas Gira, 1884-1946;
rekomenduojamosios literatūros rodyklė. Kaunas, 1957. See entry
no. 145.

--- Petras Cvirka, 1909-1949;
rekomenduojamosios literatūros rodyklė. Kaunas, 1958. See entry
no. 146.

--- Salomėja Nėris gyvenime
ir kūryboje; parodos katalogas.
[Kaunas, 1946] See entry no. 147.

ŽUKAS, Vladas. Medžiaga
Žemaitės bibliografijai. In
LTSRAMMD: Bibliotekininkystės ir bib-
lijografijos klausimai (Vilnius),
v.5, 1966, p. 177-213. See serials
consulted.

--- Salomėjos Neries kūrinių ir literatūros apie ją bibliografija. [Bibliography on Salomėja Neris and her writings] In Literatūra ir kalba (Vilnius), v.4, p.351-503. See serials consulted.

--- V. Mykolaičio spausdintų darbų bibliografija. [Bibliography of V. Mykolaitis' works] In LTSRAMMD: Literatūra (Vilnius), v.11, no.1, 1969, p. 66-89. See serials consulted.

XIII.5.b. HISTORY AND CRITICISM

XIII.5.b.1. TREATISES, ESSAYS, AND SPECIAL TOPICS

7949. AISTIS, Jonas. A sketch of free and subjugated Lithuanian literature. In Baltic Review (New York, N.Y.), no.7, 1956, p. 63-71. See serials consulted.

7950. AUGUSTAITIS, Pranas. Pierwiastki litewskie we wczesnym romantyźmie polskim. Kraków, Nakł. Autora, 1911. 89 p. PG7053.R7A92 DLC PPULC PU

7951. AURILA, Vincas. Lietuvių vaikų literatūra. [Lithuanian childrens' literature] Vilnius, Mintis, 1967. 266 p. illus., facsims., col. plates. Bibliography: p. [261]-266. PN1009.L5A9 DLC PU

7952. BEZZENBERGER, Adalbert. Die litauische Literatur. In Die Kultur der Gegenwart, ihre Entwicklung und ihre Ziele, v.1, no.9: Die osteuropäischen literaturen und die slavischen Sprachen (Berlin, 1908), p. 354-371. A23.46 v.1 pt.9 ICU CaAEU DLC MH NN WU

7953. --- Zur litauischen Literaturgeschichte. In LLGM, v.3, 1893, p. 121-129. See serials consulted.

7954. BIRŽIŠKA, Mykolas. Mūsų raštų istorija. 2. leidimas. 1. dalis ligi 1864. [History of our literature to 1864. 2d. ed.] Kaunas, Valstybės spaustuvė, 1925. 139 p. illus., ports. (Švietimo ministerijos Knygų leidimo komisijos leidinys) 891.92.B535 PU CtTMF ICCC ICLJF InU PPULC

7955. --- Obzor litovskoĭ literatury. [A review of Lithuanian literature] Vil'no [Izd. "Litvy"] 1921 22 p. Bibliography: p. [23-24] PG8708.B5 DLC

7956. --- Skrót dziejów piśmiennictwa litewskiego. [By] M. Birżyszka. Wilno, Wydawnictwo "Głosu Litwy", 1919. 68 p. PG8523.B62 CaAEU CtY

7957. BRAZAITIS, Juozas. Lietuvių rašytojai; literatūriniai straipsniai. [Lithuanian creative writers; a collection of articles. By] J. Ambrazevičius. Kaunas, Šv. Kazimiero draugija, 1938. 326 p. 891.92H.Aml4 PU ICCC

7958. ČIURLIONIENĖ, Sofija (Kymantaitė). Iš mūsų literatūros. [About our literature] Kaunas, S. Banaičio spaustuvė, 1913. 195 p. 491.922.C499 PU ICCC

7959. --- Lietuvių literatūros istorijos konspecto chrestomatija. [An outline of the history of Lithuanian literature] Voronežas, 1918. 86 p. 891.928ČI CtTMF

7960. ČIURLIONIS, Sophie. Abrégé de l'histoire littéraire de la Lithuanie. In Mercure de France (Paris), v.213, 1929, p. 5-27. See serials consulted.

7961. --- --- [Another edition] Paris, Mercure de France, 1929. 29 p. (Serie moderne) PG8703.C58 CaAEU CLU CSt MH PU

7962. DAMBRAUSKAS, Aleksandras. Meno kūrybos problemos. [The problems of the Lithuanian creative writing. By] A. Jakštas [pseud.] Kaunas, 1932. 365 p. 700.J2 CtTMF

7963. --- Mūsų naujoji poezija. [Our recent poetry. By] A. Jakštas [pseud.] In His Mūsų naujoji literatūra, 1904-1923. Kaunas, 1923. v.1, p. [11]-400. PG8701.D15 InU ICCC ICLJF

7964. --- Mūsų naujoji prozos literatūra. [Our recent prose. By] A. Jakštas [pseud.] In His Mūsų naujoji literatūra, 1904-1923. Kaunas, 1923. v.2, p. [19]-768. PG8701.D15 InU ICCC ICLJF

7965. GABRYS, Juozas. Lietuvių literatūros apžvalga. [Outline of Lithuanian literature] Kaunas, 1916. 287 p. 891.920.9.G1 CtTMF

7966. --- --- 2. pataisytas ir papildytas leidimas. [2nd ed.] Klaipėda, Spaustuvė "Rytas", 1924. xv, 314 p. 491.922.G113 PU BM(11860. b. 18.) ICLJF

7967. GAILIŪNAS, Pranas. Kristijonas Donelaitis "Keturių vėjų" poezijoje. [Kristijonas Donelaitis in the poetry of "Keturi Vėjai"] In Vairas (Kaunas), no.9, 1937, p. 33-47. See serials consulted.

7968. GINEITIS, Leonas. Klasicizmo problema lietuvių literatūroje. [On the problem of classicism in the Lithuanian literature] Vilnius, Vaga, 1972. 315 p. PG8709.G5 PU OKentU

7969. GIRA, Liudas. Kritikos raštai. [Works of literary criticism. By] E. Radzikauskas [pseud.] Įvadą parašė V. Krėvė-Miskevičius. Kaunas, Švietimo ministerija, 1928. 215 p. (Švietimo ministerijos Knygų leidimo komisijos leidinys, nr. 152) PG8701.G5 DLC CtY ICCC OCl PU

7970. --- Lietuviškos eilėdaros kūrimosi raida. [The development of the Lithuanian poetry. By] E. Radzikauskas [pseud.] In KUHMF. Darbai ir dienos, v.3, 1934, p. 130-213. See serials consulted.

7971. GRINIUS, Jonas. Laiko balsas ir lietuvių literatūra. [The current trends and the Lithuanian literature] In LKMASD, v.7, 1972, p. [309]-[326]. See serials consulted.

7972. IEŠMANTA, Marija and Antanas Iešmanta. Lietuvių literatūros istorija. [History of Lithuanian literature] Marija ir Antanas Iešmantai. Kaunas, Dirva, 1923. 143 p. 891.929I ICCC

KNYGOS; bibliografijos ir kritikos žurnalas. Kaunas, 1922-39. See serials consulted.

7973. KORSAKAS, Kostas. Straipsniai apie literatūrą. [Articles on the Lithuanian literature. By K. Korsakas Radžvilas] Kaunas, Kultūros leidinys, 1932. 400 p. 805.KR ICLJF

7974. KOSTKEVIČIŪTĖ, Irena. Kritinis realizmas lietuvių prozoje, XIX a. pabaigoje-XX a. pradžioje. [Critical realism in Lithuanian prose at the end of the 19th and the beginning of the 20th centuries] Vilnius, VGLL, 1956. 396 p. PG8709.K6 DLC NN OKentU

7975. KUBILIUS, Vytautas. Lietuvių revoliucinė poezija, 1890-1907. [Lithuanian revolutionary poetry, 1890-1907] In Literatūra ir kalba (Vilnius), v.3, 1958, p. 113-299. See serials consulted.

7976. KUZMICKIS, Zigmantas. Lietuvių literatūra; vadovėlis aukštesniosioms mokykloms. [Lithuanian literature...] Kaunas, Sakalo bendrovės leidinys, 1930-34. 5 v. illus. PG8703.K8 DLC CtTMF(2-5) OCl(2-5)

7977. --- 2. leidimas. Kaunas, 1932-36. 5 v. 891.92H.K969 PU CtTMF(1)

7978. LANKUTIS, Jonas. Lietuvių dramaturgija; kritikos etiudai. [The Lithuanian dramaturgy; a critical evaluation] Vilnius, VGLL, 1958. 322 p. PG8709.L2 DLC CaAEU CtY PU

7979. LIETUVIŲ LITERATŪRA; trumpas lietuvių literatūros istorijos kursas su chrestomatija. [Lithuanian literature; a concise course of the history of the Lithuanian literature and the reader. Chicago, Ill.] Čikagos Aukštesnioji lituanistikos mokykla, 1959-61. 4 v. illus., ports., fold. maps, facsims. Contents.--1. dalis. Tautosaka, by Domas Velička.--2. dalis. Tikybinės ir šviečiamosios literatūros laikotarpis, by Domas Velička.--3. dalis. Poaušrio laikotarpis, by Juozas Masilionis.--4. dalis. Naujosios literatūros laikotarpis, by Juozas Masilionis. PG8701.L45 DLC CaAEU CtPAM CtY ICCC ICLJF OKentU PU

7980. LIETUVOS TSR MOKSLŲ AKADEMIJA, VILNA. LIETUVIŲ KALBOS IR LITERATŪROS INSTITUTAS. Lietuvių literatūros istorijos chrestomatija; feodalizmo epocha. [Lithuanian literature; history and criticism with the extracts to 1861] Redagavo K. Korsakas ir J. Lebedys. Vilnius, VGLL, 1957. 526 p. facsims. PG8701.L52 DLC CU CtPAM CtY InU InNd ICLJF KU MH MnU NN OKentU PU TxU

7981. MACIŪNAS, Vincas. Adomas Mickevičius lietuvių literatūroje. [Adam Mickiewicz in Lithuanian literature] In Aidai (Brooklyn, N.Y.), no.10, 1955, p. 413-429. See serials consulted.

7982. --- Mickiewicz in Lithuanian literature. In Lednicki, Wacław, ed. Adam Mickiewicz in world literature; a symposium. Berkeley, Calif., 1956. p. [383]-397. PG7158.M5Z92315 1956 DLC CU CtY ICU IU KU LU MB MH NN NjP OCU PPiU PU RPB TU ViU

7983. MATULIS, Anatole C. History of the Lithuanian cultural

profile in German literature. In
Lituanus (Chicago, Ill.), v.11, no.
1, 1965, p. 18-33. See serials consulted.

7984. MAUCLÈRE, Jean. Panorama
de la littérature Lithuanienne con-
temporaines. Paris, Éditions du
Sagittaire [1938] 190 p. (Panora-
mas des litteratures contemporaines)
PG8703.M3 CSt CaNSHD CaQMM CaOTU CtY
ICU ICN InNd IaU MH NN NNC NcD NcU
NjP OCl PPiU PU

7985. MAZEIKA, Annunciata. Lithuanian attitude toward America and
American writers. Boston, Mass.,
1966. 133 leaves. Thesis (M.A.)--
Boston College, 1966. Reproduced
by xerography from typewritten
copy, 1971. PG8709.M35 1971 PU

7986. MUSTEIKIS, Antanas. The
Lithuanian heroes of the jungle.
In Lituanus (Chicago, Ill.), v.17,
no.2, 1971, p. 27-38. See serials
consulted.

7987. MYKOLAITIS, Vincas. Adomas
Mickevičius ir lietuvių literatūra.
[Adam Mickiewicz and Lithuanian li-
terature] Vilnius, 1955. 93 p.
illus., port. 891.85.M583.yMy PU
NN

7988. --- Garbinga senovė literatūroje ir praeities skriaudos ti-
krovėj. [The honorable past of
the Lithuanian literature and the
unjustice suffered in reality] In
KUHMF. Darbai ir dienos, v.3,
1934, p. 3-21. See serials consulted.

7989. --- Lietuviškoji tematika
Adomo Mickevičiaus kuryboje. [Li-
thuanian themes in the works of
Adam Mickiewicz] Kaune, Valstybinė
enciklopedijų žodynų ir mokslo
literatūros leidykla, 1949. 31 p.
(Lietuvos TSR Politinių ir mokslinių žinių skleidimo d-ja. Paskaitos, 33. AS262.L515 no.33 DLC

7990. --- Literatūros etiudai.
[Lithuanian literature in outline]
[Kaunas] Sakalas [1937] 289 p.
491.922.M994.3 PU ICLJF

7991. --- Literatūros istorija,
kritika, publicistika. [Literary
history, criticism and journalism]
Vilnius, VGLL, 1962. 696 p.
(His Raštai. T.8) PG8721.M9 v.8
1962 DLC

7992. NAUJOKAITIS, Pranas. Lietuvių literatūra; trumpas lietuvių
literatūros istorijos kursas gim-
nazijai. [Lithuanian literature; a

concise course of the history of
the Lithuanian literature for High-
School] Tübingene, Patrija [1948]
316 p. PG8703.N3 DLC CtPAM CtY
ICLJF MiD NN OKentU PU

7993. NIEMI, Aukusti Robert.
Liettualainen kirjallisuus [Lithu-
anian literature] Helsingissä,
Kustan nusosakeyhtiö otava [1925]
231 p. illus., ports. Hvc37.N555
CtY

7994. NYKA-NILIŪNAS, Alfonsas.
"Keturi Vėjai" ir keturi vėjininkai.
[The group of "Keturi Vėjai"] In
Aidai (Schwäbische Gmünde, Ger.),
no.24, 1949, p. 112-118. See
serials consulted.

7995. --- Nepriklausomos Lietuvos poezija. [The poetry in independent Lithuania] In Aidai
(Schwäbische Gmünde, Ger.), no.25,
1949, p. 172-177. See serials
consulted.

7996. PALMIERI, Aurelio. Rinas-
cita letteraria e clero in Lituania.
Firenze, Libreria editrice fioren-
tina, 1920. 34 p. PG8694.P3 DLC
PU

7997. PAULUKAT, August. Litauische Hoffnungen. Litauisch-na-
tionale Poesie und Prosa. Halle
a.S.; Berlin, Vaya Verlag, 1915.
122 p. 947.5.P28 MnU CtY NjP

7998. PETKEVIČAITĖ, Gabrielė.
Literatūros istorija. [The history
of Lithuanian literature] Vilnius,
Vaga, 1968. 589 p. (Her Raštai,
T.5) PN519.P45 ICU DLC

7999. PIGOŃ, Stanisław. Do źródeł "dziadów" kowieńsko-wileńskich.
Wilno, Skład Główny w Księgarni Sw.
Wojciecha, 1930. 126 p. (Bibljoteka "Źródeł mocy", 3)
891.85.M583P5 NNC NN

8000. PUIDA, Kazys. Mūsų dainiai;
kritikos bruožai. [Our poets...]
Chicago, Ill., Spauda ir lėšos
"Kataliko", 1913. 140 p.
805.PD ICLJF CtTMF OCl PU

8001 RUBULIS, Aleksis. Baltic
literature; a survey of Finnish,
Estonian, Latvian and Lithuanian
literature. Notre Dame, Ind.,
Notre Dame University Press, 1970.
xvi, 215. PH302.R8 PU CaAEU CaOTU
MH OKentU WaS

8002. ŠAPIRA, Nachman. Lietuva
L. Neidusa kūryboje. [Lithuania in
L. Neidus creative writings] In
KUHMF. Darbai ir dienos, v.2,

1931, p. 1-100. See serials consulted.

8003. --- Lietuvos reikšmė naujai žydų literatūrai. [The importance of Lithuania in the new Jewish literature] In KUHMF. Darbai ir dienos, v.3, 1934, p. 97-129. See serials consulted.

8004. SENN, Alfred. Storia della letteratura lituana. In Devoto, G. Storia delle letterature baltiche. [Milano, 1957] p. 299-428. PH631.D513 InNd CLU CSt CU CtY FU InU MH NN NNC NjP NcD TNJ

8005. --- --- [Another edition] In Devoto, G. Le letterature dei paesi baltici. Nuova ed. Firenze, 1969. 570 p. PH302.D4 1969 DLC PU

8006. ŠEPKUS, Lionginas. Lietuvių literatūros vadovėlis. 3. pataisytas leidimas. [Textbook of Lithuanian literature] Kaunas, Šviesa, 1969. 315 p. illus., ports. 891.92.H.Se66 PU CtY

8007. ŠEŠPLAUKIS, Alfonsas. Adam Mickiewicz and Lithuania. Putnam, Conn., Immaculata Press, 1961. 16 p. 891.86.M582.yS PU CtTMF NNC

8008. SKRUPSKELIS, Ignas. Lietuviai XVIII amžiaus vokiečių literatūroje. [Lithuanians in German literature of the 18th century] Roma, Lietuvių katalikų mokslo akademija, 1967. xix, 171 p. port. PT295.S4 1967 PU CaAEU CaOONL NN

8009. SRUOGA, Balys. Adomas Jakštas, literatūros kritikas. [Adomas Jakštas, reviewer of the literature] In His Raštai. Vilnius, 1957, v.6, p. 60-79. PG8721.S68 1957 v.6 DLC CaAEU ICU PU

8010. --- Maksimas Gorkis ir lietuvių literatūra. [Maxim Gorki and Lithuanian literature] In His Raštai. Vilnius, 1957, v.6, p. 527-556. PG8721.S68 1957 v.6 DLC CaAEU ICU PU

8011. TUMAS, Juozas. Beletristai. [Novelists. By] Vaižgantas [pseud.] Kaunas, Humanitarinių mokslų fakultetas, 1929. 318 p. (His Raštai, t.13) PG8703.T76 DLC

8012. --- Lietuvių literatūra rūsų raidėmis ir broliai Juškos-Juškevičiai. [Lithuanian literature written in cyrilic and brothers Juškos-Juškevičiai] Kaunas, 1924. 121 p. 491.922.T832 PU CtTMF

8013. --- Publicistai. [Publicists. By] Vaižgantas [pseud.] Kaunas, Humanitarinių mokslų faculteto leidinys, 1929. 301 p. (Vaižganto raštai, t.14) PN5276.A45 DLC

8014. --- Tremtiniai, romantininkai. [The exiles, novelists. By] Vaižgantas [pseud.] Kaunas, Humanitarinių mokslų fakultetas, 1929. 324 p. (Vaižganto raštai, t.11) PG8703.T8 DLC CtTMF

8015. VAIČIULAITIS, Antanas. Dvidešimties metų lyrika. [Lithuanian poetry through twenty years] In Židinys (Kaunas), v.27, no.5-6, 1938, p. 686-695. See serials consulted.

8016. --- Lietuvių literatūros problemos svetur. [The problems of Lithuanian literature abroad] In LKMASD, v.6, 1969, p. [427]-433. See serials consulted.

8017. --- La literatura guardian de la nacion; historia de las letras lituanas. In Estudios (Buenos Aires), no.376, 1943, p. [139]-161. AP63.E733 DLC PU

8018. --- Natūralizmas ir lietuvių literatūra. [The naturalism and the Lithuanian literature] Kaunas, Sakalas, 1936. 114 p. illus. Reproduced by xerography, 1970. PG8709.V33 1970 PU (xerox copy) ICCC (orig.)

8019. --- Outline history of Lithuanian literature. Chicago, Ill., Lithuanian Cultural Institute, 1942. 54 p. illus. PG8703.V3 DLC CaAEU CaBVaU CaOLU CaOTU CaSSU CtY CoU IaU ICU IEN InNd MB NN MH NNC NcD NcU OCl OKentU OrU PBm PP PU RPB ViU WU

8020. VANAGAS, Vytautas. Gotfridas Ostermejeris, pirmasis lietuvių literatūros istorikas. [Gotfridas Ostermejeris the first historian of Lithuanian literature] In Literatūra ir kalba (Vilnius), v.5, 1961, p. 395-432. See serials consulted.

8021. VAŠKELIS, Bronius. Contemporary Lithuanian drama. In Lituanus (Chicago, Ill.), v.13, no.3, 1967, p. 5-27. See serials consulted.

8022. VELIČKA, Domas, ed. Socialistinis realizmas. [Socialistic realism...] Įvado autorius Rimvydas Šilbajoris. Chicago, Ill., Pedagoginis lituanistikos institutas, 1968. xix, 586 p.

PN56.R3V45 PU

8023. WIRSCHUBSKI, Gregor. Die Entwicklung der litauischen Literatur. In Osteuropa (Königsberg in Pr.), v.4, 1928/29, p. 582-593. See serials consulted.

8024. ZABORSKAITĖ, Vanda. Realizmo klausimai 1905-1917 metų lietuvių literatūros kritikoje. [The Question of realism in the Lithuanian literary criticism during the 1905-1917 period] Vilnius, VGLL, 1957. 228 p. PG8709.Z3 DLC CtY NN PU

8025. ZAJANČKAUSKAS, Vincas. Lietuvių literatūros vadovėlis, 1400-1904. [Textbook of the Lithuanian literature, 1400-1904] Pataisytas leidimas. Vilniuje, "Rucho" spaustuvėje, 1928. 174 p. PG8703.Z3 1928 PU CtTMF

8026. ZALATORIUS, Albertas. Lietuvių apsakymo raida ir poetika. [The development of Lithuanian prose and poetry] Vilnius, Vaga, 1971. 362 p. PG8709.Z35 PU

8027. ŽEKAITĖ, Janina. Lietuvių romanas; žanro raida iki 1940 m. [The Lithuanian novel and its development until 1940] Vilnius, Vaga, 1970. 314 p. At head of title: Lietuvos TSR Mokslų akademija. Lietuvių kalbos ir literatūros institutas. PG8709.Z4 PU

8028. ŽILIUS, Jonas. Lietuviški dainiai pradžios XIX šimtmečio. Klasiškai-tautiškas perijodas. [Lithuanian creative writers at the beginning of the nineteenth century] Surinko, pataisė ir parengė į spaudą Jr. Jonas. Shenandoah, Pa., 1899. 53 p. Reprinted from "Dirva". PG8715.Z53 PU

8029. ZINKUS, Jonas, ed. Rašytojai ir religija. [Writers and religion] Vilnius, Mintis, 1966. 310 p. Hvc37+Z665 CtY OKentU

XIII.5.b.2. BY PERIOD TO 1944

8030. AUGIENĖ, Danutė (Lipčiūtė). Draudžiamojo laikotarpio grožinė literatūra. [The belles-lettres during the period of the total suppression of the Lithuanian press] In Bagdanavičius, V.J. Kovos metai dėl savosios spaudos. Chicago, Ill., 1957. p. 315-336. PN5278.L5B3 DLC CaAEU OCl

BAGDANAVIČIUS, Vytautas Jonas. Lietuviška materialistinė raštija iki nepriklausomybės paskelbimo. See entry no. 91.

8031. BIRŽIŠKA, Mykolas. Lietuvių literatūra Vilniaus universiteto metu. [Lithuanian literature during the period of the University of Vilnius] Vilnius, Lietuvių mokslo draugijos leidinys, 1921. 70 p. 891.92.B53L WaU CtTMF ICCC PU

8032. BRAZAITIS, Juozas. Literatūra spaudos draudimo laikais. [Literature during the period of the total suppression of the Lithuanian press] In Lietuvių enciklopedija. Boston, Mass., 1968, v.15, p. 607-614. See entry no. 216.

8033. --- Nepriklausomos Lietuvos literatūra. [The literature of Independent Lithuania. By] J. Ambrazevičius In Aidai (Brooklyn, N.Y.), no.2(220), 1968, p. 62-68. See serials consulted.

8034. DAMBRAUSKAS, Aleksandras. Mūsų naujoji literatūra, 1904-1923. [Our new literature. By] A. Jakštas [pseud.] Kaunas, Švietimo ministerijos knygų leidimo komisijos leidinys, 1923. 2 v. PG8701.D15 InU CtTMF ICCC ICLJF PU

8035. HERMANN, Eduard. Bemerkungen zum altlitauischen Schrifttum in Preussen. In Königliche Gesellschaft der Wissenschaften zu Göttingen. Philologisch-Historische Klasse. Nachrichten, 1923, p. 106-120. See serials consulted.

8036. MACIŪNAS, Vincas. Senoji lietuvių literatūra. [Ancient Lithuanian literature] In Lietuvių enciklopedija. Boston, Mass., 1968. v.15, p. 597-607. See entry no. 216.

8037. MYKOLAITIS, Vincas. Naujoji lietuvių literatūra, 1- . [The new Lithuanian literature, pt.1] Kaunas, Humanitarinių mokslų fakultetas, 1936. vii, 435 p. Only one vol. published. 491.922.M994.2 PU ICCC BM(Ac. 1157. e. (9.))

8038. RADAITIS, Vytautas. 1905-1907 metų revoliucijos atspindžiai lietuvių literatūroje. [The reflection of the revolution of 1905-1907 in Lithuanian literature] In Būtėnas, Julius, comp. Lietuvių literatūra... Kaunas, 1954. p. 3-[13]. PG8701.B8 DLC ICLJF

8039. SPRINDIS, Adolfas. Lietuvių literatūrinė kritika, 1861-1905.

[Lithuanian literary criticism, 1861-1905] Vilnius, VGLL, 1957. 383 p. Bibliography: p. 299-378. PN99.L5S6 DLC CaAEU CtY NN OKentU PU

8040. TUMAS, Juozas. "Apžvalga" ir apžvalgininkai. [The newspaper "Apšvalga" and its supporters] Kaunas, 1925. 132 p. 947.520.B6 CtTMF

8041. --- Aušrininkai, šviesinin- kai. [The movement of Aušra and Šviesa. By] Vaižgantas [pseud.] Kaunas, Hum. mokslų fakulteto lei- dinys, 1929. 200 p. (His Raštai, t.12) PN5276.T8A8 DLC CtTMF

8042. --- Aušrininkų grupė. [The group of "Aušra"] Kaunas, 1924. 276 p. (Lietuvių literatūros pas- kaitos. Draudžiamasis laikas) 491.922.T832.2 PU ICCC

--- Broliai Juzumai-Juzuma- vičiai ir Kazimieras Skrodzkis. See entry no.676.

--- Kun. Juozas Silvestras Dovydaitis-Šiaulėniškis senelis. See entry no. 677.

8043. --- Lietuvių literatūros paskaitos; draudžiamasis laikas. [Lectures on Lithuanian literature; a period of press' prohibition] Kaunas, 1924. 67 p. ports. PG8709.T8 DLC

8044. --- ---; "Apžvalgos grupė; Jonas Maironis-Mačiulis. Kaunas, Dirva, 1924. 272 p. 891.929.T ICCC

8045. --- Naujieji literatūros nuotykiai. [New literary experi- ences. By] Vaižgantas [pseud.] Kaunas, 1933. 326 p. (His raštai, t.19) PG8703.T78 DLC

8046. VAIČIULAITIS, Antanas. XX amžiaus pradžios ir nepriklauso- mybės laikų literatūra. [The li- terature at the beginning of the 20th century and during the period of independence] In Lietuvių en- ciklopedija. Boston, Mass., 1968. v.15. p. 615-628. See entry no. 216.

XIII.5.b.3. THE SOVIET PERIOD

8047. AISTIS, Jonas. Okupuotosios Lietuvos literatūra. [The li- terature in occupied Lithuania] In Aidai (Brooklyn, N.Y.), no.3, 1959,

p. 133-135. See serials consulted.

8048. AMBRASAS, Kazys. Literatū- ros akyračiai. [Literary horizons] Vilnius, VGLL, 1961. 293 p. PG8703.A52 DLC MH PU

8049. --- Mintys kelyje; kai kurie šiuolaikinio literatūrinio proceso bruožai. [Some character- istics of the literary process to- day] Vilnius, VGLL, 1963. 181 p. 891.Aml3.3 PU MH

8050. --- Pažangioji lietuvių kritika. [The progressive Lithu- anian criticism] Vilnius, Vaga, 1966. 359 p. Bibliography: p. 304-345. PG8703.A54 PU CtY DLC MH NN

8051. ANTANAITIS, Algirdas. New trends in the Soviet Lithuanian novel. In Lituanus (Chicago, Ill.), v.16, no.2, 1970, p. 13-19. See serials consulted.

8052. BIELIAUSKAS, Alfonsas. Apie komunistų paveikslus lietuvių Tarybinėje literatūroje. [The image of communists in the Soviet Lithuanian literature] In Būtėnas, Julius, comp. Lietuvių literatūra. Kaunas, 1954. p. 182-[189]. PG8701.B8 DLC ICLJF PU

8053. --- Keliai ir paminklai; apie gyvenimą, literatūra, rašytojus ir knygas. [... about life, lite- rature, writers and books] Vil- nius, VGLL, 1963. 305 p. PG8703.B47 DLC ICLJF MH PU

8054. BIELINIS, Jonas. Žmogaus koncepcijos bruožai dabartinėje lietuvių literatūroje. [The con- ception of man in the recent Lith- uanian literature] Vilnius, Min- tis, 1969. 186 p. PG8709.B5 PU CaOTU

8055. BŪTĖNAS, Julius and Adolfas Sprindis, comp. Lietuvių litera- tūra; straipsnių rinkinys. [Lith- uanian literature; a collection of articles] Kaunas, Valstybinė pedagoginės literatūros leidykla, 1954-1956. 2 v. PG8701.B8 DLC ICLJF OKentU PU

8056. DEKADA LITOVSKOI LITERATURY v Moskve; sbornik. [Predislov. IU. Peletskisa] Kaunas, Goslitiz- dat [1948] 86 p. ports. PG8703.D4 DLC

8057. DIDŽIOJI SPALIO SOCIALISTINĖ revoliucija ir lietuvių literatūra. The Great Socialist Revolution and Lithuanian literature. Ats. redak-

torius J. Lankutis] Vilnius, Vaga,
1967. 449 p. Summary in Russian.
PG8709.D5 DLC CaOTU CU CtY MH NjP
OKentU PU

8058. GINTAUTAS, Jurgis. Krizė
sovietinėje lietuvių literatūroje
ir kritikoje. [The crisis in the
Soviet Lithuanian literature and
criticism] In Aidai (Kennebunkport,
Me.), no.3(38), 1951, p. 131-134.
See serials consulted.

8059. GRINIUS, Jonas. Lietuvių
sovietinės literatūros pobūdis.
[The character of the Soviet Lithuanian literature] In Aidai (Brooklyn, N.Y.), no.1(87), 1956, p. 8-14;
no.2(88), p. 70-77. See serials
consulted.

8060. --- Literatur und Kunst Litauens im Spiegel der Sowjetisierung. In Acta Baltica (Königstein
im Taunus), v.3, 1963, p. 171-187.
See serials consulted.

8061. IŠ LIETUVIŲ LITERATŪROS
KRITIKOS. [From Lithuanian litera-
ture criticism. Sudarė O. Balčy-
tienė. Anotacijos J. Petronio]
Kaunas, Šviesa, 1969. 141 p.
PG8701.I7 PU CaAEU

8062. JUDELEVIČIUS, Dovydas.
Tarybinė lietuvių poezija. [Soviet
Lithuanian poetry] Vilnius, VPMLL,
1963. 51 p. (Į pagelbą liaudies
kultūros universitetams)
PG8709.J8 DLC MH

8063. KAMINSKAS, Jonas. Literatūros kryžkelėse. [Crossroads in
literature] Vilnius, Vaga, 1968.
271 p., port. "J. Kaminsko darbų
bibliografija": p. [264-269].
PG8703.K3 1968 DLC ICU IEN MH NN
OClW OrU NjP PU

8064. KAMINSKAS, J. and A. Radzevičius. Stiliaus ir charakterio
problēmos lietuvių tarybinėje prozoje. [The problems of style and
character in the Soviet Lithuanian
prose] Vilnius, Vaga, 1966. 287
p. PG8709.K25 DLC CaAEU CtY MH NN
NIC PU

8065. KAVOLIS, Vytautas. Images
of young people in Soviet Lithuanian literature. In Lituanus
(Chicago, Ill.), v.16, no.2, 1970,
p. 38-48. See serials consulted.

8066. KIRKILA, Juozas. Amžininkų
balsai. [The voices of contemporary writers] Vilnius, VGLL, 1961.
198 p. Hvc37.K635 CtY

8067. KORSAKAS, Kostas. Litera-

tūra ir kritika. [Literature and
criticism. Kaune] VGLL, 1949.
533 p. PG8701.K6 DLC

8068. --- The literature of
Soviet Lithuania. In Soviet Literature (Moskva), no.9, 1961, p.
121-165. PG2901.S72 CaAEU CSt-H
CU CaBVaU CaQMM MH NN NNC WaU

8069. --- Literatūrų draugystė;
studijos, straipsniai, pranešimai...
[The friendship of literatures...]
Vilnius, VGLL, 1962- . facsims.,
ports. Bibliography: p. 623-626,
v.1. PG2981.L5K6 DLC CaAEU ICLJF
MH NN PU

8070. ---, comp. Vekovaia nenavist'; litovskaia literatura v
bor'be protiv nemetskikh zakhvat-
nikov. Moskva, Gos. izd-vo khudozh. lit-ry, 1943. 47 p.
PG8771.R1K6 DLC NNC NN RPB WU

8071. KOSTKEVIČIUTĖ, Irena. Literatūros dienovydžiai. [Contem-
porary Lithuanian literature]
Vilnius, Vaga, 1964. 329 p.
891.92H.K848.2 PU CtY MH OClW

8072. KRITIKA IR LITERATŪROS
mokslas. [Criticism and literature]
In LTSRMAIKLI. Lietuvių literatūros istorija. Vilnius, 1968. v.
4, p. 717-741. PG8703.L72 v.4
CaAEU CSt CU CtY DLC ICU InU MH
MiU MiD NN WU

8073. KUBILIUS, Vytautas. Mūsų
rašytojai. [Our writers] Vilnius, VGLL, 1958. 301 p.
PG8709.K8 PU

8074. --- Naujų kelių ieškant.
[Looking for new ways] Vilnius,
VGLL, 1964. 377 p.
Balt 9615.264.5 MH

8075. --- Sovremennaia litovskaia
poeziia. Perevod s litovskogo B.
Zalesskoi. Moskva, Znanie, 1969.
30 p. PN35.N6 1969 no.5 PU MH

8076. LANDSBERGIS, Algirdas.
Communist novels of the postwar
struggle in Lithuania. In Baltic
Review (New York, N.Y.), no.12,
1957, p. 67-79. See serials
consulted.

8077. LANKUTIS, Jonas. Litera-
tūra ir humanistiniai idealai.
[Literature and humanistic ideals]
Vilnius, VGLL, 1963. 272 p.
PG8703.L3 DLC InNd MH PU

8078. --- Naujo mūsų literatūros
raidos etapo bruožai; 1959-1960
metų lietuvių tarbynės literatūros

apžvalga. [The outline of our new
literary development; a review of
the Soviet Lithuanian literature of
1959-1960] In Literatūra ir kalba
(Vilnius), v.5, 1961, p. 44-86.
See serials consulted.

8079. --- Socialistinis realizmas
lietuvių literatūroje. [Socialis-
tic realism in Lithuanian litera-
ture] Vilnius, VGLL, 1959. 321 p.
PG8709.L23 DLC MH PU

8080. LIETUVIŲ LITERATŪRA DIDŽIOJO
Tėvynės karo metais. [Lithuanian
literature during the Great Patriotic War] In LTSRMALKLI. Lietuvių literatūros istorija. Vilnius, 1968. v.4, p. 79-123.
PG8701.L515 v.4 DLC CSt CU CaAEU
CtY ICU InU MH MiD MiU NN WU

8081. LIETUVIŲ LITERATŪROS IR
meno dekada Maskvoje, 1954. [The
decade of Lithuanian literature and
art in Moscow, 1954] Vilnius,
VGLL, 1956. 229 p. illus.
PG8701.L5 DLC NNC OKentU PU

8082. LIETUVIŲ LITERATŪROS ISTO-
RIJA. [History of Lithuanian literature. Ed. by Kostas Korsakas]
Vilnius, VPMLL, 1957-1968. 4 v. in
5, illus., ports., facsims.
Bibliography: v.1, p. 571-575; v.2,
p. 619-630; v.3, pt.2, p. 680-[707];
v.4, p. 887-913. Contents.--T.1.
Feodalizmo epocha.--T.2. Kapitalizmo
epocha, 1861-1917.--T.3. pt.1. Kapitalizmo epocha, 1917-1940.--T.3.
pt.2. Kapitalizmo epocha, 1917-
1940.--T.4. Tarybinis laikotarpis,
1940-1967. PG8701.L512 DLC CSt CU
CaAEU CaOTU CtPAM CtY ICU InU
ICLJF(v.1-3) InNd MH MiD MiU NN NNC
OClW OKentU PPiU PU WaU WU

8083. LIETUVIŲ TARYBINĖ LITERATŪRA,
1957-1958. [Soviet Lithuanian literature. 1957-1958] Vilnius,
VGLL, 1958-59. 2 v. At head of
title: Lietuvių TSR Mokslų akademija. Lietuvių kalbos ir literatūros institutas. PG8701.L513 DLC
CaAEU CtY MH NN

8084. LIETUVOS TSR MOKSLŲ AKADE-
MIJA, VILNA. LIETUVIŲ KALBOS IR
LITERATŪROS INSTITUTAS. Lietuvių
literatūros kritika. [Critical re-
view on Lithuanian literature.
Redagavo K. Korsakas, K. Doveika]
Vilnius, Vaga, 1971- .
PG8709.L53 PU OKentU

8085. --- Literatūrinio gyvenimo
kronika, 1940-1960. [A chronicle
of the literary life, 1940-1960.
Redagavo J. Lankutis] Vilnius,
Vaga, 1970. 441 p. illus., ports.

PG8709.L5 DLC OKentU

8086. --- Ocherk istorii litovs-
koi sovetskoi literatury. Red.
kollegiia: M.K. Dobrynin, K.P. Kor-
sakas, A.T. Ventslova, I.I. Simkus,
M.I.Fetisov, L.T. Bliumfeld.
Moskva, Izdatelstvo Akad. nauk
SSSR, 1955. 258 p. PG8701.L56
DLC CaAEU CaOWtU CoU CtY HU ICU IEN
MH NIC NN NNC InNd NjP OClW PU WU

8087. --- Tarybinės lietuvių
literatūros istorijos apybraiža.
[An outline of the history of Soviet Lithuanian literature. Redakcinė kolegija: M. Dobryninas et al.]
Vilnius, VGLL, 1956. 240, [4] p.
PG8701.L53 DLC CtY PU

8088. LITERATŪROS RAIDA POKARIO
LAIKOTARPIU. [The development of
literature after the 1945 war] In
LTSRMALKLI. Lietuvių literatūros
istorija. Vilnius, 1968. v.4,
p. 201-231. PG8701.L515 v.4 DLC
CSt CaAEU CtY CU ICU InU MH MiD MiU
NN WU

8089. LITERATŪROS RAIDA, 1956-1966
m. [The development of literature,
1956-1966] In LTSRMALKLI. Lietuvių literatūros istorija. Vilnius,
1968. v.4, p. 742-886.
PG8701.L515 v.4 DLC CSt CU CaAEU
CtY ICU InU MH MiD MiU NN WU

8090. MOKSLINĖ KONFERENCIJA LIE-
TUVIŲ LITERATŪROS 1957 METŲ REZUL-
TATAMS APTARTI, VILNA. 1958. 1957
metų lietuvių tarbinė literatūra.
[Soviet Lithuanian literature in
1957. Redagavo J. Lankutis] Vil-
nius, VGLL, 1958. 323, [4] p.
PG8701.M58 DLC OKentU PU

8091. PIRMIEJI TARYBINĖS LIETUVIŲ
literatūros žingsniai. [The first
steps of Soviet Lithuanian litera-
ture] In LTSRMALKLI. Lietuvių
literatūros istorija. Vilnius,
1968. v.4, p. 30-56. PG8701.L515
v.4 DLC CSt CU CaAEU CtY ICU InU
MH MiD MiU NN WU

8092. PRANSKUS, Bronius. Lietuvių literatūros gretose; straipsnių
rinkinys. [Side by side in Lithuanian literature; a collection of
articles] Vilnius, VGLL, 1959.
533 p. PG8703.P7 DLC MH OKentU PU

8093. --- Proletarinė lietuvių
literatūra. [Lithuanian proletarian literature] Vilnius, Vaga,
1964. 500 p. ports. PG8709.P68
DLC CtY MH NN OKentU PU

8094. PRĖSKIENIS, Bronius. Literatūrinė kritika lietuvių komunis-

tinėje spaudoje, 1917-1940. [Li-
terary criticism in the Lithuanian
communist press, 1917-1940] Vilnius,
Vaga, 1966. 193 p. PG8709.P7 DLC
CSt CaAEU NN PU

8095. SIETYNAS, Andrius. The
condition of a free prisoner; poetry and prose of Vincas Mykolaitis-
Putinas. In Lituanus (Chicago, Ill.)
v.11, no.1, 1965, p. 48-69. See
serials consulted.

8096. ŠILBAJORIS, Rimvydas Pranas.
Soviet cultural imperialism in post-
war Lithuanian literature. [By]
Frank R. Silbajoris. New York, N.Y.,
1955. 172 p. Thesis--Columbia
University. NNC

8097. ŠIMKUS, Jonas. Naujo kelio
pradžia. [Beginning of a new way.
Paruošė J. Būtėnas] Vilnius, Vaga,
1970. 463 p. PG8703.S54 PU

8098. --- Realizmo kryptimi.
[Toward realism. Paruošė J. Būtė-
nas] Vilnius, Vaga, 1970. 455 p.
PG8703.S55 PU OKentU

8099. ŠIUOLAIKINĖS LIETUVIŲ LITE-
RATŪROS BRUOŽAI. [An outline of
contemporary Lithuanian literature.
Straipsnių rinkinys. Red. V. Ku-
bilius] Vilnius, Vaga, 1969. 516
p. PG8703.S5 DLC CaAEU MH OKentU
PU

8100. SLUCKAITĖ, Aušra. Kritikos
štrichai. [Literary criticism.
Pirmoji knyga] Vilnius, VGLL,
1963. 98 p. port. PG8703.S55 DLC

8101. SLUCKIS, Mykolas. Dekada
litovskoi literatury i iskusstva v
Moskve 1954 g.; spravochnik po
literature. Vil'nius, Gos izd-vo
polit. i nauch. lit-ry, 1954. 142
p. illus. PG8701.S5 DLC ICU

8102. --- Sunkiausias menas; literatūrinės pastabos. [The most
difficult art; literary remarks]
Vilnius, VGLL, 1960. 321 p.
PG8701.S53 DLC MH

8103. STAKNYS, Alina. The official line and creative ideas. In
Lituanus (Chicago, Ill.), v.6,
no.2, 1960, p. 80-84. See serials
consulted.

8104. TARYBINĖ LIETUVIŲ POEZIJA.
[Soviet Lithuanian poetry] In
LTSRMAIKLI. Lietuvių literatūros
istorija, Vilnius, 1968. v.4, p.
447-486. PG8701.L515 v.4 DLC CSt
CU CaAEU CtY ICU InU MH MiD MiU NN
WU

8105. TAUTŲ DRAUGYSTĖ LIETUVIŲ IR
rusų literatūrose;straipsnių rinkinys. [The friendship of nations
in Lithuanian and Russian literature. Redaktorius J. Macaitis]
Vilnius, VPMLL, 1963. 307 p.
Bibliography: p. 290-[308].
PG8703.T3 DLC CtY MH PU

8106. VAIKŲ LITERATŪRA. [Chil-
dren's literature] In LTSRMALKLI.
Lietuvių literatūros istorija.
Vilnius, 1968. v.4 DLC CSt CaAEU
CU CtY ICU InU MH MiD MiU NN WU

8107. TRUMPA, Vincas. Dawn of
free criticism in Soviet Lithuanian literature. In Lituanus
(Brooklyn, N.Y.), v.4, no.4, 1958,
p. 126-129. See serials consulted.

8108. VĖLAIKIS, Jonas. Lithuanian literature under the Soviets.
In Lituanus (Chicago, Ill.), v.12,
no.3, 1966, p. 25-43. See serials
consulted.

8109. VENCLOVA, Antanas. Epochos
vėjas; literatūriniai straipsniai
ir atsiminimai. [The wind of the
era; literary articles and reminis-
censes] Vilnius, VGLL, 1962. 414
p. PG8703.V4 DLC ICLJF PU

8110. --- Laikas ir rašytojai.
[The time and the writers. Straipsnių apie literatūrą,knygas ir rašytojus rinkinys] Vilnius, VGLL,
1958. 766 p. PG8703.V42 DLC CtY
ICU PU

XIII.5.b.4. LITHUANIAN LITERATURE
ABROAD

8111. BABRAUSKAS, Benys. The new
Lithuanian literature. In Books
Abroad (Norman, Okla.), v.29, no.
2, 1955, p. 144-148. See serials
consulted.

8112. BRADŪNAS, Kazys, ed. Lie-
tuvių literatūra svetur, 1945-1967.
[Lithuanian literature outside
Lithuania, 1945-1967] [Chicago,
Ill.] Į laisvę fondas lietuviškai
kultūrai ugdyti, 1968. 697 p.
(Leidinys, nr. 8) PG8703.B73 CaOTU
CaAEU PPULC PU

8113. KAUPAS, Julius Viktoras.
Our literature in exile. In Lituanus (Brooklyn, N.Y.), v.4, no.
3, 1958, p. 87-92. See serials
consulted.

8114. ŠILBAJORIS, Rimvydas Pranas.
Ausserhalb der Heimat entstandene

litauische Literatur. In Acta Baltica (Königstein im Taunus), v.6, 1966, p. 221-236. See serials consulted.

8115. --- Lithuanian poets; strangers and children of their native land. In Lituanus (Chicago, Ill.), v.17, no.1, 1971, p. 5-16. See serials consulted.

8116. --- Perfection of exile; fourteen contemporary Lithuanian writers. Norman, Okla., University of Oklahoma Press, 1970. 322 p. ports. PG8740.S5 DLC CaAEU CaOTU PU WaS

8117. VAIČIULAITIS, Antanas. Lietuvių literatūra svetur. [Lithuanian literature in exile] In Lietuvių enciklopedija. Boston, Mass., 1968. v.15, p. 629-636. See entry no. 216.

8118. --- Lithuanian literary happenings, 1942. In Books Abroad (Norman, Okla.), v.17, no.2, 1943, p. 130-131. See serials consulted.

XIII.5.b.5. LIFE AND WORKS OF INDIVIDUAL AUTHORS

ALEKSAITĖ, Irena. Borisas Dauguvietis; režisūros bruožai. Vilnius, 1966. See entry no. 456.

8119. ALEŠKEVIČIUS, A. Fausto Kiršos kūryba. [Creative works of Faustas Kirša] In Naujoji romuva (Kaunas), no.1, 1934, p. 7-11. See serials consulted.

8120. BALTARAGIS, Andrius. Numaironintas Maironis; jo sovietinio traktavimo raida. [The Soviet treatment of Maironis] In Aidai (Brooklyn, N.Y.), no.4-5, (159-160), 1963, p. 157-169; 205-214. See serials consulted.

8121. BANEVIČIUS, Mikas. V. Krėvės realistinės novelės; kritikos etiudas. [The realistic novels of V. Krėvė; a critical essay] In KUHMF. Darbai ir dienos, v.2, 1931. 113 p. See serials consulted.

BIČIŪNAS, Vytautas Pranas. Vinco Krėvės likimo kelias; pastabos ir komentarai. Kaunas, 1930. See entry no. 471.

8122. BILIŪNAS, Jonas. Annotated edition of the Jonas Biliūnas material in the Šaulys archives of

the University of Pennsylvania library [edited] by Kostas Ostrauskas. [Philadelphia] 1958. xvi, 456 leaves. Thesis--University of Pennsylvania, Philadelphia. Typescript. 891.92.B494 PU

BIRŽIŠKA, Mykolas. Barono gyvenimas ir raštai. Kaunas, 1924. See entry no. 476.

--- Donelaičio gyvenimas ir raštai. Kaunas, 1927. See entry no. 478.

8123. BLEKAITIS, Jurgis, Balio Sruogos teatro bruožai. [An outline of the theatre of Balys Sruoga] In His Kazimieras Sapiega. Chicago, Ill., 1940. p. i-[xii] PG8721.S68K3 1940z DLC

8124. --- Balys Sruoga; keli kūrybos bruožai. [Balys Sruoga; a short outline of his creative writing] In Aidai (Brooklyn, N.Y.), no.1, 1958, p. 10-17. See serials consulted.

8125. BRAZAITIS, Juozas. Vaižgantas; apmatai kūrybos studijai. [Vaižgantas; an outline of his creative writing. By] Ambrazavičius, Juozas. Kaunas, V.D.U. Teologijos--filozofijos fakultetas [1936] 190 p. (Kaunas. Universitetas. Teologijos-filosofijos fakultetas. Leidinys, kn.24) Reproduced by xerography, 1971. PG8721.T77Z67 1971 PU

8126. BRENSZTEJN, Michał Eustachy. Dionizy Paszkiewicz. Pisarz polsko-litewski na Żmudzi. Wilno, 1934. 112 p. plate. (Wydawnictwo Towarzystwa Pomocy Naukowej im E.I.E. Wróblewskich) Bibliographical references included in "Przypisy": p. 87-106. 491.922.P844.yB PU CU PPULC

BULOTA, Jonas. A. Jasutis; Gyvenimo ir kūrybos bruožai. Vilnius, 1961. See entry no. 496.

BŪTĖNAS, Julius. Žemaitė. Kaunas, 1938. See entry no. 500.

ČIBIRAS, Kazimieras. Gyvenimo menininkė Marija Pečkauskaitė. Kaunas, 1937. See entry no. 503.

8127. CIPLIJAUSKAITĖ, Birutė. Kazys Binkis and the poetic traditions of the 1920s. In Lituanus (Chicago, Ill.), v.16, no.1, 1970, p. 43-51. See serials consulted.

DAMBRAUSKAITĖ, Romana. Ieva

Simonaitytė. Vilnius, 1968. See entry no. 506.

8128. --- Ievos Simonaitytės kūryba. [The creative works of Ieva Simonaitytė] Vilnius, VPMLL, 1958. 38 p. PG8721.S5Z57 DLC CaAEU OKentU.

8129. DONELAITIS, Kristijonas. Kristijonas Donelaitis, 1714-1964; Donelaičio kūrybos vertimų pavyzdžiai. [Kristijonas Donelaitis and samples of his works in translation. Vilnius, VGLL, 1963] 81 p. illus., port. PG8721.D7J3 DLC

8130. DOVEIKA, Kostas. Kristijonas Donelaitis. Vilnius, VGLL, 1963. 112 p. PG8721.D7Z65 PU

GALINIS, Vytautas. Antanas Venclova; monografinė apybraiža. Vilnius, 1958. See entry no. 521.

GINEITIS, Leonas. Kristijonas Donelaitis ir jo epocha. Vilnius, 1964. See entry no. 525.

8131. --- Kristijonas Donelaitis ir jo poema "Metai". [Kristijonas Donelaitis and his poem "Metai-Seasons"] Vilnius, VGLL, 1955. 31 p. 891.95.D713.yG PU NN

8132. --- Kristijono Donelaičio "Metai". [The poem "Metai-Seasons" of Kristijonas Donelaitis] Vilnius, VGLL, 1954. 266 p. illus., facsims. PG8721.D7M37 DLC NN

8133. GOŠTAUTAS, Stasys. Jonas Mekas; a portret of a poet and a film-maker. In Lituanus (Chicago, Ill.), v.12, no.1, 1966, p. 54-73. See serials consulted.

8134. GRINIUS, Jonas. Putino lyrika. [The poetry of Putinas] Kaunas, Vytauto Didžiojo universiteto, Teologijos-filosofijos fakulteto leidinys, 1932. 107 p. port. PG8721.M94Z66 CU ICCC MH NN

8135. --- Vincas Mykolaitis-Putinas als Dichter zu seinem 70. Geburtstag. Bonn, Baltisches Forschungsinstitut, 1964. 82 p. (Commentationes Balticae, Bd. 10-11, no.4) See serials consulted.

IEŠMANTA, Albinas. Kudirka; rašytojo siluetas aukštesniajai mokyklai. Kaunas, 1927. See entry no. 540.

8136. JACIKEVIČIUS, Balys. Pragaro pošvaistės atošvaistėse...; recenzijų ir atsiliepimų rinkinys apie Vytauto Alanto romaną Pragaro pošvaistės. New York, N.Y., author, 1955.

230 p. PG8721.A45P77 PU

JURGELIONIS, Kleofas. Kun. A. Vienožinskis ir jo dainos. Scranton, Pa., 1911. See entry no. 562.

8137. KAVOLIS, Vytautas. Faith in exile; the decomposition and reconstitution of God in the poetry of Algimantas Mackus. In Lituanus (Chicago, Ill.), v.12, no.3, 1966, p. 5-24. See serials consulted.

8138. KELIUOTIS, Juozas. Milžino paunksmės recenzija. [The review of Milžino paunksmė] In Naujoji romuva (Kaunas), no.36, 1932, p. 760-762. See serials consulted.

8139. KORSAKAS, Kostas. A. Vienuolio romanas "Puodžiūnkiemis"; kritikos studija. [A critical study of the novel "Puodžiūnkiemis" of A. Vienuolis] Vilnius, 1953. 178 p. PG8721.V5P85 PU

8140. KRISTIJONAS DONELAITIS, literatūrinio realizmo pradininkas; jo gimimo 250 metų sukakčiai paminėti. [Kristijonas Donelaitis, the initiator of the literary realism... Redagavo Domas Velička. Įžanginės pastabos: Mykolas Drunga] Čikaga, Pedagoginis lituanistikos institutas, 1964. 56 p. illus., facsims. PG8721.D7Z78 CaOTU

KRISTIJONAS DONELAITIS; pranešimai, straipsniai, archyvinė medžiaga. Vilnius, 1965. See entry no. 571.

8141. KUBILIUS, Vytautas. A. Venclovos kūryba. [The creative writing of A. Venclova] In Būtėnas, Julius, comp. Lietuvių literatūra. Kaunas, 1954. v.1, p. 149-[165]. PG8701.B8 DLC ICLJF PU

8142. --- Balio Sruogos dramaturgija. [The art of dramatic composition of Balys Sruoga] In Pergalė (Vilnius), no.12, 1957, p. 74-90. See serials consulted.

--- Julius Janonis. Vilnius, 1962. See entry no. 574.

8143. --- Salomėjos Neries lyrika; trys etiudai. [Poetry of Salomėja Nėris; three studies] Vilnius, Vaga, 1968. 376 p. PG8721.N44Z7K95 CaAEU NN

--- Teofilis Tilvytis. Kritiko-biograficheskii ocherk. Moskva, 1958. See entry no. 576.

8144. LANKUTIS, Jonas. E. Mieželaičio poezija. [Poetry of E. Mie-

želaitis] Vilnius, Vaga, 1965.
268 p. PG8721.M45Z7 DLC PU CtY MH

8145. --- Eduardo Mieželaičio
poezija. [Poetry of Eduardas Mie-
želaitis] 2. papildytas leidimas.
Vilnius, Vaga, 1971. 216 p.
PG8721.M45Z7 1971 PU

8146. --- V. Mikolaititis-Putinas;
kritiko-biograficheskii ocherk.
Moskva, Sovetskii pisatel', 1967.
161 p. PG8721.M9Z73 DLC PU CaAEU
CaOTU

8147. --- V. Mykolaičio-Putino
kūryba. [The creative writings of
V. Mykolaitis-Putinas] Vilnius,
VGLL, 1961. 477, [6] p. illus.,
front. (port.) Bibliography: p.
472-[475]. PG8721.M9Z75 DLC CaAEU
ICLJF NN PU

8148. LITHUANIAN LITERARY SOCIETY
OF CHICAGO. Vincas Krėvė-Mickevi-
čius; rašytojo 70 metų sukaktis.
[Seventieth anniversary of the
writer Vincas Krėvė-Mickevičius]
[Chicago, Ill.] 1953. 187 p. port.
PG8721.L7Z74 DLC CaAEU PU

8149. LITUANUS. [Commemorative
issue of Lituanus on the 250th
anniversary of the classic Lithuanian poet Kristijonas Donelaitis.
Chicago, Ill., 1964] 96 p. illus.
(Lituanus, v.10, no.1) Bibliography: p. 87-96. See serials consulted.

8150. LUKŠIENĖ, Meilė. Jono
Biliūno kūryba. [The creative
works of Jonas Biliūnas] Vilnius,
VGLL, 1955. 479 p. illus., front
(port.) facsims. 891.92.B494.yL
PU ICLJF

8151. MACIŪNAS, Vincas. From
native Lithuania to the distant
orient; a survey of the literary
heritage of Vincas Krėvė. In
Lituanus (Chicago, Ill.), v.11,
no.3, 1965, p. 18-68. See serials
consulted.

8152. --- Motiejaus Valančiaus
"Giwenimai Szwentuju Diewa" stilius.
[The style of "Giwenimai Szwentuju
Diewa" of Motiejus Valančius] In
Vairas (Kaunas), nr. 7-8, 1935,
p. 273-286. See serials consulted.

8153. --- Vincas Krėvė savo laiš-
kuose, 1944-1954. [Vincas Krėvė in
his letters, 1944-1954. Chicago,
Ill., 1970. Reprint from "Draugas"
kultūrinis priedas. Chicago, Ill.,
July 26; Aug. 2, 9, 16, 23 and 30,
1969. PG8721.K7Z79 PU

8154. --- Vincas Krėvė's place
in Lithuanian literature. In Studi
Baltici (Roma) n.s., v.1(9), 1952,
p. 11-23. See serials consulted.

8155. --- Vincas Kudirka. In
Lituanus (Brooklyn, N.Y.), v.4, no.
4, 1958, p. 119-122. See serials
consulted.

8156. --- Žemaitė Amerikoje; iš-
traukos iš nespausdintų laiškų.
[Chicago, Ill., 1971] 18 leaves.
Xerox copy of clippings from "Draugas" Chicago, Ill., 1971, no. 290
and 296. PG8721.Z9Z7 PU

--- Makarov, Aleksandr
Nikolaevich. Eduardas Mezhelaitis.
Moskva, 1966. See entry no. 599.

--- Merkelis, Aleksandras.
Juozas Tumas-Vaižgantas. Čikaga,
1955. See entry no. 611.

MIKUTAITIS, Petras. Julius
Janonis: gyvenimas ir kūryba.
Kaunas, 1959. See entry no. 617.

8157. MIKŠYTĖ, Regina. Antano
Baranausko kūryba. [Literary works
of Antanas Baranauskas] Vilnius,
Vaga, 1964. 311, [3] p. illus.,
port., facsims. Bibliography: p.
295-306. PG8721.B325Z75 DLC CaAEU
CtY ICU MH NN PU

8158. --- Teofilis Tilvytis [and
his works] In Būtėnas, Julius,
comp. Lietuvių literatūra. Kaunas,
1954, p. 131-[148]. PG8701.B8 DLC
ICLJF

8159. MYKOLAITIS, Vincas. Vydūno
dramaturgija. [The dramatic compo-
sitions of Vydūnas] Kaunas, V.D.U.,
Humanitarinių mokslų fakultetas,
1935. 117 p. (KUHMF. Darbai ir
dienos, v.4, 1935) 891.920.9M3
CtTMF

8160. NARBUTIENĖ, Ona. Eduardas
Balsys; kūrybos apybraiža. [Lite-
rary works of Eduardas Balsys]
Vilnius, Vaga, 1971. 83 p.
ML410.B185N3 PU

8161. NESSELMANN, Georg Heinrich
Ferdinand. Noch einmal Donalitijus.
In Altpreussische Monatsschrift
(Königsberg in Pr.), v.4, 1867, p.
65-79. See serials consulted.

ORINTAITĖ, Petronėlė. Ką
laumės lėmė; atsiminimai apie Salomėją Nerį, 1904-1945. [Chicago,
Ill.] 1965. See entry no. 630.

8162. PAKALNIŠKIS, Ričardas. Poezija, asmenybė, laikas; Justino

Marcinkevičiaus kūryba. [Poetry, personality, time; literary works of Justinas Marcinkevičius] Vilnius, Vaga, 1969. 331 p.
PG8721.M35Z8 PU

PETRAS CVIRKA GYVENIME IR kūryboje. Vilnius, 1953. See entry no. 634.

8163. PETRULIS, Juozas. Balio Sruogos lyrika. [Poetry of Balys Sruoga] In Skaitymai (Kaunas), no. 23, 1923, p. 135-149. See serials consulted.

8164. --- Donelaičio poetika. [Poetry of Donelaitis] In Švietimo darbas (Kaunas), no.1, 3, 1927, p. 36-43; 247-256. See serials consulted.

PRANSKUS, Bronius. Pranas Vaičaitis. Vilnius, 1956. See entry no. 636.

8165. --- V. Kudirkos literatūrinis palikimas. [The literary heritage of V. Kudirka] In Pergalė (Vilnius), no.12, 1958, p. 122-152. See serials consulted.

8166. RABAČIAUSKAITĖ, A. Balio Sruogos kūryba. [The creative writing of Balys Sruoga] In Sruoga, Balys. Raštai. Vilnius, 1957. T.1: įvadas, p. 5-[35].
PG8721.S68 1957 v.1 DLC CaAEU ICU PU

RIMANTAS, Juozas. Žemaitė gyvenime ir kūryboje. Vilnius, 1956. See entry no. 643

8167. RŪKAS, Antanas. Balys Sruoga kurėjas. [Balys Sruoga, the creative writer] In Naujienos (Chicago, Ill.), Oct. 17, 1953. See serials consulted.

SAMULIONIS, Algis Romualdas. Balys Sruoga, dramaturgijos ir teatro kritikas. Vilnius, 1968. See entry no. 652.

8168. SAUKA, Donatas. Salomėjos Nėries kūryba, 1921-1940. [The works of Salomėja Nėris, 1921-1940] Vilnius, VGLL, 1957. 205 p.
PG8721.N4Z86 DLC

8169. SENN, Alfred. Vincent Krėvė. Lithuania's creator of heroes. In World Literatures. Pittsburgh Press, 1956. p. 170-184.
PN501.W6 DLC AU CU CtY GAU FTaSU IU KyU LU MiU MoU MsU MB MsSM MoSW NN NcD NjP OkU PPiU PPD TxU TU WaU

8170. ŠEŠELGIS, Aleksandras. Žemaitės raštų tekstologiniai klausimai.

[The textualism of the works of Žemaitė] Vilnius, 1968. 156 p. At head of title: Lietuvos TSR Mokslų akademija. Lietuvių kalbos ir literatūros institutas.
PG8721.Z9Z8 DLC PU

8171. ŠEŠPLAUKIS, Alfonsas. Religinis pradas Maironio kūryboje. Das religöse Element in der Dichtung Maironis'. In LKMAM, v.3, 1967, p. 133-220. Summary in German. See serials consulted.

8172. ŠILBAJORIS, Rimvydas Pranas. The tragedy of creative consciousness; literary heritage of Antanas Škėma. In Lituanus (Chicago, Ill.), v.12, no.4, 1966, p. 5-25. See serials consulted.

8173. SRUOGA, Balys. Butkų Juzė "Žemės Liepsna". [The poem of Butkų Juzė "Žemės liepsna"; a critical review] In His Raštai. Vilnius, 1957. v.6, p. 37-46.
PG8721.S68 1957 v.6 DLC CaAEU ICU PU

8174. --- Dramos velnias ir gegutė. [The devil and the cuckoo in drama] In His Raštai. Vilnius, 1957. v.6, p. 435-444.
PG8721.S68 1957 v.6 DLC CaAEU ICU PU

8175. --- Magiškas elementas Krėvės "Skerdžiuje". [The magic element in the "Skerdžius" of Krėvė-Mickevičius] In His Raštai. Vilnius, 1957. v.6, p. 94-102.
PG8721.S68 1957 v.6 DLC CaAEU ICU PU

8176. --- Vaičiūno dramaturgija. Analitiški ir kritiški eskizai. [The playwriting of Vaičiūnas; analytical and critical essays] In KUHMF. Darbai ir dienos, vol.1, 1930, 116 p. See serials consulted.

STONYS, Juozas. Antanas Vienuolis. Vilnius, 1957. See entry no. 667.

8177. --- Vienuolio realizmo problemos, 1917-1940. [The problems of realism in the writings of A. Vienuolis, 1917-1940] Vilnius, Vaga, 1966. 281 p.
PG8721.V5Z87 DLC CaAEU PU

8178. TETZNER, Franz Oskar. Christian Donalitius. In Altpreussische Monatsschrift (Königsberg in Pr.), v.34, 1896, p. 277-331, 409-441; v.36, 1900, p. 305-310; v.39, 1901, p. 138-139. See serials consulted.

TUMAS, Juozas. Antanas Baranauskas. Kaunas, 1924. See entry no. 675.

--- Lietuvių literatūros paskaitos... Jonas Maironis-Mačiulis. Kaunas, 1924. See entry no. 8044.

8179. VAITIEKŪNIENĖ, Aldona. Vaižganto apysaka "Dėdės ir dėdienės". [The short story "Dėdės ir dėdienės" of Vaižgantas] Vilnius, VGLL, 1964. 272 p. PG8721.V3215V3 DLC PU

VANAGAS, Vytautas. Antanas Strazdas. Vilnius, 1968. See entry no. 685.

8180. VAŠKELIS, Aleksas. Pietist spirit in Donelaitis poetry. In Lituanus (Chicago, Ill.), v.11, no. 3-4, 1964, p. 80-92. See serials consulted.

8181. VAŠKELIS, Bronius. Jurgis Baltrušaitis; a Lithuanian and Russian symbolist. In Lituanus (Chicago, Ill.), v.11, no.3-4, 1964, p. 45-68. See serials consulted.

8182. --- Vincas Krėvė, the Lithuanian classic. In Lituanus (Chicago, Ill.), v.11, no.3, 1965, p. 5-17. See serials consulted.

VENCLOVA, Antanas. Salomėja Nėris, poetės atsiminimui. [Kaunas, 1946] See entry no. 689.

VIENOŽINSKIS, Justinas. Straipsniai, dokumentai, laiškai. Amžininkų atsiminimai. See entry no. 692.

ZABORSKAITĖ, Vanda. Maironis. Vilnius, Vaga, 1968. See entry no. 697.

8183. ŽEKAITĖ, Janina. Antano Vienuolio kūryba iki 1917. [The creative works of A. Vienuolis until 1917] In Literatūra ir kalba (Vilnius), v.2, 1957, p. 7-157. See serials consulted.

8184. ŽIUGŽDA, Juozas. Žemaitės kūryba. [The creative writings of Žemaitė] In KUHMF. Darbai ir dienos, vol.4, 1935, 72 p. See serials consulted.

XIII.5.c. BELLES LETTRES

XIII.5.c.1. ANTHOLOGIES, COLLECTIONS, ETC.

8185. AISTIS, Jonas, comp. Lietuvių poezijos antologija. [An anthology of Lithuanian poetry. Comp. by J. Aistis and A. Vaičiulaitis] Chicago, Ill. Lietuviškos knygos klubas, 1951. 832 p. illus. PG8715.A5 DLC CaOONL CaOTU CaOTP CtTMF CtY IEN InNd ICCC IU MH MB MiD NN NB NNC OCl OKentU PPULC PP PU

8186. ANGLICKIS, Stasys, ed. Žemaičiai; žemaičių rašytojų prozos ir poezijos antologija. [Žemaičiai; an anthology of Samogitian prose and poetry. Kaunas, Sakalas, 1938] 246 p. ports. 491.922C.An44 PU ICCC OCl

8187. BALTRUŠAITIS, Juozas, ed. Atžalos; Amerikos Lietuvių darbininkų, rašytojų tvarinių rinkinys. Brooklyn, N.Y., "Laisvė", 1921. 349 p. illus., ports. MiD PU PPULC OCl

8188. BARĖNAS, Kazimieras, ed. Sauja derliaus; skaitymai augantiems ir suaugusiems. [...readings for juveniles and adults] London, Nida Press [c1957] 558 p. (Nidos knygų klubo leidinys, no.20-21) PG8713.B3 DLC CaOTP CtTMF

8189. BINKIS, Kazys, ed. Antrieji vainikai; naujosios poezijos antologija. Kaunas, Spaudos fondas, 1936. 356 p. 891.92C.B517.2 PU CtTMF ICCC

8190. --- Vainikai; naujesniosios poezijos antologija. [Garlands; the anthology of more recent Lithuanian poetry] Kaunas, Švyturio bendrovės leidinys, 1921. 230 p. ports. PG8715.B62 InU CtTMF CtY ICCC MiD NB NN OCl PPULC PU

8191. BRADŪNAS, Kazys. Žemė; naujosios lietuvių poezijos antologija. Los Angeles, Calif. Lietuvių dienos, 1951. 193 p. 4PG Lith.89 DLC CtTMF OKentU PPULC PU

8192. BRAZDŽIONIS, Bernardas, ed. Lietuvių beletristikos antologija. [Chicago, Ill.] Lietuviškos knygos klubas [1957]-1965. 2 v. PG8713.B74 DLC CaOONL CaOTU CtTMF MH

8193. BUIVYDAITĖ, Bronė, ed.

Aukštyn; moterų kūrybos almanachas.
Įvadą parašė. G. Petkevičaitė.
Kaunas, 1930. 208 p. port.
491.922.B867 PU OCl

8194. DEVYNI VILKAI; humoras ir
satyra. Vilnius, Vaga, 1970. 326
p. PG8713.D4 PU

8195. GABIJA; literatūros metraštis spaudos atgavimo penkiasdešimtmečiui ir tremties dešimtmečiui paminėti. [A literary yearbook to
commorate the 50th anniversary of
the re-establishment of the free
press and the ten years of exile.
Redaktoriai; Jonas Aistis ir Stepas
Zobarskas] Brooklyn, N.Y., Gabijos
leidykla, 1954. 550 p.
PG8737.G3 DLC ICCC MH NN PU

8196. ---; rinktinė knyga, paauko-
ta Lietuvos dainiaus Vyskupo Antano Baranaucko atminimui. [Gabija.
Selected works compiled in remembrance of Bishop Antanas Baranaus-
kas] Krokuvoje, Gebethner i Wolff,
1907. 77 p. 491.922C.G114 PU CtY
CtTMF ICCC MiD NB

8197. GIRA, Liudas. Cit, paklau-
sykit! Parinktosios lietuvių poetų
eilės. Tilžėje, O. v. Mauderodės
spaustuvės [1922] 190 p.
891.92C.G448.4 PU ICC NN OCl

8198. ---, comp. Lietuva pava-
sarį, vasarą, rudenį ir žiemą; parinktieji skaitymėliai iš lietuvių
raštijos apie Lietuvos metalaikius
ir jų dalis. [Reader on the four
seasons of the year] Kaunas, Švyturio bendrovės leidinys [1924],
124 p. Hvc40.G44 CtY CtTMF ICLJF
OCl PU

8199. ---, ed. Sveika, Nepriklausomoji! Pirmojo Lietuvos Nepriklausomybės dešimtmečio parinktieji lietuvių poetų eilėraščiai apie nepriklausomybę, kovas dėl jos ir Vilnių. [Poetry on Lithuania's in-
dependence] Kaunas, Šv. Kazimiero
d-jos leidinys, 1928. 111 p.
891.92C.G448.3 PU CtTMF ICCC

8200. ---, comp. Šventoji Lietuva; religinės lietuvių poezijos antologija. [An anthology of religious poetry. 1. Knyga] Kaunas,
Šviesos spaustuvė, 1930. 176 p.
891.92C.G448.2 PU CtTMF ICCC

8201. GRAŽI TU, MANO BRANGI TE-
vynė; antologija. [My homeland,
how beautiful you are; anthology.
Sudarė Vytautas Kazakevičius]
Vilnius, Vaga, 1967. 558 p. illus.
PG8713.G7 DLC CaAEU InNd NN OKentU
PU

8202. IŠ TARYBINĖS LIETUVIŲ PRO-
ZOS. [From Soviet-Lithuanian
fiction. Redaktorė E. Subačienė]
2. leidimas. Kaunas, Valstybinė
pedagoginės literatūros leidykla,
1958. 205 p. (Mokinio biblioteka) PG8715.I8 OKentU NN

8203. KELIUOTIS, Juozas. Grani-
tas; naujosios literatūros almanachas. [Granit; selections from
contemporary literature] Kaunas,
1930. 110 p. 891.928.K4 CtTMF

8204. KORSAKAS, Kostas. Lietuva ugnyje; Lietuvos rašytojų kūriniai apie lietuvių tautą vokiečių
okupacijoj antro pasaulinio karo
metu. [... Works of Lithuanian
writers on the Lithuanian nation
during the German occupation, 1941-
1944] Brooklyn, N.Y., 1944. 287
p. 891.92C.K845 PU CtTMF OKentU

8205. KUBILEVIČIUS, Petras, ed.
Pirmas dešimtmetis: 18 poetų...
Kaunas, Gudaitis, 1929. 264 p. OCl

8206. LIETUVIŲ POEZIJA. Sudarė
V. Vanagas, red. komisija: V. Kubilius [et al] Vilnius, Vaga,
1967. 2 v. Bibliography: v.1, p.
632-641. Vol. 2 compiled by V.
Galinis. PG8715.L5 InNd CtPAM(v.1)
CtY MH PU

8207. --- --- 2. leidimas. Vilnius, Vaga, 1969. 2 v.
PG8715.L72 1969 CaAEU OKentU WaU

8208. LIETUVIŲ POEZIJA XIX AM-
ŽIAUS. [Lithuanian poetry of the
19th Century. Comp. and ed. by
Bronius Pranskus] Vilnius, VGLL,
1955. 698 p. 891.921.P ICCC
CtPAM ICLJF NN

8209. --- --- [Another edition]
Vilnius, VGLL, 1965. 698 p.
Balt 9625.21 MH

8210. LIETUVIŲ POEZIJA IŠEIVIJOJE,
1945-1971. Redagavo Kazys Bradūnas.
Chicago, Ill., Ateitis, 1971. 671
p. (Literatūros serija, nr.5)
Bibliography: p. [640]-644.
PG8715.L52 DLC

8211. LIETUVIŲ TARYBINĖ NOVELĖ.
[Soviet-Lithuanian short stories.
Editors: J. Baltušis, J. Mikelins-
kas, A. Pocius, M. Sluckis and A.
Zalatorius. Comp. by Z. Zalatorius]
Vilnius, Vaga, 1969. 459 p.
PG8719.L72 1969 CaAEU CtY OClW PU

8212. MANOJI LIETUVA: tarybinės
poezijos rinktinė. [Selections of
Soviet Lithuanian poetry. Comp.
by V. Rudokas] Vilnius, Vaga,
1965. 438 p. illus. PG8715.M27

DLC CtPAM PU

8213. MIGLINAS, Simas, ed. Motina; lietuvių poezija ir beletristika apie motiną. [Anthology of Lithuanian poetry and prose, dedicated to "Mother"] 1. dalis. Įžgangą parašė Liudas Gira. Kaunas, Žinija, 1932. 193 p. 891.92.M583 PU CtTMF

8214. --- Mūsų Vilniaus poezija; iliustruota Vilniaus poezijos antologija. [Poetry on our Vilnius] Kaunas, Sakalas, 1932. 223 p. illus. 891.92C.M583.2 PU CtTMF ICCC

8215. MIKUCKIS, Juozas. Derliaus vainikas; Poezijos rinktinė. [Selections of poetry] London, Nida, 1964. 368 p. 891.92.K584De PU CaAEU OKentU

8216. PAPEČKYS, Kazys, ed. Du vardai granite; poezijos antologija apie Darių ir Giriną [Poetry on Darius and Giranas] Įvado žodį parašė Liudas Gira. Kaunas, 1936. 63 p. 891.92C.P198 PU CtTMF

8217. --- Prisikėlusi Lietuva; poezijos antologija. Kaunas, Dirvos bendrovės leidinys, 1939. 175 p. 891.92C.P198.2 PU CtTMF ICCC

8218. PRADALGĖ; literatūros metraštis. 1- ; 1964- . [London, Nida Press] (Nidos knygų klubo leidinys) Annual. Editor Kazimieras Barėnas. PG8713.P7 DLC CaAEU(1-2) CaOTP CaOTU ICU(1-) IEN(1-) PU(1-) 891.921S ICCC

8220. TYSLIAVA, Juozas, ed. Sūduva; suvalkiečių poezijos antologija. Kaunas, 1924. 160 p. 891.92C.T988 PU CtTMF ICCC

8221. VARPAI; literatūros almanachas 1944. [Redaktorius J. Jankauskas] Šiauliai, Šiaulių meno ir mokslo centras, 1944. 400 p. PG8713.V3 1944 PU

XIII.5.c.2. COLLECTED AND SELECTED WORKS

8222. ANDRIUŠIS, Pulgis. Rinktiniai raštai. [Boston, Mass.] Lietuvių enciklopedijos leidykla, 1968- . PG8721.A54R5 DLC CaAEU NN PU

8223. ARMINAS, Petras. Raštai. Išleidimas 3. papildintas naujomis eilėmis. Vilnius, J. Zavadzkis, 1907. 60 p. 891.92.Ar58 PU

CtTMF ICCC

8224. AŽUKALNIS, Valerijonas. Raštai lietuviški. [Parašė V. Ažukalnis, paruošė J. Girdzijauskas] Vilnius, Vaga, 1968. 364 p. facsims. (Lituanistinė biblioteka) PG8721.A98A16 1968 CaOTU

8225. BARANAUSKAS, Antanas. Iš Barono poezijos mokykloms parinko M. Biržiška. Kaunas, Dirva, 1924. 104 p. PPULC PU

8226. --- Raštai. [Red. komisija: K. Korsakas (pirm.) ir kiti. Paruošė, komentarus parengė: R. Mikšytė] Vilnius, Vaga, 1970. 2 v. illus., facsims. PG8721.B325 1970 DLC PU CaAEU

8227. --- Vyskupo Baranausko raštai. Seinai, Žmonių knygyno išleidimas, 1912. 102 p. 891.921B ICCC

8228. BILIŪNAS, Jonas. Raštai... Redagavo A. Janulaitis ir Juozas Žiugžda. Kaunas, Spaudos Fondas, 1937. 308 p. illus., ports. (Lietuvių klasikai) 891.922.B494 PU PPULC

8229. --- Raštai. Kaunas, VGLL, 1947. 310 p. 4PG Lithuanian 31 DLC

8230. --- Raštai. Vilnius, VGLL, 1954-55. 2 v. illus., ports. 891.92.B494.3 PU NN OKentU PP

8231. --- Rinktiniai raštai... Gunzenhausen, Ger., 1946. 158 p. illus., ports. 891.92.B494.2 PU CaOONL ICCC PPULC

8232. BORUTA, Kazys. Suversti arimai; devynios eilių ir poemų knygos. [M. Bulakos medžio raižiniai] Vilnius, Vaga, 1964. 338 p. PG8721.B6S8 PU

8233. BRAZDŽIONIS, Bernardas. Per pasaulį keliauja žmogus; rinktinė poezija. 3. laida. [Fellbach, Ger., Lux, 1949] 448 p. PG8721.B82P42 CaAEU CaOTU IU DLC PPULC PU

8234. --- Poezijos pilnatis. Los Angeles, Calif., Lietuvių dienos, 1970. 592 p. Selected poetry to commemorate the anniversary of the author's 60th birthday. PG8721.B7 1970 PU CaOONL

8235. BURBA, Aleksandras. Prozaiški raštai. Naujas perspausdinimas. Kaštais A.M. Miluko. Shenandoah, Pa., J.V. Stevero spaustuvė, 1900-1901. 2 v. 891.92.B896P PU CtTMF

PU CtTMF

8236. BUTKUS, Juozas. Butkų Ju-
zės raštai. Redagavo G. Paulaus-
kaitė. [Chicago, Ill.] P. Šulo
leidinys, 1954. 154 p. illus.
PG8721.B83 1954 DLC ICCC MiD PPULC
PU

8237. --- Rinktinė. [Compiled by
J. Butėnas] Vilnius, VGLL, 1962.
206 p. facsims., ports.
PG8721.B83R5 1962 DLC CtPAM PU

8238. ČIURLIONIENĖ, Sofija (Kymar-
taitė). Rinktiniai raštai. [Re-
daktorius P. Margevičius. 1. lei-
dimas] Vilnius, VGLL, 1956. 3 v.
ports. 891.92.C4985.9 PU NN

8239. CVIRKA, Petras. Raštai.
Vyriausias redaktorius A. Venclova;
redakcinė komisija K. Korsakas, J.
Šimkus, A. Venclova. [Vilnius]
VGLL, 1949-1957. 13 v. illus.
PG8721.C8 1949 DLC NN PU

8240. --- --- [Redakcinė komisija
K. Korsakas, J. Šimkus, A. Venclova
(pirm.)] Vilnius, VGLL, 1959. 8
v. 891.92.C998.2 PU

8241. DAUGUVIETIS, Borisas.
Rinktinė. Vilnius, VGLL, 1955.
283 p. music. PG8721.D35R5 DLC

DONELAITIS, Kristijonas.
Donelaičio gyvenimas ir raštai.
3. leidimas. Kaunas, 1927. See
entry no. 514.

8242. --- Kristijono Donelaičio
rankraščiai. [Vyr. redaktorius K.
Korsakas. Spaudai paruošė L.
Gineitis. Vilnius] VGLL, 1955.
vi, 48 p. of facsims. At head of
title: Lietuvos TSR Mokslų akademija. Lietuvių kalbos ir literatūros institutas. PG8721.D7Z53 DLC
CaOTU ICCC ICU IU MiU MH NN

8243. GIRA, Liudas. Liudo Giros
raštai. I. tomas, 1908-1918 lyrika. Kaunas, Universitetas, 1928.
203 p. 891.921.G ICCC

8244. --- Raštai. [Sudarė ir tekstus paruošė Eug. Matuzevičius]
Vilnius, VGLL, 1960-63. 5 v.
illus. PG8721.G5 1960 DLC CaAEU NN

8245. --- Rinktinė. [Redakcinė
komisija: Kostas Korsakas, Jonas
Šimkus, Antanas Venclova. Vilniuje]
VGLL, 1951. 296 p. illus.
PG8721.G5R5 DLC PU

8246. GUDAITIS-GUZEVIČIUS, Aleksandras. Raštai. Vilnius, VGLL,
1960-1963. 5 v. illus., port.

PG8721.G8 1960 DLC ICU NN OKentU
(2,6) PU

8247. JANONIS, Julius. Janonio
raštai. Kaunas, Varpas, 1921. 111p.
(Koperacijos bendrovės Šviesos leidinys, nr. 20) CtPAM IEN

8248. --- Raštai. Kaunas, Varpas,
1927. 112 p. (Koperacijos bendrovės Šviesa leidinys, nr. 28)
891.52.J268 PU

8249. --- --- [Another edition.
Eilėraščiai ir proza. Ed. by. V.
Kapsukas] Vilnius, VGLL, 1945. 216
p. NN

8250. --- --- [Another edition.
Redakcinė komisija: K. Korsakas, K.
Umbrasas, J. Zinkus] Vilnius, VGLL,
1957. 2 v. 891.92.J268.2 PU

8251. --- Rinktinė. Kaunas, VGLL,
1947. 111 p. (*Q p.v. 1394)NN

8252. --- --- [Another edition.
Vilniuje] VGLL, 1952. 183 p. illus.
PG8721.J3R5 DLC

8253. KORSAKAS, Kostas. Piūtis;
rinktinė. [Dailininkė L. Paškaus-
kaitė] Vilnius, Vaga, 1969. 287 p.
illus. PG8721.K865M5 CaOTU

8254. KRĖVĖ-MICKEVIČIUS, Vincas.
Raštai. Kaunas, Švyturio bendrovė,
1921. 2 v. PG8721.K7 1921 DLC

8255. --- --- [Another edition]
Kaunas, Švietimo ministerijos leidi-
nys, 1923. 5 v. PG8721.K7 1923
DLC PU

8256. --- --- [Another edition]
Kaunas, Ryto bendrovės spaustuvė,
1929. 8 v. PG8721.K7 1929 DLC

8257. --- --- [Another edition]
Kaunas, 1921-30. 10 v.
891.93.K21-30 CtTMF

8258. --- --- [Another edition.
Redagavo Vincas Maciūnas. Boston,
Mass.] Lietuvių enciklopedijos lei-
dykla, 1956-1963. (v.1, 1960) 6 v.
PG8721.K7 1960 DLC CaAEU CaOTU
CaOONL CtPAM CtTMF ICCC(2-6) NN
OKentU PU

8259. KUDIRKA, Vincas. Raštai.
[Collected and edited by J. Gabrys,
Illus. by K. Loevy and A. Braks]
Tilžėje, O. Mauderodė, 1909. 6 v.
illus., port. (Tėvynės mylėtojų
draugystė. Leidinys nr. 16)
PG8721.K8 1909 DLC CtPAM CtTMF CtY
ICCC MB OCl PU RPB WaS

8260. --- --- [Another edition]

Spaudai paruošė Simas Miglinas. [Me-
mmingen, Ger.] Tremtis [1953] 487 p.
port. PG8721.K8 1953 DLC CaOTU
CtTMF IU MB NN

8261. LANDSBERGIS, Gabrielius.
Raštai. [Paruošė A. Žirgulys] Vil-
nius, Vaga, 1972. 322 p. illus.
At head of title: Gabrielius Lands-
bergis-Žemkalnis. PG8721.L31 1972
PU

8262. MAČYS, Jonas. Raštai. [Re-
dakcinė komisija: V. Kubilius, VL.
Mozūriūnas ir B. Pranskus] Vilnius,
VGLL, 1961. 359 p. ports.
PG8721.M27 1961 DLC NN PU

8263. MAIRONIS, Jonas. Raštai.
Kaunas, 1927-30. 6 v. PG8721.M3
DLC CtTMF PU(v.1-5)

8264. --- Rinktiniai raštai. Vilnius, VGLL, leidykla, 1956. 2 v.
illus., ports., facsims.
PG8721.M3A6 1956 DLC CaAEU CtPAM
CtTMF ICCC NN OKentU PU

8265. MARCINKEVIČIUS, Jonas. Raštai. [Redakcinė komisija: A. Gricius, E. Mieželaitis, J. Šimkus.
1. leidimas] Vilnius, VGLL, 1955.
3 v. 891.92.M334 PU(v.1, 3) ICCC
NN

8266. MOZŪRIŪNAS, Vladas. Raštai.
[Sudarė, paaiškinimus parašė Romana
Dambrauskaitė] Vilnius, Vaga, 1971.
2 v. PG8721.M6 1971 PU

8267. MYKOLAITIS, Vincas. Raštai.
Kaunas, Švyturio bendrovė, 1921.
2 v. 891.92.M994 PU(v.2) CtTMF(v.1)
ICCC

8268. --- --- [Another edition]
Vilnius, VGLL, 1959-69. 10 v.
PG8721.M9 1959 DLC CtPAM NN OKentU
PU

8269. NĖRIS, Salomėja. Raštai.
[Kaunas] VGLL, [1957] 3 v. illus.,
port. 891.92.B124 PU MiU NN

8270. PAKALNIŠKIS, Kazimieras.
Raštai. [By] Dėdė Atanazas [pseud.]
Tilžė, Sargas, 1898. 891.92.K8690IK
PU

8271. PEČKAUSKAITĖ, Marija. Raštai. [By] Šatrijos Ragana [pseud.]
Kaunas, 1927-1939. 8 v.
891.93.S9-12 CtTMF

8272. PENKAITIS, Pranas. Raštai.
Kaunas, 1922-1923. 3 v. 891.93.P6
CtTMF CtY ICCC OCl(1) PU(2)

8273. PETKEVIČAITE, Gabrielė.
Raštai. Kaunas. VGLL, 1947. 273

p. 891.92.P444 PU

8274. --- --- [Another edition]
Paruošė A. Žirgulys] Vilnius,
Vaga, 1966-68. 6 v. At head of
title: Gabrielė Petkevičaitė-Bitė.
PG8721.P43 1966 PU(3-6) CaAEU DLC
ICLJF MH OCl OKentU

8275. PIETARIS, Vincas. Raštai.
Kaunas, 1921-1922. 891.93.P16-17
CtTMF(3-4)

8276. POŠKA, Dionizas. Raštai.
[Vilnius] VGLL, [1959] 742 p.
facsims. Bibliographical references included in "Pastabos ir
paaiškinimai", p. [679]-[740].
PG8721.P66 1959 DLC CtPAM PU

8277. PŠIBILIAUSKIENĖ, Sofija
(Ivanauskaitė). Raštai. Kaunas,
Švyturio b-vė, 1921-22. 4 v.
491.92.P958 PU CtTMF ICCC

8278. --- --- [Another edition]
Kaunas. Dirvos b-vės, leidinys,
1928. 244 p. 891.928.I ICCC

8279. --- --- [Another edition.
Vilnius] VGLL, 1954-55. 7 v.
illus. PG8721.P7 DLC OKentU

8280. ŠIKŠNYS, Marcelinas. Rinktinė. [By] M. Šiaulėniškis [pseud.]
Vilnius, Vaga, 1967. 269 p.
891.92.Si27.9V PU

8281. SIMONAITYTĖ, Ieva. Raštai.
[Kaune] VGLL, 1956-58. 6 v. illus.
PG8721.S5 1958 DLC CaAEU NN OKentU
PU(1-6)

8282. ŠKĖMA, Antanas. Raštai.
Chicago, Ill., Santara-Šviesa,
1967-70. 2 v. PG8721.S53R3 DLC
CaAEU CaOTU OKentU PU

8283. SRUOGA, Balys. Raštai.
[Redakcinė komisija: J. Baltušis
et al.] Vilnius, VGLL, 1957. 6 v.
PG8721.S68 1957 DLC CaAEU(1-3, 5-6)
ICU PU

8284. STANEVIČIUS, Simonas. Raštai. Vilnius, Vaga, 1967. 654 p.
facsims, music. (Lituanistinė
biblioteka) Bibliography: p. [511]-
[543]. PG8721.S69A6 1967 DLC NN PU

8285. STEPONAITIS, Edmundas. E.
Steponaičio raštai; pilnas pomirti-
nis eilių ir prozos rinkinys.
Tvarkė Liudas Gira. Kaunas, 1912.
128 p. 891.928.S ICCC

8286. STRAZDAS, Antanas. Raštai.
Surinko ir spaudai parengė J.
Gabrys. Chicago, Ill., Lietuva
Publishing Co., 1914. 77 p.

(Tėvynės mylėtojų draugijos leidinys) 891.92.St82 PU DLC ICCC NN OCl

8287. --- --- [Another edition.
Ed. by A. Rimkūnas] Vilnius, VGLL,
1952. 176 p. DLC

8288. --- --- [Another edition]
Vilnius, VGLL, 1957. 145 p.
PG8721.S75R3 1957 DLC CtPAM PU

8289. TAUTKAITĖ, Eugenija. Raštai. Vilnius, Vaga, 1965. 725,
[3] p. illus., ports. PG8721.T37
1965 DLC MH

8290. TILVYTIS, Teofilis. Raštai.
Kaunas; Vilnius, VGLL, 1954-1955.
3 v. PG8721.T55 DLC NN PU

8291. TUMAS, Juozas, 1869-1933.
Rinktiniai raštai. [By] Vaižgantas [pseud.] Vilnius, VGLL, 1957.
2 v. PG8721.T77A6 1957 DLC CaAEU
NN PU

8292. --- Vaižganto raštai. Kaunas, Švyturio b-vės leidinys, 1922-
26. 9 v. Contents.--T.1. Vokiečių
okupuotan Vilniun sugrįžus 1918 metais.--T.2. Lenkų okupuotame Vilniuje 1919 m.--T.3. Steigiamajame
Kaune 1920-21 m.--T.4 Aplink nepriklausomybės veikėjus.--T.5. Karo
vaizdai. Scenos vaizdai.--T.6.
Alegorijų vaizdai.--T.7-9. Pragiedruliai. PG8721.T77 1922 DLC CU
CtTMF(1-5) CtY ICCC PU

8293. --- --- [Kaune] Akc. "Spindulio" b-vės spaustuvė, 1929-1939.
10 v. Contents.--T.10. Dėdės ir
dėdienės.--T.11. Tremtiniai, romantininkai.--T.12. Aušrininkai.--T.13.
Beletristai.--T.14. Publicistai.--
T.15. Šeimos vėžiai.--T.16. Su bėgliais ir tremtiniais.--T.17. Kelionių vaizdai.--T.18. Iš kaimo buities.
--T.10. Naujieji literatūros nuotykiai. PG8721.T77 1929a DLC

8294. VAIČAITIS, Pranas. Prano
Vaičaičio raštai. 3. leidimas.
Kaunas, Švyturio b-vė, 1921. 197 p.
891.91.V3 CtTMF ICCC OCl

8295. --- Rinktinė. Vilnius,
VGLL, 1956. 230 p. illus.
891.92.V188.2 PU CtPAM CtY MiU

8296. VALANČIUS, Motiejus. Raštai. Redagavo ir žodynėlį pridėjo
J. Balčikonis. Kaunas, 1931. viii,
487 p. port. PG8721.V327A6 1931
DLC CtTMF OCl

8297. VALSIŪNIENĖ, Valerija.
Rinktiniai raštai. Vilnius, VGLL,
1957. PG8721.V33A6 1957 DLC MiD

8298. VANAGĖLIS, Ksaveras. Raštai. Kaunas, 1921. 189 p.
891.93.V54 CtTMF

8299. VIENUOLIS, A., pseud. Raštai. Kaunas; Klaipėda, Švyturio
bendrovė [etc.] 1920-22. 2 v.
PG8721.V5 DLC PU

8300. --- --- [Another edition]
Šiauliai, Kultūros bendrovė, 1922-
30. 5 v. PG8721.V5 1925 DLC(1-3)
CtTMF(1-3) BM(3-5)

8301. --- --- [Another edition]
Kaunas, Vairo bendrovės leidinys,
[1928-37] v. 4-11 PG8721.V5 1928
DLC CtTMF(4-11) ICCC OCl

8302. --- --- [Another edition]
Kaunas, Sakalas, 1935- . Contents.
--T.7-8. Viešnia iš Šiaurės. 2.
pataisytas leidimas, 1937-38.--T.9.
Ministeris, 1935. PG8721.V5 1935
DLC OCl CtTMF

8303. --- --- [Another edition.
Vilnius] VGLL, [1953]-1955. 7 v.
illus. PG8721.V66 1953 CaAEU(2-7)
DLC ICCC PU

8304. --- Rinktiniai raštai.
Kaunas, Švietimo ministerijos knygų
leidimo komisijos leidinys, 1937.
479 p. 891.92.Z89.9S PU CtTMF

8305. VIŠINSKIS, Povilas. Raštai.
[Surinko A. Sprindys. Spaudai paruošė ir redagavo A. Žirgulys] Vilnius, Vaga, 1964. 621 p. illus.,
port. PG8721.V54 1964 DLC CaAEU PU

8306. ŽILIUS, Jonas. Veikalai,
veikalėliai ir vertimai eilėmis.
Tilžėje, Spauda spaustuvės "Lituania" [19--] 3 v. PG8721.Z5V4
DLC OKentU PU

8307. ŽYMANTIENĖ, Julija (Beniu-
ševičiūtė). Raštai. [Red. komisija: K. Korsakas, A. Venclova, J.
Žiugžda] Vilnius, VGLL, 1957-58.
6 v. illus. PG8721.Z5 1957 DLC
CaAEU ICCC NN OKentU PU

8308. --- Rinktiniai raštai.
[Kaunas] VGLL, [1946] 552 p.
port. (*QY) NN

8309. --- Žemaitės raštai. Vilnius, J. ir P. Leonų leidimas,
1913-1914. 8 v. PG8721.Z9 1913
DLC PU

8310. --- --- [Another edition]
Kaunas; Marijampolė, Dirvos, 1924-
1931. 4 v. PG8721.Z99 CaAEU CtTMF
ICCC

8311. --- --- [Another edition.

Redaktorius A. Kalnius] Kaunas,
VGLL, 1948. 4 v. PG8721.Z9 1948 PU

XIII.5.c.3. PROSE

8312. ABRAMAVIČIUS, Faivušas.
Mirties nuosprendis; dokumentinė
apysaka. Vilnius, VGLL, 1960. 413
p. PG8722.1.B7M5 DLC

8313. ABRAMAVIČIUS, Girša. Išti-
kimybė; dokumentinė apysaka. Vilnius, Vaga, 1965. 386 p.
PG8722.1.B7217 PU DLC

8314. AISTIS, Jonas. Milfordo
gatvės elegijos. London, Nida Press,
1969. 200 p. PG8721.A4M5 PU CaOTU

8315. ALANTAS, Vytautas. Amžina-
sis lietuvis; romanas. [London,
Nida] 1972- . PG8721.A45A5 PU

8316. --- Nemunas teka per Atlantą; noveles. [London, Nida, 1970]
263 p. (Nidos knygų klubo leidinys,
nr. 79) PG8721.A45N4 PU

8317. --- Pragaro pašvaistės romanas. Memmingen, Ger., Tremtis,
1951. 432 p. 891.92.Al2P PU

8318. --- Šventaragis; istorinis
romanas. [Cleveland, Ohio] Viltis, 1972- . PG8721.A45S9 PU

8319. --- Svetimos pagairės; novelės. London, Nida, 1954. 254 p.
(Nidos knygų klubo leidinys, nr. 3)
891.92.Al.12S PU CtTMF ICCC

8320. --- Tarp dviejų gyvenimų.
Chicago, Ill., Lietuviškos knygos
klubas, 1960. 462 p.
PG8721.A45T3 DLC NN PU ICCC

8321. ALMĖNAS, Kazys. Bėgiai;
novelės. London, Nida, 1965. 197
p. 891.92.Al.63B PU IEN

8322. --- Gyvenimas tai kekė vyš-
nių; novelės. Chicago, Ill. [Algi-
manto Mackaus vardo knygų leidimo
fondas] 1967. 214 p.
PG8749.A4G9 DLC

8323. --- Upė į rytus, upė į
šiaurę. Romanas. Chicago, Ill.,
Lietuviškos knygos klubas, 1964. 2
v. 891.92.A .63U PU MH OCl

8324. ALŠĖNAS, Pranys. Talismanas;
novelės. Bambergas, Ger., [1946].
59 p. PG8721.A47T3 DLC ICCC

8325. ANDRIUKAITIS, Vladas. Audra
Žemaičiuose; Vytauto Didžiojo laikų

apysaka. [2. leidimas. Brooklyn,
N.Y., Gabija, 1954] 215 p.
891.92.An24A PU CtTMF ICCC OKentU

8326. --- Kovų aidai. Kaunas,
Lietuvos šaulių sąjungos leidinys,
1931. 159 p. 891.92.A24K PU

8327. --- Kruvina laisvė; romanas. Kaunas, Šaulių sąjungos leidinys, 1933. 254 p. 891.923A ICCC

8328. --- Martynas Skroblas; ro-
manas iš klaipėdiškių gyvenimo.
Kaunas, J. Plieninis, 1935. 213 p.
PG8721.A5 DLC CtTMF PU

8329. ANDRIUŠIS, Pulgis. Anoj
pusėj ežero; lyrinės apysakos. [2.
leidimas. Brooklyn, N.Y.] Gabija
[1953] 101 p. PG8721.A54A7 1953
DLC CtY ICCC PU

8330. --- Daina iš kito galo.
Humoristiniai ir satyriniai pasakojimai. London, Nida, 1962. 135 p.
(Nidos knygų klubo leidinys, nr. 37)
891.92.An26D PU CaAEU ICCC OCl

8331. --- Ir vis delto-juokimės!
Feljetonai... Gunzenhausenas, Ger.,
P.A.V. Sulaičiai, 1946. 54 p.
891.92.An26I PU PPULC

8332. --- Purienos po vandeniu;
novelės. London, Nida, 1963. 158
p. PG8721.A57P98 CaAEU OCl PU

8333. --- Rojaus vartai; apysaka.
[London] Nida [c1960] 198 p. (Ni-
dos knygų klubo leidinys, nr. 28)
PG8721.A54R6 DLC PU

8334. --- Sudiev, kvietkeli! Apysaka. Adelaide, Australijos lietuviai, 1951. 181 p. 891.92.An26S
PU PPULC OCl

8335. --- Tipelis; humoristinis
romanas. [Brooklyn, N.Y.] Gabija
[1953] 240 p. PG8721.A54T5 DLC
ICCC PU PPULC

8336. AVYŽIUS, Jonas. Į stiklo
kalną. Vilnius, VGLL, 1961. 423 p.
PG8721.A85I2 DLC NN PU

8337. --- --- 2. leidimas. Vilnius, Vaga, 1968. 462 p. illus.
PG8721.A85I2 1968 DLC

8338. --- Kaimas kryžkelėje; romanas. Vilnius, Vaga, 1964. 497 p.
891.92.Av99K PU CaOTU

8339. --- --- 2. leidimas. Vilnius, Vaga, 1966. 525 p.
PG8721.A85K3 1966 DLC

8340. --- Sodybų tuštėjimo metas;

romanas. Vilnius, Vaga, 1970. 593
p. PG8721.A85S6 PU CaOTU

8341. --- Žmogus lieka žmogum.
Vilnius, VGLL, 1960. 354 p.
PG8721.A85Z35 DLC

8342. BALČIŪNAS, Juozas. Eldora-
do; apysakaitės ir vaizdeliai.
Hanover, Ger., Bendrija, [1953]
150 p. 891.92.B183E PU

8343. --- Jo sužadėtinė; premijuotas romanas. [Chicago, Ill.]
Lietuviškos knygos klubas [1959]
394 p. PG8721.B27J6 DLC PU

8344. --- Knygnešių pėdsakais;
romanas. [Weinheim, Ger. Bendrija,
c1955] 295 p. PG8721.B27K6 DLC
PPULC PU

8345. --- Paskutinį kartą tave
klausiu; romanas. [Würzburge, Ger.]
L. Vismantas [1948] 169 p.
PG8721.B27P3 DLC PPULC ICCC PU

8346. --- Petras Širvokas; nuotykių nuotykiai žemėje... parašytas
lietuvių pasakų motyvais. J. Svais-
tas. Chicago, Ill., Lietuvių literatūros draugija, [1952] 228 p.
891.92.B18Pe PU CLU PPULC

8347. --- Trys žodžiai; arba, Gyvenimo magija. [By] J. Švaistas
[pseud.] Chicago, Ill., Draugo
spaustuvė, c1958. 176 p.
PG8721.B27T7 DLC PU

8348. --- Žiobriai plaukia; romanas. [By] J. Švaistas [pseud.]
[Chicago, Ill.] Lietuviškos knygos
klubas [1962] 233 p. PG8721.B27Z3
DLC OKentU PU

8349. BALTRŪNAS, Aleksas. Lietus;
apsakymai. Vilnius, VGLL, 1960.
222 p. PG8721.B28L5 DLC PU

8350. --- Tolimi keliai; apysaka.
Leid. 1. Vilnius, VGLL, 1958. 2 v.
891.92.B217T PU NN

8351. BALTRŪNIENĖ, A. Gintaras;
apsakymai. Vilnius, VGLL, 1963.
181 p. PG8722.12.A43G5 DLC

8352. BALTUŠIS, Juozas. Baltieji
dobiliukai; rinktiniai apsakymai.
[Vilnius] VGLL, 1951. 92 p.
PG8721.B32B3 PU

8353. --- Nežvyruotu vieškeliu;
apsakymų rinktinė. Vilnius, Vaga,
1971. 449 p. PG8721.B32N4 PU

8354. --- Parduotos vasaros; novelių romanas. Vilnius, VGLL, 1957- .
PG8721.B32A15 1947 DLC(1) CtPAM(1)

NN OKentU

8355. --- --- 4. laida. Vilnius,
Vaga, 1966-69. 2 v. PG8721.B32A15
1966 DLC NN OKentU PU

8356. --- Tėvų ir brolių takais.
Vilnius, Vaga, 1967. 325 p.
184.L7B35 PU MH

8357. --- Valiusei reikia Alekso;
novelės apie meilę. [Dailininkė
L. Paškauskaitė] Vilnius, Vaga,
1965. 200 p. PG8721.B32V3 PU DLC
OKentU

8358. BARANAUSKAS, Albinas. Kark-
lupėnuose. Draugo premijuotas romanas. [Chicago, Ill.] Lietuviškos
knygos klubas, 1965. 224 p.
PG8721.B324K3 DLC CaOONL CaOTU MH
PPULC PU

8359. --- Sniego platumos; nove-
lės. [London] Nida [c1955] 273 p.
(Nidos knygų klubo leidinys nr. 12)
PG8721.B325S6 DLC CaAEU CaOTU CtTMF
ICCC PPULC OKentU PU

8360. BARĖNAS, Kazimieras. Atsi-
tiktimai susitikimai. [By] K.
Baras. London, Nida, 1968. 219 p.
PG8721.B33A9 DLC PU

8361. --- Dvidešimt viena Veronika.
[London] Nida [1971] 458 p.
PG8721.B33D9 PU

8362. --- Giedra visad grįžta;
novelės. [Memmingen, Ger.] Tremtis [1953] 215 p. PG8721.B33G5
DLC OCl PU

8363. --- Karališka diena; novelės.
[London] Nida [c1957] 254 p. (Ni-
dos knygų klubo leidinys nr. 17)
PG8721.B33K3 DLC CaAEU CaOONL PU

8364. --- Tuboto Gaidžio metai.
London, Nida, 1970. 433 p. (Nidos
knygų klubo leidinys nr. 76)
PG8721.B33T8 PU CaOTU

8365. BARONAS, Aloyzas. Antrasis
krantas; novelės. London, Nida,
1954. 132 p. (Nidos knygų klubo
leidinys nr. 5) PG8721.B34A58 DLC
ICCC OCl PU PPULC

8366. --- Debesys plaukia pažemiu.
[Chicago, Ill., Terra, 1951] 223 p.
PG8721.B34D4 DLC CaAEU PPULC PU

8367. --- Išdžiūvusi lanka; novelės. Chicago, Ill., Lietuviškos
knygos klubas, 1970. 233 p.
PG8721.B34I5 PU

8368. --- Lieptai ir bedugnės;
premijuotas romanas. [Chicago, Ill.]

Lietuviškos knygos klubas [1961] 279 p. PG8721.B34L5 DLC CaOONL CaOTU ICCC PU

8369. --- Mėnesiena; romanas. Chicago, Ill., Karvelis, 1957. 202 p. PG8721.B34M4 DLC CaAEU PU

8370. --- Pavasario lietūs; romanas. London, Nida, 1967. 261 p. (Nidos knygų klubo leidinys, nr.61) PG8721.B34P3 PU CaOTU

8371. --- Saulės grįžimas; novelės. [London] Nida [1964] 141 p. (Nidos knygų klubo leidinys, nr.48) PG8721.B34S3 DLC PU

8372. --- Sodas už horizonto; romanas. Chicago, Ill., Lietuviškos knygos klubo leidinys, 1955. 254 p. PG8721.B34S6 DLC CaAEU CaOONL CtTMF ICCC NN OCl PPULC PU

8373. --- Trečioji moteris; premijuotas romanas. [Chicago, Ill.] Lietuviškos knygos klubas [1966] 196 p. PG8721.B34T7 DLC PU

8374. --- Trejos devynerios. Chicago, Ill., Lietuviškos knygos klubas, 1961. 64 p. Author's pseudonym, Dr. S. Aliunas, at the head of title. 891.92.B268T PU

8375. --- Užgesęs sniegas; romanas. [Viršelis Pauliaus Augiaus] Torontas, Tėviškės žiburiai, 1953. 285 p. (Tėviškės žiburių priedas, nr.3) PG8721.B34U9 DLC CaAEU OCl PPULC PU

8376. --- Valerijono lašai. Chicago, Ill., Nemunas [1954] 64 p. 891.92.B268V PU PPULC

8377. --- Vėjas lekia pažemiu; romanas. [Chicago, Ill.] Laisvosios Lietuvos knygų leidykla, 1971. PG8721.B34V4 PU

8378. --- Vieniši medžiai; romanas. [n.p.] 1960. 117 p. PG8721.B34V5 DLC PU

8379. --- Žvaigždės ir vėjai; novelės. [Schweinfurt, Ger.] Venta [1951] 238 p. PG8721.B34Z48 DLC NN OCl PPULC PU

8380. BARTUŠKAITĖ, V. Pionierės dienoraštis. [Žemaitytės piešiniai] Vilnius, VGLL, 1961. 225 p. PZ70.L52B3 DLC

8381. BAUŽA, Aleksandras. Kur mėlynas dangus; apsakymų rinktinė. Vilnius, Vaga, 1971. 362 p. PG8721.B37K8 PU

8382. BAVARSKAS, Medardas. Klajū-

nas; novelės. Schweinfurt, Ger., [J. Šlajus] 1946. 135 p. 891.B329K PU

8383. --- Pilkieji namai; romanas. Schweinfurt, Ger. [J. Šlajus] 1947. 200 p. 891.92.B29P PU

8384. BIELIACKINAS, Simanas. Prie teisėtumo aruodo; humoreskos apysakos. Kaunas, Progresas, 1934. 224 p. (*QY)NN

8385. --- Žmonės ir likimas; novelės. Kaunas, Progresas, 1934. 170 p. (*QY)NN

8386. BIELIAUSKAS, Alfonsas. Darbo gatvė; apysaka. Vilnius, VGLL, 1966. 318 p. 891.92.B473D PU

8387. --- Kauno romanas; romanas. Vilnius, Vaga, 1966. 442 p. illus. PG8721.B43K3 DLC IU MH

8388. --- --- 2. leidimas. Vilnius, Vaga, 1969. 427 p. port. PG8721.B43K2 PU CaAEU NN

8389. --- Mes dar susitiksim, Vilma! Romanas. Vilnius, VGLL, 1962. 422 p. PG8721.B43M4 DLC

8390. --- Rožės žydi raudonai; romanas. 2. leidimas. Vilnius, 1960. 451 p. 891.92.B473R PU

8391. --- --- 3. leidimas. Vilnius, Vaga, 1965. 439 p. PG8721.B43R6 DLC

8392. BILIŪNAS, Antanas. Puntuko akmuo; praeities atspindžiai apsakymuose. Vilnius, Vaga, 1970. 165 p. PG8722.12.I4P8 PU OKentU

8393. BILIŪNAS, Jonas. Beletristika. Kaunas, Spaudos fondas, 1937. 310 p. 891.928B ICCC

8394. --- J. Biliūnas. Sudaryta pagal Lietuvos TSR Švietimo ministerijos programą. 3. papildytas leidimas. Kaunas, Valstybinė pedagoginės literatūros leidykla, 1958. 99p. illus. (Mokinio biblioteka) PG8721.B47A6 1958 DLC

8395. --- Ivairūs apsakymėliai. Tilžė, Otto v. Mauderode, n.d. (Aušros išleidimas) 64 p. 891.92.B494I PU QCl PPULC

8396. --- Lazda...[Dailininkas V. Galdikas, Kaune] VGLL, 1959. 329 p. illus. PG8721.B47L3 DLC NN

8397. --- Lazda. Ubagas. Svečiai. Brisiaus galas. Parašė J. B-nas. Vilnius, J. Zavadzkis, 1906. 31 p. NN

8398. ––– Liūdna pasaka. Medžio raižiniai M. Bulakos. [Vilnius, VGLL, 1963] 49 p. PG8721.B47L5 DLC MH OU

8399. ––– Nemunu... Kaune, VGLL, 1947. 97 p. 891.92.B494N PU DLC NN PPULC

8400. ––– Paveikslai; pasakos ir eilės. Tilžė, J. Biliūnas, 1913. 143 p. ports. 891.92.B494P PU

8401. ––– Piestupys; Jonukas... Vilnius, J. Zavadzkio, 1906. 16 p. CtY NN OCl

8402. ––– Žvaigždė. [Iliustravo R. Gibavičius] Vilnius, Vaga, 1965. 69 p. PG8721.B47Z9 DLC

8403. BINKIS, Kazys. Kriaučius Motiejus. Vilnius, VGLL, 1947. 253 p. 891.92.B517K PU CaAEU

8404. BORIKAS, S. Neramios širdys. Vilnius, VPMLL, 1956. 90 p. illus. PG8721.B56N4 DLC

8405. BORUTA, Kazys. Baltaragio malūnas; arba Kas dėjosi anuo metu Paudruvės krašte. Iliustravo medžio raižiniais J. Kuzminskis. [2. leidimas. Chicago, Ill., Terra, 1952] 255 p. illus. PG8721.B6B3 1952 DLC CaOTU ICCC OKentU PPULC PU

8406. ––– Drumstas arimų vėjas. Ryga, Audra, 1928. 90 p. NN

8407. ––– Jurgio Paketurio klajonės su visokiais pavojais; arba, šventa teisybė, melo pasakos, kartais juokai ir linksmos ašaros. Iliustravo Algirdas Steponavičius. Vilnius, VGLL, 1963. 279 p. illus. PG8721.B6J8 DLC OKentU PU

8408. ––– Kelionės po šiaurę... [Kaunas] Spaudos fondas, 1938. 2 v. in 1. OCl

8409. ––– Mediniai stebūklai; arba Dievadirbio Vinco Dovinės gyvenimas ir darbai. Kaunas, Sakalas, 1938. 317 p. 891.923.B ICCC

8410. ––– ––– 2.[leidimas] Vilnius, Vaga, 1971. 241 p. PG8721.B6M4 1971 CaOTU PU

8411. ––– Namas Nr.13; romanas. 1. Dalis. Kaunas, Audros, 1928. NN

8412. ––– Neramūs arimai. Vilnius, Vaga, 1970– . facsims., ports. PG8721.B7P4 CaOTU

8413. ––– Sunkūs paminklai; apysaka-kronika. Vilnius, VGLL, 1960.

378 p. PG8721.B6S8 DLC CtPAM NN PU

8414. BRAZYTĖ-BINDOKIENĖ, Danutė. Mieste nesaugu; premijuota apysaka jaunimui. Čikaga, JAV LB Kultūros fondas, 1970. 169 p. PG8749.B7M5 PU

8415. ––– Viena pasaulyje; romanas. [Chicago, Ill.] Lietuviškos knygos klubas [1971] 241 p. PG8749.B7V5 PU

8416. BUBNYS, Vytautas. Alkana žemė; romanas. Vilnius, Vaga, 1971. 397 p. PG8722.12.U2A5 PU

8417. ––– Arbonas; apysaka. [Iliustravo Ada Skliutauskaitė] Vilnius, Vaga, 1969. 174 p. PG8722.12.U2A7 PU

8418. ––– Gegužio nemiga; apsakymai. Vilnius, Vaga, 1969. 209 p. PG8722.12.U2G4 PU CaAEU

8419. ––– Lapams krintant; apysaka. Vilnius, Vaga, 1966. 200 p. PG8722.12.U2L3 DLC IU MH NN

8420. BŪDAVAS, Stasius. Loreta; mergaitės likimo romanas. 2. peržiūrėta laida. [London, Eng., Bendrija, 1952] 172 p. PG8721.B8L6 1952 DLC ICCC IU OCl PPULC PU WU

8421. ––– Mokytojas Banaitis; romanas. Kaunas, Sakalas, 1935. 199 p. 891.93.B22 CtTMF ICCC ViU

8422. ––– Rūsti siena; apysaka. [Hamilton, Ont.] Rūta [1959] 193 p. PG8721.B8R8 DLC CtTMF PU

8423. ––– Uždraustas stebūklas; romanas. Brooklyn, N.Y., Gabija, 1954. 247 p. PG8721.B8U9 OCl ICCC MB OKentU PU

8424. ––– Varpai skamba; apysaka. Los Angeles, Calif., Lietuvių dienos, 1952. 180 p. PG8721.B8V3 DLC CaAEU ICCC MH MB OCl PPULC PU

8425. BUDRYS, Rimantas. Gyvos žemės mintys. Vilnius, Mintis, 1966. 110 p. PG8721.B814G9 DLC

8426. ––– Liepsnelė, Saulės spindulys; girios novelių romanas. Vilnius, Vaga, 1969. 372 p. PG8721.B814L5 PU CaAEU

8427. ––– Tėtis ir jo vaikai; penkiolikos vaizdų apysaka. Vilnius, Vaga, 1970. 190 p. PG8721.B814T4 PU

8428. BUIVYDAITĖ, Bronė. Auksinis batelis. Kaunas, Sakalas, 1937.

195 p. illus. 891.923.B ICCC

8429. --- Trys bičiuliai; apysaka.
Kaunas, Sakalas, 1937. 197 p.
illus. 891.923.B ICCC

8430. BULOTA, Juozas. Kulinukų
klausimas; feljetonai, humoreskos
ir panfletai. Vilnius, Vaga, 1966.
116 p. PG8722.12.U55K8 DLC IU MH

8431. --- Papt: feljetonai, hu-
moreskos, pamfletai. Vilnius,
Vaga, 1969. 117 p. PG8722.12.U55P3
PU

8432. --- Prieš plauką; feljetonai,
humoreskos, pamfletai. Vilnius,
VGLL, 1961. 152 p. illus.
PG8721.B82P7 DLC

8433. BŪTĖNAS, Julius. Mėlynieji
kareiviai; apsakymai. Vilnius,
Vaga, 1968. 264 p. PG8721.B82M4
1968 PU DLC ICCC

8434. ČALNARIS, Antanas. Tas
vienas vakaras; apsakymai. Vilnius,
VGLL, 1962. 54 p. port.
PG8722.13A4T3 DLC

8435. ČIPLYS, Adomas. Lapalių
mokytoja. Vilnius, VGLL, 1961.
229 p. PG8721.C49L3 DLC

8436. ČIURLIONIENĖ, Sofija (Kymantaitė). Šventmarė. Kaunas,
1937. 297 p. illus. PG8721.C5S8
DLC

8437. --- --- [Another edition.
Iliustravo Kastytis Juodikaitis]
Vilnius, 1969. 182 p. illus.
PG8721.C5S8 1969 PU CaAEU

8438. CVIRKA, Petras. Apysakos
ir autoriaus biografiniai bruožai.
Brooklyn, N.Y., 1949. 286 p.
891.92.C998Ap PU OKentU

8439. --- Ąžuolo šaknys. [Kaune]
VGLL [1945] 245 p. illus.
PG8721.C8A9 DLC PU

8440. --- Cukriniai avinėliai.
Kaunas, Sakalas, 1935. 167 p.
illus. 891.923C ICCC

8441. --- --- [Another edition]
Kaunas, VGLL, 1947. 101 p. illus.
DLC PU

8442. --- --- [Another edition]
Iliustravo D. Tarabildienė. [Kaune]
VGLL, [1952] 32 p. illus.
PZ70.L52C83 DLC NN PU

8443. --- Frank Kruk. Iliustravo
J. Kėdainis. [Kaune] VGLL, 1948.
576 p. illus. PG8721.C8F7 DLC MnU

NN OCl

8444. --- --- [Another edition]
Vilnius, Vaga, 1966. 516 p.
PG8721.C8F7 1966 DLC

8445. --- Meisteris ir sūnus.
Vilnius, VGLL, 1957. 349 p. illus.
PG8721.C8M4 1957 PU NN OKentU

8446. --- Mikučio vargai. Iliustravo D. Tarabildienė. [Kaunas,
VGLL, 1955] 348 p. PG8721.C8M5 PU

8447. --- Saulėlydis Nykos valsčiuje. Lino raižiniai A. Kučo.
Vilnius, Vaga, 1967. 217 p. illus.
port. PG8721.C8S2 1967 DLC OKentU

8448. --- Žemė maitintoja. Kaunas, VGLL, 1946. 193 p.
PG8721.C8Z25 DLC OCl

8449. --- --- [Another edition]
V. Galdiko medžio raižiniai.
[Kaune, VGLL] 1956. 245 p. illus.
PG8721.C8Z25 1956 DLC

8450. --- --- [Another edition]
Vilnius, Vaga, 1971. 250 p.
PG8721.C8Z4 1971 CaOTU

8451. DABULEVIČIUS, Andrius.
Mano tėvynė. [Sudarytojas, įvado
ir komentarų autorius: B. Pranskus]
Vilnius, VGLL, 1960. 210 p. illus.
ports. PG8721.D25M3 1960 DLC

8452. DAMBRAUSKAS, Aleksandras.
Šypt-šypt! jumoristiškų straipsnių
ir jų vertimų rinkinys. Kaunas,
"Žinijos", 1931. 2 v. in 1.
891.93.J1 CtTMF ICCC OCl

8453. --- Trys pašnekėsiai ant
Nemuno kranto. Parašė Adomas Jakštas [pseud.] Kaunas, M. Sokolovs-
kis ir Butrimas, 1906. 62 p.
891.92.D183 PU CtTMF

8454. DAUNORAS, Bronius. Mėlyna
suknelė; apysaka. Londonas [Nida]
1954. 154 p. PG8721.D37M4 DLC PU

8455. --- Neramu buvo Laisvės alė-
joj...; apysaka, [By] Br. Daubaras
[pseud.] London, Nida, 1952. 113
p. 891.92.92.D274N PU OCl OKentU

8456. --- Uždangai nusileidus;
apsakymas [By] Br. Daubaras [pseud.]
[London] Nida [1955] 120 p. (Nidos knygų klubo leidinys, nr. 6)
891.92.D274 PU

8457. DAUTARTAS, Vladas. Auksinio lyno vaišės. Teka upė pro šalį.
Mano tėtis partizanas; apysakos.
[Iliustravo N. Kryževičiūtė-Jurge-
lionienė] Vilnius, Vaga, 1968.

298 p. PG8722.14.A8 PU

8458. --- Jūros spalvos. Vilnius,
VGLL, 1960. 164 p. PG8722.14.A8J8
DLC CaAEU PU

8459. --- Kai nurausta putinas;
novelės. Vilnius, VGLL, 1963. 109
p. PG8722.14.A8K3 DLC MH NN PU

8460. --- Lakštingalų naktis;
novelės. Vilnius, Vaga, 1965. 157
p. PG8722.14.A8L3 DLC MH

8461. --- Miškinukas ir senelis
kaukas; apsakymai. [Iliustravo Edmundas Žiauberis] Vilnius, Vaga,
1971. 125 p. PG8722.14.A8M5 PU

8462. --- Pokalbis su upokšniu;
novelių rinktinė. Vilnius, Vaga,
1971. 417 p. illus.
PG8722.14.A8P6 CaOTU PU

8463. --- Prakeikimo vartai; apysaka. Vilnius, Vaga, 1966. 244 p.
PG8722.14.A8P7 DLC PU

8464. DIRGĖLA, Povilas. Žaibai
gęsta rudenį. Vilnius, Vaga, 1971.
367 p. ports. PG8722.14.I7Z3
CaOTU PU

8465. DOVYDAITIS, Jonas. Aerodro-
mo apysakos. Vilnius, Vaga, 1967.
356 p. PG8722.14.09A68 DLC PU

8466. --- Apsakymai. [Kaune]
VGLL [1947] PG8721.D74A8 DLC NN PU

8467. --- Dvylika vėjų; apsakymai
ir apybraižos. Vilnius, Vaga, 1970.
249 p. PG8722.14.C9D9 PU OKentU

8468. --- Gūdžioje girioje; apsakymai. Vilnius, VGLL, 1963. 294
p. PG8722.14.09G8 DLC MH OKentU

8469. --- Nakties vartai; nuotykių
apsakymai. Vilnius, Vaga, 1968.
252 p. PG8722.14.C9N3 PU CaOTU
OKentU

8470. --- Pilies skersgatvis.
Kietas riešutas. Vilnius, Vaga,
1968. 365 p. PG8722.14.09P5
OKentU NN PU

8471. --- Po audros; romanas.
[Kaune] VGLL, 1948. 309 p.
PG8721.D74P6 DLC PU OKentU(1953 ed.)

8472. --- Skaudi šviesa; romanas.
Vilnius, Vaga, 1966. 308 p.
PG8722.14.09S58 DLC PU

8473. --- Stikliniai balandžiai;
apysaka. Vilnius, VGLL, 1960. 224
p. PG8722.14.09S7 PU

8474. --- Velnio slenksčiai; apy-

saka. Vilnius, Vaga, 1966. 211 p.
PG8722.14.09V4 DLC

8475. --- Žmogaus sparnai. Vilnius, Vaga, 1971. 275 p.
GV765.L5D6 PU

8476 --- Žydrieji ežerai; romanas.
Vilnius, Vaga, 1964. 472 p.
PG8722.14.09Z9 DLC IU MH

8477. DOVYDAITIS, Juozapas Silvestras. Šiaulėniškis senelis. 1-5
dalys. Redaguota J. Tumo. Kaunas,
1925. 224 p. 947.520.Š4 CtTMF

8478. DOVYDĖNAS, Liudas. Broliai
Domeikos; romanas. Kaunas, 1936.
259 p. CtTMF ICCC

8479. --- --- [2. leidimas. Chi-
cago, Ill.] Terra [1952] 259 p.
PG8721.D75B7 1952 DLC CaAEU CaOTU
NN PU

8480. --- Jaujos pasakos. Kaunas,
Spaudos fondas, 1938. 2 v. illus.
891.923.D ICCC

8481. --- Kelionė į pievas. Kaunas, Sakalas, 1936. 210 p. illus.
891.923.D ICCC

8482. --- Mes ieškom pavasario.
[Schweinfurt, Ger.] L. Vismantas,
1948. 227 p. PG8721.D75M4 DLC ICCC
NN OCl PU

8483. --- Per Klausučių ūlytėlę;
apysaka. [Brooklyn, N.Y.] Gabija
[1952] 176 p. PG8721.D75P4 DLC OCl
PU OKentU

8484. --- Žmonės ant vieškelio.
Ingolstadt, Ger., 1949. 190 p.
PG8721.D74Z3 CaAEU PU

8485. FRANKIENĖ-VAITKEVIČIENĖ,
Vanda. Užburtos kanklės; pasakojimai apie senovę. [Čikaga, Laiškai
lietuviams, 1971] 166 p.
PG8721.F7U9 PU

8486. GIEDRA, Vincas. Eina į
mišką medžiai. Vilnius, Vaga, 1971.
104 p. PG8722.17.I43E5 PU

8487. GIEDRAITIS, Antanas. Aišvy-
do pasakos. [By] Antanas Giedrius
[pseud.] Iliustracijos Onos Bau-
žienės. [Chicago, Ill., Lietuviškos
knygos klubas, 1971] 140 p.
PG8721.G47A5 PU

8488. GIRDZIJAUSKAS, Vytautas.
Trys moterys ir vienas vyras. Vil-
nius, Vaga, 1971. 240 p.
PG8722.17.17T7 PU

8489. GLIAUDYS, Jurgis. Agonija;
romanas. [By] J. Gliauda [pseud.]

London, Nida, 1966. 408 p. (Nidos
knygų klubo leidinys, nr. 55)
891.92.G492Ag PU

8490. --- Aitvarai ir giria; romanas. [By] J. Gliauda [pseud.
Chicago, Ill.] Lietuvos atgimimo
sąjudis, 254 p. PG8749.G6A5 PU
OKentU

8491. --- Broliai; romanas. [By]
J. Gliauda [pseud.] Chicago, Ill.,
Draugas, 1949.

8492. --- Delfino ženkle; premijuotas romanas. [By] J. Gliauda
[pseud. Chicago, Ill.] Lietuviškos
knygos klubas, [1966] 234 p.
PG8749.G6D4 DLC CaOTU PU

8493. --- Gęstanti saulė; metmenys.
[By] J. Gliauda [pseud. Chicago,
Ill.] Lietuviškos knygos klubas
[1954] 218 p. PG9749.G6G4 DLC
CaAEU CaOONL MiD PU

8494. --- Ikaro sonata; romanas.
[By] J. Gliauda [pseud. London, Nida
Press, 1961] 194 p. (Nidos knygų
klubo leidinys, nr. 35) PG8749.G6I4
DLC CaAEU CaOONL CaOTU ICCC OCl
OKentU PU

8495. --- Liepsnos ir apmaudo aso-
čiai; premijuotas romanas. [By]
J. Gliauda [pseud.] Chicago, Ill.,
Lietuviškos knygos klubas, 1969.
304 p. PG8749.G6L5 PU CaOONL

8496. --- Namai ant smėlio. [By]
J. Gliauda [pseud.] Chicago, Ill.
["Draugo" Bendradarbių klubas] 1952.
221 p. PG8749.G6 DLC CaOTU ICCC MB
PU

8497. --- Raidžių pasėliai. [By]
J. Gliauda [pseud. Chicago, Ill.]
Lietuviškos knygos klubas [1955]
311 p. PG8749.G6R3 DLC ICCC OKentU
PU

8498. --- Šikšnosparnių sostas;
premijuotas romanas. [By] J. Glau-
da [pseud. Chicago, Ill.] Lietuviškos knygos klubas [1960] 268 p.
PG8749.G6S5 DLC CaOTU OCl PU

8499. GRAŽULIS, Balys. Brydė ru-
giuose; novelės. Tübingen, Ger.,
Patria, 1947. 190 p. 891.92.G799.B
PU CaOONL DLC ICCC OCl

8500. --- Sudužęs vaizdas. [Lon-
don] Nida [1958] 244 p. (Nidos
knygų klubo leidinys, nr. 25)
PG8721.G62S8 DLC ICCC

8501. GRICIUS, Augustinas. Kepu-
rės nenukelsim. [Vilnius, Vaga,
1971] 240 p. PG8721.G635K4 PU

8502. --- Vyrai, nesijuokit! Kaunas, "Naujo žodžio" leidinys, 1929.
159 p. 891.927.G ICCC

8503. --- --- [Another edition]
Vilnius, Vaga, 1969. 424 p.
PG8721.G635V9 PU CtPAM OKentU

8504. --- Žmonės; apsakymai. Vilnius, VGLL, 1960. 429 p.
PG8721.G635Z4 DLC

8505. GRIGAITYTĖ, Kotryna. Veidu
prie žemės; novelės. [Chicago, Ill.]
Lietuviškos knygos klubas [1962]
205 p. PG8721.G64V4 DLC CaOONL CtY
OCl PU

8506. GRINCEVIČIUS, Česlovas. Ge-
roji vasara. Chicago, Ill., Draugas, 1970. 261 p. PG8721.G66G4 PU

8507. --- Vidurnakčio vargonai;
neįtikėtinos istorijos. [Chicago,
Ill.] Lietuviškos knygos klubas
[1953] 131 p. PG8721.G65V5 DLC
CaOONL ICCC MB OCl PU

8508. GRUŠAS, Juozas. Karjeris-
tai; romanas. [2. leidimas. Lon-
don] Nida [1956] 2 v. (Nidos knygų
klubo leidinys, nr. 14-15)
PG8721.G7K3 DLC CtTMF NN OCl PU

8509. --- --- [Another edition]
Vilnius, Vaga, 1971. 288 p.
PG8721.G7K3 1971 PU

8510. --- Pabučiavimas; novelės.
[n.p., Gabija, 1953] 155 p.
PG8721.G7P3 DLC NN PU

8511. --- Rūstybės šviesa. Vilnius, Vaga, 1969. 196 p. illus.
PG8721.G7R8 PU CaAEU CaOTU

8512. --- Sunki ranka. Kaunas,
Sakalas, 1937. 205 p.
891.92.G925S PU CtTMF ICCC

8513. --- Žmogus be veido. Vilnius, Vaga, 1970. 200 p.
PG8721.G7Z6 CaOTU

8514. GUDAITIS-GUZEVIČIUS, Aleksandras. Broliai. Iliustravo medžio raižiniais V. Galdikas. [Vil-
niuje] VGLL, 1951. 4 v. illus.
PG8721.G8B7 DLC

8515. --- Juodoji torpeda; apysaka. Vilnius, Vaga, 1966. 191 p.
PG8721.G8J8 PU

8516. --- --- 2. papildytas leidimas. Vilnius, Vaga, 1970. 245 p.
PG8721.G8J8 1970 PU

8517. --- Kalvio Ignoto teisybė.
Kaunas, 1948-49. 2 v.

891.92.G999.K PU

8518. --- Sąmokslas; romanas.
Vilnius, Vaga, 1964-65.   2 v.
PG8721.G8S2 1964 DLC PU

8519. --- Spalio komisaras; istorinė apysaka. Vilnius, Vaga, 1967.
357 p. PG8721.G8S65 PU

8520. IGNATAVIČIUS, Eugenijus.
Pradalgių tyla. Vilnius, Vaga,
1971. 176 p. PG8722.19.G5P7 PU

8521. IGNATONIS, Jeronimas. ...ir
nevesk į pagundą; premijuotas romanas. [Chicago, Ill.] Lietuviškos
knygos klubas [1958] 314 p.
PG8749.I35I7 DLC CtTMF PU

8522. --- Lūžiai; romanas. [Chi-
cago, Ill.] Lietuviškos knygos klubas [1963] 301 p. PG8749.I35L8
DLC CaAEU CaOTU PU

8523. INČIŪRA, Kazys. Ant ežerė-
lio rymojau...; romanas. Kaunas,
Sakalo bendrovės leidinys, 1930.
324 p. 891.923.I ICCC

8524. --- Obelys žydi. Kaunas,
Sakalo bendrovės leidinys, 1937.
348 p. 891.923.I ICCC

8525. JACKEVIČIUS, Mykolas. Bran-
denburgo vartai; romanas. Vilnius,
VGLL, 1964. 193 p. PG8722.2.A31B7
PU

8526. JAKUBĖNAS, Kazys. Bundanti
žemė; rinktinė. Vilnius, Vaga,
1972. 318 p. PG8721.J25B8 PU

8527. JANKUS, Jurgis. Naktis ant
morų; romanas. Tübingen, Ger., Patria, 1948. 345 p. illus.
PG8749.J33N3 CaAEU CaOONL CtTMF ICCC
PU

8528. --- Namas geroj gatvėj.
[Nördlingen, Ger.] Venta [1954] 266
p. PG8749.J3N3 DLC NjN ICCC PU

8529. --- Paklydę paukščiai.
[Brooklyn, N.Y.] Gabija [1952] 2 v.
PG8749.J3P3 DLC CaAEU CaOTU CtTMF
ICCC IU OCl PU

8530. --- Pirmasis rūpestis. [Chi-
cago, Lietuviškos knygos klubas,
1955] 213 p. PG8749.J3P5 DLC
CaOONL CaOTU CtTMF ICCC OCl PU

8531. --- Po raganos kirviu.
[Brooklyn, N.Y.] Gabija [1953] 102
p. illus. PG8749.J3P6 DLC OCl

8532. --- Senas kareivis Matatu-
tis; pasakojimas apie nepaprastą
žemaitį kuris daug nuostabių dalykų

padarė, tik nepadarė vieno, kurį
tikrai turėjo padaryti. [Chicago,
Ill.] Terra [1955] 239 p.
PG8749.J3S4 DLC ICCC OCl OKentU PU

8533. JANKUS, Martynas. Žiemos
vakare adynėlė. Broliams lietuwi-
ninkams ant naudos ir pamokslo suraszė Jankų Martynas. Tilžėje,
Kasztu Jankų Martyno, 1895. 139 p.
891.92.J255Z PU

8534. JANUŠYTE, Liūnė. Iki pasi-
matymo! Feljetonai. Vilnius, Vaga,
1964. 126 p. PG8722.2.A57.I52 DLC
IU MH

8535. --- Važiuojam. Kaunas, Sakalas, 1936. 188 p. 891.923J ICCC

8536. JASIUKAITIS, Konstantinas.
Basi vaikai; apsakymai. Vilnius,
Vaga, 1969. 243 p. PG8721.J375B3
PU CaAEU

8537. JOERG, Irena (Matulionytė).
Laimės ieškotojai; novelės. [Lon-
don] Nida [1962] 262 p. (Nidos
knygų klubo leidinys, nr. 36)
PG8721.J6L3 DLC ICCC PU

8538. --- Taika ateina į slėnį;
romanas. [London] Nida [1952] 138
p. 891.92.J595T PU OCl

8539. JONYNAS, Antanas. Laimės
ratas. Vilnius, Vaga, 1965. 261 p.
PG8722.2.O5L3 DLC IU MH

8540. --- Paskutinė vakarienė; satyrinė apysaka. Vilnius, VGLL, 1962.
133 p. PG8722.2.O5P3 DLC

8541. --- Puodai savo vietose; satyra ir humoras. Vilnius, Vaga,
1969. 427 p. PG8722.2.O5P8 PU
CaOTU

8542. --- Šventieji žiedžia puo-
dus; satyrinė apysaka. Vilnius,
Vaga, 1965. 213 p. illus.
PG8721.J66S9 DLC NN

8543. --- Tu-mano kraujas gyvas.
[Apipavidalinimas ir iliustracijos
A. Vitulskio] Vilnius, VGLL, 1961.
177 p. illus. PG8722.2.O5T8 DLC
MH NN

8544. JURKŪNAS, Ignas. Aš dar
kartą grįžtu. [By] Ignas Šeinius
[pseud.] Kaunas, 1937. 291 p.
891.93.S16 CtTMF ICCC

8545. ---.Bangos siaučia; apysaka.
[By] Ignas Šeinius [pseud.] 1914.
211 p. OCl

8546. --- Kriaušės dukterys. [By]
Ignas Šeinius [pseud.] Kaunas,

1939. 100 p. 891.93.Š22 CtTMF

8547. --- Kuprelis; apysaka. [By] Ignas Šeinius [pseud.] Brooklyn, N.Y., Vienybės lietuvininkų, 1913. 258 p. 891.92.J979K 1913 PU ICCC NjP OCl

8548. --- --- [Another edition] Kaunas, 1932. 214 p. 891.93.Š17 CtTMF

8549. --- --- [Another edition. n.p.] 1951. 162 p. PG8721.J77K8 1951 CaOTU CtTMF

8550. --- Siegfried Immerselbe atsijaunina; romanas. [By] Ignas Šeinius [pseud.] Kaunas, 1934. 327 p. 891.93.Š20 CtTMF ICCC OCl

8551. --- Šventoji Inga; novelės. [By] Ignas Šeinius [pseud.] Chicago, Ill., 1952. 226 p. 891.93.Š23 CtTMF

8552. --- Tėviškės padangėje. [By] Ignas Šeinius [pseud.] Kaunas, 1938. 264 p. 891.93.Š21 CtTMF

8553. --- Vasaros vaišės. Kuprelis. [By] Ignas Šeinius [pseud.] Vilnius, Jono Rinkevičiaus leidinys, 1914. 140 p. 891.923J ICCC

8554. --- --- [Another edition] Vilnius, Vaga, 1970. 299 p. PG8721.J77V3 1970 PU

8555. --- Vyskupas ir velnias; apysakos. [Los Angeles, Calif. Lietuvių dienos] 1959. 230 p. PG8721.J77V9 DLC CaAEU CaOTU CtTMF CtY NN OCl OKentU PU

8556. JURKUS, Paulius. Ant Vilnelės tilto; Vilniaus legendos. Chicago, Ill., Lietuviškos knygos klubas, 1968. 200 p. PG8721.J8A55 PU CaAEU CaOONL OKentU

8557. --- Pavasaris prie Varduvos. [Chicago, Ill., Lietuviškos knygos klubas, 1954] 175 p. 891.92.J982P PU CaOONL

8558. --- Smilgaičių akvarelė; premijuotas romanas. [Chicago, Ill.] Lietuviškos knygos klubas [1957] 527 p. PG8721.J8S6 DLC ICCC NN OCl PU

8559. KAIRYS, Anatolijus. Ištikimoji žolė; romanas. [Chicago, Ill.] 1971. 254 p. PG8721.K217 PU

8560. KARPAVIČIUS, Kazimieras S. Juodas karžygis; senovės pasaka. Cleveland, Ohio, Spauda "Dirvos", 1927. 2 v. in 1. 891.92.K148J PU

8561. --- Jūros merga; istoriška apysaka. Iliustravo T.J. Mažeika. Cleveland, Ohio, Spauda "Dirvos", 1931. 298 p. illus. PZ63.K3 DLC PU

8562. --- Merunas, juodo karžgio sūnus; apysaka iš Apuolės išgriovimo laikų. Cleveland, Ohio, Spauda "Dirvos", 1934. 512 p. PG8749.K3M4 DLC ICCC PU

8563. KAŠAUSKAS, Romualdas. Senojo miesto amžius; apysaka. Vilnius, Vaga, 1966. 182 p. PG8722.21A715S4 DLC

8564. --- Šiaurės krantas. [Iliustravo A. Skliutauskaitė] Vilnius, Vaga, 1967. 80 p. illus. PG8722.2.A715S5 DLC

8565. --- Žmonės iš arti; apsakymai. Vilnius, VGLL, 1961. 169 p. illus. PG8721.K285Z2 DLC NN

8566. KATILIŠKIS, Marius. Išėjusiems negrįžti. [Chicago, Ill.] Terra [c1958] 537 p. PG8721.K29.I8 DLC NN PU

8567. --- Miškais ateina ruduo; romanas. [Chicago, Ill.] Terra [1957] 514 p. PG8721.K29M5 DLC NN PU

8568. --- Prasilenkimo valanda; novelės. [Schweinfurt, Ger.] Liudas Vismantas [1948] 247 p. 891.92.K158P PU NN

8569. --- Šventadienis už miesto. [Chicago, Ill., Terra, 1963] 355 p. PG8721.K29S9 DLC CaOTU PU

8570. --- Užuovėja. [Viršelis, titulinis puslapis ir iliustracijos Romo Viesulo. Chicago, Ill.] Terra [1952] 360 p. illus. PG8721.K29U9 DLC CaAEU CaOTU OCl PU

8571. KAUPAS, Julius Viktoras. Daktaras Kripštukas pragare, ir kitos nemažiau įdomios pasakos, surašytos slaptose Kauno miesto kronikose. [Iliustravo Adolfas Vaičaitis. Freiburgas, Ger.] P. Abelkio lietuviškų knygų leidykla [1948] 101 p. illus. PZ70.L5K3 DLC CaOONL ICCC InNd OCl PU

8572. KEMEŽAITĖ, Birutė. Sudiev! Aš išeinu...; romanas. [Chicago, Ill.] Laisvosios Lietuvos knygų leidykla, 1971. 295 p. PG8749.K43S8 PU

8573. KORSAKAS, Kostas. Paukščiai grįžta. [Kaunas] VGLL, 1945. 206 p. PG8721.K6P3 PU

8574. KORSAKIENĖ, Halina (Nastop-kaitė). Gimtajam mieste; apsakymai. Kaunas, VGLL, 1949. 891.92.K845G PU

8575. --- Neapšviestoji mėnulio pusė; apsakymai. Vilnius, Vaga, 1969. 221 p. PG8721.K8N4 CaAEU

KRALIKAUSKAS, Juozas. Min-daugo nužudymas; premijuotas roma-nas. Chicago, Ill., 1964. See entry no. 6276.

8576. --- Šviesa lange; romanas. London, Nida, 1960. 248 p. (Nidos knygos klubas, nr. 29) 891.92.K852S PU CtTMF OCl

8577. --- Titnago ugnis; premi-juotas romanas. [Chicago, Ill.] Lietuviškos knygos klubas [1962] 205 p. PG8721.K65T5 DLC CaAEU CaOONL PU

8578. --- Urviniai žmonės. [Chi-cago, Ill.] Lietuviškos knygos klubas [1954] 280 p. PG8721.K65U7 DLC CaOONL OCl PU

8579. --- Vaišvilkas; romanas. [Chicago, Ill.] Lietuviškos kny-gos klubas, 1971. 234 p. PG8721.K65V3 PU

8580. KRĖVĖ-MICKEVIČIUS, Vincas. Bedievis. [V. Galdiko medžio rai-žiniai] Vilnius, Vaga, 1966. 46 p. illus. PG8721.K7B4 1966 DLC PU

8581. --- Bobulės vargai. [Lino raižiniai A. Kučo] Vilnius, Vaga, 1968. 165 p. PG8721.K7B6 1968 PU

8582. --- Likimo žaismas. Vil-nius, Vaga, 1965. 269 p. PG8721.K7L5 1965 PU DLC IU MH NN

8583. --- Raganius; prieškarinių laikų sodžiaus gyvenimo šešėliai. 3. leidimas. [Nördlingen, Ger.] Sudavijos leidinys [1948] 192 p. PG8721.K7R3 1948 DLC OCl PU

8584. --- --- [Another edition] Vilnius, VGLL, 1958. 276 p. illus. PG8721.K7R3 1958 DLC PU

8585. --- Raganius. Žentas. Vil-nius, Vaga, 1968. 314 p. PG8721.K7K3 1968 PU NN PPULC

8586. --- Rytų pasakos. [Chicago, Ill.] Terra [1954] 216 p. PG8721.K7R9 1954 PU DLC NN

8587. --- Šiaudinėj pastogėj. Kaunas, 1921-22. (In His Raštai, v.2-3). 891.92.K889S PU OCl

8588. --- --- 3. leidimas. Augs-burg, Ger., Sudavia, 1948. 315 p. PG8721.K7S52 1948 DLC CtTMF PU

8589. --- --- [Another edition] Vilnius, VGLL, 1964. 235 p. PG8721.K7S5 1964 DLC IU MH MiD NN

8590. KRUMINAS, Juozas. Naktis viršum širdies; vieno susitikimo istorija. Brooklyn, N.Y., Gabija, 1950. 141 p. 891.92.K944N PU ICCC OKentU

8591. --- Šeštasis medis; romanas. [London] Nida [1963] 367 p. (Nidos knygų klubo leidinys nr. 45) PG8721.K77S4 DLC CaAEU OKentU PU

8592. KUDIRKA, Vincas. Satyros. [Nördlingen, Ger.] L.T.B. Gunzen-hauseno skyrius, 1947. 213 p. illus. PG8721.K8S3 DLC PU

8593. LANDSBERGIS, Algirdas. Il-goji naktis; novelės. [London] Nida [c1956] 175 p. (Nidos knygų klubo leidinys nr. 16) PG8721.L314 DLC CaAEU CaOTU CtTMF OKentU PU

8594. --- Kelionė; premijuotas romanas. [Chicago, Ill., Draugo bendradarbių klubo leidinys, 1954] 258 p. PG8721.L3K4 DLC CtTMF IU OCl PU

8595. LANKAUSKAS, Romualdas. Džiazo vežimas; apysaka, novelės. Vilnius, Vaga, 1971. 149 p. PG8721.L315D9 PU

8596. --- Kai nutyla trompetas. Vilnius, VGLL, 1961. 125 p. PG8721.L315K3 DLC

8597. --- Klajojantis smėlis; [apysaka, novelės]. Vilnius, VGLL, 1960. 193 p. PG8721.L315K5 DLC PU

8598. --- Nuo ryto iki vakaro. Vilnius, Vaga, 1965. 322 p. PG8721.L315N8 DLC

8599. --- Pilka šviesa. Vilnius, Vaga, 1968. 148 p. illus. PG8721.L315P5 PU DLC

8600. --- Šiaurės vitražai; nove-lės. Vilnius, Vaga, 1970. 216 p. PG8721.L31S5 CaOTU PU

8601. --- Vidury dedelio lauko; romanas. Vilnius, VGLL, 1962. 157 p. PG8721.L315V5 DLC MH PU

8602. LAUCEVIČIUS, Bronius. Apsa-kymai. [By] Br. Vargšas. [pseud.] Vilnius, VGLL, 1962. 304 p. ports. PG8721.L348A6 DLC CtPAM MH PU

8603. LIULEVIČIENĖ, Monika. Aidas tarp dangoraižių; romanas. O. Nendrė [pseud.] Chicago, Ill., 1968. 365 p. PG8749.L5A5 PU DLC

8604. --- Antroji banga; romanas. O. Nendrė [pseud.] Chicago, Ill., 1970. 202 p. PG8749.L5A53 PU

8605. LUKINSKAS, Romualdas. Mano draugai. Vilnius, VGLL, 1958. 189 p. PG8722.22.U4M3 PU

8606. --- Mėlynas laukas. Vilnius, Vaga, 1971. 619 p. PG8722.22.U4M4 PU

8607. LUKŠYTĖ, Agnė. Kalnų velnias; novelės. [Sidney, Australia] H. Meiliūnas, 1970] 172 p. PG8722.22.U5K3 PU

8608. MAČIUKEVIČIUS, Jonas. Rojaus kampelis; apysaka. Vilnius, Vaga, 1971. 251 p. PG8722.23.A295R6 PU

8609. MARCINKEVIČIUS, Jonas. Benjaminas Kordušas; [romanas. Kaunas, Spaudos fondas, 1937] 335 p. 891.93.M17 CtTMF NN

8610. --- --- [Another edition. Kaunas] VGLL, 1945. 891.92.M334B PU

8611. --- --- [Another edition] Vilnius, VGLL, 1960. 282 p. illus. PG8721.M34B4 1960 DLC OC1 OKentU

8612. --- Gyvenimas dega; rinktinės apysakos. [Kaune] VGLL [1946] 163 p. PG8721.M34G9 DLC

8613. --- Sukaustyti latrai; romanas. Kaunas, Sakalo b-vės, 1931. 219 p. 491.922.M334 PU CtTMF

8614. --- Pušis kuri juokėsi; apysaka. Vilnius, VGLL, 1961. 178 p. PG8721.M35P87 DLC

8615. MARGERIS, Algirdas. Čikagos šešėliai; žiaurios tikrovės vaizdai. Chicago, Ill., "Naujienos", 1952. 316 p. illus. 891.92.M336C PU OC1 OKentU

8616. --- Mėlynos akys; tikrovės vaizdai. Vilnius, VGLL, 1961. 363 p. PG8749.M3M4 DLC

8617. --- Mirties kvieslys; romanas. Vilnius, Vaga, 1966. 202 p. PG8722.23.A68M5 DLC

8618. --- Širdies rūmai; romanas. Chicago, Ill., Spaudė "Naujienos", 1951. 449 p. 891.92.M336Si PU

8619. --- Šliuptarniai; Amerikos lietuvių tautinio ir kultūrinio atgimimo laikų istorinis romanas. Chicago, Ill., 1949. 652 p. port. PG8749.M3S5 DLC CtTMF OKentU PU

8620. --- Už jūrų marių; romanas. Vilnius, VGLL, 1958. 410 p. NN

8621. MARKEVIČIUS, Anelius. Krizas Saulėtekis. Vilnius, VGLL, 1957. 164 p. PG8721.M355K7 PU

8622. --- Plakatas restorano lange. Vilnius, Vaga, 1967. 113 p. PG8721.M355P5 DLC PU

8623. --- Šūvis miške. Iliustravo J. Naginskaitė. Vilnius, VGLL, 1960. 289 p. illus. PG8721.M355S8 DLC

8624. --- Vaistininko duktė. Vilnius, VGLL, 1964. 118 p. PG8721.M355V3 DLC PU

8625. MARTINKUS, Vytautas. Akmenys; romanas. Vilnius, Vaga, 1972. 314 p. PG8722.23.A72A5 PU

8626. MARUKAS, K. Kam patekės saulė; romanas. Vilnius, Vaga, 1966. 221 p. illus. PG8721.M36K3 DLC NN PU

8627. --- Naktigonėje. [Vilnius] VGLL, 1953. 135 p. illus. PG8721.M36N3 DLC

8628. --- Žaliakalny šluoja gatves. Vilnius, VGLL, 1962. 351 p. PG8721.M36Z2 DLC PU

8629. MAZALAITĖ, Nelė. Apversta valtis. [Nördlingen, Ger.] Sudavija, 1948. 199 p. PG8721.M38A8 DLC CaAEU CaOTU CtTMF PU

8630. --- Gintariniai vartai; [pasakojimų rinkinys. Chicago, Ill., LKSD knygos klubas, 1952] 248 p. PG8721.M38 DLC CaOONL CtTMF MB NN OKentU PU

8631. --- Mėnuo vadinamas medaus; [apysaka. Brooklyn, N.Y.] Gabija [1951] 220 p. PG8721.M38M4 DLC OC1 PU

8632. --- Miestelis, kuris buvo mano. Brooklyn, N.Y., Darbininkas, 1966. 183 p. PG8721.M38M5 CaOTU PU

8633. --- Negęstis. Chicago, Ill., Lietuviškos knygos klubas [1955] 206 p. 891.92.M458N PU OC1

8634. --- Saulės takas. [Chicago, Ill., Lietuviškos knygos klubas, 1954] 417 p. PG8721.M38S37 DLC CaAEU CaOONL CtTMF OC1 PU

8635. MIKELINSKAS, Jonas. Lakštingala, pilkas paukštelis; apsakymai ir apysaka. Vilnius, Vaga, 1968. 286 p. PG8722.23.I35L3 PU OKentU

8636. --- O laikrodis eina; romanas. Vilnius, Vaga, 1966. 221 p. PG8722.23.I33O55 DLC

8637. --- Pažinai tu jį? Vilnius, VGLL, 1963. 157 p. PG8722.23.I35P3 DLC

8638. --- Rugpiūčio naktį; apsakymų rinktinė. Vilnius, Vaga, 1971. 377 p. PG8722.23.I35R8 PU

8639. --- Vandens nešėja; romanas. Vilnius, Vaga, 1964. 315 p. PG8722.23.I34V3 DLC IU MH

8640. --- Žiupsnis smėlio; apsakymai. Vilnius, Vaga, 1965. 199 p. illus. PG8722.23.I35Z39 DLC IU

8641. MILIŪNAS, Viktoras. Pirmoji meilė, arba nusikaltimas; apsakymai. Vilnius, Vaga, 1968. 257 p. PG8721.M47P5 PU

8642. MIRONAS, Andrius. Be namų; premijuota apysaka jaunimui. Chicago, Ill., JAV LB Kultūros fondas, 1970. 260 p. PG8721.M51B4 PU

8643. --- Naujas veidas; novelės. Chicago, Ill., Autoriaus leidinys, 1956. 273 p. 891.92.M675N PU

8644. MISEVIČIUS, Vytautas. Kryžiuočio kapas; apysaka. [Iliustravo Ulbikaitė] Vilnius, Vaga, 1966. 189 p. PG8722.23.I72K7 DLC

8645. --- Makaronda-anikonda; humoristiniai ir satyriniai apsakymai. Vilnius, Vaga, 1965. 167 p. PG8722.23.L72M3 PU

8646. --- Vampyrų maištas; dokumentinė apysaka. Vilnius, VGLL, 1963. 153 p. BX1775.L55M5 DLC

8647. --- Vėjas nuo marių. Vilnius, VPMLL, 1963. 84 p. PG8722.23.I72V4 DLC

8648. --- Žmonės praranda rojų. Vilnius, Mintis, 1964. 156 p. BX1775.L55M52 DLC

8649. MIZARA, Rojus. Algio Lumbio nuotykiai; romanas. Vilnius, VGLL, 1958. 300 p. 891.92.M699A PU OKentU

8650. --- Bernardo Gavelio klaida; romanas. Chicago, Ill., 1945. 351 p. 891.92.M699B PU OKentU

8651. --- --- [Another edition] Vilnius, VGLL, 1956. 285 p. (*QY)NN

8652. --- Mortos Vilkienės divorsas; romanas iš Amerikos lietuvių gyvenimo. Brooklyn, N.Y., 1936. 334 p. PG8749.M56M6 PU OKentU

8653. --- --- [Another edition] Vilnius, VGLL, 1955. 245 p. (*QY)NN

8654. --- Sliakeris; romanas iš Amerikos lietuvių gyvenimo. Brooklyn, N.Y., Laisvė, 1930. 891.92.M699S PU OKentU

8655. --- --- [Another edition] Vilnius, VGLL, 1956. 281 p. (*QY)NN

8656. --- Ūkanos; romanas. Brooklyn, N.Y., Laisvė, 1938. 342 p. 891.92.M699 PU OKentU

8657. --- --- [Another edition. Kaunas] VGLL, 1956. 270 p. (*QY)NN

8658. MORKUS, Albinas. Baltasis miestelis. Vilnius, Vaga, 1962. 225 p. PG8722.23.O7B3 DLC MH OKentU

8659. --- Susitikimas. Vilnius, Vaga, 1965. 133 p. PG8722.23.O7S9 DLC OKentU

8660. MYKOLAITIS, Vincas. Altorių šešėly. Kaunas, 1933-38. 3 v. PG8721.M9A67 CaOTU CtTMF

8661. --- --- [Another edition. Kaune] VGLL, 1946. 3 v. PG8721.M9A67 DLC NN

8662. --- --- [Another edition] Memmingen, Ger., 1951. 613 p. 891.92.M994A PU

8663. --- --- [Another edition. Vilnius, VGLL, 1967] 597 p. NN

8664. --- --- 5. leidimas. Vilnius, Vaga, 1971. 613 p. PG8721.M9A67 1971 PU

8666. --- Sukilėliai; kovų dėl žemės ir laisvės vaizdai, 1861-1864. Vilnius, VGLL, 1957-1959. 2 v. illus. PG8721.M9S8 DLC OKentU PU

8667. --- --- [Another edition] Vilnius, Vaga, 1967. 682 p. PG8721.M9S8 1967 DLC

8668. NAREČIONIS, Romualdas. Pasmerkimas; apysaka. Vilnius, Vaga, 1967. 183 p. PG8722.24.A7P3 DLC OKentU

8669. --- Vėžys; humoreskos. Vilnius, Vaga, 1965. 75 p.
PG8722.24.A7V4 DLC

8670. NARVYDAS, Pranas. Gimtinės
takais; pasakojimai. Parinko Juozas
Valakas. [New York, N.Y., 1968]
243 p. PG8749.N37G5 PU

8671. NAUJOKAITIS, Pranas. Ilūžę
tiltai; romanas. [Brooklyn, N.Y.]
Vaga, 1961. 237 p. PG8721.N35.I4
DLC OCl PU

8672. --- Pasisėjau žalią rūtą;
romanas. [Brooklyn, N.Y.] Darbininkas, 1972. 232 p. PG8721.N35P3 PU

8673. --- Upeliai negrįžta į kalnus; [romanas. Chicago, Ill.]
Lietuviškos knygos klubas [1959]
510 p. PG8721.N35U6 DLC CtY CtTMF
NN PU

8674. --- Žydinčios dienos; premijuotas romanas. Chicago, Ill.,
Lietuviškos knygos klubas, 1967.
250 p. 891.92.N224Z PU

8675. NĖRIS, Salomėja. Pavasario
daina. Iliustracijos D. Tarabildi-
nės. [Vilnius] VGLL [1953] 35 p.
illus. PG8721.N4P3 DLC

8676. NEVERAVIČIUS, Fabijonas.
Blaškomos liepsnos; istorinis buities
romanas. [London] Nida [1959]- .
2 v. (Nidos knygų klubo leidinys
nr. 26) PG8721.N44B5 DLC CaAEU
CtTMF NN PU

8677. --- Dienovidžio sūtemos;
apysakos ir novelė. Kassel-Mattenberg, Ger., Aistia, 1949. 187 p.
PG8721.N44D5 DLC NN PU

8678. ORINTAITĖ, Petronėlė. Dau-
biškės inteligentai; romanas. [Lon-
don] Nida [1962] 2 v. (Nidos knygų
klubo leidinys nr. 39-40)
PG8721.07D3 DLC CaAEU CaOTU CtTMF NN
OCl PU

8679. --- Grožvilės meilė; apsakymai ir apybraižos. [London] Nida
[1955] 165 p. 491.92.0r44G PU
CaAEU NjN OCl

8680. --- Liepalotų medynuose.
[London] Nida [1971] 216 p.
PG8721.07L5 PU

8681. --- Marti iš miesto; novelės. Tübingen, Ger., Patria, 1949.
90 p. 891.92.0r44M PU CaQONL CtTMF

8682. --- Paslėpta žaizda, jauna-
martės takas; romanas. 2 leidimas.
[Chicago, Ill.] Nemunas [1955] 179
p. 891.92.0r44P PU CtTMF NjN OCl

8683. --- Vitrakių vaikai. [Iliu-
travo P. Osmolskis. By] Palė Vai-
vorytė [pseud. Bielefeld, Ger.]
1952. 111 p. illus. (PLB Vokietijos krašto valdybos knygų leidyklos leidinys, nr. 3) 891.92.0r44V
PU

8684. PAKŠTIENĖ, Janina. Sutemos;
dienoraštiniai posmai. [By] Janina
Narūnė-Pakštinė. [pseud. Miami,
Fla., Išleido J. Pakštinė, 1963]
48 p. PG8749.P33S8 PU

8685. PALECKIS, Justas. Gyvenimas prasideda. Vilnius, Vaga, 1967.
PG8721.P3G89 DLC PU

8686. --- Paskutinis caras. Kaunas, Sakalas, 1937. 2 v. in 1. OCl

8687. PAUKŠTELIS, Juozas. Apyniai
kvepėjo; apsakymai. Vilnius, Vaga,
1971. 432 p. PG8721.P37A7 PU

8688. --- Čia mūsų namai; romanas.
Vilnius, Vaga, 1969. 453 p. illus.
PG8721.P37C5 PU CaAEU OKentU

8689. --- Jaunystė; romanas. Vilnius, Vaga, 1967. 413 p.
PG8721.P37J3 DLC NN PU

8690. --- Kaimynai; romanas. [2
leidimas. n.p.] Talka [1956] 238 p.
PG8721.P37K3 1956 DLC CtTMF NN
OKentU(1966 ed.) PU

8691. --- Netekėk, saulele!; Romanas. Vilnius, Vaga, 1968. 473 p.
PG8721.P37N4 DLC PU

8692. --- Pirmieji metai; romanas.
Vilnius, Vaga, 1965. 350 p. port.
PG8721.P37P5 1965 PU CtTMF IU MH NN
OCl

8693. PAŽĖRAITĖ, Karolė. Anapilio
papėdėje; romanas. [Chicago, Ill.,
Lietuviškos knygos klubas, 1971]
286 p. PG8721.P38A5 PU

8694. --- Didvyrių žemė. São
Paulo [J. Kaseliūnas] 1954. 133 p.
891.92.P299D PU

8695. --- Nusidėjėlė; apysaka.
2. laida. Adelaide, Australijos
lietuvis, 1952. 254 p.
PG8721.P38N8 1952 DLC PU

8696. PEČKAUSKAITĖ, Marija. Į
šviesą. [By] Šatrijos Ragana
[pseud.] Vilnius, 1908. 50 p.
891.93.S3 CtTMF

8697. --- Irkos tragėdija. [Pa-
ruošė A. Zalatorius] Vilnius, Vaga,
1969. 352 p. illus., ports.
PG8721.P4.I7 1969 PU CaAEU CtPAM

8698. --- Istorijos pasakos. [By]
Šatrijos Ragana [pseud.] Seinai,
1907. 54 p. 891.93.Š5 CtTMF

8699. --- Pančiai. [By] Šatrijos
Ragana [pseud.] Kaunas, Rašto, 1920.
45 p. 891.92.P336Pa PU CtTMF CtY
OCl

8700. --- Saulei nusileidžiant;
Iš mūsų karionės; Kalėdų vakaras.
[By] Šatrijos Ragana [pseud.] Shenandoah, Pa., 1908. 62 p.
891.93.Š2 CtTMF

8701. --- Sename dvare; apysaka.
[By] Šatrijos Ragana [pseud.] 3.
leidimas. Toronto, Ont., Baltija,
1951. 176 p. (Baltijos leidinys
nr. 1) PG9048.P4S4 1951 DLC CaOTU
OCl

8702. --- --- [Another edition]
Vilnius, Vaga, 1969. 430 p.
CtPAM PU

8703. --- Viktutė. [By] Šatrijos
Ragana [pseud.] Shenandoah, Pa.,
1903. 90 p. 891.93.Š4 CtTMF

8704. --- --- [Another edition.
London] Nida [1964] 143 p. (Nidos
knygų klubo leidinys, nr. 50)
PG8721.P4V5 1964 DLC CaOTU PU

8705. --- Vincas Stonis. [By]
Šatrijos Ragana [pseud.] Vilnius,
"Vilniaus žinios" spaustuvė, 1906.
143 p. 891.92.P336V PU

8706. PETKEVIČAITĖ, Gabrielė. Ad
astra; dviejų tomų romanas. Kaunas,
1933. 2 v. in 1. 891.93.P9 CtTMF
PU

8707. --- --- [Another edition.
Pabaigos žodis: A. Vaitiekūnienė.
Paruošė A. Žirgulys] Vilnius, Vaga,
1967. 532 p. (Her Raštai, v.3) MH

8708. --- Karo meto dienoraštis,
1914-1916. Kaunas, 1925. 178 p.
891.93.P8 CtTMF PU

8709. --- --- [Another edition]
Kaunas, Varpo b-vės leidinys, 1927-
1931. 2 v. OCl

8710. --- --- [Another edition.
Paruošė A. Žirgulys] Vilnius, Vaga,
1966. 839 p. illus. (Her Raštai,
v.2) MH

8711. --- Krislai; karo meto dienoraštis. [By] Gabrielė Petkevičaitė-Bitė. [Įvadas: P. Česnulevi-
čiutė] Vilnius, Vaga, 1966. 772
p. illus. (Her Raštai, v.1)
D640.P49 CaAEU DLC MH PU

8712. --- Laiškai. [By] Gabrielė
Petkevičaitė-Bitė. [pseud.] Vil-
nius, Vaga, 1968. 550 p. (Her
Raštai, v.6) D640.P465 CaAEU DLC
MH PU

8713. --- Pasikalbėjimai. [Įva-
das: J. Jurginis. Surinko ir paruošė A. Žirgulys] Vilnius, Vaga,
1967. 780 p. (Her Raštai, v.4) MH

8714. PETKEVIČIUS, Vytautas.
Apie duoną, meilę ir šautuvą; romanas. Vilnius, Vaga, 1967. 577
p. illus. PG8722.26.E8A8 DLC PU

8715. --- Baltas šešėlis; apsakymai. Vilnius, 1970. 244 p.
PG8722.26.E8B3 PU OKentU

8716. --- Ko klykia gervės; apy-
saka. Piešiniai E. Žiauberio.
Vilnius, VGLL, 1963. 302 p. illus.
PG8722.26.E8K6 DLC

8717. --- Speiguoti pavasariai;
apsakymai. Vilnius, Vaga, 1965.
376 p. PG8722.26.E8S6 DLC IU MH

8718. PETRĖNAS, Juozas. Vilniaus
rūbas; romanas. London, Nida, 1965.
495 p. (Nidos knygų klubo leidinys,
nr. 60) At head of title: Petr.
Tarulis. PG8721.P4527V5 DLC CaOTU

8719. PIETARIS, Vincas. Algimantas, arba Lietuviai XIII szimtmetyje.
Istoriszka apysaka. Shenandoah, Pa.
Lietuvių katalikų spaudos bendrijos
spaustuvėje, 1904-1905. 5 v. in 1.
891.92.P618 PU CtTMF NN(1 v.)

8720. --- --- [Another edition]
Kaunas, 1921-22. 2 v. (His Raštai,
v.3-4) 891.92.P618 1921 PU

8721. --- Algimantas; istorinė
apysaka. 4. leidimas. [Nördlingen,
Ger.] Suduva, 1948. 2 v. illus.,
port. PG8721.P5A68 1948 DLC OKentU

8722. POCIUS, Algirdas. Šešiolika
raktų; apsakymai. Vilnius, VGLL,
1960. 168 p. illus. PG8721.P6S4
DLC

8723. --- Verpetas; apsakymai.
Vilnius, VGLL, 1963. 185 p.
PG8721.P6V4 DLC MH

8724. POLIS, Algimantas. Tik
viena naktis; apsakymai ir apysaka.
Vilnius, Vaga, 1971. 154 p.
PG8722.26.O5T5 PU

8725. POŽĖRA, Juozas. Auksas;
dvi apysakos. Vilnius, Vaga, 1971.
250 p. PG8722.26.O9A8 PU

8726. --- Baltos saulės diena;

medžiotojo užrašai. [Dailininkas
A. Tarabilda. Vilnius, Mintis,
1966] 162 p. PG8722.26.09B3 DLC
NN

8727. --- Man vaidenasi arkliai;
apsakymai. Vilnius, Vaga, 1967.
128 p. PG8722.26.09M3 PU DLC NN

8728. --- Mano teismas; apysaka.
Vilnius, Vaga, 1968. 234 p.
PG8722.26.09M33 PU DLC

8729. --- Mano vienintelis rūpestis. Vilnius, Vaga, 1967. 261 p.
PG8722.26.09M35 DLC PU

8730. PŠIBILIAUSKIENĖ, Sofija
(Ivanauskaitė). Ir pražuvo kaip
sapnas; apysakos. [By] Lazdynų
Pelėda [pseud. Kaune] VGLL [1947]
305 p. PG8721.P7.I7 DLC NN PU

8731. --- Klajūnas. [Bitėnai, M.
Jankus] 1903. 63 p. (Kudirkos
iždas, nr. 4.) NN

8732. --- --- [Another edition]
Vilnius, Vaga, 1967. 316 p.
PG8721.P7K5 PU

8733. --- Motulė paviliojo.
[Brooklyn, N.Y.] Gabija [1951] 43 p.
illus. PG8721.P7M6 DLC

8734. --- Pirmoji tarnystė.
[Kaune] VGLL [1947] 283 p.
PG8721.PA14 1947 DLC

8735. --- Stebuklingoji tošelė.
[Vilnius, VGLL, 1961] PG8721.P7S8
1961 DLC

8736. PUIDA, Kazys. Apysakos.
Brooklyn, N.Y., Spauda ir lėšos
Vienybės lietuvninkų, 1915. 237 p.
PG9119.P8 DLC CtTMF NN PU

8737. --- Ruduo. Knyga I. Vilnius, "Vilniaus Žinios", 1906. 112
p. 891.92.P963R PU

8738. --- Žemės giesmė; apysaka.
Dalis 1-2. Brooklyn, N.Y., Vienybės lietuvninkų, 1911-1913. 2 v.
(Its Raštų rinkinys, t.3)
891.92.P963Z PU CtTMF NN

8739. PŪKELEVIČIŪTĖ, Birutė. Aš-
tuoni lapai; premijuotas romanas.
Chicago, Ill., Lietuviškos knygos
klubas, 1956. 392 p. 891.92.P967A
PU CtTMF OCl OKentU

8740. --- Metūgės. [Toronto, Ont.,
Baltija] 1952. 95 p. 891.92.P967M
PU

8741. --- Rugsėjo šeštadienis;
premijuotas romanas. [Chicago, Ill.]
Lietuviškos knygos klubas, 1970.
237 p. PG8749.P8R8 DLC CaOONL PU

8742. RADAITIS, Vytautas. Kryžiai lieka šešėly; pasakojimai apie
kunigus. Vilnius, VGLL, 1962. 118
p. PG8722.28.A3K7 DLC PU

8743. --- Mano Galilėjus. Vilnius, Vaga, 1965. 142 p. illus.
PG8722.28.A3M3 DLC

8744. RAMONAS, Vincas. Dailinin-
kas Rauba. [2. laida. Cleveland,
Ohio] Viltis [1963] 240 p.
PG8721.R3D3 DLC NN PU

8745. --- Dulkės raudonam saulė-
leidy; romanas. [Chicagoje, Liet.
knygos klubas, 1951] 306 p.
PG8749.R3D8 DLC CtTMF MB OKentU PU

8746. --- Kryžiai; romanas. [Tü-
bingen, Ger.] Patria, 1947. 286 p.
PG8721.R3K7 DLC CaOONL CtTMF OCl
OKentU PU

8747. --- Miglotas rytas; apysakos. [Chicago, Ill.] Lietuviškos
knygos klubas [1960] 166 p.
PG8721.R3M5 DLC CaOONL CaOTU NN PU

8748. RIMKEVIČIUS, Vytautas. Kaimo kronikos. [Dailininkas V. Kali-
nauskas] Vilnius, Vaga, 1967. 349
p. illus. PG8722.28.I58K3 DLC NN
PU

8749. RŪKAS, Antanas. Sužaliotie-
ji; romanas. [London] Nida [c1958]
245 p. (Nidos knygų klubo leidinys,
nr.24) PG8721.R9S8 DLC CtTMF PU

8750. RŪTA, Alė, pseud. Broliai;
romanas. [London] Nida [1961] 319
p. (Nidos knygų leidinys, nr.32)
PG9119.R8B7 DLC PU

8751. --- Duktė; apysaka. [Hanover,
Ger.] Bendrija, 1953. 249 p.
891.92.N147D PU NjN OCl PP

8752. --- Į saulėtekį; romanas.
London, Nida, 1960. 298 p.
891.92.N147.I PU

8753. --- Kelias į kairę; premijuotas romanas iš JAV senosios kartos lietuvių gyvenimo. [Cleveland,
Ohio] Viltis [1964] 248 p.
PG9119.R8K4 DLC CaOTU PU

8754. --- Likimo keliu; novelės.
Göttingen, Ger., Atžalynas, 1947.
140 p. 891.92.N147L PU OKentU

8755. --- Motinos rankos. [Chi-
cago, Ill.] Lietuviškos knygos klubas [1961] 397 p. (Her Didžioji
meilė, 4) PG9119.R83 DLC CaOONL PU

8756. --- Priesaika; romanas. [Chicago, Ill.] Lietuviškos knygos klubas [19-] PG9119.R8P7 DLC CLU CtY MH

8757. --- Trumpa diena; premijuotas romanas. [Chicago, Ill., Lietuviškos knygos klubas, 1955] 434 p. 891.92.N147P PU CaOONL OC1 PP

8758. --- Vieniši pasauliai; romanas. Chicago, Ill., Lietuviškos knygos klubas, 1968. 265 p. PG8721.R82V5 PU OKentU

8759. --- Žemės šauksmas; apysaka. Los Angeles, Calif., Lietuvių dienos, 1966. 307 p. 891.92.N147Z PU

8760. --- Žvaigždė viršum girios; romanas. [New York, N.Y., Darbininkas, 1960] 374 p. (Her Didžioji meilė, 1) PG9119.R86 DLC CaAEU OC1 PU

8761. SAJA, Kazys. Jurgis ant stogo, Palangoj ir kitur; humoristinė nuotykių apysaka. Vilnius, VGLL, 1963. 197 p. PG8722.29.A38J8 DLC MH NN

8762. --- Vaistai nuo strazdanų; apsakymai. Vilnius, VGLL, 1963. 197 p. PG8722.29.A38V3 PU

8763. ŠALČIUVIENĖ, Antanina (Gustaitytė) Juozukas; romanas. Kaunas [1933] 176 p. PG8721.S3J8 DLC

8764. --- Laiko laiptais; romanas. Kaunas [1931] 311 p. PG8721.S3L3 DLC CtTMF

8765. --- Vingiai; romanas. Kaunas [1932] 294 p. PG8721.S3V5 DLC

8766. --- Voras; romanas. [Kaunas, Sakalas, 1935] 213 p. 8721.S3V6 DLC

8767. ŠALTENIS, Saulius. Riešutų duona; apysakos. Vilnius, Vaga, 1972. 176 p. PG8722.29.A43R5 PU

8768. SAVICKIS, Jurgis. Novelės. Vilnius, Vaga, 1967. 297 p. ports. PG8721.S37N6 1967 DLC CaOONL NN PU

8769. --- Raudoni batukai; novelės. [Brooklyn, N.Y.] Gabija [1951] 134 p. 891.92.Sa99R PU CtTMF NN.

8770. --- Šventoji Lietuva; romanas. [Memmingen, Ger.] Tremtis [1952] 248 p. PG8721.S37S8 DLC CtTMF OC1 OKentU PU

8771. ŠIMKUS, Jonas. Apie žmones, įvykius ir save; dienoraščiai, laiškai, atsiminimai. [Paruošė K. Doveika] Vilnius, Vaga, 1971. 538 p.

PG8721.S48Z5 PU

8772. --- Mes iš Šventosios. Vilnius, Vaga, 1968. 35 p. PG8721.S48M4 PU OKentU

8773. --- Narsi širdis. [Paruošė J. Butėnas] Vilnius, Vaga, 1969. 305 p. PG8721.S48N3 PU

8774. --- Ryt bus gražu. Vilnius, VGLL, 1962. 268 p. PG8721.S48R9 DLC PU

8775. SIMONAITYTĖ, Ieva. Apysakos. [Kaune] VGLL, 1948. 51 p. PG8721.S5A7 DLC

8776. --- Aukštujų Šimonių likimas; Mažosios Lietuvos buities romanas. 2. laida. Kaunas, 1936. 437 p. 891.93.S5-6 CtTMF

8777. --- --- [Another edition. Kaune] VGLL, 1948. 343 p. PG8721. S5A9 1948 DLC CaAEU(1956 ed.) PU

8778. --- --- 3. leidimas. Toronto, Ont., Baltija, 1952.43 437 p. PG8721.S5A9 1952 CaOTU MH NN OC1 OKentU(1966 ed) PU

8779. --- Gretimos istorijėlės. Vilnius, Vaga, 1968. 125 p. PG8721.S5G73 PU

8780. --- Nebaigta knyga. [Raižiniai V. Kalinausko] Vilnius, Vaga, 1965. 425 p. illus. PG8721.S5N42 PU IU MH

8781. --- ... o buvo taip. Vilnius, VGLL, 1960. 373 p. illus. PG8721.S502 DLC MiD MH OKentU PU

8782. --- Paskutinė Kūnelio kelionė; romanas. Vilnius, Vaga, 1971. 271 p. PG8721.S5P29 PU

8783. --- Pavasarių audroj; Mažosios Lietuvos laisvės kovos. Kaunas, 1938. 228 p. 891.93.S8 CtTMF

8784. --- --- [Another edition. Chicago, Ill.] Terra [195-] 228 p. PG8721.S5P3 DLC OC1

8785. --- --- 2. laida. Chicago, Ill, Terra, 1966. 228 p. 891.92.S154P PU

8786. --- Pikčiurnienė. 2. laida. Vilnius, VGLL, 1955. 311 p. illus. port. 891.92.S154 Pi PU OKentU

8787. --- Vilius Karalius; romanas. Vilnius, VGLL, 1956. 2 v. 891.92.S154V PU OKentU

8788. --- --- [Another edition.

Iliustravo K. Juodikaitis] Vilnius,
Vaga, 1967. 606 p. illus.
PG8721.S5V5 DLC CaOONL NN OKentU PU

8789. SIRIJOS GIRA, Vytautas.
Buenos Aires; romanas. Vilnius,
VGLL, 1956. 220 p. PG8721.S52B52
PU

8790. --- Ekranas; rinktinė. Vilnius, Vaga, 1967. 210 p. illus.
PG8721.S52E4 DLC PU

8791. --- Štai ir viskas; romanas.
Vilnius, VGLL, 1963. 273 p.
PG8721.S52S7 DLC OKentU

8792. --- Susitikimas su Brunhilda;
apsakymai ir apysakos. Vilnius, Vaga, 1971. 216 p. PG8721.S53B3
CaOTU PU

8793. --- Voratinkliai draikos be
vėjo; romanas. Vilnius, Vaga, 1968.
305 p. PG8721.S52V58 PU DLC

8794. ŠKĖMA, Antanas. Balta drobu-
lė; romanas. [London, Nida Press,
1958] 192 p. (Nidos knygų klubo
leidinys, nr.23) PG8721.S53B3 DLC
CaAEU CaOTU CtTMF OCl PU

8795. --- Celesta, poezija prozoje.
[London] Nida, 1960. 69 p.
PG8721.S53C4 DLC

8796. --- Šventoji Inga. [Chicago,
Ill.] Terra [1952] 226 p.
PG8721.S53S8 CaOTU NN PU

8797. ŠLAPELIENĖ, Laura. Dvi lie-
tuvaitės Amerikoj; apysaka. [Kaunas,
1939] 179 p. PG8721.S53D8 PU CtTMF

8798. SLUCKIS, Mykolas. Adomo obuo-
lys; romanas. Vilnius, Vaga, 1966.
448 p. PG8721.S56A64 PU DLC NN

8799. --- Geri namai; romanas. [2.
leidimas] Vilnius, VGLL, 1960.
488 p. illus. PG8721.S6G4 1960 DLC
PU

8800. Geriau mums nesusitikti; novelės. Vilnius, VGLL, 1961. 455 p.
illus. PG8721.S56G43 DLC PU

8801. --- Merginų sekmadienis; apsakymai ir apysakos. Vilnius, Vaga,
1971. 425 p. PG8721.S56M4 PU

8802. --- Stebuklingoji rašalinė;
apysaka apie nepaprastus Pagrandėlio
ir Liepinuko žygius bei apsakymus.
[Iliustravo A. Skliutauskaitė] Vilnius, Vaga, 1965. 203 p.
PG8721.S56S75 PU

8803. --- Uostas mano neramus; romanas. Vilnius, Vaga, 1968. 497 p.
PG8721.S56U65 PU OKentU

8804. --- Vėjų pagairėje; novelės.
Vilnius, VGLL, 1968. 315 p.
891.92.S153V PU

8805. SPALIS, Romualdas. Alma Ma-
ter; apysaka. [Cleveland, Ohio]
Viltis [1960] 433 p. PG8721.S64A75
DLC NN PU

8806. --- Angelai ir nuodemės; no-
velės. [London] Nida [1963] 252 p.
(Nidos knygų klubo leidinys, nr.44)
PG8721.S64A7 DLC PU

8807. --- Ant ribos; apysaka. [Me-
mmingen, Ger.] Tremtis [1954] 482 p.
PG8721.S64A8 DLC OCl PU

8808. --- Didžiosios atgailos; novelės. [Memmingen, Ger.] Tremtis
[1952] 352 p. PG8721.S64D5 DLC
CtTMF IU OCl PU

8809. --- Rezistencija; romanas.
Cleveland, Ohio, Viltis, 1969. 430
p. PG8721.S64R4 PU

8810. --- Tarp dangaus ir žemės;
feljetonai. London, Nida [1965]
142 p. (Nidos knygų klubo leidinys,
nr.54) PG8721.S64T3 DLC CtTMF PU

8811. --- Trylika nelaimių; feljetonai. Coventry, Eng., Pradalgė,
1950. 167 p. 891.92.G365T PU

8812. SPRINDIS, Adolfas. Ateina
šeštadienis; apsakymai. Vilnius,
Vaga, 1964. 160 p. PG8722.29.P7T7
DLC

8813. --- Trylika zuikių. Vilnius
Vaga, 1967. 129 p. PG8722.29.P7T7
DLC

8814. SRUOGA, Balys. Bangų vir-
šūnės; [Iliustravo L. Paškauskaitė]
Vilnus, Vaga, 1966. 402 p. illus.
PG8721.S68B3 DLC NN OKentU PU

8815. --- Kas bus, kas nebus, bet
žemaitis nepražus; kaip Jonis Mažri-
mukas 1812 metais iš Viekšnių Kau-
nan nusikraustė ir Napoleoną regėjo
ir kas iš to išėjo. [2. leidimas.
Chicago, Ill.] Terra [1954] 205 p.
illus. PG8721.S68K28 DLC CaOTU OCl
PU

8816. TAMULAITIS, Vytautas. Naktis ant Nemuno. Kaunas, 1938. 201
p. 891.93.T4 CtTMF

8817. --- Raguvos malūnininkas.
[Iliustravo Z. Žilinskas, Rodney,
Ont.] Rūta [1951] 60 p. illus.
PG8721.T3R3 DLC PU

8818. --- Sugrįžimas. [Iliustravo
P. Osmolskis] Tübingen,Ger., Patri-

ja, 1948. 143 p. 891.93.T6 CtTMF
CaAEU OCl PU

8819. TARASENKA, Petras. Rambyno
burtininkas. Vilnius, VGLL, 1958.
257 p. illus. PG8721.T35R3 DLC
ICCC PU

8820. TAUTKAITĖ, Eugenija. Pirmieji. Vilnius, VGLL, 1959. 220 p.
illus., port. PG8721.T37P5 DLC

8821. TILVYTIS, Teofilius. Kelionė aplink stalą. Kaunas, 1936.
238 p. 891.93.T10 CtTMF

8822. TININIS, Juozas. Dailinin-
ko žmona; romanas. Chicago, Ill.,
Lietuviškos knygos klubas, 1970.
218 p. PG8749.T5D3 PU

8823. --- Nuskandintas žiedas; novelės. [London] Nida, 1970. 200 p.
PG8749.T5N8 PU

8824. --- Sužadėtinė. [Chicago,
Ill.] Terra [1957] 180 p.
PG8749.T5S8 DLC PU

8825. TREINYS, Pranas. Ančiuko
kryžius; romanas. Vilnius, Vaga,
1970. 247 p. PG8722.3.R4A8 PU

8826. --- Banko balandžiai; apsakymai. Vilnius, VGLL, 1963. 158 p.
PG8722.3.R4B3 DLC IU

8827. --- Ragana, pelė ir Faustas;
teatrinis romanas, apsakymai. Vilnius, Vaga, 1971. 259 p.
PG8722.3.R4R3 PU

8828. --- Saulėgražos pasaka.
[Iliustravo N. Kryževičiūtė-Jurge-
lionienė] Vilnius, Vaga, 1966. 193
p. illus. PG8722.3.R4S2 PU DLC

8829. --- Saulėlydžio vieversys.
[Dailininkė L. Ramonienė] Vilnius,
Vaga, 1965. 213 p. illus. IU MH

8830. TULYS, Antanas. Aš bučiavau
tavo žmoną; Amerikos lietuvių buities novelės. n.p., Spaudos fondas,
1935. 224 p. Hvo48.T81 CtY

8831. --- Inicialai po tiltu; novelės. London, Nida, 1965. 156 p.
891.92.T825I PU PPULC

8832. --- Tūzų klubas; novelės.
[Chicago, Ill.] Terra [1960] 196 p.
PG8749.T8T8 DLC NN PU

8833. TUMAS, Juozas, 1869-1933.
Alegorijų vaizdai. Šiaip jau vaizdai. [By] Vaižgantas [pseud.] Kaunas,Švyturio bendrovės leidinys,
1922. 247 p. (Vaižganto raštai,
t.6) PG8721.T77A75 DLC CtTMF

8834. --- Dėdė lapę nušovė. [Ilius-
travo I. Žemaitytė. By] Vaižgantas
[pseud.] Vilnius, VGLL, 1957. 198
p. illus. PZ70.L5T8 DLC

8835. --- Dėdės ir dėdienės. Kassel-Mattenberg, Ger., Aistia, 1948.
175 p. illus., ports. (Vaižganto
raštai, t.10) 891.92.T832D PU
CtTMF MiD

8836. --- --- [Another edition]
Vilnius, 1963. 97 p. 891.93.V20
CtTMF

8837. --- --- [Another edition]
Vilnius, 1967. 93 p.
PG8721.T77D4 1967 PU

8838. --- Iš kaimo buities. [By]
Vaižgantas [pseud.] Kaunas, Šv.
Kazimiero draugijos leidinys, 1938.
318 p. (Vaižganto raštai, t.18)
PG8721.T77.I7 1938 DLC

8839. --- Jaunam veikėjui; 20 fel-
jetonų. Kaune, Švyturio bendrovės
spaustuvė, 1925. 150 p.
BJ1668.L5T8 DLC CtTMF ICLJF OCl

8840. --- Karo vaizdai. Scenos
vaizdai. [By] Vaižgantas [pseud.]
Kaunas, Švyturio bendrovės leidinys,
1922. 199 p. (Vaižganto raštai,
t.5) PG8721.T77K3 DLC PU

8841. --- Kelionių vaizdai. [By]
Vaižgantas [pseud.] Kaunas, 1931.
301 p. (Vaižganto raštai, t.17)
PG8721.T77 1922 v.17 DLC CtTMF

8842. --- Pragiedruliai. Vilnius,
1918-20. 3 v. in 1. 891.93.V22
CtTMF OCl PU

8843. --- --- [Another edition]
Kaunas, Svyturio spaustuvė, 1926.
3 v. (Vaižganto raštai, t.7-9)
898.93V34 CtTMF

8844. --- --- [Another edition]
Kassel-Mattenberg, Ger., Aistia,
1948. 3 v. illus. (His Raštai)
PG8721.T77P7 DLC CtTMF NN OKentU(1,
3) PU

8845. --- ---; vaizdai kovos dėl
kultūros. Vilnius, Vaga, 1969. 2
v. PG8721.T77P7 1969 PU CtPAM

8846. --- Rimai ir Nerimai. [By]
Vaižgantas [pseud. Redagavo Domas
Velička. Žodynėlį sudarė Rimas
Černius] Chicago, Ill., Pedagogikos
lituanistinis institutas, 1969. 35
p. PG8721.T77R5 PU

8847. --- Šis-tas; trys Vaižganto [pseud.] apysakėlės. Shenandoah,
Pa., Lietuvių katalikų spaudos drau-

gijos spaustuvėje, 1906. 18 p.
Offprint from "Dirva" Shenandoah,
Pa., 1909, no.2.   891.92.T832Si PU

8848. --- Vaizdai. [Kaune] VGLL,
1947. 580 p. PG8721.T77 1947 DLC
CaOTU NN PU

8849. --- Valiulio pasaka. [By]
Vaižgantas [pseud. Iliustravo Birutė Demkutė] Vilnius, 1969. 238
p. PG8721.T77V3 PU

8850. URBONAS, Simas. Sūkuriai
ir žmonės; žmogaus kančių pynė.
[Würzburge, Ger.] 1947. 206 p.
PG8721.U7S8 DLC CtTMF PU

8851. URBONAVIČIUS, Kazimieras.
Biurokratai; apysaka. Jonas Kmitas
[pseud.] Shenandoah, Pa., "Žvaigždės" spaustuvė, 1907. 79 p.
891.92.Url3Bu PU

8852. --- Vaizdeliai. Jonas
Kmitas [pseud.] So. Boston, Mass.,
Darbininkas, 1917. 891.92.Url3V PU

8853. --- Vytis ir erelis; apysaka. [By] Jonas Kmitas [pseud.] So.
Boston, Mass., Darbininkas, 1946.
xvi, 576 p. 891.92.Url3Vy PU

8854. USAČIOVAS, Jonas. Nemunas
laužia ledus; romanas. Vilnius,
VGLL, 1956. 445 p. PG8721.U75N4 PU

8855. VAIČIULAITIS, Antanas.
Gluosnių daina; padavimai. [So.
Boston, Mass., spaudė Lietuvių
enciklopedijos spaustuvė] 1966.
127 p. illus. 891.V193G PU CaAEU
CaOTU OKentU

8856. --- Italijos vaizdai.
Stuttgart, Ger., Venta, 1949. 91 p.

8857. --- Kur bakūžė samanota.
[New York, N.Y.] Kultūros institu-
to leidinys [1947] 288 p.
PG8721.V3K8 DLC CaOTU CtTMF OKentU
PU

8858. --- Mūsų mažoji sesuo.
[London, 1970] 104 p. PG8721.V3M8
1970 PU

8859. --- Nuo Sirakūzų iki šiaurės
elnio. Kaunas, Šv. Kazimiero draugija, 1937. 205 p. 891.93.V7
CtTMF

8860. --- Pasakojimai; rinktinės
novelės. [Nördlingen, Ger.] Venta
[1955] 342 p. PG8721.V3P3 DLC
CaAEU CaOTU NjN NN OCl PU

8861. --- Vakaras sargo namely.
Kaunas, Sakalas, 1932. 129 p.
891.93.V2 CtTMF

8862. --- Valentina; romanas.
Kaunas, 1936. 219 p. 891.93.V3
CtTMF

8863. --- --- 2. pataisyta laida.
[Schweinfurt, Ger.] Venta [1951]
141 p. PG8721.V3V3 1951 DLC CaOONL
CtTMF NN PU

8864. VAIČIŪNAS, Petras. Milda,
meilės deivė; mytologijos pasaka.
Vilnius, Švyturio b-vė, 1920. 67
p. 891.92.V194M PU CaOONL CtTMF
DLC ICCC

8865. VAINEIKIENĖ, Stasė. Grafas
ir žmonės; romanas. Vilnius, VGLL,
1955. 284 p. NN

8866. --- Vaišvila, žemaičių
baudžiauninkų vadas; romanas. Vilnius, VGLL, 1959. 209 p.
891.92.V1945V PU CtPAM CtTMF

8867. VAITKUS, Mykolas. Čirikšas
siaube; novelė. [Iliustravo P.
Osmolskis. Brooklyn, N.Y.] Vagos
leidinys [1951] 87 p. illus.
PG8749.V3C5 DLC CtTMF PU

8868. --- Iš įvairių pasaulių;
apysakaitės. Kaunas, 1929. 216 p.
891.93.V18 CtTMF CaOONL OKentU

8869. --- Tvanas; senovinių amžių
apysaka. [2. leidimas. London]
Nida [1954] 205 p. (Nidos knygų
klubo leidinys nr. 4) PG8749.V3T85
1954 DLC CtTMF OCl PU

8870. VALANČIUS, Motiejus. Palą-
gos Juze. [Palangos Juzė] Vilnius,
1863. 112 p. BM(20011. e. 51.)

8871. --- --- [Another edition]
Wilniuje, 1863 [i.e. Tilžė, 1873]
112 p. PG8721.V327P3 1970 PU
(Xerox copy, 1970)

8872. --- --- 4. pataisytas leidimas. Tilžė, 1902. 132 p.
891.92.V232P PU CtTMF OCl
BM(12431. bbb. 45.)

8873. --- --- [Another edition.
Kaune] VGLL [1947] 186 p.
PG8721.V327P3 DLC

8874. --- --- [Another edition]
Vilnius, Vaga, 1965. 206 p.
PG8721.V327P3 1965 DLC CtPAM IU
MH PU

8875. --- Pasakojimas Antano Tretininko. Plymouth, Pa., 1891.
Title varies: Antano Tretininko pasakojimas. BM(012403. df. 34.)

8876. --- --- Naujas išleidimas.
Brooklyn, N.Y., Žvaigždė, 1901. 99

p. 891.92.V232Pas PU CtTMF

8877. --- --- [Another edition]
Vilnius, 1906. 112 p. OCl

8878. --- --- [Another edition]
Meerbach, Ger., J. Narbutas ir F.
Indreika, 1948. 68 p.
891.92.V232A PU CtTMF

8879. VENCLOVA, Antanas. Draugystė; įžanga į subrendusį amžių:
romanas. [Naujas leidimas] Vilnius, Vaga, 1966. 416 p. illus.
PG8721.V4D7 DLC IU MH PU

8880. --- Gimimo diena; romanas.
Vilnius, VGLL, 1959. 614 p.
PG8721.V495 1959 PU

8881. --- --- 2. leidimas. Vilnius, VGLL, 1960. 619 p. illus.
PG8721.V4G5 1960 DLC

8882. --- --- [Another edition.
Iliustracijos St. Krasausko] Vilnius, 1965. 648 p. PG8721.V4G5
1965 PU

8883. --- Jaunystės atradimas.
Vilnius, Vaga, 1966. 621 p. illus.,
facsims., ports. PG8721.V4J3 DLC
CaOTU MH OKentU PU

8884. --- Medis ir jo atžalos;
rinktiniai apsakymai. [Kaunas]
VGLL, 1947. 308 p. illus.
(*QY)NN

8885. --- Pavasario upė. Vilnius,
Vaga, 1968. 456 p. illus.
PG8721.V4P3 DLC OKentU PU

8886. --- Šalys ir žmonės. Vilnius, Vaga, 1972. 355 p.
PG8721.V4S32 PU

8887. --- Vakarinė žvaigždė.
Vilnius, Vaga, 1971. 206 p.
PG8721.V4V3 PU

8888. --- Vidurdienio vėtra.
Vilnius, Vaga, 1969. 653 p. illus.
PG8721.V4V5 PU CaAEU DLC OKentU

8889. VIENUOLIS, A., pseud. Am-
žinasis smuikininkas; apsakymai,
apysakos, legendos. Vilnius, Vaga,
1969. 519 p. PG8721.V5A5 PU

8890. --- Astronomas Šmukštaras;
apsakymai ir atsiminimai. Vilnius,
VGLL, 1962. 403 p. PG8721.V5A89
DLC

8891. --- Kryžkelės; romanas.
[Kaunas] VGLL [1945] 399 p.
(*QY)NN OCl

8892. --- --- [Another edition.

Iliustracijos V.K. Jonyno] Stamford,
Conn., Patria [1952] 401 p. illus.
PG8721.V5K7 DLC NN PU

8893. --- Padavimai ir legendos.
Vilnius, VGLL, 1957. 148 p.
PG8721.V5P25 PU

8894. --- --- [Another edition.
Iliustravo Albina Makūnaitė] Vil-
nius, Vaga, 1971. 148 p.
PG8721.V5P25 1971 PU

8895. --- Paskenduolė; apsakymai
ir apysakos. Vilnius, M. Kuktos
spaustuvė, 1913. ("Aušrinės" išleidimas, nr.3) (*QYN p.v. 379 no.7)
NN

8896. --- --- [Another edition]
Vilnius, VGLL, 1962. 473 p.
PG8721.V5P3 DLC MH PU

8897. --- Prieš dieną; romanas.
Vilnius, VGLL, 1964. 256 p.
PG8721.V5P7 DLC

8898. --- Puodžiūnkiemis; romanas.
Vilnius, VGLL, 1961. 502 p.
PG8721.V5P8 DLC OKentU

8899. --- --- [Another edition]
Vilnius, Vaga, 1966. 426 p. MH NN

8900. --- --- [Another edition]
Vilnius, Vaga, 1968. 426 p. NN

8901. --- --- [Another edition]
Vilnius, Vaga, 1970. 426 p.
PG8721.V5P8 1970 PU

8902. --- Užkeiktieji vienuoliai;
gruzinų liaudies motyvais. Daili-
ninkė Sigutė Valiuvienė. [Vilnius,
Vaga, 1964] 34 p. PG8721.V5U87 PU

8903. --- Užžėlusiu taku. [Kaune]
VGLL [1946] 257 p. PG8721.V5U9
DLC NN

8904. --- Viešnia iš šiaurės.
[Chicago, Ill.] Terra [1957]- .
2 v. PG8721.V5V5 DLC NN OCl PU

8905. VITAITIS, Stasys E. Gyvenimo dumble; apysaka iš realio
Amerikos lietuvių gyvenimo. Brooklyn, N.Y., Spauda "Vienybės", 1924.
364 p. NN

8906. VOLERTAS, Vytautas. Gyvenimas yra dailus. [Chicago, Ill.]
Lietuviškos knygos klubas [1964]
242 p. CaOONL MH

8907. --- Pragaro vyresnysis;
premijuotas romanas. [Chicago, Ill.]
1971. 273 p. PG8749.V6P7 PU

8908. --- Sąmokslas; premijuotas

romanas. [Chicago, Ill.] Lietuviškos knygos klubas [1968] 279 p.
PG8749.V6S2 DLC CaOONL PU

8909. --- Upė teka vingiais. romanas. [Chicago, Ill.] Lietuviškos knygos klubas [1963] 332 p.
PG8749.V6U7 DLC CtTMF MH PU

8910. ŽILINSKAITĖ, Vytautė. Angelas virš miesto; humoras, satyra,
parofijos. Vilnius, Vaga, 1967.
236 p. PG8722.36.I4A5 PU

8911. --- Humoreskos. Vilnius,
Vaga, 1971. 150 p. PG8722.36.I4H8
PU

8912. --- Karusėlėje; satyros ir
humoro rinktinė. Vilnius, Vaga,
1970. 309 p. PG8722.36.I4K3 PU

8913. --- Romantikos institutas;
arba, pafilosofavimai. Satyros.
Vilnius, Vaga, 1968. 122 p. illus.
PG8722.36.I4R6 DLC CaAEU OKentU PU

8914. ZOBARSKAS, Stepas. Doleris
iš Pitsburgo. [Brooklyn, N.Y., Gabija, 1952] 57 p. 891.92.Z78D PU
OCl

8915. --- Moters stiprybė; beletristika. Kaunas, 1938. 186 p.
891.93.Z3 CtTMF

8916. --- Per šaltį ir vėją. Tübingen, Ger., Patria, 1948. 42 p.
891.93.Z7 CtTMF CaAEU

8917. --- --- 2. laida. Tübingen, Ger., Patria, 1949. 45 p.
891.92.Z78P PU

8918. --- Savame krašte; novelės.
Tübingen, Ger., Patria, 1946. 248
p. 891.92.Z78S PU CtTMF

8919. ŽYMANTIENĖ, Julija (Beniuše-
vičiūtė). Marti. [By] Žemaitė
[pseud. Iliustravo A. Kučas] Vilnius, Vaga, 1964. 46 p. illus.
PG8721.Z9M3 DLC PU

8920. --- Petras Kurmelis. Gera
galva. Mieste. [Kaune] VGLL [1946]
121 p. PG8721.Z9P4 DLC

8921. --- Rudens vakaras. Dailininkas V. Jurkūnas. [Kaune, VGLL,
1960] 416 p. illus. PG8721.Z9R8
DLC CaOONL CaOTU PU

XIII.5.c.4. DRAMA

8922. ALANTAS, Vytautas. Dramos
veikalai. Čikaga, Srovė [1963]

385 p. illus., port. PG8721.A45D7
DLC CtY ICCC MiD PU

8923. ANGLICKIS, Stasys. Rūmai
be pamato; penkių, veiksmų drama.
Kaunas, 1933. 91 p. 891.92.Al
CtTMF

8924. AUDRONIS, Juozas. Teta iš
Amerikos; trijų veiksmų komedija.
Kaunas, 1938. 96 p. 800.Al3 CtTMF

8925. BAGDAS, Pranas Julius. 3
dramos veįkalai; Baisusis birželis;
Varpinė; Šiaurės pašvaistė. [By]
Pranas J. Naumiestiškis [pseud.]
Dailininkas Vytautas Ignas. [Put-
nam, Conn.] Immaculata Press,
1965. 238 p. PG8721.B24T7 DLC
CaOTU PU

8926. BALTRUKONIS, Jonas V.
Meilės paslaptys. Drama. Vaizdelis
iš lietuvių gyvenimo Rusijoje.
Boston, Mass., Darbininko spauda,
1918. 60 p. 891.92.B218M PU OCl
PPULC

8927. --- Brolžudys; penkių veiksmų tragedija. Kearny, N.Y., 1919.
49 p. With this are bound Vargšas
Tadas and other poems. 891.92.B218B
PU PPULC

8928. BALTUŠIS, Juozas. Gieda
gaideliai; keturių veiksmų drama.
[Kaunas, VGLL, 1947] 148 p.
891.92.B218G PU DLC

8929. BIELIAUSKAS, Antanas. Ne-
baigtas portretas; 4 vieksmų 5 paveikslų drama. Vilnius, VGLL, 1961.
114 p. PG8721.B45N4 DLC PU

8930. BINKIS, Kazys. Atžalynas:
penkių veiksmų pjesė. Kaunas, 1938.
177 p. 891.92.B4 CtTMF

8931. BUBNYS, Vytautas. Kaltė;
trijų veiksmų pjesė. Vilnius, Vaga,
1971. 58 p. PG8722.12.U2K3 PU

8932. ČIURLIONIENĖ, Sofija (Kymantaitė). Aušros sūnūs; keturių
veiksmų drama. Kaunas, Valstybės
spaustuvė, 1926. 114 p.
491.922.C499.3 PU ICCC

8933. --- Komedijos: Pinigėliai.
Karalaitė. Tikroji teisybė. Gegužis. Kuprotas oželis. Vilnius,
Švyturio bendrovė, 1920. 155 p.
891.92.C2 CtTMF CtY OCl

8934. DAUGUVIETIS, Borisas. Nauja vaga; septynių paveikslų pjesė.
[Kaune] VGLL [1947] 168 p.
891.92.D269 PU DLC

8935. --- Žaldokynė. Vilnius,

Vaga, 1967. 458 p. Contents.--Nauja vaga. --Laimė.--Uždavinys.--Žaldokynė.--Mokytoja.--Apie teatrą ir dramaturgiją. PG8721.D35A6 1967 PU

8936. DOVYDAITIS, Jonas. Geležinis trejetas; drama. Kaunas, 1938. 149 p. 891.92.D2 CtTMF

8937. DVI MOTERI, pseud. Litvomanai. Drama keturiuose veikimuose. Tilžė, M. Saunus, 1905. 58 p. Authors' names are: Gabrielė Petkevičaitė and Julija Žymantienė. 891.92.D4 CtTMF NN

8938. --- Velnias spąstuose; dramatiškas paveikslėlis iš trijų veiksmų. [Tilžė, 1902] 38 p. Authors' names are: Gabrielė Petkevičaitė and Julija Žymantienė. PG8721.D87V4 PU

8939. FROMAS, Aleksandras. Eglė žalčių karalienė. Dramatizuotas penkiuose apsireiškimuose. Iš mitologiško senovės lietuvių gyvenimo. [By] Gužutis. 2. laida. Plymouth, Pa., Vienybė Lietuvninkų, 1906. 56 p. 891.922 ICBM

8940. --- Palocius ežero dugnuose; trijų veiksmų drama. Brooklyn, N.Y., Spauda ir lėšos "Vienybės lietuvinkų", 1911. 49 p. 891.92.F924P PU CtTMF

8941. --- Ponas ir mužikai; drama. Vilnius, Zavadzkio, 1864. 72 p. [Tilžė, 1893] Author's pseud., Aleksandras Gužutis, at head of title. 891.92.J314A PU OCl

8942. GIRA, Liudas. Beauštanti aušrelė; pjesė. Vilnius, J. Rinkevičius, 1913. 20 p. 891.922.G ICBM

8943. GLINSKIS, Juozas. Grasos namai; trijų veiksmų drama. Vilnius, Vaga, 1971. 71 p. PG8722.17.L5G7 PU

8944. GRINIUS, Jonas. Gulbės giesmė; šešių veiksmų istoriška drama. Chicago, Ill., Lietuviškos knygos klubas, 1962. 222 p. PG8721.G67G8 DLC MiD PU

8945. --- Sąžinė; penkių veiksmų ir prologo drama. Kaunas, Šv. Kazimiero draugijos leidinys, 1929. 98 p. PG8721.G67S3 PU

8946. --- Žiurkių kamera; trijų veiksmų drama. [Brooklyn, N.Y.] "Aidų" leidinys [1954] 120 p. 891.92.G888Z PU CaOONL NN

8947. GRUODIS, Petras. Pajūrio

auka; dviejų veiksmų vaidinimas su prologu iš Klaipėdos atvadavimo. Kaunas, 1936. 62 p. 891.92.G8 CtTMF

8948. GRUŠAS, Juozas. Dūmai; keturių veiksmų penkių paveikslų komedija. Vilnius, VGLL, 1956. 891.92.G925D PU

8949. --- Meilė, džiazas ir velnias; tragiška komedija. Vilnius, VGLL, 1962. 105 p. PG8721.G7M4 PU

8950. INČIŪRA, Kazys. Painiava; trijų veiksmų vaidinimas. Kaunas, Žinija, 1929. 100 p. 891.92.In24Pa PU

8951. --- Pasiilgę Aušros Vartų; trijų veiksmų ir prologo veikalas. Chicago, Ill., Draugas, 1929. 92 p. Edition in Kaunas, Šviesos spaustuvė, 1929, has title: "Savanorio duktė" 891.92.In24P PU OCl

8952. --- Trys talismanai; trijų dalių pasaka. misterija su prologu. Kaunas, Sakalas, 1936. 104 p. 891.92.I CtTMF ICCC

8953. --- Žemaitė; šešių paveikslų pjesė. Vilnius, VGLL, 1964. 82 p. 891.92.In24Z PU IU

8954. JANKUS, Jurgis. Peilio ašmenimis; trijų veiksmų drama. [Brooklyn, N.Y., Darbininkas, 1967] 261 p. PG8749.J3P4 DLC CaOONL PU

8955. JASIUKAITIS, Konstantinas. Alkani žmonės; keturių aktų drama. Vilnius, "Vilniaus Kanklių" išleidimas, 1908. 48 p. 891.92.J314A PU

8956. KAIRYS, Anatolijus. Diagnozė; trijų veiksmų komedija. [Chicago, Ill.] Terra [c1956] 150 p. PG8721.K2D5 DLC CaAEU PU

8957. --- Du broliukai; trijų veiksmų pasaka. [Chicago, Ill.] 1970. 78 p. PG8721.K2D8 PU

8958. --- Laisvės medis; keturių veiksmų istorinė pjesė. Chicago, Ill., Menunas [1955] 120 p. 891.92.K127L PU OCl

8959. --- Palikimas; vieno veiksmo trijų paveikslų drama. Chicago, Ill., Laiškai lietuviams, 1969. 73 p. illus. PG8721.K2P3 PU DLC

8960. --- Sidabrinė diena; trijų veiksmų operetė. [Chicago, Ill.] Lietuvių meno ansamblis Dainava [1972] 155 p. PG8721.K2S5 PU

8961. --- Šviesa, kuri užsidegė;

trijų veiksmų tragedijėlė. [Chicago, Ill.] Terra [1968] 142 p. PG8721.K2S9 DLC PU

8962. --- Viščiukų ūkis; trijų veiksmų satyrinė komedija. [Chicago, Ill.] Terra [c1965] 91 p. PG8721.K2V5 DLC CaAEU CaOTU CaOONL NN PU

8963. KARPAVIČIUS, Kazimieras S. Baudžiauninkė; keturių veiksmų melodrama iš baudžiavos laikų. Cleveland, Ohio, Dirva, 1931. 76 p. PG8749.K3B3 PU

8964. --- Birutė ir kuprelis; trijų veiksmų tragedija iš lietuvių kovų su krikščionimis. Cleveland, Ohio, Spauda "Dirvos", 1927. 94 p. PG8749.K28B5 DLC CtTMF OCl

8965. --- Galiūnas; drama iš lietuvių pasakiškų kovų su žmogėdžiais gilioj senovėj. Cleveland, Ohio, Spauda "Dirvos", 1927. xii, 67 p. illus. PG8749.K28G3 DLC OCl PU

8966. KRĖVĖ-MICKEVIČIUS, Vincas. Dangaus ir žemės sūnūs; žemės vingiais. [Augsburg, Ger.] Sūdava [1949] 206 p. PG8721.K7D3 DLC PU

--- Mindaugo mirtis; drama. Kaunas, 1935. See entry no. 6284.

--- Šarūnas, Dainavos kunigaikštis; 4 dalių su įžanga dramatizuota apysaka. See entries no. 6285 - 6288.

--- Skirgaila. Mindaugo mirtis. Vilnius, 1967. See entry no. 6289.

8967. LANDSBERGIS, Algirdas. Meilės mokykla; trijų veiksmų komedija. Chicago, Ill. [Santara-Šviesa] 1965. 109 p. PG8721.L3M4 DLC CaAEU CaOTU PU

8968. --- Penki stulpai turgaus aikštėje; drama. Chicago, Ill. [Santara-Šviesa] 1966. 83 p. PG8721.L3P4 DLC CaAEU CaOTU PU

8969. LAUCEVIČIUS, Bronius. Kryžius; keturių veiksmų drama. [By] Br. Vargšas [pseud.] Chicago, Ill., 1916. 57 p. PG8721.L348K7 PU

8970. LAUCIUS, Stasys. Raudonoji melodija. Šeši scenos veikalai. [London] Bendrija [1953] 89 p. PG8721.L35R3 DLC OKentU PU

8971. --- Respublika. [n.p.] Pašvaistė [1960] unpaged. PG8721.L35R4 DLC PU

8972. --- Signalas; keturių veiksmų

laisvės kovų drama. Kaunas, 1938. 159 p. 891.92.L3 CtTMF

8973. LAURINČIUKAS,Albertas. Vidutinė moteris; 3 veiksmų pjesė. Vilnius, Vaga, 1971. 96 p. PG8722.22.A9V5 PU

8974. MAIRONIS, Jonas. Kame išganimas; libretto keturiais aktais. 4. kartą atspausta. Tilžė, 1920. 37 p. 891.92.M187T PU CtTMF

8975. --- Vytautas pas kryžiuočius; penkių aktų istoriškoji drama. Kaunas, 1925. 113 p. 891.92.M1 CtTMF

8976. MARCINKEVIČIUS, Justinas. Katedra; 10-ties giesmių drama. Vilnius, Vaga, 1971. 154 p. PG8721.M35K3 PU

--- Mindaugas; dviejų dalių drama-poema. Vilnius, 1968. See entry no. 6296.

8977. MIČIULIS, Pius. Eržkėčių taku; penkių veiksmų drama. Vilnius, 1913. 181 p. 891.92.M583 PU CtTMF

8978. --- Sugriuvęs gyvenimas; trijų veiksmų drama. Vilnius, M. Šlapelienė, 1913. 70 p. 891.92.M5835 PU NN

8979. MILIŪNAS, Viktoras. Charakteristikos; pjesės saviveiklai. Vilnius, Vaga, 1965. 165 p. PG8721.M47C45 PU

8980. --- Karuselė; dviejų dalių pjesė. Vilnius, Vaga, 1970. 92 p. PG8721.M47K3 PU

8981. --- Neramūs žmonės; vieno veiksmo komedija saviveiklai. Vilnius, VGLL, 1953. 84 p. (Pjesės saviveiklai) PG8721.M47N4 DLC

8982. --- Še tau, kad nori! 4 veiksmų 5 paveikslų komedija. Vilnius, VGLL, 1956. 94 p. 891.92.M597S PU

8983. --- Žuvėdros palydi; trys pjesės. Vilnius, VGLL, 1960. 240 p. PG8721.M47Z9 PU

8984. MYKOLAITIS, Vincas. Valdovas; penkių veiksmų šešių paveikslų drama. Kaunas, 1930. 126 p. 891.92.P11 CtTMF

8985. NAGORNOSKIS, Vincas. Vytis kankinys; penkių veiksmų drama. Boston, Mass., 1936. 170 p. PG8749.N32V9 PU

8986. NARĖČIONIS, Romualdas. Prieš nuosprendį; trijų veiksmų drama.

Vilnius, Vaga, 1966. 104 p.
PG8721.N34P7 DLC

8987. --- Sentimentali istorija;
trijų veiksmų drama. Vilnius,
Vaga, 1968. 80 p. PG8722.24.A7S4
PU

8988. OSTRAUSKAS, Kostas. Kana-
rėlė; trijų veiksmų drama. Chicago,
Ill., Lietuvių studentų santara,
1958. 84 p. 891.92.Os78K PU DLC

8989. --- Kvartetas; dramos.
Chicago, Ill. [Algimanto Mackaus
knygų leidimo fondas] 1971. 170
p. PG8749.08K9 PU OKentU

8990. --- Žaliojoj lankelėj; dvi
vienaveiksmės dramos. Chicago, Ill.
[Santara-Šviesa] 1963. 63, 36a-63a
p. PG8749.08Z2 DLC NN PU

8991. PALIONIS, Mykolas. Prieš
vėją nepapūsi; komedija trijuose
aktuose. Chicago, Ill., Turtu
"Lietuvos", 1911. 52 p.
PG8721.P3P7 DLC

8992. PAUKŠTELIS, Juozas. Audra
ateina; keturių veiksmų penkių paveikslų pjesė. Vilnius, VGLL,
1956. 106 p. 891.92.P284.2 PU NN

8993. PEČKAUSKAITĖ, Marija. Ne-
pasisekė Marytei; komedijėlė dvie-
juose aktuose. [By] Šatrijos Ragana [pseud.] Seinai, Laukaičio
spaustuvėje, 1906. 28 p.
891.92.P336N PU

8994. PETRULIS, Juozas. Pirmasis
prizas; dviejų veiksmų komedija.
Kaunas, 1935. 47 p. 891.92.P3
CtTMF

8995. --- Preiš srovę; šešių paveikslų kronikinė pjesė. Kaunas,
1938. 189 p. 891.92.P2 CtTMF

8996. PUIDA, Kazys. Dramos.
Brooklyn, N.Y., "Vienybės Lietuv-
ninkų" lėšomis, 1912. 120 p.
(Its works t.4) 891.92.P693D PU
CtTMF ICCC

8997. PŪKELEVIČIŪTĖ, Birutė.
Aukso žąsis; pasakiška trijų veiksmų komedija. [Chicago, Ill., Lietuviškos knygos klubo leidinys,
1965] 159 p. illus. PG8749.P8A8
DLC

8998. RIMKEVIČIUS, Vytautas. Rytas; [pjesė. Kaunas] VGLL, 1964.
118 p. PG8722.28.I58V9 DLC

8999. RŪKAS, Antanas. Bubulis
ir Dundulis; linksmas trijų veiksmų nutikimas. Svajonių šalis; pen-

kių veiksmų vaidinimas mažiems ir
dideliems. Čikaga [E. Rūkienė,
1970] 180 p. Cover title: Veikalai scenai. PG8721.R79B8 PU

9000. --- Vieno kiemo gyventojai;
3 veiksmų drama. Cleveland, Ohio,
1961. 34 p. 891.92.R855V PU

9001. SAJA, Kazys. Baimė; dvi
vienaveiksmės pjesės. Vilnius, Lietuvos TSR kultūros ministerijos,
Liaudies meno rūmų leidinys, 1966.
70 p. PG8722.29.A5B3 DLC PU

9002. --- Dvi pjesės. Vilnius,
Vaga, 1965. 180 p. PG8722.29.A38D9
DLC MH PU

9003. --- Klumpės. [Vilnius]
VGLL, 1958. 188 p. PG8722.29.A38K5
PU

9004. --- Mažosios pjesės... Vilnius, Vaga, 1968. 239 p.
PG8722.29.A38A6 1968 PU

9005. --- Nerimas; 6 paveikslų
pjesė. Vilnius, VGLL, 1963. 109
p. PG8722.29.A38N4 PU MH

9006. --- Šventežeris; trijų
veiksmų pjesė. [Vilnius, Vaga,
1971] 88 p. PG8722.29.A38S9 PU

9007. ŠKĖMA, Antanas. Pabudimas;
drama. [Chicago, Ill.] Terra [1956]
64 p. PG8721.S53P3 DLC CaAEU CaOTU
NN OCl PU

9008. --- Žvakidė; dviejų veiksmų
vaidinimas. [Brooklyn, N.Y., Darbininkas, c1957] 101 p.
PG8721.S53Z47 DLC CaAEU CaOTU CaOONL
NN OCl PU

9009. SKLIUTAUSKAS, Jokūbas.
Širdies liga; 5 veiksmų drama. Vil-
nius, Vaga, 1967. 82 p.
PG8722.29.K55S5 PU DLC

9010. SKUČAITĖ, Ramutė. Septinta
kėdė; 6 paveikslų pjesė. Vilnius,
Vaga, 1971. 70 p. PG8722.29.K8S4
PU

9011. SRUOGA, Balys. Aitvaras tei-
sėjas; trijų veiksmų pjesė. Kaunas,
1935. 131 p. PG8721.S68A5 PU CtTMF
NN

9012. --- --- [Another edition]
In His Raštai. Vilnius, 1957. v.
2, p. 353-462. PG8721.S68 1957 v.
2 DLC CaAEU ICU NN PU

9013. --- Apyaušrio dalia. [Kaune]
VGLL [1945] 244 p. illus.
PG8721.S68A8 DLC PU

9014. --- --- [Another edition]
In His Raštai. Vilnius, 1957. v.3,
p. 5-218. PG8721.S68 1957 DLC CaAEU
ICU NN PU

9015. --- Baisioji naktis; trijų
veiksmų šešių paveikslų drama. Kaunas, 1935. 223 p. 891.92.S9 CtTMF

9016. --- --- [Another edition] In
His Raštai. Vilnius, 1957. v.2,
p. 165-352. PG8721.S68 1957 DLC
CaAEU ICU NN PU

--- Giesmė apie Gediminą.
See entries no. 6323-6325.

9017. --- Kazimieras Sapiega; 4
veiksmų 9 paveikslų istoriška kronika. [Chicago, Ill.] Terra [194-]
257, xi p. PG8721.S68K3 DLC CtTMF
ICCC MiD NN OCl OKentU PU

9018. --- --- [Another edition] In
His Raštai. Vilnius, 1957. v.3,
p. 219-444. PG8721.S68 1957 DLC
CaAEU ICU NN PU

9019. --- Milžino paunksmė; trilo-
giška istorijos kronika. 3 veiksmai
9 paveikslai. Kaunas, 1932. 172 p.
OCl

9020. --- --- [2. leidimas. Chicago, Ill.] Terra [1954] 173 p.
PG8721.S68M5 1954 DLC CaAEU NN PU

9021. --- --- [Another edition] In
His Raštai. Vilnius, 1957. v.2,
p.5-163. PG8721.S68 1957 DLC CaAEU
ICU NN PU

9022. --- Pavasario giesmė; 3 veik-
smų lyrinė drama. In His Raštai.
Vilnius, 1957. v.3, p. 445-547.
PG8721.S68 1957 v.3 DLC CaAEU ICU PU

9023. --- Radvila Perkūnas. 2.
laida. Chicago, Ill., Terra, 1970.
129, [3] p. PG8721.S68R3 1970 PU

9024. STOROST, Wilhelm. Amžina
ugnis; dramatiška trilogija. [Dra-
ma. By] Vidūnas [pseud.] Tilsit,
Rūta, 1912-1913. 327 p. illus.
891.92.St28 PU CtTMF ICCC NN

9025. --- --- Prabočių šešėliai.
Pasaulio gaisras. [by] Vydūnas
[pseud.] Vilnius [VGLL] 1968. 666
p. music. PG8721.S7A6 1968 PU CtPAM
CaOONL NN OKentU(1908 ed)

9026. --- Birutininkai; dviveiksmė
komedija. Tilžė, Rūta, 1910. 79 p.
PG8721.S7B5 DLC CtTMF NN

9027. --- Jonuks; dviveiksmė Joni-
nių komedija. 2. taisitas leidimas.
Tilžė, Rūta, 1920. 64 p. illus.

PG8721.S7J6 DLC CtTMF

9028. --- Jūrų varpai; triveiksmė
mysterija. [By] Vidūnas. Tilžė,
Rūta, 1920. 126 p. 891.93.V53
CtTMF

9029. --- Kur protsǃ Komēdija
vienū veiksmū. [By] Vidūnas [pseud.]
Tilžė, Rūta, 1907. 64 p.
PG8721.S7K8 DLC

9030. --- Laimės atošvaista; pen-
kiū veiksmū tragaidē su atvarta ir
užvarta. [By] Vidūnas [pseud.]
Tilžē, Rūta, 1934. 132 p.
PG8721.S7L3 DLC

9031. --- Lietuvos pasakēlē. [By]
Vidūnas [pseud.] Tilžē, Rūta, 1913.
30 p. 891.93.V79 CtTMF

9032. --- Ragana; vieno veiksmo
tragedija. [By] Vidūnas [pseud.]
Tilžē, Rūta, 1918. 38 p.
891.92.St78R PU CtTMF

9033. --- Sigutē; iš lietuvių pasakos; vienveiksmē mysterija. [By]
Vidūnas [pseud.] Tilžēje, Rūta,
1914. 32 p. 891.922.St78.4 PU ICCC

9034. --- Tēviškē; vienveiksmis
dramatiškas veikalas. [By] Vidūnas
[pseud.] Tilžēje, Rūta, 1908. 52
p. PG8721.S7T4 DLC CtTMF NN OCl PU

9035. --- Varpstis; triveiksmē
drama. [By] Vidūnas [pseud.] Tilsit, Rūta, 1923. 72 p.

9036. --- Vergai ir didikai; ke-
turiū veiksmū tragedija. [By] Vi-
dunas [pseud.] Tilžē, Rūta, 1919.
126 p. 891.93.V83 CtTMF ICCC

9037. --- Žvaigždžiū takai; triveiksmē drama. [By] Vidūnas [pseud.]
Tilžē, Rūta, 1920. 891.92.St78M PU

9038. URNEVIČIŪTĖ, Dalia. Vadink
mane motina; dviejų dalių drama.
Vilnius, Vaga, 1966. 89 p.
PG8722.31.R6V3 DLC IU MH

9039. VAIČIŪNAS, Petras. Aukso
gromata; 4 veiksmų pjesė. Kaunas,
Sakalas, 1935. 214 p. 891.92.V194A
PU CtTMF

9040. --- Buridano asilas; trijų
veiksmų komedija. Kaunas, 1923.
104 p. 891.92.V1 CtTMF

9041. --- Dramos. Vilnius, VGLL,
1956. 476 p. port. 891.92.V194D
PU PAtM

9042. --- Dramos ir komedijos.
Vilnius, Vaga, 1971. 2 v.
PG8721.V32A19 1971 PU

9043. --- Giedrėjanti sąžinė. 3
veiksmų dramos kurinys. Kaunas,
Vaiva, 1924. 83 p. 891.92.V174G
PU CtY

9044. --- Mano taurė. Kaunas,
Švyturys, 1939. 120 p.
891.92.V194Ma PU CtTMF

9045. --- Naujieji žmonės; penkių
veiksmų komedija. Kaunas, 1937.
271 p. 891.92.V8 CtTMF

9046. --- Nuodėmingas angelas;
penkių veiksmų drama. Kaunas, 1927.
125 p. PG8721.V32N8 PU CtTMF

9047. --- Pražydo nuvytusios gė-
lės; 2 veiksmų 4 paveikslų pjesė.
Kaunas, 1923. 35 p. 891.92.V194P
PU OKentU

9048. --- Stabai ir žmonės; penkių veiksmų pjesė. Kaunas, 1929.
219 p. 891.92.V2 CtTMF

9049. --- Sudrumstoji ramybė; keturių veiksmų drama. Kaunas, 1927.
115 p. PG8721.V32S8 PU CtTMF

9050. --- Tuščios pastangos; 4
veiksmų drama. Kaunas, Valstybės
spaustuvė, 1926. 121 p.
891.92.V194P PU CtTMF ICCC

9051. VAITKUS, Mykolas. Vilnius
mūsų! Penkių veiksmų drama. Kaunas, Vilniui vaduoti s-ga, 1930.
44 p. L970.31ŽE ICLJF

9052. --- Žvaigždės duktė; 4
veiksmų drama. Kaunas, J. Reylenderio, 1924. 170 p. 891.92.V12
CtTMF ICCC OCl

9053. VIENUOLIS, A., pseud. 1831
metai; istorinės 1831 metų Lietuvos
sukilimo tragedijos aštuonių paveikslų dramatizuota kronika. Kaunas, Sakalas, 1937. 205 p. OCl

9054. VILKUTAITIS, Juozas. Ameri-
ka pirtyje; komedija iš trijų dalių.
[By] Robertas Keturakis. Tilsit, J.
Schoenke, 1895. 43 p. 860.V ICBM
NN

9055. --- --- Spausta 2. atvėju.
Peterburge, Imp. Mokslų akademijos
spaustuvėje, 1904. 49 p. (Lietuviškas teatrališkas knygynas, no.1)
Author's pseud., Keturakis, at head
of title. PG8721.V53A8 DLC

9056. --- --- [Another edition]
Kaunas, 1921. 891.92.V214A 1921 PU

9057. --- --- [Another edition]
Vilnius, Vaga, 1966. 118 p. facsims., ports. PG8721.V53A8 1966

DLC PU

9058. VITAITIS, Stasys E. Susi-
prato; dviveiksmė tragikomedija.
New York, N.Y., Tėvynė, 1919. 62 p.
(Susivienijimas lietuvių Amerikoje.
Leidinys, no.42) NN

9059. ŽEMKALNIS, Gabrielius.
Blinda svieto lygintojas; Žemaičių
razbaininkas. Keturių veiksmų ir
vieno paveikslo drama. Vilnius, J.
Zavadzkio spaustuvė, 1908. 127 p.
891.922.Z ICBM

9060. ŽIDANAVIČIUS, Juozas. Ba-
joras Gaidys; 5 veiksmų komedija.
[By] Seirijų Juozas [pseud.] Klaipėda, Ryto b-vės spaustuvė, 1926.
64 p. PG8721.Z5B3 PU

9061. --- Lietuvos likimas; scenos
vaizdai trijų atidengimų. Parašė
Seirijų Juozas [pseud.] Chicago,
Ill., Draugo spaustuvė, 1930. 48 p.
891.92.Z631L PU

XIII.5.c.5. POETRY

9062. AISTIS, Jonas. Be tevynės
braugios. Thompson, Conn., Mari-
anapolio kolégijos leidinys, 1942.
60 p. 891.92.Ai85B PU CaOONL MH
MiD NN

9063. --- Kristaliniam karste;
eilės. [Brooklyn, N.Y.] 1957. 45
p. port. PG8721.A4K7 CaOTU DLC NN
OKentU

9064. --- Nemuno ilgesys. Greene,
Me. [Darbininkas] 1947. 78 p.
(Lietuvos Pranciškonų leidinys, nr.
4) PG8721.A4N4 DLC PU ICCC

9065. --- Pilnatis; parinktos
eilės. Redagavo ir žodį parašė
Bern. Brazdžionis. Schweinfurt,
Ger., 1948. 159 p.
891.92.Ai85P PU ICCC OKentU

9066. --- Poezija. [2. laida.
New York, N.Y.] Romuva [1961] 420
p. PG8721.A4P6 1961 DLC CaAEU CaOTU
ICCC NN OKentU PU

9067. --- Sesuo buitis; poezija.
[Putnam, Conn.] 1951. 45 p.
PG8721.A4S4 DLC CaOTU ICCC MH NN
OKentU PPULC PU

9068. ALEKNAVIČIUS, Kajetonas.
Kikilis laibakojis. [Paruošė J.
Pilypaitis] Vilnius, Vaga, 1971.
234 p. PG8721.A46K5 1971 PU

9069. ANDRIEKUS, Leonardas. At-

viros marios; lyrika. Brooklyn,
N.Y., Franciscan Fathers, 1955.
134 p. illus. 891.93.An23A PU
CaOONL ICCC NN OKentU

9070. --- Naktigonė; lyrika.
Brooklyn, N.Y., Tėvai Pranciškonai,
1963. 111 p. PG9119.A5N3 DLC
CaOONL PU

9071. --- Saulė kryžiuose. Brooklyn, N.Y., Išleido Pranciškonai,
1960. 208 p. PG9119.A5 DLC CaOONL
CtY ICCC PU

9072. ANGLICKIS, Stasys. Karklai
žydi; eilėraščiai. Vilnius, Vaga,
1969. 114 p. PG8721.A58K3 PU
CaOTU OKentU

9073. --- Metūgės linksta į saulę.
Vilnius, Vaga, 1965. 85 p.
PG8721.A58A6 1965 DLC

9074. --- Po atviru dangum; eilėraščiai. Vilnius, VGLL, 1960. 146
p. illus. PG8721.A58P6 DLC

9075. ARMINAS, Petras. Eilės.
[By Trumpinėlis, pseud. Paruošė K.
Nastopka] Vilnius, Vaga, 1970.
122 p. PG8721.A75A17 1970 PU
OKentU

9076. BABICKAS, Petras. Dramblio
kojos. Iliustravo Vladas Vijeikis.
[Chicago, Ill.] Teviškėlė, 1957.
118 p. illus. PG8749.B3D7 DLC PU
OKentU

9077. --- Svetimoj padangėj.
Buenos Aires, 1947. 63 p.
891.92.B112S PU

9078. --- Toli nuo tėvynės. 2.
papildytas leidimas. Rome, 1946.
105 p. Bound with Aistis, Jonas.
Sesuo buitis. Putnam, Conn. 1951.
891.92.A85S PU

9079. BALČIŪNIENĖ, Ona. Beržų pasakos, poezija. Iliustravo L. Vi-
limas. Stamford, Conn., 1952. 96 p.
illus. Author's pseud., O.B. Au-
dronė, at head of title.
891.92.B184B PU PPULC

9080. --- Tik tau ir man. O. Au-
dronė [pseud.] London, Nida, 1969.
199 p. PG8721.B28T5 PU

9081. BALTAKIS, Algimantas. Ke-
liaujantis kalnas; eilėraščiai.
Vilnius, Vaga, 1967. 124 p. illus.
PG8722.12.A4K4 DLC PU

9081a --- Keturios stygos. [Vil-
nius, VGLL, 1959] 159 p.
PG8722.12.A4B42 PU

9082. ---Požeminės upės; eilėraš-

čiai. Vilnius, Vaga, 1965. 230 p.
PG8722.12.A4P6 DLC

9083. --- --- [2. leidimas] Iliustravo Em. Katilius. Vilnius, Vaga,
1967. 282 p. illus.
PG8722.12.A4P6 1967 DLC NN

9084. --- Stebuklinga žolė; eilėraščiai. Vilnius, Vaga, 1971. 421
p. PG8722.12.A4S75 PU

9085. --- Velnio tiltas. [2. papildytas leidimas] Vilnius, VGLL,
1961. 309 p. illus.
PG8722.12.A4V4 1961 DLC OKentU PU

9086. BALTRUŠAITIS, Jurgis. Po-
ezija. Spaudai parengė J. Aistis.
[So. Boston, Mass.] P.M. Juras,
1948. 270 p. port., facsim.
PG8721.B3P6 DLC CaAEU CtY ICCC MiD
OKentU PPULC PU

9087. --- --- [Another edition]
Leidinį parengė įvadą ir paaiškinimus parašė Vytautas Kubilius. Vilnius, 1967. 354 p. PG8721.B3A6
1967 PU DLC OKentU

9088. BARANAUSKAS, Albinas. Pa-
saga ir vyšnios; eilėraščiai.
Chicago, Ill., Lietuviškos knygos
klubas, 1969. 64 p.
PG8721.B324P3 PU

9089. BARANAUSKAS, Antanas.
Anykščių šilelis. Tilžė, E. Jagomasto, 1920. 16 p. illus., ports.
891.92.B2995An PU CtY PPULC

9090. --- --- [Another edition]
J. Kuzminskio medžio raižiniai.
[Redaktorius A. Žirgulys] Vilnius,
VGLL, 1954. 62 p. illus., port. NN

9091. --- --- [Another edition.
Dalininkas V. Valius. Vilnius,
VGLL, 1959] 28 p. illus.
PG8721.B325A8 DLC PU

9092. --- --- [Another edition]
Iliustravo Pranas Lapė. [Ed. by
Vincas Maciūnas. New York, N.Y.]
Romuva, 1961. 1 v. (unpaged) col.
illus. 891.92.B2296An 1961 PU CtY
NN

9093. --- Ostlitauische Texte. 1
Hft. Weimar. H. Böhlau, 1882.
xxxv, 23 p. 491.922.B2321 PU CU
ICN ICRL IU MdBJ MiU NjP NNU PPULC
WU

9094. --- Pasikalbėjimas giesmini-
ko su Lietuva. Spaudon prirengė ir
prakalbą pridėjo Antanas Jakštas.
Kaunas, Šv. Kazimiero d-ja. 1907.
141 p. PG8721.B325P3 PU

9095. BAVARSKAS, Medardas. Sunkios

valandos; pirmoji eilėraščiu knyga. Schweinfurt, Ger. [Tėviškė] 1948. 111 p. 891.92.B329S PU

9096. BERNOTAS, Albinas. Karšti laiptai. Vilnius, Vaga, 1968. 78 p. PG8722.12.B7K3 PU

9097. BINKIS, Kazys. Eilėraščiai; poezijos bandymų sąsiuvinys. Kaunas, J. Raupys, 1920. 50 p. 891.92.B517E PU OCl

9098. --- Kiškų sukilimas; poema kiškių draugams. Kaunas, Spaudos fondas, 1937. 25 p. col. illus. MiD

9099. --- Lyrika. Redagavo ir įvadą parašė Jonas Aistis. [Chicago, Ill.] Terra [1952] 116 p. PG8721.B5L9 DLC ICU NN OCl PU

9100. BLEKAITIS, Jurgis. Vardai vandenims ir dienoms; eilėraščiai. [Chicago, Ill.] Terra [1954] 70 p. PG8721.B55V3 DLC NN PPULC PU

9101. BLOŽĖ, Vytautas. Iš tylinčios žemės; eilėraščiai. Vilnius, Vaga, 1966. 85 p. PG8722.L618 DLC

9102. --- Žemės gėlės; eilėraščiai. Vilnius, Vaga, 1971. 68 p. PG8722.12.L6Z4 PU

9103. BOGUTAITĖ, Vitalija. Lietus ir laikas. Brooklyn, N.Y., Ateitis, 1969. 59 p. PG8749.B62L52 PU

9104. --- Veidrodis jūros dugne; eilėraščiai. Brooklyn, N.Y. Ateitis, 1960. 58 p. 891.92.B634V PU CaOONL OCl

9105. BORUTA, Kazys. Dainos apie svyruojančius gluosnius; lyrika ir poemos. Kaunas, Žalia vėtra, 1927. 31 p. PG8721.B6D3 PU

9106. BRADŪNAS, Kazys. Devynios baladės. [Chicago, Ill., Lietuviškos knygos klubo leidinys, 1955] 141 p. PG8749.B67D4 DLC CaAEU CaOONL CaOTU ICCC MB OCl PPULC PU

9107. --- Donelaičio kapas. Čikaga, M. Morkūnas, 1970. 94 p. PG8749.B67D6 PU OKentU

9108. --- Maras; poema. Iliustracijos T. Valius. n.p., 1947. 43 p. illus. 891.92.B722M PU CaOONL

9109. --- Morėnų ugnys. [Toronto, Ont.] Literatūros lankai [1958] 78 p. PG8749.B67M6 DLC CaOTU PU

9110. --- Sidabrinės kamanos. [Chicago, Ill.] Lietuviškos knygos klubas [1964] 94 p. PG8749.B67S5

DLC CaOONL CaOTU PU

9111. --- Sonatos ir fūgos; susitikimai su Čiurlioniu... kompozicijos padarytos Vytauto O. Virkau. Chicago, Ill., M. Morkūnas, 1967. 59 p. PG8749.B67S6 DLC CaOTU PU

9112. --- Vilniaus varpai; sonetai. Tübingen, Ger., Patria, 1947. 29 p. illus. 891.92.B722V PU CaOONL DLC ICCC

9113. BRAZDŽIONIS, Bernardas. Amžinas žydas. Kaunas, 1931. 127 p. 891.921.B ICCC

9114. --- Didžioji kryžkelė. [Chicago, Ill.] Terra [1953] 111 p. PG8721.B7D5 DLC MiD MH OCl PPULC PU

9115. --- Šiaurės pašvaistė. Schweinfurt; Würzburg, Ger., 1947. 70 p. 891.921.B ICCC

9116. --- Svetimi kalnai. [Tübingen, Ger., A. Urbonas] 1945. 190 p. 891.92.B739S PU ICCC MiD

9117. --- Vidudienio sodai. Los Angeles, Calif. [Lietuvių dienos, 1961] 126 p. PG8721.B7V5 DLC CaAEU CaOTU CtY NN PU

9118. --- Ženklai ir stebuklai. [Kaunas] Sakalas, 1936. 94 p. 891.921.B ICCC

9119. BUČYS, Algimantas. Aukštupiai; eilėraščiai. Vilnius, Vaga, 1967. 82 p. PG8722.12.U25A8 PU

9120. --- Prie skambančių plytų; eilėraščiai. Vilnius, VGLL, 1963. 30 p. ports. (Pirmoji knyga, 1963) PG8722.12.U25P7 DLC MH

9121. BUIVYDAITĖ, Bronė. Vasaros šnekos; eilėraščiai. Vilnius, Švyturio bendrovė, 1921. 82 p. 891.92B857V PU OCl

9122. CHURGINAS, Aleksys. Ir tavo širdy. Vilnius, Vaga, 1970. 173 p. PG8721.C45I7 PU

9123. --- Ugnis. [Kaune] VGLL [1946] 183 p. PG8721.C45U4 DLC NN

9124. ČIPKUS, Alfonsas. Balandžio vigilija; eilėraščiai. Alfonsas Nyka-Niliūnas [pseud.] Chicago, Ill., 1957. 96 p. PG8721.C48B3 DLC PU

9125. --- Orfėjaus medis; eilėraščiai. Alfonsas Nyka-Niliūnas [pseud. 2. laida. Čikagoje, 1954] 127 p. PG8721.C48O7 1954 DLC CtY CtTMF ICCC IU MdBE OCl PU

9126. --- Praradimo simfonijos; poezija. [Iliustravo Kazys Janulis. Tübingen, Ger.] Patrija [c1946] 127 p. illus. At head of title: Alfonsas Nyka-Niliūnas. PG8721.C48P7 DLC PU

9127. DAMBRAUSKAS, Aleksandras. Adomo Jakšto rudens aidai; eilės. [By] Adomas Jakštas [pseud.] Kaunas, 1911. 100 p. PG8721.D78R8 PU

9128. --- --- 2. pataisytas leidimas. Kaunas, "Šviesa", [1920] 99 p. PG8721.D28A7 DLC CaOTU PU

9129. --- Dainų skrynelė. [By] Adomas Jakštas [pseud.] Peterburgas, 1905. 140 p. illus. 891.91.J4 CtTMF ICCC

9130. --- Lyrika. [By] Adomas Jakštas [pseud.] Kaunas, Šv. Kazimiero draugijos leidinys, 1930. [384] p. 891.91.J2 CtTMF ICCC OCl

9131. --- Rudens aidai; eilės. [By] Adomas Jakštas [pseud.] Kaunas, Š. Banaičio spaustuvė, 1911. 100 p. 891.91.J5 CtTMF CtY

9132. DEGUTYTĖ, Janina. Ant žemės delno. Vilnius, VGLL,1963. 97 p. PG8722.14.E35A7 DLC

9133. --- Dienos-dovanos; eilėraščiai. Vilnius, VGLL, 1960. 189 p. illus. PG8722.14.E35D5 DLC PU

9134. --- Mėlynos deltos; rinktinė. Vilnius, Vaga, 1968. 242 p. PG8722.14.E35M4 PU MH PPULC

9135. --- Pilnatis. Vilnius, Vaga, 1967. 118 p. PG8722.14.E35P5 PU

9136. --- Šiaurės vasaros. Vilnius, Vaga, 1966. 106 p. PG8722.14.E35S5 DLC NN PU

9137. --- Žalia ugnelė. [Iliustravo M. Ladigaitė] Vilnius, Vaga,1966. 42 p. illus. DLC

9138. DONELAITIS, Kristijonas. Duonelaičio raštai, mokykloms parinko ir paaiškino M. Biržiška. Kaunas, Švyturys, 1921. 88 p. 891.921D ICCC OCl

9139. --- Jau saulelė vėl... [Dailininkas V. Kalinauskas. Vilnius, VGLL, 1963] 81 p. Lithuanian, German, Polish, etc. 891.92.D713J PU NN

9140. --- K. Donelaitis. Sudaryta pagal Lietuvos TSR Švietimo ministerijos programą. Kaunas, Valstybinė pedagoginės literatūros leidykla,

1955. 84 p. illus. (Mokinio biblioteka) PG8721.D7A17 1955 MiU

9141. --- Kristijono Donelaičio raštai. Pagal Rėzos, Šleicherio ir Neselmano... sutaisė J. Šlapelis. 5. išleidimas. Vilnius, M. Piaseckaitės-Šlapelienės knygyno išleidimas, 1909. 88 p. 491.22.D713.95 PU

9142. --- Metai. [The seasons. Ed. by J. Ambrazevičius, illus. by V.K. Jonynas] Kaunas, Švietimo ministerijos leidinys, 1940. 191 p. illus. Reproduction and impression: Offenburg (Baden), Ger., F. Burde, 1948. PG8721.D7M3 DLC CaAEU ICCC MiD OCl OKentU PU

9143. --- --- [Another edition] Iliustravo V. Jurkūnas. [Kaunas, VGLL, 1956] 157 p. illus. port. PG8721.D7M3 1956 DLC NN PU ViU

9144. --- --- [Another edition] Kaunas, 1966. 132 p. illus., port. PG8721.D7M3 1966 DLC PU

9145. DRILINGA, Antanas. Rankos ir betonas. Vilnius, VGLL, 1962. 118 p. illus. PG8722.14.R5R3 DLC

9146. --- Šiluma; eilėraščiai. Vilnius, Vaga, 1968. 127 p. illus. PG8722.14.R5S5 DLC NN OKentU PU

9147. GAIDAMAVIČIUS, Zigmas. Gėlynas; rinktinė. Vilnius, VGLL, 1963. 237 p. illus., facsim., port. PG8721.G28G4 1963 DLC

9148. GIRA, Liudas. Dūl-Dūl Dudelė; eilės. Vilnius, 1909. 54 p. CtTMF

9149. --- Ne margi sakalėliai. Lino raižiniai D. Tarabildienės. Vilnius, VGLL, 1963. 62 p. PG8721.G5N4 DLC

9150. --- Šilko gijos; lyrika. Kaunas, Dirvos leidinys, 1929. 80 p. illus. 891.921.G ICCC

9151. --- Tėvynės keliais. Kaunas Švyturio b-vės leidinys, 1922. 64 p. 891.92.G448.2 PU ICCC

9152. --- Tolimuos keliuos. [Kaune] VGLL, 1945. 81 p. illus. PG8721.G5T6 DLC

9153. --- Žalgirio Lietuva. Maskva, LTSR Valstybinė leidykla, 1942. 28 p. PG8721.G5Z2 DLC

9154. --- Žiežirbos; 1912-20 m. poezijos. Kaunas, Švyturio, 1921. 109 p. PG8721.G42Z2 CaAEU CtY ICCC NN OCl PU

9155. GRIGAITYTĖ, Kotryna. Paslaptis; lyrika. [Bielefeld, Ger.] Venta [1950] 77 p. illus.
PG8721.G64P3 DLC MH PU

9156. --- Rudens sapnai; premijuotas poezijos rinkinys. Chicago, Ill., Lietuviškos knygos klubas, 1963. 80 p. PG9048.G67R8 DLC CaOONL CaOTU PU

9157. --- Širdis pergamente; lyrika. [n.p.] Venta [1956] 74 p.
PG8721.G64S5 DLC

9158. --- Trapus vakaras; lyrika. Putnam, Conn., Immaculata, 1968. 108 p. PG8721.G64T7 PU PPULC

9159. GUSTAITIS, Antanas. Anapus teisybės; humoristiniai eilėraščiai. Teisingą kritikos žodį taria Pulgis Andriušis. [Brooklyn, N.Y.] Gabija [195-] 143 p. PG8721.G8A7 DLC CaAEU OCl PU

9160. --- Ir atskrido juodas varnas. Chicago, Ill., Santara-Šviesa, 1966. 119 p. PG8721.G85.I7 DLC PU

9161. --- --- 2. laida. Chicago, Ill., [Santara-Šviesa] 1968. 121 p. PG8721.G85I7 1968 CaOTU

9162. HERBAČIAUSKAS, Juozapas Albinas. Dievo šypsenos. T.1. Kaunas, Universitetas, 1939. 203 p. 491.922.H418.2 PU

9163. --- Erškėčių vainikas. [By] Jaunutis Vienuolis [pseud.] Krokuvoje, 1908. 84 p. 491.922.H418 PU

9164. INČIŪRA, Kazys. Prie Kauno marių. Vilnius, VGLL,1962. 291 p. illus. PG8721.I5P7 DLC

9165. --- Tyliųjų saulėlydžių žemėj; eilėraščių ir dainų knyga. [Kaunas] Šv. Kazimiero draugijos leidinys, 1930. 118 p. 891.921I ICCC

9166. JAKŠTAS, Jonas. Metų laiptais; eilėraščiai. Vilnius, Vaga, 1969. 116 p. PG8722.2.A55M4 PU

9167. JAKUBĖNAS, Kazys. Užia melsvas šilas; poezija. [Redakcinė komisija: A. Jonynas, E. Mieželaitis, Vl. Mozūriūnas] Vilnius, VGLL, 1957. 448 p. port. PU CaOONL

9168. JANONIS, Julius. Ave vita... Medžio graviūros Vlado Žiliaus. Vilnius, Vaga, 1964. 134 p. illus. PG8721.J3A9 DLC

9169. --- Eilėraščiai vaikams. [Įžanga ir komentarai Justino Marcinkevičiaus. Iliustracijos D. Tarabildienės ir R. Ulbikaitės] Vilnius, VGLL, 1953. 81 p. illus.

PZ70.L52J29 DLC

9170. --- Naujas rytas. Vilnius, VGLL, 1960. 157 p. illus., port. PG8721.J3N3 DLC

9171. --- Puslėtosioms rankoms. [Dailininkas Rimt. Gibavičius] Vilnius, Vaga, 1966. 232 p. illus. PG8721.J3P8 DLC IU MH PU

9172. JASILIONIS, Stasys. Bešvintantis rytas; eilių rinkinys. Brooklyn, N.Y., "Laisvė", 1936. 288 p. illus. OCl

9173. JOKIMAITIS, Gediminas. ... su naktim kalbėsiu. Vilnius, Vaga, 1971. 83 p. PG9722.2.O4S8 PU

9174. JONYNAS, Antanas. Ateina įkvėpimas; lyrika. Vilnius, Vaga, 1965. 270 p. illus. PG8722.2.O5A83 DLC IU MH

9175. JŪRA, Klemensas. Tremtinio ašara; lyrika. [n.p.] 1948. 70 p. PG8721.J73T7 PU

9176. JUŠKAITIS, Jonas. Ir aušros ir žaros; eilėraščiai. Vilnius, Vaga, 1962. 34 p. port. PG8722.2.U8I7 DLC

9177. KAIRYS, Anatolijus. Auksinė sėja; eilėraščiai. Chicago, Ill. [Nemunas] 1954. 85 p. PG8721.K2A9 DLC PU

9178. KARALIUS, Vytautas. Šviesa ir akys. Vilnius, VGLL, 1960. 39 p. port. PG8722.21.A7S9 DLC PU

9179. KAŠKAITIS, Jonas. Augo beržas. Vilnius, Vaga, 1964. 131 p. port. PG8722.21.A72A8 DLC

9180. --- Prošvaistės; eilės ir poemos. Richmond Hill, N.Y., 1950. 311 p. 891.92.K154P PU

9181. KATILIŠKIENĖ, Zinaida (Nagytė) Bevardė šalis. [By] Liūnė Sutema [pseud] Chicago, Ill., [Santarosšviesos federacija] 1966. 64 p. PG8749.K35B4 DLC CaOTU PU

9182. --- Tebūnie tarytum pasakoj. [Viršelį ir vinjetes piešė V. Ignas. Chicago, Ill.] Terra [1955] 54 p. illus. At head of title: Liūnė Sutema. PG8749.K35T4 DLC

9183. KĖKŠTAS, Juozas. Diena naktin; eilėraščiai. Buenos Aires, Argentinos jaunimo draugija, 1947. 62 p. 947.52.K267D PU DLC

9184. --- Etapai; poezija, 1933-1953. [Nördlingen, Ger.] Venta

[1953] 143 p. illus.
PG8721.K43E8 DLC CaAEU CaOTU PU

9185. --- Lyrika. Vilnius, VGLL,
1964. 138 p. port. PG8722.21.E55L9
DLC PU

9186. --- Ramybė man; poezijos lan-
kas. [Brooklyn, N.Y.] Gabija [1951]
45 p. PG8721.K43R3 DLC PU

9187. --- Rudens dugnu; antroji
lyrikos knyga. Roma, 1946. 62 p.
891.92.K267R PU

9188. --- Staigus horizontas; trečioji lyrikos knyga. Roma, 1946.
50 p. 891.92.K267S PU

9189. KETURAKIS, Robertas. Balti
sparnai. Vilnius, Vaga, 1965. 72 p.
PG8721K5B3 DLC IU MH

9190. --- Saulėtekis kely. Vilnius, VGLL, 1961. 58 p. illus.
PG8721.K5S2 DLC

9191. KIRŠA, Faustas. Maldos ant
akmens; penkta eilių knyga. [Kaunas]
Sakalas [1937] 80 p. PG8721.K57S8
DLC CtTMF ICCC

9192. --- Palikimas; eilėraščiai,
nebaigti eilėraščiai, Aidų aidužių
aidai, Pelenai III ir IV, Pabėgėliai,
užrašai ir kt. Leidinį spaudai parengė Stasys Santvaras. [Boston,
Mass.] Lietuvių enciklopedijos leidykla [1972] 318 p. PG8721.K57P3 PU

9193. --- Pelenai; poezijos rinktinė. Vilnius, Vaga, 1969. 265 p.
illus. PG8721.K61P4 DLC OKentU PU

9194. --- Piligrimai. Kaunas, Žinija, 1939. 104 p. 891.921.K ICCC

9195. --- --- 2. leidimas. Kaunas,
1940. 104 p. 8721.K57P5 1940 PU

9196. --- Šventieji akmenys; didak-
tiniai eilėraščiai. Brooklyn, N.Y.,
1951. 112 p. PG8721.K57S8 DLC
CaAEU CaOONL CaOTU CtTMF NN PU

9197. --- Tolumos. Viktoras Petravičius: lino raižiniai. [Dillingen-
Donau, Ger.] Mūsų kelio leidinys
[1947] 189 p. illus. PG8721.K57A17
1947 DLC CtTMF ICCC MiD OKentU PU

9198. --- Verpetai; pirmas eilių
rinkinys. Vilnius, 1918. 112 p.
891.92.K635V PU

9199. KRIKŠČIŪNAS, Jonas. Eilės
ir dainos. [Kaune] VGLL [1947] 135
p. port. PG8721.K47E5 DLC PU

9200. --- Neliūdėk, berželi. [Kau-

nas,VGLL, 1961] 218 p. illus.,
port. PG8721.K74N4 DLC PU

9201. --- Pirmieji žiedai. [By]
Jovaras [pseud.] Chicago, Ill.,
Turtu ir spauda "Lietuvos", 1909.
27 p. 891.92.K894P PU

9202. --- Širdies balsai; eilių
rinkinėlis. [By] Jovaras [pseud.]
Tilžėje, 1908. 891.92.K894 P PU

9203. --- Tėvynės laukuose; apysa-
kų rinkinys. Parašė Jovaras [pseud.]
Pittsburg, Pa., 1909. 891.92.K894T
PU

9204. LASTAS, Adomas. Poezijos
rinktinė. Vilnius, VGLL, 1957. 297
p. port. 891.92.L335 PU

9205. MACEINA, Antanas. Gruodas;
eilėraščiai. [Brooklyn, N.Y., Ateitis, 1965] 94 p. PG8721.M23G7 DLC
CaOTU PU

9206. MAČERNIS, Vytautas. Poezija.
Redagavo Kazys Bradūnas, iliustravo
Paulius Augius. [Chicago, Ill.]
Lietuvių fondas lietuviškai kultūrai
ūgdyti [1961] 238 p. PG8721.M25A17
1961 CaOTU CtTMF CtY NN PU

9207. MACEVIČIUS, Juozas. Ato-
švaistės; rinktinė. Vilnius, Vaga,
1971. 305 p. PG8722.23.A27A8 CaOTU
PU

9208. --- Kasdieniška knyga; [ei-
lėraščiai] Vilnius, Vaga, 1968.
86 p. PG8722.23.A27K3 CaOTU

9209. MAIRONIS, Jonas. Jaunoji
Lietuva; poema. 2. laida, bent kiek
pataisyta. Kaunas, 1920. 131 p.
891.92.M187J PU CtTMF ICCC

9210. --- --- [Another edition.
Nida [1963] 118 p. (Nidos knygų
klubo leidinys, nr. 43)
PG8721.M3J3 CaOTU

9211. --- Jūratė ir Kastytis.
Iliustravo D. Tarabildinė. [Kaune,
VGLL, 1957] [24] p. (chiefly
illus.) PG8721.M3J8 DLC

9212. --- --- [Another edition]
Iliustravo L. Barisaitė. Vilnius,
1967. 38 p. PG8721.M3J8 1967 PU

9213. --- --- [Another edition]
V. Galdiko medžio raižiniai. Vilnius, 1968. 16 p. PG8721.M3J8
1968 PU

9214. --- Maironis. Sudaryta pagal
Lietuvos TSR Švietimo ministerijos
programą. 2. leidimas. Kaunas,
Valstybinė pedagoginės literatūros

leidykla, 1958. 86 p. (Mokinio
biblioteka) PG8721.M3A6 1958 DLC

9215. --- Mūsų vargai; poema pen-
kiose dalyse. Kaunas, 1920. 151
p. 891.92.M187M PU CaOONL CtTMF
ICCC

9216. --- Pavasario balsai.
Tilžė, 1895. 78 p. 891.91.M22
CtTMF

9217. --- --- 4. leidimas. Kaunas, 1913. 109 p. 891.91.M23
CtTMF

9218. --- --- 5. leidimas. Tilžė;
Kaunas, Šv. Kazimiero draugija,
1920. 119 p. 891.91.M25 CtTMF ICCC

9219. --- --- 10. laida. Würzburg, Ger., 1947. 301 p. illus.
PG8721.M22P33 1947 CaAEU PU

9220. --- --- 17 laida. Roma
[1952] 307 p. illus. (His Kūryba,
1) PG8721.M3P3 DLC CaAEU CaOONL
CaOTU CtTMF OCl MH

9221. --- --- [Another edition]
J. Kaminskio medžio raižiniai.
Vilnius, VGLL, 1958. 179 p. illus.
PG8721.M3P3 1958 DLC CtPAM OKentU PU

9222. --- --- [Another edition]
Dailininkas Valerijonas Galdikas.
Vilnius, Vaga, 1970. 222 p.
illus. PG8721.M3P3 1970 PU OKentU

9223. --- Pavasario balsai ir Kur
išganymas. 3. kartą atspausta,
pataisyta ir padauginta. Parašė
Maironis (J. M-lis). Peterburgas,
Lietuvių laikraščio kaštais, 1905.
891.92.M187P 1905 PU

9224. --- Poezija; rinktinė.
[Redakcinė komisija: K. Korsakas,
E. Mieželaitis ir A. Venclova. Su-
darė A. Sluckaitė. Vilnius, VGLL,
1962] 308 p. illus. PG8721.M3P6
DLC NN PU

9225. --- --- [2. leidimas] Vilnius, Vaga, 1966. 310 p. illus.
PG8721.M3P6 1966 DLC OKentU

9226. --- Raseinių Magdė. 2.
laida. Kaunas, 1917. 31 p.
891.91.M7 CtTMF

9227. --- Tarp skausmų į garbę;
poema isz dabartinių laikų. [By]
Garnys [pseud.] Tilžė, Spausta
kasztu E. Jagomasto, 1895. 91 p.
891.92.M187T PU CtTMF

9228. MALDONIS, Alfonsas. Auga
medžiai; eilėraščiai. Vilnius, Vaga,
1965. 133 p. illus., ports.
PG8721.M33A8 DLC IU NN PU

9229. --- Saulėti lietūs; eilėraščiai. [Vilnius, VGLL, 1962]
150 p. illus. PG8721.M33S3 DLC

9230. --- Šitie metai; eilėraščiai.
Vilnius, Vaga, 1966. 294 p.
PG8722.23.A5S5 DLC

9231. --- Veja vėtra debesį;
eilėraščiai. [Vilnius, VGLL, 1960]
147 p. illus. PG8721.M33V4 DLC

9232. --- Viduvasaris; eilėraščiai.
Vilnius, VGLL, 1958. 102 p. illus.
PG8721.M33V5 DLC

9233. MARCINKEVIČIUS, Justinas.
Duoną raikančios rankos; eilėraščiai.
Vilnius, VGLL, 1963. 110 p.
PG8721.M35D85 DLC

9234. --- Dvidešimtas pavasaris;
poema. [Kaune] VGLL, 1960. 328 p.
illus. PG8721.M35D9 DLC

9235. --- --- [Another edition]
Vilnius, 1970. 328 p.
PG8721.M35D9 1970 PU CaOTU

9236. --- Kraujas ir pelenai;
herojinė poema. [Raižiniai ir iliustracijos S. Krasausko] Vilnius,
VGLL, 1960. 144 p. illus.
PG8721.M35K7 DLC

9237. --- Liepsnojantis krūmas.
Vilnius, Vaga, 1968. 90 p.
PG8721.M35L5 DLC CaAEU

9238. --- Mediniai tiltai; eilėraščiai. Vilnius, Vaga, 1966. 138
p. illus. PG8721.M35M4 PU DLC NN

9239. --- Prašau žodžio; eilėraščiai. [Kaunas] VGLL, 1955. 108
p. NN

9240. --- Publicistinė poema.
[Medžio raižiniai ir apipavidalini-
mas A. Skliutauskaitės. Vilnius]
VGLL, 1961. 69 p. illus.
PG8721.M35P8 DLC

9241. --- Siena; miesto poema.
Vilnius, Vaga, 1965. 149 p.
PG8721.M35S5 DLC IU MH NN

9242. --- Sena abėcėlė; eilėraščiai. Vilnius, Vaga, 1969. 348 p.
PG8721.M35S4 PU CaOTU

9243. MATUZEVIČIUS, Eugenijus.
Draugystės daina; eilėraščiai. Vil-
nius, VGLL, 1953. 122 p.
PG8721.M37D7 DLC

9244. --- Mėnesienos krantas;
eilėraščiai. Vilnius, Vaga, 1965.
97 p. PG8721.M37M4 DLC

9245. --- ed. Mylimoms sesėms.
Vilnius, VGLL, 1954. 154 p.
PG8715.M3 DLC NN

9246. --- Vasarvidžio tolumos;
eilėraščiai. Vilnius, Vaga, 1968.
326 p. illus. PG8721.M37V DLC NN
PU

9247. MEKAS, Jonas. Gėlių kal-
bėjimas; eilėraščiai. Chicago,
Ill. [Lietuvių studentų Santara]
1961. 52 p. illus. PG8749.M4G4
DLC PU

9248. --- Pavieniai žodžiai;
eilėraščiai. Chicago, Ill. [Algi-
manto Mackaus Vardo knygų leidimo
fondas, 1967. 95 p. PG8749.M4P3
DLC OKentU PU

9249. --- Semeniškių idilija.
Brooklyn, N.Y. [Aidų leidinys]
1955. 62 p. 891.92.M478S PU NN

9250. MIEŽELAITIS, Eduardas.
Antakalnio barokas. Vilnius, Vaga,
1971. 298 p. PG8721.M45A53 PU

9251. --- Atogrąžos panorama.
Vilnius [VGLL] 1963. 206 p. illus.
PG8721.M45A93 DLC CtY PU

9252. --- Autoportretas. Aviaeski-
zai. Vilnius, VGLL, 1962. 294 p.
illus. PG8721.M45A96 DLC MH

9253. --- Broliška poema. 2.
leidimas. [Dailininkas V. Valius.
Vilnius, VGLL, 1960] 275 p. illus.
PG8721.M45B7 1960 DLC

9254. --- Čia Lietuva; poetinė
publicistika. [Dailininkas V. Va-
lius] Vilnius, Vaga, 1968. 575 p.
illus. PG8721.M45A6 1968b DLC CaAEU
CaOTU OKentU PU

9255. --- Duona ir žodis. [Daili-
ninkas Vytautas Valius] Vilnius,
Vaga, 1965. 269 p. illus.
PG8721.M45D8 DLC MH PU

9256. --- Era. Dailininkas S. Krasauskas. Vilnius, Vaga, 1967. 101
p. illus. PG8721.M45E7 PU DLC

9257. --- Horizontai. Vilnius,
Vaga, 1970. 271 p. PG8721.M45H6
CaOTU OKentU

9258. --- Lyriniai etiudai. [Dail.
Rimt. Gibavičius] Vilnius, Vaga,
1964. 270 p. illus. PG8721.M45L9
DLC CtY MH NNC PU

9259. --- Naktiniai drugiai; mono-
logas. Vilnius, Vaga, 1966. 242 p.
port. PG8721.M45N3 DLC PU

9260. --- Poezija. [Vilnius, VGLL,

1968] 2 v. ports. PG8721.M45A17
1968 PU NN

9261. --- Saulė gintare; eilėraščiai, apmąstymai. Vilnius, VGLL,
1961. 309 p. illus. PG8721.M45S3
DLC PU

9262. --- Svetimi akmenys. [Me-
džio raižiniai P. Rauduvės] Vilnius, VGLL, 1957. 187 p. illus.
PG8721.M45S85 PU CtY NN

9263. --- Žmogus. [Raižiniai ir
iliustracijos S. Krasausko] Vilnius,
VGLL, 1962. 125 p. 891.92.M5832Z
PU

9264. MIKUCKIS, Juozas. Aušros
rasos; eilės. Kaunas, A. Petronio
knygynas, 1920. 87 p.
PG8721.M46A92 DLC ICCC

9265. --- Lyrikos kraitis. [Chi-
cago, Ill.] Terra [1954] 174 p.
PG8721.M46L9 DLC ICCC PU

9266. MIKUTA, Algimantas. Gėlės
braižykloj; eilėraščiai. Vilnius,
VGLL, 1962. 51 p. port.
PG8722.23.I4G4 DLC

9267. --- Paukščių žemė. Vilnius,
Vaga, 1968. 91 p. PG8722.23.I38P3
PU DLC

9268. MIŠKINIS, Antanas. Arti
prie žemės. Vilnius, Vaga, 1965.
142 p. PG8721.M53A9 PU DLC

9269. --- Eilėraščiai. Vilnius,
VGLL, 1960. 217 p. illus.
PG8721.M53E35 DLC NN PU

9270. --- Keturi miestai. 2. leidimas. Kaunas, 1938. 155 p.
891.91.M37 CtTMF

9271. --- Poezija. Vilnius, Vaga,
1970. 2 v. PG8721.M53 1970 PU

9272. --- Svajonė ir maištas; devynių giesmių lyrinė poema. Vilnius, Vaga, 1967. 72 p. illus.
PG8721.M53S9 DLC OKentU PU

9273. --- Varnos prie plento.
Kaunas, 1936. 126 p. 891.91.M36
CtTMF

9274. MONTVILA, Vytautas. Eilė-
raščio šūvis. [Iliustracijos R.
Gibavičiaus] Vilnius, VGLL, 1961.
266 p. illus. PG8721.M56E35 DLC PU

9275. --- Į saulės taką. Vilnius,
VGLL, 1963. 126 p. illus.
PG8721.M56.I2 DLC NN

9276. --- Poezija. [Kaunas]
VGLL, [1945] 207 p. port. NN

9277. --- Vainikas Tarybų Lietuvai; eilėraščiai. [Kaune] VGLL
[1946, i.e. 1947] 61 p.
PG8721.M56V2 DLC

9278. MOZŪRIŪNAS, Vladas. Jūros
posmai. [Iliustracijos Arūno Tara-
bildos] Vilnius, Vaga, 1965. 90
p. illus. PG8721.M6J8 DLC

9279. --- Lyrika. Medžio graviūros V. Žiliaus. Vilnius, Vaga,
1967. 174 p. illus. PG8721.M6L9
DLC IU

9280. --- Šaltinis prie kelio;
eilėraščiai. Vilnius, VGLL, 1957.
231 p. PG8721.M6S3 PU

9281. --- Vilniaus etiudai; eilėraščiai. Vilnius, VGLL, 1958. 71
p. illus. PG8721.M6V5 DLC

9282. --- --- Antra knyga. [Dai-
lininkas V. Kalinauskas] Vilnius,
VGLL, 1963. 60 p. illus. NN

9283. --- --- [Another edition]
Vl. Sparnaičio nuotraukos, daili-
ninko V. Kalinausko iliustracijos]
Vilnius, Mintis, 1967. 48 p.
illus. NN

9284. MYKOLAITIS, Vincas. Būties
valanda. Vilnius, VGLL, 1963. 157
p. PG8721.M9B8 DLC

9285. --- Keliai ir kryžkeliai;
lyrika. [Chicago, Ill.] Terra
[1953] 299 p. PG8721.M9K4 DLC
ICCC IU MiD PU

9286. --- Kunigaikštis Žvainys;
poema, ir Raudoni žiedai; eilės.
[By] Putinas. Petrapilis, Lietuvių
spaustuvė, 1916. 110 p.
491.922.M994 PU

9287. --- Langas. [Dailininkas
Vytautas Valius] Vilnius, Vaga,
1966. 111 p. illus. PG8721.M9L3
DLC NN OKentU PU

9288. --- Poezija. Vilnius, VGLL,
1956. 271 p. PG8721.M9A17 1956 PU

9289. --- Rūščios dienos. Kaunas,
Sakalas [1944] 75 p. Photo-mecha-
nical reproduction-Xerox.
PG8721.M9R8 1944 PU

9290. --- --- [Another edition.
By] Mykolaitis-Putinas, V. [pseud.
Redagavo Domas Velička. Čikaga,
Pedagoginis Lituanistikos institu-
tas, 1972] 40 p. PG8721.M9R8 1972
PU

9291. --- Vivos plango. [Redagavo
Domas Velička] Chicago, Ill. [Pe-

dagoginis Lituanistikos institutas]
1968. 23 p. PG8721.M9V5 PU CaOONL
CaOTU

9292. NAGYS, Henrikas. Broliai
balti aitvarai. Chicago, Ill., Algimanto Mackaus knygų leidimo fondas, 1969. PG8721.M3B7 PU

9293. --- Lapkričio naktys; lyrika. Freiburg, Ger., P. Abelkis,
1947. 112 p. 891.92.N136L PU
CtTMF ICCC

9294. --- Mėlynas sniegas; poezija.
[Boston, Mass., Lietuvių enciklope-
dijos leidykla, 1960] 87 p.
PG8721.N3M4 DLC CaAEU CaOONL CaOTU
PU

9295. --- Saulės laikrodžiai;
poezija. [Iliustravo Telesforas
Valius. Chicago, Ill.] 1952. 80
p. illus. PG8721.N3S3 DLC CaAEU
CaOONL ICCC MB NN OCl PU

9296. NAUJOKAITIS, Pranas. Akmens
širdis; elegijos. Brooklyn, N.Y.,
Ateitis, 1960. 104 p.
891.92.N224A PU

9297. --- Prie svyruojančių beržų;
pirmieji etiudai. Kaunas, 1930. 68
p. 891.921.N ICCC

9298. --- Šviesos mergaitė; lyrinė poema. [Brooklyn, N.Y., Ateitis, 1959] 72 p. PG8721.N34S9 DLC
OCl PU

9299. NĖRIS, Salomėja. Baltais
takeliais bėga saulytė. [Iliustra-
vo B. Demkutė] Vilnius, VGLL, 1956.
160 p. illus. PZ70.L5N4 DLC ICCC
PU

9300. --- Dainuok, širdie, gyvenimą; eilėraščiai ir poemos. Maskva,
LTSR Valstybinė leidykla, 1943. 38
p. PG8721.N4D3 PU

9301. --- Diemedžiu žydėsiu; knyga, laimėjusi 1938 m. Valstybinę
literatūros premiją. 2-ras leid.
Kaunas, Sakalas, 1939. 69 p.
891.921.B ICCC

9302. --- Eglė žalčių karalienė.
[2. leidimas. Kaune] VGLL [1946]
96 p. illus. PG8721.N4E4 1946 DLC
NN PU

9303. --- Laumės dovanos. Iliustravo M. Ladigaitė. Vilnius, Vaga,
1966. [26] p. illus. PG8721.N4L3
1966 DLC PU

9304. --- Mama! Kur tu? [Ilius-
travo Kastytis Juodikaitis] Vilnius, Vaga, 1971. [36] p.

PG8721.N4M3 PU

9305. --- Pavasaris per kalnus
eina. Vilnius, VGLL, 1961. 510 p.
PG8721.N4P28 1961 DLC PU

9306. --- Poezija. Antano Venclo-
vos red., įvadas ir paaiškinimai.
[Kaune] VGLL [1946] 2 v. illus.
PG8721.N4A17 1946 DLC NN

9307. --- --- [Another edition]
Vilnius, VGLL, 1954. 499 p. illus.
PG8721.N4A17 1954 DLC PPULC PU

9308. --- --- [Another edition]
Vilnius, Vaga, 1966. 2 v.
PG8721.N4 1966 DLC CaAEU CtPAM IU
MH NN PU

9309. --- --- [Another edition]
Vilnius, Vaga, 1972. 2 v.
PG8721.N4 1972 PU

9310. --- Širdis mana-audrų daina.
Vilnius, VGLL, 1959. 473 p.
PG8721.N4S46 DLC CtY NN OKentU

9311. --- Žalčio pasaka. Illus.
by Paulius Augius. [n.p.] "Forma",
1947. 112 p. 891.92.B124E PU
ICCC WyU

9312. NEVARDAUSKAS, Jonas. Užrūs-
tinti dievai. Montreal, Que., Nepi-
klausoma Lietuva, 1949. 111 p.
891.92.N412U PU

9314. ONAITIS, Vytautas. Nerimo
pasakos; eilėraščiai. Vilnius,
Vaga, 1971. 186 p. PG8722.25.N3N4
PU

9315. ORINTAITĖ, Petronėlė. Lietuvos keliu; istorinė poema jaunimui. Augsburg, Ger., Sudavija,
1948. 20 p. 491.92.0r44V PU

9316. --- Tafilė nuo Kražantės;
eiliuota apysaka. Avellanada, Argentina, 1959. 110 p. illus.
891.92.0r44T PU

9317. PALECKIS, Justas. Atgimi-
mas. Vilnius, VGLL, 1953. 166 p.
PG8721.P3A8 DLC

9318. --- Gyvenimo vardu. [Vil-
nius, VGLL, 1961] 109 p. illus.
PG8721.P3G9 DLC

9319. --- Sveika, Tarybų Lietuva!
[Kaune] VGLL, 1960. 43 p. illus.
PG8721.P3S9 DLC

9320. PAPEČKYS, Juozas. Eilės-
dainos. South Boston, Mass., "Ateities" spauda, 1917. 32 p.
891.92.P198E PU

9321. PLAČINSKAITĖ, Violeta.

Kreidos bokštai. Vilnius, Vaga,
1969. 69 p. PG8721.P27K7 PU

9322. --- Žemė kėlė žolę. Vilnius, VGLL, 1961. 53 p. illus.
PG8721.P27Z28 DLC

9323. POŠKA, Dionizas. Mužikas
Žemaičių ir Lietuvos. Paruošė A.
Žirgulys. Kaunas, 1947. 38 p.
PG8721.P66M8 1947 PU NN

9324. --- --- [Another edition]
Iliustravo V. Jurkūnas. Sudarė A.
Paraščiakas. Vilnius, Vaga, 1965.
14 p. illus. MH

9325. PRANSKUS, Bronius. Į ateitį šviesią; eilėraščiai. [By] B.
Zalionis [pseud.] Vilnius, VGLL,
1959. 189 p. PG8721.P68.I2 PU

9326. --- Kovų poemos. Vilnius,
VGLL, 1961. 201 p. illus.
PG8721.P68K6 DLC PU

9327. RADAUSKAS, Henrikas. Eilėraščiai. Chicago, Ill.[Vytautas
Saulius] 1965. 237 p.
891.92.R112E PU CaAEU CaOTU MH

9328. --- Strėlė danguje; eilėraščiai. Chicago, Ill.[V. Saulius]
1950. 110 p. illus. PG8721.R26S8
DLC PU

9329. --- Žiemos daina; eilėraščiai. Chicago, Ill.[Draugas]
1955. 77 p. PG8721.R26Z3 DLC ICCC
NN PU

9330. RASTENIS, Nadas. Trijų ro-
žių šventė. [Iliustracijos autoriaus. Baltimore, Md., N. Rastenis,
1956] 147 p. illus., (part. col.)
port. PG8749.R35I7 OKentU DLC NN

9331. REIMERIS, Vacys. Delnai;
eilėraščiai. Vilnius, Vaga, 1968.
150 p. illus. PG8721.R79D4 CaAEU

9332. --- Pilnaties ratas. Vilnius, VGLL, 1962. 158 p.
PG8721.R4P5 DLC

9333. RUDOKAS, Vytautas. Nežino-
mas kareivis; dramatinė poema.
Vilnius, Vaga, 1965. 50 p. illus.
PG8722.28.U3N4 DLC MH

9334. --- Proskyna. Vilnius,
Vaga, 1967. 135 p. illus.
PG8722.28.U3P7 DLC NN PU

9335. --- Saulėgrąžų vasara. Vilnius, Vaga, 1963. 119 p.
PG8722.28.U3S3 DLC MH NN

9336. RŪKAS, Antanas. Bokštai,
meilė ir buitis; eilėraščiai.

[Lino rėžiniais iliustravo Ž. Mikšys. Chicago, Ill., Terra] 1951. 111 p. illus. PG8721.R79B6 DLC ICCC PU

9337. --- Mano tautos istorija; lyrika. [Iliustravo Viktoras Petravičius. Chicago, Ill., 1966] 117 p. illus. PG8721.R79M3 DLC OKentU PU

9338. RŪTA, Alė. Be Tavęs; poezija. Stuttgart, Ger., A. Urbonas, 1946. 132 p. PG9119.R8 DLC CtTMF ICCC OKentU

9339. SADŪNAITĖ, Danguolė. Kai tu arti manęs; eilėraščiai. Los Angeles, Calif., Lietuvių dienos, 1965. 38 p. 891.92.S135K PU

9340. --- Laiškai Dievui; eilėraščiai. [Brooklyn, N.Y., 1970] 72 p. PG8749.S29L3 PU

9341. --- Tu esi mano žemė. Boston, Mass., J. Kapočius, 1968. 45 p. PG8749.S29T8 PU CaOTU

9342. --- Vasaros medžiuose; eilėraščiai. Chicago, Ill., Ateitis, 1961. 46 p. 891.92.S135V PU OKentU

9343. SANTVARAS, Stasys. Atidari langai; rinktinė lyrika. Boston, Mass., Lietuvių enciklopedija, 1959. 167 p. PG8721.S32A8 CaOTU CaAEU NN

9344. --- Aukos taurė; penktoji lyrikos knyga. [Boston, Mass.] Lietuvių enciklopedijos leidykla [1962] 152 p. PG8721.S32A17 1962 DLC CaAEU CaOTU PU

9345. --- Laivai palaužtom burėm; ketvirtoji lyrikos knyga. [Tübingen, Ger.] Patrija [1945] 172 p. illus. PG8721.S32A17 1945 DLC CaOONL CtTMF ICCC OKentU PU

9346. ŠEŠPLAUKIS, Alfonsas. Laukų liepsnos; sonetai. [By] Alfonsas Tyruolis [pseud.] [Nördingen, Ger.] Venta [1953] 44 p. PG8721.S4L3 DLC ICCC NN NNC PU

9347. --- Metų vingiai; lyrikos rinktinė. [By] Alfonsas Tyruolis [pseud. Chicago, Ill.] Lietuviškos knygos klubas [1963] 176 p. PG8721.S4M4 DLC CaOONL PU

9348. --- Nemarioji žemė; Lietuva pasaulinės poezijos posmuose. Antologija. [By] Alfonsas Tyruolis [pseud.] So. Boston, Mass., Lietuvių enciklopedijos leidykla, 1969. 176 p. PG8761.A3S4 PU

9349. --- Sacra via; Romos sonetai. [By] Alfonsas Tyruolis [pseud. Chi-

cago, Ill., Ateitis] 1961. 47 p. PG8721.S4S2 DLC NN PU

9350. ŠIMKUS, Vladas. Geležis ir sidabras. [Dailininkas V. Žilius] Vilnius, Vaga, 1968. 102 p. PG8722.29.I55G4 PU DLC

9351. --- Gražiausia sekundė. Vilnius, VGLL, 1960. 49 p. port. PG8722.29.I55G7 DLC PU

9352. --- Kranto konturai. Vilnius, VGLL, 1963. 85 p. PG8722.29.I55K7 DLC IU NN

9353. SIRIJOS-GIRA, Vytautas. Pro amžių bėgu. Kaunas, VGLL, 1947. 79 p. illus. PG8721.G52P7 CSt-H DLC PU

9354. ŠLAITAS, Vladas. Aguonų gaisras; eilėraščiai. Brooklyn, N.Y., Ateitis, 1969. 56 p. PG8722.29.L3A3 PU

9355. --- Ant saulėgražos vamzdžio; eilėraščiai. London, D. Britanijos lietuvių sąjungos leidinys, 1959. 48 p. 891.93.S112An PU CLU

9356. --- Be gimto medžio. [London] D. Britanijos lietuvių sąjungos leidinys, 1962. 43 p. PG8722.29.L3B4 DLC PU

9357. --- Širdies paguodai; eilėraščiai. London, Nida, 1965. 48 p. 891.92.S112S PU

9358. --- 34 eilėraščiai. [Boston, Mass.] J. Kapočius, 1967. 44 p. PG8722.29.L3T7 PU

9359. --- Žmogiškosios psalmės; eilėraščiai. Detmold, Ger., 1949. 110 p. PG8722.29.L3Z35 DLC PU

9360. SRUOGA, Balys. Deivė iš ežero. Vilnius, Švyturys, 1919. 891.52.Sr85D PU

9361. --- Dievų takais. Klaipėda, 1923. 167 p. PG8721.S68D52 PU ICCC

9362. --- Poezija. Vilnius, VGLL, 1957. 370 p. illus. (His Raštai, t.1) PG8721.S68 1957 v.1 DLC CaAEU ICU PU

9363 --- Saulė ir smiltys; poemos. Vilnius, 1920. 156 p. 891.92.Sr85S PU CtY ICCC

9364. STANEVIČIUS, Simonas. Pasakėčios. Iliustravo A. Kučas. [Redaktorius A. Žirgulys. 1. leidimas] Vilnius, VGLL, 1959. [37] p. illus. PG8721.S69P3 DLC NN PU

9365. STRAZDAS, Antanas. Poezija. Vilnius, VGLL, 1963. 102 p. PG8721.S75 1963 PU

9366. TILVYTIS, Teofilis. Artojėliai. [Kaune] VGLL, 1947. 97 p. PG8721.T55A8 DLC NN PU

9367. --- Baltijos vėjas. [Kaune] VGLL [1948] 114 p. PG8721.T55B3 DLC PU

9368. --- Dičius; poema. Vilnius, VGLL, 1955. 1 v. 891.92.T479D PU

9369. --- --- [Another edition] Dailininkas Arūnas Tarabilda. Vilnius, Vaga, 1967. 213 p. illus. PG8721.T55D5 DLC NN OKentU

9371. --- Nameliai mano brangūs; eilėraščiai. Vilnius, VGLL, 1958. 108 p. PG8721.T55P7 DLC NN OKentU PU

9372. --- Pradalgės. Vilnius, Vaga, 1968. 230 p. illus. PG8721.T55P7 DLC NN OKentU PU

9373. --- Sonetai apie laimę. [Vilniuje] VGLL, 1951. 32 p. PG8721.T55S6 DLC

9374. --- Teofilis Tilvytis. Sudaryta pagal Lietuvos TSR Švietimo ministerijos programą. 3. leidimas. Kaunas, Valstybinė pedagoginės literatūros leidykla, 1958. 76 p. (Mokinio biblioteka) PG8721.T55A6 1958 DLC

9375. --- Tėvynės laukuos. Vilnius, VGLL, 1953. 81 p. PG8721.T55T4 DLC

9376. --- Trejos devynerios; satyriniai eilėraščiai. Vilnius, Vaga, 1972. 470 p. PG8721.T55T7 PU

9377. --- Usnyne; poema. 4. leidimas. Vilnius, VGLL, 1962. 213 p. illus. MH

9378. TULAUSKAITĖ, Gražina. Po svetimu dangum; poezija. [n.p.] Venta, 1951. 60 p. 891.92.G976T PU ICCC OKentU

9379. --- Rugsėjo žvaigždės; lyrika. [Chicago, Ill.] Terra [1957] 62 p. PG8721.T75R8 DLC PU

9380. --- Vakarė banga; lyrika. [Hollywood, Calif., Lietuvių dienų leidykla, 1968] 127 p. PG8721.T75V3 DLC PU

9381. TYSLIAVA, Juozas. Nemuno rankose; poezijos rinktinė. Kaunas, Varpo bendrovės leidinys, 1924. 78 p. 891.921.T ICCC

9382. --- --- [Another edition] Vilnius, Vaga, 1967. 254 p. PG8722.3.Y73N4 DLC OKentU PU

9383. --- Poezija. New York, N.Y., 1935. 60 p. PG8721.T92A6 1935 PU

9384. URBONAVIČIUS, Kazimieras. Kvieslys į laisvę; eilėraščių rinkinys. So. Boston, Mass., Darbininkas, 1947. 351 p. Author's pseud., Jonas Kmitas, at head of title. PG8749.U7K9 PU OKentU

9385. URNEVIČIŪTĖ, Dalia. Gegužio lietus. Vilnius, VGLL, 1960. 54 p. port. PG8722.31.R6G4 DLC PU

9386. VAIČAITIS, Pranas. Eilės. Plymouth, Pa., "Vienybės lietuvninku" spauda, 1903. 165 p. 891.921V ICCC OCl

9387. --- --- [Another edition] Philadelphia, Pa., Žvaigždės sp., 1912. 157 p. port. 891.92.V188 PU

9388. --- Yra šalis. Vilnius, VGLL, 1964. 142 p. illus. PG8721.V29Y7 1964 DLC CtTMF

9389. VAIČIŪNAITĖ, Judita. Pavasario akvarelės. Vilnius, VGLL, 1960. 53 p. port. PG8722.32.A5P3 DLC PU

9390. --- Per saulėtą gaublį. Vilnius [Vaga] 1964. 51 p. PG8722.32.A5P4 DLC OKentU

9391. --- Po šiaurės herbais. Vilnius, Vaga, 1968. 97, [2] p. illus. PG8722.32.A5P6 DLC CaAEU

9392. --- Vėtrungė. Vilnius, Vaga, 1966. 90 p. PG8722.32.A5V4 DLC PU

9393. VAIČIŪNAS, Petras. Gimtuoju vieškeliu; trečias eilėraščių rinkinys. Kaunas, 1927. 52 p. 891.921V ICCC

9394. --- Gyvenimo preliūdai. Vilnius, VGLL, 1962. 239 p. PG8721.V32G9 PU

9395. --- --- [Another edition] Vilnius, Vaga, 1969. 338 p. PG8721.V32G9 1969 CaAEU

9396. --- Paukščių taku. [Sudarė J. Macevičius] Vilnius, VGLL, 1962. 198 p. 891.92.V194Pa PU MH

9397. --- Rasoti spinduliai; poezijos. Kaunas, 1923. 93 p. 891.921.V ICCC

9398. --- Rinktinė. [Kaune] VGLL
[1946] 128 p. PG8721V32R5 DLC PU

9399. --- Saulės lobis; ketvirtas
eilėraščių rinkinys. Kaunas, Spaudos fondas [1935] 112 p.
891.921.V ICCC

9400. --- Tekanti saulė; antras
eilėraščių rinkinys. [Kaunas]
1925. 126 p. 891.921.V ICCC

9401. VAITKUS, Mykolas. Alfa ir
Omega; eilėraščiai, 1947-1949.
Putnam, Conn., Immaculata Press,
1963. 891.92.V155A PU CtTMF
OKentU

9402. --- Aukso ruduo; 1950-1952
eilėraščiai. [Chicago, Ill., Lietuviškos knygos klubo leidinys,
1955] 119 p. PG8749.V3A85 DLC
CaOTU ICCC PU

9403. --- Brėkšta; poema. Tilžėje,
Jagomasto spaustuvė "Lithuania",
1915. 38 p. illus. PG8749.V3B7
CaOTU PU

9404. --- Dienoraštis; 1916 metų
eilėraščiai. Putnam, Conn., Immaculata Press, 1966. 160 p.
891.92.V195D PU

9405. --- Laimė; poema. Chicago,
Ill., Spauda ir lėšomis "Kataliko",
1911. 166 p. PG8749.V3 DLC ICCC
NN PU

9406. --- Nuošaliu taku; godos,
vaizdai, svajos, 1934-1944. [Chi-
cago, Ill.] Terra [1955] 98 p.
PG8749.V3N8 DLC ICCC NN OCl PU

9407. --- Nušvitusi dulkė. Kaunas, 1933. 198 p. 891.921.V ICCC

9408. --- Šerksno sidabras; 1953-
1954 m. Chicago, Ill., Lietuviškos
knygos klubas, 1965. 86 p.
891.92.Vi95Se PU CaOONL CaOTU

9409. --- Šviesūs krislai. Vilnius, Kuktos spaustuvė, 1913. 111
p. 891.921.V ICCC

9410. --- Vienatvė; eilėraščiai,
1944-1945. [Putnam, Conn.] Immaculata [1952] 182 p. PG8749.V3V5
DLC ICCC OCl PU

9411. VALSIŪNIENĖ, Valerija.
Šviesi diena; eilės ir poemos.
[Kaune] VGLL [1947] 118 p.
PG8721.V33S9 DLC PU

9412. --- Veronika; poema. [Vil-
niuje] VGLL, 1952. 145 p. illus.
PG8721.V33V4 DLC MH-L

9413. --- Žemė audžia pavasario

dainą. Vilnius, VGLL, 1962. 269
p. illus. PG8721.V33A6 1962 DLC
MH

9414. VENCLOVA, Antanas. Ar tu
žinai tą šalį; eilėraščiai apie
Italiją. [Dailininkas St. Krasaus-
kas] Vilnius, Vaga, 1964. 69 p.
col. plates. PG8721.V4A8 DLC

9415. --- Kovoti, degti, nenurim-
ti! Vilnius, VGLL, 1953. 166 p.
PG8721V4K6 DLC

9416. --- Mėlyno Nemuno vingiai;
poezija. Vilnius, Vaga, 1969.
586 p. illus. PG8721.V4M4 PU
CaOTU DLC

9417. --- Obelis kur augalota.
[Kaunas] VGLL, 1945. 210 p. port.
NN

9418. --- Žemė gera; rinktinė
poezija. Vilnius, VGLL, 1963. 302
p. illus. PG8721.V4Z4 DLC MH

9419. VIENAŽINDYS (VIENOŽINSKIS),
Antanas. Dainos parašytos kun. A.
Vienožinskio. Brooklyn, N.Y.,
Spauda ir lėšos "Vienybės lietuv-
ninkų", 1914. 50 p. 784.8.V ICCC

9420. --- Ilgu, ilgu man ant svieto. Vilnius, VGLL, 1958. 129 p.
illus., ports., facsims.
891.92.V673I PU CtY ICCC

9421. --- Lietuvos tėvynės dainos.
[Tilžė] 1897. 48 p.
BM(011586. df. 48.)

9422. VITKAUSKAS, Arėjas. Numi-
rėlis iš karsto; Lietuvos prisikėlimo poema. Chicago, Ill. [1930]
31 p. PG8721.V55N8 DLC PU

9423. --- Spinduliai ir šešėliai;
eilės. Pirmoji kregždė. Kaunas,
Išleido J. Vitkauskienė, 1926. 64
p. PG8721.V57S7 PU CaOONL

9424. YLA, Stasys. Sutriptame
kely; kaceto poezija. [By] Juozas
Yluvis [pseud.] Kirchheim-Teck,
Ger., 1947. 62 p. illus.
891.92.Y64S PU ICCC

9425. ŽILINSKAITĖ, Vytautė. Nesu-
stok, valandėle. Vilnius, VGLL,
1961. 35 p. port. PG8722.36.I4N4
DLC

9426. ŽITKEVIČIUS, Leonardas.
Daiktai ir nuorūkos; lyrinės ironi-
jos. [Brooklyn, N.Y.] Gabija [1954]
46 p. PG8749.Z5D3 DLC PU

9427. --- Saulutė debesėliuos.
[Chicago, Ill.] Draugo, 1953. 63 p.

illus. OCl CaOONL

9428. --- Šilkai ir vilkai; dainos
vietinės ir svetimos. Brooklyn,
N.Y., Balys Pavabalys, 1960. 62 p.
891.92.Z57S PU

9429. ŽITKUS, Kazimieras. Ašarė-
lės; eilėraščiai. [By] Vincas Stonis [pseud.] Kaunas, Ateitininkų
susišelpimo fondo leidinys, 1924.
118 p. 891.92.Z675A PU

9430. --- Lyrika; rinktinė. [By]
Vincas Stonis [pseud.] Vilnius,
Vaga, 1970. 162 p. PG8721.Z53A17
1970 PU

9431. ŽUKAUSKAS, Albinas. Anti-
vandenė. Vilnius, Vaga, 1967. 63
p. illus. PG8722.36.U4A83 DLC

9432. --- Atodangos; eilėraščiai.
Vilnius, Vaga, 1971. 163 p.
PG8722.36.U4A9 PU

9433. --- Ilgosios varsnos. Vilnius, VGLL, 1962. 162 p. illus.
PG8722.36.U4.I4 DLC OKentU PU

XIII.5.c.6. TRANSLATIONS INTO
FOREIGN LANGUAGES

9434. ANDRIEKUS, Leonardas.
Amens in amber. Versions from the
Lithuanian by Demie Jonaitis. Fore-
word by Charles Angoff. Illus. by
Telesforas Valius. New York, N.Y.,
Manyland Books [c1968] ix, 85 p.
illus. PG9119.A5A25 DLC CaOTU
CaOONL IEG NN PP PU

9435. BALDAUF, Lucia, tr. & ed.
Litauische Lyrik; eine Anthologie
litauisch-deutsch. Ausgewählt und
übersetzt von Lucia Baldauf. München, W. Fink, 1972. 306 p.
PG8715.B3 PU

9436. BARANAUSKAS, Antanas.
Anikshchiaiskii bor. Perevod s litovskogo Nikolaia Tikhonova. Vil'-
nius, Gos. izd-vo khudozh. lit-ry,
1952. 34 p. 891.92.B2295A.RT PU

9437. --- The forest of Anykščiai.
The original Lithuanian text with
English translation. Translated by
Nadas Rastenis; edited by Juozas
Tininis. [1st limited ed. Los
Angeles, Calif.] Lithuanian Days,
1956. 41 p. illus.
PG8721.B325A813 DLC CaAEU CaOTU
CtPAM NN OCl PU

9438. --- Der Hain von Anykščiai.
Nachdichtung von Hermann Buddensieg.

München, W. Fink, 1967. 37 p.
PG8721.B235A815 DLC PU

9439. BARONAS, Aloyzas. Foot-
bridges and abysses. Introd. by
Charles Angoff. [Translated from
Lithuanian by J. Žemkalnis] New
York, N.Y., Manyland Books [1965]
229 p. PZ4.B2656Fo DLC CaAEU CaOTU
NN OCl PU

9440. --- The third woman; a
novel. Authorized translation from
the Lithuanian by Nols M. Zobarskas.
Introd. by Charles Angoff. New
York, N.Y., Manyland Books [1968]
169 p. PG9747.B3T713 CaOTU CaAEU
CaOONL DLC NN PU

9441. BERMAN, Hannah. Ant hills;
an introduction by Paul Goodman.
New York, N.Y., Payson & Clarke
[c1927] xi, 300 p. PZ3.B45585An2
DLC OCl

9442. BIELIAUSKAS, Alfonsas. Wir
sehen uns wieder, Wilma. [Ins
Deutsch übertragen von Ewald Jurkschat und Helmut Komp. Gekürzte
Fassung] Berlin, Verlag Neues Leben [1966] 272 p. PG8721.B43M45
DLC

9443. BILIŪNAS, Jonas. Svetoch
schast'ia; povesti i rasskazy.
[Perevod s litovskogo B. Zalesskoi
i. O. Iodelene. Ill. V. Galdikas]
Vil'nius, Vaga, 1964. 205 p. illus.
At head of title: Ionas Biliunas.
PG8721.B47S9 1964 DLC

9444. BOBROWSKI, Johannes. Li-
tauische Claviere. Roman. Berlin,
Wagenbach [1967] 170 p.
PT2665.O2L5 1967 DLC CaOTU CtY FA
FU IEN NcU PPiU PU ViU

9445. BORUTA, Kazys. Mel'nitsa
Baltaragisa; ili, Chto tvorilos' vo
vremena ony v Priudruv'e; starin-
naia povest'-predanie. Perevod s
litovskogo El'gi Kaktyn'. [Moskva,
Khudozh. lit-ra, 1966] 237 p.
PG8721.B6B37 DLC

9446. --- Vetra vol'nogo volia.
Stikhi i poemy. Perevod s litovskogo. [Predisl. L. Ozerova] Moskva
Sovetskii pisatel', 1967. 240 p.
illus. PG8721.B6V4 1967 DLC

9447. BŪDAVAS, Stasius. The for-
bidden miracle; [a novel]. New York,
N.Y., Comet Press Books [1955] 186
p. PZ3.B8579Fo DLC NN OKentU

9448. CHURGINAS, Aleksys. Stikhi
o druzhbe. Perevod s litovskogo P.
Shubina i dr. Moskva, Sovetskii
pisatel', 1948. 104 p.

PG8771.R9C5 DLC

9449. CVIRKA, Petras. Izbrannoe.
Perevod s litovskogo. Moskva, Gos.
izd-vo khudozh. lit-ry, 1950. 418
p. port. PG8771.R9C8 1950 DLC PU

9450. --- Izbrannye proizvedeniia;
rasskazy. Zemlia kormilitsa; roman.
Perevod s litovskogo [pod red. Zi-
naidy Shishovoi] Moskva, Gos. izd-
vo khudozh. lit-ry, 1948. 518 p.
port. PG9048.C9A55 DLC CaOTU CU NN

9451. --- --- [Another edition.
Perevody] Vil'nius, Gos. izd-vo
khudozh. lit-ry Litovskoi SSR,
1954. 675 p. illus. PG8721.C8A57
1954 DLC

9452. --- Sobranie sochinenii.
V trekh tomakh. perevod s litovskogo. Red. kollegiia: A. Ventslova
[i dr.] Moskva, Khudozh. lit-ra,
1968-69. 3 v. port. PG8721.C8A57
DLC CaOTU

9453. DAUTARTAS, Vladas. Stuchus'
v dver'; novelly. [Perevel s litovskogo G. Kanovich] Vil'nius, Vaga,
1966. 385 p. PG8722.14.A8S717 DLC
PU

9454. DEGUTYTĖ, Janina. Kapli
ognia; stikhi. Perevod s litovskogo
S. Mar. Moskva, Sovetskii pisatel',
1960. 96 p. CLU MH

9455. DONELAITIS, Kristijonas.
Christian Donalitius littauische
Dichtungen, nach den Königsberger
Handschriften mit metrischer Über-
setzung, kritischen Anmerkungen und
genauem Glossar herausgegeben von
G.H.F. Nesselmann. Königsberg in
Pr., Hübner & Matz, 1869. 368 p.
Lithuanian and German on opposite
pages. 891.92.D713 PU CtY ICN InU
MH NcU NNU-H NjP

9456. --- Izbrannoe. Perevel s
litovskogo D. Brodskii. Moskva,
Gos. izd-vo khudozh. lit-ry, 1951.
109 p. PG8721.D7A57 DLC

9457. --- Das Jahr in vier Gesän-
gen. Übertragen von L.G. Rhesa.
Königsberg in Pr., 1818. 162 p.
BM(011528.g.25.)

9458. --- Die Jahreszeiten. Nachdichtung von Hermann Buddensieg.
[Holzschnitte: Vytautas Kazys Jonynas, u.a.] München, W. Fink,
1966. 156 p. Translation of Metai. PG8721.D7M315 DLC CtY CoU
InNd MH OKentU PU

9459. --- Litauische Dichtungen.
1. volständige Ausg. mit Glossar,

von Aug. Schleicher. Sanktpeter-
burg, Commissionäre der Kaiser-
lichen Akademie der Wissenschaften,
Eggers und Co., 1865. 336 p.
"Glossar": p. [163]-331.
PG8721.D7 DLC CU ICU ICN IEN KU MH
NIC NN PU WU

9460. --- --- [Another edition]
Übersetzt und erläutert von L.
Passarge. Halle a.S., Verlag der
Buchhandlung des Weisenhauses,
1894. [7], 372 p. PG8699.D7A4P3
ICU ICBM IEN OCl PU(xerox copy,
1972)

9461. --- Rok; obrazy z życia
chłopów XVIII-go wieku. Opowiedział
Christian Donalitius. Warszawa,
1933. 112 p. 891.92.D713.3 PU

9462. --- The Seasons. Rendered
from the Lithuanian into English
verse by Nadas Rastenis. Introduc-
tion and editing by Elena Tumas.
Los Angeles, Calif., Lithuanian
Days, 1967. 127 p. illus.
PG8721.D7M313 1967 DLC CLU CaAEU
CaOWtU CaOTU InNd IU OrU PU

9463. --- Vremena goda. [Perevel
s litovskogo D. Brodskii] Moskva,
Gos. izd-vo khudozh. lit-ry, 1955.
105 p. illus. PG8721.D7M317 DLC

9464. --- --- Basni. Perevod s
litovskogo D. Brodskogo. 3. izd.
Leningrad, Sovetskii pisatel',
1960. 229 p. (Biblioteka poeta.
Osnovana M. Gor'kim malaia seriia)
KU

9465. --- --- [Another edition]
Moskva, Khudozh. lit-ra, 1964.
149 p. 891.92.D713.3 MB CtY PU

9466. DOVYDAITIS, Jonas. Bol'-
shie sobytiia v Nauiamestise; roman.
Avtorizovannyi perevod s litovskogo
M. IUfit. Moskva, Sovetskii pisatel', 1951. 490 p. PG8721.D74 DLC

9467. --- Liubov' i nenavist';
rasskazy. Avtorizovannyi perevod s
litovskogo. Moskva, Sovetskii
pisatel', 1956. 250 p.
PG8721.D74A55 DLC

9468. DOVYDĖNAS, Liudas. We will
conquer the world. New York, N.Y.
[Romuva] 1971. 219 p.
DK511.L27D6513 PU

9469. FISCHE HABEN KEIN GEDÄCHTNIS;
litauische Erzählungen aus sieben
Jahrzehnten. [Ausgewählt von Welta
Ehlert und Rainer Eckert. Mit einem
Nachwort und biographischen Notizen
von Algimantas Bučys] Berlin,
Kultur und Fortschritt [1970]

411 p. PG8771.G8F5 PU

9470. GIRA, Liudas. Stikhi. Perevod s litovskogo pod red. V. Levika. Moskva, Khudozh. literatura, 1940. 108 p. (*QDH)NN

9471. GLIAUDYS, Jurgis. House upon the sand, by Jurgis Gliauda [pseud.] Translated from the Lithuanian by Raphael Sealey and Milton Stark. [Woodhaven, N.Y.] Manyland Books [1963] 168 p. PG8721.G55H84 CaAEU CaOONL CaOTU DLC NN OCl OKentU PU

9472. --- The sonata of Icarus, by Jurgis Gliauda [pseud.] Translated from the Lithuanian by Raphael Sealey. Introd. by Charles Angoff. Illus. by Mikalojus K. Čiurlionis. New York, N.Y., Manyland Books [1968] 169 p. illus. PG8749.G6I42 PU CtY DLC NN OKentU

9473. GORECKI, Antoni. Peozyie Litwina. Wydanie A. Jałowieckiego. Paryż, 1834. viii, 276 p. Slav 7111.4.381 MH BM(11585. bb. 33.)

9474. GUDAITIS-GUZEVIČIUS, Aleksandras. Brat'ia; roman. Perevod s litovskogo L. Levinene, N. Pan'shinoi, IU. Shishmonina. Moskva, Sovetskii pisatel', 1957. 814 p. PG8721.G8B77 DLC

9475. --- Pravda kuznetsa Ignotasa; roman. Avtorizovannyi perevod s litovskogo. Moskva, Sovetskii pisatel', 1951. 594 p. illus. PG8721.G8P7 1951a DLC CaAEU PU NN

9476. JANONIS, Julius. Izbrannoe. V perevode A. Kleneva. Pod red. N. Tikhonova i A. Ventslovy. Vil'nius, Gos. izd-vo khudozh. lit-ry, 1952. 232 p. port. (Dekada literatury i iskusstva Litovskoi SSR)

9477. --- --- [Another edition] Perevod s litovskogo. Moskva, Gos. izd-vo khudozh. lit-ry, 1953. 150 p. PG8721.J3A57 DLC

9478. --- --- [Another edition] Moskva, Gos. izd-vo detskoi lit-ry, 1955. 109 p. illus. PG8721.J3A572 DLC

9479. JANUŠYTĖ, Liūnė. Tri subboty; odnoaktnaia komediia v trekh kartinakh. Moskva, Iskusstvo, 1958. 23 p. illus. PG8721.J35T77 DLC

9480. JURKŪNAS, Ignas. I väntan på undret; roman. [Av] I. Scheinius [pseud.] Stockholm, Faherantz & Gumaelius [1942] 367 p.

PT9875.J8.I2 DLC PU

9481. --- The ordeal of Assad Pasha. [By] Ignas Šeinius [pseud.] Translated by Raphael Sealey. [Woodhaven, N.Y.] Manyland Books [c1963] 61 p. Translation of "Sunkiausia Assad Pašos užduotis". PZ3.J9750r DLC CaAEU CaOTU PU

9482. --- Rejuvenation of Siegfried Immerselbe, a novel, by Ignas Šeinius. Translated from the Lithuanian by Albinas Baranauskas. New York, N.Y., Manyland Books [1965] 247 p. Translation of "Siegfried Immerselbe atsijaunina". PZ3.J975Re DLC CaAEU CaOTU NN OCl PU PPULC

9483. KAIRYS, Anatolijus. Curriculum vitae; a comical tragedy in two acts. [From the Lithuanian translated by A. Milukas. Hollywood, Calif., 1971] 87 p. PG8721.K2C813 PU

9484. KAŠAUSKAS, Raimondas. Igry vzroslykh; povesti. [Perevela s litovskogo Alisa Berman] Vil'nius, Vaga, 1970. 339 p. PG8722.21.A7S817 PU

9485. KORSAKAS, Kostas. Izbrannoe. Perevod s litovskogo pod red. M. Petrovykh. Vil'nius, Goslitizdat, 1953. 164 p. (Dekada literatury i iskusstva Litovskoi SSR)

9486. KORSAKIENĖ, Halina (Nasopkaitė). Vremennaia stolitsa; roman. [Perevela s litovskogo Zinaida Fedorova] Vil'nius, Vaga, 1964. 472 p. illus. PG8721.K62V7 DLC

9487. KRĖVĖ-MICKEVIČIUS, Vincas. Gilshe. Tr. from the Lithuanian... In American Slavic and East European Review (Menasha, Wis.), v.6, no.16-17, 1947, p. 102-115. See serials consulted.

9488. --- The herdsman and the linden tree [by] Vincas Krėvė. Translated from the Lithuanian by Albinas Baranauskas, Pranas Pranckus and Raphael Sealey. Introd. by Charles Angoff. New York, N.Y., Manyland Books [1964] 128 p. PZ3.K8865He DLC CaAEU CaOTU NN OCl PU

9480. --- The temptation [by] Vincas Krėvė. Translated from the Lithuanian by Raphael Sealey. Introd. by Charles Angoff. New York, N.Y., Manyland Books [1965] 102 p. PZ3.K8865Te DLC CaAEU CaOTU MH NN PU

9490. KUDIRKA, Vincas. Memoirs of

a Lithuanian bridge. Edited by
Stepas Zobarskas. New York, N.Y.,
Manyland Books, 1962 [c1961] 42 p.
illus. PZ3.K9525Me2 DLC CaAEU
CaOTU NN OKentU PU WaS

9491. LANDSBERGIS, Algirdas. Five
posts in a market place. Introd. by
Robert Payne. New York, N.Y., Manyland Books, 1968. 76 p.
PG8721.L3P41 PU CaAEU CaOTU

9492. LANDSBERGIS, Algirdas and
Clark Mills, ed. The green oak; se-
lected Lithuanian poetry. [In Eng-
lish translation by 23 American and
British poets. 1st ed. New York,
N.Y.] Voyages Press [1962] 117 p.
PG8771.E3L3 DLC CU CaAEU CaOTP CaOTU
CtY FU IC IEN IaU InNd LU MH MnU NIC
NNC NbU NcU OCl PPiU PU RPB TxU WaU

9493. LITOVSKIE POETY XIX VEKA.
Predislovie A. Ventslovy. Vstup.
stat'ia B. Pranskusa-Zhalionisa.
Sostavlenie, biograf. spravki i primechaniia P. Chiurlisa. Red. perevod. L.A. Ozerova. Moskva, Sovetskii
pisatel', 1962. 467 p. (Biblioteka poeta. Bol'shaia ser. 2. izd.)
PG8771.R3L5 CU CaAEU CaOWtU CoU CtY
ICU InNd MH NN NcD NcU NjP PU RPB
WaU WU

9494. LITOVSKIE POETY XX VEKA.
[Sbornik] Vstup. stat'ia, sostavlenie i primechaniia V. Galinisa. Red.
poeticheskikh perevodov N.L. Brauna
i L.A. Ozerova. [Leningrad] Sovietskii pisatel', Leningradskoe otd-nie,
1971. 590 p. PG8721.R3L5 PU

9495. LITOVSKIE RASSKAZY. Perevod
s litovskogo. Moskva, Sovetskii pisatel', 1953. 364 p. "Svedeniia ob
avtorakh": p. 356-363.
PG8771.R8L5 DLC

9496. --- Sbornik. Perevod s litovskogo. Moskva, Sovetskii pisatel',
1961. 438 p. illus. "Korotko ob
avtorakh": p. 429-437.
891.92.L716 NNC

9497. MAČIUKEVIČIUS, Jonas. Chasy
ne ostanavlivaiutsia; povest'. Perevel s litovskogo Feliks Dektor.
[Moskva, Molodaia gvardiia, 1971]
222 p. At head of title: Ionas Ma-
chiukevichius. PG8722.23.A295C5 PU

9498. MAIRONIS, Jonas. Izbrannoe;
perevody s litovskogo. [Moskva] Gos.
izd-vo khudozh. lit-ry, 1949. 231 p.
PG8721.M3 1949 DLC NN

9499. --- Izbrannoe; stikhotvoreniia. Perevod s litovskogo. [Vstup.
stat'ia L. Gineitisa. Perevody pod.
red. L. Ozerova] Moskva, Gos. izd-
vo khudozh. lit-ry, 1962. 174 p.

illus. PG8721.M3A57 DLC

9500. MALDONIS, Alfonsas. Stikhi.
Perevod s litovskogo. Moskva, Khudozhestvennaia literatura, 1971.
190 p. illus., port. PG8721.M33A55
1971 CaOTU

9501. MAR, Susanna. Poety Litvy;
perevody s litovskogo. Moskva, Sovetskii pisatel', 1947. 158 p.
PG8771.R3M3 DLC CU CtY NIC NNC NjP

9502. ---, comp. Poety Sovetskoi
Litvy. Moskva, Gos. izd-vo khudozh.
lit-ry, 1945. 891.92C.M328 PU

9503. --- --- [Another edition]
Moskva, Gos. izd-vo khudozh. lit-ry,
1948. 383 p. PG9145.R3M3 DLC CaOTU
CSt-H CU ICU MH NN NIC NNC NjP WaU

9504. MARCINKEVIČIUS, Justinas.
Dereviannye mosty; stikhi. Perevod
s litovskogo. Moskva, Sovetskii pisatel', 1970. 127 p. illus., port.
PG8721.M35M417 CaOTU

9505. --- Krov' i pepel; geroiches-
kaia poema. [Perevel s litovskogo
Aleksandr Mezhirov] Vil'nius, Gos.
izd-vo khudozh. lit-ry, 1964. 159
p. illus. PG8721.M35K717 DLC

9506. --- --- [Another edition]
Vil'nius, Vaga, 1965. 163 p.
891.92.M335K PU

9507. --- --- [Another edition.
Moskva, Khudozh. lit-ra, 1966] 212
p. illus. PG8721.M35K717 1966 DLC

9508. MIEŽELAITIS, Eduardas. Ale-
liumai; litovskaia siuita. [Perevod
s litovskogo] Moskva, Sovetskii pisatel', 1970. 214 p. illus., port.
PG8721.M45A517 CaOTU PU

9509. --- Aviatiudy; stikhi, napi-
sannye v samolete. Perevod s litovskogo. Khudozhnik S. Krasauskas.
[Moskva, Khudozh. lit-ra, 1966] 310
p. illus. PG8721.M45A97 DLC

9510. --- Bratskaia poema. Avtorizovannyi perevod s litovskogo An-
dreia Kleneva. Moskva, Sovetskii
pisatel', 1956. 210 p. illus.
PG8721.M45B717 DLC

9511. --- Chelovek. Graviury na
dereve Stasisa Krasauskasa. [Pere-
vod s litovskogo. Moskva, Khudozh.
lit-ra, 1964] 120 p. illus.
PG8721.M45Z357 DLC CtY NIC

9512. --- --- [Another edition]
Moskva, Khudozh. lit-ra, 1971. 94
p. PG8721.M45Z357 1971 PU

9513. --- Kardiogramma; stikhi.
Perevod s litovskogo. Pod red. Bo-
risa Slutskogo. Moskva, Sovetskii
pisatel', 1963. 215 p. illus.
PG8721.M45K37 DLC PU

9514. --- Liricheskie etiudy. [Pe-
revod s litovskogo I. Kaplanasa. Mos-
kva] Molodaia gvardiia, 1969. 256 p.
illus. PG8721.M45L97 CaOTU

9515. --- Poety Sovetskoi Litvy.
[Red. P. Antokol'skogo, V. Mozuriu-
nasa] Moskva, Gos. izd-vo khudozh.
lit-ry, 1953. 382 p. Bio-bibliogra-
phy: p. 367-374. PG8771.R3M5 DLC MH

9516. MIKELINSKAS, Jonas. Gorst'
peska. Rasskazy. [Perevod s litovs-
kogo] Vil'nius, Vaga, 1968. 315 p.
PG8722.23.I35G617 DLC

9517. MILIŪNAS, Viktoras. Ne tot
put'; p'esa v odnom deistvii. Perevod s litovskogo. Moskva, Iskusstvo, 1959. 22 p. illus. (Repertu-
ar khudozhestvennoi samodeiatel'nosti, 28) PG8721.M47N337 DLC

9518. --- Nochnye ptitsy; komediia
v odnom deistvii. Perevod s litovskogo I. Kaplanasa. Moskva, Iskusstvo, 1961. 18 p. (Odnoaktnye p'esy)
PG8721.M47N6 DLC

9519. MONTVILA, Vytautas. Tuda,
gde solntse. [Stikhi. Perevod s litovskogo L. Ozerova. Graviury na
dereve V. Zhiliusa] Vil'nius, Vaga,
1965. 102 p. illus.
PG8721.M56I217 DLC

9520. MOZŪRIŪNAS, Vladas. Stikhi.
Avtorizovanyi perevod s litovskogo.
Moskva, Sovetskii pisatel', 1952.
159 p. PG8721.M6S8 DLC

9521. MYKOLAITIS, Vincas. Dar by-
tiia. [Perevod s litovskogo pod.
red. D. Samoilova] Vil'nius, Vaga,
1966. 242 p. At head of title:
Vintsas Mikolaitis-Putinas.
PG8721.M9B87 PU

9522. --- Povstantsy; [roman] Perevod s litovskogo I. Kaplanasa.
[Posleslovie IU. IUrginisa. Khudozhnik V. Valius. Moskva, Izvestiia,
1962] 454 p. illus. (Biblioteka
istoricheskikh romanov narodov SSSR)
At head of title: Vintsas Mikolaitis-
Putinas. PG8721.M9S87 DLC

9522a.--- --- [Another edition]
Vil'nius, Vaga, 1970. 711 p. At
head of title: Vintsas Mikolaitis-
Putinas. PG8721.M9S87 PU

9523. --- V teni altarei; roman.
[Perevod s litovskogo S. Aksenovoi i

Z. Fedorovoi. Ill. A. Kuchas] Vil'-
nius, Gos. izd-vo khudozh. lit-ry,
1958. 717. p. illus. At head of
title: Vintsas Mikolaitis-Putinas.
PG8721.M9A677 DLC

9524. --- --- [Another edition]
Vil'nius, Gos. izd-vo khudozh. lit-
ry, 1960. 720 p. PG8721.M9A677
1960 DLC

9525. NĖRIS, Salomėja. Izbrannoe.
[Vil'nius] Gos. izd-vo khudozh. lit-
ry Litovskoi SSR, 1950. 199 p. port.
PG8721.N4A57 1950 DLC

9526. --- Lirika. Perevod s litovskogo. [Moskva, Khudozestvenna-
ia literatura, 1971] 229 p. port.
PG8721.N4A55 1971 CaOTU

9527. --- Moi krai. [Perevod s
litovskogo pod red. Susanny Mar,
Mikh. Zenkevicha. Kaunas] Gos. izd-
vo khudozh. lit-ry Litovskoi SSR,
1947. 152 p. port. PG8721.N4M618
DLC

9528. PAUKŠTELIS, Juozas. Sosedi.
Perevod s litovskogo I. Sokolova i
K. Kely. Ill. E. IUrenas. Vil'nius,
Gos. izd-vo khudozh. lit-ry [1959]
333 p. illus. At head of title:
IUozas Paukshtelis. CU

9529. PETKEVIČIUS, Vytautas. O
khlebe, liubvi i vintovke; roman.
Perevod s litovskogo N. Shaforenko.
[Moskva, Sovetskii pisatel', 1971]
518 p. At head of title: V. Petkia-
vichius. PG8722.26.E8A817 PU

9530. POEZIIA LITVY: antologiia.
[Glav. redaktor Pavel Antokol'skii.
Vil'nius, Gos. izd-vo khudozh. lit-
ry Litovskoi SSR] 1950. 490 p.
PG8771.R3P6 DLC CaOKQ InNd NNC PU

9531. POŠKA, Dionizas. Muzhik
Zhemaitii i Litvy. Khudozhnik V.
IUrkunas. Vil'nius, Gos. izd-vo khu-
dozh. lit-ry, 1962. 56 p. illus.
PG8721.P66M815 PU

9532. RAMONAS, Vincas. Crosses;
now first completely done into Eng-
lish from the original Lithuanian of
Vincas Ramonas by Milton Stark. [1st.
English ed.] Los Angeles, Calif.,
Lithuanian Days Publishers, 1954.
329 p. illus. PZ4.R175Cr DLC CaAEU
CaOTU NN PU

9533. REIMERIS, Vacys. Litovskaia
vesna; stikhi. Avtorizovannyi perevod s litovskogo. Moskva, Sovetskii
pisatel', 1952. 162 p. illus.
PG8721.R4L5 DLC

9534. SIMONAITYTĖ, Jeva. Buse and

her sisters; a novel. [Translated from the Russian by E. Manning] Moscow, Foreign Languages [1957] 295 p. (Library of Soviet literature) PG8721.S5B913 CaOTU CtY DLC MH NN PU

9535. --- V chuzhom dome. [A bylo tak; kn. 2, avtobiograficheskaia povest'. Perevod s litovskogo V. Chepaitisa. Khudozhnik V. Kalinauskas] Vil'nius, Vaga, 1965. 422 p. illus. PG8721.S5N417 DLC PU

9536. --- Vysshe i ee sestry. [Perevod s litovskogo O. Iodelene i V. Finka] Moskva, Sovetskii pisatel', 1955. 263 p. PG8721.S5B87 DLC

9537. SIRIJOS-GIRA, Vytautas. Vot i vse; roman. Perevod s litovskogo E. Mal'tsa. Moskva, Sovetskii pisatel', 1964. 261 p. illus., port. PG8721.S52V6 DLC MH

9538. SLUCKIS, Mykolas. Die Himmelsleiter; Roman. [Aus dem Litauischen übersetzt von Irene Brewing] Berlin, Aufbau-Verlag [1966] 363 p. PG8722.29.L8L315 DLC

9539. --- Ulybki i sud'by. Rasskazy i povesti. Perevod s litovskogo. [Ill. A. Smiling] Moskva, Sovetskii pisatel', 1968. 432 p. illus. At head of title: Mikolas Slitskis. PG8721.S56A57 DLC

9540. --- Zhazhda; roman. Avtorizovannyi perevod s litovskogo Feliksa Dektora. [Moskva, Molodaia gvardiia, 1970] 315 p. At head of title: Mikolas Slutskis. PG8721.S56U637 PU

9541. SOVETSKAIA LITOVSKAIA DRAMAturgiia. [Sbornik. Vstup. stat'ia I. Lankutisa] Moskva, Iskusstvo, 1954. 308 p. illus. Contents.-- Lankutis, I. Sovetskaia litovskaia dramaturgiia.--Baltushis, IU. Rannom utrom.--Baltushis, IU. Poiut petukhi.--Gudaitis, A. Pravda kusnetsa Ignotasa.--Dauguvietis, B. Novaia boroda.--Gritsius, A. Nakanune. PG8771.R5S7 CLU CtY ICU NNC WU

9542. SRUOGA, Balys. La forêt des Dieux; roman. Moscou, 1967. 355 p. D805.G3S775 PU

9543. TENISON, Zenta, comp. & tr. Een steen heeft geen hart; bloomlezing uit de hedendaagse litouse poezie. Met een inleiding van Antanas Vaičiulaitis. [Oudenaarde, Orion, 1971] 83 p. PG8772.F5T4 PU

9544. TILVYTIS, Teofilis. Stikhi. Perevod s litovskogo. Moskva, Khud. lit-ra, 1964. 182 p. port. (Bib-

lioteka sovetskoi poezii) PG8721.T55A57 1964 DLC

9545. TUMAS, Juozas, 1869-1933. Diadi i detki. [Povest'. Perevod s litovskogo S. Vasi'eva. Ill. S. Krasauskas] Vil'nius, Vaga, 1968. 100 p. PG8721.T77D46 PU DLC

9546. --- Sin at Easter, and other stories [by] Vaižgantas. Translated from the Lithuanian by Danguolė Sealey [and others] Biographical outline by Antanas Vaičiulaitis. Edited by Nola M. Zobarskas. Introd. by Charles Angoff. New York, N.Y., Manyland Books [c1971] xv, 131 p. port. Contents.--Sin at Easter.-- Rimas and Nerimas.--The Misfit.-- Aleksiukas' father and mother. PG3.T8315Si3 DLC PU

9547. VAIČIULAITIS, Antanas. Noon at the country inn; short stories. Translated from the Lithuanian by Albinas Baranauskas [and others]. Foreword by Clark Mills. New York, N.Y., Manyland Books [1965] 142 p. Translation of Vidudienis kaimo smuklėje. PZ4.V128No DLC CaAEU CaOTU OCl NN OKentU PU

9548. VAIČIŪNAS, Petras. Flaming hearts; a translation of a Lithuanian play by Catherine Simonaitis. Washington, D.C., Catholic University of America, 1951. 1 v. (various pagings) Thesis(M.A.)--Catholic University of America. Typewritten. PG8749.V12E5 DCU

9549. VAITKUS, Mykolas. The Deluge, a love story of ancient times. Authorized translation from the Lithuanian by Albinas Baranauskas. Introd. by Charles Angoff. New York, N.Y., Manyland Books [c 1965] x, 172 p. PZ4.V141De DLC CaOTU NN PU

9550. VALSIŪNIENĖ, Valerija. Zvezda schast'ka. Stikhi i poemy. Perevod s litovskogo. Moskva, Sovetskii pisatel', 1957. 179 p. illus. PG8721.V33A57 DLC

9551. VENCLOVA, Antanas. Druzhba; vstuplenie v zrelyi vozrost. Roman. Avtorizovannyi perevod s litovskogo I. Kaplanasa i F. Shuravina. Moskva, Gos. izd-vo khudozh. lit-ry, 1962. 341 p. illus. (Biblioteka sovetskoi prozy) At head of title: Antanas Ventslova. PG8721.V4D77 DLC

9552. --- Izbrannoe. Avtorizovannyi perevod s litovskogo. Moskva, Sovetskii pisatel', 1957. 564 p. port. At head of title: Antanas Ventslova. PG8721.V4A58 DLC

9553. --- Stikhotvoreniia. Perevod s litovskogo. Moskva, Gos. izd-vo khudozh. lit-ry, 1953. 222 p. illus. At head of title: Antanas Ventslova. PG8721.V4A58 DLC

9554. --- --- [Another edition] Moskva, Molodaia gvardiia, 1966. 246 p. At head of title: Antanas Ventslova. PG8721.V4A6 1966 PU

9555. VIENUOLIS, A., pseud. Ausgespielt; Roman. [Übersetzt von F. Schüler] Berlin, Verlag Kultur und Fortschritt, 1955. 459 p. DLC

9556. --- Izbrannoe. [Povesti. Rasskazy. Legendy. P'esy] Perevod s litovskogo. Moskva, Gos. izd-vo khudozh. lit-ry, 1959. 518 p. illus. PG8721.V5A57 DLC

9557. --- Usad'ba Puodzhiunasov; roman. Avtorizovannyi perevod s litovskogo O. Iodelene i L. Slavina. Moskva, Sovetskii pisatel', 1953. 354 p. PG8721.V5U8 DLC

9558. --- Utoplennitsa; povesti. Vil'nius, Gos. izd-vo khudozh. lit-ry, 1955. 76 p. PG8721.V5P317 PU

9559. YAKSTIS, Frank, tr. Translations of Lithuanian poetry. Pub. by LDS. Ozone Park, N.Y., Assoc. of Lithuanian Workers, 1968. 111 p. illus. PG8771.E3Y34 TU GU HU MH NjR NmU OCl OClW OrU TxU WaS

9560. ZELINSKII, Kornelii Liutsianovich. Litovskie novelly. Moskva, Sovetskii pisatel', 1948. 341 p. PG8711.R8Z4 DLC

9561. ŽILINSKAITĖ, Vytautė. Angel nad gorodom; iumoristicheskie rasskazy. Perevod s litovskogo F. Dektora. Moskva, Sovetskii pisatel', 1972. 182 p. At head of title: Vitaute Zhilinskaite. PG8722.36. I4Z51 PU

9562. --- Maiskii zhuk [Perevod s litovskogo S. Vasil'ev] Vil'nius, Vaga, 1966. 343 p. At head of title: Vitaute Zhilinskaite. PG8722.36.I4M3 DLC

9563. ZOBARSKAS, Stepas. Das Lied der Sensen. Erzählungen. Übersetzt von R. Gladel und St. Tyschkus, mit Bildern von Hanna Nagel. Tübingen, Patria, 1947. 156 p. 891.92.Z78.9P PU

9564. ---, ed. Lithuanian quartet [by] Aloyzas Baronas [and others] Introd. by Charles Angoff. 1st ed. New York, N.Y., Manyland Books, [1962] x, 211 p.

PZ1.Z8Li DLC CaOONL CaOTU CaOTP CtY CaAEU CtPAM FU HU ICU KU LU MH MnU NcU NoU NcD NB OCl PP PU RPB ViU

9565. --- --- [Another edition] New York, Manyland Books, 1963 [c1962] 211 p. CaOTU CtY NN OCl

9566. --- The Maker of Gods, ten Lithuanian stories. With an introd. by Alastair Guinan. [1st ed. New York, N.Y.] Voyages Press [1961] 131 p. PZ4.Z85Mak DLC CaAEU CaOTU CaOTP OCl PPiU

9567. --- Selected Lithuanian short stories. Introd. by Charles Angoff. [New York, N.Y.] Voyages Press [1959] 263 p. PZ1.Z8Se DLC CaAEU CaOONL CLU CtY ICU IU InU LU MoSW MnU NIC NN NjR NcU OO OCl PU WU

9568. --- --- 2d rev. and enlarged ed. [1960] 280 p. PZ1.Z8Se DLC CaOTU CU KU GEU NcU ViU

9569. --- --- 3d ed. 1963. PG8771.E8Z63 1963 CaOTU WaU

9570. ŽYMANTIENĖ, Julija (Beniusevičiūtė) Izbrannye sochineniia. Perevod s litovskogo [F. Shuravina] Moskva, Gos. izd-vo khudozh. lit-ry [1951] 2 v. illus. At head of title: Zhemaite [pseud.] PG8721.Z9A582 DLC CaAEU CaOTU PU

9571. --- Poimannyi bes; rasskazy. [By] Zhemaite [pseud.] Perevod s litovskogo F. Shuravina. Moskva, Goslitizdat, 1961. 158 p. illus. (Massovaia seriia) MH

XIII5.c.7. ORIGINAL WORKS IN FOREIGN

LANGUAGES ON LITHU-

ANIAN THEME

9572. ERNST, Else. Das Spukhaus in Litauen. Seltsame Begebenheiten. Berlin, Neff, 1933. 370 p. PT2609.R7S7 1937 DLC MA OCl OClW OCU OEac NjP

9573. SCHROETER, Adam. 400 metų pirmajai Nemuno poemai. [Four centuries since the wording of the poem about the Nemunas River] A. Schroeterio 1553 metų "De fluvio Memela Lithuaniae". Įžanga parašė Steponas Kolupaila. [Redaktorius Bronius Kviklys. Chicago, Ill.] Akademinis skautų sąjudis, 1952. 20 p., facsims [15] p. illus. Text in Latin; preface in Lithuanian language. Summary in English. PA8577.S32D4 DLC OKentU PU

9574. SHKLIAR, Evgenii. Letuva,
zolotoe imia. Kniga stikhov shestaia. Paris. Novyi prometei,
1927. 491.922.Sh67 PU

9575. SUDERMANN, Hermann. The
Excursion to Tilsit; tr. from the
German by Lewis Galantiere. [1930]
371 p. Contents.--The Excursion to
Tilsit.--Miks Bumbullis.--Jons and
Erdma.--The Hired Girl. PZ3.S943Ex
DLC OCl

9576. --- Jons und Erdme. [Gü-
tersloh] Im Pertelsmann Lesering
[196-] 127 p. (Kleine Lesering-
Bibliothek, Bd.35) MiEM

9577. --- Litauische Geschichten.
Stuttgart, J.G. Cotta [1960] 375 p.
CU KyU MWH MoSU PPiU RPB ViU (1917 ed.)

9578. --- Miks Bumbillis, der
Wilderer, eine Geschichte aus Litau-
en. Mit einem Nachwort von Kuno
Felchner. Leipzig, P. Redlam, Jun.
[1944, c1917] 72 p. (Reclams Uni-
versal-Bibliothek, nr. 7476)
PT2640.M5 1944 DLC InU (1960 ed.)
AzU (1958 ed.)

9579. WEYSSENHOFF, Józef. The
sable and the girl; tr. from the
original Polish by Kate Zuk-Skar-
szewska. London, G. Allen & Unwin
Ltd. [1929] 307 p. PG7158.W54S6E5
CaAEU OCl

9580. --- Soból i panna; cykł
myśliwski. Warszawa, Bibljoteka
polska, 1921. 338 p. PG7158.W4S5
DLC

9581. --- ---; powieść. [Another
edition] Poznań, Wydawn. Polskie,
193- . 331 p. (His Dzieła zebrane, t.7) (*QPM) NN

9582. --- --- [Another edition]
Kraków, Wydawn. Literackie [1957]
317 p. (Biblioteka polska) MiDW
OU CSf

9583. WICHERT, Ernst. Ansas und
Grita und andere litauische Geschichten. Berlin, Deutsche Buch-Gemein-
schaft, 1937. 479 p. illus.
PT2558.A8 ICU

--- Litauische Geschichten.
See entry nos. 7812-6816.

9584. ZATORSKI, Franciszek. Znicz
nad Niewiażą, czyli, Nawrócenie
Żmudzi. Siedlce; Warszawa, J.A.
Rył; S. Orgelbrand, 1845. 2 v.
(*QPH)NN(1)

XIII.6. THEATRE

9585. ANDRIUŠIS, Pulgis. The
folk theatre. In Lithuanian Bulletin (New York, N.Y.), v.6, no.3-4,
1948, p. 29-31. See serials consulted.

9586. BIČIŪNAS, Vytautas Pranas.
Liaudies teatras. [People's
theatre] Kaunas, 1936. 333 p.
891.920.9.Bl CtTMF

9587. BLEKAITIS, Jurgis. Balys
Sruoga; asmuo ir teatro kūrėjas.
[Balys Sruoga; as a person, and as
the founder of the theatre] In
Aidai (München), no.19-20, 1948, p.
402-408. See serials consulted.

9588. --- Balys Sruoga and the
Lithuanian theatre. In Lituanus
(Brooklyn, N.Y.), v.6, no.3, 1960,
p. 108-112. See serials consulted.

9589. BRENSZTEJN, Michał Eustachy.
Teatr szkolny w Krożach na Żmudzi.
In Ateneum Wileńskie (Wilno), v.3,
1925, p. 46-70. See serials consulted.

9590. BUTĖNAS, Julius. Lietuvių
teatras Vilniuje, 1900-1918. [Li-
thuanian theatre in Vilna, 1900-
1918] Kaunas, 1940. 104 p. Offprint from "Mūsų senovė", 1937-
1939. DK511.L2A3 no. 6-9 DLC CU PU

9591. CHICAGOS LIETUVIŲ OPERA:
pirmasis dešimtmetis, 1957-1967.
[The first decade of the Lithuanian
opera in Chicago] Redaktorius
Vladas Butėnas. Chicago, Ill.,
1968. 71 p. E184.L7C45 PU PPULC

9592. "DAINOS" PIRMOJO VIEŠOJO
spektaklio 20 metų sukaktuvės, 1914-
1924. [The 20th anniversary of the
first public performance of "Daina"]
Kaunas, "Dainos" draugijos leidinys,
1924. 40 p. 491.922.D144 PU

9593. KAUNAS. VALSTYBINIS MUZIKI-
NIS DRAMOS TEATRAS. Kauno Valstybinio muz.-dramos teatro dramos
trupė, 1920-1955. [The State Theatre of music and drama, 1920-1955.
Leidinį paruošė A. Gabrėnas. Kaune,
1956] 1 v. (unpaged, chiefly illus.,
ports.) PN2859.L5K3 DLC MH

9594. KUTKUS, Aleksas. Dainininko
dalia, atsiminimai. [A singer's
lot; recollections] Boston, Mass.,
Lietuvių enciklopedijos leidykla
[1960] 159 p. illus.
ML420.K97A3 DLC CaAEU NN PU

9595. LANDSBERGIS, Algirdas. Prob-

lems of the theatre in Soviet-occupied Lithuania. In Baltic Review
(New York, N.Y.), no.15, 1958, p.
34-41. See serials consulted.

9596. LIETUVOS SCENOGRAFIJA.
[Lithuanian scenography. Tekstas
Jono Mackonio. Sudarė Gražina
Aleksienė] Vilnius, Vaga, 1968.
149 p. illus., ports. Summaries
in Russian, English and German.
DN2885.L5 DLC CtY ICBM MH OKentU PU

9597. LÜHR, Georg. 24 Jesuiten-
dramen der litauischen Ordenspro-
vinz. In Altpreussiche Monatschrift
(Königsberg in Pr.), v.38, 1901, p.
1-61. See serials consulted.

9598. MACIŪNAS, Vincas. Inci-
dentas dėl Skirgailos premjeros;
keli lietuvių kritikos istorijos
puslapiai. [An indicent relating
to the opening night of Skirgaila;
a few pages on the history of Lithuanian criticism] In Metmenys
(Chicago, Ill.), no.10, 1965, p.
40-60. See serials consulted.

9599. MAKNYS, Vytautas. Lietuvių teatro raidos bruožai. [The
development of the Lithuanian the-
atre] Vilnius, Mintis, 1972. v.1.
PN2859.L5M3 PU

9600. MAŽEIKA, Vytautas. Opera;
lietuvių tarybinio operos teatro
raida, 1940-1965. [The development of the Soviet Lithuanian opera
theatre, 1940-1965] Vilnius, Mintis, 1967. 207 p. illus. (part.
col.) ports. ML1751.L58M4 1967
DLC CaOTU ICBM OKentU PU

9601. MUSTEIKIS, Mečys. Teatras
pavergtoje Lietuvoje. [The theatre in captive Lithuania] In
Lietuvių dienos (Los Angeles, Calif.),
no.6, 1960, p. 12-13, 17. See
serials consulted.

9602. PANĖVĖŽYS, LITHUANIA. DRA-
MOS TEATRAS. Panevėžio Dramos
teatras, 1940-1955; 15 metų sukaktis nuo įkūrimo dienos. [Fifteenth
anniversary of the drama theatre in
Panevėžys Nuotraukos V. Krulicko ir
K. Vitkaus] Vilnius, Lietuvos TSR
teatro draugija, 1955. 19 p. illus.
ports. PN2859.L5P3 DLC

9603. PETKEVIČAITĖ, Gabrielė. Iš
mūsų vargų ir kovų; paminėti Palangos spektaklio 25 metų sukaktuvėms.
[Twenty-fifth anniversary of the
drama play in Palanga] Kaunas,
Varpo b-vės spaustuvė, 1927. 133
p. (Varpo bendrovės leidinys, nr.
64) 491.92.P442.2 PU

9604. PETUCHAUSKAS, Marksas.
Premjerų keliais; Lietuvos dramos
teatrų 1956-1965 m. apžvalga. [A
review of Lithuanian drama theatres,
1956-1965] Vilnius, 1967. 213 p.
illus. PN2859.L5P42 PU MH

9605. --- Teatras-amžininkas.
Kauno Dramos teatras, 1940-1964.
[The contemporary drama theatre in
Kaunas, 1940-1964] Vilnius, Mintis,
1965. 173 p. illus., ports.
792.475.P459 PU CtY MH

9606. RUZGAITĖ, Aliodija. Lietuviško baleto kelias. [The development of Lithuanian ballet] Vilnius,
Mintis, 1964. 70 p. illus. (part.
col.) GV1787.R8 DLC CtPAM PU

9607. SANTVARAS, Stasys. Dramos
teatras. [Drama theatre] In Lietuvių enciklopedija. Boston, Mass.,
1968. v.15, p. 649-673. For
holdings see entry no. 216.

9608. --- Operos teatras. [Opera
theatre] In Lietuvių enciklopedija.
Boston, Mass., 1968. v.15, p. 673-
683. For holdings see entry no. 216.

9609. SODEIKA, Antanas. Mano kelias į muzikos meną; atsiminimai.
[My road to the art of music; me-
moirs] Vilnius, VGLL, 1958. 190 p.
illus. ML420.S678A3 DLC PU

9610. SRUOGA, Balys. Lietuvių
teatras Peterburge, 1892-1918.
[Lithuanian theatre in Peterburg in
1892-1918] Kaunas, Humanitarinių
mokslų fakulteto leidinys, 1930.
139 p. incl. tables. PN2726.L4S77
PU BM CU ICBM NN

9611. --- "Šarūnas" Valstybės Te-
atre. [The play, Šarūnas, in the
State Theatre] In His Raštai.
Vilnius, 1957. v.6, p. 395-434.
PG8721.S68 1957 v.6 DLC CaAEU ICU
PU NN

9612. SUTKUS, Antanas, 1892-1968.
Vilkolakio teatras. [Vilkolakis,
the satyrical theatre in Lithuania]
Vilnius, Vaga, 1969. 358 p.
ports., photos. PN2859.L5V5 PU
CaAEU

9613. TARYBINIO MENO KELIU. [The
way of Soviet art. Vilnius, Mintis, 1968] 269 p. illus. (Iš
lietuvių kultūros istorijos,5)
Balt 7849.58.5(5) MH

9614. TEATRINĖS MINTIES PĖDSAKAIS.
Sudarė ir redagavo Ant. Vengris.
Specred. M. Petuchauskas. Vilnius,
Lietuvos TSR Kultūros ministerijos
liaudies meno rūmai, 1969. 406 p.

PN2053.T4 PU

9615. VILNA. LIETUVOS TSR VALSTY-
BINIS AKADEMINIS OPEROS IR BALETO
TEATRAS. Lietuvos TSR Valstybinis
akademinis operos ir baleto teatras,
1920-1955. [Lithuanian State Opera
and Ballet, 1920-1955] Vilnius,
Lietuvos TSR Teatro draugija, 1955.
47 p. illus., ports. ML1738.L5V5
DLC

9616. YLA, Stasys, 1913- , ed.
Lietuvių nacionalinė opera. [Lith-
uanian National Opera] Vilnius,
VPMLL, 1960. 103 p. illus.
ML1738.L5Y4 DLC PU

9617. ZABARAUSKAS, V. Panevėžio
dramos teatras. [Drama theatre in
Panevėžys] Vilnius, Mintis, 1966.
117, [2] p. illus. Bibliography:
p. 114-[118]. PN2726.P32D7 DLC

9618. ŽALINKEVIČAITĖ, Elena.
Kauno valstybiniai dramai 25 metai.
[Twenty-five years of the Kaunas
State drama] In Žiburiai (Augsburg,
Ger.), no.2,(14), 1946, p. 4. See
serials consulted.

XIII.7. MUSIC

XIII.7.a.GENERAL WORKS

9619. **AKADEMIJA IR KONCERTAS;**
profesoriui, kompositoriui ir Mu-
zikologijos archyvo organizatoriui
Juozui Žilevičiui pagerbti, 1966 m.
gruodžio 4 d. ... [Symposium and
concert in honour of Juozas Žilevičius... Edited by Antanas Giedrai-
tis] Chicago, Ill. [Vykdomasis Ko-
mitetas] 1966. 22 [10] p. illus.
ML200.8.L7A32 CaAEU CaOONL

ALANTAS, Vytautas, ed.
Antanas Vanagaitis, jo gyvenimas ir
veikla. [Cleveland, Ohio, 1954]
See entry no. 454.

AMBRASAS, Algirdas. Kompozitorius Juozas Gruodis; gyvenimo
ir kūrybos bruožai. Kaunas, 1960.
See entry no. 458.

9620. BANAITIS, Walter C. Ein
halbes Jahrhundert litauischer Mu-
zik. In Baltische Gesellschaft in
Deutschland. Die baltischen Völker
in ihrer europäischen Verpflichtung.
Hannover-Döhren, 1958. p. 35-63.
DK511.B3B285 DLC MiU PU

9621. ČIURLIONIS, Mikalojus Konstantinas. Apie muziką ir dailę,
laiškai, užrašai ir straipsniai.

[About music and art; letters, notes
and articles. Comp. by V. Čiurlionytė-Karužienė. Ed. by A. Žirgu-
lys] Vilnius, VGLL, 1960. 337 p.
illus., music. ML60.C536A6 DLC
CtPAM CtY MH OKentU PU

GAUDRIMAS, Juozas. Balys
Dvarionas. Moskva, 1960. See
entry no. 523.

9622. --- Iš Lietuvių muzikinės
kultūros istorijos, 1861-1965.
[From the history of Lithuanian mu-
sical culture, 1861-1965] Vilnius,
VPMLL, 1958-1967. 3 v., illus.,
ports., facsims., music.
LG309.L5G39 DLC CaAEU CtPAM(v.3)
CtY ICLJF MH NN PU

9623. --- Iz istorii litovskoi
muzyki, 1861-1917. Moskva, Muzyka,
1964. 211 p. music.
ML309.L5G39I8 DLC NN NcU NjP

9624. --- Lietuvių tarybinė muzika; apybraiža. [Soviet Lithuanian
music] Vilnius, VGLL, 1960. 229
p. 780.9475.G233.2 PU MH

9625. --- M.K. Chiurlenis. [Pere-
vod s litovskogo A. German, V. Ger-
man] Vil'nius, Vaga, 1965. 119 p.
col. illus., facsims., music. NN

9626. --- M.K.Čiurlionis. Vilnius,
Vaga, 1965. 107 p. illus.
ML410.C6G4 DLC CaAEU CaOTU MH PU

9627. --- Muzykal'naia kul'tura
Sovetskoi Litvy, 1940-1960; ocherk.
[By] IUozas Kazimierovich Gaudrimas.
Leningrad, Sovetskii kompozitor,
1961. 138 p. illus., ports.
ML309.L5G42 DLC PU

GROŽINĖ LITERATŪRA; katalogas: literatūra, dailė, muzika,
1940-1960. Vilnius, 1961. See
entry no. 7936.

GRUODIS, Juozas. Straips-
niai, laiškai ir užrašai. Amžininkų atsiminimai. Vilnius, 1965.
See entry no. 534.

9628. JAKUBĖNAS, Vladas. Istorinė
lietuvių muzikos apžvalga. [A his-
torical review of Lithuanian music]
In Lietuvių enciklopedija. Boston,
Mass., 1968. v.15, p. 684-701.
For holdings see entry no. 216.

9629. --- The evolution of Lithuanian music. In Lithuanian Bulletin
(New York, N.Y.), v.5, no.11, 1947,
p. 7-12; no.12, p. 13-14. See
serials consulted.

9630. --- Lietuvių muzika per 20
Nepriklausomybės metų. [Lithuanian

music during the twenty years of independence] In Kemežys, V., ed. Lietuva, 1918-1938. Kaunas, 1938. p. 237-258. 947.52.L625 PU CtTMF ICLJF

JASINSKAS, Kazys. Stasys Vainiūnas. Vilnius, 1960. See entry no. 552.

9631. KATKUS, Donatas. Lietuvos kvartetas. [Lithuanian quartet] Vilnius, Vaga, 1971. 126 p. ML1157.L5K3 PU

9632. MIKĖNAITĖ, Rima. Harmonizuota lietuvių liaudies daina. [Harmonized Lithuanian folk songs] Vilnius, Mintis, 1972. 248 p. PU

NARBUTIENĖ, Ona. Juozas Naujalis; straipsniai, laiškai, dokumentai, amžininkų atsiminimai. Vilnius, 1968. See entry no. 628.

PALIONYTĖ, Dana. Valanda su kompozitorium Antanu Račiūnu. Vilnius, 1970. See entry no. 631.

9633. ŠIMUTIS, Leonardas Juozapas. Lithuanian music prior to 1918. In Lituanus (Brooklyn, N.Y.), no.4(9), 1956. p. 10-13. See serials consulted.

9634. --- Music during the years of independence. In Lituanus (Brooklyn, N.Y.), v.4, no.1, 1958, p. 16-20. See serials consulted.

STASYS ŠIMKUS; straipsniai, dokumentai, laiškai, amžininkų atsiminimai. Vilnius, 1967. See entry no. 665.

9635. TAURAGIS, Adeodatas. Lithuanian music; past and present. [Translated by M. Ginsburgas and N. Kameneckaitė] Vilnius, Gintaras, 1971. 223 p. ML309.L5T35 PU

9636. VOROB'EV, Nikolai. M.K. Čiurlionis; der litauische Maler und Musiker. Kaunas, Pribačis, 1938. x, 95 p. illus. Includes scores of piano music by M. K. Čiurlionis. ML410.C6V6 DLC MH NN NNC PU

9637. ŽILEVIČIUS, Juozas. Amerikos lietuvių įnašas į lietuvių muziką. [The American-Lithuanians' contribution to Lithuanian music] In Aidai (Brooklyn, N.Y.), no. 7-8 (93-94), 1956, p. 352-362. See serials consulted.

9638. --- Aušra ir lietuviškoji muzika. ["Aušra" and Lithuanian music] In Židinys (Kaunas), v.21,

no.3, 1935, p. 285-295. See serials consulted.

--- Česlovas Sasnauskas. Brooklyn, N.Y., 1953. See entry no. 701.

9639. --- Muzikos kultūra Lietuvoje. [Musical culture in Lithuania] In Židinys (Kaunas), v.21, no.5-6, 1935, p. 515-521. See serials consulted.

XIII.7.b. SCORES AND MUSIC

9640. BALYS, Eduardas. Dramaticheskie freski; dlia skripki, fortepiano i simfonicheskogo orkestra. Leningrad, Muzyka, 1967. Score. (144 p.) M1040.B23D7 CaOTU

9641. BANAITIS, Kazys Viktoras. [Sonata, violin & piano, D. minor] Sonata, D min., piano & violin. Somerville, Mass., I. Vasyliūnas [c1964] Score (43p.) and part. M219.B3S6 CaOTU

9642. BRAZYS, Teodoras. [Masses. (Jėzau prie manęs ateiki) With Organ] Missa ad duas voces aequales, organo comitante, thematibus devotae cantilenae Lithuanicae. Kaunas, Švyturio bendrovės leidinys, 1922. 3 pts. in 1 v. NN

9643. BUDRIŪNAS, Bronius. Mišios Šv. Kazimiero garbei skirtos lietuvių jaunimui. [St. Cazimir's Mass devoted to Lithuanian youth] Chicago, Ill., Laiškai lietuviams, 1967. 16 p. scores. 784.B ICBM

9644. ČIULIONIS, Mikalojus Konstantinas. [Works, piano. Selections] Fugos, kanonai ir preliudai. Vilnius, Vaga, 1965. 51 p. M22.C585V3 DLC

9645. --- [Quartet, strings, C minor] Styginis kvartetas. Vilnius, Vaga, 1966. Miniature score (50 p.). M452.C586Q3 CaOTU

9646. DVARIONAS, Balys. [Pieces, piano] 12 pjesių fortepijonui. Vilnius, Vaga, 1971. 34 p. M25.D888P4 CaOTU

9647. --- [Concerto, horn; arr.] Kontsert dlia violoncheli s orkestrom. Leningrad, Muzyka [Leningradskoe otd-nie] 1966. Score (36 p.) and part. M1017.K724 CaOTU

9648. --- [Scherzo oboe & piano] Skerco obojui (birbynei) su forte-

pijonu. [Vilnius, Vaga, 1967]
Score (9 p.) and part. M246.D88S3
CaOTU

9649. --- [Sonata-ballade, violin
& piano] Sonata-ballada dlia skripki s fortepiano. Leningrad, Muzyka,
1968. Score (35 p.) and part.
M219.D974S6 CaOTU

9650. --- Vil'nius; paradnyi marsh
dlia dukhovogo orkestra. [Lenin-
grad], S[ov.] k[ompozitor, 1969]
Score (23 p.) M1247.D83V5 CaOTU

9651. GRUODIS, Juozas. [Works,pi-
ano. Selections] Kūriniai fortepijonui. Vilnius, VGLL, 1960. 126 p.
M22.G88V3 DLC

9652. --- [Suite, orchestra] Siuita, dlia simfonicheskogo orkestra.
Leningrad, Muzyka [Leningradskoe otd-
nie] 1966. Miniature score (127 p.)
M1003.G925 CaOTU

9653. HYMNS IN HONOR OF OUR BLES-
sed Mother at the National Shrine.
[Washington, D.C.] Nauji muzikos kūriniai Šiluvos Marijos koplyčios de-
dikacijos ir lietuvių religinio kon-
greso prisiminimui, Washington, D.C.,
1966. [New York, N.Y., New Yorko ir
New Jersey Kunigų Vienybės Provinci-
ja, 1969] Score (32 p.)
M2142.L5H99 CaAEU

9654. KARNAVIČIUS, Jurgis. Gražina. Piano-vocal score. Lithuanian
Gražina; keturių veiksmų opera. Li-
bretas: Kazys Inčiūra... Gražina;
opera in four acts... [Chicago, Ill.]
Chicagos Lietuvių opera [1966] vii,
262 p. M1503.K184G757 1966 DLC
CaOTU

9655. KLOVA, Vytautas. [Concerto,
violoncello; arr.] Kontsert dlia
violoncheli s orkestrom. Leningrad,
Muzyka [Leningradskoe otd-nie] 1966.
Score (36 p.) and part. M1017.K724
CaOTU

9656. KUDIRKA, Vincas. Lietuvių
Himnas. Žodžiai ir melodija V. Kudirkos; fortepionui paruošė A. Kačanauskis. [Lithuanian anthem;
words with music] Ryga, Lėšomis A.
Macejevskio. 1906. 21 p. NN

9657. --- Lithuanian national anthem; voice and piano. Words [i.e.
English translation] by Nadas Rastenis. Piano version by Vytautas Bacevičius. [New York, N.Y.] Paragon
Music Publishers [c1945] 3 p.
M1767.L4K DLC MH

9658. KUPREVIČIUS, Viktoras. S
pervogo vzgliada; muzykal'naia komediia v trekh deistviiakh. Muzyka

Viktora Kuprevicha. Moskva, Otdel
raspostraneniia dramaticheskikh proizvedenii VUOAP, 1967. 71 leaves.
ML50.K9725S27 1967 DLC

9659. LANDSBERGIS, Vytautas. Pavasario sonata. Vilnius, Vaga, 1965.
351 p. illus., music. ML410.C6L4
DLC CaOTU PU

9660. PETRAUSKAS, Mikas. Lietuviškas milijonierius; vieno veiksmo
operette. Žodžius parašė V. Sta-
garas [pseud. Lithuanian million-
aire; operetta in one act] Shenandoah, Pa., "Darbininkų Vilties"
spauda, 1915. 24 p. Libretto.
(*MZ)NN

9661. SASNAUSKAS, Česlovas. Lietuviška muzika; requiem ir kita.
[Lithuanian music; requiem and
others. Redagavo Juozas Žilevičius.
Viršelį piešė dailininkas Teofilius
Petraitis. Harrison, N.H., L. Voi-
siekauskas] 1950. Scores (133 p.)
port. M1495.S25 CaAEU ICBM NIC NNC

9662. VAINIŪNAS, Stasys. Kontsert
nr.3, dlia fortepiano s simfoni-
cheskim orkestrom [soch.33] Leningrad, Muzyka, 1967. Score [75 p.]
M1011.V34 op.33 DLC

9663. ŽILEVIČIUS, Juozas. Vytauto Didžiojo 500 metų mirties sukaktuvių minėjimo kantata. [Cantata
to commemorate fifth centenary of
the death of Vytautas the Great.
A. Jakšto žodžiai. Baritonui,
mišriam kvartetui, mišriam chorui,
trims trimitams ir pianui parašė
Juozas Žilevičius. Brooklyn, N.Y.]
D.K.L. Vytauto Didžiojo 500 metų
sukaktuvių minėjimo New Yorko ir
New Jersey, Vytauto komiteto leidinys, 1933. Score (50 p.)
M1531.Z69 CaAEU ICBM MB NN

XII.7.c. HYMNS AND HARMONIZED
FOLK SONGS

9664. BAČIŪNAS, Juozas J., ed.
Šaulių trimitai; šaulių chorams
giesmių bei dainų rinkinys įvairių
lietuvių kompozitorių. [Choral
selections of folk songs from many
composers] Išleido Juozas J. Bačiūnas. Sodus, Mich., Lietuvos
šaulių sąjungos leidinys [1932].
32 p. NN

9665. BANAITIS, Kazys Viktoras.
Liaudies dainos mišriam chorui.
[Folk songs for the mixed choir.
n.p.] Išleido P.M. Juras, 1951.

1 v. music. M1766.L4B24 DLC OC1

9666. --- 100 liaudies dainų.
[One hundred Lithuanian songs]
Brooklyn, N.Y., P.M. Juras, 1951.
133 p. music. M1766.L4B26 DLC
ICBM InU OC1 PPULC PU

9667. BANAITIS, Valteris Kristupas. Lietuvių evangelikų liaudies giesmės. [Lithuanian Protestant hymns] Ludwigsburg, Ger., Jaunimo ratelis, 1951. 55 p. 784.B ICBM

9668. BIRŽIŠKA, Mykolas, comp. Karo istorijos dainynėlis. [Songs on history of war] Kaunas, K.A.M. Karo mokslo skyriaus leidinys, 1923. 32 p. PG8715.B48 DLC

9669. BRAZYS, Teodoras, comp. Mūsų dainelės... [Our folk songs] Kaunas, Švyturio b-vės leidinys, 1923. 4 v. 784.8.B ICCC(v.3-4)

9670. DAINŲ KRAITIS; 200 lietuviškų dainų su gaidomis. [A dowry of songs; 200 Lithuanian songs with music. Chicago, Ill.] Karvelis [1957] 224 p. music and text. 780.D ICBM ICLJF

9671. DAINOS VASAROS GROŽYBIŲ. [Songs of summer splendours] 2. laida. Chicago, Ill., 1914. 33 p. 784.D1 CtTMF

9672. DAINUOJAM; dainų rinkinys. [Let's sing; a collection of songs] Kaunas, Kariuomenės štabo leidinys, 1935. 152 p. 874.D2 CtTMF

9673. DAINUOKIME. [Let's sing. Putnam, Conn., Immaculate, n.d.] 86 p. 784.D6 CtTMF

9674. Daug daug dainelių. [Many, many songs] Paruošė Jonas Račkauskas. Išleido Sukurys. Chicago, Ill., 1960. 112 p. 784.D7 CtTMF

9675. EREMINAS, Leonas, comp. Dainos; sutaisytos ant keturių balsų. [Folk songs for four-voice choir] Tilžė, Išleido P. Mikolainis, 1902. 82 p. 784.4.E ICCC

9676. GRAŽIAUSIOS IR MEGIAMIAUSIOS sodiečių dainos... Surinko B. J-nė. [The most beautiful and the best loved folk songs] Kaunas, Vairo b-vės knygynas, 1927. 168 p. 784.8.G ICCC

9677. GRUODIS, Juozas. Aguonėlės. [Poppies; folksongs] Vienam balsui prie fortepijono. [Kaunas] Aušros b-vė knygyno leidinys [1921] 3 p. NN

9678. GUDAVIČIUS, Juozapas. Že-

maitiškos dainos. [Lithuanian folk songs] Tauragė, author, 1912. 23 p. (*MOSlavic)NN

9679. JURGA, J., comp. Saulė tekėjo; žinomiausios lietuvių liaudies dainos. [The best known Lithuanian folk songs] Vilnius, VGLL, 1960. 95 p. M1766.L4J75 DLC

9680. LIETUVIŲ CHORINĖS LITERATŪROS CHRESTOMATIJA. Khrestomatiia khorovoi literatury. [Redakcinė komisija: A. Budriūnas, K. Kaveckas ir A. Gimžauskas. Sudarytojas VI. Raupėnas] Vilnius, VGLL, 1963- . M1579.4.L54 DLC(1-) PU(1-)

9681. LITUANICA, LIETUVIŲ SKAUTŲ TUNTAS, CHICAGO. 101 daina. (One hundred and one songs] Chicago, Ill., 1955. 122 p. illus. M1766.L4L5 DLC

9682. NAUJOS DAINOS. [New songs] Tilžė, 1892. 80 p. 947.5.A1 CtTMF

9683. PETRAUSKAS, Mikas. Lietuviškos dainos. [Lithuanian folk songs] Šeši sąsiuviniai; keturiems mašytiems balsams. So. Boston, Mass., Broliai Devėniai, 1922. 89 p. Lithuanian works with music for two to four voices, some with piano accompaniment. (*MP(Lithuanian))NN

9684. --- Rinktinės Miko Petrausko dainos kompozitoriui įamžinti. [Vocal works; selected] Brooklyn, N.Y., Komitetas Miko Petrausko kūriniams leisti, 1940. 63 p. illus., music. M1497.P48V6 DLC

9685. REIKALINGIAUSIOS GIESMĖS lygiems balsams, vargonams pritariant. [Hymns...] Chicago, Ill., Šv. Kazimiero seserys, 1951. 168 p. words with music. 783.R ICBM

9686. --- --- [Another edition] Chicago, Ill., Šv. Kazimiero seserys, 1959. 159 p. words with music. 783.R ICBM

9687. ŠIMKUS, Stasys. "Dainų dainorėlis"; 30 liaudies dainų trims ir dviems lygiems balsams. Skiriamas mūsų mokykloms. [Thirty folk songs for the public schools] Kaunas, Išleido J. Petronio knygynas, 1919. 56 p. illus. 784.4S ICCC

9688. --- 33 rinktinės lietuvių liaudies dainos. [33 selected Lithuanian folk songs] Boston, Mass., P.M. Juras, 1950. 60 p. music. A784.475.Si44 PU

9689. SODEIKA, Stepas. Kas sugrį-

žęs ant Nemuno kranto... Stepo So-
deikos dainos ir giesmės. [On the
shores of Nemunas; songs by Stepas
Sodeika. Chicago, Ill., Draugo
spaustuvė, 1968. Score (32 p.)
port. M1547.S67 CaAEU

9690. STRELEZKI, Anton. [Lithu-
anian song] Lithuanian song. Litauisches Lied (German version by
Helen D. Tretbar) Paroles de Maurice Sagarez. Milwaukee, Wis., W.
Rohlfing, 1887. 7 p.
sVM1621S.914L ICN

9691. TALLAT-KELPŠA, Juozas.
Kariagos aidai; tėvynės gynėjams
dainų rinkinėlis. [Collection of
war songs by J. Tallat-Kelpša]
Tilžė, O.v. Mauderodė, 1920. 29
p. 784.8.T ICCC

9692. --- Lakštutė; dainų rinkinėlis pradedantjai mokyklai.
[Nightingale; a collection of folk
songs...] Helsinkai, Suomių literatūros draugijos spaustuvė, 1917.
46 p. 491.922.T144 PU

9693. --- Tėvužėli, sengalvėli.
Sakė mane šiokia. Dvi liaudies
dainos vienam balsui su fortepijo-
nu. [Songs for one voice with
piano accomp. Kaunas] Švyturys
[192-] 3 p. (*MPbox)NN

9694. TĖVYNĖS MYLĖTOJŲ DAINOS.
[National songs...] Bitėnai, 1907.
48 p. 784.T1 CtTMF

9695. VAIČIŪNAS, Antanas. Mūsų
kariuomenės dainos, 20 dainų.
[Army songs] Tilžė, spauda, 1924.
30 p. 784.Vi CtTMF NN

9696. VANAGAITIS, Antanas. Dainuok; dainų vadovėlis skirimas
liaudies mokykloms. [A textbook
of songs for elementary schools]
Pirma dalis. Kaunas, Onos Vit-
kauskytės knygyno leidinys, 1922.
30 p. music with text.
VM1758.V21d ICN ICLJF

9697. VYTURĖLIS, B. Dainuokim
sesutės. [Let's sing sisters]
Kaunas, 1937. 63 p. 784.V5 CtTMF

9698. ŽILEVIČIUS, Juozas. Dainos
chorui à capella. [Songs without
accompaniment for chorus] Serija
I & II. Kaunas, Švyturio b-vė leidinys, [192-] 7 v. in one.
(*MP(Lithuanian)NN

9699. --- Lietuviais esame mes
gimę; lietuvių dainynas. [A song
book for voice and piano] Daina-
vimui arba pianui. Sudarė Juozas
Žilevičius. Chicago, Ill., J.

Karvelis, 1964. 110 p. music.·
M1766.L4Z69 ICU

XIII.8. ART

XIII.8.a. GENERAL WORKS

9700. BUDRYS, Stasys. Lietuvių
dailė, 1930-1940. [Lithuanian art,
1930-1940] In Pergalė. Vilnius,
1969. no.2, p. 116-130. See
serials consulted.

9701. CHERVONNAIA, Svetlana Mi-
khailovna. Iskusstvo sovetskoi
Pribaltiki i zhivopis', skul'ptura,
grafika. Moskva, Znanie, 1965.
39 p. (Novoe v zhizni, nauke, tekh-
nike. VI Seriia. Literatura i
iskusstvo, 1965., 9) AS261.N6 no.9
DLC PU

DAILĖ; tapyba, skulptūra,
grafika, taikomoji dailė. See
entry no. 1470.

9702. ELEVEN LITHUANIAN ARTISTS
in Australia. [Editor Vaclovas
Ratas] Sydney, Lithuania Community
in Australia, 1967. 91 p. plates,
ports. N7401.E4 PU CaAEU

9703. GALAUNĖ, Paulius. Vilniaus
meno mokykla, 1793-1831, jos istorija, profesoriai ir mokiniai.
[School of arts in Vilnius, 1793-
1831; its history, professors and
students] Kaunas, Humanitarinių
mokslų fakulteto leidinys, 1928.
130 p. N332.V55G3 DLC CU CtTMF
NN PU

9704. --- L'Art lithuanien Malmö
[1934]. See entry no. 7111.

9705. --- Die Entwicklung der
Kunst in Litauen. In Revue Baltique
(Tallinn), v.1, no.2, 1940, p. 254-
264. See serials consulted.

9706. GRINIUS, Jonas. Istorinė
lietuvių dailės apžvalga. [His-
torical Review of Lithuanian Art]
In Lietuvių enciklopedija. Boston,
Mass., 1968. v.15, p. 701-708.
See entry no. 216.

9707. --- Lietuvių menas sovieti-
nėj tarnyboj. [Lithuanian art in
the Soviet service] In Lietuva
(New York, N.Y.), no.8, 1956, p.
27-40. See serials consulted.

GOŠTAUTAS, Stasys. Antolo-
giá biográfica del arte lituano.
Medellin, 1959. See entry no. 435.

GROŽINĖ LITERATŪRA; katalogas: literatūra, dailė, muzika,
1940-1960. Vilnius, 1961. See
entry no. 7936.

9708. IZOBRAZITEL'NOE ISKUSSTVO
Litovskoi SSR. Moskva, Sovetskii
khudozhnik, 1957. 36 p. illus.
N6995.L519 DLC CaOWtU IEN NN NcD
PU WaU

9709. JONYNAS, Vytautas Kazys.
Art in occupied Lithuania. In
Lituanus (Brooklyn, N.Y.), v.6, no.
2, 1960, p. 85-88. See serials
consulted.

JUNGFER, Victor. Litauen,
Antlitz eines volkes. Leipzig
[1938]. See entry no. 6561.

9710. JURGINIS, Juozas. Lietuvos meno istorijos bruožai. [A
historical outline of Lithuanian
art] Vilnius, VGLL, 1960. 492 p.
illus., ports. Bibliography: p.
471-474. N6995.L5J8 DLC ICBM ICLJF
NN PU

9711. KURAUSKAS, Algirdas. A
glance at the development of Lithuanian art and the xylography of
Paulius Augius. In Lituanus (Chicago, Ill.), v.14, no.1, 1968, p.
40-64. See serials consulted.

9712. LIETUVIŲ DAILĖ. [Lithuani-
an art. Redakcinė komisija: T.
Cerniauskas et al. Dailininkas V.
Jurkūnas. Sudarė P. Gudynas, E.
Jurėnas] Vilnius, VGLL, 1954.
xxxv, 107 p. illus. Lithuanian
and Russian. N7255.L5L5 DLC CtPAM
NN PU

9713. LIETUVOS TSR DAILĖ. The art
of Soviet Lithuania. [Įžanginio
straipsnio autoriai ir albumo sudarytojai J. Umbrasas, L. Jasiulis.
Leningradas, Aurora, 1972] 31 p.
and 70 plates. N6995.L5L52 PU

9714. LITHUANIAN ART IN EXILE.
[Managing editor: Paulius Augius,
in collaboration with Viktoras Pe-
travičius and others. Tr. by W.
Rickmer Rickmers] München, T.J.
Vizgirda, 1948. 78 p. (p.[17]-78
illus. (part. col.)) (Lithuania,
country and nation, 12) N6995.L5L5
DLC CaAEU CaOKQ CaOONL ICBM IEN MH
NbU OCl PP PU NSyU OClW

9715. REKLAITIS, Povilas Viktoras. Die bildende Kunst der litauischen Emigration, 1945-1966. In
Acta Baltica (Königstein im Taunus)
v.6, 1966, p. 237-255. See
serials consulted.

9716. --- Einführung in die Kunst-

geschichtsforschung des Grossfürstentums Litauen; mit Bibliographie
und Sachregister. Marburg-Lahn,
1962. v, 217 p. map. (Wissenschaftliche Beiträge zur Geschichte
und Landeskunde Ost-Mitteleuropas,
nr.59) DR10.W5 Bd.59 DLC CaOTU CU
CtY ICU MnU NNC NcD NjP PU

9717. --- Zur Kenntnis der älteren Tafelmalerei in Litauen. In
Zeitschrift für Ostforschung (Marburg-Lahn), no.4, 1962, p. 713-718.
See serials consulted.

9718. RESPUBLIKINĖ DAILĖS PARODA
Lietuvos TSR 20-mečiui paminėti,
1960. Katalogas. [The catalogue
of the exhibition of arts to commemorate the 20th anniversary of the
Lithuanian SSR. Sudarė Pr. Gudynas
ir S. Jakštas. Redaktorius S. Jakš-
tas] Vilnius, 1960. 333, 78 p.
illus., ports. N7275.L5R4 1960 DLC
PPiU

9719. VALIUŠKEVIČIŪTĖ, Apolonija.
Kauno Meno mokykla. [The Academy
of Arts in Kaunas] Vilnius, Vaga,
1971. 152 p., 32 leaves of illus.
At head of title: Lietuvos TSR Mokslų akademija. Istorijos institutas.
N332.L753K38 DLC OKentU

9720. VIESULAS, Romas. Dainos;
ten original lithographs on the
themes of ancient Lithuanian folk
songs. Pref. by Henrikas Nagys.
Paris, 1959. [10] plates (in portfolio) NE2415.V5N3 DLC

9721. VILNA. VALSTYBINIS DAILĖS
MUZIEJUS. Jubiliejinė dailės paroda didžiojo Spalio 40-mečiui paminėti, 1957. Katalogas. [Jubilee
exhibition to commemorate 40 years
since the October revolution. Vil-
nius] Valstybinis dailės muziejus,
1957. 290 p. illus., plates.
CtPAM ICA

9722. --- Respublikanskaia khudozhestvennaia vystavka. K 20-le-
tiiu Litovskoi SSR, 1960; katalog.
[Sost. P. Gudinas i S. IAkshtas.
Red. S. IAkshtas] Vil'nius, Vil'-
niuskii gos. khudozh. muzei, 1960.
285 p. ports., 74 plates.
Fogg art Mus. MH

ŽILIUS, Jonas. Albumas
lietuviškos parodos Paryžiuje 1900
metuose... Plymouth, Pa., 1902.
See entry no. 1236.

XIII.8.b. PAINTING

9723. BROWN, Gordon. Petras

Kiaulėnas and the art of modern colour. In Lituanus (Brooklyn, N.Y.) v.4, no.4, 1958, p. 113-118. See serials consulted.

9724. CHIURLENIS. [Perevod s litovskogo] Moskva, Iskusstvo, 1971. 111 p. ND699.C6C45 PU

9725. ČIURLIONIS, Mikalojus Konstantinas. Bičiulystė; aštuonios M.K. Čiurlionio kūrinių reprodukcijos su Salomėjos Nėries eilėraščiais. [Friendship; eight reproductions of works of M.K. Čiurlionis with the poetry of Salomėja Nėris] Vilnius, Vaga, 1965. 1 v. (unpaged, in portfolio) col. plates. ND699.C6N4 DLC PU

9726. --- --- 2. leidimas. Vilnius, Vaga, 1966. ND699.C6N4 1966 PU

9727. --- M.K. Čiurlionis. 32 reprodukcijos. [M.K. Čiurlionis. 32 reproductions. Redakcinė komisija: V. Čiurlionytė-Karužienė et al.] Vilnius, VGLL, 1961. xxiv p., 32 plates (in portfolio). ND699.C6V4 DLC MH PU

9728. --- Pasaulio sutvėrimas. [Creation of the world] Vilnius, Vaga, 1971. 10 p., 13 col. plates. Text by Vytautas Landsbergis. ND699.C6L31 PU

9729. --- 16 fluorofortų. [Sixteen etchings] Vilnius, VGLL, 1963. 17 p., 16 plates (in portfolio). NE2210.C55K3 DLC PU

ČIURLIONYTĖ, Jadvyga. Atsiminimai apie M.K. Čiurlionį. Vilnius, 1970. See entry no. 505.

9730. COPENHAGEN. DANSKE KUNSTINDUSTRIMUSEUM. Litauisk Folkenkunst, Udstilling udlaant af Čiurlionies Museum i Kaunas, Apr.-Maj 1931. Kjøbenhavn, E.G. Petersen Kgl. Hof-Bogtrykkeri, 1961. 24 p., 64 pl. NNMM

9731. ETKIND, Mark Grigor'evich. Mir kak bol'shaia simfoniia; kniga o khudozhnike Chiurlenise. [Leningrad, Iskusstvo, 1970] 157 p. illus. ND955.L53C53 CaOTU

9732. GALAUNĖ, Paulius, ed. M.K. Čiurlionis. Rašo: S. Čiurlionienė et al. Kaunas, Vytauto Didžiojo kultūros muziejus, M.K. Čiurlionies galerija, 1938. 134 p. illus., mounted ports., plates. A759.75.C499.yG PU CtTMF

--- Tapytojas Juozas Oleške-

vičius. See entry no. 521.

GUDYNAS, Pranas. Petras Kalpokas. Kaunas, 1962. See entry no. 536.

9733. --- V. Eidukevičius: 24 reprodukcijos. [Twenty-four reproductions of V. Eidukevičius] Vilnius, Vaga, 1968. 21 p. 24 col. plates. Summaries in English, French, German and Russian. CtY NN

9734. --- Vladas Eidukevičius,1891-1941. Vilnius, Vilniaus valstybinės dailės muziejus, 1963. 48 p. illus., 23 plates. Lithuanian and Russian. MH

9735. --- Vytautas Mackevičius. Vilnius, Vaga, 1971. 111 p. illus. Summary in Russian, English and German. ND699.M22G78 DLC

9736. HANFMANN, George M.A. M.K. Čiurlionis; the Lithuanian painter. In Lituanus (Brooklyn, N.Y.), v.7, no.2, 1961, p. 34-36. See serials consulted.

9737. IVANOV, Vyacheslav. Čiurlionis and the problem of the synthesis of art. In Lituanus (Brooklyn, N.Y.), v.7, no.2, 1961, p.45-58. See serials consulted.

9738. JONYNAS, Vytautas Kazys. The artist Adomas Varnas. In Lituanus (Brooklyn, N.Y.), v.5, no.2, 1959, p. 58-62. See serials consulted.

JUODAKIS, Virgilijus. Balys Buračas. Vilnius, 1971. See entry no.559.

9739. JURKUS, Paulius. Adomas Galdikas- nature's painter. In Lituanus (Brooklyn, N.Y.), no.4(9), 1956, p. 19-21. illus. See serials consulted.

9740. --- The artist Povilas Puzinas. In Lituanus (Brooklyn, N.Y.), v.5, no.1, 1959, p. 18-20. See serials consulted.

9741. --- Vytautas Kasiulis, painter of the joy and life. In Lituanus (Brooklyn, N.Y.), no.1(10), 1957, p. 23-26. illus. See serials consulted.

KAIRIŪKŠTIS, Vytautas. Kajetonas Sklėrius-Šklėrys, 1876-1932. Kaunas, [1938] See entry no.565.

9742. KALPOKAS, Petras. 32 reprodukcijos. [Thirty two reproductions

of Pranas Kalpokas' works. Redakci-
nė komisija: A. Gudaitis et al.]
Text by Pranas Gudynas. Vilnius,
1966. 11 p., 32 plates. Lithuanian,
Russian, English, French and German.
ND955.L53K3 PU

9743. KIAULĖNAS, Petras. Petras
Kiaulėnas. Préf. de Maurice Scherer.
Tübingen, Ger., Patria, 1948. 71 p.
illus. Text also in English and German. ND699.K84S4 DLC InNd NN PU

9744. --- --- [Another edition]
Introd. by Gordon Brown. [n.p.] B.
A. Thrania [c1958] 7 p., 12 col.
plates (in portfolio) ND699.K48B7
DLC MB PU

9745. KUZMINSKIS, Jonas. Jonas
Kuzminskis; dailės parodos katalogas.
[Jonas Kuzminskis; catalogue of art
exhibition. Comp. by B. Pakštas]
Vilnius, Lietuvos TSR dailės muzie-
jus, 1966. 58 p. illus., ports.
Lithuanian and Russian. NE678.K84P3
DLC

9746. LEMAN, Boris Alekseevich.
Chiurlianis; tekst B.A. Lemana.
Sanktpeterburg, Izd. N.I. Butkovskoi,
1912. 28 p. 947.52.C497.yL PU

9747. --- --- 2. izd. Petrograd,
Izdanie N.I.Butkovskoi [1916] 29 p.,
plates, port. ND699.C55L4 1916 DLC
NN

9748. LIETUVOS TAPYBA XVI-XIX.
[Parengė Petras Juodelis. Lithuanian paintings of the 16th to 19th cen-
turies] Vilnius, Vaga, 1970. 112 p.
illus. Lithuanian text by P. Svičiu-
lienė and P. Juodelis; summary in
Russian, English and German.
ND695.L5L5 DLC CaOTU OKentU

9749. MACKEVIČIUS, Vytautas, Vytautas Mackevičius; [a biography.
Text by P. Gudynas. Vilnius] VPMLL,
1961. xi p., 20 p. of illus. (in
portfolio) (Lietuvių tarybinių dailininkų monografijos) Summaries in
English and Russian. ND699.M22G8
DLC PU WU

MACKONIS, Jonas. Antanas
Žmuidzinavičius. Vilnius, 1957.
See entry no.597.

9750. MAKOVSKII, Sergei Konstantinovich. N.K. Chiurlionis. In Apollon (sanktpeterburg), 1911, p. 23-
29. See serials consulted.

NĖRIS, Salomėja. Žalčio pasaka. Illus. by Paulius Augius. [n.
p.] 1947. See entry no.9311.

9751. PILLEMENT, Georges. Vytau-

tas Kasiulis. [Par Eric Persson,
ed.] Paris-Helsingborg, 1959. 84 p.
illus. Contains introduction in
French, 12 reproductions in colour,
32 in black and white, and 2 drawings
NN

9752. PIVORIŪNAS, Juozas. A Lithuanian individualist; the art of
M.K. Čiurlionis. In Lituanus (Chicago, Ill.), v.11, no.4, 1965, p. 5-24.
See serials consulted.

PUZINAS, Jonas. Tadas Daugirdas ir jo darbai. Kaunas, 1929.
See entry no. 640.

9753. RANNIT, Aleksis. Čiurlionis
seen as a symbolist. In Lituanus
(Brooklyn, N.Y.), v.7, no.2, 1961,
p. 37-44. See serials consulted.

9754. --- M.K. Čiurlionis, pion-
nier de l'art abstrait. Paris,1949.
46 p. 759.75.C499.yR PU

9755. --- M.K. Čiurlionis, the
first abstract painter of modern times. In Lituanus (Brooklyn, N.Y.),
no.3(13), 1957, 1957, p. 15-21.
illus. See serials consulted.

9756. --- Vytautas Kasiulis; un
peintre lithuanien. Baden-Baden,
Ger., Waldemar Klein, 1948. 22 p.,
16 plates. Text in French and German. 789.75.K164.yR PU CtTMF DLC
NN

9757. REKLAITIS, Povilas Viktoras.
The development of monumental art in
ancient Lithuania. In Lituanus
(Brooklyn, N.Y.), no.2(11, 1957,
p. 9-21, illus. See serials consulted.

RIMŠA, Petras. Petras Rimša
pasakoja. [Surašė Juozas Rimantas]
Vilnius, 1964. See entry no. 646.

9758. SAVICKAS, Augustinas. Pei-
sažas lietuvių tapyboje. [The landscape in Lithuanian painting] Vilnius, Vaga, 1965. 326 p. illus
(part. col) ND1360.S3 DLC OKentU PU

9759. SKLERIUS, Kajetonas. K.
Sklerius. 32 reprodukcijos. [Thir-
ty-two reproductions of paintings by
K. Sklerius. Redakcinė komisija:
P. Gudynas et al. Sudarė Jonas Um-
brasas] Vilnius, 1964. xviii p.,
plates. ND955.L53S55 PU WU

9760. Šlapelis, Ignas. Juozas
Pautienius. [Juozas Pautienius, his
life and works. Chicago, Ill.] Lietuviškos knygos klubas [1955] 87 p.
31 plates. English and Lithuanian.
ND237.P255S5 DLC CtPAM ICBM ICCC PU

9761. TAPYBA. [Paintings, 1940-
1960. Redakcinė komisija: P. Gudynas, S. Jusionis, J. Švažas] Vilnius, VPMLL, 1961. 33 p., 147 p. of
illus., (part. mounted col.) ports.
(Lietuvių tarybinė dailė)
ND695.L5T3 DLC PU

9762. --- [Paintings. Redakcinė
komisija: P. Gudynas et al.] Vilnius, Vaga, 1966. 8p., 84 p. of
illus. ND695.L5T28 DLC

9763. --- [1967-1968. Sudarė J.
Čeponis, V. Kisarauskas. Lithuanian
painting] Vilnius, Vaga, 1968. 122
p. Introductory text by G. Vaitkū-
nas. ND695.L5T29 DLC ICBM OKentU PU

9764. TAPYBA. [Sudarė B. Uogintas]
Vilnius, Vaga, 1971. 118 p.(chiefly
illus.) ND695.L5T31 PU

9765. VIENOŽINSKIS, Justinas. 24
reprodukcijos. [Twenty-four reproductions... Redakcinė komisija: P.
Gudynas et al.] Vilnius, Vaga, 1965.
xi p., 24 plates. Lithuanian, Russian,English and German.
ND955.L53V5 PU

9766. VILNA. VALSTYBINIS DAILĖS
MUZIEJUS. Justinas Vienožinskis;
dailės paroda, 1961; katalogas.
[Justinas Vienožinskis: art exhibition, 1961; catalogue. Comp. by P.
Juodelis and L. Cieškaitė. Ed. by
P. Gudynas and S. Jakštas] Vilnius,
1961. 69 p. illus., 23 plates (inl.
ports) ND699.V54V5 DLC

VOROB'EV, Nikolai. M.K.
Čiurlionis; der litauische Maler und
Musiker. Kaunas, 1938. See entry
no.9636.

ŽMUIDZINAVIČIUS, Antanas.
Antanas Žmuidzinavičius; Lietuvos
TSR liaudies dailininkas. Vilnius,
1957. See entry no.707.

9767. --- 24 reprodukcijos. [Twen-
ty-four reproductions. Redakcinė
komisija: S. Jusionis, J. Mackonis,
A. Petrulis] Vilnius, Vaga, 1966.
11 p., 24 col plates. ND699.Z6A44 PU

XIII.8.c. SCULPTURE, GRAPHIC ART,
WOODCARVING, AND
APPLIED ART

9768. ADAMONIS, Juozas. Dailioji
keramika. [Ceramics] Vilnius,LTSR
Liaudies meno rūmai, 1966. 75 p.
illus. NK4112.L5A6 DLC

ADOMONIS, Tadas. Juozas Mikėnas. Vilnius, 1969. See entry
no.452.

9769. ---, comp. Taikomoji-deko-
ratyvinė dailė: keramika, tekstilė,
interjeras, baldai, metalas, gintaras, oda, stiklas. [Applied decora-
tive art: ceramics, textiles, interior decorating, furniture, metals,
amber, leather and glass. Sudarytojas T. Adomonis] Vilnius, Mintis;
Vaga, 1965-1969. 2 v. illus. (Lietuvių tarybinė dailė) NK976.L5A3
DLC CaAEU(v.2) ICBM MH OKentU PU

9770. AUGIUS, Paulius. Paulius
Augius. Spaudai paruošė Algirdas
Kurauskas ir Vytautas Saulius. [1st
ed. Works of Paulius Augius] Chicago, Ill. [D. Augienė] 1966.
lxxvii p. illus., port., 283 p. of
plates. Introduction and table of
contents also in English. NE121.
A83K76 DLC CaAEU CaOTU CtPAM ICBM PU

BUDRYS, Stasys. Bronius
Pundžius. Vilnius, 1969. See entry
no.489.

--- Gediminas Jakubonis.
Vilnius, 1963. See entry no.490.

--- Juozas Zikaras. Vilnius,
1960. See entry no.492.

--- Robertas Antinis. Vilnius, 1968. See entry no.493.

9771. --- Lietuvių vitražas. [The
stained glass art of Lithuania]
Vilnius, Vaga, 1968. [49] p. 71
leaves of illus., plates, part. col.
Summaries in Russian, French, Englsh
and German. NK5356.A2B8 DLC CtY
ICBM OKentU PU

9772. BULAKA, Mečys. Graviury na
dereve. Woodcuts. Vilnius, Vaga,
1968. 18 p. of text and 31 plates
in portfolio. NE1217.B82A5 DLC PU

9773. DAGYS, Jacob. Dagys; sculp-
tures and paintings; introduction
by Otto Schneid. Toronto, American-
Lithuanian Art Association, 1967.
[144] p. illus. NB249.D3A44 DLC
CaAEU PU

9774. DIDŽIOKAS, Vladas. Dvidešimt plastinio meno metų. [Twenty
years of plastic art] In Kemėžys,V.,
ed. Lietuva, 1918-1938. Kaunas,
1938. 947.52.L625 PU CtTMF ICLJF

9775. 40 WOOD-CUTS. Text by Paulius Jurkus. Edited by "Žiburiai"
Augsburg, Ger., 1946. [12 p., 40
plates] Represented are the following artists: Paulius Augius, Vikto-

ras Petravičius, Vaclovas Ratas, and
Telesforas Valius. 769.75.F778 PU

9776. GRAFIKA. Sudarė ir apipavi-
dalino Ed. Jurėnas. [Graphic arts.
Edited by Ed. Jurėnas] Vilnius,
VPMLL, 1960. xxv, 197 p. illus.
(Lietuvių tarybinė dailė)
NC268.L5G7 DLC MH

9777. GRAFIKA. TAPYBA. [Graphic
art and painting. Albumas. Sudarė
ir paruošė P. Galaunė] Vilnius, Vaga, 1968. xxxvii, 286 p. illus.
(Lietuvių liaudies menas, t.7)
N6995.L5G7 DLC CtPAM CtY ICBM PU

    GUDYNAS, Pranas. Kai praby-
la medis; monografinė apybraiža apie
liaudies menininką Juozą Laurinkų.
Vilnius, 1959. See entry no.535.

9778. JASIULIS, Leonas. Vytautas
Jurkūnas. [Works of Vytautas Jurkū-
nas. Dailininkas R. Gibavičius]
Vilnius, Vaga, 1969. 67 p., 95
illus. (part col.), port. Summaries
and list of illustrations in Russian,
English, French and German.
NE678.J8J3 DLC ICBM PU

9779. JASKŪNAITĖ, O. Petras Rimša.
Vilnius, Mintis, 1966. 1 portfolio
(34 p., 31 plates) (Lietuvių tarybinių dailininkų monografijos)
NB699.R5J3 DLC

9780. JONYNAS, Vytautas Kazys.
V.K. Jonynas, un xylographe lithua-
nien; a Lithuanian wood-engraver.
[Version française de Bernadette et
Pierre Moortgat. By] Aleksis Ran-
nit. Baden-Baden, Ger., Verlag für
Kunst und Wissenschaft [c1947] 93 p.
(p. 41-89 full page plates) illus.
French, English and German.
NE1217.J6R3 DLC CtPAM CtTMF ICBM NN
PU

9781. JUODIKAITIS, Kastytis. Eks-
librisai. [Ex libris] Vilnius,
VGLL, 1963. 37 p. of illus.
Z996.J84 DLC

9782. JURKUS, Paulius. The art of
Telesforas Valius. In Lituanus
(Brooklyn, N.Y.), v.4, no.2, 1958,
p. 47-52. See serials consulted.

9783. --- The new Lithuanian gra-
phic arts. In Lituanus (Brooklyn,
N.Y.), no.2(7), 1956, p. 20-24.
See serials consulted.

9784. KERAMIKA. [Ceramics. Comp.]
P. Galaunė. Vilnius, VGLL, 1959.
vi, 322 p. (Lietuvių liaudies menas,
t.5) IaU PU

9785. KORSAKAITĖ, Ingrida. Gyvy-

binga grafikos tradicija. [Lithua-
nian graphic art] Vilnius, Vaga,
1970. 236 p. illus. Bibliography:
p. 209-[227] NC998.6.L5K6 DLC

9786. --- Jonas Kuzminskis. [Bio-
graphy of Jonas Kuzminskis] Vilnius,
Vaga, 1966. 125 p. illus., ports.
Bibliography: p. 108-[111] Summa-
ries in English, German, Russian.
NE678.K84K6 DLC NN PU

9787. KOSTKEVIČIŪTĖ, Irena. Vincas Svirskis. [Dail. Rimt. Gibavi-
čius] Vilnius, Vaga, 1966. 169 p.
illus., maps. (163 illus.)
NK9798.S85K6 DLC ICLJF NN PU

9788. KRASAUSKAS, Stasys and G.
Kanovičius. Linksma akim; šaržai
ir epigramos. [Through joyful eye.
Caricatures] Vilnius, Vaga, 1964.
70 p. illus. T741.59475K CaOTP CtY

9789. KURAUSKAS, Algirdas. Sculp-
tor Antanas Mončys. In Lituanus
(Chicago, Ill.), v.11, no.2, 1965,
p. 63-72. See serials consulted.

9790. KUZMINSKIS, Jonas. Medžio
raižiniai lietuvių liaudies dainų
motyvais. [Wood-cuts representing
motifs of Lithuanian folk songs]
Vilnius, Vaga, 1968. 14 plates.
NE678.K84A25 PU

9791. LIETUVIŲ GRAFIKA. [Lithua-
nian graphic art] 1- ; 1960/62- .
Vilnius, VGLL; Vaga. illus. annual;
irregular. DLC(1963-) CU(1963-)
IU(1966/67-) MH(1963-) MdBJ(1963-)
MnU(1963-) NIC(1963-) OKentU(1971)
PU(1963-) WU(1963-)

9792. LIETUVIŲ GRAFIKA, 1960, 1961
1962. [Lithuanian graphic art 1960,
1961 and 1962. Meninis redaktorius
ir sudarytojas R. Gibavičius] Vilnius [VGLL, 1962] [9] p., [66] p.
of illus. (part col.) Lithuanian
and Russian. NE676.L5L5 DLC PU

9793. LIETUVIŲ GRAFIKA, 1963. [Li-
thuanian graphic art, 1963. Sudarytojas: Rimtautas Gibavičius] Vilnius [Vaga, 1964] [11] p., 93 pl.
of illus.,(part col.) Lithuanian
and Russian, list of illustrations
also in English. NE676.L5L5 CaOTU
ICA MH PU

9794. LIETUVIŲ GRAFIKA, 1966, 1967.
[Lithuanian graphic art, 1966 and
1967. Leidinį parengė Rimtautas Gi-
bavičius] Vilnius, Vaga, 1968.
123 p. illus. (part. col.) Lithuanian, Russian and English.
NE676.L5L53 DLC CtY ICBM ICU PU

9795. MAKOVSKII, Sergei Konstantinovich. Grafika: M.V. Dobuzhinsko-

go. Tekst S.K. Makovskogo i F.F. Notgafta. Berlin, Petropolis, 1924. 78 p. illus. NC269.D6M3 DLC

9796. MEDŽIO DIRBINIAI. Dereviannye izdeliia. [Sudarė ir paruošė P. Galaunė] Vilnius, VGLL, 1956-58. 2 v. (chiefly illus.) (Lietuvių liaudies menas, t.1) NK9756.M4 DLC CtPAM ICU NN PU

9797. MIKĖNAS, Juozas. Juozas Mikėnas; [biography and the illustrations of his sculptures] Vilnius, VPMLL, 1961. 23 p., 47 p. of illus. (Lietuvių tarybinių dailininkų monografijos) NB699.M5B8 DLC MH

9798. MINKEVIČIUS, Jonas. Lietuvos TSR interjerai. Inter"ery Litovskoi SSR. [Redaktorius Ar. Medonis] Vilnius, VPMLL, 1963. 1 v. (unpaged) NK2056.M5 DLC

9799 --- Soviet Lithuanian Interiors. Vilnius, State Publishing House for Political and Scientific Literature, 1963. [32] p. illus. Parallel text in German. NK2056.M513 DLC

9800. RANNIT, Aleksis. Petravičius, die "Dainos" und die Seele der Litauer. Freiburg im Br., E. Burda [1948?] 8 p. A supplement to G. Krivickienė, Dainos. PG8721.P47Z8 DLC

9801. --- V.K.Jonynas, a master of wood engraving. In Lituanus(Broklyn, N.Y.), v.4, no.3, 1958, p.80-86. illus. See serials consulted.

9802. --- Vier litauische Holzschneider. In Kunstwerk (Baden-Baden), 1948. v.2, no.1-2, p.39-46. See serials consulted.

9803. RAUDUVĖ, Petras. Grafika. [Graphic art] Vilnius, VPMLL, 1964. 15 p. [32] plates (in portfolio) Text also in Russian, English and French. NE678.R3A44 DLC

9804. REKLAITIS, Povilas Viktoras. Du Vilniaus vaizdo tipai XVI-XIX amžių grafikoje. [Two different views of Vilnius from 16th to 19th centuries portrayed in graphic art] In LKMASD, v.7, 1972, p. 290-304. See serials consulted.

9805. SKULPTŪRA. [Sculpture. Sudarytojas ir įžangos autorius: St. Budrys] Kaunas, VPMLL, 1961. xxxii p., 143 illus. (lietuvių tarybinė dailė) NB955.L5S6 DLC CaAEU CaOTP CtY ICLJF MH NN PU

9806. SKULPTŪRA. [Sculpture. Sudarė ir paruošė P. Galaunė. Redakcinė komisija: Juozas Mikėnas, L. Vaineikytė ir A. Venclova. Vilnius, VGLL, 1963-1965] 2 v. chiefly illus., part. col. (Lietuvių liaudies menas, t.6, kn.1-2) Lithuanian and Russian. NB695.L5S55 DLC CaAEU CaOTP CtPAM ICLJF PU

9807. STROLIS, Liudvikas. Liudvikas Strolis: [his life and works] Vilnius, Vaga, 1966. 30 p. illus., plates (part. col.) (Lietuvių tarybinių dailininkų monografijos) Lithuanian, Russian, English and German. NK4210.S7A5 DLC

9808. UMBRASAS, Jonas. Petras Aleksandravičius. [A biography of P. Aleksandravičius] Vilnius, VPMLL 1961. xv p., 22 plates. Sp735.75.AP26.yU PU

9809. VARNAS, Adomas. Ant politikos laktų; šaržai. [Political cartoons] Kaunas, Vaivos bendrovės leidinys, 1922. 15, xxxiii p. illus. Q947.52.V437 PU CtTMF ICBM

9810. VILNA. VALSTYBINIS DAILĖS MUZIEJUS. Antroji respublikinė ekslibrisų paroda. Katalogas. [The catalogue of the second national exhibition of ex libris. Sudarė A. Laucius. Spaudai paruošė P. Gudynas ir S. Jakštas] Vilnius, 1963. (31 p.) Z994.L52V5 PU
9811. --- Jubiliejinė taikomosios dekoratyvinės dailės paroda; katalogas. [The catalogue of the exhibition of applied arts. 2. laida. Sudarė J. Šerienė. Spaudai parengė S. Jakštas] Vilnius, 1968. 127 p. NK976.L5V5 PU

9812. --- Juozas Mikėnas; dailės darbų paroda. Katalogas. [Juozas Mikėnas; the catalogue of art exhibition. Sudarė S. Budrys] Vilnius, 1962. 49 p. illus., 12 plates. MH

9813. VILNIUS-GRAFIKA-TAPYBA. [Vilnius-graphic art-painting. Leidinį parengė Jonas Čeponis, R. Gibavičius, V. Kiserauskas] Vilnius, Vaga, 1968. 108 p. illus. N6995. V5V5 ViU CaBVaS DLC ICBM OKentU PU

9814. ZIBOLIS, J., comp. Lietuvos TSR mokyklų interjeras... [Interior decoration of schools in Soviet Lithuania. Kaunas, Šviesa, 1967] [8] p., [63] p. of illus. (part.col.) Lithuanian, Russian and English. LB3261.Z5 DLC

XIII.9. ARCHITECTURE

XIII.9.a. GENERAL WORKS

9815. ARCHITEKTŪRA, I-II KNYGA. [Architecture, book I-II. Sudarė F. Bielinskis, N. Čerbulėnas et al. Redakcinė kolegija: T. Černiauskas, Juozas Mikėnas et al.] Vilnius, VGLL, 1957-65. 3 v. illus. (Lietuvių liaudies menas, t.3) Q720.9475 PU ICBM ICCA ICLJF ICU IEN PPiU

9816. BIELINSKIS, Feliksas. Architektūra perspektyviniame Lietuvos kraštovaizdyje. [Architecture in the perspective of the Lithuanian landscape] In Lietuvos TSR Architektūros klausimai (Vilnius), v.2, 1964, p. 81-116. illus., map. See serials consulted.

9817. BUDREIKA, Eduardas. Arkhitektura Sovetskoi Litvy. Leningrad, Stroiizdat, 1971. 111 p. NA1195.L5B8 PU

9818. ČERBULĖNAS, Klemensas and V. Zubovas. Lietuvos vėlybojo baroko architektūros bruožai. [An outline on the late baroque style in Lithuanian architecture] In Lietuvos TSR Architektūros klausimai(Vilnius), v.2, 1964, p. 207-244. See serials consulted.

9819. GALAUNĖ, Paulius. Naujas architektūros kurinys; bažnyčios projektas Karmelave. [New architectural work; the church project in Karmelava] In Dainava (Kaunas), v.1, 1920, p. 104-109. 891.92C.D144 PU CtTMF ICCC OCl

9820. GETNERIS, Jurgis. Lietuviškas sodžius, mūsų urbanistų mokytojas. [Lithuanian village, the teacher of out urbanists] In Naujoji romuva (Kaunas), no.11, 1940, p.221-223. See serials consulted.

9821. --- Lietuvos miesteliai, mūsų urbanistinės kultūros šaltiniai. [Lithuanian towns; sources of our urban culture] In Naujoji romuva (Kaunas), no.7-8, 1939, p. 151-152; 177-181. See serials consulted.

9822. GIMBUTAS, Jurgis. Lietuviškoji architektūra mažojoje Lietuvoje. [Lithuanian architecture in Lithuania Minor] In Aidai (München, Ger.), 1946, no.3(15), p. 38-41; no.4(16), p.58-60. illus., map. See serials consulted.

9823. IVANAUSKAS, Mikalojus. Arquitetura lituana. São Paulo, Author, 1957. 1 v., (chiefly illus.) 788Iv. ICBM

9824. --- Pirmoji apžvalginė Lietuvos architektūros paroda. [The first exhibition reviewing Lithuanian architecture] In Tautos praeitis (Chicago, Ill.), v.1, no.1, 1959, p. 94-108. See serials consulted.

9825. JASĖNAS, Kazimieras. Barokas ir subarokinti pastatai Lietuvoje. [Baroque style and pseudo-baroque buildings in Lithuania] In Židinys (Kaunas), v.19, no.3, 1934, p. 255-262. See serials consulted.

9826. --- Dailioji Lietuvos architektūra viduramžiais. [The beautiful Lithuanian architecture in the middle ages] In Židinys (Kaunas), v.18, no.10, 1933, p. 265-274. See serials consulted.

9827. --- Renesansas Lietuvos sostinėse ir provincijoje. [The renaissance in the Lithuanian capital and the country] In Židinys (Kaunas), v.10, no.12, 1933. See serials consulted.

9828. JONYNAS, Vytautas Kazys. Lietuviškoji architektūra. [Lithuanian architecture] In Aidai (Brooklyn, N.Y.), no.8(74), 1954, p. 346-352. See serials consulted.

9829. KRIŠČIUKAITIS, Kazys. Architektūros stilių raida ir lietuviško stiliaus klausimas. [The development of styles in architecture and the question of the Lithuanian style] In Aidai (Augsburg, Ger.), no.7, 1947, p. 307-315. See serials consulted.

9830. KUNDZINŠ, Pauls. Architektonische Schmuckformen des frühen Mittelalters an den Volksbauten des Ostseegebietes. In Die Gelehrte Estnische Gesellschaft, Tartu. Verhandlungen, v.30, no.1, 1938, p. 311-320. See serials consulted.

9831. LIETUVOS TSR MOKSLŲ AKADEMIJA, VILNA. ISTORIJOS INSTITUTAS. Lietuvos pilys. [Lithuanian castles. Ats. redaktorius J. Jurginis. Red. G. Gustaitė. Dailininkas K. Katkus. Spalvotos nuotraukos Z. Kazėno. Vilnius, Mintis, 1971] 304 p. illus. DK511.L21L72 CaAEU DLC OKentU PU

9832. ŁOPACIŃSKI, E. Nieznane dane archiwalne i wiadomości źródłowe do historji sztuki Wilna i... Wielkiego Xięstwa Litewskiego od XVII do początków XIX w. In Towarzystwo Przyjaciół Nauk w Wilnie. Wydział I: Filologii, Literatury i

Sztuki. Sekcja Historji Sztuki.
Prace i Materjały, v.3, 1938-1939,
p. 49-107, 319-334. See serials
consulted.

9833. LORENTZ, Stanisław. Jan
Krzystof Glaubitz architekt Wileński
XVIII wieku; materiały do biografii
i twórczości. Warszawa, Nakł. Towarzystwa Naukowego Warszawskiego,
1937. 44 p. illus. (Prace z Historii Sztuki, Towarzystwo Naukowe
Warszawskie, 3) NA1199.G5L6 DLC NN

9834. MAŽOJI ARCHITEKTŪRA. [Archi-
tecture of smaller buildings. Sudarė ir parengė K. Čerbulėnas, F. Bielinskis, K. Šešelgis. kn. 1-] Vilnius, Vaga, 1970- . illus. (Lietuvių liaudies menas, t. 9)
NA1195.L5M37 PU ICBM ICCC OKentU

9835. MINKEVIČIUS, Jonas. Naujoji
Tarybų Lietuvos architektūra. [The
new Soviet Lithuanian architecture.
Vilnius, Mintis, 1964] 30 p. illus.
NA1195.L5M5 DLC MnU NN PU

9836. --- Die neue Architektur Sowjetlitauens... Übersetzer I. Vladi-
mirovienė. Vilnius, Mintis, 1964.
30 p. illus. NA1193.L5M5R3 DLC NIC

9837. MORELOWSKI, Marian. Zarysy
syntetyczne sztuki wileńskiej od go-
tyku do neoklasycyzmu. Wilno, Grafika, 1939. 1 v. illus. (*QPZ)NN

9838. --- Znaczenie baroku wileń-
skiego XVIII stulecia. Wilno [Nakład
Autora] 1940. 80 p. xxxiii, illus.
(*QY)NN

9839. POŽĖLAITĖ, M. and Klemensas
Čerbulėnas. Baroko architektūra Lietuvoje, 1600-1790. [Baroque architecture in Lithuania, 1600-1790]
In Pergalė (Vilnius), no.7, 1970, p.
138-148. illus. See serials consulted.

9840. REKLAITIS, Povilas Viktoras.
Die Burgkirchen in Litauen. In Commentationes Balticae (Bonn), v.6-7,
1959, p. 209-247. See serials consulted.

9841. --- Lietuvos mūro architektūra ligi XXamžiaus pradžios. [The
architecture of masonry in Lithuania
until the beginning of the twentieth
century] In Lietuvių enciklopedija.
Boston, Mass., 1968. v.15, p. 713-
734. See entry no.216.

9842. --- Moksliniai darbai apie
viduramžio mūro architektūrą Lietuvoje. [Scientific research on the
medieval brick architecture in Li-
thuania] In Aidai (Brooklyn, N.Y.),

no.5(120), 1959, p. 209-217. See
serials consulted.

9843. --- The problem of the Eastern borders of Gothic architecture.
In Lituanus (Chicago, Ill.), v.10,
no.2, 1964, p. 33-49. See serials
consulted.

9844. SCHMID, Bernard. Burgen in
Litauen. In Burgwart (Berlin), no.
43, 1942, p. 1-12. illus. See
serials consulted.

9845. SOKOŁOWSKI, Marian. Daw go-
tycyzmy, wileński i krakowski w ar-
chitekturze i złotnictwie i żródła
ich znamion charakterystycznych. In
Sprawozdania Komisji do Badania Historji Sztuki w Polsce. Polska Akademia Umiejętności, Kraków. v.8,
no.1-2, 1907. 40 columns. illus.
N6991.P63 DLC CU

9846. ŠVIPAS, Vladas. Nepriklau-
somosios Lietuvos architektūra. [Ar-
chitecture of independent Lithuania]
In Lietuvių enciklopedija. Boston,
Mass., 1968. v.15, p. 734-741.
See entry no.216.

9847. TATARKIEWICZ, Władysław.
Dwa klasycyzmy warszawski i wileński.
Warszawa, E. Wende i S-ka, 1921. 32
p. mounted illus. (Towarzystwo Straży Kresowej, Warsaw. Biblioteka Wydziału Zabytków, Tom 1) NN

9848. ZEITUNG DER 10. ARMEE. Wil-
na-Minsk, Altertümer und Kunstgewer-
be; Führer durch die Zustellung der
10. Armee. Bearb. von A. Ippel.
Wilna, 1918. 40 p. 947.52.P194 PU

XIII.9.b. URBAN ARCHITECTURE

9849. BARŠAUSKAS, Juozas. Gyvenamieji ir kai kurie visuomeniniai go-
tiniai pastatai Kaune. [Some private and public buildings in Gothic
style in Kaunas] In Lietuvos TSR
architektūros klausimai (Kaunas),
v.1, 1960, p. 156-203. See serials
consulted.

9850. BATŪRA, Romas. XIV a. Vilniaus miesto gynybiniai įtvirtinimai. Iš architektūros istorijos.
Oboronitel'nye ukrepleniia g. Vil'-
niusa v XIV v. In Statyba ir architektūra (Vilnius), liepa 1964, p.
13-15. Summary in Russian. See serials consulted.

9851. GRINIUS, Jonas. Vilniaus
miesto paminklai. [Art monuments in
Vilnius] Kaunas, 1940. 134 p.

NA5697.V48G7 PU ICBM

9852. JACYNIENĖ, Halina (Kairiūkštytė) Pažaislis, ein Barockkloster in Litauen. In Tauta ir žodis (Kaunas), v.6, 1930, p. 1-172, 78 plates. See serials consulted.

9853. JANKEVIČIENĖ Algė. Vilniaus senamiesčio ansamblis. [The old part of the City of Vilnius. Fotonuotraukos H. Liandsbergo, M. Sakalausko] Vilnius, Vaga, 1969. 183 p. (36 p., 134 full page illus.) NA5697.V48J32 PU CaAEU CtPAM

9854. JASĖNAS, Kazimieras. Baroko styliaus monumentai Lietuvos sostinėse. [The monuments of baroque style architecture in Lithuanian capitals] In Židinys (Kaunas), v.21, no.3, 1935, p. 278-284. See serials consulted.

9855. KRIŠČIUKAITIS, Kazys. Lietuvos urbanizmas. [Urbanism in Lithuania] In Lietuvių encyklopedija. Boston, Mass., 1968. v.15, p. 741-744. For holdings see entry no. 216.

9856. MIESTO GYVENVIETĖS, VISUOMEniniai pastatai. [Urban and public buildings. Sudarė J. Baršauskas] Vilnius, Mintis, 1968- . (Lietuvių liaudies architektūra, t.2) NA4110.L73 DLC MH PPiU PU

9857. REKLAITIS, Povilas Viktoras. Die gotische St. Annekirche in Vilnius; eine kunstgeschichtliche Frage im Osten. Bonn, Baltisches Forschungsinstitut, 1955. 42 p. illus. (Commentationes Balticae, II:4) PG8001.C6 v.2 DLC CtY ICU MH NIC NN NNC PU

9858. --- Gotiškojo Perkūno namo Kaune kilmės klausimu. [The origin of the Gothic Perkūnas House in Kaunas] In Aidai (Brooklyn, N.Y.), no.2, 1961, p. 76-88. See serials consulted.

9859. --- Die Kunstdenkmäler der litauischen Hauptstadt Vilnius (Wilna) nach dem letzten Kriege. In Baltische Hefte (Gross-Biewende, Ger.), v.3, no.1, 1956, p.21-36. See serials consulted.

9860. --- Die St. Nicolaikirche in Wilna und ihre stadtgeschichtliche Bedeutung. In Zeitschrift für Ostforschung (Marburg-Lahn), v.8, no.4, 1959, p. 500-522. See serials consulted.

9861. ROSIAK, Stefan. Gmachy pofranciszkańskie w Wilnie a architekt

O. Kazimierz Kamieński i malarz O. Franciszek Niemirowski. In Towarzystwo Przyjaciół Nauk w Wilnie. Wydział: Filologii, Literatury i Sztuki. Sekcja Historji Sztuki. Prace, v.2, 1935, p. 315- . See serials consulted.

9862. ŚLEDZIEWSKI, Piotr. Kościol Św. Anny, Św. Barbary intra muros castri Vilnensis. In Ateneum Wileńskie (Wilno), v.9, 1933-1934, p. 1-25. See serials consulted.

9863. SPELSKIS, Antanas. The baroque gem of Vilnius. [Photographer J. Grikienis] Vilnius, Mintis, 1964. [16] p. illus. (chiefly photos) Pam Coll.30159 NcD NIC

9864. --- Lithuanian towns; past and present. [English version by Normantas and M. Ginsburgas] Vilnius, 1970. 109 p. DK511.L2S71 PU

9865. --- Po baroko skliautais. [Baroque art of Vilnius. Fotonuotraukos J. Grikienio] Vilnius, Vaga, 1967. 183 p. illus. Lithuanian, Russian, English, French and German. NA5697.V48S58 DLC CtPAM PU

9866. --- Zhemchuzhina vil'niusskogo barokka. Vil'nius, Mintis, 1964. [16] p. (chiefly illus.) NA5697.V48S6 DLC

9867. TAUTAVIČIUS, Adolfas. XVI-XVII amžiaus gyvenamieji pastatai Vilniaus žemutinės pilies teritorijoje. [The 16th-17th centuries wooden dwellings in the area of the lower castle of Vilnius] In LTSRMAIILKI, v.2, 1959, p.21-29. See serials consulted.

9868. --- Vilniaus žemutinės pilies mediniai pastatai XIII-XIV amžiais. [The wooden buildings of the Lower castle of Vilnius from the 13th-14th centuries] In LTSRMAIILKI, v.4, 1964, p. 171-187. illus. See serials consulted.

9869. V. K. F. Panevėžio bažnyčios. [The churches of Panevėžys] Panevėžys, 1936. 39 p. 914.47.F5 CtTMF

9870. VEBLAUSKAS, Petras. Kauno Šv. Kryžiaus bažnyčia ir Kauno bazilika. [The church of the Holy Cross and the Basilica in Kaunas] In Naujoji romuva (Kaunas), no. 16-19, 1935. See serials consulted.

9871. VILNIUS: architektūra iki XX amžiaus pradžios. [The architekture of Vilnius until the beginning of the 20th century. Redakcinė ko-

misija: V. Bytautas et al. Sudarytojas A. Janikas. Dailininkas E. Jurėnas. Kaune] VGLL, 1955. 227 p.
(chiefly illus.) On leaf preceding
t.p.: Architektūros reikalų valdyba
prie Lietuvos TSR Ministrų Tarybos.
Lithuanian and Russian. NA1197.V5A5
DLC CaAEU CaOTU CtY

9872. --- --- [Another edition.
Redakcinė komisija: V. Bytautas et
al. Dailininkas E. Jurėnas] Kaunas
VGLL, 1958. 244 p. (chifly illus.)
On leaf preceding t.p.: Lietuvos
TSR Ministrų Tarybos Valstybinis sta-
tybos ir architektūros reikalų komi-
tetas. Lithuanian and Russian.
NA1197.V5V52 DLC CaOTU ICU IEN InU
IU ICLJF MH MiD NN OkU PU TxHR

9873. VOROBJOVAS, Mikalojus. Vilniaus menas... [Art of Vilnius...
Kaunas] Spaudos fondas [1940] 71 p.
plates. FA2545.1555 MH

9874. WEBER, Paul. Wilna; eine
vergessene Kunststätte. Wilna, Verlag der Zeitung der 10. Armee; München, für Deutschland R. Piper, 1917.
131 p. illus., 2 col. plates, fold.
map. N6997.V5W4 DLC CaAEU CaBVaU
CSt MH NN NjP PU

XIII.9.c. RURAL ARCHITECTURE

9875. BARŠAUSKAS, Juozas. Lietuviškų svirnų architektūra. [The architecture of the Lithuanian grana-
ries] In Lietuvos TSR architektūros
klausimai (Vilnius), v.1, 1960, p.
66-117. See serials consulted.

9876. BEZZENBERGER, Adalbert. Bemerkungen über den Hausbau im russischen Litauen und in einem Theile
Kurlands. In Altertumsgesellschaft
Prussia, Königsberg in Pr. Sitzungsberichte, v.19, 1895, p. 130-135.
tables. See serials consulted.

9877. --- Über das litauische Haus.
In Altpreussische Monatschrift (Königsberg in Pr.), v.23, 1886, p. 34-
79; 629-633, illus. See serials
consulted.

9878. BIELINSKIS, Feliksas. Litovskoe narodnoe zodchestvo. Moskva,
Gos. izd-vo lit-ry po stroitel'stvu,
arkhitekture i stroit. materialam,
1960. 76 p. NA1195.L5B5 DLC PU

9879. BUDKUS, Pranas. Žemaičių
tvoros. [The fences in Žemaitija
(Samogitia)] In Gimtasai kraštas
(Šiauliai), v.3, no.1, 1936, p. 19-
23. See serials consulted.

9880. BUGAILIŠKIS, Feliksas. Senovės pirtis. [The ancient sauna]
In Gimtasai kraštas (Šiauliai), no.
2, 1934. See serials consulted.

9881. BUTKEVIČIUS, Izidorius. Gyvenvietės ir sodybos. [Bauernsied-
lungen und Bauernhöfe] In LTSRMAII.
Lietuvių etnografijos bruožai. Vilnius, 1964. p. 170-[209] illus.,
map, plans. HD725.7.L488 DLC CaAEU
ICLJF ICU MH NN PU CtY

9882. --- Kuršių neringos žvejų
gyvenamieji namai. [The dwellings
of the fishermen on the Curonian
Narrows] In LTSRMAIILKI, v.1, 1958,
p. 174-184. illus. See serials
consulted.

9883. --- Lietuvos valstiečių ūkiniai pastatai. [The farm buildings
of the Lithuanian peasants] In
LTSRMAIILKI, v.2, 1959, p. 237-256.
illus. See serials consulted.

9884. --- Nauji duomenys apie
XVIII a. žemaičių valstiečių pasta-
tus. [New data on the buildings of
the Samogitian peasant in the 18th
century] In LTSRMAIILKI, v.3, 1961
p. 158-172. See serials consulted.

9885. --- Osnovnye tipy traditsion-
nogo litovskogo krest'ianskogo zhi-
lishcha. In Voprosy etnicheskoi istorii narodov Pribaltiki (Moskva),
v.1, 1959, p. 396-407. See serials
consulted.

9886. --- Tradiciniai lietuvių
valstiečių gyvenamieji namai. [Tra-
ditional dwellings of the Lithuanian
farmer] In LTSRMAIILKI, v.1, 1958,
p. 157-173. illus. See serials
consulted.

9887. --- Valstiečių gyvenamieji
namai. [Dwellings of the Lithuanian
farmer] In LTSRMAII. Lietuvių
etnografijos bruožai. Vilnius, 1964.
p. 210-[253] illus. HD725.7.L488
DLC CaAEU CtY ICLJF ICU MH NN PU

9888. --- Valstiečių ūkiniai pastatai. [Peasants' farm buildings]
In LTSRMAII. Lietuvių etnografijos
bruožai. Vilnius, 1964. p. 254-
[285] illus. HD725.7.L488 DLC CtY
CaAEU ICLJF ICU MH NN PU

9889. --- Vidurio Lietuvos valstiečių tradicinių trobesių savitumai]
[The peculiarities of the traditional peasant buildings in central Li-
thuania] In LTSRMAD. Seria A, v.2
(21), 1966, p. 225-241. illus.
See serials consulted.

9890. ČERBULĖNAS, Klemensas. Apie

lietuviškų dvigalių gyvenamųjų namų
sudarymą. [On the development of
the Lithuanian farmhouse with living
quarters at both ends] In Lietuvos
TSR Architektūros klausimai, v.2,
1964. p. 173-191. See serials consulted.

9891. --- Namas (numas); pirminis
lietuvių gyvenamojo pastato tipas.
[Numas; the primal type of Lithuanian dwelling] In LTSRMAIILKI, v.1,
1958, p. 104-145. illus. See
serials consulted.

9892. DETHLEFSEN, Richard. Bauern-
häuser und Holzkirchen in Ostpreussen. Berlin, E. Wasmuth, 1911. 66
p. illus., plates. NA1077.D4 DLC
MB MH PU

9893. ERIXON, Sigurd Emanuel. The
North-European technique of corner
timbering. In Folk-Liv (Stockholm),
v.1, no.1, 1937, p. 13-60. See
serials consulted.

9894. FRÖLICH, Gustav. Dachgiebel-
verzierungen in Preussisch-Litauen.
In Zeitschrift der Altertumsgesellschaft, Insterburg, no.3, 1893, p.33-
46. 60 fig. on 16 fold. pages. See
serials consulted.

9895. GERAMB, Viktor. Die Kulturgeschichte der Rauchstuben. In
Wörter und Sachen (Heidelberg), v.9,
1924, p. 1-67. See serials consulted.

9896. GIMBUTAS, Jurgis. Das Dach
des litauischen Bauernhauses aus dem
19. Jahrhundert; ein Beitrag zur Geschichte des Holzbaues. Stuttgart,
1948. 104 p. illus., 24 plates,
diagrs., maps. Thesis--Technische
Hochschule, Stuttgart. NA8206.G5
DLC CU CtY ICLJF MH NN NNC PU

9897. --- Kaimo architektūra ir
statyba. [Rural Architecture and
Buildings] In Lietuvių enciklopedija. Boston, Mass., 1968. v.15,
p. 513-533. See entry no.216.

9898. --- Lietuvių sodžiaus architektūra Mažojoje Lietuvoje. [Archi-
tecture of Lithuanian peasant buildings in Lithuania Minor] In Lithuanian Reasearch Institute, New
York. Mažoji Lietuva. New York,
N.Y., 1958. p. 153-213.
DK511.L2L715 DLC CaAEU CLU PU

9899. --- Lietuvos miestelių var-
pinės. [The belfries in small towns
of Lithuania] In Technikos žodis
(Chicago, Ill.), no.3(93), p. 15-19.
See serials consulted.

9900. --- The outline of rural
settlements from the 16th century to
the present. In Lituanus (Brooklyn,
N.Y.), v.5, no.4, 1959, p. 114-117.
illus. See serials consulted.

9901. --- Senosios lietuvių kaimo
statybos savybės ir jų reikšmė. [The
peculiarities and their meaning in
ancient Lithuanian rural architec-
ture] In Aidai (Brooklyn, N.Y.),
no.1(156), 1963, p. 15-23. See
serials consulted.

9902. --- Ūkininko sodyba Mažojoje
Lietuvoje. [Peasant's farmyard in
Lithuania Minor] In Aidai (Augsburg
Ger.), no.18, 1948, p. 374-388.
illus. See serials consulted.

9903. GOZINA, G.I. Zhilishche i
khoziaistvennye stroeniia vostochnoi
Litvy XIX i nachala XX v. In Baltiiskii etnograficheskii sbornik. Moskva, 1956, p. 95-126. (Akademiia
nauk SSSR. Institut etnografii. Trudy. Novaia seriia, tom 32)
GN2.A2142 DLC CaOONM ICMILC MnU NIC
OU

9904. JURGINIS, Juozas. Alytaus
ekonomijos dvarų pastatai 1649 metais.
[Buildings in the district of Alytus]
Vilnius, LTSRMAII, 1972. 54 p.
NA8206.L5J8 PU

9905. KAIMO GYVENVIETĖS IR GYVENA-
mieji namai. [Dwellings and rural
living sites] Vilnius, Mintis,1965.
(Lietuvos liaudies architektūra, t.1)
NA4110.L73 DLC CaOTU ICU PU

9906. MAŽIULIS, Antanas Juozas.
Dusėtų krašto statyba ir jos papročiai. [The construction in the district of Dusėtai and its customes]
In Gimtasai Kraštas (Šiauliai), no.
1, 1937, p. 1-17. See serials consulted.

9907. MICKEVIČIUS, Juozas. Senovės žemaičių pirtys. [The ancient
saunas of Samogitia (Žemaitija)] In
Gimtasai Kraštas (Šiauliai), no.2/4
(10/12), 1936, p. 470-479. See serials consulted.

9908. MILIUS, Vacius. Platelių
apylinkės gyvenamieji namai. [The
living houses of the district of
Plateliai] In LTSRMAIILKI, v.2,
1959, p. 214-236. See serials consulted.

9909. MINKEVIČIUS, Jonas. Kai kurie akmens mūro architektūros ypatumai XVIII-XIX amžiuje. [Some characteristic features in stone masonry
of the Lithuanian farm buildings of
the 18th and 19th centuries] In

Lietuvos TSR Architektūros klausimai, v.1, 1960, p. 118-141. See serials consulted.

9910. NAUMANN, Hans. Bauernhaus und Kornkammer in Litauen. In His Primitive Gemeinschaftskultur. Jena, 1921. p. 148-167. plans. GR65.N3 DLC CtY MiU NjP OCU OCl OU PBm PSC

9911. RÄNK, Gustav. Die Bauern-hausformen im baltischen Raum. Würzburg, Holzner, 1962. xvi, 120 p. illus., maps, plans. (Marburger Ost-forschungen, 17) Bibliography: xiii-xvi. NA8204.R3 DLC CLU CU ICU InU MH MiU NIC NcD NjP PU WU

9912. --- Das System der Raumein-teilung in den Behausungen der nord-eurasischen Völker. Stockholm, Ins-titut för folklivsforskning, 1949-51. 2 v. GN2.I632 DLC

9913. REISONAS, Karolis. Žemės ūkio statyba. Lietuvos tautiniai mo-tyvai paruošti prof. arch. V. Dube-neckio ir dail. P. Galaunės. [The rural architecture and buildings...] Kaunas [Švyturio bendrovės spaustu-vė] 1926. 254 p. illus., plans. NA8206.R4 DLC

9914. SOEDER, Hans. Das Dorf Tritschuny im litauisch-weissruthe-nischen Grenzgebiet; ein Beitrag zur Geschichte des Holzbaues. Darmstadt, 1918. 29 p., 25 plates. NA8206.S62 PU(xerox copy, 1972)

9915. STRAZDŪNAITĖ, R. Valstiečių grūdų magazinai Lietuvoje. [Pea-sants' collective grain storehouses in Lithuania] In LTSRMAIILKI, v.1, 1958, p. 234-242. See serials con-sulted.

9916. TALVE, Ilmar. Bastu och torkhus i Nordeuropa. [The sauna and drying-house in Northern Europe] Stockholm, Nordiska Museet, 1960. xii, 544 p. illus., maps, diagrs. (Stockholm. Nordiska Museet. Hand-lingar, v.53) TH4920.T3 DLC CLU CoU CLSU CtY MH MnU NIC ViU

9917. TETZNER, Franz Oskar. Haus und Hof der Litauer. In Globus (Brunswick), v.72, 1897, p. 249-254. illus. See serials consulted.

9918. --- Klete und Swirne. In Globus (Brunswick), v.79, 1901, p. 252-255. See serials consulted.

9919. --- Die Tolminkemischen Kir-chenbauten aus der Zeit des Chris-tian Donalitius. In Altpreussische Monatsschrift (Königsberg in Pr.),

v.33, 1896, p. 190-201. See se-rials consulted.

9920. VILIAMAS, Vladas. Lietuvos kaimų sodybos ir jų problėmos. [The farmsteads of the Lithuanian villa-ges and their problems] In Židinys (Kaunas), v.23, no.1, 1936, p. 44-56. See serials consulted.

9921. ŽILĖNAS, Vincas. Lietuvių liaudies tradicinių gyvenamųjų namų susiformavimas. [The development of the traditional Lithuanian farm-house] In LTSRMAIILKI, v.1, 1958, p. 146-156. See serials consulted.

XIII.10. EDUCATION

XIII.10.a. HISTORY OF EDUCATION

XIII.10.a.1. GENERAL STUDIES

9922. ERINGIS, Stephen Anthony. Education as the cultural agency of Lithuania. [Seattle, Wash.] 1932. iv, 68 leaves. table. Thesis(M.A) --University of Washington. Type-written. Bibliography: leaves 64-68. 947.5.Er4e WaU

9923. GVILDYS, Juozas. Lietuvos švietimas praeityje. [The history of education in Lithuania] In Lie-tuvos mokykla (Kaunas), no.2-3, 1929, ·p. 47-56,113-119,164-167,363-377. See serials consulted.

9924. IŠ LIETUVOS PEDAGOGINĖS minties istorijos. [From the histo-ry of Lithuanian educational philo-sophy. Redagavo A. Gučas ir K. Si-maška] Vilnius, 1969. 212 p. At head of title: LTSR Aukštojo ir spe-cialiojo vidurinio mokslo ministeri-ja. Vilniaus Valstybinis V. Kapsu-ko universitetas. Pedagogikos ir psichologijos katedra. LA853.I48.I8 DLC

9925. JUŠKA, Antanas. Lietuviškos mokyklos augimas. [The development of the Lithuanian school] In Židi-nys (Kaunas), v.27, no.5-6, 1938, p. 674-782. See serials consulted.

9926. KIRLYS, Jonas. Šimtametė mokykla. [A century-old school] Vilnius, Mintis, 1967. 77 p. LF4446.M3K5 PU

9927. KRAUJALIS, Petras. Lietuvių švietimo draugija "Rytas". [Lithua-nian educational society "Rytas" By] P. Vieštautas [pseud.] Vilnius,

"Vilniaus Varpo" leidinys, 1927. 46 p. 947.52.K8885 PU

9928. KRIKŠČIŪNAS, Matas. Lietuvos mokytojas. [The teacher in Lithuania] In Lietuvių enciklopedija. Boston, Mass., 1959. v.19, p. 131-138. See entry no. 216.

9929. LIETUVOS MOKYKLOS. [Schools in Lithuania. By M. Krikščiūnas et al.] In Lietuvių enciklopedija. Boston, Mass., 1959. v.19, p. 117-130. See entry no. 216.

9930. ŠAPOKA, Adolfas. Mokslo ieškančių senovės lietuvių keliai. [The ways of ancient Lithuanians in seeking education] In Židinys (Kaunas), v.22, no.10-11, 1935, p. 316-327; 417-430. See serials consulted.

9931. TRINKA, Vladas. Daraktoriai. [Tutors] In Gimtasai kraštas (Šiauliai), v.1, 1936, p. 54-55. See serials consulted.

XIII.10a.2. EDUCATION BEFORE 1795

9932. BALIŃSKI, Michał. Uchebnyia zavedeniia Litvy do prisoedneniia eia k Rossii. In ZMNP, 1862. Chast' 116. Neofits. chast', otdel 1, p. 65-97, 196-215, 310-346. See serials consulted.

9933. BIRŽIŠKA, Mykolas. Lietuvių mokykla ligi XVIII amžiaus pabaigos. [Lithuanian school system until the end of the 18th Century] In His Iš mūsų kultūros ir literatūros istorijos, v.2, 1938. PG8703.B48 DLC CU ICU MH PU

9934. GVILDYS, Juozas. Edukacijos komisijos švietimo darbai Lietuvoje. [The work by the Education Commission in Lithuania] In Židinys (Kaunas), v.13, no.5-6, 1931, p. 478-494. See serials consulted.

9935. JOBERT, Ambroise. La commision d'education nationale en Pologne (1773-1794). Paris, Les Belles Lettres, 1941. 500 p. ports., fold. map. Sources et bibliographie: p. 1-24. LA841.J6 DLC CtY IaU NNC NN

9936. LUKASZEWICZ, Józef. Historya szkól w Koronie i w Wielkim Księstwie Litewskim aż do roku, 1794. Posnań, Nakładem Księgarni J.K. Zupańskiego, 1849-1851. 4 v. 947.52.L964.3 PU MH BM(8355. dd. 38.)

9937. RAČKAUSKAS, John A. The first national system of education in Europe - The Commission for national education of the Kingdom of Poland and the Grand Duchy of Lithuania, 1773-1794. In Lituanus (Chicago, Ill.), v.14, no.4, 1968, p. 5-53. See serials consulted.

9938. ŠIDLAUSKAS, A. Mokyklų reforma Lietuvoje XVIII amžiaus pabaigoje. [The school reform in Lithuania at the end of the 18th century] In LTSRMAD. Serija A, no.2, 1962, p. 32-57. See serials consulted.

9939. SUŽIEDĖLIS, Simas. Švietimas Didžiojoje Lietuvos Kunigaikštijoje. [Education in the Grand Duchy of Lithuania] In Lietuvių enciklopedija. Boston, Mass., 1968. v.15, p. 744-751. For holdings see entry no. 216.

9940. VENSKUS, D. Skatinamos priemonės lietuvių lenkų mokyklose ir jos drausmė XVIII amžiuje. [The methods of encouragement and discipline in the Lithuanian and Polish schools of the 18th Century] In Švietimo darbas (Kaunas), v.11, 1929, p. 1096-1099. See serials consulted.

9941. WIERZBOWSKI, Teodor. Komisya Edukacyi Narodowej, 1773-1794. Monografia historyczna. Tom. 1. Warszawa, Drukarnia J. Cotty, 1911. 186 p. No more published. Z5815.P6W5 DLC NN

9942. --- Szkoły parafialne w Polsce i na Litwie za czasów Komisji Edukacji Narodowej, 1773-1794. Kraków, Książnica Polska, 1921. 244 p. (Poland. Komisja do Badania Dziejów Wychowania i Szkolnictwa w Polsce. Serja I: Prace monograficzne z Dziejów Wychowania i Szkolnictwa w Polsce, nr.1) BM IU MH

XIII.10.a.3. EDUCATION, 1795-1918.

9943. BAKŠYTĖ, Veronika (Karvelienė). Beitrag zur Geschichte des Kampfes um die Schulsprache in Litauen mit besonderer Berücksichtigung der Zeit der grossen Reformen, 1855-1864. Memel, "Rytas", 1930. 120 p. Thesis--University of Königsberg. LA1040.B17 DHEW CtY DLC MH NcD PU

9944. BARSOV, Nikolai Pavlovich. Narodnye shkoly v iugozapadnom

kraie, ocherk ikh uchrezhdeniia
ustroistva i sovremennago sostoia-
niia. [Sanktpeterburg, 1864] 103
p. BM(8355 eee. 2(1).)

9945. BUDRYS, Stasys and V. Bu-
drienė. Piešimo mokykla Vilniuje,
1866-1915 metais. [School of Fine
Arts in Vilnius, 1866-1915] In
LTSRMAIILKI, v.2, 1959, p. 333-337.
See serials consulted.

9946. BARKEVIČIUS, Vilhelmas. Iš
mūsų kovų dėl Lietuvos mokyklų,
1863-1915] Kaunas, 1939. 64 p.
370.9475.B917 PU

9947. GOTTHOLD, Fredrich. Ein
Blick auf Ostpreussens und Litthauens Bildungsanstalten vor dem
Jahre 1810. In His Schriften, Bd.
4, pt.2, Königsberg in Pr., 1864.
p. 30-168. BM(12251. ee. 2.)

9948. GRABAUSKAS, Juozas. Švietimo darbas Lietuvoje prieš karą ir
dabar. [Education in Lithuania before World War I and at the present
time] In Švietimo darbas (Kaunas),
no.2, 1928, p. 109-117. See
serials consulted.

9949. GRAŽEVIČIUS, A. Lietuvos
mokykla po Caro letena. [Lithu-
anian school under the Czar's paw]
In Lietuvos mokykla (Kaunas), 1935.
See serials consulted.

9950. IUNITSKII, Nikolai. Fundu-
shi i stipendii Vilenskago uchebnago okruga... Vil'na, Tip. A.G.
Syrkina, 1884. 1 v. Lap6.F4-884i
CtY

9951. KURCZEWSKI, Jan. Wiadomości o szkołach parafjalnych w
djecezji Wileńskiej. In Roczniki
Towarzystwa Przyjaciół Nauk w Wilnie, v.2, 1908. See serials consulted.

9952. LUKŠIENĖ, Meilė. Lietuvos
švietimo istorijos bruožai XIX a.
pirmojoje pusėje. [An outline of
the history of education in Lithuania in the first part of the 19th
Century] Kaunas, Šviesa, 1970.
514 p. with maps, 2 leaves of
tables. (Lietuvos TSR švietimo
ministerija. Mokyklų mokslinio
tyrimo institutas. Pedagogikos
darbai, 4) LA853.L3L8 DLC PU

MATUSAS, Jonas. Lietuvių
rusinimas per pradžios mokyklas.
Kaunas, 1937. See entry no. 5292.

9953. OSTERMEYER, Gottfried.
Über die Schullehrer bei den Kirchen in Littauen. In Preussisches

Archiv (Königsberg in Pr.), v.9,
1798, p. 430-453. See serials consulted.

9954. PAISTRIETIS, K. Maskoliš-
kos maldos vidutinėse mokyklose.
[Russian prayers in the High Schools]
In Tėvynės sargas (Tilžė), no.2,
1897, p. 7-18. See serials consulted.

9955. RUSSIA. MINISTERSTVO NA-
RODNAGO PROSVIESHCHENIIA. Sbornik
materialov dlia istorii prosvieshcheniia v Rossii izvlechennykh iz
arkhiva Ministerstva narodnago
prosvieshcheniia. Sanktpeterburg,
1893-1902. 4 v. LA830.A43 DLC NN

9956. ŠAKENIS, Konstantinas.
Lietuviškos mokyklos prieš šimtą
metų. [Lithuanian schools one
hundred years ago] In Švietimo
darbas (Kaunas), no.10-11, 1929,
p. 1096-1099. See serials consulted.

9957. SHESTOV, A. I. Opisaniie
ekskursii uchashchikhsia Vilenskago uchebnago okruga za 1910 god.
Vil'na, Upravleniie vilenskago
uchebnago okruga, 1911. ix, 238 p.
plates. L970.31.SE ICLJF

9958. SUŽIEDĖLIS, Simas. Mokyklos
vokiečių okupacijos laikais, 1915-
1918. [Schools during the period
of German occupation, 1915-1918]
In Lietuvių enciklopedija. Boston,
Mass., 1968. v.15, p. 764-767.
See entry no. 216.

9959. --- Švietimas carinės Rusi-
jos valdžioje. [Education under
the rule of czarist Russia] In
Lietuvių enciklopedija, Boston,
Mass., 1968. v.15, p. 752-760.
See entry no. 216.

9960. URBŠIENĖ, Marija (Mašiotaitė). Lietuvos mokykla Didžiojo
karo metu. [The education in Lithuania during the First World
War] In Židinys (Kaunas), v.25,
no.3-4, 1937, p. 314-326; 454-469.
See serials consulted.

9961. VILENSKII UCHEBNYI OKRUG.
Istoricheskii obzor dieiatel'nosti
Upravleniia Vilenskago uchebnago
okruga 1803-1903 gg. Pod obshch.
red. A.V. Beletskago. Vil'na,
1903- . LA853.L48V5 DLC

9962. WOLDEMAR, C. Zur Geschichte
und Statistik der Gelehrten und
Schulanstalten. Sanktpeterburg,
Assmann, 1865. 7, 271 p. tables.
6863.982 NjP PBm

9963. ZEMKE, Hans. Der Oberbefehlshaber Ost und das Schulwesen
in Verwaltungsbereich Litauen
während des Weltkrieges. Berlin,
Junker und Dünnhaupt, 1936. 120 p.
Thesis--University of Berlin.
947.52.Z44 PU CtY

9964. ŽUKAUSKAS, Kazys. Iš Lietuvos mokyklos istorijos, 1905-
1907. [The history of the Lithuanian school in 1905-1907] Kaunas,
Valstybinė pedagoginės literatūros
leidykla, 1960. 69 p.
LA853.L48Z8 DLC

XIII.10.a.4. EDUCATION, 1918-1940,
1941-1944

9965. BRENSZTEJN, Michał Eustachy.
Nauka w respublice Litewskiej. In
Nauka Polska (Warszawa), v.19, 1934,
225-308. See serials consulted.

9966. ČIŽIŪNAS, Vaclovas and Simas
Sužiedėlis. Švietimas nepriklausomoje Lietuvoje. [Education in independent Lithuania] In Lietuvių
enciklopedija. Boston, Mass., 1968.
v.15, p. 767-778. See entry no.
216.

9967. MALDEIKIS, Petras. Nepriklausomos Lietuvos švietimo reforma.
[The reform of education in independent Lithuania] In Draugas (Chicago, Ill.), March 22, 1958. See
serials consulted.

9968. --- The trend of education
in independent Lithuania. In Lituanus (Brooklyn, N.Y.), no.2(11),
1957, p. 22-24. See serials consulted.

9969. MISIŪNAS, Kazimieras. Education in Lithuania. In School
Life (Washington, D.C.), v.24,
1939, p. 171-173. See serials consulted.

9970. NIEMI, Aukusti Robert.
Medžiaga Lietuvos mokyklų reformai.
[Research on the reform of Lithuanian schools] Kaunas, Švietimo
ministerijos komisijonieris "Švyturio" b-vė, 1920. 126 p.
370.5.N1 ICLJF CtTMF CtY

9971. PAPEČKYS, Pijus. Mūsų laimėjimai švietimo dirvoje. [Our
successes in the field of education]
In Kemežys, V., ed. Lietuva, 1918-
1938. Kaunas, 1938, p. 267-290.
947.52.L625 PU CtTMF ICLJF

XIII.10.a.5. EDUCATION IN SOVIET
LITHUANIA

9972. AISTIS, Jonas. Bendrojo
lavinimo mokyklos okupuotoje Lietuvoje. [Elementary and secondary
education in occupied Lithuania]
In Aidai (Brooklyn, N.Y.), 1958,
no.6(111), p. 251-256; no.7(112),
p. 298-304. See serials consulted.

9973. BENDŽIUS, Antanas. Liaudies
švietimas Tarybų Lietuvoje. [Pub-
lic education in Soviet Lithuania]
Vilnius, Mintis, 1967. 128 p.
Lithuanian, Russian and English.
LA853.L48B4 DLC

9974. BITINAS, Bronius. Visuoti-
no mokymo vykdymas, pedagoginė
problema. [The implementation of
compulsory education is a problem]
Kaunas, Valstybinė pedagoginės literatūros leidykla, 1962. 87 p.
LB3081.B5 DLC

9975. GRINIUS, Jonas. Erziehung
der Jugend in Sowjetlitauen. In
Acta Baltica (Königstein im Taunus),
v.1, 1961, p. 168-179. See
serials consulted.

9976. GUNTHER, Woldemar. Vom
Hochschulwesen in heutigen Litauen.
In Acta Baltica (Königstein im Taunus), v.5, 1965, p. 96-111. See
serials consulted.

9977. KNYVA, Albertas. Švietimas
Tarybų Lietuvoje. [Education in
Soviet Lithuania] Vilnius, VPMLL,
1950. 145 p. LA853.L48K6 DLC NN

9978. KOVOJE UŽ NAUJĄ ŽMOGŲ. [In
the struggle for the development of
a new man] Vilnius, VPMLL, 1963.
236 p. LC1030.K66 DLC

9979. LIAUDIES ŠVIETIMAS TARYBŲ
Lietuvoje; straipsnių rinkinys.
[The education of the masses in Soviet Lithuania; a collection of
articles. Compiled by S. Pupeikis]
Kaunas, Valstybinė pedagoginės literatūros leidykla, 1960. 115 p.
illus., ports. LA853.L48L46 DLC
CtPAM IEN MH PU

9980. LIETUVOS TSR MOKSLŲ AKADE-
MIJA, VILNA. VISUOTINIS SUSIRINKI-
MAS. Mokslas Tarybų Lietuvoje.
[Education in Soviet Lithuania.
Redakcinė kolegija: J. Matulis et
al.] Vilnius, VPMLL, 1961. 334 p.
diagrs. DK511.L27L495 DLC CtY MH PU

9981. LIETUVOS TSR MOKYTOJŲ SU-
VAŽIAVIMAS, VILNA. 1960. Lietuvos
TSR Mokytojų suvažiavimo ir Lietu-

vos TSR Liaudies švietimo darbuotojų respublikinio pasitarimo medžiaga. [Proceedings of the Conference of the Soviet Lithuanian
teachers and the staff of educational institutions] Kaunas, Valstybinė pedagoginės literatūros
leidykla, 1962. 157 p. illus.,
ports. At head of title: Lietuvos TSR Švietimo ministerija.
L106 1960.L5 DLC

9982. LITHUANIAN S.S.R. AUKŠTOJO
IR SPECIALIOJO VIDURINIO MOKSLO
MINISTERIJA. Lietuvos TSR Aukštosios mokyklos. [The High Schools
of Soviet Lithuania] Vilnius,
1966. 119 p. L942.L5A5 DLC PU

    LITHUANIAN S.S.R. CENTRINĖ
STATISTIKOS VALDYBA. Prosveshchenie
i kul'tura Litovskoi SSR; statisticheskii sbornik. Vil'nius, Statistika, 1964. See entry no. 394.

9983. MATULIS, Juozas. Mokslas
Tarybų Lietuvoje; trumpa istorinė
apybraiža. [Science in Soviet
Lithuania...] Vilnius, Mintis,
1970. 151 p. Q127.L5M3 PU

9984. PETKUS, J. Liaudies mokytojas; apybraiža. [Description of
a country teacher] [Vilniuje]
VPMLL, 1950. 48 p. PG8721.P45L5
DLC

9985. PROCUTA, Ginutis. The
transformation of higher education
in Lithuania during the first decade of Soviet rule. In Lituanus
(Chicago, Ill.), v.13, no.1, 1967,
p. 71-92. See serials consulted.

9986. REMEIKIS, Thomas. General
education in Soviet Lithuania. In
Lituanus (Brooklyn, N.Y.), v.5,
no.2, 1959, p. 41-49. tables.
See serials consulted.

9987. RESPUBLIKINIS KULTŪROS-
ŠVIETIMO darbo mokslinis-metodinis
kabinetas. Kultūros-švietimo įstaigose. [In the cultural and educational institutions. Sudarytoja:
B. Pociūtė] Vilnius, VPMLL, 1961.
79 p. illus., ports., diagrs.
DK511.L212R4 DLC

9988. VAITIEKŪNAS, Vytautas.
Sovietized education in occupied
Lithuania. In Vardys, V.S., ed.
Lithuania under the Soviets. New
York, N.Y., 1965. p. 171-196.
DK511.L27V35 DLC CSt CSt-H CU IC
MoU MWalB MU PPi TU AzU

9989. --- Švietimas okupuotoje
Lietuvoje. [Education in occupied
Lithuania] In Aidai (Brooklyn,

N.Y.), no.1(126), 1960, p. 11-20.
See serials consulted.

9990. VILNA. RESPUBLIKINIS MOKYTO
JŲ TOBULINIMOSI INSTITUTAS. Internationalinis moksleivių auklėjimas
mokykloje (iš mokyklų darbo patirties) [The education of students
in schools towards internationalism]
Vilnius, Laikraščių ir žurnalų
leidykla, 1963. 100 p.
LC1090.V5 DLC

9991. VILNA. VALSTYBINIS PEDAGO
GINIS INSTITUTAS. Liaudies švietimas ir komunistinis auklėjimas;
dokumentų rinkinys. Sudarė V. Mikėnas. [Communist education of
people...] Vilnius, 1960. 390 p.
LC1030.V45 DLC

9992. ZUNDĖ, Pranas. Allgemeinbildende Schulen in Sowjetlitauen.
In Commentationes Balticae (Bonn),
v.6-7, 1959, p. 351-392. See
serials consulted.

XIII.10.a.6. LITHUANIAN EDUCATION
IN OTHER COUNTRIES

9993. CHICAGO. PEDAGOGINIS LI
TUANISTIKOS INSTITUTAS. Reguliaminas ir programos. [Regulations
and programs] Chicago, Ill., 1968.
47 p. E184.L7C44 PU

9994. ČIKAGOS AUKŠTESNIOJI LITU
ANISTIKOS MOKYKLA. Daigeliai:
Moksleivių metraštis, 1964-1965,
ČALM 15 metų veiklos apžvalga.
[... history of the Institute for
Lithuanian studies] Redagavo Juozas Masilionis. Chicago, Ill.,
1965. 248 p. illus. LD7501.C4C73
DLC ICLJF

9995. JANČAUSKAS, Raimundas C.
Tautinės kultūros galimumai J.A.V.
mokyklose. The possibility of a
national culture in education in
the United States. In LKMASD, t.5,
1964, p. 281-289. Summary in
English. See serials consulted.

9996. KRIKŠČIŪNAS, Matas and Petras Maldeikis. Lietuviškoji mokykla išeivijoje. [The Lithuanian
school in exile] In Lietuvių enciklopedija. Boston, Mass., 1968.,
1968. v.15, p. 786-793. See entry
no. 216.

9997. LIULEVIČIUS, Vincentas.
Lietuvių švietimas Vokietijoje...
mokyklų...veikusių, 1944-1950 m.
apžvalgos. [Educations of Lithuanians in Germany, 1944-1950; a

review] Chicago, Ill., 1969. 640
p. illus. D809.G3L56 PU

9998. --- Švietimo židiniai tremtinių stovyklose. [The centres of
education in the refugee camps] In
Tautos praeitis (Roma), v.1, no.1,
1959, p. 78-93; v.1, no.2, 1960, p.
269-274; v.1, no.3, 1961, p. 449-
467; v.1, no.4, 1962, p. 616-629;
v.2, no.1(5), 1964, p. 122-137;
v.2, no.2(6), 1965, p. 161-180;
v.2, no.3-4(7-8), 1967, p. 287-310.
See serials consulted.

9999. NAUSĖDAS, Vladas. Lietuviškos mokyklos Prūsijoje, XVI-
XVIII amžiuje. [Lithuanian schools
in Prussia in the 16th, 17th and
18th Centuries] In LTSRMAIILKI, v.
2, 1959, p. 320-332. See serials
consulted.

10000. PINNEBERG, GER., BATLIC
UNIVERSITY. Baltic University in
figures and pictures, 1946-1949.
Pinneberg, Ger., 1949. v.1, 24 p.
BM(8358. c. 161.)

10001. PLUME, R. Documents concerning Baltic University, 1945-
1947. n.p., [1947] p. 49. Typescript. BM(8357.I.22.)

10002. RYGOS LIETUVIŲ GIMNAZIJA.
10 metų sukaktuvėms paminėti.
[The tenth anniversary, 1923-1933,
of the Lithuanian High School in
Riga] Rīgā, Pirmais tipografijas
kooperatīvs, 1933. 47 p. illus.,
tables, ports. (*Qp.v.462)NN

10003. SAKALAUSKAS, B. Mokyklos
ir Prūsų mokyklų politika naujuo-
siuose Rytų Prūsuose. [The
schools and the policy of the
Prussian schools in the new East
Prussia] In Praeitis (Kaunas), v.
1, 1930, p. 139-165. See serials
consulted.

10004. WOTSCHKE, Theodor. Pol-
nische und Litauische Studenten in
Königsberg. In Jahrbücher für
Kultur und Geschichte der Slaven.
N.F.(Breslau), v.6, 1930, p. 428-
447. See serials consulted.

XIII.10.b. EDUCATIONAL INSTITUTIONS

XIII.10.b.1. PRIMARY, SECONDARY AND SPECIAL SCHOOLS

BURKEVIČIUS, Vilhelmas.
Iš mūsų pradžios mokyklų praeities.
In Lietuvos praeitis, v.1, 1941.

See entry no. 9946.

10005. KUDIRKA, Juozas. Veiverių
mokytojų seminarija (1866-1918).
[Teacher's college in Veiveriai,
1866-1918] Vilnius, Laikraščių ir
žurnalų susivienijimas "Periodika",
1970. 83 p. LF4446.V4K8 PU

10006. LOMANAS, P. and J. Sluoksnaitis, comps. Pradžios mokyklų
įstatymai, taisyklės, instrukcijos,
aplinkraščiai ir programos; surinko P. Lomanas ir J. Sluoksnaitis.
[Laws, by-laws, instructions, cir-
culars, and programs of primary
education] Kaunas, Dirvos b-vės
leidinys, 1930. 200 p. 372.L ICCC

10007. RŪGIS, Jonas. Palangos
progimnazija. [Junior High School
of Palanga] In Tautos praeitis
(Roma), v.1, no.1, 1959, p. 55-62.
See serials consulted.

10008. ŠALKAUSKAS, Stasys. Spe-
cialinis mokslas. [Professional
education] In Kemėžys, V., ed.
Lietuva, 1918-1938. Kaunas, 1938.
p. 299-304. 947.52.L625 PU CtTMF
ICLJF

10009. ŠVENČIONIŲ LIETUVIŲ GIMNA-
ZIJA; 15-kos metų sukaktuvėms paminėti, 1919-34. [The 15th Jubilee
of the Lithuanian High School in
Švenčionys] Vilnius, 1935. 47 p.
370.S5 CtTMF

10010. TOTORAITIS, Jonas. Dešimtmečio ir 60 metų Rygiškių Jono Gim-
nazijos sukaktuvės. [The tenth and
sixtieth anniversaries of the
Rigiškių Jonas High School] Mari-
ampolėje, Šaltinio, 1928. 13 p.
illus. MB.

10011. --- Marijampolės gimnazi-
jos praeitis. [The history of the
High School in Marijampolė] In
Švietimo darbas (Kaunas), no.1-2,
1921, p. 96-97. See serials consulted.

10012. VILNIAUS LIETUVIŲ GIMNAZI-
JA 10-ties metų sukaktuvėms paminė-
ti. [The tenth anniversary of the
Lithuanian High School in Vilnius]
Vilnius, 1925. 53 p. 370.Vl
CtTMF BM(8358. f. 47.)

10013. ZABUTIS, Henrikas. Higher learning in Lithuania. [Trans-
lated by Vl. Grodzenskis and V.
Normantas] Vilnius, Gintaras, 1968.
114 p. illus., ports.
LA853.L48Z33 DLC NcD PU

XIII.10.b.2. UNIVERSITIES,
ACADEMIES, ETC.

10014. AUKŠTOSIOS MOKYKLOS KŪRIMA-
sis ir vystymasis Kaune. [The
founding and the development of the
University in Kaunas. Atsakingasis
redaktorius S. Biziulevičius]
Vilnius, Mintis, 1967. 114 p.
illus. LA853.L48A9 DLC PU

10015. AVIŽONIS, Petras. Lietuvos Universiteto medicinos fakultetas. [The Faculty of Medicine
at the University of Lithuania]
Kaunas, 1923. 20 p. 370.L4 CtTMF

10016. BALIŃSKI, Michał. Dawna
Akademia Wileńska. Próba jéj historyi od założenia w roku 1579 do
ostatecznego jéj przekształcenia w
roku 1803. Petersburg, J. Ohryzko,
1862. xi, 606 p. plate, diagr.
LF4425.V5B2 NN BM(8355. dd. 36.)
DLC ICU KU MH NIC NNC PPULC PU

10017. BEDNARSKI, Stanisław.
Dwieście lat Wileńskiej Akademji
jezuickiej. In Powszechny Zjazd
Historyków Polskich w Wilnie, 1935.
Pamiętnik VI. Referaty (Lwów), v.
1, 1935, p. 289-294. See serials
consulted.

10018. BIELIŃSKI, Józef. Stan
nauk lekarskich za czasów akademii
medyko-chirurgicznéj Wileńskiéj,
bibliograficznie przedstawiony.
Warszawa, Towarzystwo Lekarskie,
1888. 907, iii p. WZ70.GP6B5s
1888 DNLM NN(1889 ed.)

10019. --- Uniwersytet Wileński
(1579-1831). Kraków, W.L. Anczyc i
Spółka, 1899-1900. 3 v. front.,
plates, ports. (Fontes et commentationes historiam scholarum su-
periorum in Polonis illustrantes,
2, 4.) 947.52.B476 PU ICLJF(v.1-2)
NN NNC PPULC

10020. BIRŽIŠKA, Mykolas. Pe-
rimant Vilniaus Universitetą.
[Taking over the University of Vil-
nius] In Naujoji romuva (Kaunas),
no.10, 1940, p. 197-200. See
serials consulted.

10021. --- Senasis Vilniaus Universitetas; vardų ir veikalų atran-
ka. [The old University of Vilna;
a selection of names and works.
2d ed., London] Nida [1955] 178 p.
illus. (Nidos knygų klubo leidinys,
nr.11) LF4425.V5B5 1955 DLC CaAEU
CaOTU CaOTP CtTMF CtY ICCC ICLJF
MB MH NjP PU

10022. --- Vilniaus Universitetas,
1940-1941 m. [The University of
Vilnius in 1940-41. Memmingen,
Ger., Mintis, 1948] 64 p.
LF4425.V56B5 DLC CtTMF CtY ICLJF
MH NN OKentU PU PPULC

10023. BULAVAS, Juozas, ed. Vilniaus universitetas. [The University of Vilnius] Vilnius, VPMLL,
1956. 109 p. illus., ports.
LF4425.V5B8 DLC ICU MH NN NNC NcU
PPiU PU

10024. ČEPĖNAS, Pranas, ed. Lietuvos universitetas, 1579-1803-1922.
[University of Lithuania, 1579-1803-
1922] Chicago, Ill., Lietuvių profesorių draugija Amerikoje, 1972.
xvi, 896 p. LA853.L48C4 PU DLC

10025. DOVGIALLO, Dmitrii Ivanovich. Posliedniaia stranitsa istorii Vilenskago universiteta. Vil'-
na, Izd. Sievero-Zapadnago otdiela
Russkago geogr. ob-va, 1914. 20 p.
LF4425.V5D65 DLC PU

10026. DZIKOWSKI, Mikołaj. Wystawa jubileuszowa Uniwersytetu
Stefana Batorego, 1579-1929, w Uniwersyteckiej Bibljotece Publicznej
w Wilnie, 9-20.X. 1929. Wilno,
1931. 13 p. illus.
LF4425.V591D9 DLC

10027. GRINIUS, Jonas. Iš universiteto gyvenimo. [Activities at
the University] In Ateitis (Kaunas),
no.8, 1922, p. 182-185. See serials
consulted.

10028. HOLOWACHYI, Romanus R.
Seminarium Vilnense SS. Trinitatis
(1601-1621). Ed. 2. Romae, PP.
Basiliani, 1957. xix, 157 p. (Ana-
lecta OSBM, ser. 2. Sectio 1,
Opera, v.8) Div.S.271.79.A532AN
Sec.1, v.8 NcD CtY MH DLC-P4

10029. JANOWSKI, Ludwik. Histo-
riografija Uniwersyteta Wileńskiego.
In Towarzystwo Pszyjaciól Nauk w
Wilnie. Rocznik, v.7, 1922, p. 7-
139. See serials consulted.

10030. --- Wszechnica Wileńska,
1578-1848. Wilno, L. Chomiński,
1921. vi, 60 p. LF4425.V56J3 DLC

10031. --- Zbiór ułamkowych wiadomości o Uniwersytecie Wileńskim.
In Pismo Zbiorowe Wilenskie (Wilno),
1859, v.1, p. 132-150; v.2, p. 117-
132. See serials consulted.

10032. KAUNAS. UNIVERSITETAS.
Lietuvos Universitetas. [The University of Lithuania] Kaunas, 1923.
113 p. fold. table. LF44445.A5 1923
DLC DHEW CtPAM MH PU

10033. --- Lietuvos Universitetas, 1922.II.16-1927.II.16; pirmųjų penkerių veikimo metų apyskaita. The University of Lithuania, Feb 16, 1922-Feb. 16, 1927. [Kaunas, Valstybės spaustuvė, 1927] [3]-370 p. illus., diagrs. LF4445.A5 1927 DLC CaOTU CaQMM CtY ICU MH MiU NN NNC PU ViU WaU

10034. --- Lietuvos Universitetas, 1927-1928 mokslo metais. [University of Lithuania; academic year 1927-1928] Kaunas, 1928. 76 p. LF4445.A3 1927-28 DLC CtTMF PU

10035. --- Lietuvos Universitetas, 1928-1929 mokslo metais. [University of Lithuania; academic year 1928-1929] Kaunas, 1929. 1 v. FL4445.A3 1928-29 DLC CtTMF PU

10036. --- Lietuvos Universitetas, 1929-1930 mokslo metais. [University of Lithuania; academic year 1929-1930] Kaunas, 1930. 1 v. LF4445.A3 1929-1930 DLC

10037. --- Lietuvos Universiteto veikimo apyskaita, 1922-1924. Report of the University of Lithuania, 1922-24. Kaunas, 1925. 292, vi p. illus., facsim. Text in Lithuanian with abstracts in English. LF4445.A3 MH DLC

10038. --- Vytauto Didžiojo Universitetas 1922-1932; trumpa 10 metų veikimo apžvalga. [University of Vytautas the Great, 1922-1932; a short review of its ten years of operation] Kaunas, 1932. 48 p. LF4445.A3 1922-1932 DLC CtTMF

10039. --- Vytauto Didžiojo Universitetas; antrųjų penkerių veiklos metų. 1927. II.16 - 1932.IX.1, apžvalga. [University of Vytautas the Great: a review of its second quinquennial operation, 1927, Feb. 16 - 1932, Sept. 1. Kaunas] Spindulio spaustuvė [1933] 527 p. illus., plates, ports., facsims, tables. LF4445.A3 1927-1932 DLC CU MiU NN PU

10040. --- Vytauto Didžiojo Universitetas 1930-1931 mokslo metais. [University of Vytautas the Great; academic year 1930-1931] Kaunas, 1931. 127 p. 378.475.Lie.4 PU CtPAM CtTMF DLC

10041. --- Vytauto Didžiojo Universiteto kalendorius, 1934. Tretieji metai. [The calendar of the University of Vytautas the Great for 1934] Kaunas, 1934. 240 p. 378.475.Lie.6 PU NN

10042. KRYSHANOVSKII, O. Uchebno-prosvietitel'noe dielo v Pol'shie nakanune posliednei reformy Vilenskago Universiteta, 1803 g. Sankt-peterburg, Tip. A.I. Lopukhina, 1899. 127 p. LA843.7.K7 DLC

10043. LIETUVOS TSR MOKSLŲ AKADEMIJA, VILNA. Akademiia nauk Litovskoi SSR. kratkii ocherk. [Podgotovil A. Ivashkevichius] Vil'nius, 1967. 31 p. illus. L Soc 2690. 20.35 MH

10044. --- Lietuvos TSR Mokslų akademija; trumpa apybraiža. [Soviet Lithuanian Academy of Sciences; an outline. Parengė A. Ivaškevičius] Vilnius, 1967. 38 p. illus., ports. AS262.L4836 DLC

10045. --- Lietuvos TSR Mokslų akademija, XXV. [Soviet Lithuanian Academy of Sciences - 25 years. Redakcinė kolegija; pirmininkas J. Matūlis] Vilnius, Mintis, 1967. 466 p. illus., ports. Bibliography: p. 453-463. AS262.L4826 DLC CtY ICU MH NN PU

10046. --- Statutas. Patvirtintas Lietuvos TSR Liaudies Komisarų Tarybos 1945 m. balandžio 14 dienos nutarimu nr.208. [Statutes as endorsed by the Council of the Peoples Commissars of the Lithuanian SSR on the 14th of April, 1945, nr.208] Vilnius, 1945. 18 p. (Its Leidinys nr.1) AS262.L4824 nr.1 DLC

10047. --- --- [Another edition. Patvirtintas Lietuvos TSR Ministrų Tarybos 1956 m. lapkričio 28 d. nutarimu nr.574. Statutes as endorsed by the Council of the Peoples Commissars of the Lithuanian SSR on Nov.28, 1956, nr.574] Vilnius, 1957. 54 p. AS262.L4843 DLC DNLM

10048. MACIŪNAS, Vincas. Senojo Vilniaus universiteto istorijos bruožai. [The historical outline of the old University of Vilnius] In Dirva (Cleveland, Ohio), no.4, 1954. See serials consulted.

10049. MASIONIS, Antanas. Vytauto Didžiojo Universiteto, teologijos-filosofijos fakultetas. [University of Vytautas the Great, Faculty of Theology and Philosophy] Kaunas, 1933. 13 p. L289.8MA ICLJF CtTMF

10050. MICELMACHERIS, Viktoras. Vilnius-senasis medicinos mokslo židinys. [Vilnius, the ancient centre of medical sciences] Vilnius, VPMLL, 1956. 52 p.

R804.L5M5 DLC MH

10051. POPŁATEK, Jan. Powstanie
seminaryum Papieskiego w Wilnie,
1582-1585. In Ateneum Wileńskie
(Wilno), v.6, 1929, p. 47-71;
429-455. See serials consulted.

10052. --- Wykaz alumnów Seminaryum Papieskiego w Wilnie,
1582-1773. In Ateneum Wileńskie
(Wilno), v.11, 1936, p. 218-282.
See serials consulted.

10053. --- Zarys dziejów Seminaryum Papieskiego w Wilnie, 1585-
1773. In Ateneum Wileńskie (Wilno),
v.6, 1929, p. 47-71; 429-455; v.7,
1930, p. 170-228; v.11, 1936, p.
218-282. See serials consulted.

10054. RABIKAUSKAS, Paulius.
Medžiaga senojo Vilniaus universiteto istorijai. Informatio de novo
collegio Vilnensi facta mense Sep-
tembri 1570. In LKMAM, v.3, 1967,
p. 221-266; v.4, 1968, p. [321]-
368. Lithuanian and Latin. See
serials consulted.

10055. --- Mokslinė pažanga Vilniaus akademijoje. [Scholarly
progress in the Academy of Vilnius]
In LKMASD, v.7, 1972, p. 203-234.
See serials consulted.

10056. --- Vilniaus Academija
(Academia Vilnensis; Collegium Aca-
demicum Vilnense; Collegium Vilnense Societatis Iesu) In Lietuvių enciklopedija. Boston, Mass.,
1966. v.34, p. 132-144. See entry
no. 216.

10057. --- The Vilnius Academy
during its period of growth. In
Lituanus (Chicago, Ill.), v.16, no.
4, 1970, p. 5-20. See serials
consulted.

10058. STANKA, Vladas. The Baltic University in figures and pictures, 1946-1949. Pinneberg, Ger.,
1949. 78 p. 378.43 PE PU

10059. SUKIENNICKI, Wiktor. Le-
genda i rzeczywistość; wspomnienia
i uwagi o dwudziestu latach Uniwersytetu Stefana Batorego w Wilnie.
Paryż, Instytut Literacki, 1967.
135 p. (Biblioteka "Kultury", 147,
Dokumenty, 20) CT1232.S82A3 DLC
CaAEU CaOTU MH NNC NjP PU WaU

10060. TARULIS, Albert N. Sor-
rows of the young Baltic University.
In American Association of University Professors. Bulletin, v.34,
no.4, 1948, p. 723-742. See
serials consulted.

10061. TUR, Ludwik. Uniwersytet
Wileński i jego znaczenie. Lwów,
Macierz Polska, 1903. ports., col.
plates, illus. Educ 5245.620 MH

10062. VILNA. UNIVERSITETAS.
Studentų priėmimo i Vilniaus val-
stybinį V. Kapsuko vardo universitetą taisyklės ir stojamųjų egzaminų programos. [The regulations
for acceptance of students into the
University of Vilnius] Vilnius,
[n.d.] 1 v. LF4425.V52 DLC

10063. VILNA. UNIVERSYTET. Księga pamiątkowa ku uczczeniu CCCL
rocznicy założenia i x wskrzeszenia
Uniwersyteta Wileńskiego. Wilno,
1931. 2 v. illus. LF4425.V56A5
DLC CaBVaU(v.1) MH NcD PU

10064. VILNIAUS UNIVERSITETAS.
[University of Vilnius. Board of
Editors: A. Bendorius, J. Kubilius,
J. Žiugžda] Vilnius, Mintis, 1966.
319 p. illus. LF4425.V56V5 DLC
CaOTU MH NjP OKentU PU

10065. WOROTYŃSKI, Wiktor. Semi-
naryum główne w Wilnie...1803-1816.
Wilno, Z zasiłku Funduszu Kultury
Narodowej, 1935. 323 p. Thesis--
University of Vilnius.
M40.St99v.7 CtY

10066. ŻONGOŁŁOWICZ, Bronisław.
Ustrój Uniwersyteta Wileńskiego.
In Rocznik Prawniczy Wileński, v.1,
1925, 194-232. See serials consulted.

XIII.10.b.3. LEARNED SOCIETIES

10067. ADAMOWICZ, Adam Ferdinand.
Krótki rys początków i postępu
anatomii w polsce i Litwie skreś-
lony na pamiątkę 50 letniego trwa-
nia Cesarskiego Towarzystwo Lekars-
kiego Wileńskiego dnia 12. Grudnia
1855 roku. Wilno, J. Zawadzki,
1855. 109 p. DNLM

10068. KRASAUSKAS, Rapolas. Lietuvių katalikų mokslo akademijos
veikimo ir darbų apžvalga, 1954-
1965. Compte rendu de l'activité
de l'Académie. In LKMAM, v.1,
1965, p. 329-342. See serials consulted.

10069. MIENICKI, Ryszard. Wileńska Komisja Archeologiczna, 1864-
1915. Wilno, Nakładem Towarzystwa
Przyjaciół Nauk w Wilnie, 1925.
vi, 222 p. tables. (Rozprawy
Wydziała III. Tom 1. zeszyt 1)
DK1.V56 DLC CtY NN

10070. VALAITIS, Antanas. Iš
Lietuvių mokslo draugijos istorijos.
[The history of the Lithuanian
Science Society] Vilnius, Ruch,
1932. 63 p. tables. Offprint
from Lietuvių Tauta. Vilnius, kn.
4, sąs. 3, 1963. Q947.52.V228 PU
NN

10071. VILENSKAIA KOMISSIIA DLIA
RAZBORA I IZDANIIA DREVNIKH AKTOV.
Kratkii istoricheskii ocherk Vilenskoi Komissii dlia razbora i
izdaniia drevnikh aktov, 1864-1906.
Sostavil chlen Komissii Ar. Tur-
tsevich. Vil'na, Tip. A.G. Syrkina,
1906. 66 p. DK1.V54 DLC NNC

10072. VILNA. LIETUVOS TSR VAL-
STYBINIS DAILĖS INSTITUTAS. Lietuvos TSR Valstybinis dailės institutas. [The Lithuanian SSR State Institute of Art. Redaktorius V.
Mackevičius. Sudarytojas ir įžangos autorius T. Adomonis. Dailininkas A. Kučas] Vilnius, VPMLL,
1960. 186 p. illus. N332.V55A5
DLC MH PU

10073. YLA, Stasys, 1908- .
Lietuvių katalikų mokslo akademija;
bendras žvilgsnis į praeitą kelią.
[Lithuanian Catholic Academy of
Sciences; general review] In
LKMASD, v.5, 1964, p. 3-[28] See
serials consulted.

10074. ZIEDONIS, Arvids, Jr. On
the advancement of Baltic Studies
by the AABS. In Lituanus (Chicago, Ill.), v.17, no.4, 1971, p.
35-43. See serials consulted.

XIII.10.b.4. ARCHIVES, GALLERIES,
LIBRARIES AND MUSEUMS

10075. BALZEKAS MUSEUM OF LITHU-
ANIAN CULTURE. Progress report.
Chicago, Ill., Balzekas Museum,
1971. 32 p. illus. ICBM

10076. BERNOTIENĖ, Stasė. Lietuvos TSR Istorijos-etnografijos muziejus. [The historico-ethnogra-
phical museum of Soviet Lithuania]
Vilnius [Mintis] 1970. 140 p.
illus. At head of title: S. Bernotienė, O. Mažeikienė, B. Tautavi-
čienė. GN37.V66B4 DLC PU

10077. BRENSZTEJN, Michał Eustachy. Bibljoteka Uniwersytecka w
Wilnie do roku 1832-go. Wilno,
Nakład J. Zawadzkiego, 1922. [8]
146 p. plates, ports. Bibliography:
p. [113]-135. Z818.V77B8 1922 DLC
CtY PU PPULC

10078. --- --- Wyd. 2., uzup. Z
przedmową Stefana Rygla. Wilno,
1925. 160 p. illus. (Wydaw.
Bibljoteki Publicznej i Uniwersyteckiej w Wilnie, 2) B8901.7.10 MH
CtY DLC ICU NNC

10079. BURKEVIČIUS, Vilhelmas.
Kauno notariato archyvas (vyresnio-
jo notaro įstaiga); keli bruožai
iš įstaigos veikimo ir sutvarkymo.
[Archives of Notary Public of Kaunas; its organization and opera-
tion] Kaunas, 1928. 20 p.
947.52.B8335 PU

10080. CHICAGO. ČIURLIONIO VARDO
GALERIJA. Čiurlionio galerijos
Čikagoj trijų metų sukaktis ir dailės paroda, 1960, gruodžio 3-12 d.
[Čiurlionio gallery in Chicago;
exhibition on the occasion of the
third anniversary...] Chicago,
Ill., Čiurlionio galerijos direkci-
ja, 1960. 64 p. N531.C5A3 PU

10081. GALAUNĖ, Paulius. Muzie-
jininko novelės. [Curator's notes]
Vilnius, Vaga, 1967. 162 p. illus.
AM61.L5G3 DLC MH PU

10082. GOLUB, Vladimir Kuz'mich.
Piatidesiatiletie Vilenskago tsentral'nago arkhiva drevnikh aktovykh
knig, 2 aprielia 1852-1902; istoricheskii ocherk. Vil'na, Tip. A.
G. Syrkina, 1902. viii, 117 p.
tables. CD1735.V5G6 DLC MH NN

10083. GUDYNAS, Pranas and Stasys
Pinkus. Palangos gintaro muziejus.
[The museum displaying amber in
Palanga] Vilnius, Mintis, 1964.
64 p. illus. Bibliography: p. 63-
64. NK6000.G8 DLC PU

10084. --- Vilniaus valstybinis
dailės muziejus. [The State Art
Museum of Vilnius] Vilnius, VPMLL,
1957. 47 p. illus., ports.
708.9475.G933 PU CtPAM ICLJF

10085. --- Vil'niusskii gosudarstvennyi khudozhestvennyi muzei.
Vil'nius, Gos. izd-vo polit. i
nauch. lit-ry Litovskoi SSR, 1958.
46 p. illus. N3690.R9V5 DLC

10086. IVAŠKEVIČIUS, Adolfas,
comp. Vilniaus bibliotekos; vadovas. [A guide to the library of
Vilnius] Vilnius, Mintis, 1966.
151 p. illus. Z821.7.V55.I9 DLC
MH PU

10087. JAKUBOWSKI, Jan. Archivum
Państwowe W. X. Litewskiego i jego
losy. In Archeion (Warszawa), v.
9, 1931, p. 1-18. See serials
consulted.

10088. JURKUS, Paulius, ed. Art
collection of the Lithuanian Franciscan Fathers. [English translation by Joseph Boley] Brooklyn,
N.Y., Franciscan Fathers, 1963.
127 p. illus., plates.
709.475.J978.EB PU CaOTU CtPAM
CtTMF DLC MH

10089. KASPERAVIČIUS, J. Lietuvos TSR muziejai. [The museums of
Soviet Lithuania] Vilnius, Mintis, 1968. 90 p. illus.
AM61.L5K3 DLC CaAEU

10090. KAUNAS, VALSTYBINIS M.K.
ČIURLIONIO VARDO DAILĖS MUZIEJUS.
Kauno Valstybinis M.K. Čiurlionio
dailės muziejui 30 metų. [Thirty
years of the M.K. Čiurlionis State
Art Museum in Kaunas. Comp. by
P. Galaunė et al. Ed. by P.
Stauskas] Kaunas, 1956. 36 p.
N3315.45.A55 DLC PU

10091. --- Kauno valstybinis M.
K. Čiurlionio vardo dailės muzie-
jus. [The M.K. Čiurlionis State
Museum of Arts in Kaunas. Su-
darė: I. Andrulytė-Aleksienė et al.
Redaktorius P. Stauskas] Vilnius,
VPMLL, 1959. 87 p. illus.
N3315.45.A55 DLC ICA MH PU

10092. --- Pirminės kultūros
skyriaus ekspozicijos vadovas. [The
guide to the exposition of the
ancient culture. Parengė R. Ja-
blonskytė-Rimantienė. Kaune] 1956.
50 p. illus. DK511.L21K3 DLC MH

10093. KAUNAS. VYTAUTO DIDŽIOJO
KULTŪROS MUZIEJUS. M.K. ČIURLIO-
NIES GALERIJA. M.K. Čiurlionies
galerija, 1925. XII. 13-1930; pen-
kerių metų darbo apyskaita. Sudarė
P. Galaunė. [The Art Gallery of
M.K. Čiurlionis; report for 1925-
1930] Kaunas, 1931. 28 p.
A708.9475.K164.2 PU

10094. KONFERENTSIIA BIBLIOTEK
AKADEMII NAUK PRIBALTIISKIKH SOVETS-
KIKH RESPUBLIK, VILNA, 1969. Ma-
terialy konferentsii bibliotek AN
Pribaltiiskikh sovetskikh respublik
(Vil'nius, 17-21 iiunia 1969 g.)
[Sostavitel' A. Ivashkiavichius]
Vil'nius, 1970. 215 p.
Z819.B3K6 1969 PU

10095. LIETUVOS TSR MOKSLŲ AKADE-
MIJA, VILNA. CENTRINĖ BIBLIOTEKA.
Lietuvos TSR Mokslų akademijos
Centrinė biblioteka. [The Central
Library of the Lithuanian Academy
of Sciences. Comp. by A. Ivaške-
vičius. Ed. by J. Galvydis et al.]
Vilnius, 1959. 82 p. illus.
Summaries in Russian and English.

Z821.7.L5 DLC CaOTU CtY CU ICU MH
NN NNC NcD PPiU PU RPB WaU

10096. LIPSKI, Jacek, ed. Archi-
vum Kuratorji Wileńskiej X. Ad.
Czartoriskiego. Kraków, Nakł. M.
Arcta w Warszawie, 1926. xiv, 308
p. port. LA61.B33 nr.2 DLC MH NN
NNC

10097. LISOWSKI, Stanisław. Uni-
wersitecka biblioteka publiczna w
Wilnie w latach, 1919-1929. Wilno,
Druck J. Zawadzkiego, 1931. 28 p.
diagr. Bibliography: p. 22-28.
Z818.V77L5 DLC

10098. LITHUANIAN AMERICAN ART
CLUB, CHICAGO. Art gallery of
Čiurlionis, 1957-1958. [Text by M.
Šileikis et al.] Chicago, Ill.
[1958] 1 v. (chiefly illus.)
N531.C5L53 DLC PU

10099. MIENICKI, Ryszard. Archi-
wa Wielkiego Księstwa Litewskiego.
In PZHP w Wilnie 17-20 września
1935. Pamiętnik VI. Referaty
(Lwów), v.1, 1935, p. 403-413. See
serials consulted.

10100. --- Archivum akt dawnych
w Wilnie, w okresie od 1795 do
1922 roku. Rys historyczny opracował Ryszard Mienicki... [Warsza-
wa] Nakł. Archiwów państwowych,
1923. vii, 138 p. illus., fold.
plan. (Wydawnictwa Archiwów państwowych, 1) CD1757.V5M5 DLC CtY

10101. --- Archiwum Murawjenskie
w Wilnie. 1898-1901-1936. Wilno,
1937. 84 p. (Poland. Ministerstwo
Wyznań Religijnych i Oświecenia
Publicznego) BM(11900. l. 35.)

10102. PETRAUSKIENĖ, Zofija.
Bibliothek der Universität Vilnius.
Vilnius, Mintis, 1970. 47 p.
illus. Z821.7.V55P49 CaAEU

10103. --- Vilniaus universiteto
biblioteka. [The University Library in Vilnius] Vilnius, Mintis,
1970. 45 p. illus. Z821.7.V55P46
DLC PU

10104. --- The Vilnius University
Library. [Translated by M. Gins-
burgas] Vilnius, 1970. 46 p.
Z821.7.V55P45 PU

10105. SINKEVIČIUS, K. Iš Lietuvos TSR masinių bibliotekų istorijos.
[From the history of Soviet Lithuanian Public Libraries] In VUBMBM,
1958-1959. Vilnius, 1961. p. 107-

127. Z821.7.V5 1958-1959 DLC InU
MH NN PU

10106. SOKOŁOWSKI, August. Archiwum domu Radziwiłłów... Kraków,
A. Radziwiłł, 1885. (Scriptores
rerum polonicarum, T.6) DK402.S4
DLC CU MH NNC PU

10107. VAIDINAUSKAITĖ, S. Vilniaus Valstybinio V. Kapsuko v.
Universiteto mokslinė biblioteka,
1958-1959 m.; ataskaitos duomeni-
nis. [The library report of the
University of Vilnius, 1958-59] In
VUBMBM, 1958-59 m. Vilnius, 1961,
p. 5-14. Z821.7.V5 1958-1959 DLC
InU MH NN PU

10108. VALATKA, Vitas. Telšių
kraštotyros muziejus. [Folk Art
Museum in Telšiai] Vilnius, Mintis,
1971. 53 p. DK511.L2V335 PU

10109. VILNA. GORODSKOI SOVET.
ISPOLNITEL'NYI KOMITET. OTDEL
KUL'TURY. Biblioteki Vil'niusa...
[comp.] S. Vaidinauskaitė et al.
Vilnius, Mintis, 1968. 159 p.
illus. MH

10110. VILNA. LIETUVOS TSR VAL-
STYBINĖ RESPUBLIKINĖ BIBLIOTEKA.
1919-1969. [National library of
Lithuania, 1919-1969. Fotonuo-
traukos Č. Montvilos ir L. Opulskio.
Sudarė ir red. St. Elsbergas, A.
Lukošiūnas, St. Skrodenis] Vilnius,
1969. 161 p. illus. Summaries in
Russian, English, German and French.
Z821.7.V477 DLC MH

10111. VILNA. PUBLICHNAIA BIBLIO-
TEKA. Otchet Vilenskoi publichnoi
biblioteki i muzeia za 1903 god.
Vil'na, 1904. 142 p. Z821.7.V55
1903 PU

10112. --- Putevoditel' po Vilens-
koi publichnoi bibliotekie. Vil'na,
Tip. A.G. Syrkina, 1904. 28 p.
Cyr.4.2291 DLC CtY

10113. VILNA. UNIVERSITETAS. BIB-
LIOTEKA. Vilniaus valstybinio V.
Kapsuko vardo universiteto mokslinės
bibliotekos vadovas. [A guide to
Scientific Library of the V. Kapsukas State University of Vilnius.
Sudarė: S. Vaidinauskaitė, I. Vaitkevičiūtė ir L. Vladimirovas] Vilnius, 1958. 68 p. illus. diagrs.,
forms. Summary in Russian, English
and German. Z821.7.V54 DLC MH NNC
PU

10114. VLADIMIROVAS, Leonas. [Vil-
niaus universiteto biblioteka. [The
Library of the University of Vilnius]
Vilnius, VPMLL, 1958. 104 p.
Z821.7.V55V53 DLC PU

10115. --- Visuomeninių bibliotekų vystymasis Lietuvoje 1861-1917 m.
[The development of the community
libraries in Lithuania, 1861-1917]
In VUBMBM, 1958-1959. Vilnius,
1961. p. 67-106. Z821.7.V5 1958-
1959 DLC InU MH NN PU

XIII.11. HISTORY OF THE BOOK;
        LITHUANIAN PUBLISHING
        AND JOURNALISM

10116. ABRAMOWICZ, Ludwik. Czte-
ry wieki drukarstwa w Wilnie (1525-
1925) Wilno, L. Chomiński, 1925.
149 p. illus., facsims. Bibliography: p. 141-144. 947.52.Ab82 PU NN

10117. ANUSHKIN, Aleksandr Ivanovich. Na zare knigopechataniia v
Litve. Vil'nius, Mintis, 1970. 196
p. illus. Z168.L7A65 CaOTU

10118. --- Vo slavnom meste vilenskom; ocherki iz istorii knigopechataniia. Moskva, Iskusstvo, 1962.
170 p. Bibliography: p. 169-171.
Z166.V5A65 DLC PU

10119. BANDTKIE, Jerzy Samuel.
Historia drukarń w Królewstwie Polskim i. W.K. Litewskim. W Krakowie,
Drukarnia J. Mateckiego, 1826. 3 v.
947.52.B223 PU CtY PPULC

10120. BAUDOUIN DE COURTENAY, Jan
Ignacy Niecisław. Kwestya alfabetu
litewskiego w państwie Rosyjskiem i
jej rozwiązanie. W Krakowie, Nakładem Antoniego Cołonniewskiego. 1904.
44 p. 3297.40 MH BM(ol2902. ff.
8.(7))

10121. BIRŽIŠKA, Vaclovas. The
American-Lithuanian publications,
1875-1910. In Journal of Central
European Affairs (Boulder, Colo.),
v.18, no.4, 1959, p. 396-408. See
serials consulted.

10122. --- Iš lietuvių laikrašti-
jos praeities. [On the history of
Lithuanian periodical literature] In
Bibliografijos žinios (Kaunas),1931,
no.6, p. 221-224; 1932, no.1, p. 1-
16, no.2, p. 57-72, no.5, p. 181-195,
no.6, p. 221-239. See serials consulted.

10123. --- Iš mūsų laikraščių praeities. [From the past of our news-
papers] Kaunas, 1932. 71 p. Reprint from Bibliografijos žinios,
1931-1932. Z2537.B58 DLC NN NNC

10124. --- Lietuviškų knygų istorijos bruožai. [The outline of the

history of Lithuanian books] Kaunas, Spaudos fondas [1930] 131 p. illus., facsims. Supplement to "Bibliografijos žinios", 1929-1930. Z8.L5B48 DLC ICCC PPULC PU WaS

10125. --- Martin Mažvydas und seine Mitarbeiter; zur Erinnerung an das Bestehen des litauischen Buches. Heidelberg, 1948. 31 p. (Sonderbeilage der Zeitschrift "Scholar", no. 2-3) 491.922.M459.yB PU DLC PPULC

10126. --- Senųjų lietuviškų knygų istorija. History of the ancient Lithuanian books. Chicago, Ill., The Lithuanian Literary Society of Chicago, 1953-1957. 2 v. Z8.L5B5 DLC CaAEU CtPAM ICCC(v.1) NN ICLJF(v.1) MH MiD OCl PU

BRUOŽIS, Ansas. Prūsų lietuvių laikraščiai. In Draugija (Kaunas), 1914. See entry no. 176.

10127. BŪČYS, Pranciškus Petras. Apie apšvietą. [About education] Chicago, Ill., Draugo [n.d.] 60 p. DK511.L713B926 InNd PU

10128. DAMBRAUSKAS, Aleksandras. Apie katalikiškus lietuviškus šventraščio vertimus ir vertėjus. [On the Lithuanian Catholic translations of the Holy Scriptures and their translators. By] Adomas Jakštas [pseud.] Kaunas, 1933. 26 p. 947.520.J4 CtTMF

10129. --- Ką yra pasakęs A. Jakštas? Jo pastarais laikais, 1924-30 m. parašytų publicistiškų straipsnių rinkinys. [What did A. Jakštas say?] Kaune, Mokytojos Raudonaičių Mortos lėšomis, 1930. [153] p. 891.92.D183K PU OCl

10130. --- Šv. Kazimiero Draugija; jos kūrimasis ir pirmųjų XXV metų veikimas, 1906-1931. [The Society of St. Casimir...] Kaunas, Šv. Kazimiero Draugija, 1932. 149 p. illus., ports. (Šv. Kazimiero draugijos jubiliejinis leidinys, 553 nr.) DK511.L2A27 DLC CtTMF ICCC PU(Xerox copy, 1971)

10131. DIRVA, PUBLISHERS, MARIJAMPOLĖ. Dirva; dešimt metų sėjos barų 1918/19-1929. [Dirva, the 10th anniversary of publication] Marijampolė, 1929. 98 p. 891.92H.D264 PU

FALKENHAHN, Viktor. Der Übersetzer der litauischen Bibel Johannes Bretke und seine Helfer. Königsberg in Pr., 1941. See entry no.6487.

10132. GEDMINAS, Antanas and Rim-

tautas Gibavičius. Knyga ir dailininkas. [The book and the artist] Vilnius, Vaga, 1966. 158 p. illus., ports. Summaries in Russian, English and German. NC985.G42 DLC CtPAM OKentU

10133. GRYCZOWA, Alodia (Kawecka). Drukarze dawnej Polski od XV do XVIII wieku. Zesz, 5: Wielkie Księstwo Litewskie. Wrocław, Zakład Narodowy im Ossolinskich, 1959. 1 v. (Książka w dawnej kulturze polskiej, 10, zesz.5) Z163.G68 DLC PU

10134. IVINSKIS, Zenonas. Die Druckerei der Jesuiten in Vilnius und die ersten litauischen katholischen Bücher. In Commentationes Balticae (Bonn), v.1, 1954, p. 27-67. See serials consulted.

10135. JACOBY, Karl Rudolf. Zur Geschichte der litauischen Übersetzung des kleinen Lutherischen Katechismus. In LLGM, v.1, 1880, p.118-129. See serials consulted.

JUODIKAITIS, Kastytis. Ekslibrisai. Vilnius, 1963. See entry no.9781.

10136. JURGĖLA, Constantine R. 400 anniversary of the first Lithuanian book. In Lithuanian bulletin (New York, N.Y.), v.5, no.12, 1947, p.1-12. See serials consulted.

10137. KORSAKAS, Kostas. Lietuviškos knygos 400 metų kelias. [The Lithuanian book trough 400 years. Kaunas] VGLL, 1948. 32 p. PG8709.K65 PU

LAVINSKAS, Frank. Amerikos lietuvių laikraščiai, 1879-1955. Long Island City, N.Y. [c1956] See entry no.178.

10138. LIETUVOS TSR KNYGŲ RŪMAI. Lietuvos TSR spaudos statistika, 1940-1955. [Statistics of the Soviet Lithuanian press, 1940-1955. Comp. by T. Čyžas, A. Madeikis, P. Ulpis. Ed. by A. Madeikis] Vilnius, VPMLL, 1957. 115 p. PN5278.L5L5 DLC CaAEU CtY InU MH PU WU

10139. --- Lietuvos TSR spaudos statistika, 1956-1957. [Statistics of the Soviet Lithuanian press,1956-1957] Vilnius, 1958. 30 p. PN5278.L5L5 1956-1957 DLC MH

10140. LIETUVOS TSR MOKSLŲ AKADEMIJA, VILNA. CENTRINĖ BIBLIOTEKA. Rūsų knygos spausdinimo pradžia ir Lietuva. [The beginnings of Russian book publishing and Lithuania] Vilnius, Mintis, 1966. 231 p. illus.

(Bibliotekininkystė ir bibliografija,
t.3) Added title page in Russian;
introduction and summaries in English and Russian.
Z228.R8L6 Ref. CaOONL

10141. LIETUVOS TSR MOKSLŲ AKADE-
MIJA, VILNA. LIETUVIŲ LITERATŪROS
INSTITUTAS. Senoji lietuviška knyga; pirmosios lietuviškos knygos
400 metų išleidimo sukakčiai paminėti. [The ancient Lithuanian book...
Redakcinė kolegija: K. Korsakas, P.
Pakarklis, J. Kruopas. Atsakingasis
redaktorius V. Mykolaitis. Kaunas]
Valstybinė enciklopedijų, žodynų ir
mokslo literatūros leidykla [1947]
338 p. plates. BX8080.M36L5 DLC
CaAEU NN PU

10142. LINGIS, Juozas. The Lithuanian emigrant press. In Baltic Review (Stockholm), v.1, no.6, 1946,
p. 299-303. See serials consulted.

LUTHER, Martin. Pirmoji
lietuviška knyga. [The first book
in Lithuanian language. Redaktorius
Jonas Kruopas, dailės redaktorius
Mečislovas Bulaka. Kaunas] Valstybinė enciklopedijų, žodynų ir mokslo
literatūros leidykla [1947] xv, 182
p. facsims., music. Translation
of Kleiner Catechismus, translated
and first published by Martynas Mažvydas under title: Catechismusa
prasty szadei. At head of title:
Lietuvos TSR Mokslų akademija, Vilna. Lietuvių kalbos institutas.
BX8070.L727K7 DLC NN

10143. MACIŪNAS, Vincas. Mūsų
pirmoji pasaulinė grožinės literatūros knyga. [Our first book of bel-
les-lettres] In Aidai (Augsburg,
Ger.), no.4, 1947, p. 145-150.
See serials consulted.

MAŽVYDAS, Martynas. Die
ältesten litauischen Sprachdenkmäler
bis zum Jahre 1570. Hrsg. von Georg
Gerullis. Heidelberg, C. Winter,
1923. xxxx, 592 p. facsims. (Indogermanische Bibliothek. 5 Abt.:
Baltische Bibliothek, Bd.2) At head
of title compiler's name: Mosvid.
Consists of Catechismusa prasty szadei, the first book printed in Lithuanian, a translation of Luther's
Shorter catechism; Giesme S. Ambra-
seijaus bey S. Augustina, kurę wadin
Te Deū laudamus; Forma chrikstima,
a translation of Die Form aber wie
man teuffen soll, ist diese, ...
Kirchenordnung wie es im Hertzog-
thumb Preussen... gehalten wird
[vom] 1558; Paraphrasis, a translation of Paraphrasis des Vater unser
in the Kirchenordnung of 1558 (this
Lithuanian version has previously

been ascribed to Bretkunas), and
Giesmes chriksczoniskas.
PG8701.M3 1570a DLC CLU CSt CaBVaU
CaBVaS CaOHM CaOONL CU CtTMF ICN ICU
KU MH MnU MiU NN NcD NcU NjP OrU OU
PBm PU TxU WU WaU

--- Martynas Mažvydas, pirmosios lietuviškos knygos autorius
jo mirties 400 metų sukakčiai paminėti. Chicago, Ill., 1963. See
entry no. 607.

10144. MIELCKE, Christian Gottlieb
and Georg Adam Meissner. Bedenken
über einen Entwurf zu einem neuen
littauischen Gesangbuch... Ans Licht
gestellt von G. Ostermeyer. Königsberg in Pr., 1786. 55 p.
BM(11825. 1. 4. (2.))

10145. MILUKAS, Antanas, ed. "Aušros" 40 metų sukaktuvės, 1883-1823.
[The fortieth anniversary of "Aušra"]
Philadelphia, Pa., Žvaigždė, 1923.
265 p. facsims, ports. Offprint
from "Žvaigždė" 1923. PN5279.T57A85
DLC CtTMF ICCC ICLJF PU

10146. --- "Aušros 50 metų sukaktuvės. [The fiftieth anniversary
of "Aušra"] Philadelphia, Pa.,
Žvaigždė, 1933. 33 p. Offprint
from "Žvaigždė", 1933.
891.92H.M649.4 PU

10147. --- 30 metų spaudą atgavus,
1904-1934. [The thirtieth anniversary of reestablishment of the free
Lithuanian press] Pranaičių Julės
ir bendraleidėjų leidinys. Philadelphia, Pa., Žvaigždės spauda,
1935-1936. 2 v. 891.92H.M649.5 PU
ICCC ICLJF

10148. MUSTEIKIS, Antanas. Freedom of the press in both Czarist
and Soviet Russia. In Baltic Review
(New York, N.Y.), no.4, 1955, p.64-
75. See serials consulted.

10149. MYKOLAITIS, Vincas. Pirmoji lietuviška knyga. [The first book
in Lithuanian. Kaunas] Valstybinė
grožinės literatūros leidykla, 1948.
40 p. illus. BX8070.L72M9 DLC PU

10150. OSTERMEYER, Gottfried.
Erste litauische Liedergeschichte
ans Licht gestellet. Königsberg
in Pr., Gedrückt mit Drietischen
Schriften, 1793. xii, 206 p.
BM(11825. 1. 4. (1.))

10151. PAJAUJIS, Juozas. Varpas;
literatūros, politikos ir mokslo
mėnesinis laikraštis. [Varpas (a
Bell); a monthly journal of literature, politics and science] In
Lietuvių enciklopedija. Boston, Mass.,

1965, v.33, p. 167-176. See entry no. 216.

10152. PENKI METAI AKCINĖS "VARPO" bendrovės darbuotės, 1920-1924. [The fifth anniversary of "Varpas" Ltd., Co.] Kaunas, 1924. 37 p. illus. 970.4VA ICLJF

10153. 50 METŲ SPAUDOS DARBUOSE. [Fifty years in the publishing business] Offprint from Žvaigždė, 1940, no.1, p. [26]-47. 891.92.M649.yP PU

10154. PRANSKUS, Bronius. The 400th anniversary of printing in Lithuania. Moscow, 1948. 13 p. At head of title: The U.S.S.R. Society for cultural relations with foreign countries. (*DAH p.v. Z92)NN

10155. PRUNSKIS, Joseph. Amerikiniai lietuvių laikraščiai. [The American Lithuanian newspapers] In Bagdanavičius, V.J. Kovos metai dėl savosios spaudos. Chicago, Ill., 1957. p. 297-314. PN5278.L5B3 DLC CaAEU OC1

PRŪSŲ KALBOS PAMINKLAI. Vilnius, 1966. See entry no. 7238.

10156. REMEIKIS, Thomas. A note on book publishing statistics as an index to Soviet cultural policy. In Lituanus (Brooklyn, N.Y.), v.9, no.2, 1963, p. 43-48. See serials consulted.

10157. ŠAKENIS, Konstantinas. "Auszra" ir jos gadynė; penkių dešimtų metų "Aušros" sukaktuvėms paminėti. ["Auszra" and its era; to commemorate the fiftieth anniversary of "Auszra"] Kaunas, 1933. 75 p. DK511. L25S33 1970 PU(xerox copy 1970) ICCC

10158. SCHWEDE, R. Zur Geschichte der litauischer Gesangbücher. In LLGM, v.3, 1893. PG8503.L7 v.3 DLC CtY ICU MH NN NjP MiU

10159. SKRUPSKELIS, Enata. The Lithuanian immigrant press in the U.S. after World War II. Chicago, Ill., 1961. 90 leaves. Thesis(M.A.)--University of Chicago. Z10999 ICU

ŠLIŪPAS, Jonas. Lietuviszkiejie rasztai ir rasztininkai. Tilžėje, 1890. See entry no. 73.

10160. ŠMOTELIS, Juozas. "Naujienų" istorijos bruožai. [A historical outline of the publishing house "Naujienos"] Chicago, Ill. [n.d.] 22 p. 691.92.B219M PU

10161. SPAUDOS DARBUOTOJŲ KOOPEratyvinė bendrovė "Raidė". [Annual report of the cooperative publishing company "Raidė"] Kaunas, 1930. (*QYA)NN

10162. STANKIEWICZ, Maurycy. Wiadomość o biblii litewskiej drukowanej w Londynie 1663 r., i o wrzekomym jej tłumaczu Samuelu Bogusławie Chylińskim. Kraków, 1886. (Studya bibliograficzne nad literaturą litewską, nr.1) Z9545.84 ICN PU

10163. TAUTRIMAS, R., pseud. Cultural discrimination in Lithuania; the problem of cultural press. In Lituanus (Chicago, Ill.), v.12, no. 1, 1966. p. 21-32. See serials consulted.

10164. --- Literatūrinės periodikos problema Lietuvoje. [The problem of literary periodicals in Lithuania] In Metmenys (Chicago, Ill), no.11, 1966, p. 137-148. See serials consulted.

TAUTVILAS, Danutė Dana J. The Lithuanian press in America. Washington, D.C., 1961. See entry no. 187.

10165. TURKOWSKI, Stanisław. Materyaly do dziejów literatury i oświaty na Litwe i Rusi z Archivum Drukarni i Księgarni Józefa Zawadzkiego w Wilnie z lat 1805-1865. Wilno, 1933-1937. 3 v. (Źródła i materjały historiczne Wydziału III Towarzystwa Przyjaciół Nauk w Wilnie, t.2-4) 947.52.T844 PU BM(Ac.1156.i.(5)) NN

10166. ŪKININKAS. Penkiolika metų sukakus. Bruožai is "Ūkininko" gyvenimo. [An anniversary of periodical "Ūkininkas"] Tilžė, M. Saunus, 1905. 16 p. (*QYL p.v.1, no.13)NN

10167. "VIENYBĖS LIETUVNINKŲ 25 metų sukaktuvių jubiliejus, 1884-1911. Historiški atsiminimai mūsų praeities...[The twenty fifth anniversary of "Vienybė Lietuvninkų"] Brooklyn, N.Y.,"Vienybė lietuvninkų" 1911. vi, 218 p. ports. 891.92C. V674 PU CtPAM

10168. VILEIŠYTĖ, Barbora. Kultūrinė Seinų spaustuvės veikla, 1906-1915. [Lithuanian printing house in Seinai.] In LKMAM, v.4, 1968, p. 51-161. See serials consulted.

A.B. Klaipėdiškis, pseud. see
 Bruožis, Ansas.
Aarne, Antti Amatus, 6638.
Abelkis, Povilas, 2477.
Åberg, Nils F., 4202.
Abraham, Władysław, 3043, 3100.
Abramavičius, Faivušas, 8312.
Abramavičius, Girša, 449, 8313.
Abramavičius, J., 2731.
Abramavičius, Vladas, 89, 193-195,
 450-451, 3525.
Abramowicz, Ludwik, 5305, 10116.
Abramson, A., 2758.
Adamowicz, Adam Ferdinand, 6478,
 10067.
Adamus, Jan, 2639, 2660, 2759, 3044,
 4423, 4537, 4701, 4804.
Adamus Bremensis, 4621-4624.
Adomavičius, Vladislovas, 2210.
Adomonienė, O., 4181-4182.
Adomonis, Juozas, 9768.
Adomonis, Tadas, 47, 452.
Adrianova-Peretts, V.P., 4610.
Afanas'ev, Dimitrii Fedorovich,
 5966.
Agaras, A., 4424.
Aistis, Jonas, 1006, 6823, 7949,
 8047, 8185, 8195, 8314, 9062-9071,
 9972.
Akademiia nauk SSSR. Institut Arkhe‐
 ologii, 2093.
Akademiia nauk SSSR. Institut etno‐
 grafii, 3745.
Akademiia nauk SSSR. Institut geo‐
 grafii, 1863.
Akademiia nauk SSSR. Institut isto‐
 rii, 3335.
Akademiia nauk SSSR. Institut sla‐
 vianovedeniia, 5186-5188.
Akelaitis, Vincas, 2776, 2780, 3641.
Akielewicz, Mikołaj, 2019, 7476.
Aksenova, S., 9523.
Alantas, Vytautas, 454, 8315-8320,
 8922.
Albertrandi, Jan Chrzciciel, 4926.
Alekna, Antanas, 455, 4508-4512,
 5189, 6391-6392.
Aleknavičius, B., 1193.
Aleknavičius, Kajetonas, 9068.
Aleknavičius, T., 2760.
Aleksa, Jonas, 1007, 3828.
Aleksa, O., 1232.
Aleksa-Angarietis, Zigmas, 848,
 5662-5663, 7010.
Aleksaitė, Irena, 456.
Aleksandravičienė, E. 46.
Aleksandravičius, J., 7477.
Aleksandravičiūtė, L., 5687.
Aleksandrov, Aleksandr Ivanovich,
 7268, 7679, 7759.
Aleksandrov, V.A., 3500.
Aleksienė, Gražina, 9596.
Aleksynas, K., 5984, 6910, 7680.
Aleškevičius, A., 8119.
Alexandrowicz, S., 3976.
Alikhova, Tat'iana Nikolaevna, 1951.
Ališauskas, Kazys, 2430, 2852,2853,
 3694, 5450.
Almėnas, Kazys, 8321-8323.
Alminas, Kazys, 236, 7834.

Alminauskis, Kazys see Alminas,
 Kazys.
Almquist, Helge Knut Hjalmar, 5017.
Allied Powers (1919-) Conference
 of Ambassadors, 2979.
Allied Powers (1919-) Treaties,
 etc., 2980-2982.
Alseika, Danielius, 959, 3299, 5967.
Alseika, Vytautas, 2317, 2761.
Alšėnas, Pranys, 457, 8324.
Ambainis, O., 6639.
Ambrasas, Kazys, 8048-8050.
Ambraška, Jurgis, 7528.
Ambrazas, Algirdas, 458.
Ambrazas, Vytautas, 7326, 7681-7683.
Ambrazevičius, Juozas, 960, 9142.
Ambrazevičius, Juozas see also Bra‐
 zaitis, Juozas.
Ambraziejus, Juozupas, see Ambroze‐
 wicz, Józef.
Ambrose, Aleksas, 2336.
Ambrozewicz, Józef, 237.
Amerbiuras, 3755.
American Lithuanian Engineers and
 Architects of New York, 1469.
Amerikos lietuvių rymo katalikų ku‐
 nigų sąjunga, 218.
Amerikos lietuvių rymo-katalikų ku‐
 nigų vienybė, 2340.
Amerikos lietuvių tautinė sąjunga,
 2341.
Anderson, Edgar, 2952-2953.
Anderson, Herbert Foster, 756.
Andrée, Karl, 1864-1865.
Andreev, A., 6258.
Andreev, A.M. 5629.
Andriekus, Leonardas, 9069-9071,
 9434.
Andriukaitis, Vladas, 8325-8328.
Andrius, Juozas, 1632-1633, 1646.
Andriušis, Pulgis, 2466, 8222,8329-
 8335, 9585.
Andziulytė-Ruginienė, Marija, 6393.
Angelaitis, T., pseud. see Narbutas
 Titas.
Anglickis, Stasys, 8186, 8923, 9072-
 9074.
Angoff, Charles, 9434, 9439-9440,
 9488-9489, 9549, 9564,9567.
Angrabaitis, Juozas, 1.
Aničas, Jonas, 3392, 6342-6343.
Anskaitis, Vincas, 319.
Antanaitis, Algirdas, 8051.
Antokol'skii, Pavel, 9515, 9530.
Antoniewicz, Jerzy, 90, 3977, 5994,
 6163-6166.
Antonovich, Vladimir Bonifat'evich,
 4321-4323, 4650, 4745.
Anushkin, Aleksandr Ivanovich,10117-
 10118.
Anusiewicz, Marian, 5088.
Anysas, Martynas, 3121, 4974, 6547.
Anysienė, Valerija, 6547.
Apyvala, Stasys, 5521.
Arkhangelogorodskii letopisets,4567.
Arkheologicheskii s"ezd, 2094-2095.
Arminas, Petras, 8223, 9075.
Arminas-Trupinėlis, Petras see Ar‐
 minas, Petras.
Armon, Witold, 2211-2212.

Gabrėnas, A., 9593.
Gabris, Paul, 2467.
Gabrys, Jerzy see Gabrys, Juozas.
Gabrys, Joseph see Gabrys, Juozas.
Gabrys, Juozas, 882-885, 969, 1069-
   1070, 2817, 3052, 3302,4211, 4437,
   5272, 5315- 5320, 5356-5357, 6351,
   7965- 7966, 8259, 8286.
Gaerte, Wilhelm, 2102, 6084, 6604.
Gaida, Pranas, 2443
Gaida, Pranas see also Gaidamavi-
   čius, Pranas.
Gaidamavičius, Pranas, 2322.
Gaidamavičius, Zigmas, 9147.
Gaidžiūnas, Balys, 5476, 5534.
Gaigalaitė, Aldona, 3553, 4646,
   5577, 5631, 6015, 6352-6353.
Gaigalas, Algirdas, 1707-1708,
   1910, 1937-1940.
Gaigalat, Wilhelm, 778, 823, 1016,
   2970, 6488, 6489, 7425.
Gailiūnas, Pranas, 7296, 7600, 7746-
   7747, 7967.
Gailius, P., 1122.
Gailius, Valentinas, 6490.
Gailius, Viktoras, 250-251.
Gaillard, Gaston, 4257.
Gaižutis, Vladas, 5867.
Galantiere, Lewis, 9575.
Galęska, S., 2676.
Galaunė, Paulius, 521, 6557, 7076,
   7111-7115, 7126, 9705, 9732, 9777,
   9784, 9796,9806, 9819,10081.
Galdikas, Valerijonas, 8396, 8449,
   8514, 8580, 9213, 9443.
Galinis, Vytautas, 246, 461, 522,
   8206-8207, 9494.
Gallogly, Inman Gray, 2030.
Galnaitytė, D., 6681.
Galter, Albert, 5762.
Galvanauskas, Ernestas, 2992, 3161.
Galvanauskas, Gediminas, 3939.
Galvydis, J., 194.
Ganss, Johannes, 6016-6o17.
Gar, Josef, 5477.
Garbaliauskas, Česlovas, 1752, 1759,
   1761.
Gargasas, Petras, 824, 886, 3907-
   3909, 4095, 4107, 4109-4110.
Garliauskas, Stasys, 2482.
Garmiza, Vadim Vladimirovich, 3870.
Garmus, Antanas, 6201.
Garmus, Paulius, 1709.
Garnys, pseud. see Maironis, Jonas.
Garšva, Pranas, 2468.
Gartman, V.G., 4005.
Garunkštis, Aleksas, 1710, 1825-
   1826, 1832-1835.
Gąsiorowski, Janusz Tadeusz, 4186.
Gasiūnas, Ipolitas, 1770.
Gasiūnas, Vytautas, 5925.
Gaška, Ignas, 5695.
Gasparavičius, Kazimieras, 359.
Gatterer, Johann Christoph, 887.
Gaučys, Povilas, 7613.
Gaudrimas, Juozas, 9622-9627.
Gaul, Dietrich, 3839.
Gause, Fritz, 418.
Gautherot, G., 5598-5599.
Gauthiot, Robert, 7877.
Gavėnas, Petras, 3643.

Gawełek, Franciszek, 2225.
Gazeł, Antoni, 3982.
Gečys, Kazys, 888, 3746-3747, 4985.
Geda, Sigitas, 1220.
Gedainis, Irvis, pseud. see Jurkū-
   nas, Ignas.
Gediminas, Antanas, 1765, 10132.
Gediminas, Grand Duke of Lithuania,
   4708, 4787.
Gedroits, A.E., 1887.
Gedvilas, Zigmontas, 2358.
Gehrmann, Karlheinz, 779.
Geisler, V., 7032.
Geitler, Leopold, 7297-7298, 7878.
Geležinius, Vytautas, 3053.
Gelumbis, Francis A., 434.
Gelžinis, Martin, 4096, 5763.
Gentizon, Paul, 780.
Genzelis, B., 5204.
Geograficheskoe obshchestvo Severo-
   Zapadnyi otdel, 1503, 3377.
Geograficheskoe obshchestvo SSSR,
   889, 2260.
Geramb, Viktor, 9895.
Gerasimov, Georgii, 843, 6861.
Gerikas, T., 289.
Gerlach, Jan, 2665.
German, A., 9625.
German, V., 9625.
Germanavičius, Adomas, 6901.
Germanicus, pseud. see Tornius, Va-
   lerian Hugo.
Germany. Auswärtiges Amt, 2894,
   4647-4648.
Germany. Heer. Generalstab, 1787.
Germany. Heer. Oberbefehlshaber
   Ost, 3135, 5329.
Germany. Publikationsstelle Berlin-
   Dahlem, 890, 2278-2279.
Germany. Reichsamt für Weterdienst,
   1742.
Germany. Reichsarchiv, 5321.
Germany. Treaties, etc., 1919-1925
   (Ebert), 3340.
Gersdorf, Harro, 4986.
Gerullis, Georg, 419, 6018, 6085,
   7426-7427, 7445, 7493, 7837, 7879-
   7881.
Gerutis, Albertas, 2554, 2555, 4349,
   5753.
Gervydas, A., pseud., 5717.
Gessen, Sergei Iakovlevich, 4258.
Getneris, Jurgis, 9820-9821.
Giannini, Amedeo, 2608, 2993, 3337,
   4259, 6354.
Gibavičius, Rimtautas, 1965, 6783,
   8402, 9258, 9274, 9778, 9792-9794,
   10132.
Gibbons, Herbert Adams, 5358.
Gibbons, John, 781.
Gidžiūnas, Viktoras, 4542, 4839,
   4987, 5926, 6401-6404, 6437-6439,
   6533- 6535.
Giedra, Vincas, 8486.
Giedraitis, Antanas, 6743, 8487,
   9619.
Giedraitis, Juozapas Arnulfas, 7390,
   7396, 7398.
Giedrius, Antanas, pseud. see Gie-
   draitis, Antanas.

Gielgud, Adam, 4638.
Giere, Werner, 4260.
Gierszyński, Henryk, 3054, 5091.
Giertych, Jędrzej, 3055.
Gieysztor, Jakób Kazimierz, 5106, 6202-6203.
Gilbert, Eleazar, 6492.
Giller, Agaton, 5205.
Gilvydis, J., 195.
Gimbutas, Jurgis, 131, 524, 3519, 6405, 7116, 9822, 9896-9902.
Gimbutas, Marija (Alseikaitė), 782, 2105, 3940, 4212-4217, 6605-6606, 6904, 7117-7120.
Gimžauskas, Silvestras, 970.
Gineitis, Kazys, 2359, 3834.
Gineitis, Leonas, 525, 7968, 8131, 8132, 8242, 9499.
Ginet-Piłsudzki, Bronisław, 7120.
Ginsburgs, G., 3446-3447.
Ginsburgas, M., 10104.
Gintautas, Jurgis, 8058.
Gintneris, Antanas, 3941, 6204.
Gira, Liudas, 526, 7614, 7969, 7970, 8197-8200, 8243-8245, 8942, 9148-9154, 9470.
Girdenis, A., 7882.
Girdvainis, J.V., 527.
Girdzijauskas, J., 7770, 8224.
Girdzijauskas, Vytautas, 8488.
Girdžius-Klausutis, Jonas, 5635.
Girėnas, pseud. see Sauerveinas, Jurgis Julius Justus.
Girgensohn, Joseph, 4709.
Girnius, Juozas, 2082, 2360, 3056.
Gisevius, Eduard Karl Samuel, 6744-6747, 6852.
Gizbert, W., 1123.
Gizbert-Studnicki, Wacław see Studnicki, Wacław Gizbert.
Giżycki, Jan Marek Antoni, 6449-6451.
Gladel, R., 9563.
Glaser, Stefan, 5322.
Glebov, Ivan, 2160.
Glemžaitė, Michalina, 7033, 7064, 7069-7070.
Gliauda, Jurgis, pseud. see Gliaudys, Jurgis.
Gliaudys, Jurgis, 2303, 2441, 2483, 3266, 7131, 8489-8498, 9471, 9472.
Glinka, Jan, 718.
Glinskis, Juozas, 8943.
Glogau, Karl Wilhelm Otto, 825.
Gloger, Kurt, 783, 2994.
Gloger, Zygmunt, 1071, 3478.
Glušauskas, Jurgis, 5478.
Gobbato, Imero, 6792.
Goetz, Bruno, 784.
Goidánich, Pietro Gabriele, 7449.
Goldas, M., 24.
Gol'dshtein, Severian Mavriki'evich, 891.
Gołębiowski, Eugeniusz, 4939.
Gołębiowski, Łukasz, 4807.
Goltz, Rüdiger von, 5452.
Golub, Vladimir Kuz'mich, 10082.
Gomer, Abba, 3594.
Goodman, Paul, 9441.
Gorbachevskii, Nikita Ivanovich, 322, 4187-4188.

Gorczyński, Władysław, 1743.
Gorecki, A., 9473.
Gornung, E., 7203.
Górski, Konstanty, 4940.
Gorzuchowski, Stanisław, 2031, 2436.
Gorzuchowski, Xavier, 3057.
Goshkevich, I.I., 2280.
Goštautas, Stasys, 435, 8133.
Gotthold, Friedrich, 9947.
Gotthold, T.A., 7979.
Goyski, Maryan, 4840.
Gožanskis, Jokūbas, 3395.
Gozina, G.I., 9903.
Grabau-Grabauskas, Juozas see Grabauskas, Juozas, (1895-).
Grabauskas, Juozas, (1895-), 2772.
Grabauskas, Juozas, (1873-), 9948.
Grabiański, Alexandre, 3058.
Grabowski, Ignacy, 4900.
Graham, Malbone Watson, 2524, 2921, 4438, 4649, 5826.
Grappin, Henri, 3136.
Grašis, Vincas, 6205.
Gratianskii, Nikolai Pavlovich, 4988.
Graužinis, Casimir, 3137.
Graževičius. A., 9949.
Gražiūnas, Albinas, 5536.
Gražulis, Balys, 8499-8500.
Great Britain. Department of Overseas Trade, 3760.
Great Britain. Foreign Office, 3341-3343, 5206.
Great Britain. Foreign Office. Historical section, 4439.
Great Britain. Naval Staff. Naval Intelligence Division, 1624.
Great Britain. Treaties, etc., 3344-3350.
Great Britain. War Office. General Staff. Geographical Section, 323.
Gregor, Josef, 6870.
Gregorauskas, Marijonas, 4138.
Grewingk, Constantin Caspar Andreas, 2103-2104.
Gricius, Augustinas, 1980, 8265, 8501-8504.
Griciūtė, Angėlė, 1744-1746, 3681.
Griessinger, Bruno, 3138.
Grigaitytė, Kotryna, 8505, 9155-9158.
Grigas, Kazys, 528, 6665, 6682, 6694, 6748-6751, 6910.
Grigas, Napalys, 7615-7616.
Grigat, Christian, 6019.
Grigat, Fritz, 4218.
Grigat, Martin, 1072.
Grigelis, Algimantas, 1888, 1896, 1898, 1930, 1954.
Grigelytė, M., 1845, 1853, 1855.
Grigolaitis, Jonas Endrikis, 5537.
Grigonis, Matas, 3664-3666.
Grinaveckienė, Elena, 420, 7883-7885, 7908.
Grinaveckis, Vladas, 7886-7895.
Grincevičius, Česlovas, 4192, 8506-8507.
Grinevičius, Adomas, 529.
Grinius, Jonas, 530, 5538, 7121-7122, 7971, 8059-8060, 8134, 8135, 8944-8946, 9851, 9975.

Jonynas, Ambraziejus, 6560, 6667-6670, 6794, 6877-6878, 6910.
Jonynas, Antanas, 8539-8543, 9174.
Jonynas, Ignas, 3141, 4513, 4759-4760.
Jonynas, Vytautas Kazys, 6806, 8892, 9142, 9458, 9709, 9738, 9780, 9828.
Jonynienė, Sofija, 7622, 7623,
Jopson, N.B., 7751.
Jordan, Karl August, 7314.
Jordan, Wilhelm, 6879.
Jovaišas, Albinas, 555, 6671.
Jozefowicz, Antoni see Juozapavičius, Antanas.
Jučas, Mečislovas, 3526, 3539, 3986, 4547-4550, 4715, 4716, 4849, 4908-4909.
Jucewicz, Ludwik Adam, 1021, 5933, 5977, 6755, 6880.
Jucys, V., 6959.
Judelevičius, Dovydas, 8062.
Juknevičius, D., 1188.
Juknevičius, J., 1189.
Jundzill, Stanislaw Bonifacy, 1975,
Jungfer, Victor, 898, 899, 1022, 3766, 6561, 6562, 6672, 6881, 6882.
Juodakis, Virgilijus, 557.
Juodelis, Petras, 9748, 9766.
Juodikaitis, Kastytis, 8788, 9304, 9781.
Juodis, Simonas Egidijus, 127, 130.
Juonienė, S., 5642.
Juozapavičius, Antanas, 2565.
Juozapavičius, Pranas, 558.
Jūra,, Klemensas, 9175.
Jurčiukonienė, A., 32, 97.
Jurėnas, Eduardas, 5574, 9528, 9712, 9776, 9871, 9872.
Jureviz, Jekob, 402.
Jurevičius, A., 326.
Jurevičius, Stanislovas, 33.
Jurevičiūtė, I., 7936-7937.
Jurga, J., 9679.
Jurgaitis, Algirdas, 1711, 1941.
Jurgaitis, Kazys, 5718.
Jurgėla, Constantine Rudyard, 2365, 2366, 2971, 3282, 4514, 4910,4911, 5210, 10136.
Jurgėla, Kostas Rudaminas see Jurgėla, Constantine Rudyard.
Jurgėla, Peter Vincent, 561.
Jurgelionienė, N. (Kryževičiūtė), 8457.
Jurgelionis, Kleofas, 562, 6756, 7903.
Jurgeliūnas, Antanas, 2231.
Jurginis, Juozas, 563, 828, 1023, 1028, 1125, 2739, 2861, 3469, 3488, 3489, 3564, 3540- 3542, 4761, 5588-5590, 5638, 6413, 9710, 9831, 9904
Jurgutis, J., 2252.
Jurgutis, Vytautas, 3518.
Jurkėnas, J., 7787.
Jurkschat, Christoph, 6757.
Jurkschat, Ewald, 9442.
Jurkūnas, Ignas, 2084, 2895, 5480-5483, 6564, 8544-8555, 9480-9482.
Jurkūnas, Vytautas, 8921, 9324, 9143, 9531, 9712, 9778.

Jurkus, Paulius, 8556-8558, 9739-9741, 9775, 9782, 9783, 10088.
Jusaitis, Antanas, 4151-4156.
Jusėnaitė, J., 3682-3683.
Jusionis, Stasys, 9761, 9767.
Juška, Antanas, (1902-), 9925.
Juška, Antanas, (1819-1880), 255, 6883-6887, 6894, 6981, 7036-7038.
Juška, Jonas, 7624.
Juškaitis, Jonas, 9176.
Juškevičius, Adomas, 5978.
Juškevičius, J., 3668.
Juškienė, E., 290.
Juškytė, Jadvyga, 6817.
Juzumowicz, Tadeusz, 7625.
Juzumowicz, Wincentas, 7430.

Kaasik, Nikolai, 2324, 2955, 3352.
Kabailienė, M.V., 1936, 1955-1956.
Kabelka, Jonas, 349, 360, 703, 7764.
Kaczmarczyk, Zdzisław, 2694, 2719.
Kačanauskis, A., 9656.
Kadžiulis, A., 5546.
Kadžiulis, M., 4101.
Kaelas, Aleksander, 2922, 5719.
Kahle, Wilhelm, 6503.
Kairiūkštis, Leonardas, 3887-3888.
Kairiūkštis, Vytautas, 565.
Kairiūkštytė, Silvija, 273.
Kairys, Anatolijus, 8559, 8956-8962, 9177, 9483.
Kairys, Steponas, 975, 2819, 3919, 5361, 5362, 6210.
Kajeckas, Juozas, 2923, 5484, 5601.
Kakies, Martin, 1190-1191, 2008.
Kakliauskas, S., 2282.
Kaktyn', El'gi, 9445.
Kalijarvi, Thorsten, 3002, 3003, 6063.
Kalinauskas, Vytautas, 8748, 8780, 9282-9283.
Kalinka, Walerian, 2566-2569, 5033-5034.
Kaliński, Wilhelm, 1024.
Kalme, Albert, 5720-5721.
Kalninš, Brūno, 4270.
Kalnius, A., 8311.
Kalpokas, Petras, 9742.
Kalugin, S.F., 6271.
Kalvaitis, Bruno, 2341.
Kalvaitis, Jonas, 2441.
Kalvaitis, Vilius, 6888-6889, 7125, 7788.
Kalvelis, Leonas, 6695.
Kalwaitis, Wilius see Kalvaitis, Vilius.
Kamantauskas, Viktoras, 327-328, 7498, 7613, 7626-7629.
Kamieniecki, Witold, 1025, 2529, 3520, 4295, 4457, 4459, 6357.
Kaminskas, Jonas, 6743, 8063, 8064, 9221.
Kancedikas, S., 5593.
Kaminski, Aleksander, 6173-6175.
Kanados lietuvių katalikių moterų draugija, 2449.
Kanner, L.F., 900.
Kanovich, G. see Kanovičius, G.
Kanovičius, G., 9453, 9788.

Lietuvos TSR Kraštotyros draugija,
6565, 6568.
Lietuvos TSR Kultūros darbuotojų suvažiavimas, 6569.
Lietuvos TSR Liaudies meno rūmai,
7132.
Lietuvos TSR Mašinų ir prietaisų gamybos pramonės darbuotojų ekonominė konferencija, 4105.
Lietuvos TSR Mokslų akademija, Vilna, 837, 1552, 1555, 4383, 10043-
10047.
Lietuvos TSR Mokslų akademija, Vilna. Archyviniams dokumentams skelbti redakcija, 5552-5556, 5802,
5803.
Lietuvos TSR Mokslų akademija, Vilna. Biologijos institutas, 1556,
1778, 2013.
Lietuvos TSR Mokslų akademija, Vilna. Botanikos institutas, 332,
589, 1557, 1978.
Lietuvos TSR Mokslų akademija, Vilna. Centrinė biblioteka, 47-60,
159, 190, 193-195, 204, 1558,3525,
7167-7168, 10095, 10140.
Lietuvos TSR Mokslų akademija, Vilna. Ekonomikos institutas, 1029,
1559, 3378, 4077, 4106-4110,4146-
4149.
Lietuvos TSR Mokslų akademija, Vilna. Energetikos ir elektrotechnikos institutas, 1800.
Lietuvos TSR Mokslų akademija, Vilna. Energetikos ir elektrotechnikos institutas. Terminologijos Komisija, 333-336.
Lietuvos TSR Mokslų akademija, Vilna. Fizikos ir matematikos institutas, 337, 1561.
Lietuvos TSR Mokslų akademija, Vilna. Fizikos-technikos institutas,
1560.
Lietuvos TSR Mokslų akademija, Vilna. Geologijos ir geografijos institutas, 1562, 1629, 1874,1897-
1898.
Lietuvos TSR Mokslų akademija, Vilna. Geologijos ir geografijos institutas. Lietuvos TSR fizinė geografija see Basalykas, Alfonsas.
Lietuvos fizinė geografija.
Lietuvos RSR Mokslų akademija, Vilna. Istorijos institutas, 1563,
1564, 2120, 2232, 3492, 3493, 3526,
4518, 4519, 6570.
Lietuvos TSR Mokslų akademija, Vilna. Istorijos ir teisės institutas, 4586.
Lietuvos TSR Mokslų akademija. Vilna. Lietuvių kalbos ir literatūros institutas, 420, 1565, 5787,
6682-6684, 6703, 6704, 6910,7557,
7709,7849, 7909, 7938- 7942,7980,
8084-8087.
Lietuvos TSR Mokslų akademija, Vilna. Lietuvių literatūros institutas, 5787, 10141.
Lietuvos TSR Mokslų akademija, Vilna. Melioracijos institutas,1960.

Lietuvos TSR Mokslų akademija, Vilna. Visuotinis susirinkimas, 9980.
Lietuvos TSR Mokslų akademija, Vilna. Zoologijos ir parazitologijos institutas, 1842.
Lietuvos TSR Mokytojų suvažiavimas, Vilna, 1960., 9981.
Lietuvos TSR Paminklų apsaugos ir kraštotyros draugija, 5937-5939,
5983, 5984.
Lietuvos TSR Zoologų konferencija,
1567.
Lietuvos turizmo draugija, 1113,
1140-1141.
Lietuvos Ūkininkas, 5290.
Lietuvos ūkininkų partija, 2828.
Lietuvos žemės ūkio kooperatyvų sąjunga, 4055.
Lieven, Wilhelm, 4274.
Ligue des droits des peuples, 2929.
Likas, Albinas, 3411.
Likowski, Edward, 6539-6541.
Limanowski, Bolesław, 3285, 4384,
4466, 5157, 5223.
Linčius, Augustinas, 1899.
Lincke, Barnim, 2189.
Linde, Gerd, 5380.
Linde, Samuel Bogumił, 2667, 7218.
Lingis, Juozas, 2235, 7133, 1o142.
Lingys, Juozas, 6977, 6982-6989..
Linksch, Erich, 908.
Linkus, Anicetas M., 2490.
Liobytė, Aldona, 6752, 6760, 6783.
Lipčius, Mykalojus, 3779.
Lipkin, Maksim, 4818.
Lipmanas, D.M., 3610.
Lipnitskii, I., 5985.
Lipski, A., 6350.
Lipski, Jacek, 10096.
Lirov, V. P., 209.
Lisowski, Stanisław, 10097.
Litauische Literarische Gesellschaft,
Tilsit, 1568.
Litauische Literarische Gesellschaft,
Tilsit. Bibliothek, 160.
Literskis, Vladas, 3949.
Lithuania. Army, 2865.
Lithuania. Automobile Club see
Lietuvos automobilių klubas.
Lithuania. Centralinis statistikos biuras, 369-380, 2285.
Lithuania. Constitution, 2610-2618.
Lithuania. Consulate, New York, 62.
Lithuania. Delegation to the League of Nations, 3161-3162.
Lithuania. Finansų departamentas,
3780-3781, 4019.
Lithuania. Finansų ministerija,
3782-3784, 4020-4024.
Lithuania. Geležinkelių valdyba,
3950-3954, 5847-5848.
Lithuania. Hidrometrinis biuras,
1819-1821.
Lithuania. Karo ministerija, 2773.
Lithuania. Krašto apsaugos ministerija, 340, 2804.
Lithuania. Kredito įstaigų ir kooperatyvų inspekcija, 4056.
Lithuania. Kommissyja Skarbu, 4025.

8096, 8114-8116, 8172.
Šilde, Ādolfs, 5737-5738.
Šileikis, Mikas, 10098.
Silich, M.V., 1822.
Šilietis, J., 5342.
Silvanto, Reino, 936.
Silvestravičius-Davainis, Mečislo-
vas see Davainis-Silvestravičius,
Mečislovas.
Simaška, Klemensas, 9924.
Šimkūnaitė, E., 1995.
Šimkūnas, V., 128.
Šimkus, Jonas, 634, 8097-8098, 8239-
8240, 8245, 8265, 8771-8774.
Šimkus, S., 5636.
Šimkus, Stasys, 9687-9688.
Šimkus, Vladas, 9350-9352.
Šimoliūnas, Jonas, 3970.
Simon, Fritz, 3936.
Simon, Walter, 248.
Simonaitis, Catherine, 9548.
Simonaitytė, Ieva, 8281, 8775-8788,
9534-9536.
Šimonis, Kazys, 657, 6785.
Šimtakojis, pseud. see Čaplikas,
Juozas.
Simutis, Anicetas, 18, 230-231, 3817.
Šimutis, Leonardas, 2414.
Šimutis, Leonardas Juozapas, 9633-
9634.
Sinha, S.P., 3459.
Sinjoras, A., 444.
Sinkevičius, K., 10105.
Sinkevičius, V., 5566.
Šinkūnas, Peliksas, 1630, 5953,
7053.
Šipelis, J., 2882.
Sirijos-Gira, Vytautas, 8789-8793,
9353, 9537.
Sirvaitis, Casimir Peter, 1049.
Širvydas, Joseph Otto, 4484.
Širvydas, Konstantinas, 318, 7457-
7459.
Širvydas, Vytautas, 72, 486, 659,
4192.
Sitnikaitė, A., 49-54, 118, 190.
Sittig, Ernst, 7511, 7928.
Siuchiński, Mateusz, 4913.
Sjögren, Anders Johan, 6180.
Skałkowski, Adam, 5096, 5098.
Skalweit, August Karl Friedrich,
6122.
Skalweit, Bruno, 3855.
Skardzis, Vikentsii, Iosifovich,
2452.
Skardžius, Pranas, 362, 6903, 7355-
7364, 7512-7515, 7612, 7724-7726,
7817-7822, 7841.
Škema, Antanas, 8282, 8794-8796,
9007-9008.
Škerys, Antanas, 3898.
Skipitis, Rapolas, 6234-6235.
Skirius, Antanas F., 2415.
Skirmuntt, Konstancja, 4415, 4485-
4488, 4768-4769, 6236.
Škirpa, Kazys, 5504, 5831-5832.
Sklėrius, Kajetonas, 9759.
Škliarskaitė, Feigė, 5651.
Skliutauskaitė, A., 8417, 8564,
8802, 9240.
Skliutauskas, Jokūbas, 9009.

Skorupskis, Vladas, 2883-2884.
Skrodenis, S., 5938, 6682, 10110.
Skrupskelis, Enata, 10159.
Skrupskelis, Ignas, 8008.
Skučaitė, Ramutė, 9010.
Svireckas, Juozapas Jonas, 7385-
7386, 7399-7401, 7407.
Šlaitas, Vladas, 9354-9359.
Slančiauskas, Motiejus, 6944.
Šlapelienė, Laura, 8797.
Šlapelis, Ignas, 9760.
Šlapelis, Jurgis, 304-306, 347,
6796.
Šlapelis, Skaistutis, 1675.
Šlapoberskis, D., 238-240, 272, 290,
308, 317.
Šlapšinskas, Juozas see Rimantas,
Juozas.
Slavėnas, Julius Paulius, 5571,
5740.
Slavėnas, P., 107.
Slaviūnas, Zenonas, 6945, 6987,
7003-7006, 7153.
Sławoczyński, Salomon M., 6381.
Šlaža, M., 250.
Śledziewski, Piotr, 9862.
Sleinis, Indrikis, 937.
Šlekys, Vincas, 9660.
Šležas, Paulius, 988, 3106, 4530,
4879-4883, 5246, 6050, 6382, 6427.
Šleževičius, Kazys, 1948-1949.
Sliesoriūnas, F., 5172.
Šliogeris, Vaclovas, 660.
Šliubauskienė, J., 89.
Šliūpas, Jonas, 73, 661, 938-940,
989, 2089, 2989, 2960, 3107, 4416,
5077, 5389, 6123, 6628, 6803.
Śliwiński, Artur, 2945, 5097, 5173,
5247.
Slizień, A., 4489.
Sližys, Balys, 3971.
Slonimskis, S., 3657.
Sluchevskii, Konstantin Konstantino-
vich, 1104.
Sluckaitė, Aušra, 9 8100, 9224.
Sluckis, Borisas, 9513.
Sluckis, Mykolas, 460, 8101-8102,
8211, 8798-8804, 9538-9540.
Sluoksnaitis, J., 10006.
Smetona, Antanas, 990-992, 2068,
2838, 3108, 5390, 5438-5439, 5505,
6237-6238.
Smiling, A., 9539.
Smirnov, Anatolii Filippovich, 5248-
5249.
Smogorzewski, Kazimierz Maciej,
3238, 4307.
Smokowski, Wincenty, 5954.
Smoleński, Władysław, 2592-2593,
3109.
Smołka, Stanisław, 4734, 4825.
Šmotelis, Juozas, 10160.
Šmulkštys, Julius Joseph, 5506-5507.
Šnaideraitienė, Magdalena, 6696.
Šnapštys, Juozas, 6797.
Snarskis, Povilas, 1996-1998.
Šniukšta, Petras, 3740.
Sobieski, Wacław, 2594, 4308, 6519.
Šoblinskas, Adomas, 7641.
Sobolevitch, Elias, 2946.

TITLE INDEX

Miškų ūkio organizavimas kolūkiuose, 3886.
Mįslės, 6801.
Mįslės surinktos Alytaus, Niedzingės Perlojos, Kabelių ir Merkynės parapijose, 6766.
Mįslės surinktos Lazdūnų parapijoj, 6796.
Mįslių knyga, 6756.
Missa ad duas voces, 9642.
Mistinės literatūros studijos, 1521.
Miting predstavitelei litovskogo naroda, Moscow, Apr.,1942., 5557.
Mistiniame sode, 6247.
Mittelalterliche Grenzen in Osteuropa, 4490.
Mituvos upyno tarmės fonetika, 7884.
Młode lata Zygmunta Starego, 4962.
Młodzierz litewska i dekabriści, 3731.
Moi krai, 9527.
Mokinių ateistinio auklėjimo metodikos klausimai, 5798.
Mokslas ir gyvenimas, 1359.
Mokslas ir technika, 1577.
MOKSŁAS skaitima raszta lietuwiszka dieł mažu wayku, 7646-7647.
Mokslas Tarybų Lietuvoje, 9980, 9983.
Mokslinė pažanga Vilniaus akademijoje, 10055.
Mokslinės bibliotekos metraštis,1596.
Moksliniai pranešimai, 1562.
Mokslingo miškininko Antano Rukuižos spausdintų darbų sąrašas, 141.
Moksliniai darbai apie viduramžio mūro architektūrą Lietuvoje, 9842.
Mokslo dienos, 1360.
Mokslo ieškančių senovės lietuvių keliai, 9930.
Mokykla ir gyvenimas (Šiauliai),1361.
Mokyklos ir Prūsų mokyklų politika, 10003.
Mokyklos vokiečių okupacijos laikais 1915-1918., 9958.
Mokyklų reforma Lietuvoje XVIII amžiaus pabaigoje, 9938.
Mokytojas Banaitis; romanas, 8421.
Monetnoe dielo v Litvie, 4012.
Monografii po istorii Zapadnoi i IUgozapadnoi Rossii, 4322.
Months names in Lithuanian and Lettish, 7802.
Motiejaus Valančiaus "Giwenimai Szwentuju Diewa" stilius, 8152.
Monumenta medii aevi historica res gestas Poloniae illustrantia, 4659.
Monumenta Poloniae Vaticana, 4660.
Monumenta Reformationis Polonicae et Lithuanicae, 4661.
Der Moorleichenfunde von Drobnitz... Ostpreussen, 2188.
The more important works on the Baltic States, 9.
Morėnų ugnys, 9109.
Morfologiia, stroenie i genezis rel'-efa sredne-litovskoi nizmennosti, 1725.
Mortos Vilkienės divorsas, 8652-8653.
Moskiewskie na Litwie rządy, 5104.

Moskovskii letopisnyi svod kontsa XV veka, 4593.
Moters stiprybė, 8915.
Moterų išeiginiai dėvimieji drabužiai, 7068.
Moterų kūrybos almanachas, 8193.
Motiejus Valančius; Žemaičių vyskupas, 624.
Motiejus Valančius kaip istorikas, 606.
Motiejus Valančius politiškas auklėtojas, 582.
Motina, 8213.
"Motinėlės" draugija, 2394.
Motinos rankos, 8755.
Motives of West Russian nobles in deserting Lithuania, 3474.
Les mots d'origine commune des langues slaves et baltiques, 7838.
Motulė paviliojo, 8733.
Mourawieff et les archives du Tzarisme, 5241.
Le mouvement coopératif en Lithuanie, 4063.
Mowa do ludu w Wilnie, 6422.
Mówią kamienie Wilna, 5702.
Die Münzen und das Papiergeld Estlands, Lettlands, Litauens, 4029.
Muitinių įstatai, 2805.
Munką Wieszpaties Jezaus, 7453.
Muraviovo veikimas Lietuvoje, 5246.
Murinė statyba pas senovės lietuvius, 3924.
Mūrinės statybos ugdymo planas, 3915.
Music during the years of Independence, 9634.
La musique et la dansé, 7008.
Muślimowie, czyli tak zwani Tatarzy litewscy, 3635.
Mūšos Dobilas; kunigui J. Lindei Dobilui atminti, 626.
Mūsų bajorai ir lietuvystė, 2087.
Mūsų dainelės, 9669.
Mūsų dainiai; kritikos bruožai, 8000.
Mūsų darbai, 2388.
Mūsų girios, 1362.
Mūsų įžymieji žmonės, 442.
Mūsu kaiminu valstis un Baltijas jūra, 937.
Mūsų kalbos ūgdymas, 7372.
Mūsų kalendorius, 1610.
Mūsų kariuomenės dainos, 9695.
Mūsų keliai, 2449, 2822.
Mūsų kelias, 1363.
Mūsų kovos dėl kalbos Vilniaus krašto bažnyčiose, 3261.
Mūsų kovos dėl Vilniaus, 5878.
Mūsų krašto fauna lietuvių tautosakoje, 6661.
Mūsų krašto ropliai lietuvių folkloro šviesoje, 6662.
Mūsų laikraštis, 1364.
Mūsų laimėjimai švietimo dirvoje, 9971.
Mūsų Lietuva, 1365.
Mūsų lietuviškieji vardai, 7807.
Mūsų mažoji sesuo, 8858.
Mūsų naujoji literatūra 1904-1923 m., 8034.
Mūsų naujoji poezija, 7963.

Studya bibliograficzne nad literatū-
ra litewską, 77.
Studya nad dziejami Żmudzi, 6000.
Studya nad dziejami Żmudzi wieku
XIII, 4780.
Studya i szkice z czasów Kazimieza
Jagiellończyka, 4961.
Studya nad stosunkami narodowoścío-
wemi na Litwie, 2036.
Stumbrų radiniai Lietuvoje ir jų
rūšiavimo klausimas, 2011.
Styginis kvartetas, 9645.
Su bėgliais ir tremtiniais, 2457.
Su Minija į Baltiją, 6250.
...su naktim kalbėsiu, 9173.
Su Lietuva ar prie Lenkijos, 2092.
Subsidium reipublicae generalis
contributionis od stanów koron-
nych, y W.X. Litewskiego, 2704.
Sud'by narodov Rossii; Litva, 4311.
Sudebnik korolia Kazimira IAgello-
vicha, dannyi Litvie 1468 goda,
2740.
Sudiev! aš išeinu, 8572.
Sudiev, kvietkeli! apysaka, 8334.
The Sudovians, 6165.
Sudrumstoji ramybė, 9049.
Sūduva, 8220.
Sūduvos praeitis, 6003.
Sūduvos-Suvalkijos istorija, 5997.
Sudužęs vaizdas, 8500.
Suffragia Woiewodztw y Ziem Koron-
nych y W.X. Litewskiego, 2595-
2596.
Sugriuvęs gyvenimas, 8978.
Sugrįžimas, 8818.
Sukaustyti latrai, 8613.
Sukilėliai, 8666-8667.
Suktinis; liaudies šokiai, 7007.
Sūkuriai ir žmonės, 8850.
Sumarinė saulės ir dangaus skliauto
radiacija Lietuvos TSR teritori-
joje, 1761.
Sumariusz i inwentarze Metryki Li-
tewskiej, 4730.
Sumienie Polski; rzecz o Wilnie i
kraju wileńskim, 3216.
Sunki ranka, 8512.
Sunkiaisiais laikais, 6231.
Sunkiausias menas, 8102.
Sunkios valandos, 9095.
Sunkūs paminklai; apysaka-kronika,
8413.
Sur le débit maximal des fleuves de
la Lithuanie, 1815.
Sur le prétendu recensement de
Vilna, en 1916., 2287.
Sur le transport de l'armée polo-
naise de Haller par la Lituanie,
3094.
Sur l'unité linguistique balto-
slave, 7368.
Sur les confins de deux mondes,
1048.
Sur quelques toponymes lituaniens,
7813.
Surinktos dainos isz visos Lietu-
vos, 6954.
Survey of developments in occupied
Lithuania, 5615-5618.
Survey of international affairs,

1920-1923., 2913.
A survey of recent developments in
nine captive countries, 3374.
A survey of the Bronze Age culture
in the South-Eastern Baltic area,
2105.
A survey of the literary heritage
of Vincas Krėvė, 8151.
Susiprato, 9052.
Susiekimo ministerijos 1937 metų
metraštis, 3961.
Susitelkimas lietuvių Amerikoje,
2416.
Susitikimas, 8659.
Susitikimas su Brunhilda, 8792.
Susivienijimo lietuvių Amerikoje
auksinio jubiliejaus albomas,
2382.
Susivienijimo lietuvių Amerikoje
istorija nuo 1886 iki 1915 metų,
2383.
Susivienijimo lietuvių Amerikoje
42-ras seimas, 2384.
Suskaita arba statistika visų lie-
tuviszkų knygų atsaustų [sic]
Prusuose nuo 1864 metų iki pa-
baigos 1896 metų, 1.
Suskaita arba statistika visų lie-
tuviszkų knygų atspaustų Ameri-
koj...iki 1900 metų, 88.
Sutartinės; daugiabalsės lietuvių
liaudies dainos, 7005.
Sutartinės ir mūsų muzikos įrankiai,
7001.
Sutemos; dienoraštiniai posmai,8684.
Sutriptame kely, 9424.
Suvalkų mieste 1882-1914 metais;
Juozą Marčiukaitį prisimenant,632.
Suvalkų rėdybos pilekalniai, 2131.
Suvalkų trikampis ir raštai apie
jį, 124.
Suvažiavimo darbai, 1527.
Suversti arimai; devynios eilių ir
poemų knygos, 8232.
Šūvis miške, 8623.
Sužadėtinė, 8824.
Sužalotieji, 8749.
Svadebnye obriady u litovtsev v
Shadovskom prikhode Shavel'skogo
uiezda, 7032.
Svajonė ir maištas; devynių giesmių
lyrinė poema, 9272.
Svatovstvo i svad'ba u litovtsev
Sesikskoi volosti, 7027.
Sveika, Nepriklausomoji! 8199.
Sveika, Tarybų Lietuva! 9319.
Sveikatos apsauga; nepriklausomieji
1918-1940 metai, 3658.
Sveikatos apsauga; okupaciniai 1940-
1944 metai, 3652.
Sveikatos apsauga Tarybų Lietuvoje,
3750.
Sveikatos draudimas ir socialinis
saugumas, 3644.
Švėkšnos praeitis, 5949.
Švenčionių lietuvių gimnazija, 15-
kos metų sukaktuvėms paminėti,
10009.
Šventadienis už miesto, 8569.
Šventaragis, 8318.
Šv. Kazimieras, 4944, 4968.

LIST OF SERIALS CONSULTED, WITH LOCATIONS AND HOLDINGS

ACADÉMIE IMPÉRIALE DES SCIENCES DE ST. PÉTERSBOURG. Mémoires 6-e série, seconde partie see Akademiia nauk SSSR. Mémoires... sér. 6, t.3-10. Seconde partie.

ACTA ARCHAEOLOGICA. v.1- ; [1930- . København, Levin & Munksgaard. illus., plates, maps. Three numbers a year. CCl.A2 DLC(1-) CU(1-) CaOTU (1-) CtY(1-) ICU(1-) IU(1-) InU(1-) MH(1-) MdBJ(1-) MiU(1-) MnU(1-) NN(1-) NNC(1-) NNU(1-) NbU(1-) NjP(1-) OCl(1-) OCU(1-) OrU(1-) PPiU(1-) RPB(1-) TxU(1-) CaAEU(1-)

ACTA BALTICA, v.1- ; 1960/61- . Königstein im Taunus, Institutum Balticum. Annual. DK511.B25A5 DLC(1-) AzTeS(1-) CaAEU(1-) CaOTU(1-) CLU(1-) CU(3-) ICU(1-) MH(1-) MnU(1-) NIC(1-) NN(1-) PU(1-) OKentU(1-)

ACTA BALTICO-SLAVICA. 1- ; 1964- . Białystok, Białostockie Towarzystwo Naukowe. illus. Annual. DK511.B25A612 DLC(1-) CaAEU(1,3-) CaOTU(1-) CU(1-) CtY(1-) CLU(3,7-) GU(1,3-) ICU(1-) MH(1-) MiU(1-) NN(1-) NNM(1-) NNC(1-) PU(1-) WaU(1-)

ACTA ETHNOLOGICA. 1-3; 1936-38. Copenhagen, Levin & Munksgaard. Merged into Folk-liv. CU ICF ICU MH MH-P MnU NN PPAP(1-2) PPT

ACTA GEOLOGICA POLONICA. t.1- ; 1950- . Warszawa. Quarterly. QE1.W27.3 DLC CoU CoDGS KU NmU NN WyU

ACTA PHAENOLOGICA. 1-3; Jan.1931-March 1935. The Hague, 1931-35. CLSU CU CU-A CaOLU CaOON CaOTU CtY ICU MH-A MiU OCl OClW OO(1-2) OrCA PPAN TNG WU

AIDAI; mėnesinis kultūros žurnalas. [Echoes: cultural magazine] München, Ger.; Kennebunkport, Me.; Brooklyn, N.Y., 1945- . Monthly. In United States published by Franciscan Fathers, Kennebunkport, Me. since Oct. 1949 and in Brooklyn, N.Y. since Oct. 1952. AP95.L5A4 DLC(1952-) CtTMF(1946, no.9(21)-1963) CtY(1957-) ICCC(1945-1946,no.6,7,8; 1947-1949,no.22-23, 25-26; 1950-1956) ICLJF(1945-1946,1951,1957-1970) MH(1957-) NN(1-) PU(1947-) OKentU(1947-); (1945-1946 on microfilm)

AKADEMIE DER WISSENSCHAFTEN, BERLIN. Sitzungsberichte. Bd. 1- ; Berlin, 1882-1921. Monthly. Supersedes its Monatsberichte and continued in classes. AS182.B35 DLC(1-) CLU(1-) CSt(1-) CU(1-) CaQMM(1882-1896,1915-1921) CaOTU(1-) CtY(1-) DSG(1-) ICU(1-) MH(1-) MiU(1-) NN(1-) NNC(1-) NbU(1-) NjP(1-) OCU(1-) PU(1-) WaU(1-)

AKADEMIE DER WISSENSCHAFTEN, GÖTTINGEN. Philologisch-historische Klasse. Nachrichten. 1894-1933;n.F 1941- . Göttingen, 1894- . Prior to October 1940 as Gesellschaft der Wissenschaften in Göttingen. AS182.G823 DLC CU(1894-) CSt(1894-1903, 1906-1933) CaOTU(1894-1931, 1933) CtY(1894-[1941]-) ICN(1894-1924) ICU(1894-) IEN([1895], 1917-1933) IU(1942-) IaU(1894-1898, 1900-1933) MH(1942-) MdBJ(1894-) MiU(1-) MnU(1894-1913,1915-1933) NIC NN (1894-[1918-1919]-[1921]-1933 NNC NjP(1942-1944) PU(1894-) RPB([1908, 1929] 1930,[1933]) TxU(1894-1924) WU(1894-1933)

AKADEMIE DER WISSENSCHAFTEN, VIENNA. Philosophisch-historische Klasse. Sitzungsberichte. Bd.1- ; 1848- . AS142.A313 DLC(1-) AzU(214-) CLU(12-[142-213]-)CSt(1-) CU(1-) CaAEU(1,4-31,34,41,43-44,47-48,50-52,54-56,58-63, 65-72,74-129,132-148,150-152,154,156,162-166,170-183,185-199,201-248,250-256,261-264,267,269-270-) CaOTU(1-) CtY(1-) ICN(1-) IU(1-) IaU(1-39,41-211) InU(124-) MB(1-) MH(1-) MdBJ(1-) MiU(1-) NIC(1-) NN(1-) NNC(1-[99]-[208]-) NbU(1-172) NcD(1-) NcU(199-) NhD(1-) Njp(1-) OClW(1-[96]-) PU(1-63,67-125, 127-131,133-) RPB([142.168,170.177,212,214]) TxU(4,6,-[158-197],199-) WU(1-) WaU(1-)

Akademie zur wissenschaftlichen Erforschung und zur Pflege des Deutschtum. Deutsche Akademie, Munich. Deutsche Kultur im Leben der Völker see Deutsche Kultur im Leben der Völker.

AKADEMIIA NAUK SSR. Izvestiia. Seriia istorii i filosofii. v.1-9, no.3; 1944-May/June 1952. Moskva, 1944-52. 9 v. AS262.A6247 DLC(1-) CSt-H([1]-[3]-[5]-) CU(1-[3]-) CaOTU([1]-[3-4]-[6]-) IaU(1-) MH(1-) MiDW(5-) NIC(1-)

NN(1,[2]-[4]-) NNC(1944-[1946]-) NSU([1946-1948]-) NcD(4,6-) PPAP(4-) PU(3,
[4],6-) WaU([1-4]-)

AKADEMIIA NAUK SSSR. Mémoires de l'Académie impériale des sciences de St.
Pétersbourg. Sér.6, t.1-10; 1831-1859. Sanktpeterburg, 1831-59. 10 v.
plates, tables, diagrs. Beginning with vol.3, divided into two parts:
Mémoires... sér.6, t.3-9. Première partie. Sciences mathématiques et
physiques. t.1-7; and Mémoires... ser.6, t.3-10. Seconde partie. Scien-
ces naturelles. t.1-8. Each volume has title page for the general series,
and one for the special series. AS262.A618 DLC(1-) CSt([1],6) CU(1-[3]-10)
CaOOG(6,[9]) CaTR([1,-3[-10) CaOTU(1,5) CtY DGS([1,3-8]-10) ICF([1-10])
ICU([1-4,6-7]) IU IaAS MB MH MdBJ(1-9) MiU NN NNC NcD NjP(3,5,7,9,) OClW(3)
PPAN([1]-[3-4]-[10]) WaU

AKADEMIIA NAUK SSSR. Zapiski. T.1-76; 1862-95. Sanktpeterburg, 1862-95.
76 v. in 58. illus., ports., maps. Supersedes Uchenyia zapiski of the
academy's Otdelenie fiziko-matematicheskikh nauk and Otdelenie istoricheskikh nauk i filologii, and Uchenyia zapiski of its Otdelenie russkogo iazyka
i slovesnosti. Absorbed by the Academy's Mémoires, Sér.8. AS262.S328 DLC
CU([1-75]) CtY DSG(1-7) MH NN NNC(1-[61]) NjP(1-75) PPAN(1-8)

AKADEMIIA NAUK SSSR. INSTITUT ARKHEOLOGII. Kratkie soobshcheniia o
dokladakh i polevykh issledovaniiakh. T.1- ; 1939 . Moskva. DK30.A173
DLC(9-) CaOONM(no.[6-50]-) DDO(11-30,34-35,37-) ICU(2-3,5-6,10) MH-P(4-)
NIC([13-34]-) OU(11-16,48-) PU-MU([2-27]-)

AKADEMIIA NAUK SSSR. INSTITUT ETNOGRAFII. Kratkie soobshcheniia. T.1- ;
1946- . Moskva. GN2.A2144 DLC(1946-1947, 1949) CU(3-) CtY(1-3,6-)
CaOONM(1-2,4-13) IU(2-) IaU(1-) NNC(1-) OU4-26) PU-Mu(1-)

AKADEMIIA NAUK SSR. INSTITUT ETNOGRAFII. Trudy. Moskva, 1934-37. 16 v.
GN2.A2142 DLC(2-7) CU(1-2,4,8-12,14-) CaOOG(1-) CaOTU(1-) CtY(9-12) DSI-E(1-)
ICF(1-) MH(1-15) MH-P(1-) NN(1-4,8-10,12-16) WaU(9-12,14-)

AKADEMIIA NAUK SSSR. INSTITUT ETNOGRAFII. Trudy. Novaia seriia. t.1- ;
1947- . Moskva. GN2.A2142 DLC(1-3,5,7-) CtY(1-2) CaAEU(1,11,14,18,22,38,
49,55,66,69,81,86,90) CaOONM(1,5-6,8-) InU(1-2) MiU(1-3) MnU(1-2,5-)
NN(1-2,5) NIC(1-) OU(1-)

AKADEMIIA NAUK SSR. ISTORIKO-ARKHEOGRAFICHESKII INSTITUT. Materialy po
istorii narodov SSR. Moskva, 1930-36. 7 v. DLC93-7) CtY([6]) InU MH(5-6)
NN(1-6) NNC NcU

AKADEMIIA NAUK SSSR. OTDELENIE RUSSKAGO IAZYKA I SLOVESNOSTI. Izvestiia.
T.1-10; 1852-1895; 1896- . Sanktpeterburg, Prodaetsia u kommissionerov I.
Akademii nauk J.J. Glazunova. PG2013.A63 DLC(1-s2,v.4,7-9,12-[14]-32)
CU(3,5-10-s2,v.[3-4],7-[9]-[11-12],13-[18]-[20],21-32) CtY(1-s2,v.[1-2],
7-[21-24]-27) MH(1,3-10; s2,v.3-[5]-[15-16]-32) NN(3,[4]-10; s2,v.7-32)
NNC(3-10; s2,v.13-32) NjP(3-s2,v.[4]-32)

AKADEMIIA NAUK SSSR. OTDELENIE RUSSKAGO IAZYKA I SLOVESNOSTI. Sbornik.
Petrograd; Sanktpeterburg; Leningrad, 1867-1928. 101 v. CSt(50,58,60-65,
69-80,[95]-[100-101]) CU CtY(1-[61]-[95]) DLC MH(4,[5],10-41,43-46,51-54,
56-58,60-100) MiU([2-99]) NN NNC([1-101]) NjP(1-[101]) OCl([22-93])

Akademiia nauk, Sanktpeterburg. Otdielenie russkogo iazyka i slovesnosti.
Izvestiia see Akademiia nauk SSSR. Otdelenie russkogo iazyka i slovesnosti. Izvestiia.

Akademiia nauk, Sanktpeterburg. Otdielenie russkogo iazyka i slovesnosti.
Sbornik see Akademiia nauk SSSR. Otdelenie russkogo iazyka i slovesnosti.
Sbornik.

ALMA MATER VILNENSIS. Prace społeczności Akademickiej Uniwersytetu Stefana
Batorego na obczyźnie. Zesz.1- ; 1949- . LF4425.V55A4 DLC(1-) CtY(1-)
CU(3) CaBVaU(1951) IaU(1-) InU(2) MH(1,11) NIC(1-2,4-) PU(1-) WU(1-) WaU(1-)

ALTERTUMSGESELLSCHAFT INSTERBURG, Insterburg, Prussia. Bd.1- ; 1881- .
Insterburg, Pr. MH(1-19) NjP(1-3) CtY(1)

ALTERTUMSGESELLSCHAFT PRUSSIA, KÖNIGSBERG. Sitzungsberichte. Bd.1- ;

1874/75-   . Königsberg in Pr., 1875-   . GN814.P8A3 DLC(1-21,27-28,31,33)
MH(1-22) MH-P(2,5-6,8-) NN(3-6,8,10-18) NNC(1-22) PU-Mu(22-24)

ALTPREUSSISCHE FORSCHUNGEN. Bd.1-20; 1923/24-1943. Königsberg in Pr.,
Gräfe und Unzer, 1924-43. 20 v. Semiannual. At head of title: Histo-
rische Kommission für ost- und west-preussische Landesforschung. Includes
"Bibliographie der Geschichte von Ost- und Westpreussen". DD491.04A17
DLC(15-) MH([1]-) NN([12]-) NNC(1-) PU(1,7-15,16,no.1,17-20)

ALTPREUSSISCHE MONATSSCHRIFT. Bd.1-3; 1864-1866; neue Folge der Neuen
preussischen Provinzial-Blätter, 4. Folge. Bd.4-59 (der Preussischen Provinzial-Blätter. Bd.70-125; 1867-1923. Königsberg in Pr., 1864-1923.
59 v. plates, ports, maps, plans, facsims, tables. Eight numbers annually,
1864-76; four double numbers annually, 1877- . Vol.1-3 have title: Altpreussische Monatsschrift zur Spiegelung des provinziellen Lebens in Literatur, Kunst, Wirtschaft und Industrie. Inhaltsverzeichniss von Bd.1-40.
Königsberg in Pr., 1905. 4 p.l., 154 p. DD491.04A3 DLC IU(1-42,51,54-57,
59) MH MH-Z([4]-[9]-10) NNC NjP(4-28,30,32-50) PU(23,26-27)

AMERICAN ACADEMY OF POLITICAL AND SOCIAL SCIENCE, PHILADELPHIA. Annals...
v.1- ; July 1890- . Philadelphia, Pa. H1.A4 DLC(1-) AzU(1-) CLU(1-)
CU(1-) CaAEU(1-39,45,47-80,84-85,89-92,94-96,99-149,152-398-) CaOTP(1-)
CaOTU(1-) CaBViP(1-) CtY(1-) IaU(1-) KU(1-) MH(1-) MdBJ(1-) NN(1-)
TxDaM(1-) WaU(1-)

AMERICAN ANTHROPOLOGIST. v.1-11;1888-1898; New Series. v.1- ; 1899- .
Washington, D.C.; New York, N.Y.; Lancaster, Pa: Menasha, Wis., The American Anthropological Association. GN1.A5 DLC(1-) BM(1-59) CLU(1-3,5-9; ns,
v.1-) CU(1-) CaAEU(1-73-) CaBVaU(1-) CaOOP(1-) CaOG(1-) CaOTU(1-[3]; ns,
v.1-) CaBViP(2-11; ns,v.28-34) CtY(1-) ICU(1-) IU(1-) NN(1-) NNC(1-) NjP(1-)
MH(1-) MiU(1-) OCl(1-) OClW(1-) OU(1-) PPAN(1-) PU(1-) TxU(1-) WaU(1-)

AMERICAN ASSOCIATION OF UNIVERSITY PROFESSORS. Bulletin. 1- ; Dec.
1915- . Boston, Mass. LB2301.A3 DLC(1-) AzU(1-) CSt(1-) CU(1-) CaAEU(3-4,
8,10,13,20-25,40-50,52-53) CtY(1-) GU(1-) IaU(1-) InU(1-) KU(1-) KyU(1-)
MH(1-) NIC(1-) NN(1-) NNU(1-) OCl(1-) PU(1-) TU(1-) TxDaM(1-) WaU(1-)

AMERICAN JOURNAL OF INTERNATIONAL LAW. Washington, D.C., 1907- Quarterly.
JX1.A6 DLC(1-) CSt(1-) CU(1-) CaAEU(1-) CtY(1-) CLU(1-) ICN(1-) InU(1-)
MH(1-) MdBJ(1-) MnU(1-) NN(1-) NNC(1-) NjP(1-) OClW(1-) PsT(1-) TxDaM(1-)
WaU(1-)

AMERICAN JOURNAL OF SOCIOLOGY. v.1- ;1896- . Chicago, Ill., University
Press. HM1.A7 DLC(1-) CLU(1-) CaAEU(1-) CU(1-) CSt(1-) CaBVaU(1-) CaOKQ(1-)
CaOLU(1-) CaQMM(1-) CaOTU(1-) CaOTP(1-) CaBViP(1-) CaMWU(1-) CtY(1-)
CoDU(1-) MH(1-) NN(1-) TxU(1-) WaU(1-)

American Slavic and East European review see Slavic review.

ANNALES DE GÉOGRAPHIE. 1- ; 1891- . Paris. G1.A6 DLC(1-) CaAEU(1-79-)
CaOG(22-) CaOTU(8-) CaBViP(1-18) CLU(1-) CSt(1-[18,22]-) CU(1-) CtY(1-)
ICU(1-7,9-) IU(1-) InU(7) MH(1-) MiU(1-) MnU(1-) NIC(1-) NN(1-) NNA(1-)
NNC(1-) PPAN(1-) PU(2-8,10-34) WU(1-)

APOLLON. Sanktpeterburg; Petrograd, 1909-17. 24 v. illus., plates.
Monthly except June and July. N6.A5 DLC CSt-H CU CtY FU KU MH MiU NN NNC NhD

ARCHAEOLOGY; a magazine dealing with the antiquity of the world. v.1- ;
1948- . Cambridge. GN7000.A725 DLC(1-) CLU(1-) CU(1-) CaAEU(1-) CaBVa(1-)
CtY(1-) ICU(1-) InU(1-) NN(1-) NNC(1-) OCl(1-) OU(1-) NIC(1-) TU(1-)
TxU(1-) WU(1-) WaU(1-)

ARCHEION; czasopismo naukowe poświęcone sprawom archiwalnym. 1- ; 1927-
. Warszawa. irregular. CD1740.A5 DLC(1-) ICU(4-5,8-) NNC(1-) MH(1-6/7)
NN(1-15)

ARCHIV FÜR REFORMATIONSGESCHICHTE, TEXTE UND UNTERSUCHUNGEN. In Verbind-
ung mit dem Verein für Reformationsgeschichte hrsg. von Walter Friedensburg.
Bd.1- ; 1904- . Berlin: Leipzig, C.A. Schwetschke und Sohn; M. Neinsius
Nachfg. BR300.A5 DLC(1-) CaAEU(1-) CSt(1-20) CtY(1-) ICT(1-) ICU(1-)
MdBJ(1-) MiU(1-) MnU(1-) NN(35-) NjPT(1-) OCl(1-) OU(1-) WU(1-)

ARCHIV FÜR RELIGIONSWISSENSCHAFT VEREINT MIT DEN BEITRÄGEN ZUR RELIGIONS-
wissenschaften Gesellschaft in Stockholm. Bd.1-37,no.1-2- ; 1898-1941- .
Freiburg i. Br., J.C.B. Mohr;[etc] BL4.A8 DLC(1-) CU(1-) CaQMM(1-17,21-31)
CaOTU(7-18) CtHC(1-) CtW(1-) CtY(1-) CtY-D(15-16) DSI-E(1-[6],7,9-20) ICF(7-
18) ICM(11-20) ICT(1-14) ICU(1-) IU(1-) IaU(1-) MA(1,3-) MB(1-33) MH-AH(1-)
MNS(7-) MdBJ(1-) MiU(1-) MnU(1-) NIC(1-) NN(1-7,9-) NNC(1-) NNMM(1-) NNUT(1-)
NbU(1-) NcD(7-) NjP(1-20) NjPT(1-) OCH(1-) OCU(1-3,7-27) OCl(1-4,7-) OU(1-)
PU(1-21,23-) WU(1-)

ARCHIV FÜR SLAVISCHE PHILOLOGIE.Berlin, 1876-1929. 42 v. illus., plates.
ports., facsims. Quarterly; irregular. Was suspended May 1920 till Oct.
1922. Index for volumes 1-34. PG1.A8 DLC(1-) CU(1-) CaAEU(no.1-482 on
microfilm) CtY(1-) ICN(1-) ICU(1-) MB(1-) MH(1-) MdBJ(26-42) MiU(1-) MnU(1-)
NIC(1-) NN(1-) NNC(1-) NbU(1-31) NjP(1-) WU(1-42)

ARCHIVES D'ÉTUDES ORIENTALES. v.1- ; 1910- . Uppsala, K.W. Appelberg,
1911- . DLC(10,13,15,20) CU(1-17,19-) CtY(1-) CtY-OS(1-) ICU(1-12,14-20)
MH(1-[20]) NN(1-) NNC(1-[5]-[18]-[20]) NjP(1-[5]-) OCl(1-2,4,[5],6,8-9,11,
14-) PU(1-20)

ARCHIVUM DO DZIEJÓW LITERATURY I OŚWIATY W POLSCE. Serja 1,1878- ;Serja
2, 1925- . Kraków, Nakład Polskiej Akademii Umiejętności. AS142.K868
DLC(1-14) CU(13-) MH(1-19) NN(1-) NNC(1-10)

ARCHIVUM FRANCISCANUM HISTORICUM. v.1- ; 1908- . Quaracchi; Firenze,
Collegia D. Bonaventura. Quarterly. BX3601.A7 DLC(1-) CSt(1-) CU(1-)
CaOTU(28-) CtY(1-) ICN(1-) IU(1-) MH(1-) MH-AH(22-) NN(1-) NNC(1-) NNF(1-)
NjPT(1-) OU(1-) PU(1-)

ARCHIVUM PHILOLOGICUM. Commentationes ordinis philologorum Universitatis
Vitauti Magni. Kaunas, Humanitariniu Mokslu Fakultetas, 1930-39. 8 v.
illus. Contains articles on Baltic linguistics in Lithuanian, French or
German. P9.A7 DLC(1-) BM CU(1-) CaAEU(5) ICU(1-5) MH(2-) MoK(1-) MoU(1-)
NN(1-) PU(1-6,8) ICCC(5)

ARKHEOLOGICHESKII S"EZD. Trudy. v.1-15; 1869-1911. Moskva, 1871-1916.
15 v. DK30.A72 DLC([2-8,12,14]) CU(1,[4],6,[8-9],10,[11]) MB(7) MH NN NNC
NjP OrU

ARKHEOLOGICHESKII S"EZD. 9th, Vilna, 1893. Trudy Vilenskago otdieleniia
Moskovskago predvaritel'nago komiteta po ustroistvu v Vil'nie IX Arkheologicheskago s"iezda. Moskva, Imperatorskoe Arkheologicheskoe Obshchestvo,
1895. DK30.A75 1893 DLC CU MH NNC NjP OrU

L'ART VIVANT; revue... des amateurs des artistes. 1-234. Paris, Nou-
velles littéraires [1925]-39. illus. Semimonthly. N2.A65 DLC CaOTP(1-2)
CtY(3-) ICR(no.144-191) IU(no.180-) MH(4-6; no.145-171,174) MiD(6-) MiD-A(2,
4-5; no.145-155) NBuG(1,[5]-) NN(1-) NNC(1-) NNCoo(no.180-234) NNMM(1-)
NjNbN(no.145-) PPiU(1-) PPPM(no.92-104,106-107,109-112) PSt(no.156-167,174-)

ARYAN PATH. v.1- ; Jan.1930- . [Bombay] Monthly. PB500.A8 DLC(1-)
CSd(8-) CL(1-) CaOLU(7-) CaLP(8-) CaQMM([8]-) CtY([1]-) MH(1-) NBuU(7-)
NN(1-) NNC(1-) NcD(6-) NjP(1-) OCl(7-)

ATEITIS; katalikiškojo jaunimo žurnalas. Nr.1- ; vasaris 1911- . Kaunas;
München, Ger.; Tübingen, Ger.; Schwäbische Gmünde, Ger.; Brooklyn, N.Y.,
illus., ports. Monthly except July and August. AP95.L5A8 DLC(1953,1953-)
CaOONL(1954,no.2-10; 1955-1958; 1960-1963; 1965-1966) CSt-H([2-4]-7; 1914-
1918) CtPAM(1911,no.2,5,11-12; 1912,no.4,6-7,8; 1913,no.1-4,9-12; 1914, no.
2-3,7-12; 1915,1916,no.2,4; 1917-1922,1923,no.1; 1924,no.2-3,5-6; 1925-1927,
1928,no.1,4-10,12; 1929-1930, no.1-7,11-12; 1932,no.6; 1933,no.6-7,9-10,11-
12; 1934,no.3-4,6-8,12; 1935,no.1,2,8-9,11; 1936,no.1-6,10,11; 1937,no.1-2,
4,11-12; 1938,no.1(13),2(14),3(15); 1939,no.1-2,5,8; 1940,no.5. 1946-1970-)
CtTMF(1911-1914,1919-1940,1946-1970-) ICCC(1911-1912) 1913,no.1-7,9; 1914,
1916,no.2-6; 1917,no.2-6,8,12; 1918,no.6,9-12; 1919,no.1-2; 1920-1922-1924,
[1925],1926-1936; 1938,no.1-6; 1938/39-1939/40; 1946-1956-) ICLJF(1911,
1937-1939, 1951-1965, 1967-1970-) NN(1914, 1950-) PU(1911,no.1-12) OKentU

ATENEUM WILEŃSKIE; czasopismo naukowe, poświęcone badaniom przeszłości
ziem Wielkiego Księstwa Litewskiego. Wilno, Towarzystwo Przyjaciół Nauk,
1923-39. 14 v. illus., plate, maps, tables. Quarterly. DK511.L2A77

DLC(2-[6]) CLU(8-) CU(1-) CtY(1-) CaBVaU CoU(v.7,no.3-4) ICU ICLJF(v.6,no.
1-4) KU MH(1-14) MiU(1-) NN(1-[6-7]-) NNC(7-8) PU(1-13)

ATHENAEUM; kalbos, literatūros, istorijos ir geografijos žurnalas.
Kaunas, Teologijos-filosofijos fakultetas, 1930-38. 9 v. CU(1-) ICCC(1931,
1933-1934) ICU MH NN(1-5,7-) NNC(1-5,7-[11]-) PU(1-) WaU(1,4-)

AUSTRIA. GEOLOGISCHE BUNDESANSTALT. Jahrbuch. Jahrg.1- ;1850- . Wien.
illus. maps, diagr. Annual. Issued by the institution under various names:
1850-1917, Kaiserlich-Königl. Geologische Reichsanstalt; 1918-1919, Geologische Reichsanstalt; 1920-1921, Geologische Staatsanstalt. Indexes for
vol. 1-10, 1850-59. QE226.A165 DLC DI-GS CoDGS FU KU ICU ICJ LU MB MiU
OrU OClW OU PPAN PPULC TxU

BALTIC AND SCANDINAVIAN COUNTRIES. Thorn (Toruń); Leyden; [etc.], Baltic
Institute, 1935-39. 5 v. Title varies: vol.1-2, 1935-Dec.1936 as Baltic
countries. D965.A1B3 DLC(1-) CLSU(1-) CLU(1-) CU(1-)_CaoC(1,[2],3) CtY[1]-
[5]) ICU(1-4) IEN(3-5) MB(1-) MH(1-) MiU(1-) McM([2-5]) MnHi(1-) MnU(4-5)
NN(1-) NNC(1-) NNU(1-2) NR(1-) NcD(1-) NjP(1-) OCU(1-[4],5) OCl(1-) OU(1-)
PU([1]-[4]) WU(1-)

BALTIC REVIEW. v.1-2, no.1-3; Dec.1945-Sept.1949. Stockholm, Baltic Hu-
manitarian Association. 2 v. illus., maps. Irregular. Supersedes Revue
Baltique and superseded by the Baltic review published in New York, N.Y.
DK511.B25B32 DLC PU(v.1,no.1-8; v.2,no.1-3) CSt-H CU CtY ICU IEN IU IaU InU
MB MH MdBJ MiU MnU NN NNC NjP PPiU TxDaM WU(1) WaS

BALTIC REVIEW. No.1- ; Dec.1953- . New York, N.Y. Committee for a
Free Estonia, Latvia and Lithuania. Supersedes The Baltic review published
in Stockholm, 1945-49. Nos.1-10, Dec.1953-March 29,1957, with numbers 6-10
printed. DK511.B25B318 DLC(1-) AMAU(1-) AzU(1-) CLU(9-)_CU(4-) CaAEU(1-3,
5,7-8,10,12,15-16,19-31-) IEN(1-) MH(1-) MdBJ(4-) MnU(1,5-) NN(1-) NcU(1-)
NjR(19-) NIC(8-) NNC(1-) NjP(1-) OU(1-) OKentU(5,8-9,12,16,18,23,25,27,28,
29, 32, 34, 36, 37) PU(1-) ViU(4-) WaU(1-3) WU(1-) KU(2-) CtY(1-) CaOTU(1-)
LU

BALTICOSLAVICA. Wilno, Instytut Naukowo-Badawczy Europy Wschodniej, 1933-
38. 3 v. (Its Bulletin) Irregular. PG1.B2 DLC(1-3) DSI-M(1) NN(1-) PU(1-2)

BALTIJAS UNIJA. L'Union Baltique. Bulletin. Riga, [1933-34] 2 v. illus.
ports. English or French translations appear in parallel columns with the
text in Lettish or Estonian. DK511.B25B34 DLC CtY ICU(1) NN(1-) NjP(1-)
MH(1)

BALTISCHE HEFTE. Bd.1- ; Oct. 1954- . Grossbiewende, Ger. illus.,
plates, ports. Quarterly. Began publication with Oct. 1954 issue. Issued
in 1951 as supplement to Baltische Briefe; 1952-53, as supplement to Baltische Rundschau. Includes section Baltische familiengeschichtliche Nachrichten. DK511.B25B36 DLC(4-) CLU(5-) CtY(2-) ICU(1-) MH(1-) NN(1-) PU(2-)

BALTISCHE STUDIEN. Hrsg. von der Gesellschaft für pommersche Geschichte
und Altertumskunde. Bd. 1-46; 1832-1896; NF1- ; 1897- . Stettin, 1932- .
DD491.P7G4 DLC(27-) CLU(1-ns,v.10) CU(1-) CSt(18-23) CaAEU(44-56-) CtY(1-ns,
v.16,18-) ICN(ns.v.1-) ICU(1-) MH(1-) MdBJ(1-) NIC(1-17,19-ns,v.26) NN(1-ns,
v.[30]-[33]-38,40-) NNC(1-ns,v.31) PU(1-ns,v.17) WU(1-)

BALTISTIKA. 1- ; 1965- . Vilnius, Mintis. Annual. An annual consist-
ing of two parts, issued at intervals of six months. Text in Lithuanian,
Latvian, Russian, English, German and French with summaries in one or two of
these languages. Vol.3(1967) called vol.3(1). QE260.B25 DLC(1-) CaAEU(1-)
CaOTU(1-) ICU(1-) CLU(1-) CSt([1-3]) CU(1-) CtY(1-) InNd(2-) MH(1-) MiU(1-)
NIC(1-) PU(1-) NjP(3-) WU(1-) OKentU(1969, no.1; 1970, no.1)

BEITRÄGE ZUR KENNTNISS DES RUSSISCHEN REICHES UND DER ANGRENZENDEN LÄNDER
Asiens. Sanktpetersburg, Kaiserliche Akademie der Wissenschaften, 1839-96.
CLU([2-15],25) CSt(1,s3,v.1,7) CU(1-) CtY(1-) DGS(1-s4,v.1) DLC(1-s3,v.6,
8-s4,v.2) ICJ(23,s2,v.1,5,s3,v.1-3) MB(12,23,25,s4,v.1-2) MBA(1-s3,v.7)
MH-A(1-s3,v.2) MH-Z(s2,v.1,5-8,s3,v.1-s4,v.2) MnU(s2,v.1-4,7-8,s3,v.[1-s4,
v.2]) NIC(1-[23]-s3,v.7) NN NNC(1-s3,v.6) PPAN(1-22) WU WaU(1-3)

BEITRÄGE ZUR KUNDE DER INDOGERMANISCHEN SPRACHEN. Göttingen, R.Peppmuller,

1877-1906. 30 v. in 25. P501.B4 DLC(1-) CLU(1-) CSt(1-) CU(1-) CaQMM(1-28)
NIC(1-) NN(1-) NbU(1-) NjP(1-) OCU(1-) PU(1-) TxU(1-) WU(1-)

BEITRÄGE ZUR KUNDE PREUSSENS. Bd.1-7; 1818-1824; NS v.L, 1837. Königsberg
in Pr., 1818-37. 8 v. illus. irregular. MH(1-[6],7) NNC(1-7) BM(107,ns1.)

BEITRÄGE ZUR NAMENFORSCHUNG. Bd.1-16,no.3, 1949/50-1965; NF1- , 1966- .
Heidelberg, 1949- . maps. Three numbers a year. P769.B45 DLC(2-) CSt
CU-Riv(1-[2]-) GU(9-) LU(1,3-) MnU(1-) MdU(1-) MiDW(1,3) NIC(1-) NN(1-)
PU(1-) ViU(1-) WaU(1-) CaAEU(1-16,ns1-)

BEITRÄGE ZUR NATURKUNDE PREUSSENS. Königsberg in Pr., 1868-1912. 10 v.
QE821.P79 DLC(1-7) CSfA(1-9) CaOTU(1-7) MBN(1-7) MH-Z(1-) NNC(2,5) NMM(1-)
PPAN(1-)

BERICHTE ÜBER LANDWIRTSCHAFT. Nr.1-41, 1907-1919; NF 1- ,1923- . Hamburg, 1907- . HD1951.A3 DLC(7-14,ns,v.5-) DA(1-) CSt(ns,v.1-) CtY(ns,v.1-)
CaAEU(45-) ICU(ns,v.1-) WU(ns,v.1-) NIC(1-)

BIAŁOSTOCKIE TOWARZYSTWO NAUKOWE. Prace. t.1- ; 1963- . Białystok,
Państwowe Wydawnictwo Naukowe. AS262.B47A14 DLC(1-) CU(2-) MH(1-)

BIBLIOGRAFIJOS ŽINIOS. 1-16 metai. Kaunas, 1928-44. 16v. illus. bimonthly. Issued by the University Library, Lithuanian Bibliographical Institute
and Lithuanian Librarians' Association. Z2537.B58 DLC(1-13) BM CtY(1928-
1943-microfilm) ICU(1-16) NN(1-13,no.6;14-16-Microfilm) MH(1-16,no.5) NNC
PU(1928-1944-microfilm)

BIBLIOTEKA DLIA CHTENIIA. Sanktpeterburg, 1834-65. 186 no. Monthly.
AP50.B5 DLC(1-128,135-152,158-174) CU(11,15,20,22) CtY(1-140) NN(1-[17]-
[26],27,29-40,42-55,59,[62]-104,111-116,123-126,141-152,158-18-)

BIBLIOTEKA WARSZAWSKA; pismo miesięczne, poświęcone nauce, literaturze,
sztukom i sprawom społecznym. Warszawa, 1841-1914. 295 v. AP54.B5 DLC
CU(274-275) IC(257-294) ICJ(249-250,253,254,259-260) MH N(251-252,255-258,
[264]) NBu(249-254,257-259,261-271) NN(1-168,213-[295]) NNC(270-295)
BM(1-295)

BLÄTTER FÜR INTERNATIONALES PRIVATRECHT. Leipzig; München, 1926-31. 6 v.
Supplement to Leipziger Zeitschrift für deutsches Recht. DLC-L CtY-L MH-L
MiU-L NNC NNU

BOOKS ABROAD. v.1- ; Jan. 1927- . Norman, Okla., University of Okla-
homa. Z1009.B717 DLC(1-) CLU(2-) CSt(1-) CU(1-) CaAEU(3-44-) CaBVaU(1-)
CaOLU CaOTP(8-) CaOTU(1-) CtY(1-) ICU(1-) IaU(1-) InU(1-) KU(1-) MH(1-)
MdBJ(1-) MiU(1-) NIC(1-) NNC(1-) NjR(1-) TxU(1-9,11-) WaU(1-)

BOTANICHESKII ZHURNAL. T.1- ; 1916- . Moskva; [etc.] illus., plates,
ports, maps. Frequency varies. Title varies: 1916-31, Zhurnal russkogo
botanicheskogo obshchestva; 1932-47, Botanicheskii zhurnal SSSR. Vols. 1-32
no.4 have summaries in English, German or French. QK1.V713 DLC(1-) CU(1-)
CU-I CSt CaBVaU CaOTU CaOON(24-) DA(1-) GU ICJ(1-3,9,[10]-15) ICF(27-)
ICU([8-16]) InIA(1-) MH-A([15]-[17]-[20]-[23-26]-[28]) MnU(1-[21]-) MdBJ
MoSB(1-) NcD NIC-A(1-) NYBT(12-) OCl(1-5) PPAN(1-)

BRUSSELS. UNIVERSITÉ LIBRE. INSTITUT DE PHILOLOGIE ET D'HISTOIRE ORIEN-
TALES ET SLAVES. Annuaire. T.1- ; 1932/33- . Annual. Bruxelles; [etc.]
illus., plates, ports, maps, facsims. Annual. PJ4.B92 CaAEU(1-7,9-19-)
CU(1-) CtY(1-) IU(1-) MH(1-) MiU(1-) NN(1-) NNC(1-) NNMM(1-) NbU(1-) NhD(1-)
NjP(1-) WU(1-) WaU(1-)

Bulletin of bibliography _see_ Bulletin of bibliography and dramatic index.

BULLETIN OF BIBLIOGRAPHY AND DRAMATIC INDEX. v.1- ; April 1897- .
Boston, Mass. Z1007.B94 DLC(1-16) CL(1-) CLU(1-) CSt(1-) CU(1-) CaBVaU(1-)
CaQMM(1-) CaOTU(1-) CaBViP(8-14) CoD(1-2,5-) CoU(1-) CtY(1-) DA(1-) GA(1-)
GU(4-) ICJ(1-) ICU(1-15) ICN(1-) IEN(1-) IaU(1-) IU(1-) InU(1-) KU(1-)
KyU(1-) LU(1-) MB(1-) MH(1-) MdBJ(1-) MiU(1-) MnU(1-) NBu(1-) NIC(1-) NN(1-)
NNC(1-) NcU(1-) NjP(1-) OCU(1-) OCl(1-) OClW(1-) OU(1-) OrU(1-) PPi(1-)
PU(1-) TxU(1-) WaU(1-)

Bulletin of bibliography and magazine notes see Bulletin of bibliography and dramatic index.

Bulletin of bibliography and magazine subject-index see Bulletin of bibliography and dramatic index.

BULLETIN OF INTERNATIONAL NEWS. London, Royal institute of international affairs, 1925-45. 22 v. in 27. maps. Biweekly; irregular. D410.B8 DLC(1-) CaAEU(17-22) CLU([7-9]-[11-15]-) CSt-H([4-5],8-) CU(6-) CaOTU([4-7]-) CaBViP([4]-[9],13-) CaMW([11]-) CaMWU(4-5,10-11-[13]-) CtY([5-6]-) CtY-L([1-3]-) ICU([9]-) IEU([16]-) IU(11-) MH-L(1-) MH(7-[10]-[16]-) MdBJ([4-6]-11, [16]-) MiU(6-) NN([1-2]-) NNC(1-) NjP[1]-) OCl(7-) WU(15-) WaU([4-7]-)

BURGWART. Bd.1- ; 1899- . Berlin, Vereinigung zur Erhaltung deutschen Bürgen. MnU(1-[13-15]) NN(1-[3]-7) NNC(12-)

CATHOLIC WORLD; a monthly magazine of general literature and science. v.1- ; 1865- . New York, N.Y., L. Kehoe; [etc.]. Monthly. AP2.C3 DLC(1-) CU(1-) CaOTP(1-) CtY(1-) CaBVaU(1-) CaBViPA(1-) ICN(1-) MoS(1-) NIC(1-) NN(1-) NNC(1-) MH(1-) MiU(1-) TxU(1-) WaU(1-)

COMMENTATIONES BALTICAE. Bd.1- ; 1953- . Bonn, Baltisches Forchungs- institut. illus., maps. Annual. At head of title: Jahrbuch des Balti- schen Forschungsinstituts. PG8001.C6 DLC(1-) CaOTU(1-) CtPAM(1-) CtY(1-) CLU(8 9-) CaOLU ICU(1-) MH(1-) MiU NcD NIC(1-) NN(1-5-) OU(1-) NNC(1-) PU(1-) OKentU(1953-1966)

CONGRÉS DES GÉOGRAPHES ET ETHNOGRAPHES SLAVES. 2ND, KRAKÓW, 1927. Comtes- rendus. Kraków, Nakład Komitetu Organizacyjnego, 1929-30. 2 v. in 1. G56.C64 1927 ICU BM

CONGRESSUS SCOTICUS INTERNATIONALIS, 2d, OXFORD AND EDINBURGH, 1966. De doctrina Ioannis Duns Scoti. Acta Congressus... Cura Commissionis Scotisti- cae. Romae, 1968. 4 v. plate. (Studia scolastico-Scotistica, 1-4) English, French, German, Italian, Latin, and Spanish. B734.S85 DLC(1-4) MH-AH NNG NN

CONTEMPORARY REVIEW. v.1- ; 1886- ; London. AP4.C7 DLC(1-158) CL(1-) CLU(1-3,19,21-22,24-29,66-109,111-112,117-) CSt(1-) CU(1-) CaBVaU(1-) CaAEU(105-) CaQMM(1-) CaOTP(1-84,86-) CaBVa(1-) CoD(1-) CtY(1-) ICN(1-) ICU(1-) IEN(1-) IU(1-) IaU(1-) InU(1-) MB(1-) MH(1-) MdBJ(1-) MiU(1-) MnU(1-) MoS(1-) NBu(1-) NIC(1-) NN(1-) NNC(1-) NcD(1-8,10-) NcU(19-) NjP(1-) OCl(1-) OClW(1-) OU(1-) OrU(1-) PPi(1-) PU(1-) RPB(1-) TxU(1-100,102-) TxDN(1-) VtU(1-) WaU(1-)

CZASOPISMO PRAWNO-HISTORYCZNE. T.1- ; 1948- . Poznań; [etc.], Pań- stwowe Wydawnictwo Naukowe; [etc.] Annual; semiannual. Supersedes Prze- wodnik historyczno-prawny. DLC-L(1-) CLU(1-) CU(1-) CtY(1-) MH-L(1-) MiU-L (1-) NIC(1-) NN(1-) NNC(1-) ICJ InU NcU IEN WaU

Chteniia v Istoricheskom Obshchestve see Moscow. Universitet. Ob- shchestvo istorii i drevnostei rossiiskikh. Chteniia.

DEUTSCHE GEOLOGISCHE GESELLSCHAFT, BERLIN. Zeitschrift der deutschen geo- logischen Gesellschaft. Bd.1- ; 1849- . Berlin; [etc.], W. Hertz; [etc.]. illus., plates, maps, tables. Quarterly. QE1.D4 DLC(1-66,69-70,73-78,80-88) CSt(1-) CaQMM(1-86) CaOG(1-15,24-) CaOTU(1-) CtY(1-) DI-GS(1-) ICU(1-) IU(1-) InU(21-48,56-) MH-Z(1-) MdBJ(1-) MiU(1-) MnU(2,4-) NIC(1-) NN(1-) NNC(1-) NjP(1-) OClW(1-16,24-) OU(1-) PPAN(1-) PU(3-4,8-9,11-12,[42]) TxU(1-) WaU(1-)

DEUTSCHE GESELLSCHAFT, KÖNIGSBERG. Historische und litterarische Abhand- lungen. Königsberg in Pr., 1830-38. 4v. AS182.K782 ICU CLD IEN OCl OClW

DEUTSCHE HEFTE FÜR VOLKS-UND KULTURBODENFORSCHUNG. Langensalza; [etc.], 1930-34. 4 v. maps. G1.D35 CU(1-4)

DEUTSCHE KULTUR IM LEBEN DER VÖLKER; Mitteilungen der Deutschen Akademie. Bd.1- ; Juni, 1925- . München, C. Wolf. illus. Three numbers a year. DD1.D465 DLC CU(11-) CaBVaU CtY([1-4]-) ICU([8-14]) IEN(7-) KU([11]-) MB MH([4-5,11,13]) MnU([11]-) NN(1-) NNC(5-) WU(20,27)

Schriften. Bd.1- ; 1931- . DLC(1,4,9,12,16,22,28) CSt-H([3-24]) CU(1, 4,9,12,20) CtY(2,6,11-14,16) ICU(11) IEN(3,12,16,28) MH(1-) MiU(13) NIC(21) NN(1-14,23) NNC(1-) Index for vol. 1-15 in v.16.

DEUTSCHE VOLKSKUNDE. München; Berlin, Arbeitsgemeinschaft für Deutsche Volkskunde, 1939-44. 6 v. GR1.D4 DLC(1-) CtY([1-3,5]) ICN([2-5]) ICU(1-[5]) NN([1-5]) NhD([1-3],5)

DEUTSCHES ARCHIV FÜR LANDES- UND VOLKSFORSCHUNG. Leipzig, 1937-44. 8 v. DD1.D5 DLC(1-) CU(1-) ICU(1-) IU(1-) MH(1-) NN(1-) NNA(1-) NNC(1-) NjP(1-) MiU(1-)

DEUTSCHES AUSLAND INSTITUT, STUTTGART. Schriften. Reihe A. Kultur-historische Reihe. Stuttgart, 1919-32. 32 v. Unclassified DLC(1-9,11-32) CSt(5) CSt-H(1-2,4,11,16,19) CLU(13) CU CaQMM(2,7,18,31) CtY(27,30) ICJ(7) ICU(4,10,12) IU(12,25) MH(19,29) MdBJ(26-27) MnU(19,24-25) NN NNA([2-29]) NNC(10,12,34) NhD(3,31) NjP(9,12) OClW WaU(30)

DEUTSCHES JAHRBUCH FÜR VOLKSKUNDE. Bd.1- ; 1955- . Berlin, Akademie-Verlag. illus. GR165.D4 DLC(1-) CaAEU(1-) CU(1-) CSt(9-) IU(1-) InU(1-) ICU(8) KU(1-) KyU(1-) MH(1-) MiU(1-) MoU(1-) NN(1-) NIC(1-) NcU(2-) NjP(6-) OCl(1-) PU(1-) TxU(1-)

DIRVA [Field]; Lithuanian quarterly publication. Shenandoah, Pa., 1898-1906. 9 v. Merged in 1903 with Žinyčia, Tilsit and was published: Dirva-Žinynas for Lithuania and Dirva for United States. BM(kn.1-5,8-14,16-18, 20,21) CtPAM(1903-1904) CtTMF(1898-1906) ICCC(1898,nr.2,3,4; 1899,nr.2-4; 1900,nr.2,4; 1901,nr.1; 1902,nr.2; 1903,nr.1-2; 1904,nr.1-4; 1905-1906)

DIRVA; tautinės minties savaitraštis. [Field] Nr.1- ; rugpiūtis 1916- . Cleveland, Ohio. Weekly; twice a week. OKentU(1957-1961,1963,1964, 1952)

DORPATER JAHRBÜCHER FÜR LITERATUR, STATISTIK UND KUNST, BESONDERS RUSS-LANDS... Bd.1-5; Juli 1833-Dez. 1835. Riga; Dorpat, Verlag von Eduard Frantze's Buchhandlung, 1833-36. 5 v. tables. Monthly. AP30.D72 ICU(1-5) DF InU MH MnU NN

DRAUGAS; lietuvių katalikų laikraštis. 1- ; Liepa 1909- . Wilkes Barre, Pa; Chicago, Ill. Weekly; daily since 1916. CtTMF(1,no.3-8,20,21; 2,no.5-9,1722,25,27,32) ICCC(1909; liepa gruodis) ICD IU([1917]-[1929]) DLL OKentU(1919,1920,1923,1924,1944, 1972, 1973)

DRAUGIJA; literatūros, mokslo ir politikos mėnesinis laikraštis. Nr.1-153; 1907-1923; Nauja serija. T.1, nr.1-10, sausis-spalis 1932. Kaunas, Šv. Kazimiero draugija; "Šviesos" spaustuvė, 1907-23. Suspended 1915-1919. AP95.L5D7 DLC(v.1,no.1-2) MH(ns1,no.1-2) MH-AH(ns1,no.3-4) BM ICBM(1909, 1911) ICCC(no.1-84,1907-1913; no.97-108, 1914; no.109-114,117-118, 1920; no. 121-124,127-128,1921; no.145-147,150-151,1923) ICLJF(no.1-12,1907; no.25-28, 45-60,69-92, 1909-1914)

DRAUGIJA; Kauno arkivyskupijos organas. Kaunas, 1937-40. Biweekly. CtPAM(1937-1940) CtTMF(1937-1940) ICCC(1937,no.1, 1938,no.1-10,17-18,20-24; 1939; 1940,no.1-14)

EAST AND WEST; a quarterly review of Soviet and Baltic problems. No.1-35. London, Markham House Press, 1954-61. 5 v. DK266.A2E25 DLC(1-) AMAU(1-) DS(1-) CLU(1-) IaU(1-) IEN(1-) MH(1-) NN(1-) NhD(1-) NIC(1-) NNC(1-) NjP(1-) PU(1-7) WaU(1-)

EAST EUROPE. v.1- ; Jan. 1952- . New York, N.Y., Free Europe Committee. Title varies: vol.1-5, Jan.1952-Dec.1956, News from behind the Iron Curtain. Supersedes News from behind the Iron Curtain, 1950-51. DR1.N363 DLC(1-) AzU(1-) CLU(1-) CtY(1-) DS(1-) FU([1]-) IaU([4]-) InU(1-) KU(2-) MH-PA([1]-) MnU(1-) MoS(1-) NN(6-) NNC(1-) NcD(1-) NjP(1-) OCU(6-) OU([1-4]-) OClW(1-) OKentU(6-) PPi(1-) PU(1-) ViU([1]-) WaU([1]-[3])

EAST EUROPEAN QUARTERLY. v.1- ; March 1967- . Boulder, Col., University of Colorado. DR1.E33 DLC(1-) CLU(1-) CSt-H(1-) CaAEU(1-) CaOTU(1-) CaOOU(1-) CaOKQ(2-) CaOWA(1-) CtY(1-) FU(1-) GU(1-) IaU(1-) InU(1-) ICU(1-) IEN(1-) IU(1-) KU(3-) MiU(1-) MnU(2-) MH(1-) MdBJ(1-) NcD(1-) NcU(1-) NNC(1-) NjP(1-) NjR(1-) OCU(1-) OClW(1-) OrU(1-) PU(1-) PPiU(2-) WU(1-)

EASTERN QUARTERLY. London, 1949-53. 6 v. DR1.E366 DLC(2-) CSt-H(2-) CU(1-) CtHC(3-) IEN(2-) InNU(3) IU(2-) KyU(3-) MH2-) NIC(2-) NN(2-) NhD(2-) NjP(2-) WaU(3-)

ÉCRITS DE PARIS; revue des questions actuelles. no.1- ; cot. 1944- . Paris. AP20.E355 DLC(1946-) CaAEU(1961-) CaQMM(1947-48) CaOOU(1-99) NN(1-21,23-55,57-58) DCU(1-115) RPB([1947]-) CaQMU([1947-1948]-)

EKONOMIKA; ekonomisty žurnalas. Kaunas, Ekonomisty draugija, 1935-40. NN(1-)

English Folk Dance and Song Society, London. Journal. V.1- ; 1932- . London. CLU(1-) CU(1-) DLC(1-) ICN(1-) IU(1-) ICU(1-) MB(1-) MH(1-) MnU(1-) MoU(1-) NN(1-) NNC(1-) NcD(1-) NjP(1-) OCl(1-) OU(1-) VU(1-)

ESPRIT INTERNATIONAL. The International Mind. Paris, 1927-40. 14 v. Quarterly. JC362.A1E8 DLC(1-) AzU(1-) CLU(1-) CSt(1-) CU(1-) CaVaU(1-) CaOLU(1-) CaQMM(1-) CaOOP(1-) CaOTU([1-2]-) CaViP(2-) CtU(1-) CtY(1-) FU(1-) ICN(1-) ICU(1-) IEN(1-) IU(1-) IaU(1-) InU(1-) MB(1-) MH(1-) MdBJ(7-) MiU(1-) MnU(1-) MoS(1-) NIC(1-) NN(1-) NNC(1-) NNU(1-) NSU(1-) NcD(1-) NcU(1-) NjP(1-) NjR(1-) OCU(1-) OCl(1-) OClW(1-) OU(1-) OrU(1-) PPi(1-) PU(1-) TU(1-) TxU(1-) VtU(1-) WU(1-) WaS(1-) WaU(1-)

ETNOGRAFIA POLSKA. T.1- ; 1958- . Wrocław, Zakład Narodowy im. Ossolińskich. GN585.P6E8 DLC(1-) CU(1-) IU(5-) ICU(1-) MB(1-) MiU(3-4) NIC(12-) NSyU(10-) PU(5-) TxHR(4-) WaU(1-)

ETNOGRAFICHESKOE OBOZRENIE. Moskva, Obshchestvo Liubitelei Estestvozaniia, Antropologii i Etnografii, 1889-1916. 28 v. Index for vol.1-21, 1889-1909. GN1.E885 DLC(1-3,16) CU(20-[25]) CtY(1-24) ICF([5-7]-[10-13,15]-28) MH(1-14) MnU(1-[1-[12-19]-[26-28]) NN(1-) PU(1-) PU-MU(7-9,11-28) WaU(21-22)

ÉTUDES SLAVES ET ROUMAINES. Budapest, 1948-49. 2 v. in 1. illus. Published by the Institut de philologie slave and the Institut des langues romanes of the Université de Budapest. Superseded by the Studia Slavica. PG1.E7 CU(1-2) CaBVaU(1-2) CtY(1-2) ICU(1-2) NIC(1-2) NN(1-2) NNC(1-2) OCl(1-2) OClW(1-2) OrU(1-2)

ÉTUDES TRADITIONNELLES. T.1- ; 1896- . Paris. B2.E88 DLC CtY([52]) MH([42],44-) MH-P([44]) PU(53-)

ERGON. T.1- ; 1958- . Warszawa, Państwowe Wydawnictwo Naukowe. DK401.E7 CtY(1-2) MH(6-) ViU(1)

EUROPA-ARCHIV. Ausgabe B. Bd.1- ; 1946- . Frankfurt am Main. Quarterly. D839.E862 DLC(1-) CSt-H(1-) CaBVaU CtY ICU(1-) MH(1-) NN(1-) NNC(1-) NjP(1-) OrU

L'EUROPA ORIENTALE; revista mensile pub. a cura dell' Instituto per l'Europa orientale. Anno 1- ; guigno 1921- . Roma, Libreria di Cultura. DR1.E8 DLC(1-) CSt-H(1) CtY(1-[5]-23) DCU([2-3]) ICU(1-2,4-7,9-17) MH(1-) MnU(1-9) MH-AH([3-4]-8) NN(1-) NNA([8-9]) NNG(1-)

EUROPÄISCHE OSTEN. Jahrg.1- ; 1955- . München; [etc.], Joerg Verlag, illus., ports. Monthly. DR1.E83 DLC(2-) CaAEU(13-) CaOTU(5-) LU(1-) MH(1-) NN(1-) NNC(1-) NNF(4-) PU(3-) TxU WaU

EZHEGODNIK PO GEOLOGII I MINERALOGII ROSSII. Annuaire géologique et minéralogique de la Russie. Warszawa; Novo Alexandria, 1895-1917. 17 v. Vol.11, no.10; v.12, no.9-10; v.13, no.8-10, and v.15, no.8-10 never published. QE1.E9 CU(1-3,no.1-8,10-7-17,no.1-8) CaOOG(1) DGS(1-[11-15]) DLC([1-5]-[7]-10) ICJ(1-[16]) IU([11-15]) MH-Z(1-[7-9]) MdBJ(1-[5-6]-11-13]) NN(2-[16]) NNM(1,[2-4]-[11-15]) PPAN(1-16)

FEDERAL BAR NEWS. v.1- ; June 1940- . Washington, D.C. Federal Bar Association. 10.99.A3F32 NBuU-L DLC([1940-1942,1944-1949]) DBB DS DT PU GEU LU-L MH-L([1944]-[1947]) NcU NbU NbH NNC OU OClW OrU-L PPT TU WaU-L ViU

FENNIA; bulletin de la Société géographique de Finlande. T.1- ; 1889 . Helsingfors. G23.G4 DLC(1-47,49-61,63-64) CaAEU(4-29,31-) CSt(1-40,[46,51, 55,60,62]) CU(17,40-) CaOTU(1-) CtY(30,48,55,[59-60,62,66]) DI-GS(1-)

ICU(6-65) MH(1-) MnU(1-) NN(1-) NNC(44,47-48,50,[55,60],63-64) NjP(1-) WU(1-)

FOLKLIV, Review of Nordic and European Ethnology. Acta etnologica et
folkloristica europea. T.1- ; 1939 . Stockholm, K. Gustav Adolfs Akademi
för Folklivsforskning. GN1.F6 DLC(1-) CLU(1-) CaOTU(1-) ICU(1-) IEN(2-)
ICN(1-) IU(1-) MH(1-) MH-P(1-) NBuG(1-) NN(1-) NNC(1-) OCU(1-) PPAP(1-)

FOLKLORE FELLOWS, Helsingfors. F F Communications. No.1- ; 1911- .
Helsingfors. GR1.F55 DLC(1-) CLU(1-) Cst(1-) CaOG(1-) CaOTU(74,91,118-)
CtY(1-) DCU(1-) ICN(1-) IEN(1-) IU(1-) IaU(1-) InU(1-) LU(1-) MH(1-)
MdBJ(1-) MiU(1-) MnU(1-) NIC(1-) NN(1-) NNC(1-) NMM(1-) NcD(1-) NhD(1-)
OCl(1-) OU(1-) PU(1-) WU(1-124,126-) WaU(1-)

FOLK-LORE; a quarterly review of myth, tradition, institution and custom.
V.1- ; 1890- . London, Folk-lore Society. GR1.F5 DLC(1-) CaAEU(1-80-)
CLU(1-) CU(1-) CtY(1-) ICU(1-) InU(1-) McBJ(1-) MnU(1-) NN(1-) NNC(1-)
NbU(1-) NjP(1-) OCl(1-) PP(1-) TU(1-) WHi(1-)

FOREIGN AFFAIRS; an American quarterly review. V.1- ; 1922- . New York,
N.Y., Council on Foreign Relations. Quarterly. Supersedes Journal of In-
ternational Relations. Index for vol. 1-10, 1922-32. D410.F6 DLC(1-)
CLU(1-) CaAEU(1-49-) CaOKQ(1-) CaOLU(1-) CaQMM(1-) CaOOP(1-) CaOG(1-)
CaOTP(1-) CaOTU(1-) CaBVa(14-) CaBViP(1-) CtY(1-) CSt(1-) ICU(1-) KU(1-)
MH(1-) MiU(1-) NIC(1-) NNC(1-) NjP(1-) OCl(1-) TxU(1-) WaU(1-)

FOREIGN POLICY REPORTS. New York, N.Y., Foreign Policy Association, 1925-
51. 27 v. maps. Frequency varies. D410.F65 DLC([1],3-) CaOLU(2-) CaSSU([
12]-) CLU(1-) CSt-H([1]-) CU([1-2]-) CtY([1]-) CaOTU(8-14 CaBViP(8-)
FU([2-5]-) ICU([2]-) IEN([1]-) IEN-L(1-) IU([1]-) IaU(2-) KU(2-) KyU(2-)
MH([1-2]-) MdBJ([1-2]-) MiU([1]-) MnU(2-) NIC([2]-) NN([1]-) NNC([1]-)
NcD([1-3],6-) NcU(3-) NjP(1-) OCl(1-) OClW([2-4]-) OU([2]-) PPiU([5-11]-)
PU(7-) RPB([1]-[9-10]-) TxU(3-) WU([2]-) WaU[1]-)

FORSCHUNGEN UND FORTSCHRITTE; Korrespondenzblatt der deutschen Wissen-
schaft und Technik. Berlin, 1925-50. 26v. Semimonthly; three numbers a
month. Suspended between Jan/Feb., 1945 and April 1947. Q3.F6 DLC(1-[26])
CLSU(3-) CSt(1-) CU([3]-[14]-) CaBVaU([2]-[15]) CaQMM(2-) CaOTU([2-15])
CtY([3,6]-) DCU(4-) ICJ([1]-) ICU(1-) IEN([2]-) IU(1-) IaU(6-) InU(1-)
KU(2-) MCM(3-) MH(1-) MiU([1-3]-) MnU(1-) NN(1-) NNC(1-) OCU(5-)
OCl([3]-[6]) OClW(1-) TxU(3-) UPB(3-) WM(1-) WU(7-)

FORSCHUNGEN ZUR DEUTSCHEN LANDESKUNDE. Im Auftrage der Zentralkommission
für wissenschaftliche Landeskunde von Deutschland. Bd.1- ; 1885- . Leipzig; Stuttgart, S. Hirzel; J. Engelhorn; [etc.], 1886- . Title varies:
1886-1939, Forschungen zur deutschen Landes- und Volkskunde. G58.F73 DLC(1-)
CLU([19-25]) CtY([1-2]-[4]-[21]) CaAEU(60,73,131; cat. as monographs) ICU(1,
[2-10]-) IEN(1-10) MB(1-) MH(1-) MiU([1-8]-) MoU(1-23) NIC([2,7,12-22])
NN([2,13,17-22,26]) NNA(1-) NNC(1-) NjP(1-) OCl(3,[9,16]) PPAN(1-28)

FORTSCHRITTE DER GEOLOGIE UND PALÄNTOLOGIE. Nr.1-48. Berlin, 1923-43.
14 v. QE1.F6 DLC(1-) CLU(4,13-14,21-23,27,38) CPT(1-) ICU(1-39,42-) CU(1-38)
IaU(1-) MdBJ(1-) NIC(1-) NN(1-) NNC(1-39,42-) NNM(1-) NjP(1-) OU(1-) PPAN(1-)

GENERAL LINGUISTICS. V.1- ; 1955- . Lexington, Ky. P1.A1G32 CaAEU(1-
10-) CaQMM(1-) CLU(1-) CU(1-) CoU(1-) CtY(1-) DLC([2]-) GU(5-) ICU(1-)
IU(1-) InU(1-) IaU(1-) KU(1-) KyU(1-) LU(1-) MnU(1-) MdBJ(1-) MH(1-) MoU(1-)
NIC(1-) NNC(1-) NN(1-) NjP(1-) OU(1-) OClW(1-3) PPiU([4],6-) PU(1-) TxU(1-)
ViU(1-) WU(1-)

GEOGRAFICHESKOE OBSHCHESTVO SSSR. Izvestiia. T.1- ; 1865- . Leningrad;
Petrograd; Sanktpetersburg. illus., plates, ports., maps, diagr. Frequency
varies. Title varies: Izviestiia. Issued by the society under its earlier
names: Imp. Russkoe geograficheskoe obschestvo, 1865-1924; Gosudarstvennoe
russkoe geograficheskoe obshchestvo, 1925-1930; Gosudarstvennoe geograficheskoe obshchestvo, 1931-1939 and under its alternate name: Vsesoiuznoe
geograficheskoe obshchestvo, 1940- . Summaries in English or French.
G23.G16 DLC(1-[7-8]-[18]-) CSt-H([7,18],33-35,40,[41]44,49,53,[54]-) CU(1-
[9]-[17],19-) CaOTR([2-29]-[48-61]) ICF([40-42],46,50-[52],55-57,61-66,
68-) ICU(28,41,[42,44-45]) MBA(8-10.[14-18]-27,29-[44]-48-50-[53-54]-)
MH([1-11]-[28]-[40-41]-[44]-[54]-[62],63,66-[69]) MH-Z([13-18]-20,22-[44-45-
65]-) NN(12-15,17-[49-50]-[54]-) NNA(1-) NNC([1,14,18-19]-[24-27]-[33-35]-

42-65],66) PPAN(11-)

GEOGRAFICHESKOE OBSHCHESTVO. Severo-Zapadnyi otdel. Zapiski. Sankt-peterburg, 1911-13. 4 v. CSt(1-4) CU(1-3) MH(1-2,4) NN(1-4) PU(1-4)

GEOGRAFINIS METRAŠTIS. 1- ; 1958- . Vilnius. Added title page in English; The Geographical Year-Book. Issued by Geologijos ir geografijos institutas of the Lietuvos TSR Mokslų akademija, and Lietuvos TSR Geografinė draugija. In Lithuanian with summaries in Russian and English. Gl.G3135 DLC(1-) CU(1-) CtY(1-) CtPAM(1-) DI-GS InU(1-) MH(1-) NN(1-) NNC NNM(1-) PU(1-) PPAN(1-) WyU(6-)

GEOGRAPHISCHE ZEITSCHRIFT. Leipzig; Wiesbaden, 1895-1944. 50 v. Suspended, 1945-1962. Index: vol.1-10, 1895-1904; vol.11-20, 1905-1914; vol. 21-30, 1915-1924. Gl.G37 DLC(1-) CLU(1-) CU(1-) CtY(1-[22-23]-) DGS(1-) ICU(1-) IEN(1-19) InU[1-24]-) MB(1-[20-23],25-) MH(1-) MiU(1-) MnU(1-21,24-) NN(1-22,24-) NNA(1-) NjP(1-) OCl(1-) WU([16]-20,36-)

GEOLOGISCHES ARCHIV. Zeitschrift für die gesamte Geologie und deren Nachbargebiete. Königsberg in Pr., 1923-27. 4 v. Monthly. CU ICJ([3],4) MdBJ(1-3) NNM(1-3) NjP OU PPAN

GEOLOGISCHES JAHRBUCH. Bd.1- ; 1880- . Hannover; [etc.] Title varies: 1880-1905, Jahrbuch der Königlich preussischen Landesanstalt und Bergakademie zu Berlin; 1906-1939, Jahrbuch der Preussischen geologischen Landesanstalt zu Berlin; 1939- , as Jahrbuch des Reichsamts für Bodenforschung. Indexes: vol.1-20,1880-1899; vol.21-31,1900-1909. QE269.A19P3 DLC(1-49,51-57) CaBVaU CU(1-57) CaOG(10-) CtY(1-[32],34-[36]-) DI-GS GU ICJ(1-53) ICU(1-26,28-) IaU(1-43,52-) KU(12-[31-34]-57) LU MH-Z(1-[36]) MdBJ([1-50]) MiU(1-[35],50,52,56-57) NN(1-26,28-34,37-) NNA(7-) NNC NNM(1-) OClW(10-57) OU(1-) PPAN(1-) PSt

GEOLOGISKA FÖRENINGEN, STOCKHOLM. FÖRHANDLINGAR. Bd.1- ; 1872- Stockholm. illus., plates, port., maps, plans, tables, diagr. Seven nos. a year, 1872-1920. Quarterly since 1921. QE1.G497 DLC CaBVaU DI-GS CU-Riv FU GU IaAS IU ICJ MiU MBdAF NcU NN NjP PPAN PBm PPWa OU RPB TU TxDaM

Gesellschaft der Wissenschaften in Göttingen. Nachrichten see Akademie der Wissenschaften, Göttingen. Philologisch-historische Klasse. Nachrichten.

GESELLSCHAFT FÜR GESCHICHTE UND ALTERTUMSKUNDE ZU RIGA. Mitteilungen aus der livländischen Geschichte. Riga, 1836-1937. 25 v. irregular. Title varies: vol.1-20, 1836-1910 as its Mitteilungen aus dem Gebiete Liv-, Ehst-, und Kurlands. Superseded by its Mitteilungen aus der baltischen Geschichte. Neue Folge. DK511.B25M63 DLC(1-[20-21]25) CLU([9],17,23) CSt(24) CSt-H([21]) CU DSI-E([13]-[18-25]) ICU(1-23) MH MnU(1-2,4-25) NN(1-[21-24],25) PU(17-20)

Gesellschaft für Geschichte und Altertumskunde zu Riga. Mitteilungen aus der livländischen Geschichte see also Mitteilungen aus der baltischen Geschichte.

GESELLSCHAFT FÜR GESCHICHTE UND ALTERTUMSKUNDE, RIGA. Sitzungsberichte. Riga, 1874- . illus., plates, port. Name varies: Gesellschaft für Geschichte und Altertumskunde der russischen Ostsee-Provinzen. Suspended 1915-1929. DLC(1873-1914), 1930-1934) CLU(1873-1907,[1911]-1912, 1914) CSt(1873, 1875,1877-[1889]-1890,1893) CU(1873-1914, 1930 31-) CtY(1873-) MH(1873 74-1914, 1930 31-) MnU(1873-[1914]) NN(1873-[1914]) PU(1896-1912)

GIMTASAI KRAŠTAS; kraštotyros organas. Šiauliai, Kraštotyros draugija; Lietuvos Mokslų akademija, 1934-44. illus. irregular; quarterly. 572.9475 G427 PU(1934-37, nos.1-17) OKentU(1934, no.3-4; 1935, no.5-6)

GIMTOJI KALBA. Kaunas, 1933-41. 9 v. Ten nos. a year. PG8509.G54 PU(1-9, no.1-3) ICCC(1933-1938,1939,no.1-5,7-10; 1940,no.2,3,5)

GIMTOJI KALBA; bendrinės kalbos laikraštis. Lietuvių Kalbos Draugijos organas. Nr.1-11; liepa/rugsėjis 1958-1968. Riverside, Ill., JAV LB Kultūros Fondas. Quarterly. 491.92 G427 PU(1958-1966,no.1-33) DLC(1958-1968, no. 1-2) CLU(1965-) NNC(1959-) OKentU(1958,no.2; 1959,no.1-4; 1960, no.1-4; 1961-1965)

GLOBUS. Hildburghausen; Brunswick, 1861-1910. 94 v. Gl.G57 DLC(1-)
CU(1-) CaOG(1-96) CaOTU(1-12) ICU(1-) IU(1-) MH(1-) MnU(1-) NIC(1-) NN(1-5,
7-98) NNC(1-98) NhD(1-98) NjP(1-98) OClW(1-98)

Gosudarstvennoe geograficheskoe obshchestvo see Geograficheskoe obshchestvo SSSR.

Gosudarstvennoe russkoe geograficheskoe obshchestvo see Geograficheskoe
obshchestvo SSSR.

DAS GRÖSSERE DEUTSCHLAND; Wochenschrift für deutsche Welt- und Kolonial
politik. Weimar; Dresden, 1914-18. 5 v. Weekly. NJ3934.A3 DLC([1]-5)
CSt-H(1-[5]) CtY([1-2,4]) ICN([1]-5) ICU([1-2]) IEN([1-2]) MB(v.1,no.24,26,
28,35) MH(1-[4]) NN(1,[2-4]) NjP(1-3) OU(1) TxU([4])

HEBREW UNION COLLEGE. Annual. v.1- ; 1924- . Cincinnati, Ohio. illus.,
plates, ports, facsims. Annual. Supersedes Journal of Jewish lore and
philosophy. BM11.H4 DLC(15-11) CU(1-) CaOTU(1-) CoDU([2-13]) CtHT(11-)
CtY(1-) ICP(1-4,6-7,10) ICU(1-) IU(2-) MWelC(1-) MdBJ(1-9,11) NN(1-) NNC(2-)
NNG(1-9) NIC(1-9) NNJ(1-) NRCR(1-) NcD(1-) NjPT(1-) OCH(1-) OCU(5-) OCX(2-)
OO(1-) OrU(1-) PCC(1-) VRT(1-)

HAROLD POLSKI; czasopismo naukowe illustrowane... poświęcone heraldyce
polskiej. Kraków, Wydawn. S.z. Ruszczy Rusieckiego na Trojance. CR613.P7 H43
DLC

HIGHLIGHTS OF CURRENT LEGISLATION AND ACTIVITIES IN MID-EUROPE. V.1- ;
June 1953- . Washington D.C. Monthly. Z663.55.H5 DLC([1-8]) AU(1-) CU(2-)
FU([2]-) IU(1-) IaU(3-) MH-L(1-) MH-PA(1-) MiU-L(2-) NIC(2-) NjP(5-) NN([2]-)
NNC-L(2-) OU(2-) PU(5-) TxU(3-) WaU([2-3])

I LAISVE; lietuvių Fronto bičiulių politikos žurnalas. 1- ; 1941- .
Kaunas; Los Angeles, Calif.; [etc.], Lietuvių Frontas; Friends of the Lithu-
anian Front. June 25,1941-December 31,1942 daily newspaper. Suspended by
German occupational authorities; 1943-1944 published in Marijampolė, Utena,
Telšiai, etc. as underground irregular newspaper, total 34 nos.; 1948 in
Germany published 3 nos. since Dec. 1953 published in United States.
320.5 I12 PU(nr.1-56, 1953-1972) DLC(20-) ICLJF(6-33,1955-1963) CaOONL(47-48,
[84-85], 1969-1970 OKentU(no.1-13,15-23,27-30,35,1953-1962; **1964-1972**)

IAZYK I LITERATURA. Leningrad, Nauchno-issledovatel'skii institut re-
chevoi kul'tury, 1926-32. 8 v. Unclassified (Yudin P105,S319) DLC KU NN NNC

Imperatorskoe Moskovskoe arkheologicheskoe obshchestvo. Trudy...arkheolo-
gicheskago s"ezda see Akheologicheskii s"ezd. Trudy.

Imperatorskoe russkoe geograficheskoe obshchestvo see Geograficheskoe
obshchestvo SSSR.

INDOGERMANISCHE FORSCHUNGEN; Zeitschrift für indogermanische Sprach und
Altertumskunde. Bd.1- ; 1891- . Strassbourg, Berlin, K.J. Trübner; [etc.]
illus., plates. Suspended between June 1944 and May 1948. P501.I4 DLC(1-)
CLU(1-37) CSt(1-) CU(1-) CaOG(1-) CaOTU(1-) CtY(1-) DCU(1-) ICN(1-) IEN(1-)
IU(1-) IaU(1-) InU(1-) KU(1-) MB(1-) MH(1-) MdBJ(1-) MiU(1-) MnU(1-)
NIC(1-) NN(1-) NNC(1-) NbU(1-) NcD(1-) NcU(1-) NhD(1-) NjP(1-) OCU(1-) OCl(1-
36,44-45) OClW(1-10,33-37,40-) OU(1-) PBM(1-) PU(1-) TNV(1-) TxU(1-) WaU(1-)

DAS INLAND; eine Wochenschrift für Liv-, Esth- und Curland's Geschichte,
Geographie, Statistik und Litteratur. Dorpat, 1836-63. 28 v. NN(no.1-15,
17-28, 1836-1863) BM

INTERNATIONAL FOLK MUSIC COUNCIL. Journal. V.1- ; March 1949- . Cambridge, Eng. ML26.I544 DLC([1]-) ClSU(1-) CLU(1-) CU(1-) ICN(1-) ICU(1-)
IEN(1-) MH(1-) MiU(1-) MnU(1-) NIC(1-) NN(1-) NNC(1-) RPB(1-) TxU(1-) WaS(1-)

INTERNATIONAL GEODETIC AND GEOPHYSICAL UNION; Association of Geodesy.
Bulletin géodésique, organe de la section de géodesie de l'Union géodésique
et géophysique internationale. V.1- ; 1924-41-42; New Series. V.1- ;
July 1946- . Toulouse. QB294.I53 DLC(1-44,53-) CSt(1-) CU(1-2,4-) CaBVaU
(7-17,24-25,27-42) CaQMM(2,7,9,18-) CaOG(1-7,9,12-16) CaOTU(5-) CtY(1-)

DGL(4-) DGS([1-28]-42,51-) ICU(1-) MdBJ(7-17,24-30,54-56) NN(1-) NNA(1-)
NjP(57-) OCU(1-)

INTERNATIONAL JOURNAL OF SLAVIC LINGUISTICS AND POETICS. v.1- ; 1959- .
The Hague, Mouton & Co. Irregular. PG1.I5 DLC(1-) CSLU(1-) CU(1-) CLU(1-)
CSt(1-) CaOTU(1-) CtY(1-) ICU(1-) IEN(3-) IU(1-) IaU(1-) KyU(1-) LU(1-)
MH(1-) MdBJ(1-) MiU(1-) NIC(1-) NN(1-) NNC(1-) NNF(1-) NNU(1-) NcD(1-)
NjP(1-) OU(1-) PU(1-) RPB(1-) WU(1-) WaU(1-)

INTERNATIONAL LABOUR OFFICE. Industrial and Labour Information. Geneva,
1922-40. 74 v. HD4811.I62 DLC(1-) CLSU([1]-) CLU(9-) CSt-H(1-) CU(1,[2]-)
CaBVaU(25-[45]) CaQMM(17-20,29-) CaOTU(1,3,23-) CaBViP([2]-) Cty(1-) IU(1-)
IaAS(5-74) IaU(1-) InU(1-16,18-74) KU(25-) KyU(29-) LU(1-) MA(25-) MB(33-)
MH MH-BA([1-19]-74) MiU(1-) MiU-L(1-) MnU(1-) NN(1-) NNC(1-) NNU(1-) NjP(1-)
OCU(1-) OCL OC1W([1-15],22-48,50-[57]-) OU(1-16,[18]-[21]-) PSC(1-) PU(5-)
TxU(1-64,65-71) WU(1-16,18-) WaS(1-) WaU(1,[2]-)

INTERNATIONAL PEASANT UNION. Bulletin. V.1- ; 1950- . Washington, D.C.
HD103.I752 DLC(1-) CLU(1-) CU(1-) CtY(1-) CSt-H(1-) MH(1-) MH-PA(1-) NN(1-)
MdBJ(1-) NcD(1-) OC1(1-) OCU(1-) AzU(1-) DA(1-)

INTERNATIONALES RECHT UND DIPLOMATIE. Bd.1- ; 1956- . Hamburg. Articles in German, French, English and Russian. JX5.I6 ICU-L(1-15-) CLL(1-)
DCU(11-) DLC(1-) IU(1-) MH-L(1-) MiU(1-) NN(1-) NNC-L(1-) NjP(1-)

INTERNATIONAL REVIEW OF HISTORY AND POLITICAL SCIENCE. V.1- ; June 1964-
. Meerut, India, Review Publications. Semiannual. D839.I54 DLC(1-)
CaOWA(1-) CLU(4-) CSt(1-) CtY(1-) GEU(1-) InNd(1-) ICU([1]-) InU(1-) MiU(1-)
MH([1]-) MnU(1-) MoU([1]-) NIC(1-) NhD(1-) NjP(1-) PU(1-) UU(1-) ViU(1-)
WU(1-) WaU(1-)

INTERNATIONAL REVIEW OF AGRICULTURE. Revue internationale d'agriculture.
New Series. Rome, 1931-46. 37 v. AzU CLU CU CaAEU CaOOAg CtY DLC MH NN
NNC NjP OC1 PU TxU WU WaU

Iš lietuvių klutūros istorijos see Lietuvos TSR Mokslų Akademija, Vilna.
Istorijos institutas. Iš lietuvių kultūros istorijos.

ISTORICHESKII VIESTNIK; istoriko-literaturnyĭ zhurnal. g. 1-38. Petrograd; Sanktpeterburg, Tip. A.S. Suvorina, 1880-1917. 150 v. in 152. illus.,
ports. Monthly. AP50.I9 DLC CLU(1-[142-143]) CSt-H CU(1-148) CtY(1-126,
130, 135-138) MH NIC(1-3) NN NNC(1-3,7-[14]-[39]-[62]-150)

ISTORICHESKIE ZAPISKI. T.1- ; 1937- . Moskva, Akademiia nauk SSSR.
Institu istorii. irregular. DK1.I8 DLC(1-) CU(1-) CtY(1-7,10) CaAEU(15,18,
20-22,26,29,34,37-40,42-45,47-51,54-69,72-79)

ISTORICHESKIĬ ZHURNAL. Moskva, Pravda; [etc.] 1931-45. 15 v. in 30.
illus., ports., maps. Monthly. Superseded by Voprosy istorii. D1.I75
DLC(1-) CSt-H([1]-4,7-) CU[1]-) MH(1-) MnU(9-10) NN(1-) NNC(113,115,116)

ISTORIIA SSSR. T.1- ; mart/apr. 1957- . Moskva, Izd-vo Akademii nauk
SSSR. DK1.A3275 DLC(1957-) AzU(1959-) CU(1957-) CSt-H(1957-) CtY([1958]-)
ICU([1958]-) IaU(1957-) IU(1959-) MdBJ(1957-) MH(1957-) NIC(1959-) NjP(1958-)
NjR(1959-) NN(1957-) PSt(1959-) RPB(1957-) WaU(1960-)

JABLONOWSKI, HORST, ed. Forschungen zur osteuropäischen Geschichte. Bd.
1- ; 1954- . Berlin, Osteuropa Institut. In Kommission bei O. Harrassowitz, Wiesbaden. (Osteuropa-Institut an der Freien Universität Berlin.
Historische Veröffentlichungen) DR1.J12 DLC(1-) CLU(1,3-) CU(1-) DDO(1-)
ICU(1-) IEN(1-) MH(1-) MH(1-) MiU(1-) MiDW(1-) NIC(1-) NjP(1-) WU(1-)

JABRBUCH DER ALBERTUS UNIVERSITÄT ZU KÖNIGSBERG IN PR. Bd.1- ; 1951- .
Freiburg in Br., Dickreiter Verlagsgesellschaft. (Der Göttinger Arbeits-
kreis. Veröffentlichungen) LF2901.C53 DLC(1952-) CLU(1-) CU(1-) CSt(1951-)
CaAEU(2-10) CtY(1954/55-) ICU(2-) IU(1-) MoU(1-) NIC(2-) NNC(1-) NN(1-)
NCU(1-) NcD(2-)

Jahrbuch der Königlich preussischen Landesanstalt und Bergakademie zu
Berlin see Geologisches Jahrbuch.

Jahrbuch der Preussischen geologischen Landesanstalt zu Berlin see
Geologisches Jahrbuch.

JAHRBUCH DES ÖFFENTLICHEN RECHTES DER GEGENWART. Bd.1- ; 1907- . Tü-
bingen, J.C.B. Mohr (P. Siebeck). JF13.031 DLC(1-) CLU(1-) CSt-H(2,9)
CtY-L(1-) ICJ(1-20) ICU(1-) IEN(1-10) IEN-L(1-) MH(1-22) MH-L(1-) MdBJ(1-)
MiU(1-) MiU-L(1-) NN(1-) NNC(1-) NcD(1-18) NjP(1-) OClW(1-) OU(1-) OrU(1-19)
TxU(9-) WU(1-)

Jahrbuch des Reichsamts für Bodenforschung see Geologisches Jahrbuch.

JAHRBUCH FÜR INTERNATIONALES RECHT. Bd.1- ; 1948- . Hamburg; Kiel;
Göttingen. JX21.J33 DLC CaAEU(3,4,12) CtY-L InNU MH-L MMet-F MiU-L NNC-L
NjP PU-L RPB WaU

JAHRBUCH FÜR VOLKSLIEDFORSCHUNG. Berlin; Leipzig, Deutsches Volkslied-
archiv, 1928-44. 7 v. ML3630.J2 DLC(1-) CLU(1-) CU(1-) CaOTU(1-) CtY(1-)
FU(6-) ICN(1-) ICU(1-) IU(1-) NN(1-) NNC(1-) NRU(1-) NjP(1-4) IaU(1-) InU(1-)
MB(1-) MH(1-) MiU(1-) MnU(1-6) OCl(1-) OU(1-) WU(1-)

JAHRBÜCHER FÜR GESCHICHTE OSTEUROPAS. Bd.1-6; 1936-41; Neue Folge. Bd.1-
; 1953- . Breslau. Supersedes Jahrbücher für Kultur und Geschichte der
Slaven. D1.J3 DLC(1-) CaAEU(ns14-) CSt(1-) CtY(1-) CU(1-) MH(1-) MiU(1-)
NN(1-) NNC(1-) NIC(ns1-)

JAHRBÜCHER FÜR KULTUR UND GESCHICHTE DER SLAVEN. Bd. 1, Hft.1; 1924; Neue
Folge. Bd.1-11; 1925-1935. Breslau; Priebatsch. CB231.A3 DLC CST(ns1-11)
CU CtY(-ns2-7) ICJ(ns1-2) ICU(ns1-11) MH MdBJ(1-ns7) MiU(1-ns1,3-11) NN
NNC OCl(1-ns11)

JOMSBURG; Völker und Staaten im Osten und Norden Europas. Leipzig. S.
Hirzel, 1937-42. 6 v. illus., plates, maps. Quarterly. D1.J53 DLC(2-)
CtY(1-) ICU(1-) MH(1-) NNC(1-) NcD(1-) NjP(1-)

JOURNAL OF CENTRAL EUROPEAN AFFAIRS. V.1- ; Apr. 1941- . Boulder, Col.
Quarterly. D1.J57 DLC(1-) CLU(1-) CSt-H(1-) CU(1-) CaAEU(1-) CaBVaU(1-)
CtY(1-) ICU(1-) MoU(1-) MH(1-) NIC(1-) NN(1-) NNC(1-) NjP(1-) OCl(1-) PU(1-)
TxU(1-) WaU(1-)

JUS PONTIFICUM; seu, Ephemerides Romanae ad canonicas disciplinas spec-
tantes. Annus 1-20; Oct. Dec. 1921-1940. Romae, 1921-40. 20 v. in 7.
illus., ports, maps, facsims. Quarterly. Q947.53 PU(1-) MoS(1-) CaOOU(1-)
CtY-L(1-) DCU(1-) DD(1-) DLC(1-) IMS(1-) KAS(1-) MH(1-) MH-L(1-) NNC(1-)
NNUT(1-) NStC(1-)

KALBA; bendrinès kalbos žurnalas. Kaunas, Sakalo bendrovè, 1930. 3 nos.
in 1 v. (208 p.) 491.92 K127 PU(1,no.1-3) ICCC(1, no.1-3)

KARYS; pasaulio lietuvių karių-veteranų mènesinis žurnalas. [The Warrior]
Metai 1- ; 1950- . Brooklyn, N.Y. 10 nos. a year. CtPAM(1952, 1954,
1956-1961, 1963-1964) DLC(1951-1953) NN(1950-) OKentU(1950-1952;[1953],1967)

KARO ARCHYVAS. Kaunas, Krašto apsaugos ministerija, Karo mokslo skyrius,
1925-39. 11 v. D552.L5A5 DLC(1,2,11) ICCC(7) PU(2-4,6-8)

Kaunas. Antano Smetonos lituanistikos institutas. Lietuvos istorijos
skyrius. Lietuvos praeitis see Lietuvos praeitis.

KAUNAS. LIETUVOS ŽEMÈS ŪKIO AKADEMIJA. Žemès ūkio akademijos metraštis.
Kaunas, 1926-40. 13 v. illus., plates, plans, tables, diagrs. S13.D6
DLC(1924/26-1927, 1929/30-1933, 1935-1937) CU(1924/26-) CaOTU(1924-1927,
1929/30) DA(1924/25-[1938]-) ICU(1924/25-1927, 1929-1931, IU(1933, 1935-)
MH(1924/26, 1929/30, 1931) MdBJ(1924/26) MiU(1924/26) NIC-A(1924/26-)
NN(1924/26, 1929/30) NjP(1924/26-1927) PU(1924/26, 1929/30, 1935) TxU(1927,
1929/30, 1931, 1933, 1935-)

KAUNAS. POLITECHNIKOS INSTITUTAS. Darbai. Trudy. T.1- ; 1949- . Kaunas.
diagrs. Vol.1, 1949 published as Kaunas. Universitetas. Techniniai fakultetai. Darbai and continued vol.2, 1953. TA7.K3 DLC(9-) MCM(3-)

KAUNAS. UNIVERSITETAS. BOTANIKOS SODAS. Raštai. Kaunas, 1931-39. 6 v.

DNAL(1-3,5-) MH(1-3) MH-G(5,7,9) PU(1-2)

KAUNAS. UNIVERSITETAS. HUMANITARINIŲ MOKSLŲ FAKULTETAS. Darbai ir dienos. Acta et commentationes ordinis philologorum. Kaunas, 1930-40. 9 v.
illus. PN9.D22 CaAEU(1,3,6,7) BM DSI CU(1-) ICCC(1-) ICU(1-5) MH(2-)
MoU(1-) NN(1-4) PU(1-6)

KAUNAS. UNIVERSITETAS. MATEMATIKOS-GAMTOS FAKULTETAS. Darbai... Mémoires de la Faculté des sciences de L'Université de Vytautas le Grand.
Kaunas, 1923-39. 13 v. illus., plates, maps, facsims, tables, diagrams.
Text in Lithuanian, German, or English. Summaries in German for Lithuanian
articles. Q60.K14 DLC(1-) CU(1-6) CtY(3-) DNAL(1-) DGS(5-7,9,13) DSI(6,no.
2-3;7-9;10,no.2;11; 12, no.1) ICU(3-11) MH-G(5,7,9) NIC-A(1-) NN(1-5)
NbU(2-) NNC(1-3) NBG(1,3-) NNM(3,5-) NjP(1923,1929) RPB(2;6,no.2-3;7-9;10,
no.1;11;13)

KAUNAS. UNIVERSITETAS. TEISIŲ FAKULTETAS. Darbai. Ouvrages de la Faculté de droit de l'Université de Lithuanie. Kaunas, Valstybės spaustuvė,
1924-39. 10 v. (*QYA) NN(1-3,4,no.2-6,no.12,14) CaAEU(T.2,no.4; T.8, no.2)
MH(T.5,kn.5; T.6,kn.1,3-4,6,8-12,14-15) MoU(5-6)

KIEV. UNIVERSYTET. Universitetskiia izviestiia. T.1-59, pt.4; 1861-
1919; novaia seriia. T.1-2; 1935-1936. Kiev, 1861-1936. DNAL(ns1-2)
DLC(11-58) DSG(24-32,37-54) ICU(1-52) MH(7,[9,13,19,31],36,43-59) MiU(11-
[13]) NN([1,3-6]-[8-12]-15,17,20-[23]-[52]-[54]-59) NNC(1-[3]-[5-6]-15,17,
20-22,24,[25]-[28]-36,38-59)

KIEVSKAIA STARINA. G.1-25(t.1-94); ianv. 1882-noiab./dek. 1906. Kiev,
1882-1906. 94 v. illus., plates, ports., maps, plans. Monthly. DK508.A2K5
DLC(1-) CaAEU(1-94; microfiche) CU(29-31,36-47) CSt-H(5-7,11-13,17-23, 28-
35,40-47,56-79,84-94) NN(1-19,24-27,32-35,40-[70-71]-94)

Königliche Gesellschaft der Wissenschaften zu Göttingen. Philologisch-
historische Klasse. Nachrichten see Akademie der Wissenschaften,
Göttingen. Philologisch-historische Klasse. Nachrichten.

KOMUNISTAS; Lietuvos komunistų partijos žurnalas. T.1- ; 1946- . Vilnius, Lietuvos KPCK laikraščių ir žurnalų leidykla. illus., ports. Monthly.
HX8.K588 DLC(38-) OKentU(1963, no.10,12; 1972)

KNYGŲ LENTYNA. Memmingen, Ger.; Danville, Ill., 1948-66. 19 v. Irregular.
Z2537.K76 DLC CaOTU ICCC(1951-1955) ICLJF(no.4-17) ICU MH(4,no.7-12;5-7)
NN(1,no.2,5-3,no.1,3-6,11,12-7,no.9-10;8-9,no.4-8;10;12,no.7-8;13,no.1-2;
14,no.2,4-15,no.4; 16,no.2; 17-19,no.1) NNC(4-10,no.1-9; 11-18) OKentU(4,
no.1-12; 6,no.1-12; 7,no.1-4,7-12; 9,no.4-12; 10,no.7-12; 11-13; 14,no.1,
3,5; 15-16) PU(4-18,19,no.1)

KOSMOS; gamtos ir šalinių mokslų iliustruotas žurnalas. Kaunas, 1920-40.
Monthly. ICBM(1.no.2-3(1920-1921); 3-4,no.2(1922-1923) ICCC(1920-1925,no.
1-2,4-6; 1926-1927,no.1-3,6-12; 1928,no.1; 1929-1931; 1938,no.1-3)

KOSMOS; czasopismo Polskiego Towarzystwa Przyrodników im. Kopernika. Lwów,
1876-1927. 52 v. Annual; quarterly(irregular) Q4.K7 DLC(1-) CU(1-) NN(34-
50) NNM(2-6,8,10-24,27,29,34,36-52) NjP(2-52)

KRASNYI ARKHIV; istoricheskii zhurnal. Moskva, Gospolitizdat, 1922-41.
106 v. in 35. ports., maps, facsims. Frequency varies. DK1.K7 DLC(1-)
CLSU(3-91) CLU(3-31,[33-47]-) CSt-H(1-) CU(1-) CtY(1-) ICU(1-) IU(2-) MH(1-)
MH-L(1-) MdBJ(2-) NIC(4-22,81-96,98-104) NN(1-) NNC(1-) NjP(1-48,50,51-67)
OCl(2-[10]-[34]-) PU(2-) TxU(1-79) WaU(2-20,22-23,25,28-30,47-48,65-)

KRYTYKA; miesięcznik poświęcony sprawom społecznym, nauce i sztuce.
Kraków, 1899-1914. 16 v. illus., plates. Semimonthly. Beginning with Jan.
1909, in two sections: Dział polityczno-społeczny; Dział artystyczno-liter-
acki. AP54.K8 DLC(5-[11]-16) NN([7]-[16])

KULTŪRA; mėnesinis iliustruotas, mokslo, visuomenės, literatūros žurnalas.
Šiauliai, Kultūros bendrovė, 1923-41. Monthly. 57.92 K954 PU(1925-1926;
1928-1929; 1932,no.6-12; 1933,no.1-8; 1934,no.1-3,8-10,12) ICBM(1939,no.5)
OKentU(1930)

DAS KUNSTWERK; eine Zeitschrift über alle Gebiete der bildenden Kunst.
Bd.1- ; 19- . Baden-Baden, W. Klein. illus. Monthly. N3.K95 DLC([1-
2]-) CLU(4-) CU(3-) CtY([1]-) ICU(1-) IEN(1-) MnU([1]-) MH(1-) NN(1-)
NNC(1-) TxU(3-) WU(1-)

KURYBA; literatūros žurnalas. Kaunas, 1943-44. 5 nos. 57.92 K968
PU(1943,no.1; 1944,no.1-4)

KWARTALNIK HISTORII KULTURY MATERIALNEJ. T.1- ; 1953- . Warszawa.
Polska Akademia Nauk. Instytut Historii Kultury Materialnej. Summaries in
English and Russian. DK401.K9 DLC(2-) CU(4-) ICU(5-) MiDW(3-) MH(2-) MiU(2-)
NN(2-) NNC(4-)

KWARTALNIK HISTORYCZNY. T.1- ; 1887 . Lwów, Polskie Towarzystwo Histo-
ryczne. Quarterly. D1.K85 DLC(10-12,16-32,34-) CU(1-41) CaAEU(66-) CtY(1-)
IUC(65-) KU(66-) MH(1-) MdBJ([8-12,19-26]-33,46-52) MnU(1-) NIC(62-) NN(1-)
OCl(51-) PU(65-)

KWARTALNIK LITEWSKI. Edited by Jan Obst. Sanktpeterburg, 1910. 4 nos.
(160 p.) Quarterly. 947.P K979 PU ICLJF(1,no.1-2)

LAIŠKAI LIETUVIAMS. Metai 1- ; 1950- . Chicago, Ill., Lithuanian
Jesuit fathers. 11 nos. a year. CaOONL(1967-1969) CtPAM(1950-1970-)
CtTMF(1950-1970-) ICLJF(1950-) OKentU(1950-1952,1954-1964,1966-1969) DLC(5-)

LATVIA. IZGLĪTIBAS MINISTRIJA. Izglītibas ministrijas mēnešraksts. T.1-
; 1920- . Riga. Monthly. L466.L3A3 DLC

LATVIEŠU LITERARISKA BIEDRĪBA, RIGA. Magazin.   Riga, 1828-1936. 21 v.
Suspended 1914-1935. German name: Lettisch-Litterärische Gesellschaft,
Riga. Magazin. PG8803.L5 DLC([16],17[19-20]) ICN NIC(6,[9-11]) NN([3,7,14],
21) PU([5,14-17])

LEKSIKOGRAFICHESKII SBORNIK. Vyp.1- ; 1957- . Moskva, Gos. izd-vo
inostrannykh i natsional'nykh slovarei. Issued by Institut iazykoznaniia of
the Akademiia nauk SSSR. P327.L4 DLC(1-) CaAEU(4-) CaOTU(1-) CU(1-) CoU(3-)
CtY(1-) DS(1-) IU(1-) IaU(1-) IEN(1-) InU(1-4) LU(1-5) MH(1-) MiU(1-) NN(1-)
NIC(1-) NNC(1-2) PSt(2-) PU(1-) ViU(1-3)

Lettisch-Litterärische Gesellschaft, Riga. Magazin see Latviešu literariska biedrība, Riga. Magazin.

THE LIBRARY CHRONICLE. V.1- ; 1933- . Philadelphia, Pa., Friends of
the Library, University of Pennsylvania. Z733.P418 DLC(1-) CU(1-) CaOTU(1-)
CtU(1-) ICN(1-) ICU(1-) IEN(1-) IU(1-) IaU(1-) MB(1-) MiU(1-) MnU(1-)
NN(1-) NNC(1-) NjP(1-) PU(1-)

LIETUVA; politikos žurnalas. New York,N.Y., 1952-56. 8 nos. in 2 v.
ports. Frequency varies. Nos. 1-4 called also v.1-2. Summaries in English.
No.1 published by the Lithuanian Consultative Panel; nos.2-8 by the Committee
for a Free Lithuania. Published in cooperation with the Research and Publication Service, National Committee for a Free Europe. DK511.L2A24 DLC(1-8)
NN(1-8) MH(1-8) OKentU(1-8) PU(1-8) ICLJF

LIETUVIŲ DIENOS. LITHUANIAN DAYS. Metai 1- ; 1946- . Los Angeles,
Calif., A.F. Skirius. illus. Monthly except July and August. CaOONL([1952,
1954,1958-1959], 1963-1965) CLL CtTMF(1-14-) DLC(4-) ICCC(1950-) ICLJF(1956-
1957,1960-1965) IU(6-) MiD(3) NN(7-) OCl(9-) OKentU(1951-1973) OkU(9-) PU

LIETUVIŲ KALBOTYROS KLAUSIMAI. T.1- ; 1957- . Vilnius, Valstybinė poli-
tinės ir mokslinės literatūros leidykla. Summaries in Russian. PG8501.L5
DLC(1-) CU(1-) CLU(1-) CaAEU(1-4,6) CaOTU(6,7) CtY(1-) ICU(1-) InU(1-) IU(2-)
MH(1-) NN(1-) OKentU(1,2,4) PU(3) TxU(1-) WaU(1-6)

LIETUVIŲ KATALIKŲ MOKSLO AKADEMIJA, ROME. Metraštis. 1- ; 1965- .
Roma. (Its Leidinys) Some articles have summaries in English or French.
AS222.L5A2 DLC(1-) CaAEU(1-) CtPAM(1-) CtY(1-) ICU(1-) MB(2-) NN(1-) PU(1-)

LIETUVIŲ KATALIKŲ MOKSLO AKADEMIJA, ROME. Suvažiavimo darbai. 1- ;
1957- . Roma. Ports. (Its Leidinys) Summaries in English, French, or
German. Each vol. has also a distinctive title. BX839.R6L49 DLC(4-5)

CaAEU(4-) ICU(4-) MB PU

LIETUVIŲ TAUTA; Lietuvių mokslo draugijos raštai. Vilnius, Ruch'o spaustuvė, 1907-35. 5 v. illus., ports. DK511.L2A245 DLC BM BN(1-4) CtPAM(4, no.3) ICBM(3,no.1) ICCC(1,no.1-2,4) NN(2,no.4-4,no.1-3) NNC(1) PU(1-5)

Lietuvių tautosakos lobynas see Treasury of Lithuanian Folklore. Lietuvių tautosakos lobynas.

LIETUVOS AIDAS. Metai 1-2,nr.1-214; rugsėjis 1917-gruodis 1918. Vilnius, 1917-18. 2 v. Film News 82 PU(1.10.1917-23.10.1918)

LIETUVOS AIDAS. Nr.1(215)-335(5544); 1.2.1928-15.6.1940. Kaunas, Pažangos bendrovė, 1928-40. Supersedes "Lietuva" and also previously published "Lietuvos aidas" in Vilnius. CtPAM(1935-1938) CtTMF(1930-1939, 1940(Jan.-July) DLL NN NNCL PU(Feb.1, 1928-Dec.23, 1936; microfilm)

LIETUVOS MOKYKLA; katalikiškosios krypties mėnesinis pedagogikos žurnalas. Kaunas, Lietuvių katalikų mokytojų sąjunga, 1918-40. Monthly. CtPAM(1919, 1921,[1930-1934], 1937-1938) ICCC(1919-1923; 1924,no.1-3,8; 1925; 1926, no. 1-11; 1927-1933,no.1-5,7-20; 1934-1936,no.1-2; 1937,no.12; 1938,no.1-3)

LIETUVOS PRAEITIS. T.1, sąs.1-2. Kaunas, Lituanistikos institutas, Lietuvos istorijos skyrius, 1940-41. DK511.L2A233 DLC NN

LIETUVOS TSR AUKŠTŲJŲ MOKYKLŲ MOKSLO DARBAI: Bibliotekininkystės ir bibliografijos klausimai. T.1- ; 1961- . Vilnius, Mintis. Z671.L722 CaAEU(1, 2,4) CU(1-) ICU(1-) NN(1-3) NjP MH PU(1-) WaU(1-2) CLU(1-) InU(3-5) MCM(1-) MiU(1-5)

LIETUVOS TSR AUKŠTŲJŲ MOKYKLŲ MOKSLO DARBAI: Filosofija. 1- ; 1960- . Vilnius. Irregular. This title commences with vol.2, continuing numbering of subseries "Filosofija" of Vilna. Universitetas. Mokslo darbai. Vol. 1(1960) Text in Russian and Lithuanian. B6.L72 CaAEU(5) CLU(1-) DLC(2-) InU(1-7) MH(1-) MiU(1-) NjP(5-)

LIETUVOS TSR AUKŠTŲJŲ MOKYKLŲ MOKSLO DARBAI: Geografija ir geologija. 1- ; 1962- . Vilnius, Valstybinė politinės ir mokslinės literatūros leidykla. illus., maps. QE1.L447 DLC(1-) CU CaAEU(3-) ICU(1-) IU(1-) MH(1-) MiU(1-4) PU(2-)

LIETUVOS TSR AUKŠTŲJŲ MOKSYKLŲ MOKSLO DARBAI: Istorija. 1- ; 1958- . Vilnius, Valstybinė politinės ir mokslinės literatūros leidykla. DK511.L21423 DLC(3-) CLU(1-) ICU(1-) InU KU(1-) IU(1-) MH NjP(1-) PU(1-10)

LIETUVOS TSR AUKŠTŲJŲ MOKYKLŲ MOKSLO DARBAI: Kalbotyra. 1- ; 1958- . Vilnius, Valstybinė politinės ir mokslinės literatūros leidykla. illus. Irregular. Text and summaries in Lithuanian or Russian. Title varies: vol. 1-2, Kalbotyra issued 1958-1960 by Vilnius Valstybinis V. Kapsuko vardo Universitetas as its Mokslo darbai. P9.L52 CU(1-) CLU(1-) CaAEU(1-7,10,12-) CaOTU(11,13-14) ICU(10-) InU(3-8-) KU(1-) MH(1-) NNC(15-) OKentU(3-7,11-12) PSt(1-) PU(16-)

LIETUVOS TSR AUKŠTŲJŲ MOKYKLŲ MOKSLO DARBAI: Statyba ir architektūra. 1- ; 1962- . Vilnius, Valstybinė politinės ir mokslinės literatūros leidykla. Text in Russian or Lithuanian with summaries in the other language. Unclassified DLC(1-5)

LIETUVOS TSR ARCHITEKTŪROS KLAUSIMAI. 1- ; 1960- . Kaunas. Irregular. At head of title: Lietuvos TSR Mokslų akademija. Statybos ir architektūros institutas. Summaries in Russian. NA1195.L5L53 DLC(1-) CU(1-) CtY(1-) IU(1-) MH(1-) NN(1-3)

LIETUVOS TSR MOKSLO AKADEMIJA, Vilna. Darbai. Serija A. T.1- ; 1955- . Vilnius, Valstybinė politinės ir mokslinės literatūros leidykla. illus., maps. Semiannual. Supersedes in part the Academy's "Žinynas" (1947-1953). Text in Lithuanian and Russian with summaries in the other language. AS262.V422 DLC CLU(1962-) CaOTU(1968-) CtY(1-29-) ICU(1-) KyU(1-) MH(1-) NN(1955-) NIC(1964-) NcU NcD NNC(1967-) PPiU(1966-) PU(1-) PSt(1967) RPB(1966-) ViU WU(1966-) WaU(1957-) OKentU(1972)

LIETUVOS TSR MOKSLŲ AKADEMIJA, VILNA. Darbai. Serija B. T1- ; 1955- .
Vilnius, Valstybinė politinės ir mokslinės literatūros leidykla. illus.,
maps. 3 nos. a year. Supersedes in part the Academy's "Žinynas" (1947-
1953) Text in Lithuanian or Russian with summaries in the other language.
Q4.L52 DLC(1955-) CLU(1962-) CU(1955-) CU-A(1963-) CU-Riv(1963-) CtY(1955-)
DNAL(1955-) ICRL(1955-) IU(1962-) ICU(1965-) IaAS(1966-) MH(1955-) MWHB(1957-)
NN(1955-) NNC(1962-) NcU(1962-) NcD OrU(1955-) PU(1955-) SCU(1956-)

LIETUVOS TSR MOKSLŲ AKADEMIJA, VILNA. Darbai. Serija C. T.1- ; 1960- .
Vilnius, Valstybinė politinės ir mokslinės literatūros leidykla. 3 nos. a
year. Text in Lithuanian or Russian with summaries in the other language.
QH301.L52 DLC CU(1960-) CtY(1961-) CLSU-H(1960-) DNAL(1960-) DNLM(1960-)
IaAS(1966-) IU(1966-) MoKL(1967-) MH(1960-) NN(1960-) NIC(1960-) OKentU(1972)

LIETUVOS TSR MOKSLŲ AKADEMIJA, VILNA. Žinynas. Vestnik. Kaunas, Valstybinė enciklopėdijų, žodynų ir mokslo literatūros leidykla, 1947-55. 12 v.
ports. Superseded by Its Darbai, Serija A and B. Summaries in Russian.
As262.V42 DLC PU(3-5,9)

LIETUVOS TSR MOKSLŲ AKADEMIJA, VILNA. BIOLOGIJOS INSTITUTAS. Darbai.
Trudy. Vilnius, 1951-59. 4 v. No more published. QH301.L53.DLC(1-)
DNAL(1-) CU(1-) PPAN(1-)

LIETUVOS TSR MOKSLŲ AKADEMIJA, VILAN. CENTRINĖ BIBLIOTEKA. Bibliotekininkystė ir bibliografija. 1- ; 1961- . Vilnius, Valstybinė politinės ir
mokslinės literatūros leidykla. facsims. Summaries in English and Russian.
Z674.L5 DLC CLU CU CaAEU(1-2) ICU CaOONL(3-) DNAL MH NN NjR PPiU

LIETUVOS TSR MOKSLŲ AKADEMIJA, VILNA. EKONOMIKOS INSTITUTAS. Darbai.
1- ; 19 . Vilnius. HC337.L5L45 DLC(3-) CU(2-) MH(2-) NN(8-)

LIETUVOS TSR MOKSLŲ AKADEMIJA, VILNA. GEOLOGIJOS IR GEOGRAFIJOS INSTITUTAS
Moksliniai pranešimai. 1- ; 1955- . Vilnius, Valstybinė politinės ir
mokslinės literatūros leidykla. Illus., maps. QE1.L448 DLC(1-) CU(1-)
CaOOGB(1-) CtY(1-8,12-14-) ICU(1-) InU(5-8-) MWHB(1-) NN(1-) PPAN(1-)
WyU(4,12-)

LIETUVOS TSR MOKSLŲ AKADEMIJA, VILNA. ISTORIJOS INSTITUTAS. Darbai. 1- ;
1951- . Kaunas; Vilnius. CLU CtY(1-) PU(1-)

LIETUVOS TSR MOKSLŲ AKADEMIJA, VILNA. ISTORIJOS INSTITUTAS. Iš lietuvių
kulturos istorijos. 1- ; 1958- . Vilnius, Valstybinė politinės ir mokslinės literatūros leidykla. In Lithuanian with summaries in Russian.
DK511.L212L5 DLC(2-) CLU(2-) CU(1-) ICU(2-) InU(1-) KyU(1-) NN(1-) PU(1-)

LIETUVOS ŪKIS; mėnesinis visuomenės ūkio ir finansų laikraštis. Finansų
ministerijos leidinys. T.[1]-6,(Metai[1]-7; gruodis 1921-gruodis 1928.
Kaunas, Valstybės spaustuvė [etc.], 1921-28. 6 v. in 2. Monthly.
HC337.L5A16 DLC CtPAM(no.1-75) NN(no.1-67,69-75)

LIETUVOS ŽINIOS; politikos, visuomenės ir literatūros laikraštis.
19.6.1909-15.8.1915 (Vilnius); 16.2.1922-18.1940 (Kaunas) Vilnius; Kaunas,
1909-40. Twice a week; three times a week; daily. CtPAM(1924-1925) NN(1910,
1915) OKentU(1909, no.1-59; 1912, no.1-152; 1913, no.1-154 [1914]1915,no.1-87)

LINGUA: International Review of General Linguistics. 1- ; Dec.1947-
Haarlem, Netherlands, J.H.Gottmer. Irregular. Suspended between 1950 and
Feb. 1952. P9.L47 DLC(1-) CLU(1-) CU(1-) CaBVaU([1]-) CoU(1-) CtY(1-)
ICN(1-) ICU(1-) IEN(1-) IU(1-) IaU(1-) InU(1-) KyU(1-) OClW(1-) OkU(1-)
MH(1-) MdBJ(1-) MiDW(1-) MiU(1-) MnU(1-) NIC(1-) NN(1-) NNC(1-) NNU(1-)
NjP(1-) PSt(1-) PU(1-) RPB(1-) TxDaM(1-) TxU(1-) WU(1-)

LINGUA POSNANIENSIS; cazaopismo poświęcone językoznawstwu porównawczemu i
ogólnemu. T.1- ; 1949- . Poznań, Poznańskie Towarzystwo Przyjaciół Nauk.
Wydział Filologiczno-Filozoficzny. Komisja Filologiczna. P25.L55 DLC(1-)
CtY(1-) IaU(1-) IU(1-) MiU(1-) NIC(1-) TxU(1-)

LITAUISCHE LITERARISCHE GESELLSCHAFT, TILSIT. Mitteilungen. Bd. 1-6
(Heft 1-31) 1880-1912. Heidelberg, C. Winter, 1883-1912. 6 v. illus.,
plates, maps, plans. Irregular. PG8503.L7 DLC([1]-6) BM(1-6) CtY(v.2,no.10)
ICU HH MiU(1-6) NN(1-6) NNU-H(4-6) NjP(1-[5],6) OClW(1-6) PU(no.2-11,13-14,

17,23-24-30)

LITERATŪRA; lietuvių literatūros, meno ir mokslo metraštis. Redagavo
Martynas Gudelis. Kn.1-2. Chicago, Ill. Lietuvių literatūros draugija,
1950-54. 2 v. Balt. 9601.258.5 MH(1950-1954) PU

LITERATŪRA IR KALBA. T.1- ; 1956- . Vilnius, Valstybinė grožinės literatūros institutas. PG8503.L6 DLC(1-) CaAEU(1-7,9-) CLU(1-) CU(1-) CtY(2-
10-) InU(1-) IU(1-) ICU(1-) ICLJF(5) KyU(1-) MH(1-) NN(1-) OClW(1-) PU(1-)

LITERATŪRA IR MENAS. 1- ; liepa 1946- . Vilnius, Lietuvos TSR Rašytojų
sąjunga. Weekly. AP95.L5L77 ICU(1967-) DLC(1955-) InU(1968-) MH(1964-)
NN(1955-) OKentU(1957, no.25,29-31,36,39,41; 1958, no.27,29-34,36-49,51;
1959, no.1,3-17,19-23,25-29,3135,37-52; 1962, no.47; 1968, no.27, 1969, no.
22-27,30; 1972) PU(1955-)

LITHUANIAN BULLETIN. V.1-9,no.7; April 15,1943-July 1951. New York, N.Y.,
Lithuanian American Council, 1943-51. 9 v. First, Bulletin was published by
Lithuanian National Council, Apr.1943-Jan.1946. DK511.L2A26 DLC([1]-) AU(1-)
CLSU(1-) Cst-H([1]-) CU(1-) CtY(1-9) CtPAM(1943-1951) DCE(1-) FTS(1-)
FU([1-5],6-8) GU(1-) IaU(1-) InU(1-) IU(1-9) IEN(1-6) MH(1-9) MdBJ(1-)
MnU(1-) MoS([2]-) NBuU(1-) NIC(1-) NN(1-9) NNC(1-) NNHi(1-) NcD(1-) NjP(1-)
NjR(1-) OCl(1-) OClW OOxM(1-) PPi PPT(1-) WaS(1-9) WaU(1-)

LITUANISTIKOS DARBAI. Lithuanian Studies. 1- ; 1966- . Čikaga, Lituanistikos institutas. illus. Irregular. "Yearbook of the Institute of
Lithuanian Studies" DK511.L2A264 DLC CaAEU(1-) CaOTU FU ICU MH NIC NN PU WU

LITUANUS. V.1- ; 1954- . Brooklyn, N.Y., Lithuanian Student Associa-
tion. Quarterly. Issues for Nov., 1954-Dec., 1957 lack volume numbering
but constitute volumes 1-3. DK511.L2L78 CaAEU(7-) CaOWA(4-) CaBVaU(3-)
CaSSU CaMWU(10-) CaNSHD CaOLU CaSRU(14-) CaOTU CoFS(8-) CtY([106]-) CSt
InNd(4-) InU(8-) IaU IEN([2],12-) LU MH(1-) MsU MShM MdBJ MWalB NN NIC
NdU(11-) NcU NNC(1-) NmU NSyU OCl OKentU(1-) PU TxU TxDaM WU WaU

LÓDZ, POLAND. UNIWERSYTET. Zeszyty Naukowe. Seria 1.; Nauki Humani-
styczno-Społeczne. Zesz.1- ; 1955- . Lodz, Państwowe Wydawnictwo Naukowe.
illus., ports. Irregular. Summaries in English, French, or other languages.
AS262.L6A18 DLC(1-) CU(5-) CaAEU(64-) CoU(7-) CtY(1-) ICU(2-) IU(7-)
MH-L(6-) NNC(7-) WU(1-)

LOODUSUURIJATE SELTS, AASTARAAMAT. Köide [1]- ; 1953/60- . Tallin.
illus., maps. Title varies: 1853/60-1898, Sitzungsberichte; 1899-19 , Pro-
tokoly, and also Aruanded; 1899-1933, have title also in German. Q60.T26
DLC(1-23,26-) CLU([39]-) CU(1-) CaOTR(1-[3]-[16]-) DGS(4-) ICJ(1-43) IU(12-)
IaAS(1-) IaU(39-) MH(3,[4]) MH-A(1-) MiU(1-) MnU(1-33) NIC-A(5-8,12-)
NNC([13-33]) NNM(1-) NbU(1-[40-41])

LUD. Organ Towarzystwa Ludoznawczego we Lwowie. T.1-20, 1895-1903; NS 1-
15(21-35), 1904- . Lwów, [etc.], Towarzystwo Ludoznawcze, 1895- . illus.,
plates. Monthly, 1895; quarterly, 1896- . GR1.L8 DLC(1-17,21-38) CLU(25,
31,33-36,38-) CU(1-) CaQMM(38) CtY([3-6],9-10,13-16,[21],23,36-44) ICU(1-35,
37-41) MiU(21,37-) NIC(36-) NNC(36,39) NbU(38-) NjP(11-[3]-32,36-38,41) PU-
MU(36-)

LUX CHRISTI; trimėnesinis kunigų biuletenis. 1- ; 1951- . New Britain/
Putnam, Conn., Kunigų vienybė. Quarterly. 262.05 L979 PU(1-) ICCC(1951-)
DLC(4-) ICLJF(1951-1955,1962-) OKentU(1951-1959; 1968-1972)

LVOV. UNIVERYTET. Naukovi zapysky. 1- ; 1946- . L'viv. QE1.L96
DLC(no.[2-46]) CaOOG(6-8) CU(1-) NNC(12,24,26,31,40,43) PPAN(6-) RPB(4)

Magazin der lettisch-litterärischen Gesellschaft see Latviešu literariska biedrība, Riga. Magazin.

MATERIALY STAROŻYTNE. 1- ; 1956- . Warszawa, Państwowe Muzeum Archeologiczne. Annual. DK409.M3 DLC(2-) CU(1-) CaOTU(1-) CtY(1-) MiU(2) MH-P(1-)
NN(1-) NMM(1-) PU-Mu(1-) WU(1-)

MAŁOPOLSKIE STUDIA HISTORYCZNE. T.1- ; 1958- . Kraków, Państwowe

Wydawn. Naukowe. 4 nos. a year. At head of title: Polskie Towarzystwo
Historyczne. Title varies. DK511.M24M3 DLC(4-) CU(10-) CaOTU(1-) CtY(6-)
IU(1-) MH(2-) MiU([1-8]) NjP(10-)

MANNUS; Zeitschrift für Vorgeschichte. Würzburg, Reichsbund für deutsche
Vorgeschichte, 1909-44. 34 v. GN700.M3 DLC(1-) CU(1-) CaOOG(1-5,7-13)
CtY(1-) ICU(1-) MH-P(1-) MdBJ(1-) MiU(1-) MnU(1-) NN(1-) NNC(1-) NjP(1-)
PU(1-5,7) TxU(1-)

MARGUTIS; mėnesinis... žurnalas. Metai 1- ; 1928- . Chicago, Ill., A.
Vanagaitis; Margutis Publishing Co. Monthly. (*QYA-)NN([1]-) CtPAM(1928-
1961) ICCC(1928-1929; 1931,no.7; 1932,nr.21; 1934,no.14,16; 1936,no.11,15;
1937,no.14; 1939,no.7-16,18-24; 1940,no.1-10,12-24; 1941-) OKentU(1928-1930,
no.9,12; 1931,no.1; 1951,no.1-4,8-9,11-12; 1952,no.1-3,5,8-12; 1953,no.2;
1956,no.10; 1958,no.2-6,9,12; 1959,no.2; 1963,no.7)

MERCURE DE FRANCE. Sér. moderne. T.1- ; jan.1890- . Paris. illus.,
plates, ports., facsims. Monthly, Jan.1890-Dec.1904; semimonthly, Jan.
1905- . AP20.M5 DLC(1-) CLU(1-) CSt([2-3,5,17,19,28-29,31,35,38-40,65-)
CU(1-) CaBVaU(1-7-) CaQMM(101-) CaSSU(241-) CaOTU(53-) CoU(59-) CtW(1-)
CtY(1-[294]-) ICN(47-) ICU(77-) IEN(1-) IU(1-) IaU(1-) KyU(1-[194]-[247]-)
LU(1-) MB(3,7-40,42-137,140-) MH(1-) MNS(1-) MWiW(1-) MiU(1-) MnU(1-275,285-)
MoSW(77-) NBC(37-) NIC([1]-) NN(59-) NNC(1-34,39-234-243,245-) NRU(1-)
NcD(1-160,169-) NcU(153-) NhD(7-) NjP(1-16,18-) OCU(1-) OCl(1-) OU(1-)
OKU(1-) PU(1-38,125-130,132-) TxU(29-32,37-40,59-64,95-) WU(1-) WaU(1-)

METMENYS; jaunosios kartos kultūros žurnalas. 1- ; 1959- . [Chicago],
Ill. AP95.L5M4 DLC(1-) CLU(7-) CtY(1-) MH(1-) NN(1-) OU(1-2,6-7,9,12,14,16-)
PU(1-) OKentU(1959-1972, no.1-24)

MIESIĘCZNIK HERALDYCZNY. 1- ; 19- . Warszawa, Nakł. Oddziału Warszawskiego Polskiego Towarzystwa Heraldycznego. Illus., ports., maps. 9 no. a
year; monthly, 1931- . CS870.M5 DLC

MINSK. UNIVERSITET. Pratsy. Trudy. Mensk, 1922-32. 26 nos. AS262.M52
DLC(2-26) CSt(6-26) CU CtY(6 7-12,16-20,22,24) ICU(1925-1926,1928) IU(1-3,
6-12,14-15,17-26) MH(6-16) NN NNC(4-24,26) NNC(4-10) OCU(4-22) OrU(1-19,21,
23-24)

MINSK. UNIVERSITET. Uchenye zapiski. 1- ; 1939- . Minsk. AS262.M522
DLC(24,26) NNC(2)

MITTEILUNGEN AUS DER BALTISCHEN GESCHICHTE. Bd.1- ; 1938- . Riga, E.
Bruhns. "Neue Folge der Mitteilungen aus der livländischen Geschichte"
Supersedes its Mitteilungen aus der livländischen Geschichte. DK511.B25M63
DLC CU(1-) DSI-E(1-) MH(1-2)

Mitteilungen der Litauischen literarischen Gesellschaft, Tilsit see
Litauische Literarische Gesellschaft, Tilsit. Mitteilungen.

MOKYKLA IR GYVANIMAS. Šiauliai; Kaunas, Lietuvos mokytojų profesinė sąjunga, 1920-40. Monthly. ICCC(1920-1921, no.2-12; 1922,no.2-8; 1923-1924,
no.3-12; 1925,no.1,4; 1926-1932,no.1-9; 1933,no.1-7)

DER MONAT; eine internationale Zeitschrift für Politik und geistiges Leben.
Bd.1- ; Okt. 1948- . München; Berlin. Subtitle varies slightly.
AP30.M56 DLC(1-) CLU(1-) CSt-H(1-) CtY(1-) ICU(1-) IEN(1-) IU(1-) IaU(1-)
InNU(1-) MCM([3]-) MH([1]-) MNS(1-) MdBJ([1-2]-) MiU(1-) MnU(1-) NNC(1-)
NcU(1-) NjP([1,15,18,20]-) OCl(1-) OClW([3]-) OU([1-2]) OrU(1-) PSt([1-2]-)
RPB(2-)

LE MONDE SLAVE. Année 1-2; juil. 1917-sept.1918; NS1-15, v.1-3,no.[7],
nov.1924-juil.1938. Paris. Monthly. D461.M7 DLC CSt-H(1-ns yr. 6,13-15)
CU(1-ns yr[15]) CaQMM(nr yr[2-4]-[6]-10) CtY(ns yrl-15) ICU(1, ns yr1-15) MH
MiU(1-ns yr[1]-15) MnU(ns ur3-15) NN(ns yrl-15) NNA(1, ns yr[1-2,6]-15)
NNC(ns yrl-15) OCl(ns yr2-[6]-15) RPB([1], ns yrl-[9]-[12],14) TxU(1-2)

MOSCOW. UNIVERSITET. OBSHCHESTVO ISTORII I DREVNOSTEI ROSSIISKIKH.
Chteniia. G.1-64(kn.1-264); 1846-1918. Moskva. illus., plates, ports.,
maps, plans. Quarterly(irregular) Supersedes Russkii istoricheskii sbornik.
Superseded, 1849-57 by Vremennik of the Society; resumed publication in 1858

continuing its former numbering. DK1.M672 DLC(1-) CLU([241-245]) CSt-H([1-255]) CU([1-22]-260) CtY([1-264]) ICU([1846-1848]-[1896-1897]-[1910]-1918]) MH(1-) NN(1-) NNC(5-21,24-244,246-264)

MRÓWKA; czasopismo illustrowane. Lwów, 1869-71. 3 v. BM

MŪSŲ GIRIOS; miškininkystės, gamtos apsaugos ir medžioklės žurnalas. Nr. 1-104, 1929-1940; nr.1-4,1942/43; nr.1- , 1957- . Kaunas; Vilnius, Lietuvos Miškininkų sąjunga; Lietuvos TSR Miškų ūkio ir miško pramonės ministerija. illus. Monthly. Publication suspended by Soviet and German occupational authorities, 1940-42; 1944-57. Volumes for 1957 called also no. 108 continuing the volume numbering of the previous publication. SD1.M8 DLC(1957-) ICLJF(1958,no.1-4) OKentU(1960, no.1,3; 1962, no.6, 10)

MŪSŲ SENOVĖ; žurnalas Lietuvos istorijos medžiagai rinkti. Kaunas, Švietimo ministerijos leidinys, 1921-22. 1937-40. 10 v. Irregular. DK511.L2A3 DLC(no.1-5,9) CU(6-9) CtY(v.3,no.10) PU(no.1-6) ICCC(1921-1922,1937)

MŪSŲ TAUTOSAKA. Kaunas. Humanitarinių mokslų fakultetas, 1930-35. 10 v. Irregular. CU(1-8) CtTMF(1,3) ICCC(1-10) ICU MH(2-7) MoU(1-8) NN(1-5)

MŪSŲ ŽINYNAS; karo mokslo ir istorijos žurnalas. Kaunas, Krašto apsaugos ministerija, Karo mokslo skyrius, 1921-40. 38 v. Quarterly, 1921-1928; monthly, 1929-1940. U4.M8 DLC (1-7,10-13,16-23) CtTMF(1921-1925) NN(28-32)

NACHBARN; Jahrbuch für vergleichende Volkskunde. Bd.1- ; 1948- . Göttingen. CU(1-) InU(1-) MH NIC(1-) OCl(1-) PU(1-)

NATION UND STAAT; deutsche Zeitschrift für das europäische Minoritätenproblem. Wien, W. Braumüller, 1927-44. 17 v. illus. Monthly. D410.N3 DLC(1-[12-13]-) CSt-H(1-) CaAEU(5-6,8-9,11,14) CtY-L(1-) ICU(1-) IEN(1-) MH([1-3]) MH-L(1-) NBuG(1-) NN(1-) NjP(1-2,4-) OCl([1]-[3]-)

NATURWISSENSCHAFTLICHE WOCHENSCHRIFT. Berlin; Jena, Deutsche Gesellschaft für volkstümliche Naturkunde, 1887-1922. 37 v. Weekly. Q3.N9 DLC(1-[10]-37) CLU(32-33) CSt(21-37) CU CaQMM(17-37) DNAL([15],17-37) ICF(4-14,17-37) ICJ(17-37) IU([8,13],17-29) MB MdBJ([4,6,10,14-15]-29) MoSB(17-[31]) NIC-A(5-37)

NAUJIENOS. 1- ; Vasario 19d, 1914- . Chicago, Ill., Lithuanian News Publishing Co. Weekly; daily. F71.L714N PU(20-35,37-44; 1934-1958)DLL ICN

NAUJOJI AUŠRA. Chicago, Ill., Lietuvių kultūros institutas, 1947-49. 13 nos. Q59.9192 N224 PU(1-13) OKentU(1-13)

NAUJOJI ROMUVA. Kaunas, Naujosios Romuvos bičiulių draugija, 1931-1940. 10 v. illus. Weekly; monthly. CtPAM(1931-1940,no.1-15) CtTMF(1931-1940,no.1-15) DLL ICCC(1931-1936,no.1-36,38-50; 1937-1938,no.1-28,31-52; 1939,no.1-2,4-12,14-52; 1940,no.1-8,10-15) NNCL

NEUE ZEIT; Wochenschrift der deutschen Sozial-Demokratie. Stuttgart, J.H.W. Dietz Nachf.[etc.], 1883-1923. 41 v. Monthly; weekly. Supersedes Geografische Nachrichten für Welthandel und Volkswirtschaft HX6.N6 DLC(1-[38]) CSt(1-[25]-34,36-[41]) CU(1-[34]-[38]-41 CaQTU(1-[29-38]) CtY(1-40) ICU(8-[34],36-41) IEN(9-15,[17]) IU IaU MB(13-[35],38-41) MH(1-[41]) MiU MnU NN(1-[34]-[36]-[41]) NNC(1-[35]-[38-39]-[41]) NcD(1-[41]0 NjP(9-38) OClW TxU(1-7,9-41) WU(1-[34]-[37-41])

NAUKA POLSKA, jej potrzeby, organizacja, rozwój. T.1- ; 1918- . Warszawa, Institut Popierania Nauki. AS262.W274 DLC(1,4-24) AzU(1-) CSt-H(6-) ICU(7-12) MH91-17,22) MiU(3-5) NN(1-) NNE(24) NhD(4-20) RPB(13-15,18,20) WU(15,17,19,21)

NEPRIKLAUSOMA LIETUVA; demokratinės minties Kanados lietuvių savaitraštis. 1- ; rugpiūtis 1940- . Toronto, Ont.; Montreal, Que.; Kanados lietuvių taryba; "Nepriklausoma Lietuva" spaudos bendrovė. Weekly. CtTMF(1949, 1952-1953) ICCC(1942,no.1-4,6-10; 1943,no.11-21; 1944,no.25-31; 1945,no.32-43; 1946-1948,no.44-78) OKentU(1959,no.[1-52])

NEUE PREUSSISCHE PROVINZIAL-BLÄTTER. Bd.1-12, 1846-1851; Folge 2, Bd.1-12, 1952-1857; Folge 3, Bd.1-11, 1858-1866. Königsberg in Pr., In Commis-

sion bei Tag & Koch [etc.], 1846-66. 35 v. in 18 plates, maps, tables.
Monthly, 1846-1861; quarterly, 1864-1866. Supersedes Preussische Provin-
zial-Blätter. Suspended 1862-1863. Series 2 has added title page:
Preussische Provinzial-Blätter. Merged into Altpreussische Monatsschrift.
DD491.04A2 DLC(1-) ICN(s2-v.[12],s3-v.[1]-4) IEN(1-s3-v.2) IU(1-) MH(1-)
MH-Z(1-s3-v.11) MnU(1-) NNC(1-) NNUT(1-) NjP(1-)

Neue Preussische Provinzial-Blätter see also Altpreussische Monatsschrift.

NEUES JAHRBUCH FÜR MINERALOGIE, GEOLOGIE UND PALEONTOLOGIE. Stuttgart;
[etc.], E. Schweizerbart, 1830-1949. Superseded in 1950 by Zentralblatt
für Mineralogie. QE1.N4 DLC(1833-[1917]) CLU(1830-[1917]-) CSt(1830-1893,
1899-) CU(1830-) CaAEU(1943,1944) CaOTU(1933-1914, 1920,[1921]-) CtY(1830-)
ICU(1830-) IEN(1901) IU(1830-) IaU(1831-1914, 1922, 1925-) InU(1895-1932)
MH(1830-) MiU(1830-) MnU(1830-[1901-1925], 1928-) NN(1830-) NNC(1830-)
NjP(1876-) OClW(1892-[1914]) PPAN(1830-) TxU(1839-1913, 1915-[1920]-)
WU(1871-[1917]-) WaU(1863-)

NIEPODLEGŁOŚĆ; czasopismo poświęcone dziejom polskich walk wyzwoleńczych w
dobie popowstaniowej. Warszawa, Wydawnictwo Instytutu Badania Najnowszej
Historji Polski, 1930-39. 20 v. plates, ports. Irregular. DK401.N5
DLC(1-[3]) CSt-H(1-3) CtY(7) MiU NN(1-[3]-) NjP(1-2) VU(1-6)

NIWA POLSKA. Warszawa, 1872-1903. 32 v. NN(6,[8],[30]-32)

NORSK TIDSKRIFT FOR SPROGVIDENSKAB. 1- ; 1928- . Oslo. P25.N86
CaAEU(1-) CLU(1-) CU(1-) ICU(1-) IEN(1-) IU(1-) IaU(1-) MH(1-8) MdBJ(1-)
MiU(1-) NIC(1-) NN(1-) NjP(1-) OCU(1-) TxU(1-10)

NUOVA ANTOLOGIA DI LETTERE, SCIENZE ED ARTI. 1- ; 1866- . Firenze;
Roma. illus., plates, ports., maps. Monthly, 1866-1877; semimonthly, 1878-
. AP37.N8 DLC(1-[409]-) CSt(1-) CU(1-) CaOTU(1-20,22,24,105,107,109-)
CaAEU(37-145,147-150,157-180,182-400,404-430,439-447,460,464-468,470,472,
481-510-) CtY(1-) ICU(1-) IEN(1-) MB(1-) MH(1-) MiU(1-) NIC(1-) NN(1-[108-
109]-[296]-) NNC(1-[222]-[241]-360,362-) NjP(1-) OCl(1-) PU(1-) TxU(1-)

OBSHCHESTVO LIUBITELEI ESTESTVOZNANIIA, ANTROPOLOGII I ETNOGRAFII, MOSKVA.
Antropologicheskii otdel. Trudy. Moskva. 1866-1914. Appears in the Society's "Izviestiia" CtY(6,10,[14],24) ICF(18-29) NNC(2-7,9-19,21-22,28)

ÖSTERREICHISCHE GESELLSCHAFT FÜR ANTHROPOLOGIE, ETHNOLOGIE UND PRÄHISTORIE.
Mitteilungen. Bd.1- ; 1870- . Wien. GN.0422 DLC(1-42,44-49) CSt(2-51)
CU(1-) CaOTR(2-) CtY(1-) DSG(1-) ICF(1-) ICJ(1-63) IU(1-) MnU(1-) NN(1-)
NNA(1-) NNC(1-) NNM(1-) NjP(1-) PPAP(1-) WaU(1-)

ONOMASTICA; pismo poświęcone nazewnictwu geograficznemu i osobowemu. Rocz.
1- [zesz.] 1- ; 1955- . Wrocław [etc.], Zakład Narodowy im. Ossolińskich.
illus., ports., maps. Semiannual. Summaries in French. G104.057 DLC(1-)
CLU(5) CaQMM([6]) CaQMU([2-7]) CaAEU(12-) CaBVaU(9-10-) CtY(1-) CU(1-)
InU(1-2) KU(1-) MB(1-) MH(1-) NN(1-) NNC([2]-) NcD(1-) NcU(1-) TxHR(1-)
WaU(8-)

LE OPERE E I GIORNI; ressegna mensile di politica, lettere, arti, etc.
Genoa, 1922-38. 17 v. Monthly. (*DO)NN(7-17) NNC(8-11)

ORIENTALIA CHRISTIANA PERIODICA; commentarii de re orientali setatis
christianae sacra et profana. 1- ; 1935- . Roma, Pontificio instituto
orientale. illus., plates, plan. Quarterly. BX100.074 DLC(1-5) CaAEU(30-)
CtY(1-) CaOTU(12) ICU(1-) MH(1-) MiU(1-) NN(1-) NNC(1-) WU(1-)

OSTEUROPA. Bd.1- ; 1951- . Stuttgart, Ost-Europa Verlag. Supersedes
Osteuropa; Zeitschrift für die gesamten Fragen des europäischen Ostens.
D410.07 DLC(1-) CU(1-) CaBVaU(6-) CLU(1-) CSt-H(1-) CtY(1-) IU(1-) INU(1-)
MH(1-) MdBJ(1-) NN([1]-) NIC(1-) NNC(1-) NjP(1-) PSt(1-) TxU(1-)

OSTEUROPA; Zeitschrift für die gesamten Fragen des europäischen Ostens.
Jahrg. 1-14; 1924 25-Aug. Sept., 1939. Königsberg in Pr., Deutsche Gesellschaft für Osteuropakunde, 1925-39. 14 v. Superseded by "Osteuropa" in
1951. D410.07 DLC(1-14) CLU(1-) CSt-H([1]-[14]) CU(1-) CaAEU(1-14) MH(1-)
MiU(1-9) MnU(1-12) NcU(7-8,11) NN(1-) NNA(4,9,11-12) NNC(2-)

Osteuropa Institut an der Freien Universität Berlin. Historische Veröffentlichungen. Forschungen zur osteuropäischen Geschichte <u>see</u> Jablonowski, Horst, ed. Forschungen zur osteuropäischen Geschichte.

OST-EUROPA MARKT. Königsberg in Pr., Ost-Europa Verlag, 1919-44. 24 v.
"Zeitschrift des Wirtschaftsinstituts für die Oststaaten, Königsberg in
Pr." HC240.A1 O77 DLC CSt-H(12-13) CU(3-) MdBJ(5-) NN([12]-14)

OSTLAND. REICHSKOMMISSAR. Statistische Berichte für das Ostland...
Jahrg. 1-4; Nov./Dec. 1941-Mai/Juli 1944. Riga, 1944-44. 4 v. Monthly.
HA1448.B307 DLC BM NN

OST-PROBLEME. Bad Nauheim, 1949-69. 21 v. weekly. DK266.A207 DLC
([1951-1952]) CSt-H(1-) CU([2]-[4]-) CaAEU(2-3,5-21) CtY([3]-) ICU(1,[2-5]-)
IEN([2-6]-) IaU(6-) InU(5-) MdBJ(1,5-) MiU([5-6]-[8-11]-) MnU([1]-) NIC([1]-)
NN(2-) NNC(11-) TxU([4]-[8]-) WaU(6-)

OSTDEUTSCHE MONATSHEFTE. Bd.1- ; Feb. 1920- . Salzburg, A. Pustet.
plates. monthly. Suspended 1941-1951, 1953-1954. AP30.08 DLC(1-20,[22-
23]-) CSt-H(4-5) LU MoU(15-[19-20]) MH(1-) MiU(1-)

OXFORD SLAVONIC PAPERS. v.1- ; 1950- . London. PG2025.096 DLC(1-)
CL(1-) CLU(1-) CLSU(1-) CU(1-) CU-Riv(1-) CoU(1-) CtY(1-) FU(1-) ICU(1-)
ILS(1-) KyU(1-) LU(1-) MB(1-) MH(1-) MCM(1-) MWelC(1-) MdBJ(1-) MoS(1-)
NN(1-) NNF(1-) NIC(1-) NcD(1-) NhD(1-) NCU(1-) NjR(1-) OCl(1-) OU(1-) PU(1-)
PSt(1-) RPB(1-) ViU(1-)

PAMIĘTNIK FIZJOGRAFICZNY. T.1-27; 1881-1922; T.1- ; 1955- . Warszawa,
Wydawn. Geologiczne. illus., fold. col. maps. QE276.5.P3 DLC MH-P(1-3,
9,12-16,18-20,23,25-27) MBdAF(1-2,23-25) NN(12-15,18-19,26-27) NNM(2-3,9,12-
16,18-20,22-27) PPAN(26-27)

PANTEON. Sanktpeterburg, 1840-56. 17 v. DK37.P3 DLC([1840],1841,1843-
1844,1850-1851,1954,[1955]) CtY(1840-1841) NN(1840,1853)

PERGALĖ; literaturos, meno ir kritikos žurnalas. 1- ; 1942- . Vilnius.
illus., ports. Monthly. PG8501.P4 DLC([1945-1947]) CtY(1957-) OKentU(1948,
no.5; 1955, no.3,6; 1957, no.5-8,10,11; 1958, no.7-8,12; 1959, no.1-2,6-8,
10-12; 1961, no.1,6,10; 1962, no.3,5,7-9; 1963, no.8-12; 1964,no.2,3,5; 1965,
no.1; 1966, no.11-12; 1967-1969; 1970, no.5-8; 1971-1972) PU(1953, no.1-3,
5-12; 1954, no.2-10,12; 1955-) NN(1957, 1964-)

PETERMANNS MITTEILUNGEN AUS JUSTUS PERTHES' GEOGRAPHISCHER ANSTALT.
Jahrg.1- ; Feb. 1855- . Gotha, J. Perthes. plates, maps, charts. Month-
ly. G1.P43 DLC(1-) CSt(1-51,[62-72]-) CU(1-) CaAEU(1-) CaOG(1-60,68-)
CaOTU(1-) CaQMAI(1855-1900-) CtY(1-) ICN(1-) ICU(1-) IEN(1-) IU(1-) IaU(1-)
InU(1-56) KyU(1-33,48-) MH(1-) MdBJ(1-) MiU(1-) MnU(1-) NIC(1-) NN(1-) NNC
(1-) NjP(1-) OClW(1-) PU(1-) TxU(1-) WU(1-)

PHYSIKALISCH-ÖKONOMISCHE GESELLSCHAFT, KÖNIGSBERG. Schriften der Physikalisch-ökonomischen Gesellschaft zu Königsberg. Königsberg in Pr., 1860-
1941. 72 v. Title varies: vol.1-13 (1860-1872), Schriften der Königlichen
physikalisch-ökonomischen Gesellschaft zu Königsberg. Each volume comprises
"Abhandlungen" und "Sitzungsberichte". General-Register zu den Publikationen... for 1860-1884 im Jahrgang 23(1884). Q49.K7 DLC(1-66) CLU(64-) CU(1-)
CaQMM(1-7,12-16) CaOG(17-35,36-) CaOTR(6-51,53) CaOTU(20-31) CtY(1-65)
DNAL(1-) DGS(1-) ICU(1-32,36-52) MH-Z(1-) MdBJ(1-15,17-44,48-) MnU(1-)
NN(1-) NNC(1-64) NNM(1-) NhD(1-60) NjP(1-65) PPAN(1-) WU(1-) WaU(1-21,27-29)

PINNEBERG, GER. BALTIC UNIVERSITY. Contributions. Hamburg-Pinneberg,
1946-48. 67 no. in 3 v. diagrs., tables, maps. AS182.P5 DLC(1-3,5-10,
12-24,26-32,34-36,38,40-42,44-45,47,49-62,64-67) AzU BM(1-62,64-67) CaOTU
CU(1-) CtY(1-) DGS IEN IaU InLP MA MH(1-) MnU NhD(1-) NNC NNRI(1-) PPi WU
WaU

PISMO ZBIOROWE WILEŃSKIE. Wilno, 1859-62. 2 v. BM(1859,1862)

PLAIN TALK. v.1- ; 1947- . New York, N.Y. D839.P56 DLC(1-) CU(1-)
CtY(1-) MH(1-) NN(1-) WaU(1-)

POLEN; Wochenschrift für polnische interessen. Jahrg.1-4(no.1-201),

1915-Nov. 1918. Wien, 1915-18. 4 v. Weekly. CSt-H(no.1-160,[161-120])
CtY(1-[9]) ICU([1-70]) MH(1-50,52,54-56,60-62,64-65,68-69]) NN(1-157)

POLICIJA; Lietuvos policijos mėnesinis laikraštis. Nr.1-148. Metai 1-9;
rugėjis 1924-1932. Kaunas, Piliečių apsaugos departamentas, 1924-32. 9 v.
illus. Monthly. HV7551.P6 DLC(no.1-40,43-148)

POLISH REVIEW. v.1-2, no.3; Jan. 1917-Dec. 1918. London, G. Allen & Unwin, 1917-18. 2 v. ports., facsims. DK401.P82 DLC CSt CU(1-2) CtY ICU MH
NN NNC OCl RPB(1-4) TxU(1-2,4) WU

POLISH INSTITUTE OF ARTS AND SCIENCES IN AMERICA. Bulletin. v.1-4; Oct.
1942-1945/46. New York, N.Y. Quarterly. AS36.P84 DLC(1-) CST-H(1-) CU(1-)
CaQMM(1-) CaOTU(1-) CoU(1-) CtY(1-) DCU(1-) ICJ(1-) ICU(1-) IEN([2]-)
IaU(1-) MH(1-) MWC(1-) MdBJ([1]-) MiU(1-) MnU(1-) NBuU(1-) NIC(1-) NN(1-)
NNC(1-) NNU(1-) NcD(1-) NhD(1-) NjP(1-) NjR(1-) OU(1-) PPi(1-) PU(1-)
RPB(1-) WMM(1-)

POLITIQUE ÉTRANGÈRE. T.1- ; 1936- . Paris, Centre d'études de politique
étrangère. Quarterly. DLC(2-[5]) CaOOND(1946-) CaQMM(24-) CaAEU(33-)
CtY([1-3]-) DCE(1-) MH(1-) MH-L(1-) MnU([1,3]-) NN(1-) NNA([1]-) NNC([1]-)
OU([1] 5-) PP(1-) RPB([1]-)

LA POLOGNE; revue mensuelle. Année 1-15, no.6; fév. 1920-juin 1934.
Paris, Association France-Pologne, 1920-34. 15 v. Monthly. DK401.P84 DLC
CSt MH(6-15) NN NjP(1-[3]-15)

POLSKA AKADEMIA UMIEJĘTNOŚCI, KRAKÓW. Sprawozdania z czynności i posiedzeń. T.1- ; 1896- . Kraków. Vol.1-24, 1896-1919, issued under the
Society's earlier name: Akademia Umiejętności. AS142.K82 DLC(3-5,7,15,16)
IaAS(1-[4-5]-[10]-[15]-[25]-48,50-52) ICJ(19-[29-30]-[42]-[44]) MH([3] 26-
30) NN(19-15) OCl(43-)

POLSKA AKADEMIA UMIEJĘTNOŚCI, KRAKÓW. KOMISJA ANTROPOLOGICZNA. Ma-
teryały antropologiczno-archeologiczne i etnograficzne. T.1-14; 1896-1919.
Kraków, Nakład Akademii Umiejętności, 1896-1919. 14 v. illus. Supersedes
its Zbiór Wiadomości do Antropologii. Superseded by its Prace i materyały.
.. GN2.P582 DLC(1-13) CU CtY(1-4) ICU(1-11,14) ICJ(1-11,14) MH MnU NN NNC
NNM(14)

--- Prace i materyały antropologiczno-archeologiczne. Kraków, Nakład
Akademii Umiejętności, 1920-27. 4 v. Supersedes its Materyały antropolo-
giczno-archeologiczne i etnograficzne. Superseded by the Academy's Komisja
Antropologji i Prehistorji. Prace and Materjały Prehistoryczne.
GN2.P582 DLC CU ICJ MH(1-2) NNM

POLSKA AKADEMIA UMIEJĘTNOŚCI, KRAKÓW. KOMISJA DO BADANIA HISTORII, FILO-
sofii w Polsce. Archivum. Kraków, Nakład Akademii Umiejętności; Skł. Gł.
w Księg. Gebethnera i Wolffa, 1917-37. 6 v. in 3. B99.P62P6 DLC(6) CtY
MB(1-6) NCJ(1-5) NN(1-2) NNC(1-2,4-6) WaU

POLSKA AKADEMIA UMIEJĘTNOŚCI, KRAKÓW. KOMISJA PRAWNICZA. Archivum. Col-
lectanea ex Archivo. T.1- ; 1895- . Kraków, Nakład Akademii Umiejętności;
Skład Główny w Księgarni Spółki Wydawniczej Polskiej. DLC(1-) CU(1,3,5-9)
IEN-L(1-5,7-9) IU(2,4) MH(1-5;7-9) MH-L(1-11) NN(1-)

POLSKA AKADEMIA UMIEJĘTNOŚCI, KRAKÓW. WYDZIAŁ HISTORICZNO-FILOZOFICZNY.
Bulletin international de l'Académie des sciences. Classe de philologie.
Classe d'histoire et de philosophie. T.1- ; 1901- . Kraków, Nakład
Akademii Umiejętności. AS142.K835 DLC(1901-) CLU(1914-1916) CSt(1916-1933)
CU(1901-) CaQMM(1930-1938) CaOTU(1901-) CoDM(1930-1938) CoU(1901) DSI-M(1-)
ICJ(1901,[1904-1905]-[1911]-1912-1914-1922,1924-1938) ICN(1901-1922)
IU([1901,1925], 1929-) IaAS(1901-1926) MdBJ(1901-1904,1919-1922) MiU(1901-)
NNC(1901-[1931]-[1936]-) OU(1901-1922) WU(1901-) WaU(1901-)

--- Rozprawy. T.1- ; 1874- . Kraków, Nakład Akademii Umiejętności;
Skład Główny w Księgarni G. Gebethnera. Vol.1-25, 1874-1891 include the
Society's reports of its meetings: Sprawozdania z posiedzeń. AS142.K85
DLC(1-s2,v.44,46-) CU(s2,v.6,8,11-12,14-21,24-42) CaOTR(22-s2,v.30,32-41)
DGS(1-) ICU(16) MH(1-) NN(s2,v.8,11,38) NNC(s2,v.38,41) PPAP(21-24;s2,v.3-5,
7-[31-33]-)

POLSKA AKADEMIA UMIEJĘTNOŚCI, KRAKÓW. WYDZIAŁ MATEMATYCZNO-PRZYRODNICZY.
Pamiętnik. Kraków, Skład Główny w Księgarni Spółki Wydawniczej Polskiej,
1874-94. 18 v. in 9. illus., fold. map, plates. Q60.P74 DLC(1-s2,v.[1-2])
DGS(2-18) DSG(1-17) ICJ(2-17) MBdAF(2-17) NN(12-18) NNM(2-17)

POLSKIE TOWARZYSTWO GEOLOGICZNE. Rocznik. T.1- ; 1921/22- . Kraków.
Annual (*QPA)NN CU(1-) CaOOG(1-) DLC(1-14) IU(1-11) MiU(2) NNM(1-)
NjP(1-) OClW(1-14) PPAN(1-14) WU(3-[8-9])

POWSZECHNY ZJAZD HISTORYKÓW POLSKICH. Referaty. 1- ; Warszawa, Polskie
Towarzystwo Historyczne. Irregular. Title varies; Pamiętnik Zjazdu His-
toryków Polskich. DK401.P8943 DLC(4-5) CSt-H(9) ICU(9) MH(9) MiU(9)
NN(2,4-5,9) NNC(9) OU(9) PU(5-6) RPB(9) WU

POSEN. UNIWERSYTET. Historia. Zesz.1- ; 1956- . Poznań. illus.,
tables. (Its Zeszyty Naukowe) Summaries in German, French, or English.
DK401.P892 DLC(2,5-) MH(1-2,5)

Pozen. Uniwersytet. Wydział Filozoficzno-Historyczny. Prace. Seria:
Historia. (Its Zeszyty Naukowe) see Posen. Uniwersytet. Historia.

PRÄHISTORISCHE ZEITSCHRIFT. Bd.1- ; 1909- . Berlin. GN700.P825.
DLC(1-) CU(1-) CtY(1-) ICU(1-) IU(1-) MH-P(1-) MiU(1-) NN(1-) NNC(1-)
NNM(1-) NjP(1-) OCU(1-) PPiU(1-) WU(1-25)

PRAEITIS. Kaunas, Lietuvos istorijos draugija, 1930-33. 2 v. illus.,
maps. DK511.L2P75 DLC(1-2) CaAEU(1-2) ICU(1-2; microfilm) KU(1-2) PU(1-2)

PREUSSISCHE JAHRBÜCHER. Berlin, G. Reimer[etc.], 1858-1935. 240 v.
AP30.P8 DLC CLU CSt CSt-H([159-183]) CU(1-163,165-183,185-240) CaAEU(1-240)
CaQMM(155-158,199-240) CaOTU(64-158,175-176,182-240) CtY(1-240) ICN IEN IU
IaU InU(39-204,207-210) MH MiU MnU NN(1-240) NNC NjP OClW PU WU

PREUSSISCHE PROVINZIAL-BLÄTTER. Bd.1-27, 1829-Juni 1842; Neue Folge.
Bd. 1-7, Juli 1842-Dec.1845. Königsberg in Pr., 1829-45. 34 v. Monthly
(irregular). Title varies: vol.1-12, 1829-1834. Preussische Provinzial-
Blätter; vol.13-27, 1835-1842, Vaterländisches Archiv für Wissenschaft,
Kunst, Industrie und Agrikultur oder Preussische Provinzial-Blätter; NS
v.1-7, 1842-1845, Archiv für Vaterländische Interessen oder Preussische
Provinzial-Blätter. Superseded by Neue Preussische Provinzial-Blätter.
DD491.04A2 DLC ICU(1-15,17-18,[20-21]-[27]) IEN(12) MH(1-27) IU MnU(15-ns7)
OCl(15)

Preussische Provinzial-Blätter see also Altpreussische Monatsschrift.

PREUSSISCHES ARCHIV. Königsberg in Pr., K. Deutsche Gesellschaft, 1790-
98. 9 v. Annual. NNC(1-9)

Prussia. Altertumsgesellschaft Prussia, Königsberg see Altertumsgesellschaft Prussia, Königsberg in Pr.

Prussia. Geologische Landesanstalt. Jahrbuch see Geologisches Jahrbuch.

Prussia; Zeitschrift für Heimatkunde und Heimatschutz, Königsberg in Pr.
see Altertumsgesellschaft Prussia, Königsberg in Pr. Sitzungsberichte.

PRZEGLĄD ANTROPOLOGICZNY. T.1- ; 1926- . Poznań, Polskie Towarzystwo
Antropologiczne. GN2.P65 DLC(1-) MH-P(1-) NNN(1-5) NIC(17-) OU(19-)
PU-Mu(16-19,21-)

PRZEGLĄD GEOGRAFICZNY. Revue polonaise de géographie. T.1- ; 1918/19- .
Warszawa, Nakładem Polskiego Towarzystwa Geograficznego. illus., maps.
G1.P7 DLC(1-4,6-18) CSt-H(1-5) CU(1-) DGS(6-) CaQMM(21,23,26-) CtY(24-)
MBdAF(1-21,27-29) MWhB(26-) NN(1-) NNA(1-) OCU([9]-[14]) TxHR(29-) ViU(24-)

PRZEGLĄD HISTORYCZNY. T.1- ; 1905- . Warszawa, Państwowe Wydawn.
Naukowe [etc.] Suspended 1940-1945. Vol. 21-35 also called Series 2, v.1-
15. DK401.P915 DLC CtY(45-) ICU(47,49-) CaAEU(50-) MiU(46) NIC(46-)
NN(1,[2]-) NNC PU

PRZEGLĄD POLSKI. Rok 1-48; 1866-1914. Kraków, 1866-1914. 192 v.

(*QPA)NN([6]-[15] 38-48)   NNC

PRZEGLĄD POWSZECHNY; miesięcznik poświęcony sprawom religijnym, kultu-
ralnym i społecznym. Rok 1- ; 1898- . Warszawa, Wydawn. Księży Jezui-
tów. Monthly. Publication suspended 1940-1946.   AP54.P78 DLC BM(59,
no.175,177; 60,no.178,179; 230,no.10(703), etc.) CaOTU(209)

Przewodnik Historyczno-Prawny see Czasopismo Prawno-Historyczne.

PRZEWODNIK NAUKOWY I LITERACKI. Lwów, Nakł. Gazety Lwowskiej, 1873-1913.
41 v. Monthly. Supersedes Gazeta Lwowska; Dodatek miesięczny.
AP54.P823 DLC MH(yr.2,v.1)

RASSE; Monatsschrift der nordischen Gedanken. Jahrg. 1- ; 1934- .
Leipzig, Teubner. Title varies slightly. GN1.R3 DLC(1-) CtY(1,4) MH(1-)
MnU(1-) NN(1-) NNN(1)

REFORMACJA W POLSCE. Warszawa, Skład Główny w Księgarni Trzaska, Evert
Michalski, 1921-38. 18 v. Summaries in French. BR20.P7R4 DLC(1-8)
CtY(7-8) MiU(4,no.13-16) NN(1-8)

REVIEW OF REVIEWS. No.1-553. London, 1890-1936. 87 v. AP4.R4 DLC(1-
[87]) CU(1-[57]) CaQMM(1-13,15-16,18-23,26-28,76-[87]) CaOTU(1-2,5-[80-81]-
87) CaBVa(1-2,4-41,43-49,83-87) CaBViP([2]-[86]) CtY(1-40) IC(1-80) ICN(1-
50,81-87) ICU(1-34) Ia(1-52) InI(1-48) MB(1-17,19-87) MnM(1-84) MoS(1-[64]-
87) NB(3-87) NCH(1-3,15-20,30-42,69-87) NIC(1-42) NN(1-12,14-87) NcU(1-52)
NjP(63-64,66-87) OCl(1-52,82-87) OrU(1-58) TNF(1-33,35-53,55-60,63-64,80-83,
85-86) TxU(1-47) WHi(1-55)

REVISTA BALTICA. 1- ; 1957- Buenos Aires. Semiannual. DLC RPB(1-)

REVUE BALTIQUE; organe de la collaboration des États Baltes. No.1-2;
fév.-juin 1940. Tallin, 1940. 1 v. Edited by the Bureau for Estonian,
Latvian and Lithuanian Cooperation. Articles in French, English or German.
Superseded in Dec. 1945 by the Baltic Review published in Stockholm.
DK511.R25R42 DLC(1-) MH(1-) NN(1) NNC(1)

REVUE DE DROIT INTERNATIONAL. Année 1-13, (T.1-25); jan.1927-1940. Paris,
1927-40. 25 v. Quarterly. JX3.R35 DLC(1-23) CLU(1-) CU(1-) CtY(1-)
DCE(1-) MH-L(1-) MdBJ(1-) NIC(1-) NjP(1-)

REVUE DE DROIT INTERNATIONAL ET DE LÉGISLATION COMPARÉE. T.1-30, 1869-
1898; 2. sér., T.1-16, 1899-1914; 3. sér., T.1- ; 1920- . Bruxelles.
Quarterly, 1869-1877; 6 no. a year (irregular), 1878-1928; 4 no. a year
1929- . CLU(s3,v.1-) CSt(1-s2,v.9,11-s3,v.20) CU(1-) CaOOP(1-27,29-s2,v.8,
10-) CaOOSC(1-s3,v.18) CoDU(7-) CtY(1-) CtY-L(1-) DCE(1-) DLC-L(1-) ICU(1-
s3,v.16,18-) IEN(1-) IU(1-) IaU(s3,v.1-) LU-L(1-s2,v.15; s3,v.1-) MB(1-s2,
v.14) MH(1-) MH-L(1-) MdBJ(1-) MiU(1-s2,v.12,15-) MiU-L(1-) MnU(1-) MoU(1-)
NIC(1-) NN(1-7,9-s2,v.[16]-s3,v.[1]-) NNC(1-s3,v.2,4-) NcD(1-) NhD(1-)
NjP(1-) OU(1-s2,v.2,8-) PPB(1-) PU(1-s3,v.3,7-) RPB(1-s3,v.[3]-) TxU(1-)
WU(1-) WaU(1-)

REVUE DE PSYCHOLOGIE DES PEUPLES. T.1- ; 1946- . [Le Havre] Quarterly. Official organ of Institut havrais de sociologie économique et de psychologie des peuples. BF732.R48 DLC(3-[5]) CLU(1-) CaOOG(1-) CtY(1-) IEN(1-)
MoKL(1-) NN(1-) NNA(1-) NNC(1-) NcD(4-)

REVUE DES DEUX MONDES. T.1-s14, v.1-81; 1831-sept.15, 1944. Paris, 1831-
1944. Semimonthly. Superseded by Revue; littérature, histoire, arts et
science. Supersedes Revue des deux mondes (1829-1830) AP20.R243 DLC(1-
s14,v.56) CLU(1-) CU(1-) CaOTU(1-) CSt(1-) IaU(1-) IEN(1-) MiU(s4,v.21-)
MH(1-) MB(1-) MBAt(1-) NIC(1-) NN(1-s3,v.4; s4,v.8,12,14-s14,v.55-) NHC(1-)
NNC(s4,v.1-) NcU(1-) NcD(1-) NhD(1-) NjP(1-) NRU(1-) TxHR(1-) WU(1-) WaU(1-)

Revue des sciences politiques see Sciences politiques.

REVUE DES ÉTUDES SLAVES. Paris, Impr. nationale [etc.] 1921-68. 47 v.
PG1.R4 DLC(1-19) CSt(1-) CU(1-) CaAEU(1-47) CaQMM(1-21,27,31-33) ICU(1-)
IU(1-) MH(1-) MiU(1-) NN(1-) NjP(1-) OCl(1-) PU(2-5) WU(1-) WaU(1-)

LA REVUE DES VIVANTS. Année 1-9; fév.1927,-nov./déc.1935. [Paris, 1927-

1935] 9 v. in 33. illus., plates, ports. Monthly. AP20.R36 DLC CSt-H(1-
[6]) CU([3-5]) CtY ICL([2-3,5]) IU([6,8]) NN PP([4-5]) PU

REVUE ÉCONOMIQUE INTERNATIONAL. No.1-2; avril-15 juin, 1930. Paris, 1930.
2 no. HB3.R5 DLC CU NN

REVUE GÉNÉRALE DE DROIT INTERNATIONAL PUBLIC. Année 1- (T.1-); 1894- .
Paris, A. Pedone. Biamonthly. JX3.R56 DLC(1-46) CLU(1-) CSt(1-) CU(1-)
CaAEU(s2,v.7-8; s3,v.1-13,17-33,38-) CaQMM CaOOSC(1-46) CaOTU(1-) CtY-L DCE
MH(1-) MdBJ(1-) MiU(1-) MnU(1-) NIC(1-) NN(1-) NNB(1-) NNC(1-) NNU(1-)
NjP(1-) OClW(1-) PU(1-) TxU(1-) WU(1-) WaU(1-)

REVUE HEBDOMADAIRE. Année 1-48, no.3/4; mai 28,1892-août 26,1939. Paris,
1892-1939. 48 v. AP20.R55 DLC(1-[27]-[42]-[48]) CLU([1-48]) CU(24-48)
CaOOU(2-48) CaQMM(22-[45]) CaOOP(15-48) CaMWU(33-) CtY(1-11,17-48) IEN([1-
5]-48) IaU(1-48) MH([17-19]21-[23]-48) MiU(1-[10]-48) MnU(1-12,18-48) NN(1-
48) NNC(1-48) NjP([23-29]34-48) OClW([1-2]-8,17-30,32-48) PU([6-8,17-19,28]
33-[37,39]-48) TxU(28-48) WU(26-48) WaS([27]-31)

Revue internationale d'agriculture see International Review of Agriculture.

REVUE INTERNATIONALE D'HISTOIRE POLITIQUE ET CONSTITUTIONNELLE. Ns no.
1/2-27/28; 1951-1957. Paris, Academie internationale de science politique
et d'histoire constitutionnelle, 1951-57. 28 no. Superseded by Politique;
revue internationale des doctrines et des institutions. JA11.R4 DLC
CaOOP(13-) CoU(1-) KyU([1]5-) LU(2-) MH-L(1-) MiU-L(1-) MiDU(1-) MnU(1-)
MoSW(1-) NIC(4-) NCU(1-) NN(1-) NjR(7-) PU(1-)

REVUE INTERNATIONALE D'ONOMASTIQUE. T.1- ; mars 1949- . Paris.
CS2300.R4 DLC(1-) CU(1-) CaQMM(1-) IEN(1-) IU(1-) MH(1-) MdBJ(3-) NNC(1-)
NhD(1-)

REVUE INTERNATIONALE FRANÇAISE DU DROIT DES GENS. T.1- ; jan.15, 1936- .
Paris, E. Müller. Irregular. JX3.R57 DLC(1-) CU(1-) CtY-L(1-) DCE(1-)
MH-L(1-) MiU-L(1-) NN(1-) NNC(1-) NNU(1-) NjP(1-)

REVUE PARLEMENTAIRE ÉCONOMIQUE ET FINANCIÈRE. T.1- ; 1935- . Paris
Title varies. DLC(16-[36]) DS(47-) MH([25,27]) MnU(1-12) NN(1-30,[32])

REVUE POLITIQUE ET PARLEMENTAIRE. T.1- ; juil. 1894- . Paris, A. Colin
& Cie. col. plates, maps, plan, tables. Monthly. H3.R4 DLC(1-182) CLU(1-)
CSt(1-) CU(1-) CaOOP(1-) CtY(1-) DCU(1-26) ICN(15-) ICU(1-80,82-) IU(1-)
IaU(1-) MB(1-) MH(1-) MdBJ(1-) MiU(43-) MnU(1-) MoSW(1-) MoU(1-) NIC(1-)
NN(1-) NNC(1-) NcD(1-) OClW(51-) PU(43-) TxHR(1-) WU(1-74,77-) WaU(1-)

RICERCHE SLAVISTICHE. v.1- ; 1952- . Roma, G. Casini. DR25.R5 DLC(1-)
CU(1-) CLU(6-) CtY(1-) ICU(1-) MH(1-3) NN(1-) NjP(1-) NcD(1-2) PU(1-)
RPB(1-)

ROCZNIK BIAŁOSTOCKI. T.1- ; 1961- . Białystok, Museum. DK401.R54
DLC(1-) CaOTU(1-) CU(1-) CtY(1-) DSI(1-) IU(1-) ICU(1-) InU(1-) MH(1-) NN(1-)
NNC(1-2) NjP(1-) PU(2-) PU-Mu(1-)

ROCZNIK OLSZTYNSKI. T.1- ; 1958- . Olsztyn, Pol. Museum Mazurskie.
Summaries in English and Russian. DK511.O47R6 DLC(1-) MH(1-) NN(1-)
NNC(1-) WU(1-)

ROCZNIK PRAWNICZY WILEŃSKI; organ Wydziału Prawa... Uniwersytetu... oraz
Towarzystwa Prawniczego im. Daniłowicz. T.1- ; 1925- . Wilno, J. Zawadzki. DLC-L(1-6) BM(3-) MH-L(1-5) NNC-L(1-5)

ROCZNIK TATARSKI. T.1- ; 1932- . Warszawa. Irregular. DK412.R55
DLC(1-) CtY(1-) NN(1-) OCl(1-)

ROCZNIK WOLYŃSKI. T.1- ; 1930- . Równe, Nakł. Zarządu Wolyńskiego
Okręgu, Związku Nauczycielstwa Polskiego. illus., maps. DK511.V7R6 DLC

ROCZNIKI DZIEJÓW SPOŁECZNYCH I GOSPODARCZYCH. Annales d'histoire sociale
et économique. T.1- ; 1932- . Lwów; Poznań, Poznańskie Towarzystwo Przyjaciół Nauk. Publication suspended 1939-1945. HC337.P7A255 DLC(9) CLU(12-)

CU(7-) CaAEU(1959-) CtY(8-) MH(2-5,8) NN(5-6,8-) NjR(12-) NIC(12-)

ROCZNIKI HISTORYCZNE. T.1- ; 1925- . Poznań, Towarzystwo Miłośników Historii. Vol. 15 covers period 1939-1946. DK401.R63 DLC(15-18-) CU(15-) CtY(15-) NN(15-) NNC(4,6,8) NIC(18-) WU(18-)

RUSSIA. ARCKHEOLOGICHESKAIA KOMISSIIA. Izviestiia. Vyp. 1-66. Petrograd; Sanktpeterburg, 1901-18. 66 v. in 47. illus., ports., maps. Annual. DK30.A32 DLC

RUSSIA. MINISTERSTVO NARODNOGO PROSVESHCHENIIA. Zhurnal. Ch.1-362; 1834-1905. Novaia seriia. Ch.1-72; 1906-1917. Petrograd; Sanktpeterburg, 1834-1917. Quarterly; monthly; bimonthly. L451.A55 DLC NN

Russia. Ministerstvo narodnogo prosveshcheniia. Vilenskii uchebnyi okrug see Vilenskii uchebnyi okrug.

RUSSIA (1917-R.S.F.S.R.) GLAVNOE UPRAVLENIE TORFIANOGO FONDA. Sbornik statei po izucheniiu torfianogo fonda. Vyp.1- ; 1956- . Moskva. illus., maps. Title varies: vol.1, Sbornik statei po izucheniiu torfianykh mestorozhdenii. TN840.R9A28 DLC(2-)

RUSSKII ANTROPOLOGICHESKII ZHURNAL. Moskva, Gos. izd-vo, 1900-30. 19 v. Quarterly. GN1.R85 DLC(1-[3] 5-[9] 12-19) CU([14,16]-19) CtY(1-3 [12-14]) DSG(1-3) DSI-E(1-9,12-17) MH(1-) MH-P(1-) MiU([14-15] 17-18) MnU(1-9,[13]-18) NN(1-9,12-[16-17) NNC(1-8,[13,15]) NNM(1-9,12-19)

RUSSKII FILOLOGICHESKII VIESTNIK. G.1-39 (T.1-78); 1879-1918. Varshava (Warszawa) 1879-1918. 78 v. Quarterly. PG2003.R84 DLC(1-2,4-11-) CaAEU(1-78; microfiche) CtY(1-62,67-72) InU MH(1-2,4-77) NN(29-32,63-72)

RUSSKII ISTORICHESKII SBORNIK. Moskva, 1837-44. 7 v. plates. (Moscow. Universitet. Obshchestvo istorii i drevnostei rossiiskikh) Supersedes the Society's Trudy i lietopisi. Superseded by its Chteniia. DK1.M6725 DLC CU MH NN

Russkoe geograficheskoe obshchestvo see Geograficheskoe obshchestvo SSSR.

RUSSKOE SLOVO. G.1-8; ianv.1859-ianv.1866. Sanktpeterburg, 1859-66. 8 v. in 40. illus., ports., maps. Monthly. Publication suspended June-Dec. 1862. AP50.R87 DLC NN(1859-[1861]-1865)

SAECULUM; Jahrbuch für Universalgeschichte. Bd.1- ; 1950- . Freiburg in Br.; München, Verlag Karl Albert. 4 no. a year. D2.S3 DLC(1-) AzU(10-) CU(1-) CU-Riv(1-) CaAEU(1-) CtU(8-) CtY(1-) DDO(1-) ICN(1-) ICU(1-) IU(1-) IEN(1-) KyU(9-) MH(1-) MdBJ(1-) NN(1-) NCU(1-) NcD(1-) OCU(1-) OU(1-) PPiU(11-) PU(1-) RPB(1-) TxU(1-) WaU(1-)

SANTARVĖ; rezistencinis visuomeninių ir kultūros reikalų žurnalas. London, Lietuvių Rezistencinė Santarvė, 1953-58. 42 no. Irregular. AP95.L5S26 PU(6-42) DLC(1953) OKentU(1953, no.3; 1954, no.3,6,10;[1955-1958])

SAVIVALDYBĖ; mėnesinis Lietuvos savivaldybių laikraštis. Metai 1-18; birž. 1923-liepa 1940. [Kaunas], Savivaldybių departamentas [etc.], 1923-40. illus., ports., diagrs. Monthly. Subtitle varies. JS6130.5.A1S3 DLC(1923-1937) CtPAM(1931-1938)

SCANDOSLAVICA. v.1- ; 1954- . Copenhagen. International publication for Slavonic and Baltic philology, literature, history and archaeology belonging to the Association of Scandinavian Slavists. Text in English, French, Italian, German, or Russian. PG1.S28 CaAEU(1-) CLU(1-) CU(1-) CSt(1-) CtY(1-) DLC(1-) KyU(1-) MH(1-) MnU(1-) NNC(1-2) MiU(1-) NIC(1-) NcD(1-) NjP(1-) OkU(4-)

SCHOLAR; the magazine... No.1-2/3; Nov.1947-1948. Heidelberg, 1947-48. 3 no. AP1.S36 PU(1-3) CSt-H(2/3) MH(1) ICLJF(1)

SCHOOL LIFE. Washington, D.C., Govt. Print. Office, 1918-64. 47 v. illus. L11.S378 CaAEU(45-47) AzU(1-) CLU(1-) CSt(1-) CU(1-) CaBViP(1-) CtY(1-) DLC(1-) ICN(1-) MH(1-) NNC(1-) NN(1-) OCl(1-) PU(1-) TxDaM(1-) WaU(1-)

SCHWEIZERISCHE ZEITSCHRIFT FÜR GESCHICHTE. Revue Suisse d'histoire.
Jahrg.l- ; 1951- . [Zürich] Quarterly. Dl.S34 DLC(1-) CLU(1-) CU(1-)
CU-Riv(10) CaAEU(11-) CtY(1-) CoU(1-) ICN(1-) ICU(1-) IU(1-) KyU(12-)
InU(1-) MH(1-) MdBJ(1-) MiU(9-) MnU(1-) NN(1-2) NIC(1-) NcD(1-) NcU(1-)
OU(1-) OrU(10-) PU(1-) WU(1-)

SCHWEIZERSCHES ARCHIV FÜR VOLKSKUNDE. Bd.l- ; 1897- . Basel [etc.],
Schweizerische Gesellschaft für Volkskunde. illus. (part. col.) maps,
music. Quarterly (irregular). Some numbers have title: Archives Suisses
des traditions populaires. GR1.S4 DLC(1-) CU(1-32) CaAEU(1-3,5-50,53-56,
63-64) CtY(1-) ICN(1-) ICU(1-) IU(1-) IaU(1-) MH(1-) MiU(1-32) MnU(1-32)
NIC(1-) NN(1-) NNC(1-) NbU([1]-) NcD(1-27) NjP(1-) OCl(1-) PU(1-) WU([35]-)

SCIENCES POLITIQUES. Année 1-26; jan.1886-nov./déc.1911; Année 27-51
(T.27-59); jan./fév. 1912-oct./déc. 1936; Année 52- (nouv. sér. no.1-);
mars 1937- . Paris, F. Alcan; Recueil Sirey. Quarterly, 1886-1893; bimonthly, 1894-1920; quarterly, 1921-1936; 5 no. a year, 1937; bimonthly,
1938- . H3.R35 DLC(1-ns,no.16-) CLU(1-) CSt(1-) CU(1-) CaBVaU(1-46,49-
[56]) CaOOP(1-36) CaOTU(1-) CtW(1-) CtY(1-) ICU(1-[40]-) IEN-L([26-59]-)
IaAS(1-59) IaU(1-) InU(13-) MH(1-) MH-L(1-) MNS(1-) MdBJ(1-[44-45]-) MiU(1-
[48]-) MiU-L(1-) MnU(1-59) MoU(1-[38]-) NIC(1-) NN(1-) NNC(1-) NjP(1-)
PSC(5-) PU(1-) WaU(1-)

SENOVĖ. Kaunas, Humanitariniu mokslu fakultetas, 1935-38. 4 v. illus.
Annual. 908.K164 PU(1-4) DSI(4) CU(1) ICCC(1-2)

SKAITYMAI; literatūros ir kritikos žurnalas. Kaunas, Švietimo ministerijos leidinys, 1920-23. 24 no. in 4 v. Monthly. AP95.L5S4 DLC(1-24)
CtY(1a,1b,4,10-12,14,17,19-20) ICCC(1-24) MH(7-20) NN(1-24) NNC(1-24)

SLAVIC REVIEW: American quarterly of Soviet and East European studies.
v.4- (no.8/9-); Aug.1945- . Menasha, Wis., G. Banta Publ. (American
Association for the Advancement of Slavic Studies, Inc.) Semiannual;
quarterly. Formerly The American Slavic and East European Review. Issues
for 1941-1943 (vol.1-3) were published as vol.20-22 of the Slavonic and
East European Review. American series. D377.AlA5 CaAEU(4-30-) CLU(4-)
CSt(7-) CU(4-) CaBVaU(4-) CaOLU(4-) CaOTU(4-) CaOOU(9-) CaMWU(5-) CtY(4-)
DLC(4-) ICU(4,6-) IEN(4-) IU(4-) IaU(4-) InU(4-) MH(4-) MdBJ(4-) MiU(4-)
NIC(4-) NN(4-) NNC(4-) NcD(4-) NjP(4-) OU(4-) PU(4-) TxU(4-5,7-) WaS(4-)
WaU(5-) WU(5-)

SLAVICA; Beiträge zum Studium der Sprache, Literatur, Kultur, Volkskunde
und Altertumskunde der Slawen. Heidelberg, 1919-37. 13 v. CU(2-7,12)
CaBVaU(1,3-13) ICU(1-13) MH(1-13) NN(1-13) NNC(1-13) PU(1-9)

SLAVONIC AND EAST EUROPEAN REVIEW. American series. v.1-3- 1941-1944.
Menasha, Wis., 1941-44. 3 v. Published as vol.20-22 of Slavonic and East
European Review. Vol.4- , separately published as American Slavic and
East European Review. D377.AlS65 DLC(2-3) CSt-H(1-3) CU(1-3) CaBVaU(1-3)
CaOTU(1-3) CaOTP(1-3) CtY(1-3) IEN(1-3) IaU(1-3) MH(1-3) MdBJ(1-3) NIC(1-3)
NN(1-3) OCl(1-3) PU(1-3) WaU(1-3)

THE SLAVONIC AND EAST EUROPEAN REVIEW; a survey of the peoples of Eastern
Europe, their history, economics, philosophy and literature. v.1- ;
June 1922- . London [etc.] Eyre & Spottiswoode; [etc.]. 3 no. a year,
1922-Jul.1939; annual, 1939/40-1941; Semiannual, Mar.1943- . Title varies:
June 1922-Dec.1927, The Slavonic Review; Mar.1928-Dec.1930, The Slavonic
(and East European) Review; Mar.1931- . The Slavonic and East European
Review. Imprint varies. D377.AlS65 DLC(1-) CLU(1-) CU(1-) CaOTP(1-)
CaAEU(4,6-7,20,22,25-31,33-38,40-41,44) CaOTU(1-) CtY(1-) ICU(1-) MH(1-)
MdBJ(1-) MnU(1-) MoU(1-) NN(1-) NNC(1-) NjP(4-) OCl(1-) PP(1-) TxU(1-)
WaS(1-)

Slavonic Review see Slavonic and East European Review.

SOCIAL SCIENCE. v.1- ; Nov.1925- . Winfield, Kan., Pi Gamma Mu, Na-
tional Social Science Honor Society. H1.S55 DLC(1-) AzU([2-6]-[8] 10-)
CLU(2-) CSt-L([1-10]) CStoC(1-) CU(6-) CtU([6-7]-) CtY[1-2]-) ICP(4-)
IEN([8],11-) IU(1-) IaU(4-) InU(6-7,11-) KU(1-) MH(1-) MiU(1-) MnU(1-)
MoU(1-) NN(1-) NNC(1-) NjR(1-) NNU(6-[8-9]-[11-13]-) OCl(6-) OU(1-) OrU(1-)
PBL(1-) PU(1-8) TxU(1-) WU([1-4]-) WaS(6-7) WaU([2-3] 4,6-) PPiU(6-7,10-13)

SOCIETA GEOGRAFICA ITALIANA, ROME. Bollettino. T.1- ; 1869- . Roma.
Semiannual (irregular); monthly. G17.S67 DLC(1-[77]-) CLU(1-s5,v.12; s6,
v.9-) CU(1-) CaQMM(10-) CaOG(s2,v.9-) CaTR(3-16,18-) CtY(1-) DSI-M(4-)
ICJ(1-70) IU(1-5,52-) IaU(32,34,[37]-[40]-[50]-[71]-[73]) MB(1-64,66-)
MH(1-) MiU(1-) MnU(1-58) NBuG(1-62) NN(1-) NNA(2-) NNU(1-55,64-69) NhD(1-49,
52-) NjP(1-) OCU(60-) PPAN(s2,v.9-)

SOCIÉTÉ DE LINGUISTIQUE DE PARIS. Mémoires. Paris, 1868-1935. 23 v.
illus., fold. plates. P12.S45 DLC CLU CSt CU CaOOG(1-22) CaOTU CtY ICU
ICN(1-22) IEN IU(1-[7,16]-23) InU MB(1-21) MH MdBJ MiU MnU MoSW(1-15) MoU
NIC NN NNC(1-[23]) NcU NhD(1-23) NjP OCU OCl(1-20) OU PU RPB TxU WU

SOTER; religijos mokslo laikraštis. Kaunas, Teologijos-filosofijos fakultetas, 1924-39. 28 no. Mostly twice a year. BL9.L8S6 DLC CU(1-)
ICCC(1928,1931,no.1)

SOUTHERN FOLKLORE QUARTERLY. v.1- ; March 1937- . Jacksonville, Fla.,
Southern Folklore Society. GR1.S65 DLC(1-) CLU(1-) CSt(1-) CU(1-) CoDU(1-)
CtY(1-) FU(1-) GU(1-) ICN(1-) ICU(1-) IEN(1-) IU(1-) IaU(1-) KU(1-) KyU(1-)
LU(1-) MB(1-) MH(1-) MdBJ(1-) MiD(3-) MiU(1-) MnU(1-) MoU(1-) NIC(1-)
NN(1-) NcD(1-) NcU(1-) NhD(1-) NjP(1-) OC(1-) OCl(1-) OU(1-) OrU(1-) PU(1-)
RPB(1-) TNF(1-) TU(1-) TxU(1-) ViU(1-) WaU(1-)

SOVETSKAIA ARKHEOLOGIIA. Moskva [etc] Akademiia Nauk SSSR, 1936-59. 30
v. illus., plates, maps, plans, tables. Published by the Akademiia nauk
SSSR. Institut antropologii, arkheologii i etnografii. DK30.Q17 DLC(1-30)
CaBVaU(8,11,13,15-) CaOOG(5-) ICF(1) MH-P(1-) MiU(2) NN(1-) NNMM(1-)
NNM(1-4,6-7) NjP(1-4) PBm(2-4)

SOVETSKAIA ARKHEOLOGIIA. G.1- ; 1957- . Moskva, Izd-vo Nauka, illus.
Quarterly. DK30.A1733 (DLC 1957-) AzU([1960]-) CaAEU(1959-) CtY(1957-)
DSI(1957-) ICU(1960-) InU([1961]-) IaU(1962-) MnU(1965-) MiU([157-1958]-)
NNC([1957,1958])

SOVETSKAIA ETNOGRAFIIA. T.1- ; 1931- . Moskva; Leningrad, Akademiia
nauk SSSR. Bimonthly. GN1.S65 DLC(1931-1937) CSt(1933-1937) CSt-H(1934-
1935) CU(1932-) CaAEU(1960-)

SOVETSKAIA MUZYKA. G.1-9, 1933-1941; G.10- ; 1946- . Moskva, Komitet
po delam iskustv. Suspended between Aug.1941 and 1946; replaced by Sovetskaia muzyka; sbornik statei. 1946 called year 10. ML300.S75 DLC(1-
[9-13]-) CU(1-) CLU(1-) CtY(12-) MH([3-4] 10-[13-14]-) NN(2-[4-6]-[8]-)

SOVIET STUDIES; a quarterly review of the social and economic institutions
of the USSR. v.1- ; June 1949/50- . Oxford, Blackwell. Quarterly.
DK266.A2S74 DLC(1-) CLU(1-) CaAEU(1-) CaOOAG(1-) CaOKF(1-) CaQMM(1-)
CaOTU(1-) CtY(1-) ICN(1-) ICU(1-) IEN(1-) IU(1-) InU(1-) KyU(1-) MdBJ([1]-)
MH(1-) MiU(1-) NN(1-) NNC(1-) NcD(1-) NjP(1-) OClW(1-) OU(1-) PU(1-)
TxU(1-) WU([1]-) WaU(1-)

SOZIALISTISCHE MONATSHEFTE. Jahrg.1-39, Heft.2; Jan.1897-Feb.4,1933.
Berlin, Verlag der Sozialistischen Monatshefte, 1897-1933. 37 v. in 71.
illus., plates, ports. Monthly; biweekly (irregular) Supersedes Sozialistische Akademiker. yr 1-16, 1897-1912 also as its yr 3-18. yr 22-39 also
as v.44-77, no.2. HX6.S6 DLC-CLU(v.52,60-62) CSt-H(v.47-[58-59]-77)
CU(1-5,7-[24]-[39]) ICU(5-22,[25]-39) IaU(1-39) MH(3-39) MdBJ(1-39)
MnU(v.58-59) NN(1-39) NNC(1-39) NjP(4-[26]-39) WU([1-2]-4,[5]-16 [19-23] 26-
38)

Sprawozdania Towarzystwa Naukowego we Lwowie see Towarzystwo Naukowe we
Lwowie. Sprawozdania.

Sprawozdania z czynności i posiedzeń Polskiej Akademii Umiejętności w
Krakowie see Polska Akademia Umiejętności, Kraków. Sprawozdania z
czynności i posiedzeń.

Sprawozdania z posiedzeń (Wydziału I-IV) Towarzystwa Naukowego Warszawskiego see Towarzystwo Naukowe Warszawskie. Sprawozdania z posiedzeń
Wydzialu I-IV.

SPRAWY OBCE; piśmo kwartalne. T.1-2(no.1-8); październik 1929- październik

1931. Warszawa, Drukarnia W. Łazarskiego, 1929-31. 2 v. D410.S6
DLC(no.1-4,7) CSt-H(no.1-7) NN(1-8)

Statyba ir architektūra see Lietuvos TSR Aukštųjų mokyklų mokslo darbai: Statyba ir architektūra.

STIMME DER FREIHEIT; unabhängige Zeitung für Demokratie, aktive Frei-
heitspolitik und Wiedervereinigung. Hrsg. von Aktion Freier Staatsbürger
e.V., Saarbrücken; Volksbund für Frieden und Freiheit. Jahrg. 1- ; 1959 .
Saarbrücken, Verlag Stimme der Freiheit. Monthly. Title varies: vol.1-7,
1959-1965, Saarländische Stimme der Freiheit. DLC(4-)

STUDI BALTICI. 1-8, 1931-1940; [New series] 1(9)- , 1952- . [Roma]
L.S. Olschki. (Academia toscana di scienze e lettere "La Colombia".
Studi, 2) PG8001.S8 DLC CaOTU CtY(1-) CtPAM(1-4,6,9-10) NN(1-) NNC(1-)
NjCA(1-) OU(1,9) PU(1-) WU(1-)

Studia Historyczne Polskiej Akademii Nauk... Kraków see Małopolskie
Studia Historyczne.

STUDIA I MATERIAŁY DO HISTORII WOJSKOWOŚCI. T.1- ; 1954- . [Warszawa]
Wydawn. Ministerstwa Obrony Narodowej. illus., maps. DK417.S8 DLC(4-)
MH(1-) NN(1-)

STUDIA Z FILOLOGII POLSKIEJ I SŁOWIAŃSKIEJ. T.1- ; 1955- . Warszawa,
Panstwowe Wydawnictwo Naukowe. Issued by Komitet Sławianoznawstwa (called
in 1955 Komitet Sławistyczny i Rusicystyczny) of the Polska Akademia Nauk.
PG6001.S8 DLC(1-) CSt-(2-) CLU(1-) CaAEU(1-9) IU(1-) MnU(5-) NN(1-) PSt(2-)

SUOMALAINEN TIEDEAKATEMIA, HELSINGFORS. Sitzungsberichte. Bd.1- ; 1908-
. Helsingfors. Q60.H5 DLC(1908-1935) CSt(1908-1936) CaQMM(1908-)
CtY(1952) DSI-M(1908-) MiU(1946-1948) MnU(1908-1930) NNC(1908-1933)
PPAN(1908-1912) RPB(1908-1912)

SUOMALAINEN TIEDEAKATEMIA, HELSINGFORS. Suomalaisen tiedeakatemian toimituksia. Annales Academiae scientiarum fennicae. Ser. B. T.1-60; 1909-
1946. Helsinki, Suomalaisen tiedeakatemian kustantama, 1909-46. 60 v.
Q60.H53 DLC(1-34,36-49,51-) CSt(1-) CLU(38-49,51-) CU([8,21,28]) CaOON(1-)
CaQMM(1-) CaOG (6,8-9,[14-34],36-49,51-) CaOTU(17,42-) CtY(1-) IU([29] 34-
49,51-) KU(34-) MH(1-) McBJ(1-41,43-49,51-) MiU(19,21,23-) MnU(1-[38] 42,
[45]) NIC(34-49,51-) NN(17,19-49,51-) NNC(1-) NcD(33-) NhD(1-) NjP(1-)
OU(1-) RPB(1-) PPAN(1-) WU(1-)

SURVEY OF INTERNATIONAL AFFAIRS. v.1- ; 1920/23- . London; New York,
N.Y., Oxford University Press [etc.]. Irregular. D422.S8 DLC(1-) CL(1924-)
CaOTU(1-) CtY-L(1-) FTS(1-) IaAS(1-) IEN(1-) MdBP(1920/23-1933) MiU(1-)
MiU-L(1-) NNC(1-) PU(1930-) TNV(1925-) WyU(1920-1925,1927-1933) WM(1920-1938)

ŠVIETIMO DARBAS; mėnesinis Švietimo ministerijos žurnalas. Kaunas, 1919-
30. 12 v. Monthly. L51.S8 DLC ICCC(1919,no.2-3; 1920,no.2-5,8-12; 1921,
no.1-4,7-12; 1922-1930) NN(1919-1930)

ŚWIATOWIT; rocznik poświęcony archeologii i badaniom pierwotnej kultury
polskiej i słowiańskiej. T.- ; 1899- . Warszawa, Państwowe Wydawnictwo
Naukowe. Annual. Suspended 1914-1923 and 1940-1944. GN845.P7S9 DLC
CU(17) CtY(1-4,6-12) ICF(14-17) MH-P MiD-A(15) MiU(13-17) NN(2,14-17)
NNM(1-10,12-16) OClMA(15) WaU(12-17)

TARTU. ÜLIKOOL. ÕPETATUD ESTI SELTS. Toimetused (Verhandlungen). Commentationes litterarum societatis esthonicae. 1- ; 1840- . Tartu (Dorpat, IUr'ev). illus., plates, ports., maps, plans, facsims. Irregular.
Title varies: vol.1-23,1840-1925, Verhandlungen der gelehrten estnischen
Gesellschaft zu Dorpat; vol.24-28, 1927-1936, Toimetused... Verhandlungen..;
vol.29- , 1938- , Toimetused. Commentationes... AS262.T225T6 DLC(1-
[16]-) CU(25) ICN(1-3,5-[7-8],10-12) MBN([5]-[8]-[21]) MH(1-31) MnU(1-25,27-)
NN(1-2,9,13-15,17-22) NNC([1-5]-[8]-15,17-[20]-22) NNM(1-3,5-25)

TAUTA IR ŽODIS. Epe lituana; sumptibus Ordinis philologorum Universitatis
lituaniensis edita. Kn.1-7; 1927-1931. Kaunas, Humanitarinių mokslų fakulteto leidinys, 1927-31. 7 v. illus., ports. Irregular. PG8501.T3
DLC BM(1,3,6-7) CU ICU(1-5,7) ICCC(1-7) MH(1-7) MoU(6) NIC(6) NN(1-7)

NNC(1-5) PU(1-6) WU(1-7) CaAEU(1,7)

TAUTOS PRAEITIS; istorijos ir gretimųjų sričių neperiodinis žurnalas.
T.1- ; 1959- . Chicago, Ill., Lietuvių istorijos draugija. illus.,
facsims. Irregular. In Lithuanian with summaries in English. Each book
has 4 no. DK511.L2A276 DLC(1-) CaOONL(no.1-8) CaOTU(1-) ICCC(v.1,kn.1-2)
ICBM(v.2,kn.1-2,5-6) ICLJF(kn.1-4; 1959-62) InU([2]) KU(v.1,kn.1) MH(1-),
NN(1-) OKentU(1-2) PU(1-)

TAUTOS ŪKIS. Metai 1-11; sausis 1930-liepa 1940. Kaunas, Ekonominių
studijų draugija, 1930-40. 11 v. Monthly; weekly. CtPAM(1931-1939)

TAUTOS ŪKIS; Volkswirtschaft. Beilage der wöchentlichen Wirtschaftszeitung Tautos ūkis. Nr.1-16; gegužis 1938-rugp. 1940. Kaunas, 1938-40.
16 no. Monthly (irregular). HC337.L5A36 DLC

TAUTOSAKOS DARBAI. Kaunas, Lietuvių tautosakos archyvas, 1935-40. 7 v.
In Lithuanian, German, or English. GR203.L68T2 CLU(1-) BM CaAEU(1-5)
ICCC(1,3,5) ICBM(3,6,7) ICU(1-) PU(1-7)

TECHNIKA. Edition periodique de la Faculté technique à l'Université
Lithuanienne... Kaunas, 1924-40. 11 v. (Kaunas. Universitetas. Techni-
kos fakultetas) Articles in Lithuanian with summaries in French. T4.T2
DLC(1-9) CSt(1-7) CU(1-) CaOTU(1-7) ICU(5-6) IaAS(1-) InLP(1-7) MiU(1-5,7)
MnU(1-8) MH(1-6) MoSA(6) NIC(1-7) NN(1-6) NNC(1-) NbU(1-7) MoU(1-8) OU(1-7)
PSt(1-6) WU(1-7)

TECHNIKA IR ŪKIS. La technique et l'économie. Kaunas, Lietuvos inžinierių draugija, 1929-40. illus., maps, diagrs. 3-6 no. a year (irregular).
947.59 T226 WaU(1930,no.2) CU(1-9,30-)

TECHNIKOS ŽODIS. 1- ; balandis 1951- . Chicago, Ill., American Lithuanian Engineers and Architects. Monthly; bimonthly. DLC([3]) ICCC(1952,
no.1-4,6-8,10; 1953,no.1-4,6,7) OKentU(1960, no.5-6; 1961, no.1-5; [1965])

TEISĖ; teisės mokslų ir praktikos žurnalas. Nr.1-52. Kaunas, Lietuvos
teisininkų draugija, 1922-40. 52 no. Quarterly. ICBM(1-35)

TEISININKŲ ŽINIOS. Nr.1-26; lapkr.1952-gruod.1958. Chicago, Ill., Lietuvių teisininkų draugija, 1952-58. 26 no. Irregular. DLC-L(1-)
ICCC(1953,no.2) MH-L(1-) OKentU(1953, no.3)

TEKA WILEŃSKA. Wilno, Drukiem Teofila Glücksberga, 1857-58. 6 v.
491.922 T237 PU(1-6) BM(1-6)

TEKI ARCHIWALNE. 1- ; 1953- . Warszawa, Państwowe Wydawn. Naukowe.
DK402.T36 DLC(3-) ICU(1-) MH(2) MiU(4) MiDW(1-2,5-) NIC(2-) NN(1-) NNC(1-)
NNU(3) OU(1-) WU(1-)

TEKI HISTORYCZNE. T.1- ; czerw.1947- . Londyn. Quarterly. Issued
by Polskie Towarzystwo Historyczne w Wielkiej Brytanii. DK401.T4 DLC([1-2])
CSt-H([1]-[3]) DCU(2-) NN(1-) NIC(1-) OU(1-) ViU(1-) WU(1-)

TERRA. Suomen maantieteellisen seuran aikakauskirja; Geografiska sällska-
pets i Finland tidskrift. Årg.1- ; 1888- . Helsingfors, 1889- .
illus., plates, port., maps, diagrs. Title varies: 1888/89-1912, Geografiska föreningens tidskrift; 1913-1921, Terra. Geografiska föreningens
tidskrift; maantieteellisen yhdistyksen aikakauskirja. G28.G5 DLC(1-[14]-
52-) CaQMAI([58-59]-) IU([44-45] 47-) MH-Z(42,[43]-[46] 49,[50-52]-)
MiU(44-) NN([1-2]-[12]-) WU(1-)

TĖVIŠKĖS ŽIBURIAI. Metai 1- ; gruodis 1949- . Toronto, Ont., Kanados
lietuvių katalikų kultūros draugija. Weekly. DLC(3-) OKentU(1959)

TĖVYNĖS SARGAS; mėnesinis laikraštis paskirtas dvasiškam ir medžiagiškam
lietuvių tautos sulaikymui par jos apšvietimą. Metai 1-9; sausis 1896-
gegužis 1904. Tilžė. Monthly. CtPAM(1897-1901) ICCC(1897,no.4,6,9,10-11;
1898,no.5-8; 1899,no.11-12; 1900,no.2-3; 1901,no.6-10; 1902,no.1-3,6,2-3B;
1903,no.2-4,7-10,9-10B; 1904,no.1) MePKF(1901-1904)

TĖVYNĖS SARGAS; politikos ir socialinių mokslų žurnalas. No.1- ; 1947- .

Reutlingen, Ger.; Chicago, Ill., Lietuvių krikščionių demokratų partija.
Irregular. DK511.L2A57 PU(1-) ICCC(1947-1948, 1951-1954) ICLJF(1947-1949,
1951-1955) MH(2,no.1-2/3,5-6/7) OKentU(1-4,8-10,15-16,2-31)

TIESOS KELIAS; religijos bei doros mokslo ir visuomenės gyvenimo žurnalas. Nr.1-186; sausis 1925-birž.1940. Kaunas, 1925-40. 186 no. Monthly.
CtPAM(1925-1939) ICCC(1925-1933,no.1-8,11-12; 1934-1937,no.1-5,8-12; 1938-
1940,no.1-6) ICLJF(1926-1933) OKentU(1936,1938) PU(1935,no.2-12; 1936,no.
1-10,12; 1937-1940,no.1-6)

TOWARZYSTWO NAUKOWE W TORUNIU. Roczniki. Rok 1- ; 1878- . Toruń.
DLC(54-) MiU(58-) NN(1,4-11,16-39,42-) NNC(35-36)

TOWARZYSTWO NAUKOWE W TORUNIU. Wydział Nauk Historychnych, Prawniczych
i Społecznych. Zapiski Historyczne; kwartalnik poświęcony historii Pomorza. T.1- ; 1908- . Toruń. Monthly (irregular); quarterly. 1939-1945
suspended. DD491.P71T6 DLC(6) InU(23) NN(1-10) NNC(20-)

TOWARZYSTWO NAUKOWE WE LWOWIE. Sprawozdania. T.1- ; 1921- . Lwów.
3 no. a year. AS262.L926 DLC(1-) CU(1-13) IU(1-2) MH([1-3]-5,[12,14])
NN([15]-) NNA(2-[13-14,16) OCl(6-) PPAN(15-)

TOWARZYSTWO NAUKOWE WE LWOWIE. WYDZIAŁ II: historyczno-filozoficzny.
Archivum. T.1- ; 192 - . Lwów. Irregular. D1.T68 DLC

TOWARZYSTWO NAUKOWE WARSZAWSKIE. Sprawozdania z posiedzeń Wydziału I-IV.
Rok 1-31,1-36,no.6; 1908-1938. Warszawa. Monthly. Vol.1,no.9 never pub-
lished. Suspended 1918-1925. AS262.W323 DLC(1-31) CU(6,19-31) CaTR(29-30)
CtY(1-24,26-31) ICJ(1-31) MH(1-31) NN(1-31) NNC(24-29) NNM(1-31) NcD(19-31)
RPB(1-31) WaU(6-31)

TOWARZYSTWO NAUKOWE WARSZAWSKIE. WYDZIAŁ II: Nauk Historycznych i Filozoficznych. Prace... Warszawa, 1910-36. 24 v. AS262.W34 DLC(1-18,21-24)
MBA(4-10) MH(19) MH-P(6,10,14,17-18) NN(1-2,4-24) NNC(23-25) NjP(17)

TOWARZYSTWO PRZYJACIÓŁ NAUK W WILNIE. Rocznik. Rok 1-7; 1907-1921.
Wilno, 1908-21. 7 v. illus., maps. 943.8 T6591 NNC(1-2) CU(7) NN(1,3-7)

TOWARZYSTWO PRZYJACIÓŁ NAUK W WILNIE. WYDZIAŁ I. Rozprawy i materiały...
Rok 1- ; 1928- . Wilno. BM(1,no.3-) CU([3]-[7-8]-) CtY([3-4] 6,8)
ICU(6,9) IEN([6]) MH([6,8-9]) MiU([1]-[3]) NN([1]-[9]-) NNC(9)

TOWARZYSTWO PRZYJACIÓŁ NAUK W WILNIE. WYDZIAŁ II: MATEMATYCZNYCH I
PRZYRODNICZYCH. Prace Towarzystwa Przyjaciół Nauk w Wilnie. Travaux de la
société des sciences et des lettres de Vilno. Classe des sciences mathématiques et naturelles. T.1- ; 1923- . Wilno. illus., plates (part.
col.) map, diagrs. AS262.V452 DLC(2-5) CU(1-) CtY(6-8) IU(7-11) MH(12-13)
NIC-A([1-10]-[13]) NN(1-3,5-) RPB(1-11)

TOWARZYSTWO PRZYJACIÓŁ NAUK W WILNIE. WYDZIAŁ III: HISTORII, FILOZOFII I
NAUK SPOŁECZNYCH. Rozprawy... T.1- ; 1925-1938. Wilno, 1925-38. illus.,
fold. maps. Irregular. 943.8.T658 NNC CU(5-) CtY(5-8) MiU(1-6,9-)
NN([1]-4,6-10)

TRIMITAS. Metai 1-21; birž. 1920-birž. 1940. Kaunas, Lietuvos šaulių sąjunga 1920-40. 21 v. illus. Weekly. CtPAM(1923-1924,1929-1931,1935-1937,
1939-[1940]) CtTMF(1930-1933,1936,1939) DLL ICCC(1929,no.13,25; 1930,no.28,
50; 1931,no.2-4; 1936,no.5; 1938,no.40; 1940,no.20) NCCL

UNITED STATES. LIBRARY OF CONGRESS. Quarterly journal of current acqui-
sitions. v.1- ; July/Sept.1943- . Washington, D.C., plates, ports.,
maps, facsims., music. Z881.U49A3 DLC(1-) ClSU(1-) CtHW(1-) CtY(1-)
MBU(1-) MdBU(1-) Mid-B(1-) MnHi(1-) NNC(1-) NNN(1-) PPC(1-) WaWW(1-) VHS(1-)

UPPSALA. UNIVERSITET. Årsskrift. Årg.1- ; 1861- . Uppsala.
AS284.U71 DLC(1-) CU(1-) CaOON(1886-) CaOTU(1861-1867,1869-1883,1885-)
CtY(1-) KMK(1887-1890,1892-) MH(1-) MdBJ(1861-1938) MiU(1887-) NbU(1-)
NjP(1-) WU(1-)

VARPAS; literatūros, politikos ir mokslo mėnesinis laikrasztis. Metai 1-
17; sausis 1889-kovas 1906. Tilžėje; Ragainėje, 1889-1906. 17 v. Monthly.

Merged in "Lietuvos ūkininkas". 57.92 V436 PU(1889-1891; 1892,no.6-12; 1893-1905) CtY(2) NN(1-3,5,no.4,6-8,10-11; 6-7,no.11; 8,no.3,5-10; 13, no.3,5; 14-17)

VARPAS; neperiodinis žurnalas. Nr.1- ; 1953- . Brooklyn, N.Y., Varpininkų leidinių fondas. Irregular. 57.92 V438 PU(1-5-) DLC(1-) ICLJF(6) NN(1-)

LE VIE DEL MONDO. 1- ; mar. 1929- . [Milano] Touring club italiano, illus., maps. Monthly. G1.V53 DLC(13-) IU([22]-) MWelC(7-15) MdBCN([7-8]) NN([12]-) NNA(1-[11])

VIENNA. INSTITUT FÜR ÖSTERREICHISCHE GESCHICHTSFORSCHUNG. Mitteilungen. Bd.1- ; 1880- . Innsbruck; Wien. CU(1-) CtY(1-) DLC(1-[35]) ICN(1-) ICU(1-52) MH(1-) MiU(1-31) MnU(1-49) NIC(1-) NN(1-) NNC(1-) OCl(1-) OU(1-)

VIERTELJAHRSHEFTE FÜR ZEITGESCHICHTE. Jahrg.1- ; 1953- . Stuttgart. Quarterly. D410.V66 CaAEU(1-) AMAU(2-) AzU(5-) CLS(8-) CLU(1-) CSt-H(1-) CtY(1-) ICU(1-) IU(1-) KU(1-) KyU(4-) MH(1-) MdBJ(1-) MnU(1-) MCU(1-) NNC(1-) NRU(1-) NcD(1-) NjP(1-) NN(1-) OCU(1-) OU(1-) PU(1-) WU(1-)

VIERTELJAHRSSCHRIFT FÜR SOZIAL- UND WIRTSCHAFTSGESCHICHTE. Bd.1- ;1903-. Leipzig; Stuttgart, C.L. Hirschfeld; W. Kohlhammer. H5.V6 DLC(1-) CaAEU(1-) CaOTU(1-) CaBVaU(1-) CU(1-) CtY(1-) ICU(1-) IU(1-) IaU(1-) MH(1-) MnU(1-) NN(1-) NNC(1-) NjP(1-) PU(1-) TxU(1-) WU(1-) WaU(1-)

VIESTNIK EVROPY. Moskva, Universitetskaia tipografiia, 1802-30. 174 v. Semimonthly. Superseded by Viestnik Evropy, Sanktpeterburg. AP50.V48 DLC(1802-1829) CtY'1802-1830) NN[1803],1813-1819,[1824]-1826)

VIESTNIK EVROPY; zhurnal nauki, politiki, literatury. G.1-53 (no.175-434) mart 1866-ianv./apr. 1918. Petrograd; Sanktpeterburg, D.N.Ovsianniko-Kulikovskii [etc.] 1866-1918. 260 v. Quarterly; monthly. Supersedes Viestnik Evropy, Moscow. AP50.V5 DLC(1-[52-53]) CSt-H(1-52) CU(1-52) CtY(1-47,[49]) ICU(15-52) MH(1-[46]-53) NNC(1-46,48-49,51,53)

VIESTNIK ZAPADNOI ROSSII; istoriko-literaturnyi zhurnal. G.1-9,no.4; iiul' 1862-1871. Kiev [etc.], 1862-71. 9 v. Monthly. Title varies: 1862-July 1864, Viestnik IUgo-Zapadnoi i Zapadnoi Rossii. Microfiche. Tumba, Sweden. International Documentation Centre. 409 cards. 947.7005VIE IU(1-[6-8]-9,no.4; microfiche) CSt(1862) DLC(1870) CaAEU(1-9,no.1-4; microfiche) NN(1-[9])

VILENSKII KALENDAR. Vil'na, Tip. Russkii Pochin, 1884-1914. 947.52 V713 PU(1904-1905) MH(1899-1900)

VILENSKII VREMENNIK. T.1-6. Vil'na, Murav'evskii Muzei, 1904-13. 6 v. Bw93W68+A15 CtY(1-3,5-6) DLC(1-6) NN(1-[5-6])

VILNA. UNIVERSITETAS. Biologija, geografija, geologija. 1- ; 1949- . Vilnius, Valstybinė politinės ir mokslinės literatūros leidykla. (Its Mokslo darbai) This is a subseries of Vilna. Universitetas. Mokslo darbai. Vol.1-2,1949-1954, are unnumbered and have title: Seriia estestvenno-matematicheskikh nauk. Title varies: vol.3-4,1955-1957, Biologijos, geologijos ir geografijos serija. DLC(3-4)

VILNA. UNIVERSITETAS. Ekonomika. T.1- ; 1955- . Vilnius. Irregular. Title varies: vol.1, 1955, Ekonomikos ir teisės mokslų serija. vol.2, 1957, and vol.3,1958, Ekonomikos mokslų serija. H31.V5 DLC(2-3) MH

Vilna. Universitetas. Ekonomikos ir teisės mokslų serija see Vilna. Universitetas. Ekonomika.

Vilna. Universitetas. Ekonomikos mokslų serija see Vilna. Universitetas. Ekonomika.

Vilna. Universitetas. Filosofija see Lietuvos TSR Aukštųjų mokyklų darbai: Filosofija.

Vilna. Universitetas. Istorija see Lietuvos TSR Aukštųjų mokyklų mokslo darbai: Istorija.

Vilna. Universitetas. Istorijos-filologijos mokslų serija _see_ Lietuvos TSR Aukštųjų mokyklų mokslo darbai: Istorija.

Vilna. Universitetas. Kalbotyra _see_ Lietuvos TSR Aukštųjų mokyklų mokslo darbai: Kalbotyra.

VILNA. UNIVERSITETAS. Mokslo darbai. T.1- ; 1949-1961. Vilnius. L Soc.2690.25 MH(1-4,6-13,17,20-21,23-36) RPB(8,11,16,25)

VILNA. UNIWERSYTET. Studium Historii Prawa Litewskiego. Wiadomości. T.1- ; 1938- . Wilno. DLC-L NNC-L PU(1)

VILNA. VALSTYBINIS PEDAGOGINIS INSTITUTAS. Mokslo darbai. T.1- ; 1955- . Vilnius. illus., diagrs. Articles in Lithuanian or Russian. Summaries in Lithuanian, Russian, English, or German. AS262.V442 DLC(9-) MH(1955-)

VILNA. WOJEWÓDZKI KOMITET REGIONALNY. Wilno i ziemia Wileńska. Wilno, 1930-37. 2 v. DK651.V4A57 DLC

VISA LIETUVA; informacinė knyga. 1922- . Kaunas, Spaudos Fondas. Irregular. Articles in Lithuanian and German. HC337.L7A2 ICU CSt-H(1925) CtPAM(1922) DLC(1922,1925,1931) PU(1925)

VÖLKERBUND UND VÖLKERRECHT. Berlin, Deutsche Gesellschaft für Völkerbundfragen, 1934-38. 4 v. Merged to Europäische Revue. JX5.V5 DLC CSt-H CtY-L DCE MH-I MiU-L NN NNC NjP

VOLK UND RASSE. München; Berlin, 1926-44. 19 v. GN1.V6 DLC CU(1-8) DSG(1-) ICU(1-) MH(1-) MH-P(1-10) MdBJ(14-) NN(1-) NNC([5-6.9]) NjP(1-)

VOPROSY IAZYKOZNANIIA. 1- ; ianv./fevr. 1952- . Moskva, Akademiia nauk SSSR. P9.V6 DLC(1952-) CLU(1952-[1953]) CaAEU(1-7,9-17,19-) CtY(1952-) IU(1959-) IaU(1953-) InU(1952-) MH(1952-) MdBJ(1952-) MiU([1953]-) NN(1955-) NIC(1952-) NjP(1959-) PU(1952-) RPB(1953-) WU(1960-)

VOPROSY ISTORII. 1- ; 1945- . Moskva. Monthly. At head of title: Akademiia nauk SSSR. Institut istorii. Supersedes Istoricheskii zhurnal. DK1.V6 DLC CLU([1946]-) CSt-H(1945-) CU([145]-) CaAEU(1945-) CaSSU([1947]-) CaOTU(1945-[1947-1948]-) CtY(1945-) ICU([1946]-) IaU(1945-) InU(1945-) MH(1945-[1949]-) MdBJ(1950-) MiU([1947]-1949) NIC(1945-) NN(1945-[1938]-) NNC([1945]-) NcD([1946]-1948) OCl(1946-1948) OU(1949-) PU([1945]-) RPB(1945-) TxU[1946]-[1948]-) WU([1947-1948]-) WaU([1945-1948]-)

VOPROSY SLAVIANSKOGO IAZYKOZNANIIA. 1- ; 1954- . Moskva, Akademiia nauk SSSR, Institut slavianovedeniia. PG1.V6 DLC(1-) CU(1-) CSt(1-) CLSU(1-) CLU(1-) CaAEU(1-) CoU(7-) CtY(4-) ICU(1-) IaU(2-) IU(1-) InU(4) KyU(1-) MH(1-) MnU(1-) MiU(1-) NNC(4-) NjP(3-) PSt(1-) PU(1-) RPB(2-) ViU(1-3)

VORGESCHICHTLICHE FORSCHUNGEN. Bd1- ; 1924- . Berlin. CU([1-2]) CtY(1-) ICJ(1-2) ICU(1-) MH(1-) MH-P,[2]-) MnU(1-) MdBJ([2]) NN(1-) NNC(1-) NNM(1-) NjP([1-2]-)

VORONEZHSKII ISTORIKO-ARKHEOLOGICHESKII VESTNIK. Voronezh, 1921. 2 no. CSt-H(1-2)

VSESOIUZNYI GIDROLOGICHESKII S"EZD. Trudy. 1- ; 1931- . Leningrad, Gidrometeorologicheskoe izd-vo, maps. Irregular. GB651.V83 DLC(3-)

VYTIS. The Knight. v.1-6, 1915-1918; New series. v.1-15, 1919-1933; 1934-1935; v.22- ; 1936- . Chicago, Ill., Lietuvos Vyčiai. In English and Lithuanian. CtPAM(1915-) ICCC([1915-1930, 1936-1940] 1941-) ICBM(1921-1922) ICLJF(1921-1927, 1962-1963) ICJ(1-[6]; ns v.[1]-4,8) ICN([3]-6; ns v.1-2,5-7) NN(ns v.5,[6] 7,12,[13]-) OKentU(oct.15, 1915-1921; 1925, no. 15,19; 1929, no.17; 1931, no.1-6,20-22; 1932, no. 2-4,7,9-12,14-16; 1933, no.1,3,5,7,9,10,12,14,15,17; 1934, no.1-4,6-12; 1935-1940, 1943-1973)

WARSAW. INSTYTUT GEOLOGICZNY. Biuletyn. no.1-; 1938- . Warszawa.
Formed by the union of its Sprawozdania and Posiedzenia... QE276.5.W362
DLC(no.[1-161]-) CLU(no.[1-142]-) CU[1-136]-) CtY([1-44) IaU([24-60]-)
IU([1-79]-) KU([1-24]-) KyU(97-) MdBJ([1-90]-) MiD([13-32]-) NIC([71-107]-)
NbU([8-132])

--- Posiedzenia naukowe Państwowego Instytutu Geologicznego. Comptes-
rendus des seances du service geologique de Pologne. Nr. 1-48; stycz.
1922-lip.1937. Warszawa, 1922-37. 48 no. in 2 v. Irregular. United
with its Sprawozdania to form its Biuletyn. QE276.5.A32 DI-GS

--- Sprawozdania. Bulletin. T.1-9, zesz.2; 1920-1938. Warszawa, 1920-
38. 9 v. in 12. illus. maps. United with its Posiedzenia Naukowe to
form its Biuletyn. Summaries in French, English or German. QE276.5.W36 DLC

Warsaw. Państwowy Instytut Geologiczny see Warsaw. Instytut Geologiczny.

WARSAW. UNIVERSYTET. Izviestiia. Varshava, 1870-1915. CU(1911-[1915])
DLC(1878-[1882]-[1915]) MH(1908-[1910]) NN(1871-1873,[1875]-[1878]-[1883,
1889,1896-1902,1906-1908]-[1914-1915]) NNC(1905,[1906-1908]-[1913])
RPB(1870,1879,1884-1892,1914-1915)

DIE WELT DER SLAWEN; Vierteljahrsschrift für Slavistik. 1- ; 1956- .
Wiesbaden. Quarterly. PG1.W4 DLC(1-) CSt(1-) CU(1-) CaQMM(1-) CaOTU(1-)
CtY(1-) DDO(1-) ICN(1-) ICU(1-) IEN(1-) IU(1-) INU(1-) InNd(1-) IaU(1-)
KyU(1-) KU(1-) MH(1-) MB(1-) MiU(1-) NIC(1-) NN(1-) NNC(1-) NcU(1-) NjR(1-)
OCl(1-) PU(1-) RPB(1-) ViU([1] 4-) WU(1-) WaU(1)

WELTWIRTSCHAFTLICHES ARCHIV; Zeitschrift für algemeine und spezielle
Weltwirtschaftslehre. Bd.1- ; Jan.1913- . Jena, S. Fischer. Each vol.
consists of sections: Abhandlungen; Chronik und Archivalien; Literatur.
H5.W4 DLC(1-) CSt-H(1-) CU(1-) CaAEU(88-) CtY(1-) IEN(1-) MH(1-) MdBJ(1-)
MiU(1-) MnU(1-) NN(1-) NNC(1-) NjP(1-) OCU(1-) TxU(1-) WU(1-)

WIADOMOŚCI ARCHEOLOGICZNE. T.1- ; 1873- . Warszawa, Państwowe Muzeum
Archeologiczne. Suspended 1883-1919. CU(2-) CtY(1-3,5-15) DLC(5-14)
DSI-M(1-[8]-12) IU(5-6) MH-P(1-) MiU(5-7) NN(2,5-12) NNM(2-) NjP(5-7)

WIADOMOŚCI NUMIZMATYCZNO-ARCHEOLOGICZNE. Kraków, Towarzystwo Numizma-
tyczne, 1892-1949. 21 v. illus., ports. Monthly (irregular). CJ9.W5
DLC(4-21) CtY(19) NNAN(1-5,[7]-19)

WIENER ARCHIV FÜR GESCHICHTE DES SLAWENTUMS UND OSTEUROPAS. Bd.1- ;
1955- . Graz, Institut für osteuropäische Geschichte und Südostforschung
der Universität Wien. CU(1-) CaBVaU(1-) DDO(2) DLC(1) ICU(1-) IU(1-)
KyU(1-) MH NNC(1-) NjR PSt(1-) PU(1-) WU(1-)

WIENER PRAEHISTORISCHE ZEITSCHRIFT. Jahrg.1-30. Wien, Praehistorische
Gesellschaft, 1914-43. 30 v. illus. GN700.W5 CU(1-26) CtY(1-12)
ICU(11-20) MH-P(1-) MiU(1-17) NNC(1,6) NNM(1-) NjP(1-18) PPAN(1-16)

Wilno i Ziemia Wileńska see Vilna. Wojewódzki Komitet Regionalny.

WINGST, GER. ERDMAGNETISCHES OBSERVATORIUM. Jahrbuch. Nr.1- ; 1949- .
Hamburg, Ger. QC830.W553 DLC

WISŁA; miesięcznik geograficzno-etnograficzny. T.1-21. Warszawa,
Polskie Towarzystwo Etnologiczne, 1887-1922. 21 v. Monthly. Suspended
1918-1921. DK401.W55 DLC(2-19) DSI-E(1-19) MH(1-19) NN(12-[17]-19)
NNC(1-[13-14,16-17]) NhD(1-19) OCl(1-8)

WISSENSCHAFTLICHER DIENST FÜR OST-MITTELEUROPA. Jahrg. 1- ; Juli 1951- .
Marburg, Lahn, Johann Gottfried Herder-Institut. Monthly. AS181.J6
DLC(2-) MH([1]-) NN(5-)

WIZERUNKI I ROZTRZĄSANIA NAUKOWE. T.1-12; Nowy poczet 1-24; Drugi
poczet 1-24. Wilno, J. Zawadzki, 1834-43. 60 v. BM(1-60)

WÖRTER UND SACHEN; Zeitschrift für indogermanische Sprachwissenschaft,
Volksforschung und Kulturgeschichte. Heidelberg, C. Winter, 1909-44.

23 v. maps. 4 no. a year. P501.W6 DLC CSt(1-) CU(1-) CaAEU(1-8,10-17)
CaOTU(1-) CtY(1-) MH(1-) MdBJ(1-) NN(1-18,20-23) NjP(1-) OU(1-) PU(1-)
TxU(1-) WU(1-)

WORLD AFFAIRS. No.1- ; Sept. 1939- . London, Federal Union. Title
varies. JX1.L6 DLC(1943-) CoU(1-7,9-) CtY(1,4-52,54-61,63-) IaU(1-)
MH(1-3,16-24,26-84,86-88,90-) NN(1-) NjP(80-)

Zapiski Historyczne; kwartalnik poświęcony historii Pomorza see Towarzystwo Naukowe w Toruniu. Wydział Nauk Historycznych, Prawnych i Społecznych. Zapiski Historyczne.

Zeitschrift der Altertumsgesellschaft, Insterburg see Altertumsgesellschaft, Insterburg. Prussia.

ZEITSCHRIFT FÜR AUSLÄNDISCHES ÖFFENTLICHES RECHT UND VÖLKERRECHT. Bd.
1- ; 1929- . Berlin; Leipzig, Institut für ausländisches öffentliches
Recht und Völkerrecht. Suspended between September 1944 and February 1950.
CU(1-) CtY-L(1-) DCE(1-) DLC(1-) ICU(1-8) MH-L(1-) MiU-L(1-) NN(1-)
NNB(1-) NNC(1-) NNU(1-) NjP(1-) PU-L(1-) RPB(1-)

ZEITSCHRIFT FÜR DAS GESAMTE HANDELSRECHT UND KONKURSRECHT. Bd.1- ;
1858- . Erlangen; Stuttgart, F. Enke. Irregular. Title varies: Zeitschrift für das gesamte Handelsrecht, vol.1-59, 1858-1907. DLC(1-106,
112-114) CU(1-) CtY(1-[3]-[5]) CtY-L(1-) ICU(1-) IEN-L(1-112) IU(1-)
MiU-L(1) NNC-L(1-) NNU(1-79,92-98) OCU(1-58,60-78,80-88)

ZEITSCHRIFT FÜR DEUTSCHE MUNDARTEN. Berlin, Deutscher Sprachverein,
1906-24. Wiesbaden, 1970. 19 v. Supersedes Zeitschrift für Hochdeutsche
Mundarten. Superseded by Zeitschrift für Mundartforschung. Reprint of
the journal published in Berlin by Deutscher Sprachverein. PF3003.Z47
CaAEU(1-19; reprint) CSt CU CtY ICU IEN IU InU MH MiU MnU(1-18) NN NhD
NjP(1-18) OClW PU RPB TxU WU WaU

ZEITSCHRIFT FÜR DEUTSCHKUNDE. Bd.1- ; 1887- . Leipzig. Bimonthly.
Title varies: Vol.1-33, 1887-1919, Zeitschrift für den deutschen Unterricht.
CLSU(43-) CLU(1-) CSt(1,3,5-[7]-[31]-[34]-) CU(1-30,32-[34]-) CaSSU(27-28,
35-41) CaOTU(7-28,34-) CaMWU(45-) CtY(1-[31]-[34]-) ICN(6-28) ICU(1-[32]-)
IEN(1-[31]-) IU(1-) IaU(1-[31]-[34]-) INU([3-21]) KU(39-) LU(1-) MH(1-)
MNS(1-) MdBJ(1-[51]-) MiU(1-) MnU(1-) MoSW(1-) MoU(16-30,35-) NIC(30,[31]-
[34]-[37]-) NN(1,3,8-12,16-20,23-26,28,36-) NNC(1-) NNU(1-13,42-)
NbU(1-31,33-) NcD(38-) NcU(38-) NhD(21-) NjP(1-29,32-) OCU(1-) OClW(15-)
OU(1-[31-42]-) PBm(1-) PU(1-) TxU(1-12,17-[31]-[54]) WaU(1-)

ZEITSCHRIFT FÜR DIE GESCHICHTE DES OBERRHEINS. Bd.1-39; 1850-1885; Neue
Folge. Bd.1- ; 1886- . Karlsruhe; Heidelberg. DD801.B11B2 DLC(1-31,34-
40,45-[71]-) CtY(1-) ICN(1-) ICU(1-71,73-) KyU(107-) MH(1-74,76-91) NN(1-)
NIC(107-) NjP(1-31,34-ns,v.35,37-) WU(ns,v.1-)

ZEITSCHRIFT FÜR ERDKUNDE; neue Folge der geographischen Wochenschrift.
Frankfurt am Main, M. Diesterweg; [et.] 1933-44. 12 v. Weekly (irregular),
1933-1935; semimonthly, 1936- . Title varies: Geographische Wochenschrift;
wissenschaftliche Zeitschrift für das Gesamtgebiet der Geographie, 1933-
1935. G1.Z46 DLC(1-) ICU(1-) CtY([1] 4-[7]-8) NN(1-) NNA(1-)

ZEITSCHRIFT FÜR ETHNOLOGIE. Bd.1- ; 1869- . Berlin, Berliner Ge-
sellschaft für Anthropologie, Ethnologie und Urgeschichte. Bimonthly.
Suspended 1945-1949. Subtitle varies. GN1.Z4 DLC(1-57,60-69,72-73,75)
CLU(1-45,51-64,71-) CSt(1-53) CU(1-) CaOOG(1-52,54-[70]) CaTR(34-45)
CaOTU(2-[12-13]-) CtY(1-[71-72]) ICF(1-) ICJ(1-[65]) ICN(1-) ICU(1-[71]-)
IU(1-) LU(1-2,4-) MB(1-) MiU(1-) MH-P(1-) NNM(1-) NbU(1-) NhD(1-) NjP(1-)
OCU(7-39,41-42) OClW(1-) PU(1-40) PPAP(1-) TNV(1-) WaU(1-)

ZEITSCHRIFT FÜR FISCHEREI UND DEREN HILFSWISSENSCHAFTEN. Berlin, Reichs-
verband der deutschen Fischerei, 1893-1944. 42 v. illus., maps. SH1.Z5
DLC(1-16) IU(1-) MH(1-13) NN(9-31,33-) NIC-A(1-) WaU(1-)

ZEITSCHRIFT FÜR KOMMUNALWIRTSCHAFT. Oldenburg, 1910-33. 23 v.
JS5301.Z4 DLC(18-23) CLU(19-23) ICU(19-23) MiU-G(16-23) MnU(21,22) NN(3-7,
9-23) PBm(16-22) PP(15,19-22) ViU(19-22)

ZEITSCHRIFT FÜR OSTEUROPÄISCHES RECHT... Jahrg. 1-3, Mai 1925-Mai 1927;
Neue Folge. 1- ; Juli 1934- . Berlin; Breslau, H. Sack; C. Heymann.
6 no. a year; monthly. Published by Osteuropa-Institut in Breslau.
DLC-L(1-) CtY-L(1-) ICU(1-) MH-L(1-) MdBJ(1-) MiU-L(1-) NN(ns,v.1-)
NNC(1-) NNB(ns,v.[1]-) OrU(1-3)

ZEITSCHRIFT FÜR OSTFORSCHUNG: Länder und Völker im östlichen Mittel-
europa. Jahrg. 1- ; 1952- . Marburg/Lahn, Johann Gottfried Herder-
Forschungsrat; N.G. Elwert. illus., maps. 4 no. a year. DR1.Z4 DLC(1-)
AMAU(2-) ClU(8-) CU([1-4] 5-) CaAEU(1-) CaQMM(1-) CtY([1]-) InU(1-) MH(1-)
MiDW(1-) NIC(1-) NN(1-) NjP(1-) OCl(10-) PSt(1-) PU(1-) TxHR(9-)

ZEITSCHRIFT FÜR OSTRECHT. Berlin, C. Heynemann, 1927-34. 8 v. Monthly.
Formed by merging of Ostrecht and Zeitschrift für osteuropäisches Recht.
CtY-L DLC-L ICU MH-L MdBJ MiU-L NN(1-[7]-8) NNB NNC OrU

ZEITSCHRIFT FÜR PHONETIK, SPRACHWISSENSCHAFT UND KOMMUNIKATIONSFORSCHUNG.
Bd.1- ; Apr./Juni 1947- . Berlin, Akademie Verlag. illus. Frequency
varies. Title varies: Zeitschrift für Phonetik und allgemeine Sprach-
wissenschaft. Supersedes Archiv für vergleichende Phonetik. P1.Z4
DLC([1]) CU(1-) CtY(1-) ICU(1-) IEN(1-) IU(1-) MH(1-) MdBJ(1-) MiU([1]-)
NN(1-) NNC(1-) NcU(1-) OClW(1-) OU(1-) PU(1-)

ZEITSCHRIFT FÜR POLITIK. Bd.1-35, 1907-1945; Neue Folge. Bd.1- ;
1954- . Berlin, C. Heymann. JA14.Z67 CaAEU(ns,1-3,5-13,15-17-) CU(12-)
CtY(1-) DLC(1-) MH(1-) MiU(1-) MdBJ(1-) MnU(1-) MoU(1-) NN(1-) NNC(1-)
NjP(1-) OClW(1-) WU(1-)

ZEITSCHRIFT FUR RASSEN-PHYSIOLOGIE. Mitteilungen der Deutschen Gesellschaft für Bluttgruppenforschung. München,J.F. Lehmanns Verlag, 1928-43.
13 v. Quarterly. CU(1-) DSG(1-) ICJ(1-6) MWhB(1-) MdBJ(1-7) MdBW(1-)
MiEM(1-) MiU(9-) NNM(1-) NNN(1-) PPC(1-6) TNV-M(1-)

ZEITSCHRIFT FÜR SLAWISCHE PHILOLOGIE. Bd.1- ; [1924]- . Leipzig, Mar-
kert & Petters, 1925- . plates, diagrs. 2 double no. a year. PG1.Z4
DLC(1-6,18-20) CU(1-) CaAEU(1-) CtY(1-) ICN(1-) IU(1-) IaU(1-3,9) MH(1-)
MdBJ(1-) MiU(1-) MnU(1-) NoU(1-) NN(1-) NNC(1-) NNU-H(1-) NjP(1-) OCU(1-)
OCl(1-) OClW(1-) WU(1-)

ZEITSCHRIFT FÜR SLAVISTIK. Bd.1- ; 1956- . Berlin, Akademie-Verlag.
ports. Quarterly. PG1.Z43 DLC(1-) ClU(4-) CU(1-) CaAEU(9-) CtY(1-) ICU(1-)
KU(1-) MiU(1-) MH(1-) NIC(1-) NN(1-) NNC(1-) NjP(1-) NjR(5-) PU(1-) WU(1-)

ZEITSCHRIFT FÜR VERGLEICHENDE SPRACHFORSCHUNG AUF DEM GEBIETE DER INDO-
germanischen Sprachen. Bd.1- ; 1852- . Berlin [etc.] F. Dümmler;
[etc.]. Bimonthly. Title varies: Bd.21-40 called also Neue Folge, Bd.1-20.
P501.Z5 DLC CSt(1-) CU(1-) CaAEU(1-58) CtY(1-) IU(1-) KyU(1-) MH(1-)
MnU(1-) NN(1-) NNC(1-) NbU(1-) OCU(1-) RPB(1-)

ZEITSCHRIFT FÜR VÖLKERRECHT. Breslau, 1906-39. 23 v. 6 no. a year.
JX5.Z5 DLC(1-) CSt-H(1-[9] 10) CU(13-) CtY-L(1-) DCE(1-) ICJ(1-10) ICU(1-)
IEN(1-) IU(1-) IaU(13-) MH(1-) MH-L(1-) MdBJ(1-18) MiU(1-18) MiU-L(1-) NN(1-)
NNB(1-) NNC(1-) NcD(1-) NjP(1-) OU(13-) PU(1-) WU(1-) WaU(1-)

ŽEMĖS ŪKIS; dvisavaitinis iliustruotas žemės ūkio mokslo žurnalas. Nr. 1-
210(1925-1941)- ; spalis/gruodis 1925-1944. Kaunas, Žemės ūkio ministerija; Žemės ūkio rūmai, 1925-44. 11 v. Irregular. 20.Z42 DNAL(Metai 12,
no.149-172(1937)) CtPAM(1927-1931)

ŽEMETVARKA IR MELIORACIJA. Kaunas, Lietuvos matininkų ir kultūrtechnikų
sąjunga, 1926-40. Quarterly; bimonthly. TC801.Z4 DLC(1930-1940) DNAL

Zentralblatt für Mineralogie, Geologie und Paläontologie see Neues
Jahrbuch für Mineralogie, Geologie und Paläontologie.

ZHIVAIA STARINA; periodicheskoe izdanie. Sanktpeterburg; Petrograd,
Gosudarstvennoe Russkoe geograficheskoe obshchestvo. Otdielenie etnografii,
1890-1916. 25 v. GN1.Z5 DLC CSt-H(23-24) CU(1-24) CtY(1,[2,4-5]-[7-11]-
[16-22]-24) MH(1-27) MnU([1-22]) NN(1-27) NNC([1]-25)

ZHIVOPISNAIA ROSSIIA. Otechestvo nashe v ego zemel'nom, istoricheskom, plemennom, ekonomicheskom i bytovom znachenii, pod obshchei redaktsiei P.P. Semenova... Sanktpeterburg, Izd. T-va M.O. Vol'fa, 1879-1901. 12 v. illus., ports., plans, plates, maps. Monthly. DKl.Z5 DLC(1-2,5-8,11-12) CSt-H(1-12) MH([1]-[3]-7,12) NN(1-9,11-12) PU(3)

Zhurnal ministerstva narodnogo prosveshcheniia. Zhurnal.

ŽIBURIAI. Augsburg, Ger.,1945-49. 261 no. Weekly. CtPAM(no.1-110) OKentU(1-261) ICLJF(1-261)

ŽIDINYS; literatūros, mokslo, visuomenės ir akademinio gyvenimo mėnesinis žurnalas. Metai 1-17, no.1-6; gruodis 1924-birž. 1940. Kaunas, Studentų ateitininkų sąjunga, 1924-40. Monthly. 57.92 Z67 PU(25-31,no.1-4) CtPAM(1924-1940) CtTMF(1925-1940) ICCC(1924-1940,no.1-4) OKentU(1928, no. 5-6; 1929, no.1-7,10,11; 1930; 1931, no.1,2,4,7-9,12; 1932, no.1,5-6; 1933, no.2,7; 1934, no.1-10,12; 1935; 1936, no.10; 1937, no.7,10,11; 1938, no.1-3,11,12; 1939, no.1-4,7-11; 1940, no.1-4)

ŽINYČIA; kvartalinis laikraštis, paskirtas apšviestesniesiems lietuviams. Tilžė, Kaštu Tėvynės Sargo, 1900-02. 5 no. Quarterly. In 1903 merged with Dirva of Cleveland, Ohio. CtPAM(1900, no.1-2; 1901, no.3; 1902, no.4-5) CtTMF(1-3) ICCC(1-5)

Znicz; noworocznik wydany przez J. Kraszewskiego. Wilno, 1834-35. 2 v. BM(P.P. 4865. ee.)

ŻYDOWSKI INSTYTUT HISTORYCZNY, WARSAW. Biuletyn. T.1- ; 1951- . Warszawa. 1951-1952, 2 no. a year; quarterly since 1953. Summaries in English, French and Russian. DS135.P6Z9 DLC([1-2]) CSt-H(10-) NN(1-) NNC(1-)